UNITED STATES HISTORY

FIFTH EDITION

Joseph Jarrell

bju press
Greenville, South Carolina

Note: The fact that materials produced by other publishers may be referred to in this volume does not constitute an endorsement of the content or theological position of materials produced by such publishers. Any references and ancillary materials are listed as an aid to the student or the teacher and in an attempt to maintain the accepted academic standards of the publishing industry.

UNITED STATES HISTORY
Fifth Edition
 Joseph Jarrell, MS, MA

Contributing Writers
 Dennis Bollinger, PhD
 Sarah Weaver, MEd

Consultants
 Carl Abrams, PhD
 Mark Sidwell, PhD

Editors
 Leigh Kosin
 Ben Sinnamon, MA, MLIS

Biblical Worldview
 Brian Collins, PhD

Cover & Book Design
 Drew Fields

Design
 Dan VanLeeuwen
 Ciara Weant

Page Layout
 Katherine Cooper
 Jessica Johnson

Project Coordinator
 Dan Berger

Permissions
 Sharon Belknap
 Tatiana Bento
 Sylvia Gass
 Sarah Gundlach
 Carrie Walker

Illustration
 Preston Gravely, Jr.
 Del Thompson
 Ciara Weant

Photograph credits appear on pages 697–701.

Text acknowledgments appear on-page with text selections.

All trademarks are the registered and unregistered marks of their respective owners. BJU Press is in no way affiliated with these companies. No rights are granted by BJU Press to use such marks, whether by implication, estoppel, or otherwise.

© 2018 BJU Press
Greenville, South Carolina 29609

Fourth Edition © 2012 BJU Press
First Edition © 1982 BJU Press

Printed in the United States of America
All rights reserved

ISBN: 978-1-62856-207-1

15 14 13 12 11 10 9 8 7 6

CONTENTS

Pronunciation Guide ix

UNIT I: HORIZONS

Chapter 1: New and Old Worlds Meet 2

Chapter 2: Thirteen Colonies 19

Chapter 3: Colonial Life 38

Chapter 4: Religion in the American Colonies 54

UNIT II: FORGE

Chapter 5: The Rising Storm (1689–1770) 74

Chapter 6: Independence (1770–1783) 92

Chapter 7: The Critical Period (1781–1789) 119

Chapter 8: The Federalist Years (1789–1801) 138

UNIT III: NATION

Chapter 9: The Jeffersonian Era (1801–1825) 158

Chapter 10: The Age of Jackson (1820–1840) 180

Chapter 11: The Growth of American Society (1789–1861) 202

Chapter 12: Manifest Destiny (1840–1848) 231

UNIT IV: CRISIS

Chapter 13: A House Dividing (1848–1861) 254

Chapter 14: The Civil War (1861–1865) 278

Chapter 15: Reconstruction (1865–1877) 310

UNIT V: QUEST

Chapter 16: The Gilded Age (1877–1896) 334

Chapter 17: America Expands (1850–1900) 361

Chapter 18: The Progressive Era (1890–1920) 388

Chapter 19: The Great War (1914–1920) 417

UNIT VI: LEADERSHIP

Chapter 20: The Twenties (1920–1929) 442
Chapter 21: The Thirties (1929–1939) 464
Chapter 22: The World at War (1939–1945) 490

UNIT VII: CHALLENGE

Chapter 23: The Postwar Era (1945–1963) 524
Chapter 24: The Shattered Society (1963–1973) 552
Chapter 25: A Nation with Challenges (1973–1980) 573
Chapter 26: Resurgence of Conservatism (1981–1992) 593
Chapter 27: Facing a New Millennium (1993–2017) 612

Appendices 640
Glossary 657
Index 679
Photo Credits 697

FEATURES OF THE BOOK

HORIZONS 1488–1760

CHAPTERS
1. NEW AND OLD WORLDS MEET
2. THIRTEEN COLONIES
3. COLONIAL LIFE
4. RELIGION IN THE AMERICAN COLONIES

Timeline events:
- 1488 Dias rounds the Cape of Good Hope
- 1492 Columbus lands in the New World
- 1498 Da Gama reaches India by sailing around Africa
- 1519 Cortés arrives in Mexico
- 1519–1522 Magellan's fleet sails around the world
- 1588 Defeat of the Spanish Armada
- 1607 Founding of Jamestown
- Pilgrims come to the N[ew World]
- 1630–40 Great Migration of Puritans to Massachusetts Bay
- 1664 England conquers New Netherland
- 1682 William Penn settles Pennsylvania
- ca. 1720 – ca. The Great Awakening
- 1733

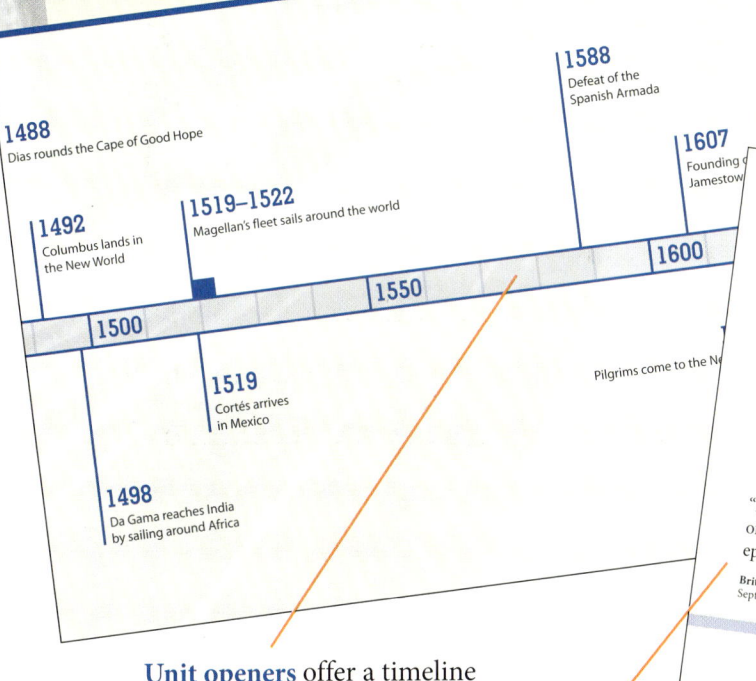

22 THE WORLD AT WAR 1939–1945

> "Not in vain" may be the pride of those who survived and the epitaph of those who fell.
>
> **British Prime Minister Winston Churchill**
> September 28, 1944

U.S. Marines raise the American flag atop Mount Suribachi on Iwo Jima.

Big Ideas
1. How did the dictators seize power, and what territories did each conquer?
2. How did the United States transition from a neutral state to an active participant in the war?
3. What role did American forces play in Europe?
4. What role did American forces play in the Pacific?

I. A Time of Tyrants
II. Isolation and Infamy
III. The Fight for Fortress Europe
IV. Pushing Back the Axis

Unit openers offer a timeline of major events covered in associated chapters.

Thought-provoking **quotations** give insight into the issues discussed in the chapter.

Each chapter includes **Big Ideas** to engage student learning.

The **chapter outline** lists the major topics that will be covered.

Amazing **color photographs and artwork** assist the students in "seeing" the sites, people, and events discussed in the text.

Guiding questions focus the students and prepare them for reading the sections within the chapter.

Feature boxes provide a deeper look at people, events, or concepts mentioned in the text.

Page 3 — NEW AND OLD WORLDS MEET

Iron shackles clanked in the musty prison cell as huddled forms awakened. One prisoner, gathering quill and parchments from beneath his pillow, continued his writing. In happier times he had been a writer of romances and chivalric legends who had enjoyed modest acclaim. Now, during a war in 1298, he found himself cast into prison with a living legend named **Marco Polo**.

Though a prisoner of war, Polo was still free to tell the most fantastic stories. His adventures in China had spanned nearly twenty years, during which time he had been a favorite of Kublai, the grand khan of the Mongols.

Polo described mysterious Asia as a world of shimmering silks, fragrant spices, and unlimited gold. In a land that would someday be called Japan, Polo had heard that gold was so common it was used for pavement.

In that prison cell, Marco Polo's new friend, Rustichello da Pisa, penned the words of one of history's greatest travelers, later published under the imposing title *Description of the World*. Polo's narrative became the definitive work on Asia for the next three centuries. Its vivid descriptions enticed men to see the region for themselves, and this enticement prepared men to experience sweeping change. Asia offered Europeans a chance to experience sweeping growth, personally in wealth and nationally in power and prestige. Seeking this growth eventually led to the discovery of another world—a world that would make all they had known seem old.

I. Changes in the Old World
China, Innovations, and Mercantilism

Early European explorers saw China as the source of great riches and opportunities for their countries. The first peoples to take advantage of access to China (and the East Indies islands of South Asia) were the Muslims, who for decades held a virtual monopoly on all trade in the region. Soon, however, Europeans determined to get their share of trade in the Indies, and that area became the focus of exploration before the discovery of the New World. Several innovations made it possible for the Europeans to compete with the Muslims and eventually to discover the New World.

Marco Polo

Guiding Questions

1. How did Europeans become interested in the riches of Asia?
2. How did European explorers travel to Asia?
3. How did the Protestant Reformation prompt many Europeans to travel to the New World?

Page 113 — INDEPENDENCE

American leader arose out of the war in the West—**George Rogers Clark**.

Clark, a native Virginian, had come to the Ohio River Valley in 1772. As a resident of Kentucky, Clark recognized the threat that the frontier faced from the British and the Indians. In 1778, the twenty-five-year-old Clark won Virginia's approval to lead an attack on British trading posts north of the Ohio River in the region then known as the Northwest. With a tiny force of approximately 175 men, Clark sailed down the Ohio River to what is now Illinois. From there Clark marched his men overland to the Mississippi River town of Kaskaskia (kus KAS kee uh). The town, populated mostly by French settlers who did not care for the British anyway, happily surrendered. Several other trading posts quickly fell, including the most important—Vincennes on the Wabash River in what is now Indiana.

Clark's Campaign

"I Have Not Yet Begun to Fight"

John Paul Jones (left) commander of the Bonhomme Richard is shown here battling the Serapis.

The American navy in the War for Independence was pitifully small, particularly in contrast to the mighty British fleet. Most American naval victories consisted of the capture of unarmed British merchant ships so the cargo could be confiscated. At least one triumph at sea, however, was big enough, as one historian wrote, "to set a tradition of victory" for the U.S. Navy.

Scottish-born Captain John Paul Jones was the ablest commander in the American fleet, and he needed all of his talent on September 23, 1779. Jones was commanding the *Bonhomme Richard* (named in honor of Benjamin Franklin and his *Poor Richard's Almanac*) off the coast of Great Britain when he encountered two British warships, the *Serapis* and the *Countess of Scarborough*. The *Serapis* alone outgunned the *Bonhomme Richard*, and the presence of the *Countess* only increased the odds against Jones. Nonetheless, Jones joined battle.

The three-and-a-half-hour fight started poorly for the Americans when two of their largest cannons exploded, killing several men. Jones tried to overcome the British advantage in cannons by coming close to board the *Serapis*. The British crew held off the Americans, however, and their guns tore gaping holes in the side of the American ship. At one point, an officer of the *Bonhomme Richard*, thinking that Jones was dead, called out to the British, offering to surrender. Jones refused to surrender, rose, and supposedly cried out, "I have not yet begun to fight!"

Although his ship was sinking slowly, Jones continued by sheer grit to pound at the British. Finally, the captain of the *Serapis*—his mainmast fallen—surrendered; the smaller *Countess* fled. Jones and his crew boarded the shattered *Bonhomme Richard* sink beneath the waves. The Americans took their prize to the Netherlands, and Jones visited Paris, where the French greeted him with an uproarious celebration. John Paul Jones had given America its first great victory at sea.

Terms in bold type draw attention to important facts, ideas, people, or definitions.

Section reviews help the students remember what they have learned so far.

Margin boxes offer intriguing bits of information.

CHAPTER 10 — page 196

John Ross was the principal chief of the Cherokees from the late 1820s until his death in 1866. He was one-eighth Cherokee.

Trail of Tears

Believing the earlier promises contained in their treaties with the United States that they would be left to govern themselves, the Cherokees resisted removal. They soon found that Christian missionaries to their tribe were their strongest defenders. The leader of the mission board that supported many of these missionaries petitioned Congress and wrote many newspaper articles in support of the Cherokees' rights.

In response, the Georgia legislature passed a law targeting missionaries. It forbade white people to live among the Cherokees without government approval. Several missionaries were arrested for continuing their ministry among the Cherokees without such approval. Two were sentenced to serve four years hard labor in a state prison. These two, Samuel Worcester and Elizur Butler, appealed to the U.S. Supreme Court, and the Supreme Court ruled in favor of the missionaries. In *Worcester v. Georgia*, Chief Justice John Marshall ordered Georgia to release the missionaries and also told President Jackson to send troops into Georgia to remove white settlers who had moved onto Cherokee lands. But Georgia and President Jackson ignored the Court. Jackson reportedly said, "John Marshall has made his decision. Now let him enforce it."

Many Cherokees still resisted. But by 1838 troops had forcibly moved those who had not already gone west to the Indian Territory (now Oklahoma). U.S. soldiers dragged the Cherokees from their homes—sometimes at gunpoint—and placed them in detention camps until the marches west began.

These forced marches west began in the summer, and sickness and drought killed many of the travelers. Several groups waited until fall, but heavy rains became a problem. Travel was difficult and food was scarce. As winter set in, frigid weather and bad water caused more disease. About four thousand of the fifteen thousand Cherokees died en route to the Indian Territory. The sick, the aged, and the very young suffered the most. The Indians called the location the **Trail of Tears**.

"The Trail Where They Cried"
Perhaps the saddest event in the Indian resettlement process was the Trail of Tears, the forced removal of more than ten thousand Cherokees from North Carolina, Georgia, and Tennessee to the Indian Territory (located in what is now Oklahoma) in 1838 and 1839. The Cherokee phrase for "trail..."

Section Review
1–3. What were the three new political ideas introduced in the presidential election of 1832?

4–5. How did the reactions of the Seminoles and the Cherokees to Indian removal differ? What was the result for each tribe?

★ Evaluate the idea of a protective tariff.

★ Who was responsible for the forced removal of the Cherokees? Explain your answer.

RECONSTRUCTION — page 313

Johnson's plan for Reconstruction was a modification of Lincoln's. In addition, it offered **amnesty** (a pardon for offenses) to Southerners who would swear loyalty to the Union. But Johnson excluded those whose property was worth more than $20,000. Those people, mostly former large-plantation owners, had to apply to him personally for a pardon. Unpardoned Southerners could not vote, hold office, or reclaim property seized by the government.

Next, each former Confederate state was required to hold a state convention. That body would draft a new state constitution that would revoke its declaration of secession, refuse to pay Confederate debts, and ratify the **Thirteenth Amendment** (which abolished slavery).

Implementation of Johnson's Plan
Changes in Southern States
At the end of the war, the South lay devastated. Nearly 300,000 Southern men had died in battle, in prison camps, or from disease. The economy of the South was in shambles, devastated by the heavy fighting that had taken place throughout the region. Some Northern observers touring the region said that morale was so low that Southerners would accept almost any government that the North chose to impose on them. Andrew Johnson's lenient approach, however, encouraged the South. Perhaps, thought Southerners, recovery would not be as painful as they had feared.

By the winter of 1865, most of the former Confederate states had met most of Johnson's terms. As they organized their new governments and elected members to Congress, Johnson began granting pardons to thousands of Southerners.

Black Codes
The new Southern legislatures passed a series of laws known as **black codes**. These severely limited the rights of black people. Though the codes varied from state to state, all seemed intended to keep African Americans in a condition similar to slavery.

In some states, black people could work only as household servants or farmers. Some codes forbade them to live in towns or cities. The codes restricted many blacks to the same fieldwork they had done as slaves. Those who wanted to practice trades or do anything besides farming had to be apprenticed and often had to obtain costly licenses. Few black Americans had enough money to pay these fees.

Blacks who were not employed could be arrested. Those who could not pay fines could be hired out to anyone who would pay their fines. Some black codes forbade them to carry weapons and other codes limited where they could own property. In some states, they were prohibited from voting, holding office, suing whites, or serving on juries.

Southerners defended the codes by arguing that the uneducated former slaves could be easily manipulated and thus should not be granted equal rights. Many Northerners strongly disagreed and insisted that black Americans should be treated as equal members of society.

Congressional Response
When Congress gathered for its next session in December 1865, the newly elected Southern legislators arrived to take their positions. Dozens of them had been members of the Confederate

As Reconstruction progressed, African American men were given the right to vote. In this November 1867 illustration, some are doing so for the first time. Unfortunately, many Southern states later instituted laws and regulations designed to make it difficult for black men to have access to the ballot box.

Black Codes
The following codes were instituted in Opelousas, Louisiana, in 1865.

No negro or freedman shall be allowed to come within the limits of the town of Opelousas without special permission from his employers.... Whoever shall violate this provision shall suffer imprisonment and two days' work on the public streets, or shall pay a fine of two dollars and fifty cents....

No negro or freedman shall be permitted to rent or keep a house within the limits of the town under any circumstances....

No negro or freedman shall reside within the limits of the town of Opelousas who is not in the regular service of some white person or former owner....

No public meetings or congregations of negroes or freedmen shall be allowed within the limits of the town....

No freedman who is not in the military service shall be allowed to carry firearms, or any kind of weapons....

No freedman shall sell, barter, or exchange any articles of merchandise... within the limits of Opelousas without permission in writing from his employer.

viii

reaped $17 billion in revenue. Movie celebrities such as Douglas Fairbanks and Mary Pickford appeared at huge rallies to boost bond sales. Even schoolchildren saved their pennies to fill Liberty Books with 25¢ stamps appropriately captioned "Lick a Stamp and Lick the Kaiser."

The war touched every area of life. Artists used their pens and paints in the war effort, producing posters to recruit men and raise money. And in a day before radio and television, families often gathered around the piano in the evening to sing such sentimental ballads as "I'm Hitting the Trail for Normandy, So Kiss Me Good-bye" or George M. Cohan's spirited "Over There," the unofficial anthem of the American "**doughboy**," or soldier.

Politics of Patriotism

The national zeal for the war effort contributed toward widespread anti-German sentiment. Many high schools dropped German language courses, and "liberty" replaced virtually everything connected with the hated Hun—German measles became "liberty measles," German shepherds were renamed "liberty dogs," and sauerkraut was now "liberty cabbage."

The anti-German attitude led to changed laws as well, often at the cost of constitutionally guaranteed liberties. For example, the **Espionage and Sedition Acts** made it a criminal offense to criticize the war effort in any way. Such acts must be understood in their wartime context. A number of German spy plots, including the successful sabotage of a New Jersey munitions plant, prompted lawmakers to enact stiff laws to safeguard national security. Undoubtedly though, some of the enforcement of the Espionage and Sedition Acts, which resulted in more than a thousand convictions, was the result of unfounded fears and hysteria. Despite

---

THE GREAT WAR 429

"Over There!"

This song, written in 1917, became popular with both the military and the public. It was used to encourage young men to enlist in the army.

Over there, over there, send the word, send the word, over there,
That the Yanks are coming, the Yanks are coming,
The drums rum-tumming ev'rywhere.
So prepare, say a prayer, send the word, send the word to beware:
We'll be over, we're coming over,
And we won't come back 'til it's over over there!

World War I in Europe

Maps, charts, and diagrams help the students visualize geographic locations and information.

THE CIVIL WAR 309

CHAPTER REVIEW 14

Making Connections

1. Why was life on the home front more difficult in the South than in the North?
2. Why did many state governments in the South oppose conscription?
3. How did the Lincoln administration keep Maryland in the Union?
4–6. List three of the reasons South Carolina provided when it seceded from the Union.
7. Why did the South assume at first that Great Britain would come to the aid of the Confederacy?

Developing History Skills

1. Explain briefly why each side in the war thought it was right.
2. Conduct an online search for the declarations of secession of Georgia, Mississippi, and Texas. List three of the basic reasons these states provided for seceding from the Union.

Thinking Critically

1. Consider William Sherman's statement: "War is cruelty, and you cannot refine it." Is that statement true? Is there a potential danger in such an attitude?
2. Why was the Emancipation Proclamation significant even though it only applied to slaves in areas not under Union control?

Living as a Christian Citizen

1. If you were actively involved in the effort to end abortion in the United States, what lessons would you draw from Lincoln's approach to emancipation of the slaves?
2. Imagine that you are a Christian congressional representative from the North. How should your Christian faith influence your response to the conduct of Sherman?

People, Places, and Things to Remember

states' rights
Anaconda Plan
Thomas J. Jackson
First Battle of Bull Run
George B. McClellan
ironclad
USS *Merrimack*
USS *Monitor*
Robert E. Lee
J.E.B. Stuart
Second Battle of Bull Run
Clara Barton
Battle of Antietam
Battle of Fredericksburg
Battle of Chancellorsville
Pickett's Charge
Battle of Gettysburg
Gettysburg Address
Ulysses S. Grant
Battle of Shiloh
David Farragut
Vicksburg
Braxton Bragg
Battle of Chickamauga
Battle of Chattanooga
blockade runners
conscription
New York draft riot
border states
West Virginia
Copperheads
Trent affair
Emancipation Proclamation
Wilderness Campaign
William Tecumseh Sherman
Battle of Atlanta
March to the Sea
Petersburg
Appomattox Court House
John Wilkes Booth

The **Chapter Review** asks students about terms, people, places, and concepts to help them prepare for assessments.

PRONUNCIATION GUIDE

Vowels			
symbol	example	symbol	example
a	cat = KAT	aw	all = AWL
a_e	cape = KAPE	o	potion = PO shun
ay	paint = PAYNT	oa	don't = DOANT
e	jet = JET	o_e	groan = GRONE
eh	spend = SPEHND	oh	own = OHN
ee	fiend = FEEND	u	some = SUM
i	swim = SWIM	uh	abet = uh BET
ih	pity = PIH tee	oo	crew = CROO
eye	icy = EYE see	oo	push = POOSH
i_e	might = MITE	ou	loud = LOUD
ah	cot = KAHT	oy	toil = TOYL
ar	car = KAR		

Consonants			
symbol	example	symbol	example
k	cat = KAT	th	thin = THIN
g	get = GET	*th*	then = THEN
j	gentle = JEN tul	zh	fusion = FYOO zhun

The pronunciation key used in this text is designed to give the reader a self-evident, acceptable pronunciation for a word as he reads it from the page. For more accurate pronunciations, the reader should consult a good dictionary.

Stress: Syllables with primary stress appear in LARGE CAPITAL letters. Syllables with secondary stress and one-syllable words appear in SMALL CAPITAL letters. Unstressed syllables appear in lowercase letters. Where two or more words appear together, hyphens separate the syllables within each word. For example, the pronunciation of Omar Khayyám appears as (O-mar keye-YAHM).

HORIZONS
1488 – 1760

1488
Dias rounds the Cape of Good Hope

1492
Columbus lands in the New World

1519–1522
Magellan's fleet sails around the world

1588
Defeat of the Spanish Armada

1607
Founding of Jamestown

1500 — 1550 — 1600

1519
Cortés arrives in Mexico

1620
Pilgrims come to the New World

1498
Da Gama reaches India by sailing around Africa

CHAPTERS

1 NEW AND OLD WORLDS MEET
2 THIRTEEN COLONIES
3 COLONIAL LIFE
4 RELIGION IN THE AMERICAN COLONIES

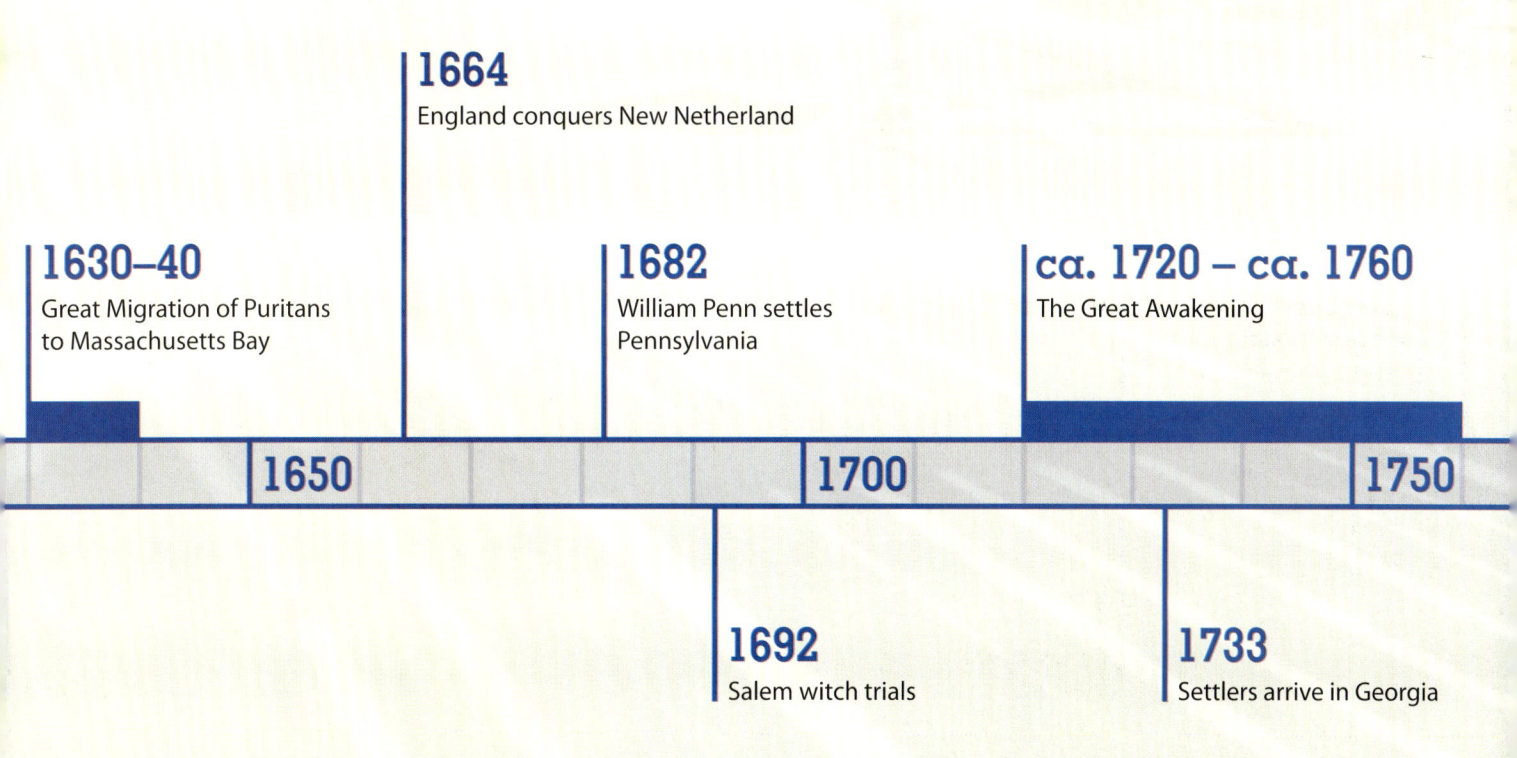

1630–40
Great Migration of Puritans to Massachusetts Bay

1664
England conquers New Netherland

1682
William Penn settles Pennsylvania

ca. 1720 – ca. 1760
The Great Awakening

1650 — 1700 — 1750

1692
Salem witch trials

1733
Settlers arrive in Georgia

1 NEW AND OLD WORLDS MEET

At two hours after midnight appeared the land…

Christopher Columbus
October 12, 1492, Captain's Log Entry

Columbus erroneously thought he had reached Asia when he landed on an island he called San Salvador.

Big Ideas

1. What changes in the Old World led to exploration of the New World?
2. What did Europeans discover in the New World, and what changes did they bring to the New World?

I. Changes in the Old World

II. Contacts in the New World

Iron shackles clanked in the musty prison cell as huddled forms awakened. One prisoner, gathering quill and parchments from beneath his pillow, continued his writing. In happier times he had been a writer of romances and chivalric legends who had enjoyed modest acclaim. Now, during a war in 1298, he found himself cast into prison with a living legend named **Marco Polo**.

Though a prisoner of war, Polo was still free to tell the most fantastic stories. His adventures in China had spanned nearly twenty years, during which time he had been a favorite of Kublai, the grand khan of the Mongols.

Polo described mysterious Asia as a world of shimmering silks, fragrant spices, and unlimited gold. In a land that would someday be called Japan, Polo had heard that gold was so common it was used for pavement.

In that prison cell, Marco Polo's new friend, Rustichello da Pisa, penned the words of one of history's greatest travelers, later published under the imposing title *Description of the World*. Polo's narrative became the definitive work on Asia for the next three centuries. Its vivid descriptions enticed men to see the region for themselves, and this enticement prepared Europe to experience sweeping change. Asia offered Europeans a chance to experience remarkable growth, personally in wealth and nationally in power and prestige. Seeking this growth eventually led to the discovery of another world—a world that would make all they had known seem old.

Marco Polo

I. Changes in the Old World
China, Innovations, and Mercantilism

Early European explorers saw China as the source of great riches and opportunities for their countries. The first peoples to take advantage of access to China (and the East Indies islands of South Asia) were the Muslims, who for decades held a virtual monopoly on all trade in the region. Soon, however, Europeans determined to get their share of trade in the Indies, and that area became the focus of exploration before the discovery of the New World.

Several innovations made it possible for the Europeans to compete with the Muslims and eventually to discover the New World.

Guiding Questions

1. How did Europeans become interested in the riches of Asia?
2. How did European explorers travel to Asia?
3. How did the Protestant Reformation prompt many Europeans to travel to the New World?

The astrolabe and other new navigational instruments made it easier for explorers to sail the unknown oceans of the world more accurately.

Caravel

Mercantilism Versus Free Market

Free market economics, in contrast to mercantilism, sees trade as a mutually beneficial arrangement in which both sides emerge as winners. Each side gives up something it considers less valuable to gain something it considers more valuable.

One was the development of the **compass**, which enabled sailors to know in which direction they were heading. Another invention was the **astrolabe**, which allowed them to determine their ship's latitude on the ocean.

Another important innovation was a Portuguese ship called a **caravel**. This small light ship sported two or three triangular sails that made it easy to maneuver. The swiftness of the caravel, combined with its overwhelming cannon power, enabled not only the expansion of European trade with China and the Indies but also the discovery of the New World. The confrontation between Muslims and Europeans in the Indies was the second major conflict between the Muslim and the Christian European cultures. The first confrontation was the Crusades (1095–1291). Those wars sparked an increase in trade, as the European participants returned home with products from Asia.

Perhaps as important as such innovations was a shift in economic thinking that occurred in Europe about the time explorations began, and it greatly spurred exploratory efforts. Monarchs in Europe were gradually shifting from the feudal, or manorial, economic thinking prevalent during the Middle Ages to a nationalistic economic system of thought known as **mercantilism**. Although that shift in thinking might have been a step toward free market capitalism, it most certainly was not capitalism or free trade.

Mercantilism was an economic system that was designed to enhance the wealth and power of a nation. It operated on two basic assumptions:

1. Mercantilists believed that a nation's wealth consisted of precious metals, especially gold. The value of a product, they thought, was determined by how much gold (or other precious metal) people were willing to give in exchange for it.

2. Mercantilists were nationalists who believed that a country could increase its wealth by increasing its surplus of gold. For one nation to increase its wealth (gold), they thought, another country had to lose it. Mercantilism saw a world of winners and losers. The monarchs' desire for gold led to numerous conflicts between nations, possibly accounting in large measure for the desire of France and England to separate Spain from its treasures of gold found in the New World.

Mercantilism also led to national desires to build colonial empires that would serve both as sources of riches and raw materials from which to manufacture goods and as markets for those goods once they were made in the mother country. In practice, mercantilism led to the government's granting of special charters, subsidies, and bounties for some companies or individuals while it discouraged imports and encouraged exports. Mercantilists sought to achieve a "favorable balance of trade," that is, to export more than they imported, thereby collecting even more gold. An understanding of mercantilism is necessary for understanding both the intense competition among the major European powers and the conflict that eventually arose between England and its New World colonies.

Sugar and Spice

Marco Polo's account of China in the 1200s fired the imaginations of Europe's merchants and adventurers. But the overland route to China was costly and dangerous. Muslim merchants, who controlled the eastern silk and spice trade, choked the highways, prompting Western Europeans to find a waterway to China in order to bypass the Muslim monopoly.

The Portuguese led the way in 1488 when **Bartolomeu Dias** (DEE ahz) sailed southward along the west coast of Africa and rounded its southern cape, which he optimistically called Good Hope. A decade later, **Vasco da Gama** (dah GAH mah) followed up Dias's discovery by sailing to India. Da Gama returned to Portugal with a cargo of spices worth sixty times the cost of his expedition.

Such fantastic profits signaled the end of the Muslim monopoly on the spice trade and the beginning of the European scramble for wealth. Ships laden with cinnamon, gold, ivory, and sugar revolutionized Europe's economy, politics, and worldview.

As Portugal, Spain's neighbor, was dominating trade in the Indian Ocean, Spaniards looked in another direction for trade with Asia. Like most educated Europeans of the fifteenth century, the Italian-born **Christopher Columbus** believed that the world was round. Basing his calculations—or, as it turned out, his miscalculations—on the circumference estimates of the second-century Greek mathematician Ptolemy, Columbus reasoned that the shortest route to the East was west. Columbus and Ptolemy, though correct about the earth's shape, were incorrect about its size. Columbus figured that by sailing three thousand miles west, he could reach Japan and its fabled riches. (Actually, Japan is more than twelve thousand miles west from the coast of Spain.)

When the king of Portugal refused to underwrite a westward voyage, Columbus turned to the Spanish for help. After receiving the reluctant support of Queen Isabella, Columbus set out in early August 1492 with three ships and a letter of greeting from the Spanish crown to the king of Cipango (Japan). The letter was to be personalized after Columbus learned the name of the distant ruler.

On the evening of October 11, Columbus wrote in his ship's log, "the Admiral, at ten o'clock in the night, being on the sterncastle, saw a light.... like a small wax candle.... the Admiral was certain that they were near land." By 2:00 a.m. the light proved to be land, and though Columbus did not realize it, he had stumbled not onto an island of Cipango but onto a sliver of sand in the Bahamas. That day Columbus went ashore and named the island San Salvador (Holy Savior) in gratitude for the merciful ocean passage that God had given his expedition. Curious natives gathered about the strange band of pale visitors and offered gifts of parrots and raw cotton. Columbus was certain that he was on an island of the Indies, off the coast of mainland Asia; thus, he called the people *los indios*—Indians. Many more misunderstandings between the two cultures would occur in the centuries to follow.

If he were an explorer looking for new lands, Columbus could not have been in a better location, since there are literally thousands of islands in the Caribbean archipelago. But as an explorer looking for Asian riches, Columbus could not have been in a more frustrating position. He would make three more voyages to the region in a vain search for China and Japan, and it appears that he went to his grave believing he had reached the outskirts of Asia. In addition, much confusion occurred because he used the inaccurate term "Indian" for the native peoples of the region.

Vasco da Gama

Christopher Columbus

Amerigo Vespucci

Other men, however, came to realize what Columbus did not—that there was a new world across the ocean. One of those men was **Amerigo Vespucci** (vehs POO chee), who made at least two voyages to the Caribbean and South America. One of history's interesting ironies is that in 1507 a little-known German mapmaker was so bold as to name this area not Columbus, but "America" in honor of Amerigo.

England was not idle during the race for the Asian region. In 1497, the Italian explorer Giovanni Caboto—known to the English for whom he sailed as **John Cabot** (KAB uht)—reached Newfoundland in his search for a passage to China. The following year, he once again sailed west for the East, but he never returned. His fate remains a mystery; yet his initial discovery changed the course of history, for it provided the basis for England's claim to and colonization of North America.

Two continents were now added to the world map. Yet the Americas seemed more of an obstacle to sail around than a land to settle. Explorers set about finding a way to bypass it, believing riches lay just beyond the new world horizon. **Ferdinand Magellan** (muh JEHL uhn) determined that he could reach the Spice Islands of the East by sailing south around the Americas. In what would be one of the the greatest sea voyages of all time, Magellan sailed from Spain in 1519 with five ships and a crew of about 270 men. While stopped on the coast of present-day Argentina, a mutiny occurred. Magellan crushed the rebellion and executed its leaders. Afterwards, one of the ships sank in a terrible storm. As he neared the area where the Atlantic and Pacific Oceans converge, fierce storms and huge waves tossed the ships. The crew on one ship abandoned the expedition and returned to Spain. Unfortunately, this ship contained a large portion of the fleet's supplies.

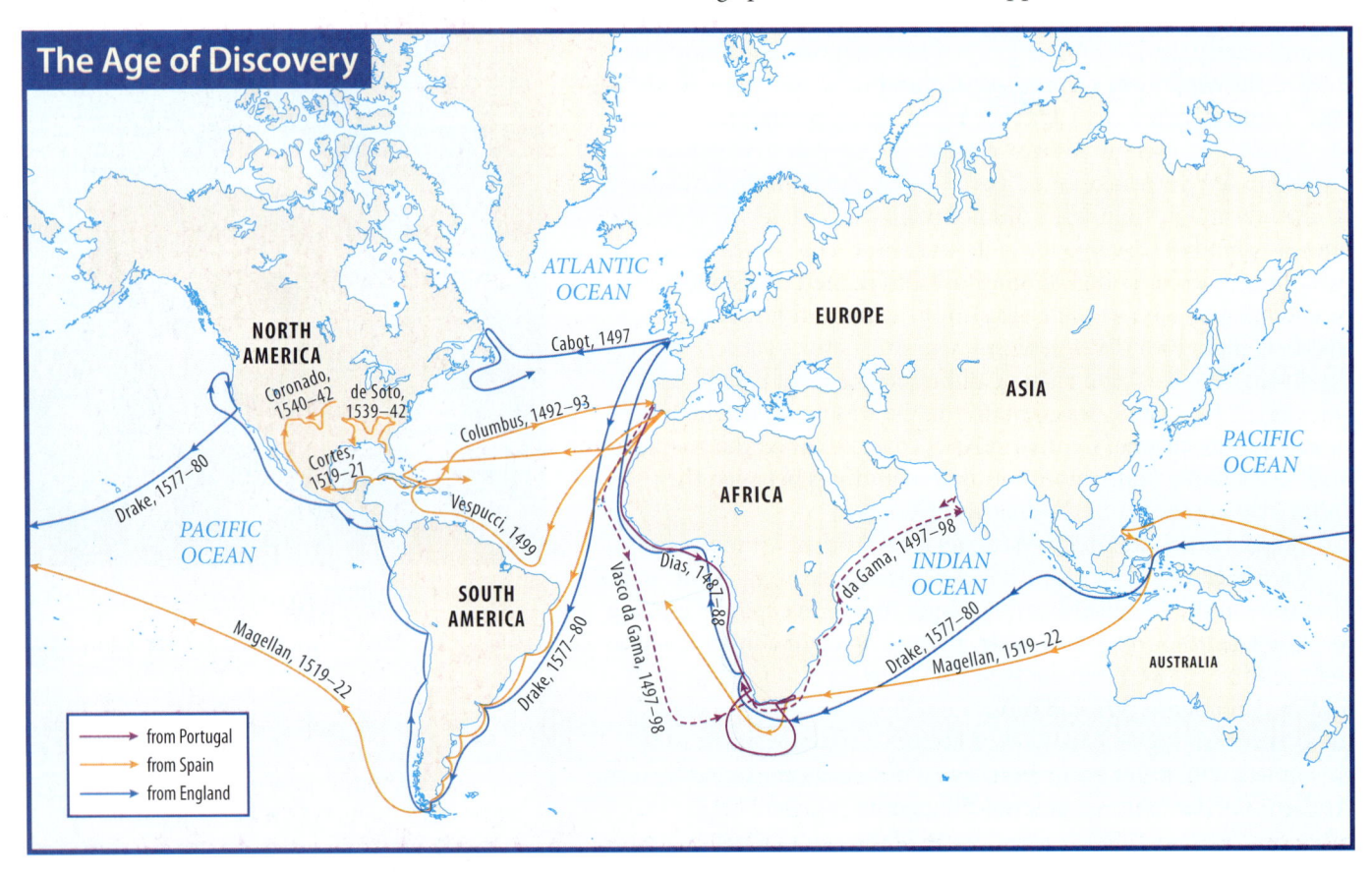

The Age of Discovery

The three remaining ships sailed through waters never before traversed by Europeans. A few years earlier, the Spanish explorer Balboa had first seen that blue expanse from a hillside in Panama, but Magellan's little fleet was now plunging through its waves. However, Asia did not lie just beyond the Americas. As Magellan continued to pursue an ever-receding horizon, provisions ran low.

For almost a hundred days the crew languished on the difficult sea. The stench of foul water and death hung heavy about the ships. Gnawing hunger drove the sailors to eat sawdust and leather from the ships' rigging. Rats became a prized dish. Although the three ships eventually reached present-day Guam, where the survivors obtained needed supplies, it was now painfully clear that a western route to Asia was impractical.

The ships sailed on to the Philippines, where a tribal squabble resulted in Magellan's death by poisoned arrows. Although he never lived to see it, one of his ships reached the Spice Islands and continued the voyage westward for home. Three years after Magellan's fleet left Spain, that ship, the *Victoria*, returned with only eighteen of the original fleet's crew. Their daring feat was stunning—they were the first to **circumnavigate** (sail completely around) the world!

Nearly five centuries later, the first circumnavigational voyage remains an incredible achievement. Magellan had revealed the size of the globe, yet for the time its vastness set limits on western trade routes. Increasingly, the focus would be on the Americas, a new world that offered new promise.

Religious Change

While Magellan's ships were making their global trek, a German monk named **Martin Luther** (1483–1546) was gaining the attention of all Europe. For centuries Roman Catholicism had dominated every aspect of European society. But by Luther's time the corruption of the Roman Catholic Church was apparent. Luther stood against these corruptions, but he was different from many others who sought reform.

Luther came to realize that the root of these problems was a false view of how people could be saved from their sins. The Catholic Church taught that God's grace flowed to sinners only through the Church's system of penance. Luther, however, preached that salvation was a work of God. God justified (declared to be righteous) those who trusted in Jesus' death on the cross and resurrection and who called out for salvation from their sin.

Eventually, Luther and others like him formed their own churches. These churches emphasized that Christians were free from the authority of Roman Catholicism. They also emphasized that Christians should not depend on others for their spiritual well-being. All Christians should learn to read the Scriptures for themselves and should know how to apply God's Word to their lives.

Luther's teaching called into question much about the Roman Catholic Church. And since the Church played a role in all aspects of European society, Luther's influence led to great changes in the culture of Europe. The movement that pressed for these changes was the **Protestant Reformation**. England, Switzerland, Scandinavia, and parts of Germany were the places most influenced by this movement. France and Spain were the most opposed to it. As the Reformation spread across Europe, theological battle lines often became actual battle lines. Some of the competition between

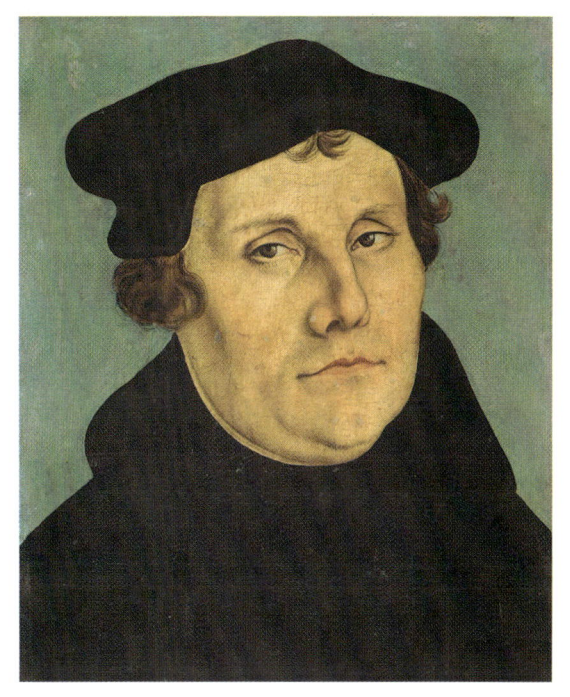

Martin Luther

This is an artist's portrayal of Martin Luther nailing his Ninety-Five Theses to the church door in Wittenberg, Germany.

John Calvin

English explorers and French and Spanish explorers was motivated by a rivalry between Protestantism and Roman Catholicism. Both religious groups saw the discovery of these new lands as an opportunity to spread their influence.

Geneva, Switzerland, soon became one of the leading centers of the Reformation. **John Calvin** (1509–1564) was Geneva's most influential teacher. Like Luther, Calvin taught that salvation was God's work and that sinners needed simply to trust in Christ. Calvin also attempted to restructure the society of Geneva so that every part of human life experienced the renewal of the Reformation.

Believing that a solid education was the best way to produce effective leaders for church and society, Calvin and many other reformers reorganized their educational systems. They emphasized universal literacy as well as advanced education for the clergy.

Calvin and other reformers also taught that every vocation was a sacred calling. For this reason the merchant, weaver, and carpenter needed to work steadily, waste no time, and do everything in moderation. As a result, cities that implemented these reforms, like Geneva, enjoyed a great increase in wealth and influence. Many Protestants interpreted this growth—seen by some historians and sociologists as an early success for capitalism—as God's blessing for obeying His will.

Although Calvin and other reformers emphasized that Christians should submit to their governmental leaders, Calvin did speak critically of certain kinds of government. Many reformers believed that monarchy tended toward abuse and corruption. A better form of government—one that would protect the liberty of the people—was a series of assemblies elected by the citizens. Geneva and a few other cities developed this kind of government.

Calvin's ideas proved to be very influential in Europe. In England especially, many Protestants desired not only to free themselves from traces of Roman Catholicism but also to reshape their society. Geneva was seen by many as a model city—the pattern for a new world.

Section Review

1–2. Who was responsible for stirring European interest in China before the Age of Discovery? How did he do so?

3. How did the Crusades affect European trade?

4. What name was given to the economic system during the age of exploration and colonization whereby colonies were exploited for the benefits and wealth they could bring to the mother country?

5. How did Columbus's plan for reaching Asia differ from da Gama's?

6. What was Martin Luther's main disagreement with the Roman Catholic Church?

★ Explain the innovations in technology that made exploration much easier for the Europeans.

★ How did the teachings of men such as Luther and Calvin support the ideals of (a) freedom, (b) individualism, and (c) equality?

II. Contacts in the New World

First Peoples

While these various Europeans were discovering and exploring unknown (at least to them) oceans and lands, other non-Europeans were living in their own developed civilizations in South, Central, and North America. In South America lived the Incas. In Central America, the Mayas and the Aztecs developed civilizations. And across North America were numerous thriving groups of American Indians.

Where had they come from? In the Far North, near the Arctic Circle, the massive continents of Asia and America each taper into slender fingers of land that stop just short of touching. Some historians think that sometime after the Flood, the ancestors of the American Indians entered the Western Hemisphere there. Some historians think they crossed the narrow **Bering Strait** in small boats or on foot over a bridge of ice. Other historians think that a land bridge connected the two continents, and that the peoples perhaps simply walked over it.

However they came, those Asian immigrants moved slowly southward. Eventually, their descendants settled the entire hemisphere down to the tip of South America. When the European explorers arrived in the New World, they found it already teeming with humans living in developed civilizations. Millions of American Indians were living in North America before Columbus made his discovery.

Historians of American Indians usually group them into tribes (several families sharing common customs) and culture areas (several tribes living near each other and sharing similar customs, means of livelihood, and levels of civilization). When the Europeans arrived in the New World, it was already inhabited by several major groups, each in its own culture area. For example, in the Southwest was the Pueblo civilization. In the middle Atlantic region and the Northeast was the Eastern Woodlands civilization. These groups of peoples shared certain common characteristics. Yet, each of them was different from the others in many ways.

Guiding Questions

1. What civilizations did Europeans discover in the New World?
2. What Spanish explorers made discoveries in the New World, and why was Spain's approach to governing its colonies unwise?
3. How did other European nations settle the New World, and how did English settlements differ from the Spanish and the French?

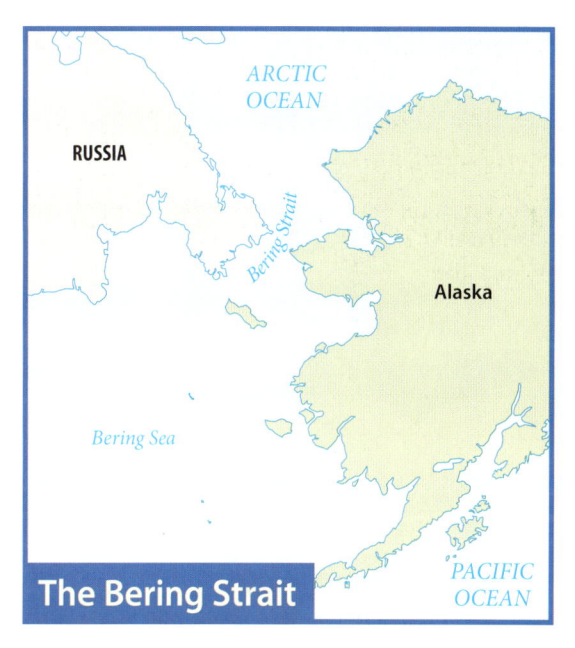

The Bering Strait

One difference among the various Indian tribes was the types of homes in which they lived.

The ruins at Tuzigoot National Monument in Arizona were the homes of Sinagua Indians, who lived in pueblos.

Other Pueblo Indians lived under overhanging rocks, such as these at Mesa Verde, Colorado.

Basic Groups of American Indians

The Pueblos—Probably the first North American Indians the Spanish explorers of the Southwest encountered were the pueblo dwellers. The word *pueblo* means "town." The **Pueblo Indians** lived in small villages made up of two or three family groups or clans. Some of the Pueblo Indians lived in caves along the rims or under ledges of canyons of the Southwest and became known as the cliff dwellers. Some of the tribes among the Pueblos were the Zuni, the Hopi, and the Taos.

The pueblos were independent of each other, and each town was ruled by a council of elected elders. The villages, though sometimes quite large, never developed into cities because of the lack of food caused by the dry climate of the Southwest. When one of the men married, he moved in with his wife's clan, perhaps building a new room onto or above the existing adobe (mud brick) house. Families that had too many sons dwindled, and those that had many daughters grew.

Pueblo Indians were farmers, growing maize (corn), squash, and beans. They also made baskets and pottery. They were basically a stationary people, but occasionally, they were forced to move to ensure an adequate supply of water. The Pueblos reached their "golden age" around AD 1000, but lack of water and frequent raids by neighboring tribes took a toll. A severe drought occurred from about 1275 to 1310. By the time Columbus arrived in the New World, the Pueblo civilization had declined significantly.

The Mound Builders—Two successive cultures developed in what is now called the Midwest: the Adena culture (1000 BC to AD 200) and the Hopewell culture (AD 500 to 1600). Their civilizations developed in villages along the Ohio River Valley and later spread eastward to the Chesapeake Bay area, New York, and New England.

These peoples lived in fixed agricultural settlements where they grew squash, gourds, and sunflowers. They also grew tobacco. Their agricultural pursuits produced bountiful harvests, and that large food supply sparked population growth.

These peoples lived in large dome-shaped structures of bent saplings covered with animal skins or bark. They were noted for the hundreds of large mounds they built; hence, they were called the **Mound Builders**. In the mounds, some of which measured more than 30 feet high and around 200 feet in circumference, they often buried their dead. The Indians also buried many artifacts in the mounds, but most of them, except for pottery and stone or iron tools, rotted in the damp soil. The most famous mound visible today is the Great Serpent Mound in southern Ohio, about fifty miles east of Cincinnati. It portrays a slithering snake more than 1,300 feet long. The snake's mouth is open, apparently swallowing a small round mound.

The Great Serpent Mound in southern Ohio is a splendid example of a burial mound.

The Mound Builders developed an extensive, almost continent-wide trading network. They obtained copper from Indians in the Great Lakes area, seashells and shark teeth from Indians along the Atlantic and Gulf coasts, quartz and grizzly bear teeth from the Rocky Mountains, and freshwater pearls from surrounding rivers.

Eastern Woodlands Indians—Another diverse American Indian civilization developed in the Southeast and along the Atlantic coast into the Northeast. These tribes were called the **Eastern Woodlands Indians** and were probably the first Indians the English, French, Dutch, and Swedish settlers encountered in the New World. The civilization's development began around AD 700 between the areas of Memphis and St. Louis and spread quickly throughout the Southeast, especially after 1200. They tended to settle along the rich bottomlands of the Mississippi, Ohio, and Tennessee rivers and developed tight-knit agricultural communities. The women grew corn, beans, squash, and sunflowers while the men were hunters and, when necessary, warriors.

These Indians had a matriarchal society, meaning that the women held power in the social structure and political decision making. They were a politically skillful people, not unorganized and uncivilized. In the Southeast, this group included the Cherokees, Chickasaws, Choctaws, Creeks, and Seminoles. Northern tribes of Eastern Woodlands Indians included the Mohawks, Oneidas, Senecas, Cayugas, Onondagas, and Tuscaroras.

At various times in early American history, these tribes were sometimes friends and sometimes enemies of the European explorers and colonists. Sometimes they helped the early settlers and sided with the colonists against the colonists' enemies. Other times they helped the settlers' enemies and warred against the colonists. As we shall learn in later chapters, the group as a whole gradually declined over the centuries as a result of droughts, famines, European diseases (e.g., smallpox, chicken pox, and measles), infighting, wars with the colonists, enslavement, and intermarriage.

The Spanish Century

Throughout the sixteenth century, the Spanish dominated the exploration and exploitation of the New World. From their Caribbean settlements on Hispaniola (begun by Christopher Columbus and his brother), Puerto Rico, and Cuba, the Spanish launched their conquests of the mainland. There in Mexico and Central and South America, the conquistadors discovered advanced civilizations, vast cities, and incredible treasure. Within a quarter century, the Spanish vanquished the Indian populations, amassing an empire that was virtually unrivaled both in terms of size and wealth.

Hernando Cortés was the first great **conquistador** (conqueror). In 1519, he and his fleet of 11 ships reached Mexico with strict orders from the governor of Cuba to explore the mainland coast and proceed no farther. Cortés disobeyed. To reduce the potential for mutiny against his unsanctioned mission, and knowing he would be hanged for insubordination if he were ever forced to return to Cuba, Cortés ordered his ships run aground.

He marched inland with more than 500 men, numerous dogs, several cannons, and 16 horses. As he proceeded, he enlisted support from many Indian tribes that had been conquered by the strongest tribe in the region, the Aztecs. Many welcomed the Spaniards as deliverers from Aztec rule. Those tribes despised the Aztecs for requiring heavy tribute (payments) from them and especially for taking the best of their young warriors to offer as human sacrifices in their bloody rituals.

The great Aztec king, **Montezuma**, hearing of the Spanish arrival, sent representatives offering gifts. It appears that he thought that Cortés might be an Aztec god. The enticing gleam of turquoise masks, intricate gold figurines, and massive disks of hammered gold made Cortés decide he would conquer the Aztecs. He commented that he had a "disease of the heart that only gold can cure."

Cortés marched to Tenochtitlán (tay nahch tee TLAHN), the Aztec capital located on the site of modern Mexico City. He eventually crushed the Aztec resistance there.

Despite the advanced cultures of the Aztecs and other Indian tribes in Central and South America, they were no match for the military superiority of the Europeans. Cortés's experiences in Mexico were indicative of the clash of cultures that would lead to European dominance in that hemisphere. At one battle, Cortés's army was outnumbered an estimated one hundred to one; yet they were able to fight to a draw. Indians, equipped with spears and clubs, faced soldiers armed with muskets and artillery. Some of the Spanish soldiers were mounted on animals that the Indians had never seen—horses.

Far more devastating to the native populations than firearms were the European diseases, to which the Indians had little immunity. The Indian population dropped by an estimated 90 percent between the sixteenth and seventeenth centuries. In the West Indies, the destruction of whole Indian populations by disease created a labor shortage for the Spanish that would be forcefully remedied with the arrival of more newcomers—African slaves.

Spain did not confine its New World interests to Mexico and Central and South America. A number of conquistadors explored the vast hinterland of North America (southeastern, southwestern, and Gulf coast regions) hoping to repeat Cortés's seizure of Indian wealth. **Francisco de Coronado**, for example, commanded an

Hernando Cortés meeting Montezuma

Indians and European Diseases

The Indians had one enemy against which they had no known defense: diseases spread by the Europeans who landed in the New World. What we call common childhood diseases today—such as measles, mumps, and whooping cough—are generally manageable, fairly easily treated, and rarely fatal. Among a population that has never been exposed to them, however, those same diseases are often deadly. In addition to the diseases already mentioned, the Indians were exposed to typhus, cholera, influenza, and others. Perhaps the most deadly among them was smallpox, a disease that was finally eradicated in the late twentieth century.

West African Culture

From about 600 to 1600, a succession of empires—first Ghana, then Mali, and later the Songhai—flourished in West Africa. Each of the three was progressively larger than the previous one. West Africa was a land of thriving trade, diverse societies, and many rich states.

The empire of Ghana was located between the salt mines of the Sahara and the gold mines to the south. Ghana prospered by taxing goods that traders carried through the territory. Frequent wars, exhaustion of the soil due to continued cultivation, and the opening of new trade routes that bypassed Ghana led to the empire's collapse by the early 1200s.

East of Ghana, the empire of Mali arose. Its wealth and power resulted from controlling the salt and gold trade. Mali's empire reached its peak in the 1300s under the leadership of Mansa Musa (ca. 1280–ca. 1337). Musa's capital, Timbuktu, was a center of trade and scholarship. The prosperous city attracted doctors, religious leaders, and scholars. Timbuktu became known for its bustling prosperity and intellectual climate.

Along the Niger River, the empire of Songhai emerged. When Mali began to decline, the ruler of Songhai seized Timbuktu in 1468. He then pushed north into the Sahara and south along the Niger River; thus the empire extended farther than Ghana or Mali. With wealth from the north and south trade routes, various rulers of Songhai raised large armies and conquered new territory. They also built cities, administered laws, and supported art, architecture, and education. The Songhai became the largest West African empire in history. Songhai remained a powerful empire until 1591, when Moroccan troops shattered its army.

As in other parts of the world, slavery existed in African society. Often prisoners of war were held for ransom or became slaves of the conquering people. West African slavery changed with the arrival of Muslim traders who exchanged horses, cotton, and other goods for enslaved people.

West Africans knew little about Europeans before the 1400s. In that century, Portuguese traders established outposts on their coast. Unfortunately, in addition to trading a variety of goods, the Portuguese began purchasing slaves. At first, such transactions were limited to a small number of people bought from village chiefs, usually captives from rival groups. By the 1700s, that number rose dramatically as the demand for slave labor in the New World increased.

---

expedition that left Mexico in 1540 to explore what would later be the southwestern United States. Believing the Indian tales about the mythical Seven Cities of Gold, Coronado explored Arizona, New Mexico, Texas, and Kansas. That anyone in Coronado's expedition survived the four-thousand-mile trek in the extreme temperatures of the Southwest was an extraordinary accomplishment. His expedition did not find gold, but one of its parties did discover and explore the Grand Canyon.

Before the Spanish knew about what is today Florida, they had already established scores of settlements throughout the West Indies. There, and later in Central and South America, they discovered wealth, which they sent back to Spain in treasure fleets. Spaniards also made a number of attempts to settle the southeastern United States.

In 1513, **Juan Ponce de León** sailed northwest from Puerto Rico in search of more rumored wealth. He sailed up the east coast of the Florida peninsula and landed near present-day St. Augustine, claiming the area for Spain and naming it Florida. Some accounts say that he was searching for the legendary Fountain of Youth, although some historians have disputed this claim. Years later, in 1565, the Spanish established the settlement of **St. Augustine**. It

Juan Ponce de León

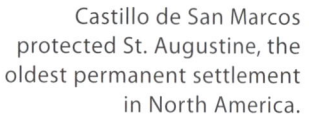

Castillo de San Marcos protected St. Augustine, the oldest permanent settlement in North America.

King Philip II of Spain

Sir Francis Drake

is the oldest permanent city settled by Europeans in the present United States.

In 1539, **Hernando de Soto** landed at present-day Tampa Bay, Florida, where he began a meandering trek through Florida. De Soto's journey took him as far north as modern Charlotte, North Carolina. Then, traveling through the Deep South, he eventually discovered the Mississippi River.

In later decades, the Spanish built settlements and outposts along the coast of Florida, Georgia, South Carolina, and Virginia's Chesapeake Bay, and as far west as Tennessee's Great Smoky Mountains. However, disease, hunger, and hostile Indians prevented Spain from becoming firmly established in North America.

Through their exploration and settlement efforts, the Spanish claimed much of what is now the United States. But Spanish rule was not beneficial to the new land; the Spanish preferred exploiting the land to developing it. To Spain, the New World was little more than a treasure chest to be looted, not a resource to be cultivated. Also, the government that Spain brought to the New World was harsh and dictatorial.

The Spanish and Portuguese also introduced to the New World a practice which would create problems that would not be resolved until the American Civil War—slavery. Not only did the Spanish enslave Indian captives, but the Spanish and the Portuguese captured and brought African slaves to their Caribbean island settlements. Eventually, those slaves were sold to colonists on the mainland of North America. The repercussions of that slave trade would be felt for centuries afterward.

International Competition

By the late sixteenth century, it was clear that it was easier for Spain to claim territory than to keep it. The shiploads of gold and silver that Spain was siphoning out of the New World heightened French, English, and Dutch envy of Spain and their interest in America. In addition, Spain's Catholic king **Philip II** (ruled 1556–98) was bent on crushing Protestantism in western Europe—and he had much success in doing so. Subsidized by Mexican gold and Peruvian silver, Philip's army was the largest, best-equipped in Europe, and thousands of Protestants were killed in its bloody wake. Bitterness over Catholic Spain's military threat made Spanish New World outposts a tempting target for Protestant sea captains, such as England's Sir **Francis Drake**.

Drake was the most famous admiral during Queen **Elizabeth I**'s rule. He and other commanders attacked and often robbed Spanish ships in the New World. They called themselves **Sea Dogs**. The Spanish viewed them as pirates. In 1577, Drake followed the course around South America that Magellan had first steered a half century earlier. Drake looted Spanish outposts in the Pacific and, failing to find a northern sea route back to the Atlantic, sailed from California westward to England. The circumnavigator reached England again in 1580, his ship laden with Spanish treasure.

In 1493, to settle a dispute over who could explore and claim new lands in the Western Hemisphere, Pope Alexander VI had divided the world in half, giving Portugal rights to lands east of the "line of demarcation" and giving Spain the lands west of the line. Protestant England scorned the pope's presumption that the world was his to divide. His ruling would have shut the English out of the New World. Drake was a strong Protestant and an ardent English patriot. Sailing for the honor of England, he was determined to challenge Spain's monopoly in America. After his circumnavigation of the globe, however, Drake's concerns about Spain would be much closer to home. In 1586, Philip II began amassing a huge fleet to conquer Protestant England. The outcome of this conflict would determine not only the fate of the island kingdom but also who would colonize most of North America—Catholic Spain or Protestant England.

In 1588, the **Spanish Armada**, 130 ships and about 30,000 men, entered the English Channel. Drake used fire ships to break up the Spanish formation, sinking a number of vessels. The Spanish admiral's attempt to outrun the English guns by sailing around Ireland ended when a fierce storm, which the relieved English later called the "Protestant Wind," destroyed much of Spain's fleet. Philip's dream of conquering Protestant England lay amid the wreckage floating off the rugged Irish coast.

The defeat of the Spanish Armada was both dramatic in its scope and decisive in its results. It secured the future for Protestants in England. In addition, it brought about the end of the Spanish century and the beginning of English dominance on the seas and eventually in North America.

The English Foothold

In the 1580s, a number of Englishmen, including Sir **Walter Raleigh**, compiled for Queen Elizabeth a list of arguments favoring the colonization of North America. They presented a number of advantages to settling the New World, including expanding Protestantism, boosting trade and national influence, reducing unemployment, and establishing military outposts to thwart Spanish dominance.

In 1584, the queen gave Raleigh permission to plant a colony in the land he called Virginia in honor of the unmarried virgin queen. Although Raleigh himself never came to North America, he sponsored an expedition of colonists to settle on **Roanoke Island**, located along North Carolina's Outer Banks. The colony was short-lived. After wintering on the island, the colonists encountered rough treatment from neighboring Indians and threats of a Spanish attack. As a result, the English abandoned the lonely outpost in the summer of 1586.

The determined Raleigh financed a second group to Roanoke Island in 1587 under the command of John White, a veteran of the

Queen Elizabeth I of England

Sir Walter Raleigh

This current road sign welcomes visitors to Roanoke Island.

John White returned to Roanoke in 1590.

Henry Hudson landed in present-day New York.

first expedition. White's group numbered about 115 and for the first time included women and children. Among them were White's daughter and her husband. White's daughter gave birth to a child shortly after arriving in the New World. That baby, Virginia Dare, was the first English child born in America.

Unfortunately, the colonists arrived too late in the summer to plant crops. With the prospect of a lean winter, they urged White to return to England for supplies. After he reached England, however, the war with Spain delayed his return until 1590. When White returned, the little colony had disappeared. All he found was a single word carved on a tree where the village had once stood—"Croatoan." The Croatans were an Indian tribe in the area. The fate of the "**Lost Colony**" has never been determined. Perhaps they were killed or captured by Indians. Perhaps they joined a nearby tribe. When Elizabeth I died in 1603, no trace of her colonizing efforts remained in the hostile wilderness that bore her name.

New France

The British colonies were significantly different from the Spanish and French settlements in the New World. Spanish America was a rigidly structured plantation society controlled directly and completely by the monarch, run for its profit and the benefit of the Catholic Church. Relatively few Spaniards came to the New World to live, and fewer families migrated there.

Similarly, the sparse French settlements in Canada, or **New France**, were largely dependent on the mother country for their success. The French king determined colonial policies and exercised complete control over his colonial subjects. In addition, the economic realities of New France did not encourage growth and independence. The long Canadian winters reduced most farming to a subsistence level, leaving little to export. And though the French fur trade was profitable, it was more suited for frontiersmen than farmers and merchants, which are key participants in a mature, productive settlement.

New Netherland

The area of the North Atlantic coast of North America that is now New York was discovered and claimed for the Dutch by **Henry Hudson** in 1609. The area was named

New Netherland, and its main town was named New Amsterdam (now New York City). The colony became a province of the Dutch Republic in 1624.

The most famous governor of New Netherland was a one-legged firebrand named Peter Stuyvesant (STY vih sent). He took control in 1647 and sought to protect the colony from potential Indian attacks. He became very unpopular for his heavy-handed rule.

In 1664, the English seized the colony, promising the citizens freedom of life, liberty, and property in return for their surrender. Stuyvesant signed the treaty ceding the colony, and it was officially renamed New York. The population of the area had grown from 270 in 1628 to about 9,000 (700 of which were black slaves) by 1664.

English Dominance in North America

As we shall see in the next chapter, the English came in greater numbers than their rivals to the south and north, and by the 1620s they were coming as families. They brought their English heritage with them. Their books were printed in London, their houses were styled after English architecture, and their schools were patterned after those in England. They also brought English political institutions. Significantly, in Queen Elizabeth's original charter authorizing an American settlement, colonists and their succeeding generations were granted the full rights of English citizenship—in the words of the charter, "as if they were borne and personally residuante within our sed Realme of England."

English patterns of self-government became an early, integral part of colonial life. In 1619, the Virginia colony at Jamestown (discussed in Chapter 2) established the House of Burgesses, an assembly modeled after the English Parliament. As other colonies developed, so did their political institutions. Living in relative isolation from the mother country, generations of colonists gained practical experience in self-government under a local political system that for them held more relevance than the royal government on the other side of the ocean.

Peter Stuyvesant was the one-legged, hard-nosed, and heavy-handed ruler of New Netherland until he lost the colony to the English.

Section Review

1–3. What were the three basic groups of American Indians that explorers encountered in the New World, and where was each generally located?

4. What European nation first dominated the exploration of the New World?

5–6. What great Indian empire formerly ruled Mexico? What Spaniard is responsible for conquering it?

7–8. Who financed the first two English attempts to settle North America? Where were these settlements located?

9. Which European power furthered its control over North America by promising Dutch colonists preservation of life, liberty, and property in return for their surrender?

★ Assess the impact of European diseases on Indians in the New World.

★ Why was the defeat of the Spanish Armada in 1588 important to the history of European settlement in North America?

People, Places, and Things to Remember

Marco Polo
compass
astrolabe
caravel
mercantilism
Bartolomeu Dias
Vasco da Gama
Christopher Columbus
Amerigo Vespucci
John Cabot
Ferdinand Magellan
circumnavigate
Martin Luther
Protestant Reformation
John Calvin
Bering Strait
Pueblo Indians
Mound Builders
Eastern Woodlands Indians
Hernando Cortés
conquistador
Montezuma
Francisco de Coronado
Juan Ponce de León
St. Augustine
Hernando de Soto
Philip II
Francis Drake
Elizabeth I
Sea Dogs
Spanish Armada
Walter Raleigh
Roanoke Island
Lost Colony
New France
Henry Hudson
New Netherland

CHAPTER 1 REVIEW

Making Connections

1. For the ten explorers listed below, answer the following two questions: For what country did he sail? Why is he most remembered?

   a. Bartolomeu Dias
   b. Vasco da Gama
   c. Christopher Columbus
   d. John Cabot
   e. Ferdinand Magellan
   f. Hernando Cortés
   g. Francisco de Coronado
   h. Juan Ponce de León
   i. Hernando de Soto
   j. Francis Drake

2. Why did many European nations practice mercantilism?

3. How did Martin Luther differ from others who sought to reform the Roman Catholic Church?

4–5. Why did the Protestant sea captains make raids on Spanish shipping? (List two reasons.)

Developing History Skills

1. Evaluate the cultural achievements of the Pueblos, the Mound Builders, and the Eastern Woodlands Indians. What do you believe were their greatest accomplishments?

2–4. Give three ways the English settlements in the New World differed from those of the French and the Spanish.

Thinking Critically

1. Respond to the following statement: "The defeat of the Spanish Armada had nothing to do with divine providence. We have no historical proof that God was fighting for England and Protestantism. It is true that this defeat helped Protestants, but many events in the 1500s hurt the Protestant cause. If God was fighting for Protestantism in 1588, why did He not protect the thousands of French Huguenots [Protestants] who were killed in 1572 at what became known as St. Bartholomew's Day massacre?"

2. Evaluate the exploits of Drake and the Sea Dogs (include the good and the bad about their endeavors).

Living as a Christian Citizen

1. You are Hernando Cortés. How should you deal with the native inhabitants of the Americas?

2. You are an English nobleman attempting to organize a colonizing effort in North America. You are trying to convince a group of devout Protestants to plant a colony in Virginia. Write an essay designed to persuade them to cross the ocean and establish this colony.

THIRTEEN COLONIES 2

An illustration of the Jamestown fort

> Being thus arrived in a good harbor, and brought safe to land, they fell upon their knees and blessed the God of Heaven.
>
> **William Bradford**
> ca. 1650, recalling the Pilgrims' arrival in the New World

I. Why the English Came

II. English Settlements Made Permanent

III. The New England Colonies

IV. The Middle Colonies

V. The Southern Colonies

Big Ideas

1. What motivated English settlement?
2. How did English settlements differ from other European settlements?
3. What characterized the New England colonies?
4. How did the middle colonies differ from other English colonies?
5. What characterized the southern colonies?

Guiding Question

What five motivations resulted in English settlers coming to the North American colonies?

The Lure of Land

The promise of abundant land drew many colonists to America. The charter colonies in Virginia and Massachusetts began under an arrangement whereby individuals were to work and share alike for the good of the colony. The absence of private ownership of property robbed the colonists of incentive and productivity, so the system was a failure. The companies soon reorganized to provide for land ownership. By 1614, each Jamestown colonist received three acres of land. With a seemingly endless supply of land rolling to the west, the Virginia Company later offered **headrights** (land grants) of fifty-acre tracts to those who paid for their passage or who fulfilled an **indenture** (work contract) for a specified period, usually between four and seven years. Nearly half of the arrivals to the colonies outside of New England came in this latter manner and were known as indentured servants. A man who was willing to work, no matter how poor he was when he arrived, received land, tools, seed, and, above all, opportunity.

King John signing the Magna Carta in 1215

Twice the English had tried to establish colonies on the Atlantic coast of North America. First, they had attempted to build a settlement on Roanoke Island, only to be discouraged by threats from the Indians and the Spanish. The next year they tried again to establish a colony there, only to have the inhabitants mysteriously disappear, leaving only the hint "Croatoan" carved on a tree. By 1700, however, the east coast of North America had become a "new England," dotted with many thriving English settlements. The story of this change is a remarkable one, and it has done much to define American culture. But to understand this story, one must begin by learning something about how the English viewed the New World and the opportunities there.

I. Why the English Came

Englishmen came to the New World for many reasons. Many of them were fortune seekers drawn by dreams of quick riches. The gold and silver never materialized, however, so the settlers took advantage of the many resources found in the New World. Tobacco, rice, lumber, pine tar, indigo, and furs became valuable exports, enriching both England and the colonies.

Some Englishmen traveled to the colonies for the opportunity to own land. In England, wealthy families held much of the land. Tradition kept a family from selling their land to anyone else, and only the firstborn inherited land. Younger family members and most other Englishmen had little hope of owning their own property. However, America had an abundance of available land.

Still other Englishmen desired political freedom, even though some already had a limited voice in their government. The Magna Carta, a document signed by King John in 1215, had limited the power of the English monarch. It also guaranteed certain basic rights to the nobility, but most Englishmen remained unprotected from government abuse. For example, James I and Charles I tried to strengthen royal power at the cost of personal liberty. As a result, many Englishmen went to America to escape oppressive leaders.

Religious freedom also became a powerful force in attracting settlers to America. Most of those who traveled to the New World for religious liberty wanted the freedom to structure their society so that every part of life experienced the renewal of the Protestant Reformation.

Many of those who became settlers had been frustrated when England's official church, the **Church of England** (also known as the Anglican Church), embraced aspects of the Reformation while continuing several Roman Catholic practices. Christians quickly discovered that English rulers were not interested in fully implementing the work of the Reformation. As a result, they viewed the New World as a haven where they could establish communities and complete the Reformation. This reason for settlement distinguished the colonial heritage of the United States from that of new colonies established in other regions.

One other reason some settlers came to America was a longing for adventure. However, most found hardships and great difficulty. While many of America's early settlers found plenty of adventure, the cost of life and success proved to be very high for the first colonists.

Section Review

1–5. List five reasons why the English and others came to America.

6. What political document guaranteed certain basic rights to some Englishmen?

★ Why did English believers become frustrated with the Church of England?

II. English Settlements Made Permanent

Sir Walter Raleigh's Roanoke expedition was the last individual effort of an Englishman to establish a colony. Later attempts were made by companies of individuals who shared the expenses of founding a colony, with the understanding that profits would also be shared.

Joint-stock companies, whose investors shared profits, provided a means whereby enterprises could obtain large monetary resources and remain free from the government control that accompanied government-sponsored projects. These companies provided a vehicle through which individuals could work together to establish new institutions in a new land. In 1606, King James I granted a charter to such a group, the London Company, permitting them to colonize Virginia.

Jamestown

The London Company (later renamed the Virginia Company) sent 104 men and boys to America. After a rough ocean passage, they reached the Chesapeake Bay in May 1607, where they found a wide inlet that they cautiously entered and went ashore. The Englishmen named both the river and their little fort after their monarch. **Jamestown** became the first permanent English settlement in the New World.

The first years were bitter ones for the colony. Malaria, typhoid fever, and dysentery (an intestinal disorder) took a devastating toll. By the end of the first winter, over half of the colonists had died in this hostile land.

Guiding Questions

1. What struggles did members of the Virginia colony endure and what is the significance of the year 1619 to this colony?

2. What three types of colonial administrations were developed by the British?

Jamestown

Captain John Smith

Indians of the Powhatan Confederacy also complicated the settlers' existence. At first, relations between the two peoples were friendly enough, but as the colonists began to clear more land, the Indians sent war parties to attack. A shaky peace came to the area in 1614 with the marriage of **Pocahontas** (POH kuh HAHN tus), the daughter of the Powhatan chief, to Englishman John Rolfe.

Typhoid was not the only fever to wreak havoc among the colonial ranks; gold fever consumed much of the settlers' time and resources. As a result, they neglected and even scorned planting and hunting. That attitude threatened the colony with starvation. Captain **John Smith**, however, enforced the kind of discipline necessary for the survival of Jamestown, drawing from the biblical principle of 2 Thessalonians 3:10—that only those who work should eat. Smith also improved the settlers' relations with Powhatan's men, who taught the settlers how to grow maize and melons.

In 1609, hundreds of new colonists arrived in Jamestown. Unfortunately, that same year a gunpowder explosion had severely injured John Smith and forced his return to England. The winter of

The Swashbuckling Career of Captain John Smith (1580–1631)

Captain John Smith is justly famous for his role in helping establish the Virginia colony, but his adventures there were only a part of his sensational exploits. As a teenager, Smith fled the dull life of a farm laborer in England to seek adventure as a soldier of fortune. He fought for the Dutch in their war for independence against Spain and afterward traveled around Europe looking for another war and an army in need of an experienced hand.

In 1600, he joined the Austrian and Hungarian forces fighting the Turks in Hungary, where he eventually rose to the rank of captain. In one glorious but gory incident, Smith took on three Turks in separate one-on-one combats and killed and beheaded all three. He was later captured by the Turks and sold into slavery. Sent to work in the fields of what is now southern Russia, Smith killed his Turkish master with a club used for threshing. After hiding the body, Smith donned his dead master's clothes, took his horse, and escaped into Russia. From there, he was able to make his way back to Europe, eventually ending up in England in time to join the Jamestown expedition.

As one of the leaders of the Jamestown colony, Smith had a number of encounters with the Indians. On one occasion, he and fifteen men on a trading trip were surrounded in an Indian village by more than seven hundred Indians. Quickly, Smith seized the chief of the Indians by the hair and clapped a pistol to the chief's chest. Fearing for their leader's safety, the Indians disarmed and traded peacefully with the Englishmen.

The most famous episode between Smith and the Indians (one which some historians still question) involved the Indian princess Pocahontas. As Smith related the story, the Indians captured him while he was exploring. The Indian chief had ordered his braves to club Smith to death when the chief's daughter, Pocahontas (only about thirteen years old), dashed out, cradled Smith's head in her arms, and begged that his life be spared. A somewhat indulgent father, the chief agreed, and Smith was spared.

Smith's adventures did not end when he left Virginia. French pirates captured him, and Smith spent several months sailing with them as they preyed on ships in the Atlantic. For the most part, however, Captain Smith spent his last years living in England, writing of his exploits, dispensing advice on colonizing to whomever would listen, and wishing that he could return at least once more to the New World for more adventure.

Pocahontas supposedly saved the life of John Smith.

"Precious Stink"

"Precious stink." That is how an early Virginian settler described pungent and profitable tobacco, America's first cash crop. The Spanish discovered the New World plant when they encountered Caribbean natives smoking *tabacos*—rolled leaves that they lit and inserted into both nostrils.

The Virginia settlers were the first to compete with the Spanish tobacco trade when, in 1614, John Rolfe sent a shipload of tobacco to England, where it received mixed reviews. Tobacco had reached England as early as Raleigh's first colonizing effort, but Rolfe's crop was a milder variety owing to his introduction of a sweeter strain of West Indies tobacco.

Many people believed that tobacco actually had medical benefits. A popular couplet of the time went "Divine tobacco! which gives ease / To all our pains and miseries." Actually, today we know that it is the source of a great deal of pain and misery. King James I objected to the colonial crop as a "noxious weed." Yet, despite its harmful effects, the "jovial weed" remained popular. Just five years after Rolfe's first shipment, Virginia exported forty thousand pounds of tobacco, and by the late 1630s that figure had skyrocketed to 1.5 million pounds per year.

Tobacco became so crucial to the Virginia economy that the price of goods was measured not in shillings or dollars but in pounds of tobacco. One person aptly declared that Virginia "was founded upon smoak."

1609–10 was possibly the worst trial the Jamestown colonists faced. It was known as the "**starving time**" because death due to hunger became a way of life. Settlers ate horses, dogs, cats, mice, and snakes. Some even ate the bodies of the dead. Roughly 90 percent of the colony died during that terrible winter.

In the spring of 1610, survivors planned to abandon Jamestown. However, when three supply ships arrived, they decided to remain. Although many more hardships awaited the settlement, the starving time was the toughest one, and they had grimly endured it.

In 1618, the Virginia Company of London granted colonists the right to elect a law-making body. That group, the **House of Burgesses**, became the first self-governing assembly in the New World.

A month after the representatives, called burgesses, undertook the business of governing the colony, a Dutch ship arrived at Jamestown. No one there could have foreseen its significance. John Rolfe simply recorded in his journal that "about the last of August . . . twenty [Africans]" arrived. The first Africans in British North America were treated like indentured servants, working for a period and then receiving their freedom. Gradually, though, racial distinctions were made among indentured servants, and blacks were placed in permanent bondage. Slave labor was later used throughout the colonies from New England to Georgia. That day in 1619, when those Africans were deposited by force on the banks of the James River, signaled the beginning of tremendous social division and moral tension for succeeding generations of Americans.

Another ship's arrival in 1619 held more immediate significance. Ninety eligible women arrived, available for purchase as wives for the cost of their passage. The price was 125 pounds of tobacco (which served as currency at the time), and sales were brisk. The establishment of families in Virginia brought a more settled aspect and a steadier growth to the colony.

One source of difficulty for the Virginians was Indian relations. As mentioned earlier, the initial tension between the Indians and the English eased with the marriage of Pocahontas to John Rolfe. The Indian princess converted to Christianity and even made a celebrated tour of England. Unfortunately, the trip ended tragically

Pocahontas

Virginia's governor sent Pocahontas, who had received the Christian name Rebecca, to England along with her husband, John Rolfe. She was an impressive advertisement for the London Company of Virginia. Dressed in rich fabric and lace, the Indian princess became a social sensation in London and even met King James I.

In 1617, she died and was buried in England. She was about twenty-one years old. Her infant son, Thomas Rolfe, received his education in England but then returned to Virginia, where he gained prominence.

Slavery in the New World

Shortly after arriving in the Americas, the Spanish began enslaving thousands of Indians. Unfortunately, many Native American tribes practiced some form of slavery long before the arrival of Europeans. In fact, it was not unusual for a conquering tribe to enslave war captives. As disease reduced the number of native peoples in the Americas, European settlers turned elsewhere for slaves.

Africans were soon transported in large numbers to North and South America. The truth about how these innocent people were forced to work as slaves is a shameful and tragic story. Their trip typically began with a forced march, often led by traders who were also Africans, to the West African coast. As they boarded ships, they were crammed as closely as the captains thought possible without causing them to smother. For weeks they were chained together, enduring dirty, stifling, and wretched conditions. They were given little food and drink. Sometimes contagious diseases, such as smallpox, spread throughout the ship. The death toll was often enormous, and those who died or became ill were thrown overboard.

Historians estimate that between ten and twelve million Africans were enslaved and sent to the Americas in the centuries after Columbus arrived. On the way, roughly two million died at sea. The Africans' journey to the New World was later called the **Middle Passage** because it was the middle part of the trade route taken by many of the ships.

Of the eight to ten million who reached the two American continents, more than three million went to Portuguese Brazil, while about 1.5 million went to the Spanish colonies. The British, French, and Dutch colonies in the Caribbean imported over three million to work on their plantations. Approximately 500,000 Africans were transported to the thirteen British colonies.

African captives in the hold of a slave ship

Middle Passage

Olaudah Equiano survived the horrors of the Middle Passage. Years later, after obtaining his freedom, he wrote an autobiography. The following is an excerpt from that book.

> At last, when the ship we were in had got in all her cargo, they made ready with many fearful noises, and we were all put under deck.... The stench of the hold while we were on the coast was so intolerably loathsome, that it was dangerous to remain there for any time, and some of us had been permitted to stay on the deck for the fresh air; but now that the whole ship's cargo were confined together.... The closeness of the place, and the heat of the climate, added to the number in the ship, which was so crowded that each had scarcely room to turn himself, almost suffocated us. This produced copious perspirations, so that the air soon became unfit for respiration, from a variety of loathsome smells, and brought on a sickness among the slaves, of which many died.

when she died from disease (possibly smallpox, pneumonia, or tuberculosis) on the eve of her return voyage to Virginia.

Not long afterwards, Pocahontas's father died. His brother became the new chief. On Good Friday morning, March 22, 1622, Indian warriors attacked and killed more than three hundred colonists. The battered Virginians gathered their forces and exacted heavy revenge. Later, another Indian attack on white settlers resulted in a treaty that restricted the area where the English could settle. The English soon violated that treaty, and the atmosphere of animosity continued between the two groups. Because of the Indian uprisings and the bickering among the Virginia Company's leadership, Charles I had the company dismantled, and Virginia became a royal colony in 1624.

There were three types or categories of English colonial administration: charter, proprietary, and royal. A **charter colony** was one governed by a trade company (such as the Virginia Company) that received its authorization from the king. Charter colonies usually enjoyed the most independence in their government. Under the **proprietary** arrangement, the king appointed a proprietor or proprietors (ultimately responsible to him) to govern a colony. A **royal colony** was controlled directly by the king, which meant that the monarch and his advisers appointed the governor directly. As the seventeenth century progressed, a number of charter and proprietary colonies became royal colonies as the king assumed increasing control over colonial affairs.

Section Review

1. Which Englishman tried to establish a colony on Roanoke Island?
2. What was the first permanent English settlement in the New World?
3. Who ensured the survival of that settlement by enforcing a biblical principle, and what was that principle?
4–6. Name and define the three categories of colonial government.
* After rereading "Precious Stink" in the margin of this section, assess the importance of tobacco to Virginia.
* How did the trials and successes of Jamestown manifest the core values of freedom, individualism, equality, and growth? What contradictions to these values began to develop?

III. The New England Colonies

The differences and similarities of the English colonies can best be studied by arranging and examining them geographically. The four northernmost colonies were known as New England. The four colonies immediately to the south of New England were known as the middle colonies. The remaining five were called the southern colonies.

Massachusetts

In 1614, Captain John Smith, who had been commissioned by the Virginia Company to explore the coast far north of Jamestown, found a region rich with furs and fish. Smith's account of that land, which he called **New England**, stimulated interest in the region.

The Pilgrims

The first English settlers to New England arrived in November 1620. The ***Mayflower***, swept off its course to Virginia by a fierce storm, anchored off Cape Cod, Massachusetts. On board the ship were a number of Christians known as **Pilgrims**. They had left their houses and lands and crossed an ocean to worship God freely. They showed extraordinary faith in the midst of the hardships they faced and the sacrifices they made.

To study the settling of Massachusetts by the Pilgrims and a decade later by the Puritans, one must understand the religious situation in England at that time. As mentioned earlier, the official church was a Protestant one, the Church of England. However, England's official break with Roman Catholicism resulted largely from political rather than spiritual concerns. This is not to say that the Reformation failed to have a spiritual impact on England. For example, William Tyndale translated the Scriptures into English. The psalmist wrote that "the entrance of thy words giveth light" (Ps. 119:130), and so it was in England. Thousands of copies of Tyndale's translation were distributed, and as the gospel was preached throughout the country, many came to trust Christ as their Savior.

However, many traces of Roman Catholicism remained in the rituals of the Anglican Church and in the conduct of its ministers. Two groups, the Puritans and the Separatists, emerged in opposition to those problems. The **Puritans** were a group of Anglicans who wanted to purify the state church from within by pushing for

Guiding Questions

1. How did the Pilgrims differ from the Puritans?
2. How were each of the New England colonies founded?

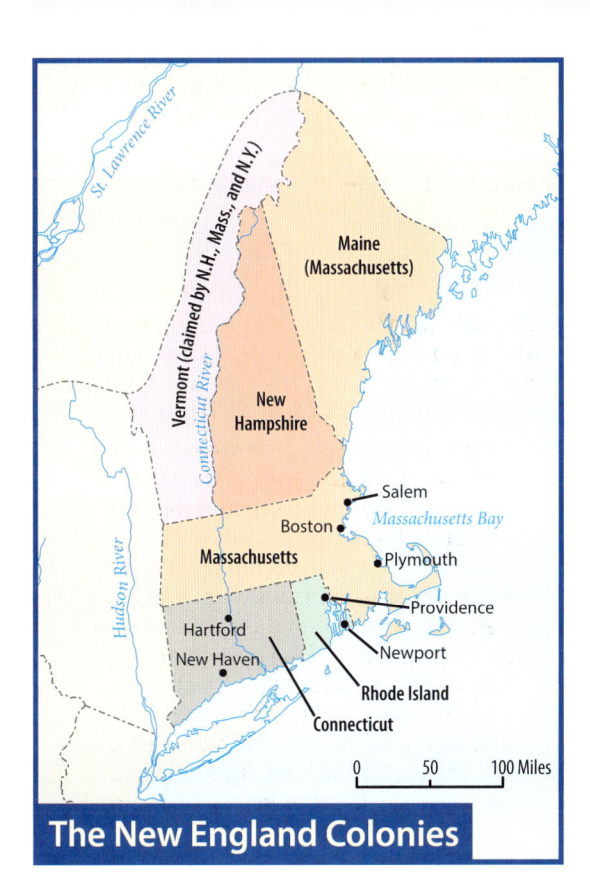

The New England Colonies

reforms that would rid England of Roman Catholic influences and bring greater spiritual vitality to the nation.

The **Separatists**, though agreeing with many of the spiritual goals of the Puritans, believed that Christians needed to separate from the official church. They thought each congregation should be independent of all other churches, free to worship and serve God without interference. Because the Separatists refused to attend Anglican churches and recognize the authority of the state church, they were harassed, and many were jailed.

In 1607, one congregation of Separatists from England migrated to the Netherlands (also called Holland) because religious tolerance there allowed them to preach and practice their faith freely. After a decade in Holland, however, they noticed that the Dutch language and customs threatened the preservation of their own language and culture among their children. In addition, the worldly atmosphere in Holland threatened the spiritual well-being of their children and their congregation. Because of these concerns and their desire to spread the gospel, they obtained a land grant from the Virginia Company to settle in the New World. Under the terms of the agreement, they would receive land and, most importantly to them, the right to worship freely.

The Pilgrims prayed for God's help as they set out for the New World.

A replica of the *Mayflower*

In September 1620, the *Mayflower* left Plymouth, England, bound for America. Aboard were 102 passengers, about half of whom were Separatists. Because of their travels, this particular group of Separatists became know as the Pilgrims. The Pilgrims referred to the other travelers as "strangers."

The ocean passage was stormy, and the little *Mayflower* was blown far north of the Virginia colony to Cape Cod, Massachusetts. From there, a second attempt to reach Virginia was also beaten back by a tempest. By then, it was November and scant provisions remained. Consequently, the Pilgrims decided to settle in Massachusetts. A scouting party went ashore and chose a site that Captain John Smith had named "Plymouth" during his New England trip six years earlier.

Because they were outside the area claimed by the Virginia Company, the leaders devised a contract of government to guide them. The agreement, known as the **Mayflower Compact**, bound the settlers to submit to the colony's laws and duly elected leadership. It was the first document of self-government in America.

Signing of the Mayflower Compact

William Bradford

William Bradford, who became governor of Plymouth in 1621, later wrote the history of the colony. In *Of Plymouth Plantation*, completed around 1650, he recorded the spirit, courage, and faith of those stalwart Christian families:

> Being thus arrived in a good harbor, and brought safe to land, they fell upon their knees and blessed the God of Heaven who had brought them over the vast and furious ocean, and delivered them from all the perils and miseries thereof, again to set their feet on the firm and stable earth, their proper element.

As the Pilgrims stood in the winter's chill at the edge of a hostile wilderness, Bradford recorded their plight as well as their quiet confidence in God.

> This poor people's present condition. . . . no friends to welcome them nor inns to entertain or refresh their weatherbeaten bodies; no houses . . . to repair to. . . . which way soever they turned their eyes (save upward to the heavens) they could have little solace. . . . summer being done, all things stand upon them . . . and the whole country, full of woods and thickets, represented a wild and savage hue. If they looked behind them, there was the mighty ocean. . . . What could now sustain them but the Spirit of God and His grace?

The first months at Plymouth were devastating ones. Half of the little group died before spring, including their first governor. Following that first winter, however, the colony began to prosper. Friendly Indians helped the colony raise native crops of maize (corn), pumpkins, squash, and tomatoes. Under the wise and godly leadership of their new governor, William Bradford, Plymouth gained a firm foothold.

Plymouth Colony grew steadily, though after 1630 it was surpassed in size and influence by the Puritans' Boston settlement. In 1691, Plymouth merged with the rest of Massachusetts, which by then had become a royal colony. The Plymouth Colony, however, had an influence that extended far beyond the bounds of seventeenth-century Massachusetts. As Bradford put it, "As one small candle may light a thousand, so the light here kindled hath shone unto many, yea in some sort to our whole nation." The enduring legacy of the

WILLIAM BRADFORD GOVERNOR AND HISTORIAN OF THE PLYMOUTH COLONY

BORN IN AUSTERFIELD, ENGLAND-1590
DIED IN PLYMOUTH, NEW ENGLAND-1657

Squanto and Samoset

In mid-March 1621 the settlers in Plymouth received a surprise visit from an Indian named Samoset. They were probably stunned when he greeted them in broken English he had learned from contact with English fishermen. A few days later, Samoset returned to Plymouth with another Indian named **Squanto**. Squanto had been in contact with the English since 1605 and had lived in England for a few years. In 1619 he had returned to his homeland and discovered that his tribe and neighboring tribes had been wiped out by a plague.

Squanto provided the settlers with life-saving information about crop fertilization in order to increase food production. He also led them to areas where they could catch fish and eels to supplement their diet.

In addition, Squanto worked to establish peace between the settlers and the neighboring Wampanoag tribe. His efforts led to a peace that endured for nearly fifty years.

The Pilgrims and Thanksgiving Day

Faith in God sustained the members of the Plymouth Colony through their tribulations. When God delivered them from such trials, they were quick to follow Paul's command to give "thanks always for all things unto God and the Father in the name of our Lord Jesus Christ" (Eph. 5:20). After the bitter winter of 1620–21, the harvest of 1621 was a welcome relief to the colonists. In gratitude to God for His mercy, Governor William Bradford proclaimed a time of thanksgiving in the colony, celebrated in October 1621. For three days, the colony celebrated reverently but joyfully. They feasted on the bounty that God had provided for them—vegetables (such as cabbages, carrots, turnips, onions, and beets) and wild game (perhaps including turkeys, but this is not certain). Around ninety friendly Indians joined the Pilgrims, providing fresh venison as their contribution to the feast.

A day of special thanksgiving to God by His people was by no means unusual. The Israelites' Feast of Pentecost and Feast of Tabernacles, for example, were both celebrations of thanksgiving for the blessings of harvest. Moses wrote, "And thou shalt rejoice in thy feast. . . . because the Lord thy God shall bless thee in all thine increase, and in all the works of thine hands" (Deut. 16:14–15). Christians throughout history have set aside special days of prayer, thanksgiving, and feasting to commemorate the blessings of God. However, the Plymouth feast—popularly regarded as "the first Thanksgiving" in America despite earlier such celebrations in Virginia—has become a part of the nation's heritage, an almost legendary event as famous as Washington's crossing the Delaware.

Though the annual celebration of Thanksgiving Day in America owes its inspiration to the Pilgrims, the official holiday is much more recent. President George Washington proclaimed the first day of national thanksgiving on November 26, 1789. Thanksgiving became a regular annual holiday in 1863 when President Abraham Lincoln made the last Thursday in November Thanksgiving Day. This remained the standard date until 1939 when President Franklin Roosevelt moved it back one week to lengthen the Christmas shopping season. Finally, in 1941 Congress officially set the fourth Thursday in November as America's Thanksgiving Day.

Pilgrims lies in their godly testimony, their pioneering spirit, and the way in which they defined America—as a refuge, a land of liberty for the worship of God and the preaching of His Word.

The Puritans

In 1629, the Massachusetts Bay Company received a royal charter to settle on land in the New World. In 1630, a fleet of about a dozen ships, carrying a thousand Puritans, arrived in America to establish the Massachusetts Bay Colony. This began a new phase of the colonization of North America. Over the next decade, some fifty thousand settlers sailed from England to various colonies in America and the West Indies. With the flood of new arrivals, a number of towns quickly emerged in Massachusetts: Salem, Dorchester, Charlestown, and Boston, the colony's seat of government.

The driving force behind the Puritan colony was its governor, **John Winthrop**. The well-educated leader dreamed of establishing a Puritan commonwealth where the Scriptures would direct the affairs of both church and state.

Winthrop's vision for Massachusetts was set forth in a sermon he preached aboard ship before going ashore. In his message, titled "A Model of Christian Charity," the governor underscored the purpose of the colony: it was to be a Christian community in the most thorough sense of both of those words—*Christian* and *community*. Every member of the community—pastor and parishioner alike—would contribute to the success of the whole. It was God's purpose that "they might be all knit more nearly together in the bonds of brotherly affection." Winthrop further declared that the colony had been given an extraordinary opportunity and responsibility to represent God: "We shall be as a city upon a hill. The eyes of all people

John Winthrop

are upon us. So that if we shall deal falsely with our God in this work we have undertaken, and so cause him to withdraw his present help from us, we shall be made a story and a by-word through the world" [from the Winthrop Society].

At the heart of this goal of establishing a community of believers was the Puritans' belief in the **covenant**. They believed they were in a covenant (legally binding relationship) with God. They were bound to obey this covenant if they were to receive His blessings. As a result they committed to build a holy commonwealth.

The Puritans set out to apply biblical principles to every aspect of their society, including their government and educational systems. In 1636, **Harvard College** was established near Boston to train young men for the ministry. One book about New England, written in 1643, included a section explaining the reason America's first college was founded:

> After God had carried us safe to New England, and we had builded our houses, provided necessaries for our livelihood, reared convenient places for God's worship, and settled the civil government: One of the next things we longed for and looked after was to advance learning and perpetuate it to posterity; dreading to leave an illiterate ministry to the churches, when our present ministers shall lie in the dust.

The Puritans emphasized the scriptural principles of working hard and not being lazy (Prov. 12:24; 13:11; 21:25; 1 Thess. 4:11; 2 Thess. 3:10, 12). They viewed economic prosperity as God's blessing and reward for their diligence. Some even concluded that this success implied they were God's chosen people. Sadly, many in the second and third generations did not establish a personal relationship with Christ and maintain the spiritual covenant of their fathers. Material prosperity replaced spiritual inquiry and dependence upon God. Just as Israel had done in the past, the Puritans failed to heed God's warning in Deuteronomy 6:10–15 about prosperity and the tendency to forget the Lord.

If the Bay Colony was, in Winthrop's words, "a city upon a hill," then it was a city that resembled those of England, an ocean away. Many Puritan officials in England immigrated to Massachusetts with their family and friends. These officials received town land grants from the Massachusetts Bay Company, which included authority to lay out the town and make property allotments. As a result, the settling of Massachusetts was more organized than that of other colonies.

Settlers continued to come to the Puritan commonwealth. As many as twenty thousand arrived in Massachusetts in the 1630s, and Boston soon became the largest city on the continent. Those colonists did not all stay in Massachusetts, however. Two factors—expansion and disagreement—led to the settlement of other colonies throughout New England.

Connecticut

Not everyone wanted to live in Boston. The boundless expanse of forest laced with rivers drew settlers farther west.

One of the most significant migrations took place in 1636, when the Puritan minister Thomas Hooker moved three congregations under his leadership into the Connecticut River Valley. Eventually, the settlements there united politically under the provisions of the Fundamental Orders of Connecticut (1639). This document,

One of the present buildings on the Harvard University campus

which has been called the first written constitution in America, established a framework for representative self-government in Connecticut. Although the Massachusetts Bay Company provided a well-organized system of self-government, Connecticut developed a more democratic order by not making church membership a requirement for voting.

There were some tragic events associated with the founding of the Connecticut colony. In 1636, several settlers in Connecticut were brutally murdered, possibly by members of the nearby Pequot Indian tribe. Colonial forces, assisted by Indians that were their allies, marched on a large Pequot village. They reduced the village to ashes and murdered four hundred men, women, and children. Pequots who escaped the fire and sword were captured and sold into slavery.

Rhode Island and New Hampshire

The expansion that resulted from a massive influx of settlers was one reason for the development of new colonies. In addition, disagreement with the Puritan leadership in Massachusetts contributed to the formation of Rhode Island and New Hampshire.

In 1631, **Roger Williams** arrived in Massachusetts and soon gained a reputation as a troublemaker for his unusual ideas. Williams declared that it was a "national sin" for England to take Indian land without paying. He also denounced his fellow Puritans for not severing all ties with the Anglican Church.

Williams preached about a "pure church." He was convinced that unbelievers should not participate in worship services. Williams taught that families should not pray together if some of the children were not believers. According to Williams, preaching and praying were worship activities reserved only for true Christians.

Since Puritans believed that their society had a special covenant with God, as was true of Israel in the Old Testament, they felt obligated to ensure a godly society. Williams disagreed. He thought God's relationship with Israel was a model for the church, not the state (government). Though he did believe that government should enforce laws prohibiting theft, murder, adultery, and other immoral acts, he advocated complete separation of church and state.

Williams did not want the state to support a specific church or doctrinal system. He also argued that a person's religious views should not affect his influence in society.

Several of Williams's ideas angered Puritan leaders. As a result, in 1635 the colony's General Court ordered his arrest and return to England. Instead, Williams fled the colony and wintered with Indians. In the spring, he and his followers established a settlement on land he purchased from the Narragansett tribe. Providence, the town Williams founded, later became the capital of Rhode Island.

Roger Williams was a key figure in the development of the modern idea of religious liberty. He felt that every person should be free to worship according to his conscience. Williams's radical idea was for the state to tolerate any religious belief. This concept does

Roger Williams with Indians who befriended him

not seem unusual today because it is the standard view of most Americans, Christians and non-Christians alike. Williams's idea of religious freedom was later included in the Constitution, and it prepared the way for the emergence of a religiously diverse United States of America.

In addition to Roger Williams, another leading dissenter (one who opposes official policy), **Anne Hutchinson**, eventually fled to Rhode Island. Hutchinson arrived in Massachusetts in 1634. Soon, she hosted regular gatherings at her home to discuss Sunday sermons.

Later, Hutchinson went far beyond simply reviewing sermons. She was teaching what Puritan leaders considered to be heresy (religious beliefs contrary to Christian teachings). For example, she proclaimed that outward obedience to the Scriptures was unnecessary to demonstrate an inward relationship to God. Furthermore, she taught that God had given her direct revelation that was more important than the Bible.

When the Puritan leaders attempted to counsel her, she was unresponsive. The General Court then voted to banish her from the colony. A few of her supporters went with her to Rhode Island, where they established a small settlement in 1638.

That same year, the first significant settlement in New Hampshire was established. However, it did not become a separate colony until 1679, when the king made it a royal colony. Before that time, it was controlled by Massachusetts.

Anne Hutchinson

Section Review

1. What was the difference between Puritans and Separatists?
2. Why did the English Separatists leave the Netherlands (Holland)?
3. Which dissenter settled in Rhode Island on land he purchased from Indians?
4. Which other dissenter also fled to Rhode Island after being banished from Massachusetts?
★ Reread the 1643 explanation regarding the establishment of Harvard College (see p. 29). Analyze that statement.
★ Since the Puritans had come to the New World to worship as they saw fit, why did they not allow dissenters the same freedom of worship?

IV. The Middle Colonies

No other segment of the colonies reflected the cultural diversity of British North America quite like the **middle colonies**. English, Dutch, Germans, French, Finns, Scots, and Swedes all found a home in the stretch of land from Long Island to the Delaware Bay.

New York and New Jersey

As previously mentioned, New York began as a Dutch settlement. In 1609, Henry Hudson sailed into an inlet and up the river that now bears his name. Although he did not find the Pacific Ocean he was seeking, he claimed the land for the Dutch (people from Holland), and it became known as New Netherland. In 1626,

Guiding Questions

1. What role did the Dutch and English have in establishing the colonies of New York and New Jersey?
2. Who was William Penn and why did he establish a colony?
3. How did Delaware become a colony?

Peter Minuit meeting with Indians.

a Dutchman named Peter Minuit "purchased" Manhattan Island from a group of Indians with cloth and trinkets that were worth about twenty-four dollars, and New Amsterdam (now New York City) was born. There were some problems with this "purchase." First, the Indian concept of ownership did not include fences or property deeds; land was often viewed as a common resource to be used by all. Second, the tribe that "sold" the land was not the tribe that controlled most of the island. Those Indians, therefore, must have thought it strange that Minuit paid them for something that they did not even own.

England was not content to have the Dutch as neighbors in the New World. Consequently, they invaded New Netherland in 1664. The Dutch chose to surrender rather than resist the larger force. The area was renamed New York, to honor James, the duke of York, who was the brother of King Charles II.

The duke of York gave the southern portion of his new territory to two friends. Eventually, that area became a royal colony and was named New Jersey.

Pennsylvania

More than any other colony, Pennsylvania was the product of one man's vision and labor—**William Penn**. He was a member of a religious group called the Society of Friends, or Quakers. Like the Puritans, the Quakers objected to the teachings of the Church of England. However, unlike the Puritans, the Quakers abandoned many biblical teachings. For example, they taught that all men have a spark of grace that makes them able to achieve salvation by doing the right things. They also rejected the office of pastor and the unique authority of Scripture in favor of guidance by an "inner light." Furthermore, some Quakers refused to respect the authority of government officials.

The English authorities were concerned about the social disruption such beliefs would cause, and they began to persecute the Society of Friends. Officials imprisoned Penn for a time. Following his release, he continued to write and preach. In 1681, as payment for a debt owed to Penn's late father, King Charles II granted the Quaker leader sole proprietorship (ownership) over a large section

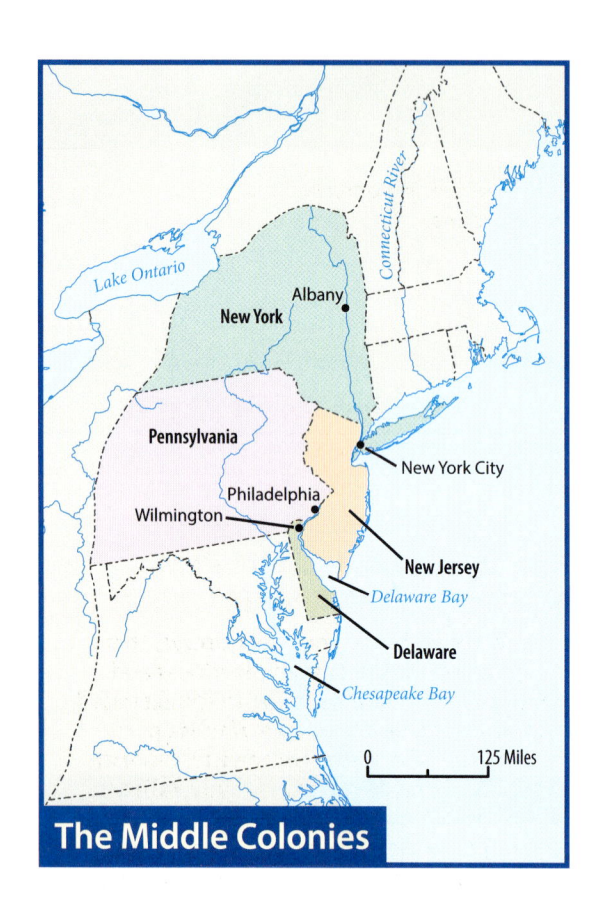

The Middle Colonies

William Penn arriving in Philadelphia

William Penn signing a treaty with the Indians

of land north of Maryland. The king appropriately named the forested area Pennsylvania (meaning "Penn's woodland") in honor of William Penn's father, a naval hero. That grant was the beginning of Penn's "Holy Experiment" in America. He sought to establish a society based on love, peace, and toleration.

Penn's constitution, Frame of Government of Pennsylvania, provided religious toleration and political liberty for the colony. His Quaker convictions concerning equality were reflected in his respectful treatment of the Indians. In fact, he paid the Indians for the land the king had granted him. He made friends with them and thereby avoided the attacks that were common in other colonies.

The open political and religious environment, the fertile land, and Penn's shrewd advertising in England and Germany attracted thousands to the colony. Philadelphia—the "city of brotherly love"—rapidly became an important trading center. As more and more non-Quakers moved into the colony, the Quaker ideals became less evident. The harmony that Penn hoped to achieve gave way to the hard realities of a diverse society. Even social evils such as slavery and the mistreatment of Indians began to intrude on Penn's dream of a blissful colony.

Excerpt from William Penn's Letter to the Indians

"Now I would have you well observe, that I am very sensible of the unkindness and injustice that hath been too much exercised towards you by the people of these parts of the world, who sought themselves, and to make great advantages by you, rather than be examples of justice and goodness unto you, which I hear hath been matter of trouble to you, and caused great grudgings and animosities, sometimes to the shedding of blood, which hath made the great God angry; but I am not such a man, as is well known in my own country; I have great love and regard towards you, and I desire to win and gain your love and friendship, by a kind, just, and peaceable life, and the people I send are of the same mind, and shall in all things behave themselves accordingly."

Delaware

William Penn's land also included what is now called Delaware. However, the settlers there resisted being ruled by Quakers in Philadelphia. The colony was eventually granted the right to form its own legislature and it became a separate colony in 1704. However, it continued to have the same governor as Pennsylvania until 1776.

Section Review

1. What nationality originally settled New York?
2. Which nation eventually took control of New York?
3. Describe William Penn's relationship with the Indians.
4. What was another name for the city of Philadelphia?
* Compare William Penn's treatment of Indians with that of Roger Williams.
* Why was Pennsylvania unable to maintain the Quaker ideals that William Penn envisioned for the colony?

Guiding Questions

1. How did the Carolinas become colonies?
2. What were two purposes for the founding of Georgia?

The Southern Colonies

V. The Southern Colonies

The third geographical division of the English colonies was the South. The colonies in this division were Virginia, Maryland, the Carolinas, and Georgia. Since Virginia has already been covered, this section will focus on the other **southern colonies**.

Maryland

In the 1600s, Separatists, Puritans, and Quakers were not the only groups that faced religious persecution in England. Roman Catholics also lacked religious freedom since the official church in England continued to be the Anglican Church.

The first group of settlers arrived in Maryland in 1634. Their proprietor was **Cecilius Calvert**, who held the title **Lord Baltimore**. His father, a Roman Catholic, received a large grant from the English king, Charles I. However, Calvert's father died before he could settle the land.

Calvert had two motives for planting a colony in Maryland: to provide a refuge for English Catholics and to make the colony a commercial success. In order to give liberty to the Catholics and still attract Protestant settlers, the colony's leaders established religious toleration through the Toleration Act of 1649, which provided that everyone professing a belief in Christ would have religious freedom. Since Protestant settlers outnumbered the Catholics from the very beginning of the colony's settlement, the act was indeed sensible.

The Carolinas

In 1663, the English king, Charles II, gave the land between Virginia and Spanish Florida to eight noblemen. The region these eight proprietors controlled was named in honor of the king's father, Charles I, and thus called Carolina (from the Latin *Carolus*, or Charles). Two areas of settlement emerged: the area to the north, called Albemarle, and the area to the south at a harbor settlement named Charles Town (later called Charleston).

The two regions grew separate from one another. In 1719, South Carolina became a royal colony. Proprietors continued to rule North Carolina until 1729, when it, too, became a royal colony.

Georgia

Settlement of this southernmost colony of British North America did not begin until 1733. It was the last of England's thirteen colonies. The British established Georgia for two purposes: to create a military buffer against Spanish Florida and to provide a colony where debtors, who often languished in English jails, could start a new life.

Georgia's founder, James Oglethorpe, wanted to focus more on reforming prisoners than on punishing them. He wanted to build a colony that would provide rehabilitation through opportunity and hard work. The first settlers in Georgia established Savannah, and a variety of settlers quickly followed the initial migration. Surprisingly, few debtors actually came to the colony.

The Emerging America

The vast Atlantic separated the thirteen colonies from England, and wilderness isolated them from one another. Isolation strengthened their love of freedom and encouraged their individualism. Every colony founded in America was the result of private, even individual, effort. Smith, Bradford, Winthrop, Williams, Calvert, Penn, and Oglethorpe had individual dreams of what America was to be, and they wanted to be free to live out those dreams. Of course, freedom and individualism can cause problems, as the Puritan fathers learned when dissenters, like Roger Williams and

Skull and Crossbones

"Blackbeard," whose real name was Edward Teach, was the most notorious of the pirates who plagued the settlements along the Carolina coasts. He had a long, black beard that he twisted together and tied with ribbons into little "tails." When he entered a fight, he carried a belt with six guns draped from one shoulder diagonally across his chest. He wore a fur hat and stuck a lighted match on each side of it to make himself look more frightful.

The Wesleys in Georgia

In 1736, John and Charles Wesley went to the new Georgia colony at James Oglethorpe's request. Both were still members of the Anglican Church. These brothers were two of the nineteen children born to Susanna Wesley.

On the voyage to Georgia, John Wesley was impressed by the faith of the Moravians aboard the ship. These Protestants, who traced their origins to the present-day Czech Republic, were courageous and kind. At one point, a violent storm nearly sank the ship. While the English panicked, the Moravians calmly sang psalms.

John pastored in Savannah but returned to England after a little less than two years. On his voyage home, he wrote in his journal, "I went to America, to convert the Indians; but oh! who shall convert me? . . . I have a fair summer religion. I can talk well; nay, and believe myself, while no danger is near; but let death look me in the face, and my spirit is troubled. Nor can I say, 'To die is gain!' I have a sin of fear. . . . Oh! who will deliver me from this fear of death? What shall I do? Where shall I fly from it?"

John Wesley

Charles Wesley

In May 1738, a few months after returning to England, he had a true conversion experience. Three days later Charles, who had spent only four months in Georgia, was converted in England. He wrote thousands of hymns in his lifetime.

Estimated Population of the American Colonies

	1640	1660	1680	1700	1720	1740
Virginia	10,400	27,000	43,600	58,600	87,800	180,400
Massachusetts*	9,900	22,100	46,200	55,900	91,000	151,600
Rhode Island	300	1,500	3,000	5,900	11,700	25,300
Connecticut	1,500	8,000	17,200	26,000	58,800	89,600
New Hampshire	1,100	1,600	2,000	5,000	9,400	23,300
New York	1,900	4,900	9,800	19,100	36,900	63,700
New Jersey	—	—	3,400	14,000	29,800	51,400
Maryland	500	8,400	17,900	29,600	66,100	116,100
Pennsylvania	—	—	700	18,000	31,000	85,600
Delaware	—	500	1,000	2,500	5,400	19,900
North Carolina	—	1,000	5,400	10,700	21,300	51,800
South Carolina	—	—	1,200	5,700	17,000	45,000
Georgia	—	—	—	—	—	2,000
Total	25,700	75,100	151,500	250,900	466,200	905,600

*The population for Massachusetts includes the population of Plymouth Colony before 1700.

Anne Hutchinson, insisted on their freedom to worship differently than the Puritans.

A stubborn streak of independence and a firm commitment to equality were common among the colonists. They believed that if people in England had their Parliament, it was only right for the colonies to have their own legislatures.

Life in the colonies could be hard—even short—but there was a newness about it, a sense of hope and opportunity that attracted thousands to America's shores to build their cities in the wilderness. There were certainly risks. But many considered the opportunity to own land and increase the influence of Christ's kingdom to be worth the risks.

Yet, full equality—at least as it is defined today—did not exist. Political power in some colonies rested only in adult white male property owners who were church members; only they could vote or hold office. Black males, whether free or slave, and Indians could not participate. Indentured servants did not own property, so they could not take part. Neither could women. Nonetheless, political freedom and power in the English colonies were open to more common people than in any other time or place.

Section Review

1. Who was the proprietor of Maryland?
2. What was the religious motive in planting the Maryland colony?
3-4. What were the two purposes the British had in founding Georgia?

★ Analyze the entry from John Wesley's journal and the information provided about the Wesleys. Why are their experiences so unusual?

★ Using the four core values of individualism, freedom, growth, and equality, briefly describe the emerging America revealed in this chapter.

CHAPTER 2 REVIEW

> **People, Places, and Things to Remember**
>
> Church of England
> headrights
> indenture
> joint-stock companies
> Jamestown
> Pocahontas
> John Smith
> starving time
> House of Burgesses
> charter colony
> proprietary (colony)
> royal colony
> Middle Passage
> New England
> *Mayflower*
> Pilgrims
> Puritans
> Separatists
> Mayflower Compact
> William Bradford
> Squanto
> John Winthrop
> covenant
> Harvard College
> Roger Williams
> Anne Hutchinson
> middle colonies
> William Penn
> southern colonies
> Cecilius Calvert (Lord Baltimore)

Making Connections

1. What role did religious freedom play in American settlement?
2–3. What consumed much of the Jamestown settlers' time and resources? Discuss the problems caused by this attitude.
4. In what way were the Mayflower Compact, the Fundamental Orders of Connecticut, and William Penn's Frame of Government each an important step in the development of American government?
5. Which geographic division of the thirteen colonies was the most culturally diverse?
6. With which of the thirteen colonies was each of the following men most closely associated?
   a. John Smith
   b. William Bradford
   c. John Winthrop
   d. Roger Williams
   e. William Penn
   f. Cecilius Calvert (Lord Baltimore)

Developing History Skills

1–2. Near what geographic feature did colonies tend to be established? Why?
3. Referring to Deuteronomy 6:10–15, describe how the Puritans failed to heed the warning that God gave the Israelites.
4. How does the above passage apply to your generation?

Thinking Critically

1. The Massachusetts Bay Colony and Pennsylvania took very different approaches to religious liberty. What are the benefits and liabilities of each approach?
2. Why was William Penn's dream of a blissful society in the New World destined to fail? Use Scripture to justify your answer.

Living as a Christian Citizen

1. In light of what you have learned about religion and liberty, use the Bible to respond to the argument that denying homosexuals the right to marry would be denying them fundamental liberties that heterosexuals possess.
2. Imagine that you are the founder of a new colony. Write a constitution that will provide the rationale and form of the government.

3 COLONIAL LIFE

"You would Do well to advise all poor people whom you wish well to take currage and Com to this Country it will be of Benefit to ther riseing generation."

Immigrant Alexander McAllister
ca. 1772, advising his cousin in Scotland to join him in North Carolina

The Copley Family by John Singleton Copley, one of the most famous colonial artists, portrays his wife, children, father-in-law, and himself.

Big Ideas

1. What characterized the early colonial population?
2. What types of diversity existed regarding colonial housing, diet, and education?
3. What occupations were common among the early colonial population?
4. What types of recreation were available to the early colonial population?

I. The Rhythms of Life

II. At Home

III. At Work

IV. At Play

Winston Churchill wrote, "History with its flickering lamp stumbles along the trail of the past, trying to reconstruct its scenes, to revive its echoes, and kindle with pale gleams the passion of former days."

Churchill, who is most remembered for his work as Britain's prime minister during World War II, was trying to describe the difficult but rewarding task of both the writer and reader of history. This chapter reconstructs the colorful scenes of daily life in colonial America. The colonial era, like any period past or present, is far more than the sum of its great leaders. The farmer and the merchant, the butcher, the baker, and the chandler—all of these played a role in colonial society. Observing their daily routines in their homes and getting a glimpse of their responsibilities as they work to make a living reveals much about them.

I. The Rhythms of Life

Patchwork Population

It would not have been unusual while walking the streets of the British colonial cities of New York, Philadelphia, or Charleston to hear conversations of German, Dutch, or French mingling with English. Although English colonists constituted a clear majority, there was a remarkable degree of ethnic diversity in the colonies, particularly after 1700.

The two largest groups of non-English settlers were **Scots-Irish** (also called "Scotch-Irish") and Germans. The Scots-Irish were Presbyterian Scots from the Protestant colony of Ulster in northern Ireland. Economic hard times and religious intolerance sent as many as a quarter-million Ulstermen to the colonies. Many arrived in Philadelphia, but most did not stay. Hungry for land, they migrated west and southwest, funneling down the Shenandoah Valley into the Virginia and Carolina backcountry. Their avenue through the wilderness was an old Iroquois Indian trail dubbed the **Great Wagon Road**. The trail, as significant as any of its better-known successors, such as the National Road or the Santa Fe Trail, was the chief access to backcountry settlements from Virginia to Georgia. Tens of thousands of settlers traveled the rutted pass by foot or jostled down the rugged road in wagons built by Germans from Pennsylvania's Conestoga Valley. A string of inns along the seven-hundred-mile road grew into backcountry towns such as Frederick and Hagerstown, Maryland; Winchester, Staunton, and Fincastle, Virginia; Salisbury and Charlotte, North Carolina; Camden, South Carolina; and Augusta, Georgia.

The Scots-Irish and the Germans were generally the leaders of Appalachian expansion in the early eighteenth century. Most of the Germans were Protestants from southwestern Germany. Thousands of them arrived in Pennsylvania, attracted by the religious freedom of

Guiding Questions

1. How and why did the Scots-Irish and the Germans settle in the British colonies?
2. Why did large families become common in the colonies?
3. What were some of the common causes of death in the colonies?

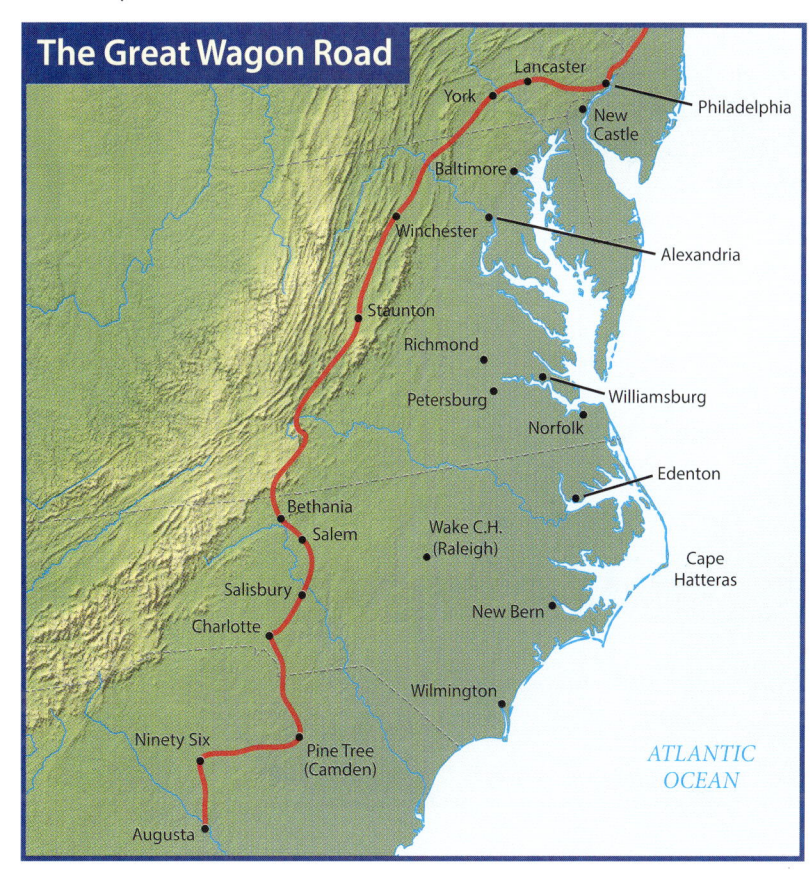

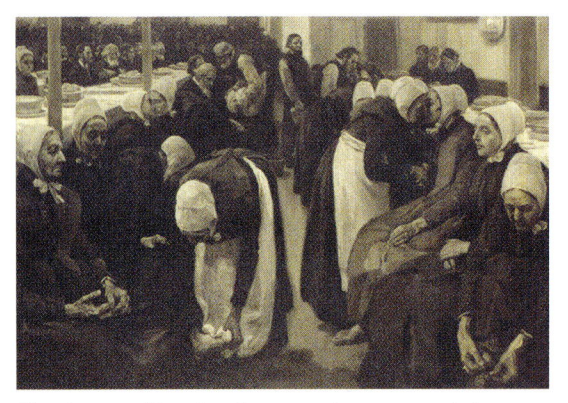

The German "Dunkers" were unique not only in immersing their converts but also for their "love feasts," or their commemoration of the Lord's Supper, and their practice of footwashing.

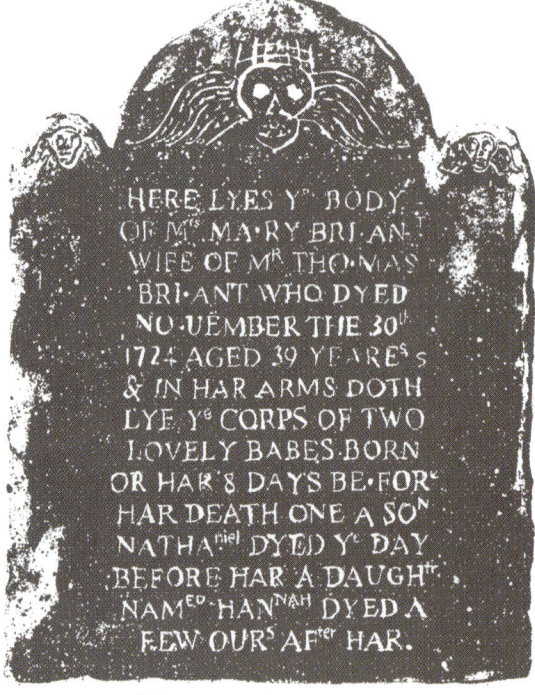

This 1724 epitaph of a Massachusetts wife tells an all-too-familiar story of the day.

This tombstone honors three children from the same Massachusetts family. They all died in April 1792.

Penn's Quaker commonwealth and the rich farm country that was so much like their homeland. This included German Baptists who were also called "Dunkers."

A number of German immigrants remained in Pennsylvania, where they became known as **Pennsylvania Dutch**. In this context, the word "Dutch" does not refer to people from the Netherlands, but to Germans. (*Deutsch* is the German word for "German.") Other Germans, however, followed the Scots-Irish into Virginia.

The rapid growth of German settlements bothered their English neighbors. The Scots-Irish at least spoke the same language as the English did. But Germans were different. However, German and most other European immigrants quickly adapted to English ways while maintaining their own traditions.

The blending of non-English cultures into the social landscape was an important influence in the development of America. A diverse society developed in which ethnic and religious differences existed together.

Marrying and Burying

The colonial population was not only varied but was also growing. In 1700, the population stood at roughly 250,000, and it increased during the next three-quarters of the century to 2.5 million at the outset of the Revolutionary War. Immigration was, of course, a contributing factor, but equally important was the high birthrate, which was twice that of Europe. In fact, in the 1790 census, more than half of all Americans were under sixteen years of age.

A key reason for the increase was that colonial women married at a younger age, usually around twenty. By contrast, their European counterparts married in their late twenties, if they married at all. Earlier marriages were prompted by the reversed gender ratio between the Old World and the New. In England, for example, women outnumbered men. But in the colonies, particularly in the late seventeenth-century South, men outnumbered women two or three to one. As a result, few women remained single, and earlier marriages meant more childbearing years.

Earlier marriages and large families were also favored because they provided an important labor source for the home. Ninety percent of the colonists depended on farming for their livelihood, and children provided helping hands and strong backs to put food on the table and in the market. Consequently, families with six to eight children were common, and it was not unusual for families to have a dozen or more children.

Unfortunately for our founding mothers, childbearing could prove fatal. Infections and difficult deliveries sent many women to an early grave, and their babies often followed them.

As serious as the infant death rate was in the colonies, it was dramatically lower than that experienced in Europe during the same period. The mortality rate there was grim—25 percent at birth and another 25 percent before the age of fifteen. Thus, half the children in eighteenth-century Europe never reached adulthood. By contrast, records from late seventeenth-century Massachusetts reveal that nine out of ten children survived infancy. The scattered settlements of the New World and America's productive and plentiful land restrained the disease and famine that were prevalent in Europe's crowded conditions.

This fact offers an important clue as to why epidemics were more prevalent in eighteenth-century America than in the previous century. As cities grew, crowded urban centers spawned contagious diseases. The problems of the Old World resurfaced in the New. Roads from the cities carried both settlers and germs to the frontier. Farmers bringing goods to the coastal market picked up not only exotic stories from the sailors they met there but also exotic diseases.

Fighting Smallpox

One of the first men in America to urge the use of inoculations to combat deadly smallpox was Rev. Cotton Mather, a godly Puritan pastor in Boston. Mather read that exposing a person to a mild strain of smallpox would enable him to resist the full effects of the disease. However, early inoculation attempts were risky, even fatal, and opposition to Mather's new ideas was intense. Even leading physicians of the day opposed it. Finally, Mather was put to the ultimate test when his son Samuel developed the dreaded disease after being inoculated. In the following excerpts from his 1721 diary, Mather recorded the opposition to his pioneering efforts and his own personal struggle over the fate of his son.

[May] 26. The grievous Calamity of the *Small-Pox* has now entered the Town. The Practice of conveying and suffering the *Small-pox* by *Inoculation*, has never been used in *America*, nor indeed in our Nation. But how many Lives might be saved by it, if it were practiced? . . .

[June] 13. What shall I do? what shall I do, with regard unto *Sammy*? He comes home, when the *Small-pox* begins to spread in the Neighbourhood; and he is lothe to return unto *Cambridge*. I must earnestly look up to Heaven for Direction. . . .

[July] 16. At this Time, I enjoy an unspeakable Consolation. I have instructed our Physicians in the new Method used by the *Africans* and *Asiaticks*, to prevent and abate the Dangers of the *Small-pox*, and infallibly to save the Lives of those that have it wisely managed upon them. The Destroyer [the devil], being enraged at the Proposal of any Thing, that may rescue the Lives of our poor People from him, has taken a strange Possession of the People on this Occasion. They rave, they rail, they blaspheme; they talk not only like Ideots but also like *Franticks*. And not only the Physician who began the Experiment, but I also am an Object of Fury. . . .

[August] 1. Full of Distress about *Sammy*; He begs to have his Life saved, by receiving the *Small-Pox*, in the way of *Inoculation*, whereof our Neighbourhood has had no less than ten remarkable Experiments; and if he should after all die by receiving it in the common Way, how can I answer it? On the other Side, our People, who have Satan remarkably filling their Hearts and their Tongues, will go on with infinite Prejudices against me and my Ministry, if I suffer this Operation upon the Child. . . .

15. My dear *Sammy*, is now under the Operation of receiving the *Small-Pox* in the way of *Transplantation*. The Success of the Experiment among my Neighbours, as well as abroad in the World . . . [has] made me think, that I could not answer it unto God, if I neglected it. . . .

25. Friday. It is very critical Time with me, a Time of unspeakable Trouble and Anguish. My dear *Sammy*, has this Week had a dangerous and threatening Fever come upon him, which is beyond what the *Inoculation* for the *Small-Pox* has hitherto brought upon my Subjects of it. In this Distress, I have cried unto the Lord, and He has answered with a Measure of Restraint upon the Fever. The Eruption proceeds, and he proves pretty full, and has not the best sort, and some Degree of his Fever holds him. His Condition is very hazardous. . . .

[September] 5. *Sammy* recovering Strength. I must now earnestly put him on considering, what he shall render to the Lord! Use exquisite Methods that he may come Gold out of the Fire. . . .

[November] 19. Certainly it becomes me and concerns me, to do something very considerable, in a way of Gratitude unto GOD MY SAVIOUR, for the astonishing Deliverance, which He did the last Week bestow upon me, and upon what belong'd unto me.

When the epidemic was over, Mather was largely vindicated. His son, Samuel, had been inoculated and survived. Although the vaccine had proved fatal for 3 percent of those who received it, 15 percent of those who were not inoculated had died. Unfortunately, in 1758 the great Puritan minister, Jonathan Edwards, was one of those who died as a result of a smallpox inoculation.

Epidemics of smallpox and dysentery, an intestinal infection, reduced the population in New England by as much as 10 percent during major outbreaks. Diphtheria, a serious infection of the nose and throat, began in New Hampshire and spread southward into the middle colonies from 1735 to 1737. The epidemic left thousands dead. Children were particularly susceptible to the virus; nearly all of the victims were under twenty years of age.

Despite such problems, the colonies generally flourished. The abundance of land invited expansion, and young men reaching adulthood usually married and moved on. The majority of families were isolated and largely self-sufficient. The husband, his wife, and their children shared the hardships and the rewards of building a home in the wilderness.

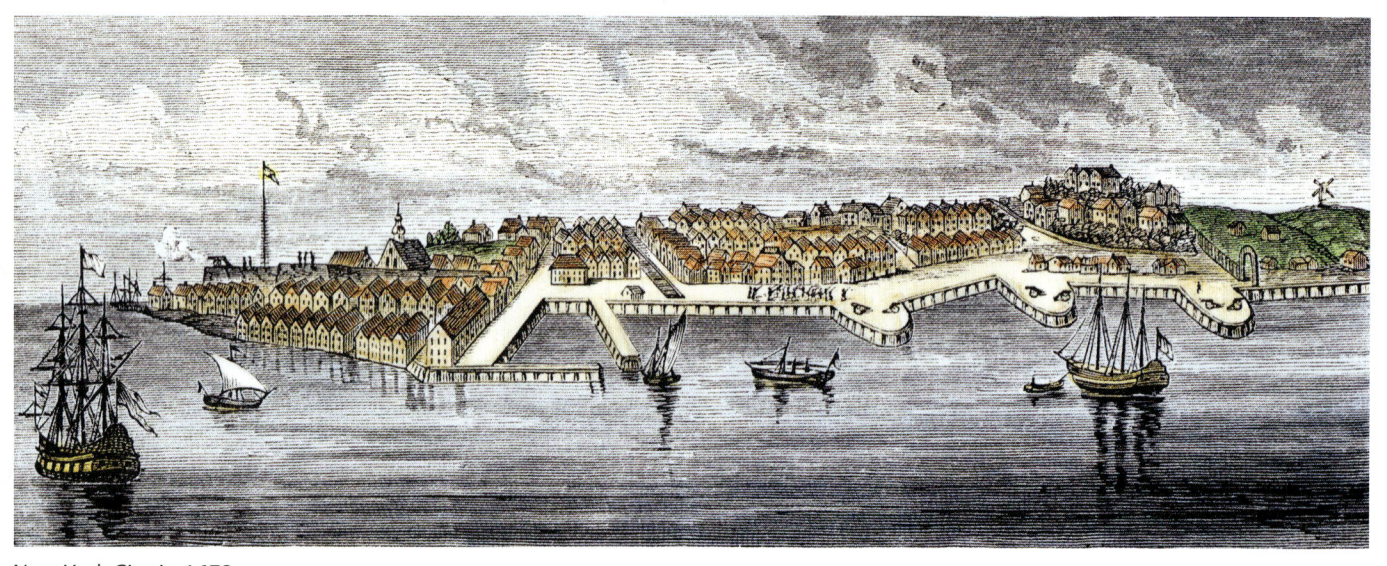

New York City in 1673

Section Review

1. What were the two largest groups of non-English settlers in the colonies?
2–3. Who were the "Pennsylvania Dutch"? Why did they settle in Pennsylvania?
4. Why did so many colonists prefer large families?
★ Why were epidemics more prevalent in eighteenth-century America than in the previous century?
★ What effect do you think the prominence of death and disease had on the colonists?

II. At Home

Housing

Styles of colonial houses changed based on the time period, region, and the cultural heritage of each house's occupants. With the earliest houses, however, survival was more important than style. To weather their first wilderness winter, many Plymouth settlers dug out caves and lined the walls with bark, or some copied their Indian neighbors by constructing wigwams.

As a colony took on a more settled aspect, its residents built houses patterned after the styles they had known in England. Isolated by an ocean from the old country, the colonists were out of

Guiding Questions

1. What characterized colonial housing?
2. How was the colonial diet influenced by the New World and Europe?
3. Why was education important to the colonists, and what were the typical forms of colonial education?

touch with the architectural trends of seventeenth-century England. As a result, what is now considered **colonial-style** or Williamsburg-style architecture—steep gabled roofs, tall brick chimneys, brick arches over doors and windows, and interiors with exposed beam ceilings—was really the century-old English Tudor-style construction.

The image of all Southern plantation homes as sprawling, white mansions accented with magnolias and stately, wide verandas is inaccurate. Since a plantation was a large farm, the planter's house could best be described as a large farmhouse. Of course, there were elaborate exceptions, particularly in the early nineteenth century, but most Southern planters lived in a simple log or clapboard house. As their families and incomes grew, they added more rooms and elaborated on the structure—for example, replacing the translucent oiled paper windows with glass. Another popular addition to colonial plantation houses was the *piazza*, or roofed porch, that provided some protection from the hot southern sun.

In the backcountry, shelters reflected the roughness of the land and its people. One observer recorded that during the first year or two, the Scots-Irish lived in crude and cold "open Logg Cabbins," open-faced, three-sided log structures with a roof. After they were established, they generally built a cabin of notched logs, filling the cracks with moss and clay. German settlers generally squared up their logs and located the chimney in the middle of the cabin to centralize the heat source. The result was a tighter, tidier house.

Diet

The adage "you are what you eat" would certainly hold true in the colonial period, at least in terms of social standing. At a 1769 meeting of the Old Colony Club in Plymouth, Massachusetts, the menu featured nine courses: baked Indian whortleberry pudding, steaming succotash (a soup containing fowl, pork, and corned beef), a dish of clams on the half shell, a dish of oysters and codfish, roasted venison, a dish of duck, a dish of cod and eels, spiced apple pies, and a final course of succulent cranberry tarts and cheese.

Such dinners were, of course, for the wealthy. On the farm, meals were much simpler. The standard fare for most families, particularly on the frontier, was salt pork, corn meal, Indian beans, and greens in the summer. The more settled farms often had an apple or peach orchard, a source of both food and drink. Hard cider and brandy were common beverages in the colonies; rum was more prevalent on the coast, where ports provided inlets for the West Indies liquor.

In terms of colonial cuisine, a great deal of trading took place. The first Europeans in America discovered a new world of food. Corn, a variety of beans (such as snap and lima), cacao (chocolate), tomatoes, squash, pumpkins, peppers, potatoes, and peanuts were all Native American contributions to the colonial diet.

Europeans also introduced foods to America: bananas, melons, rice, wheat, oats, and a favorite American beverage after the Boston Tea Party, coffee. An array of farm animals were also transplanted to America: cows, pigs, sheep, and chickens.

The Van Cortlandt House was built in 1748. It is the oldest building in the Bronx, New York City.

This colonial house is located near Lexington and Concord in Massachusetts.

Venison

A colonial meal

A hornbook

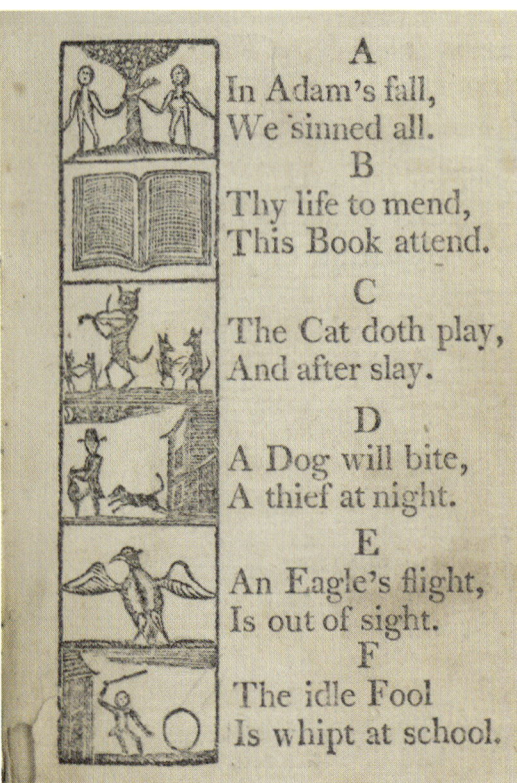

The *New England Primer*, the standard reading textbook in New England, tried to communicate the truths of Scripture while teaching the basics of reading.

In what rightly has been called a "green revolution," transplanted Indian crops of corn and sweet potatoes sustained burgeoning populations across the Eurasian landmass from Beijing to Belfast. From the early days of its discovery, America became a breadbasket to the world. Clearly God's providential hand has been at work in providing the blessing of food to a world population that has increased tenfold during the past four centuries. The psalmist rejoiced that the Lord "giveth food to all flesh: for his mercy endureth for ever" (Ps. 136:25).

Education

Whether children received their schooling at home or attended a village school, the primary reasons for education during the colonial period were to teach basic skills and the ability to read the Bible. This emphasis reflected the Protestant character of America. As one historian stated, "It was the Protestant Reformation, and the Protestant insistence that every man have free access to the Word, without priestly interference, that finally broke the Church's monopoly on literacy." The completeness of the church's medieval monopoly on reading and writing is underscored by the fact that during the five hundred years from the sixth to the eleventh century, very few English kings could sign their own names.

The Reformation not only created a spiritual revolution but also triggered an educational one, because an obvious prerequisite for reading the Scriptures is learning to read. In England, Puritan zeal for the Word of God and widespread spiritual hunger produced a boom in education in the early 1600s. This fact is particularly important in understanding the educational climate in Puritan New England.

It has been estimated that there was a greater percentage of college graduates in Massachusetts during the 1630s than there is today. Despite the hardships of the wilderness, the founders were determined that their children would not be deprived of an education. The home was the original schoolhouse in America.

A child's first "book," the **hornbook**, was a board shaped like a paddle. On its face was a card containing the alphabet and the Lord's Prayer. It was covered with a thin sheet made from an animal's horn for durability. A child usually graduated from using the hornbook to using a primer (PRIHM er) for more thorough reading training. The *New England Primer* served as the standard text throughout the colonial period. It provided basic grammar and vocabulary accented with moral lessons and also included a short catechism (instruction regarding Christian beliefs).

Not all colonial parents were capable of or interested in teaching their children at home. Particularly in New England, the concentrated pattern of village settlements contributed to the development of the village school. Such schools, open to boys and girls, were often called **dame schools** since they were generally taught by women.

Outside New England, two factors—geography and the lack of a Puritan presence with its enthusiasm for the printed page—limited the scope of colonial literacy. In the middle colonies and the South, farms were more scattered and families more isolated. As late as 1860, Virginia had 14 residents per square mile, whereas Massachusetts had 127.

The majority of people living in the rugged backcountry did not have the luxury of a village school; most of them lived days from the nearest settlement. If parents were illiterate, their children likely would be as well. Many parents, however, made extraordinary efforts and sacrifices to have their children taught, even if only through infrequent contact with literate travelers, indentured servants, or missionaries. Devereux Jarratt, born in poverty in colonial Virginia, recorded that the highest ambition of his parents "was to teach their children to read, write, and understand the fundamental rules of arithmetic." Jarratt, like others, after learning the rudiments of reading, would walk miles to borrow even a single book.

Although education in the backcountry was often inconsistent, those who could afford it hired private tutors for their children. A number of towns with greater resources made efforts to establish schools. Charleston, South Carolina, for example, sponsored two free schools for the education of the poor. Charleston also led the way in 1698 by establishing one of the first public libraries in America.

Old Deluder Satan Act

Leaders of the Massachusetts colony passed three laws dealing with public education in the 1640s. The most famous began with the words "that Old Deluder, Satan" and explained that illiteracy enabled Satan to prevent men from direct access to God's Word. The Puritans, along with other Protestants, saw the importance of being able to read and viewed a basic education as essential to an informed and Christian-influenced society. Other colonies passed similar laws. These laws became the foundation upon which others built compulsory public education.

Section Review

1–4. List at least four of the Native American foods that Europeans found in the New World.

5. Why was the literacy rate higher in New England than in the other regions?

6. According to the Old Deluder Satan Act, what enabled Satan to prevent men from direct access to God's Word?

★ Do you think including religious instruction in the *New England Primer* was a good method of instruction? Why or why not?

★ Evaluate the significance of the Old Deluder Satan Act.

III. At Work

The following section uses four fictional characters to portray work life in the colonies.

Louis Timothy, Rice Farmer
(Edisto Island, South Carolina, 1718)

Louis Timothy felt justly proud as the carpenters put the finishing touches on the clapboards which covered his log house. His wife wanted them white-washed, but that could wait until next year. Besides the cost, it would take time away from his work in the rice fields. For the young planter, the new face on an old house was a fitting sign of the success that had marked his path in recent years.

Though successful, they had not been easy years. Louis had arrived at Charles Town, South Carolina (later known as Charleston) as a lad with his family among a shipload of refugees. His father, the elder Louis Timothée, was one of the Huguenots. They were French Protestants who followed the Reformation ideas of John Calvin. Thousands of them fled France because of religious persecution. From Charles Town, the Timothée family made their way down the coast and found a niche of cheap land on the Edisto River.

Guiding Question

What types of labor characterized colonial life?

Their three-hundred-acre tract was not a pretty prospect when they arrived. Before them lay a tangle of swamp and sand covered with scrubby pines and imposing cypress trees. That first year their house was no more than a two-room cabin with a roof of palmetto palms and a floor of sand. Aside from a table, benches, and straw bedding, the house was bare of furnishings. During the first year, food, not shelter, was the priority. Vegetables were the first things planted to feed a hungry family. The daylight hours were spent wrestling a farm out of the wilderness.

The coastal flats had rich, productive soil, but the land had to be cleared by cutting trees and burning and digging out stumps. It was exhausting work, and the merciless sun beat down on the laborers, while mosquitoes and biting sand fleas, or sand flies, usually joined them in the field—sometimes giving them deadly fevers.

Louis's younger brother died during their second spring on the land. He was the family's first, but not its last, victim of malaria. The elder Timothée died of the fever in 1710 and was buried between his son and his wife. Charlotte Timothée had died in childbearing six years earlier.

Louis Timothy now stood surveying the land his father had conquered. He liked innovation. He had changed his last name and had moved from merely growing food for his family to cultivating rice to sell. That cash crop was suited not only to his land but also to the needs of his growing family and his own rising expectations.

Preparing the land for growing rice had been a tiring, back-breaking task. To undertake the work, Timothy had purchased three slaves in Charles Town, and they joined him and his eldest son in the field, along with two slaves that he had inherited from his father. Their first task was to turn the stream that flowed through the land into an irrigation canal that was needed to grow rice. The land itself had to be leveled and divided by a grid of ditches for flooding and draining. All of this labor had been done with hoes, shovels, and muscles.

In the spring, they planted the tiny rice seeds and then flooded the fields for a few days as the life in the seeds took hold beneath the warm cover of water. Through the summer the green shoots ripened to golden grain. By September, the rice was ready for harvest. With sickles flashing, Timothy, his son, and their slaves moved slowly through the fields cutting the rice. Sometimes the black men sang harvest songs in the strange tongues of Igbo and Mandingo, the languages of their native Africa in the happier years before they fell into the hands of an enemy African chieftain, then Dutch and British middlemen, and finally, Master Timothy.

This year's harvest would amount to forty bushels per acre. The cutting was only the beginning, however. The slaves would work until Christmas on the monotonous routine of flailing and husking the kernels. Timothy would oversee their work, as well as the cutting of timber and irrigation repairs. In late winter, he would gather his finished grain on flatboats for the Charles Town market. Louis Timothy would return with money in his pocket, as well as cloth, shoes, nails, tools, and a bucket of paint for his patient wife.

A rice field in South Carolina

This man is harvesting rice near Charleston, South Carolina. He is using the same methods used in colonial times.

COLONIAL LIFE

Debora Riedhauser, House Servant
(Germantown, Pennsylvania, 1747)

As the coals glowed and fired the crackling wood, Debora could see her breath in the frosty November air. The sun was not yet up over the Pennsylvania countryside when she began to prepare breakfast. The house was quiet—though it would not be for long when the children awoke! It was Debora's favorite time of her busy day, especially this morning because it was her sixteenth birthday.

Her master had promised her a pennysheet on her next trip to the market. After learning the hornbook, Debora had only dreamed of owning a book. The pennysheet was no book but was merely a page with pictures and words of wisdom from *Poor Richard's Almanack* by that witty Mr. Franklin of neighboring Philadelphia. Nonetheless, it would still be quite a treasure.

However, Debora's master, Josiah Hastings, had said nothing about her birthday. She figured he was probably thinking about her birthday in two years when her time as an indentured servant would end. Well, Debora was also thinking about that day—with mixed emotions. This had been her home for three years since she had arrived in Philadelphia from her native Germany. Debora was an orphan; her mother's death was only a vague memory, and her

Poor Richard's Almanack

One of the most popular reading pastimes of the late colonial period was the almanac, and none surpassed Benjamin Franklin's **Poor Richard's Almanack**, which he published from 1733 to 1758. In addition to the usual astronomical and weather predictions, it was filled with sayings that emphasized thrift, honesty, and diligence. Even today, Franklin's sayings flavor our conversation. Here are a few examples.

- Fish and visitors stink in three days.
- Well done is better than well said.
- A spoonful of honey will catch more flies than a gallon of vinegar.
- The used key is always bright.
- Little strokes fell great oaks.
- If your head is wax, don't walk in the sun.
- Beware of little expenses; a small leak will sink a great ship.
- Pay what you owe, and you'll know what's your own.
- Three may keep a secret, if two of them are dead.
- Lost time is never found again.
- Haste makes waste.
- Early to bed and early to rise, makes a man healthy, wealthy, and wise.
- Keep your eyes wide open before marriage, half shut afterwards.
- Forewarn'd, forearm'd.
- Creditors have better memories than debtors.
- Glass, china, and reputation are easily crack'd, and never well mended.
- If Jack's in love, he's no judge of Jill's beauty.
- Plough deep, while sluggards sleep.

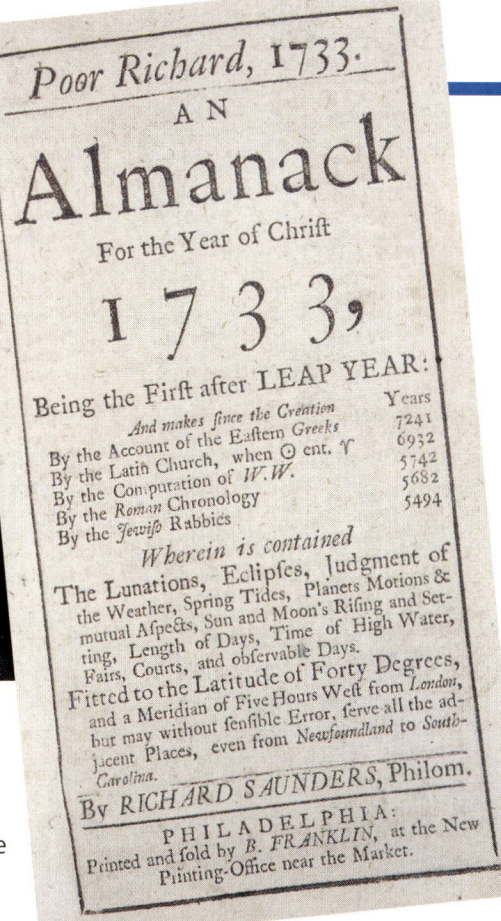

A plantation owner's family is shown visiting slave quarters in Virginia.

TO BE SOLD on board the Ship *Bance-Island*, on tuesday the 6th of *May* next, at *Ashley-Ferry*, a choice cargo of about 250 fine healthy NEGROES, just arrived from the Windward & Rice Coast. —The utmost care has already been taken, and shall be continued, to keep them free from the least danger of being infected with the SMALL-POX, no boat having been on board, and all other communication with people from *Charles-Town* prevented.
Austin, Laurens, & Appleby.

N. B. Full one Half of the above Negroes have had the SMALL-POX in their own Country.

This newspaper advertisement announces the forthcoming sale of Africans and stresses their freedom from smallpox.

father had been killed during one of the frequent wars that swept the German countryside. Her uncle, not wanting any more mouths to feed, had sent Debora and her two brothers to America. Their passages were paid in Philadelphia in return for five years of service. The purchasers, however, were indifferent to keeping the family together. One brother lived twenty-five miles away. Being a full day's journey apart, they usually only saw each other at Christmas. Her other brother had left with his new master down the Great Wagon Road and had not been heard from since.

Master Hastings needed young Debora as a house servant during his wife's long and uncertain recovery from complications with her last pregnancy. The baby had died, and Mrs. Hastings had been left far too weak to care for her four other children.

Stirring noises upstairs shook Debora out of her thoughts. She adjusted the Dutch oven, a three-legged covered pot, and dropped a cut of 'possum fat into it. Over the sizzling grease she poured a batter of cornmeal and sour milk to make flat johnnycakes.

The table was set with seven wooden plates, seven wooden cups, and seven wooden spoons. Debora had never even seen a china plate or a silver spoon.

The noon meal would be hearty but simple: dried apples, cold mush (cornmeal pudding), and hot cider. Supper would fill the house with smells of cabbage, cheese, sausage, and maybe a strong roasted chestnut brew to warm them before the night chill set in.

Between meal preparations Debora would milk the cow, churn its milk for butter, and weave linsey-woolsey (a mixture of linen and wool) for shirt cloth. Yet as little feet scampered down the stairs to breakfast, all of these things, like her life, lay ahead of her. For on her sixteenth birthday, this German orphan thought not so much about what the past had given her as what the future offered her in this new land.

Akachi, Former Slave
(Virginia and New York, 1750s)

Sweat pouring down his brow, Akachi heaved a barrel into the ship's hold. Only ten barrels were left, and then he could go take care of some of his other business. The New York sun was setting, and he would have to hurry if he was going to be on time to his meeting with the merchant.

Akachi was grateful to God to now be a free man, but the road that he had taken to get here was one of terrible suffering. When he was a boy, he was torn from his home in Africa by a neighboring Igbo tribesman and sold to Dutch slave traders. The "middle passage" of the journey from Africa to the New World was the worst time of his life. The slave traders kept Akachi chained and crammed in the ship's hold with many other slaves. Hunger, thirst, and the fear of death were constant. Akachi watched many of his fellow slaves die before they could reach the New World. In those dark days he had wished for death, but the providence of God had preserved him for a purpose.

Once in the New World, Akachi was sold and resold to several Virginia planters, and he labored long days growing tobacco under the hot sun. Some of his masters were kind, but one master in particular was especially cruel. He demanded that Akachi change his name to the European name Henry. When Akachi refused, his master forced him to work wearing chains until Akachi submitted to the new name.

Eventually a naval officer purchased Akachi. During this time Akachi learned to read. Few slaves were given this privilege. He learned much about the navy, and also during this period, Akachi became a Christian. He had heard the powerful preaching of George Whitefield in Philadelphia, and the message moved Akachi to learn more of Christ. He was converted and baptized. However, because he was a slave, Akachi had to sit in the balcony of church with the other slaves and could not truly fellowship with all the Christians in the church.

Later a New York sea merchant, John Bradfield, bought Akachi. Bradfield was a Quaker, and slavery bothered his conscience. So he allowed Akachi to do some trading on his own, and he promised to free Akachi if he could get enough money. Akachi worked hard because he could see an end to his bondage. After years of hard work, he eventually purchased his freedom.

Akachi often thought of his native Africa. He prayed that his friends and relatives there would hear the gospel. Perhaps some day missionaries would tell the story of Jesus to his people. He hoped they would be spared the horrors of both physical and spiritual bondage. He was grateful that he was no longer a slave to another man nor to sin.

Jeremy Shrimpton, Wigmaker
(Boston, Massachusetts, 1735)

The list of accounts in the large ledger brought a smile to Jeremy Shrimpton's lips—business had been good. His decision to move his business from his native London to the colonies five years earlier had paid off handsomely. Wigmakers were as much in demand in America as they were in Europe. Ever since French royalty started wearing wigs a century earlier, the powdered hairpieces had remained the fashion rage for upper-class males.

Now, however, even men with thick locks were being fitted for wigs. For many it was as essential to their business attire as a coat and tie would be at a later time period. Well, such attitudes were good for business too, Shrimpton mused, and the rising merchant class in Boston was as fashion conscious as any he had fitted in England.

Looking up from his shop window, Shrimpton could see the gleaming masts of ships anchored in Boston Harbor. Their owners were his best customers, so he always enjoyed seeing a busy harbor. A sharp rap on the door, however, interrupted his thoughts. Shrimpton opened the door to a rumpled farmer, probably in town selling produce. The wigmaker eyed his visitor coolly. He sniffed contemptuously and thought, *A backwoods bumpkin, he certainly has no use for a wig!*

In his thoughts, the poor farmer sniffed back, *Now here's a fancy little fellow, a real dandy.*

In their own way, both men were too professional to give words to such thoughts—the visit was strictly business. "Do you buy hair?" the farmer began. "My wife's going to sell hers."

Shrimpton nodded and followed him to a wagon where a tense little woman sat. The wigmaker ran his bony fingers through her

Typical cabin for slaves

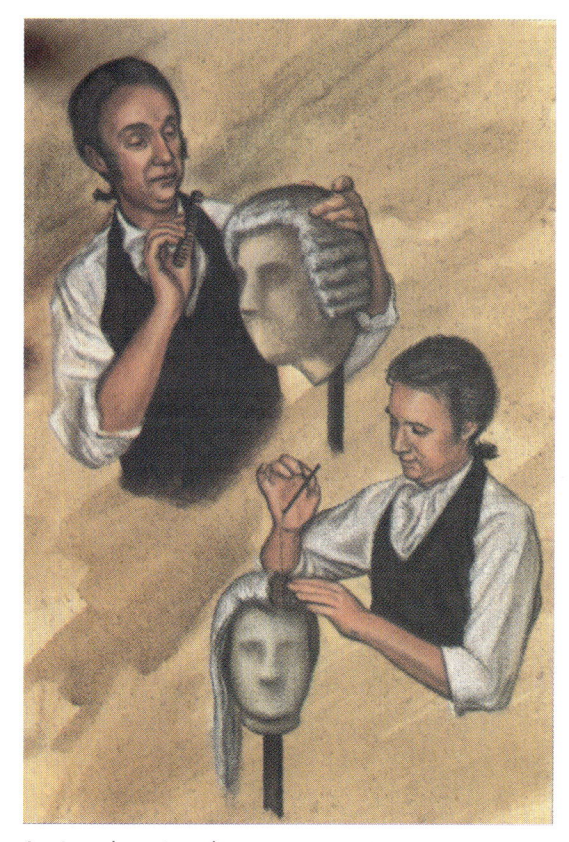

A wigmaker at work

George Washington did not wear a wig; however, he did powder his hair.

hair and held it up with an experienced hand. "Three shillings," he said to the farmer. With a nod the locks were snipped. After Shrimpton had applied his craft to these long locks, the hair would adorn the head of a merchant or minister who, unlike the farmer's wife, had more money than hair.

Jeremy Shrimpton made a variety of wig styles to suit the tastes and incomes of his clients. Common folks who wanted budget fashions could purchase a simple curled wig. The wealthy had several choices. All of the hair pieces were large, flowing extravagances. Their owners were not called bigwigs for nothing.

Wigmaking was a careful, customized process. First, a client would arrive at Shrimpton's shop for head measurements and style selection. Next, purchased hair was cleaned, combed, rolled, and baked in rye dough to temper and strengthen the hair. In the finishing stage, Shrimpton shaped the curls and "dressed" the wig with powder and perfume. The powder was added for coloring, of which there were a variety of shades from white or blonde to chestnut or black.

Despite the time and talent invested in making a wig, it seemed that a wigmaker's work was never done. Not only did he have new orders to fill but also old wigs to care for. On Saturdays, Shrimpton sent his two apprentices out to make house calls to rescue drooping curls and to refresh smelly wigs in time for Sunday worship.

For another generation, wigs remained essential to the well-dressed man. By the end of the century, though, wigs became a curious relic of the past.

Section Review

1. Which of the four fictional characters in this section—Louis Timothy, Debora Riedhauser, Akachi, or Jeremy Shrimpton—had the easiest time surviving in colonial America?
2. Which of the four characters had the brightest, most promising future?
★ Examine the many changes that occurred in Akachi's life. Summarize how these affected him.
★ How are the values of freedom and growth discussed in Chapter 2 seen in these narratives?

IV. At Play

Guiding Question

What forms of recreation did colonists enjoy?

People have several misconceptions about colonial leisure that must be corrected. First, colonial leisure time existed. Naturally, in the early years of settlement along the coast, the priority was survival; virtually the only contact among pioneers, in a nonwork setting, was on Sundays at church. When life became more settled, more leisure time was possible. This pattern occurred repeatedly as the frontier progressively moved farther west. This explains some of the differences between leisure activities in the cities and in the backcountry settlements during the later colonial period.

Second, early Americans did enjoy life during the colonial period. Modern views of the colonists (particularly the Puritans) as sour, gloomy people with dark clothes and dreary looks are inaccurate. Puritans had colorful wardrobes, listened to music, and enjoyed literature and wholesome games. The word *pleasure* was definitely in a Puritan's vocabulary. But what was also in his vocabulary was *consistency*. A godly believer did not forget his relationship to Christ during his leisure moments; rather, he honored Christ in them. He believed that God was to be revered in all things, not just at church.

As stated previously, leisure activities in the city areas and those in the backcountry differed. Since those living in cities were closer together, they had more opportunities to socialize and organize clubs and activities. Those who lived in the country, however, were scattered and isolated by many miles and sometimes swollen rivers and dense forests. Yet the backwoodsmen, being innovators by necessity, found ways to combine work and play.

Barn raisings, corn huskings, and quiltings gave opportunities for frontier families to gather and socialize while sharing the workload. At such events, adults exchanged news and children played with one another. The gatherings often culminated in a bonfire where people played music, danced, and spun tall tales.

Even worship services were social occasions in the backcountry. One Anglican missionary to the Carolinas, Charles Woodmason, complained in his journal, "No making of them sit still during Service—but they will be in and out—forward and backward the whole Time (Women especially) as Bees to and fro to their Hives."

Such infrequent social gatherings in the isolated backcountry stood in sharp contrast to the eastern cities of Charleston, Williamsburg, Philadelphia, New York, and Boston, where wealthy planters and merchants kept a full social calendar through countless clubs, balls, and parties. In Charleston, where wealthy planters escaped their swampy lands from May to December, a 1773 diary reveals a number of clubs that the movers and shakers could join, including the Smoking Club, Laughing Club, Beef-Steak Club, Monday-Night Club, Friday-Night Club, and the Fort Jolly Volunteers.

However, not everyone in the city was rich and famous enough for such exclusive merrymaking. Other city dwellers enjoyed bowling games on the village green, picnics, or trips to the tavern, where they could hear the news either through the usual story swapping or from a patron reading a newspaper aloud. Such newspapers, which became a part of colonial life in the second quarter of the eighteenth century, featured colonial happenings, advertisements, obituaries, and humor, as well as the "latest" news (usually several months old) from London.

Colonial newspapers were published in all the major cities; they included Boston's *New-England Courant*, Philadelphia's *American Weekly Mercury* and *The Pennsylvania Gazette* (published

Ben Franklin and His Water Tools

A little-known fact about Benjamin Franklin is that he conducted many experiments with tools for use on or in the water. An avid swimmer himself, he experimented with various flotation devices (he called them "swimmies") to help swimmers stay afloat or to rescue foundering swimmers. He also windsurfed using a kite for propulsion.

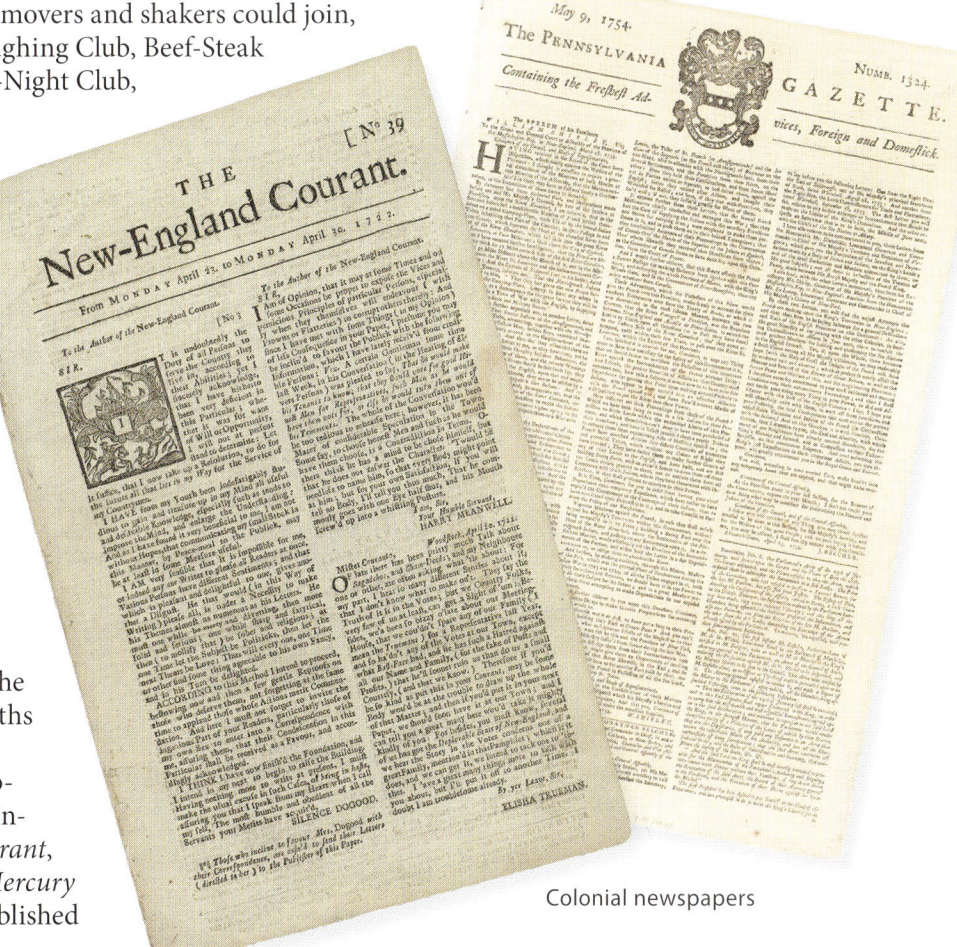

Colonial newspapers

by Benjamin Franklin), and Charleston's *South Carolina Gazette*. The papers filtered to backcountry communities by horse and rider, providing a much-needed break in the isolation of wilderness living.

The toys and games of colonial children included marbles, hoops, dolls, puzzles, hopscotch, shuffleboard, shuttlecock (badminton), and whoop-and-hide (hide-and-seek). Most toys were homemade, simple, and highly prized because a child generally had very few of them. A girl, for example, usually had only one doll during her childhood, often carved from a stick or made from a corncob. Swimming and fishing were popular in the summer, as were ice skating and sleigh rides in the winter when possible. Children of the wealthy could even take trips to the beach for swimming.

Children in colonial times played just as children today do, but they also worked at household chores much more.

The growing, varied leisure time of the period revealed an underlying fact—the colonies were maturing and prospering. Political and economic freedom led to material prosperity and the invention of time- and labor-saving devices, which allowed more time for the development and pursuit of the finer things of life and culture. The "starving times" seemed to be just a distant memory as the following generations built upon the foundation of their fathers. As future president John Adams explained to his wife:

> I must study politics and war that my sons may have liberty to study mathematics and philosophy. My sons ought to study mathematics and philosophy, geography, natural history, naval architecture, navigation, commerce, and agriculture, in order to give their children a right to study painting, poetry, music, architecture, statuary, tapestry, and porcelain.

Adams had a great deal of politics and war to study in the late colonial period. The colonies were blossoming, Britain's grip on them was loosening, and Americans were gaining a greater sense of independence.

John Adams

Section Review

1. What is the typical modern view of the Puritans? Why is that view inaccurate?
2. What are some examples of social gatherings on the frontier?
3. What are some examples of social gatherings in a colonial city?
4. List some of the toys and games of colonial children.
★ How did the Puritans reflect a Christian view of leisure?
★ Examine John Adams's quote. What do you think he meant by his statement?

CHAPTER REVIEW

People, Places, and Things to Remember

Scots-Irish
Great Wagon Road
Pennsylvania Dutch
colonial-style architecture
hornbook
New England Primer
dame schools
Poor Richard's Almanack

Making Connections

1. How did the Great Wagon Road help to develop the American frontier?
2. Why was the birthrate higher in America than in Europe in the 1700s?
3–5. Name at least three deadly diseases that American colonists faced.
6. Why was education so important to the Puritans?
7. What role did colonial newspapers play in spreading news to cities and backcountry areas?

Developing History Skills

1. Describe colonial-style architecture.
2. Considering that most frontier people lived several days' journey from the nearest trading outpost, how would that affect their daily lives?

Thinking Critically

1. Considering the danger of smallpox inoculation, would you have undergone such treatment if you had lived in colonial days?
2. Was it in the best interest of the Massachusetts Bay Colony to provide public education?
3. Is it generally good for government to provide education?

Living as a Christian Citizen

1. Choose a saying from *Poor Richard's Almanack* and write a brief paragraph telling why it would or would not be sound advice for a Christian to follow.
2. Review the quotation from John Adams and the story of Louis Timothy. What common principle can be drawn from them?

4 RELIGION IN THE AMERICAN COLONIES

And we are evidently a people blessed of the Lord! And here in this corner of the world, God dwells, and manifests his glory.

Jonathan Edwards
1736, *A Faithful Narrative of the Surprising Work of God*

Pilgrims Going to Church by George Henry Boughton

Big Ideas

1. What is an established denomination and what is a non-established denomination?
2. Which non-established denominations were prominent in the American colonies?
3. How did colonial Christians worship?
4. Was the evangelization of Indian tribes effective?
5. How did the Great Awakening affect the American colonies?

I. Established Denominations

II. Non-Established Denominations

III. Worship and Indian Missions

IV. The Great Awakening

RELIGION IN THE AMERICAN COLONIES

The tall, lean minister stood behind the wooden pulpit and faced his audience. He began his sermon, speaking in careful, measured tones. His words astounded his listeners. "There is nothing that keeps wicked men at any one moment out of Hell," he declared, "but the mere pleasure of God." He continued,

> O sinner! Consider the fearful danger you are in: it is a great furnace of wrath, a wide and bottomless pit that you are held over in the hand of that God, whose wrath is provoked and incensed as much against you, as against many of the damned in hell. You hang by a slender thread, with the flames of divine wrath flashing about it, and ready every moment to singe it, and burn it asunder; and you have . . . nothing to lay hold of to save yourself, nothing that you ever have done, nothing that you can do, to induce God to spare you one moment.

As the minister preached, some in the congregation cried out in fear, struck with overwhelming conviction. Others grew solemn. As the fear of divine judgment began to grip the audience, the preacher exhorted his listeners, "Therefore, let everyone that is out of Christ now awake and flee from the wrath to come."

The year was 1741, the speaker was Jonathan Edwards, and the sermon was "Sinners in the Hands of an Angry God." The Pilgrims' first Thanksgiving and Edwards's preaching of this sermon are two of the most famous events in colonial American history. The sermon was a climax to religious development in colonial America. Behind "Sinners in the Hands of an Angry God" lay more than a century of diverse, complex, and intriguing religious history.

Jonathan Edwards, the outstanding theologian of the Great Awakening

I. Established Denominations

Denominations that enjoyed state (government) support and protection were called **established denominations**. The concept of a state-supported church began with Roman emperor Constantine in the fourth century and continued for centuries. The established denominations included the Puritans in New England and the Anglicans in Virginia and the Carolinas. State support included financial aid from taxes and exclusive rights enforced by the state.

Guiding Questions

1. What religious struggles occurred in the English church under English kings?
2. What were the main factions within the Anglican Church?
3. What was the Puritan view of the covenant? Why did Puritanism decline?
4. What conditions resulted in the Salem witch trials?

English Background

The heritage of the American colonies was predominantly English. Understanding the religious history of England, therefore, helps us understand the religious history of the colonies. During the 1500s, England swung back and forth like a pendulum from Catholicism to Protestantism. King Henry VIII (ruled 1509–47) broke from the Roman Catholic Church and established the Church of England (Anglican Church). Though he left the Catholic Church because the pope refused to allow him to divorce his wife, Henry's beliefs were still predominately Catholic. Under Henry's son, Edward VI (ruled 1547–53), Protestant leaders pushed for a thorough

King Henry VIII *(left)* and King Edward VI *(right)*, his only son

Queen Mary I, Henry VIII's older daughter

Queen Elizabeth I, Henry VIII's younger daughter

reform, insisting on drastic and immediate changes that offended many English people. Edward's successor, the Roman Catholic Queen Mary (ruled 1553–58), attempted to reinstate Catholicism in England. She burned some three hundred Protestants at the stake and became known as "Bloody Mary." After Mary's death, her sister, Queen Elizabeth I (ruled 1558–1603), made the Anglican Church the official English church again.

Three important groups emerged within the Church of England. The **Puritans** were staunch Protestants who agreed wholeheartedly with the Anglican creed. However, they thought that the Anglican ceremonies and practices, such as its use of bishops and elaborate garments for priests, were too similar to the Roman Catholic Church. The Anglican Church, they argued, must be "purified" of such corruptions.

Low-church Anglicans agreed doctrinally with the Puritans but saw no problem with the church's ceremonies and structure. Such matters were unimportant, the low-churchmen held, as long as the church was doctrinally sound. **High-church Anglicans** believed that the church's traditional practices, notably its rule by bishops, were divinely ordained. They were less opposed to Catholicism than the Puritan and low-church groups.

Another group, the **Separatists,** believed that the whole Church of England was corrupt and that true Christians must completely separate from it. Separatist groups included the Pilgrims, and later, Baptists, Quakers, and Presbyterians.

Puritanism in America

Although Virginia was the site of America's earliest settlement, New England was more influential in religious matters. The Puritan views of the settlers in Massachusetts Bay Colony and the surrounding regions affected every other colony and later shaped the religious character of the United States. Thus, New England Puritanism was the most influential religious movement in colonial history.

Puritan Beliefs

Like other Protestants, the Puritans believed the basic doctrines of the Reformation: the authority of the Bible alone, justification by faith alone, and that all believers could serve as their own priests. But several features set the Puritans apart from other Protestants. One was at the heart of Puritan theology—the idea of the covenant. Puritans believed that God deals with mankind through a series of covenants, or agreements. For example, the Puritans held that in salvation the believer enters into a "covenant of grace" with God. God saves an individual, and in return the believer fulfills his "covenant obligations" by obeying God's law.

The covenant idea affected every aspect of Puritan society. Like Israel in the Old Testament, the Puritans believed that as a community they had made a social covenant with God to establish a model society ruled by God's laws. The settlers hoped not only to establish a society in accordance with God's standards but also to demonstrate to England how such a godly society should operate.

The covenant idea also affected the personal lives of individual Puritans. Because each Christian is in a covenant with God, he has certain responsibilities to fulfill. Of course, the Puritans did not believe that salvation resulted from good works but that good works were the natural result of salvation. Puritans emphasized Romans 12:1 and its teaching that Christian dedication was simply the "reasonable service" of one who had received the "mercies of God."

Another distinguishing feature of New England Puritanism was its system of government in the church. In the Church of England, the monarch was the leader and thus appointed important church officials. However, New England Puritans adopted a **congregational form of church government**. Each congregation elected its own officers, and each church remained independent of other churches. Other groups, notably the Baptists, also adopted this system. Eventually, most of the Puritans in America came to be called simply **Congregationalists**.

Puritan Decline

Like the children of Israel after the deaths of Joshua and the elders who outlived him (Judg. 2:7–10), the Puritans declined in religious fervor after the original generation of settlers died. Later generations built a prosperous colony and usually remained outwardly moral, but most lacked the passionate faith of their forefathers. Materialism, the love of possessions and wealth, replaced a love for God in the lives of many Puritans. This decline created a serious problem in the Congregationalist churches.

Converted, or regenerated, adults formed the first Congregational churches. Others later joined upon profession of faith in Jesus Christ. The pastor baptized the children of church members as infants. These children were then considered members of the church but could not become full members and take the Lord's Supper until they "owned the covenant," declaring their personal faith in Christ. As the years passed, fewer and fewer members of the later generations owned the covenant.

The early Puritans were committed to constructing a holy commonwealth. This meant maintaining a pure church in a pure society. Though this had not been possible in England, the Puritans believed it could be a reality in New England. But as subsequent generations failed to own the covenant, the Puritans worried that the society was becoming impure, just as it was in England. They reasoned that it would be better to have non-professors filling the church pews than to exclude them and have empty pews. The leaders remained convinced that the church would be able to exercise a positive influence in society by rebuking and disciplining those whose lives became openly sinful.

The presence of unconverted church members led to another issue. Could the children of these unsaved members be baptized? Eventually, the ministers of New England devised what became known as the **Half-Way Covenant**. Church members who had not owned the covenant but whose lives were outwardly moral could present their children for baptism. Initially, neither the parents nor the children could become full members and take the Lord's Supper until they professed a personal faith in Christ. Despite its purpose of keeping people in the church and under sound preaching, the Half-Way Covenant increased the number of unconverted church

The Truth about the Salem Witch Trials

In 1692 in Salem Village, Massachusetts, a group of young girls began having hysterical fits. They claimed that witches were afflicting them and began to name certain people in the village as witches. Based almost entirely on the testimonies of those girls alone, authorities began to arrest and then to try several Salem citizens who were astonished at the accusations. Nineteen people were hanged, one man was pressed to death with heavy weights, and several died in prison.

Ironically, only the accused who maintained their innocence were executed; those who confessed were imprisoned. Realizing this fact, some of the accused confessed to save themselves. Authorities hoped those in jail would identify other witches. Some innocent people refused to make a false confession. Mary Easty said to her judges, "I know not the least thing of witchcraft, therefore I cannot [confess], I dare not belie my own soul. I beg your honors not to deny this my humble petition from a poor dying innocent person." Though Easty was hanged anyway, her petition may have contributed to the end of the Salem witch trials.

Several factors are ignored in the blast of accusations hurled at the Puritans. Concerning the trials, the ministers of Massachusetts, rather than being persecuting fanatics, actually counseled caution and restraint to the more zealous civil authorities. It was the opposition of some of the clergy, in fact, that helped end the witch trials. Boston pastor Increase Mather said, "It were better that ten suspected witches should escape than that one innocent person should be condemned."

Often forgotten too is the fact that some people in Massachusetts actually were practicing witchcraft—although it is difficult to tell whether that practice was mere superstition or real demonic activity. Even if this activity was only superstition, nearly everyone at that time—not just the Puritans—believed that it was genuine witchcraft and that it must be relentlessly punished. In the century before the Salem witch trials, for example, more than three thousand accused witches were burned in Vaud, a region in Switzerland. Furthermore, tens of thousands of Europeans were executed for witchcraft from the fifteenth to the eighteenth centuries.

And finally, critics of the Puritans also ignore the repentance of many in Salem. Within five years the citizens of Massachusetts held a day of prayer and fasting to implore God's pardon for their actions. One of the judges in the trials, Samuel Sewall, was overcome with guilt when his son read Matthew 12:7 during the family's devotions: "But if ye had known what this meaneth, I will have mercy, and not sacrifice, ye would not have condemned the guiltless." Sewall, in remorse, went to church, confessed his guilt to the congregation, and asked for forgiveness. Ann Putnam, one of the hysterical girls, likewise stood before the congregation in Salem Village and apologized for being "an instrument for the accusing of several persons of a grievous crime, whereby their lives were taken away from them, whom now I have just grounds and good reason to believe they were innocent persons."

What, exactly, happened in Salem Village? No one today can be quite sure. It is certain, however, that innocent people died because of fear and hysteria, and the reputation of Massachusetts Puritans was blemished. Regrettably, the worthy contributions of early American Puritanism have been obscured by the wild fanaticism of a few and by a willingness of later generations to believe only the worst.

High emotions and hysteria characterized the Salem witch trials.

members. It was a serious compromise of the principles of the original Puritans.

Several other factors contributed to the spiritual decline in New England. For example, in 1691 the Massachusetts colony received a new charter that required religious freedom. This diminished the Puritan influence and encouraged a diversity that included many unbelievers. In addition, financial success lulled many Puritans into valuing material wealth more than spiritual prosperity. The rapidly growing population also resulted in a large increase of unbelievers in Massachusetts. Finally, Harvard College, which produced many pastors and other leaders in the colony, significantly reduced its emphasis on spiritual matters.

The low point in Puritan history came in 1692. Having forsaken much of the faith of their fathers, some Massachusetts colonists sank into fanaticism and hysteria. The **Salem witch trials** resulted from the claims of several young girls in Salem Village, Massachusetts, that witches were afflicting them. The authorities took the charges seriously and began to try those who were accused. Before the hysteria was over, at least twenty people were dead, and the reputation of Massachusetts suffered permanent damage. The spiritually chilling influences of the Half-Way Covenant, the Salem witch trials, and the reaction to those trials left New England spiritually depressed until the Great Awakening in the 1700s.

Anglicanism in America

Anglicanism came to North America in 1607 with the settlers at Jamestown, and it became, after Puritanism, the most widespread religious force in seventeenth-century America.

Beginnings

Virginia has sometimes mistakenly been viewed as a secular, materialistic colony in contrast to the more spiritually minded Massachusetts. In reality, some of the early settlers of Virginia were just as devout as the Puritans. For example, with the original settlers came Anglican minister Robert Hunt to serve as chaplain. One of his first acts on arriving at Jamestown was to hold a service to thank God for a safe arrival. He continued to preach weekly to the settlers, holding his services under an awning made from an old sail. He visited and served the many sick in the early days of the colony. Hunt's strenuous labors may have contributed to his death within two years of his arrival. Captain John Smith wrote, "He was an honest, religious, and courageous divine. He preferred the service of God . . . to every thought of ease at home."

The early Virginians were usually low-church Anglicans, agreeing doctrinally with the Puritans but having no objection to Anglican forms of worship. They were less interested in establishing a new holy commonwealth like the Puritans. Later, the Anglicans of Virginia, as was true of the Puritans, declined spiritually.

Realizing that Anglicans in America needed guidance, church leaders in England sent additional ministers to the colonies. In 1693, Anglicans also established the College of William & Mary. One of its missions was to train Anglican ministers.

Expansion

The Anglican Church grew throughout the colonies. By the Revolutionary War, Anglican churches existed in every colony, and Anglicanism had become the established (government-supported)

Samuel Sewall, who presided over the Salem witch trials, later apologized for the town's zealous but misguided pursuit of innocent people.

church in Virginia, Maryland, the Carolinas, Georgia, and parts of New York and New Jersey.

Expansion, however, did not always bring spiritual growth. Anglican churches constantly suffered from a shortage of academically and spiritually qualified pastors. Expansion also brought spiritual coldness as more high-church Anglican influences entered the colonies. When the Great Awakening swept the colonies in the 1700s, the Anglican Church was the Protestant denomination that was least affected by the revival.

Section Review

1. From what did Puritans want to "purify" the Church of England?
2. What is the "heart" of Puritan theology?
3. Explain the type of church government adopted by New England Puritans.
4. What were the provisions of the Half-Way Covenant?
★ Why did the Puritan commonwealth fail?
★ Examine the information about the Salem witch trials. What do you think were the major reasons they occurred?

II. Non-Established Denominations

Several Protestant groups in America were officially separate from the Church of England. The Pilgrims of Plymouth were the first of these to arrive in the New World. However, because of their size and influence, some of the other Separatist groups—such as the Baptists, the Quakers, and the Presbyterians—were ultimately more important. The Separatists and the Roman Catholics formed the **non-established denominations**. These groups did not have state (government) support and protection.

Baptists

When **Roger Williams** fled from Massachusetts and founded Rhode Island, he sought to create a more pure church than those in the rest of New England. In 1639, he founded what is considered the first Baptist church in America.

The **Baptists** grew slowly at first, and they suffered persecution from colonial authorities, particularly in Massachusetts and Virginia. Nonetheless, they succeeded in founding churches throughout the colonies and had their largest numbers in religiously tolerant Pennsylvania.

As their name suggests, Baptists differ from other groups regarding the doctrine of baptism. Like the Congregationalists, the Baptists practice a congregational form of church government and believe that only the regenerate should be church members. Unlike the Congregationalists, who allowed baptism of infants, Baptists baptize only professing believers and then only by immersing them in water.

Quakers

The **Quakers**, or the Society of Friends, originated with the Englishman **George Fox**. Fox claimed to have received guidance by

---

Guiding Questions

1. Who were the leading English Separatists and what did they teach?
2. In addition to the Separatists, what other non-established religious groups developed in America?

George Fox, founder of the Quakers

the "inner light," an illumination from God found in every man. Quakers teach that this "inner light" is some kind of spark of divinity and that man is saved through obeying its leading rather than through the atonement of Christ. Most (but not all) early Quakers opposed participating in war, taking oaths, or holding political office. They preferred to be called Friends rather than Quakers. The name Quaker originated from the practice of some Quakers who shook while worshipping. Those opposed to the Quaker movement assigned them this name.

The Quakers practiced an extremely plain method of worship. Believers sat in silence—often in a circle—and waited for the "inner light" to move one member to give a word of testimony or exhortation. The early Quakers did not have regular ministers and did not practice baptism and communion.

Quakers did not receive a warm welcome in the colonies. The Puritans in New England quickly arrested and deported any Quaker who entered their colonies. Between 1659 and 1661, authorities in Massachusetts hanged four Quakers for returning to the colony after repeated warnings.

Many of the Quakers lived in Rhode Island, but the center of colonial Quakerism was Pennsylvania, where William Penn established his colony as a "Holy Experiment" in religious diversity. Many Quakers who did not believe in the prohibition against holding office became influential political leaders in that colony.

Lutherans

The **Lutherans**, followers of the teachings of the great German reformer Martin Luther, came to America in trickles rather than in floods. The Swedish Lutherans of New Sweden (Delaware) were among the first, and many Dutch Lutherans settled in New Amsterdam. Most Lutherans who came to America, however, originated in Germany. Like many of the other small groups, the Lutherans flocked to Pennsylvania because of its religious freedom and abundant land.

Anabaptist Groups

The Anabaptists arose during the Reformation in protest of what they considered the incomplete reforms of other Protestants. Most Anabaptists refused to have anything to do with the state; they refused to serve in the military, vote, or hold office. They also stressed the importance of a holy, simple life. The **Mennonites**, followers of the Dutch teacher Menno Simons, were the largest Anabaptist group. The **Amish** were a more conservative branch of the Mennonites.

These Amish buggies are traveling along a road in present-day Lancaster County, Pennsylvania.

Persecuted by governments in Europe, many of the Mennonites and Amish fled to the New World and established farms and towns in Pennsylvania. By thrift and hard work, they built prosperous farms that their descendants continue to farm even today. Both groups tried to preserve their old ways of life by rejecting modern changes and having little contact with outsiders. Even today, some Mennonites and Amish still use only a horse and buggy for transportation and follow farming practices that date back to the 1700s.

Other Protestant Groups

Like the Puritans, **Presbyterians** originated in the British Isles. Many came to the American colonies seeking religious freedom.

The Dutch Reformed came to the New World with the settling of New Amsterdam, though not in great numbers. Because the Netherlands was the most religiously tolerant nation in Europe, few people there had religious reasons to migrate to America. The Dutch who came were often more interested in wealth than in religion.

The French Reformed, also called **Huguenots** (HYOO guh nots), settled throughout the colonies, especially after the French king, Louis XIV, abolished their freedom of worship in 1685. The largest concentrations of Huguenots were in Virginia and South Carolina; however, the French Reformed were rarely concentrated in any one colony. Many eventually became Presbyterians.

The German Reformed Church, from southern Germany, also migrated to the American colonies. Unlike the Huguenots, the Germans preserved their identity by concentrating in one colony, Pennsylvania.

The **Moravians** were followers of the teachings of preacher John Huss of Bohemia (modern-day Czech Republic). Huss was burned at the stake in 1415 for rejecting Roman Catholic teachings. Persecution in Europe led many Moravians to flee to America. They emphasized the importance of conversion, the need for personal piety (devoutness), and the necessity of living a holy life. Evangelism was also a primary concern; thus, they conducted mission work among the slaves in the Caribbean and among the Indians in America. As mentioned in an earlier chapter, John Wesley credited his conversion in part to his contact with Moravians. Later, the denomination's membership and influence declined.

One of the Moravian settlements was Salem, North Carolina.

Roman Catholics

Most Protestants in the colonies feared Roman Catholicism. Some of that feeling was simple prejudice, but much of it resulted from opposition to the unbiblical teachings of the Roman Catholic Church and from the persecution of Protestantism in Catholic countries. Also, Roman Catholic Spain and France threatened the existence of the English colonies.

The center of colonial Catholicism was Maryland, the colony established as a haven for Catholics. Even there, however, Catholics were still a minority. Some Catholics lived in Pennsylvania, and a few settled in New York, but virtually none were found elsewhere in the colonies. In the early 1700s, the British government eliminated the limited toleration Catholics had enjoyed. The government's act placed Roman Catholics in a difficult position until the Revolutionary War, and their numbers remained small in America until the massive Irish immigration of the 1840s.

Section Review

1–4. What were the four most important Separatist groups to settle in the colonies?
5. In what colony did the German Reformed settle?
6. Which colony was the center of Catholicism?
★ From the four core values (freedom, individualism, equality, and growth), choose two and explain how they encouraged the development of non-established denominations.
★ Explain the statement given above: "Most Protestants in the colonies feared Roman Catholicism."

III. Worship and Indian Missions

Often Christian worship in the colonial era varied depending on each denomination. Some groups, such as the Anglicans, practiced more formal worship, whereas others, such as the Quakers, were much more informal. But some of the worship practices were similar for most or all of the different groups. The following section provides a broad, generalized description of how colonial Christians worshiped.

Guiding Questions

1. What were the main features of a typical colonial church building?
2. What was the typical order of service in a colonial church?
3. What methods were used to evangelize the Indians? How effective were those efforts?

Buildings

Settlers built church buildings near the center of town to indicate the importance of religion to the community. Structurally, many early churches resembled barns. (In fact, some of the earliest American churches were actually barns.) The building also served as a hall for public meetings. Patrick Henry, for example, gave his famous "liberty or death" speech to an assembly of colonial delegates gathered in St. John's Church in Richmond, Virginia.

The interiors of early colonial churches were likewise plain. The earliest pews were simple benches with no padding or backs. Later, churches constructed pews paid for by monetary gifts from members of the congregation. Those pews were then reserved for the people who had purchased them. In some churches, members reserved pews by paying an annual rental fee. The higher one's social standing, the nearer to the front of the church one sat. Those front pews were elaborate box pews, closed on three sides to reduce drafts and having a door that opened into the aisle.

Pulpits also grew more elaborate as the colonies grew more settled. The early rough-hewn boxes gave way to graceful and elaborate pulpits. Above the later pulpits was a sounding board, a wooden structure designed to bounce sound waves out so that the minister could be clearly heard.

The WEST PARISH Meetinghouse
West Barnstable, Massachusetts built in 1717

The interior of the parish meeting house in West Barnstable, Massachusetts

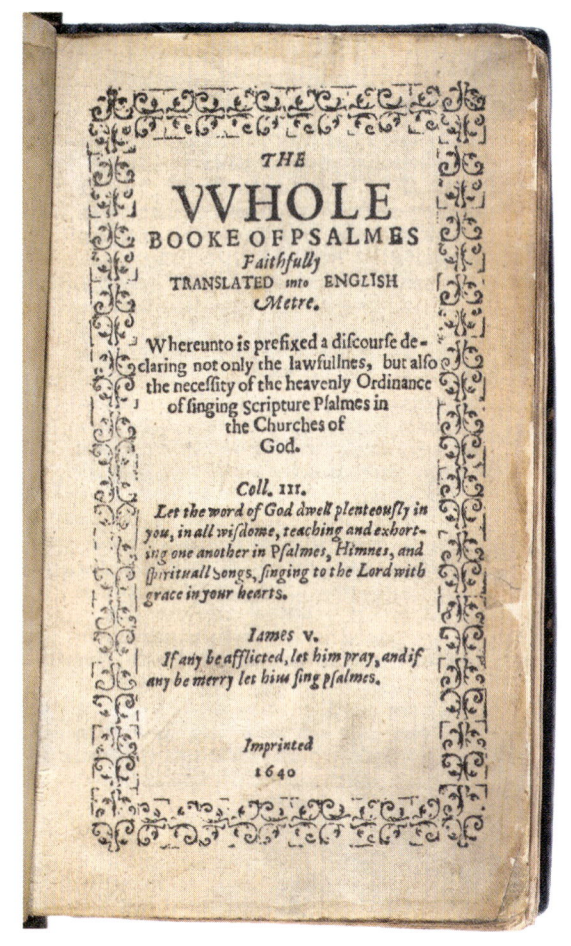

The title page of the *Bay Psalm Book*, the hymnal of the Puritans and the first book published in the British colonies

Many colonial churches also contained a balcony. Churches often reserved the balcony for certain groups such as servants, slaves, and free blacks. It was not uncommon for slaves to be required to enter by climbing a set of stairs or a ladder outside the church that led directly to the balcony.

Services

A drum, or later a bell, summoned the colonists to worship. Churches usually held two services on Sunday, one in the morning and one in the afternoon. Sunday school was not developed until the late 1700s, but children often attended catechism class between the two services. A catechism is a summary of a denomination's doctrine using a question-and-answer format. Children memorized and recited the answers to the questions. For example, the Westminster Shorter Catechism, which was the Presbyterian catechism, begins as follows:

Question: What is the chief end of man?
Answer: Man's chief end is to glorify God, and to enjoy Him forever.

The first part of the services contained a long prayer by the pastor ("bills of request" were laid on the pulpit ahead of time for the pastor's notice) and the reading of the Scripture. Singing was, of course, an essential part of the service. At first, most colonists sang adapted versions of the psalms.

The early churches, particularly those of the Puritans, contained no instruments. Some colonial Christians, citing passages such as Amos 5:23, believed that the Bible forbade instruments in church. Others simply could not afford to import instruments from England. By the end of the colonial period, however, organs were in widespread use.

The sermon was the centerpiece of the church service. Most Puritan and Separatist sermons lasted at least an hour. Anglican sermons varied. Sleeping or talking during the sermon was strongly discouraged. In the early Puritan churches, in fact, ushers walked around during the sermon looking for sleepy saints. They carried a long pole with a feather at one end for tickling the women as a warning and a knob at the other end for striking the men.

The preacher might memorize his sermon for delivery, preach with only a few notes, or write the message out completely and read it to the congregation. Reading a sermon did not necessarily lessen its impact. Jonathan Edwards, who was mentioned at the beginning of this chapter, might have read "Sinners in the Hands of an Angry God" to his listeners; however, the sermon stirred the congregation with great conviction. Generally, despite their own distinctives, colonial denominations believed the Bible was the authoritative Word of God.

Indian Missions

From the very beginning, a goal of many colonists was to convert Indians to the gospel. The charter for Virginia stated that the settlers aimed at "propagating [the] Christian religion to such people, as yet live in darkness and miserable ignorance of the true knowledge and worship of God." The charter of Massachusetts likewise obligated the colonists to "win and incite the natives of the country to the knowledge and obedience of the only true God

Missionaries to the Indians

While pastoring a Puritan church in New England, John Eliot (1604–1690) became concerned about the Algonquin Indians. With the help of an Indian who knew English, Eliot learned their language and began to preach to them.

He translated various devotional works and finally the entire Bible into the Algonquin tongue. (The Algonquin Bible was the first Bible printed in America.) His success was remarkable; it appears that some four thousand Indians were converted under Eliot's ministry. Those converts, called "praying Indians," formed communities appropriately called "praying villages," with Indians often serving as pastors.

That effective ministry came to an end, however, during a war between the English settlers and the Indians in 1675–76. The praying Indians sided with the English, a fact that caused the other Indians to hate them. Unfortunately, the colonists also distrusted them and even disbanded some of their villages.

David Brainerd (1718–1747), a close friend of Jonathan Edwards and his family, conducted a brief work among the Indians in New York, New Jersey, and Pennsylvania, until his death from tuberculosis at the age of twenty-nine. Although Brainerd's ministry was not successful numerically, his *Journal*, published after his death, inspired many other young men to enter mission work, and their efforts were successful.

John Eliot

David Brainerd

and Savior of mankind, and the Christian faith." Some historians consider these statements an attempt to conceal exploitation of the Indians by Europeans. The evidence, however, demonstrates otherwise: many colonists were genuine in their concern for the spiritual state of the Indians.

Thus, throughout the colonial era, many devout Christians attempted to reach the Indians with the gospel. Sometimes personal contact resulted in the conversion of an individual, such as Pocahontas. Ministers often preached to the Indians in addition to their other duties. Roger Williams, for example, was one of the first white men in New England to preach to the Indians. Jonathan Edwards worked with an Indian mission in the latter part of his ministry. John and Charles Wesley came to Georgia in 1736 to evangelize the Indians. (However, the Wesleys themselves were unconverted at the time, and the work was a dismal failure.)

A chief shortcoming of some missionary efforts was the tendency to think that Indians had to be "civilized" before they could be converted. It is true that certain Indian customs could not be reconciled with biblical morality, but some colonists believed that Indians needed European standards in dress and housing as much as they needed the gospel. Despite these difficulties, colonial Indian missions were not a failure. Thousands of Indians who had never heard the gospel were converted as a result of these efforts.

Section Review

1. What is a catechism?
2. Why did many colonial churches lack musical instruments?
* What was the central focus of the typical colonial worship service? Evaluate this focus.
* Some have criticized missionary efforts during this period for attempting to "civilize" the people to whom the missionaries ministered. What are some positive and negative aspects of this attempt?

IV. The Great Awakening

Religious revivals have occurred a number of times in American history. The first significant one became known as the **Great Awakening**. It was not simply a revival, however; it was a powerful social, political, and religious force that permanently altered the course of American history. Some historians limit the Awakening to the 1730s and 1740s, the years of greatest fervor and activity. But closer study reveals that the whole Great Awakening and its effects covered nearly a half century, from the 1720s to the early 1770s.

Background

Religious life in the North American colonies had begun to wither by the early 1700s. Although some religious groups experienced growth, most were in a spiritual lull. Secular historians in search of causes of the Great Awakening recognize the desire for security created by economic and political uncertainty of the times, and they focus on that as the primary reason for the revival. Those factors might indeed have contributed to the revival, but ultimately it was simply, in the words of Jonathan Edwards, "a surprising work of God."

The colonies needed a spiritual awakening. In New England, the Half-Way Covenant was slowly filling the Congregationalist churches with unconverted members. Some areas, such as the frontier regions of the Carolinas, had almost no religious life. Many who attended church did so because of traditions, but they lacked the spiritual zeal that had motivated their forefathers. It appears that even some of the colonial ministers were not converted.

Voices Crying in the Wilderness

Early Stirrings

In 1720, Dutch Reformed pastor Theodore J. Frelinghuysen (FREE ling hi zun) came to New Jersey. He preached about practical Christian living. He emphasized personal conversion and the holiness of life that an awareness of God's holiness brings. Frelinghuysen's faithful preaching was rewarded in the 1720s by a series of revivals in his churches. The Great Awakening had begun.

Another New Jersey minister, Presbyterian Gilbert Tennent, was also an early light in the Awakening. Encouraged by Frelinghuysen, Tennent began to preach about the need for conversion and holy living. Like Frelinghuysen, Tennent saw fruit for his labor in converted souls and rededicated saints. Tennent was soon in demand by other churches. He and other preachers carried the revival throughout the colonies.

Guiding Questions

1. What were the spiritual conditions in the colonies prior to the Great Awakening?
2. Who were the leaders of the Great Awakening?
3. What were the results of the Great Awakening?

The Log College

Presbyterian Gilbert Tennent graduated from an unusual college. For example, Tennent did not receive instruction from a wide array of learned professors; he had only one teacher—his father, William Tennent Sr., who wanted a school to prepare his four sons for the ministry. Otherwise, they would have had to go to New England or even back to England for their education.

Furthermore, the college was merely a large log building near Tennent's Pennsylvania home. It began with thirteen students—Tennent's brothers and nine others who wanted to study for the ministry. Enemies derisively called the school "the Log College," but there was nothing crude about the quality of the education provided there. The students worked diligently at their studies under Tennent's direction and gained practical experience by serving in his church.

The heritage of the Log College was rich. Gilbert Tennent, his brothers, and the other graduates of the school became effective supporters of the Great Awakening, leading hundreds—perhaps thousands—of souls to Christ. Ironically, the often-despised Log College spawned an increase in higher education. Many colleges claim their descent from the ministry of the Log College and its graduates. Among those schools was the College of New Jersey (now Princeton University), which was chartered the year that William Tennent died (1746). George Whitefield even compared the humble cabin college to schools like Harvard and Yale, saying that it "seemed to resemble the school of the old prophets."

Jonathan Edwards

The greatest theologian of the Great Awakening—and perhaps of American history—was **Jonathan Edwards**. A brilliant man (he entered Yale College before he was thirteen), Edwards lived with a constant sense of the presence of God. He did not simply practice an outward piety (devotion); he was consumed with love for God. As pastor of a Congregationalist church in Northampton, Massachusetts, Edwards sought to instill in his people the same passionate dedication that he felt in his own heart.

In 1734, Edwards began preaching a series of sermons on justification by faith. The sermons sparked a series of awakenings in the church that, Edwards admitted, surprised even him. Edwards soon became the leader of the Awakening in New England and was its staunchest and ablest defender in print. He wrote glowingly of the revival's results, but he also cautioned that some individuals overemphasized emotion. He warned against excessive shouting in services, working oneself into a trance, or claiming to have received visions from God.

In his sermon, "Sinners in the Hands of an Angry God," Edwards said,

> You have an extraordinary opportunity, a day wherein Christ has thrown the door of mercy wide open, and stands calling, and crying with a loud voice to poor sinners; a day wherein many are flocking to Him, and pressing into the kingdom of God; many are daily coming from the east, west, north, and south; many . . . are now in a happy state with their hearts filled with love to Him who has loved them, and washed them from their sins in His own blood, and rejoicing in hope of the glory of God.

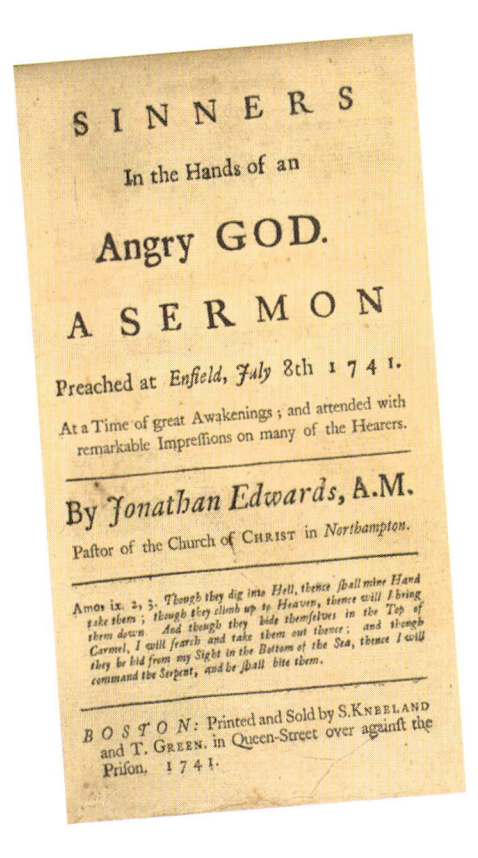

Edwards documented the impact of the Great Awakening in his book *A Faithful Narrative of the Surprising Work of God*. He also wrote *Religious Affections* to help people discern the difference between the work of the Holy Spirit reviving their love for God and mere emotionalism.

George Whitefield

If Edwards was the outstanding theologian of the Great Awakening, then **George Whitefield** (WHIT feeld) was its outstanding evangelist. Born in England, Whitefield became a friend of John and Charles Wesley while studying at Oxford. Like them, he was later converted and became a powerful preacher. But often the doors of England's churches were closed to him by ministers who did not share his passion, so Whitefield began to preach outdoors wherever he could gather a crowd.

After seeing remarkable results from his preaching in Britain, the twenty-four-year-old Whitefield came to America for the first time in 1738. Over the next thirty years, he made seven preaching tours of the colonies. He preached in Savannah, Charleston, Philadelphia, New York, Boston, and hundreds of villages and crossroads, carrying the revival throughout the colonies. In 1740, the year of his greatest tour, Whitefield preached to thousands daily, and many of those thousands were converted. Whitefield's tours also united the revivalists throughout the colonies, and he became a close friend of Jonathan Edwards.

Whitefield was a gifted preacher. He had a powerful, melodious, persuasive voice. Philadelphia printer Benjamin Franklin, who published some of Whitefield's sermons in America, testified to the power of that voice. Once, Franklin attended one of Whitefield's meetings, determined not to give any money for the offering to support Whitefield's orphanage in Georgia. Franklin later wrote,

George Whitefield

George Whitefield *(left)* preached throughout the colonies.

Benjamin Franklin *(right)* estimated that Whitefield's voice could be heard by thirty thousand people.

> I had in my pocket a handful of copper money, three or four silver dollars, and five pistoles in gold. As he [Whitefield] proceeded I began to soften, and concluded to give the coppers. Another stroke of his oratory made me ashamed of that, and determined me to give the silver; and he finished so admirably, that I emptied my pocket wholly into the collector's dish, gold and all.

On another occasion, Franklin did an experiment during one of Whitefield's outdoor sermons. Franklin walked away from the minister as he preached and measured how far he could go and still hear Whitefield's voice. By his reckoning, Franklin figured that Whitefield could reach a crowd of thirty thousand—without the help of any modern electronic amplification equipment.

Results of the Awakening

Though the Great Awakening began in the northern colonies, it soon spread. The South was the last section to experience the Awakening, but the revival's impact in that region was no less profound. This movement had several effects on the religious, social, and political life of colonial America.

First, the effects on America's churches were dramatic. Church growth was the most visible result. Because of the large number of conversions and the spiritual renewal of many Christians, both churches and church members increased markedly. Presbyterians and Baptists experienced the greatest growth.

Second, the number of religious colleges increased. Princeton, Brown, Rutgers, and Dartmouth were all established as a result of the revival and each became a training center for the ministry. Yale College experienced a renewed spiritual emphasis. Harvard College, however, continued its move away from its spiritual roots as a Puritan institution that emphasized the Bible.

Third, the Awakening transformed the spiritual life of the churches. The Half-Way Covenant began to vanish; increasingly, churches in America required personal regeneration for membership. The revival also promoted unity among the churches. Different congregations and even different denominations overlooked their minor doctrinal differences in the interest of evangelism. This tendency toward religious unity helped to pave the way for a political uniting of the colonies in the coming break with England.

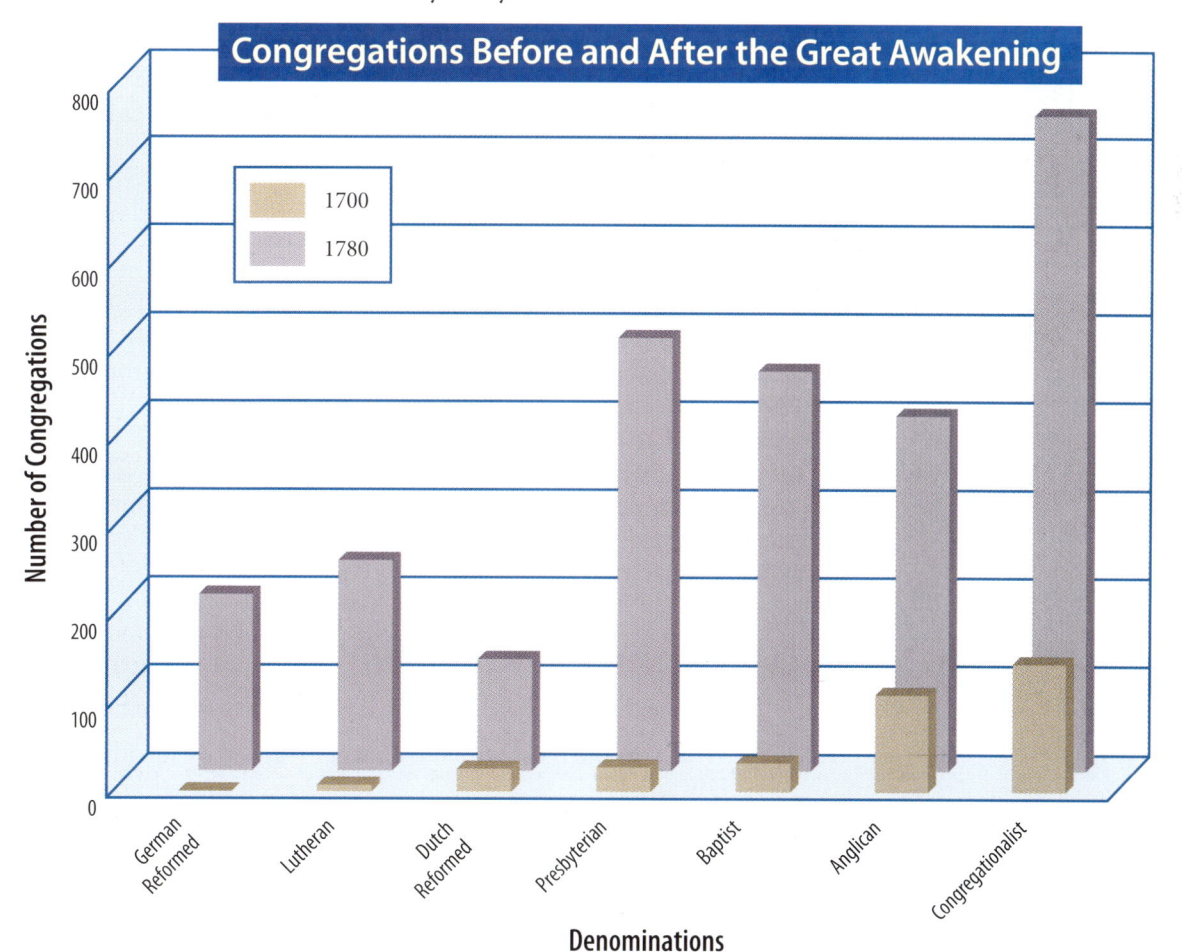

On the other hand, the Great Awakening also brought division to America's churches. Nearly every denomination had disagreement between those who favored the revival and those who opposed it. Not all of the "antirevivalists" were necessarily against revivals; some were simply offended by, at least in their view, the fanatical extremes of some people. Many of the opponents, though, were theologically opposed to the revival. They disliked the emphasis on personal experience, the criticism of unconverted pastors, and the general upsetting of "good church order."

The Anglican Church was the denomination most generally opposed to the Awakening, despite the fact that many individual Anglicans supported it. That church was powerful, especially in the southern colonies; however, many colonists resented its close association with the British government. Such dislike intensified when the British tightened their control over the colonies. As other denominations grew, Anglican officials and their friends in colonial governments passed some restrictions for licensing of preachers, building of new churches, and printing of religious material.

The Great Awakening also had political effects on the colonies. It was the first truly national movement in American history. The revival cut across sectional lines and touched every colony and nearly every class of people. The Great Awakening was not southern or northern, Presbyterian or Congregationalist, upper class or lower class; it was *American*.

The Awakening also advanced personal liberty. By reaffirming the equality of men before God, the revival stressed the equality of all men. The work of revivalists resulted in greater freedom of worship for the colonists. A democratic influence swept into the churches; power moved away from the wealthy and the educated within the congregations, and all laymen began to share equally in the rule of the church. Also, by holding large meetings—opposed by some church leaders—Whitefield and others set a precedent for the constitutional rights of free speech and assembly.

However, not all effects of greater democracy proved to be positive. As democracy and individualism became stronger forces, some Americans began to doubt traditional Christian doctrines. Before the Great Awakening, people usually respected the expertise of their pastors in understanding the Scripture. Now, many thought their own unstudied opinions were just as valid. This led to problems in the nineteenth century. For example, during that period there was a large increase in the establishment of groups that identified themselves as Christian but actually departed from traditional Christian beliefs.

Many movements that were unleashed in the Great Awakening saw their full development in the American Revolution. Foremost was an awakening of both the spirit of democracy and the spirit of religious liberty.

Old Ship Church in Hingham, Massachusetts, was built in 1681. It is the oldest continually used church in America.

Section Review

1. Who was the greatest theologian of the Great Awakening?
2. What was the most famous sermon preached by Jonathan Edwards?
3. Who was the most outstanding evangelist of the Great Awakening?
★ Assess the spiritual results of the Great Awakening.
★ Assess the political results of the Great Awakening.

CHAPTER REVIEW

Making Connections

1. What is the difference between Puritans and low-church Anglicans?
2. What is the difference between low-church and high-church Anglicans?
3. Why was the Half-Way Covenant dangerous to the Congregationalist churches in New England?
4–6. List at least three distinctive beliefs of the Quakers.
7. Describe the order of a typical service in a colonial church.

Developing History Skills

1. Why do you think Pennsylvania was the most religiously diverse colony?
2. Secular historians minimize or eliminate the supernatural from their consideration of historical events. If you were a Christian historian, how would you determine the cause or causes of the Great Awakening?

Thinking Critically

1. Had you lived in Queen Elizabeth's day, would you have been a Puritan, a low-church Anglican, a high-church Anglican, a Separatist, or a member of one of the other groups mentioned in this chapter? Why?
2. How were the Baptists like the Congregationalists? How were they unlike them?

Living as a Christian Citizen

1. A chief shortcoming of some missionary efforts was the belief that Indians needed to be "civilized" before they could be converted. What are your thoughts about this? How is this issue still a relevant one today?
2. Imagine a legislator in your state is proposing a bill to ban prayer before the legislative session on the grounds that such prayers are an establishment of religion. Based on what you learned in this chapter about established and non-established churches, write a letter in response to the legislator.

People, Places, and Things to Remember

established denominations
Puritans
low-church Anglicans
high-church Anglicans
Separatists
congregational form of church government
Congregationalists
Half-Way Covenant
Salem witch trials
non-established denominations
Roger Williams
Baptists
Quakers
George Fox
Lutherans
Mennonites
Amish
Presbyterians
Huguenots
Moravians
Great Awakening
Jonathan Edwards
George Whitefield

FORGE
1689–1801

1754–63
The French and Indian War

1765
The Stamp Act

1770
The Boston Massacre

1755　　　1760　　　1765　　　1770

1767
The Townshend Acts

CHAPTERS

5 THE RISING STORM (1689–1770)

6 INDEPENDENCE (1770–1783)

7 THE CRITICAL PERIOD (1781–1789)

8 THE FEDERALIST YEARS (1789–1801)

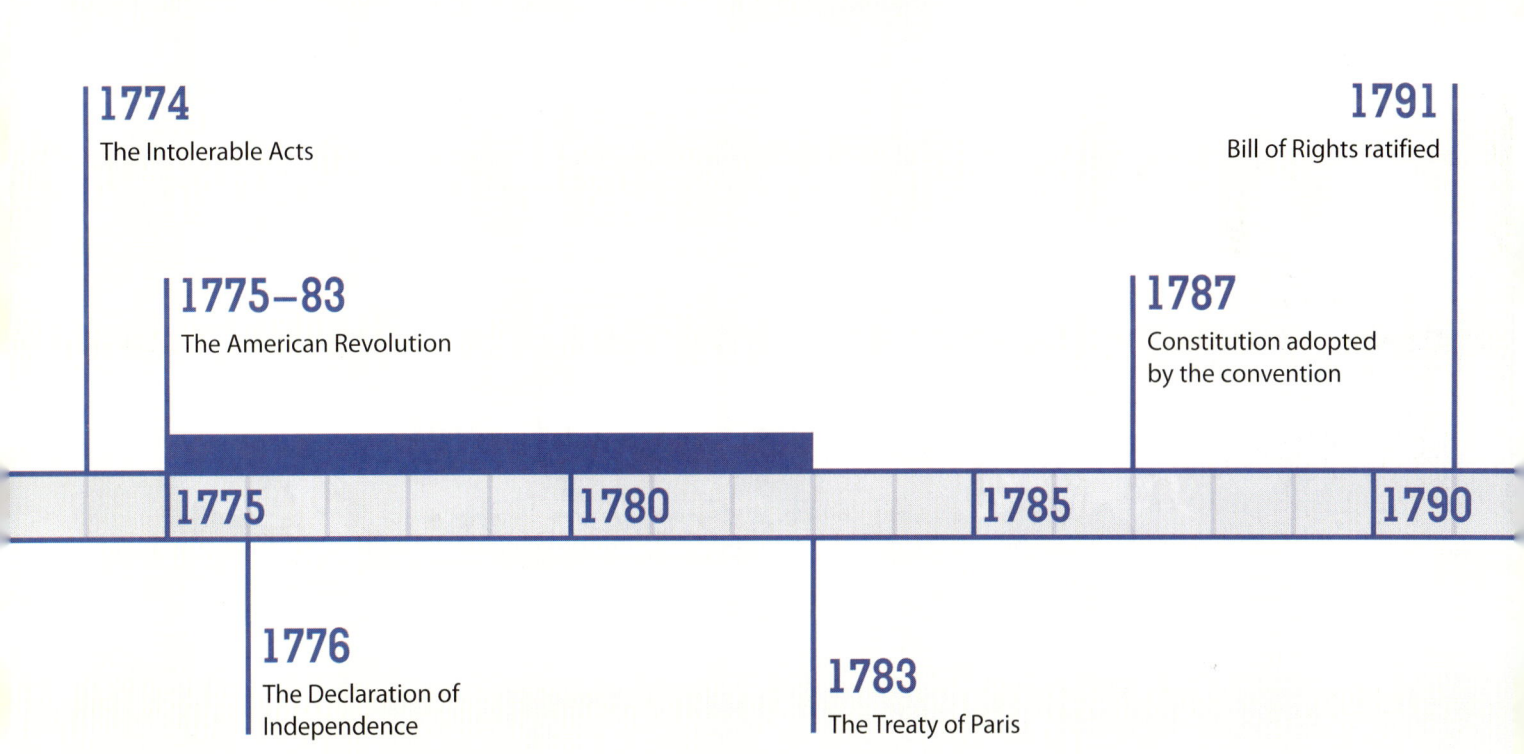

1774
The Intolerable Acts

1775–83
The American Revolution

1776
The Declaration of Independence

1783
The Treaty of Paris

1787
Constitution adopted by the convention

1791
Bill of Rights ratified

5 THE RISING STORM (1689–1770)

> My lads, they will not fire.
>
> **Samuel Gray**
> March 5, 1770, last words before being killed by the first British volley during the Boston Massacre

The Death of General Wolfe by Benjamin West

Big Ideas

1. What was the significance of the early conflicts that arose between the British and the French?
2. What were the consequences of a British victory in the French and Indian War?
3. What events resulted in a movement toward American independence from Britain?

I. Frontier Feuds

II. The French and Indian War

III. The Growing Rift

From the 1680s to the 1760s, recurring wars raged on the American frontier. Two colonial empires—the English and the French—fought from the sandy beaches of Florida to the snowy plains of Canada.

For many years, the English were able to safely ignore their French neighbors in the New World. Though they first explored North America in 1534, the first permanent French settlement was not established until 1608. In that year, Samuel de Champlain founded Quebec, Canada. However, "New France" amounted to little more than a scattered string of outposts.

By the late 1600s, the French decided to build an empire that would surpass that of their rivals, the English. In 1682, Robert de LaSalle (lah SAL) set out to explore the length of the Mississippi River. At the river's mouth, he named the vast region **Louisiana** in honor of the French king, Louis XIV. LaSalle made a comprehensive claim of "all the nations, peoples, provinces, cities, towns, villages, mines, minerals, fisheries, streams, and rivers" as possessions of France.

However, the French learned that it was easier to claim than to colonize. New France was never heavily populated with French settlers. For example, in the 1660s, the number of French settlers in Canada was approximately 3,000. Although the colony grew to about 80,000 by 1750, that was only a small number compared to the more than one million people who lived in British America.

The French posed a serious threat to the thirteen colonies for several reasons. First, the French had strong Indian alliances that greatly expanded their military capabilities. The prospect of well-armed Indian warriors was more worrisome to the colonists than facing French troops. However, one weak link in the French and Indian alliances was their inability to win over the powerful Iroquois. The French were aligned with the Algonquins, with whom the Iroquois were feuding. As a result, the Iroquois became allies of the British-American forces during the colonial wars.

A second factor that worked to the advantage of the French was the nature

The Indian Perspective

As colonies expanded, they settled on lands that Indian tribes had inhabited for generations. Sometimes colonists paid Indians for lands on which they settled—often they did not. Even when colonists did pay, the purchase of that land reduced Indian access to sources of food, including deer and fish.

The Indians also sensed a growing threat as more Europeans arrived, many of whom brought powerful weapons. Some Indian leaders even experienced diminishing authority over their own people. Indians became dependent on trade with colonists. Over time, colonists and Indians often resorted to capturing or killing each other.

European Claims in North America (ca. 1700)

of the frontier. The British colonies had a vaguely defined western boundary of isolated farms and villages that invited attack. Finding the enemy in the dense wilderness was difficult, and effectively defending the scattered American settlements was nearly impossible. Thus, settlers in some areas lived in constant fear of attacks by both the Indians and the French.

The French held a third advantage—the failure of the American colonies to unite. Petty jealousies and shortsightedness often divided the colonies, making them easy targets for French attacks.

I. Frontier Feuds

As the French expanded their claims in Canada, the Great Lakes region, and the Mississippi River basin, and as the English moved farther west, friction was inevitable. Furthermore, when France and England were at war in Europe, their colonists fought

Guiding Questions

1. How did the French threaten the British colonies?
2. What four wars were fought in America between the French and the British?

A Redeemed Captive

The colonial wars often turned quiet backwoods settlements into the frontlines of battle, catching settlers in savage crossfire. During Queen Anne's War, one man, Reverend John Williams, faced such a crisis with courage and faithfulness, leaving an enduring testimony to the sustaining grace of God.

Early on the morning of February 29, 1704, a war party of French soldiers and Indian warriors attacked the frontier town of Deerfield, Massachusetts. Reverend Williams and his family were still in bed when the attackers began to break open the doors and windows of their house with axes. Williams seized his pistol and aimed it at the nearest Indian, but the gun misfired. The Indians quickly captured Williams and his family. They killed two children and a slave and then marched their captives through the winter snow back to Canada.

The French and Indians killed thirty-eight settlers and captured more than one hundred citizens of Deerfield. The number of captives dwindled as the group slogged through the frigid wilderness. Anyone who could not keep up was killed. Williams's wife, who had given birth only a few weeks earlier, was one of the victims. When her strength failed, an Indian ended her life with a blow from a tomahawk. Williams suffered from the forced march as well. He recorded that each night he had to wring the blood from his socks.

When the Indians chose a Sunday to rest on the long march, they allowed Williams to preach. He spoke from Lamentations 1:18. "The Lord is righteous; for I have rebelled against his commandment: hear, I pray you, all people, and behold my sorrow: my virgins and my young men are gone into captivity."

In Montreal, the French governor took Williams and several others from the Indians. In many ways, the captives' situation improved. The French were kind and sympathetic, caring for the captives and giving them food and shelter. However, the captives faced a different and more subtle kind of persecution. The Jesuit priests were determined to convert the captives to Catholicism by any means possible.

Williams noted that the Indians had allowed the captives to keep their Bibles and hymnbooks, but the priests had quickly taken them away. The Catholics worked relentlessly to convert Williams. They tried arguments, pleas, and even blackmail and bribery. Some captives were beaten for refusing to convert, but the priests seemed to realize that such treatment would not move the Massachusetts pastor. Knowing that Williams's surviving children were separated from him, the priests told Williams that he could have them back if he would convert. They also said that the governor would give him a generous pension. Williams refused. "I told them my children were dearer to me than all the world," he wrote, "but I would not deny Christ and his truths for the having of them with me; I would still put my trust in God, who could perform all things for me."

Finally, in 1706, the British rescued fifty-seven Deerfield captives and returned them to Boston. Williams and all but one of his surviving children were among them. (One daughter had become a Catholic and joined an Indian tribe; she refused to return despite her father's pleas.) Williams returned to the pastorate, and all of his sons eventually followed him into the ministry. Williams's widely read account of the ordeal, *The Redeemed Captive Returning to Zion*, first appeared in 1707. Despite his sadness for those left behind, Williams wrote, "We have reason to bless God who has wrought deliverance for so many."

in America as well. Between 1689 and 1763, these two rival nations were involved in four wars. In the colonies, the first three bore the names of the English monarch at the time each conflict occurred: King William's War, Queen Anne's War, and King George's War. In America, the fourth conflict was called the French and Indian War, while in Europe it was known as the Seven Years' War.

King William's War (1689–97)

In Europe, this war became known as the War of the League of Augsburg, but the Americans named their frontier version after England's newly crowned king, William III. French settlers and Indians inflicted considerable damage and fear upon the English settlements. Though the English colonies had the advantage of numbers, they did not cooperate with one another well enough to raise funds for military supplies.

In Europe, a peace treaty was finally signed in 1697 that returned all captured territory in North America to its pre-war owners. But the rivalry between the French and English only deepened as the French continued to build forts along the Mississippi and St. Lawrence Rivers.

Queen Anne's War (1702–13)

Peace was short-lived. Europeans called the next struggle the War of the Spanish Succession, but American colonists named it after the reigning monarch of England, Queen Anne. In America, the war often consisted of sporadic, but bloody, fights on the frontier and along the coasts. France's Indian allies attacked several New England settlements, and the English colonists responded by raiding Canadian villages.

England won a series of decisive victories in Europe. Therefore, the peace treaty that ended the fighting in 1713 cost France control of much of eastern Canada. There was a shaky peace for a generation, but the feud between England and France was far from over.

King George's War (1744–48)

In Europe, the next conflict was called the War of the Austrian Succession. In America, it was fought under the name of Great Britain's King George II. A truce was declared in Europe in 1748, and the fighting ended.

The peace, however, was a mere pause in the conflict between Great Britain and France. Open conflict would erupt again in 1754 and would not only settle old problems in America but also create new ones.

George II

Different Names for the Same Wars		
Colonial Name for the War	**European Name for the War**	**Duration of the War**
King William's War	War of the League of Augsburg	1689–97
Queen Anne's War	War of the Spanish Succession	1702–13
King George's War	War of the Austrian Succession	1744–48
French and Indian War	———	1754–63
———	Seven Years' War	1756–63

Section Review

1–2. Which two European nations became the most bitter rivals in North America?

3–5. What three factors increased the danger of the French threat to the thirteen colonies?

6. Why was friction between England and France inevitable in North America?

★ Assume you were Reverend John Williams in the story given in this chapter entitled "A Redeemed Captive." How do you think you would have reacted in this situation? Would your actions be justified in view of biblical principles?

II. The French and Indian War

Although considerable blood was shed in the three major wars that occurred from 1689 to 1748, neither England nor France gained much land from the other in America. In 1754, a fourth struggle began and became known as the **French and Indian War** (1754–63). Unlike the three earlier conflicts, it began in the New World. It spread to Europe two years later, and there it was called the **Seven Years' War** (1756–63).

The Seven Years' War eventually saw Britain and Prussia allied against Austria, Russia, France, Spain, and several other nations. With fighting on three continents among several nations and tribes, the war was perhaps the first "world war." The conflict began in the backwoods of western Pennsylvania with a small incident involving a twenty-two-year-old untested Virginian colonel named **George Washington**.

Outbreak

The Spark

In 1752, the French governor of Canada ordered the construction of a chain of forts extending from Lake Erie to the Ohio River. These were designed to keep the English from crossing into territory claimed by France. In the spring of 1754, Lieutenant Colonel George Washington led his men toward this region. Virginia's governor had ordered Washington to clear the territory of the French who, according to the English, had illegally entered the area. On the way, Washington and his troops surprised a small group of French soldiers. In the ensuing skirmish, ten Frenchmen were killed and the remainder were captured—even though Britain and France were officially at peace.

A much larger force of French soldiers and Indian warriors, however, was waiting at the newly constructed **Fort Duquesne** (doo KANE). Realizing that he was outnumbered, Washington retreated and hastily built defenses. This structure, aptly named Fort Necessity, showed Washington's inexperience. Located in a low area, the fort allowed the French to fire directly into it from nearby heights. Washington was forced to surrender, but the French were surprisingly gracious. They allowed the Virginians to march home after Washington naively signed a note of surrender that put the blame for the whole affair on the British. The British government repudiated Washington's note, and Britain and France went to war.

Guiding Questions

1. What were the causes and the events of the French and Indian War?
2. What were the strengths and weaknesses of each nation relating to the war?
3. What were the results of the war?

Colonel George Washington at the time of the French and Indian War

The Two Sides

In the early stages of the war, the French enjoyed a friendlier relationship with their Indian allies than the British had with their Indian allies. The French also had an important advantage in that they understood the Indians and Indian warfare better than the British army did. The French borrowed methods of forest fighting from the Indians and practiced **guerrilla warfare**—sudden surprise attacks by small, hidden groups—against the British, whereas the British originally tried to fight in the open, ordered style used in Europe.

Strengths of the French and the British in the French and Indian War

French	British
Had better relations with the Indians	Outnumbered the French twenty to one
Had better understanding of guerrilla warfare	Controlled the waterways
Benefited from the disunity among the British colonies	Had significant material investments in the colonies

However, the British possessed some advantages. British colonists outnumbered French colonists by more than twenty to one. British colonists also had invested much in the New World. They had roots in America—land, businesses, and families. Many of the French, by contrast, were isolated traders and trappers who took products such as furs out of the New World but put little into it. Above all, the British navy could control the waterways and thereby hinder the arrival of French reinforcements and supplies.

The chief British disadvantage was the lack of unity in the colonies. As the war was about to begin, the **Albany Congress** attempted to establish political unity when it met at Albany, New York. Delegates from most of the colonies north of Virginia attended this meeting in June 1754. On the second day, **Benjamin Franklin** proposed his "Albany Plan" for centralized colonial rule, including a president chosen by the king and a congress chosen by the separate colonies. The plan was finally rejected, however, because the colonists feared that it would establish a government that was too strong. Many colonists feared centralized political control even more than they feared France.

British Setbacks

Braddock's Defeat

The early years of the war were disastrous for the British in North America. The government sent General **Edward Braddock** and a thousand seasoned British troops to capture Fort Duquesne. Braddock was joined by colonial forces and by Colonel Washington, who was eager to atone for his defeat at Fort Necessity. To move his men and supplies, Braddock painstakingly cut a road through the wooded wilderness to a spot within a few miles of the French fort. Washington tried in vain to warn Braddock that the French and Indians would not fight in the open, organized fashion that the general knew in Europe.

This 1754 appeal by Ben Franklin for cooperation among the colonies is the earliest political cartoon in American history.

General Braddock's burial

William Pitt, British leader

Site of Fort Duquesne and Fort Pitt in present-day Pittsburgh

On July 9, 1755, the French and Indians attacked. They hid in the trees and thick brush and poured deadly fire into the British ranks. The red-coated British regulars stood in close, ordered lines and braved the hail of bullets for three hours. "We would fight," some said, "if we could see anybody to fight with." Braddock, who was riding bravely about the field, overseeing the battle, was shot through the lungs. Eventually, the officers led by Colonel Washington organized a retreat. Over half of the British force was killed or wounded. Braddock died during the retreat after muttering, "Who would have thought it?"

Montcalm

The French assigned command of their forces in America to the **Marquis de Montcalm** (mar-KEE deh mahnt-KAHM). Montcalm, a talented soldier and commander, engineered a series of stinging defeats on the British from 1756 to 1758. In addition, pro-French Indians raided the frontier, terrorizing the British colonists. Up to this point, the British had bungled their response to the French threat.

British Successes

Pitt's Plan

The situation brightened for the British in 1757 when **William Pitt** became leader of the British government. Though he did not officially hold the title, he was essentially the prime minister. "I am sure that I can save this country, and that nobody else can," Pitt declared. Although this statement may seem arrogant, he proved as good as his word. Pitt quickly adopted a plan to win the war. He decided to let his ally, Prussia, bear the brunt of the fighting in Europe. Meanwhile, Britain used its superb navy to isolate the French forces in America and India. Pitt also replaced old, incompetent commanders with young, energetic officers who would lead the army to victory.

Turnaround

Among those new, dynamic commanders was General **James Wolfe**. With his thin body and upturned nose, Wolfe did not look like an inspiring commander. His military talents, however, were tremendous. The government soon entrusted Wolfe with the key campaign of the war, the attack on the French Canadian capital, Quebec.

By this time, English troops had captured Fort Duquesne and renamed it Fort Pitt, in honor of the British leader. The site is now part of Pittsburgh, Pennsylvania.

Battle of Quebec

In 1759, the two greatest commanders of the war, Montcalm and Wolfe, fought the **Battle of Quebec**. Montcalm knew that Quebec, high on cliffs above the St. Lawrence River, was a natural fortress; if the French could hold out against the enemy, the bitter Canadian winter would force the British to retreat.

A determined Wolfe, however, devised a plan to capture the city. Under cover of darkness, British soldiers scaled the cliffs and swarmed the Plains of Abraham, a field just outside Quebec. Montcalm led the French response. In the brief but deadly battle, the British won a great victory. However, Wolfe did not live to savor the victory; both he and Montcalm were severely wounded and died. The British triumph at Quebec and another in Montreal ended the war in North America.

Results of the War

The Treaty of Paris

The fighting in North America ended in 1760, but the war in Europe continued until 1763. The **Treaty of Paris (1763)** drastically changed the geography of North America. France had to surrender its land in Canada and all its claims to the Mississippi and Ohio River Valleys to Britain. The British also acquired Florida from Spain, a French ally. Spain gained the French lands west of the Mississippi River, including the city of New Orleans.

For the victorious British, the cost of both the war and the administration of the new possessions was high. The British had borrowed heavily to fight, and now the debts needed to be repaid. In addition, Parliament wanted to station thousands of troops in the colonies to protect against the Indians. Not surprisingly, the government thought the colonies should share this expense. In addition, when **George III** came to the throne in 1760, the British government announced its intention to carefully analyze the financial and political affairs of the colonies.

The colonies, after almost a century and a half of semi-independence, resented the interference. Furthermore, some Americans suspected that the British troops were intended to enforce government policies more than they were intended to guard against Indian attacks. Skillful statesmen such as William Pitt might have been able to calm the

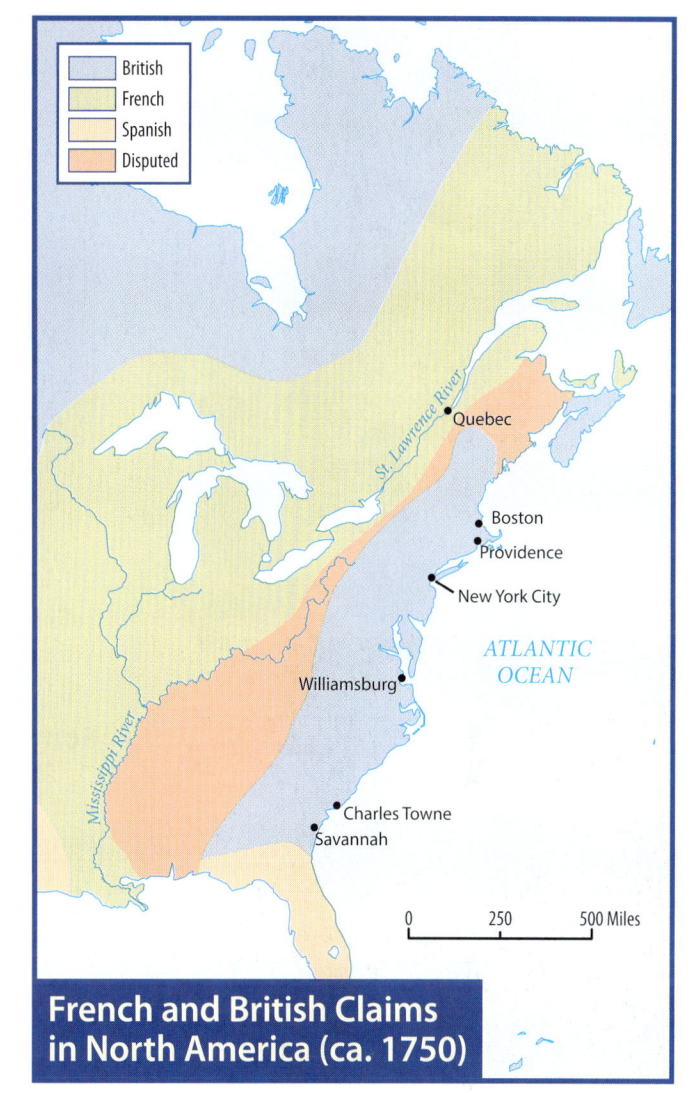

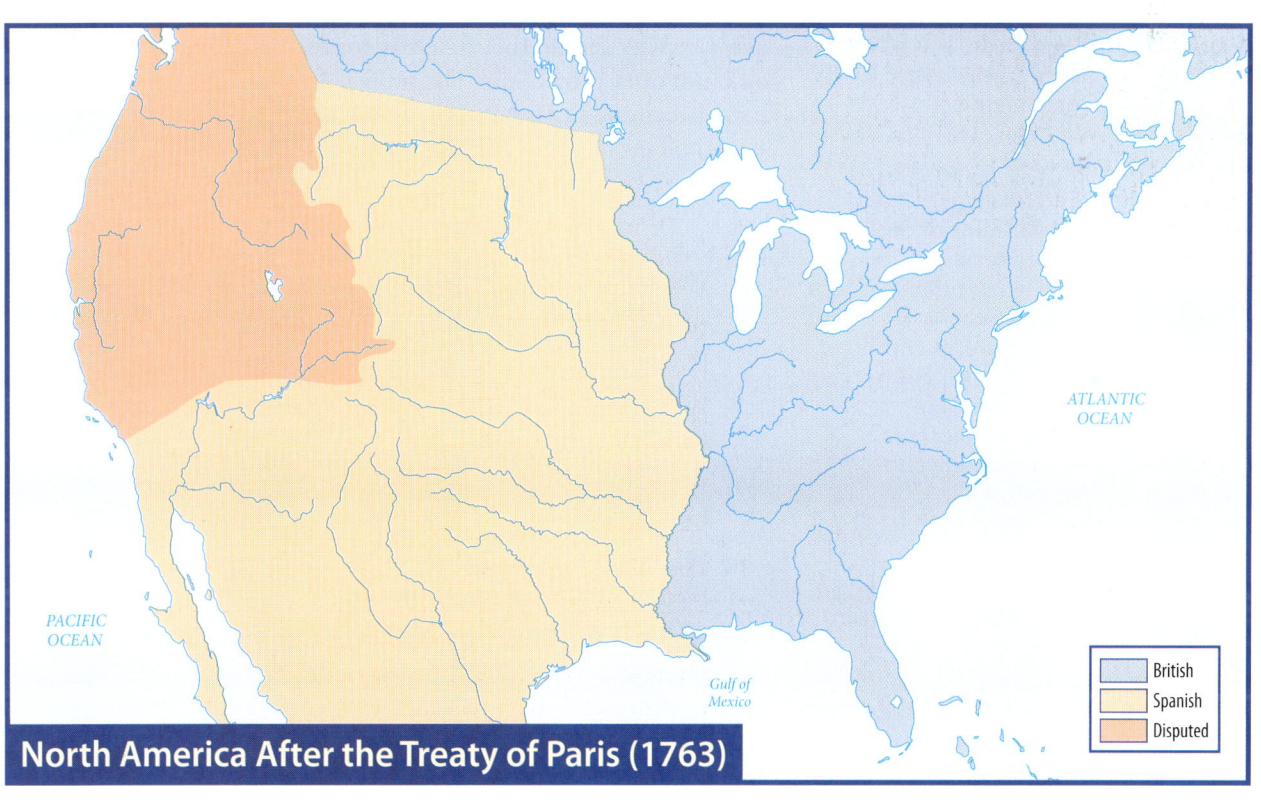

French and British Claims in North America (ca. 1750)

North America After the Treaty of Paris (1763)

Pontiac *(above)* meeting in a tribal council and *(right)* meeting with a British commander

Pontiac's Speech

In May 1763, Chief Pontiac addressed a gathering of Indian leaders. He stated:

> It is important for us, my brothers, that we exterminate from our lands this nation [Great Britain] which seeks only to destroy us. You see as well as I do that we can no longer supply our needs, as we have done, from our brothers, the French. The English sell us goods twice as dear [much] as the French do, and their goods do not last. Scarcely have we bought a blanket or something else to cover ourselves with before we must think of getting another; . . .
>
> When I go to see the English commander and say to him that some of our comrades are dead, instead of bewailing their death, as our French brothers do, he laughs at me and at you. If I ask for anything for our sick, he refuses with the reply that he has no use for us. From all this you can well see that they are seeking our ruin. Therefore my brothers, we must all swear their destruction and wait no longer. Nothing prevents us; they are few in numbers, and we can accomplish it.

colonies, but Pitt had resigned in 1761. The twenty-two-year-old king and his circle of policymakers scarcely understood the growing troubles in America and failed to resolve them.

Pontiac's War (Pontiac's Rebellion)

After the war, the French army returned home, leaving the Indians on their own. However, as early as 1762, a brilliant Ottawa Indian chief named **Pontiac** had formed an alliance with other Indian tribes. Enraged by the Treaty of Paris, Pontiac and his forces waged a devastating war against British soldiers and settlers from 1763 to 1766. They hoped to protect their land by driving settlers back across the Appalachian Mountains. Eight of Britain's twelve frontier forts fell to the Indians, and hundreds of people—both soldiers and civilians—were killed. Yet Pontiac was unable to hold his alliance together, and he eventually made peace with the British.

Pontiac's success raised a serious question in the minds of the colonists: why should they help pay for the costly British army if it could not offer protection? The French and Indian War settled matters between the British and the French, but it also created a host of new problems between Britain and its colonies.

Section Review

1. What was the French and Indian War called in Europe?
2. What was the chief British disadvantage in the French and Indian War?
3. Why was General Edward Braddock defeated so decisively at Fort Duquesne?
4–6. What was William Pitt's three-part plan to win the French and Indian War?
7–8. Who were the two greatest military commanders of the French and Indian War?
9. How did the Treaty of Paris change North America?
★ List and assess the French advantages during the French and Indian War.
★ List and assess the British advantages during the French and Indian War.

III. The Growing Rift
A Sense of Nation

For a century and a half, forces were at work creating a new type of citizen in the New World—an *American*. Viewed in isolation, those factors could easily be overlooked, but their cumulative effect began to create a national consciousness in the 1760s and 1770s.

Geography was an important factor in breaking the ties with the Old World. Isolated by an ocean, the colonists were forced to fend for themselves. The years of settlement forged in them self-reliance, ingenuity, and independence. The mother country seemed more like a distant cousin when problems arose in the colonies. The colonies independently dealt with threats from Indians, pirates, the French, and the Spanish. Britain did not take an active role in the defense of the colonies until King George's War in the 1740s.

The way the land was settled also helped shape American attitudes. Private ownership of property was an attractive incentive for settlers from Europe. A man who owned property had a stake in society, and on his land he was the master of all he possessed. This power gave him greater independence and broader horizons than he or his father had ever known in the old country. One immigrant put it thus:

> An European, when he first arrives, seems limited in his intentions, as well as in his views; but he very suddenly alters his scale; . . . he no sooner breathes our air than he forms schemes, and embarks in designs he never would have thought of in his own country.

Another factor that influenced American attitudes toward Britain was the diversity of the colonists. Not everyone was British. Although English language and institutions prevailed, many settlers had a non-English heritage. The thousands of settlers who were German, French, Dutch, Swedish, and Finnish composed a significant portion of the population of British North America. Most of them had little or no loyalty to the British king. Some non-English Americans actively supported the independence of their new homeland. For example, Apollos Rivoire, a French Huguenot, made many sacrifices for his new country, not the least of which was his name. Altering his name, as he noted, "merely on account that the bumpkins pronounce it easier," he became known as Paul Revere. His son, Paul Jr., became the famous midnight rider and a hero of the Revolutionary War.

A fourth factor that influenced the formation of a national consciousness was the Great Awakening. This religious revival was trans-colonial, not merely of a local nature. The religious unity resulted in a cultural unity as well.

Another crucial force in the development of American nationalism was the strength of colonial self-government. Colonial governments consisted of a governor, his advisors, and an elected assembly. With few exceptions, colonial governors were not a strong political force because they usually owed their jobs to the king but their salaries to the colonial assembly. Thus, by the beginning of the eighteenth century, the elected houses (such as the House of Burgesses in Virginia, the House of Representatives in Massachusetts, and the House of Delegates in Maryland) were clearly the most powerful forces in the governing of their respective colonies.

Guiding Questions

1. What events led many American colonists to become alienated from Britain?
2. How did British and American views of Parliament's actions differ?
3. How did colonists respond to new Parliamentary laws in general and to the Boston Massacre in particular?

George III

These assemblies held the all-important **power of the purse**, which meant that salaries for royal officials, military appropriations, and taxes had to obtain the approval of elected officeholders. In addition, the assemblies had the power to initiate their own legislation. They were not mere puppets for decrees from the royal governor.

The colonies were aware of their political clout. Nurtured by geographic remoteness and official neglect from Britain, generations of colonists gained experience in representative government, and the assemblies jealously guarded their power. Attempts to curb the self-governing power of the colonial legislatures were seen as threats to cherished rights and liberties.

Following the French and Indian War, the many forces that shaped America's growing sense of *nation* would be magnified by a sense of confidence and optimism. American troops had helped oust the French, clearing the way for western expansion. The Americans had also stood shoulder to shoulder with British regular troops and had left unimpressed. The British failure at frontier fighting, General Braddock's humiliating defeat at Fort Duquesne, and the offensive presence of troops during peacetime caused resentment. Americans came to view the British troops less as defenders and more as invaders. The battle lines were quietly being drawn.

Taxes and Tensions

After the French and Indian War, the relationship between Britain and the colonies changed significantly. Although British troops had helped to eliminate the threat of French domination, the successful conclusion of the war decreased colonial dependence on Great Britain. Increasing attitudes of independence and even hostility to Britain reflected the heritage of self-government in the colonies.

At the same time, however, attitudes in Britain were changing toward the nation's colonial offspring. Britain had just defeated France in a global war on land and sea, assembling an empire that would have made the ancient Roman emperors envious. The triumph was a source of great pride for the British, and many decided that it was time to "be an empire"—time to gain greater control over the thirteen colonies. In one parliamentary act after another during the 1760s and 1770s, the British pursued a policy of coercion instead of cooperation. That proved to be a costly mistake for Britain.

The Proclamation Line (1763)

Parliament issued the **Proclamation of 1763** in October of that year. It prohibited the colonists from settling beyond the Appalachian Mountains. The British government viewed this Proclamation Line as a way to diminish conflicts with the Indians. American colonists, however, denounced it as interference with their local governments; it denied westward expansion into lands the colonists viewed as their own.

Nevertheless, expansion continued. There was little concern in America for a law passed halfway around the world. Land-hungry settlers defied the prohibitions and pushed into the forbidden region. A number of towns, including Pittsburgh, were established during the decade after the line was drawn.

The Sugar Act (1764)

In 1764, following the lead of **George Grenville**, the nation's prime minister, the British Parliament passed the **Sugar Act**. This act placed a tariff, or tax, on certain goods (such as sugar, molasses, and coffee) that were imported into the colonies. The stated purpose of the Sugar Act was to raise revenue "for defraying the expenses of defending, protecting, and securing" the colonies. Such external tariffs (taxes on goods imported by Americans) had been levied before, but Parliament had seldom enforced them. This time, however, the British government clearly intended to collect the money. The colonists protested that since Parliament could now enforce such taxation with the standing army, the colonists and their legislatures were virtually powerless.

The Stamp Act (1765)

Grenville sought other ways to raise needed funds. In February of 1765, he proposed to Parliament a stamp tax required for newspapers, diplomas, and a variety of legal and commercial documents. Actual stamps or special stamped paper had to be purchased and attached to each of these items. The **Stamp Act** levied the first **internal**—or direct—**tax** (a tax on items produced and consumed entirely within the colonies) ever imposed on the colonies. For Americans, the issue was not the amount of the tax but that they were being taxed without their consent and that the traditional power of the colonial legislatures was being bypassed.

The little stamp seemed innocent enough to Parliament; only a handful of members opposed it, among them Colonel Isaac Barré, a veteran of Wolfe's Quebec campaign and a man who understood America. Barré stood in the House of Commons and declared that Britain's infringement on the rights of the colonists had "caused the blood of these sons of liberty to recoil within them." In America, colonists received word of Barré's speech enthusiastically. A growing body of opponents to British rule snatched Barré's phrase and proudly called themselves the **Sons of Liberty**.

The Quartering Act (1765)

Parliament passed the Stamp Act on March 22, 1765. Two days later, they passed the **Quartering Act**, which officially subjected the colonies to a standing army in peacetime and further required that the colonists feed and house them. Even Prime Minister Grenville admitted that the quartering clause was "by far the most likely to create difficulties and uneasiness . . . especially as the quartering of soldiers upon the people against their will is declared by the petition of Right [passed by Parliament in 1628] to be contrary to law." The almost simultaneous passage of the Stamp Act and the Quartering Act led the colonists to conclude that they were being oppressed by an unlawful military occupation to enforce illegal taxation.

Colonial Opposition

These parliamentary decisions, particularly the Stamp Act, sparked a firestorm of protest in America. On May 29, 1765, **Patrick Henry**, a member of the Virginia House of Burgesses, presented resolutions to that body declaring that Virginians possessed all the rights and privileges of Englishmen and that to grant the right of taxation to any group other than the Virginia Assembly was an act of tyranny. Though accounts differ about Henry's exact words,

Two of the hated stamps

Patrick Henry

Patrick Henry, "Voice of the Revolution"

Among the voices raised in defense of American liberty, few were as eloquent as that of Patrick Henry. After one speech, a listener said that the audience was "taken captive; and so delighted with their captivity, that they followed implicitly, whithersoever he led them; that, at his bidding, their tears flowed from pity, and their cheeks flushed with indignation."

In his early years, however, Henry showed little sign of possessing unusual talent. In fact, his first ventures into making a living proved to be dismal failures. He twice went bankrupt trying to operate a store. (Some people claim that he preferred engaging his customers in debates to selling goods.) An effort at farming proved so troublesome that Henry seemed almost relieved when his farmhouse burned and he had to seek other employment. Almost in desperation, Henry turned to law. Even then, his study was so hurried that another lawyer signed his license only after Henry solemnly promised to pursue further study as he practiced.

Henry proved far more diligent in law than in his earlier pursuits, and his extraordinary speaking ability was a tremendous advantage in arguing cases before a jury. He became a prosperous, much-sought-after attorney.

He was elected to Virginia's House of Burgesses in 1765. Later that year, he gave his fierce denunciation of the Stamp Act.

Patrick Henry must have learned some of his oratorical skills from the speakers he heard as a young man. Some historians think that young Patrick may have heard George Whitefield, the English evangelist who helped carry the Great Awakening throughout the colonies. In addition, Henry heard Samuel Davies, a Presbyterian leader of the Awakening in Virginia.

The effect of Davies, other ministers, and the Bible itself on Henry was profound. The Virginia statesman's speeches were filled with the literary style of Scripture and with numerous allusions to the Bible. Few speeches show that tendency more clearly than Henry's most famous oration, given in March 1775. A decade had passed since his Stamp Act speech. As war with England brewed, he raised his eloquent voice in a ringing call for liberty. His fiery declaration that "Gentlemen may cry peace, peace—but there is no peace" echoes the prophet Jeremiah (Jer. 6:14; see also 8:11). Likewise, Henry's rhetorical question posed in the same speech a few moments later—"Why stand we here idle?"—alludes to Jesus's words in the parable of the laborers in the vineyard (Matt. 20:6).

> Gentlemen may cry, peace, peace—but there is no peace. The war is actually begun! The next gale that sweeps from the north will bring to our ears the clash of resounding arms! Our brethren are already in the field! Why stand we here idle? What is it that gentlemen wish? What would they have? Is life so dear, or peace so sweet as to be purchased at the price of chains and slavery? Forbid it, Almighty God! I know not what course others may take, but as for me, give me liberty, or give me death!

Patrick Henry became the voice of resistance to British oppression in the colonies.

it appears that he gave a blunt warning to King George III about the consequences of such tyranny. He apparently made references to two earlier leaders who had been killed by opponents. Henry told the Assembly, "[Julius] Caesar had his Brutus, [King] Charles the First his [Oliver] Cromwell, and George the Third . . ." He was interrupted midsentence by the Speaker of the House of Burgesses who is said to have cried, "Treason!"

Indeed many present thought Henry was implying that the king should be assassinated. Though he later apologized for his remarks and assured his fellow legislators that he was loyal to the king, the tension evident that day was spreading throughout the colonies.

A few months later, in October 1765, the first example of genuine colonial unity occurred. Delegates from nine colonies met in New York for the **Stamp Act Congress**. They formally denounced the Stamp Act and the seizure of colonial rights that it represented. Elsewhere, matters became violent. In Boston, the Sons of Liberty, led by **Samuel Adams**, hung an effigy (crude likeness of a hated person or group) of the royal stamp distributor for Massachusetts. More radical members of the opposition ransacked his home, smashing windows and furniture. Although Samuel Adams distanced himself from the vandalism, he was generally pleased with the protest. The tax official resigned as the Sons of Liberty organizations in other colonies began staging similar protests.

In March of 1766, Parliament repealed the hated Stamp Act. However, at the same time, it passed the **Declaratory Act**. It stated that Parliament had the right to pass any law regarding the colonies that it desired. Because the repeal of the Stamp Act was being celebrated, many colonists paid little attention to the new act. Others feared, quite accurately, that more taxes would be forthcoming.

Sam Adams led the Sons of Liberty in Boston.

Effigy of a Stamp Act official hung by protesting colonists.

Victorious colonists celebrated the repeal of the Stamp Act by conducting a mock funeral for it.

Townshend Acts (1767)

An uneasy calm followed the repeal of the Stamp Act, but the quiet was soon shattered by a new revenue plan in Parliament. In 1767, Charles Townshend, the head of the British Treasury, proposed a series of taxes and enforcement measures that had far-reaching political consequences. The **Townshend Acts** placed taxes on glass, paint, paper, and tea. Furthermore, the acts strengthened the writs of assistance, which were general search warrants used and often abused by customs officials in their search for taxable goods. It was proposed that the revenue raised from those taxes should pay the salaries of royal officials, including the governor. This was in direct conflict with the traditional "power of the purse" that many colonial assemblies had maintained for nearly a century.

An optimistic Charles Townshend told Parliament that the colonies should submit to this unprecedented power-grab because they were "planted with so much tenderness, governed with so much affection, and established with so much care and attention." However, Barré retorted, "We did not plant the colonies. Most of them fled from oppression. They met with great difficulty and hardship, but as they fled from tyranny here they could not dread danger there. They flourished not by our care but by our neglect. They have increased while we did not attend to them. They shrink under our hand."

Opposition to the Townshend Acts grew. Colonists organized **boycotts**, or refusals to buy British goods. In Boston, the hotbed of the resistance movement, a riot broke out in 1768 when customs officials seized a ship belonging to one of the city's leading businessmen, John Hancock. In the fall, British troops and artillery arrived to police Boston and to quash the growing unrest.

The English government, through the Sugar Act, the Stamp Act, and the various Townshend measures, was moving not only to raise money but also to centralize authority in London. These new taxes outraged the colonists. Their fury did not center primarily on the cost of the taxes but rather on the fact that they had no voice in the approval of them. "**No taxation without representation**" became a rallying cry for many colonists. They repeatedly complained that there were no colonial representatives in Parliament; however, Parliament insisted that every member of their body represented everyone who resided in the British Empire. But many colonial leaders argued that the colonists were being deprived of their freedoms and their rights of self-government.

First Bloodshed

Lord North became the British prime minister in 1770. Two years earlier he had told Parliament, "America must fear you before she can love you. . . . I will never think of repealing [the Townshend Acts] until I see America prostrate at my feet." However, in 1770, all of the Townshend duties (taxes) were repealed except for a small tax on tea. Nevertheless, North's words had a prophetic ring to them in ways the prime minister did not expect. In the late winter of 1770, Americans would indeed be lying at the feet of the British—cut down, not with taxes, but with lead shot in the **Boston Massacre**.

With the arrival of a thousand British troops in Boston in 1768, the atmosphere in the city had grown from tense to explosive. The sight of the British force and its fleet of warships overseeing a city at peace irritated Bostonians. It outraged Samuel Adams and his

Boston Massacre Engraving

Paul Revere was a Boston silversmith and engraver. Just three weeks after the Boston Massacre, he created the engraving shown here. However, it is not an accurate portrayal of what really happened. Revere deliberately presents the colonists in a sympathetic light. For example, the British soldiers appear to be cold and determined while the colonists' faces reflect pain and horror. Additional inaccuracies include:

- Soldiers are shown as though they are moving in a line of attack, as they would do on the battlefield. In reality, the scene was chaotic, and the soldiers were separated from each other by the crowd.
- A sniper (circled) is erroneously shown in a second story window.
- On the right of the engraving is a building Revere labels as "Butcher's Hall." It was the location of a British government office, the Customs House.
- The British commander, Captain Preston, appears to be giving the order to fire by waving his sword. In truth, he was trying to calm the situation and gave no such command.
- The colonists, mostly laborers, are dressed as gentlemen. Elevating their status could affect the way people perceived them.
- No snow or ice is shown, though some in the crowd had hurled snowballs at the soldiers.

Crispus Attucks, a former slave, was one of the five killed in the first clash between the colonists and British soldiers.

fellow Patriots (those who opposed the British). The spark that ignited the powder keg of conflict came in late February 1770.

On a Friday afternoon, February 23, an informant for British customs officials took it upon himself to pull down a boycott sign that the Sons of Liberty had placed near his home. A small crowd gathered and began hurling stones and exchanging insults with him. He retreated to his house, vowing revenge. When a rock smashed through his window, hitting his wife, the informant took his musket and fired into the crowd, killing an eleven-year-old boy.

Over the weekend a blizzard struck Boston, so it was not until Monday that a funeral procession could make its way through the snowdrifts to bury the boy. Despite the February cold, tempers were hot.

By the end of the week, a few minor confrontations between dockworkers and British soldiers heightened tensions. The soldiers vowed to settle the score. On March 5, a band of Patriots gathered in the square outside the British barracks to demand the departure of the unwelcome soldiers. The angry crowd hurled sticks and snowballs at seven soldiers. One of the soldiers was struck by a stick and fell on the ice. While getting up, he fired his musket into the mob—whether in anger or by accident cannot be determined. Following his shot, however, the other British soldiers spontaneously fired into the crowd.

As the smoke from the muskets cleared, five colonists lay dead or dying in the square. Several others were also wounded. Among those killed was Crispus Attucks, a former slave. As news of the shooting spread, many in Boston were wild with anger. Soon the event was being called a "massacre."

Several months later, after tempers had cooled somewhat, nine British soldiers were placed on trial for murder. One of the attorneys defending them was Samuel Adams's cousin, **John Adams**. Though he had been critical of Parliament's actions and considered himself a Patriot, John Adams believed that everyone was entitled to a fair trial. Eventually, all soldiers, except two, were acquitted. Those two were found guilty of manslaughter, rather than murder. Their thumbs were branded, and they were released.

Though some colonists resented John Adams's defense of the soldiers, he was recognized as an outstanding lawyer. Over the next decade, he was heavily involved in the colonial struggle for independence. In 1789, he became the new nation's first vice president and later was elected as the second president.

Section Review

1. What is "the power of the purse"?
2–3. Why did Parliament establish the Proclamation Line of 1763? Why did the colonists oppose it?
4–9. Name six acts of Parliament after the French and Indian War that created tension between Great Britain and its colonies.
10. What city was the site of a "massacre" in 1770?
* Explain a possible reason for the power and eloquence of Patrick Henry's "liberty or death" speech.
* Assume you were John Adams. Defend your decision to work as an attorney for the British soldiers charged with murder in the Boston Massacre.

CHAPTER 5 REVIEW

Making Connections

1-2. Which two European nations fought recurring wars from the 1680s to the 1760s?

3-4. What mistaken tactic did the British follow that led to the tragic defeat of Braddock as he marched his troops toward Fort Duquesne? What tactic did their enemy practice?

5. How did acts of Parliament following the French and Indian War lead to increased tensions between Britain and the colonies?

Developing History Skills

1. List and then summarize five reasons the colonists were feeling more like Americans and less like Englishmen by the mid-1700s.

2. Explain Franklin's Albany Plan for colonial unity.

Thinking Critically

1. If you had lived at the time of the Proclamation Line of 1763, would you have viewed it as a security from Indian attacks or as interference in local government and a hindrance to expansion? Why?

2. Who was responsible for the Boston Massacre—the assembled colonists; the soldiers who fired on the crowd; or Lord North, who urged Parliament not to repeal the Townshend Acts "until [he saw] America prostrate at [his] feet"? Support your answer.

Living as a Christian Citizen

1. Imagine you are a pastor in New England. Write a brief address instructing your congregation about how to respond to the conflict between the colonies and England.

2. Imagine you are writing a newspaper editorial during the time leading to the War for Independence. Write an article describing the new type of citizen emerging from the New World—the American. Organize your article around the core values of freedom, individualism, equality, and growth.

People, Places, and Things to Remember

Louisiana
French and Indian War
Seven Years' War
George Washington
Fort Duquesne
guerrilla warfare
Albany Congress
Benjamin Franklin
Edward Braddock
Marquis de Montcalm
William Pitt
James Wolfe
Battle of Quebec
Treaty of Paris (1763)
George III
Pontiac
power of the purse
Proclamation of 1763
George Grenville
Sugar Act
Stamp Act
internal tax
Sons of Liberty
Quartering Act
Patrick Henry
Stamp Act Congress
Samuel Adams
Declaratory Act
Townshend Acts
boycotts
no taxation without representation
Boston Massacre
John Adams

6 INDEPENDENCE (1770–1783)

> We fight, get beat, rise, and fight again.
>
> **General Nathanael Greene**
> 1781

Continental soldiers continued their drills during the harsh winter at Valley Forge, Pennsylvania.

Big Ideas

1. How did colonists react to British actions?
2. What were two major colonial views about independence?
3. What were the significant early military campaigns?
4. What were the significant battles in the South?

I. The Eve of War

II. Declaring Independence

III. Early Campaigns

IV. The War in the South

"The Revolution was effected before the war commenced," John Adams, Founding Father and future president, reflected years afterward. "The Revolution was in the minds and hearts of the people. . . . This radical change in the principles, opinions, sentiments, and affections of the people, was the real American Revolution."

This revolution in the heart was in many ways an evolution that began at Jamestown and Plymouth more than a century earlier. Escalating events, however, gradually moved the revolution from the heart to open conflict. The question for many Americans became not whether they would submit to taxes but whether they would submit to tyranny.

One interview with an old veteran minuteman, Levi Preston, conducted more than fifty years after he fought the British, cuts to the crucial issue behind the war. The interviewer asked Preston to describe the British oppressions that led to independence. The ancient warrior replied, "Oppressions? I didn't feel them."

"What, were you not oppressed by the Stamp Act?"

"I never saw one of those stamps. . . . I am certain I never paid a penny for one of them."

"Well, what then about the tea-tax?"

"Tea-tax! I never drank a drop of the stuff; the boys threw it all overboard."

"Then I suppose you had been reading Harrington or Sidney and Locke about the eternal principles of liberty."

"Never heard of 'em" the old man answered. "We read only the Bible, the Catechism, Watts's Psalms and Hymns, and the Almanack."

The puzzled questioner demanded, "Well, then, what was the matter? And what did you mean in going to the fight?"

"Young man, what we meant in going for those Redcoats was this: we always had governed ourselves, and we always meant to. They didn't mean we should."

The Pennsylvania State House, later known as Independence Hall, was the site of the adoption of the Declaration of Independence in July 1776.

I. The Eve of War

After the Boston Massacre, tensions relaxed in the colonies. The calm, however, was merely the eye of the storm. In June 1772 an armed British customs ship, the **Gaspee**, ran aground near Providence, Rhode Island. The ship's captain, who had previously searched ships without a warrant and had sent his crew ashore to seize food without paying for it, was not welcome in Rhode Island. On the night of June 9, local citizens boarded the *Gaspee*, captured and removed the crew, and burned the ship.

This attack on one of His Majesty's ships prompted the British to send a commission to investigate and make arrests. In the past, such matters had been handled by colonial courts. At the same time, the Massachusetts governor announced that his salary would now come from the king, not the colony. No longer would the legislature be able to limit the governor or other royal officials by using the "power of the purse." More and more, the colonists came to believe that their rights were being stripped away.

Another development in 1772 furthered this belief. In November, the Boston Town Meeting authorized the formation of a **Committee of Correspondence**. Under the guidance of Samuel Adams, the committee provided information on British threats to liberty to other areas of the colony.

Guiding Questions

1. What events led to Britain and the American colonies going to war?
2. What were the purposes for the Tea Act and the Intolerable Acts?
3. What was the significance of the First Continental Congress?
4. Do you think the colonial response to Britain's actions was scriptural?

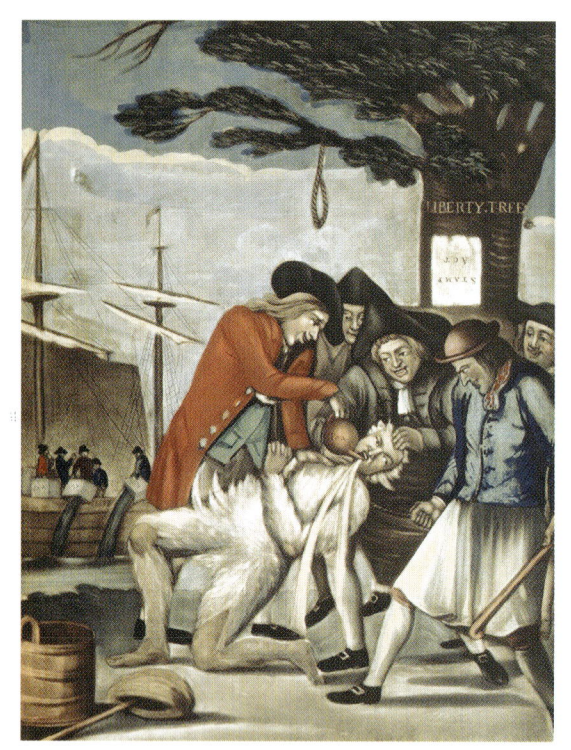

The king's tax collectors often felt the brunt of the colonists' anger over British policies. In this picture a tax collector is being tarred and feathered.

The Boston committee also successfully encouraged the formation of a network of Committees of Correspondence. Within three months, eighty new committees had formed in Massachusetts alone. In March 1773 the Virginia legislature voted to establish a permanent Committee of Correspondence, and other colonies quickly followed. The committees provided not only information but also a model of intercolonial cooperation that would be an important step toward a united political and military response to British actions.

The Boston Tea Party

The Tea Act

The East India Company had been one of the most profitable businesses in Britain, but the company was facing a crisis: its warehouses were stuffed with seventeen million pounds of tea. The company, verging on bankruptcy, turned to its powerful friends for help. At the urging of the prime minister, Lord North, Parliament passed the **Tea Act of 1773**, which basically granted the East India Company a monopoly on the shipment and sale of English tea in America. The British tea was still cheaper to buy than the smuggled Dutch tea; however, colonists were enraged. If Parliament could grant a monopoly on tea, what next? In port cities from Boston to Charleston, opposition to the tea shipments was intense. In New York and Philadelphia, for example, tea agents resigned, and sea captains returned their cargoes home to England for fear of their lives and property. Tea, like the hated stamp nearly a decade earlier, became a symbol of tyranny. Coffee replaced the British beverage on Patriot tables.

"Boston Harbor—a Teapot Tonight"

When tea arrived in Boston Harbor aboard the *Dartmouth* on November 28, 1773, Patriots made every effort to have it returned to England. The governor refused to allow the ship's return, and the confrontation became a stalemate. The Patriots were determined that the tea would not be unloaded in Boston; the governor was determined that it would be.

On the evening of December 16, 1773, thousands gathered for the Boston Town Meeting in the Old South Church, not far from the waterfront. Shortly afterwards, to shouts of "Boston harbor—a teapot tonight," approximately 150 men and boys crudely disguised themselves as Mohawk Indians and boarded the *Dartmouth* and two other newly arrived tea ships.

In the **Boston Tea Party**, the group dumped 342 large cases of tea into the harbor in under three hours. To clarify the purpose of their protest, the raiders took great care to avoid damaging anything except the tea. Even a broken padlock was anonymously replaced the next day. Only one man was caught stealing tea, and he was promptly kicked off the ship. When the ships had been emptied of tea, the participants cleaned them and released their crews. The Patriots then lined up at attention on deck, emptied any loose tea from their boots, swept it into the harbor, and marched away singing,

Rally, Mohawks! Bring out your axes,
And tell King George, we'll pay no taxes
On his foreign tea.

The Boston Tea Party

Tea in Other Ports

Boston was not the only colonial port that protested the tea tax. The "tea party" was copied in New York. Charleston stored its tea until the war broke out and then sold it at auction to help pay for colonial forces. Philadelphia let its tea rot in warehouses.

Even pro-British colonists, or **Loyalists**, admitted that the tea party "had been conducted as correctly as a crime could be." Across the Atlantic, however, the incident was not regarded lightly. A law had been disregarded and property had been destroyed. King George III instructed Lord North that it was time for strong measures against the colonies. "The colonies must either submit or triumph," the king declared. On this, at least, the Patriots and the king were in agreement.

The Intolerable Acts

The Boston Tea Party spurred the British government to action against Massachusetts. In 1774, Parliament passed four acts, known collectively as the **Coercive Acts**, intended to punish the troublesome colony.

The first act closed the harbor, effective June 1, 1774, until the cost of the destroyed tea was repaid. The second act revoked the Massachusetts colonial charter. Now officials would be appointed by the royal governor rather than elected, and town meetings were allowed only with the governor's approval. The third act dictated

> *Political Protest by Colonial Women*
>
> Another protest to the Tea Act occurred in Edenton, North Carolina, on October 25, 1774. A group of fifty-one women pledged not to drink any more tea (or buy British-made cloth and other British imports). Their action was the earliest-known instance of political activity on the part of American women in the colonies.

A Heritage of Resistance

Even before the Boston Tea Party, Americans made numerous violent attempts to vent their anger against perceived government abuses. Three specific groups are noteworthy.

First were the **Paxton Boys**, a large group of Scots-Irish living in the backcountry of Pennsylvania near the village of Paxton (near present-day Harrisburg). During Pontiac's War, they thought that Pennsylvania's colonial government was not doing enough to protect the people of the colony, especially those in the backcountry. Believing that the government would not defend them, they decided to defend themselves. They formed a vigilante group. (Vigilantes are civilians who act in a law enforcement capacity without the legal authority to do so.)

The nearest hostile Indians were about two hundred miles away, but the Paxton Boys took out their frustrations on the nearest Indians, the peaceful Conestogas (also known as the Susquehannocks). Many of these Indians were Christians and even lived among the settlers. But the Paxtons accused them of being spies, murdered six of them, and burned the cabin where the murders had occurred.

Though the government of Pennsylvania offered a reward for the murderers, no one would report them to authorities. Unchallenged, the Paxton Boys went after other peaceful Indians in eastern Pennsylvania. In January 1764 some of the Indians fled to Philadelphia, and hundreds of the Paxtons followed. Benjamin Franklin and other prominent Philadelphians negotiated with the Paxtons and thereby prevented any further bloodshed. About half of the rescued Indians died, however, when they contracted smallpox in the crowded city.

Another violent group was the **Regulators**. These North Carolina residents were dissatisfied with the colony's wealthy, upper-class leaders, whom they considered cruel and corrupt and who imposed high taxes on the colonials. The Regulators rose up in armed rebellion. Their goal was to set up a better government and reduce taxes. They dominated the backcountry of North Carolina from 1764 to 1771. Eventually, colonial leaders suppressed the rebellion. It is worth noting that the Regulators directed their violence against local and colonial leaders, not against the British.

A third group that turned to violent protest was the Sons of Liberty. This secret group was formed in 1765 in reaction to the Stamp Act. Their actions were directed against the symbols and representatives of British authority, including the property of customs agents and Loyalists (colonists who supported the British king). They burned officials in effigy and tarred and feathered tax collectors (literally placing hot tar on the person and covering him in feathers). They dumped the tea into Boston Harbor and intimidated those who seemed to support the king's rule, policies, and agents.

The Sons of Liberty were not officially or formally organized. Their leaders tended to come from the middle and upper levels of society; the regular members came from all social levels. Almost all the colonies had some such group, but Boston's was probably the most prominent. As mentioned in the previous chapter, the leader of the Boston Sons of Liberty was Samuel Adams.

that British officials accused of committing crimes be tried not in Massachusetts but in another colony or in England. In a new Quartering Act, the fourth act required the housing and feeding of British soldiers in private homes. With the arrival of a military governor, General Thomas Gage, to replace the existing governor, Bostonians knew that their city was under military occupation.

If colonial submission was the purpose behind the Coercive Acts, they were clearly a failure. In America these measures, called the "**Intolerable Acts**" by Patriots who refused to be coerced, hardened opposition and created an unprecedented sense of unity among the colonies.

In addition, Parliament passed the **Quebec Act**, which was directed at British Canada, not the thirteen colonies. The timing, however, could not have been worse. The Quebec Act set up a rigid political system, made Roman Catholicism the official religion of Quebec, and extended the territorial boundaries of Quebec southward to the Ohio River. The possibility of Catholicism rising in the West with the approval of Parliament enraged many American Protestants who had fled Catholic persecution in Europe. They also feared that the act might set a precedent for Parliament to establish Anglicanism as the state religion throughout the colonies. The Quebec Act encouraged many Christians to join the growing chorus of dissent out of fear of centralized religious authority.

First Continental Congress (1774)

Sympathy for beleaguered Boston spread throughout the colonies. In the House of Burgesses in Williamsburg, a thirty-one-year-old Virginian named Thomas Jefferson called for a day of fasting and prayer as a show of support for Boston Patriots. The royal governor, upon hearing of the resolution, dissolved the House. Unperturbed, the legislators simply reconvened in a nearby tavern, where they adopted a resolution calling for the meeting of a Continental Congress. Similar calls came from other colonies. The Massachusetts House of Representatives called for the Colonial Committees of Correspondence to meet in Philadelphia in September.

On September 5, representatives from all the colonies except Georgia gathered in Philadelphia's Carpenter's Hall for the **First Continental Congress**. Far from being a gathering of radicals, the fifty-five delegates had been elected by their colonial assemblies or by provincial congresses and included some of the most distinguished men in America, including George Washington and Patrick Henry of Virginia, as well as John Adams and Samuel Adams of Massachusetts.

The changing times required new thinking, and the delegates showed themselves equal to the task. The geographic and historical features that divided the colonies had to give way to united thinking. Patrick Henry declared, "The distinctions between Virginians, Pennsylvanians, and New Yorkers and New Englanders are no more. I am not a Virginian, but an American."

A spirit of cooperation existed among the delegates. When one member proposed that the sessions open with prayer, the idea was at first opposed on the grounds that Congregationalists, Presbyterians, Quakers, Anglicans, and Mennonites, all represented

The First Continental Congress in prayer

among the delegates, could not possibly worship together. Samuel Adams, who as a young man had sat under the preaching of George Whitefield, favored the prayer proposal and declared that his faith did not prevent him from hearing anyone pray as long as the man was devout in his religious beliefs and a patriot. The other delegates conceded the point, and the next day an Anglican pastor arrived. During the night, word reached the city that General Gage's troops had opened fire on civilians in Boston. In light of the tragedy in Boston, the minister read Psalm 35:1–2: "Plead my cause, O Lord, with them that strive with me: fight against them that fight against me. Take hold of shield and buckler, and stand up for mine help." Then he prayed powerfully for ten minutes for the people of Boston. When he had finished, the assembly was visibly moved and many delegates wept openly.

Although the report of Boston casualties proved to be false (Gage had confiscated a stock of Patriot gunpowder, but there were no deaths), the delegates proceeded with business. They adopted a Declaration of American Rights that stated the colonies must be self-governing in nearly every respect. Although they maintained their allegiance to the king, they asserted that his actions had to be consistent with American rights. As self-governing states, the colonies had the right to raise militias to defend themselves.

After seven weeks of work, the delegates agreed to reconvene the Congress in May 1775. None of them could foresee that by then the course of events would take a decidedly bloody turn.

"Shot Heard Round the World"

When the delegates returned to their homes, they set about putting their words into action. In October 1774 Massachusetts had already established a Provincial Congress that was elected by the people. This assembly, in addition to the usual legislative functions, prepared Massachusetts for the conflict that loomed over Boston. They authorized the organizing, drilling, and supplying of Patriot militias. Special units of militiamen called **minutemen** formed a quick first line of defense in case the British invaded the countryside.

Throughout the colonies, the Patriots gathered their forces militarily and politically. At a gathering of the Virginia Convention in late March 1775, the delegates discussed the issue of organizing volunteer militias. **Patrick Henry** rose to address his fellow legislators

Religious Changes in America

Religious life was altered dramatically both during and after the war. Government support of religion gave way to complete freedom of religion and the separation of church and state. The Anglican Church suffered because of its association with England. In all the colonies where it had been the established church—with the exception of Virginia—tax support for the Anglican Church ended during the war. Virginia continued to provide tax support until the Virginia Statute of Religious Freedom was adopted in 1786. Government support for the Congregational (Puritan) Church lingered in New England until the early 1800s. But overall it was clear that the war had made religion in America diverse and voluntary.

Militia vs. Regulars

Militia were "citizen soldiers," part-time fighters who were prepared to leave their farms and businesses to fight in emergencies. The famous "minutemen" of the War for Independence (citizens supposedly ready to fight on a minute's notice) are an example of American militia. Although militia units might serve for months or even years at a time, they remained nonprofessionals, serving only as long as the emergency lasted.

Regulars, on the other hand, were professional, full-time soldiers who made the military their career. The British army in the War for Independence consisted of regulars, although some Loyalist militia units fought alongside them. The Continentals were America's regulars in the war, serving as the veteran core of Washington's army. Although militiamen often performed valiantly in battle, most generals—including Washington—preferred regulars. These seasoned professional soldiers often proved more dependable in battle.

Patrick Henry delivered a fiery speech to the Second Virginia Convention. Representatives from the colony had assembled to discuss their response to British policy.

with powerful words that would soon be confirmed with blood. As noted in the last chapter, he said:

> Gentlemen may cry peace, peace—but there is no peace. The war is actually begun! The next gale that sweeps the north will bring to our ears the clash of resounding arms. Our brethren are already in the field! . . . I know not what course others may take, but as for me, give me liberty or give me death!

In April 1775 General Gage decided to suppress the growing militia strength in the Massachusetts countryside. Based on spy reports, Gage learned that a large stock of Patriot munitions (ammunition and other military supplies) was stored in Concord, a town sixteen miles west of Boston. In what he hoped would be a quiet show of force, he ordered 700 soldiers to seize the stockpile.

On the night of April 18, 1775, the British quietly rowed across the bay to Cambridge and assembled for the march to Concord. Along the way, they planned to stop in Lexington to arrest two Patriot leaders, John Hancock and Samuel Adams.

When Patriots learned of the plan, they sent **Paul Revere** (who had made the Boston Massacre engraving) and William Dawes to warn colonists. These two men, following separate routes, made it to Lexington. A third man, Dr. Samuel Prescott, joined them as they rode to Concord. Each was stopped by the British, but Prescott managed to reach Concord.

About seventy Lexington minutemen were waiting on the village green when the British arrived on the morning of April 19. Just as the sun was breaking through the chill morning mist, Major John Pitcairn, commanding the British advance, spotted the thin line of Patriot militia. Pitcairn ordered his troops to hold their fire and advance as he galloped forward, shouting to the Americans to disarm and disband. The minutemen's commander, Captain John Parker, had ordered them not to open fire either, only to stand in a show of defiance to the king's troops. Having accomplished this, the militia began to disperse. At

Paul Revere "spread the alarm / through every Middlesex village and farm."

Famous Order

"Don't fire unless fired upon, but if they want to have a war, let it begin here."

—Captain John Parker at Lexington

The minutemen faced the British on the village green at Lexington.

Differences Between Revolutions

Addressing the United Nations in 1988, Soviet Premier Mikhail Gorbachev declared, "Two great revolutions, the French Revolution of 1789 and the Russian Revolution of [November] 1917, exerted a powerful impact on the very nature of history." Gorbachev correctly considered the French and Russian Revolutions together, because they had similar causes and consequences. Yet Gorbachev ignored an important revolution—the American War for Independence. These three events are separated by far more than time and place. The French and Russian Revolutions began with legitimate grievances, but the leaders engaged in bloody struggles for power. However, the American War for Independence, which was fought to obtain freedom from political oppression, avoided similar bloodshed among its participants.

In both the French and the Russian Revolutions, a narrow, ruthless minority, the Jacobins in France and the Bolsheviks in Russia, seized the reins of power in the name of the people. These fierce factions overthrew the existing institutions of God and government and replaced them with atheistic dictatorships. Those who opposed were often taken to a guillotine or a firing squad.

The American War for Independence, however, was fundamentally different from either of the other two revolutions. The United States was settled in the early modern period and, unlike Europe, did not have the strong class divisions of feudalism. Also unlike Europe, the United States enjoyed widespread land ownership.

Some Americans do not feel comfortable calling their War for Independence a "revolution" because they associate revolutions with thuggery. The War for Independence was a revolution in the sense that it brought profound political and social changes to America. It was an overthrow of a recognized political power by those who had previously submitted to it. However, as a revolution, it was radically different from the French and Russian versions.

France and Russia had rejected the Protestant Reformation. In stark contrast, many Protestants fled persecution in Europe and came to the American colonies. Enlightenment ideas influenced both France and the American colonies. However, the French accepted these ideas without the biblical restraints recognized by many American colonists. Many Russian leaders embraced humanistic concepts that denied biblical truths, such as the fallen nature of people.

The French and Russian Revolutions also opposed religion; thus, they established secular states. However, the American colonists were encouraged, supported, and often led by their religious leaders. In addition, the American colonies experienced a great spiritual awakening prior to the war and an extended period of revival during and following the war. In striking contrast, French revolutionaries exalted the goddess Reason, and Russian revolutionaries persecuted organized religion.

Alexander Hamilton, observing the French Revolution in the 1790s, noted, "There is no real resemblance between what was the cause of America and what is the cause of France; that the difference is no less great than that between liberty and licentiousness [lawlessness]."

In 1787, just a few years after the American Revolution ended, the U.S. Constitution was written. This remarkable charter has lasted over two centuries. France, on the other hand, had four constitutions between 1791 and 1799.

To maintain their iron-fisted grip on power, revolutionary leaders in France and Russia resorted to executions rather than elections. Approximately forty thousand French citizens were executed during their revolution. Millions of Russians were killed by leaders such as Joseph Stalin. Little wonder that the Russian revolutionaries had to keep their subjects behind barbed wire and guarded borders, lest the people see the freedoms that had resulted from the American Revolution.

---

that point, a shot rang out—who pulled the trigger has never been determined—but the British regulars then unleashed two volleys on the scattered band of soldier-farmers, killing eight and wounding ten. Most of them were shot in the back. Pitcairn, angered that his men had disobeyed orders, rebuked his troops. Only one of his men had been wounded in the skirmish. The British then proceeded to Concord.

Alerted to the British advance, hundreds of minutemen converged on the outskirts of Concord. Uncontested, the British entered the town in search of munitions. Most munitions had been removed, but the British burned items they found. The Patriots, seeing smoke rising from the village, assumed that the British were torching their homes. As a result, a number of Americans advanced

The "shot heard round the world" was fired at the Old North Bridge in Concord.

Patriot minutemen harassed the British troops relentlessly as the British returned to Boston after having fired on the Patriots at Lexington and Concord.

on the British at the North Bridge that led into Concord. Fatal shots were exchanged, and the British were pushed back. Years later, author Ralph Waldo Emerson wrote of the skirmish at Concord Bridge:

> By the rude bridge that arched the flood,
> Their flag to April's breeze unfurled,
> Here once the embattled farmers stood,
> And fired the shot heard round the world.

For the king's men, the march back to Boston was a nightmare as Patriots fired from the cover of stone walls, trees, and barns. Although most of the minutemen had never had formal military training, they were experienced wild game hunters, so they found the bright red uniforms of the British to be even easier targets.

Although many Patriots lost their lives in the battles of **Lexington and Concord**, the Americans had clearly won the day. Forty-nine Americans had been killed and about forty more wounded. But the British regulars had been hurt badly by farmers. Not only were 73 British soldiers killed and 174 wounded, but Patriot forces now had them bottled up in Boston. The war had begun.

Section Review

1. Why were the colonists offended by the decision to have the king pay the Massachusetts governor's salary?
2. Why did the colonists oppose the Tea Act of 1773 even though it provided tea at lower prices?
3–6. Describe each of the four Coercive Acts.
7. What did the colonists call the Coercive Acts?
8. Why did the British army send a force to Concord?
★ Do you think the colonists who resisted the British government had biblical justification for doing so? Refer to the following passages as you consider this question: 2 Kings 11; Acts 5:29; Romans 13:1–7; 1 Peter 2:13, 21–23.
★ Explain some differences between the American War for Independence and the French Revolution (1789) and Russian Revolution (November 1917).

II. Declaring Independence

Divided Loyalties

The undeclared war that had erupted deeply divided the colonies. Many colonists answered the call to arms as **Patriots**, fighting for the cause of independence. Others, however, were Loyalists, or **Tories** (named after the political party in Parliament that supported the king), because they continued to support the king. The division cut across regions and social classes. It tore communities and even families apart, pitting father against son (such as Benjamin Franklin and his son William) and brother against brother. In some areas (such as South Carolina), the War for Independence was fought almost entirely between American Patriots and American Loyalists.

It is impossible to know how many Americans supported the king during the Revolution, but they were numerous. At least one hundred thousand Loyalists left America by the end of the war.

Guiding Questions

1. How was colonial opinion divided regarding the war?
2. What impact did *Common Sense* have on support for independence?
3. How did the Olive Branch Petition and the Declaration of Independence differ?

Some historians believe that Loyalists comprised about 20 percent of the population. Others estimate that allegiances were divided almost equally among the colonists: one-third Loyalists, one-third Patriots, and one-third apathetic or uncommitted to either side.

Sympathy for the Patriot cause was not confined to America. When the war finally came, the British were also divided over waging war against their colonial cousins. Partly because of such attitudes, King George III was forced to find German mercenaries (professional soldiers who are paid to fight) to fill the ranks of British forces in America. These mercenaries were called **Hessians**

Taking Sides

Loyalists (Tories)

Some colonists were loyal to England for political, religious, and economic reasons. Many believed that they were fairly represented by Parliament and that taxes to fund the defense of the colonies were just. Others thought that Parliament had exceeded its bounds with various acts; however, they did not think that those mistakes justified war. Furthermore, many Loyalists feared that independence would lead to mob rule and tyranny.

Some Tories saw the king as God's authority over them, and they believed that it was wrong to rebel. For them, Romans 13:2 settled the matter: "Whosoever . . . resisteth the power, resisteth the ordinance of God: and they that resist shall receive to themselves damnation." They also feared that cutting ties with Britain would remove the colonies from profitable trade relations in the British Empire. Others remained loyal to Britain because of family connections.

Many Loyalists fled to England, Canada, or the British West Indies. One such individual was Isaac Wilkins, a member of the New York Assembly. Before leaving America he said, "It has been my constant maxim through life to do my duty conscientiously, and to trust the issue of my actions to the Almighty. May that God in whose hands are all events, speedily restore peace and liberty to my unhappy country."

But most Loyalists stayed in the American colonies, probably because they did not want to risk losing their property. To avoid trouble, some kept their opinions to themselves. Other Tories fought for Britain, especially when it seemed to be winning. These colonists also aided the British by selling them food and other supplies.

Patriots

The Patriots also had political, religious, and economic reasons for their cause. They believed that their political right to a representative government was at stake. The colonists were accustomed to representing themselves locally by creating many of their own laws and taxes. When a distant Parliament began to tax the colonies, many Americans saw this as a loss of their liberty. Those who were influenced by the ideas of John Locke and other writers believed it was justified to overthrow a government that had become oppressive. In their thinking, such a government was no longer legitimate.

Religious beliefs also greatly influenced the Patriots. In fact, the war might not have been as popular without the influence of preachers, many of whom called for independence. Religious colonists, many of whom had read what Romans 13 says about rebellion, wrestled to decide to which authority they should submit. Jonathan Mayhew, a noted minister in Boston, wrote this in reference to Romans 13, "Common tyrants and public oppressors are not entitled to obedience from their subjects by virtue of anything here laid down by the inspired Apostle [Paul]."

For more than a century, the colonists had established their own local governments. Patriots did not want to defy these authorities. They resisted the king and Parliament because Patriots believed British leaders were taking away their rights. The colonists cited Scripture passages (such as 2 Kings 11:13–16 and 2 Chronicles 26:14–21) and claimed they allowed submission to local governments, or "lesser magistrates," rather than to the British government. These colonists did not view their actions against Britain as rebellion (and thus did not think they were acting contrary to Scripture).

Some became Patriots for economic reasons. Parliament's new policies hurt many prosperous American merchants. Colonists thought they should be allowed to trade with whomever they wished.

Neutral colonists

The remaining colonists joined neither side. Some were neutral for business reasons, fearing that they would suffer financial loss if they chose sides. Others lived in remote areas and were not greatly concerned about the conflict unless it came near their homes. Others, such as the Quakers and Moravians, rejected all participation in war.

Philosophical Underpinnings of the War for Independence

Economic questions initially dominated relations between the colonists and Britain leading up to the War for Independence. Colonists resisted taxation and regulation of trade by the British. This resistance led, in turn, to political debate over representation in Parliament. Also, some of Jefferson's arguments in the Declaration of Independence were political, borrowed from the Enlightenment (specifically from John Locke). Ideas such as life, liberty, pursuit of happiness, and natural rights reflected contemporary secular philosophy.

While Jefferson referred to philosophers like John Locke, religious Americans were influenced by the political thoughts of John Calvin and other Protestant reformers. Though these reformers emphasized obedience to rulers, they noted that some political systems had certain governmental officials (like the tribunes in Rome) whose job was to protect the people from tyranny.

Later theologians developed the idea that the rulers and the people were bound together in a covenant. A ruler who violated the covenant lost the right to rule, and certain governmental officials should ensure that he left office. Locke also spoke of a contract between the people and their rulers. By the 1770s, Americans believed they could justify their separation from England.

Capture of Fort Ticonderoga

Benedict Arnold proposed a plan to capture Fort Ticonderoga, a British fort, which guarded the link between Lakes George and Champlain on the La Chute River in northeast New York. The Green Mountain Boys caught the British by surprise. Entering the fort at night, they awoke the commandant. He surrendered the fort without a shot. The fort's cannons were later moved to Boston.

because most were from the German province of Hesse-Cassel. In addition, some of the most eloquent voices in the British Parliament were raised in opposition to the king's hard-line policies against the thirteen colonies. William Pitt, Edmund Burke, and Charles James Fox repeatedly warned their colleagues and king of the hazards of ignoring American rights. Their published speeches also excited the Sons of Liberty with words such as those Pitt delivered in 1777.

> If I were an American as I am an Englishman, while a foreign troop was landed in my country I never would lay down my arms—never—never—never!

Second Continental Congress

When the delegates gathered in Philadelphia on May 10, 1775, for the **Second Continental Congress**, they found themselves in an awkward situation. War in the Massachusetts countryside had erupted three weeks earlier, and thousands of New England militia had the British army pinned down in Boston. In addition, on the day of the opening session, the British-held **Fort Ticonderoga** in New York fell to Patriot forces known as the "Green Mountain Boys" under the leadership of **Ethan Allen** and Benedict Arnold.

The original purpose of the Continental Congress was not to make laws and supply armies but to debate and deliver cooperative resolutions concerning British colonial policies. Now, however, necessity thrust the matter of governing upon the shoulders of the assembly.

General Washington

The assembly's first priority was dealing with the military situation around Boston. The delegates appointed one of their own as commander in chief. **George Washington** had arrived in Philadelphia in uniform to offer his services in command of Virginia's militia forces. Now he was being asked to take charge of a continental army—a shabby collection of farmers and shopkeepers facing the best-trained, best-equipped army in the world.

Washington was a natural choice for commander in chief. His appointment proved to be one of the best decisions of the Second Continental Congress. As a southerner, the forty-three-year-old Virginian would help link the Patriot cause in New England with the rest of the country. As commander of the Virginia forces during the French and Indian War, Washington had emerged from the conflict as a local hero, though with a war record not unmixed with failure. His greatest strength, however, was not his resumé but his commanding presence, coolness under fire, and keen ability to lead and inspire—all essential to the seemingly impossible task to which the Continental Congress had unanimously elected him.

The Siege of Boston

As Washington traveled from Philadelphia to Cambridge (just outside Boston) to take charge of the army, word came of a major battle near **Bunker Hill** on the Charlestown peninsula north of Boston. On June 16, 1775, Patriot forces had hastily built fortifications there. The British commander Thomas Gage, with contempt for the soldier-farmers opposing him, ordered a frontal assault on the entrenched Patriots the next day. In an attempt to conserve their limited ammunition, Patriot leader William Prescott reportedly ordered the troops, "Don't fire until you see the whites of their eyes." When the British charge failed, their commander ordered a second assault; when that one failed, he ordered a third. The Patriots, having used all of their ammunition, were then forced to retreat. The British won, but the victory was costly. They suffered more than a thousand casualties among the two thousand soldiers sent up the slope of **Breed's Hill** (located near Bunker Hill), where most of the fighting took place. By contrast, of the 1,500 soldiers in the Continental army, 115 were killed and 300 wounded or captured. Most American casualties came after the colonists had used all their ammunition. Though the British won the engagement, inaccurately named the Battle of Bunker Hill, the encounter showed that the colonial militia could stand up to the British army.

When Washington arrived to take command of the army, the siege of Boston had returned to an uneasy standoff. He decided to break the deadlock. In December, he ordered Colonel **Henry Knox** to go to Fort Ticonderoga and retrieve the captured British cannons. Knox, overweight and good-natured, seemed an unlikely choice for the task. His knowledge of artillery had come entirely from books he had read at his Boston bookstore. Nonetheless, Knox was a man who got things done, even colossal things. He and his men used oxen, sleds, and rafts to transport fifty-nine pieces of heavy artillery on a wintry, mountainous, three-hundred-mile trek.

When Knox's cannons arrived in late January 1776, Washington put them to good use. On the evening of March 4, he fortified Dorchester Heights, overlooking Boston and its harbor. When the British awoke on March 5, they found themselves in an indefensible position and soon were forced to evacuate Boston. For Colonel Knox, that day had a double significance. On March 5, 1770, he had stood at the front of the crowd in a snowy Boston Square when a volley of British bullets claimed its first victims. Now, exactly six years after the Boston Massacre, the British found themselves on the muzzle-end of Knox's heavy guns.

The British commander decided his soldiers should withdraw from Boston. He warned the Americans that if they did not allow

Henry Knox and his men moved captured British cannons from Fort Ticonderoga to Boston.

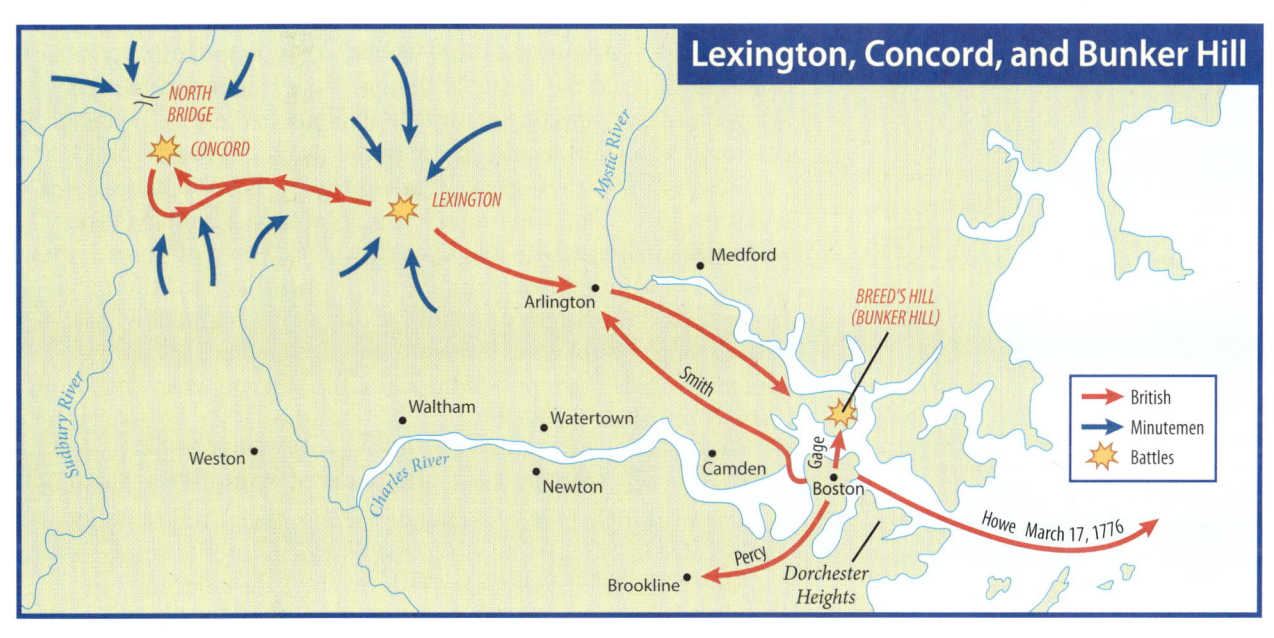

Thomas Paine

Common Sense

Even after sending Washington to Boston to take command of the army, delegates of the Second Continental Congress still hoped to reconcile with Great Britain without sacrificing American rights. On July 5, 1775, the delegates adopted the **Olive Branch Petition** (an olive branch is a symbol of peaceful intentions), which pledged loyalty to the king and requested his intervention in curbing Parliament's abusive exercise of power. The next day the Continental Congress issued a "Declaration of the Causes for Taking Up Arms," in which they stated that British actions had left the American people with only two choices—"unconditional submission to the tyranny of irritated ministers or resistance by force." They had chosen to fight. Yet they emphasized that their purpose was to gain recognition of American rights not to pursue any "ambitious designs of separating from Great Britain and establishing independent states."

The Olive Branch Petition was an attempt to settle matters peacefully. But King George III refused to even read it. Instead, he issued a Proclamation of Rebellion and instructed his Boston army to treat the Americans as "open and avowed enemies." Parliament sent twenty-five thousand more troops to suppress the American cause, authorized the hiring of thousands of Hessian mercenaries, and ordered the confiscation of all American exports. For the Patriots, the last ties of allegiance to the Crown were snapping.

Public opinion was greatly influenced by the 1776 publication of a pamphlet called **Common Sense**. Its author, **Thomas Paine**, was an Englishman who had lived in America for a little more than a year, yet he put Patriot thinking into words that fired their will. He described monarchy as a foolish form of government whose path through history was strewn with human wreckage. Paine concluded that "the blood of the slain, the weeping voice of nature cries, 'TIS TIME TO PART.'"

Sales of Common Sense quickly reached a half million copies. George Washington wrote in April 1776, "I find that Common Sense is working a powerful change there in the minds of many men." Later in 1776, Paine wrote the first in a series of sixteen papers entitled The American Crisis. In these, he continued to argue the Patriot cause. Despite his support for the cause of inde-

him to leave peacefully, he would destroy the city. Washington wisely agreed to let the British withdraw.

Excerpts by Thomas Paine

In *Common Sense* (January 1776), Paine wrote:

> A government of our own is our natural right: And when a man seriously reflects on the precariousness [uncertainty] of human affairs, he will become convinced, that it is infinitely wiser and safer, to form a constitution of our own in a cool deliberate manner, while we have it in our power, than to trust such an interesting event to time and chance.

In *The American Crisis* (December 1776), Paine wrote:

> These are the times that try men's souls. The summer soldier and the sunshine patriot will, in this crisis, shrink from the service of their country; but he that stands by it now, deserves the love and thanks of man and woman. Tyranny, like hell, is not easily conquered; yet we have this consolation with us, that the harder the conflict, the more glorious the triumph. What we obtain too cheap, we esteem too lightly; it is dearness only that gives every thing its value. Heaven knows how to put a proper price upon its goods; and it would be strange indeed if so celestial an article as FREEDOM should not be highly rated.

pendence, Paine opposed Christianity and advocated a unrestrained form of democracy that John Adams thought dangerous.

"Free and Independent States"

During the spring and summer of 1776, one colony after another changed its constitution to a republican form of government. On June 7, 1776, Richard Henry Lee of Virginia presented a resolution to the Second Continental Congress calling for complete independence from Britain: "These United Colonies are, and of right ought to be, free and independent States."

Such a final and potentially fatal resolution required serious consideration, and debate continued throughout June. In the meantime a committee of five men—**John Adams** of Massachusetts, Benjamin Franklin of Pennsylvania, Roger Sherman of Connecticut, Robert Livingstone of New York, and **Thomas Jefferson** of Virginia—were appointed to draw up a declaration in support of Lee's resolution. Most of the work on the draft, however, was shouldered by the brilliant and eloquent Jefferson.

On July 2, the Congress approved the independence resolution. Two days later, July 4, 1776, Congress approved the final draft of the **Declaration of Independence**. It not only listed the grievances that Americans had against the king but also stated universal principles that would shape the character and direction of the emerging nation.

> We hold these truths to be self-evident, that all men are created equal; that they are endowed by their Creator with certain unalienable Rights, that among these are Life, Liberty and the pursuit of Happiness.—That to secure these rights, Governments are instituted among Men, deriving their just powers from the consent of the governed.

Benjamin Franklin, John Adams, and Thomas Jefferson (*left to right*) writing the Declaration of Independence.

John Locke and the Right of Rebellion

John Locke, whose ideas were used extensively in the Declaration of Independence, taught that citizens have the right to overthrow tyrants. (He also recognized the danger that frequent rebellions pose to society.) Locke said that a tyrant violates the contract between himself and those he rules, and therefore, he is not a lawful ruler. This theory raised the issue of how to identify a tyrant. Locke said that a ruler who makes an error or who occasionally oppresses the people is not a tyrant. He said that tyrants are those who commit a series of abuses. Many Americans believed that King George III's actions demonstrated that he was a tyrant. A list of his abuses was recorded in the Declaration of Independence.

The Declaration of Independence being presented to Congress

Fifty-six delegates from thirteen colonies inscribed their names on the document. Their signing was an act of bravery unsurpassed on the battlefield. Each man knew the British government would view this document as treason. If the cause failed, he was signing his death warrant and could face execution. Yet these courageous men found the cause worth the risk. They sealed their commitment with ink and were no less willing to seal it with their blood. As Jefferson's closing words of the document state, "We mutually pledge to each other our lives, our fortunes, and our sacred honor."

Section Review

1. What was a Hessian?
2. Why did the Continental Congress choose George Washington as commander in chief?
3–4. Who helped break the deadlock at Boston by bringing artillery? From where did he bring the artillery?
5. Who was primarily responsible for the original draft of the Declaration of Independence?
6–7. According to the quotation from the Declaration of Independence, what rights do all people have and how did they receive those rights?
* Assume you were a Patriot. Why would William Pitt's ideas and words appeal to you?
* Assume you were a Loyalist. Why would you disagree with William Pitt?

III. Early Campaigns

Disaster in New York

When the British army evacuated Boston in March 1776, Washington's temporary relief was mixed with apprehension. Where would the British go next? A few months later, when the British turned their attention to New York City, Washington marched his army to that city and began its defense.

New York was not really defensible, however. The Americans had no navy, and the city was bordered by the East and Hudson Rivers and could be entered by a large harbor. The British fleet could land troops at numerous points on the river and march against the American forces. Although it would have been militarily wise to abandon the city, it would also have been politically disastrous. Washington and Congress both knew that the Americans could not simply give up one of their most important cities without a fight. The American people, still divided about the war, would see such an act as a sign of weakness and cowardice. Washington, therefore, prepared for the worst when General **William Howe**, General Thomas Gage's replacement, landed his forces on Staten Island (see map on p. 108) in July of 1776.

From the summer of 1776 to late fall, the British gave the Americans a painful lesson in warfare. On Long Island, Manhattan Island, and the mainland, the British won a series of easy victories. Washington's inexperience as a commanding general, the inexperience of the American troops, and the superiority of the British navy combined to contribute to the defeat of American forces. During one typical skirmish, Washington watched in disgust as some of his soldiers abandoned their positions and ran from the British without firing a shot. The general hurled his hat to the ground in frustration and exclaimed, "Are these the men with whom I am to defend America?"

A few bright spots relieved the gloom for the Continental army. After a disastrous defeat in the Battle of Long Island (August 27, 1776), Washington conducted a brilliant night retreat across the East River. Although retreats would not win the war, they helped

Guiding Questions

1. What were the successes and failures of the early campaigns?
2. What were the results of the Battle of Saratoga?
3. What contribution did Baron von Steuben make to the American army?

save the army from destruction. By November, New York was in British hands, and the Continental army was in New Jersey.

Trenton and Princeton
Trenton

The onset of winter in late 1776 found the Continental army in great despair. They had been driven from New York, and the enlistments of many of the troops would expire at the end of the year. Most of them appeared unwilling to re-enlist in a losing cause. Faced with this disheartening situation, Washington decided on a move as dangerous as it was daring. He would attack.

Washington's forces were on the Pennsylvania side of the Delaware River. In **Trenton** (see map on p. 108), on the New Jersey side, lay a force of approximately 1,500 Hessians. On Christmas night of 1776, Washington led some 2,400 men across the river during a howling storm. Snow and freezing rain pelted them as they then marched to Trenton through the darkness. At least two men froze to death during the march.

Washington crossing the Delaware

The abominable weather gave the Americans some advantages, however. The storm hid their movements from the Hessian forces. Furthermore, the Hessians were comfortably sleeping off their Christmas merry-making. They never expected that anyone would attack in such weather. As dawn neared, Washington attacked Trenton; he caught the astonished Hessians completely unprepared. After a brief and confused resistance, they surrendered. Nearly one thousand Hessians were killed or captured. Washington did not lose a single man in the actual fighting.

Princeton

Flushed with unaccustomed success, Washington followed the brilliant stroke at Trenton with an equally daring move. About a week after his Trenton victory, he left a small group of American soldiers to keep the campfires burning and to make noise. Meanwhile, the remainder of his army slipped away and attacked British troops at **Princeton** (see map on p. 108).

The attack on Princeton on January 3, 1777, did not begin well. The Americans, although more numerous than the British, were disorganized. As the small but disciplined British force advanced, Washington and his officers rode into the confused American lines to restore order. General Washington himself rode in front of his lines and directed the attack. To the horror of his aides, Washington stayed between the two opposing lines and ordered the Americans to fire. One aide covered his own face with his hat, fully expecting to see his commander soon lying dead on the ground. But when the smoke cleared, Washington was unharmed, and the shattered British forces ran.

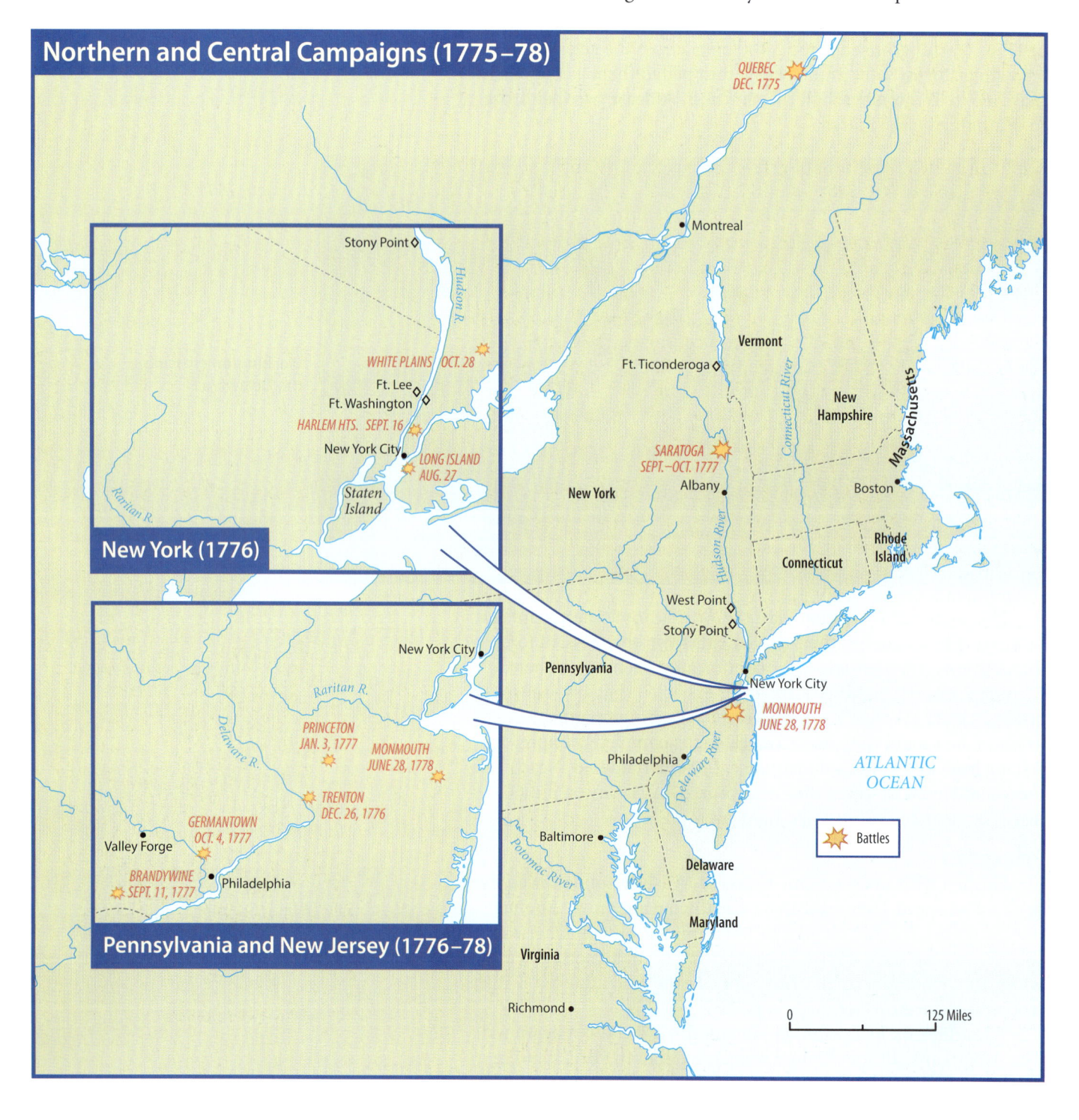

Trenton and Princeton were minor affairs militarily, more like raids than battles. But their effect on American morale was dramatic. After earlier disasters, any victory would have been welcome. Such overwhelming victories only made the triumph sweeter. There was a visible result as well. Many of the soldiers whose enlistments had expired rejoined the army. The Americans had an army and hope with which to continue the fight.

Fight for Philadelphia

The British launched a plan in 1777 that had the potential to win the war. They planned a three-pronged assault on New York. A British force in Canada under General John Burgoyne would move south down Lake Champlain and through the wilderness of upstate New York, while General Howe would send a force north from New York City up the Hudson River to the city of Albany. Meanwhile, a third British force was to take a different route from Montreal to Albany. With these moves, the British would isolate New England from the other colonies.

Fortunately for the Americans, Howe did not cooperate with the plan. Instead, he moved against the American capital, Philadelphia. Howe's action proved embarrassing to the United States initially, but in the long run it resulted in an American victory.

Instead of marching across New Jersey to Philadelphia, the British used their fleet to sail up the Chesapeake Bay and land in Maryland, some fifty miles from the American capital. As Howe marched from Maryland through northern Delaware and into Pennsylvania, Washington placed the Continental army behind Brandywine Creek, south of Philadelphia, to await the enemy. At the Battle of Brandywine (September 11, 1777), Howe outmaneuvered Washington and the Continental Army retreated. The British entered Philadelphia unopposed on September 26. On October 4, Washington made an attempt to recapture the city by attacking the British forces stationed at Germantown, north of Philadelphia. The attack failed, and the American capital remained in enemy hands.

A Turning Point—Saratoga

While Howe was preparing his blow against Philadelphia, General Burgoyne was marching down Lake Champlain in impressive order. He easily seized Fort Ticonderoga. At this point, however, the British plan for a three-pronged attack began to break down. Howe's decision to attack Philadelphia meant that only a small force would even attempt to move up the Hudson River. The third British force that was marching toward Albany to help Burgoyne was pushed back by an American force.

Following these indirect setbacks came several defeats inflicted directly on Burgoyne's forces. Then in two separate battles south of Saratoga, New York (September 19 and October 7, 1777), the Americans dealt heavy blows to the British. The American commander, General Horatio Gates, received much of the glory for these victories, but the real credit belonged to Gates's subordinates, General Benedict Arnold and Colonel Daniel Morgan.

The British attempted to retreat to Canada. However, the Americans, who were more experienced woodsmen, overtook and surrounded them near Saratoga. On October 17, Burgoyne surrendered to Gates. The **Battle of Saratoga** (see map on p. 108) was a major turning point of the war. First, an entire British invasion force of more than six thousand men had been killed or captured. Second, France entered the war.

France was eager to see Americans win their independence because it would weaken France's rival, Great Britain. The French

Benedict Arnold

Benedict Arnold: The American Traitor

In a secluded spot on the site of the Battle of Saratoga stands an odd memorial. Its inscription honors "the most brilliant soldier of the Continental Army winning for his countrymen the decisive battle of the American Revolution." The sculptor dared not mention the hero's name. The soldier was **Benedict Arnold**, who became one of the most infamous traitors in American history.

Arnold's war record was one of the finest in the Continental army. As joint commander with Ethan Allen, he had captured British-held Fort Ticonderoga in New York in one of the earliest American triumphs of the war. In an otherwise ill-fated attack on Canada in 1775, Arnold conducted a brilliant march across the winter wilderness of Maine, and he was wounded while supervising a night attack on Quebec during a howling winter storm. At Saratoga, Arnold had injured his leg leading a charge that broke the British lines and turned the tide of battle.

But Arnold was dissatisfied. He was often passed over for promotion by a Continental Congress that was more interested in rewarding an officer's political connections than his bravery in battle. George Washington recognized Arnold's obvious abilities and gave him command of Philadelphia after the British retreated. But politicians and jealous fellow officers criticized Arnold and sought to undermine his authority.

Arnold became bitter. He seems to have felt some genuine patriotic fervor, but he also loved power, wealth, and glory. Dealing with an ungrateful Congress dampened his patriotism. Soon Arnold began to look for ways to fill his purse and feed his ego. In 1779, he secretly offered his services to the British.

Washington valued Arnold, and in 1780 he wanted to honor Arnold by giving him command of a section of the Continental army. Arnold instead asked to be given command of West Point, an important fort on the Hudson River (now the site of the United States Military Academy). Washington was puzzled that a bold and dashing officer should request such an inactive post. Arnold pleaded that the pain from his wound at Saratoga required an undemanding command. In reality, Arnold had plotted with the British to turn the fort over to them for a large sum of money. Unaware of Arnold's treachery, Washington granted his request.

But Arnold's plans went disastrously wrong. Americans captured his contact, British Major John André, with incriminating papers in his possession after he and Arnold had met secretly. Arnold fled to the British in New York; André was hanged as a spy.

Arnold traded his country for a reward and a red coat. He spent the rest of the war leading bloody but unimportant raids for the British in Virginia and Connecticut. After the war, he fled to Britain. Although financially comfortable (he received a reward and a pension for his treason), Arnold was shunned by British society. He died unhappy in London in 1801, no longer known as the hero of Ticonderoga and Saratoga. Rather, Washington described him as having "sullied [disgraced] his former glory by the blackest treason."

Monument to Benedict Arnold's injured foot at Saratoga

---

had been providing war materiel and loans to America. After the surprising American victory at Saratoga, France officially recognized the United States as a separate nation and then entered the war against its old enemy, the British. America now had a powerful ally in its struggle for independence.

A Winter of Discontent and Hope

Valley Forge

Word of the French alliance did not reach America until spring of 1778. Meanwhile, Washington and his army went through perhaps the darkest period of the war. With the British controlling the former capital Philadelphia, the American army made its headquarters for the winter of 1777–78 some twenty-five miles away at **Valley Forge**. The

Washington and Lafayette at Valley Forge

army had to build a camp there. A "city" of wooden barracks and huts soon sprouted in Valley Forge, but the soldiers were hungry and ill-clothed. Few men had whole uniforms, and even fewer had shoes. Washington grimly observed that "you might have tracked the army from White Marsh to Valley Forge by the blood of their feet."

Washington could do little to relieve the suffering of his men. For one thing, the general had only the worthless paper currency of the Continental Congress to buy supplies. Farmers and merchants found it far more profitable to sell their goods to the British in Philadelphia, who paid in gold and silver. Despite the hardships, Washington's men endured surprisingly well. Some even joked about their ragged condition.

Baron Friedrich von Steuben drilling Continental troops at Valley Forge

Drill and Discipline

In February of 1778, **Baron Friedrich von Steuben** (STOY bun) came to Valley Forge in a splendid German uniform to serve as a drillmaster for the Continental army. Von Steuben did not know English, but he knew how to train men and how to instill pride and discipline. By memorizing a few English phrases, the German was able to drill the American forces. He taught them to march properly and showed them how to maneuver in battle. Building on the experience that the Patriots had gained in past battles, von Steuben transformed the disorganized horde that had fled from New York into a reasonably efficient fighting force. When spring brought news of the French alliance, Washington looked at his newly drilled men and decided the time had come to strike a major blow to the British.

Battle of Monmouth

When the French entered the war, the British decided to adjust their strategy. First, they would focus more attention on the southern colonies (where more Loyalists lived). Second, they would withdraw from Philadelphia to New York. When the British left Philadelphia in June 1778, Americans attacked them at Monmouth (MAHN muth) Court House in New Jersey (see map on p. 108).

The Battle of Monmouth vindicated von Steuben's work. Despite the early disorder, the Americans quickly and professionally took

Legend or Reality?

At the Battle of Monmouth, the temperature was oppressively hot—over 100 degrees. In fact, more men appear to have died from the heat than from bullets. Stories say that the wife of a member of an American artillery crew, Mary Hays, carried pitchers of water to the troops (earning herself the nickname "Molly Pitcher"). When her husband was wounded, it is said she took his place and helped fire the cannon. Did "Molly Pitcher" really exist? Historians continue to debate the story.

Lafayette, the Republican Aristocrat

Several European officers served with distinction in the Continental army. Among them were Baron Friedrich von Steuben, the German drillmaster; Baron de Kalb, another German, who was the hero of the Battle of Camden; and Count Casimir Pulaski, veteran of a valiant but failed Polish war for independence. Perhaps the most famous of these international heroes was the French Marquis de Lafayette (1757–1834).

Born of wealthy aristocracy in France, Lafayette seemed an unlikely candidate for honor in a republican revolution. When Lafayette was two, his father died in battle. Young Lafayette read widely, especially military books, and he too became an officer in the French army. When he was eighteen, Lafayette attended a dinner where the American War for Independence was discussed. The American cause fired his imagination. When an American representative came to France in 1776 seeking officers for the Continental army, Lafayette enthusiastically volunteered. Because he was already wealthy, Lafayette declined to take a salary. He said that he would only take compensation for his expenses.

When General Washington learned that he was receiving a nineteen-year-old major general in his command, he was unenthusiastic. Upon meeting the young officer, however, Washington's doubts melted. Lafayette was gracious, humble, and eager both to learn and to serve. Lafayette became like a son to Washington. For Lafayette, Washington became the father he had never known.

Lafayette served bravely with the Continental army. Of his education as a soldier, he wrote, "I read, I study, I examine, I listen, I reflect, and the result of all is the endeavor at forming an opinion, into which I infuse as much common sense as possible." Despite his studious nature, Lafayette was no armchair soldier; he was always in the thick of the fighting. He was wounded at the Battle of Brandywine, and a small force under his command constantly harassed Cornwallis and the British in Virginia. At Yorktown, he led an attack on a major British fortification. When he returned to France after the war, Lafayette left behind a group of veterans who had been impressed with the young man's unflagging cheerfulness and courage.

Back in France, Lafayette became a leader for reform in his own country. He dreamed of making his native land a model of republican virtue just like his adopted nation. When the French Revolution broke out in 1789, the marquis assisted in devising and adopting a new constitution for France. At one point, Lafayette was probably the most popular leader in France. The revolution turned ugly, however, and violence erupted. When Lafayette tried to moderate the conflict, radicals denounced him as a traitor to the revolution. In dismay and disgust, Lafayette left France with hopes of traveling to America; however, he was arrested by Austrians and imprisoned for five years.

After his release from prison, Lafayette returned to France. He continued to fight for his republican ideals, but his battlefield was the French legislature. He made one last visit to America in 1824. To his astonishment, hordes of enthusiastic admirers and graying veterans greeted him. Hailed as a hero, Lafayette found that his efforts on behalf of the American republic were cherished and honored by a grateful people.

---

their places in the battle lines. Although the battle was a draw, it showed how much Washington's army had improved since the disasters earlier in the war. The British withdrew to New York.

The War in the West

While George Washington was trying to build an army that could fight the British regulars, a different kind of warfare was taking place on the frontier along the Ohio River. There the fighting resembled the guerrilla tactics of the French and Indian War. A group of British soldiers and fierce Indian tribes engaged in a brutal struggle with hardy but scattered American frontiersmen. One

American leader arose out of the war in the West—**George Rogers Clark**.

Clark, a native Virginian, had come to the Ohio River Valley in 1772. As a resident of Kentucky, Clark recognized the threat that the frontier faced from the British and the Indians. In 1778, the twenty-five-year-old Clark won Virginia's approval to lead an attack on British trading posts north of the Ohio River in the region then known as the Northwest. With a tiny force of approximately 175 men, Clark sailed down the Ohio River to what is now Illinois. From there Clark marched his men overland to the Mississippi River town of Kaskaskia (kus KAS kee uh). The town, populated mostly by French settlers who did not care for the British anyway, happily surrendered. Several other trading posts quickly fell, including the most important—Vincennes on the Wabash River in what is now Indiana.

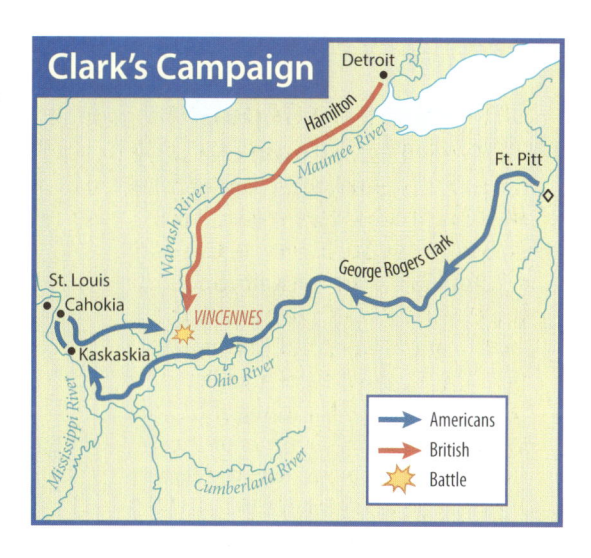

"I Have Not Yet Begun to Fight"

John Paul Jones (left) *commander of the* Bonhomme Richard *is shown here battling the* Serapis.

The American navy in the War for Independence was pitifully small, particularly in contrast to the mighty British fleet. Most American naval victories consisted of the capture of unarmed British merchant ships so the cargo could be confiscated. At least one triumph at sea, however, was big enough, as one historian wrote, "to set a tradition of victory" for the U.S. Navy.

Scottish-born Captain John Paul Jones was the ablest commander in the American fleet, and he needed all of his talent on September 23, 1779. Jones was commanding the *Bonhomme Richard* (named in honor of Benjamin Franklin and his *Poor Richard's Almanac*) off the coast of Great Britain when he encountered two British warships, the *Serapis* and the *Countess of Scarborough*. The *Serapis* alone outgunned the *Bonhomme Richard*, and the presence of the *Countess* only increased the odds against Jones. Nonetheless, Jones joined battle.

The three-and-a-half-hour fight started poorly for the Americans when two of their largest cannons exploded, killing several men. Jones tried to overcome the British advantage in cannons by coming close to board the *Serapis*. The British crew held off the Americans, however, and their guns tore gaping holes in the side of the American ship. At one point, an officer of the *Bonhomme Richard*, thinking that Jones was dead, called out to the British, offering to surrender. Jones refused to surrender, rose, and supposedly cried out, "I have not yet begun to fight!"

Although his ship was sinking slowly, Jones continued by sheer grit to pound at the British. Finally, the captain of the *Serapis*—his mainmast fallen—surrendered; the smaller *Countess* fled. Jones and his crew boarded the British warship and watched the shattered *Bonhomme Richard* sink beneath the waves. The Americans took their prize to the Netherlands, and Jones visited Paris, where the French greeted him with an uproarious celebration. John Paul Jones had given America its first great victory at sea.

George Rogers Clark accepting surrender of the British forces at Vincennes.

Later, the British recaptured Vincennes. In February 1779 Clark marched a small force some 150 miles through icy rivers and flooded prairies to face the British there. He retook Vincennes.

Clark's victories in the Northwest were not as significant as the battles in the East in terms of numbers, but they had great strategic importance. Clark's expedition reduced Indian attacks, and his presence helped the United States lay claim to the territory north of the Ohio River. Much of the credit for securing Kentucky and the Northwest belongs to him.

Section Review

1. What militarily indefensible city did the Continental army try to defend for reasons of politics and morale?
2. Why were the victories at Trenton and Princeton so important to the American cause?
3. Why was the Saratoga campaign a turning point of the war?
4–5. Who was a drillmaster of the Continental army? What battle demonstrated the success of his work?
6. Why were George Rogers Clark's victories in the Northwest strategically important?
★ Reread "Benedict Arnold: The American Traitor." Assess some of Arnold's character flaws.
★ What do you think the winter at Valley Forge revealed about the American Patriots?

Guiding Questions

1. How did the role of southern colonies change during the course of the war?
2. What significant battles occurred in the South?
3. What was the significance of the Treaty of Paris?

IV. The War in the South

During the early years of the war, the southern colonies poured men and supplies into the military and political ranks of the Patriot cause. But the British largely ignored the region in favor of fighting Washington's Continentals and isolating New England. In 1776, they had tried to quell the rebellion in the South, beginning with a naval attack on Charleston, South Carolina. They made no further attempts until 1778, after the British defeat at Saratoga.

In late 1778, the British attacked Georgia and began a drive through the South. They hoped that the presence of His Majesty's troops would awaken Loyalist sentiment in the backcountry, soften opposition, and sever the South from the rest of the country. The plan worked so well at first that British commanders failed to see its flaws. The southern campaign would be Britain's last.

The British Advance

Charleston

By early 1779, all of Georgia—including Savannah, its chief city and port—had fallen into British hands. Georgia became a staging area for the more important **siege of Charleston**, South Carolina. If the British could conquer Charleston, they would not only capture one of the most populated and important cities in America but also gain access to the Carolina heartland through the navigable rivers that the city defended.

In late March 1780, British forces besieged Charleston. Most of the Continental forces in the South, an army of about five thousand, occupied the city. The American commander, General Benjamin

Lincoln, heeded the pleadings of Charlestonians to hold the city at all cost. Considering the Americans were outnumbered more than two to one and their supply lines cut by the British cavalry, the outcome was not surprising. On May 12, 1780, Lincoln surrendered his entire army to the British. It was America's worst defeat of the war.

With the fall of Charleston, the Carolinas lay invitingly open to the British. General **Charles Cornwallis** now commanded the British troops that were marching through the South Carolina low country. In August 1780 he defeated Patriot forces in Camden, South Carolina. After the double disasters at Charleston and Camden, the Patriot cause looked grim.

Swamp Surprises

One small band of South Carolinians kept the war alive in the British-occupied low country of South Carolina. The group was "distinguished by small black leather caps and the wretchedness of their attire; their number did not exceed twenty men and boys, some white, some black, and all mounted, but most of them miserably equipped." The leader of this motley assortment of guerrillas was the elusive General **Francis Marion**, who soon earned the nickname "Swamp Fox."

Marion and his men would slip out of the swamps and sand flats to attack British outposts and supply lines. Such small guerrilla bands, of course, could not beat a British army in open battle. Their strategic importance lay in pressuring the enemy. Marion's successful hit-and-run operations pinned down British troops, kept them from joining the main British force, and forced Cornwallis to keep looking over his shoulder. One British commander declared that "the devil himself could not catch" Marion.

The forces of Francis Marion, the Swamp Fox, harassed British troops in South Carolina.

Kings Mountain

A surprising turn of events occurred in October 1780 that gave Patriots cause for encouragement. Cornwallis sent Major Patrick Ferguson to lead an all-Tory detachment of more than a thousand men into the western foothills of South Carolina. Ferguson warned the "over-mountain men" in the backcountry settlements of the western Carolinas and in what is now Tennessee that unless they pledged their loyalty to George III, he would lay waste to their

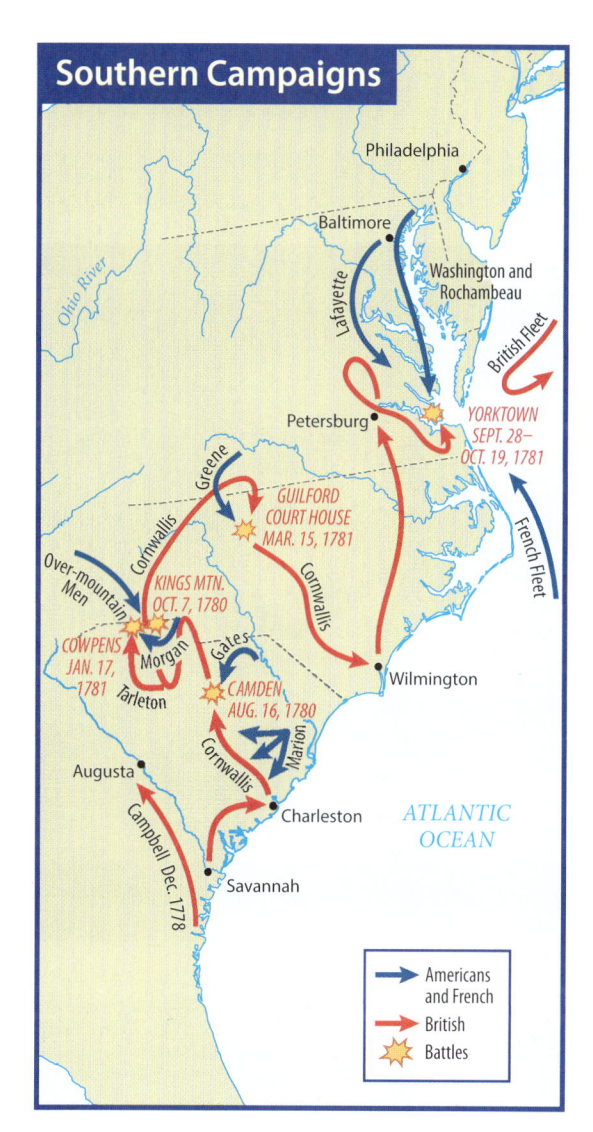

Southern Campaigns

The "over-mountain men" dealt the Tories a decisive blow at the Battle of Kings Mountain.

fields, burn their homes, and hang their leaders. Unfortunately for Ferguson, these frontiersmen did not respond well to threats. A buckskinned force of nine hundred men, nearly half of whom were from Tennessee, caught Ferguson and his Tories on the wooded slopes of Kings Mountain, There, on the border of North and South Carolina, they killed Ferguson. Almost his entire army was killed, wounded, or captured. The victory at the **Battle of Kings Mountain** strengthened Patriot resolve.

Nathanael Greene

Toward the end of 1780, Congress appointed a new commander for the region. On Washington's advice they sent the "Fighting Quaker" from Rhode Island, General **Nathanael Greene**. Greene took a small, threadbare, penniless, demoralized army and—by courage, resourcefulness, and military genius—made it the terror of Cornwallis's army.

Greene's first move was to divide his outnumbered army and send a detachment south under General Daniel Morgan. Morgan left with six hundred Continentals, hoping that Cornwallis would also divide his force and pursue him.

Cornwallis sent Lieutenant Colonel Banastre Tarleton and his Tory legion to catch the Continentals. The Americans hated Tarleton for his reputation of killing his prisoners after they had surrendered. Tarleton, however, would more than meet his match in Daniel Morgan. On the rolling meadows of South Carolina in a place known as the Cowpens, the two armies clashed. On January 17, 1781, Morgan displayed his exceptional military skill. In less than an hour, the battle was over. The British suffered over 900 casualties; the Americans had fewer than 100. The Battle of Cowpens was the first major step toward eventual British defeat.

After the unsettling losses at Kings Mountain and Cowpens, Cornwallis determined to crush Greene. He and his troops were the only serious obstacle to a conclusive conquest of the Carolinas. In mid-March 1781, the American army faced Cornwallis at a little crossroads in North Carolina called Guilford Court House. The British won a victory, but Cornwallis lost one-fourth of his men there.

After exhausting battles in the Carolinas, Cornwallis decided to march north to Virginia where he was joined by reinforcements. He established his headquarters at a port on Virginia's York River, which was only a few miles from Jamestown, the site of the first permanent English settlement in 1607. Little did he realize that this port, **Yorktown,** would be the scene of a humiliating defeat.

Victory at Yorktown

Cornwallis Cornered

By late summer of 1781, Cornwallis had amassed a force of 7,200 troops. The **Marquis de Lafayette**, commanding the outnumbered Continental forces in Virginia, watched with alarm. Although he shouldered the burdens of leadership well, the young Lafayette confided in a letter at the time, "When one is twenty-three, has an army to command and Lord Cornwallis to oppose, the time that is left is none too long for sleep."

At the end of August, the French fleet under Admiral de Grasse sailed up the Chesapeake Bay, landed three thousand French troops to join Lafayette, and defeated the British fleet. Suddenly Cornwal-

Nathanael Greene

Charles Cornwallis

lis found himself in trouble. Not only was he cut off by sea, but also the arrival of Washington's Continentals and a large force of French regulars meant that he was outnumbered and surrounded.

Washington had been leaking false reports that said he planned to attack the British in New York, but instead he was marching to Yorktown. Admiral de Grasse's victory had been an unexpected bonus for Washington, who now caught the ill-fated Cornwallis in a trap. About 17,000 French and American troops surrounded the British and bombarded them day and night.

After desperate attempts to break the siege, Cornwallis yielded to the inevitable, asking for terms of surrender on October 17, 1781. Two days later, seven thousand British soldiers marched between two half-mile lines of American and French troops to lay down their arms.

Cornwallis was not present. He claimed he was ill. One of his subordinates carried the general's sword to the French commander, General Rochambeau. The French general shook his head and pointed him to Washington, who understood the insult of Cornwallis's absence and directed that the sword be given to General Benjamin Lincoln, Washington's subordinate.

The Treaty of Paris, 1783

Surrender of the British at Yorktown

George III was shaken by the loss at Yorktown. The king initially demanded that the war should continue, but soon he submitted to pressure from Parliament and the people to accept that the war was over. Peace commissioners were appointed to meet the American negotiators—Benjamin Franklin, John Jay, and John Adams—in Paris.

The **Treaty of Paris** was finally signed on September 3, 1783. It acknowledged that the colonies were indeed independent. The United States was awarded all the land east of the Mississippi River with the exception of Florida, which returned to Spanish control.

Yorktown was not an end, however, as much as a beginning. A costly war had secured independence; now the task of nation building lay before them. In many ways, the challenges of peace would be greater than the challenges of war. Yet the generation of Americans who rallied at Lexington, weathered Valley Forge, and besieged the defenses at Yorktown would prove that they could not only win their liberty but also preserve it.

Section Review

1. What was America's worst defeat of the war?
2–3. Who was the leader of a band of Patriot guerrillas in South Carolina? What was his nickname?
4–5. What admiral helped trap Cornwallis at Yorktown? What was his nationality?
★ Evaluate the success of Francis Marion. What did his small group accomplish?

People, Places, and Things to Remember

Gaspee
Committee of Correspondence
Tea Act of 1773
Boston Tea Party
Loyalists
Coercive Acts
Paxton Boys
Regulators
Intolerable Acts
Quebec Act
First Continental Congress
minutemen
Patrick Henry
militia
regulars
Paul Revere
Lexington and Concord
Patriots
Tories
Hessians
Second Continental Congress
Fort Ticonderoga
Ethan Allen
George Washington
Bunker Hill
Breed's Hill
Henry Knox
Olive Branch Petition
Common Sense
Thomas Paine
John Adams
Thomas Jefferson
Declaration of Independence
William Howe
Trenton
Princeton
Battle of Saratoga
Benedict Arnold
Valley Forge
Baron Friedrich von Steuben
George Rogers Clark
siege of Charleston
Charles Cornwallis
Francis Marion
Battle of Kings Mountain
Nathanael Greene
Yorktown
Marquis de Lafayette
Treaty of Paris (1783)

CHAPTER REVIEW

Making Connections

1. What did the Committees of Correspondence provide to the colonies?
2. Why did the colonists fear the Quebec Act?
3. Why was the battle of Bunker Hill (Breed's Hill) an empty victory for the British?
4. In what way did Howe's decision to attack Philadelphia eventually work to the advantage of the Americans?

Developing History Skills

1. Put the following acts of the Continental Congress in chronological order: Declaration of Independence, Olive Branch Petition, Declaration of American Rights, appointment of George Washington as commander in chief.
2. Even though between one-fifth and one-third of the American colonists favored the British in the War for Independence, why was Benedict Arnold's attempted treason still considered such a terrible act?

Thinking Critically

1. Assess the role of the French during the American War for Independence.
2. Some historians have claimed that Britain lost the war because of the incompetence of its military commanders rather than because of any accomplishments by the Americans. Do you agree or disagree and why?

Living as a Christian Citizen

1. If you were a pastor during the era of the War for Independence, how would you counsel the political leaders who attended your church? Write an essay that summarizes your advice. Be sure to ground your counsel in Scripture.
2. Many countries today are ruled by tyrants. If you were a diplomat, how would you advise an opposition group to proceed against a military dictator? Use and evaluate the ideas of John Locke that are mentioned in this chapter.

THE CRITICAL PERIOD (1781–1789) 7

Constitutional Convention

> This Country must be united. If persuasion does not unite it, the sword will.
>
> **Gouverneur Morris**
> 1787

I. Government by Confederation

II. A New Charter

III. The Struggle for Ratification

Big Ideas

1. What were the weaknesses of the Confederation government?
2. What compromises and key principles emerged from the Constitutional Convention?
3. What were significant differences between the Federalists and Anti-Federalists?

The 1780s were arguably the most critical decade in America's history. From the War for Independence to the ratification of the Constitution, those years were characterized by conflict and change. At the start of the decade, for example, British troops patrolled the streets of New York City in the name of King George III. By the decade's end, American citizens paraded through the same streets to celebrate the inauguration of another George, President George Washington.

Americans changed governments twice during the 1780s. They threw off British rule through success on the battlefield, but they then scrapped their national Confederation because of its weaknesses and set up a new form of government.

Americans made their greatest contribution to political thought and practice: the writing of the Constitution. The Constitution capped the independence movement, providing a stable national government through which the states were united in more than name only. The Constitution gave substance to the "spirit of '76."

Guiding Questions

1. What was the nature and structure of the Confederation government?
2. What were the successes and failures of the Confederation?

I. Government by Confederation

On June 7, 1776, the Second Continental Congress voted to draw up a charter for joining the colonies into a **confederation**, a close alliance of sovereign states. Congress entrusted the task to a committee headed by John Dickinson of Pennsylvania, and in a little more than a month, Dickinson's committee presented its work. After more than a year of debate and revision, Congress adopted these **Articles of Confederation**. By 1781, all thirteen states had approved the Articles, and they went into effect.

League of States

Dickinson originally proposed establishing a strong central government. However, the states—jealous of their power and fearing centralization—watered down his plan. The Articles of Confederation did little more than grant legitimacy to the loosely constructed Continental Congress and provide the minimum authority needed to conduct the war. Although the states pledged themselves to "perpetual union," they committed themselves only to "a firm league of friendship with each other." The Articles said plainly, "Each state retains its sovereignty, freedom, and independence." In effect, the central government was only as strong as the states allowed, and that was not very strong.

The legislature was the only component of the Confederation government. The Congress of the Confederation was **unicameral** (having only one house). Each state legislature could elect two to seven representatives to attend, but each state had only one vote, regardless of how many representatives it sent. Important legislation—such as declaring war, approving treaties, and coining money—had to be approved by nine states. Amending and ratifying the Articles required the unanimous consent of all thirteen states.

The chief executive, the president of Congress, was chosen by the legislature and was completely under its control. He was virtually powerless, and three officials (the superintendent of finance and the secretaries of war and foreign affairs) handled most administrative duties. A national judiciary did not yet exist.

The Articles simply formalized how the thirteen states were functioning historically, politically, and economically. Therefore, the Articles reserved to the states every "power, jurisdiction, and right" that was not "expressly delegated" to Congress. Among the most important powers reserved to the states was the power to tax. Unable to levy taxes, Congress was forced to ask the states for money, a request that the states could—and did—ignore if they wished. The central government was reduced to scraping funds together through loans from other nations (which the government usually could not repay), the sale of public lands on the frontier, and the profits from the government-owned post office ($10,000–$15,000 a year). In its years of existence, the Confederation government barely had enough revenue to cover its expenses.

Successes of the Confederation

Despite its glaring weaknesses and ultimate failure, the Confederation achieved a few successes. Chief among these were the Treaty of Paris and the settlement of the western lands dispute.

The Treaty of Paris

The Treaty of Paris (see Chapter 6) was the Confederation's greatest triumph in foreign affairs. By forcing Great Britain to recognize American independence, the treaty built enormous prestige for the young nation. At the same time, enforcement of the treaty revealed several weaknesses in the Confederation and squandered much of the reputation that the United States had carefully built.

By the provisions of the treaty, the United States was to restore the seized property of Loyalists and allow British subjects access to American courts to recover debts owed them. The American government, however, had no means of enforcing those provisions; it could only *ask* the states to comply. When the states refused, Britain used that breach of the treaty as an excuse to keep its forts in the Great Lakes region and thus protect the profitable British fur trade. When John Adams complained to the British about their violation of the treaty, the British pointed to the United States' failure to honor its obligations. When Adams tried to argue that the states would not allow the central government to do so, the British asked whether the United States was one nation or thirteen. Other governments that dealt with the young nation soon echoed the taunt.

American commissioners of the Treaty of Paris (unfinished because the British refused to pose)

Western Lands

Approval of the Articles of Confederation had been delayed until 1781 because Maryland refused to ratify them until the matter of the western lands had been settled. The Treaty of Paris left the United States in control of all territory east of the Mississippi River and north of Florida and Louisiana. Several states, notably Virginia and New York, claimed parts of that huge tract of land. Several other states, including Maryland, had no such claims and feared the power of the other states if they succeeded in claiming the land. Therefore, Maryland would not ratify the Articles unless the other states abandoned their claims and turned those lands over to the federal government. When Virginia and New York agreed to yield their claims to the federal government, the others eventually followed suit, and Maryland ratified the Articles. North of the Ohio

Western Land Claims

[Map showing western land claims of the original states, including areas claimed by Virginia, Massachusetts, Connecticut, North Carolina, Georgia, disputed claims with Britain and Spain, and Spanish-claimed Louisiana territory.]

Legend:
- Thirteen States and Maine
- Disputed Claims
- Northwest Territory
- Southwestern Claims
- Spanish Claims

River, all lands that passed into the hands of the national government became known as the **Northwest Territory**.

The question of how to develop and govern the Northwest Territory was settled by a series of ordinances. The first and most farsighted was the **Ordinance of 1784**, written by Thomas Jefferson. He proposed creating ten new states out of the territory, each of which would be equal to the other states in the Union. He also proposed banning slavery in the region and giving the land to settlers instead of selling it.

Unfortunately, the ordinance was so farsighted that it never went into effect. Too many states feared the creation of ten competing states, and some states opposed the ban on slavery. The **Land Ordinance of 1785** was far more cautious and avoided thorny political questions. Instead,

Jefferson's Vision

When Thomas Jefferson drew up his 1784 ordinance for the Northwest Territory, he also proposed the names and boundaries for ten states. The following map shows the division of the territory as Jefferson envisioned it, along with the boundaries of the states that were actually created.

The other thirteen states eventually rejected Jefferson's plan. They feared sharing their power with ten new competitors. Finally, only five states (Ohio, Indiana, Michigan, Illinois, and Wisconsin), along with a portion of Minnesota, were formed from the territory.

[Map showing Jefferson's proposed states: Sylvania, Michigania, Cherronesus, Assenisipia, Metropotamia, Washington, Illinoia, Saratoga, Polypotamia, Pelisipia.]

Land Ordinance of 1785

Township (6 miles square, or 36 square miles)

6	5	4	3	2	1
7	8	9	10	11	12
18	17		15	14	13
19	20	21	22	23	24
30	29	28	27	26	25
31	32	33	34	35	36

16 — Income from the sale of section 16 was reserved for education, but schools could be built on any of the sections.

Quarter section (160 acres)
Quarter of a quarter section (40 acres)
Half section (320 acres)
Half of a quarter section (80 acres)
Section (1 square mile)

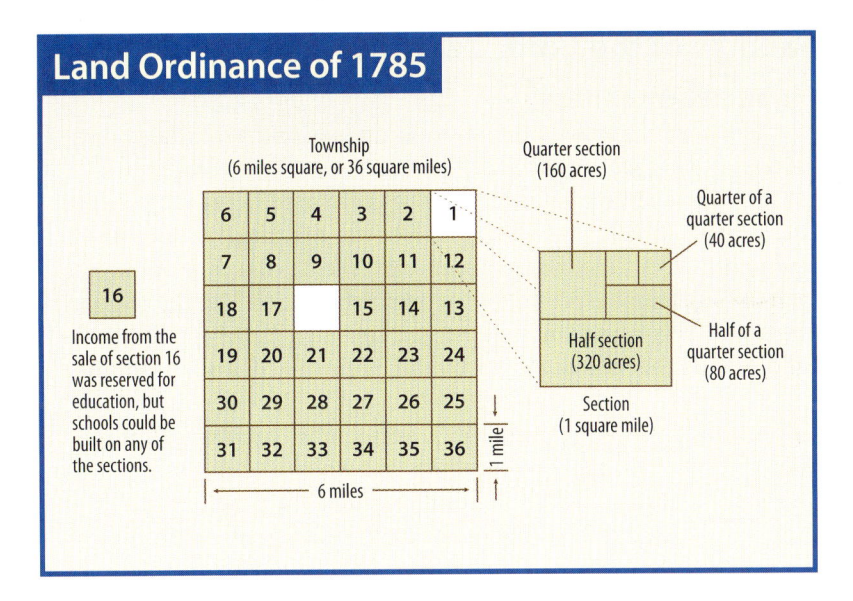

it concentrated on the settlement of the territory. The ordinance divided the new lands into orderly townships for sale and development. Each township contained thirty-six sections, or lots, of one square mile (640 acres). Each lot was to be sold for a dollar an acre ($640), contrary to Jefferson's hopes for free land for settlers. The proceeds from the sale of lot sixteen in each township were to go toward building and maintaining schools in the area.

More sweeping was the **Northwest Ordinance of 1787**. Whereas the ordinance of 1785 concerned settlement, the ordinance of 1787 concerned government. The Northwest Territory was to be divided into at least three but no more than five states. Each would-be state went through three stages. In the first stage, the region remained almost completely under the direct control of the federal government. When a region had at least five thousand free inhabitants, it entered the second stage and became a territory. The people could then elect a legislature and send a representative to Congress. However, the governor—still appointed by the national government—could veto any act passed by the territorial legislature, and the territorial representative to Congress could not vote. In the third stage, once a territory had sixty thousand free inhabitants, it could draw up a state constitution and be admitted to the Union on an equal basis with the other states.

Other provisions are noteworthy. Building on the educational provisions in the Land Ordinance of 1785, the Northwest Ordinance of 1787 explicitly emphasized the importance of education: "Religion, morality, and knowledge, being necessary to good government and the happiness of mankind, schools and the means of education shall forever be encouraged." Most importantly, the ordinance followed Jefferson's original suggestion and prohibited slavery in the new territories. Also, most states that entered the Union afterward followed the political process set down by the Northwest Ordinance.

These ordinances were the greatest success of the Confederation government. They allowed orderly settlement of the territory, and the land sales they permitted provided income for the government. Years later, Daniel Webster said that he doubted "whether one single law of any lawgiver, ancient or modern, has produced effects of more distinct, marked, and lasting character than the Ordinance of 1787."

Failures of the Confederation

Financial Weakness

The new nation's financial situation was understandably dire after a six-year war on its soil. The weakness of the Articles did not help. The national government was almost always in debt, and the individual states were not much better off. **Hard money** (silver and gold) was scarce. But paper money, the obvious answer to a lack of hard money, presented its own difficulties. During the war, the national government had printed so much money ("Continental dollars") that paper money's value plummeted, and merchants would not accept it. The expression "not worth a Continental" came to mean that something was worthless.

Compounding the problem was each state's ability to print its own currency. State currency was often as worthless as the Continental notes. Many merchants required payment in hard currency or barter (traded goods). One Massachusetts newspaper editor announced that he would accept salt pork as payment for subscriptions.

Finally, the states dealt a fatal financial blow to the Congress of the Confederation. On two occasions, Congress proposed amendments to the Articles that would permit Congress to levy small tariffs for revenue (as opposed to a protective tariff). In both instances, failure to attain the required unanimous vote for an amendment killed the measure. The second failure spurred efforts by those who desired a revision of the Articles or even a new constitution. It seemed nothing of lasting value could ever be accomplished under the Articles of Confederation.

Foreign Weakness

The separate interests of the states often hampered the national government's conduct of foreign affairs. In negotiating the Treaty

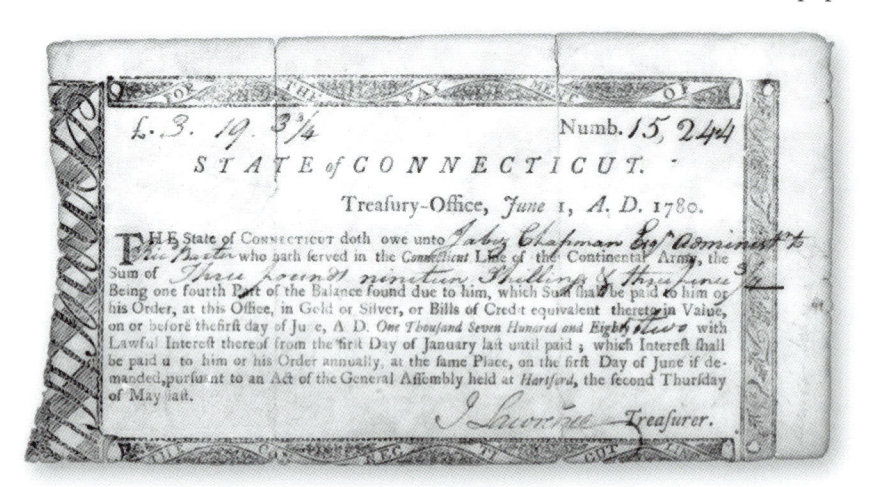

An example of paper money issued by a state

"Excesses of Democracy"?

Provincial politics is nothing new in America. Following independence from Britain, a rapid increase of qualified voters resulted, and with this expansion came a host of new people who could now run for office. Those considered common men—such as farmers, merchants, and artisans—became candidates and won elections at a rate that concerned the elites who had previously controlled colonial assemblies. However, bias against manual laborers serving in government is also nothing new. Even the Greek philosopher Aristotle believed that laboring with one's hands was not noble and that it worked against "virtue." This partiality was still popular among many of the educated in America.

A republican form of government required a change in thinking. A monarchy could prosper if the monarch was virtuous, but in a republic, virtue needed to be a widespread quality among the people.

Many leaders of the Revolutionary War began to worry that the new nation might be destroyed by what they termed "excesses of democracy." Some of those excesses were states printing large quantities of paper money with resulting inflation and frequent revision of laws to satisfy various political or economic interests. These concerns became one underlying reason for meeting to revise or replace the Articles of Confederation.

of Paris and in later treaty discussions, European powers such as Britain, Spain, and France learned that they could play on jealousies among the states to undercut the United States' bargaining position. Financial and military weaknesses only worsened matters. When the United States ran afoul of the Barbary pirates in northern Africa, the nation could not even pay the demanded bribes, let alone build and arm a naval squadron to protect American shipping.

Domestic Weakness

Internal weakness resulted in part from economic confusion. The existence of fourteen different currencies, varying tariffs, and a postwar depression weakened the financial fabric that could have bound the nation together. The most serious threat, however, was the national government's inability to keep the peace within its own borders.

In 1783, a group of officers in Newburgh, New York, grew frustrated by Congress's inability to pay salaries and pensions. The soldiers were backed by businessmen who feared the economic chaos that they saw looming before them. In this **Newburgh Conspiracy**, the officers intended to force Congress and the states to grant them their back pay. Some conspirators wanted more; they wanted to establish a new government under a king or a dictator. Washington was their first choice as the leader; but if he refused, they would find someone else.

Washington coldly rejected every offer to become a military ruler. When he learned that the officers planned a mass meeting in Newburgh to discuss their grievances, he came as an uninvited guest. He spoke kindly to the men, sympathizing with their needs but urging them not to destroy the nation they had fought for. At the conclusion of the speech, Washington started to reassure the men by reading a favorable letter from a congressman. Before reading it, he paused and with deliberation took out his glasses and put them on. "Gentlemen, you will permit me to put on my spectacles," the general said, "for, I have grown not only gray, but almost blind in the service of my country."

When Washington finished reading, tears filled the eyes of many of the men for reasons unrelated to the letter's contents. Before them stood the Patriot who had weathered the snows of Valley Forge and faced the bullets of the British, the man whose strength of character and leadership had been the greatest weapon in the American arsenal. The Newburgh Conspiracy collapsed, but it had threatened the young and fragile government.

An even more serious problem arose in Massachusetts in 1786. Instead of simply conspiring against the government, as the ringleaders at Newburgh had done, a group of men actually took up arms against the government. Daniel Shays, a veteran of the Revolution, led an insurrection of farmers against the courts in the western part of the state. The farmers had purchased land at inflated prices. In the depression that followed, they could not meet their obligations. When many of them were jailed, others retaliated by using force to close the courts. The insurrection climaxed with a vain attempt to seize weapons from an arsenal. Shortly thereafter, the militia crushed the uprising.

Shays's Rebellion was quelled only a few weeks before the delegates of the Constitutional Convention met at Philadelphia in 1787. The delegates, shaken by the violence, undoubtedly considered it a

Daniel Shays

warning. Americans had preserved their liberty from destruction by the British; after the war, they had to preserve it from destruction by themselves. The Articles of Confederation looked increasingly inadequate for that task.

Section Review

1. What was the greatest accomplishment in foreign affairs by the Confederation government?
2–3. What were the two most controversial provisions of the proposed Ordinance of 1784?
4–6. According to the provisions of the Northwest Ordinance of 1787, what were the three steps a region went through to become a state?
7–8. What were the two serious domestic threats to the government's authority under the Articles of Confederation?
★ How did the American core value of individualism cause problems in the Confederation?
★ What was the biblical root of problems in the Confederation?

II. A New Charter

The failures and weaknesses of the Confederation government caused thoughtful men to consider what could be done. Trade discussions gave them an opportunity to voice their ideas. Representatives from Virginia and Maryland met in 1785 at Alexandria, Virginia, and at George Washington's home at Mount Vernon to discuss trade disputes involving the Potomac River. The Mount Vernon meeting was so profitable that the legislatures of Maryland and Virginia called for another trade convention in Annapolis, Maryland, that would include all thirteen states. The **Annapolis Convention** was not well attended; only five states sent representatives. Alexander Hamilton, a delegate from New York, wrote a resolution calling for another convention to remedy the weaknesses of the Confederation government. Faced with growing discontent and fearful of anarchy, the Confederation Congress (which Washington described as "a half starved limping government") reluctantly seconded the idea of a convention in Philadelphia for May 1787.

The Constitutional Convention

The delegates arrived for the opening session on May 25. A cool rain offered relief from the already unbearably warm weather that had settled over the city. Old-timers agreed that it was the hottest summer in memory.

Drenched and mud-spattered, the delegates met at the Pennsylvania State House, where eleven years earlier the Declaration of Independence had been signed. Despite the wet weather, the delegates were excited. They were eager to work and enthusiastic about what could be accomplished. Virginian **James Madison**—whose ideas earned him the title "Father of the Constitution"—declared that their work would "settle forever the fate of republican government."

Thomas Jefferson, overseas at the time as minister to France, referred to the men who served in the Philadelphia Convention as

Guiding Questions

1. What circumstances brought the delegates of the Constitutional Convention together?
2. What three major compromises occurred at the convention?

James Madison

"an assembly of demigods [partly divine beings]." It was indeed a remarkable gathering of talent. Numbered among the fifty-five delegates were the best political thinkers and finest lawyers in America, well-read and well-educated. Their talents, however, were not simply the product of book learning. They were practical men of experience, many of them as skilled with the sword as with the pen. Half of them had fought in the Revolutionary War. Thirty-nine had served in the Continental or Confederation Congresses, which gave them a broad range of practical political experience. Among these men were past, present, and future governors and two future United States presidents.

The **Constitutional Convention** was more than a gathering of talent, however; it was also a collection of regional and individual interests. Twelve independent states (Rhode Island refused to participate) were represented. These states, apart from war-time emergencies, had never been very neighborly. Diverse delegate interests led to heated debates and threatened the survival of the convention. That these men represented their states' interests could hardly be considered a vice because they were elected as state representatives to the convention. However, many of them had a larger, national vision of their work and were able to compromise.

The first task was to elect a convention president to chair the proceedings. The delegates unanimously elected George Washington, whose very presence gave credibility to the meeting. Interestingly, twelve years earlier in the same room in which they were meeting, Washington had been elected commander in chief of the Continental army. He likely found his war experiences beneficial in overseeing the squabbles that soon broke out at the convention.

Crucial Compromises

The most important question that the convention delegates faced initially was why they were meeting. Were they there to revise the Articles in an attempt to breathe some life into the Confederation, or should they start over and draft a fresh agreement? The delegates answered the question on May 30. Acting on a resolution by Delegate Gouverneur Morris, they agreed that "a national government ought to be established, consisting of a supreme legislative, executive, and judiciary."

Having quickly answered that basic question, the delegates soon saw their harmony fractured over the details of how such a government should be formed. The disputes grew largely out of regional interests and would require compromises on three major issues: representation, slavery, and trade.

The Great Compromise

How the states were to be represented was the most difficult question. The battle lines were drawn between the large states (e.g., Virginia, Pennsylvania, and New York) and the smaller states (e.g., New Jersey, Delaware, and Maryland).

James Madison had carefully considered the composition and structure of the new Congress. His thorough study of political thought, both ancient and modern, and his careful planning resulted in a proposal known as the **Virginia Plan**, which would become the basis for much of the Constitution.

Madison's Virginia Plan, which was introduced to the convention by fellow Virginian Edmund Randolph, advocated a **bicameral**

> "Representatives and direct Taxes shall be apportioned among the several States which may be included within this Union, according to their respective Numbers, which shall be determined by adding to the whole Number of free Persons, including those bound to Service for a Term of Years, and excluding Indians not taxed, three fifths of all other Persons."
>
> Article I, Section 2, Clause 3 of the Constitution

(two-house) Congress, with the number of representatives based on state population. Members of the lower house, or House of Representatives, would be elected by direct popular vote. The lower house, in turn, would elect members of the upper house, or Senate, from nominees submitted by state legislatures.

In contrast to the powerless, penniless Confederation Congress, the legislature under the Virginia Plan would have greatly expanded powers. For example, the new Congress would be able to enforce its laws on the states and would be empowered to elect both the chief executive and the national judiciary. Those two branches, the executive and the judicial, could unite to veto congressional acts, but their veto could be overridden by a vote in both houses of Congress.

Since representation under the Virginia Plan was based on state population, it naturally favored the states with larger populations. The smaller states were quick to react to the proposal, setting forth a proposal of their own known as the **New Jersey Plan**. This small-state plan, presented by William Paterson of New Jersey, advocated a unicameral Congress, similar to the Confederation Congress, with each state having only one vote regardless of its population. John Dickinson, who had represented Pennsylvania in the First and Second Continental Congresses, was now living in Delaware. As a delegate from that state, he rebuked Madison, saying the New Jersey Plan was the result of Madison's stubborn refusal to change his view about representation.

The convention deadlocked over the issue of representation. Dickinson conceded that "some of the members from the small States wish for two branches in the General Legislature and are friends to a good National Government." But he told Madison, "We would sooner submit to a foreign power, than submit to be deprived of an equality of suffrage, in both branches of the legislature, and thereby be thrown under the domination of the large States." The small states feared domination by the large states; the large states feared the diminishing of their power through lack of representation, arguing that basic democratic principles favored proportional representation. In summary, the New Jersey Plan advocated each state receive one vote in Congress; the Virginia Plan advocated congressional representation based on population.

The haggling went on for weeks as hot weather and hotter debates threatened the survival of the convention. The windows were raised at times in hopes of drawing a breeze, but they usually drew only unwelcome flies and fumes—sewer construction was underway in the streets outside the State House. Irritated delegates adjusted their sweaty collars but not their positions. Some threatened to go home.

Roger Sherman of Connecticut offered the embroiled assembly a solution to its dead-end debating. Sherman was a Christian with an unwavering testimony for Christ. John Adams referred to him as "that old Puritan, honest as an angel." Sherman put together a compromise that saved both the convention and the Constitution. The **Great Compromise** (or Connecticut Compromise, as it is sometimes called) proposed that representation in the lower house be based on state population, whereas representation in the Senate be equal for all states regardless of size. Alexander Hamilton called it "a motley measure." But Sherman's proposal was a classic example of political compromise: both sides gave up something, and both sides got something. The convention continued.

Roger Sherman

The Three-Fifths Compromise

The next divisive issue that confronted the delegates of the Constitutional Convention was how to count slaves when determining representation for states. Since slavery was practiced in all of the original thirteen states, this was not yet a fully-developed North/South or a slave-state versus free-state issue. However, slavery was quickly being abolished in northern states, and southern states had a growing slave population. Therefore, a formula for counting slaves for purposes of representation was important to all. To settle the issue of how slaves should be counted, delegates established the **Three-Fifths Compromise**. Under this settlement, three-fifths of the total slave population of a state would be included for representation purposes in the House, but those states would also have to pay taxes on the slave population at the same rate. It is significant to note that the wording of the Constitution recognized slaves as *persons* rather than property. This wording established an important precedent. The compromise also sought to maintain a balance between states with a small slave population and states with a large slave population. But it did not resolve the growing debate about slavery.

Many delegates were opposed to slavery, but the issue was a thorny political question. Oliver Ellsworth of Connecticut reminded his fellow delegates that "the morality or wisdom of slavery are considerations belonging to the States themselves. . . . The States are the best judges of their particular interest." George Mason of Virginia countered, "Every master of slaves is born a petty tyrant. They bring the judgment of heaven on a Country." Yet it would be left to the children and grandchildren of the constitutional framers to resolve the slave question.

The Trade Compromise

Part of the motivation behind calling the Philadelphia Convention was the failure of the Confederation to resolve interstate trade disputes and direct international trade. Although most delegates agreed that Congress needed a role in commerce, regional interests kept them at odds over the extent of that role. Southern states, in particular, were concerned that the new Congress would ban the slave trade and raise revenue through export duties. Such duties would hurt the economies of these states, which were dependent on the export of raw goods.

A compromise settled the issue. By the terms of the agreement, Congress was given power over foreign and interstate commerce. However, the legislature was forbidden to impose any export taxes on the states, and Article V of the Constitution prevented making any amendments regarding the slave trade until 1808.

Constitutional Principles

Despite disputes over details, the constitutional framers agreed on certain basic principles. These principles have given the Constitution and the government it outlined durability.

Many of the constitutional principles grew out of the founders' understanding of human nature. They recognized that people, both the governed and the governors, are inherently sinful. As John Adams, quoting Machiavelli, pointed out, "Whoever would found a state and make proper laws for the government of it must presume that all men are bad by nature."

> ### *Context of the Three-Fifths Compromise*
>
> This compromise balanced the interests of the northern states, which had few slaves, and the southern states, which had a much larger number of slaves. Northern states strongly opposed the southern idea of counting each slave for the purpose of determining representation in the House of Representatives. Therefore, James Wilson of Pennsylvania and Charles Pinckney of South Carolina suggested the three-fifths compromise as a way to satisfy both sides in this debate. While this was initially intended only for representation, the final agreement also covered any potential taxation based on state populations.

This is not to say that the Constitution is a "Christian" document any more than its framers were all Christians. Some were moral men, some were God-fearing men, and some were neither. But what is clear is that the Constitution was written in a society where biblical principles were pervasive, and the document can be best understood in the light of those principles. These principles are not spelled out in the document itself, but they contribute to its fabric.

The key principles of the Constitution center on the issue of power—how to divide, balance, limit, and allot governmental power in view of human corruption. James Madison underscored this point in *The Federalist* (number 51) when he wrote,

> What is government itself, but the greatest of all reflections on human nature? If men were angels, no government would be necessary. If angels were to govern men, neither external nor internal controls on government would be necessary. In framing a government which is to be administered by men over men, the great difficulty lies in this: you must first enable the government to control the governed; and in the next place oblige it to control itself.

Striking a balance between liberty and order was the great challenge and triumph of the Constitutional Convention.

Republican Philosophy

The Constitution established a republic, a government run by representatives chosen by and accountable to the voters. The founders opposed a monarchy or an aristocracy but also opposed a democracy, which they feared would devolve into rule by the mob. This republican philosophy was part of the founders' thinking when they decided how various government officials would be elected: the president by the Electoral College, which through its electors represents the people of the entire nation; the House members by popular vote to represent specific local districts; and the senators by state legislators to represent state governments.

Limited Government

The underlying theme of the Constitution is **limited government**. The nation had only recently shaken off British tyranny through a bloody war, so the Philadelphia delegates fully understood the consequences of unlimited government—the very definition of tyranny.

The principle of limited government is expressed by the nature of a written constitution, the first and oldest in continuous use. Unlike the unwritten British constitution, an open-ended accumulation of laws and traditions subject to Parliamentary action, the American Constitution as a written charter clearly defined the limits of governmental power and broadened the scope of individual liberty. The principles of separation of powers and checks and balances also contributed to the limitations on governmental power.

Separation of Powers

To prevent any group or individual from gaining too much power, the founders designed the national government with the **separation of powers** in mind. That is the division of the government into three separate branches: the legislative branch (Article I of the Constitution), the executive branch (Article II), and the judicial branch (Article III). In broad terms, under the Constitu-

Constitutional Convention

tion, Congress makes the laws, the president executes and enforces the laws, and the courts interpret the laws.

Although the three branches are separate, they are not fully independent. Their responsibilities intersect in many areas, and a certain amount of cooperation is necessary to make the national government work effectively.

Checks and Balances

Although separation of powers is often thought to be synonymous with **checks and balances,** there is an important difference. If power were only divided, then one branch could expand its powers within its rightful sphere and come to dominate the other branches.

The principle of checks and balances is designed to thwart such an accumulation of power by establishing a balance of power among the three branches. For example, Congress passes a bill to become law, but the president may reject, or veto, the bill. However, his veto may be overridden by a two-thirds vote in both houses of Congress. For its part, the Supreme Court may nullify acts of both Congress and the president if a majority of justices interprets a law as unconstitutional.

Federalism

Federalism is the division of power between national and state levels of government. The federal system was a product of American historical and political realities.

Thirteen separate, sovereign states, with differing political and social backgrounds, had emerged from the colonial and early national periods. These fiercely independent states had no intention of giving up their political power. The delegates, though representing states' regional interests, also recognized the need for the strength and order of national unity. The federal system struck a crucial balance between state and national demands. Today, federalism provides needed flexibility in a large country of varying regions by giving citizens a greater voice in their affairs at the state and local level. Many people believe that the genius of the Constitution is its ambiguity. Supporters of both limited government and a strong central government can ultimately accept it. The perpetual tension that exists between these two views actually strengthens and safeguards freedoms.

Popular Sovereignty

Popular sovereignty, the idea that the ultimate source of governmental power lies in the people, is a constitutional principle that is evident in several areas of the Constitution. The **Preamble**, which introduced the charter with a full and flourishing sentence, reads:

> We the People of the United States, in Order to form a more perfect Union, establish Justice, ensure domestic Tranquility, provide for the common defence, promote the general Welfare, and secure the Blessings of Liberty to ourselves and our Posterity, do ordain and establish this Constitution for the United States of America.

Despite the dramatic "We the People," the Constitution was actually formed by the agreement of states, not individuals, and its approval was subject to state conventions, not a national referendum.

The principle of popular sovereignty is best expressed in the Constitution through the document's provisions for representation and amendment. Representation allows the people to have a voice in their republican government through their elected officials. The constitutional framers, partly because they feared the fickleness of public opinion, limited the directness of the people's voice on the national level by providing direct election only for the House of Representatives.

The president and the senators, by contrast, were elected indirectly by the people. Senators, for example, were initially elected by their respective state legislatures rather than by a direct vote from their constituents. Likewise, the president is elected through the indirect means of the **Electoral College**. Under this constitutional provision (Article II, Section 1), each state has a number of electors equal to the state's representation in Congress. In general, all the electoral votes from a state go to the presidential candidate who receives the highest number of popular votes from that state.

Constitutional **amendments**, changes to the Constitution, are also an expression of the people's sovereignty. Amendments that survive the difficult ratification process often reflect widespread popular support and always take precedence over the laws of Congress, the actions of the president, and the rulings of the courts. Chief Justice John Marshall stated, "The people made the Constitution, and the people can unmake it. It is the creature of their will, and lives only by their will."

"We the People" is an enduring declaration not only of the people's power to rule themselves but also of the people's responsibility for that rule. Self-government is no easy task. It does not occur by accident, nor is it a self-propelled machine. The members of each generation must grapple with their government—use its principles and cherish its freedoms to make it work for their day and the next.

Section Review

1. How did the Constitutional Convention reach a compromise on the issue of representation?
2. What compromise allowed the convention to settle the problem of slavery in relation to taxation and representation?
3–4. Between what two qualities did the Constitutional Convention seek a balance?
5–10. What are the six principles of government contained in the American Constitution?
   ★ Has the system of checks and balances been successful in preventing any one branch of government from expanding its powers? Use examples to support your answer.
   ★ Did the Three-Fifths Compromise encourage, discourage, or remain neutral regarding slavery? Defend your answer and propose an alternative if you think the compromise was counterproductive.

III. The Struggle for Ratification

On September 17, 1787, Washington offered the final draft of the new charter to the convention. After the delegates signed and sent it to the Confederation Congress, the document would pass to the states for their consent (ratification).

Although many of the delegates supported the final document, Edmund Randolph and George Mason of Virginia and Elbridge Gerry of Massachusetts objected to the expanded powers of the national government and the absence of a bill of rights. Mason adamantly declared that he "would sooner chop off his right hand than put it to the Constitution" because of the document's failure to guarantee civil liberties. Such objections foreshadowed a difficult ratification process that ultimately proved successful: the approval of at least nine states was required by Article VII of the Constitution.

After the signing and a celebration supper, the delegates parted company. Their work would now be scrutinized by the nation. The greatest hurdles lay before them. The Constitution-makers had put forth a remarkable effort, but privately some of them worried about ratification because the stakes were so high. Washington wrote Randolph saying, "This, or a dissolution of the Union, awaits our choice." He also wrote his fellow delegates, advising them that "the event is in the hand of God."

War of Words

Two days after the delegates went home, the text of the Constitution was published in the *Pennsylvania Packet* of Philadelphia. For the first time, Americans learned what had been devised behind the closed doors of the Pennsylvania State House, and not everyone was pleased. The battle lines were drawn between supporters of the Constitution, called **Federalists**, and those who opposed it, the **Anti-Federalists**.

Just one week after the proposed Constitution was published, a New York newspaper denounced the Constitution in an article penned under the pseudonym "**Cato**." Cato was, in fact, New York

---

Guiding Questions

1. What were the Federalists' arguments favoring ratification of the Constitution?
2. What were the Anti-Federalists' arguments opposing ratification of the Constitution?
3. Why was ratification of the Constitution significant?

Franklin's Plea

Eighty-one-year-old Benjamin Franklin, suffering from gout and kidney stones, gave a written address to a colleague to read in hopes of swaying undecided delegates to sign. Franklin acknowledged,

> I confess that there are several parts of this constitution which I do not at present approve, but I am not sure I shall never approve them: For having lived long, I have experienced many instances of being obliged by better information, or fuller consideration, to change opinions even on important subjects.... Thus I consent, Sir, to this Constitution because I expect no better, and because I am not sure, that it is not the best.

Excerpt from "Cato," Essay VII

Hitherto we have tied up our rulers in the exercise of their duties by positive restrictions—if the cord has been drawn too tight, loosen it to the necessary extent, but do not entirely unbind them.—I am no enemy to placing a reasonable confidence in them; but such an unbounded one as the advocates and framers of this new system advise you to, would be dangerous to your liberties; it has been the ruin of other governments, and will be yours.

Alexander Hamilton

Excerpt from Federalist 1
Happy it will be if our choice should be directed by a judicious estimate of our true interests, unperplexed and unbiased by considerations not connected with the public good. But this is a thing more ardently to be wished than seriously to be expected. The plan offered to our deliberations affects too many particular interests, innovates on too many local institutions, not to involve in its discussion a variety of objects foreign to its merits, and of views, passions and prejudices little favorable to the discovery of truth.

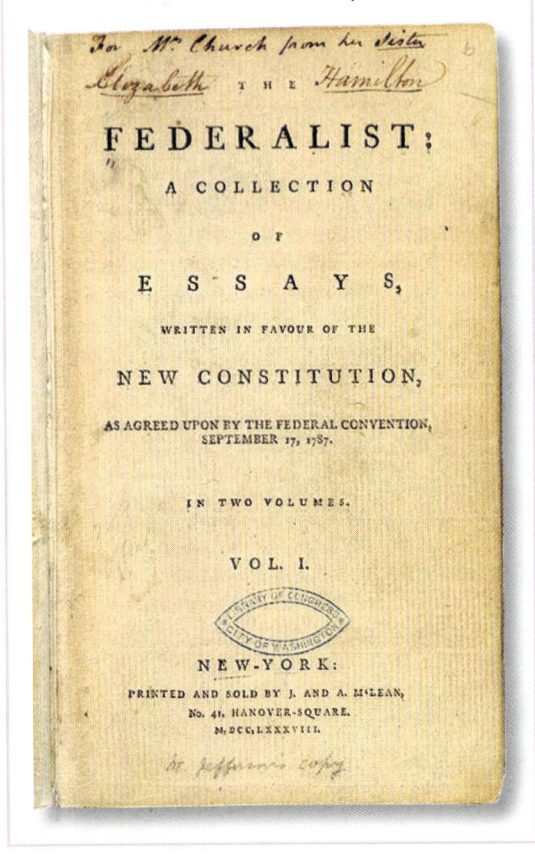

governor George Clinton. He was soon joined by "Sidney," "Brutus," and others in a series of Anti-Federalist articles.

Alexander Hamilton, the lone New York delegate who had supported and signed the Constitution, returned home to find the political winds blowing against the Constitution. He responded to the Anti-Federalist articles by writing some Federalist articles under the pen name "**Publius**." Hamilton also enlisted the help of James Madison and John Jay in a war of words. Together, the trio wrote eighty-five essays that were widely read throughout the country.

The essays were compiled and published in two volumes in May 1788 under the title **The Federalist**, or *The Federalist Papers*. This work answered Anti-Federalist objections by carefully explaining and forcefully defending constitutional provisions of power. It also predicted dangers and dismemberment for the nation if the Constitution were rejected.

The Federalist was to ratification what *Common Sense* had been to the Revolution. It was a persuasive force, particularly in those states where ratification hung in the balance. But *The Federalist* is also a comprehensive commentary on republican government. Jefferson praised it as "the best commentary on the principles of government which has ever been written." Historian Clinton Rossiter perhaps best explained the universality of *The Federalist* when he wrote that the essays are

> now valued not merely as a clever defense of a particular charter, but as an exposition of certain timeless truths about constitutional government.... The message of *The Federalist* reads: no happiness without liberty, no liberty without self-government, no self-government without constitutionalism, no constitutionalism without morality—and none of these great goods without stability and order.

Less well known are **The Anti-Federalist Papers**, the collected writings and speeches by opponents of the new Constitution. They were the response of the Anti-Federalists to the publications of the Federalists. The Anti-Federalists were not radicals who were against free government and constitutional liberties. The Anti-Federalists included patriots such as Patrick Henry, Edmund Randolph, James Monroe, George Mason, George Clinton, and William Paterson. In addition to "Cato," "Sidney," and "Brutus," the Anti-Federalists wrote under pseudonyms such as "Centinel" and "Federal Farmer."

Thirteen Battles

Delaware led the states by giving the Constitution its unanimous consent on December 7, 1787. Within a month, four more states—Pennsylvania, New Jersey, Georgia, and Connecticut—ratified the Constitution. The toughest battles, however, were in Massachusetts, Virginia, and New York, where the Anti-Federalists were better organized and had leaders of considerable stature among their ranks.

Massachusetts approved the Constitution in a close vote in February 1788 after the Federalists gained the support of John Hancock and Samuel Adams. Three more states—Maryland, South Carolina, and New Hampshire—joined the six ratifying states to make the nine necessary for the Constitution to become law. The letter of the law, however, was not enough. Practically speaking, any hopes for a national union had to include both Virginia, which was the largest state, and New York. If New York failed to ratify, then New England would be cut off geographically from the rest of the country. If Virginia refused to join, then the South would be severed.

The Anti-Federalists of Virginia were led by the fiery orator Patrick Henry and non-signing Constitutional Convention delegates George Mason and Governor Edmund Randolph. The objections of this Anti-Federalist trio represented legitimate concerns: fear of consolidated political power in an overarching national government and the absence of guarantees of personal liberty in a bill of rights. The Federalists were not opposed to personal liberty; rather, most of them thought that a bill of rights was unnecessary or even that it was too restrictive to limit rights to a written list. The Federalists also feared that the attempt to compose a bill of rights before ratification would derail both the Constitution and the necessary precondition for such freedoms—national order. After James Madison promised to introduce amendments for a bill of rights in the first session of Congress, the Virginia Federalists won a narrow victory for ratification, 89 to 79.

Madison's concession was the tie breaker in Virginia and a catalyst for the final great state battle raging in New York. There Governor Clinton and his Anti-Federalists commanded a decisive majority against backers of the Constitution, led by Alexander Hamilton. However, news of the Anti-Federalist collapse in Virginia struck a fatal blow to Clinton's edge. By a slim margin of 30 to 27, New York ratified. North Carolina and Rhode Island held out for some time, but plans for the new government proceeded. Elections for the new Congress were set, and the opening session was scheduled for March 4, 1789, at the temporary national capital, New York City.

Benjamin Franklin wrote with satisfaction, "Our new Constitution is now established, and has an appearance that promises permanency; but in the world nothing can be said to be certain except death and taxes."

A Rising Sun

The office of chief executive was one of the most significant and least controversial departures from the old Confederation government. George Washington—"first in war, first in peace, and first in the hearts of his countrymen"—was the natural choice for the nation's highest office.

On February 4, 1789, Washington was unanimously elected president by the Electoral College. His old Massachusetts ally, John Adams, was elected as the first vice president. Washington's triumphal journey from Mount Vernon to New York City for his inauguration was a swirl of speeches, suppers, and small-town serenades. The road to New York was lined with parents hoisting their puzzled children for a glimpse of the great man and thousands of other onlookers reaching out to touch the hero.

The modest Washington was taken aback by his welcome and privately admitted that he felt more like "a culprit who is going to his place of execution." He also felt the weight of responsibility growing as he approached his inauguration.

On April 30, 1789, on the balcony of New York's Federal Hall on Wall Street, the great Virginian placed his hand on the Bible and promised to preserve, protect, and defend the Constitution. With

Edmund Randolph

George Mason

Baptists and the Bill of Rights

Many Protestants, including Baptists, supported the War for Independence. One reason for their support was the anticipation of religious freedom that would result. However, when the text of the Constitution became known, Baptist leaders, including Pastor John Leland, expressed serious concerns because the document contained no guarantees of religious freedom. James Madison and others argued that these guarantees were unnecessary because the federal government could likely not attain a level of power that would threaten freedom of religion. However, Pastor Leland and many others insisted that their support for the Constitution was contingent on the addition of a bill of rights. When Pastor Leland convinced Madison to offer the suggested amendments, Leland and other Baptists supported the ratification of the Constitution and helped to ensure its passage.

From Thirteen Republics to One Republic

Under the Articles of Confederation, the thirteen states were essentially thirteen distinct republics. A decade later, the leaders had developed a document that, once ratified, would create a single republic with separate powers for the national government and state governments.

But what is a republic? Some modern definitions have reduced the meaning of the term to a national entity with no king. However, there is much more to this form of government than the absence of a monarch. A republic is a form of government where citizens elect leaders who carry out their assigned duties according to the rule of law. This system of government was designed to provide stability and yet allow for change in an orderly manner. It was intended to protect a country from the whims of a charismatic leader or the attraction of a passing idea whose consequences had not been fully considered.

One might ask why there have been so few republics in history. A republic is a fragile concept and its success depends on several factors. The citizens must be informed in order to elect the best people to represent them. In addition, the citizens must be moral in order to select the right leaders and reject the wrong leaders. This requires work and sacrifice, and these run contrary to nature.

Many have said, "The price of liberty is eternal vigilance." Perhaps the same could be said of a republic. Citizens must be engaged, informed, and subject to moral restraint. This enables them to govern themselves and to elect those who will not bribe citizens into surrendering their liberty in exchange for immediate gratification.

Republics should have another characteristic—that all of its citizens are equal. Free citizens are equal citizens, and this equality leads to opportunity for all. It does not guarantee an equality of outcome, but does promise an equality of opportunity. Engaged, informed, and equal citizens in a republic have the freedom and opportunity to preserve and advance the welfare of their families, their communities, their states, and their nation.

George Washington

that, President Washington kissed the Bible, and the city erupted with cheers, bells, and cannons.

Washington's inauguration marked both an end and a beginning. It was the end of the long struggle for liberty and self-government, and it was a national beginning. While the delegates were signing the Constitution, Madison recorded that

> Dr. Franklin, looking towards the president's chair, at the back of which a rising sun happened to be painted, observed to a few members near him that painters had found it difficult to distinguish in their art a rising from a setting sun. "I have," said he, "often and often during the course of the session . . . looked at that behind the president, without being able to tell whether it was rising or setting, but now at length I have the happiness to know that it is a rising and not a setting sun."

Section Review

1. Why did Edmund Randolph, George Mason, and Elbridge Gerry oppose the Constitution?
2. Who were "Cato" and "Publius"?
3. How did James Madison win approval for the Constitution in Virginia?
* What does the opposition of Edmund Randolph, Patrick Henry, and George Mason to the Constitution say about their beliefs on human nature?

CHAPTER 7 REVIEW

Making Connections

1. Why was the Treaty of Paris an important foreign policy achievement for the new nation?
2. How did the Confederation encourage educational growth in the young nation?
3. How was the Northwest Territory to be divided? Name the states that ultimately were created from it.
4. What principles were the foundation of the Constitution?
5. What basic biblical principle concerning human nature did the framers of the Constitution recognize when writing the Constitution?

Developing History Skills

1. Did the Constitution address the concerns of many American leaders that the new nation had developed "excessive democracy?" Explain your answer.
2. If there had been no Connecticut Compromise, which would have been better for the United States: the Virginia Plan or the New Jersey Plan? Why?

Thinking Critically

1. How are constitutional amendments an expression of the people's sovereignty?
2. How do you think the failure of the Articles might have contributed to the Constitution's success?

Living as a Christian Citizen

1. If you were a delegate to the Constitutional Convention, would you have voted for the compromises regarding slavery? Be careful to consider both the results these compromises had in history and the possible effects had these compromises failed to pass.
2. Write a constitution for an imagined nation, considering the six principles of the Constitution from a biblical perspective. Be prepared to present it to the class.

People, Places, and Things to Remember

confederation
Articles of Confederation
unicameral
Northwest Territory
Ordinance of 1784
Land Ordinance of 1785
Northwest Ordinance of 1787
hard money
Newburgh Conspiracy
Shays's Rebellion
Annapolis Convention
James Madison
Constitutional Convention (1787)
Virginia Plan
bicameral
New Jersey Plan
Roger Sherman
Great Compromise
Three-Fifths Compromise
limited government
separation of powers
checks and balances
federalism
popular sovereignty
Preamble
Electoral College
amendments
Federalists
Anti-Federalists
"Cato"
"Publius"
The Federalist
The Anti-Federalist Papers

8 THE FEDERALIST YEARS (1789–1801)

> We are not to expect to be translated from despotism to liberty in a feather bed.
>
> **Thomas Jefferson**
> 1790, in a letter to Lafayette

President Washington reviewing American troops during the Whiskey Rebellion (October 1794)

Big Ideas

1. What challenges did the new government face during its early years?
2. What differing viewpoints led to the development of political parties?
3. What led to the decline of the Federalist party?

I. Launching the New Government

II. Emerging Political Parties

III. Declining Federalist Influence

Franklin's rising sun, which Franklin observed at the end of the Constitutional Convention, shone across a rugged political landscape. Throughout the 1790s, the fledgling republic weathered one storm after another; some blew in from Europe, others from the backcountry, and some arose in the halls of power in the new government.

These difficulties, although not unlike those the country endured in the previous decade, had a completely different result. Rather than weakening the national government, they strengthened it. The Constitution proved to be a practical and powerful instrument. Despite growing pains, the Federalist years were a formative era in which personal liberties were defended, national supremacy was demonstrated, and political parties were developed. The nationalist character of Federalism, so evident throughout the decade, would not grow unchecked, however. Forces for decentralization and limited government would blunt the nationalist thrust, sparking controversy and conflict.

I. Launching the New Government

Getting Started

The first order of business in 1789 was to organize the new government in accordance with the new Constitution. The key features were the cabinet, the courts, and the Congress.

Cabinet

With congressional approval, President **George Washington** organized three departments in the executive branch—the departments of State, Treasury, and War—and appointed their secretaries, or chief officers. Washington chose **Thomas Jefferson**, recently returned from a five-year assignment as minister to France, to head the Department of State. Washington chose his wartime aide, the brilliant **Alexander Hamilton**, to be secretary of the treasury. And he selected Henry Knox, of War for Independence fame, to head the War Department. In addition, Washington appointed fellow Virginian, and former governor, Edmund Randolph as attorney general. He provided legal counsel for the new administration.

Guiding Questions

1. What were the key features of the new government?
2. What is the significance of the Bill of Rights?
3. What were the two main approaches to interpreting the Constitution?

George Washington

Washington and his cabinet (*left to right*): Washington, Knox, Hamilton, Jefferson, Randolph

The Washington family

Although the term *cabinet* in the sense of an advisory body was in neither the Constitution nor Washington's vocabulary, the department heads met regularly with the president to discuss policy decisions. Eventually, these advisors took the collective name "cabinet" and played a key role in the first and future presidential administrations.

Courts

The Constitution directly provided for only a Supreme Court but permitted Congress to establish lower federal courts. As a result, Congress passed the **Judiciary Act of 1789**. It organized thirteen district courts (one for each of the states), established three circuit courts to handle appeals, and set the number of Supreme Court justices at six. Washington appointed John Jay to be the court's chief justice. Later, the number of courts and justices increased.

Despite constitutional provisions and a working system of federal courts, the Supreme Court had little power or respect during its first few years. In fact, when the national government moved to its permanent capital of Washington, D.C., in 1800, planners failed to provide a place for the third branch of government. The president had his executive mansion, Congress met in the Capitol, and the Supreme Court justices also met in the Capitol building—in the basement.

One significant section of the Judiciary Act of 1789 would have an important ramification in the future. It provided that state court decisions could be appealed to the federal court level if constitutional questions were involved. This provision clearly declared the supremacy of the federal courts over the state courts. Though some political leaders believed this part of the measure violated the rights of individual states, the bill easily passed Congress.

Congress

The First Congress accomplished more of significance than did most later ones. During the remarkable two-year session from 1789 to 1791, Congress drafted the Bill of Rights, organized the executive and judicial branches, and passed a number of crucial measures to put the country on a sound financial footing. These achievements seem all the more outstanding considering that the First Congress was breaking new ground. **James Madison**, a leader in the House of Representatives at the time, observed, "We are in a wilderness without a single footstep to guide us. Our successors will have an easier task."

In addition to the landmark legislation passed during the original session, the congressmen also grappled with an issue that still faces our country today: how to resolve a huge national debt without raising taxes. They also discussed less serious issues, searching for a balance between respectability and royalty. On what to call the president, for example, John Adams favored "His Highness, the President of the United States and Protector of Rights of the same." Fortunately, that breathtaking title was shelved in favor of a simple "Mr. President."

The First Congress members also approved a salary for themselves, six dollars a day, which raised immediate howls from constituents over congressional extravagance. Yet considering what these congressmen were able to accomplish so quickly, particularly in drafting what would become the first ten amendments to the Constitution, their salary was a bargain.

Bill of Rights

In the summer of 1789, James Madison honored his pledge to his Anti-Federalist adversaries when he introduced amendments to the Constitution to protect individual rights. What emerged in 1791, after gaining the approval of three-fourths of the states, were the first ten amendments—the **Bill of Rights**.

The first and most fundamental of these amendments protects the freedoms of religion, speech, press, assembly, and petition. The second, third, and fourth amendments protect the rights of the individual by guaranteeing the right to bear arms (have weapons), prohibiting the forced quartering of troops in private homes during peacetime, and protecting against unreasonable searches and seizures. The fifth, sixth, seventh, and eighth amendments guarantee fair treatment for those accused of crimes. The ninth and tenth amendments place further restrictions on the extent of national power. The Ninth Amendment states that people's rights are not limited to those specifically mentioned in the Constitution. The Tenth Amendment states:

> The powers not delegated to the United States by the Constitution, nor prohibited by it to the States, are reserved to the States respectively, or to the people.

In summary, the Bill of Rights was specifically intended to restrict the power of the national government and to protect individual rights.

In 1789, Congress approved twelve amendments to the Constitution. By 1791, ten of those had been ratified by enough states to become a part of that document. They were known as the Bill of Rights.

Hamilton's Plans

War debts and nearly a decade of neglect had left the country's finances in shambles. One of the greatest challenges of the 1790s was to put America's economy in order before it collapsed. Fortunately, the first secretary of the treasury was a man whose ideas, imagination, and energy were equal to the challenge, although his critics accused him of trying to centralize government even further.

Alexander Hamilton's early life gave little indication of his destiny to be, as one historian put it, "the greatest administrative genius in America, and one of the greatest administrators of all time." Born out of wedlock on the Caribbean island of Nevis, Hamilton was abandoned by his father and later orphaned at thirteen when his mother died. Never one to let difficulties limit him, he managed to gain admission to King's College (now Columbia University) in New York with the help of some friends when he was seventeen. He later became Washington's chief of staff during the War for Independence and distinguished himself by his bravery at Yorktown.

Hamilton, having grown up in the West Indies, had none of the regional attachments that characterized many of the Founding Fathers. He viewed himself as an American, not as a New Yorker or

The First Amendment and Religion

The First Amendment did not legislate the absence of religion from government or public life. However, one of its major purposes was to prevent the establishment of a national church, such as the Anglican Church of Great Britain. Religion was, in fact, viewed as a desirable and even necessary ingredient of government, as the various inscriptions on public buildings in Washington, D.C., confirm.

a northerner. Although his background fueled his nationalist zeal, it also made it difficult for him to appreciate the sectional differences that were such a delicate and volatile aspect of American politics.

Hamilton was a key figure in setting the course of the young republic. He had been instrumental in calling the Constitutional Convention in 1787, and his appointment as secretary of the treasury at the age of thirty-two placed him in a powerful policy-making role. In four influential reports issued to Congress in 1790 and 1791, Hamilton outlined plans for resolving the nation's debt problem, establishing a national bank, and encouraging manufacturing and economic expansion. Eventually, the vast majority of Hamilton's proposals were shaped into law.

Report on Public Credit

Perhaps the most important of Hamilton's proposals was his first, the *Report on Public Credit*. This report held that for the sake of national pride and future credit, all government debt had to be paid. His ambitious plan consisted of two major aspects: funding and assumption.

Debt **funding** proposed that the federal government give bonds paying 6 percent interest to those the Continental Congress owed money for goods or military services provided during the war. The bonds were to be recognized as currency, a procedure called "monetizing the debt." Despite the enormity of the debt for that day (more than $77 million), Hamilton's funding plan was approved by Congress.

Assumption—the national government's takeover of all state debts—had a rougher passage through Congress. Most of the southern states had faithfully paid their debts, whereas the New England states were delinquent, a factor that made most southerners view assumption as unfair. This soon became a divisive issue between the North and South. Virginian James Madison, a leader in the House of Representatives, abandoned his old friend Hamilton by taking a firm stand against the assumption plan. The legislative stalemate was broken only by a major compromise. The site for a permanent national capital, to be known as Federal City, had not been determined. At a mediation meeting arranged by Jefferson, Hamilton promised to get sufficient northern votes to locate Federal City in the South, on the banks of the Potomac River, in return for southern votes on assumption. The deal was struck, and Washington himself chose the site of the capital that would one day bear his name, Washington, D.C., The new capital was to be occupied in ten years; meanwhile, Philadelphia would serve as the temporary one.

National Bank

Having dealt with the problem of past debts, Hamilton looked to the future in his second report. He proposed the formation of a national bank, which he saw as the centerpiece of a sound, strong economy. A national bank would issue a uniform currency, and its branches throughout the country would provide a source for business loans to encourage economic expansion.

The bill for a national bank with a twenty-year charter cleared Congress, but by the time it reached the president's desk to be signed into law, Madison and Jefferson were challenging the constitutionality of a national bank.

This was the opening round of what would be an ongoing controversy over constitutional interpretation. The constitutional framers produced a brief document that provided a sturdy framework but left many areas open to interpretation. A detailed, lengthy Constitution would have quickly grown outdated because its writers in 1787 could not possibly anticipate the kinds of problems the nation would face in 1887, much less in the twenty-first century and beyond. They wisely chose to draft a firm but flexible charter. How much flexibility was the thorny question. Those who advocated more flexibility on a given issue were called **loose constructionists** or broad constructionists. Those who held to a closer reading of the constitutional text were known as **strict constructionists**.

Congress had no specific authority to charter a national bank. Jefferson argued that "to take a single step beyond the boundaries thus specially drawn around the power of Congress is to take possession of a boundless field of power." President Washington, concerned over the questions of constitutionality raised by Jefferson and Madison, asked Hamilton to present his side of the debate.

Hamilton presented the chief executive with what has become the standard rationale for a loose interpretation of the Constitution. He argued that Article I, Section 8, Clause 18 of the Constitution gave Congress the authority to do whatever was "necessary and proper" to fulfill its duties. In other words, if the Constitution specified an end, then unspecified means could be used to reach that end. In contrast, Jefferson believed that what the Constitution did not permit, it prohibited. Thus, his strict interpretation of the Constitution advocated a more limited government.

Washington was persuaded by Hamilton's convincing arguments and signed the bill into law. The first **National Bank** was created. However, a serious rift had occurred within his administration.

First Bank of the United States, Philadelphia (the first National Bank)

Section Review

1–3. What three executive departments did Washington organize after taking office? Whom did he appoint to head each department?

4–5. Name and describe the two major points of Hamilton's *Report on Public Credit*.

6–7. What two benefits did Alexander Hamilton believe a national bank would bring to the United States?

★ What is the difference between a "strict constructionist" and a "loose constructionist"? Evaluate how the opposing viewpoints of Jefferson and Hamilton regarding this issue affected their positions regarding the national bank.

★ Was it a good or a bad idea for Washington to staff his cabinet with men having such opposite views of government as Jefferson and Hamilton? Support your answer.

II. Emerging Political Parties

Political parties or factions were not unknown to the Founding Fathers, but they were unwelcome. Political parties in Europe were often characterized by plots, conspiracy, and hostile division. The founders feared that parties in America would rip the young nation apart. They hoped that in free elections the best people would be

Guiding Questions

1. What two political parties developed in the 1790s?
2. How did these political parties differ regarding foreign and domestic challenges?
3. Were the philosophies of these political parties scriptural?

Hamiltonians (Federalists) vs. Jeffersonians (Democratic-Republicans)

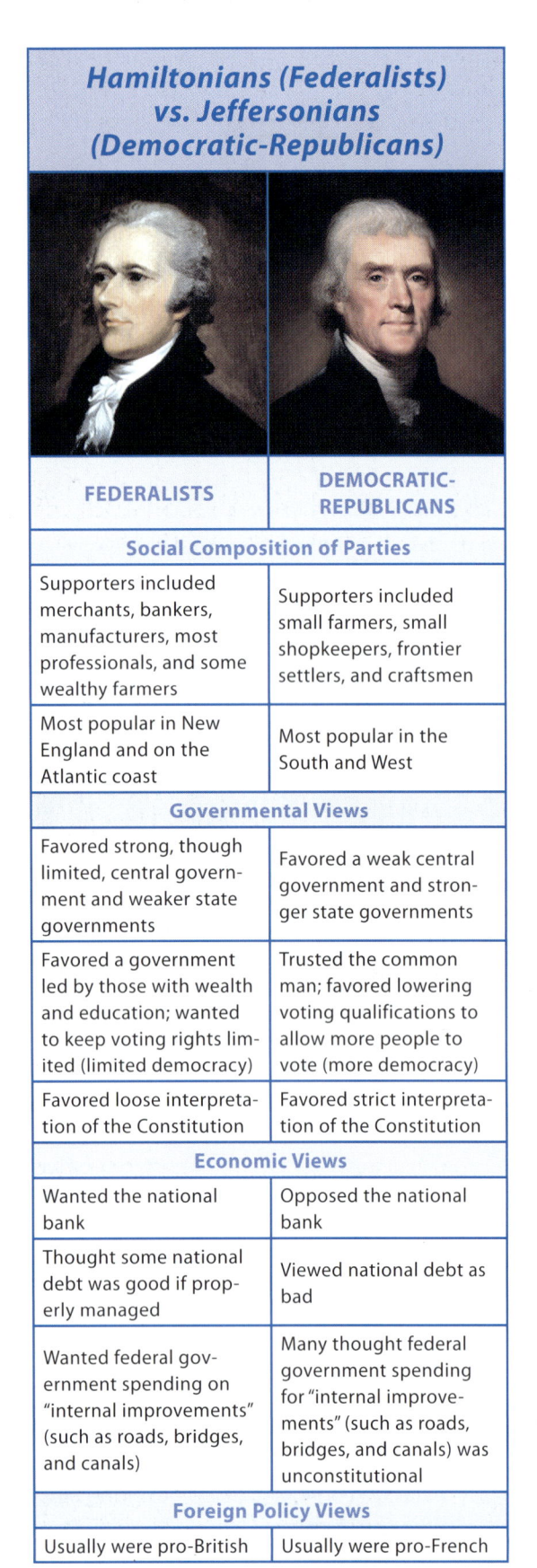

FEDERALISTS	DEMOCRATIC-REPUBLICANS
Social Composition of Parties	
Supporters included merchants, bankers, manufacturers, most professionals, and some wealthy farmers	Supporters included small farmers, small shopkeepers, frontier settlers, and craftsmen
Most popular in New England and on the Atlantic coast	Most popular in the South and West
Governmental Views	
Favored strong, though limited, central government and weaker state governments	Favored a weak central government and stronger state governments
Favored a government led by those with wealth and education; wanted to keep voting rights limited (limited democracy)	Trusted the common man; favored lowering voting qualifications to allow more people to vote (more democracy)
Favored loose interpretation of the Constitution	Favored strict interpretation of the Constitution
Economic Views	
Wanted the national bank	Opposed the national bank
Thought some national debt was good if properly managed	Viewed national debt as bad
Wanted federal government spending on "internal improvements" (such as roads, bridges, and canals)	Many thought federal government spending for "internal improvements" (such as roads, bridges, and canals) was unconstitutional
Foreign Policy Views	
Usually were pro-British	Usually were pro-French

selected. That is why in presidential elections, before the growth of parties necessitated an amendment (the Twelfth Amendment), the candidate receiving the most electoral votes would be president and the second-place candidate would be vice president. The founders assumed that leaders would act in the interest of the public, not the party. Although the idea was noble, it was not always realistic.

America had always been a land of diverse interests: southern and northern, farmer and merchant, coastal planter and backcountry frontiersman. In a society where the freedoms of speech, assembly, and petition enjoyed constitutional protection, the development of political parties was probably inevitable. In addition, the party spirit was already evident in the ratification battles in which the Constitution itself drove a wedge between Federalists and Anti-Federalists.

During the 1790s, two opposing political groups emerged: the **Federalists** and the **Republicans** (or **Democratic-Republicans**). During the early stage of party development, the labels varied considerably. Federalists might be called "Hamiltonians" or something less flattering, such as "Monarchists," if the Republicans were doing the labeling. Democratic-Republicans were called "Jeffersonians" or even "Madisonians," but they generally referred to themselves as Republicans, although they have no relation to the modern party of that name. (The modern Republican Party was established in 1854.)

For his part, Washington deplored political parties. He embodied the nonpartisan attitude to public office that had been the founders' ideal. His dismay, therefore, was profound when he discovered that the political divisions that would shake up the government began in his own cabinet.

Cabinet Conflicts

James Madison led the Republican opposition to Hamilton's treasury program in Congress. Thomas Jefferson led it within the president's cabinet.

Hamilton and Jefferson were often at odds with each other. The men's backgrounds and personalities almost destined them to clash. Hamilton had risen from poverty to power by his energy and intelligence. Jefferson was a Virginia planter living on an inherited estate. Hamilton was emotionally reserved, whereas Jefferson would reveal his feelings, particularly in letters to Washington. Jefferson viewed Hamilton as an evil genius bent on perverting the republic into a monarchy. Hamilton viewed Jefferson as a meddler, a sower of dissent who would destroy national unity. Both men could write well and persuasively. One historian has observed that "Hamilton feared anarchy [political chaos] and loved order; Jefferson feared tyranny and loved liberty."

The personality clash between Hamilton and Jefferson tends to overshadow the larger issues involved in the development of a two-party system in America. Jefferson's Republican Party and Hamilton's Federalist Party had two different views of America that reflected regional and economic differences. The Republican Party was the friend of the farmer, and in pre-industrial America that meant it had many friends. It distrusted centralized government and feared urban growth. Cities, they believed, were centers of corruption that would stain the national character. Accordingly, the key to America's future was its two great resources: its land and its people, particularly its farmers.

Federalists believed that America's future was in trade and industry, and their experiences during the Confederation period taught them that economic growth occurs only under a strong national government. The Federalists were not necessarily motivated by financial gain. They believed that power placed in the hands of those who had property and money would provide the country with a stable, conservative government.

The political division growing within the government alarmed President Washington. He had hoped to retire to his beloved Mount Vernon after one term. But with the election of 1792 looming, all sides urged him to run again. The cabinet and Congress knew that no one could hold the fledgling nation together like Washington. Jefferson reminded him that "North and South will hang together if they have you to hang on."

Reluctantly, the old general accepted the call for the sake of the nation and was unanimously reelected. For Washington, the second term would be difficult, both personally and politically. But his continuing leadership was crucial for the nation. Problems brewing in Europe were stirring unrest in America, and the new nation would need a steady hand to guide it.

Foreign Feuds

The **French Revolution** erupted in 1789, just months after America inaugurated its new constitutional government. Most Americans welcomed the news from their old ally. The French, they believed, were following the path to independence that America had pioneered. By 1792, however, it was clear that there was a definite fork in the revolutionary road. The turmoil within France had worsened. Then the year-long Reign of Terror (September 1793–July 1794) brought the execution of more than 40,000 French citizens, including King Louis XVI. This violence diminished much of the pro-French fervor in America.

When France declared war on Britain in 1793, America faced its first foreign policy crisis. According to the 1778 Treaty of Alliance, America was obligated to come to the aid of France during wartime. The United States had to decide whether to honor the treaty and support the French cause against its old enemy, Britain. Some Americans argued that the French treaty had been made with a government and a king that the revolutionary regime had destroyed. Therefore, the United States was under no obligation to go to war for France. Others disagreed.

Many Republicans favored a pro-French policy, whereas Federalists were decidedly pro-British. Federalists noted that besides being America's chief trading partner, Britain controlled Canada to the

One of the many receptions hosted by Martha Washington when she was the First Lady

Washington's second inauguration (1793)

In July 1789, French revolutionaries attacked the Bastille. The prison and armory stood in the center of Paris.

north and a number of forts to the west, and its superior navy ruled the Atlantic. Pursuing a middle course, President Washington issued a **Proclamation of Neutrality** in April 1793. He declared that the United States would pursue a policy of friendliness and impartiality toward both nations. However, challenges to American neutrality would quickly arise at home and abroad.

Citizen Genêt

The already difficult neutrality policy was further complicated by the arrival of the French ambassador, Edmond Charles Edouard Genêt, who in current French fashion rejected titles of nobility and referred to himself as simply **Citizen Genêt**. The flashy Frenchman, instead of following the accepted practice of arriving at Philadelphia to meet with American officials, landed in Charleston, South Carolina. He made a grand tour through the country, stirring up pro-French sentiment in hopes of overturning American neutrality. Genêt gathered enthusiastic followers wherever he went, including Thomas Jefferson.

Genêt, however, overrated his charm with Washington. The president gave the ambassador a courteous but cold reception, reminding him that the United States was neutral and intended to stay that way. This was not what Genêt wanted to hear. Secretly, Genêt attempted to raise an army to fight Britain's ally Spain in Florida, and he recruited private American ship captains to attack British cargo shipping. His plottings and personal attacks on Washington, published in newspapers, eventually became an embarrassment to his supporters.

When a more radical faction took over the French government, its new ambassador arrived with an arrest warrant for Genêt. His return to France would almost certainly mean his execution by guillotine. Washington graciously allowed the troublemaker to remain in America on the condition that he keep quiet. Grateful, Genêt settled in New York where he married the governor's daughter.

The Genêt episode left the country deeply divided. At the same time, British attacks on American ships further complicated Washington's efforts to keep the country out of a European war.

Jay's Treaty

In 1793, the British began attacking American ships trading in the French West Indies. Not only did the British seize cargoes to deprive the French of them, but they also practiced **impressment**, seizing American sailors and forcing them into British naval service. British violations of American neutrality especially enraged Republicans, many of whom were eager to fight England.

In 1794, Washington dispatched the chief justice of the Supreme Court, John Jay, to London to settle American and British differences. In addition to the neutrality issue, he was to discuss Britain's promises to remove all troops from the Northwest Territory and to settle prewar debts. After difficult negotiations, Jay returned with a treaty that seemed to gain little from Britain. The British promised only to remove its soldiers from American territory and offered to pay compensation for the previous year of raiding by the British navy on American shipping.

Given the United States' weak bargaining position (particularly because of the nation's lack of a navy), the **Jay Treaty** was probably the best agreement that could be reached. Republicans denounced

Citizen Genêt meeting with Thomas Jefferson and George Washington

the treaty as pro-British, and it barely received Senate approval in 1795. Despite the howls against the "Federalist" treaty, Jay's negotiations achieved one outstanding result—they avoided war with Britain.

Whiskey Rebellion

Discontent over Hamilton's economic policies had been simmering in the backcountry for some time. Hamilton had proposed raising revenue to pay the government's debt by taxing the production of liquor. Many backcountry farmers, who made their living raising corn and grain, used part of their crop to make whiskey; most hated the tax and refused to pay it. It is important to realize that this was the first time that the new government had imposed an internal tax. This was very different from external taxes such as a tariff (a tax on goods imported by Americans). Many of the farmers saw little difference between the whiskey tax and the Stamp Act. All along the frontier, the "Whiskey Boys" were grumbling and looking for ways to avoid the tax and the tax collector. In western Pennsylvania, discontent turned into violence against the government.

President Washington's response was decisive. He summoned thirteen thousand militiamen to crush the **Whiskey Rebellion** and initially took command of them personally. Alexander Hamilton rode alongside the president. When the huge army reached the western counties, the rebellion collapsed. The few that were captured and convicted were later freed by the president. Washington had made his point: the national government possessed the strength and the will to enforce the law. If citizens did not like a law, they could change it through the ballot box and the courts, not through violence. In Washington's words, Americans had to "distinguish between oppression and the necessary exercise of lawful authority." This was the only time a president personally led troops while occupying the office.

Although the rebellion ended, discontent over the tax did not. Whiskey stills, used to make the liquor, were hidden from the tax collectors.

The farmers' refusal to pay this tax was not limited to western Pennsylvania; however, farmers there received more attention because they resorted to violence. Washington and Hamilton chose to make an example of the Pennsylvanians.

Americans who disliked the Jay Treaty burned effigies of John Jay.

President Washington during the Whiskey Rebellion (October 1794)

Daniel Boone (1734–1820), Kentucky Backwoodsman

In 1792, Kentucky became the fifteenth state in the Union (Vermont, the fourteenth state, entered in 1791). Kentucky's admission was the result of the pioneering efforts of many men and women, the best known of whom was frontiersman **Daniel Boone**.

Born and bred in Pennsylvania on the edge of the wilderness, Boone explored restlessly, delighting in the rugged beauty of the land. He adopted Indian ways of hunting and tracking; few men, white or Indian, could match his skills. He was a keen marksman. He called his rifle "Ticklicker" because he boasted that it could "lick a tick" off a bear's nose at one hundred yards.

Boone began exploring Kentucky in the 1760s to scout land for settlement. He blazed a trail called the "Wilderness Road" through the Cumberland Gap, and it became the main route of early settlers to Kentucky. He also helped establish some of the first settlements in Kentucky, one of which, Boonesborough, was named for him.

The Cherokees called Kentucky "the dark and bloody ground," and few other areas of the United States saw such fierce warfare between whites and Indians. Boone experienced that conflict firsthand as settlers and Indians feuded over land. His brother and two of his sons died in such clashes. When asked about the dangers of the frontier, Boone reportedly replied, "Fear's the spice that makes it interesting to go ahead."

Always restless, Boone moved from Kentucky to Missouri in 1799, joking that someone had moved within seventy miles of him and he needed more elbow room. Actually, Boone wanted to escape the debts and lawsuits piling up in Kentucky as a result of the state's irregular settlement. In Missouri, Boone spent his time hunting, fishing, and trapping, although sometimes his rheumatism was so bad that his wife had to carry his rifle for him. In his eighties, some reports state that Boone explored as far west as the Yellowstone region of modern Wyoming. He died in his son's home in Missouri, a legend in his own time.

Washington's Farewell

In 1796, after two terms, Washington announced his plans to retire. He left a remarkable legacy. The size of the nation by the end of his two terms had been enlarged by the admission of Vermont (1791), Kentucky (1792), and Tennessee (1796). Under Washington's presidency, the country also grew in strength. Credit and commerce were stabilized, and the Constitution proved to be a workable document.

In **Washington's Farewell Address**, however, he was looking not at the past but to the future. Issued on the ninth anniversary of the signing of the Constitution, September 17, 1796, Washington urged Americans to lay aside partisan divisions. He encouraged commercial ties with Europe, but he warned against political ties to those nations.

> Europe has a set of primary interests which to us have none, or a very remote relation. Hence she must be engaged in frequent controversies, the causes of which are essentially foreign to our concerns. . . . Our detached and distant situation invites and enables us to pursue a different course. . . . It is our true policy to steer clear of permanent alliances with any portion of the foreign world . . . [but] we may safely trust to temporary alliances for extraordinary emergencies.

After serving two terms as president, Washington retired to his Virginia home, Mount Vernon.

Washington's influential Farewell Address was not delivered orally. Instead, it was printed in numerous newspapers throughout the nation. It significantly influenced America's basic foreign policy until the world wars of the twentieth century.

Section Review

1–2. Who were the two most important leaders of the Republicans during Washington's administration?

3. Why was Washington's Proclamation of Neutrality in 1793 not popular with either the Federalists or the Republicans?

4. What was the most important result of Jay's Treaty?

★ Assess the significance of Washington's response to the Whiskey Rebellion.

★ Was Washington's advice about permanent alliances good or bad?

III. Declining Federalist Influence

The election of 1796 marked the first real contest in presidential politics. During the first two elections, no one had the stature to compete with Washington. With his retirement, however, the heated partisan debate between Federalists and Republicans set the stage for a close race. The 1796 election demonstrated two features in the political maturing of the American republic that are remarkable even today: the peaceful transfer of power and also the nonviolent competition between political parties. More immediately, the close election demonstrated that the Federalist power was loosening in the face of the growing Republican challenge.

Guiding Questions

1. What was significant about the presidential election of 1796?
2. How did President Adams respond to the Quasi War and to the Alien and Sedition Acts?
3. What was significant about the presidential election of 1800?
4. How did the elections of 1796 and 1800 and the presidency of Adams affect the Federalist party?

The Election of 1796

The Federalists bypassed their most vocal leader, Alexander Hamilton, because of his many political enemies. Instead, they gave the presidential nomination to Washington's two-term vice president, **John Adams** of Massachusetts. To balance the ticket geographically, the Federalists gave the vice-presidential slot to Thomas Pinckney of South Carolina. Republicans nominated Virginian Thomas Jefferson for president with Aaron Burr of New York as his running mate.

Each elector cast two votes for president. As noted earlier, the candidate who received the most votes became president while the runner-up became vice president. Hamilton, for personal and political reasons, opposed Adams for the presidency and secretly worked to keep him as vice president. Hamilton quietly suggested to the

John Adams, second U.S. president

Abigail Adams, wife of John Adams

South Carolina electors that they should withhold their votes from Adams so that Pinckney would win the presidency. When Massachusetts electors heard of this, they refused to vote for Pinckney. Hamilton's attempt to engineer the election backfired.

As a result of Pinckney's loss of support, Republican Thomas Jefferson became vice president, falling just three electoral votes short of John Adams's tally. A mixed administration of political adversaries was certainly not what the constitutional framers had in mind fewer than ten years earlier.

The second president, John Adams, was a man whose distinguished career stretched back to the earliest days of the independence movement when Boston was a hotbed for the Revolution. Adams was educated at Harvard, unlike his predecessor, Washington, who had little formal education. Despite his credentials as a lawyer, diplomat, and statesman, Adams often felt that his achievements were underrated. In 1790, for example, he complained in a letter to a friend, "The history of our Revolution will be one continued lie from one end to the other. The essence of the whole will be that Dr. Franklin's electrical rod smote the earth and out sprang General Washington."

Yet, Adams was a man of courage and conviction. Few presidents have made decisions with less concern for their own political future than Adams. Such courage would prove crucial for the nation throughout his term.

Quasi War

During Adams's presidency the United States approached international matters very delicately. To favor either France or Britain was to risk war with the other. To continue to ignore the threats of both nations toward American trade was to irritate Americans and risk the nation's economic future.

French hostility toward the United States following the Jay Treaty was more intense than even the British raids of 1793. By 1797, the French had seized cargo on three hundred American ships. This "**Quasi War**" (a conflict resembling war in nearly every particular except a formal declaration) with France occupied much of Adams's time in office.

XYZ Affair

In 1797, French antagonism led Adams to send three diplomats to negotiate with the revolutionary government in France, at that time a five-man Directory. The French foreign minister, the shrewd Charles Maurice Talleyrand, hinted through three of his agents that he would negotiate with the Americans for a price—$250,000 for each of the Directors and a $12 million loan to the French government. One of the American representatives—C. C. Pinckney—replied, "No, no, not a sixpence."

Americans were outraged by France's request for money. When Congress later demanded to see the correspondence regarding the affair, Adams complied but substituted the letters X, Y, and Z for the names of the French agents. The episode soon became known as the **XYZ Affair**.

The XYZ Affair is the subject of this 1797 cartoon. The five-headed monster stands for the Directory, which led the French government. The three American representatives are shown at the left.

Retaliation

French arrogance in the XYZ Affair raised a cry in America: "Millions for defense, but not one cent for tribute." In 1798, as fear of war intensified, Congress authorized a larger army. That same year, Congress formed a Department of the Navy and funded a strong shipbuilding effort. Within two years, the United States Navy had more than thirty ships in its fleet.

Many of those ships were soon tested in battle during the undeclared naval war against the French. The Federalists and a growing number of Republicans, however, wanted a full-scale war against the French. Instead, President Adams put the interests of his country ahead of his party, a decision that contributed to his loss in the next election. Adams wanted to protect national honor and preserve freedom of the seas, but at the same time he believed that war would destroy the gains of the young American republic. When the French hinted at the possibility of peace negotiations, Adams seized the opportunity.

Adams sent a peace commission to France in late 1799, even though many Federalists opposed the idea and though he knew that it would further erode his support. Napoleon Bonaparte had assumed the leadership of France and was playing the role of peacemaker at the time. Under Napoleon's favorable terms, France promised to leave American ships alone and to suspend the Treaty of Alliance, signed in 1778, in exchange for an American promise not to seek compensation for shipping damages from the Quasi War.

Alien and Sedition Acts

Quieting the Critics

The anti-French sentiment that swept the country in the late 1790s provided the Federalists with an important political opportunity since Jefferson and his Republicans had identified with the French cause from the beginning. In a series of four acts, known as the **Alien and Sedition Acts**, the Federalist-controlled Congress sought to silence their political opponents. The Alien Acts placed restrictions on immigrants—particularly the French and Irish, ethnic groups that were predominantly Republican. They also gave the president greatly expanded powers to expel or imprison such individuals. The Sedition Act not only outlined penalties for antigovernment activities, such as riots, but also made it illegal to speak or write anything "false, scandalous and malicious . . . against the government of the United States . . . or the President of the United States, with intent to defame . . . or to bring them, or either of them, into contempt or disrepute." Stiff penalties of fines and imprisonment awaited anyone convicted of such "treasonous" speech.

This crude political cartoon notes the clashes between factions in Congress in the late 1790s.

It is true that Republican journalists had published lies and misrepresentations, but so had the Federalists. Although fewer than a dozen people were convicted under the Sedition Act, the Republican Party was clearly the target of the law. For example, Matthew Lyon, an outspoken Republican congressman from Vermont, was fined $1,000 and spent four months in jail for accusing President Adams of having an "unbounded thirst for ridiculous pomp, foolish adulation, and selfish avarice."

The Sedition Act was clearly unconstitutional because it ignored protections given in the Bill of Rights. At the time, however, when anti-French hysteria and the fear of chaos gripped the government, Federalists genuinely viewed it as a means to preserve order. Many Republican newspaper editors unwittingly contributed to the act's passage by printing articles that were bitter, false, and inflammatory toward the Federalists.

Kentucky and Virginia Resolutions

In November 1798, Jefferson responded to the Alien and Sedition Acts by writing the **Kentucky Resolutions**. They were approved by the state legislature there. In December, Madison further responded by writing the **Virginia Resolutions**, which later received approval from the legislature there. Both lists of resolutions opposed the Alien and Sedition Acts as a violation of the First Amendment, and both expressed the rights of the states to judge the constitutionality of a law. The resolutions held that, under the Constitution, the national government existed by consent of the states and, by extension, that the dissent of the states could nullify (declare invalid) government acts that the states considered unconstitutional. Though each of the resolutions called for other states to adopt similar declarations, none did so. Nevertheless, the nullification theory would gain importance a generation later (see Chapter 10).

The political persecution resulting from the Alien and Sedition Acts was short-lived. Jefferson urged his supporters to make their views known through the ballot box, not violence. The upcoming election of 1800 would give Republicans the opportunity to determine the future of the Alien and Sedition Acts as well as Federalist control of the government.

The Election of 1800

In the summer of 1800, John Adams moved to the new national capital. The city, soon known as Washington, D.C., was named in honor of the first president (who had died in December 1799). Adams's stay in the executive mansion, however, would be brief. Adams's efforts to make peace with France divided his own party, and the Alien and Sedition Acts had energized his opponents. The election of 1800 was one of the bitterest ever.

The Candidates

The presidential and vice-presidential candidates for both parties were very nearly repeats of the 1796 election. The Republicans chose Jefferson and Burr again, and the Federalists picked Adams and Pinckney, but this Pinckney was Charles Cotesworth Pinckney, brother of Thomas.

Ridiculous accusations swirled between the rival camps. Jefferson described the Federalist administration as a "reign of witches." Federalists warned the public that if Jefferson were elected

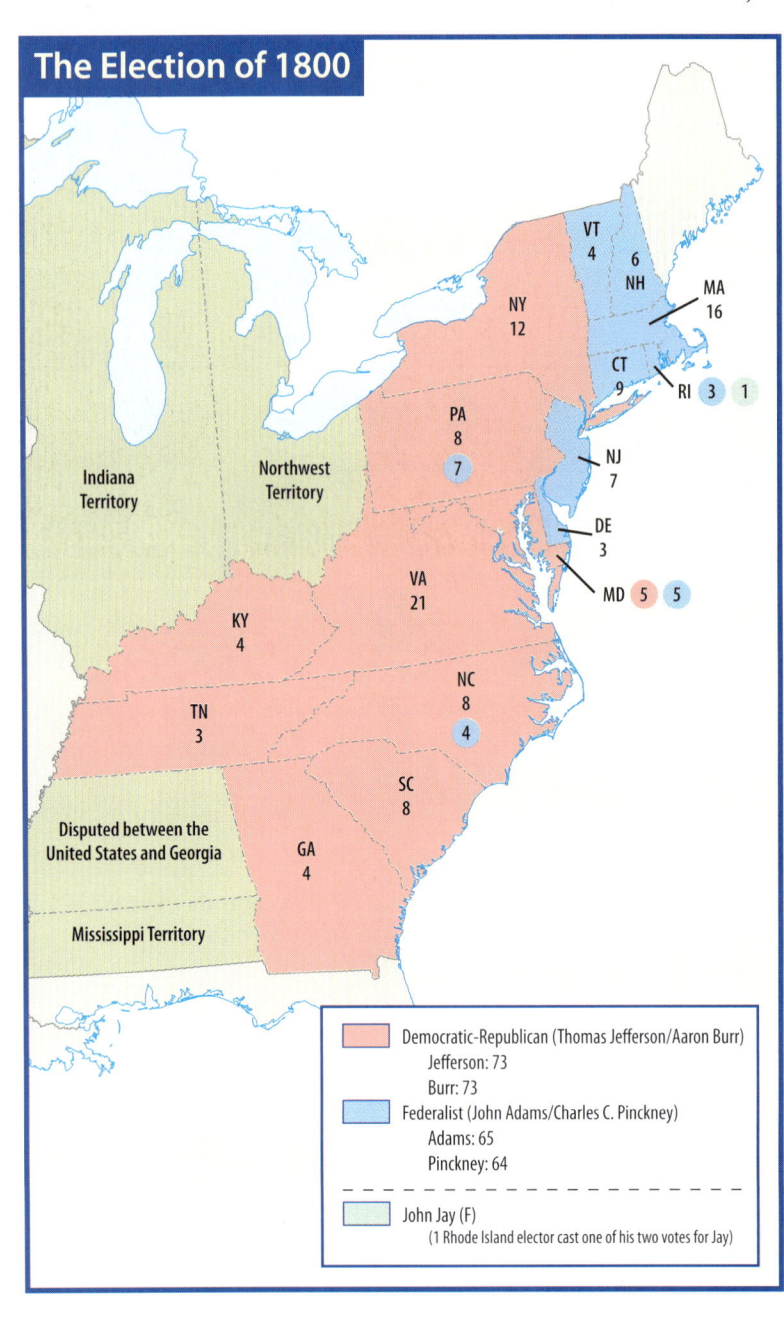

The Election of 1800

Democratic-Republican (Thomas Jefferson/Aaron Burr)
Jefferson: 73
Burr: 73
Federalist (John Adams/Charles C. Pinckney)
Adams: 65
Pinckney: 64

John Jay (F)
(1 Rhode Island elector cast one of his two votes for Jay)

VT 4
NH 6
MA 16
NY 12
CT 9
RI 3 / 1
PA 8 / 7
NJ 7
DE 3
MD 5 / 5
VA 21
KY 4
NC 8 / 4
TN 3
SC 8
GA 4

Indiana Territory
Northwest Territory
Disputed between the United States and Georgia
Mississippi Territory

the people could expect "dwellings in flames, hoary [aged] hairs bathed in blood, . . . children writhing on the pike and halberd [spears]."

The Results

The Federalist electors arranged to have one of their electors not vote for Pinckney in order to distinguish between their presidential and vice-presidential candidates; Adams received 65 electoral votes, and his running mate Pinckney received 64 votes. The Republicans should have imitated the Federalists. Instead, the Republican electors each cast their votes for both Jefferson and Burr, giving them a tie at 73 votes apiece. As stipulated in the Constitution, the election was decided by the House of Representatives. The Federalist-controlled House of Representatives was left to choose between the two Republican candidates. After a deadlock that lasted several days, Jefferson, considered to be slightly less repugnant than Burr, was elected president on the thirty-sixth ballot. Burr became vice president.

Soon after the election, the Republicans supported the Twelfth Amendment to the Constitution. It called for electors to cast separate ballots for president and vice president. This prevented a reoccurence of the complications that took place in the 1800 election.

The "Midnight Appointments"

The Federalists lost control of both the executive and the legislative branches in 1800. The only branch left to them was the judicial. After the election, but before Jefferson's inauguration, Adams took steps to strengthen Federalist control of the court system. In early 1801, he appointed the Federalist John Marshall as chief justice of the Supreme Court. Marshall, who would serve as chief justice for thirty-four years, delivered some of the court's most important decisions. He was perhaps the most enduring legacy of the Adams administration. Also, before newly elected Republican congressmen replaced the Federalists, Congress passed the **Judiciary Act of 1801**, which increased the number of federal judges. Adams, of course, filled these appointments with Federalists. He was accused of staying up until midnight the night before Jefferson's inauguration on March 4, 1801, signing commissions for the new judges. The appointments were thus called the "**midnight appointments**." Jefferson made reference to his opponents losing control of the executive and legislative branches by begrudgingly remarking that the Federalists had "retired into the judiciary as a stronghold."

A Time to Heal

When Jefferson took the oath of office, Adams did not stay to watch what he believed was the beginning of national ruin. After thirty years of public service, the old patriot returned to his home in Quincy, Massachusetts, to retire. Contrary to the predictions of Adams and the Federalists, the nation did not disintegrate following Jefferson's inauguration. Two terms later, Jefferson also retired—to Monticello, nestled in Virginia's Blue Ridge Mountains. After a few years, the two ex-presidents started corresponding and became friends again. The lengthy letters of these presidential pen pals are more than witty commentaries on national politics; they reveal true friendship, the healing of old wounds. Even in death, the two men who at one time despised each other were knit together. On the fiftieth anniversary of the Declaration of Independence, the document

Thomas Jefferson

Aaron Burr

The President's House, later known as the White House

that brought Adams and Jefferson together in 1776, both men lay on their deathbeds. Adams's last words were about his old enemy and new friend; he whispered, "Thomas Jefferson survives." Ironically, his friend had died at his home in Virginia a few hours earlier.

The relationship between John Adams and Thomas Jefferson illustrates much about the 1790s. The formative Federalist decade established national supremacy and enduring precedents, but it also produced deep political divisions. In time, those wounds would heal. After some maturing, the political parties brought healthy competition, not open conflict, to America. The fiery trials of the 1790s tempered the young nation, fitting it for a growing role at the dawn of a new century.

Section Review

1–2. Name the president and vice president, along with their political parties, who were elected in 1796.

3. What is the origin of the phrase "Millions for defense, but not one cent for tribute"?

4. What political theory did the Virginia and Kentucky Resolutions advocate?

5. How did the Judiciary Act of 1801 allow the Federalists to continue their influence in government after the election of Jefferson in 1800?

★ Assess Adams's decision to pursue peace with France. Why has it been described as a politically brave act?

★ Examine the Alien and Sedition Acts. What was the intent of the laws? What did they provoke?

CHAPTER REVIEW

Making Connections

1–2. One section of the Judiciary Act of 1789 had a powerful ramification in the future. What was it? What was the significance?

3. What did Hamilton offer the South to win southern support for assumption of state debts by the federal government?

4–5. How did the elections of 1796 and 1800 reveal flaws in the presidential election system established by the Constitution?

Developing History Skills

1. The various provisions of the Alien and Sedition Acts had either expired or were not enforced during Jefferson's presidency. If that had not occurred, how might they have "backfired" on the Federalists?

2. Compare and contrast the course and consequences of Shays's Rebellion and the Whiskey Rebellion.

Thinking Critically

1. Which view of constitutional interpretation do you think is better, loose or strict constructionism? Defend your answer.

2. How was the presence of political opponents Alexander Hamilton and Thomas Jefferson in Washington's cabinet both positive and negative for the young nation?

Living as a Christian Citizen

1. Imagine that the United States Congress was sued for opening its sessions in prayer on the grounds that such prayers amount to the establishment of religion in violation of the First Amendment. You are a lawyer tasked with defending the members of Congress in court. Outline your arguments on their behalf.

2. Construct what you believe would be an ideal political philosophy, having evaluated the strengths and weaknesses of the Federalists and Democratic-Republicans from Scripture.

People, Places, and Things to Remember

George Washington
Thomas Jefferson
Alexander Hamilton
cabinet
Judiciary Act of 1789
James Madison
Bill of Rights
funding
assumption
loose constructionists
strict constructionists
National Bank
Federalists
Republicans (Democratic-Republicans)
French Revolution
Proclamation of Neutrality
Citizen Genêt
impressment
Jay Treaty
Whiskey Rebellion
Daniel Boone
Washington's Farewell Address
John Adams
Quasi War
XYZ affair
Alien and Sedition Acts
Kentucky Resolutions
Virginia Resolutions
Judiciary Act of 1801
midnight appointments

NATION
1801–1861

1803 Louisiana Purchase

1811 Battle of Tippecanoe

1812–15 War of 1812

1820 Missouri Compromise

1823 Monroe Doctrine proclaimed

1800 1810 1820

ca. 1800–ca. 1825 Second Great Awakening

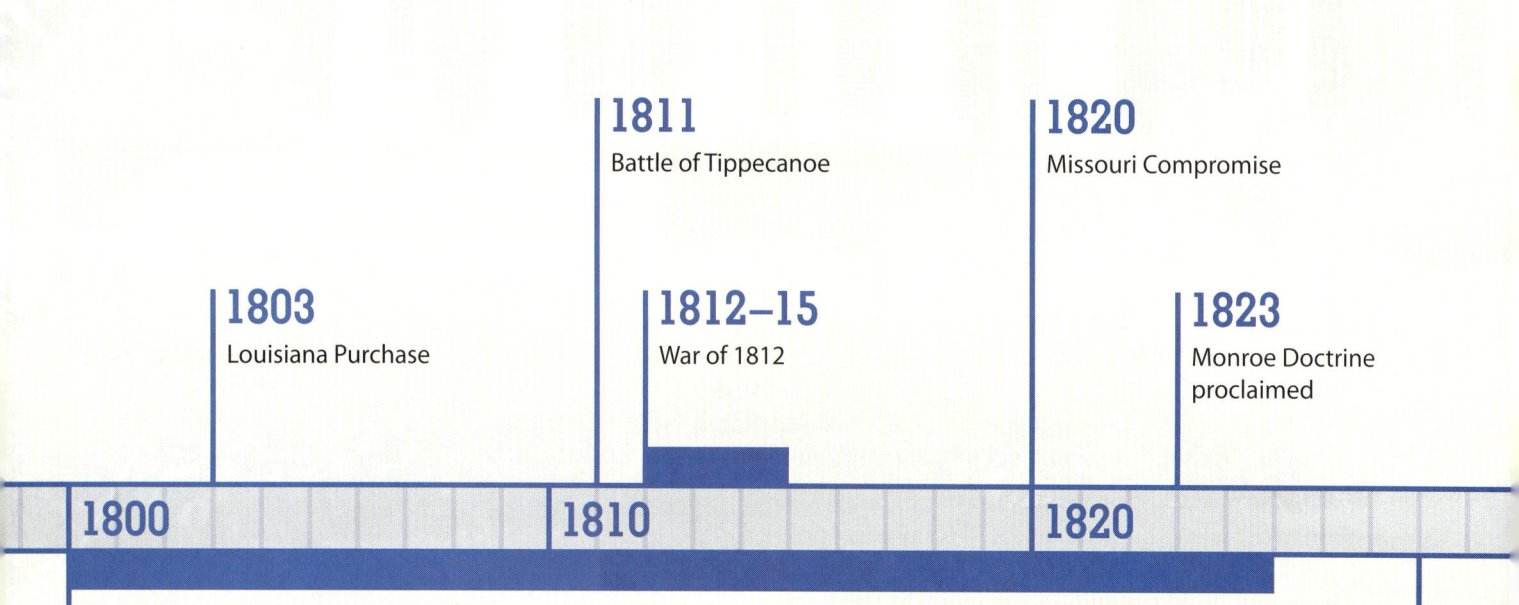

1828 The "Tariff of Abominations"

CHAPTERS

9 THE JEFFERSONIAN ERA (1801–1825)

10 THE AGE OF JACKSON (1820–1840)

11 THE GROWTH OF AMERICAN SOCIETY (1789–1861)

12 MANIFEST DESTINY (1840–1848)

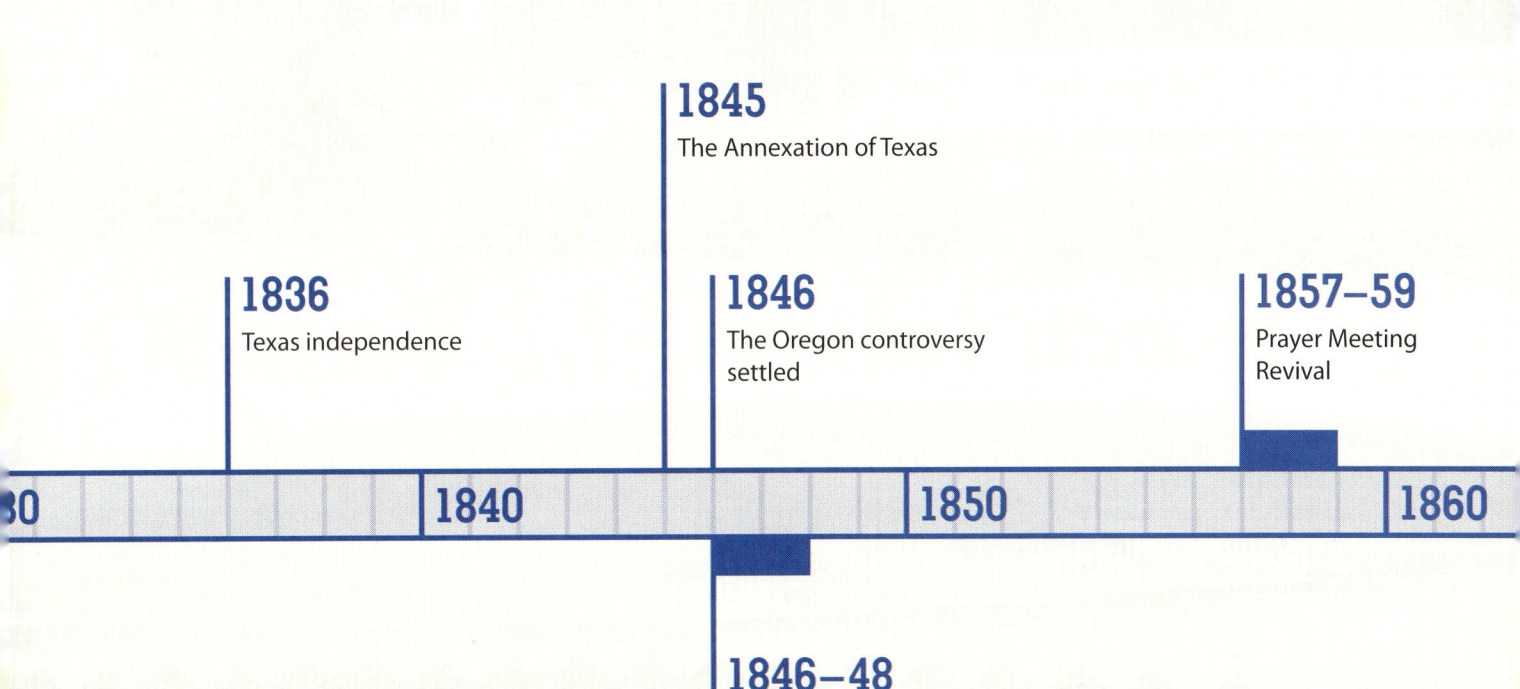

1845 The Annexation of Texas

1836 Texas independence

1846 The Oregon controversy settled

1857–59 Prayer Meeting Revival

1846–48 Mexican War

9 THE JEFFERSONIAN ERA (1801–1825)

> Our country! In her intercourse with foreign nations, may she always be in the right; but our country, right or wrong.
>
> **Stephen Decatur**
> April 1816, toast given at Norfolk

The Battle of New Orleans by E. Percy Moran

Big Ideas

1. How did the Jeffersonian Republican and the Federalist political philosophies differ?
2. Did Jefferson effectively deal with foreign powers?
3. What was the significance of the Fallen Timbers campaign?
4. What were the causes of the War of 1812?
5. What was America's foreign policy under President Monroe?

I. The Revolution of 1800

II. Jefferson and Foreign Affairs

III. Indians and the Northwest Territory

IV. War of 1812

V. The Era of Good Feelings

THE JEFFERSONIAN ERA   159

In the first year of the nineteenth century, Washington, D.C., was as raw and unfinished as the nation of which it was the capital. The country's leaders walked muddy pathways that served as streets from the ramshackle, overcrowded boarding houses in which they lived to the half-completed buildings in which they worked. On March 4, 1801, **Thomas Jefferson** left his boarding house, strolled over to the unfinished Capitol, and took the oath of office as the third president of the United States. Then he delivered his inaugural address in a whispery, indistinct voice; much of what he said was lost to his audience. The simple ceremony would not have impressed the cultured rulers of Europe, a fact that undoubtedly pleased Jefferson.

The tall, lanky president, his red hair peppered with gray, preferred a fairly simple lifestyle. He soon offended the English ambassador by greeting him while wearing a pair of carpet slippers. On another occasion, the president astounded Washington society by taking his nephew shopping around the city. Though his habits were modest, he was certainly remarkable. By 1801, his accomplishments included writing the Declaration of Independence and serving as ambassador to France, governor of Virginia, secretary of state, and vice president. He also had developed numerous inventions and architectural designs in his spare time. "Science is my passion," Jefferson reportedly said, "politics my duty." His interests and abilities ranged from politics to art to science. In 1962, President John F. Kennedy told a gathering of Nobel Prize winners, "I think this is the most extraordinary collection of talent, of human knowledge, that has ever been gathered together at the White House, with the possible exception of when Thomas Jefferson dined alone."

The administrations of Jefferson and his handpicked successors, James Madison and James Monroe, constitute the era of **Jeffersonian Republicanism** (1801–25). The period bears Jefferson's stamp and embodies his philosophy. Through events ranging from a magnificent land purchase that doubled the size of the United States to the torching of the nation's capital by a foreign power, Jeffersonian principles endured in both prosperity and adversity. By the end of the period, Jefferson's party and philosophy stood virtually unopposed on the political landscape of America.

The unfinished U.S. Capitol as it appeared in the time of Thomas Jefferson

Monticello, Jefferson's home, is near Charlottesville, Virginia.

I. The Revolution of 1800

Jefferson called his election "the revolution of 1800," suggesting that his victory marked a transformation as dramatic as that of 1776. Although time would demonstrate that the change was not as great as Jefferson imagined, it signaled a definite shift from the policies of the Federalist era.

Nature of Jeffersonian Republicanism

Republican ideas might best be understood in contrast to the ideas of the Federalists. The Federalists were the party of finance, the great defenders of the merchant class. They believed that a strong merchant and manufacturing base was necessary for the nation to be free from outside interference. On the other hand, Jefferson believed that liberty in the United States would be preserved

Guiding Questions

1. What were the political views of the Jeffersonian Republicans?
2. What were the political views of the Federalists?
3. How did the policies of the Republican-dominated branches of government differ from the Federalist-dominated judicial branch?
4. How did Supreme Court decisions during this period affect the nation?

Jefferson's Religious Views

Jefferson admired the teachings of Jesus, calling them "a system of morals" that is "the most perfect and sublime that has ever been taught by man." However, Jefferson denied most of the scriptural teaching concerning Christ. Of the virgin birth, for example, he wrote to John Adams, "The day will come when the [account of the birth of Christ] ... will be classed with the fable of Minerva [the Roman goddess]." He also believed that much of the New Testament writings were corruptions of Jesus' teaching.

Jefferson compiled his own version of the "true" teachings of Jesus. Using scissors, paste, and two English and two Greek New Testaments, he pieced together an account of Jesus' life and teaching that excluded every miracle and every reference to Christ as God. The result—variously called "The Philosophy of Jesus of Nazareth," "The Morals of Jesus," or "Jefferson's Bible"—limited itself almost entirely to the moral teachings of Jesus. Jefferson read from his edition nearly every night and called it "a document in proof that I am a real Christian, that is to say, a disciple of the doctrines of Jesus."

Jefferson played a significant positive role in the founding of the United States. American believers can appreciate his rich contribution to the development of the country; however, his devotion to the Enlightenment had negative consequences. For example, his denial of the Scripture's teaching about human sinfulness caused him to underestimate the depravity of man. When Jefferson designed the curriculum for the University of Virginia, he placed science, rather than theology, at the center of the curriculum.

---

only as long as the country remained predominantly a nation of independent, self-sufficient farmers. He thought people were naturally good, but cities and commercial activity often corrupted them. The Federalists, having seen the weaknesses under the Articles of Confederation, preferred a strong national government to protect and further national interests. The Republicans advanced the principle that the less government there is, the better. Jefferson believed that a world of small governments without standing armies or debts was the ideal.

Both parties wanted leaders who would govern with the common good in mind, rather than personal gain, but they differed on where those leaders should be found. The Federalists thought that government required the "best" individuals from the highest tier of society, finance, and trade. Republicans elected such men as Jefferson—an intelligent, cultured, and accomplished individual—but, they defended the common man as any man's equal. With the best of intentions, the Federalists overestimated the goodness of the upper class, and the Republicans overestimated the goodness of the common man.

Jefferson was right, perhaps, in seeing his election as a change, but it was no revolution. There was no wholesale repudiation of the Federalist method of governing, merely an alteration of the practices that Republicans disliked. Jeffersonian Republicanism was a transitional phase between the elitism of the Federalists and the more truly "common man" politics of Andrew Jackson that would triumph in the mid-1820s.

Making Changes

Jefferson undeniably made changes when he took office. The Republicans quickly repealed the Judiciary Act of 1801 and allowed the Alien and Sedition Acts to expire. To guard against a repetition of the deadlocked election of 1800 (see Chapter 8), Congress and the states adopted the **Twelfth Amendment**, which enabled electors to cast separate ballots for president and vice president. The extremely formal receptions that Washington and Adams had held with political leaders gave way to Jefferson's informal discussions with congressional leaders around his dinner table. Eager to reduce the size of the national government, Jefferson ordered his secretary of the treasury to devise a plan for both reducing taxes and eliminating the national debt.

Yet the Republicans did not try to force change everywhere. For example, though Jefferson had opposed the creation of the National Bank because he believed it was unconstitutional, he made no attempt to destroy it. In fact, after the bank's charter expired, a Republican Congress under Jefferson's successor, James Madison, created another bank in 1816.

John Marshall and the Supreme Court

The Supreme Court remained under Federalist control. The leader of that court, and its first great chief justice, was **John Marshall**. A Virginia Federalist and cousin of Jefferson, Marshall was appointed and took office in the closing weeks of the Adams administration. The Supreme Court was not as important then as it is today. The first chief justice, John Jay, resigned the office to become governor of New York, an office that he considered more prestigious. Marshall served for thirty-four years on the court and handed down many decisions that would strengthen the power and prestige of that body.

Marshall was a Federalist in the mold of George Washington. He envisioned a tremendous future for the young nation as long as the central government held the power to develop the new land's potential. In a series of landmark decisions, during and after Jefferson's presidency, the Marshall Court upheld the authority of the national government and increased the scope of the Court's authority. Marshall, and others who followed him, helped to establish the judiciary as an independent branch of government.

Marbury v. Madison

The first major case before the Marshall Court involved the Judiciary Act of 1801. William Marbury had received one of Adams's "midnight appointments." However, Jefferson's secretary of state, James Madison, refused to deliver Marbury's commission, meaning that Marbury could not take office. Marbury asked the Supreme Court to issue an order forcing Madison to deliver the commission. Marshall knew that he had no means of forcing Madison to obey, and some Republicans eagerly awaited the opportunity to disregard the authority of the Federalist judge.

Marshall cleverly handed down a ruling that preserved the authority of the Court without giving the Republicans an opportunity to defy it. Although Marbury was right in his complaint, Marshall said, the power to issue such orders was not one of the powers delegated to the Court by the Constitution. The law that permitted such orders, then, was unconstitutional and therefore invalid. Thus, in *Marbury v. Madison* the Supreme Court established the principle of **judicial review**, the right of the Court to declare a law unconstitutional. As Marshall wrote in handing down the decision, "A legisla-

John Marshall

William Marbury

tive act contrary to the Constitution is not law.... It is emphatically the province and duty of the Judicial Department to say what the law is." Since that decision, the Supreme Court has declared well over a thousand state and federal laws unconstitutional.

Gibbons v. Ogden

Years later, another important ruling protected the federal government's **delegated powers**, those powers specifically given to the national government by the Constitution. This case, handed down in 1824, involved one of Congress's delegated powers—the right to regulate interstate commerce. New York had granted one company the exclusive right to operate steamboat ferries between New York and New Jersey. When another steamboat company challenged this monopoly, the case was presented to the Supreme Court. In *Gibbons v. Ogden* the Court ruled that the delegated powers given to the national government by the Constitution could not be limited by state boundaries. Where the Constitution entrusted Congress with a power, the states had no right to interfere with that power.

McCulloch v. Maryland

Perhaps the most far-reaching decision of the Marshall Court was *McCulloch v. Maryland* (1819). The state of Maryland opposed the idea of a national bank and tried to tax the Baltimore branch of the Bank of the United States out of existence. Claiming that "the power to tax involves the power to destroy," the Court overruled the state's action. The Constitution is the supreme law of the land, Marshall said, referring to Article VI of that document. Therefore, the states had no authority to interfere with Congress's ability to enact legislation that is "necessary and proper" to carry out its delegated powers (Article I, Section 8, Clause 18). (These "necessary and proper" powers that enable the government to carry out the delegated powers are called **implied powers**.) In this decision, Marshall placed the Court squarely on the side of the loose constructionists and national supremacy. The Supreme Court might have been a Federalist island in a sea of Republicanism, but John Marshall ensured that it was an island that Jeffersonians could not ignore.

Section Review

1. How did the Federalists and the Republicans disagree concerning the power of the central government?
2. What is judicial review?
3–5. List three important court cases in which the Marshall Court ruled. Each case established a different long-range principle. Identify those principles.
★ Assess whether or not Jefferson's election was truly a "revolution."

II. Jefferson and Foreign Affairs

Despite his overriding concern with domestic affairs, Thomas Jefferson achieved two successes in the field of foreign affairs. Through his clash with the Barbary pirates and even more through the Louisiana Purchase, Jefferson dramatically increased the international prestige of the young nation.

Guiding Questions

1. What was the significance for the United States of fighting with the Barbary States?
2. Why was the Louisiana Purchase a difficult constitutional issue for President Jefferson?
3. How important was the Louisiana Purchase for the United States?

THE JEFFERSONIAN ERA

To the Shores of Tripoli

As part of his plan to cut federal expenses, Jefferson wanted to reduce the size of the navy. However, several small Muslim kingdoms in North Africa, where piracy and kidnapping were the chief sources of national income, forced the president to reconsider his budget cuts. The ships of these **Barbary states** raided Mediterranean shipping and occasionally ventured out into the Atlantic. These pirates captured unarmed merchant ships, enslaved the crews, and demanded ransom from the owners. Most nations found it cheaper and easier to pay ransom to the Barbary states than to send their warships.

Many countries, including the United States, began paying an annual tribute (a fee or tax) to the pirates to avoid conflict with them. When Jefferson became president, he wanted to end this practice. Thus, he sent a squadron of warships to Tripoli (see map) to frighten the most important Barbary state with a show of force. In the war that followed, ships bombarded Tripoli harbor. This later inspired a phrase in the Marine Corps' hymn—"to the shores of Tripoli."

The fighting that began in 1801 ended with an agreement in 1805. The United States paid a ransom for American prisoners to Tripoli but refused to pay additional tribute. Piracy in the other Barbary States continued for another decade, long after Jefferson left the presidency. In 1815, the American navy, with help from European warships, ended all payment of American tribute along the Barbary coast.

The Barbary States

The Louisiana Purchase

"A Noble Bargain"

In 1800, France and Spain secretly signed a treaty returning the Louisiana Territory to France. In exchange, France helped Spain obtain a part of Italy. Word of this deal leaked out and caused panic in Washington. New Orleans was vital to American interests; the western states shipped millions of tons of American goods down the Mississippi River to New Orleans and, from there, to other markets around the world. Dealing with the relatively weak Spanish had often been troublesome. Dealing with the French under their powerful new leader, **Napoleon Bonaparte**, could be potentially disastrous for the Americans.

Jefferson sent James Monroe to join Robert Livingstone, the ambassador to France. He instructed them to go to Napoleon and offer him as much as $10 million for New Orleans. Napoleon's foreign minister astounded the Americans with a counteroffer: *all* of the Louisiana Territory—a region larger than the whole United States—for $15 million. The American representatives hurriedly sent word to Jefferson and urged him to accept. Jefferson saw that this not only secured New Orleans, but it also provided land that furthered Jefferson's vision of more land for farmers. Nevertheless, the offer bothered Jefferson, who was a strict constructionist. It was certainly a splendid opportunity, but the Constitution gave the

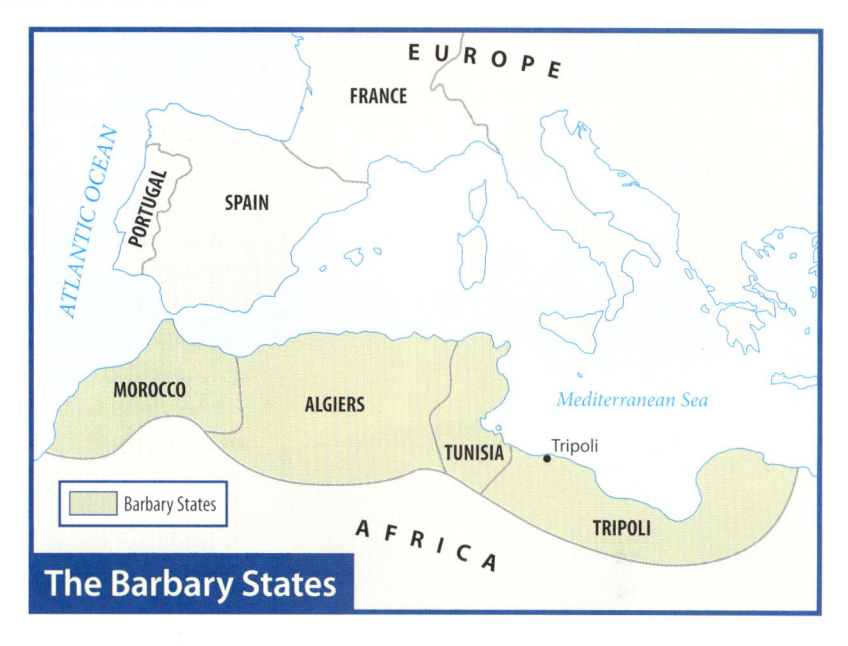

Napoleon Bonaparte

Meriwether Lewis (*above*) and William Clark (*right*)

government no specific authority to purchase land. Jefferson briefly considered requesting a constitutional amendment to permit the purchase, but his ministers in France warned him to hurry before Napoleon changed his mind. Casting his constitutional concerns aside, Jefferson submitted the treaty to the Senate. It was quickly approved. With the **Louisiana Purchase**, the United States more than doubled its size.

Why did Napoleon so eagerly sell such a huge tract of land for less than three cents an acre? Although Napoleon was then at peace, he was preparing again for war with Great Britain. When war broke out, Napoleon would be forced to defend Louisiana thousands of miles away across the Atlantic. Because France was rich in land, but in need of funds, it made more sense to sell the territory to the United States. Napoleon would have more money for his expected war with Britain, and he would increase favor with the United States—not a bad bargain in exchange for a territory that he probably could not keep anyway.

An important question remained: exactly what were the boundaries of Louisiana? The French foreign minister replied evasively to Livingstone that they were the same as those that France had received from Spain. Livingstone persisted. What were *those* boundaries then? The minister declined to answer but said simply, "You have made a noble bargain for yourselves, and I suppose you will make the most of it."

Exploring the New Lands

To help determine the size of the territory and what it contained, Jefferson asked Congress to authorize army officers **Meriwether Lewis** and **William Clark** to lead an expedition to explore the Louisiana Territory. Lewis was the president's private secretary and Clark was the brother of Revolutionary War hero George Rogers Clark.

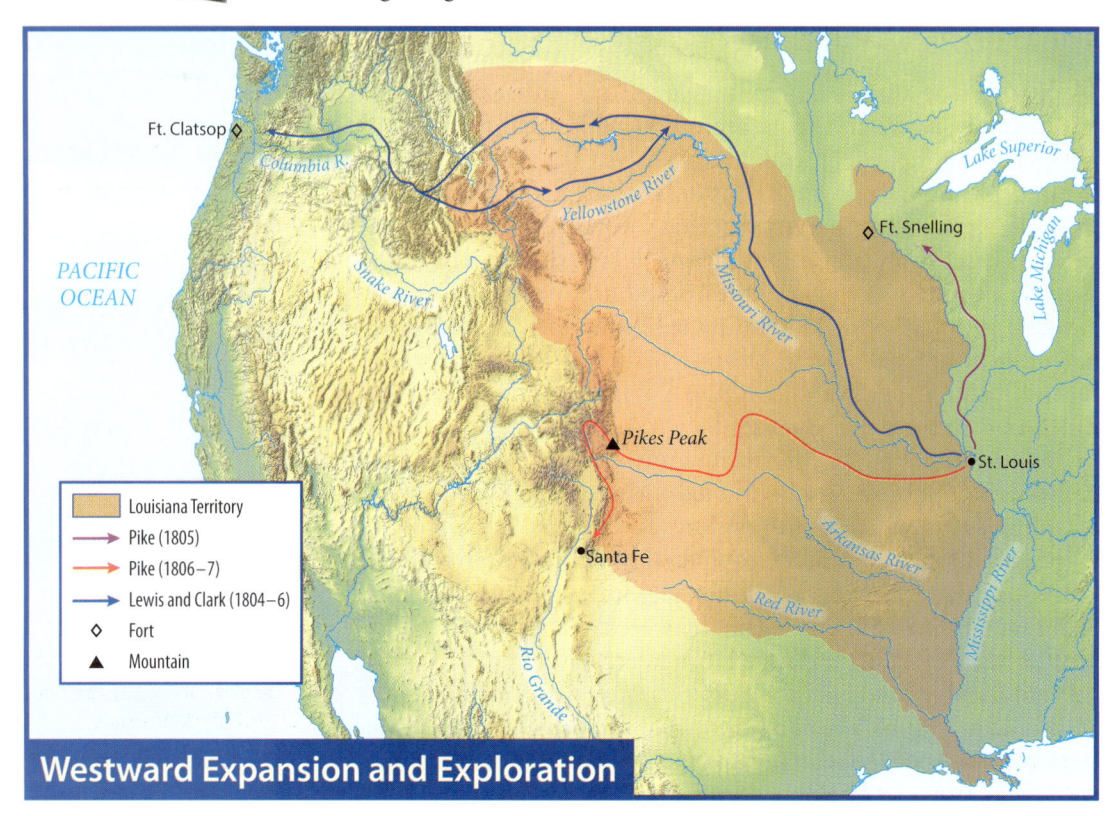

Westward Expansion and Exploration

Sacagawea

Accompanying Lewis and Clark through the Pacific Northwest was a Shoshone (shoh SHOW nee) Indian woman named Sacagawea (SAC uh juh WEE uh), wife of a French fur trader. Sacagawea had been kidnapped from the Shoshones as a young girl, and she regarded the American expedition as an opportunity to see her people again. Lewis and Clark knew that they would need horses from the Shoshones to cross the Rocky Mountains. They quickly struck a deal, and Sacagawea and her husband joined the group.

Sacagawea was already several months pregnant when she joined the expedition, and in February 1805 she gave birth to a son. Rather than being a burden to the expedition, the woman and her infant helped the explorers when they met suspicious Indians. "A woman with a party of men is a token of peace," Clark observed.

When the expedition met the Shoshones, Sacagawea interpreted for the explorers. She suddenly stopped and began to weep and ran over to the Shoshone chief, who, as it turned out, was her brother. She smoothed the way for Lewis and Clark among the Shoshones.

Contrary to popular belief, she was not a guide, although she did point out some important landmarks in Shoshone country (the Snake River area of modern Idaho).

When the expedition returned to the east, Sacagawea and her family stayed behind. A few years later, Clark showed his appreciation to her by paying for the education of her son in St. Louis.

On May 14, 1804, their group of about fifty men left St. Louis. The party traveled up the Missouri River, through the Dakotas and Montana, and across the Rocky Mountains. By December 1805 they had paddled canoes down the Columbia River to the Pacific. The explorers saw wonders of the American West previously unseen by white men. Raging, swirling rivers tumbled through the land, threatening to swallow any boat that challenged them. Strange animals, such as the fierce grizzly bear and the cougar, stalked the explorers. In the mountains, shrieking winds shot pellets of ice and snow like bullets.

In addition to the dangers were breathtaking scenes. Some of the streams were fierce, but they were also sparkling clear and fresh. The Rocky Mountains certainly held dangers, but their rugged outline and dizzying heights amazed those who were accustomed to the lower, rounded peaks of the Appalachians.

The climax of the trip must have been when the explorers stood on the shores of the Pacific and gazed at an ocean they had never seen. The explorers returned by way of the Yellowstone River and saw much of the awe-inspiring scenery now contained in Yellowstone National Park. The adventures finally ended when the party reached St. Louis again in September 1806. Few explorations in history can rival the Lewis and Clark expedition for extensive travel, spectacular sights, and fruitful discoveries.

Zebulon Pike, another army officer, directed two other important expeditions about the same time as Lewis and Clark's trip. The first (1805) went northward to the upper reaches of the Mississippi River. The second trip, in 1806 and 1807, crossed the Great Plains to the Colorado Rockies, where Pike discovered (but did not actually climb) Pikes Peak, the mountain named for him. The expedition then turned southward into Spanish-held Mexico. As a result of these and other explorations, Americans learned more about their continent and could realistically begin to envision a nation that stretched "from sea to shining sea."

Selections from Lewis and Clark journals

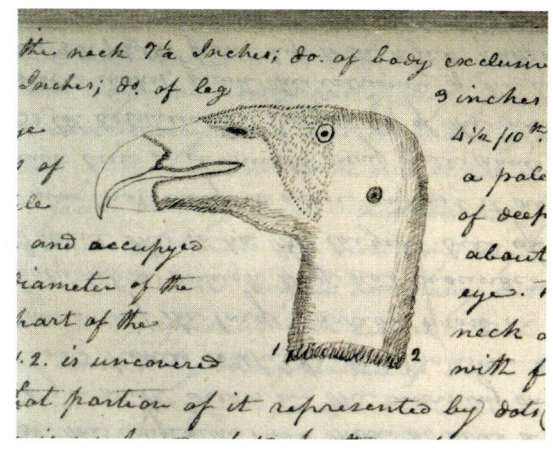

Sketch of a vulture's head and notes in the Lewis and Clark journals

Section Review

1–2. What were Jefferson's two successes in foreign affairs?
3. Why did Napoleon sell the Louisiana Territory to the United States?
4–6. Who were the three great explorers of the American West during Jefferson's administration?
* How was Jefferson's decision to buy the Louisiana Territory a violation of his principles of limited government?
* Explain why the Lewis and Clark expedition was so important.

III. Indians and the Northwest Territory

The Treaty of Paris after the War for Independence gave the Great Lakes region to the United States, but no one asked the Indians who lived there about the matter. If settlers were to move into the Ohio River Valley and north to the Great Lakes, they would have to deal with the Indians. Unfortunately, the means of dealing with them were usually violent.

Fallen Timbers and the Opening of Ohio

As early as George Washington's administration, settlers and Indians had been locked in a bloody struggle for Ohio. Treaties existed in abundance, but the Americans did not always honor them. Furthermore, many Indians shared the beliefs of Tecumseh, a Shawnee Indian chief. He said, "The land belongs to all Indians, and cannot be sold without the consent of all. . . . What! Sell a

Guiding Questions

1. How did American Indians and white Americans differ in their views of Indian land?
2. What was the wide-ranging significance of the Fallen Timbers campaign for the development of the United States?
3. Who were the major figures and what were the major events in the conflict over the Northwest Territory?

Aaron Burr

Alexander Hamilton said that the driving force in Aaron Burr's life was his "inordinate ambition." He viewed Burr as a man without principles.

Ironically, Burr had a godly heritage. He was Jonathan Edwards's grandson, and his father was a Presbyterian pastor and president of Princeton University. Unfortunately, his life was often contrary to the model of his ancestors. Though he briefly studied for the ministry, he never gave evidence that he truly professed Christ.

Burr became one of the most influential men in New York. The Republicans added him to the 1800 ticket as Jefferson's running mate. In that deadlocked election, Burr denied being interested in the presidency, but rumors abounded that he was secretly hoping to win when the House of Representatives voted. Jefferson believed the rumors and never trusted his vice president again.

In 1804, while still vice president, Burr ran for governor of New York. Partly due to Alexander Hamilton's opposition, Burr lost. Angered, Burr challenged him to a duel. In the **Burr-Hamilton duel**, on July 11, 1804, Burr shot Hamilton. Hamilton died the following day.

Later Burr began assembling supplies and weapons on an island in the Ohio River between Virginia and Ohio. Some people think that he intended to take over Mexico, and others think that he planned to lead the western states and territories out of the Union to form his own empire. Jefferson had Burr arrested and tried for treason. He was acquitted in September 1807, when Chief Justice Marshall ruled that there were not two witnesses to the alleged treason, as the Constitution required. Though Burr lived until 1836, his political career was over.

country! Why not sell the air, the clouds, and the great sea, as well as the earth?" An old Indian once complained to William Henry Harrison that the French had been friendlier to the Indians than the Americans had been. He said,

> They [the French] never took from us our lands; indeed, they were common between us. They planted where they pleased, and they cut wood where they pleased, and so did we. But now, if a poor Indian attempts to take a little bark from a tree to cover him from rain, up comes a white man and threatens to shoot him, claiming the tree as his own.

When the Indians realized that the Americans intended to keep the lands forever—and keep the Indians *off*—they went on the warpath.

Settlers, on the other hand, considered the Indians' way of living wasteful. Using the land, as the Indians did, only to raise a few crops and to hunt did not begin to tap the potential resources of the country. Many settlers used their desire to "improve" the land as an excuse to take it from the Indians. They considered themselves better managers of the land's resources. These differing philosophies of settlers and Indians only increased the potential for conflict.

In 1790 and 1791, the Indians inflicted two stinging and humiliating defeats on the American army. Faced with an increasingly dangerous situation, President Washington appointed Revolutionary War hero "**Mad Anthony**" **Wayne** to crush the Indians. Wayne, known for his reckless courage, staged a careful, meticulously planned campaign. Wayne and his force marched from Fort Washington on the Ohio River (modern Cincinnati) to a site near modern Toledo. In the **Battle of Fallen Timbers** (August 20, 1794), so called because most of the fighting occurred in a maze of tangled trees knocked down by a storm, Wayne's forces soundly defeated the Indians. In the resulting Treaty of Fort Greenville, the Indians surrendered all rights to the southern half of Ohio.

After Fallen Timbers, settlers began to pour into the Ohio region of the Northwest Territory. A series of land acts passed in 1796, 1800, and 1804 reduced the size of a minimum purchase to 160 acres and lowered the price from $2.00 to $1.64 an acre. In addition, these acts allowed the settler to purchase on credit with a down payment of $80. As a result, ordinary farmers could buy land in the Ohio Valley. By 1799, Ohio's population had grown so much that Congress separated it from the remainder of the Northwest Territory and made it a separate territory. In 1803, Ohio was admitted to the Union as the first state from the Northwest Territory.

The signing of the Treaty of Fort Greenville, which opened Ohio to white settlement

Harrison vs. Tecumseh

The men who fought under "Mad Anthony" Wayne at Fallen Timbers included Meriwether Lewis, William Clark, and Zebulon Pike. But the two most important veterans of Fallen Timbers, as far as the Northwest Territory was concerned, were young men on opposite sides—a nineteen-year-old officer named **William Henry Harrison** and an Indian scout named Tecumseh.

The Northwest Territory

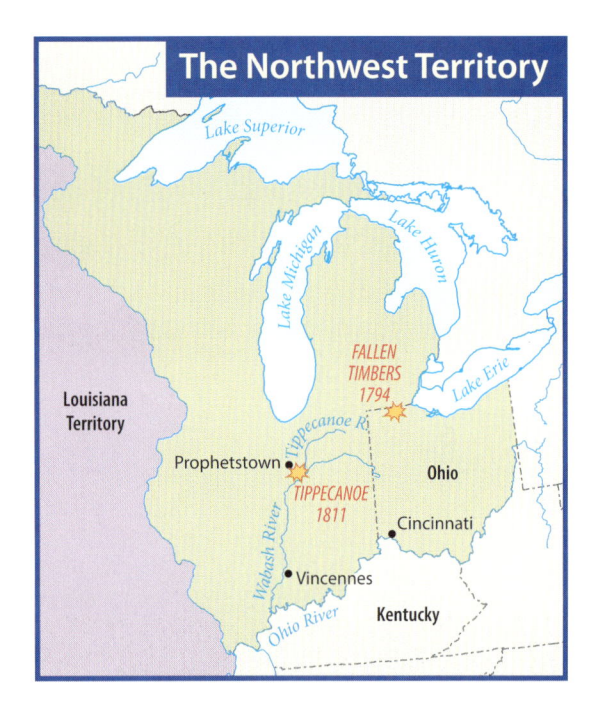

Tecumseh

William Henry Harrison

Harrison was the son of Benjamin Harrison, governor of Virginia and signer of the Declaration of Independence. Lured by the promise of glory and adventure, Harrison joined the army, serving as an aide to Wayne in the Fallen Timbers campaign. In 1798, Harrison left the army and entered politics. In 1800, he was appointed governor of the Indiana Territory (modern Indiana, Illinois, Michigan, and Wisconsin), and he served in that office until 1812.

Harrison, like President Jefferson, wanted the Indians to abandon much of their hunting and devote themselves to farming. In that way, the Indians would lead a more settled life, and they would not need large tracts of undeveloped forests in which to hunt. Should the Indians give up their traditional way of life, their lands would be open to American settlement.

Tecumseh

Harrison's chief adversary was **Tecumseh**. Born around 1768 near modern Springfield, Ohio, Tecumseh led the last great Indian challenge to the United States in the Northwest Territory. As part of the Shawnee tribe, he was reared to be a warrior. After his father and two brothers were killed in battle against the frontiersmen, he retaliated.

Tecumseh realized that, individually, the Indian tribes could never stand against the United States. Therefore, he proposed joining all the Indian tribes into a single confederation with himself as head. When Harrison protested Tecumseh's actions, the Indian replied calmly that he was simply following the example of the United States in joining his people into one nation. Although resented by some chiefs who feared him as a threat to their power, Tecumseh began building his confederation by sheer force of personality. His persuasive speeches wooed Indians to his cause. His fearlessness and code of honor won respect even among white men. (Tecumseh never tortured prisoners or attacked women and children.)

The Prophet

Contributing to Tecumseh's success was a religious movement led by his brother, a man known as **the Prophet**. Maimed (having lost an eye in an accident with a bow and arrow) and a virtual alcoholic, Tecumseh's brother claimed in 1805 to have received a revelation from the "Master of Life." After this experience, he quit drinking and began to preach to the tribes. Indians must reject the white man's ways, the Prophet said, especially his whiskey. All Indians must learn to treat each other fairly and to draw together against the settlers, who were the offspring of an evil god.

When the Prophet began to win converts among the tribes of the Northwest, Governor Harrison sent a message to the Indians, urging them to reject this so-called prophet. He said,

> Demand of him some proofs at least of his being the messenger of the Deity.... If he is really a prophet, ask of him to cause the sun to stand still—the moon to alter its course... or the dead to rise from their graves. If he does these things, you may then believe that he has been sent from God.

The message backfired. Somehow (perhaps through British agents in Canada), the Prophet learned of a total eclipse of the sun that was to occur in 1806. The Prophet announced to every Indian he could reach that he would indeed make the sun stand still. The

Indians were awed when the Prophet announced, "Behold! Darkness has shrouded the sun," and the sun apparently did vanish. Multitudes flocked to Tecumseh and his brother. At their headquarters, the brothers built a village called Prophetstown in the Indiana Territory at the juncture of the Wabash and Tippecanoe Rivers—only about a hundred and twenty miles from Harrison's territorial capital city.

The Battle of Tippecanoe

As his warrior army grew, Tecumseh announced that no more Indian lands would be opened to the white man without the consent of all the tribes. Harrison knew that this demand would mean that no more land sales would be made. The governor met Tecumseh personally in 1810, but they could reach no agreement. When Harrison suggested sending Tecumseh's demands to the president, the Indian leader replied that the president "is so far off he will not be injured by the war; he may sit still in his town and drink his wine, whilst you and I will have to fight it out."

Thinking that a clash seemed inevitable, Harrison decided to act quickly. In 1811, when Tecumseh was away in the South trying to rally the tribes there to his cause, Harrison took a force of some eight hundred men and camped near Prophetstown on the Tippecanoe River. In his brother's absence, the Prophet ordered a night attack on the American camp, promising to charm the white man's weapons so that they would not harm the warriors. In the **Battle of Tippecanoe**, Harrison's forces drove off the Indians but took heavy losses. The Indians abandoned Prophetstown, and Harrison destroyed it. When Tecumseh returned, he found that he must begin all over again. This time, however, he had an ally, Great Britain. The United States and the British were about to go to war.

Battle of Tippecanoe

Section Review

1. What battle opened the Ohio Territory to white settlement?
2–3. Who were the single most important white and Indian leaders, respectively, in the Northwest Territory?
4. How did Harrison's plea to the Indians to test the Prophet backfire?
★ Assess the quotation from Tecumseh regarding selling Indian land to white settlers.
★ Describe the Battle of Tippecanoe and its significance.

IV. War of 1812

Worsening Relations

In 1803, Great Britain and France went to war again. The British navy was too powerful for Napoleon to invade Great Britain, and Napoleon's army was too strong for Britain to defeat France in battle on land. As a result, each side tried to starve the other by destroying its trade. Unfortunately, the neutral United States was

Guiding Questions

1. What led to the War of 1812?
2. What were the major battles in the War of 1812?
3. Who were the important leaders in each military campaign?
4. What were the results of the war?

caught between the two. Both Britain and France seized American ships that they thought were bound for enemy ports, but Britain—with its powerful navy—seized more than the French. By 1807 Britain had captured more than 1000 American ships and confiscated their cargoes. France had taken about half that number.

When the British stopped American ships, they forcibly removed British deserters and put them back into service. The discipline in the Royal Navy was harsh and cruel and the living conditions despicable; so it was no surprise that British seamen (many of whom had been forced into the navy in the first place) fled to American ships. As if stopping and searching American ships were not enough, British officers—in desperate need of sailors—sometimes "mistakenly" took Americans as well. **Impressment**, seizing American sailors and forcing them to serve in the British navy, outraged the United States. Although both Britain and France disrupted American shipping, the greater number of British harassments made Britain the greater threat to the United States.

Jefferson, who had been reelected to a second term in 1804, faced serious challenges. In June 1807, the American warship *Chesapeake* was fired upon by a British warship. Three Americans were killed and more than a dozen were wounded. After the American ship surrendered, the British went aboard and impressed (seized) four sailors. Americans immediately called for retaliation. The **Chesapeake affair** nearly brought war.

Jefferson, in an attempt to avoid war, persuaded Congress to adopt the **Embargo Act**. It banned all American trade with the rest of the world. In keeping needed American goods from Europe, Jefferson hoped to force Britain and France to lift their restrictions. The embargo failed miserably. France did not need American goods as much as Jefferson thought. Britain needed the goods more, but it could not risk helping Napoleon by lifting its restrictions. Those most hurt by the embargo were Americans. Shipping dropped dramatically, and economic recession threw merchants, sailors, shipbuilders, and many others out of work. Food rotted on docks as owners could find no market for them. New England suffered the most, but all the states were economically harmed. Both political parties denounced the embargo. It was finally repealed just days before Jefferson left office in 1809.

In 1808, Jefferson had refused to run for a third term, but he persuaded the Republicans to nominate his secretary of state, **James Madison**, as his successor. Madison crushed Federalist Charles Cotesworth Pinckney in the election and became the nation's fourth president in March 1809. Though Madison was a keen politi-

Chesapeake (right) being attacked by a British warship

This political cartoon opposes Jefferson's Embargo Act of 1807. Note that *ograbme* is the reverse spelling of *embargo*.

cal philosopher (he was, after all, the Father of the Constitution) and an experienced politician, he was distracted by the continuing conflicts with France and Great Britain.

Like Jefferson, President Madison hoped to avoid war. At his request, Congress restored international trade—except with Britain and France. In 1810 Congress tried yet another approach with what was known as **Macon's Bill Number Two**. It restored *all* trade. The act further stated that if either Britain or France would repeal its anti-trade regulations, the United States would continue trade with that side and refuse to trade with the other. England and France themselves would determine which side gained the trade.

Napoleon responded by seemingly repealing his restrictions in 1810, and thus the United States resumed its embargo with Britain. The British correctly doubted Napoleon's honesty and rejected the offer. Despite Napoleon's continued interference with American shipping, the United States took Napoleon at his word and tried to force the British to comply. Both England and France viewed the American action as virtually bringing the United States into the war on France's side. The action hastened America's entering into a real war against Britain.

The War Hawks

The congressional elections of 1810 nudged America closer to war. In the West and the South several intensely nationalistic, prowar representatives were elected to the House. These "**War Hawks**," led by **Henry Clay** of Kentucky and **John C. Calhoun** of South Carolina, pushed for war with Britain. British trade restrictions hurt Southern planters and Western farmers, who earned much of their income by shipping goods overseas. They also believed that the British were supporting, and perhaps equipping, the Indians under Tecumseh in the Northwest. Some War Hawks were expansionists who wanted to seize Canada. Above all, the group saw British acts, such as impressment, as insults to American honor. The War Hawks quickly elected Clay to be Speaker of the House and began pressuring Madison toward war.

Declaration, Division, and Disarray

Madison did not need much pressure. On June 1, 1812, the president asked Congress to declare war on the British. Among the reasons he gave legislators for doing so were (1) their impressment of American sailors, (2) their interference with American trade (including seizure of American ships), and (3) their encouragement of Indians against Americans.

Debate over the declaration of war was bitter. Federalists, New Englanders, and easterners generally opposed the war. They depended on the sea for their livelihood and could see no advantage in making matters worse. If anything, they preferred a war against France.

Some Republicans opposed the war because they feared it might strengthen the national government, put the country in debt, and even result in the loss of parts of the United States. Nonetheless, many people in the South and the West, including the War Hawks, favored the war. The middle states were divided, but the prowar faction managed to build a majority in both houses. The House voted 79–49 and the Senate 19–13 for war. Ironically, only days before the declaration, Great Britain had revoked its trade

James Madison

President Madison's wife, Dolley

restrictions. If some quick means of communicating the news had existed, the war might never have occurred.

Fighting a war is a difficult endeavor even in the best of circumstances. The United States entered what became known as the War of 1812 divided and unprepared. The New England states in particular resented the war and resisted giving money or men to the war effort. They called it "Mr. Madison's War," as though the whole affair had nothing to do with them. The War Hawks were eager to fight but reluctant to pay the costs. After declaring war, they helped defeat an attempt to enlarge the navy. With only sixteen seagoing warships, America entered a war against the world's greatest naval power.

The United States Army was not ready either. Jefferson and the Republicans feared a large standing army (a permanent army that is not disbanded during peacetime) as a threat to liberty. In 1812, the army numbered a mere seven thousand men, and it would take time to raise and train new recruits. The nation had thousands of state militiamen, but they often proved undependable in real fighting. One person noted that many of the militia had come to see a show rather than fight a war. Most of the army's commanders were aged veterans of the War for Independence. Fortunately for Americans, Britain was fighting Napoleon and could not devote its full attention to the United States.

Course of the War

Disasters in Canada

Conquering British-controlled Canada was one objective of the war. It would accomplish two things: (1) eliminate British influence among the Indians and (2) provide a new area for land-hungry Americans. The fact that there were almost 8 million Americans in 1812 and only 300,000 Canadians led many to believe that victory in Canada would be a quick and easy task. Henry Clay had bragged that "the militia of Kentucky alone" would be enough to conquer Canada.

In reality, the task was far more difficult because of Canada's enormous size and pro-British population. American military leaders planned to attack Canada from Detroit in the west and from New York in the east. Brilliant British maneuvering derailed that plan. First, the British-Indian force darted into Michigan and surrounded the Americans in Detroit. By hinting that the Indian allies would be savage and uncontrollable in an attack, the British frightened the Americans into surrendering the entire force without a fight. Thus the entire Northwest was opened to the British and the Indians. The British then rushed toward Niagara Falls. In the ensuing battle, the Americans were driven back into New York. The United States' opening campaign was a fiasco.

The War at Sea

The disasters in Canada were at least partly offset by early victories at sea. In engagements with single British warships, American vessels fared quite well. The **USS Constitution** and other ships defeated British ships in combat. If fact, British cannonballs often bounced off the solid oak sides of the *Constitution*, leading Americans to nickname it "**Old Ironsides**."

The British navy, however, outnumbered the American fleet in ships by at least fifty to one. As the British tightened their block-

USS *Constitution*

ade along the coast, American victories soon ceased. But the early triumphs on the high seas had encouraged the American public.

Recovery of the Northwest

After the defeat at Detroit, the U.S. government gave William Henry Harrison command in the Northwest. Harrison realized that he could never secure the territory unless the United States controlled Lake Erie. American captain **Oliver Hazard Perry** rose to the challenge. Building his own ships, dragging cannons and ammunition through the wilderness to Lake Erie, and using as sailors Kentucky militiamen who had never been on anything larger than a flatboat, Perry defeated the British fleet in the **Battle of Lake Erie** (September 10, 1813). Perry sent a triumphant message to Harrison: "We have met the enemy and they are ours."

With Lake Erie secured, Harrison moved against the British army. The two armies met near the River Thames (TEMZ) some sixty miles east of Detroit on October 5, 1813. In the Battle of the Thames, Harrison crushed the British-Indian force. Tecumseh was killed in the battle, and with him died the dream of an Indian confederation. The Northwest was never again seriously threatened by the Indians or the British.

The British Drive for Victory

Despite Harrison's victory, the American situation remained grave early in 1814. Napoleon had surrendered, allowing Britain to turn its full attention to its former colonies. The British devised a threefold plan to win the war: (1) an army would descend from Canada and separate New York and New England from the rest of the states, (2) a naval force would attack and raid major cities on the eastern coast, and (3) another force would attack and capture New Orleans.

The first stage of the campaign ended in failure when a small American naval squadron defeated a larger British fleet on Lake Champlain on September 11, 1814. Without control of the lake, the British commander would not risk an invasion, and the force turned back.

The second stage was initially more successful. A British force landed in Maryland in August and marched toward Washington. In the **Battle of Bladensburg**, the British scattered a large force of American militia and cleared a path to the American capital. Madison had been at the battlefield and was among those who escaped. Government leaders fled in haste, and the British army marched into the city unopposed. Madison's wife, Dolley, helped save several important items from the Executive Mansion before she fled, including a famous painting of George Washington. British officers dined in the president's mansion on a meal that had been prepared for the Madisons. Soldiers soon set fire to the Capitol, the president's mansion, and several other important government buildings. Only a series of severe thunderstorms prevented the entire city from burning to the ground.

The British had no intention of holding Washington, the value of which was more symbolic than strategic, so they next turned their attention to Baltimore. That city, however, was protected by a larger, more disciplined force and by the well-designed **Fort McHenry**.

"Don't Give Up the Ship!"

When Perry won his great victory on Lake Erie, the flag flying over his ship read, "Don't Give Up the Ship!" The quotation was by a commander who had lost his life—and his ship—in battle only a few months earlier.

On June 1, 1813, the USS *Chesapeake* (the same ship that the British had humiliated in 1807) under Captain James Lawrence sailed out of Boston Harbor to meet the British warship *Shannon*. The two ships were relatively equal, but the crew of the British ship was more experienced and better trained. The *Shannon* manhandled the *Chesapeake* in battle. When a musket ball hit Captain Lawrence in the stomach, he said to his men, "Fight her 'til she sinks, and don't give up the ship."

But the British did capture it, and Lawrence died before the ship reached harbor. His words lived on, however. The phrase became a motto for the U.S. Navy. Perry's flag is now on display in Memorial Hall at the U.S. Naval Academy in Annapolis, Maryland.

Fort McHenry in Baltimore, Maryland

"By the Dawn's Early Light"

Just before the British attack on Fort McHenry, Baltimore lawyer **Francis Scott Key** and a friend sailed out to the British fleet under a flag of truce. They asked for the release of a civilian doctor, William Beanes, who had been captured by the British. The British commander agreed to release the doctor but refused to allow them to leave because the fleet was preparing to attack Fort McHenry. The Americans had to stay aboard until the battle was over.

Key watched the British fleet shell the fort. As the pounding continued into the night, the anxious lawyer strained to see what was happening. As dawn broke, he saw the American flag flying proudly above the fort, signaling that the bombardment had failed. Key gazed at the flag and was inspired. He began writing on the back of an envelope the first verse of a poem. What he called "The Defense of Fort McHenry" we know today as "The Star-Spangled Banner." He wrote the other verses after he returned to shore. Set to music, the poem became one of the most popular patriotic songs in America. Eventually, in 1931, Congress officially proclaimed "The Star-Spangled Banner" the national anthem of the United States.

The British fleet tried vainly to bombard the fort into submission. After three days of fighting, during which the British commanding general was killed, the British abandoned the task. The whole force left Chesapeake Bay and joined the effort to capture New Orleans.

The War in the South

In the South, the War of 1812 was complicated in a manner that the British never expected. As a result of Tecumseh's efforts among the southern tribes, civil war broke out among the Creek Indians in the Mississippi Territory (modern Alabama and Mississippi). The conflict between pro-American and anti-American Creeks grew sharp, and settlers bordering Indian lands began to suffer. The government authorized Tennessee general **Andrew Jackson** to help the Creeks that were friendly toward Americans and to defend the South against the British. Jackson was not a brilliant strategist, but he was a firm and unflinching leader. Jackson's men called him "Old Hickory" because he was as lean and tough as a hickory branch. Jackson knew how to handle his frontier army. When some of his militia tried to leave during the campaign, for example, Jackson laid his rifle across his horse's neck and promised to personally shoot the first man who tried to leave. Jackson's force won a series of victories against the unfriendly Creeks, climaxing in the Battle of

Horseshoe Bend (1814), in which he nearly annihilated them.

Jackson had little time to celebrate his victory, however. He marched quickly to New Orleans late in 1814 to meet the British thrust there. At New Orleans Jackson stationed his troops and artillery behind fortifications that included cotton bales. On January 8, 1815, the overconfident British, believing that their troops would easily win, marched directly on Jackson's lines. Old Hickory's massed artillery tore huge gaps in the British lines, and his frontier sharpshooters picked off those who managed to survive the cannons. The British had more than two thousand casualties; the Americans had thirteen.

The **Battle of New Orleans** was the most stunning victory of the War of 1812, but it was fought after the war was over. The **Treaty of Ghent** (signed December 24, 1814), climaxing four months of negotiations, had ended hostilities some two weeks earlier. Slow communications from Europe, however, kept that news from America for several weeks. Nonetheless, the battle made Jackson the greatest hero of the war.

Battle of New Orleans in January 1815

The Treaty of Ghent was signed on Christmas Eve in 1814.

Results of the War

The Treaty of Ghent, signed in the European city bearing that name, was a peace without victory; conditions largely returned to what they had been in 1812. Britain and the United States simply wanted to stop fighting, and both were willing to settle their differences diplomatically later. The United States did profit from the war, however. Tecumseh's confederation was finished, and the Northwest was wide open to settlement. Also, the British blockade unintentionally spurred the growth of American industry and manufacturing (discussed in Chapter 11).

The war also brought changes in attitude. For years, the United States had tried in vain to distance itself from affairs in Europe. After the war, the nation was secure enough to retreat from the rest of the world into a shell of isolationism. Not until the Spanish-American War in 1898 would Americans again become deeply involved in foreign affairs.

Perhaps the chief result was a sense of national pride and honor. In a toast after the war, naval commander Stephen Decatur captured this spirit when he said, "Our country! In her intercourse with foreign nations, may she always be in the right; but our country, right or wrong." This surge of patriotism became an important influence in shaping the period after the war, the "Era of Good Feelings" under President James Monroe.

Section Review

1–2. By what two pieces of legislation did the United States hope to apply economic pressure to avoid war with Great Britain?

3–5. Name three reasons President Madison gave for going to war against Britain.

6–8. What was Britain's threefold plan for winning the War of 1812? How did each stage of the plan fare in the actual fighting?

★ Both Britain and France seized American ships and interfered with American trade. Explain why the United States was more upset with Britain.

★ Some people have suggested that "The Star-Spangled Banner" should be replaced with a new national anthem. Do you agree or disagree? Why? If you agree, what song would you substitute as the anthem?

V. The Era of Good Feelings

The "Virginia dynasty" of presidents continued in 1816 when Secretary of State **James Monroe** was elected to succeed James Madison (of the first five presidents, only Adams was not from that state). Monroe maintained the dominance of the Jeffersonian philosophy into the 1820s. His quiet, modest manner pleased and impressed even the staunchest anti-Jeffersonians. So popular—or at least so unobjectionable—was Monroe that in the election for his second term, in 1820, he came within one electoral vote of becoming the only president besides Washington to be elected unanimously. The president's popularity and the collapse of all political opposition to the Republicans caused Monroe's two terms to be known as the **Era of Good Feelings**.

Collapse of the Federalists

One cause of the Era of Good Feelings was the collapse of the Federalist Party. In 1812, the Federalists halted their decline by joining antiwar Republicans against Madison. The election of 1812 was so close in the Electoral College that the switch of Pennsylvania alone would have given the victory to Federalist-Republican DeWitt Clinton instead of Madison. Throughout the War of 1812, the Federalists led a loud chorus of protest against the progress and conduct of the war.

During the conflict's darkest days in 1814, representatives of the New England states—mostly Federalists—met in Hartford, Connecticut. The **Hartford Convention** opposed the war and hinted that New England might secede from the Union if its demands were not met. There was widespread public disapproval of this meeting. The Treaty of Ghent and the Battle of New Orleans soon followed the Hartford Convention and removed much of the reason for its existence. If the Federalist Party was dying before the war, then it was clearly dead after. Within a few years, the discredited party disappeared.

Mending Fences with Britain

The Treaty of Ghent stopped the fighting with Britain, but it did not settle the problems between the two nations. The United States and Great Britain, therefore, carried out extensive negotia-

Guiding Questions

1. What led to the demise of the Federalist Party?
2. What was the significance of the Rush-Bagot and Adams-Onis Treaties?
3. How significant was the Monroe Doctrine?

James Monroe

tions to settle their differences. One of the first and most important of these agreements was the Rush-Bagot (BAG ut) Treaty (1817), which limited the number of British and American warships in the Great Lakes. Its provisions were eventually extended along the entire U.S.-Canadian border as the nations advanced westward. The United States and Canada have maintained peaceful relations for two centuries with no fortifications, barbed wire, or large armies between them. In 1818, the United States and Britain agreed to occupy the Oregon Territory on the Pacific Ocean jointly until they could decide how to divide it.

Conflict in Florida

Some members of Congress, especially the War Hawks, had hoped that the War of 1812 would result in the conquest of Florida. Although Spain owned the area, it exercised little control over it. Anarchy, or chaos, would be a better description of the government there. Pirates, escaped slaves, and others not only lived in Florida but also used it as a haven from which to make raids across the U.S. border. When violence occurred between the Indians and settlers in Georgia, the American government authorized General Andrew Jackson to take a force into Florida and crush the Indians. In 1818, Jackson punished the Indians in a swift campaign. He also arrested two British citizens who were accused of aiding the Indians. After speedy trials, "Old Hickory" had one hanged and the other shot. Then Jackson's army captured Pensacola, the capital of Spanish Florida.

Jackson's actions exceeded his orders; the government was certainly not interested in offending the British again. But Jackson's campaign was enormously popular in the United States. Fortunately, the British were not interested in going to war over a couple of obscure Indian traders. The Spanish were understandably angry, but Secretary of State **John Quincy Adams** decided to take a firm stand with the Spanish government. Jackson, he said, was only defending American lives and property. Adams argued the Spanish should do a better job of policing their territory. Jackson's campaign showed Spain how helpless it would be if the United States found sufficient excuse to take Florida. Rather than risk losing a war, the Spanish government decided to sell the region. Under the provisions of the **Adams-Onis Treaty**, the U.S. gained Florida in 1821 at a cost of $5 million. The United States now possessed all territory south of Canada and east of the Mississippi River, as well as its holdings in the Louisiana Territory.

The Monroe Doctrine

The impact of Napoleon's conquering armies and ideas was not limited to Europe. When Napoleon conquered Spain and Portugal, the Spanish and Portuguese possessions in Latin America leaped at the chance to be free. Led by revolutionary leaders Simón Bolívar and José de San Martín, most of Latin America broke from its European overlords and founded independent republics. After the fall of Napoleon, Spain began to look longingly at its former colonies, and the other powers of Europe indicated their willingness to help crush the "dangerous" revolutionary republics. One exception to this mood of reconquest was Great Britain. The British had established a profitable trade with the new nations and had no desire to see them become Spanish colonies again. So the British government asked the United

States if it would join Britain in proclaiming that European powers should not intervene in the Americas.

President Monroe and Secretary of State Adams considered the offer. They decided that rather than tying America to Britain, the nation should issue its own warning. In 1823, during his annual message to Congress, President Monroe declared, "The American continents, by the free and independent condition which they have assumed and maintain, are henceforth not to be considered as subjects for future colonization by any European powers." Furthermore, he added, "In the wars of the European powers in matters relating to themselves we have never taken any part, nor does it comport [conform] with our policy so to do."

With the **Monroe Doctrine**, as Monroe's statement of policy came to be called, the United States established two principles: European nations could not intervene in the Western Hemisphere (except where they already held colonies), and the United States would not meddle in European affairs. When issued, the statement was little more than a paper pledge since the United States lacked the military might to back it up. The Monroe Doctrine, however, has become a cornerstone of American foreign policy. Since 1823, numerous presidents and statesmen have defended its principles and expanded its meaning. It affects the manner in which the United States conducts its foreign policy even today.

President Monroe (*standing*) is shown with his cabinet as he discusses the Monroe Doctrine.

The Monroe Doctrine embodied one of the cherished tenets of Jeffersonianism and also solidified one result of the War of 1812—it formalized America's determination to remain isolated from Europe and its affairs. At the time, that proved to be wise. In the twentieth century, Americans found such detachment increasingly difficult to maintain.

As Monroe's term of office and his Era of Good Feelings drew to a close, the nation confronted serious internal problems and important internal developments. The young nation directed its energies toward expanding and developing the frontier, harnessing new technologies, and grappling with the problem of slavery—all of which would test the character of America's government. The Era of Good Feelings, and of Jeffersonianism in general, ended with threatening clouds of conflict on the horizon.

Section Review

1. Why was Monroe's time in office called the Era of Good Feelings?
2. Which commander's military campaign in Florida motivated Spain to sell that territory to the United States?
3. What treaty enabled the U.S. to purchase Florida from Spain?
4. Who was secretary of state when Monroe was president?
5-6. What are the two basic principles of the Monroe Doctrine?
- ★ Explain the factors that led to the collapse of the Federalist Party.
- ★ Assess why the Monroe Doctrine was necessary for the regions south of the United States but not for those north.

CHAPTER REVIEW

Making Connections

1–2. What was the view of Thomas Jefferson and William Henry Harrison concerning American Indian policy? Why was their view unsatisfactory to the Indians?

3. Explain how the Battle of New Orleans occurred after the War of 1812 ended.

4–6. Name at least three results of the War of 1812 and explain why each was important.

Developing History Skills

1. How did Tecumseh hope to slow the advance of the Americans into the Northwest Territory?

2. Do the positive results of Jackson's invasion of Florida excuse his exceeding his orders?

Thinking Critically

1. Do you think that Thomas Jefferson's dream of a dominantly agricultural America was a realistic idea?

2. Does the principle of judicial review make the Supreme Court too powerful? Defend your answer.

Living as a Christian Citizen

1. Thomas Jefferson designed the curriculum for the University of Virginia based on Enlightenment ideals. Write a paragraph outlining the core courses that a Christian university should have and how Christianity should influence the teaching of those courses.

2. Imagine that you are a settler in the Northwest Territory during the Jeffersonian era. How would you respond to the troubles in American and Indian relations?

People, Places, and Things to Remember

Thomas Jefferson
Jeffersonian Republicanism
Twelfth Amendment
John Marshall
Marbury v. Madison
judicial review
delegated powers
Gibbons v. Ogden
McCulloch v. Maryland
implied powers
Barbary states
Napoleon Bonaparte
Louisiana Purchase
Meriwether Lewis
William Clark
Zebulon Pike
Burr-Hamilton duel
"Mad Anthony" Wayne
Battle of Fallen Timbers
William Henry Harrison
Tecumseh
the Prophet
Battle of Tippecanoe
impressment
Chesapeake affair
Embargo Act
James Madison
Macon's Bill Number Two
War Hawks
Henry Clay
John C. Calhoun
USS *Constitution* ("Old Ironsides")
Oliver Hazard Perry
Battle of Lake Erie
Battle of Bladensburg
Fort McHenry
Francis Scott Key
Andrew Jackson
Battle of New Orleans
Treaty of Ghent
James Monroe
Era of Good Feelings
Hartford Convention
John Quincy Adams
Adams-Onis Treaty
Monroe Doctrine

10 THE AGE OF JACKSON (1820–1840)

> Just think, Mama! This sofa is a millionth part mine.
>
> A child to her parents as she romped on White House furniture during Jackson's inauguration, 1829

Andrew Jackson making a speech on his trip to his inauguration in Washington, D.C. in 1829

Big Ideas

1. What was the impact of nationalism, sectionalism, and democratization on the United States during this period?
2. What were the major issues that Andrew Jackson faced as president?
3. What political and economic turmoil followed the Jackson administration?

I. Crosscurrents

II. The Jackson Years

III. Party Politics

Although the period from 1820 to 1840 is often named for **Andrew Jackson**, it was actually well under way before Jackson's 1829 inauguration. Since the beginning of the century, powerful crosscurrents were tossing the political and social seas. Jackson would ride into office on its turbulent crest, but the age was shaped by forces much larger than any man. Widespread currents of nationalism, sectionalism, and democratization originated before Jackson's presidency, and they would shape America's future long after Old Hickory had gone.

I. Crosscurrents

Nationalism

The years immediately following the War of 1812 saw a growing spirit of nationalism (loyalty and devotion to one's nation). The relief and the prospects that came with peace bolstered national pride and vision. The rapid expansion of the period gave the nation seven more states by 1821: Louisiana (1812), Indiana (1816), Mississippi (1817), Illinois (1818), Alabama (1819), Maine (1820), and Missouri (1821). In addition, a new generation of intelligent and energetic leaders—men such as John Quincy Adams and Daniel Webster of New England, Henry Clay of Kentucky, and John C. Calhoun of South Carolina—were advancing the vision of a strong, prospering America.

At the heart of that new nationalism was a concern for the economic strength of the nation. **Henry Clay**, the chief advocate of this economic nationalism in Congress, called it the **American System**. Clay's system consisted of three parts: protective tariffs, renewal of the National Bank, and internal improvements.

Protective Tariff

Jefferson's Embargo Act (Chapter 9) and the trade disruptions brought by the War of 1812 had the unexpected benefit of stimulating the growth of American manufacturing. This was an important step toward economic independence from Europe. Since colonial days, America had served as both a source of raw materials for Europe, particularly Britain, and a market for British finished goods. American manufacturing brought some changes to this longstanding arrangement. The British were quick to see the threat to their own interests posed by America's infant industry, and they determined to stop it. One member of the British Parliament even urged his country to sell goods to America well below cost "to stifle [smother] in the cradle, those rising manufactures in the United States, which the war [of 1812] had forced into existence, contrary to the natural course of things."

A **tariff** is a tax on imported goods, and a **protective tariff** is an unusually high tariff designed to shield a nation's manufactures from foreign competition. The **Tariff of 1816** was America's first such protectionist legislation. When trade resumed with Britain after the War of 1812, the British sold their goods far below the cost of American merchandise. They could do so because their factories were more advanced than those in their former colonies. Consequently, few Americans bought the more expensive American products. The tax imposed by the Tariff of 1816 increased the cost of foreign goods and thereby eliminated the British price advantage.

Guiding Questions

1. What were the major national issues of this period?
2. What events resulted in greater sectionalism during this period?
3. What factors led to greater democratization of American life?
4. What were the strengths and weaknesses of nationalism, sectionalism, and democratization in this period?

Henry Clay proposed the American System.

Second National Bank was located in Philadelphia.

> ### Types of Tariffs
> Traditionally, tariffs have been of two types. *Revenue tariffs*, relatively low taxes on imports, raise income for the operation of the government but have little effect on the average consumer or the greater economy. *Protective tariffs*, however, are designed to protect one or more industries against foreign competition. They impose such high taxes on imports that they may negatively affect the entire national economy, especially the average consumer. They are aimed at the short term, not the long term. Protective tariffs may backfire in that they often lead foreign countries to retaliate with their own high tariffs on American goods, thereby stifling free trade and leading to a general economic downturn. Sometimes, they have also contributed to war. In reference to this matter, it has been said, "If goods don't cross borders, armies will."

The tariff, however, was a two-edged sword. Although it encouraged some American economic growth and increased the sale of American products, it meant higher prices for customers. Also, growth was hindered in regions of the country that produced raw goods, such as the agricultural South, or that depended upon shipping for their livelihood, such as New England. These two regions were hurt by weakened foreign trade. At first, economic independence outweighed other considerations, but protective tariffs later became a divisive issue between the regions.

Second National Bank

The charter for the first National Bank expired in 1811. State-chartered banks and private banks issued their own paper money. Without a national bank to regulate currency, prices rose rapidly. The financial problems created by this inflation were enormous.

Interestingly, the Republicans of the 1790s were vigorously opposed to both a national bank and a protective tariff. When in power, though, they tended to set aside their constitutional qualms in favor of such "Federalist" ideas. In 1816, nationalistic Republicans approved a twenty-year charter on a second Bank of the United States, patterned after Hamilton's first central bank. Such a bank would assist economic growth by providing uniform currency, a source for loans to the public and private sectors, and a place to deposit government funds.

Internal Improvements

Another key element of the American System was **internal improvements**—funding for roads, canals, and harbor developments that would bolster commerce and communications. Such improvements would help link western goods with eastern markets and provide better routes for settlement beyond the Appalachian mountains.

Despite the many advantages of internal improvements and their popularity in the growing West, they were the least successful aspect of the American System. President Madison and others believed that they lacked constitutional authority to fund such projects. Why should Maine, they reasoned, be taxed to pave a road in Maryland? Roads and canals were the responsibility of the state or local area they served. Younger Republicans complained that the president's narrow views were hindering economic growth. Calhoun, for example, protested to the president that the Constitution "was not intended as a thesis for the logician [philosopher] to exercise his ingenuity on. It ought to be construed with plain good sense."

Before the issue of internal improvements became such a controversy, one important step was approved: the building of the **National Road**. Construction of the first part of this graveled road began in 1811 at Cumberland, Maryland. Lack of funding later halted construction. After considerable debate during the Madison years, Congress appropriated additional funds to extend the route to Wheeling, Virginia (now West Virginia). Further funding in 1825 drove the road into the heart of the new western states, reaching Zanesville, Ohio, and by 1839 ending in Vandalia, Illinois. Today, motorists on Interstate 70 east of St. Louis travel basically the same route that pioneering families took in the 1830s by covered wagon, ox cart, or on foot.

Sectionalism

Monroe's Era of Good Feelings amounted to little more than that—just feelings. When problems emerged in the country and tough questions were raised in Congress, the good feelings soured and drove the sections of the country further apart. Sectional strife would have a large impact on the politics of the coming Jacksonian era.

Panic of 1819

After the War of 1812, the resumption of trade and the growth of domestic industry and western land sales brought an economic boom to the country. Yet two unrelated events an ocean apart quickly sent America's postwar prosperity tumbling, resulting in a depression, or *panic*, called the **Panic of 1819**.

In England, the price of cotton fell sharply, owing to higher American prices and the introduction of inexpensive cotton from India. The collapse of cotton prices led to a decline in demand for other American goods. The financial failure was due in part to the high protectionist Tariff of 1816, and many people, particularly in the hard-hit South, were quick to point to this. The Virginia Agricultural Society told Congress in 1820 that the tariff unfairly favored a privileged class by granting them "oppressive monopolies, which are ultimately to grind both us and our children after us 'into dust and ashes.'"

The second factor contributing to the Panic of 1819 was the irresponsible action of state banks and the National Bank. The opening of western land purchases seemed to present a golden opportunity for banks to make loans to settlers and land speculators (people who purchase land with the intent to sell later at a higher price). Banks made a large number of loans to both groups. When the economy worsened, many people could not pay their loans, and some lost their lands and homes. Fraud and scandal had occurred in the Bank of the United States, and many people, particularly

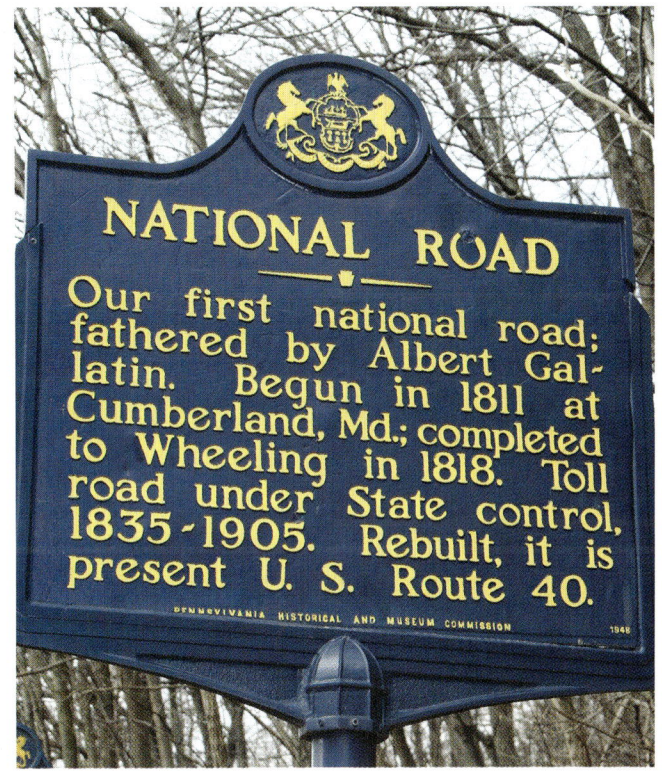

This historical marker is located in Pennsylvania.

in the South and West, blamed it for the economic difficulties. In those regions, bitterness toward the National Bank grew.

Missouri Compromise

The routine admission of new states suddenly sparked a heated controversy, one that John Quincy Adams afterward described as a "title page to a great tragic volume."

In 1819, there were eleven slave states and eleven free states. When Missouri applied for statehood that year, its constitution permitted slavery (not surprising, considering that Missouri had ten thousand slaves at the time). The question of political balance between the South and the North lay at the heart of the debate. The South, some time before, had lost control in the House of Representatives to the more populous North; balance in the Senate, therefore, remained critical to the region's political equality.

In February 1819 Representative James Tallmadge of New York proposed a resolution that prohibited slaveholders from bringing new slaves into Missouri. It also stated that enslaved children born there after Missouri received statehood would obtain freedom at age 25. The Tallmadge Amendment brought an outcry from the slave states because it interfered with a state's laws. Furthermore, because slavery would be gradually eliminated there, it threatened the balance in the Senate. Voting along sectional lines, House members approved the Tallmadge Amendment despite Southern objections. However, the amendment was defeated in the Senate.

Maine's application for statehood in the summer of 1819 and Speaker of the House Henry Clay's skillful handling of the controversy helped provide a compromise solution to the statehood stalemate. The **Missouri Compromise** of 1820 proposed that Maine be admitted as a free state and Missouri as a slave state and that in

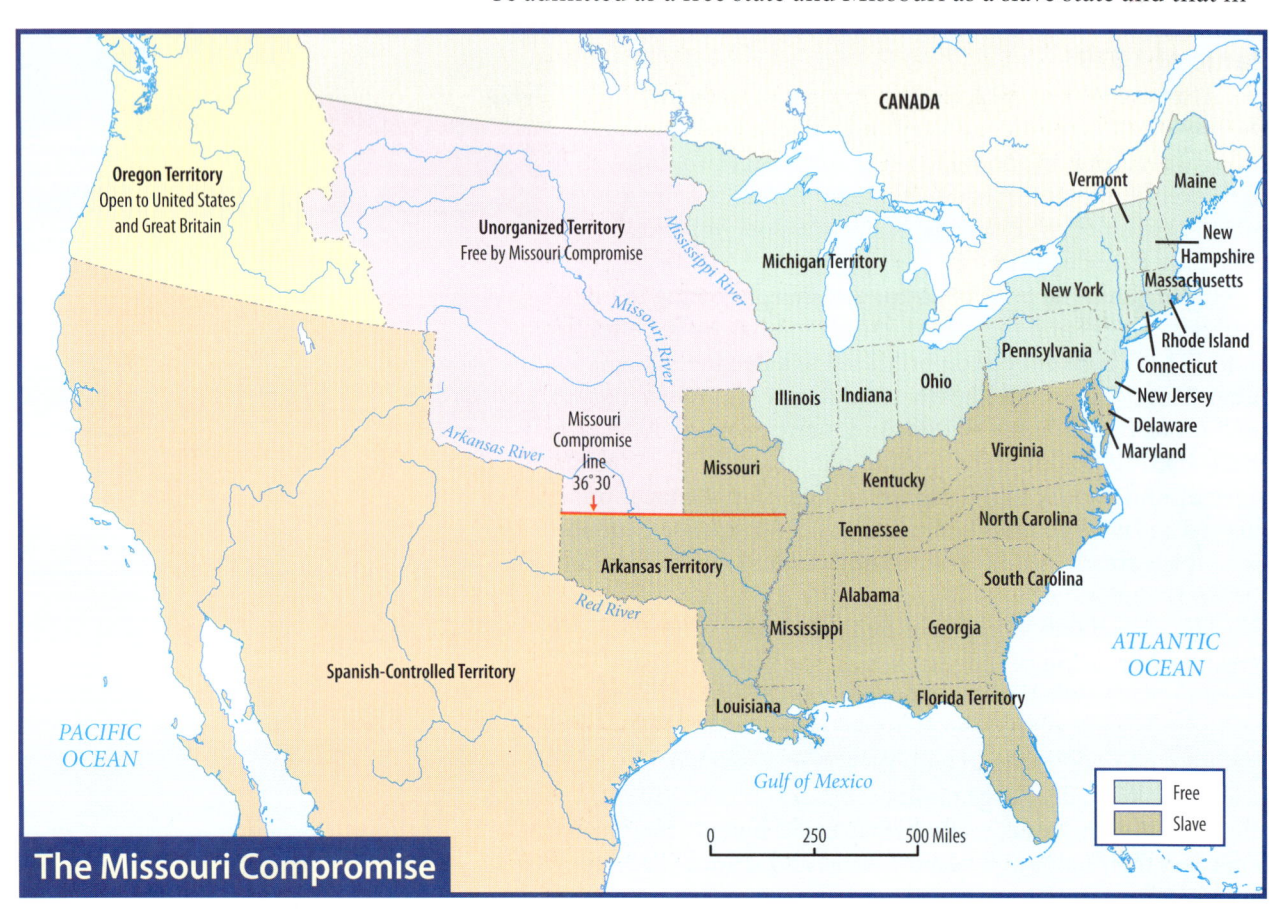

The Missouri Compromise

the rest of the Louisiana Territory slavery not be permitted north of 36° 30′, Missouri's southern boundary. By a narrow margin, Congress approved the Missouri Compromise.

The Missouri controversy exemplified the growing turmoil concerning equality and liberty. Political lines were drawn between the regions, and with the ever-expanding westward settlement, Missouri represented a problem that would not soon go away. Southern states wanted to maintain an equal number of senators with the North and wished to retain the right to own slaves. Meanwhile, a growing number of Americans objected to the fact that slaves were denied both liberty and equality.

Democratization

Another growing force during the first quarter of the nineteenth century was increasing access to the political process. This democratization gave the average citizen a greater voice in his government. Thus, there was now greater equality in participation.

Political expansion was evident in three major changes during the period. First was the emergence of universal manhood suffrage for white men (voting rights for all adult white males, not just property owners). New western states entering the Union, unbound by the political customs of the older states, drafted more democratic constitutions that helped open the way for this change by the 1830s. Some free black men also received the right to vote. Second, the people gained a greater voice in presidential elections. In the early years of the republic, most electors in the Electoral College were chosen by their state's legislature. By the 1820s, however, the majority of presidential electors were selected by popular vote, giving voters a greater influence in the choosing of their president. Even though increasing numbers of common people were able to vote, the electorate usually chose their leaders from the upper class, not from their own ranks.

In turn, these democratic changes encouraged the third important development—the fracturing of the one-party system and the emergence of a strong two-party system. Since Jefferson's 1800 victory, the Republicans had dominated national politics. In fact, the Federalists soon ceased even to be a threat in presidential contests. Without genuine competition, this single-party dominance made it seem that national politics had returned to President Washington's ideal. It became popular to criticize any hint of political division. Even Andrew Jackson, who would one day be among the most partisan of presidents, urged Monroe in 1816 "to exterminate the monster called party spirit." Nonpartisan unity, like the Era of Good Feelings of which it was a part, proved to be a fragile thing.

The Great Awakening was a democratic event that affected not just religion but politics as well (see Chapter 4). Likewise, the political democratization of the Jacksonian era affected religion. People became much more willing to value their own understanding when interpreting Scripture, more than the guidance of a minister or the writings of a Christian theologian. Taken to the extreme, this approach made human reasoning the final authority rather than Scripture itself. Many new religious groups formed during this period, as men dismissed previous generations' careful study of Scripture and developed doctrines that they personally found more reasonable.

Medal commemorating the Missouri Compromise

Death of "King Caucus"

From 1796 to 1820, a congressional caucus selected the presidential and vice-presidential nominees for its party. (A **caucus** is a closed meeting of party leaders.) Therefore, after Republicans became the dominant party, a handful of congressmen chose the president of the United States. Three members of the "Virginia Dynasty"—Jefferson, Madison, and Monroe—serving a total of twenty-four years, were selected by the closed-door caucus method.

Despite those impressive presidential choices, the reign of "King Caucus" understandably came under fire as undemocratic. As early as 1800, one newspaper criticized "this factious meeting, this self appointed, self elected, self delegated club or caucus, or conspiracy," charging that about twenty-four men were deciding "for the people of the United States who should be president and vice president."

The 1824 election proved to be a political turning point in America. The caucus system of nominating candidates was completely discredited, and the divisive presidential campaign that year ended the idea of a nonpartisan government.

A "Corrupt Bargain"

Four men threw their hats into the ring as candidates for president in 1824. William H. Crawford of Georgia was the choice of the dying congressional caucus, a fact that did him more harm than good. **John Quincy Adams**, son of the former president and Monroe's secretary of state, announced his candidacy. In addition, two westerners joined the slate of candidates: the popular Speaker of the House, Kentuckian Henry Clay, and the "Hero of New Orleans," General Andrew Jackson of Tennessee.

The four-way race was not among competing parties, since all the candidates were at least in name Republicans, heirs of Mr. Jefferson. Rather, the race was between competing personalities and regions of the country. The results were predictable—no candidate received a majority of the votes. In the Electoral College tally, Jackson polled 99, Adams 84, Crawford 41, and Clay 37. The popular vote, which was recorded for the first time, gave (in rounded figures) Jackson 154,000, Adams 109,000, Crawford 41,000, and Clay 48,000. Since no candidate had won a majority, the Twelfth Amendment required that the election be decided by the House

John Quincy Adams

William H. Crawford

Henry Clay

Andrew Jackson

of Representatives. There the president would be chosen from among the top three candidates from the Electoral College.

Clay, who finished fourth, was placed in a unique position. He could not win the election, but as the powerful Speaker of the House, he could decide who would. Clay preferred the nationalist policies of Adams, and he considered Jackson unqualified. It was an easy decision for him; he supported Adams. Consequently, Adams won on the first ballot.

Jackson's supporters were outraged. Old Hickory had won the most electoral and the most popular votes in the general election; why then was Adams president? Adams then compounded the problem by nominating Clay as secretary of state, a position that had already produced four of the six presidents (Jefferson, Madison, Monroe, and John Q. Adams). Jackson's supporters claimed that Adams and Clay had made a "**corrupt bargain**," an underhanded deal to give Adams the presidency in return for making Clay secretary. Although no proof of a prior deal exists, the charge hurt Adams personally and impaired his administration from the start.

Adams had had a distinguished political career, having served capably in several offices. His performance as secretary of state under James Monroe—particularly his settling of differences with Britain and his negotiation of the purchase of Florida from Spain—have caused some historians to rate him as one of the greatest secretaries of state in history. He was unquestionably brilliant and morally conscientious and consistent. Nevertheless, he was an ineffective president. Like his father, Adams had little patience for political maneuverings, and he often did not understand the people he was asked to lead. In his first annual address to Congress, for example, Adams urged the members to support his proposals for internal improvements, saying that they should not "fold up [their] arms and proclaim to the world that we are palsied [paralyzed] by the will of our constituents." His seemingly low regard for voters strengthened the pro-Jackson forces.

One of the key features of Adams's administration was its strong nationalist emphasis. Expanding on Clay's American System, Adams worked for higher protective tariffs to encourage American manufacturing and internal improvements. He even proposed federal funding for higher education and the arts.

That nationalist thrust became a distinguishing mark of Adams's wing of the party, which became known as the **National Republicans**. The Jackson wing kept the old name, Democratic-Republicans, but eventually dropped the "Republican" part, keeping the name by which the party is still called, the **Democratic Party**.

Rematch and Revenge

The candidates and perhaps the outcome of the 1828 election were probably determined four years earlier. It was an Adams-Jackson rematch. By that time, many of the former Crawford and Clay supporters had moved into the Jackson camp, including a

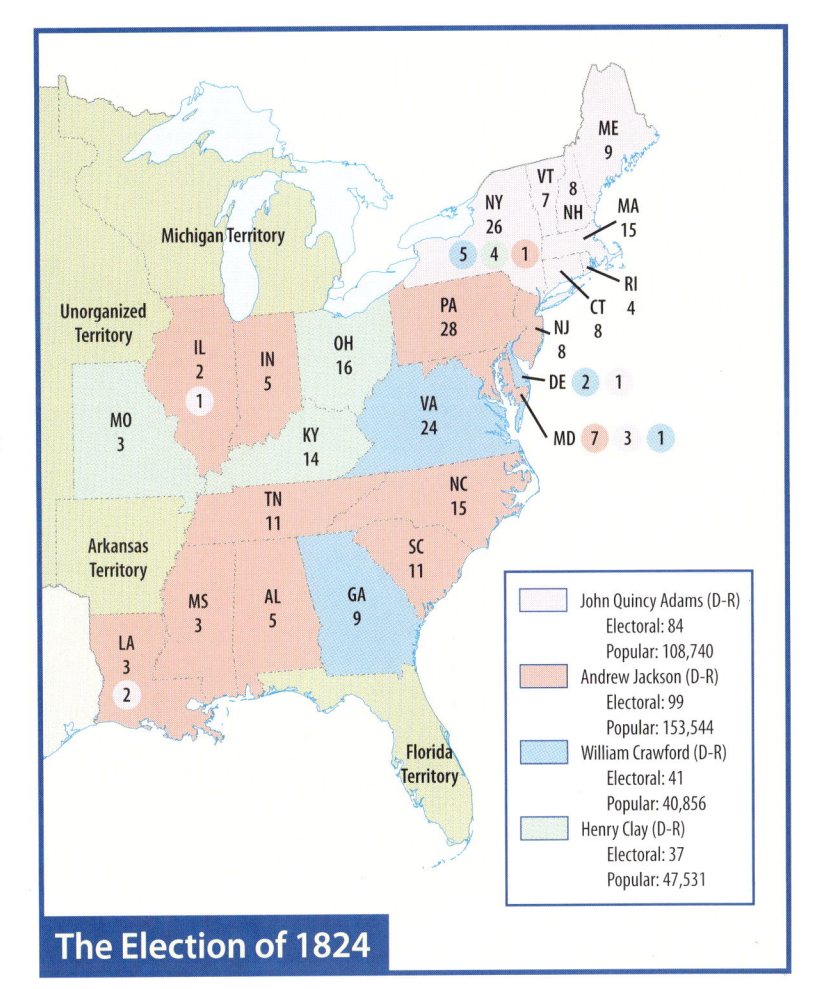

The Election of 1824

John Quincy Adams (D-R)
Electoral: 84
Popular: 108,740

Andrew Jackson (D-R)
Electoral: 99
Popular: 153,544

William Crawford (D-R)
Electoral: 41
Popular: 40,856

Henry Clay (D-R)
Electoral: 37
Popular: 47,531

The Election of 1828

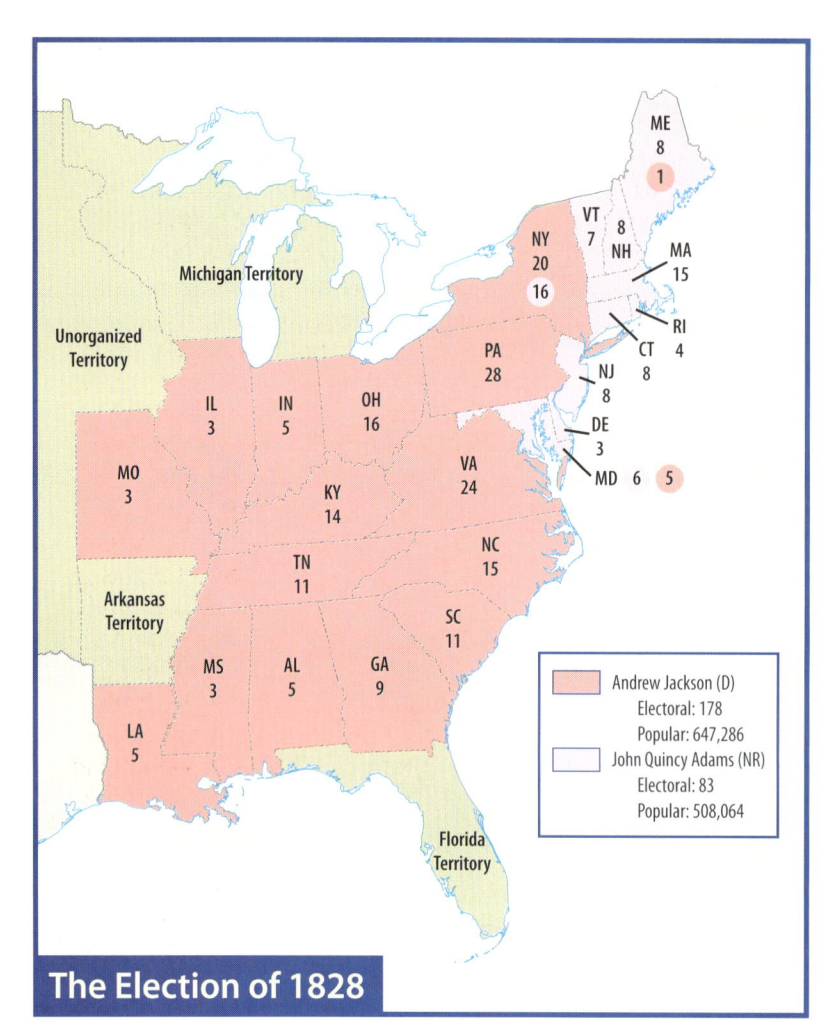

Andrew Jackson (D) — Electoral: 178, Popular: 647,286
John Quincy Adams (NR) — Electoral: 83, Popular: 508,064

shrewd New York senator named **Martin Van Buren**. Van Buren's skillful political maneuvering earned the 5′6″ native of Kinderhook, New York, the nickname "Little Magician." He helped organize the Democratic effort and urged Jackson to avoid mentioning divisive issues, emphasizing instead a *symbolic* campaign—Old Hickory, the friend of the common man.

Unfortunately the election was bitterly fought. Both sides engaged in extensive mudslinging (criticizing each other tirelessly and engaging in personal attacks). But in the end, Jackson and his running mate, **John C. Calhoun** of South Carolina, won by a landslide, getting 56 percent of the popular vote and an electoral tally of 178 to 83. The election's two-party competition also boosted voter participation. For the first time, more than one million voters cast ballots for the presidency, triple the number in the 1824 election. John Adams had been swept from the White House in 1800, and now, nearly thirty years later, his son John Quincy Adams was suffering the same fate.

In March 1829, record numbers attended the inauguration. The celebrating crowd poured into the White House. They stripped wallpaper for souvenirs, scooped out globs of melting ice cream (and dripped trails of it on the carpet), smashed furniture and glass, and gripped the hand of the mansion's newest occupant, Andrew Jackson, just before he slipped out a back door to leave the house to its fate. As one unamused observer grumbled, "The reign of King Mob seemed triumphant."

Although it is true that the invading army of Jackson's supporters could be faulted for being a bit disorderly, they should also be credited with providing a fitting start to a new American era—the age of Jacksonian democracy, the age of the common man.

Election Day in Philadelphia in the early 1800s

Eyewitness Account of Jackson's Inauguration

The most complete description of Jackson's inauguration is found in a letter by Mrs. Margaret Bayard Smith, a high-ranking member of Washington society and wife of a banker. She wrote extensively about life in the capital city during the first half of the nineteenth century.

After describing the scene at the Capitol, where Jackson took his oath before a crowd of perhaps fifteen to twenty thousand, she tells how the great multitude rushed behind the president to the White House. Smith was unable to get near the mansion for several hours because of the throng, but finally she and her escort were able to enter.

"But what a scene did we witness! . . . A mob of boys . . . women, children, [were] scrambling, fighting, romping. . . . What a pity! No arrangements had been made, no police officers placed on duty and the whole house had been inundated by the rabble mob. We came too late.

"The President, after having been *literally* nearly pressed to death and almost suffocated and torn to pieces by the people in their eagerness to shake hands with Old Hickory, had retreated through the back way or south front and had escaped. . . .

"Cut glass and china to the amount of several thousand dollars had been broken in the struggle to get the refreshments, punch and other articles [that] had been carried out in tubs and buckets, but had it been in . . . [even larger containers] it would have been insufficient, ice-creams, and cake and lemonade, for 20,000 people, for it is said that number were there, tho' I think the number exaggerated.

"Ladies fainted, men were seen with bloody noses and such a scene of confusion took place as is impossible to describe. . . . This concourse had not been anticipated and therefore not provided against. Ladies and gentlemen, only had been expected at this Levee [reception] not the [ordinary] people . . . but it was the People's day, and the People's President and the People would rule."

A portion of the crowd at the White House for Jackson's first inaugural reception in 1829

Section Review

1–3. What were the three components of Henry Clay's American System?
4. What was America's first protectionist legislation?
5–6. What two factors contributed to the Panic of 1819?
7–9. List the three provisions of the Missouri Compromise.
10–11. What two men did Andrew Jackson's supporters accuse of making a "corrupt bargain" in the presidential election of 1824?
★ Evaluate the costs and benefits of the democratization of American politics and religion.
★ Assess the significance of the election of 1828.

II. The Jackson Years

Old Hickory

The democratic movement that won Jackson the presidency was underway before Old Hickory became its popular hero. By joining the movement, Jackson brought his fame to the national political stage. His remarkable life supplied more than enough material for his hero's image. By 1828 Jackson's biography read like *A Brief History of the United States*.

Guiding Questions

1. What kind of person was Andrew Jackson?
2. What were the significant decisions of Jackson's administration?

Claims to Jackson

Andrew Jackson was born in a region known as "the Waxhaws" (after the Waxhaw Indians who originally lived there). It encompassed modern-day Lancaster County, South Carolina, and Union County, North Carolina. No one knows in precisely which section Jackson was born, so both states claim him as their native son. Perhaps the greatest claim on Jackson, however, is by Tennessee, where Jackson spent most of his life and built his mansion, the Hermitage. That home is located in present-day Nashville.

Rachel Jackson, Andrew Jackson's wife

The Preacher and the President

Peter Cartwright, a fearless Methodist preacher during the Jackson years, was invited to speak in a Nashville-area church. The pastor of the church recognized Andrew Jackson in the crowd and worried that Cartwright might offend the president, tugged on Cartwright's coat to warn him of the presence of the distinguished man.

"Who is General Jackson?" Cartwright roared. He then warned that if the general "don't get his soul converted," then "God will damn him" as quickly as He would any other sinner.

The next day, Cartwright ran into Jackson on the street, and Jackson said, "Mr. Cartwright, you are a man after my own heart. . . . A minister of Jesus Christ ought to love everybody and fear no mortal man."

Cartwright later joined Jackson's Democratic Party and served as a representative in the Illinois state legislature. In 1846 Cartwright even ran for Congress but lost to an up-and-coming figure in Illinois politics—Abraham Lincoln.

Jackson was born in the Carolina backcountry in 1767. His parents were Scots-Irish who had left Europe just two years before their son was born. Frontier life was challenging and dangerous. Andrew Sr. died in an accident while clearing his fields for spring planting. Three weeks later his grieving widow gave birth to a third son, giving him the name of her dead husband.

Young Andrew's early life was rugged and difficult. At thirteen he joined Patriot forces against the invading British, serving as a messenger. In April 1781 Andrew and his brother Robert were captured by British cavalry. When one of the officers ordered Andrew to clean his boots, Jackson refused. The enraged officer slashed the boy on his head with a sword and hacked at his raised arm. Jackson would bear the scars of his defiance for the remainder of his life.

After the war Jackson studied law in North Carolina and was admitted to the bar. The young lawyer soon became a public prosecutor in the Tennessee Territory. The opening West well suited the fiery, energetic Jackson. He acquired land, slaves, horses, and a taste for politics. Jackson became a state judge and in 1796 was elected to a term in Congress, where he gained some respect for his straightforward though sometimes harsh manner.

Jackson's reputation, however, was not made in Washington; it was forged on the frontier, fighting Indians and Redcoats. General Jackson drove his men hard, but he drove himself harder. His grit earned him the admiration of his ranks. "He's tough as hickory," they would say, and so he was.

But Jackson displayed many flaws in the years before he won the presidency. During the War of 1812, he ignored a treaty that had been negotiated with the Creek Indians. He confiscated huge portions of their land, even from those Creeks who aided him in the conflict. As noted in Chapter 9, he led soldiers into Florida, then controlled by the Spanish, in 1818. There he exceeded his orders and nearly caused a war with Spain. He was brutal in his treatment of the Seminole Indians in that region. In 1824, former President Jefferson said, "I feel much alarmed at the prospect of seeing General Jackson [become] president. He is one of the most unfit men I know of for such a place. He has had very little respect for laws or constitutions, though [he is] an able military chief."

The People's President
Spoils of Victory

Jackson's partisan victory for "the people" ushered in a change in the filling of government jobs. The new president believed that public service should not be a lifelong career. Until this time bureaucratic officials such as clerks, postmasters, revenue collectors, and court officers were appointed to serve on a fairly permanent basis. Jackson held that men who stayed in public office for too long were prone to be corrupted by their power. Accordingly, after reasonable intervals, particularly with the change of administrations, rotation in office should occur.

Jackson actually took a low-key approach to replacing officeholders. During his first year in office he turned out only 9 percent of the appointed officeholders he inherited, and less than 20 percent during his two terms.

The significance of Jackson's replacement of government officeholders was not so much what he did as what he started. This **spoils system**, giving government jobs to political supporters, would endure for half a century. While it is true that Jackson's policy did shake up an entrenched bureaucracy, it also removed some highly qualified individuals from office at times and replaced them with highly unqualified individuals. Neither did the spoils system necessarily make public servants more responsive to the public, since the bureaucrats owed their jobs to their party leaders, not to the people.

Kitchen Cabinet

Jackson's cabinet members were given their posts as political rewards for services rendered during the campaign, but they actually had little influence with the president. Jackson's real advisors were a close circle of friends that critics called his "**Kitchen Cabinet**." It included newspaper editors, prominent Democrats in Congress, and his secretary of state, Martin Van Buren—all political insiders. Increasingly the president was taking on the role of party leader.

Almost from the outset, Jackson's administration was torn by infighting, particularly the jockeying for power between Martin Van Buren and Vice President Calhoun. Van Buren increasingly sought the favor of President Jackson in an effort to limit Calhoun's influence. In addition, the sectional differences between the New Yorker and the South Carolinian heightened the dispute, particularly over the tariff question. Calhoun, who had been an ardent nationalist in the War of 1812, was becoming the major spokesman for the interests of the South.

This cartoon of Jackson's Kitchen Cabinet satirizes the disagreements among its members.

Nullification Crisis

At the time of Jackson's inauguration, the tariff controversy was raging again. In 1828 Congress passed a new higher protective tariff with rates of up to 50 percent on some imports. The more industrialized North welcomed the tariff, while the South dubbed it the "**Tariff of Abominations**."

Southern leaders recognized the constitutional right of Congress to levy modest tariffs to raise revenue (Article I, Section 8, Clause 1). However, they considered tariffs aimed at protecting a particular class or favoring one section of the country over another to be unconstitutional. The North favored a high protective tariff to curb competing foreign imports. The South, though, depended on foreign imports in exchange for its agricultural exports. Higher tariffs meant higher prices in the South and higher sales of northern goods. Revenue the government received from the tariffs therefore came largely from the South but was mostly spent to fund internal improvements in the North. In short, southerners viewed the high tariff as a discriminatory tax.

In December 1828 the South Carolina legislature officially declared the new tariff unconstitutional. It further suggested, as had

John C. Calhoun

Jefferson and Madison in the Kentucky and Virginia Resolutions, that any unconstitutional federal act could be nullified (declared invalid) by the states. Georgia declared the tariff unconstitutional that same month. Mississippi and Virginia did the same two months later.

The issue of nullification was drawn from an anti-tariff pamphlet published anonymously by Vice President Calhoun. The South Carolinian proposed the doctrine of **nullification** whereby states could nullify or reject congressional acts they deemed unconstitutional. Congress then could either change the law or send it to the states as a constitutional amendment to be ratified or rejected. Nullification was Calhoun's attempt to find a constitutional middle ground between submission and secession (withdrawing from the country).

Nullification raised both tempers and constitutional questions in Congress. In a celebrated debate in January 1830, Senator **Robert Y. Hayne**, a gifted orator from South Carolina, rebuked New England's opposition to secession as inconsistent since it had considered secession itself in the Hartford Convention of 1815 (see Chapter 9). Hayne further denounced the Tariff of 1828 and proclaimed nullification the only hope of self-preservation for the South and the West.

Daniel Webster, a senator from Massachusetts and perhaps America's finest orator, defended New England in his response to Hayne. He insisted that the people of the United States as a whole, not as individual states, had ratified the Constitution. Webster declared, "It is . . . the people's Constitution, the people's government, made for the people, made by the people, and answerable to the people."

Therefore, he said, a state could neither secede nor nullify an act. Webster's speech climaxed with the famous phrase, "Liberty *and* Union, now and for ever, one and inseparable!" His views, however, like those of others involved in the controversy, appeared inconsistent; in 1815 he too had supported the Hartford Convention's decision to secede if Congress denied its demands. Opponents charged that Webster was seeking only what was best for his state and region. In 1815 secession had appeared best for New England; in 1830 enforcement of the tariff was best for New England.

The nullification issue smoldered for a few years. A new conflict arose in 1832; in May of that year, John Quincy Adams, who had returned to Congress after his unsuccessful bid in 1828 for reelection to the presidency, proposed a revision to the Tariff of 1828. Congress passed the revised tariff, which was lower than that of 1828 but still higher than most Southerners wanted; Jackson signed it in July. The South Carolina legislature responded by calling for a special state convention that in turn declared the tariffs of both 1828 and 1832 unconstitutional and therefore null and void. The convention further declared that South Carolina would secede if there were any attempts to collect the tariff duties.

Senator Hayne resigned his Senate seat when he was elected governor of South Carolina. John C. Calhoun resigned as vice president to take Hayne's place on the Senate floor. Calhoun's resignation climaxed months of worsening relations between the president and vice president, a conflict that had become increasingly public. At a banquet in 1830, Jackson had pointedly looked at Calhoun as he raised a toast: "Our Union: it must be preserved." Without missing a beat, Calhoun rose and presented his own toast: "The Union: next to our liberty, most dear."

Despite Calhoun's maneuverings, only a little sympathy and no support could be found for South Carolina's action. An angry Andrew Jackson threatened to hang Calhoun and secured from Congress consideration and later passage of the **Force Bill**, which gave the president the power to use the military against South Carolina. In his *Proclamation to the People of South Carolina*, Jackson warned,

> The laws of the United States must be executed. I have no discretionary power on the subject; my duty is emphatically pronounced in the Constitution. Those who told you that you might peaceably prevent their execution deceived you. . . . Their object is disunion. But be not deceived by names. Disunion by armed force is *treason*. Are you really ready to incur its guilt?

Leaders in South Carolina declared that Jackson's constitutional views were "erroneous and dangerous," and despite its friendless position the state was prepared to "repel force by force, and . . . maintain its liberty at all hazards."

Behind these bare-knuckle pronouncements was an attempt on both sides to find a bloodless solution. At this juncture Henry Clay, "the Great Compromiser," proposed a new tariff that substantially, though gradually, reduced the Tariff of 1832, making it acceptable to South Carolina. Clay's proposed tariff, known as the **Compromise Tariff of 1833**, passed on March 1. In a parting shot to the president, though, South Carolina nullified the Force Bill.

War had been averted, but there was little to cheer about. The crisis heightened tensions between the sections, and throughout the South there was a growing, uneasy sense of loss of control over their destiny. As one South Carolinian observed at the time of the nullification crisis, "It is useless and impracticable to disguise the fact that the South is in a permanent minority, and that there is a sectional majority against it—a majority of different views and interests and little common sympathy."

Busting the Bank

The major campaign issue as Jackson faced reelection in 1832 was the future of the **Bank of the United States**. Jackson had little understanding of banking practices but had a distaste for banks nonetheless. The Panic of 1819 was still a vivid and bitter memory in the West and South, and the Bank was the culprit in the minds of many Americans.

In the summer of 1832, the president of the National Bank, **Nicholas Biddle**, submitted the Bank's charter to Congress for a twenty-year renewal, though the existing charter did not expire until 1836. When Jackson learned that his old political rival Henry Clay had instigated the early renewal of the charter, hoping that it would help him to be elected president, Jackson said, "The bank is trying to kill me, but I will kill it."

The Bank had such strong support in Congress that Clay believed he had a winning campaign issue. The recharter bill

This cartoon compares John C. Calhoun to Joshua. The caption indicates that Calhoun wanted to stop time so that "the nation of Carolina may continue to hold negroes & plant Cotton till the day of Judgment."

Nicholas Biddle

passed Congress; Jackson vetoed it, claiming that it was unconstitutional. The Senate was unable to gain a two-thirds majority to override Jackson's veto; thus, the Bank was to expire in four years. Clay thought the stage was now set for him to win a great victory.

The election of 1832 introduced three new political ideas. For the first time in a presidential election, a **third party** nominated a candidate. The Anti-Masonic Party arose in opposition to Masons, a controversial secret society. It also opposed Catholic immigration and supported federal funding for internal improvements. The party established two other traditions. It issued a **platform**, a written statement describing where the party stood on various issues. More importantly, it held a **national convention** where state delegates gathered to nominate the party's presidential and vice-presidential candidates. The major parties quickly followed its example, and nominating conventions have since become a standard part of the American political process. Henry Clay was chosen as the presidential candidate at the National Republican convention, while President Jackson was chosen at the Democratic convention.

The election itself was not so interesting. Clay had miscalculated badly; support in Congress for the Bank and support in the countryside turned out to be two different things. Jackson swept to victory with his old ally Van Buren as his new vice president. His reelection having convinced him more than ever that he was the choice of the people, Old Hickory turned his attention to the Bank. His terms were unconditional surrender. Jackson claimed that withdrawing federal funds from the Bank would lessen the negative effects of the charter's expiration in 1836. Two secretaries of the treasury refused to remove the federal deposits. Jackson fired both and then appointed Roger B. Taney as Treasury secretary in September 1833. The next month Taney began removing federal deposits and placing them in state banks—Jackson's "**pet banks**," as his enemies called them.

The Bank's defeat was not a victory for the common man over the wealthy financiers, as Jackson had claimed that it would be. Jackson's actions were a two-edged sword. The loss of federal deposits in the Bank of the United States led the bank president to reduce the number of loans. As a result, fewer businesses could borrow money needed to expand. Some factories closed and many workers lost their jobs. When businessmen urged Jackson to save

Bills, Bills, Bills

Jackson's successful war against the National Bank helped open a new era in American banking from 1836 to the mid–1860s. Although state banks and branch banks had been in operation before, the absence of both a national banking system and regulations on state and private banks brought a colorful period of "free banking."

Hundreds of banks opened representing towns, canal companies, insurance agencies, railroads, and factories. These diverse, largely unregulated banks issued a motley supply of money. Bills were issued in various colors, sizes, and engravings, and denominations were also varied—$1, $2, $3, $4, and $5 bills. A twenty-five cent bill and a fifty-cent bill were issued. In contrast to the somber gallery of statesmen on our currency today, bank notes of the antebellum period were adorned with birds, bees, buffaloes, children, trains, steamboats, coal miners, cotton pickers, and timber cutters.

Thousands of varieties of notes were issued throughout the country during that period. In the 1860s, however, federal banking acts were passed that imposed a uniform national currency and greater Treasury control. Three-dollar bills and other oddities became only historical curiosities and collectibles.

the country from depression, he replied, "Go to Nicholas Biddle!" Jackson blamed Biddle for the mounting problems while Biddle said Jackson was at fault. In 1836, when its charter expired, the Bank of the United States ceased to exist.

Resettlement of the Indians

In his first inaugural address, in March 1829, President Jackson promised,

> It will be my sincere and constant desire, to observe toward the Indian tribes within our limits, a just and liberal policy; and to give that humane and considerate attention to their rights and their wants, which is consistent with the habits of our Government, and the feelings of our people.

The old Indian fighter, however, pursued Indian policies that were anything but "just and liberal" and that showed a remarkable lack of "humane and considerate attention to their rights and their wants."

Indian Removal

Even before Jackson took office, the United States had discussed moving all Indian tribes in the East to lands west of the Mississippi River and east of the Rockies. Such a policy seemed fair to the government, since it wanted the Indian lands and did not want the western lands—yet. The Indians were understandably less impressed with the fairness of the idea. When he took office, Jackson pursued this **Indian removal policy** vigorously. At his urging, Congress passed the Indian Removal Act of 1830 that authorized such actions. As a result, during his administration, no less than ninety-four treaties were made with the Indians, some of them forcibly. With the treaties as legal justification, the United States began moving the Indians westward and opening Indian lands in the East to white settlement.

Indian Resistance

Not all the Indians submitted meekly to this treatment. Some responded with violence. In 1832 a group of Sauk (sahk) and Fox Indians under Chief Black Hawk crossed the Mississippi River back into northern Illinois to reclaim their land. A force of regular soldiers and Illinois militia moved to intercept the Indians. The resulting **Black Hawk War** was brief but bloody. As with most U.S.-Indian conflicts, the Indians suffered more and lost the war.

More challenging was the **Seminole War** (1835–42). The Seminoles, led by the canny Osceola (oss ee OH luh), also resisted efforts to move them west. They hid in the swamplands and marshes of Florida as American troops tried in vain to track them down. Many battles and skirmishes occurred. Over 1,500 Americans and an unknown number of Indians died in the conflict. Most Seminoles were captured and sent west, but some hid in Florida until the government gave up and left them to live in peace.

The Cherokees in the southeastern United States tried a different approach in their dealings with American settlers. They adopted many features of white civilization. They built communities with roads and schools and developed prosperous farms using European methods of agriculture. Many also converted to Christianity. A brilliant Cherokee named **Sequoyah** even developed a written Cherokee alphabet, allowing the Indians to publish newspapers and the Bible in their own language.

Sequoyah

John Ross was the principal chief of the Cherokees from the late 1820s until his death in 1866. He was one-eighth Cherokee.

Believing the earlier promises contained in their treaties with the United States that they would be left to govern themselves, the Cherokees resisted removal. They soon found that Christian missionaries to their tribe were their strongest defenders. The leader of the mission board that supported many of these missionaries petitioned Congress and wrote many newspaper articles in support of the Cherokees' rights.

In response, the Georgia legislature passed a law targeting missionaries. It forbade white people to live among the Cherokees without government approval. Several missionaries were arrested for continuing their ministry among the Cherokees without such approval. Two were sentenced to serve four years hard labor in a state prison. These two, Samuel Worcester and Elizur Butler, appealed to the U.S. Supreme Court, and the Supreme Court ruled in favor of the missionaries. In *Worcester v. Georgia*, Chief Justice John Marshall ordered Georgia to release the missionaries and also told President Jackson to send troops into Georgia to remove white settlers who had moved onto Cherokee lands. But Georgia and President Jackson ignored the Court. Jackson reportedly said, "John Marshall has made his decision. Now let him enforce it."

Many Cherokees still resisted. But by 1838 troops had forcibly moved those who had not already gone west to the Indian Territory (now Oklahoma). U.S. soldiers dragged the Cherokees from their homes—sometimes at gunpoint—and placed them in detention camps until the marches west began.

These forced marches west began in the summer, and sickness and drought killed many of the travelers. Several groups waited until fall, but heavy rains became a problem. Travel was difficult and food was scarce. As winter set in, frigid weather and bad water caused more disease. About four thousand of the fifteen thousand Cherokees died en route to the Indian Territory. The sick, the aged, and the very young suffered the most. The Indians called the relocation the **Trail of Tears**.

Trail of Tears

"The Trail Where They Cried"

Perhaps the saddest event in the Indian resettlement process was the Trail of Tears, the forced removal of more than ten thousand Cherokees from North Carolina, Georgia, and Tennessee to the Indian Territory (located in present-day Oklahoma) in 1838 and 1839. The name is derived from a Cherokee phrase describing it: *Nunna-da-ul-tsun-yi*, "the trail where they cried." Beginning in virtual prison camps in the Carolinas, the Cherokees were herded like cattle by the U.S. Army.

A small number of Cherokees escaped the army roundup and hid in the Smoky Mountains. They eventually emerged from hiding and were allowed to legally reclaim about fifty thousand of the seven million acres of Cherokee land the government had seized. This grant was an extremely small area for a people who had suffered so much and so unjustly. Today, a Cherokee Indian reservation still exists in the region.

Section Review

1–3. What were the three new political ideas introduced in the presidential election of 1832?

4–5. How did the reactions of the Seminoles and the Cherokees to Indian removal differ? What was the result for each tribe?

★ Evaluate the idea of a protective tariff.

★ Who was responsible for the forced removal of the Cherokees? Explain your answer.

III. Party Politics

A strong indication of the democratic forces at work during the Jackson years was the growing, organized, and even turbulent political competition of the era. Within a span of just a dozen years, from 1828 to 1840, two new national parties—Jackson's Democratic Party and his opposition, the Whig Party—competed effectively for the presidency and control of Congress.

Guiding Questions

1. What factors led to the emergence of the Whig party?
2. Why was the Whig party victorious in the election of 1840?

Jackson and Anti-Jackson

Andrew Jackson's strong leadership at the presidential helm often made as many foes as followers. During his second term, though Jackson was still popular, opposition to him was growing. His fight against the Bank of the United States and federal funds for internal improvements angered many nationalists allied with Henry Clay and John Quincy Adams. In addition, his willingness to lower the tariff to ease the pressure on the South angered New England business interests represented by Daniel Webster. At the same time, Jackson's gruff treatment of South Carolina also aroused opposition throughout the South.

These anti-Jackson forces, despite their differing regions and interests, formed a political alliance in the early 1830s that became known as the **Whig Party**. The Whigs derived their name from the British party that traditionally opposed royal tyranny. Jackson's intimidating methods and the manner in which he dictated his policies to Congress and his cabinet seemed to his opponents to have the appearances of monarchy. The Whigs dubbed the so-called people's president "King Andrew the First" and insisted that he did not have a monopoly on the common man's support.

Besides being anti-Jackson, the Whigs were also a nationalist party. They sought to breathe new life into Clay's American System. Whig emphasis on optimism and opportunity had a national appeal across the young republic and attracted a new crop of young leaders such as Abraham Lincoln, Horace Greeley, and William Seward. The Whig Party quickly demonstrated that it had a national organization as well as a nationalist platform when it competed in the presidential election in 1836.

An anti-Jackson cartoon

Van's Victory

Having won 98 seats in the House of Representatives in 1834, the upstart Whigs devised an ambitious strategy for the 1836 election. Due to their fledgling status, their strategy was to run several candidates, each strong in his own region, who would carry enough states to prevent Van Buren from gaining a majority of the electoral votes. The election would then go to the House of Representatives, where the Whigs hoped to be strong enough to maneuver one of their men into office. Daniel Webster from Massachusetts ran in New England; William Henry Harrison, popular Indian fighter from Ohio, ran in the West; and Tennessee's Hugh White ran in the South.

On the Democratic side, Martin Van Buren had been Jackson's hand-picked successor almost from the start. In the case of Jackson and Van Buren, it seemed true that opposites attract. Though both were born in humble circumstances, they grew up in different worlds. Jackson became a planter and an Indian fighter; Van Buren, a politician with polish. The 6'1" Jackson, with his shock of iron-gray hair, certainly contrasted with his balding, sandy-haired vice

Martin Van Buren

Whigs versus Democrats	
Whigs	**Democrats**
Followed the ideas of John Quincy Adams and the National Republicans; primary leader was Henry Clay	Followed the ideas of Thomas Jefferson and Andrew Jackson
Favored a mixed economy of commerce, manufacturing, and agriculture	Favored an economy dominated by agriculture
Supported a protective tariff to help developing American industries	Supported a small revenue tariff
Wanted federally funded internal improvements	Wanted internal improvements to be financed primarily by state and/or local governments
Supported a national bank	Opposed a national bank; favored state banks
Usually opposed territorial expansion	Usually supported territorial expansion
Were inclined to support rights of Indians	Were inclined to violate rights of Indians
Opposed the growing power of the president	Usually supported increased power of the president
Usually were pro-British	Usually were pro-French

president who was seven inches shorter. Although the two men differed in background, appearance, and temperament, Old Hickory owed the Little Magician a great deal for his political skills in winning elections. With general (though short-lived) prosperity at the time of the election, Jackson's endorsement was really the deciding vote in Van Buren's favor.

Even with Jackson's help, Van Buren won the popular vote by only 25,000 out of the 1.5 million votes cast. Van Buren became the last incumbent vice president to be elected president until 1989, when George Bush succeeded Ronald Reagan.

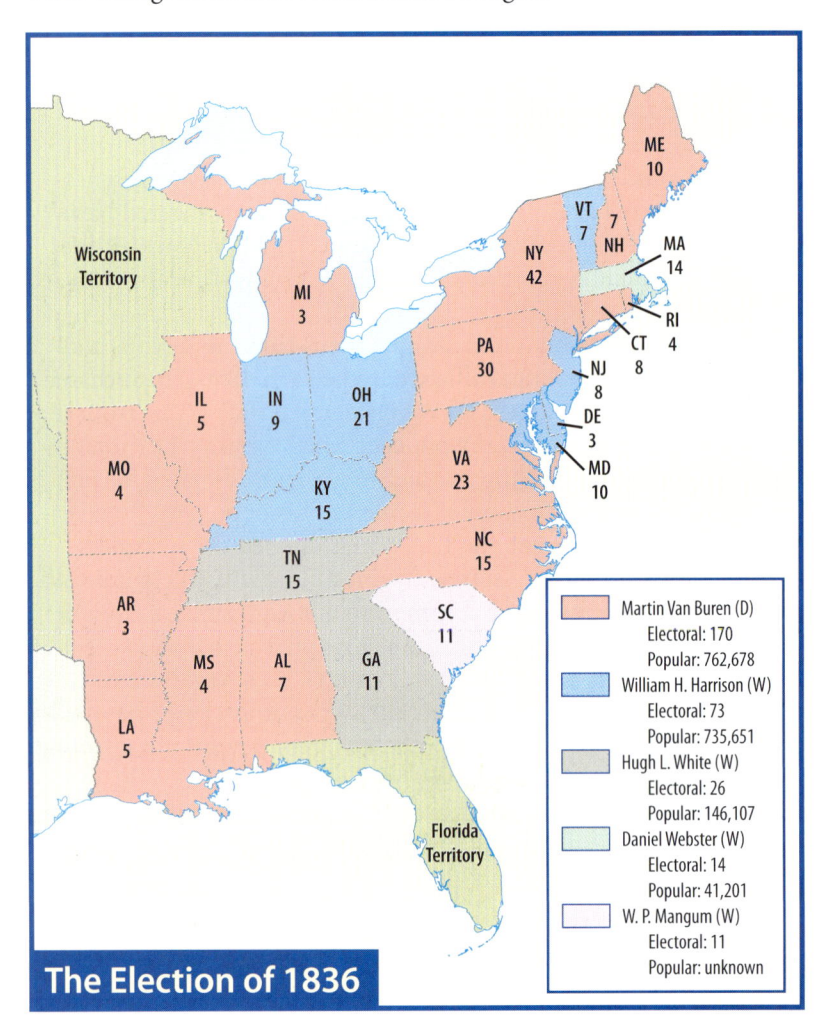

The Election of 1836

Martin Van Buren (D) Electoral: 170 Popular: 762,678
William H. Harrison (W) Electoral: 73 Popular: 735,651
Hugh L. White (W) Electoral: 26 Popular: 146,107
Daniel Webster (W) Electoral: 14 Popular: 41,201
W. P. Mangum (W) Electoral: 11 Popular: unknown

Hard Times

Just weeks after Van Buren took office, the economy collapsed, pulling the country into a deep five-year depression known as the **Panic of 1837**. Banks and businesses failed, and unemployment grew across the nation.

The economic hard times were caused by a number of factors. Jackson's economic policies, of course, had been a financial disaster. His malpractice worsened—though it did not cause—all the problems of the ailing economy. Wild, irresponsible practices among the state banks, as well as a massive wheat crop failure and the collapse of cotton prices, brought the economy to its knees. One historian argued that Jackson's shortsighted financial measures had "sown the wind, and Van Buren was to reap the whirlwind." When it came to the economy, the Little Magician had no more tricks. Blame for the depression would hinder his administration his entire term.

Van Buren had few solutions for the problems he had inherited, but he was determined at least to reorganize the government's financial structure. As a result Van Buren proposed an independent treasury to replace the state banks as a depository for federal funds. The treasury was to have only federal funds deposited in it, and only government employees were to manage it. Subtreasuries were planned for major cities throughout the nation. (Van Buren's proposal was often called the "subtreasury system.") This system would separate private banks from federal funds. The plan was proposed in 1837, but because of opposition, Congress did not pass it until 1840.

Log Cabin Campaign

The 1840 campaign was one of the most colorful in our nation's history, a remarkable fact considering the rather dull candidates that the two parties offered the country. The excitement came from the images and enthusiasm that the parties, particularly the Whigs, were able to generate.

The Democrats renominated President Van Buren and hoped to stretch General Jackson's popularity for yet another election. The Whigs realized that it would take more than the battered economy to turn the entrenched Democrats out of office. In 1840, Whigs reasoned, "If you can't beat them, learn from them." As a result they nominated an old Indian fighter, **William Henry Harrison**, the hero of the Battle of Tippecanoe nearly thirty years earlier. They added **John Tyler**, a states' rights Virginian and friend of Clay, as running mate to broaden the ticket's appeal. In the campaign to follow, the Whigs would outgeneral the general's party.

The Democrats thought bringing Harrison, who was nearing age 68, out of retirement was ludicrous. But the Whigs presented Harrison as a humble, yet heroic backwoodsman symbolized by a log cabin. He was in contrast to the aristocratic Van Buren who lived in the White House, or the "Palace," as the Whigs referred to it. Actually, Harrison was born in a mansion belonging to his prominent political family. His father, a Virginia plantation owner, was a signer of the Declaration of Independence and later a governor of the state. Van Buren, who was the son of a New York tavern keeper, hardly had a luxurious upbringing. But facts were not allowed to interfere with either party's campaign.

Torch-light parades, log cabin floats, and quantities of hard cider drew crowds for the Whigs. Throughout the country the Whigs were just as imaginative with their campaign slogans: "Tippecanoe and Tyler too!" and "Van, Van is a used-up man!" Songs often accompanied the noisy Whig parades. In this one "Tip" refers to Harrison, and "Mat" makes reference to Martin Van Buren.

> Old Tip he wears a homespun coat;
> He has no ruffled shirt-wirt-wirt.
> But Mat has the golden plate,
> And he's a little squirt-wirt-wirt.

This almanac cover celebrates the election of Harrison and Tyler. The beverage (hard cider) and the log cabin symbolized Harrison as a common man.

The Election of 1840

William H. Harrison (W)
Electoral: 234
Popular: 1,275,016

Martin Van Buren (D)
Electoral: 60
Popular: 1,129,102

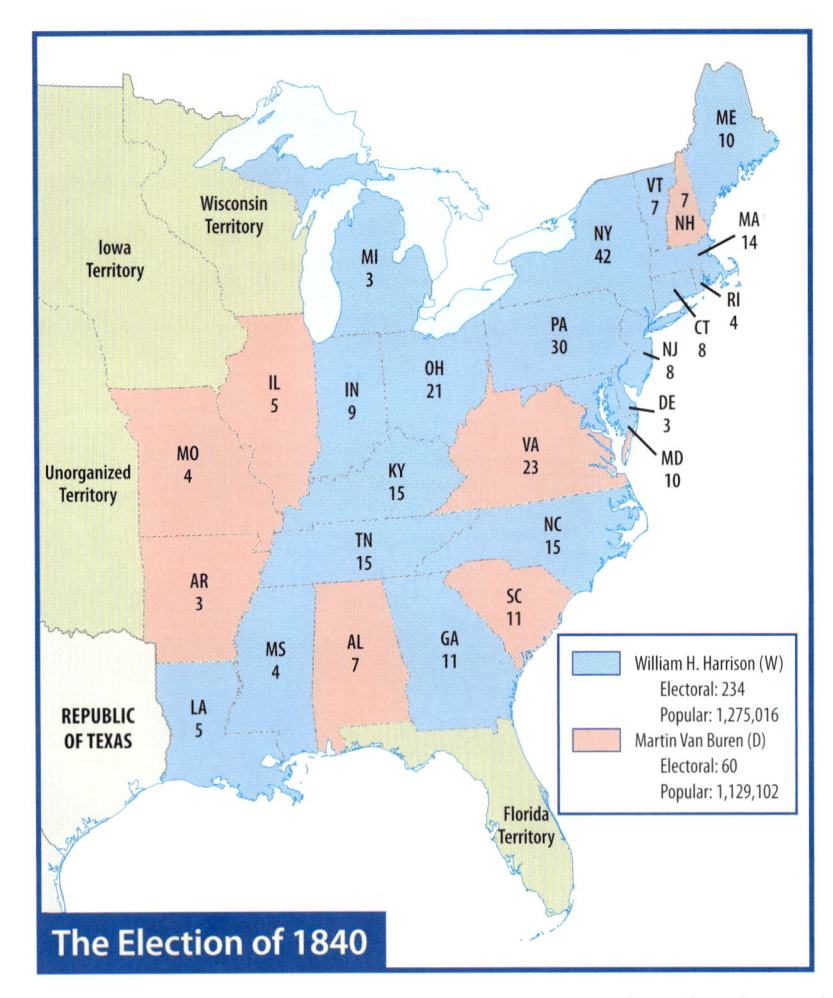

"OK"

The 1840 campaign did more than change the political landscape in America and shape the style of future campaigns; it also made an enduring contribution to our language. Van Buren's supporters rallied followers for "Old Kinderhook" (a reference to Van Buren's birthplace in Kinderhook, New York) by organizing O.K. Clubs. The Whigs declared that O.K. did not stand for Old Kinderhook but rather for "Oll Korrect" [all correct], a spelling the Whigs jokingly pinned on the backwoods Jackson, who was a poor speller. The Whigs then, ironically, took what began as a Democratic slogan and stamped it on their kegs of campaign cider.

The term "OK" may actually have originated and obtained its present meaning even before the 1840 election. However, it appears the election made it a popularly accepted term.

The Whigs rode their log cabin theme all the way to the White House, with an electoral landslide of 234 to 60.

Harrison's inauguration was certainly anticlimactic compared to his campaign. On that dreary, cold day of March 4, 1841, Old Tippecanoe stood on the east steps of the Capitol and read his speech for nearly two hours. He delivered it, the longest in American history, while wearing neither an overcoat or hat. He then rode through the streets in the inaugural parade. That evening he attended three balls.

The sixty-eight-year-old general was not well as it was, and in the days after he moved into the White House, he found the flood of office-seekers trying to take advantage of his success overwhelming. Besides, his wife, Anna, was back home in Ohio. She had not been well enough to join him on the difficult journey by steamboat, stagecoach, and train to Washington. As a result the White House was simply not in order. In the chill spring rain, he journeyed to the fish market and the butcher shop to stock the White House cupboards. A cold that had nagged him since his inaugural speech worsened. In that speech he had pointedly declared himself to be a one-term president; ironically, he was to be a one-month president. Stricken with pneumonia on April 1, Harrison died three days later, a bare month after taking office. He was the first president to die while in office.

The president's death stunned the nation. Harrison's larger-than-life campaign image suddenly turned mortal. The oldest president yet elected was now replaced by the youngest president yet to serve. The nation now faced its future under the leadership of Tyler, age 51, a man whom most had never expected would actually govern.

Section Review

1–3. Name three of Jackson's views that angered his opponents. These disagreements with him led them to form the Whig Party.

4–5. What was the Whig strategy in the presidential election of 1836? What was the result?

6–9. Name four causes of the Panic of 1837.

★ Assess the election of 1840. What do you think were the most important factors that led to Harrison's victory?

★ What important lesson does the vice presidency of John Tyler teach us about presidential elections?

CHAPTER 10 REVIEW

Making Connections

1. Why did many American leaders, such as James Madison, generally oppose federal funding of internal improvements?
2. Why did Missouri's application for statehood create controversy?
3. Why did Henry Clay favor John Quincy Adams over Andrew Jackson when the presidential election of 1824 went to the House of Representatives?
4. Why did the South oppose protective tariffs?

Developing History Skills

1. Place the following events from the nullification crisis in their proper chronological order from earliest to latest: (a) Senators Hayne and Webster debate nullification; (b) Henry Clay proposes the Compromise Tariff of 1833; (c) the Tariff of Abominations is passed; (d) President Jackson proposes the Force Bill; (e) Vice President Calhoun anonymously advocates the doctrine of nullification.
2. Why was the 1840 campaign called the "log cabin campaign"?

Thinking Critically

1. Review the toasts given by Jackson and Calhoun in 1830 (pp. 192–93). With whose statement do you most agree and why?
2–3. Do you think the Whig approach to the election of 1840 is a proper one? Why or why not?

Living as a Christian Citizen

1. Imagine that you are a Christian missionary living with the Cherokees. Write a letter to President Jackson urging him to respect the Cherokees' legal rights. Make sure to include reasons from a Christian perspective in your letter.
2. One of the religious controversies of this period was whether the post office should be open on Sunday. Write an editorial supporting one of the views.

People, Places, and Things to Remember

Andrew Jackson
Henry Clay
American System
tariff
protective tariff
Tariff of 1816
internal improvements
National Road
Panic of 1819
Missouri Compromise
caucus
John Quincy Adams
corrupt bargain
National Republicans
Democratic Party
Martin Van Buren
John C. Calhoun
spoils system
Kitchen Cabinet
Tariff of Abominations
nullification
Robert Y. Hayne
Daniel Webster
Force Bill
Compromise Tariff of 1833
Bank of the United States
Nicholas Biddle
third party
platform
national convention
pet banks
Indian removal policy
Black Hawk War
Seminole War
Sequoyah
Trail of Tears
Whig Party
Panic of 1837
William Henry Harrison
John Tyler

11 THE GROWTH OF AMERICAN SOCIETY (1789–1861)

> What hath God wrought!
>
> **Samuel F. B. Morse**
> May 24, 1844, first telegraph message

Camp meeting

Big Ideas

1. What was the impact of technology on the United States in the early nineteenth century?
2. What were some examples of early nineteenth-century American cultural achievements?
3. What role did slavery play in America?
4. What impact did American religion have on the United States in the early nineteenth century?

I. American Technology

II. American Culture

III. American Slavery

IV. American Religion

The face of the United States changed dramatically between 1789 and 1861. For example, transportation improved markedly. In 1789, George Washington traveled to his inauguration over muddy roads in a carriage; in 1861, Abraham Lincoln traveled to his over iron rails in a train. The speed of communication also increased at an incredible rate. In 1815, the United States defeated Britain at the Battle of New Orleans, unaware that the war had already ended with the Treaty of Ghent two weeks before. With the laying of the transatlantic telegraph cable in 1858, however, the time for such communications was reduced from weeks to minutes. In spite of these improvements, slavery remained a burden on the nation's conscience and became a cornerstone for reformers. At the same time the religious face of the nation changed too. From a spiritual decline after the Revolutionary War, the country soared to new spiritual heights through two major nationwide revivals. The era from 1789 to 1861 was one of remarkable cultural growth for the United States—technologically, intellectually, and spiritually.

I. American Technology

Manufacturing and Industry

The history of American manufacturing and industry is basically the history of inventions and applications of processes. But it is also the history of the people who devised the inventions and developed the processes. American industry is more than the story of machines; it is the story of the creative men and women behind the machines and the free-market economy that made those advances possible.

Textiles

In 1789, Great Britain was the world's leader in manufacturing, and the British intended to keep it that way. The British government carefully guarded not only all machinery relating to Britain's textile industry but also the blueprints for the machinery. Laws prevented skilled workers in the textile industry from emigrating. But that did not deter **Samuel Slater**. Although a successful apprentice in an English textile mill, Slater saw greater economic opportunities

Guiding Questions

1. How did manufacturing and agriculture in the United States develop during the early nineteenth century?
2. What types of improvements in transportation in the United States occurred during the early nineteenth century?
3. What kinds of changes did technology bring to American culture?

Old Slater Mill in Pawtucket, Rhode Island

for himself in America. Slater carefully memorized the construction of the textile machines, disguised himself as a farm hand, and escaped to the United States in 1789.

In Providence, Rhode Island, Slater—working entirely from memory—constructed an English-style mill with the financial support of American investors. This mill proved to be the first of a series of mills that sprouted across New England. The region, with its numerous streams and rivers to drive the water wheels used to power the machinery, was a natural site for the textile industry. The factory system was critical in the establishment and growth of the fledgling American economy. It spread throughout New England and much of the North. Textiles became America's first major industry.

Interchangeable Parts

Slater's contribution in textile machinery was only one of several advances in American manufacturing. Perhaps the most important work was by **Eli Whitney**. Although Whitney was better known in his own day for inventing the cotton gin (discussed later), his work with interchangeable parts was ultimately more important. In 1798, Whitney took an order to provide ten thousand rifles for the United States government. Until that time, guns, like most machinery, were handmade by craftsmen who individually made and fitted each part. Repairs required the craftsmen to make each replacement part by hand. Whitney designed a gun that was made of standardized, identical, machine-manufactured parts. When a piece broke, a new one could be easily inserted. Building on Whitney's process, every industry soon began to use standardized interchangeable parts.

The Colt .45 revolver

Patents and Inventors

American inventors benefited from the support of the United States government, which clearly saw the importance of developing industry. The government's most important help to industry was the passage of the first national patent law in 1790, which allowed inventors to secure patents for new devices and processes. As long as the patent was in effect, no one else could legally copy the inventor's work, and the inventor could reap the profits from a useful invention.

Spurred by the patent law and the promise of profits, inventors flooded the United States with new devices. Elias Howe, for example, perfected a mechanical sewing machine. With the improvements that Howe and others made, the sewing machine permitted the quicker, cheaper manufacture of clothing and other cloth products. Samuel Colt made his mark on the firearms industry. He patented and manufactured a "six-shooter," a pistol with a revolving cylinder which allowed a user to fire six times before reloading. Colt's sales started slowly, but his weapon became popular during the Mexican War when it became the standard sidearm of the United States Army.

Heavy Industry

Americans had dabbled in coal and iron production in colonial days, but before the War for Independence most iron products had to be imported from England. Much of the coal used in colonial days was bituminous, or "soft," coal, which smoked a great deal when burned and did not heat up enough to "smelt" (melt) iron ore properly so that the pure iron could be separated from waste materials. Americans soon discovered large deposits of anthracite, or "hard" coal, and iron ore in western Pennsylvania. With the cleaner-burning, higher-heating hard coal, American manufacturers could produce both more and better iron. As roads, canals, and railroads reached into the American interior, iron products also spread throughout the nation, and western Pennsylvania became a center of American heavy industry.

Most iron went into the growing railroad industry to provide rails and engines. Smaller amounts of iron went into producing items such as tools and cooking utensils. An efficient process of producing steel from iron was developed in the 1850s in Great Britain and spread to the United States. Although steel was much stronger and more durable than iron, its production did not become important to the United States until after the Civil War.

As America became more industrialized, towns grew up around the factories. Workers who came from the countryside and immigrated from Europe found employment in the factories. To meet the needs of these workers and their families, some entrepreneurs opened stores, inns, and other retail establishments. Others offered much-needed services, such as blacksmithing, carpentry, and saddle and harness making. Urbanization became a new way of life for many people.

Agriculture

The United States had been dominantly agrarian since its founding. The period from 1789 to 1861 saw important advances in agricultural technology. The applications of that technology led to an increasing division between the agricultural system of the South and that of the rest of the nation.

Agricultural Advances

As settlers streamed into the wilderness of the Northwest Territory and across the Mississippi River, they found an abundance of rich and fertile soil. The soil was so rich, in fact, that it produced more than farmers could easily harvest. The untapped potential of the frontier lands presented a challenge to the young nation.

The rich soil of the Northwest and of the plains on the west side of the Mississippi was sticky and covered with a tough sod. Several men experimented with iron plows that could cut through the sod and turn the soil over cleanly without letting it stick to the blades. Eventually, a blacksmith from Vermont named **John Deere** perfected the plow. He put an edge of steel over the iron blade of the plow, and his improved plow proved ideal for the new lands of the West. Reaping the harvest became simpler thanks to **Cyrus McCormick**. In 1834, McCormick received a patent for a reaping machine, a horse-drawn device that allowed one man to cut and stack ten to twelve acres of grain in a single day. Spurred by easterners who mocked his invention, McCormick moved his headquarters to Chicago, where his business made him a millionaire by 1860. A devout Christian, McCormick used his wealth to support Christian efforts such as seminaries and the work of Evangelist D. L. Moody.

Through these and other technical advances in agricultural machinery, American farm production grew at a tremendous rate.

In 1789, farmers had generally eked out only enough to feed their own families. But by 1861, the United States was producing nearly $2 billion worth of agricultural products each year.

In the Old Northwest, farmers (most of whom had migrated from New England and Pennsylvania) soon built an agricultural empire that included the production of corn, wheat, and cattle. When one combines the migration to the Old Northwest with the migration from the coastal and mid-Atlantic states to the South,

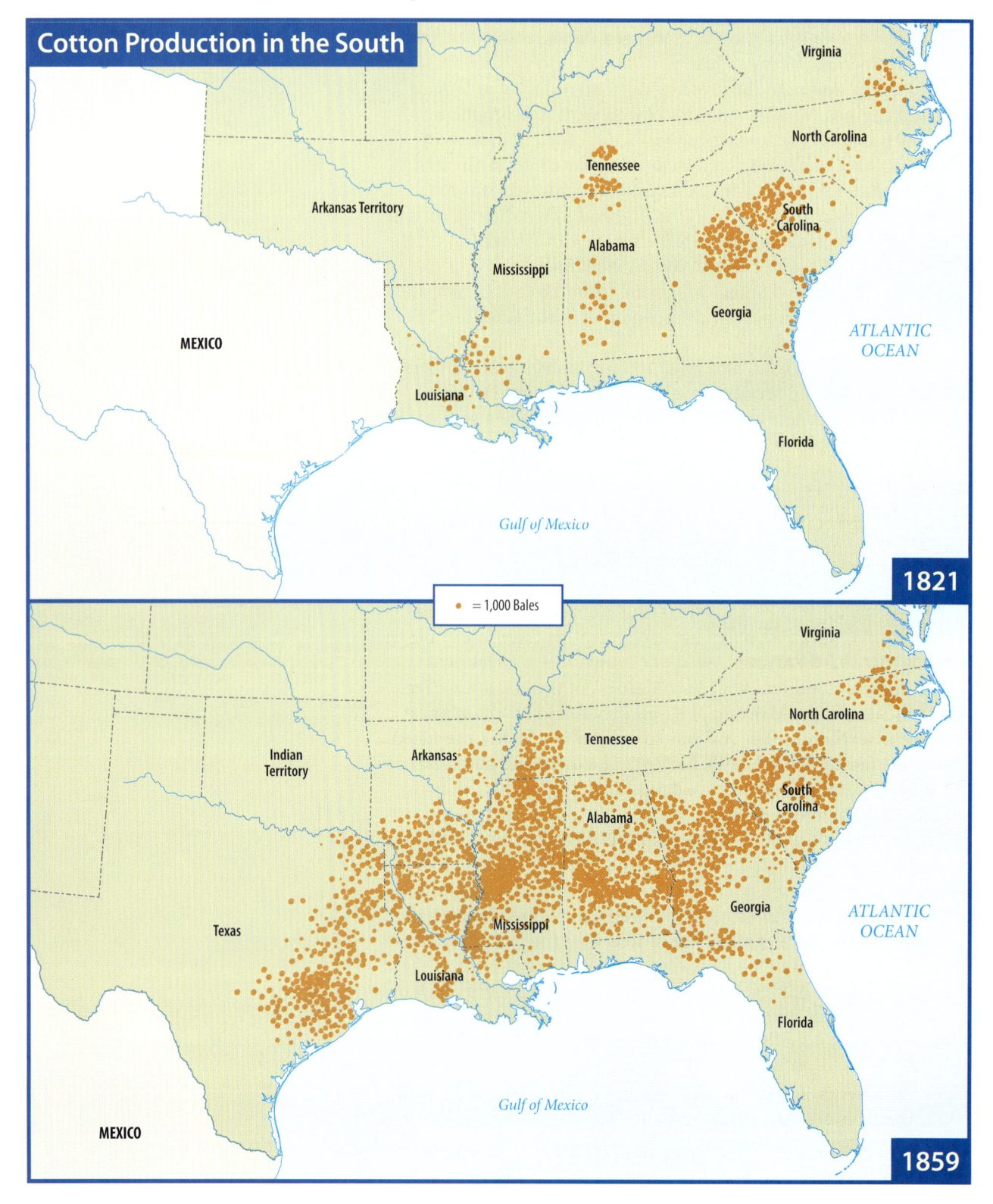

Cotton Production in the South

• = 1,000 Bales

1821

1859

which led to the development of the cotton kingdom, more than 40 percent of Americans lived west of the Appalachian Mountains by 1840.

The Cotton Kingdom

The South differed from the North and the West in that, although foodstuffs were important, the South did not produce the abundant grains of the West. Tobacco was important to some areas, particularly the states of the Upper South. Another cash crop, however, dominated the agriculture and economy of the region—cotton. "Cotton is King" was the motto of many southerners, and King Cotton placed its distinctive stamp on the culture of the South.

In 1789, cotton was a relatively unimportant crop. Most cotton grown in the South was a short-staple variety, the seeds of which clung to the cotton fibers. A slave had to work a whole day to clean just one pound of cotton. Eli Whitney changed that situation in 1793. While working as a tutor on a Georgia plantation, Whitney got the idea of making a machine to clean cotton. In just ten days, Whitney devised the **cotton gin**, a machine containing a series of metal teeth mounted on rollers that separated the cotton from the troublesome seeds. The cotton gin cleaned cotton fifty times faster than slaves working by hand.

Whitney's invention transformed the Southern economy. In response to the strong demand for cotton in the textile mills of the North and Europe, farmers in the Lower South rushed to plant cotton. In 1790, the United States produced two million pounds of cotton; in 1860, the nation produced more than two *billion* pounds—seven-eighths of the cotton produced in the world. Cotton was by far the most important export of the United States.

The growth of the cotton kingdom, however, widened the gap between the South on the one hand and the North and the West on the other. Cotton growing, for one thing, revitalized slavery. In 1790, slavery had seemed an increasingly unprofitable and dying institution. With the advent of the cotton gin, however, many planters thought that slavery was necessary again. The value of field hands soon doubled, and the South became increasingly sensitive to Northern attacks on slavery. The overwhelming value of cotton also hampered Southern industrial development. Most southerners simply saw no use in developing industry and transportation networks as the North was doing. King Cotton by itself seemed sufficient to supply the region's needs.

Section Review

1–2. What was America's first major industry? In what region of the nation did it center?

3–5. Name three of this era's important inventors and their respective inventions.

6. Why was the discovery of anthracite coal in western Pennsylvania important?

★ How did the invention of the cotton gin increase the differences between the South and the rest of the nation?

★ How did American development of industry and natural resources fulfill aspects of the Creation Mandate?

Transportation

Manufacturing products and growing crops was one matter; getting those products to market was another. The United States could not tame its frontier until it built a network of transportation and communication to unite the sections of the nation. The United States rose to that challenge during the period between the Revolution and the Civil War.

River Transportation

The oldest avenues in America were rivers and streams. Indians and early settlers used canoes on the numerous waterways

Transportation Routes in the First Half of the 19th Century

Legend:
- Roads—Early 1800s
- Major Canals by 1850
- Main Railroads by 1860

to penetrate the dense forests. Later settlers, needing some means of moving farm products to market, used flatboats and keelboats. These were sufficient for sailing downstream but were obviously of limited use in going up. The nation needed some kind of powered water transportation.

The answer to the problem was the steamboat. Several Americans had been trying since 1763 to develop a steam-powered ship. The idea was finally perfected by a talented, imaginative inventor from Philadelphia, **Robert Fulton**. In 1807, Fulton unveiled his steamboat, the *Clermont*, on the Hudson River. Critics called it "Fulton's Folly," but it successfully sailed upstream to Albany. The steamboat soon revolutionized river traffic. Goods and passengers could now move cheaply and easily through the interior wherever navigable rivers existed.

Roads

The rather obvious shortcoming of steamboats was that they could go only where rivers went. To link landlocked points, Americans built a system of roads across the countryside. Colonial roads, such as the Great Philadelphia Wagon Road (Chapter 3), had provided the earliest means of reaching the frontier. Braddock's Road, built for military purposes during the French and Indian War (Chapter 5), became an important commercial route. Pioneer Daniel Boone blazed the Wilderness Road, which carried travelers from southern Virginia, through the Cumberland Gap and into Kentucky, all the way to the Ohio River. Branches of the Wilderness Road also led to Nashville, Tennessee, and into the Carolinas.

Early roads were obviously not modern superhighways. A good road had a surface of gravel. Many consisted of a series of boards laid side by side (plank roads) or logs. Roads made of logs were called corduroy roads because of their bumpy surface. Some roads were nothing more than dirt trails—or mud in wet weather. Most roads were built by private companies that paid for them by charging tolls (fees) for their use. Such roads were called toll roads or turnpikes.

Maintenance of roads was almost nonexistent. By the time the National Road reached Vandalia, Illinois, its eastern portions were already decaying. Nineteenth-century roads were helpful in facilitating transportation, but rapid economic expansion soon outstripped the road-making technology of the day.

Canals

The canal era began in 1817, when New York, at the urging of Governor DeWitt Clinton, began building a canal from Albany to Lake Erie. With the backbreaking labor required for the task, the idea of a 363-mile canal seemed, as Thomas Jefferson said, "little short of madness." At a cost of some $6 million, the canal was a gamble for the state. Critics called it "Clinton's Big Ditch." Yet the **Erie Canal** proved such a success that it had paid for itself in tolls in less than ten years. Furthermore, the cost of shipping goods plunged. Before

Robert Fulton

Road construction

The National Road

The most important early American road was the **National Road** (also known as the Cumberland Road because it originally began in Cumberland, Maryland), begun in 1811. Following roughly the same route as modern Interstate 70 and U.S. Highway 40, the National Road eventually linked Baltimore to Vandalia, Illinois. The road was a major transportation route for early settlers of the Old Northwest. It was also the first federal highway; the federal government had spent some $7 million on it by the time the road was finished in 1839.

Canals

Canals combined some of the best features of rivers and roads. Like rivers, canals permitted pioneers to use boats, a cheaper and generally faster mode of transport than wagons. A horse pulling a canal boat, for example, could pull fifty times more weight than it could pull in a wagon. Like roads but unlike rivers, a canal could be built practically wherever it was needed.

Canals had their shortcomings though. Most of them were in the North, for example, where winter freezes rendered them useless for months at a time. Also, they were expensive to build. By the 1840s, the "canal craze" was nearly over. Canals gave way to a new and better form of transportation: the railroad.

the canal opened, it cost twenty cents a pound to ship goods from Buffalo to New York City. After the canal opened, the price dropped to less than a penny a pound. In 1827, the governor of Georgia complained that wheat from upstate New York was selling more cheaply in Savannah than wheat from central Georgia.

The success story of the Erie Canal encouraged other efforts. The Wabash and Erie Canal in Indiana and the Miami and Erie Canal in Ohio connected Lake Erie to the Ohio River. The Illinois and Michigan Canal connected Lake Michigan to the Mississippi River by way of Chicago. By the 1830s, one could travel from New York City to New Orleans completely by inland waterways.

Railroads

Nineteenth-century American transportation climaxed with the development of the railroad, which combined the flexibility of canals and roads with the dependable power of steam. The first economically successful railroad in America was the **Baltimore & Ohio** (B & O) **Railroad**. Originally, the B & O consisted of horse-drawn carriages on metal rails. Inventor Peter Cooper believed that the line could develop a steam-driven engine, like the ones British companies were using. Working mostly with scrap metal, Cooper constructed the *Tom Thumb*. This small but powerful steam engine was well designed to handle the sharp curves and steep climbs of the B & O rail line. To display the engine's capabilities, Cooper agreed to run the *Tom Thumb* in a thirteen-mile race against a horse. Although the horse won narrowly because the engine had a mechanical problem, the future of American transportation was clearly with steam power. South Carolina's Charleston-to-Hamburg line opened in 1833, and its 137-mile length made it the longest line in the world. Other lines, usually local in service, grew around major cities.

Tom Thumb train

Several inventions smoothed the way for the growth of railroads. Iron rails replaced wooden ones covered with iron strips. A cowcatcher attached to the front of an engine reduced damage from collisions with animals. The perfecting of the steam engine rendered trains faster, safer, and more powerful. Most important of all, railroads, particularly in the North and the West, began using a standard gauge (width) of track of 4′8½″. The resulting ability of trains from different companies to use the same tracks became vitally important during the Civil War in linking the war efforts of the Northeast and the West. Virtually the only drawback to railroads was that they initially cost more to build than steamboats, canals, and roads.

The Growth of Railroads

In 1830, the United States contained a total of 32 miles of track. By 1860, more than 30,000 miles of track fanned out across the country, and more than 20,000 miles of that had been built since 1850. Formerly unimportant cities such as Chicago and Indianapolis became major centers of rail traffic. Chicago, for example, mushroomed from a population of about 4,000 in 1840 to more than 100,000 by 1860. By the time of the Civil War, railroads had become not only the nation's most important means of transportation but also a growing economic, social, and political force.

Sea Transportation

American sea trade on both the Atlantic and Pacific oceans boomed in the 1840s and 1850s as a result of one of the most beautiful inventions in transportation history. The clipper ship differed from earlier seagoing vessels. With its slender, streamlined hull and its hundreds of square feet of canvas sails, the clipper was one of the fastest sailing ships ever built, and those of Donald McKay of Boston were the fastest of all. McKay's *Lightning*, for example, set a record by sailing 436 miles in a single day. From 1845 to 1860, the United States carried more sea trade than any other nation.

The clipper ship eventually fell victim to another technological advance, the steamship. At first, steam power was impractical for oceangoing vessels. They could not carry enough coal to fuel their engines for a long ocean voyage. Improvements in engine design, however, soon enabled the steamship to replace the clipper. Steam gave ships a constant source of power, one not dependent on winds and currents. Steamships were bigger and could carry more cargo. By the time of the Civil War, the British had retaken the lead in sea trade. The reign of America's clipper ships was glorious but brief.

Communication

The telegraph was the invention of **Samuel F. B. Morse**, a talented painter who studied under the famous Benjamin West in England. While he was in England, Morse's contacts with British evangelicals led to his conversion to Christ. Also while in Europe, Morse became interested in the semaphore communications system in France. The semaphore system worked by using flags to send signals from one location to another. Morse got the idea of using electricity to carry messages over wire much more quickly and over longer distances than semaphore.

Morse spent several years developing his system. A series of tests of his method impressed Congress enough to motivate members to appropriate $30,000 for constructing a model telegraph system. Stringing wire on poles from Baltimore to Washington, D.C., Morse sent the first intercity telegraph message on May 24, 1844, before a group of important political leaders in the United States Capitol. Appropriately, the first message was a Bible verse: "What hath God wrought!" (Num. 23:23). Soon telegraph lines stretched all across the United States. People living hundreds of miles apart could now communicate almost instantly. In 1858, the first successful transatlantic cable was laid between North America and the British Isles. A message between the United States and Britain would have taken weeks to deliver in 1789 when George Washington became the nation's first president. Now it was a matter of minutes. Perhaps no improvement better symbolizes the rapid changes produced by technology than this linking of continents.

The Pony Express

As fast as travel became in the period between the Revolution and the Civil War, communication became even faster. One attempt to improve communication was colorful but short-lived, and it became one of the symbols of westward movement. William Russell established the Pony Express in 1860. With a stable of 500 horses and a series of 190 stations stretching from Missouri to California, Russell promised to carry mail across the continent in the shortest possible time. A series of riders working in relays carried the mail from St. Joseph, Missouri, to San Francisco in ten to twelve days. However, the company went broke in 1861, a victim of the most important communications invention of the era, the telegraph.

Section Review

1–2. Name two methods of surfacing roads in the nineteenth century.

3. What was America's most important method of transportation by 1861?

4. What was the first economically successful railroad in America?

★ What are the advantages of government-funded roads, canals, or railroads? What are the disadvantages? What role does private business play in such projects?

Guiding Questions

1. What were the leading reform movements and artistic schools in the United States during the early nineteenth century?
2. What were the major characteristics of early nineteenth-century American culture?

II. American Culture

Balancing the economic and technological side of American life was the cultural side. American expansion in technology was matched by an expansion in art and thought. Most Americans may have thought of themselves primarily as "doers" in that era, but there were also accomplished thinkers. American achievements in art, literature, and reform were just as important as the nation's technological advances.

Reform

Paralleling American efforts to improve technology were efforts to improve society. Reform movements, attempts to eliminate evils in society, blossomed and flourished in the first half of the nineteenth century. Most of the reformers were religiously inspired; some were guided by simple humanitarian ideals. All believed that glaring evils in America should—and could—be rooted out. Many freedoms and advantages that we enjoy today resulted from the efforts of nineteenth-century reformers.

Education

Two important trends developed in the reform of American education during this period: the growth of both public education and teacher education. Most schooling since colonial days had been a private matter. Children often snatched a few months of training, usually during the winter when farm work eased, to learn the "three Rs" from someone in their church or community.

Yet despite its sporadic nature, private education was remarkably successful. The 1840 census reported that 78 percent of the entire population was able to read and write and that nine of ten whites could read and write. Despite America's having possibly the highest literacy rate in the world, a movement for change was afoot, beginning in the 1830s. Reformers argued that the states should assume a larger role in schooling their young citizens to help ensure that the rising generation of voters could make informed decisions.

One of the leading reformers in the drive for public education was **Horace Mann**. As head of the Massachusetts Board of Education, Mann brought a crusader's zeal to the task. He believed that people could find deliverance from ignorance and social problems through sound moral education. After Mann had been at his post for eleven years, every child in the state could go to school for six months out of the year, fifty new high schools had been built, and teachers' salaries increased by half. Massachusetts became a model for public education to the rest of the country.

In addition, Mann led a growing movement to train teachers. Previously, teaching was generally viewed as something a law student or seminary student did to earn money before entering his profession. But teaching as a profession itself became an important part of educational reform. Teacher colleges—called "normal schools" because they offered a uniform curriculum—developed, and more trained women began to join the profession.

Unfortunately for Horace Mann, his energetic reforms were motivated by faulty reasons. As a young man he had rejected the orthodox Christian influence of his parents and pastor and drifted to liberal Unitarianism. He believed, in the words of a friend, "If we can but turn the wonderful energy of this people into a right channel, what a new heaven and earth might be realized among us."

Sylvester Graham

One of the most eccentric reformers of the era was Presbyterian clergyman Sylvester Graham. Graham followed a strict vegetarian diet that excluded not only meat but also ketchup and mustard (as potential causes of insanity). He set up special food stores in which only healthful "Graham foods" were available. He also recommended soaking one's head in cold water as a cure for headaches. Among those who followed his teachings were Bronson Alcott (father of Louisa May Alcott, the author of *Little Women*), Joseph Smith (founder of Mormonism), and Evangelist Charles Finney. Today Graham is mainly known through "graham" (whole-wheat) flour and products made from such flour, notably graham crackers.

Noah Webster

One important Christian figure in early American education was Noah Webster. More than 100 million copies of his *American Spelling Book* (1782, commonly known as the "Blue-Backed Speller") were sold. He later published a self-study grammar book and a reader.

Webster is also known for *An American Dictionary of the English Language* (1828). In his dictionary, Webster frequently cited Bible passages to illustrate the meanings of words, and he emphasized the early American ideals of individual liberty and responsibility. His dictionary has remained the model for American dictionaries.

Although he was a lifelong churchgoer, Webster was not converted until the age of fifty, during the Second Great Awakening.

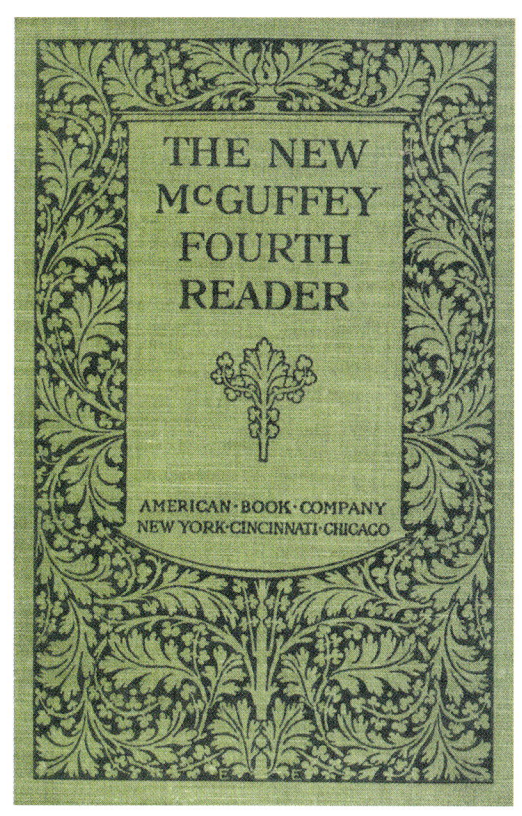

McGuffey Reader

In aiming for the head, however, Mann missed the heart. The belief that ignorance is the greatest evil misdiagnoses man's sinful nature. As the apostle Paul reminded Titus, "Unto them that are defiled and unbelieving is nothing pure; but even their mind and conscience is defiled" (Titus 1:15). Only Christ can provide deliverance as He cleanses the heart and mind through salvation.

Another person who saw the importance of the public education movement was a Christian who also realized its potential for the gospel—**William H. McGuffey**. In a series of elementary reading books, McGuffey taught generations of Americans rules for living as well as rules for grammar. By the beginning of the twentieth century, 120 million copies of his *Eclectic Readers* had been sold. McGuffey believed that biblical values had a natural and necessary role for shaping character in the classroom, and his work was enormously successful.

Prohibition

Alcohol was another social evil that reformers attacked. The problem of drunkenness had been long recognized, but efforts to reduce drinking had achieved only limited success. Reformers eventually replaced their call for temperance, or moderate drinking, with a call for the outright prohibition, or banning, of the sale and consumption of alcohol. Support for prohibition was widespread. A growing number of Christians supported temperance or prohibition as a moral principle. Social reformers supported prohibition because of the suffering that drunkenness brought to drinkers, their families, and society generally. Employers supported prohibition because drunkenness affected production and absence rates. The movement scored its first major victory in 1846 when Maine voted for statewide prohibition. The Prohibition movement's greatest success came in the early twentieth century with the passage of the Eighteenth Amendment (see Chapter 18).

Women's Rights

As demonstrated by the work of Dorothea Dix, many of the leading advocates of reform in the first half of the nineteenth century were women. In the Prohibition and abolition movements particularly, women were both numerous and active. Some reformers resented such "unladylike" activity. An antislavery convention

Dorothea Dix, Reformer in Mental Health

One of the most important reformers of the era was a quiet schoolteacher and writer, Dorothea Dix. As the head of a young women's school and author of children's books, she seemed an unlikely reformer. When she began teaching a Sunday school class in a Massachusetts prison, however, Dix was appalled to find four mentally ill persons imprisoned there. They had been thrown into prison by officials who did not know what else to do with them. Secretly, she visited numerous prisons and insane asylums to get firsthand information about conditions there. Appalled by what she found, Dix wrote and lectured, attempting to inform the public about the situation. Through her efforts, legislatures in several eastern states voted to improve the sanitary conditions and treatment of inmates in asylums.

in London, for example, refused to seat women delegates simply because of their gender. That rejection, combined with activism in other fields, led naturally to agitation for women's rights, notably women's suffrage (the right to vote). In 1848, a number of women reformers held a convention in Seneca Falls, New York, in which they passed resolutions calling for equal rights for women. Some of these resolutions could be supported by Christian women, such as woman's suffrage or the right to own property. But some leaders of the Seneca Falls Convention were also hostile to Scripture and supported resolutions that rejected the Bible's limitation of the pastoral office to men as well as the husband's leadership role in the home. The Seneca Falls Convention is now commonly regarded as the birth of the modern women's rights movement.

Utopian Reformers

Most reformers focused on a single major problem in society, such as prison reform or alcohol, and aimed at eliminating the problem throughout society. **Utopian reformers**, on the other hand, sought to establish small, perfect communities that would serve as models for the reform of society at large. (A utopia is an ideally perfect place. The word *utopia* means literally "nowhere," implying that there is no such thing as a true utopia on the earth.) Some of these reformers operated from religious motives. The Harmony Society, also known as the Rappites after their leader, George Rapp, founded a religiously based community in Harmonie, Indiana, in 1815. The Harmony Society established a society based on the idea of mutual helpfulness and support. (They also practiced celibacy, the abstaining from all sexual relations, a belief which limited their growth and eventually caused the group to die out.)

Other utopians operated from secular, rationalistic motives. British reformer **Robert Owen** purchased Harmonie from the Rappites in 1825. Renaming it New Harmony, Owen sought to establish a perfect society based on common ownership of property. After two years of internal fighting and a loss of $200,000, Owen abandoned the New Harmony project.

Another group that tried to develop utopian societies was the transcendentalists. They taught a liberal, unbiblical philosophy known as transcendentalism, which arose from Unitarianism (discussed later in this chapter). Perhaps their best-known attempt at developing a utopian society was Brook Farm, which was an experiment in communal living based on the idea that man could transcend feelings by coming into harmony with his inner being. Like all other utopian experiments, it was a failure.

Transcendentalism was primarily the creation of writer and lecturer Ralph Waldo Emerson. A graduate of Harvard, Emerson entered the Unitarian ministry but found even liberal Unitarianism too confining. He developed his own optimistic, man-centered "faith." Like Unitarianism, transcendentalism denied the miraculous, but it went even further in its teachings. Basically, it put man in the place of God. Emerson taught that man was essentially good and ultimately perfectible. He rejected the Christian view of God and taught instead that everything is part of God and that God dwells within every person. Emerson denied, as he put it, a faith "*in* Christ" in favor of a faith "*like* Christ's," which Emerson said was "faith in man." Transcendentalists were never numerous, but they were influential. Among those influenced by transcendentalism were author Henry David Thoreau and poet Walt Whitman.

The utopian reformers, whether religious or secular, all ultimately failed because of their faulty view of the nature of man. Man's inherent sinfulness dooms any human attempt to build a perfect society on earth.

The Arts

Americans in the early nineteenth century did not pursue the fine arts with the same enthusiasm that they did the technological arts. For example, Samuel F. B. Morse was an accomplished painter, but he found it far easier to put bread on the table as an inventor. However, American painters, architects, musicians, and writers produced works that displayed remarkable talent. They produced works that copied European models less and were more distinctly American in nature. This period was the real beginning of truly *American* art.

Painting and Architecture

The period from the inauguration of George Washington to that of Andrew Jackson is usually called the era of the Federalist style in art. The Federalist approach more or less duplicated the neoclassical style of Europe. It emphasized balance, emotional restraint, and a respect for the artistic styles of ancient Greece and Rome. Federalist art borrowed heavily from European models. **Benjamin West**, America's first great painter, was really more English than American, although he often painted New World subjects. He was born in Pennsylvania, but he studied in Europe and eventually settled in England. Yet he continued to influence American painting through his teaching of leading American artists.

Death of General Wolfe. Historical paintings were popular in Europe at this time, but this painting felt more American because it was of a contemporary event in North America.

Several of West's students came to dominate American art. One was **Gilbert Stuart**, one of the young nation's finest portrait painters. He is best known for his different portraits of George Washington, especially his "unfinished" portrait which appears on the $1 bill. Possibly the greatest of the Federalist artists was **John Trumbull**, another student of West's. Trumbull, in fact, specialized in the realistic historical paintings that West had pioneered.

After the rise of Jacksonian democracy, the emphasis of American art began to shift. The formal portraits of the Federalist era gave way to casual portrayals of the common man in everyday life. No one surpassed the self-described "thorough democrat" George Caleb Bingham in drawing the common man. His *Stump Speaking* and *The County Election*, for example, captured the boisterous, sometimes crude, but always lively activity of American politicking. Carrying the love of American beauty even further was the so-called Hudson River school of painters. These artists specialized in

Washington's portrait

Thomas Cole landscape

Unfinished Capitol building

Emerson—Self-Reliance
Why drag about this corpse of your memory, lest you contradict [what] you have stated in this or that public place? ... A foolish consistency is the hobgoblin of little minds, adored by little statesmen and philosophers and divines [theologians]. With consistency a great soul has simply nothing to do.

Whitman's Romantic Beliefs
Whitman expressed his belief in the nobility, unity, and brotherhood of man in his "Song of Myself":
I celebrate myself, and sing myself.
And what I assume you shall assume.
For every atom belonging to me as good belongs to you.

landscapes, capturing the land in its serene and majestic beauty. **Thomas Cole** became one of the best-known painters of the Hudson River school. His landscapes captured the beauty and sublimity of nature and subtley minimized the role of man in contrast with its majesty.

Federalist architecture also borrowed from ancient classical civilizations. The Greek revival recreated the columns and porticos of ancient Greek and Roman buildings. Charles Bulfinch, an early American architect, was so eager to further classical styles that he even drew architectural designs free of charge to encourage people to build in the Federalist style. Both Bulfinch and another American architect, Benjamin Henry Latrobe, worked at different times on the design of America's most famous Federalist-style building, the United States Capitol. Republican president and amateur architect Thomas Jefferson was a proponent of the Federalist style. Jefferson thought that Greece, the great example of ancient democracy, and Rome, the great example of ancient republicanism, provided ideal models for America's young democratic republic. Among Jefferson's designs were his home in Virginia (known as Monticello), the Virginia state capitol, and the University of Virginia rotunda.

Literature

America's most lasting contribution in culture during this era probably came in the field of literature. Although some American writers had achieved a degree of success in the colonial period, the first great age of American literature began with the romantic movement (1820–65). Romanticism rejected the balanced unemotionalism of the Federalist and neoclassical styles. Instead romanticism emphasized the emotional, the colorful, and the imaginative. Furthermore, this style placed greater stress on the love of nature and on the individual person rather than on society. (The painters of the Hudson River school, for example, were romantic in their focus on portraying nature.)

The first American writer to gain fame outside America was novelist **James Fenimore Cooper**. His Leatherstocking Tales, one of which was *The Last of the Mohicans*, created an exaggeratedly romantic view of life on the American frontier. Although Cooper's works sound dated today, his novels paved the way for later writers. Washington Irving rose to fame with *Knickerbocker's History of New York*, a comic fictional history of Dutch New York. Through his later stories, such as "Rip Van Winkle" and "The Legend of Sleepy Hollow," Irving helped put a distinctively American twist on the increasingly popular short story format.

Romanticism's central belief in the goodness—or even godhood—of man and the glory of nature, as expounded by **Ralph Waldo Emerson** in his works *Nature* and *Self-Reliance*, drew both supporters and critics. Essayist Henry David Thoreau, author of *Walden*, and poet Walt Whitman, in his work *Leaves of Grass*, both celebrated the glory and nobility of man.

Other romantics attacked the idea of man's inherent goodness. **Nathaniel Hawthorne**, for example, realized the truth of man's depravity. *The Scarlet Letter*, perhaps his finest work, attempts to deal with the problem of sin and its effects, but the novel criticizes what Hawthorne considered the narrow, hypocritical views of Puritanism. Edgar Allan Poe delved even deeper into the dark, tortured depths of man's soul in stories such as "The Tell-Tale Heart" and poems such as "The Raven." In the process, Poe became the master short-story writer of America before the Civil War.

Music

American music from 1789 to 1861 probably represents the character of American culture better than any of the other arts. In Europe, this was the period of great classical composers such as Beethoven. America had no such musical giants. Instead, popular music dominated the United States. America's most important composer of the period was **Stephen Foster**. Foster wrote lyrical ballads such as "I Dream of Jeannie with the Light Brown Hair" (written for his wife) and spirited songs about the South such as "Camptown Races," "Oh, Susanna," and "My Old Kentucky Home" (although Foster had never even visited the South).

Another great composer of the time represented the importance of religious faith to the era. Hymnwriter **Lowell Mason** published several popular hymnbooks and composed the tunes for such hymns as "Nearer, My God, to Thee" and "My Faith Looks Up to Thee." Mason constantly sought to introduce classical European ideals into American hymn music. He arranged his tune for Isaac Watts's "When I Survey the Wondrous Cross," for example, from a medieval Gregorian chant. Mason was also a leading promoter of music education, particularly the teaching of music in public schools.

Stephen Foster

Newspapers and Magazines
The fine arts were not the only examples of American cultural growth. Rising literacy rates caused by educational improvements created a market for popular literature: newspapers and magazines. Improvements in technology not only allowed printers to publish a greater number of materials but also enabled them to produce materials more quickly and more cheaply.

Section Review

1–2. What were the two important trends in American education in the early 1800s?

3. What is the difference between temperance and prohibition?

4. How did utopian reformers differ from other reformers?

★ Critique the excerpt of Ralph Waldo Emerson in the margin box on p. 216.

★ What is at the heart of the failure of every attempted utopian society?

III. American Slavery

One of the most offensive features of American society between the Revolutionary War and the Civil War was the existence of slavery. By 1775, the North American colonies held five hundred thousand slaves, of whom two hundred thousand lived in Virginia and one hundred thousand in South Carolina.

However, slavery was a national—not just a Southern—problem. Although fewer slaves were held in the North, regions such as New England also thrived economically as a result of slavery. Eight of the top ten names on the Newport, Rhode Island, tax rolls were traders in molasses, rum, and slaves. New York City became the

Guiding Question

1. How did Americans resist s
2. Who were leading abolitio America?
3. What does the Bible tea

hub of the slave trade, even after that trade was made illegal. Massachusetts textile mills wove cloth from cotton grown by Southern slaves. And Connecticut became a leader in the ivory trade, which often involved slave labor in Africa. In the South, as cotton became an important cash crop, slavery became an increasingly important part of this region's economy.

Following the Revolutionary War, more Americans looked on slavery as inconsistent with the principles of the Declaration of Independence with its claim that liberty is an "inalienable right" granted by the Creator. A declining number of Americans defended slavery as good and necessary.

Life of Slaves in America

Work

Work for the slave varied according to the kind of crops grown and the time of the year. Most slaves worked in the fields caring for cotton or tobacco. Men and women would work plowing, planting, and tending the fields. Harvest time was especially grueling. It required long hours of back-breaking work. At other times slaves would care for animals, repair fences, clear land for fields, and repair equipment. Some slaves worked in the house, cooking or caring for the master's children.

Depending on the temperament of the master, slaves worked under the threat of a whip, although whipping a slave to the point of death or incapacitation was rare. Slaves were considered too valuable to be treated this way, and some slave-owners wished to see themselves as a parent to their slaves. Even so, whipping of slaves was common for some masters.

Family and Personal Life

Though many details of the slaves' lives were controlled for them, slaves did have personal lives. Slaves developed songs and stories that could be shared as they worked or at the end of a long day. Family was very important to the slaves. Although slave marriage was not recognized or protected by law, slaves married and established families. However, slave families were markedly different from free families. Rather than depending on fathers or husbands, the slaves had to depend on their owners to meet family needs.

Slaves from different masters who married were not even allowed to live together. They had to get permission to visit their spouses. If one of the slaves was a house slave, she would probably live in the master's house rather than with the other slaves and her husband. Mothers could not personally care for their children because of their labor in the fields or the master's house. So elderly slave women tended to the slave children until they were ten years old. At this age the children were often sent to work in the fields. Perhaps the greatest fear of a slave was to have a family member sold to another region. It was not unusual for a slave to be sold at least once in his lifetime.

Slave Responses

Many slaves made the bold move to run away and seek freedom. The "**Underground Railroad**" developed as a means of hiding fleeing slaves and leading them to safety and freedom in the North. This "railroad" consisted of a secret network of people who assisted the escaping slaves with temporary housing and food then "conducted" the slaves to the next point in their journey toward freedom.

Perhaps the most famous member of the Underground Railroad was **Harriet Tubman**. Born a slave in Maryland in 1822, Tubman suffered much abuse at the hands of her masters until her escape in 1849. She not only spoke at antislavery meetings but also made some thirteen trips to the South to help lead dozens of slaves to freedom, including many of her family members. During the Civil War she served as a scout and a spy for the Union forces.

In August of 1831, a slave and radical preacher named **Nat Turner** led a slave rebellion in Southampton County, Virginia. Up to sixty white people and perhaps a hundred black people died in the rebellion and the bloody repression that followed. Turner, along with other alleged leaders, was hanged. These revolts were rare, but nervous slaveholders often resorted to sleeping with a gun. Several states even made it illegal to teach slaves to read and write in order to diminish the possibility of slave revolts.

The Bible and Views of Slavery

The longer slavery persisted in the United States, the more Americans had to think about what to do about slavery. Various views developed, and because most Americans professed Christianity, the Bible played an important role in the debate over slavery.

Defenses of Slavery

Just after the Revolution many slave-owners themselves, men such as Thomas Jefferson, voiced a negative view of slavery. They thought that slavery eventually would and should die out. Yet as slavery became more and more important to the Southern economy and culture, men began to mount defenses of the South's "peculiar institution."

Many argued that the slave-holding South was more virtuous than the money-grubbing North. What is more, they argued that slavery was more moral than the "wage slavery" they claimed was occurring in northern manufacturing. There immigrants worked at dangerous jobs in dreadful working conditions for low wages, but Southerners argued that slaves were treated with paternal care by most masters in the South. This argument was made with little consideration of the degradation that treating adult men and women like children brings to them.

Others argued that slave-holding actually promoted virtue. A few of those who owned slaves had the leisure to pursue education and refinement of manners. They could afford to be hospitable and chivalrous. They concerned themselves with duty and honor rather than with merely acquiring money. Thus to attack slavery was seen by 1 or 2 percent of the southern population as an attack on their flourishing way of life.

Some defended slavery on religious grounds. They claimed that bringing uncivilized Africans to America and exposing them to Christianity for the good of their souls was moral. (Opponents of slavery argued that concern for African souls should have resulted in sending missionaries rather than taking slaves.) Many also justified slavery by pointing to the Bible. Abraham owned slaves, and God regulated but did not forbid slavery in Israel. Nor did Christ and the apostles abolish slavery. Paul even returned the runaway slave, Onesimus, to his master, Philemon. Nonetheless, even strong

Slavery and the Churches

American Christians differed widely on the issue of slavery. Many, almost entirely in the North, called slavery a sin and slave owners sinners. Others, almost entirely in the South, defended slavery as a "positive good" for the benefit of blacks and claimed that slavery was sanctioned by the Bible. Some, in both the North and the South, tried to straddle the issue.

But the nation could not avoid the issue, as several denominations discovered to their sorrow. Two of America's largest denominations—the Methodists and the Baptists—divided over slavery in 1844. In both cases, Southern members formed new denominations—the Methodist Episcopal Church South and the Southern Baptist Convention.

However, many denominations avoided schism over the slavery issue. For example, the Congregationalists—the majority of whom were in the North, mainly New England—were both antislavery and completely unified. Other denominations that avoided division, such as the Episcopal Church, usually did so by simply avoiding the issue as much as they could.

defenders of slavery admitted that the practice did not always live up to the defense. Baptist minister James Boyce worked to evangelize slaves, but there was opposition to this effort. Boyce, a defender of slavery, wrote "I feel that our sins as to this institution have cursed us,—that the negroes have not been cared for in their marital and religious relations as they should be; and I fear God is going to sweep it away."

Abolitionism

Abolitionists desired to see slavery swept away. **Abolitionism** was the movement to eliminate slavery immediately and entirely. Part of the motivation for abolitionism came from evangelical Christians as a result of the Second Great Awakening. A church in Oberlin, Ohio, was typical of many Northern churches when it resolved that "as Slavery is a Sin, no person shall be invited to preach or Minister to this church, or any Brother invited to commune who is a slaveholder." Quakers in particular had been leading advocates of abolition since colonial days.

But not all opponents to slavery were religious. Perhaps the most important and most militant abolitionist leader was **William Lloyd Garrison**. In 1831, he launched a newspaper, the *Liberator*, dedicated to attacking the moral evil of slavery. His methods could be extreme. He once denounced the Constitution as "a league with death, and a covenant with hell" because it did not condemn slavery. On another occasion he publicly burned a copy of the Constitution. He was convinced that the Bible was a proslavery book, so he rejected it entirely. In the pages of the *Liberator*, he reported every atrocity against slaves that he could find—including a few that were not true.

Garrison enraged many Southerners with his violent attacks on both slavery and those who owned slaves. He once called slaveholders the "meanest of thieves and the worst of robbers." Nor was Garrison particularly popular in the North. His uncompromising attacks on slavery offended both those who preferred gradual reform and those who cared little for any reform at all. Furthermore, some Northerners disliked Garrison's linking his attacks on slavery with attacks on discrimination against free black Americans in the North. The editor scathingly pointed out that African Americans in some states in the North were denied access to public schools or opportunities to serve as apprentices. In short, he noted that black Americans in the North were sometimes little better off than slaves in the South.

Women also played prominent roles in the abolitionist movement. Foremost among them were the Grimké sisters, originally from a slaveholding family in Charleston, South Carolina. Sarah and Angelina were born on the same day exactly thirteen years apart. They both left the South as adults and moved to Philadelphia, where they became active with the Quakers and abolitionism—Sarah as a writer and behind-the-scenes organizer and Angelina as a speaker. Angelina was the first woman to address the Massachusetts state legislature, promoting abolition. She married fellow abolitionist Theodore Weld.

Undismayed by opposition, abolitionists pressed their cause zealously. Several former slaves helped by writing and speaking of their experiences. **Frederick Douglass** was one of the most brilliant, most eloquent, and most radical. His understandably strong hatred of slavery caused him to make statements such as: "Slaveholders not only forfeit their right to liberty but to life itself."

Gradual Emancipation

Not all who opposed slavery supported abolitionism. They believed that the abolitionists did not look at the consequences of their actions. The abolitionists were right that slavery was a moral wrong and should be ended. But if it was ended by force in an unconstitutional manner, then later groups would act unconstitutionally if they had the power to do so. And they might not act in a righteous cause. Freeing the slaves immediately would create other problems. It would harm the economy for the whole nation. Slaves would have trouble finding jobs because they would not have been given skills to have good paying jobs. The bitterness over abolition would harm the freedmen by raising racial tensions. These tensions would mean that freedmen would face opposition in their efforts to better their lives.

Men such as John Quincy Adams, Henry Clay, and Abraham Lincoln initially favored emancipating the slaves gradually. This had been done successfully in Northern states after the Revolutionary War. Those who favored gradual emancipation offered several reasons for their view. Gradual emancipation would free the slaves over time without causing catastrophic economic problems for the slaveholders. It would also allow time to educate the slaves and train them with skills so they could support themselves. Henry Clay went so far as to propose the return of excess federal revenues to the states. He intended the funds to be used to help pay for the cost to slave states of emancipating the slaves. However, many abolitionists and slaveholders opposed the idea of gradual emancipation and it was abandoned.

Richard Allen

One instrument God used in reaching African Americans was a former slave himself—Richard Allen. Born in Pennsylvania, Allen was converted under the preaching of a Methodist in Delaware in 1777. Shortly thereafter, Allen's master allowed the young slave to purchase his freedom.

Allen chopped wood, worked in a brickyard, and delivered salt to make a living. He preached in the evenings and on Sundays. Allen became a circuit rider in New Jersey and Pennsylvania.

Allen enjoyed a fruitful ministry among African Americans in Philadelphia. Allen and his converts originally attended a white Methodist church in the city, but some members resented the increased numbers of black Christians in their services. In 1787, Allen and the other African attendees walked out and started their own church—the African Methodist Episcopal (AME) Church in Philadelphia. Bishop Francis Asbury dedicated the church in 1794, and he later ordained Allen. When several other black congregations expressed an interest in closer fellowship with Allen's church, they decided to form their own denomination, and Allen became their first bishop. Under his leadership, the denomination became one of the most effective means of reaching African Americans with the gospel before the Civil War.

The Bible and Slavery

Most Americans at this time professed to be Christians, and the Bible played an important role in public debate. Even those like Garrison, who rejected the Bible, reckoned with it in their discussion of slavery. It might seem at first that those who thought the Bible supported slavery had the better argument. Slavery was regulated and not prohibited in the Old Testament, and in the New Testament Paul tells slaves to submit to their masters.

However, this is only the case on a surface reading. Closer examination of the Bible reveals that it provides no support for American slavery. First, American slaveholders did not follow the Old Testament regulations on slavery. Daniel Coker, a minister in the African Methodist Episcopal Church, pointed out that God never commanded Israel to capture innocent people and ship them across the sea in such conditions that thousands were murdered by the ill treatment they received all for the purpose of making them slaves for their entire life and for the lives of their children. Indeed, Exodus 21:16 implies that those who participate in the slave trade should suffer the death penalty, for they steal a person's life. Further, slavery in the Old Testament was not based on race, and it was not typically life-long. It was primarily a way for indebted people to work off their debts. After six years of labor the debtor was to be freed and richly provided for by his master. The hope was that the former slave could have a fresh start on life apart from debt (Deut. 15:12–14). The only time that an Israelite slave could be held for life was if he asked to remain a slave because he loved the household he was in and because of the financial security it provided (Deut. 15:16–17). The Old Testament also provided numerous protections for slaves. If a slave ran away, he was not to be returned to his master (Deut. 23:15–16). The presumption was that a slave working off his debt under a righteous man would not run away. In the United States, however, great effort was undertaken to recover runaway slaves. Israelite slaves who were harmed were also freed, even if only so much as a tooth was lost (Ex. 21:26–27).

Second, those opposed to slavery often pointed to broad biblical principles that were contrary to the practice of American slavery. For instance, the whole law hangs on the commands to love God and to love one's neighbor as one's self (Matt. 22:36–40). Similarly, Jesus said the Old Testament Law could be summarized in the teaching "whatsoever ye would that men should do to you, do ye even so to them" (Matt. 7:12). An Israelite who bought the labor of an indebted Israelite, enabled him to work off his debts, and then provided him generously with the means to begin a new life might well have wished that someone would do the same for him if ever he fell into debts he could not pay. But no American slave owner would ever desire to be torn away from his family with the knowledge that he and his children would be slaves forever. Nor would he desire to be treated as though he were an inferior human being, fit only to work for another's financial advance. American slavery could not be reconciled with the great summaries of the Law.

Third, the New Testament's commands for slaves to submit to their masters was not an endorsement of Greco-Roman slavery. In the early centuries of the church, Christians were not socially powerful. They could not change the laws and customs of the Roman Empire. Many Christians were slaves. The Christian way of changing society has never been through rebellion. Christ set a different example for Christians (1 Pet. 2:18–23). Some might wonder why the apostles did not command Christian masters to set their slaves free immediately. The answer again rests in the command to love one's neighbor as one's self. Slaves in Greco-Roman culture existed at all different social levels. Some slaves were highly skilled teachers or respected managers in government or business while others were laborers. A blanket command without the reformation of the entire society could have been detrimental to some slaves. In one case Paul implied that a slave should be given his freedom (Philem. 1:16), whereas in other places he instructed Christian masters to treat their slaves as if they were not slaves. A Christian master could not think that he was any way superior to his slave, since there is no favoritism with God. Nor could a Christian master so much as threaten his slave, let alone mistreat him in any other way (Eph. 6:9).

If these New Testament practices were followed by those Christians who claimed the New Testament justified slavery, then all prejudice against black Americans would have of necessity ceased—including paternalism. All beatings and threatening would have been outlawed. And state laws would have given opportunity for every slave who wished to be freed to go free (1 Cor. 7:21; Matt. 7:12). In other words, the institution of slavery would have ceased. It was only by ignoring what the Bible actually said that some Americans were able to persuade themselves that the Bible justified this grievous sin.

Section Review

1. Who was the most important leader of the abolitionist movement?
2–3. Name two former slaves who became active in opposing slavery.
4–5. What two skills did some slave owners oppose being taught to slaves?
★ How did American slavery differ from the slavery that God permitted in Israel?
★ Why should Americans have concluded that the Bible condemned American slavery?

IV. American Religion

Religious life in America also expanded from 1789 to 1861. Some of the expansion was only numerical, not spiritual; a few of the religious movements of the era were sources of spiritual darkness instead of spiritual light. Many of the movements, however, seem to have been genuine expressions of the work of the Holy Spirit. Significantly, this period in American history began and ended with a sweeping national revival.

The Second Great Awakening

Shortly after the ratification of the Constitution, America experienced its second great revival of religion. The **Second Great Awakening** was longer and more complex in nature than the first. It touched different regions of the nation in different ways, and its effects reached even across the sea.

Guiding Questions

1. What was the background and course of the Second Great Awakening?
2. How did the teachings of major unorthodox religions in America differ from biblical doctrine?
3. What was the background and course of the Prayer Meeting Revival?

Deism

Revolutionary War veteran Ethan Allen wrote one of the first American defenses of deism in a crude, anti-Christian work titled *Reason: The Only Oracle of Man*. Thomas Paine, author of *Common Sense*, wrote a more polished—but no more orthodox—exposition of deism, *The Age of Reason*. Other American leaders, such as Thomas Jefferson and Benjamin Franklin, also embraced deism.

Francis Asbury

Background

Christianity faced many severe challenges after the War for Independence. **Deism** was the "faith" of several American leaders. Deists believed that reason rather than Scripture was the way men came to know God. God Himself created the world but rarely, if ever, became personally involved in its affairs. Deists denied the deity of Christ, the inspiration of the Bible, the reality of miracles, and any other belief that struck them as superstitious because they could not explain it by their own reason.

Besides this "intellectual religion," some Americans lacked any religion at all. For them, the pleasures of the day—drinking, gambling, and the like—were far more important than any kind of creed, Christian or otherwise. John Marshall observed sadly that the church was "too far gone ever to be revived."

But the situation was not all darkness and despair. One of the brightest spots for Christianity was the growth of American Methodism. The **Methodists** were followers of the teachings of English minister John Wesley. After his long and desperate struggle with a sense of guilt and sin, Wesley had been converted. He began to travel around Great Britain, preaching the need for conversion to Christ and holy living. The Methodists remained technically part of the Church of England until Wesley's death, but afterwards they became a separate denomination.

Methodism in America grew slowly at first, partly because of its association with Anglicanism and partly because of Wesley's opposition to the War for Independence. Later, however, it proved enormously successful at reaching all classes of society with the gospel, including both free blacks and slaves. Much of the credit for the denomination's growth must go to the Father of American Methodism, **Francis Asbury**. Sent from England in 1772, Asbury worked for years to establish Methodist congregations. He developed the most important institution of American Methodism, circuit riding. The United States was too vast and its population too scattered for Asbury to establish a minister in every community. Asbury therefore divided the land into sections, or circuits. One minister, called a "circuit rider," traveled on horseback from settlement to settlement throughout his assigned circuit, ministering to Christians and preaching to the lost. Facing the challenges of an untamed wilderness, Methodist circuit riders were tough men with tender hearts. Asbury himself traveled nearly three hundred thousand miles on horseback. On the frontier in particular, Methodists became some of the most important contributors to the awakening.

Revival in the East

The Second Great Awakening began in the East. There the revivals centered in the churches and colleges, where Christian zeal had lapsed into apathy and even open sin. Yale, founded in 1701 to train ministers, may be an example, as one minister wrote recalling his student days before the awakening:

> College was in a most ungodly state. The college church was almost extinct. Most of the students were skeptical, and rowdies were plenty. Wine and liquors were kept in many rooms; intemperance, profanity, gambling, and licentiousness were common.

Into this situation at Yale came **Timothy Dwight**, a grandson of Jonathan Edwards. Elected president of Yale in 1795, Dwight confronted the problem of a rebellious student body. He openly challenged all comers in public debates on the truths of the Christian faith. Dwight also preached a series of sermons in chapel on basic Christian theology. The fruit of Dwight's labors was a series of revivals in which at least a third of Yale's students were converted.

Revival in other schools and churches of the East followed the pattern of Yale. Order and restraint were the key characteristics to avoid excesses that had occurred in some instances during the First Great Awakening. The Second Great Awakening was characterized by the faithful work of local pastors and laymen rather than prominent leaders like Edwards and Whitefield. The awakening endured for sixty years and influenced the nation for several generations. The preaching was urgent in its message but calm in its tone. The spiritual fervor of the revivals in the East was deep but quiet, and the results were profound.

Revival in the West

On the frontier, the awakening appeared a little later and in a different form. The chief feature of the western revivals was the **camp meeting**, a series of religious services lasting several days and often held outdoors. Usually several preachers exhorted the crowds in simple but fiery gospel sermons. The camp meeting was originated by Presbyterian James McGready in Logan County, Kentucky. In 1800, McGready, three other Presbyterians, and a Methodist preacher held an outdoor Communion service to welcome new members into the church. During this and other services that followed, hearers began to profess a deep sense of their own sinfulness and to cry out for salvation. The results in Logan County proved so remarkable that other preachers began to hold camp meetings. Probably the most significant camp meeting was held at **Cane Ridge**, Kentucky, in 1801. Estimates of the attendance at Cane Ridge range from ten thousand to twenty-five thousand. This attendance was phenomenal, especially considering that nearby Lexington, the largest city in Kentucky at that time, had a population of only eighteen hundred people.

Camp meeting revivals contrasted markedly with the orderly and careful preaching of the revivals in the East. At an increasing number of meetings some of the hearers shook, jerked, jumped, ran, barked, and fell. While some physical responses were initially the outward manifestation of inward conviction, several preachers began to encourage these outward displays. This led to a split between those ministers who cautioned against excesses that distracted from the gospel message and those who believed that these physical responses were signs of God's favor. A number of preachers began counting how many people had fallen during the preaching in an attempt to measure God's work.

The western revivals brought about mixed results. Many people were converted by the preaching of the gospel, and their changed lives provided the evidence of conversion. On the other hand, the western revivals provided an opportunity for some to stress outward physical responses at the expense of true gospel preaching.

Foreign Missions

The effects of the Second Great Awakening reached beyond the shores of the United States. The first great American missions movement resulted from this revival. Among the colleges in the East that were touched by the revival was Williams College in

Massachusetts. In 1806 a group of students from the college was holding an outdoor prayer meeting when a fierce thunderstorm blew in. Taking shelter under a nearby haystack, the little group began to discuss the need to carry the gospel throughout the world. One member of that group, Samuel Mills, decided to fulfill that dream and helped establish the American Board of Commissioners for Foreign Missions (ABCFM), America's first foreign mission board.

The ABCFM, a Congregationalist organization, sent many missionaries throughout the world, but it was not the only American mission board for long. **Adoniram Judson** and Luther Rice went to India in 1812 under the ABCFM. On the way, however, Judson and Rice decided that their theological views were more Baptist than Congregationalist. Judson remained in Asia while Rice returned to the United States to raise some support among Baptists. Judson eventually moved to Burma, where his faithful translation work and preaching made him a hero of the American missions movement. Rice helped start a Baptist mission organization that became a major force in sending missionaries overseas. Through the support of men such as Mills and Rice and through the labors of missionaries such as Judson, thousands of lost souls throughout the world came to salvation in Jesus Christ.

Charles Finney and the "New Measures"

In the 1820s, as the first wave of revivals began to subside, **Charles Finney** tried to perpetuate the revivals with innovative methods. While practicing law in upstate New York, Finney professed conversion in 1821 during a revival. After informal study with a Presbyterian pastor, Finney began preaching in small towns across New York. Reports of numerous dramatic conversions increased Finney's reputation. By the 1830s, he was preaching to huge crowds in New York City and was one of America's leading evangelists.

Finney admitted his success was not due to the miraculous working of God's Spirit. Revival, according to Finney, "is a purely philosophical result of the right use of the constituted means." He developed what others dubbed "New Measures," new and unusual methods for conducting revivals. Finney always kept an "anxious bench" in his meetings, reserved seats for sinners who sensed a conviction of sin. He also prayed publicly by name for those known to be sinners. Finney held "protracted meetings," services held daily for up to several weeks in one location. He combined elements of both eastern and western revivals. Finney insisted on order and restraint in his meetings, like those in the East. His aggressive sermons and extended meetings, however, had the flavor of the West about them. Finney's success guaranteed that many would copy him.

Finney proved influential for American evangelists, and many evangelists and preachers today use at least some of his methods. However, he also received much-deserved criticism. Finney claimed that sinners had the responsibility and ability to change their own hearts without the gracious working of God. He also denied that all humans are born guilty sinners, that Jesus received God's wrath in the place of sinners, and that justification comes by faith alone. Still, through his hugely successful campaigns and later his influential position as professor and president of Oberlin College in Ohio, Charles Finney became one of the most dominant figures in American religion in this era.

Charles Finney

Results of the Awakening

Like the colonial Great Awakening, the Second Great Awakening produced dramatic results. First and most important, multiple thousands of people were converted to Christ and joined churches. American Methodists, for example, numbered 15,000 in 1785. By 1840 their numbers had grown to 850,000, and Methodism had become the largest denomination in the United States. Second, as mentioned earlier, was the birth and growth of America's foreign missions movement. Third, moral sins declined in the wake of the revival; for example, drunkenness declined. Also, the revival fueled the drive for moral reform. Many of the leaders in the Prohibition and abolition movements were zealous converts of the revival. Fourth, new methods of evangelism resulted from the revival. The Second Great Awakening touched and transformed the lives of a large segment of the American people.

Unorthodox Religion

Not all the religious movements in the first half of the nineteenth century reflected biblical teaching. In fact, several influential movements denied scriptural truth and promoted error.

Unitarianism

One of the most prestigious unorthodox religions is **Unitarianism**. Its name derives from its basic doctrine of the "unity" of God; that is, Unitarianism denies the Trinity and therefore the deity of Christ. Jesus, to the Unitarians, was a great religious teacher, but He was only a man, so His death provided no atonement for sin. Instead, Unitarianism teaches that people should simply live moral, upright lives to please God.

The first Unitarian church in America began in 1785, but the denomination's real growth came after 1805, when Harvard appointed its first Unitarian professor. Within twenty years, Harvard had become a center of Unitarian teaching, and many of the old Congregationalist churches in the East declined from orthodoxy to Unitarianism. The denomination's influence was even greater than its numbers, in part because many wealthy and prominent leaders of eastern society became Unitarians. The denomination initially experienced little influence outside New England, however, causing one wit to remark that Unitarian preaching was limited to "the fatherhood of God, the brotherhood of man, and the neighborhood of Boston."

Millerites

Miller was a Baptist minister in New York who began to attract attention in the 1830s. Miller was a premillennialist. He believed that Christ would return to the earth and establish the Millennium, a perfect kingdom of peace lasting a thousand years. (The word *millennium* comes from two Latin words meaning "thousand years.") However, Miller strayed from Christ's declaration in Matthew 24:36 that no man can know the day and hour of His return. He set a date for Christ's return, sometime between March 21, 1843, and March 21, 1844. Thousands of people in the Northeast heard Miller, and perhaps as many as one hundred thousand became followers of his teaching.

The frenzied year of Miller's prediction came—and went. Mockers ridiculed Millerites, and they poured their scorn on premillennialism in general. Unproved rumors circulated of how

---

Finney's Methods Reflected the Society of the Time

Finney's views and the methods he used were reflective of what was occurring in politics at the same time. He allowed all, including women, to participate in his services. He encouraged women to pray publicly, to testify, and to organize and run volunteer societies, especially in urban evangelism and personal Bible studies. Similarly, Jacksonian democracy opened the doors to political participation to more people, encouraged involvement by the common man (but not yet by women), and substituted rule by an elite aristocracy for rule by "the people."

One Preacher's Testimony of the Revival's Results

One Presbyterian pastor, who earlier had been skeptical of the revival, wrote to a friend, "Study I cannot, being run down by persons, many of whom I never knew, in search of counsel. . . . The openness of thousands to doctrine, reproof, etc., is undeniable. . . . You may rest assured that there is a great awakening among us."

Millerites, dressed in white "ascension robes," waited on rooftops for the great event. Miller brought reproach on the doctrine of the Second Coming by ignoring Jesus' own words about His return: "But of that day and that hour knoweth no man, no, not the angels which are in heaven, neither the Son, but the Father. Take ye heed, watch and pray: for ye know not when the time is" (Mark 13:32–33).

While Miller abandoned his efforts to predict the Lord's return, others continued to do so. Ultimately, Seventh-Day Adventists developed from the Millerites.

Other Unorthodox Movements

Several other unorthodox groups developed in this era. Many of them were cults, groups that called themselves Christian but deviated from orthodox doctrine on one or more points. One such group was the **Shakers**, who began in England in the 1700s but enjoyed their greatest growth in America in the early 1800s. Shakers took their name from the shaking or dancing that accompanied their worship. They practiced celibacy and owned property in common. Shakers believed that their founder, Mother Ann Lee, was an incarnation of God, just as Jesus was. The Shakers built prosperous, well-ordered farms in New England, New York, Ohio, Indiana, and Kentucky. The group won many converts in the early 1800s, but it eventually died out because of its practice of celibacy.

Probably the most significant unorthodox religion to arise at this time was **Mormonism**, also known as the Church of Jesus Christ of Latter-Day Saints. Mormonism was founded by **Joseph Smith** in 1830. Smith claimed that an angel showed him some golden plates inscribed with ancient writing. With the angel's help, Smith said, he translated the plates to produce the Book of Mormon, one of the holy books of Mormonism. The Mormons say that they accept the Bible as God's Word but that the Book of Mormon is "another revelation" that takes precedence. They also teach that salvation rests primarily on good works and that one who is good enough eventually becomes a god. Mormons stirred up the most controversy, however, by their practice of polygamy, the taking of more than one wife at the same time. Non-Mormons viewed that practice as a major assault on the traditional family.

Opposition drove the Mormons from New York to Ohio to Nauvoo, Illinois. In Illinois, conflicts between Mormons and local residents led to the jailing of Smith in Carthage. There, a lynch mob attacked the jail and killed Smith. **Brigham Young** then assumed the leadership of the group. He led the Mormons on a prolonged trek west, where they founded Salt Lake City, capital of a territory that eventually became the state of Utah. The Mormons eventually abandoned the practice of polygamy officially and built a huge temple in Salt Lake City.

Mary Baker Eddy, the founder of **Christian Science**, was reared in a strict Congregationalist home. As a child, she suffered numerous physical and emotional ailments. She married and outlived three husbands.

Throughout that time, Mary Baker Eddy, as she was generally known, had been gathering material and ideas for a book she published titled *Science and Health with Key to the Scriptures*. Christian Science denies the Trinity, the inspiration of Scripture, miracles, the atonement, and other key Christian doctrines. The group also denies sickness and death. Perhaps the group's most public feature today is its national newspaper, the *Christian Science Monitor*.

Brigham Young

Mary Baker Eddy

The Prayer Meeting Revival

Despite the growth of false religious movements such as Mormonism, the first half of the 1800s was a time of triumph for many biblical groups. The climax of American religious life in that era came just before the Civil War in what was called by some the "third great awakening," or the **Prayer Meeting Revival** of 1857–59.

The revival began shortly after a serious financial crisis, the Panic of 1857. In September of that year in New York City, a lay evangelist named Jeremiah Lanphier began holding a weekly prayer meeting during the noon lunch hour. Attendance grew from six the first week, to twenty the next, to forty the next, and then more. Soon the group decided to meet daily, and the church building was full to overcrowding. Other churches, first in New York and then in other eastern cities, began to hold daily prayer meetings. Within months, churches and auditoriums across America were filled with men and women who met to pray for an hour. Every day in cities throughout the United States, life stood still for an hour as shopkeepers, laborers, and others paused to pray.

There was no formal organization to the prayer meetings. Each group usually met under the leadership of some Christian, often a layman. They sang a few hymns, shared requests, and listened to short devotionals, but mostly they prayed. Afterward, pastors and other Christian workers remained to help those who sought spiritual counsel.

The results of the revival were astounding. Nearly a million people were converted. Encouraged by the revival, Christians raised money to found Christian schools and support foreign missionaries. Established Christian organizations received floods of new volunteers whose lives had been transformed by the awakening. For example, the Young Men's Christian Association (YMCA), established in 1844 in Great Britain, was able to expand its ministry of providing wholesome recreation and fervent religious instruction for young people, primarily in the cities. The Prayer Meeting Revival also marked perhaps the first time that laymen had dominated the leadership of a revival. The overall impact of the revival was remarkable.

The revival came at a providential time. Within two years of its close, the United States would go to battle against itself in the Civil War. The blessings that God so graciously shed upon the young nation in revival would help to sustain it in the fiery furnace of war.

Section Review

1. What system did Francis Asbury develop to solve the problem of having too few ministers to cover a large area of land?
2–5. Give four results of the Second Great Awakening.
6–9. Name four unorthodox religious movements of the era.
   ★ In what ways did the revivalism of this era reflect the American values of liberty, equality, individualism, and growth?
   ★ Critique Finney's description of sinners in light of Romans 3:10–12 and Ephesians 2:8–9.

CHAPTER REVIEW

People, Places, and Things to Remember

Samuel Slater
Eli Whitney
John Deere
Cyrus McCormick
cotton gin
Robert Fulton
National Road
Erie Canal
Baltimore & Ohio Railroad
Samuel F. B. Morse
Horace Mann
William H. McGuffey
utopian reformers
Robert Owen
Benjamin West
Gilbert Stuart
John Trumbull
Thomas Cole
James Fenimore Cooper
Ralph Waldo Emerson
Nathaniel Hawthorne
Stephen Foster
Lowell Mason
Underground Railroad
Harriet Tubman
Nat Turner
abolitionism
William Lloyd Garrison
Frederick Douglass
Second Great Awakening
deism
Methodists
Francis Asbury
Timothy Dwight
camp meeting
Cane Ridge
Adoniram Judson
Charles Finney
Unitarianism
Shakers
Mormonism
Joseph Smith
Brigham Young
Mary Baker Eddy
Christian Science
Prayer Meeting Revival

Making Connections

1. Why did western Pennsylvania become an early center of American heavy industry?
2. How did reform movements affect the American public during the first half of the nineteenth century?
3-4. During the Second Great Awakening, which were more emotional, the revivals in the East or the revivals in the West? In which region did the revivals center in the schools and churches?
5. Name the religious figure described by each phrase:
   a. foreign missionary to Burma
   b. originated the camp meeting
   c. founded the African Methodist Episcopal Church
   d. sparked the Prayer Meeting Revival
   e. oversaw the Yale revivals
   f. founded Mormonism
   g. Father of American Methodism
   h. taught faith in man instead of faith in Christ
   i. practiced the "New Measures"
   j. incorrectly predicted the Second Coming

Developing History Skills

1. What were three arguments offered by Southerners in defense of slavery?
2. How could the history of America have been affected had the South developed a similar system of transportation and communication by 1860 as the North and West did?

Thinking Critically

1. Read Philemon 1:15–17 on the relationship of Paul, Philemon, and Onesimus. Although some slaveowners appealed to this passage in support of slavery, how does this passage undercut the religious arguments in support of slavery?
2. Evaluate mission work as conducted by men like Adoniram Judson and mission-support work as conducted by men like Luther Rice.

Living as a Christian Citizen

1. Perhaps you will be visiting relatives soon and your Christian education will be questioned or challenged. How will you respond? Base your answer, in part, on what you learned about Horace Mann and William H. McGuffey.
2. The Second Great Awakening was a time of expansion for the American church. Currently, the church is expanding in places such as Africa and China. What are the similarities to the Second Great Awakening, and what are the differences?

MANIFEST DESTINY (1840–1848)

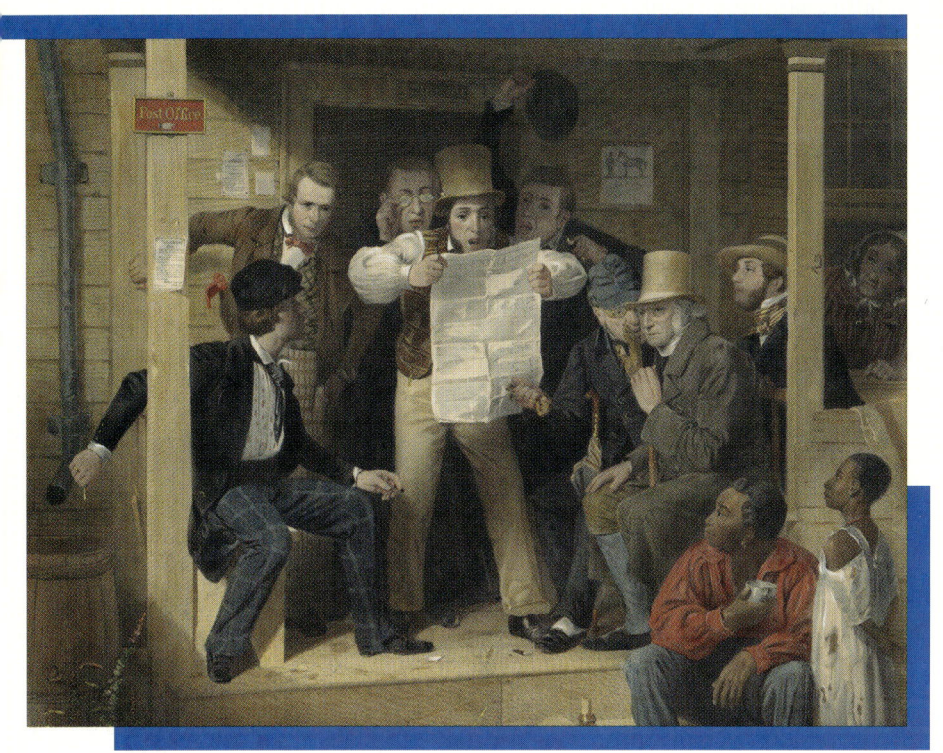

12

Mexican News by Alfred Jones (detail)

Our manifest destiny [is] to overspread and to possess the whole of the continent which Providence has given us.

John Lewis O'Sullivan
December 27, 1845, *New York Morning News*

I. Across the Wide Missouri

II. Tyler and Polk

III. War with Mexico

Big Ideas

1. What motivated increased settlement west of the Missouri River?
2. How effective were the administrations of John Tyler and James K. Polk?
3. What led to the war with Mexico?

According to a popular story, when Henry Clay was traveling through the Cumberland Gap (where the states of Tennessee, Kentucky, and Virginia meet) in 1850, he stopped and began to concentrate as though he were listening intently to something. When a curious onlooker asked what he was doing, Clay replied, "I am listening to the tread [footsteps] of the coming millions."

Since the founding of the first settlements on the Atlantic coast, Americans had been moving ever westward to settle the continent. As one pioneer wrote in her diary,

> When God made man,
> He seemed to think it best
> To make him in the East
> And let him travel west.

The 1840s saw that pattern continue with violent vigor as a burst of expansion resulted in the nation's stretching "from sea to shining sea." Supporting and motivating this growth was a controversial philosophy that urged, even demanded, expansion. In 1845, a New York journalist and prominent Democrat, John Louis O'Sullivan, both named and described this philosophy when he wrote that

> our manifest destiny [is] to overspread and to possess the whole of the continent which Providence has given us for the development of the great experiment of liberty and federated self-government entrusted to us.

The idea of **Manifest Destiny**—that America was providentially, or divinely, ordained to possess the North American continent—dominated American thinking in the 1840s. The term literally means "obvious destiny." Many Americans asserted boldly—perhaps even arrogantly—that some "higher power" had given the whole continent to the United States. The two main factors in Manifest Destiny were land and gold. Manifest Destiny also included the seeds of a future empire beyond American borders.

Daniel Boone leading families through the Cumberland Gap

Guiding Questions

1. What role did missionaries play in promoting American settlement of Oregon?
2. How did Texas change from a Mexican possession to a republic?
3. What were three major trails to the West?

I. Across the Wide Missouri

Expansion in the 1840s was not as sudden as it might have seemed at the time. The background of that dramatic decade lay in more than twenty years of dealings between the United States and Britain on the one hand and the United States and Mexico on the other. The basis of Manifest Destiny in the 1840s was the history of the territories of Oregon and Texas and the development of the western trails.

Oregon

Joint Occupation

As mentioned in Chapter 9, the United States and Great Britain agreed in 1818 to occupy the Oregon Territory jointly until the two nations could decide how to divide the area. The Oregon Territory included the present states of Oregon, Washington, Idaho, as well as parts of Wyoming and Montana. In addition, it included a sizable portion of land in present-day Canada. At first, Britain did

Narcissa Whitman

Narcissa Whitman soundly refuted the argument that the Oregon country was no place for a white woman. But in many ways Narcissa was not a typical woman. A lovely and well-educated woman from New York, she penned accounts in her letters and diary that present a vivid picture of the courage and faith of a pioneer missionary.

Several years after her conversion at the age of eleven, Narcissa became interested in the mission field, but the American Board of Commissioners for Foreign Missions refused to consider an unmarried woman missionary. When she met physician Marcus Whitman, Narcissa eagerly shared in his dream of carrying the gospel to the Indians of the Pacific Northwest. They were married, and the board approved them as missionaries.

The trip to Oregon fascinated Narcissa. She had her first encounter with buffalo meat. She also noted with amusement the westerners' figures of speech.

Like most travelers to Oregon, she had to sacrifice some of her possessions along the way. She especially hated being forced to leave her trunk in the wilderness.

Once in Oregon, the romance of mission work quickly wore off. The work of building and keeping up the mission compound/farm was heavy, and the Indians did not respond as readily as the Whitmans had hoped. Narcissa gave birth to a daughter, but the child tragically drowned in a river at the age of two. Narcissa noted that the grave of her daughter was "in sight every time [she stepped] out the door." The unvarying, unending labor wore on Narcissa both physically and spiritually.

Through the years, though, she stayed with the task. She wrote to her parents in April 1846, "There has been considerable evidence of the movings of the Holy Spirit.... For ourselves, we feel that our own souls have been greatly revived, and I hope and pray that we may never again relapse into such a state of insensibility and worldly-mindedness as we many times have found ourselves in." In November 1846, she wrote home with some optimism: "We feel that God has heard prayer, for many precious souls give evidence of having passed from death to life, some among the Indians and many more among our own countrymen." About a year later, she and her husband were murdered by Indians.

A family moving to the West

---

more toward developing the territory. Attracted by Oregon's abundance of beaver and other animals, British fur traders and trappers flocked to the region, but theirs was a wandering profession, and few of them settled down to build houses or to farm. In 1840, the number of white people living in Oregon, aside from those involved in the fur trade, was only two hundred. As the 1840s proceeded, however, that situation changed rapidly.

Missions to the Northwest

One of the more positive aspects of Manifest Destiny was an increased interest in missions. In fact, American missionaries to the Indians strongly encouraged settlers to come to Oregon. In 1833, an Indian convert to Christianity published an appeal for Christians to reach the Indians of the Northwest with the gospel. Many eagerly responded, the most famous of whom were two missionary couples: **Marcus and Narcissa Whitman**, and Henry and Eliza Spalding. The Spaldings, settling in what is today northern Idaho, enjoyed some success among the Nez Perce (NEZ PURS) Indians. They were able to establish both a church for the Nez Perces and a school for their children. Eliza handpainted visual aids, such as charts, to present the gospel pictorially to the Indians. In addition,

The Spaldings and the Whitmans

The Spaldings and the Whitmans traveled west together, but their relations were not always cordial. Henry Spalding had been in love with Narcissa Whitman before she married Marcus, and he apparently was still unhappy about her rejection. The tension was partially responsible for the couples' ministering far apart. But, as when Paul and Barnabas separated over John Mark (Acts 15:36–41), the result was two missionary teams taking the gospel to different regions.

Narcissa and Marcus Whitman, missionaries to the Indians of the Northwest, were murdered by the people they sought to reach for Christ.

Stephen F. Austin led the first American settlers into Texas.

the Spaldings attempted to help the Indians learn better methods of agriculture. Henry Spalding said, "We point them with one hand to the Lamb of God . . . with the other to the hoe as the means of saving their famishing bodies."

The Whitmans had less apparent success as missionaries but had greater impact on the settlement of Oregon. The Whitmans, soon joined by other missionaries, built a mission compound near the site of modern Walla Walla, Washington, and tried to reach the fiercely independent Cayuse (kye YOOS) Indians. Although the mission featured a thriving farm, the area proved less fertile for the gospel. The suspicious Cayuses distrusted the settlers. The missionaries did not help matters by suggesting that the Indians could better please God by abandoning hunting and fishing and becoming farmers like the whites. Thus, the Whitmans proved more successful at recruiting settlers than reaching Indians. They sent back not only calls for more workers but also exciting descriptions of the rich, unsettled lands. Marcus Whitman even served as a scout for some parties of settlers from the East.

The increasing stream of white settlers angered the Cayuses and caused them to suspect that the white man was more interested in taking Indian land than in saving Indian souls. Marcus Whitman wrote optimistically in a letter in 1844, "The Indians are anxious about the consequences of settlers among them, but I hope there will be no acts of violence on either hand." Whitman's hopes proved vain, especially when a measles epidemic, apparently carried into Oregon by settlers, wiped out nearly half the tribe despite Whitman's efforts to treat the ill. Finally, in 1847, a party of Cayuses ambushed the mission compound, murdering Marcus, Narcissa, and twelve other settlers.

Growing Numbers

The missionaries had opened the door for a flood of immigrants. A thousand settlers came to Oregon in 1841; within two years the number had tripled and continued to grow. Extravagant stories of the region's beauty and wealth filtered back to the East, such as the tall tale that "the pigs are running about . . . already cooked, with knives and forks sticking in them so that you can cut off a slice whenever you are hungry." The truth about Oregon was enough to attract most settlers: abundant land, fertile soil, and a mild climate. By the mid-1840s, southern Oregon was far more American than British, and the joint occupation agreement of 1818 no longer seemed satisfactory to many Americans.

Texas

American Settlement

As part of Spain's vast North American empire, Texas remained almost unsettled until the 1820s. In 1821, **Stephen F. Austin**, with the permission of Spanish authorities, led the first of many land-hungry American settlers into the region. Soon after arriving, Austin received news that the Mexicans had overthrown the Spanish and gained their independence. Austin quickly secured approval for his venture by pledging allegiance to the new government of Mexico. Under Austin's leadership, the transplanted Americans prospered, and others arrived to take advantage of the riches of the new land. Cotton growing and cattle raising in particular became major businesses in Texas.

Sam Houston

Sam Houston was a soldier, statesman, and adventurer whose life was even larger than his legend. Some sources say he was 6'6", though others set his height at 6'2". Texas's largest city bears his name.

As a teenager in East Tennessee, Houston ran away from home and lived with the Cherokee Indians for three years. The tribe adopted him, giving him the name "the Raven." Several years later, at age twenty-three, Houston served as a lieutenant under Andrew Jackson at the Battle of Horseshoe Bend. There he received an arrow in the thigh and two bullets in the shoulder while leading a daring charge.

When Old Hickory began his rise to national power, Houston followed as Jackson's friend. He was elected as one of Tennessee's representatives to Congress. In 1827, he was elected governor of the state. Then, suddenly, his career came crashing down. His bride of only three months left him. Angry and embittered, Houston resigned as governor and—like many other Tennesseans, including Davy Crockett—moved to Texas.

In Texas, Houston became a rowdy, moody loner who tried to drown his troubles in alcohol. The Indians gave him a new and more appropriate name: "Big Drunk." But the Texan War for Independence gave him new purpose and drive. His natural leadership and military talents won him the command of the Texan forces. After his decisive victory at San Jacinto, Houston was the most popular man in Texas.

Houston put his life back together and served two terms as the president of the Republic of Texas. After Texas joined the Union, he served the state as both U.S. senator and governor. He also married again in 1840 and proved to be a devoted family man, rearing eight children. He later professed trust in Christ and was baptized at the age of sixty-one in a Texas creek.

The final crisis of Houston's career came in 1860 when he was governor. Texas strongly favored joining the other Southern states in seceding from the Union. As loyal to the Union as he was to Texas, Houston opposed secession.

When the new Confederate government ordered all officials to take an oath of allegiance to the Confederacy, Houston refused. He resigned as governor and retired from public life. He died in 1863. The last line of the inscription on his tombstone reads, "A Consistent Christian—An Honest Man."

At first, Americans accepted Mexican citizenship, but few adopted Mexican customs or viewed Mexico as their country. It became apparent that some Americans had moved to Texas with the goal of splitting the region from Mexico. Consequently, in 1830, Mexico closed its borders to additional American immigrants. It also banned the import of slaves and placed a heavy tax on goods from the United States. Many American settlers, in spite of their earlier promise of obedience to the Mexican government, ignored the new laws. In fact, the number of settlers continued to increase and by 1835, Americans in the area numbered between twenty and twenty-five thousand—far more than the Mexican population. Many new settlers openly violated Mexican law by continuing to bring slaves with them.

Differences arose among Texans. Some, led by Stephen Austin, advocated making Texas a separate state within

This Catholic mission, located in Texas, was called the Alamo.

Davy Crockett

Davy Crockett, who died at the Alamo, is second in fame only to Daniel Boone among American frontiersmen. Born in Tennessee in 1786, Crockett was a farmer, hunter, and soldier. Crockett fought in the Creek campaign of 1813–14 and served in the Tennessee legislature and the U.S. House of Representatives as a Democrat.

A shrewd self-promoter and frontier humorist, Crockett enhanced his reputation with outlandish tales of his achievements. For example, he explained with mock seriousness how he killed raccoons by grinning them to death. On one occasion, he said he was preparing to shoot a raccoon when it turned to him and said, "Is your name Crockett?" When Crockett admitted that it was, the animal responded, "Then you needn't take no further trouble, for I may as well come down without another word."

Because he disagreed strongly with President Jackson over Indian removal and other issues, Crockett switched to the Whig Party. Defeated for reelection to Congress in 1834, Crockett led a company of Tennessee riflemen to join the Texan War for Independence. He died at the Alamo.

---

the Mexican federation. Another group, led by former Tennessee governor **Sam Houston**, was more radical, proposing a rebellion that would lead to full independence from Mexico. Houston's idea was particularly popular with newcomers and with slave owners.

"Remember the Alamo!"

A series of revolutions in Mexico City brought to power a government that was determined to retain the loyalty of the province of Texas. In 1834, General **Antonio López de Santa Anna** discarded the Mexican constitution of 1824 and declared himself a dictator. The following year, the Texans prepared to fight, at first to defend the Mexican constitution of 1824, which guaranteed them a degree of self-government within Mexico. However, when Santa Anna approached Texas with some five thousand troops, the Texans changed their demands to a call for outright independence from Mexico.

The battle at the Alamo became a symbol of the Texans' determination to gain independence.

Santa Anna planned to push through the heart of Texas, execute the leaders of the revolt, and expel the American pioneers. His first stop in this effort was San Antonio, which was defended by a Catholic mission-turned-fortress called the **Alamo**. The commander of the Texan forces, Sam Houston, ordered the tiny force holding the Alamo to destroy the fort and fall back. But the commanders at the Alamo, **Jim Bowie** and **William Travis**, decided to hold the post and block the Mexican advance. In February 1836, Santa Anna marched into San Antonio and laid siege to the Alamo. The Mexicans flew a blood-red flag, meaning that no mercy would be shown to the defenders. Almost 190 defenders—including Bowie, Travis, and the legendary Tennessee frontiersman Davy Crockett—held out for thirteen days, and they inflicted somewhere between 600 and 1,500 casualties on the Mexicans. In the end, though, the Mexicans stormed the fort and killed all the defenders. A few women, children, and slaves survived.

While the battle at the Alamo was occurring, delegates from throughout Texas had gathered more than 150 miles away. They declared independence from Mexico and began writing a constitution for the new country, the Republic of Texas. Sam Houston was named commander of the new nation's army. Despite the pleas of his men to attack the Mexicans and avenge the slaughter, Houston slowly fell back, forcing the Mexicans to stretch their supply lines. Santa Anna split his army into three forces to speed the crushing of the revolt. Seizing his opportunity, Houston attacked part of Santa Anna's divided army near the San Jacinto (juh SIN toh) River on April 21, 1836. In the brief but bloody **Battle of San Jacinto**, 800 enraged Texans—many shouting, "Remember the Alamo!"—easily defeated 1,200 Mexicans. The Texans captured Santa Anna himself and forced the dictator to sign a treaty recognizing Texan independence.

The Republic of Texas

Although the Mexican government quickly denounced the treaty, Texas was in fact free from Mexico. Most Texans would have preferred to join the United States. President Andrew Jackson, however, realized that accepting Texas into the Union might spark a war with Mexico. He also knew that antislavery forces in the United States opposed Texan annexation because Texas would almost certainly enter as a slave state. Thus, Jackson recognized the independence of Texas but did not support it becoming a new state. Thus began a ten-year history of independence for the **Republic of Texas** or "Lone Star Republic."

Trails West

One important aspect of Manifest Destiny was simply getting to the West. Traveling to the new lands of the West in the 1800s was obviously not a simple matter. The goal of the pioneers was the far West, and the means of getting there was the overland trails. *Trail* is an accurate term, for these routes were certainly not roads. At best, they consisted of the ruts left by preceding wagons. Packing all their belongings into sturdy ox-drawn wagons, settlers journeyed west seeking a new and better life. Often, as trails climbed into the steep passes through the Rocky Mountains, pioneers had to lighten their loads. Oak chests, chairs, trunks, even grandfather clocks littered the wayside, victims of the

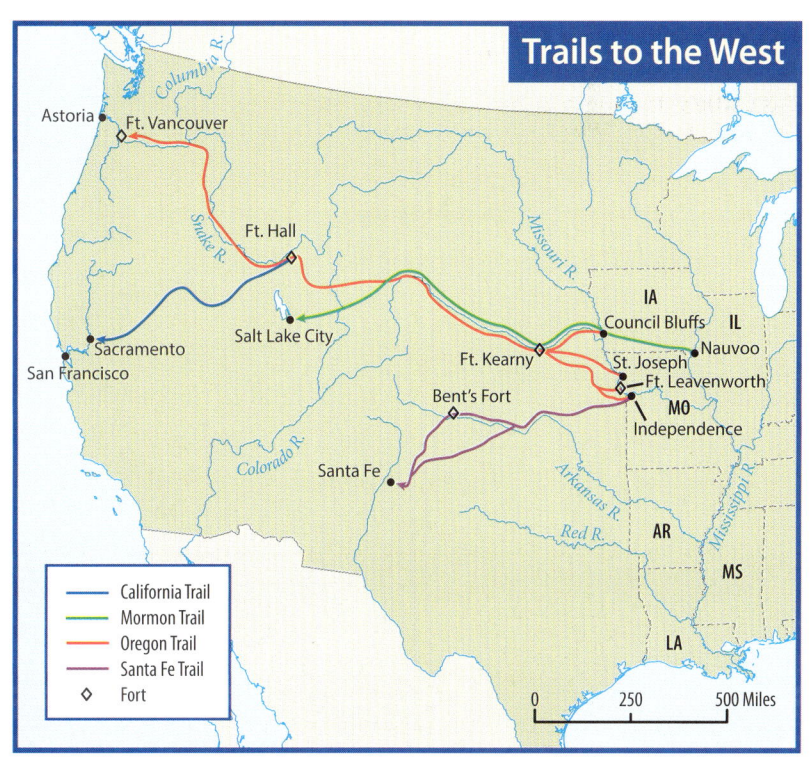

This monument, located near Truckee, California, honors the Donner Party. The statues are atop a twenty-two-foot monument shaft, which was the depth of the snow when the settlers were trapped there.

craggy heights of the Rockies. The discards could have furnished many houses—if only one had the means of carrying them.

Traveling the trails was dangerous. Indian attack, of course, was always a possibility. More mundane, but nearly as deadly, were broken axles or the death of an exhausted ox, events which could strand families in the wilderness to die.

Weather was also a factor. Storms and floods could slow the advance of a wagon train, and woe to the pioneer who did not reach his destination before winter arrived. Probably the most horrible example of the dangers of the trails was the fate of the Donner Party. Heading to California in 1846, a group under the leadership of George Donner was trapped for months in the Sierra Nevada range by the winter snows. About half of the eighty-seven members of the party survived. It appears many did so by resorting to cannibalism, eating the bodies of those that died that terrible winter.

Three main trails reached westward. The **Oregon Trail** not only led to Oregon, but it also had branches ("cutoffs") that reached into California. The **Santa Fe Trail** was also important, but it was more of a commercial route than a means of pioneer transportation. During the era of Spanish domination, American merchants began a thriving trade between Santa Fe, New Mexico, and Independence, Missouri. Even after Mexican independence, the trade flourished. Fear of growing American activity in Texas eventually caused the Mexican government to close the trail, but memories of earlier profits caused many Americans to covet New Mexico. The **Mormon Trail**, as its name indicates, was blazed by the Mormons when they fled from Nauvoo, Illinois, to Salt Lake City in 1846–47 (see Chapter 11). More Mormons followed the trail, and eventually non-Mormons found it a convenient route to California. The constant stream of pioneers along the trails began to fill the West. It also began to increase tension between the United States and both Great Britain and Mexico.

Section Review

1. Who strongly encouraged American settlers to come to Oregon?
2–4. Name three characteristics of Oregon that attracted settlers to that region.
5–6. Why did Andrew Jackson oppose annexing Texas (two reasons)?
7–10. Name four dangers of traveling on the western trails in the first half of the nineteenth century.
11. Using both the text and the map in this section, identify the western trail described by each of the following phrases:
    a. Involved thriving trade with the Spanish
    b. Was a cutoff from the Oregon Trail
    c. The southernmost trail
    d. Blazed primarily by a religious sect
* Evaluate the missionary efforts in the Oregon Territory.
* Explain the significance of Sam Houston, a native Tennessean, to the history of Texas.

II. Tyler and Polk

While Americans boldly settled in the West, politics in the East proceeded more cautiously. For example, Jackson refused to annex Texas. Political developments in Washington, D.C., in the 1840s profoundly affected affairs in far-off Oregon, California, and Texas. Numerous factors made Manifest Destiny popular among many American politicians. Some saw it as a divine mission to spread democracy, others saw it as an opportunity to expand American agriculture, and still others applauded it as a means of spreading slavery. Southerners and Democrats tended to support expansion; Whigs and New Englanders usually opposed it.

Guiding Questions

1. What were the successes and failures of John Tyler's administration?
2. What four goals did Polk set for his administration?

And Tyler Too

"His Accidency"

The sudden death of President Harrison in 1841 created confusion in the Whig Party. Their leaders had chosen **John Tyler** of Virginia as their vice presidential candidate in order to win votes in the South. They never expected him to become president. Since Harrison was the first president to die in office, some questioned Tyler's position. Was he simply "Acting President," or did he have the full powers of the presidency? At any

The Whigs never expected Vice President John Tyler to become president, and when he did, he caused great consternation.

The Tylers—An Unusual "First Family"

In March 1790, less than one year after George Washington's inauguration, future president John Tyler was born. Though his birth occurred in the eighteenth century and his death occurred in the nineteenth century, he still had grandchildren alive in the twenty-first century.

Tyler married his first wife, Letitia Christian, on his twenty-third birthday in 1813. They had eight children. She died of a stroke in the White House in September 1842 and almost two years later, Tyler wed again. Julia Gardiner and the president married in New York City when he was fifty-four years old—she was only twenty-four. Tyler, the first president to marry while in office, had three children older than his new wife. Julia and Tyler eventually had seven children. Thus, the president had a total of fifteen children, more than any other person who has occupied the White House.

John Tyler was age 63 when his thirteenth child, Lyon, was born in 1853. Lyon, who served as the president of the College of William and Mary for more than three decades, had a total of six children in his two marriages. One of those children, Lyon Gardiner Tyler Jr., was born in 1924 when his father was age 71. Another, Harrison Ruffin Tyler, was born in 1928 when his father was age 75. Both these sons, grandsons of President Tyler, were still alive as of 2016.

So, three generations of Tylers spanned over 225 years. Put in today's context, imagine someone born in 1990 who will have grandchildren alive in 2216. That would be remarkable! Like the Tylers, that would be an unusual family.

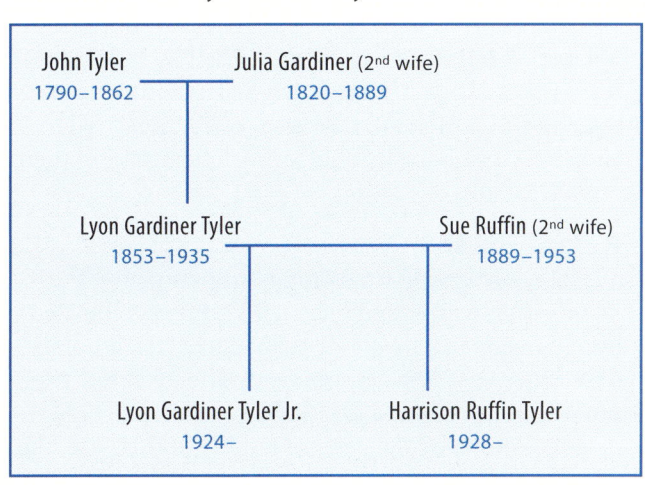

```
John Tyler          Julia Gardiner (2nd wife)
1790–1862           1820–1889
        |_____|
                  |
    Lyon Gardiner Tyler         Sue Ruffin (2nd wife)
    1853–1935                   1889–1953
        |_____|
                      |
    Lyon Gardiner Tyler Jr.    Harrison Ruffin Tyler
    1924–                      1928–
```

Maine Border Settlement

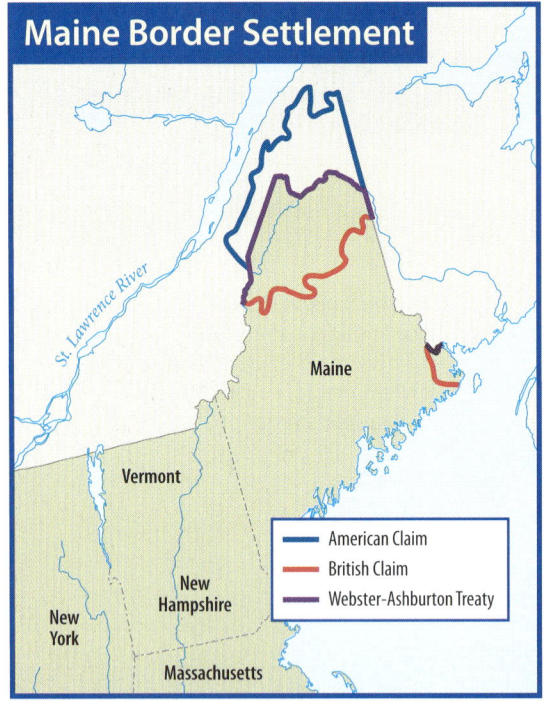

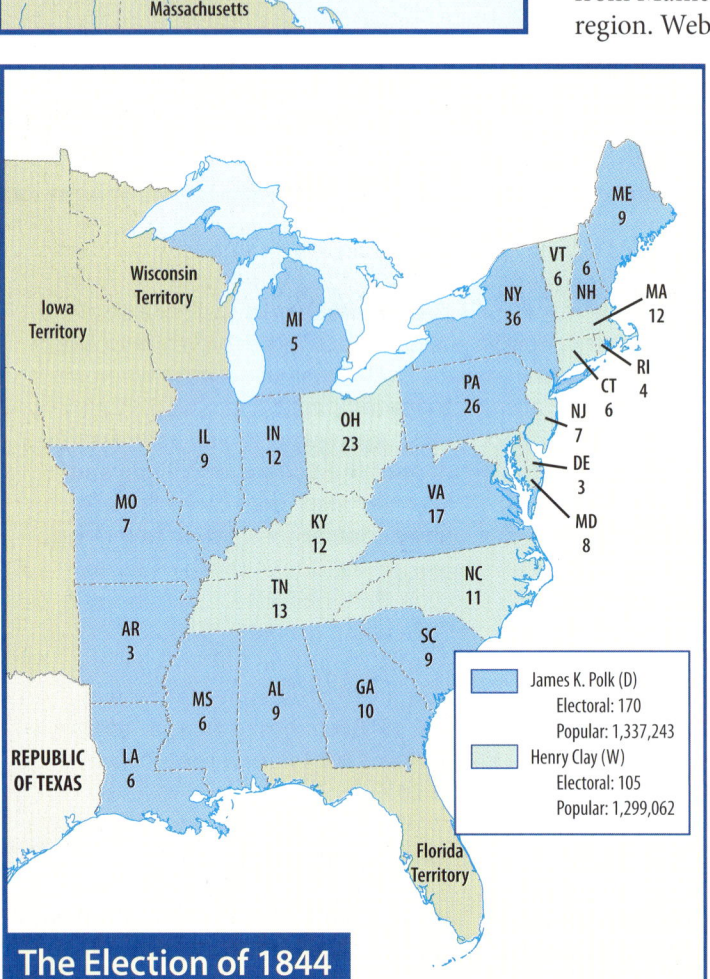

rate, most Whig leaders in Congress and the cabinet assumed that Tyler should submit to their guidance and instruction. **Henry Clay**, the real head of the party, boasted, "Tyler dares not resist me. I will drive him before me."

Tyler, however, refused to be driven. He left no doubt that he was president in the full sense of the term. Rather than follow the wishes of Clay, Tyler shocked the Whigs by his policies. At heart more of an anti-Jackson Democrat than a true Whig, Tyler vetoed bills calling for higher tariffs, a new national bank, and internal improvements. Clay, of course, supported each of those measures. The Whigs responded to Tyler by voting him out of the party. Five of his six cabinet members—all except Secretary of State **Daniel Webster**—resigned in the fall of 1841. Embittered Whigs began to refer to Tyler as "His Accidency."

Webster-Ashburton Treaty

One reason Webster remained in the cabinet was his ongoing negotiations with Great Britain over the American-Canadian border. The northern border of Maine was the main point of controversy. Due to lack of clarity in the Treaty of Paris (1783), Britain and the United States argued over some twelve thousand square miles of territory. The conflict heightened in 1840 when lumberjacks from Maine and Canada clashed over timber claims in the disputed region. Webster and the British representative, Lord Ashburton, sought to settle the issue. After much discussion, the pair hammered out the Webster-Ashburton Treaty (1842). Under the treaty, the United States received seven-twelfths of the disputed area, and the British received the remainder. The diplomats also clarified the border between Minnesota and Canada.

"Who Is James K. Polk?"

Campaign of 1844

As another presidential election approached in 1844, Clay emerged as the leading Whig candidate over the discredited Tyler. The president would have liked to run for reelection on the Democratic ticket, but the Democrats did not trust a man who had been a Whig only four years earlier. The leading Democrat was, in fact, former president Martin Van Buren. Tyler tried to rally support for himself by making the annexation of Texas (which he favored) a major issue in the campaign; Clay and Van Buren tried to eliminate that issue by publishing letters stating their opposition to annexation.

A Dark Horse

Clay easily won the Whig nomination, but the Democrats surprisingly rejected Van Buren. Pushed by expansionists, the party turned to a "**dark horse**," a nominee who is not a serious candidate before the nominating convention and about whom little is usually known by the general public. In this case, the dark horse was **James K. Polk** of Tennessee. During the campaign, Whigs derisively asked, "Who is James K. Polk?"

Though not well-known nationally, Polk was politically experienced. He had served for fourteen years in the House of Repre-

The Election of 1844

James K. Polk (D)
Electoral: 170
Popular: 1,337,243

Henry Clay (W)
Electoral: 105
Popular: 1,299,062

sentatives, including four years as Speaker of the House. He had also been the governor of Tennessee. His close association with Andrew Jackson earned him the nickname "Young Hickory." More importantly for Democratic expansionists, Polk willingly ran on a platform that called for "the reoccupation of Oregon and the reannexation of Texas."

As annexation fervor grew, Clay hedged his position. He declared that he was not necessarily opposed to annexing Texas if such an act would not result in war with Mexico. Opponents of slavery objected to Clay's shift, and many of them switched their support to a third-party candidate, James Birney. He was the nominee of the tiny antislavery Liberty Party. Polk, pledging to serve only one term, won the election by a narrow margin of 38,000 out of 2.7 million votes cast and by a count of 170 to 105 in the Electoral College. Birney drew only 62,000 votes, but he might have cost Clay the election. Polk carried New York by only 5,000 votes, and Birney polled 15,000 in that state. Had Clay not lost the antislavery vote, he might have become president.

Texas Annexed

After Texas won its independence from Mexico, the new republic still faced the possibility that Santa Anna would try to reclaim Mexico's lost northernmost state. As the first president of Texas, Sam Houston sought security from both Great Britain and the United States. If either country expressed support for the new country, Mexico would be less likely to invade. Houston thought that the British might want to retain an interest in the hemisphere through Texas. He also thought that when the United States saw the potential for British influence there, U.S. lawmakers would be more willing to consider annexing Texas to prevent British influence. His problem in dealing with Britain, however, was that the British had outlawed slavery in their empire, but many Texas settlers owned slaves. The problem he had in dealing with the United States was that many U.S. lawmakers opposed annexation, especially if it might mean going to war with Mexico. Houston pleaded with Andrew Jackson to use his influence to promote annexation.

After the 1844 election but before Polk took office, President Tyler took the election results as a mandate to push for the annexation of Texas. Tyler realized that he could not obtain the two-thirds majority needed in the Senate to ratify a treaty of annexation; so he proposed to annex the region through a **joint resolution** of Congress, an action that required only a simple majority in both houses. The resolution passed, and Tyler signed it in March 1845, just days before leaving office. Texas became the twenty-eighth state in the Union.

James K. Polk

The present-day flag of Texas

Polk's Administration

A Disciplined Executive

Polk was a hard-working and self-disciplined leader. Eighteen-hour workdays were common for him. Polk paid for that unceasing labor, however. His health declined during his time as president. He fulfilled his pledge to serve only one term and died within four months of leaving office.

One historian noted that Polk "knew how to get things done, which is the first necessity of government, and he knew what he wanted done, which is the second." A cabinet member recalled that on his inauguration day, Polk outlined four goals for his administration. He wanted to (1) lower the tariff, (2) restore the independent treasury system of Van Buren, (3) settle the Oregon question, and (4) acquire California from Mexico.

Notably, Polk achieved all four of his goals. With a Democratic majority in Congress, Polk easily attained the first two. The last two, which dealt with fulfilling the idea of Manifest Destiny, proved to be more difficult for him. Furthermore, the final objective was soon a part of a moral debate—should the United States use a war with its neighbor, Mexico, as a means of expanding American territory?

The Oregon Question

The Oregon country stretched from 42° latitude in the south to 54° 40′ latitude in the north. Many expansionists clamored for the United States to take the whole region. Their slogans were **"Fifty-four-forty or fight!"** and "All of Oregon or none!" The British, on the other hand, had long maintained that the proper boundary should be the Columbia River, a border that would have given most of the modern state of Washington to Canada. War between Britain and the U.S. was a possibility.

Polk offered to extend the U.S.-Canadian border along the 49th parallel (49° latitude), the line that formed the border from Minnesota to the Rockies. Because the fur trade had declined along the Columbia River, the British had less interest in that region and were more open to compromise. In 1846, the two nations signed a

Oregon Controversy Settled—1846

A wagon train of settlers heading west

treaty that settled the Oregon question by making the 49th parallel the international boundary to the Pacific, but Britain retained all of Vancouver Island. Polk did not please the most passionate expansionists with that compromise, but he made what most Americans considered a fair settlement.

Section Review

1. Why was Tyler unpopular with the Whig Party?
2. Who received more of the disputed territory in Maine under the provisions of the Webster-Ashburton Treaty?
3. Why did Tyler annex Texas through a joint resolution of Congress rather than a treaty in the Senate?
4–7. What were Polk's four goals for his administration?
8–10. Where did extreme American expansionists want to draw the Oregon boundary? Where did Britain originally contend that it should be drawn? What became the actual boundary?
★ Some advocates of Manifest Destiny claimed that it was God's will that the United States expand across the entire continent. Assess that idea from a scriptural viewpoint. Consider using Ezekiel 13:7–8; Exodus 20:7, 15, 17.
★ Evaluate Polk's handling of the controversy regarding Oregon.

III. War with Mexico

Polk's fourth goal, acquiring California, involved diplomatic dealings with Mexico. Affairs with that nation, however, were neither so smooth nor so peacefully settled as they had been with Britain. In fact, the American desire for California coupled with difficulties over Texas plunged the United States into war with its neighbor to the south. The **Mexican War (1846–48)** was the climax and the most violent phase of Manifest Destiny.

Background of the War

Causes

The causes of the Mexican War were complex. First, there was a history of hostility between the two nations. Americans often viewed the Mexicans as somehow crude and inferior. Many Texans angrily recalled the slaughter at the Alamo. Mexicans, on the other hand, viewed America as arrogant and feared its expansion at their expense. Mexico's unstable political situation did not help relations; the constant series of Mexican revolutions allowed little time for the two nations to handle their differences. Second, many expansionists in the United States longed for California and New Mexico. Some people wanted the rich, fertile lands of California and its fine harbors; others fondly recalled the profitable trade that had existed along the Santa Fe Trail. In addition, the instability of the Mexican government caused some expansionists to urge that the Americans seize those two areas before some other power, such as Britain tried to do so. Third, Mexico resented the annexation of Texas and had never recognized Texan independence.

> **Guiding Questions**
> 1. What events led to the Mexican War?
> 2. What were the major military campaigns of the Mexican War?
> 3. What were the results of the Mexican War?

Poet for the Opposition

Some people thought that the war was a brazen attempt to create more slave states. New England poet James Russell Lowell wrote scathingly,

They [just] want this Californy
So's to lug new slave-states in
To abuse ye, an' to scorn ye,
An' to plunder ye like sin.

A fourth cause was the failure of an attempt to reach a peaceful settlement. In 1845, Polk sent a representative to negotiate with Mexico. Polk was prepared to pay $5 million to settle the disputes about Texas and up to $30 million to purchase California and New Mexico. Mexicans considered the offer an insult to their national honor, and the Mexican government could not even discuss the offer for fear of starting another revolution among its angry population. The Mexicans' rejection of the offer drove another wedge between the nations. Polk's representative, furious at the treatment he had received, wrote back to his chief, "Depend on it, we can never get along with them until we have given them a good drubbing [beating]."

A fifth cause—the real spark of the conflict—was a dispute over the Texas-Mexico boundary. The Mexicans claimed that the southern border of Texas was the Nueces (noo AY sis) River. This had been the boundary between Texas and the remainder of the country when Mexico controlled the area. However, the Republic of Texas had claimed that the Rio Grande was the border, some fifty to one hundred miles to the south. This was the border that President Polk supported. After Texas officially entered the Union, Polk sent a force under General Zachary Taylor into the disputed area between the two rivers. The Mexicans demanded that they leave

---

Two Views of the Mexican War

It was a mistake.

James Waddell Alexander, a Presbyterian minister, wrote this about the Mexican War: "It is a war of pretexts. None of the alleged causes existed.... Never have I so much feared the judgments of God on us as a nation."

Ulysses S. Grant, who later served as U.S. president, was a lieutenant during the war. He wrote the following almost four decades after the war ended, "to this day [I] regard the war ... as one of the most unjust ever waged by a stronger against a weaker nation. It was an instance of a republic following the bad example of European monarchies, in not considering justice in their desire to acquire additional territory."

Nicholas Trist was the U.S. representative that negotiated the treaty that ended the conflict. Just prior to the treaty signing, a Mexican representative commented to him, "This must be a proud moment for you; no less proud for you than it is humiliating for us." Trist responded, "we are making peace, let that be our only thought." Later, Trist wrote to his wife, "Could those Mexicans have seen into my heart at that moment, they would have known that my feeling of shame as an American was far stronger than theirs could be as Mexicans. For though it would not have done for me to say so there, that was a thing for every right minded American to be ashamed of, and I was ashamed of it, most cordially and intensely ashamed of it."

It was a just war.

In President James K. Polk's war message to Congress on May 11, 1846, he stated, "The strong desire to establish peace with Mexico on ... honorable terms, and the readiness of this [U.S.] Government to regulate and adjust our boundary and other causes of difference with that power ... induced me ... to seek the reopening of diplomatic relations ... An envoy [representative] of the United States repaired [went] to Mexico with full powers to adjust every existing difference.... The Mexican Government not only refused to receive him or listen to his propositions, but after a long-continued series of menaces have at last invaded our territory and shed the blood of our fellow-citizens on our own soil....

"Thus the Government of Mexico, though solemnly pledged by official acts in October last to receive ... an American envoy ... refused the offer of a peaceful adjustment of our difficulties. Not only was the offer rejected, but the indignity of its rejection was enhanced by the manifest breach of faith in refusing to admit the envoy who came because they had bound themselves to receive him.... the Mexican Government refused all negotiation ...

"As war exists, and, notwithstanding all our efforts to avoid it, exists by the act of Mexico herself ...

"I [ask] the prompt action of Congress to recognize the existence of the war, and to place at the disposition of the Executive [president] the means of prosecuting the war with vigor...."

immediately and posted an army on the southern bank of the Rio Grande. On April 25, 1846, Mexican troops attacked a detachment of American cavalry across the river. More than a dozen American soldiers were killed or wounded. Polk was already preparing to ask Congress to declare war on Mexico when news reached him, on May 9, of this incident. Within days, Congress approved the president's request. War began.

Problems at Home

Although the attack in Texas enabled Polk to persuade Congress to declare war, the administration was hampered by division at home. A sizable minority of Americans considered the conflict an unjust war of conquest.

Even Southern spokesman John C. Calhoun warned against expansion by saying, "Mexico is to us the forbidden fruit; the penalty of eating it would be to subject our institutions to political death." Young Whig congressman Abraham Lincoln of Illinois introduced a resolution that called for the administration to announce the exact spot of the Mexican attack. That way Congress could decide whether the war had actually begun on U.S. soil and was truly defensive or had been provoked. His motion, popularly known as the "Spot Resolution," was never acted upon, but it earned him the nickname "Spotty Lincoln." Nor did matters improve as the war dragged on. Almost eighteen months after voting to declare war, the House of Representatives narrowly passed a resolution stating that the conflict had been "unnecessarily and unconstitutionally begun by the President of the United States." The Senate did not approve the measure. Some opponents simply referred to it as "Mr. Polk's War."

The U.S. military had not been ready for the war. The regular army was tiny, about seven thousand men. Tens of thousands volunteered to fight, but they often proved unruly and undisciplined. The two leading generals, Winfield Scott and Zachary Taylor, were Whigs whose every success created jealousy in the Democrats' ranks. Furthermore, neither Polk nor the army had any real overall strategy for winning the war. Typical of the president's ignorance of the situation was his suggestion that Taylor's army "live off the land" in northern Mexico, land that was mostly desert. The credit for the American victory ultimately rested on the nation's naval superiority, the bravery of its troops in battle, and Mexico's lack of preparedness.

Campaigns of the War

The course of the Mexican War can be divided neatly into four military campaigns: (1) Taylor's campaign in northern Mexico, (2) the New Mexico campaign, (3) the California campaign, and (4) Scott's campaign in central Mexico, which climaxed with the capture of Mexico City.

Taylor in Northern Mexico

Zachary Taylor, the commander of the troops on the Rio Grande, was a veteran of the War of 1812 and several Indian wars. Nicknamed "Old Rough and Ready" by his men, Taylor dressed

General Zachary Taylor, hero of the Mexican War

sloppily and lacked the distinguished image that many generals carefully cultivated. New recruits often failed to recognize their slouchily dressed, rumpled-looking commander on first meeting. For example, one new lieutenant, seeing Taylor sitting behind his tent cleaning his sword, unwittingly asked him if he would take a dollar to clean the lieutenant's sword too. "Sure thing," replied the general cheerfully.

Taylor's undeniable bravery and his simple, friendly manner won him the unflinching devotion of his men. But he was not a particularly good strategist, and his battles with the Indians had given him little experience in fighting a regular army. Also, his easygoing manner did not create the most organized or disciplined of camps.

However, Taylor overcame his shortcomings as a commander. He began the campaign with two important victories, driving the Mexicans from the Rio Grande. Then, gathering his force of 6,600 men, Taylor marched to Monterrey, the main city of northern Mexico, and confronted a well-entrenched force of 7,000 Mexicans. For three days (September 21–23, 1846), the Americans assaulted the fortifications of Monterrey. After the forts fell, fierce street fighting followed as the Americans battled house by house toward the city's central plaza. Realizing his hopeless situation, the Mexican commander finally surrendered.

Taylor had won a great victory, but several factors worked to undermine his position. Defeat at Monterrey was not enough to force the Mexican government in far-off Mexico City to make peace. Meanwhile, so many Whigs were speaking of running "Old Rough and Ready" for president that the Democratic administration resolved to give him no more opportunities for glory. A planned thrust on Mexico City was instead entrusted to Winfield Scott, Taylor's superior. Scott, to boost his own troop strength, took the best of Taylor's men and left him with only 4,500 volunteers. After Scott removed the troops, Taylor suddenly found himself facing a new army of 15,000 Mexicans under the leadership of the scourge of the Alamo, Santa Anna.

Santa Anna's presence on the field was the result of a diplomatic blunder by Polk. Living in exile in Cuba when the war broke out, Santa Anna convinced the Americans that if they allowed him back into Mexico, he would arrange a peace settlement. On returning to Mexico, however, he seized power again and vowed to drive the Americans from Mexican soil. After intercepting some correspondence that revealed American plans, Santa Anna marched north to crush Taylor. In the Battle of Buena Vista (February 22–23, 1847), Taylor's outnumbered army held out in a desperate defensive battle that brought the Americans as close as they came to defeat during the entire war. Finally, the exhausted Mexicans broke off the fighting and began a demoralizing retreat to Mexico City to meet the next American thrust.

Santa Anna

This photo of an American force entering Saltillo, Mexico, is one of the earliest photographs of American soldiers taken in time of war.

New Mexico Campaign

Campaign is almost too glorious a term for the capture of New Mexico; it was more a desert march than anything else. Polk appointed General **Stephen Kearny** to lead a force of 1,500 men, mostly cavalry, down the Santa Fe Trail to capture New Mexico. Kearny's army left Fort Leavenworth (in present-day Kansas) on June 5 and captured Santa Fe on August 18 after almost no resistance. Leaving most of his troops to occupy the newly conquered province, Kearny took part of his men west to aid in the conquest of California.

This flag was used by the Bear Flag Republic.

The present-day flag of California

General Winfield Scott

California Campaign

California proved much more difficult to capture than New Mexico. Although a number of Americans had settled in the province, the Spanish-speaking population outnumbered them ten to one. Furthermore, the Spanish Californians were suspicious of Americans.

Captain **John C. Frémont**, an explorer known as "the Pathfinder of the West," struck the next blow in California. Before the war broke out, Frémont had led a group of sixty men into California, supposedly to explore, but Frémont's party appeared too numerous and too well armed to be a simple exploration team. When the American settlers there revolted against Mexico and established the **Bear Flag Republic** (because their flag featured a bear) on June 14, 1846, Frémont supported them.

Frémont thought Mexico and the United States were still at peace. He had not received word that Congress had declared war on Mexico weeks earlier. A month later, the American fleet arrived at California's Monterey Bay with the news that war had started. Relieved, Frémont joined forces with the naval commander, and the new republic ended. The American forces quickly subdued California. Initially, most Californians greeted the Americans enthusiastically. The contempt and harsh treatment that some American soldiers displayed toward the Spanish Californians, however, quickly soured relations. The Spanish revolted and recaptured Los Angeles. At this point, Kearny arrived from New Mexico with his men. With an unusual army consisting of Frémont's "explorers," armed settlers, marines from the American fleet, and Kearny's cavalry, the Americans recaptured Los Angeles and crushed the revolt. The victors treated the defeated foe generously this time, and by January 1847, California was once again quiet and firmly under U.S. control.

Scott in Central Mexico

Taylor's victories in northern Mexico and the conquest of New Mexico and California meant little if Mexico would not make peace. Finally, Polk approved an attack on Mexico City in an attempt to end the war. The president assigned this task to General **Winfield Scott**. Called "Old Fuss and Feathers" because of his love for military formality and discipline, Scott lacked the warmth of Taylor and was not as popular with the rank-and-file soldiers. But he had a better grasp of strategy, and his Mexican campaign was one of the most brilliant in American military history.

Scott planned to follow the route that the Spanish *conquistador* Cortés had followed more than three hundred years before. Scott's army landed south of the Mexican port of Veracruz early in March 1847, and he captured the city in less than three weeks. Santa Anna, having recovered from his setback at Buena Vista, blocked the Americans' path. By quick movement and shrewd maneuvering, Scott drove the Mexicans back toward their capital. At least three times Scott outwitted the enemy by sending his troops over ground that Santa Anna thought impassable. In August and September, Americans and Mexicans engaged in a series of bloody battles outside Mexico City. As the Americans edged nearer, Santa Anna realized the hopelessness of his cause. With his army defeated and the populace of the capital calling for his head, Santa Anna abandoned the city. Scott led the victorious Americans into Mexico City on September 14, 1847.

Results of the War

The loss of Mexico City was the final blow to Santa Anna's government. He resigned in disgrace, and a new government began negotiating with the United States. The result was the **Treaty of Guadalupe Hidalgo** (gwah-duh-LOO-pay ee-DAHL-go) in 1848. Mexico recognized American claims to Texas southward to the Rio Grande and ceded New Mexico and California to the United States. In turn, the United States paid Mexico $15 million and agreed to pay $3.25 million in debts that Mexico owed American citizens.

Five years later, in 1853, the United States paid Mexico $10 million for territory bordering the southwestern United States. The land known as the **Gadsden Purchase** was needed for the path of

The Human Cost of the War

The cost of the war was high in more than dollars. About 1,700 Americans died in combat, and more that 11,000 perished from such diseases as dysentery (an intestinal disorder), malaria, measles, and mumps.

Mexico: Dress Rehearsal for the Civil War

The Mexican War was the first conflict in which graduates of West Point, the United States Military Academy, played a major role. It also proved to be a training ground for many of those graduates who would see exhausting service on the battlefields of the Civil War.

Many young officers gained distinction in Mexico. Captain Robert E. Lee was an engineer on General Scott's staff in central Mexico. While scouting the field at Cerro Gordo, Lee found a potential route for the Americans that would allow them to slip behind the Mexican position. As he scouted the route, Lee suddenly heard the voices of Mexican soldiers. Lee scrambled behind a log to hide. He lay completely still while a party of Mexican soldiers gathered and talked. Some of them even sat on the log behind which Lee was hiding. Insects added torment to the suspense as they crawled over the motionless American and bit him. After several hours, the Mexicans left, and Lee hurried back to Scott's headquarters. Using the information Lee supplied, the American army outflanked Santa Anna and won a smashing victory. Lee's unflinching personal discipline and his self-sacrificing character were even more evident years later when he led the Confederate Army of Northern Virginia.

Many other famous men won their first glory in Mexico. Lieutenant Ulysses Grant showed great ingenuity under Scott in central Mexico. Sixteen years later, in the siege of Vicksburg, Grant displayed the same abilities on a much larger scale.

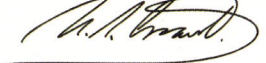

Another lieutenant, Thomas J. Jackson, also won praise for his bravery with an artillery unit in the attack on Mexico City. As bullets and shells whizzed around him, Jackson walked about in the open, calling, "There is no danger. See! I am not hit." It was that same brave determination that won Jackson the nickname "Stonewall" fourteen years later at the First Battle of Manassas (Bull Run).

However, not all the great generals of the Civil War won glory in Mexico. For example, Lieutenant William Sherman began the Mexican War as a recruiting officer in Pittsburgh and never got into the fight. In another decade, though, a different war provided more than enough action for the over two hundred Mexican War officers who later served as generals in the Civil War.

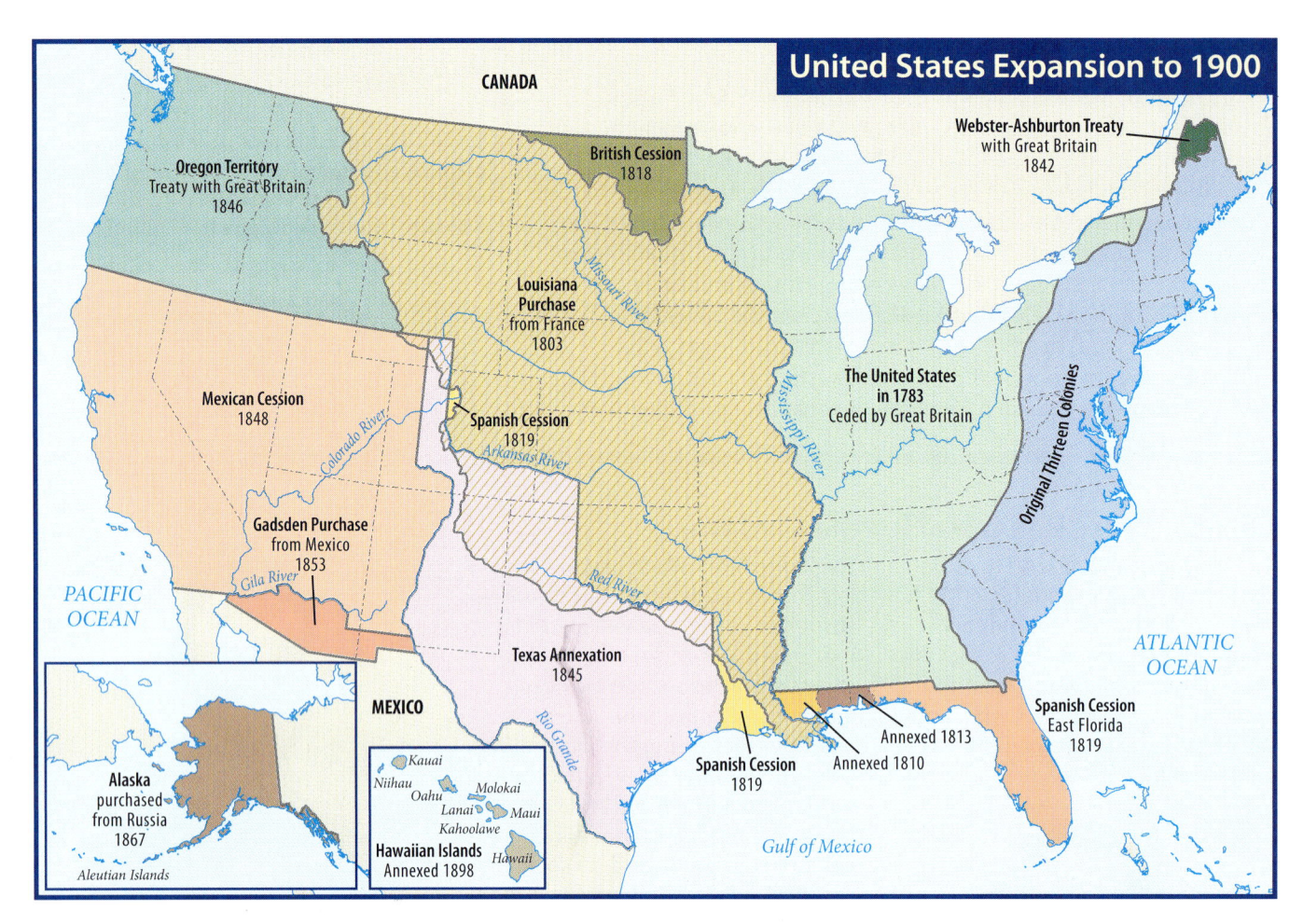

a transcontinental railroad. Ironically, the Mexican president who negotiated the purchase was Santa Anna, who had regained control of the government only months earlier. He was later overthrown, partly in reaction to the sale. The Gadsden Purchase negotiated by American representative James Gadsden finalized the continental United States at its current boundaries. It was in many ways the climax of Manifest Destiny.

Section Review

1–5. List the five causes of the Mexican War.

6–9. What were the four main military campaigns of the Mexican War?

10. How did Santa Anna return to power in Mexico during the Mexican War?

11. What were the specifics of the Treaty of Guadalupe Hidalgo?

★ Explain why many Americans opposed going to war with Mexico.

★ Analyze the feature box entitled "Mexico: Dress Rehearsal for the Civil War." Why is this title an accurate assessment?

CHAPTER REVIEW 12

Making Connections

1. How did the Santa Fe Trail differ in purpose from the Oregon and Mormon trails?
2. Give the dates for the following steps in American expansion and then place the steps in their proper chronological order.
   a. Treaty of Guadalupe Hidalgo
   b. Annexation of Texas
   c. Maine boundary settlement
   d. Gadsden Purchase
   e. Oregon boundary settlement
3. Why did Secretary of State Daniel Webster decide not to resign with the rest of Tyler's cabinet in 1841?
4. Why did the Polk administration entrust the Mexico City campaign to Winfield Scott instead of Zachary Taylor?

Developing History Skills

1. How would you evaluate the Whitmans' missionary work? What lessons can we learn from their experience?
2. How did Henry Clay's stand on Texas possibly cost him the election of 1844?

Thinking Critically

1. In his later years, Ulysses S. Grant called the Mexican War "one of the most unjust ever waged by a stronger against a weaker nation." Identify some arguments that would support this conclusion.

Living as a Christian Citizen

1. The Whitmans' missionary work included both sharing the gospel and trying to civilize the Cayuse people. Today missions work in Third World countries often includes building schools, providing medical care, and doing other development work. Write a paragraph that discusses problems and benefits of such work.
2. Many Americans disapproved of the Mexican War. What are right ways for a Christian to respond when his government does wrong? What are wrong ways to respond?

People, Places, and Things to Remember

Manifest Destiny
Marcus and Narcissa Whitman
Stephen F. Austin
Davy Crockett
Sam Houston
Antonio López de Santa Anna
Alamo
Jim Bowie
William Travis
Battle of San Jacinto
Republic of Texas
Oregon Trail
Santa Fe Trail
Mormon Trail
John Tyler
Henry Clay
Daniel Webster
dark horse
James K. Polk
joint resolution
"Fifty-four-forty or fight!"
Mexican War (1846–48)
Zachary Taylor
Stephen Kearny
John C. Frémont
Bear Flag Republic
Winfield Scott
Treaty of Guadalupe Hidalgo
Gadsden Purchase

CRISIS
1848–1877

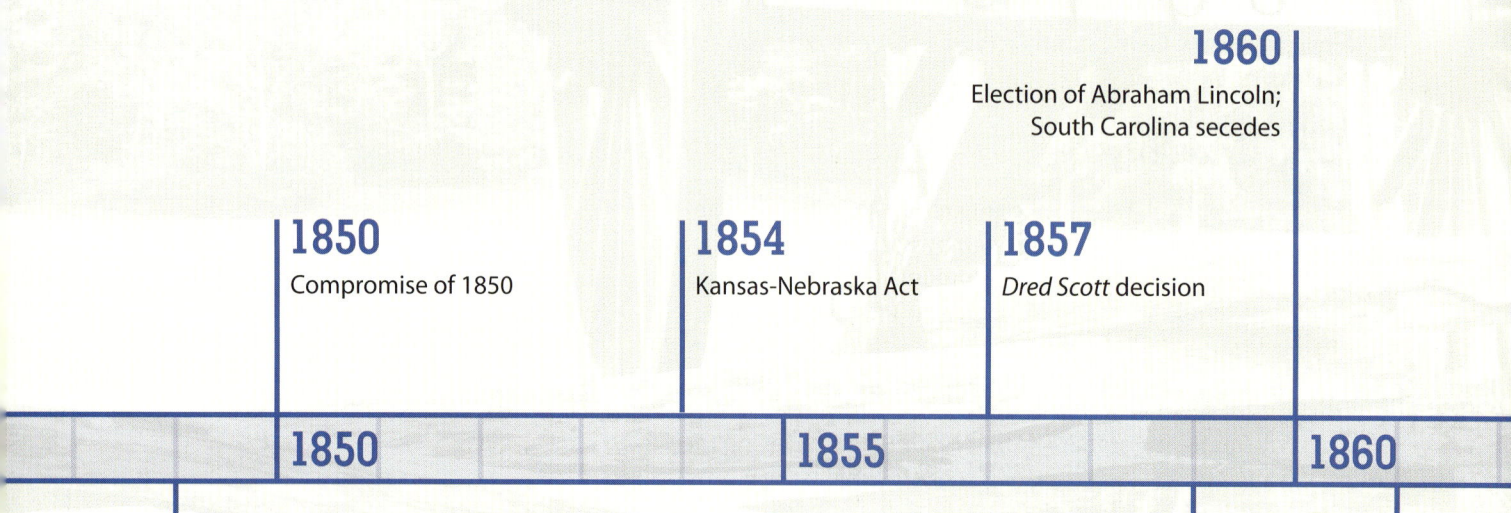

1860
Election of Abraham Lincoln; South Carolina secedes

1850
Compromise of 1850

1854
Kansas-Nebraska Act

1857
Dred Scott decision

1850 — 1855 — 1860

1849
California gold rush

1859
John Brown's raid on Harpers Ferry

1861
Firing on Fort Sumter

CHAPTERS

13 A HOUSE DIVIDING (1848–1861)

14 THE CIVIL WAR (1861–1865)

15 RECONSTRUCTION (1865–1877)

1863 Emancipation Proclamation takes effect

1866 Military Reconstruction Act

1865 Surrender at Appomattox; Lincoln assassinated

1868 Impeachment of Andrew Johnson

1877 Compromise of 1877

1865 — 1870 — 1875

13 A HOUSE DIVIDING (1848–1861)

And so we fool on into the black cloud ahead of us.

Mary Baykin Chestnut
April 11, 1861, diary entry from Charleston, South Carolina, the day before the firing on Fort Sumter

Abolitionists led slaves to freedom by means of the Underground Railroad.

Big Ideas

1. How was the slavery issue handled in the newly acquired American territories?
2. What political events set the stage for the Civil War?
3. What actions left the United States in a state of crisis by 1860?

I. Controversy

II. Conflict

III. Crisis

The 1850s was perhaps America's most *decisive* decade since nationhood, the 1860s its most *divisive*. The one decade prepared the way for the other. Although in 1858 Senator William Seward termed the coming war an "irrepressible conflict," the 1850s had actually provided many opportunities for peace and compromise. But like sand in an hourglass, these diminished with time. Americans of that day have rightly been called "the blundering generation": extremists in both the North and the South, with their often ruthless speeches, tore at the cords of union, and most people were merely content to watch them.

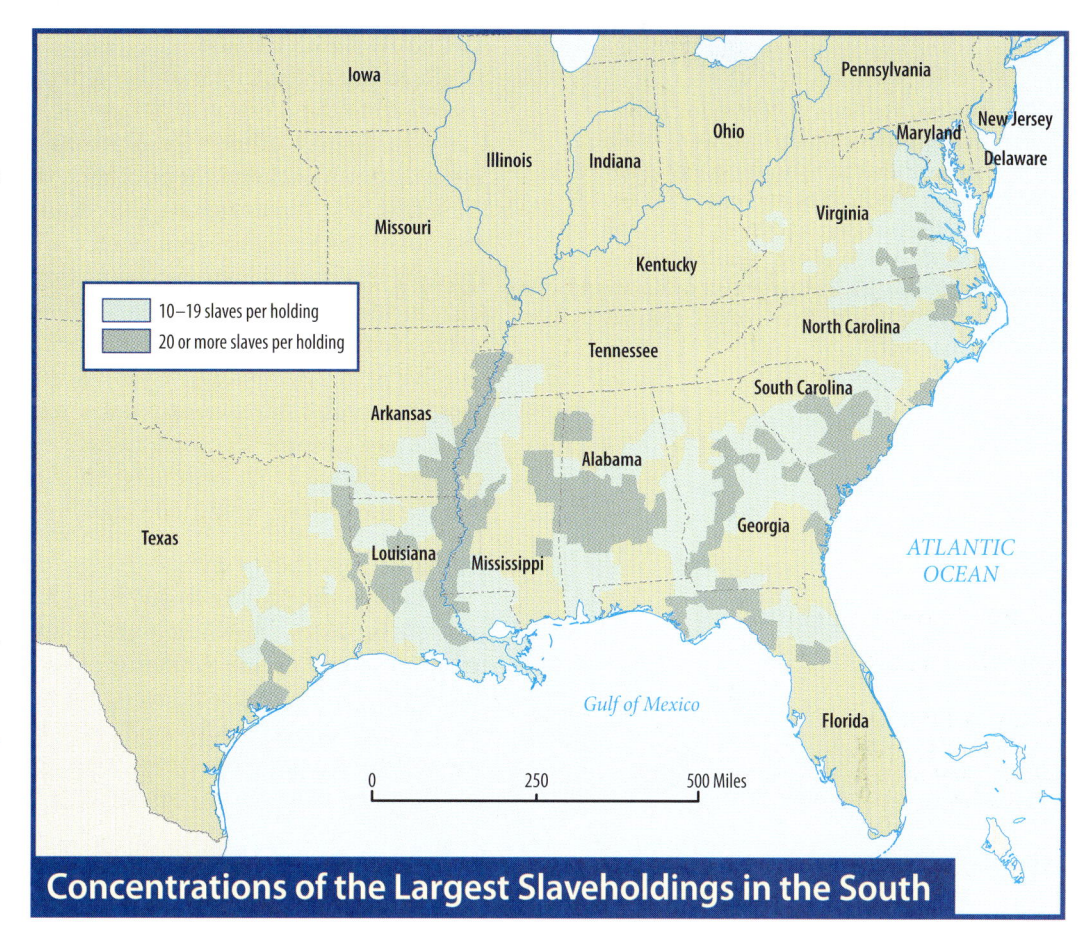

Concentrations of the Largest Slaveholdings in the South

- 10–19 slaves per holding
- 20 or more slaves per holding

I. Controversy

New Territories, Old Questions

As a result of the annexation of Texas and the Mexican War, the United States made the largest acquisition of territory in its history, larger even than the Louisiana Purchase. With the new lands came a revival of old problems. This time, however, the problems did not go away. They continued to fester throughout the 1850s and finally plunged the nation into war. Events seemed to confirm the gloomy prediction by poet and philosopher Ralph Waldo Emerson. During the Mexican War he wrote, "The United States will conquer Mexico, but it will be as the man who swallows arsenic which brings him down in turn. Mexico will poison us."

Wilmot Proviso

In 1846, President Polk sent a bill to Congress requesting funds to pursue negotiations with Mexico even while the fighting was occurring. A Democratic representative from Pennsylvania, David Wilmot, attached an amendment to the bill that became known as the **Wilmot Proviso**. It proposed that the United States prohibit slavery in any territory acquired from Mexico. The South was outraged, and Southerners in the Senate kept the proviso from becoming law. Nevertheless, Wilmot's amendment became a rallying point for antislavery forces. Over the next few years, antislavery congressmen repeatedly offered the Wilmot Proviso to Congress. Several times the act passed the House only to be rejected by the Senate.

Guiding Questions

1. What were three positions regarding slavery in the American territories?
2. How did the gold rush influence sectional divisions during this period?
3. What conflicts preceded the start of the Civil War?

David Wilmot

> **Seeds of Discord**
>
> One by one, the lines of communication were severed until Americans were talking past each other, then shouting past each other, then shooting at each other. The seeds of discord that had been in the soil since the founding of the republic were warmed in the 1850s by hateful rhetoric and watered with blood. They would soon yield a bitter harvest.

Calhoun Resolutions

Reacting to the threat of the Wilmot Proviso, many Southerners rallied to the position of Senator John C. Calhoun of South Carolina. In his **Calhoun Resolutions**, offered to the Senate in 1847, Calhoun outlined the Southern view of the status of slavery in the territories. Territories are the common possession of the states and not of the federal government, Calhoun argued. Therefore, slave owners have the same constitutional protection of their property (including slaves) in the territories as they have in their home states. Neither Congress nor territorial legislatures, Calhoun said, had the right to limit slavery. Only when a territory became a state could it prohibit slavery. Although Congress had previously prohibited slavery in some territories under the Missouri Compromise, Calhoun claimed that such measures were extraconstitutional acts that the South had permitted simply to preserve the Union.

Popular Sovereignty

Between the positions of Wilmot and Calhoun arose a compromise proposal known as **popular sovereignty**: the residents of a territory should decide the status of slavery in their territory. If the majority of voters wanted slavery, they could have it; if they did not want it, they could prohibit it. The doctrine of popular sovereignty was strongest among the Democrats. Lewis Cass of Michigan and later Stephen Douglas of Illinois became its leading proponents.

Election of 1848

In the presidential election campaign of 1848, the Democrats nominated Lewis Cass, champion of popular sovereignty. The Whigs decided to avoid the question altogether. They nominated **Zachary Taylor**, hero of the Mexican War. Although Taylor owned

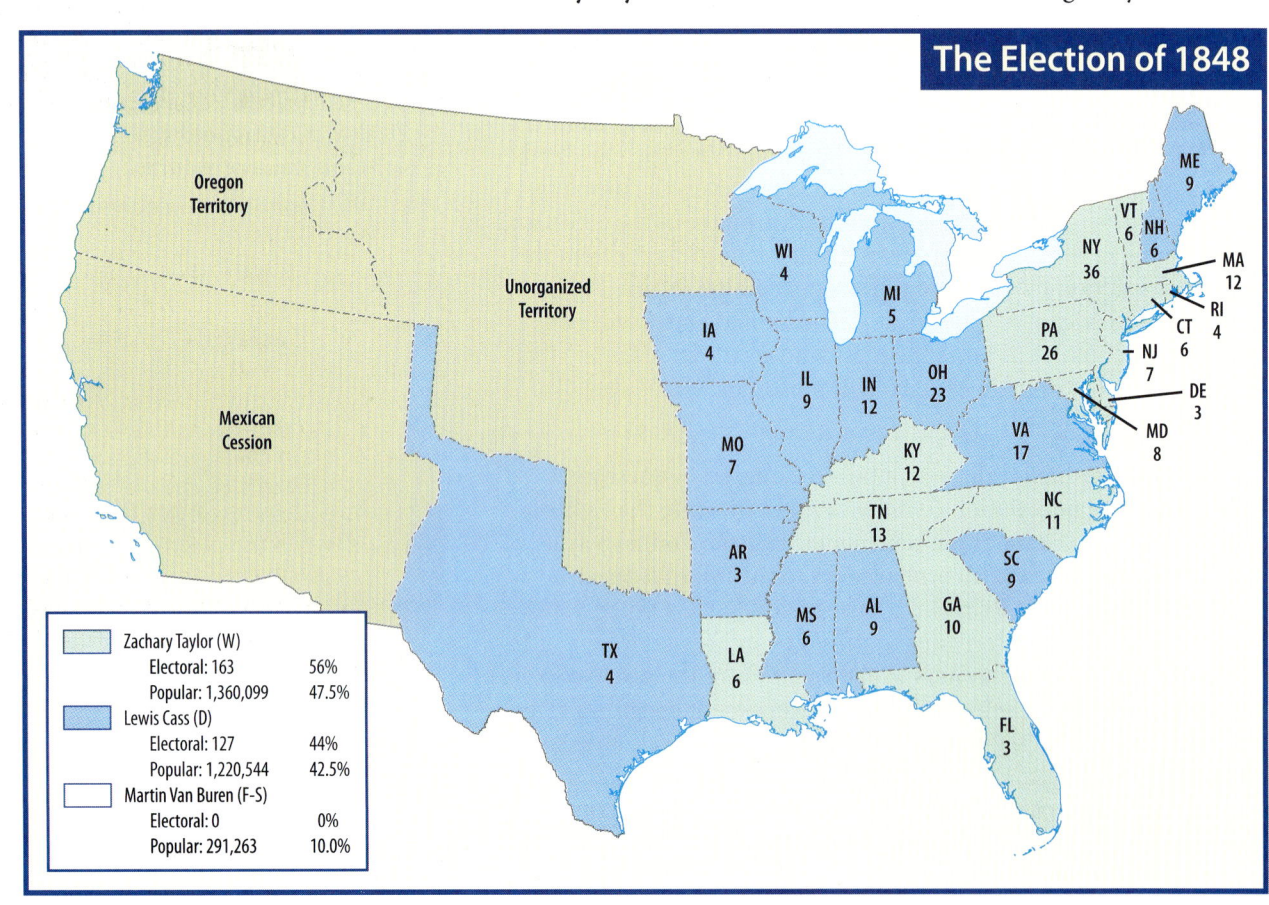

The Election of 1848

Zachary Taylor (W)
Electoral: 163   56%
Popular: 1,360,099   47.5%

Lewis Cass (D)
Electoral: 127   44%
Popular: 1,220,544   42.5%

Martin Van Buren (F-S)
Electoral: 0   0%
Popular: 291,263   10.0%

slaves on his plantation in Mississippi, his political views were little known. In fact, Taylor had never even voted in a presidential election. Copying their successful formula of 1840, the Whigs nominated a general, avoided adopting a platform, and emphasized instead the military achievements of their candidate.

The positions of Cass and Taylor were not likely to please either the antislavery forces or **Free-Soilers**, those who favored allowing slavery where it already existed but opposed its extension into the territories. The antislavery and Free-Soil groups joined forces to form a third party, the **Free-Soil Party**. Under the slogan "Free Soil, Free Speech, Free Labor, and Free Men," the new party warmly supported the Wilmot Proviso and nominated former president Martin Van Buren as its candidate. With Van Buren attracting dissatisfied Democrats in the North (particularly in New York), Taylor won a narrow victory over Cass. The new president faced a difficult situation. A dramatic discovery in California was about to spark a renewal of the sectional controversy.

California

Gold Rush

Swiss immigrant John Sutter arrived in California in 1839 while the region was still under Mexican control. After obtaining a grant of fifty thousand acres of land from the Mexican government, Sutter began building a large, self-sufficient ranch at the junction of the Sacramento and American Rivers (the site of the modern city of Sacramento). The transfer of California from Mexico to the United States in 1848 did not affect Sutter—at first. He continued his construction, planning to build a sawmill to provide lumber for his extensive ranch. In 1848, during the building of the mill, one of Sutter's foremen found some glittering stones below the mill's water wheel. The stones, he soon discovered, were gold. The foreman took the gold to Sutter, who tried to keep the matter quiet.

Such news, however, was impossible to conceal. Word spread first throughout California and then back to the eastern United States and overseas. "Gold fever" seized thousands of otherwise sensible men and drew them to California, where wealth was seemingly theirs for the taking. The **California gold rush** began. Because the first wave of gold hunters came in 1849, they all became known as **forty-niners**. Most forty-niners followed the overland route to California, like the pioneers who had followed the Oregon Trail. A number, particularly on the East Coast, went

Ships rot in the harbor of San Francisco, where crews had abandoned them to hunt for gold.

The Siren Call of Gold

The lure of wealth irresistibly drew men to California. Whole crews deserted when their ships landed on the West Coast, leaving the hulks to rot in the harbors. Some captains learned to take the precaution of putting their crews in chains before landing in San Francisco. Even many soldiers stationed in California abandoned their responsibilities and moved to the gold fields. Lieutenant William Sherman, who was later a famous Civil War general, complained bitterly, "None remain behind but we poor devils of officers who are restrained by honor."

Gold mining in California in 1849

THE WAY THEY GO TO CALIFORNIA.

This cartoon illustrates some of the fanciful ways people envisioned getting to California.

by sea. Some sailed to Central America, crossed the narrow bridge of land by mule and canoe, and tried to find a ship on the Pacific side going to California. Some took the all-water route, the long and dangerous journey around the southern tip of South America. In all, some eighty thousand men came to California in 1849, and more than four hundred thousand came in the ten years from 1848 to 1858.

Seeking gold was a gamble; only a few people were winners. Many gambled their savings, their occupations, and even their lives, believing that they would win. Some who hoped to strike it rich died in shipwrecks or on the trails without ever reaching California. Those who successfully staked claims found that standing in water all day and wielding a pick and shovel was hard, discouraging work. The few who found rich ore, however—if they were not murdered or swindled out of their claims—became wealthy and inspired stories that encouraged others to come.

Regardless of whether a prospector found gold, he seldom left California. The trip home was too long and the beauty of the region too appealing. Ironically, one man who did not share in the wealth was John Sutter. Much of his land was overrun by greedy gold hunters. He never profited from the gold rush that began there.

Statehood Question

The rush of people into California resulted in governmental chaos. The military rule installed after the Mexican War proved insufficient to govern the large number of sometimes unruly forty-niners. Out of necessity, California organized a government. Encouraged by President Taylor, California decided to skip the territorial stage, write a constitution, and apply for admission to the Union as a free state in late 1849. Southerners opposed the move. The admission of California would upset the balance between slave and free states in the Senate. Many Southern leaders also wanted Congress to clarify what would be done with the other lands taken from Mexico—the Utah and New Mexico territories. Some Southerners even talked of secession—withdrawing their states from the Union. An old, bitterly divisive controversy was heating up again.

The Great Debate

The West was driving a new wedge between the North and the South. The resulting crisis was evident on the Senate floor in what was perhaps the most extraordinary debate in congressional history. Three aging giants—Clay, Calhoun, and Webster—entered the political arena for the last time. The trio had begun their congressional careers in the days of Madison when they and the nation were young; now the old warriors were searching for a peaceful solution to calm the Republic's troubled waters.

Compromise of 1850

Henry Clay became known as "the Great Compromiser" because he had a major role in formulating three landmark agreements: the Missouri Compromise of 1820; the Compromise Tariff of 1833; and now the Compromise of 1850. As a concession to the North, he proposed that (1) California be admitted as a free state and that (2) the slave trade—but not slavery itself—be abolished in the District of Columbia. To the proslavery forces he offered (3) a new and more effective slave law, which required that all escaped slaves be returned to their masters, and (4) the protection of slavery in the District of Columbia. In addition, Clay offered the two sides

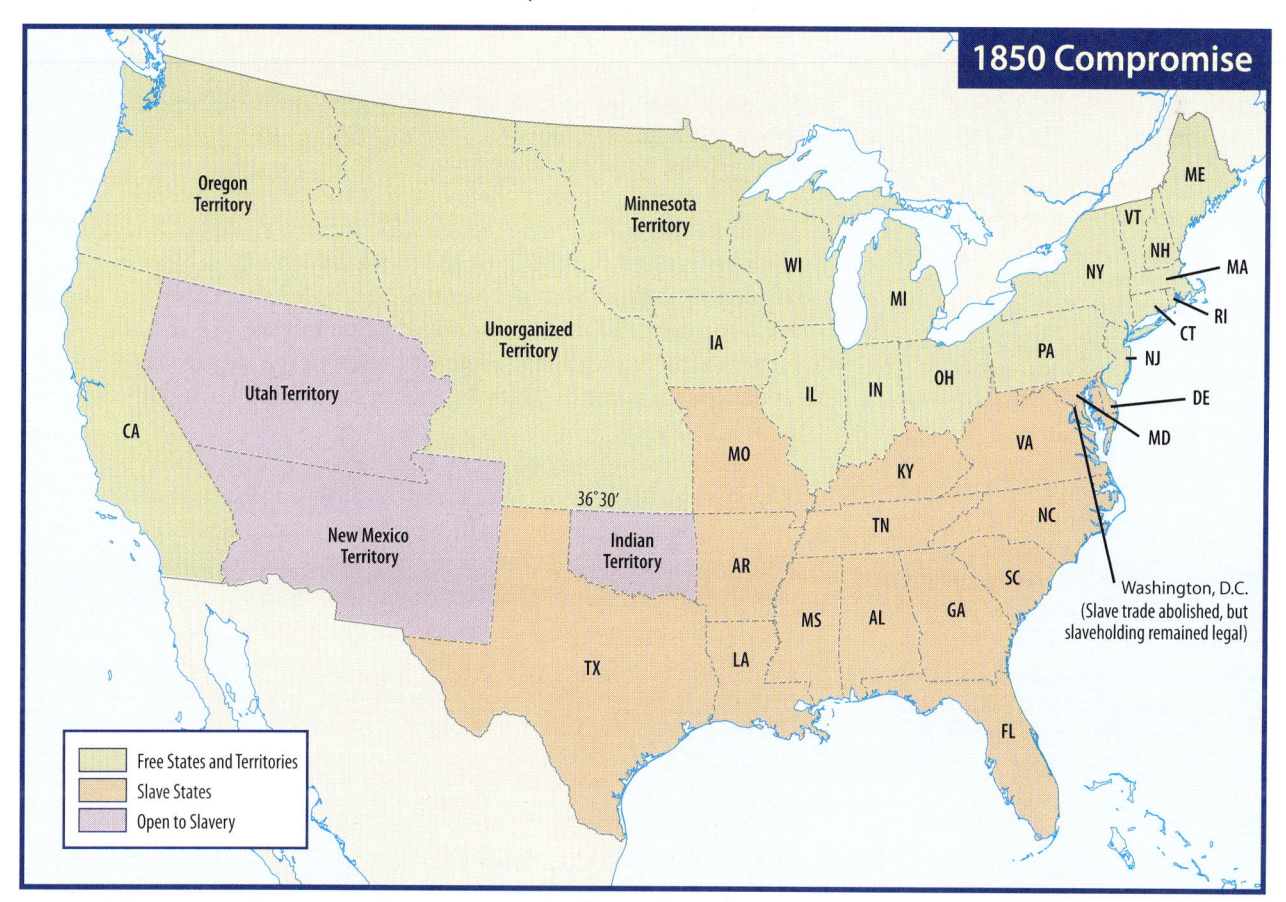

Henry Clay addresses the Senate in the historic debate about the Compromise of 1850.

The Death of Zachary Taylor

On July 4, 1850, Zachary Taylor strolled to the unfinished Washington Monument for some Independence Day speechmaking. It was a blistering day. When the president returned to the White House, hot and hungry, he ate some cherries and cucumbers and washed them down with milk and ice water.

The president quickly grew ill and suffered severe stomach pains until he died five days later. He had been in office for sixteen months. Food poisoning? Cholera (a deadly disease that could be caused by bacteria in the milk and water)? Gastroenteritis (an inflammation of the intestines that could be caused by the highly acidic cherries combined with the milk)? Murdered by means of arsenic poisoning? There has been no shortage of theories or rumors about his death.

In June 1991, some 141 years after his death, his coffin was opened and his remains were examined and subjected to a number of tests. The conclusion? Probably gastroenteritis or another intestinal ailment caused Taylor's death. No evidence of deliberate poisoning was found.

a joint concession, proposing that (5) the new territories of New Mexico and Utah be organized and the slavery question there would be decided by popular sovereignty.

Clay's proposals, collectively known as the **Compromise of 1850**, underwent intense debate from all sides. President Taylor opposed the Compromise for making concessions that might extend slavery into the territories. He thought debate on the Compromise would succeed only in deepening sectional division and delaying the admission of new territories.

The aging Calhoun came to the Senate on March 4 to present the South's position. Gravely ill and suffering intensely—he would be dead within three weeks—Calhoun was too weak to speak but gave his written remarks to a fellow senator to read. Calhoun declared that the Compromise did not go far enough in protecting Southern rights. Constitutional guarantees needed to be extended so that neither section could dominate the other. He argued that the Southern states might secede from the country.

Three days later, the eloquent Daniel Webster rose to speak. His "Seventh of March" speech was the most crucial and courageous of his distinguished career. Webster declared, "I wish to speak today, not as a Massachusetts man, nor as a northern man, but as an American. . . . I speak today for the preservation of the Union. 'Hear me for my cause.'"

Webster then noted that the bounds of slavery were already set by the Northwest Ordinance and the Missouri Compromise, as well as by geography. The barren conditions of the new territories could not support a slave economy anyway. Therefore, the Wilmot Proviso was needless and provocative.

The silver-tongued senator then turned his arguments in favor of union and compromise against the extremists in both sections. Webster blasted the abolitionists in the North and scolded the hotheaded secessionists in the South: "Secession! Peaceable Secession! Sir, your eyes and mine are never destined to see that miracle." If either extreme prevailed, Webster believed, the future was a "cavern of darkness." A far brighter future for the nation lay in "liberty and Union."

Abolitionists heaped every abusive adjective available upon Webster for his speech. Despite such criticism, Webster's support of the Compromise was a critical factor in sparing the country war and disunion. Another factor in the passage of the Compromise was the sudden removal of one of its most influential critics when President Taylor died. When the vice president, **Millard Fillmore**, succeeded to the presidency, he solidly backed Clay's proposals. By September they had passed Congress and were signed into law.

Sectional Strains

The Compromise of 1850 brought a shaky sense of relief. Tensions eased for a time even within the political parties. In 1852, the controversies over slavery expansion that had torn the Democrats apart in 1848 were laid aside. The Democrats' platform and their

The Election of 1852

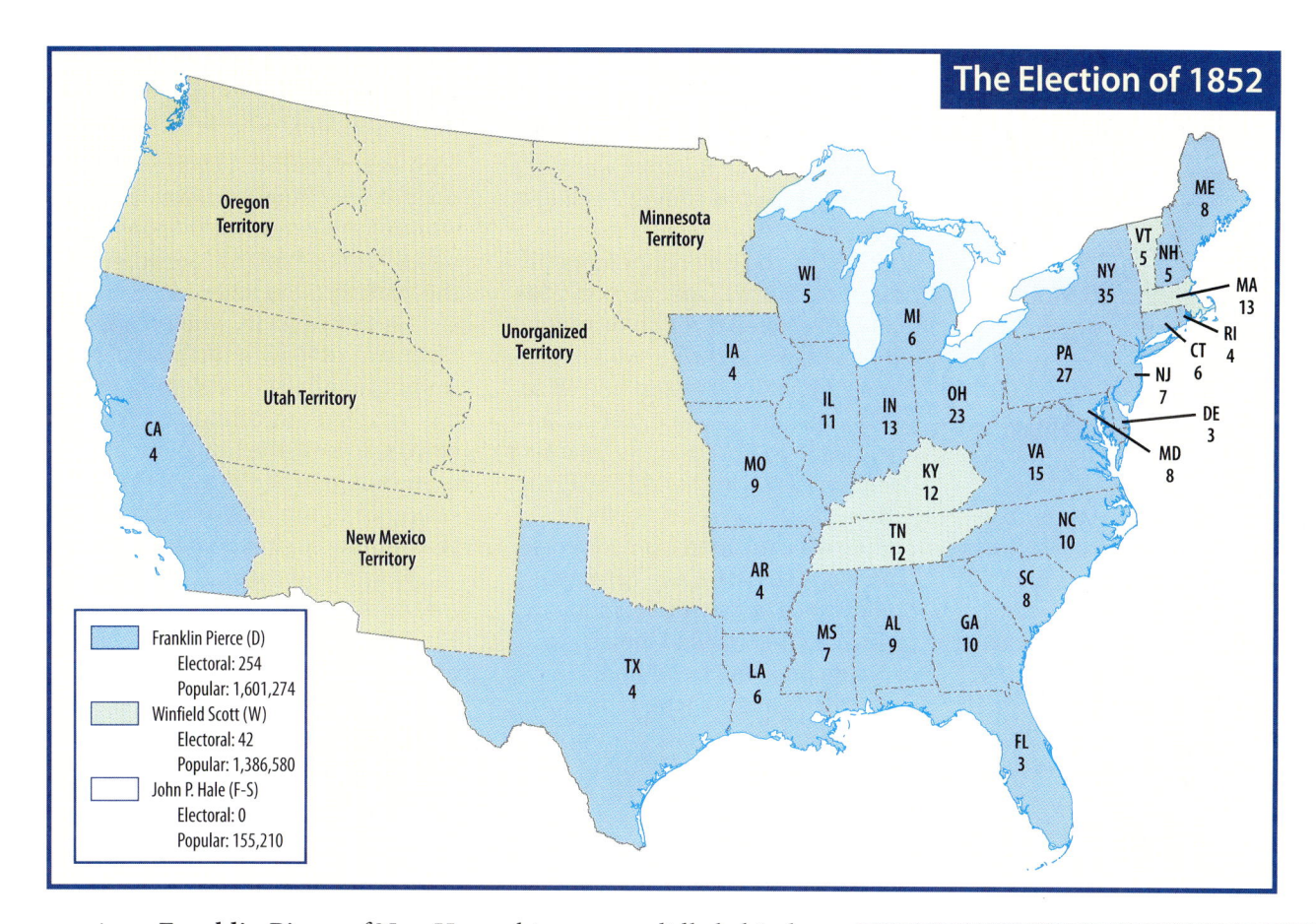

Candidate	Electoral	Popular
Franklin Pierce (D)	254	1,601,274
Winfield Scott (W)	42	1,386,580
John P. Hale (F-S)	0	155,210

nominee, **Franklin Pierce** of New Hampshire, were solidly behind the Compromise. Evidently, most of the voters were too. Pierce won a lopsided electoral victory in both the South and the North over the Whigs' candidate, General Winfield Scott. The Free-Soilers, who continued to support the Wilmot Proviso, polled only 155,210 votes of more than three million cast.

Ironically, the peace that the Compromise produced was soon shaken by the Compromise itself. One of its provisions, a concession to the South, was a new, tougher **Fugitive Slave Act**. The return of runaway slaves to bondage became a powerful emotional tool of the abolitionists in gradually turning public opinion. A number of them, such as Ralph Waldo Emerson, urged citizens to break the law on "the earliest occasion," and several Northern states practiced a version of nullification by passing "Personal Liberty" laws. These laws prohibited the imprisonment of runaway slaves and, in violation of the Fugitive Slave Act, guaranteed jury trials to them. Even some Northerners who were not abolitionists supported such measures. They feared that the lack of safeguards in the new federal law could result in free black Americans being kidnapped and sent into slavery. Of course, Southern slaveholders were furious with Northern resistance to the federal statute.

By the 1850s, some abolitionists were no longer just denouncing slavery but were attacking the South itself by portraying it as an evil culture built on the backs of black slaves. Although approximately one fourth of Southern families owned slaves, the abolitionist attacks had a decisive effect on Southerners. Many grew defensive and tried to portray slavery as positive, attempting to promote it as good and noble—stating that slaves had a better life than many of the poor in the North and in other countries. The most radical Southerners were the "Fire-Eaters," extremists who advocated the

Fugitive Slave Act (1850)

The Fugitive Slave Act proved to be the most controversial provision of the Compromise of 1850. The Constitution (in Article 4, Section 2, Clause 3) required that escaped slaves be returned to their masters. This law established a new process for doing so. Special federal commissioners now judged fugitive slave cases. They were paid ten dollars if they ruled for the slave owner and five dollars if they ruled against. The higher payment was justified on the grounds that ruling against an alleged fugitive required more paperwork, but opponents of slavery argued that the higher payment effectively was a bribe to influence the decision.

Before 1850 slave owners had to recapture fugitives with their own resources, but now they could demand the aid of U.S. Marshals. Citizens could be deputized by marshals and required to help recapture a fugitive. Marshals who refused were fined $1,000, and citizens who refused could also be punished. These provisions angered many in northern states, for they could be forced to aid slaveholders even if they opposed slavery as a moral evil. Northern resistance to the Fugitive Slave Act angered Southerners. In 1860, South Carolina listed the failure to enforce this act as one of the justifications for seceding from the Union.

The Underground Railroad

Harriet Tubman

As mentioned in Chapter 11, the Underground Railroad was an escape route for fugitive slaves through the Northern states (particularly Illinois, Indiana, Ohio, and Pennsylvania). The name's origin is uncertain. Some legends credit it to a slave owner who lost track of a fugitive slave he was pursuing. According to the story, the frustrated owner grumbled that Northerners must have an "underground railroad" to spirit off slaves. In theory, and in keeping with the railroad idea, the system consisted of a series of *safe houses* (also called *stations* or *depots*), each overseen by a *conductor*. Fugitives, called *passengers*, traveled secretly from house to house until they were safe in either the far northern states or Canada.

Actually, the Railroad was not as well organized as some tales might indicate. Escaping slaves usually had to use their own ingenuity to reach the North. One married slave couple escaped through disguise. The light-skinned wife, who could "pass" for white, dressed herself as an ailing, elderly white planter, and her husband posed as the "planter's" devoted slave. In that disguise, the couple easily traveled north. Another slave escaped from Virginia more directly. He had a carpenter build him a large wooden crate in which he then mailed himself to Philadelphia and freedom.

Once slaves reached the North, they found more help, although some slaves escaped without ever being aware of the existence of the Underground Railroad. "Conductors" gave runaway slaves food, shelter, and further directions on the route to safety. (Despite the legends, few fugitives hid in secret rooms or scurried through secret tunnels.)

Some of the best-known conductors were white abolitionists, such as Levi Coffin, a Quaker who openly aided fugitive slaves. His work was so extensive that some people called him the "president" of the Underground Railroad.

Harriet Tubman, who escaped slavery in 1849 with the help of the Underground Railroad, was perhaps the most famous conductor. William Lloyd Garrison, the noted abolitionist, nicknamed her "Moses," making reference to the prophet who led the Hebrews to freedom from Egypt.

How many slaves escaped by means of the Underground Railroad? Exact figures are almost impossible to determine. They certainly numbered in the thousands. Estimates range from 25,000 to as high as 100,000. But, in contrast to the millions of black people who remained slaves, the number is small. However, the Underground Railroad had great symbolic value. For the South, it symbolized Northern refusal to obey the fugitive slave laws. For the North, it was a protest against the injustice of slavery. For slaves, it simply meant freedom.

South's leaving the Union as the only way to preserve the Southern way of life.

Communication began to break down. Institutions that bound the regions together, such as religious denominations and political parties, fell apart along sectional lines. After 1850, the common ground of compromise would be increasingly difficult to find.

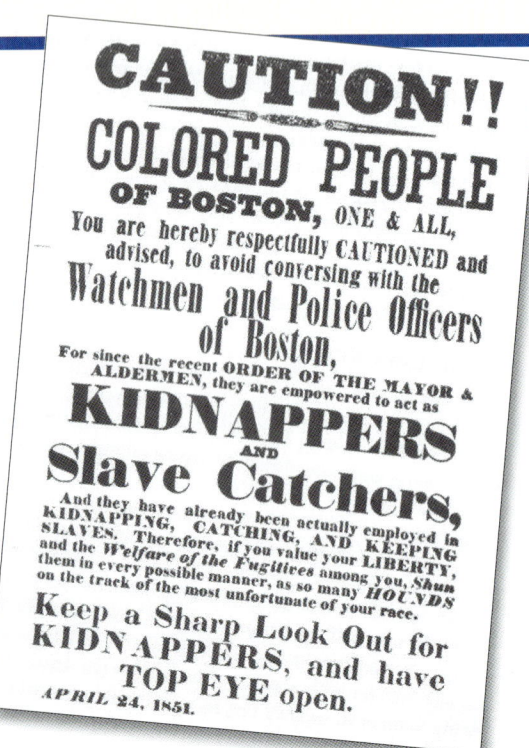

The Fugitive Slave Law gave abolitionists the opportunity to highlight the immorality of slavery to a wider public audience.

Section Review

1–3. What did each of the following state regarding slavery in the territories: Wilmot Proviso? the Calhoun Resolutions? popular sovereignty?

4–5. What two sea routes did forty-niners take to California?

6–10. What were the five provisions of the Compromise of 1850?

11. Why did some Northerners who were not abolitionists oppose the Fugitive Slave Law?

★ Should Christians have obeyed or violated the Fugitive Slave Law? Provide biblical reasons based on Romans 13 and 1 Timothy 1:10.

★ Propose a plausible alternative to the Fugitive Slave Law that would have avoided some of the act's tensions.

II. Conflict

Kansas-Nebraska Act

Despite the growing sectional conflicts and its own weaknesses, the Compromise of 1850 postponed war for several years. The overwhelming support for the pro-Compromise Democrats, led by presidential candidate Franklin Pierce in 1852, would certainly seem to indicate that most Americans wanted an end to bitter and divisive struggles. The wounds of sectional conflict were unwittingly reopened in 1854, however, by the actions of the major Democratic leader of the 1850s, Senator **Stephen A. Douglas** of Illinois.

Douglas, like many perceptive Americans of his time, envisioned the construction of a transcontinental railroad linking the East and the far West. The United States had arranged the Gadsden Purchase from Mexico, for example, as part of a potential southern route for such a line. Douglas, like most politicians, wanted his home state to benefit from the railroad by having it pass through Illinois. A transcontinental route from that state, however, would have to go through the unorganized portion of the Louisiana Purchase, which lay west of Missouri. The region would need an organized government to allow construction and maintenance of the line. Many Southerners opposed territorial organization, though, because of the still-unanswered questions about the expansion of slavery.

Douglas sought to win Southern support for his railroad by a clever piece of legislation. In the **Kansas-Nebraska Act** (1854), the Illinois senator proposed organizing two territories from the region—the Kansas Territory, just west of Missouri, and the Nebraska Territory, just west of Iowa. To settle the slavery issue, Douglas returned to the idea of popular sovereignty; each territory would decide the status of slavery for itself. To make popular sovereignty work and to please Southern congressmen, the act repealed the provision of the Missouri Compromise that banned slavery north of 36° 30′ latitude.

Southerners, of course, welcomed this opportunity to expand slavery into an area that had been previously closed to it. Northern resistance, on the other hand, was strong. Due to the large Democratic majority in Congress and the support of nearly all the South, the Kansas-Nebraska Act passed. Afterward a storm of protest erupted across the North and West as people objected to both the extending of slavery and the abandoning of the Missouri Compromise. Douglas bore much of the fury himself, but his party did not escape. More than two-thirds of the incumbent Northern Democrats in Congress lost their seats in the next election. Only seven of forty-four Northern Democrats in the House who voted for the act were reelected. More important, the Kansas-Nebraska Act resulted in two events that eventually destroyed the Democratic Party's dominance of American politics: the rise of the Republican Party and a virtual civil war in Kansas.

Rise of the Republicans

Collapse of the Whigs

The Whigs had never been a strongly unified party. It existed primarily as a coalition of various opponents to Democratic policies. The two times the party won a presidential election, 1840 and 1848, it had done so in part by refusing to adopt a platform. The poor

> **Guiding Questions**
> 1. What was the impact of the Kansas-Nebraska Act?
> 2. What were the political positions of the Whig, Know-Nothing, Republican, and Democratic parties?
> 3. What events led to the rise of the term "Bleeding Kansas"?
> 4. What was the impact of the *Dred Scott* decision?

How the Know-Nothings Got Their Name

This curious nickname arose from the secret societies, such as the Order of the Star-Spangled Banner, that were forerunners of the American Party. When people asked members about their secret group, they were taught to reply that they knew nothing about it. Outsiders soon called them "Know-Nothings."

Uncle Tom's Cabin (1852)

With the passage of the Fugitive Slave Act in 1850, **Harriet Beecher Stowe** wanted to bring the plight of slave families and runaways to public attention. In 1852, she wrote **Uncle Tom's Cabin**.

The Stowes had lived for a while in Cincinnati, Ohio, across the Ohio River from the slave state of Kentucky. There, she had met fugitive slaves. Using that experience, what she read in abolitionist papers, and her imagination, she wrote the novel. Within a year of publication, three hundred thousand copies had sold.

Stowe tried to capture the wide variety of American experience with slavery. She showed well-intentioned slave owners caught in an unjust system along with cruel masters. Northern abolitionists and Northern racists both appeared in the book. African American Christians appeared alongside non-Christian ones. But the point was consistent: the system of slavery was inescapably unjust. The book stirred opposition to slavery, but it angered many Southerners. Some accused Stowe of lying about the conditions of slaves.

Even though the novel was a best seller, more Americans heard the story as a play or musical rather than reading the book. Stowe's work had a huge impact. She was loved by many and despised by others. Some accounts say that when she visited the White House during the Civil War, Abraham Lincoln said, "So this is the little lady that started the big war."

Theatrical poster

---

showing in the presidential election of 1852 weakened the Whigs; the Kansas-Nebraska Act destroyed them. Southern Whigs almost unanimously supported the act; Northern Whigs almost unanimously opposed it. No political party could survive such a traumatic split. Within a few years, the Whigs had disappeared completely, and their collapse left a huge hole in America's political party system.

The Know-Nothings

For a time it seemed that the Whigs might be replaced by the American Party, better known as the **Know-Nothings**. The Know-Nothings arose in reaction to increasing immigration from Europe in the 1840s and 1850s. Problems such as the potato famine in Ireland and conflicts in Germany sent hundreds of thousands of Europeans fleeing to America for refuge. Many Americans feared that the immigrants would take jobs from native-born Americans. The fact that many of the immigrants were Catholic also caused uneasiness among Protestants. Some Catholic monarchs in Europe practiced tyranny and repression, and American Protestants feared that Catholics might somehow interfere with democratic institutions in the United States.

In 1854, the Know-Nothings capitalized on both fear of immigrants and resentment of the Kansas-Nebraska Act to score big gains in Congress and state legislatures. Though the Know-Nothings were stronger in the North, they displayed surprising strength in slave states such as Kentucky and Texas. The movement proved to be a passing fad, however. Simple negativism was not a strong base on which to build a party, and the Northern and Southern wings of the Know-Nothings had almost as little in common as Northern and Southern Whigs. After the 1856 presidential election, most Southern Know-Nothings eventually joined the Democrats. A number of Northern Know-Nothings joined a new party, the Republicans.

The Republicans

The real successor to the Whigs was the **Republican Party**. Although many cities compete for the title "birthplace of the Republican Party," the honor seems to go to Ripon, Wisconsin. On February 28, 1854, a rally of those opposed to the Kansas-Nebraska Act in that town called for others of like mind to join under the label of Thomas Jefferson's old party, "Republican." Soon, the Republican movement spread across the North, and the party was able to offer candidates in the 1854 election.

The Republicans began as a generally "antislavery party," but even that description covers a wide range of beliefs. Abolitionists naturally gravitated to the Republicans. Free-Soilers, those who opposed the expansion of slavery, also joined. Sadly, the party's opposition to slavery did not necessarily mean that all of its members had the interests of the slaves at heart. In fact, some Free-Soilers were more interested in preserving the territories for white settlers than in helping black slaves. The appeal of the Republicans was by no means built entirely on the slavery issue. The Republicans adopted many of the pro-business, nationalistic ideas of the Whigs, such as a protective tariff and government support of roads, railroads, and other internal improvements. Many Know-Nothings joined as well, if for no other reason than that the Democrats seemed to be the party of the immigrants. Republicans appealed to the small farmer by promising the distribution of inexpensive land to settlers in the western territories. Despite this range of interests, though, the Republicans remained strictly a sectional party; they were nonexistent in the South.

Election of 1856

The election of 1856 revealed both the strengths and the weaknesses of the Republicans and marked the decline of the Know-Nothings. Borrowing from the Whigs' tactics of choosing a hero as a presidential candidate, the Republicans bypassed their most prominent political leaders, such as New York senator William Seward. They instead nominated explorer-soldier **John C. Frémont**, "Pathfinder of the West" and a popular Mexican War commander. The Republicans also borrowed from the Free-Soil slogan of 1848 as they said that they were for "Free speech, free press, free soil, free men, Frémont and victory." The American Party (Know-Nothings) nominated former president Millard Fillmore, but his devotion to the anti-immigrant, anti-Catholic principles of the party was at best lukewarm. (In fact, Fillmore's daughter had been educated by nuns.)

The Democrats ignored their colorless incumbent, Franklin Pierce, and nominated an accomplished, though lackluster, legislator and diplomat, **James Buchanan**. As a native Pennsylvanian who was generally sympathetic to the South, Buchanan seemed the ideal candidate to unite all factions of the party. Also, he had been ambassador to Great Britain since 1853 and was therefore, unlike prominent Democrats such as Stephen Douglas, not associated with the controversial Kansas-Nebraska Act. Running on a platform defending popular sovereignty, Buchanan offered himself as the safe, sensible alternative to the "extremists," Frémont and Fillmore. Frémont proved successful in the North and West, carrying eleven states and winning 114 electoral votes. Fillmore, though winning many popular votes, carried only Maryland with its 8 electoral votes. However, Buchanan, as the head of the only party with a truly nationwide following, carried the entire South and enough Northern states to win 174 electoral votes and the election. Again the voters had chosen the moderate, middle course. Signs of trouble were evident, though. Buchanan had won only a plurality, not a majority of the votes, and several Southern leaders had threatened secession during the campaign if Frémont won.

"Bleeding Kansas"

During the 1856 campaign, Republicans repeatedly criticized the increasingly troublesome situation in the Kansas Territory. Douglas's system of popular sovereignty meant that the settlers there would decide the fate of slavery. As a result, large numbers of proslavery and antislavery advocates streamed into the territory, each side attempting to win the region for its position. Savage fighting occurred between the two factions, and the dissension-torn territory became known as "**Bleeding Kansas**."

Lawrence

The situation in Kansas steadily worsened. Thousands of proslavery Missourians—called "border ruffians" in the newspapers—

John C. Frémont

President James Buchanan

Border ruffians

Members of the Kansas Free State Battery fought proslavery groups in Kansas.

Much of Lawrence, Kansas, was destroyed in 1856.

A Northern cartoon reflects the outrage that Northerners felt over Representative Preston Brooks's beating of Senator Charles Sumner in the Senate chamber.

and antislavery forces—known as "free-staters"—clashed in open violence. In May 1856, three events within the span of five days (May 21–25) brought the Kansas conflict to national attention. First, on May 21, an army of border ruffians attacked the town of Lawrence, Kansas, a center of antislavery settlers. Because the citizens chose not to resist the attackers, only one man died, a ruffian who was killed when a collapsing building fell on him. However, the ruffians freely burned, looted, and destroyed the town. The **sack of Lawrence** outraged free-staters.

Sumner-Brooks Episode

About the same time, Senator Charles Sumner of Massachusetts, a fiery abolitionist, gave a heated Senate speech denouncing "the crime against Kansas." For two days, he verbally attacked his colleagues who supported slavery. He made particularly abusive statements about Andrew Butler, a senator from South Carolina. Butler was not present to defend himself. Two days later, just a day after the sack of Lawrence, Representative Preston Brooks of South Carolina, Butler's cousin, confronted Sumner in the nearly empty Senate chamber. The harsh language the Massachusetts senator had used was inexcusable, but Brooks's response was hardly justified. As Sumner sat at his desk, Brooks began to hit him repeatedly with a cane. Brooks continued to beat him mercilessly until Sumner was bloody and badly injured. Several senators stood idly by or kept others from interfering. To the North, Brooks's action confirmed the prejudice that Southern leaders were violent beasts. The Southern reaction did not help matters. Brooks's district overwhelmingly reelected him to the House, and admirers from all over the South sent him new canes. Brooks wrote proudly, "The fragments of the stick are begged for as sacred relics." Because of his injuries, Sumner did not return to the Senate for over two years. Brooks was later convicted of assault and assessed a fine but received no prison sentence. Many Southerns praised Brooks for his actions.

Pottawatomie Massacre

The news of the **Sumner-Brooks episode** enraged one Northerner to a murderous fury. **John Brown** was a fanatical abolitionist from Connecticut who had come to Kansas to help win the territory for the antislavery forces. A failure in every business venture he attempted, he soon dedicated himself to the antislavery cause. The sack of Lawrence infuriated Brown not only because the border ruffians had attacked the town but also because the free-staters had not fought back. Furthermore, when he received news of Brooks's beating of Sumner, Brown, in the words of his son, "went crazy—*crazy*." Gathering his followers about him on the night of May 24–25, he sought revenge by attacking several proslavery families along Pottawatomie (paht uh WAHT uh mee) Creek. In the grisly **Pottawatomie Massacre**, Brown's men butchered five proslavery settlers with razor-sharp swords.

Three episodes within a week—the sack of Lawrence, the Sumner-Brooks episode, and the Pottawatomie Massacre—highlighted how the deeply divisive issue of slavery could easily become violent. By the end of 1856, more than 200 people were killed in Kansas during the dozens of bloody incidents.

John Brown was never arrested or tried for the Kansas murders. Soon he had returned East where he was hailed as a hero among some in the abolitionist movement.

The *Dred Scott* Decision

On March 6, 1857, only two days after James Buchanan took office, the Supreme Court handed down a decision that further compounded the conflict over slavery. The case *Dred Scott v. Sandford* revealed that even the Supreme Court could not provide a solution to the problems that so troubled the nation.

Dred Scott was the slave of an army surgeon from Missouri. During the 1830s, he had taken Scott to the free state of Illinois and the unorganized free territory of the Louisiana Purchase. The owner later returned to Missouri, a slave state, with Scott. After the owner's death in 1843, Scott sought to gain his freedom on the grounds that he had become free by entering free territory and could not be reenslaved. The case eventually found its way to the Supreme Court.

With its pro-Southern majority, the Supreme Court under Chief Justice **Roger Taney** (TAW nee) welcomed the opportunity to settle the slavery question. In *Dred Scott v. Sandford* the court ruled that a slave was not a citizen and had no right to sue. According to the chief justice, the Constitution did not recognize slaves or free blacks as citizens. Black men, in Taney's words, "had no rights which the white man was bound to respect." Taney then went on to examine the Missouri Compromise, which he ruled unconstitutional on the grounds that it had unfairly deprived slaveholders of their property in territories north of 36°30′.

Of course, Taney's decision that Congress could not forbid slavery in the territories was hailed in the South and denounced in the North. It made slavery theoretically legal in all territories. It was now unclear whether or not slavery could be excluded from a territory by use of popular sovereignty. The decision only worsened sectional conflict. Animosity grew.

Dred Scott

Chief Justice Roger B. Taney

Lincoln-Douglas Debates

One man caught in the crossfire over the *Dred Scott* decision was Stephen A. Douglas. Although Douglas personally did not care whether a territory adopted or prohibited slavery, he strongly maintained under the doctrine of popular sovereignty that the citizens of a territory had the right to decide for themselves. In light of the *Dred Scott* case, Douglas had to find a way to reconcile popular sovereignty with the Supreme Court's ruling. In what became known as the **Freeport Doctrine** (after one of the cities in Illinois where he promoted the idea), Douglas argued that a territory could still prohibit slavery by refusing to adopt laws establishing and protecting it.

Douglas's Freeport Doctrine, as one would expect, drew the wrath of the proslavery forces. Douglas's political career was further threatened when he disagreed with President Buchanan regarding Kansas. Proslavery forces in that territory had managed to devise a state constitution that established slavery—although the majority of settlers were free-staters. Buchanan, eager to please the South and bring Kansas into the Union as a Democratic state, pushed Congress to accept the slavery constitution and admit Kansas. Douglas led a courageous group of

Stephen Douglas (*left*) and Abraham Lincoln (*right*) were opponents in the U.S. Senate race in Illinois in 1858 and in the presidential election in 1860.

Democrats who resisted the administration's attempts to oppose the will of the majority in Kansas. Under pressure from the Republicans and the Douglas Democrats, Congress put the constitution to a vote in the territory, and the Kansans rejected it overwhelmingly. As Douglas prepared to run for reelection in 1858, he faced opposition from his own Democratic president. In addition, the Republican Party had grown markedly stronger in Illinois and was offering a strong challenger to Douglas—Illinois lawyer **Abraham Lincoln**.

Abraham Lincoln

The story of Abraham Lincoln's life sounds like one of the classic "rags to riches" tales. He was born into the family of a poor farmer living near Hodgenville, Kentucky, in 1809. The family moved to southern Indiana when Abraham was only seven. In both places, the Lincoln family experienced the crushing poverty that burdened many settlers on the frontier. Young Lincoln spent his youth performing the backbreaking labor of a pioneer farmer—clearing and cultivating the land, splitting rails for fences, and trying to help keep his family from starving.

Lincoln's standard of living improved when the family moved to Illinois in 1830. There Lincoln was able to find work as a store clerk, postmaster, and surveyor. He had always had a desire for education but was able to attend school only infrequently; his formal education probably totaled about a year. However, Lincoln became an avid reader, eagerly consuming the works of Shakespeare, the poems of Robert Burns, and the Bible. He also began to study law on his own, and in 1836 he was licensed to practice.

Lincoln also developed a taste for politics. He joined the Whig Party, headed by his idol, Kentuckian Henry Clay, and became an influential leader in the Illinois party. He served four terms in the Illinois state legislature (1834–42) and one term as a member of the U.S. House of Representatives (1847–49). By 1850, however, Lincoln had left politics to devote himself to his profitable law practice in Springfield, Illinois.

Abraham Lincoln's character was a mixture of genuine kindness, personal ambition, and unflinching determination. His reputation for honesty earned him the nickname "Honest Abe." Even political opponent Stephen Douglas said that Lincoln "is as honest as he is shrewd." His thoughtfulness and generosity, not to mention his sense of humor and talent for telling amusing stories, charmed those who met him. The driving force behind his political thinking was that slavery was wrong. He often quoted the Declaration of Independence's famous phrase "All men are created equal." Later Lincoln said, after his election to the presidency, "I have never had a feeling politically that did not spring from the sentiments embodied in the Declaration of Independence." Primary among those sentiments, he said, was the "promise that in due time the weights should be lifted from the shoulders of all men, and that *all* should have an equal chance."

Yet Lincoln was a realist. He knew that slavery could not be easily eliminated, and he believed that the federal government had no right to interfere with slavery in the states where it already existed. Lincoln satisfied himself with the Free-Soil doctrine that slavery should not be allowed to expand any farther. He condemned popular sovereignty because it attempted to avoid the moral concerns about slavery. The territories must be kept free. Perhaps then, Lincoln thought, slavery would eventually die out.

The Kansas-Nebraska Act brought Lincoln out of his political retirement. "I was losing interest in politics," Lincoln wrote in 1859, "when the repeal of the Missouri Compromise aroused me again." Lincoln denounced the act because it offered the possibility of slavery's expansion into the territories. His eloquence and folksy, relaxed manner pleased listeners and attracted the attention of many. Conservative by nature, Lincoln tried to work within the dying Whig Party. Eventually, however, he realized that the Republicans offered him a better political future. By 1858 he was the leading Republican in Illinois and the natural choice to oppose incumbent Stephen Douglas for the U.S. Senate.

The Debates

Lincoln launched the campaign by giving one of his most famous speeches. Quoting in part from Mark 3:25, Lincoln said,

> "A house divided against itself cannot stand." I believe this Government cannot endure permanently half slave and half free. I do not expect the Union to be dissolved—I do not expect the house to fall—but I do expect it will cease to be divided. It will become all one thing or all the other.

Douglas immediately charged Lincoln with promoting conflict and discord. After all, Douglas argued, the nation had existed as half slave and half free since its founding. Why should it not continue to do so? Lincoln responded by challenging Douglas to a series of debates. Douglas accepted, and the **Lincoln-Douglas debates** became a platform for not only the Illinois election but also the national debate on slavery.

Lincoln and Douglas met seven times at different sites in Illinois. Douglas continued to promote popular sovereignty as the answer to the slavery question. He also played on the racist prejudices of his listeners by accusing Lincoln of preaching the absolute equality of the races. "I do not believe that the Almighty ever intended the negro to be the equal of the white man," said Douglas. "He belongs to an inferior race, and must always occupy an inferior position."

Put on the defensive, Lincoln—reflecting the prejudices of the day—retreated from the issue of equality. "I am not nor ever have been in favor of bringing about in any way the social and political equality of the white and black races," he told one audience. Lincoln refused to deny that slavery was immoral, however, and restated his conviction that its expansion must be prohibited. In another town, Lincoln declared,

> Notwithstanding all this, there is no reason in the world why the negro is not entitled to all the natural rights enumerated in the Declaration of Independence, the right to life, liberty, and the pursuit of happiness. . . . [I]n the right to eat the bread, without the leave of anybody else, which his own hand earns, *he is my equal and the equal of* [Stephen] *Douglas, and the equal of every living man.*

The heart of the controversy, Lincoln said, was not black equality but the immorality and expansion of slavery. "The real issue in this controversy . . . is the sentiment on the part of one class that looks upon the institution of slavery *as a wrong*, and of another class that *does not* look upon it as a wrong." Douglas, with his indifference to slavery, was in the second group. Lincoln was part of the first group, believing that slavery should "be treated as a wrong,

One of the seven debates between Lincoln and Douglas in 1858

Lincoln-Douglas Debates (1858)

1. Ottawa — August 21
2. Freeport — August 27
3. Jonesboro — September 15
4. Charleston — September 18
5. Galesburg — October 7
6. Quincy — October 13
7. Alton — October 15

and one of the methods of treating it as a wrong is to make provision that it shall grow no larger."

When the state legislature chose a senator, Douglas won the close election and continued to serve in the Senate. Although Lincoln lost, he had gained national attention for his views. Two years later, Lincoln would win a greater prize.

Section Review

1. Why did Stephen Douglas propose the Kansas-Nebraska Act?
2–4. What three events during the period of May 21–25, 1856, focused national attention on Kansas?
5. What did the *Dred Scott* decision do to the Missouri Compromise?
6. Why did Stephen Douglas break with President James Buchanan?
7. How did Abraham Lincoln and Stephen Douglas differ concerning the expansion of slavery?
★ Assess the impact of *Uncle Tom's Cabin* on the nation.
★ Explain how campaigning as Lincoln and Douglas did in 1858 was an improvement when compared to typical campaigns during that period.

III. Crisis

John Brown's Raid

While politicians debated the slavery matter, John Brown continued his work. Several months after his grisly Pottawatomie murders, he appeared in the plush parlors of Boston's elite. That Brown could gather such audiences says as much about the temper of the times as about the charisma of the man.

Between 1857 and 1859, Brown raised money and an army for his grand but ill-conceived scheme to start a slave revolt in the South. His far-fetched plan of mass murder and violence seemed to confirm Brown's strange mental state, yet a group of supporters known as the Secret Six, which included some of the most prominent clergymen and abolitionists in the Northeast, endorsed the plan. In addition, dozens of others were aware of Brown's intentions. Brown's ties with such well-placed supporters, revealed after the plot unraveled, would further poison sectional relations.

Raid on Harpers Ferry

In the fall of 1859, Brown and several followers moved secretly to a farmhouse near **Harpers Ferry**, Virginia (now West Virginia), to wait for promised supplies to arrive from supporters in New England. In October, Brown was ready to attack the federal arsenal at Harpers Ferry, strategically located at the junction of the Shenandoah and Potomac Rivers. Brown expected to capture the arsenal and its large supply of weapons for a spontaneous slave revolt. He apparently believed that enough slaves and abolitionists would join him to make the plan successful.

During the night of October 16, 1859, Brown and his gang of twenty-one raiders captured the arsenal and cut the telegraph lines.

Guiding Questions

1. How did John Brown's raid affect sectional strife?
2. What were some of the unusual aspects of the 1860 election?
3. What were arguments for and against secession?

The Secret Six

John Brown's infamous raid on Harpers Ferry was supported and largely financed by the following Northern abolitionists:

Gerrit Smith, landowner and reformer; later suffered a breakdown and was committed to Utica Insane Asylum

Samuel G. Howe, physician and husband of Julia Ward Howe (composer of the "Battle Hymn of the Republic"); fled to Canada

Thomas W. Higginson, preacher; commanded a regiment of black soldiers during the Civil War

Theodore Parker, preacher and reformer; died of tuberculosis in Italy

George Stearns, businessman; fled to Canada

Franklin Sanborn, teacher

By the next morning, alarmed citizens and militia from Harpers Ferry and nearby towns had surrounded the arsenal. As the day wore on, several people on both sides were mortally wounded, including two of Brown's sons. Ironically, the first person that Brown's raiders killed was a free black man working as a baggage man on a train.

Word of the raid spread quickly. Colonel Robert E. Lee received orders to take command of federal troops in the area and recapture the arsenal. On the morning of October 18, Lee ordered a detachment of marines under the command of Lieutenant James Ewell Brown (J.E.B.) Stuart to take Brown's stronghold. After a brief fight, Brown and his remaining raiders were captured and jailed.

This sketch of U.S. Marines storming the engine house at Harpers Ferry to capture John Brown was drawn by an artist who was at the scene when it happened.

Aftermath

At his trial, Brown was convicted of murder and treason. He spent November in prison awaiting execution. Southerners were, of course, eager for the man who had such ruthless designs against them to receive his just reward. A number of Republicans, embarrassed by Brown's ties to their party, were also eager that he be soon silenced. As for the old man himself, he eagerly awaited his execution date. The self-styled martyr saw it as a date with destiny in which he would gain greater glory than he had achieved in life. In a letter to his wife, Brown wrote, "I have been *whiped* [sic] as the saying *is*; but am sure I can recover all the lost capital occasioned by that disaster; by only hanging a few moments by the neck; & I feel quite determined to make the utmost possible out of a defeat."

On December 2, 1859, John Brown's body swung from a noose in Charlestown, Virginia, but this was no routine execution. It was the inauguration of a period of mourning in the North that shocked the South by its excess. Buildings were draped with black, church bells rang, and poets and pulpiteers poured out their most eloquent words on Brown, so recently convicted for murder and treason. Abolitionists found his death a useful symbol, and such famous writers as Ralph Waldo Emerson, Henry David Thoreau, and Louisa May Alcott compared Brown to Christ. Ironically, Thoreau also called Brown "an angel of light," apparently unaware that this is a scriptural name for Satan (2 Cor. 11:14). In that context, most Southerners would have heartily agreed with Thoreau.

The majority of Northerners, however, did not support slave revolts or Brown's methods. Lincoln noted that although Brown "agreed with us in thinking slavery wrong. That cannot excuse violence, bloodshed and treason." Others went even further, denouncing Brown's actions as "among the gravest of crimes."

These voices of moderation, however, were not being heard in the South above the increasing clamor. Understandably, unionist sympathies in the South were evaporating, and fear of both secret plots and slave revolts multiplied after Harpers Ferry. Across Dixie, Brown's ties with Republican leaders meant guilt by association.

John Brown shortly before his hanging in 1859

Stephen Douglas's height, reportedly five feet four inches, and forceful personality earned him the nickname "Little Giant."

John C. Breckinridge of Kentucky

John Bell of Tennessee

If the Republicans came to power, Southerners believed, the South was not safe. Such dark thoughts foretold ill for the future as the nation stumbled into the new and fateful year of 1860.

Election of 1860

The election of 1860 was probably the most critical contest in American politics. Perhaps, with the nation so divided following the Harpers Ferry plot, it was not a good time to be choosing a new president. But the Constitution required it. The outcome of the campaign would shatter the last truly national institution tying the sections together—the Democratic Party—and serve as a stimulus for dissolving the Union.

Democratic Division

The Democratic Party held its convention in Charleston, South Carolina, in April 1860. As it began, Stephen Douglas was generally the preferred presidential nominee over the incumbent, James Buchanan. The struggle over the party platform had created a serious rift.

Douglas supporters wanted simply to follow the 1856 platform, which called for congressional noninterference with the slave question in the territories and the use of popular sovereignty. A number of representatives from the Deep South states called for federal protection of slavery in the territories. Buchanan's supporters, trying to deny Douglas the nomination, advocated this idea. When the Northern delegates rejected the proposal, delegates from several Southern states left the convention.

Eventually, the sectional factions reconvened separately in Baltimore. Northern Democrats nominated Douglas, while Southern Democrats nominated Buchanan's vice president, **John C. Breckinridge** of Kentucky. In addition, a new group emerged. It was a coalition of conservative Southerners and Northerners, including many former Whigs, calling themselves the **Constitutional Union Party**. They nominated **John Bell**, a former U.S. senator from Tennessee for the presidency. The Constitutional Union platform was probably the most concise in American history: "The Constitution of the Country, the Union of the States and the Enforcement of the Laws." Bell's party, representing much of the sentiment in the Upper South and border states, offered a pro-Union alternative to those who believed that a Republican victory would bring disunion. Despite the attempts by all the Democratic factions to keep the Union intact in their own way, the division of their ranks virtually ensured Republican success.

Lincoln's Victory

Republicans met in Chicago for their convention. Although William Seward seemed to be the favorite for the nomination, Abraham Lincoln won the top spot on the ticket. The Republican platform reflected the coalition character of the party. The party opposed the expansion of slavery into the territories and supported a protective tariff for Northern business interests. It also endorsed a transcontinental railroad and opening of western lands to appeal to farmers and immigrants. The Republicans also tried to calm Southern fears by pledging not to interfere with slavery where it already existed.

The presidential campaign was really two sectional races: Lincoln and Douglas competing in the North, Bell and Breckinridge

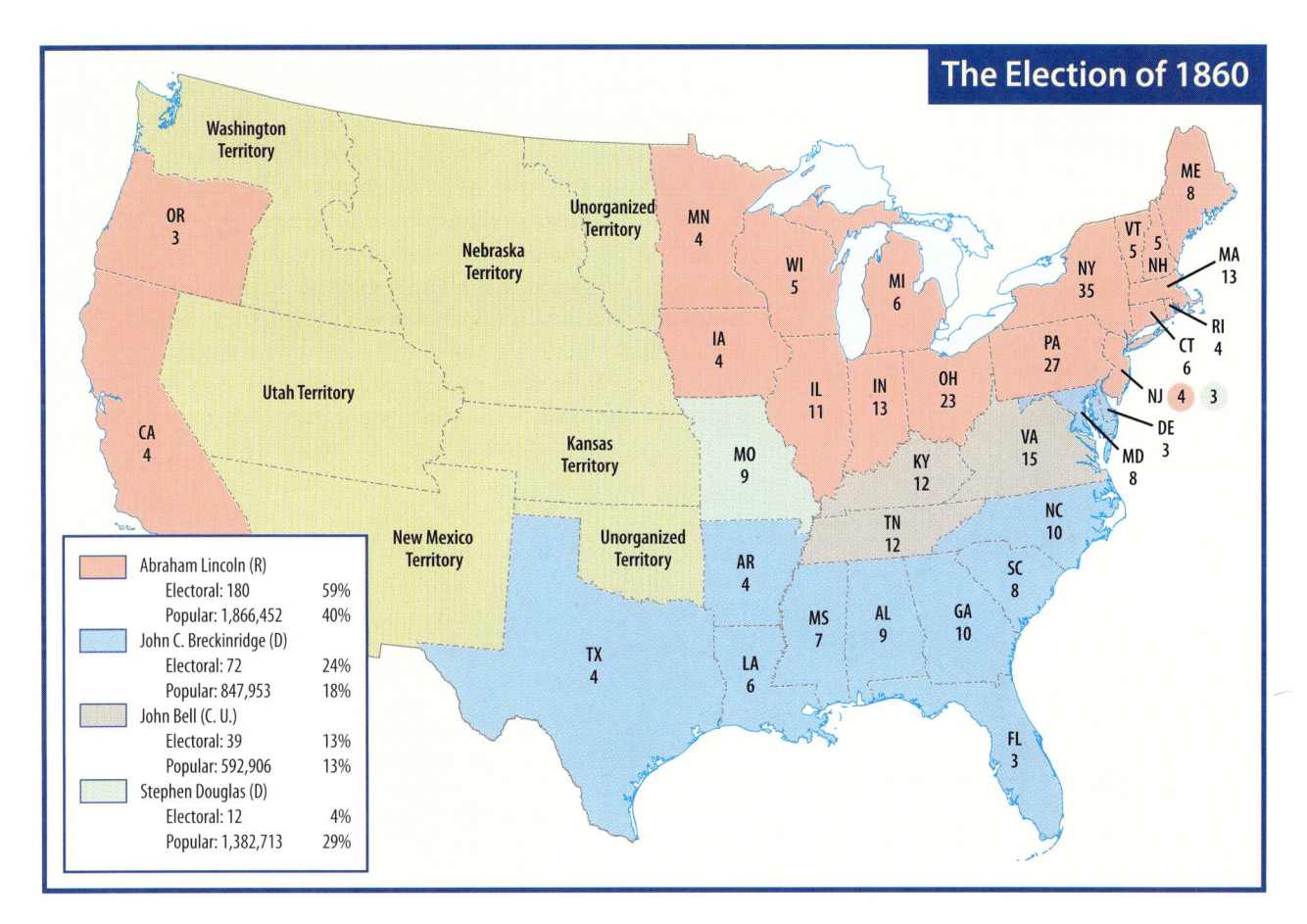

The Election of 1860

Abraham Lincoln (R)
- Electoral: 180 — 59%
- Popular: 1,866,452 — 40%

John C. Breckinridge (D)
- Electoral: 72 — 24%
- Popular: 847,953 — 18%

John Bell (C. U.)
- Electoral: 39 — 13%
- Popular: 592,906 — 13%

Stephen Douglas (D)
- Electoral: 12 — 4%
- Popular: 1,382,713 — 29%

in the South and border states. Douglas became the first presidential candidate to make a nationwide campaign tour, including the South, where he did not expect many votes. With the Democrats hopelessly divided, Lincoln won by a plurality with just under 40 percent of the popular vote. Since his sectional strength was confined to the more populous North, however, he gained a strong majority in the Electoral College.

Secession

The election results triggered disunion. Many leaders in the Deep South had promised that if Lincoln won, they would not submit themselves to what they considered a hostile, strictly Northern party. They would **secede** (leave the Union).

South Carolina led the way on December 20, 1860, by unanimously approving an **Ordinance of Secession**. It was South Carolina's Declaration of Independence. By February 1, 1861, six more states in the Deep South—Mississippi, Florida, Alabama, Georgia, Louisiana, and Texas—had joined South Carolina in seceding. On February 8 in Montgomery, Alabama, those seven Southern states formed the Confederate States of America, or the Confederacy. **Jefferson Davis**, a former senator from Mississippi and the secretary of war under Franklin Pierce, was elected president of this newly declared nation.

Attempts at Compromise

As the nation unraveled, men frantically searched for a compromise. Unfortunately Henry Clay, Daniel Webster, and John C. Calhoun were dead. Men of lesser ability now governed. Buchanan sat in the White House fretting, frustrated, and indecisive. President-elect Lincoln repeated his campaign promise not to interfere with slavery in the states where it already existed, but he refused to commit himself to any course of action until he took office and personally held the reins of power.

As precious time slipped away in the weeks following the election, Senator **John J. Crittenden** of Kentucky proposed a series of constitutional amendments that would reinstate the Missouri Compromise line of 36°30′ for the western territories and guarantee the protection of slavery where it already existed. Crittenden made a noble effort to save the Union and preserve the peace, but his compromise ultimately failed in the Republican-controlled Congress. It was the last, desperate hope of avoiding war. Its failure would cost Crittenden dearly—one of his sons would become a general in the Union army, another a general in the Confederate army.

First Fire

Only a spark was needed to bring the country to war. Anger in the North over Southern secession and fear in the South that the North would try to forcibly prohibit such a move meant neither side was eager for reconciliation. The spark was the issue of federal forts in the South, particularly **Fort Sumter**, strategically centered in the mouth of the Charleston, South Carolina, harbor. In early March 1861, that fort remained under the federal government's control. Almost all other forts in the seceding states were now controlled by the Confederacy.

On March 4, 1861, Lincoln became president. In his inauguration speech, he pledged again not "to interfere with the institution of slavery in the States where it exists. I believe I have no lawful right to do so, and I have no inclination to do so."

As Lincoln began his term, the Confederacy sent three peace commissioners to Washington to resolve the problem of federal forts. Both Lincoln and his Secretary of State, William Seward,

---

Lincoln's View of Secession

In his first inaugural address, Lincoln stated why he believed states could not leave the Union. By that time, seven states had claimed the right to do so. Four others later joined them. In his speech, the new president said,

> I hold that in contemplation of universal law and of the Constitution the Union of these States is perpetual [permanent]. . . .
>
> If the United States be not a government proper, but an association of States in the nature of contract merely, can it, as a contract, be peaceably unmade by less than all the parties who made it? One party to a contract may violate it—break it, so to speak—but does it not require all to lawfully rescind [abolish] it? . . .
>
> It follows from these views that no State upon its own mere motion can lawfully get out of the Union; that *resolves* and *ordinances* to that effect are legally void, and that acts of violence within any State or States against the authority of the United States are insurrectionary or revolutionary. . . .
>
> I therefore consider that in view of the Constitution and the laws the Union is unbroken, and to the extent of my ability, I shall take care, as the Constitution itself expressly enjoins upon me, that the laws of the Union be faithfully executed in all the States. . . .
>
> In doing this there needs to be no bloodshed or violence.

refused to meet the commissioners personally. They thought that doing so would be, in effect, recognizing the Confederate government. Seward, however, sent word that Fort Sumter would be evacuated and on April 7 confirmed his promise in writing—although it is unclear whether Lincoln knew of Seward's actions. On April 9, when the commissioners learned that a squadron of ships had been sent to take supplies to the fort, they concluded that they had been deceived. Lincoln notified the governor of South Carolina of his intentions to send food, but not military supplies, to the fort. Confederate leaders decided to stop the supplies from reaching Sumter. They believed that allowing federal troops to continue to occupy the fort would be a threat to the Confederacy's independence.

On the other hand, Lincoln had pledged in his inaugural speech to "hold, occupy, and possess" federal property in the states that had formed the Confederacy. Therefore, he was clearly opposed to surrendering Fort Sumter.

When Lincoln's naval expedition neared Charleston on April 12, 1861, Confederate General Pierre G. T. Beauregard opened fire on Fort Sumter, which was commanded by Major Robert Anderson. Ironically, when Beauregard was a cadet at West Point, his artillery instructor was the same Robert Anderson. Now Beauregard had an opportunity to show his former teacher just how well he had learned his lessons. After a two-day bombardment Anderson surrendered the garrison; Union troops were permitted to leave for New York on steamships.

On April 12, 1861, the Confederates opened fire on Fort Sumter.

Remarkably, no one on either side had been killed in the two-day fight. (Two men were killed in an accidental explosion after the battle ended.) War, however, had begun. The day after the surrender, Lincoln called for the states still in the Union to supply a total of seventy-five thousand troops to suppress the secessionist states. Many Northern states responded readily with troops. Other states were not so cooperative.

Extremists in both the North and the South welcomed the war as an opportunity to teach the other region a lesson. In the Upper South, many people had hoped for reconciliation. When Lincoln recruited soldiers to invade the South, four additional states—Virginia, Arkansas, Tennessee, and North Carolina—also seceded. They refused to fight their sister states. There were now eleven states in the **Confederate States of America (CSA)**.

Declaration of War

Confederate President Jefferson Davis wrote, "The order [by Abraham Lincoln] for the sailing of the fleet [to Fort Sumter] was a declaration of war. The responsibility is on their shoulders, not on ours. A deadly weapon has been aimed at our heart. Only a fool would wait until the shot has been fired." Lincoln, on the other hand, believed that he would be accepting the right of states to secede if he did not defend federal property in the South. As he said in his inaugural address, "The power confided to me will be used to hold, occupy, and possess the property and places belonging to the government."

Does a State Have the Right to Secede?

Talk of secession had occurred at various times for assorted reasons in both the North and the South since the earliest years of the Republic. The foundational argument was that the individual sovereign (self-governing) states had voluntarily united with other sovereign states to form a union. Having entered the Union voluntarily, they could at any time voluntarily leave it.

Furthermore, those who favored secession noted that nowhere did the Constitution prohibit it. They argued that since the Tenth Amendment stated that powers not delegated to the federal government nor prohibited to the states were reserved to the states or the people, states could leave the Union.

Opponents of secession disagreed with the theory that the states retained their sovereignty. They pointed to Article V of the Constitution and noted that it does not recognize the states as independently sovereign in terms of amending the Constitution. An individual state may object to an amendment but is nonetheless bound by it if it meets the stipulations of Article V. This position insisted that ratification of the Constitution entailed the surrender of state sovereignty.

Secessionist opponents also noted that Article I, Section 10 of the Constitution forbade states from doing things that a sovereign nation does. For example, it prohibited states from coining money and charging a state tariff. Notably, it also said, "No state shall enter into any treaty, alliance, or confederation."

America After Secession

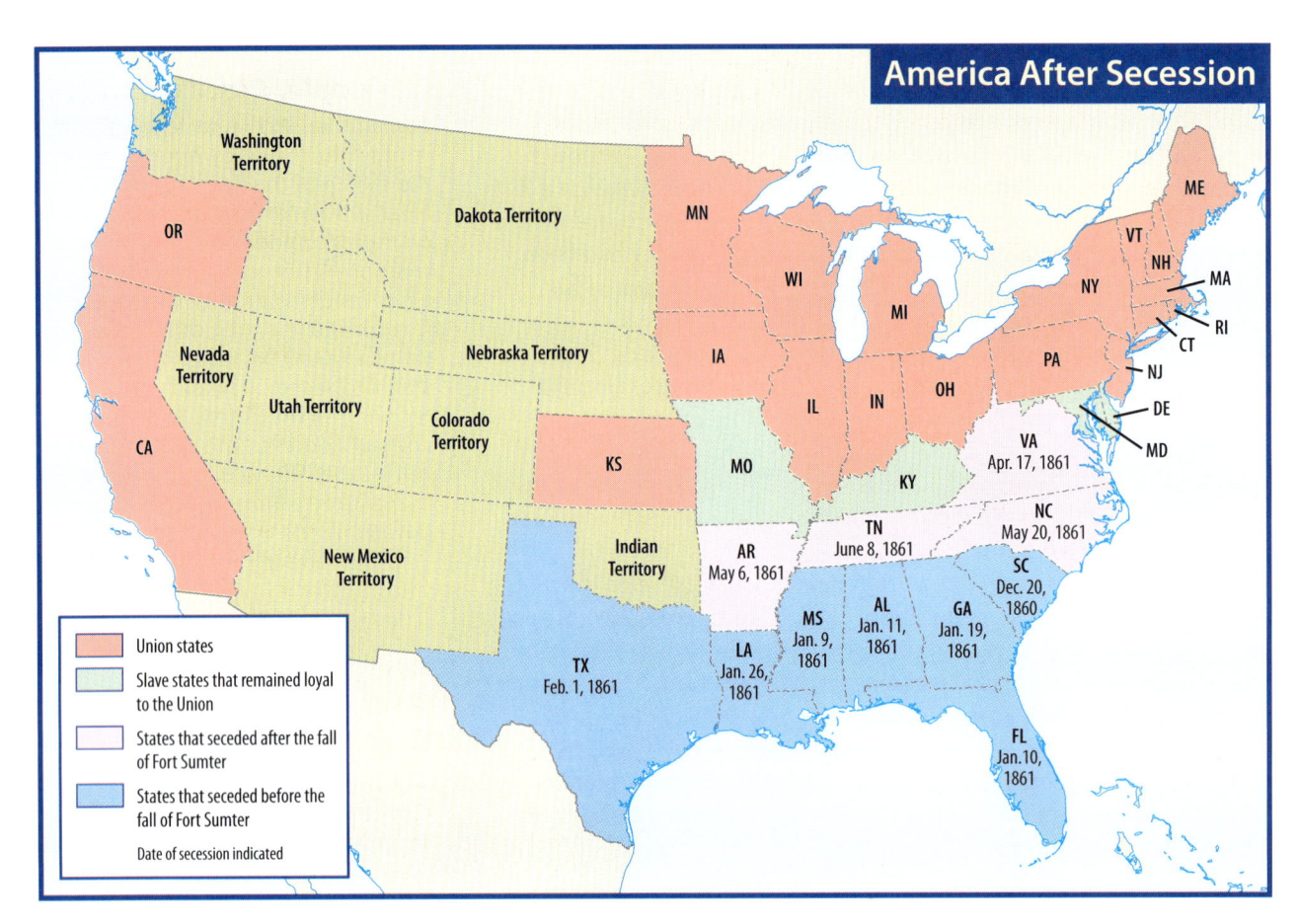

(Map showing Union states; Slave states that remained loyal to the Union; States that seceded after the fall of Fort Sumter; States that seceded before the fall of Fort Sumter, with date of secession indicated.)

- **Union states:** OR, CA, MN, WI, IA, IL, IN, OH, MI, PA, NY, VT, NH, ME, MA, RI, CT, NJ
- **Slave states that remained loyal to the Union:** MO, KY, MD, DE
- **States that seceded after the fall of Fort Sumter:** VA (Apr. 17, 1861); AR (May 6, 1861); TN (June 8, 1861); NC (May 20, 1861)
- **States that seceded before the fall of Fort Sumter:** SC (Dec. 20, 1860); MS (Jan. 9, 1861); FL (Jan. 10, 1861); AL (Jan. 11, 1861); GA (Jan. 19, 1861); LA (Jan. 26, 1861); TX (Feb. 1, 1861)
- **Territories:** Washington, Dakota, Nebraska, Nevada, Utah, Colorado, New Mexico, Indian, KS

The time for debate and compromise had slipped through the fingers of leaders. Differences would now be settled by the force of clashing arms rather than with constitutional arguments. The spring of 1861 was the beginning of desolations for the nation. Four bloody, bitter springtimes would pass before Americans had exhausted themselves in killing each other.

Section Review

1. Why did John Brown raid the federal arsenal at Harpers Ferry?
2–5. Name the four presidential candidates and their parties in the election of 1860.
6–7. Which was the first Southern state to secede from the Union? When did it secede?
8. What event marked the beginning of the Civil War?
★ Explain the essential positions in favor of and against the principle of secession.
★ Should President Lincoln have sent supplies to Fort Sumter? Explain why you think his decision was wise or unwise.

CHAPTER REVIEW

Making Connections

1. What is the difference between an abolitionist and a Free-Soiler?
2. Who owned the land where gold was discovered in 1848?
3–4. Why did Southerners resist the admission of California to the Union? (Give two reasons.)
5. Why did Southerners generally welcome the Kansas-Nebraska Act?
6. Explain the term "Bleeding Kansas."

Developing History Skills

1. Why did both abolitionist and nonabolitionist Northerners generally oppose the Fugitive Slave Law that was included in the Compromise of 1850?
2. Given the events in Kansas and the moral questions raised by Lincoln, was the doctrine of popular sovereignty a wise proposal? Defend your answer.

Thinking Critically

1. Do you think that the Free-Soilers were right in believing that Americans should tolerate slavery in areas where it already existed? Why or why not?
2. Why did the Compromise of 1850 succeed in avoiding war, whereas Senator Crittenden's compromise failed to do so?

Living as a Christian Citizen

1. Write a speech as if you were a congressman addressing the Wilmot Proviso, the Calhoun Resolutions, and popular sovereignty. Be sure to address the constitutionality and morality of each position.
2. Shared values bind nations together. But when groups within a nation interpret values differently, conflicts arise. Explain how the North and the South interpreted the American values of freedom, equality, individualism, and growth differently.

People, Places, and Things to Remember

Wilmot Proviso
Calhoun Resolutions
popular sovereignty
Zachary Taylor
Free-Soilers
Free-Soil Party
California gold rush
forty-niners
Compromise of 1850
Millard Fillmore
Franklin Pierce
Fugitive Slave Act
Stephen A. Douglas
Kansas-Nebraska Act
Know-Nothings
Harriet Beecher Stowe
Uncle Tom's Cabin
Republican Party
John C. Frémont
James Buchanan
Bleeding Kansas
sack of Lawrence
Sumner-Brooks episode
John Brown
Pottawatomie Massacre
Dred Scott
Roger Taney
Dred Scott v. Sandford
Freeport Doctrine
Abraham Lincoln
Lincoln-Douglas debates
Harpers Ferry
John C. Breckinridge
Constitutional Union Party
John Bell
secede
Ordinance of Secession
Jefferson Davis
John J. Crittenden
Fort Sumter
Confederate States of America (CSA)

14

THE CIVIL WAR (1861–1865)

Duty is ours; consequences are God's.

Thomas J. "Stonewall" Jackson
1863

Crobb's and Kershaw's Confederate troops firing from behind a stone wall at Marye's Heights, Fredericksburg.

Big Ideas

1. How did the North and South differ at the beginning of the Civil War?
2. What Civil War battles occurred in the East?
3. What Civil War battles occurred in the West?
4. What significant matters arose on the home front during the Civil War?
5. What strategies resulted in a Northern victory in the Civil War?

I. War of Brothers

II. War in the East

III. War in the West

IV. On the Home Front

V. Road to Appomattox

Dogwood blossoms and yellow jasmine danced in the warm spring breeze. Across the country, men gathered on village greens, their knapsacks laden with goodies, their cheeks with kisses, their heads with laurels. Most had seen little or none of the world beyond their horizons, and now they were eager to go teach the Yankees (Northerners) or Rebels (Southerners)—depending upon where those horizons happened to lie—a thing or two.

Shiny brass, scarlet sashes, golden trim, and glistening rifles all drew the admiration of wives and sweethearts and the envy of little boys with stick guns marching through the milling crowd. The spring of 1861 with its pageantry and patriotism gave little hint of the reality ahead. Four years later those village scenes were drained of the color and clamor of that first spring. Veterans, pale and disfigured, hobbled past their old parade ground. Black-draped widows moved about the square. The little boys so anxious to trade their sticks for swords never reached the battlefront; many of their fathers never returned home.

In the fight both sides demonstrated remarkable courage. The Southern soldier heroically fought in the face of overwhelming odds; the Northern soldier pursued victory in the face of devastating casualties. The war produced more than courage, however; the bitterness of a war in which countrymen killed each other had far-reaching consequences. The war that swept the land forever changed the face of its people and its politics. Issues that should have been handled with ballots were settled with bullets. As one historian has starkly observed, when the war was over, "Slavery was dead; secession was dead; and six hundred thousand men were dead."

> ### The Many Names for the War
> The war between the North and the South has been called many different names. The two most common are the Civil War and the War Between the States. Northern sympathizers sometimes called it the War of the Rebellion or the War Against Slavery. Southerners often called it the War for Southern Independence or the War Against Northern Aggression. However, many other names have also been used. People, then and now, disagree on what to call the war as well as the causes of it.

Jefferson Davis, president of the Confederate States of America, meeting with his cabinet

I. War of Brothers

Causes

A number of complex, competing forces converged and clashed to produce the bloodiest chapter in American history.

Union vs. Secession

The central issue that sparked the Civil War concerned the nature of the Union. Could states that voluntarily joined the Union by ratifying the Constitution voluntarily leave the Union? The issue had been hotly debated since the earliest years of the Republic. During the War of 1812, opposition to the war created strong secessionist sentiment among some disgruntled Federalists in New England. After 1830, the growing sense of frustration over the South's minority role in Congress simply renewed what was, in fact, an open constitutional question at the time: Do the states have the right to secede?

The fact that the secession question was a central cause of the war was underscored by Congress. The war resolution, approved

> ### Guiding Questions
> 1. What were the causes of the Civil War?
> 2. How did the natural and human resources differ between the North and the South in the Civil War?

Recruiting poster used in New York

A few weeks after the war began, this Tennessee poster called for volunteers to join the Confederate army.

121 to 2 in the House of Representatives on July 25, 1861, stated plainly that

> in this national emergency . . . this war is not waged . . . in any spirit of oppression, or for any purpose of conquest or subjugation, or . . . of overthrowing or interfering with the rights or established institutions of those States, but to defend and maintain the *supremacy* of the Constitution, and to preserve the Union with all the dignity, equality, and rights . . . and that as soon as these objects are accomplished the war ought to cease.

Many Southern leaders asserted the constitutional right of secession based on state sovereignty. According to the **states' rights** view, each state was largely an independent entity joined in a voluntary compact of union—but a union in which they maintained their identity and were not subordinate to a centralized national authority.

Many Northern leaders insisted that secession was unconstitutional. They believed that when states ratified the Constitution, they were surrendering state sovereignty. They believed that Article VI of that document made this clear.

Thus, the war opened with the constitutional questions and countercharges over which statesmen had wrestled for decades. The North argued that the Union must be preserved above all else; the South argued that the rights and liberties of the states must be preserved, even at the expense of the Union. Now the issue would be settled in battle.

Economics

Economic differences between the North and the South also played a vital role in bringing about the war. The foundation of the Northern economy was industry and manufacturing, whereas the foundation of the Southern economy was agriculture, especially cotton production. Sugar, rice, tobacco, hemp, and other crops were also major ingredients of the Southern economy. The South produced these raw materials and shipped them both to the Northern factories and to foreign countries. Tied to much of that agricultural economy was the practice of slavery.

One of the often overlooked contributing factors to the war was the tariff. The North favored a high tariff, not as a source of revenue (though it was a good revenue source for the government) but as a means of protecting its industries from foreign imports. The South opposed a high tariff because it had little industry. Foreign imports and trade supported its economy; a high tariff hurt trade and made foreign products more expensive. Southerners believed that they were, in effect, being forced to pay the tariff to support Northern industry.

Slavery

Slavery was an integral part of the Southern culture. A major reason Southern states seceded was that many leaders there did not believe Lincoln's assurances that he would not interfere in their way of life, which depended on slavery. The Southern farming economy relied heavily on slave labor. Thus, slavery played an important role in the decisions that led to war.

In the North, abolitionists had made gradual gains in public opinion, at least in opposition to the expansion of slavery. Of course, racial prejudice in the North and fear that freeing slaves would cause many slaves to move to the North (and compete for jobs there) made many Northerners indifferent to the plight of blacks in bondage. Nonetheless, the moral problem was difficult to ignore—there was an obvious contradiction between "the proposition that all men are created equal" and the institution of slavery.

Only about one-quarter of southern families owned slaves. However, by the time of the Civil War, many Southerners, even those who did not own slaves, argued that slavery was good. Some even insisted that the Southern slave culture cultivated the virtues of honor, courage, duty, and dignity. George McDuffie, governor of South Carolina in the 1840s, called slavery "the cornerstone of our republican edifice [government system]." As a result, Northern opposition to slavery was seen as interference with the core of Southern society.

Concerns

Not everyone understood the emotionally charged issues of secession, union, states' rights, economics, and slavery. Often, people tend to characterize each section as having uniform sympathies and motives. Not so. For example, some proslavery men fought for the Union, and some who cared little about defending slavery fought for the Confederacy.

Abraham Lincoln (*top*) and Jefferson Davis (*bottom*) served as presidents of the opposing sides.

Why Did States Secede?

Eleven states left the Union. When South Carolina became the first to do so, it passed the "Declaration of the Immediate Causes Which Induce and Justify the Secession of South Carolina from the Federal Union." Excerpts of that document are below. The other states that formed the Confederacy passed and approved similar statements.

The people of the State of South Carolina, in Convention assembled, on the 26th day of April, A.D., 1852, declared that the frequent violations of the Constitution of the United States, by the Federal Government, and its encroachments [intrusions] upon the reserved rights of the States, fully justified this State in then withdrawing from the Federal Union; but in deference to the opinions and wishes of the other slaveholding States, she forbore at that time to exercise this right. Since that time, these encroachments have continued to increase, and further forbearance [restraint] ceases to be a virtue. . . .

Thus were established the two great principles asserted by the Colonies, namely: the right of a State to govern itself; and the right of a people to abolish a Government when it becomes destructive of the ends for which it was instituted. . . .

We hold that the Government thus established [by the Constitution] is subject to the two great principles asserted in the Declaration of Independence. . . . We maintain that in every compact between two or more parties . . . that the failure of one of the contracting parties to perform a material part of the agreement, entirely releases the obligation of the other. . . .

We assert that fourteen of the States have deliberately refused, for years past, to fulfill their constitutional obligations [in Article IV of the Constitution by resisting the return of fugitive slaves to the South]. . . .

Those [nonslaveholding] States . . . have denounced as sinful the institution of slavery; they have permitted open establishment among them of societies, whose avowed object is to disturb the peace and to eloign [take] the property [that is, the slaves] of the citizens of other States. They have encouraged and assisted thousands of our slaves to leave their homes. . . .

A geographical line has been drawn across the Union, and all the States north of that line have united in the election of a man to the high office of President of the United States, whose opinions and purposes are hostile to slavery. . . . he has declared that that "Government cannot endure permanently half slave, half free," and that the public mind must rest in the belief that slavery is [on] the course of ultimate extinction.

Many soldiers were indifferent to or even ignorant of the motives with which they are often charged for fighting against their countrymen. They answered the call to arms out of a sense of duty, whether as Southern patriots or Northern patriots.

Perhaps Robert E. Lee best illustrates the dilemma that many Southerners faced at the outset of the war. Lee had a great American heritage as the son of Revolutionary War hero Henry "Light-Horse Harry" Lee, and his wife was the step-granddaughter of George Washington. Lee had already given thirty years of distinguished service to his country as an officer in the army. In April 1861, Lincoln offered him the job as commander of the Union armies. Earlier, Lee had told a friend, "If Virginia stands by the old Union, so will I. But if she secedes (though I do not believe in secession as a constitutional right, nor that there is sufficient cause for revolution), then I will follow my native State with my sword, and, if need be, with my life." When Virginia left the Union, he declined Lincoln's offer and resigned, declaring, "Save in defence of my native state, I never desire again to draw my sword."

Some have argued that the war resulted from a leadership failure that permitted extremists to take the terms of debate to their own ends. Historian James Randall summarized the issue thus:

> Let one take all the factors traditionally presented—the Sumter maneuver, the election of Lincoln, abolitionism, slavery in Kansas, prewar objections to the Union, cultural and economic differences, etc.—and it will be seen that only by a kind of false display could any of these issues, or all of them together, be said to have caused the war if one omits the elements of emotional unreason and overbold leadership. If one word or phrase were selected to account for the war, that word would not be slavery, or economic grievance, or state rights, or diverse civilizations. It would have to be such a word as fanaticism (on both sides), misunderstanding, misrepresentation, or perhaps politics.

Comparisons

Behind the massing armies of the North and the South were a number of sectional differences that would prove to be critical factors over the course of the war.

Resources

In terms of the basic resources of population, food production, and industrial output, the North had the advantage in every area. The eighteen Northern states had a population of 22 million, more than twice that of the eleven seceding states. The Confederate States of America (CSA) had 9 million people, of which 3.5 million were slaves.

Napoleon once remarked that an army "marches on its stomach." In this regard the Northern army marched farther. The agriculture of the South in terms of volume was geared toward the cash crops of cotton and tobacco, which would do little to sustain hungry troops. The North's Midwest region

General Robert E. Lee

Lee to His Sister

In a letter to his sister, Robert E. Lee explained his difficult decision: "With all my devotion to the Union, and the feeling of loyalty and duty of an American citizen, I have not been able to . . . raise my hand against my relatives, my children, my home."

Railroads were a vital way of moving troops and supplies during the war.

dominated production of wheat, corn, and oats. The two regions, however, were more balanced in their numbers of livestock.

Sharp differences existed between the sections over manufacturing ability. The North had five times the number of factories and ten times the number of industrial workers. The North also had twice the railroad mileage of the South and the capacity to produce more. In retrospect, it is difficult to see how the South fought on for four years in the face of such odds.

Leaders

One area in which the South surpassed the North, particularly in the early years of the war, was in military leadership. The South had a strong military tradition, and many Southerners attended West Point, the national military academy, and military academies in the South. As a result, many of the Confederate officers were better trained than their Union counterparts at the outset of the war. This command difference was particularly pronounced in the eastern campaigns, where Robert E. Lee, "Stonewall" Jackson, and J.E.B. Stuart displayed brilliance and resourcefulness that often bewildered their opponents.

Other leaders, despite being untrained, proved their worth militarily, especially in the West. Nathan Bedford Forrest, for example, proved to be one of the South's greatest cavalry leaders, and John Hunt Morgan and John Mosby became legendary in their feats of unconventional warfare. The North had its own share of military heroes, but when the war began, the South had an advantage in military leadership.

Strategy

The two sides also differed in their strategy for winning the war. The North would have to invade the South and defeat the Southern armies on the battlefield. General Winfield Scott, commander of the Union army at the beginning of the war, devised a plan. First, he proposed a blockade of Southern ports to make it difficult for the Confederacy to obtain necessary supplies. Second, Scott's plan called for control of the Mississippi River. This would split the Confederacy and hamper its ability to move men and supplies from west to east and to trade with the world through New Orleans.

Unlike his more enthusiastic subordinates, Scott—himself a Virginian—believed a quick military victory over the South was unlikely. Rather, his plan involved slowly eliminating the Confederacy's ability to wage war. The Northern press, reflecting the popular view that the war would last only a few weeks, mockingly called Scott's scheme the **Anaconda Plan**, after a large South American snake that slowly crushes its prey within its coils. Scott's ideas, though, would eventually prove both realistic and successful. Later, the strategy was modified to include two additional goals: to divide and conquer the Southern heartland, and to capture the Confederate capital, Richmond, Virginia.

The Confederate strategy was largely defensive, to outlast the enemy's will to fight. In general, the Southern soldier took up arms for the compelling reason that he was fighting to protect home and family from an invading force, which over the long term provided a sustaining motivation in the face of death and hardship. Defending the home front strengthened the will to fight, but the strategy risked Southern devastation by attacking forces.

General Winfield Scott's strategy became known as the Anaconda Plan.

Northern Strategy

Map legend:
1. Blockade the Confederate coasts
2. Control the Mississippi River
3. Divide/conquer the Southern heartland
4. Capture Richmond

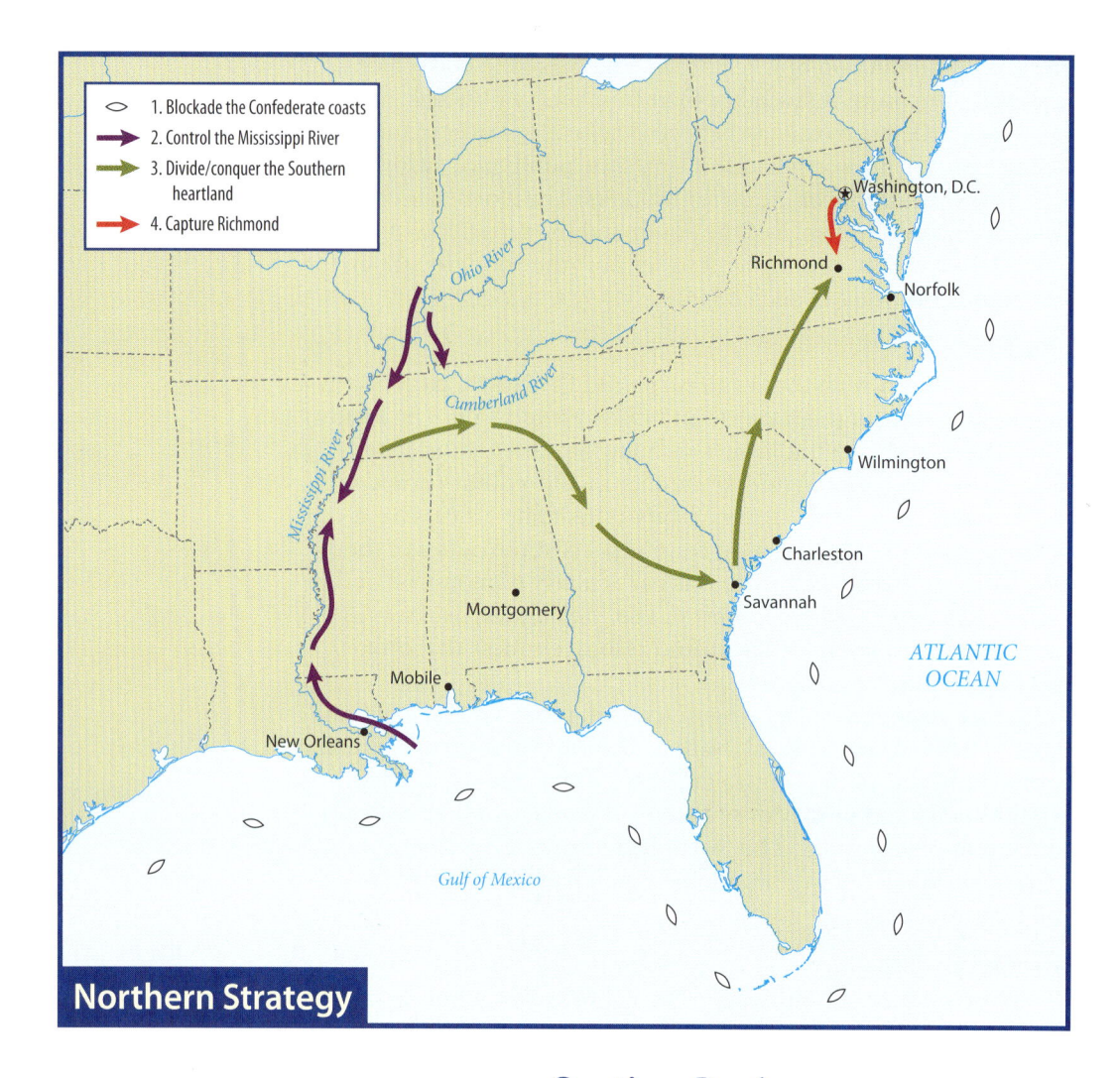

Section Review

1. What was the central issue that sparked the Civil War?
2–4. The North had more basic resources than the South. Name three of these.
5. Why was Winfield Scott's plan to win the war called the "Anaconda Plan"?
★ What core values were violated by support for slavery?
★ Explain why the South had an advantage in the area of military leadership.

Guiding Questions

1. What major battles occurred in the East?
2. Why were these battles significant?

II. War in the East

The contest in the East, fought largely in Virginia, centered on the North's attempt to defeat the Confederate army and capture the new capital at Richmond, Virginia. The Confederate government's move from Montgomery, Alabama, to Richmond linked the success of the Confederacy to the fortunes of the state that would contribute the most to the cause. "On to Richmond" was the battle cry that characterized much of the Union strategy. However, Richmond had capable and courageous defenders who would force the Union army into a long and costly campaign.

In the spring of 1861, in both North and South, most people believed that a quick, decisive battle held somewhere between

War in the East 1861–63

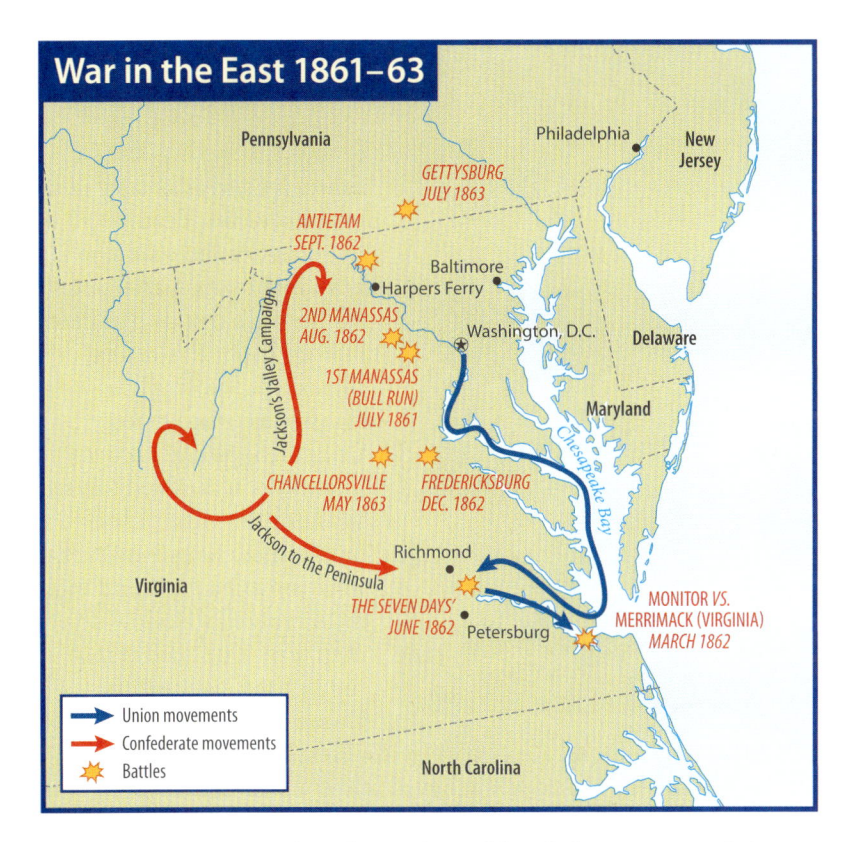

Washington, D.C., and Richmond would end the war. Lincoln's initial call for troops in April was for an enlistment of three months. These summer soldiers, like their Southern counterparts, were eager for fame and fighting. They would soon get a chance to prove themselves at a little Virginia crossroads called Manassas Junction.

First Battle of Bull Run (July 1861)

With the Northern press clamoring for something to write about and the three-month enlistments nearing an end for about 80,000 troops, Lincoln felt pressure to take the offensive. General Irvin McDowell, field commander of the Union forces, was ordered south to take Richmond. On July 18, McDowell's troops encountered the Confederate forces under General Beauregard near Manassas Junction, a railroad intersection about twenty-five miles southwest of Washington.

In Washington, news of the massing armies was the talk of the town. Hundreds of spectators, from senators to socialites, turned out in their finery with picnic baskets in hand for the gala event. This curious crowd included Illinois congressman John Logan. After arriving for the front-line festivities, he decided to join the troops. He went into battle wearing a top hat and tuxedo.

The Confederates chose to take a stand at a little stream near Manassas called Bull Run. On Sunday morning July 21, McDowell launched his attack. At first the raw Federal (Union) troops did well, pushing back the equally raw Confederates. However, the timely arrival of troops under South Carolinian Barnard Bee and Virginian **Thomas J. Jackson** stemmed the tide. Facing heavy fire and repeated assaults, Bee's troops were about to retreat. But Bee, galloping among his troops and urging them to hold the line, reportedly pointed to Jackson's brigade and shouted, "There stands Jackson like a stone wall! Rally behind the Virginians!" The name stuck; Jackson was thereafter known as "Stonewall." As for Bee, his

Names of Battles

Was the fighting that occurred on July 21, 1861, the Battle of Bull Run or the Battle of Manassas? Both names are used. Was the fighting on September 17, 1862, the Battle of Antietam or the Battle of Sharpsburg? Books use both. What about the battle in late December 1862 and early January 1863? Was it the Battle of Stones River or the Battle of Murfreesboro? Both.

Why the confusion? The Union usually named battles for natural features, such as creeks or rivers. Confederates usually used the name of the nearest town or manmade landmark. Thus, Northerners called the first major battle of the war the Battle of Bull Run (because of nearby Bull Run Creek), while Southerners referred to it as the Battle of Manassas or Manassas Junction (because of the nearby town with that name). Likewise, Antietam and Stones River were names used by the Union army, while Sharpsburg and Murfreesboro were used by the CSA.

The First Battle of Bull Run was the first major battle of the war.

General George B. McClellan

inspiring words were among his last. Riding at the front of his troops under murderous fire, he was struck down, an early casualty in a long list of war dead.

The Confederate line held, and by mid-afternoon McDowell's troops had been pushed back. The retreat turned into a complete disaster as unseasoned Union troops and panicky picnickers scrambled toward Washington. The victorious Confederates, however, were too exhausted and too disorganized to follow up their win. They celebrated rather than pursued the Union army.

After the Confederate victory at the **First Battle of Bull Run** (or Manassas), the South was relieved and confident, the North demoralized. The next day, Lincoln replaced McDowell with General **George B. McClellan**. The most significant result was that both sides were beginning to realize that the war would not be over quickly. Members of Congress, some of whom had attended the Sunday afternoon picnic near Bull Run, voted for a half million more troops for a three-year enlistment. The season for summer soldiers had passed.

Peninsular Campaign (March–July 1862)

In the months following Bull Run, McClellan took the shattered remnants of McDowell's army and the flood of raw recruits and organized and drilled them into an impressive force called the Army of the Potomac. That, however, was about all McClellan did with his army—organize and drill them.

Lincoln, eager for aggressive action, commented, "If General McClellan does not want to use the Army, I would like to borrow it for a time." By the spring of 1862, Lincoln ordered McClellan south to Richmond. The general offered an alternate plan. He would move his troops up the peninsula between the James and York Rivers and attack Richmond from the east, then send a second force from the north, and crush the capital with the two armies.

The *Monitor* and the *Merrimack* (March 1862)

McClellan's plan to use the James River as a supply line was nearly upset before the campaign began. The Confederates unveiled a new weapon, an **ironclad** (an iron-plated warship). The ugly but dangerous monster was built on the damaged hull of an abandoned Union warship, the **USS *Merrimack***, which Southerners had renamed the CSS *Virginia*. This vessel, with its heavy iron armor, ten guns, and iron ram attached to its bow, sailed out against the Union blockade fleet at Hampton Roads, Virginia, on March 8, 1862. The *Merrimack*, resistant to Union cannons, easily sank two large Northern wooden warships. Word quickly spread throughout the North about the South's new weapon.

But when the *Merrimack* returned the next day, it faced a strange opponent. Described as "a cheese box on a raft" and "a tin can on a shingle," it was the **USS *Monitor***, the Union's own ironclad. It was an unusual craft. Instead of the usual fixed guns on each side of the ship, the Union vessel had only two revolving guns that could fire in any direction. The *Monitor* battled the *Merrimack* for more than four hours without either seriously damaging the other. Although the battle was a draw, the *Monitor* had saved the Union fleet at Hampton Roads. More important, the clash was the first between iron warships, and it spelled the end of the age of wooden ships.

Monitor and *Merrimack* engaged in battle.

Diversion in the Valley (March–June 1862)

Considering the numerical advantages of the Union forces, McClellan's plan to capture Richmond might have worked if not for Stonewall Jackson and one of the most brilliant campaigns of the war. During the Valley Campaign (March 23–June 9, 1862), Jackson, with fewer than 20,000 men, ranged up and down Virginia's Shenandoah Valley, defeating two separate armies. Jackson's forces effectively pinned down 50,000 Federal troops before slipping out of the valley for Richmond to help stop McClellan.

On to Richmond!

Beginning in April 1862, McClellan, with 100,000 troops, pushed up the neck of land from Chesapeake Bay toward Richmond. The outnumbered Army of Northern Virginia under General Joseph E. Johnston delayed the Union advance, grudgingly giving ground to the overly cautious McClellan. Eventually, however, the Union forces came within sight of Richmond.

On the last day of May, Johnston struck McClellan hard at Fair Oaks on the outskirts of Richmond. The two-day fight left heavy casualties on both sides. Johnston, severely wounded, would be out of action for months. With the enemy at the gates, CSA President Jefferson Davis turned to his military advisor, **Robert E. Lee**, to command the army. Lee seized the initiative, launching what would be known as the Seven Days' Battles. From June 25 to July 1, at obscure little creeks and crossroads such as Gaine's Mill, Savage's Station, White Oak Swamp, and Malvern Hill, the Confederates pushed McClellan's grand army back to the James River, with both sides taking heavy losses. Having been outwitted by Lee, McClellan abandoned the peninsula and returned to Washington, D.C., where he planned to join General John Pope for a new drive on Richmond. Lee, however, had no intention of waiting to be attacked.

General Joseph E. Johnston

Second Battle of Bull Run (August 1862)

Lee knew that if McClellan's army joined with Pope's army, they would have an overwhelming advantage in manpower and firepower. Lee sent his cavalry commander, **J.E.B. Stuart**, to raid Pope from the rear. Stuart attacked Pope's headquarters and, while the general was away, took the Federal payroll, battle plans, and—for good measure—Pope's dress coat.

J.E.B. Stuart was a Confederate colonel early in the war but was soon promoted to the rank of general.

Clara Barton

Clara Barton (1821–1912) is one of the most famous American nurses. Born in Massachusetts, she began her career as a schoolteacher. When the Civil War began, Barton volunteered her services to the North. She gained permission to visit the front lines and was shocked at what she found there. She spent the remainder of the war helping soldiers. She was called the "angel of the battlefield."

In 1869, Barton went to Europe, where she became associated with the International Red Cross, which was founded in 1864. She returned to the United States and helped form the American National Red Cross. She was the organization's first president, holding this post for twenty-two years.

As the group's leader, Barton expanded the role of the American Red Cross to assist victims of peacetime emergencies, such as floods, hurricanes, earthquakes, and epidemics. Later, the International Red Cross made this American effort the standard for the whole organization.

In 1898, during the Spanish-American War, Barton went to Cuba. Though in her seventies, she managed nursing efforts there. Her tireless efforts were an inspiration to many.

While Stuart was creating havoc at Pope's back door, Lee sent General Jackson around Pope's army. Stonewall's men marched sixty-two miles in forty-eight hours, capturing Federal supplies at Manassas Junction and attacking Pope's lines on the evening of August 28. Just as Pope was preparing to attack Jackson the next day, the remainder of Lee's army arrived. On the second day of the battle, Southern defenders cut down brave Federal assaults with devastating effect. With a piercing "Rebel yell," the Confederates counterattacked, seeming to one retreating Federal "like demons emerging from the earth." This **Second Battle of Bull Run** sent Pope's army reeling back to Washington. Remarkably, after only two months, Lee had cleared practically all of Virginia of Federal forces.

Antietam (September 1862)

After his victory at Bull Run, Lee decided to take the war into enemy territory. In September, he crossed the Potomac River into Maryland, hoping to disrupt transportation and communication systems to Washington. He hoped that success on Northern soil would help him gain foreign assistance for the Confederacy or force the Union government into ending the war.

On September 13, a Union private found three cigars wrapped in papers. These were Lee's orders to one of his generals, orders that revealed Lee's battle plan. When McClellan was shown the orders, he was overcome with delight. He waved them and boasted, "Here is a paper with which, if I cannot whip Bobby [Robert E.] Lee, I will be willing to go home."

Within a day, Lee learned that McClellan had his battle plan and knew his positions. Lee quickly gathered his army, a force of about 30,000, and set up a defensive line at **Antietam** Creek near Sharpsburg, Maryland, where they awaited the onslaught of McClellan's 87,000 troops.

At dawn on September 17, Union forces attacked the Confederate line. At one place between the two armies stood a forty-acre cornfield, ripe and full, ready for harvest. There was, in fact, a grim harvest that day, as the cornfield became a killing field.

The day was a furious swirl of blood, sweat, and smoke as the armies held each other in a death grip. One Confederate recalled, "The sun seemed almost to go backwards, and it appeared as if night would never come." When night finally arrived, 24,000 men

The Battle of Antietam was the bloodiest single day of fighting in our nation's history.

had been killed or wounded. It was the bloodiest one-day battle in American history.

Lee slipped his battered army back across the Potomac into Virginia. Antietam was technically a Union victory because the Confederates had withdrawn. In reality, however, the battle was a draw. Even so, Lincoln used news of this battle to announce the Emancipation Proclamation.

Fredericksburg (December 1862)

After Antietam, Lincoln replaced McClellan with General Ambrose Burnside. On December 13, 1862, Burnside launched repeated attacks on entrenched Confederate positions on the outskirts of the quaint village of **Fredericksburg**, Virginia. Before the cold day ended, 12,000 Union soldiers were killed or wounded. Southern casualties were about half that number.

As a dismal December closed on 1862—the first full year of the war—Burnside, overwhelmed by his losses, broke off the assault. When Lincoln heard of the defeat, he turned command over to yet another general, "Fighting Joe" Hooker. It had been a very bloody year for both sides.

Chancellorsville (May 1863)

"Fighting Joe" was a popular, proven general. "May God have mercy on General Lee," the new commander boasted, "for I will have none."

Hooker, with a huge force of 130,000 men, returned to the Fredericksburg area to crush the Southern army. Lee had half the number of troops. Fierce fighting occurred for five days in the **Battle of Chancellorsville**. Hooker was defeated and the Union general retreated northward with his huge army.

Lee's triumph, however, was marred by the fatal wounding of Stonewall Jackson. Tragically for the South, on May 2, Confederate troops mistakenly shot Jackson while he rode at the front of his lines at dusk amid the tangled fighting. A surgeon amputated Jackson's left arm, and Stonewall died eight days later of pneumonia. The loss to Lee and the Southern cause was inestimable. Nonetheless, Lee's decisive win at Chancellorsville pushed back the Union threat, paving the way for more ambitious plans.

The Confederacy's victories in the East from First Bull Run to Chancellorsville were important for more than just military glory. First, these victories succeeded in frustrating one of the Union's chief war aims, the capture of Richmond. The only Union "victory" in the campaign was the bloody stalemate at Antietam. Even then, the battle only drove Lee back into Virginia; it did not bring the Northerners any closer to the Confederate capital. Second, the victories raised the morale of the South and lowered that of the North. Despite defeats in the West (discussed in the next section), Confederates took hope from Lee's triumphs that they might yet win the war. Northerners, on the other hand, became weary of defeat. Because all that the South needed to win was for the North to give up, Northern weariness was itself a Southern victory. Third, the longer the South inflicted defeats on the Federals, the more likely it was that a European power, such as Britain, would recognize the Confederacy and aid its cause. After Chancellorsville, Southern hopes for independence seemed close to fulfillment.

Abraham Lincoln meeting with General McClellan in September 1862 following the Battle of Antietam

Sideburns and Burnside

Union General Ambrose Burnside eventually became better known in the world of fashion than in military history. The whiskers he wore down each side of his face were soon referred to as "burnsides" and, eventually, as "sideburns."

Lee and Jackson

Generals Lee and Jackson had a special relationship. Both of them were Virginians and Christians. They worked well together militarily, and it seemed as if each could read the other's mind and predict what the other would do in a given situation. In one concise statement, Lee revealed how much he depended on Jackson. Upon learning that Jackson's left arm had been amputated, Lee lamented, "I have lost my right arm."

Spotlight on Stonewall Jackson

One of the greatest heroes of the South was also one of its most devout Christians. General Thomas Jackson, nicknamed "Stonewall," converted to Christ shortly after he served in the Mexican War. He started and taught a Sunday school class for African American people in his area. Though Jackson owned several slaves, he was not known as a passionate defender of slavery.

Jackson initially opposed secession. He believed Southerners should handle disagreements without leaving the Union. But when Virginia withdrew, he remained intensely loyal to his state. Jackson served brilliantly in the Confederate army, combining his Christian zeal with his military genius.

His faith in God carried him through many dangerous battles. An aide asked Jackson how he managed to remain so calm as bullets and shells whistled about him. Jackson replied, "Captain, my religious belief teaches me to feel as safe in battle as in bed. God has fixed the time for my death. I do not concern myself about *that*, but to be always ready no matter when it may overtake me."

Jackson was quick to express his gratitude to God for victory. After the Second Battle of Bull Run, an officer on the general's staff said, "We have won this battle by the hardest kind of fighting." Jackson disagreed: "No. No, we have won by the blessing of Almighty God."

Jackson cared for the spiritual needs of his men as well. He ordered regular religious services to be held in camp, and the general himself faithfully attended. He carried saddlebags of religious tracts for his men and welcomed Christian civilians who distributed religious literature among the troops.

Jackson's testimony impressed those who knew him. One evening during the Seven Days' Battles, General Richard Ewell and General William Whiting asked Jackson if they could change their route of march for the next day. Jackson said that he would think it over. After they left, Ewell said to Whiting, "Don't you know why 'Old Jack' would not decide at once? He's going to pray over it first!" Then, realizing he had forgotten his sword, Ewell re-entered the headquarters and found Jackson on his knees beside his bed praying.

After Jackson received his mortal wounds at Chancellorsville, his calm faith and composure deeply touched those who attended him on his deathbed. When told that he was dying, Jackson took the news calmly. A little later he said, "It is the Lord's Day. . . . My wish is fulfilled. I always wanted to die on Sunday."

On Sunday, May 10, 1863, Jackson said quietly, "Let us cross over the river and rest under the shade of the trees," and then he died. He left behind the testimony of a man who combined unflinching bravery with unflinching faith. As Jackson's wife said after his death, "The fear of the Lord was the only fear he knew."

Brutal Fighting at Gettysburg

One Massachusetts soldier, present at the height of the battle, described that day on Cemetery Ridge:

Foot to foot, body to body and man to man they struggled, pushed, and strived and killed. . . . The mass of wounded and heaps of dead entangled the feet of the contestants, and, underneath the trampling mass, wounded men who could no longer stand, struggled, fought, shouted and killed—hatless, coatless, drowned in sweat, black with powder, red with blood, . . . with fiendish yells and strange oaths they blindly plied the work of slaughter.

Gettysburg (July 1863)

Confederate armies in the West had not fared well against Union forces, and growing shortages among Lee's own troops convinced him that the South needed a victory on Northern soil to help turn the tide. In late June, the Confederate army marched through Maryland into Pennsylvania, shielded from view of the Union army by J.E.B. Stuart's cavalry. Lee was careful to order his men not to destroy private property or molest citizens. The citizens were surprised to see that the lean soldiers who had so often put the Union army to flight were poorly clothed and equipped and that many were barefoot.

Neither side chose Gettysburg, Pennsylvania, as the site for a major battle. On June 30, an advance party of Confederates neared the town and clashed with an advance unit of Federals under the command of General George Meade, who had replaced Hooker. The two armies had stumbled on each other.

On July 1, the advancing Confederate army drove the Federals back. The Union army entrenched on high ground south of Gettysburg. The next day, Lee, who by then had almost his whole army in place, renewed the assault on Meade's position, but Union reinforcements held their line.

Pickett's Charge

On July 3, Lee made one final attempt to dislodge Meade's army by ordering an assault on the center of the Union position along Cemetery Ridge. Fresh troops, mostly veteran Virginians under the command of General George Pickett, formed a line nearly a mile long and marched into the face of a murderous artillery fire. Those who survived **Pickett's Charge** and reached Union lines engaged in fierce hand-to-hand combat.

Fighting on three sides with no reinforcements, Pickett's men were quickly overwhelmed. About 6,750 men of the 12,500 who made the charge were either killed, wounded, or captured. When Pickett returned numbly to the Confederate lines, Lee ordered him to rally his division for the expected Union counterattack. Pickett reportedly replied, "General, I have no division."

Union soldiers fought the advancing Confederates during Pickett's charge at the Battle of Gettysburg.

The **Battle of Gettysburg** was over; the two sides had suffered 50,000 casualties between them. It was the single bloodiest engagement of the war. Two days later, the retreating remnants of Lee's army crossed the Potomac into Virginia, and Meade, exhausted by his costly victory, failed to stop him. The South would never recover from the loss at this battle. Yet the war was far from over. Names of sites on the Gettysburg battlefield still evoke images of the savagery of the conflict: Cemetery Ridge, Round Top, Little Round Top, Devil's Den, and the Wheatfield.

Gettysburg Address

With the human wreckage of war strewn across the Pennsylvania countryside, seventeen acres of the hotly contested ground were set aside to bury the men who had fallen there. Four months after the battle, the cemetery was dedicated. More than 15,000 spectators, including several governors, were present. The first speaker, noted orator Edward Everett, spoke for two hours. Lincoln then spoke ten eloquent sentences—his **Gettysburg Address**. He noted the common courage and sacrifice of the soldiers. Everett later wrote to Lincoln, "I should be glad, if I could flatter myself that I came as near to the central idea of the occasion, in two hours, as you did in two minutes."

Gettysburg Address— November 19, 1863

Four score and seven years ago our fathers brought forth on this continent, a new nation, conceived in Liberty, and dedicated to the proposition that all men are created equal.

Now we are engaged in a great civil war, testing whether that nation, or any nation so conceived and so dedicated, can long endure. We are met on a great battlefield of that war. We have come to dedicate a portion of that field, as a final resting place for those who here gave their lives that that nation might live. It is altogether fitting and proper that we should do this.

But, in a larger sense, we can not dedicate—we can not consecrate—we can not hallow—this ground. The brave men, living and dead, who struggled here, have consecrated it, far above our poor power to add or detract. The world will little note, nor long remember what we say here, but it can never forget what they did here. It is for us the living, rather, to be dedicated here to the unfinished work which they who fought here have thus far so nobly advanced. It is rather for us to be here dedicated to the great task remaining before us—that from these honored dead we take increased devotion to that cause for which they gave the last full measure of devotion—that we here highly resolve that these dead shall not have died in vain—that this nation, under God, shall have a new birth of freedom—and that government of the people, by the people, for the people, shall not perish from the earth.

Section Review

1. Why did the Confederates not follow up their victory at the First Battle of Bull Run?
2. How did the First Battle of Bull Run affect Northern and Southern morale?
3. What event marred for the Confederates their victory at Chancellorsville?
4–6. In what three ways were the series of Confederate victories in the East, from First Bull Run to Chancellorsville, important to the Southern cause?
* What core values did Lincoln include in the Gettysburg Address?
* Assess the significance of the clash between the *Monitor* and the *Merrimack* (*Virginia*).

III. War in the West

The Civil War in the West differed from the fighting in the East. There were two main campaigns in the West, for example, instead of the prolonged single contest between the Army of Northern Virginia (CSA) and the Army of the Potomac (USA) in the East. In the West, the war from 1861 to 1863 was divided between the Mississippi River campaign and the Kentucky-Tennessee campaign. The West also saw a large number of Union victories, in contrast to the Confederate triumphs in the East. In addition, while the South's greatest generals (Lee and Jackson) fought in the East, the North's best commanders (U. S. Grant and William Sherman) rose to fame in the West. In one respect though, the two theaters of war were identical: the fighting was hard and bloody.

Mississippi River Campaign

One of the most important goals of Winfield Scott's "Anaconda Plan" was the capture of the Mississippi River. Union control of the Mississippi would split the Confederacy in two and provide Union farmers in the Midwest a needed transportation outlet for their products. Control of the Mississippi was therefore crucial to both sides. The Confederacy sought to maintain its grip through major fortifications on the river, primarily those in Columbus, Kentucky; in Vicksburg, Mississippi; and in New Orleans, Louisiana. To win the river, the Union had to break those strongholds.

A Fleet and a General

One major Union advantage was its river fleet of gunboats. These ugly, ungainly ironclad warships were nicknamed "turtles" for their appearance and slow speed. They were the most powerful force on the western rivers. Another Union advantage in the West was the presence of one of the North's finest generals, **Ulysses S. Grant**.

Forts Henry and Donelson (February 1862)

The Union high command knew that a frontal attack on heavily fortified Columbus, Kentucky, would be foolhardy. Therefore, Grant was ordered to take his troops and the gunboat fleet and capture two important forts behind Columbus in northwest Ten-

---

Guiding Questions

1. What were the major battles of the Mississippi River campaign?
2. Who were the significant leaders on both sides in the West?
3. What were the major battles of the Kentucky-Tennessee campaign?
4. What was the significance of the Battle of Chattanooga?

nessee: Fort Henry on the Tennessee River and Fort Donelson on the Cumberland River. Grant easily captured the poorly designed Fort Henry on February 6, 1862.

Capturing Fort Donelson, only twelve miles to the east, was far more difficult. This fort was well designed and garrisoned with some 20,000 Confederate troops. The winter fighting for the fort was hard and bitter, and Grant's men outside the fort suffered terribly. Finally, on February 16, the Confederate commander sent a message asking for terms of surrender. Grant replied, "No terms except unconditional and immediate surrender can be accepted." The fort fell, and a jubilant Northern public, playing on the general's initials, honored its new hero with a nickname—"Unconditional Surrender" Grant. With Henry and Donelson in Union hands, the Confederates abandoned Columbus. Then Nashville, Tennessee, fell to the Union, opening the state to Union advances.

Shiloh (April 1862)

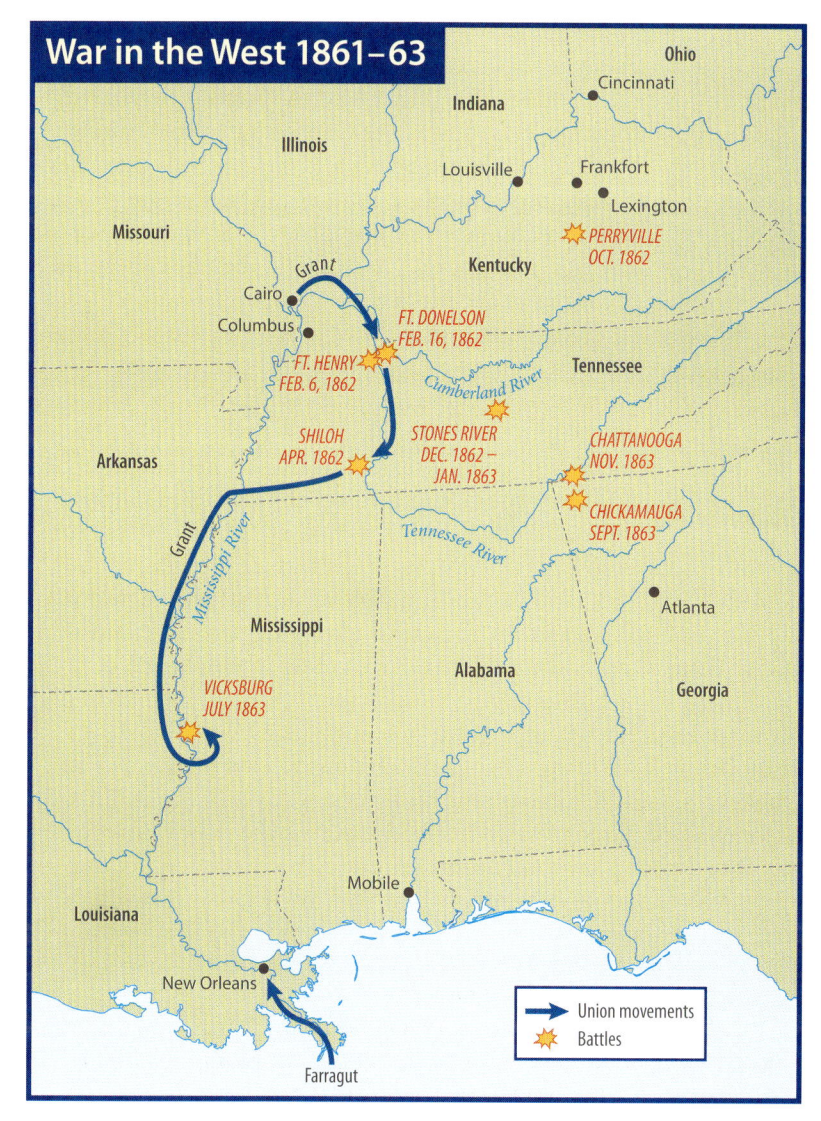

Grant's popularity lasted only until his next battle. As the Union army moved south along the Tennessee River, Confederate commander General Albert Sidney Johnston decided to strike the enemy a sudden blow. On the morning of April 6, 1862, Johnston's 40,000 soldiers surprised a Union force of about equal size near an abandoned Methodist church called Shiloh. After intense fighting, the disorganized Union forces fell back toward the Tennessee River. As darkness fell, the Union army was barely holding its positions.

During the night, however, Northern reinforcements arrived. The Confederates had taken heavy losses, including General Johnston, who had suffered a leg wound and bled to death before he realized how serious the wound was. At dawn on April 7, Grant counterattacked and drove the Confederates back. The **Battle of Shiloh** was a Union victory, but it was a costly one. Each side suffered more than 10,000 men killed and wounded. Angry newspapers and politicians called for Grant's dismissal. Lincoln refused, saying, "I can't spare this man. He fights."

New Orleans (April 1862)

April 1862 also brought some good news to the Union. Late in that month, Union naval commander **David Farragut** led the fleet up the Mississippi from the Gulf of Mexico and captured New Orleans, the South's largest city and most important seaport. One major obstacle remained for Union control of the river—the city of Vicksburg, Mississippi.

Fall of Vicksburg (July 1863)

Vicksburg was an important river port even before the war. Its high bluffs above the river made it a natural fortress, and the swampy lands near the city made it difficult for an enemy to approach. Jefferson Davis called Vicksburg "the nailhead that held the South's two halves together." As long as the Confederates held the city, they could bring supplies and troops from their western regions. Lincoln remarked, "Vicksburg is the key. The war can never be brought to a close until that key is in our pocket." Vicksburg, therefore, became the focus of the Mississippi campaign.

Despite the near-disaster at Shiloh, U. S. Grant was the Union's best general, and to him was entrusted the capture of Vicksburg. In the Vicksburg campaign, Grant revealed both a talent for experimentation and a streak of daring. When his first attack on the city in December 1862 failed, Grant decided to gather his forces north of the city and to try to find a way to bypass the guns of the forts. Throughout the winter of 1862–63, Grant tried first digging a canal and then floating his gunboats and troop transports along the bayous, swamps, and streams surrounding the city. All of these attempts failed.

Finally, Grant attempted a risky maneuver. First, he marched his men down the swampy western bank of the Mississippi to a point below Vicksburg. Then he floated his fleet of gunboats and transports past the guns on the bluffs under cover of night. This accomplished, Grant ferried his troops across the river below the city. The Union army had outmaneuvered the Confederates, but it had also abandoned its supply line. The army had only what its soldiers carried on their backs. Calmly, Grant wrote that he wanted "to get up what rations of hard bread, coffee and salt we can and make the country furnish the rest."

Grant's bold strategy worked. His move astonished the Confederates and allowed his army to sweep north and surround Vicksburg by May 1863. The defenses of the city were too strong to

Armored Union gunboats on the Mississippi River during the Battle of Vicksburg

Hardship in Vicksburg

Life in Vicksburg during the siege was so dangerous that civilians began living in caves they dug into the hillsides around the city. Conditions became so desperate that horses, cats, dogs, and even rats disappeared as the starving population sought food.

assault so Grant laid siege to Vicksburg to starve it into submission. Conditions inside the besieged city worsened. Finally, on July 4, 1863—the same day that Lee began his retreat from Gettysburg—Vicksburg surrendered. The Mississippi River was completely in Union hands. Abraham Lincoln declared with satisfaction, "The Father of Waters again flows unvexed to the sea."

Kentucky-Tennessee Campaign

While Grant was pushing slowly down the Mississippi River, an equally important, but less famous, campaign was occurring—the struggle for control of Kentucky and Tennessee.

Kentucky

Kentucky was one of the most divided border states. When the war began, for example, the governor was pro-Confederate and the state legislature was pro-Union. Faced with this drastic division, the state declared that it would remain neutral. Such neutrality was impossible to maintain, considering Kentucky's location. However, Lincoln and Jefferson Davis—each eager to win the state to his side—promised to respect Kentucky's wishes. Eventually, the need to protect the Mississippi River forced the Confederates to move into the state. The Union responded by sending troops. By February 1862, a number of Union victories had forced Confederate forces to retreat from Kentucky.

After the death of Albert Sidney Johnston at Shiloh, the Confederate government appointed General **Braxton Bragg** to head its armies in the West. Bragg devised a plan to revive the Confederate cause in the West—an invasion of Kentucky. Such a campaign, Bragg thought, would raise new troops from among the pro-Confederate citizens of Kentucky and might even bring the state into the Confederacy.

Bragg entered Kentucky in August 1862. But the campaign did not work as he had hoped. Although some Kentuckians rallied to the Confederate standard, even more volunteers enlisted in the Union cause to expel the invaders. After a number of encounters with the enemy over a period of several weeks, Bragg ordered a retreat into Tennessee. His great invasion had failed, and the Confederacy never again seriously threatened Kentucky.

Chattanooga—Climax in the West

Chickamauga (September 1863)

In 1863, Union forces moved across Tennessee. In the summer, they steadily pushed back the outnumbered Confederates through Chattanooga and into northern Georgia. General William Rosecrans, the Union commander, pushed his men on for what he thought would be the final blow against General Bragg's army. Bragg counterattacked near the banks of a creek named **Chickamauga** (Cherokee for "river of death"). In two days (September 19–20), the Confederates shattered the Union forces.

Complete disaster for the Union was avoided only through the courage of General George Thomas. He calmly held his troops on the field to protect the retreating forces and then slowly withdrew.

Despite the heroics of Thomas and his troops, the Battle of Chickamauga was a major Confederate victory and a disastrous Union defeat. The Union army was trapped in Chattanooga and Bragg threatened to starve it just as Grant had starved Vicksburg.

Music During the War

Music played a major role on both sides. Such instruments as bugles, drums, and fifes were used to communicate. Singing was a popular activity and was often used to relieve tension. For example, the night before the Battle of Stones River (fought near Murfreesboro, Tennessee, from December 31, 1862, until January 2, 1863) the bands of the two armies serenaded each other with strains of "Yankee Doodle" and "Dixie." Then the Union band began playing "Home Sweet Home," and the Confederate band joined in. For a short time, enemy soldiers were countrymen once again, united in thoughts of home. The music the next morning came from a chorus of cannons.

"The Rock of Chickamauga"

A member of Rosecrans's staff, General (later president) James Garfield, wrote that General George Thomas was "standing like a rock." Thereafter, Thomas was known as the "Rock of Chickamauga."

General Grant (*left*) and his officers on Lookout Mountain

Union Reorganization

Rosecrans's disastrous defeat forced the Lincoln administration to make changes. General George Thomas replaced Rosecrans as commander of the forces in Chattanooga. Meanwhile, Lincoln rewarded Grant by making him chief of all Union forces in the West. Grant and part of his troops left the Mississippi region for Chattanooga. First, Grant broke the siege that Bragg had laid and got supplies into the hungry city. Then he prepared to drive the Confederates from their strong positions south of the city on Lookout Mountain and Missionary Ridge.

Fighting for Chattanooga (November 24–25, 1863)

As the **Battle of Chattanooga** began, Union soldiers captured Lookout Mountain on November 24. The mist-enshrouded encounter became known as "the Battle Above the Clouds." But the Southerners still held the more formidable position on Missionary Ridge. None of Grant's plans in the battle for the ridge (November 25) worked as he had envisioned. When attacks on the Confederate line failed, Grant ordered General Thomas's men to create a diversion by capturing enemy trenches at the base of Missionary Ridge. The troops not only captured the trenches but also spontaneously swept beyond them, swarming up the ridge toward the main Confederate positions. Watching from a distance, an unpleasantly surprised General Grant asked, "Thomas, who ordered those men up the ridge?" "I don't know," replied General Thomas. "I did not." After watching for a few minutes, Grant muttered, "It's all right, if it turns out all right. If not, someone will suffer."

The Union attack, however, surprised the outnumbered Southerners almost as much as it had Grant. Missionary Ridge was soon in Northern hands, and Bragg's troops were again retreating into Georgia. General Bragg had earned a reputation for angering easily, refusing to listen to suggestions, and failing to act decisively. He now resigned his command, and President Davis replaced him with Joseph E. Johnston. Three months later, President Lincoln promoted Grant to commander of all Union forces. Georgia was open to invasion, and the tide in the West was definitely flowing in the Union's favor.

Grant—Unlikely Military Genius

He was short and slight and usually unkempt in appearance. On first meeting Grant's staff, Secretary of War Stanton unknowingly bypassed the general, shook hands with the staff surgeon, and said, "How are you, General Grant? I knew you at sight from your pictures." Nor was Grant particularly accomplished. His record at West Point had been mediocre, and he had resigned from the army in the 1850s under threat of a court-martial for drunkenness.

In civilian life, Grant had failed as a farmer and a real-estate salesman, and when the war occurred, he was working in his father's leather shop in Galena, Illinois. After volunteering for the army, Grant was made a brigadier general and entrusted with a command at Cairo, Illinois, the point at which the Ohio and Mississippi Rivers join. General Grant soon surprised his superiors with his abilities.

Section Review

1–2. What were the two main campaigns of the Civil War in the West?

3–4. For what two reasons did the Union want to control the Mississippi River?

5. How did the South seek to maintain control of the Mississippi River?

6. The capture of what city was the key to the Mississippi River campaign?

7–8. What were the two goals of Braxton Bragg in his invasion of Kentucky in 1862?

★ Evaluate Ulysses S. Grant. Consider his personal life as well as his military abilities.

IV. On the Home Front

War consists of more than the dramatic clash of arms on the battlefield. In addition to the suffering of the wounded was the quieter but no less real suffering of those at home. Behind the lines of battle lay large civilian populations and their governments, all of which tried to function as effectively as possible in the strained circumstances of war.

Life Behind the Lines

In the South

Because most of the fighting took place on Southern soil, life in the South was far more difficult than life in the North. In addition, the Confederate leaders had to assemble a central government and thus confronted problems that the Lincoln administration never faced. The South, for example, possessed very little gold and silver. The Confederacy, therefore, found itself printing paper money with little to support it except confidence in the government. As people realized the worthlessness of the money and as Confederate successes on the battlefield dwindled, prices soared. By late 1864, hams were selling in Richmond for as much as $350 apiece, and by the following January, flour was $425 a barrel. By the end of 1864, Confederate money was worth one-fortieth of its face value. After the war, of course, it

Guiding Questions

1. How did life differ on the home front in the North and South?
2. What constitutional questions arose as a result of the Civil War?
3. What was the significance of the Emancipation Proclamation?

Confederate currency

Christ in the Camp

Christians served on both sides in the war. The Christian testimonies of Southern Generals Robert E. Lee and Stonewall Jackson are well-known, and several Union officers were likewise followers of Christ. For example, Admiral Andrew Foote, commander of General Grant's gunboat fleet, was a devout Christian who was known to preach to his men on the deck of his ship. Lay evangelists, such as Northerner Dwight L. Moody, labored among the soldiers, preaching, witnessing, and ultimately leading many of them to Christ.

Revivals in the Confederate ranks of Lee's Army of Northern Virginia occurred throughout the war, but the most sweeping came during the fall and winter of 1862–63 and after the defeat at Gettysburg. During that time, Confederate chaplains and Southern preachers saw a remarkable number of conversions.

Nearly all Southern denominations joined hands in promoting the revival. One preacher noted of one meeting, "We had a Presbyterian sermon, introduced by Baptist services, under the direction of a Methodist chaplain, in an Episcopal church!"

Estimates of the number of converts vary. Virginia chaplain J. W. Jones, in his book *Christ in the Camp*, estimated conservatively that as many as 15,000 men in Lee's army were converted during the four-year war. The number might have been even higher. After the war, Jones tried to follow up on the 410 soldiers he personally had baptized. He found that only three had abandoned their faith and returned to their sinful ways.

During the fall and spring of 1863–64, a similar revival swept through the Army of Tennessee under General Joseph Johnston. One historian estimates that more than 100,000 Confederate soldiers were converted during the course of the war.

There were many stories of conversions in the Union army as well. One of the revivals that occurred was in April 1864 among Union troops in Ringgold, Georgia (just outside Chattanooga, Tennessee). Services were crowded to overflowing. Reports stated that "the doors and windows were filled, and the crowds extended out into the street, straining their ears to catch the words of Jesus. Sometimes hundreds of persons would go away unable to get within hearing distance."

was worth nothing. Many who invested heavily in the Confederate cause lost everything they possessed.

Some goods were extremely scarce, and both civilians and soldiers suffered from shortages of food and clothing. People learned to make do with what was available. Newspapers in Vicksburg printed their issues on wallpaper when supplies of newsprint ran out. A Memphis newspaper used shoe polish when it had no more ink. Sometimes the shortages resulted in anger and violence. In April 1863, hungry women in Richmond started a riot because of bread shortages. Mobs smashed windows, broke into stores, and stole food. Only when Jefferson Davis personally confronted the rioters and persuaded them to disperse did the violence stop.

The primary cause of shortages was the Union blockade of the Confederacy. Some daring merchant ships, called **blockade runners**, risked the wrath of the Union navy to bring supplies into Southern ports, where those goods were sold for enormous profits. Many blockade runners, usually operating at night, were successful. Historians have noted that the Confederate effort was well organized and administered and that Southern defeat might have come much sooner without blockade running. Nonetheless, Southern trade dropped below prewar levels. One of the primary reasons for this drop was the fact that the British—with the mightiest navy in the world—chose to accept the blockade. Had Britain been determined to trade normally with the South, the North could not have stopped the British short of declaring war on them. As the war progressed, the Union built more ships and captured more Confederate seaports. As a result, the effectiveness of the blockade increased, and blockade running became too hazardous to be profitable.

In the North

The situation on the Northern home front was easier, but it was not without problems. Inflation and shortages also plagued Northern families, but neither became as severe as in the South. In fact, after the first shock of secession, the North actually entered a period of prosperity. With most farm workers away fighting, farmers learned to rely more heavily on machinery, such as McCormick's reaper, to do the work. As a result, Northern farms produced more foodstuffs during the war than they had before. Likewise, heavy industries, such as ironworking, profited from the Union army's need for cannons, iron for ships, and other war supplies. At the close of the war, an increasingly prosperous North stood in marked contrast to a devastated and war-torn South.

Government in Time of War
Filling the Ranks

The main challenge for both the Union and the Confederacy was assembling an army. At first, volunteers were more than enough to fill the ranks. As the war dragged on, however, men became less willing to serve in the army as they saw the casualty lists and realized how their families back home were suffering. Eventually, first the Confederacy and then the Union adopted **conscription**, the "drafting," or compulsory enrollment, of men into military service. Unfortunately, the resulting draft laws were not always fair. Anyone drafted could avoid serving by hiring a substitute or paying an exemption fee. Such provisions led to mutterings that it was "a rich man's war and a poor man's fight."

Blockade runners helped provide needed supplies for Southerners.

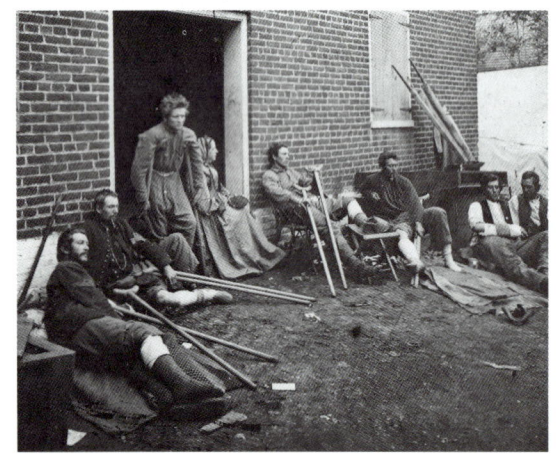

Wounded soldiers being treated during the war

Resistance to the draft arose in both sections. In the South, a surprising amount of the opposition came from state government officials. Having gone to war over the issue of states' rights, many officials resisted giving the central government the power to draft recruits. Especially troublesome were the governors of Georgia and North Carolina. Because the draft law exempted justices of the peace from the draft, for example, the governor of Georgia appointed hundreds of new "justices" to save them from conscription. In all, North Carolina and Georgia accounted for more than 90 percent of the exemptions granted in the Confederate draft.

Although a few Southerners resisted the draft with violence, the North faced scenes of violent resistance. The most vicious example was the **New York draft riot** in July 1863. The city of New York was home to many recent immigrants; many of whom did not understand the war, and few of whom wanted to fight in it. In four days of rioting, mobs attacked not only government officials but also the city's African American population. For example, one mob burned an orphanage for black children, and another seized a crippled black coach driver and hanged him from a lamppost. By the time the riots were suppressed, 119 people had died and about 300 had been injured. But the New York riots were about more than the draft. Under the surface was racial animosity. Some New Yorkers, especially Irish and German immigrants, were becoming unwilling to risk death in battle for what they were coming to see as a war to free blacks. Many were worried that freed slaves would swell the number of competitors for their jobs.

Black people provided a valuable pool of recruits for the work needed to conduct war. The South used some free black men in nonmilitary roles such as wagon drivers and in the construction of fortifications. Some Confederate generals proposed using black men in combat roles. At the very end of the war, Robert E. Lee even suggested granting slaves their freedom in return for fighting for the Confederacy, but the idea came too late to be enacted. Most African Americans who saw combat fought in the Union army, fighting for the freedom of their race. Blacks provided about 10 percent of the Union army's soldiers and about one-fourth of the navy's sailors. Their brave performance in battle did much to dispel prejudices that black people were inferior to white people, and they proved important to the Union cause.

Border States

Of interest to both the Union and the Confederacy were the **border states**, slave states that did not secede from the Union (Missouri, Kentucky, Maryland, and Delaware). Missouri, despite guerrilla warfare among its citizens, remained in the Union. Delaware never seriously considered seceding, and Kentucky, after an initial declaration of neutrality, joined the Union cause.

Maryland was a special case. The loyalty of its citizens was about evenly divided, and no one knew for certain what the state would do. If Maryland seceded, however, Washington, D.C., would be left rather uncomfortably within the Confederacy. To avoid this risk, Lincoln ordered the military occupation of the state. The national government jailed pro-Confederacy leaders without trial and stationed troops in secessionist "hot spots," such as Baltimore. Only in the middle of 1862, after the first crisis had passed, did Lincoln order the release of the political prisoners.

An ambulance crew removing wounded soldiers from a battlefield

Draft riots in New York City in 1863

The two camps shown above were typical of those used during the war.

Another border state owed its existence to the war. When Virginia seceded from the Union, citizens in the mountainous western portion of the state refused to follow. With the help of the Union army and the federal government, western Virginia established its own state government. Though the Constitution states that "no new state shall be formed or erected within the jurisdiction of any other state . . . without the consent of the legislatures of the states concerned" (Article IV, Section 3), the federal government recognized the pro-Union state, and Congress admitted it to the Union on June 20, 1863, as the state of **West Virginia**. (Pro-Union East Tennesseans tried to form their own state too, but before they could do so, Confederate troops occupied the area and held it for the South.)

Lincoln and the Constitution

As the situations in Maryland and West Virginia indicate, the war led to strong disagreements regarding the federal government's actions. In fact, some of Lincoln's Northern opponents complained that the president was making himself a dictator and ignoring the Constitution. Lincoln, for example, suspended writs of *habeas corpus*, meaning that the government could arrest a person without charging him with a crime or bringing him to trial. Thousands of such arrests were made. Lincoln defended his actions by noting that the Constitution allowed suspending writs of *habeas corpus* "in cases of rebellion or invasion" (Article I, Section 9). Critics replied that such power belonged only to Congress, since Article I deals with the power of the legislative branch.

Like all wartime leaders, Lincoln faced the challenge of balancing the desire to win the war with protection of citizens' rights. As the war progressed and the Union government felt more secure, such conflicts became less common. In March 1863, to eliminate questions of constitutionality, Congress officially gave the president the power that he had been exercising.

Copperheads

One reason for Lincoln's actions was his fear of Southern sympathizers in the North. Such men were called **Copperheads**, after the poisonous snakes of that name. In the border states and the southern parts of Illinois, Indiana, and Ohio, Copperhead sentiment was strong. In reality, the Copperheads may not have been as numerous as the administration feared, and many of them were interested in securing peace rather than in directly helping the Southern cause. Their presence, however, was a constant worry for the Lincoln administration.

Diplomatic Maneuvers

The war was fought largely within the borders of the United States, but its impact was international. The main goal of Southern diplomacy was to persuade a European power—preferably Great Britain—to accept the independence of the Confederacy, just as France had recognized the United States during the Revolutionary War. The North, obviously, sought to keep Europe out of the affair.

Lincoln versus a Copperhead

The best known of the Copperheads was Democrat Clement Vallandigham of Ohio. He opposed the war and was outspoken in his condemnation of Lincoln. His views resulted in arrest, trial, and imprisonment. Lincoln later reduced his sentence to banishing him to the Confederacy. Vallandigham, however, slipped out of the South and into Canada, and then, in disguise, back to Ohio, where he supported the 1864 presidential campaign of George McClellan.

Southern Efforts

Southerners hoped at first that simple economics would force Britain to recognize the Confederacy. The British textile industry depended heavily on Southern cotton to supply its mills. The South thought that when the British lost their source of cotton, they would come to the South's aid. Yet Great Britain was not eager to risk war with the United States over what seemed—to the British, at least—a purely internal American matter. The use of cotton from India and Egypt enabled the British to do without the South's cotton.

The South came closest to receiving British help not because of its diplomacy but because of Union mistakes. In November 1861, an incident on the sea nearly brought Britain into the war on the side of the Confederacy. The Confederate government had commissioned two agents, John Slidell and James Mason, to go to Europe to negotiate for aid. They were sailing on a British mail ship, the *Trent*, when the U.S. Navy forced the British ship to surrender the agents.

The **Trent affair**, as it was called, outraged the British, who demanded an apology and the release of Mason and Slidell. Secretary of State Seward freed the agents and managed to apologize in a way that satisfied the British but did not offend the Northern public. The Union thus narrowly avoided British intervention.

Ultimately, Britain would recognize the Confederacy only if it thought the South could actually win. This fact led many Southerners to hope that a great military victory would bring Britain to their side, much as the Battle of Saratoga had persuaded France to help the United States during the War for Independence. Thus, one of the motives for Lee's Maryland campaign was to win a victory that would impress the British. The uncertain results of the Battle of Antietam, however, dashed those hopes. Despite numerous victories in the early years of the war, the South could never seem to gain the decisive victory that it needed to win British recognition.

Emancipation Proclamation

When the Civil War began, Lincoln indicated that the conflict was a war to preserve the Union, not a battle against slavery. As the fighting progressed and as casualties continued to increase, Lincoln concluded that he could end some slavery through his war powers. In September 1862, shortly after the Battle of Antietam, Lincoln issued the **Emancipation Proclamation**. As of January 1, 1863, Lincoln declared, all slaves in rebel-controlled territory would be freed. The proclamation, therefore, excluded slaves in the border states and in Confederate territories already under Union control, such as New Orleans.

The president had four main purposes in issuing the proclamation. He wanted (1) to keep Britain from recognizing the South by appealing to the strong British antislavery feeling, (2) to encourage black people

The Union political cartoon (*top*) portrays a thoughtful Lincoln writing the Emancipation Proclamation; the Constitution and the Bible are on his lap. The Confederate cartoon (*below*) shows a deranged Lincoln with his foot on the Constitution and his inkwell held by the devil.

Lincoln and his cabinet discussing the Emancipation Proclamation

Lincoln's Thoughts on the War

Although Lincoln opposed slavery, his 1860 campaign focused on his opposition to its expansion. He had pledged not to interfere with it where it already existed. On August 22, 1862, Lincoln wrote to newspaper editor Horace Greeley, "My paramount object in this struggle is to save the Union, and is not either to save or to destroy slavery. If I could save the Union without freeing any slave I would do it; and if I could save it by freeing all the slaves, I would do it; and if I could do it by freeing some and leaving others alone, I would also do that."

But as the war continued, Lincoln concluded slavery had to end. At the time he wrote the reply to Horace Greeley, he had already quietly discussed the Emancipation Proclamation with his cabinet. He was waiting for a Northern victory to set the stage for his announcement. That victory came in September 1862 at the Battle of Antietam.

---

to join the war effort and fight for the Union, (3) to revive failing spirits in the North by giving Northerners another reason for fighting the war in addition to preserving the Union, and (4) to take the first step toward freeing slaves.

Lincoln achieved his goals. Britain did not recognize the Confederacy, and thousands of black men joined the Union forces. Although some Northerners initially resisted fighting "to free the slaves," by the end of the war most were describing their fight as a battle for freedom.

As noted, the proclamation did not apply to border slaves. Lincoln feared freeing slaves there might risk losing the loyalty of the border state governments. Thus, since the Confederacy did not recognize Lincoln as its leader, the decree technically did not free *any* slaves. However, later as the Union army advanced, slaves in captured areas were freed.

Also, Lincoln presented the Emancipation Proclamation as a war-time emergency act, like his suspension of *habeas corpus*. Otherwise, of course, the president had no power to make such a sweeping act without the consent of Congress. The president anticipated that, whatever happened, those who were later freed by Union soldiers were not likely to be re-enslaved.

Regardless of its limitations, the Emancipation Proclamation was an important step toward eliminating slavery. By its existence, the proclamation transformed the conflict from a war to save the nation to a war of liberation. "We shout for joy that we live to record this righteous decree," rejoiced Frederick Douglass.

Section Review

1. How did the fact that so many farm workers became soldiers actually help the growth of agriculture in the North?
2–5. List the four border states at the beginning of the war.
6. What was the main goal of Southern diplomacy during the Civil War?
7. What event in 1861 nearly brought Great Britain into the war on the side of the Confederacy?
8–11. What were Lincoln's four main purposes in issuing the Emancipation Proclamation?
★ Explain how the war adversely affected people on the home front in both the North and the South.
★ What factors might have contributed to the prevalence of the revivals in Northern and Southern armies during the war?

V. Road to Appomattox

War in the Wilderness

As mentioned earlier, Grant's successes in the West resulted in Lincoln giving him command of all Union forces. When Grant assumed his new position in March 1864, General Meade warned him "that Lee and the Army of Northern Virginia are not the same as Bragg and the Army of Tennessee." In other words, Grant's new opponent—Lee—would provide a greater challenge than he had previously faced.

Guiding Questions

1. What were the significant battles in the 1864 Wilderness and Georgia campaigns?
2. How was total war implemented against the South?
3. How did Northern victories affect the outcome of the presidential election in 1864?
4. What events led to the defeat of the Confederate forces?

Wilderness Campaign

With a force of 122,000 troops, Grant marched south toward Richmond. Lee, with half that number, blocked his advance near the scene of his Chancellorsville triumph a year earlier. In the dense woods and tangled underbrush appropriately called "the Wilderness," the two armies began a month-long series of battles. The **Wilderness Campaign** resulted in some of the costliest and most desperate fighting of the war.

In the battles of the Wilderness (May 5–6, 1864), Spotsylvania Court House (May 8–12), and the North Anna River (May 16–23), the Confederates dealt punishing blows to the Union forces. Yet Grant kept up the pressure. Unlike previous Union commanders, such as McClellan, Grant did not retreat after a major setback. At Spotsylvania he wrote, "I propose to fight it out along this line if it takes all summer."

Cold Harbor

At a dusty crossroads called Cold Harbor, east of Richmond, Grant made his costliest mistake of the campaign. The battle there (June 1–3) climaxed on the final day with a massive assault on entrenched Confederate positions that left 7,000 Union soldiers dead or dying before the sun had fully risen. When the soldiers were ordered to renew the suicidal assault, they simply refused. Between the two armies lay acres of bodies, what soldiers from both sides dubbed "Grant's Slaughter Pen." A survivor later described it as "not war but murder."

Cold Harbor capped a month of devastation for the battered Union army. In four weeks of nearly continuous fighting, Grant had lost more men than Lee had in his entire army. The difference, however, was that Grant could replace his numbers; Lee could not. Every assault on the thin Southern lines made them thinner yet. In addition, while the Union supply lines had more than enough food and clothing, some Southern soldiers were literally starving. In late May, for example, many Confederates received a ration of only one biscuit, with perhaps a slice of bacon, every two days.

War in Georgia

When Grant was made commander of all the Union forces, he left the troops in Chattanooga under the command of his most trusted officer, General **William Tecumseh Sherman**. His task was to destroy General Joseph Johnston's Southern army and to capture Atlanta, Georgia, one of the South's most important remaining railroad and manufacturing centers. Sherman approached the job with a grim determination. "War is cruelty," he said, "and you cannot refine it."

A burial party gathering the grisly remains from the Battle of Cold Harbor

General William T. Sherman

Sherman's soldiers heated and then twisted railroad rails into loops. These became known as "Sherman's neckties."

Atlanta Campaign (May–September 1864)

In May 1864, Sherman began his campaign a hundred miles from his goal. Between the Union forces and Atlanta stood a smaller but resolute force under General Joseph E. Johnston. A master of defensive tactics, Johnston carefully constructed fortifications of earth, timber, and stone and waited for his adversary to make a mistake. Sherman usually knew better than to attack such strong positions. Instead, he would use his superior numbers to slip around the Southerners, forcing them to retreat or be overwhelmed.

Johnston's slow and skillful retreats frustrated Sherman, but they also irritated Jefferson Davis. The Confederate president thought that the Southern general was afraid to fight and was risking the loss of Atlanta. In July, when the Union armies forced Johnston back just north of Atlanta, Davis replaced him with the fiery, energetic John B. Hood. True to his reputation as a fighter, General Hood attacked the more numerous Union forces in the **Battle of Atlanta** (July 20–22, 1864). The attack surprised Sherman, but the Federals recovered quickly. The Southerners suffered heavy casualties. Slowed, but not halted, Sherman continued to encircle the city. Faced with destruction if he stayed, Hood abandoned Atlanta on September 2.

The March to the Sea (November–December 1864)

As Sherman sat in Atlanta, he devised an idea to hasten the end of the war. He would wage total war on the South, destroying not only its armies but also its economy and its will. He marched his army three hundred miles across Georgia to Savannah, on the coast. Along the way, he fought against soldiers and civilians alike. The march served two purposes. First, Sherman's men could destroy food, animals, and other supplies that supported the Confederate army. Second, the march would show Southerners that the Confederacy was rapidly losing the ability to resist. As Sher-

Oliver O. Howard

Oliver O. Howard had an impressive list of accomplishments. He was a Union general in the war, the head of Howard University and West Point, the director of the Freedmen's Bureau in the South after the war, and a peace negotiator with the Indians.

Although Howard had attended church all his life, he had no inner peace. After graduating from West Point in 1854, he was assigned to a lonely outpost at Tampa, Florida. There, through meditating on the verse "the blood of Jesus Christ . . . cleanseth us from all sin" (1 John 1:7), Howard was converted.

During the war, Howard fought in more major battles than nearly any other Union general. He lost his right arm fighting in Virginia. Afterward, General Philip Kearny, who had lost his left arm in the Mexican War, tried to comfort Howard. The wounded Howard replied, "There is one thing that we can do, general; we can buy our gloves together!"

As a commander, Howard was deeply concerned about the spiritual needs of his men. He ensured that services were held each Sunday, and the general himself substituted as speaker when a chaplain was unavailable. General Howard held sessions of prayer and Bible study for his officers, even on the mornings of battles. Howard also visited the wounded after battles to comfort them.

Even those who did not sympathize with Howard's religious views learned to respect him. When the mayor of Columbia, SC, came to General Sherman to ask for help for his devastated city in 1865, the irreligious Sherman replied, "Go to Howard. Howard runs the religion of this army."

man himself said, "If the North can march an army right through the South, it is proof positive that the North [will] prevail." As he prepared what became known as his "**March to the Sea**," Sherman told his superiors in Washington, "I can make the march and make Georgia howl!"

Sherman began marching toward Savannah on November 15. As he did so, he left a trail of destruction fifty to sixty miles wide from Atlanta to Savannah. Anything that could be used to support the Confederate war effort—crops, livestock, railroad lines, personal valuables—was either seized for the Union forces or destroyed. They burned houses and barns by the hundreds. For decades to come, the Georgia countryside was punctuated by lone blackened chimneys, all that remained of once-elegant homes. With only loose control by their officers, some men became little more than vandals, wrecking, looting, and destroying.

When Sherman reached Savannah in December (which he offered as "a Christmas gift" to Lincoln), the general estimated that his army had done $100,000,000 worth of damage to Georgia. The March to the Sea was a deadly blow to the provisions and morale of the Confederate war effort, and it left deep emotional scars on the Southern people.

Election of 1864

Sherman's success almost came too late for Abraham Lincoln. Grant's bloody battles with Lee in northern Virginia and Sherman's slow advance in northern Georgia were creating weariness with the war in the North. No end to the fighting seemed to be in sight, and by the summer of 1864, Lincoln's chances for reelection looked slim. On August 23, Lincoln wrote, "This morning, as for some days past, it seems exceedingly probable that this Administration will not be re-elected." Facing Lincoln as the Democratic nominee was none other than George McClellan, former head of the Army of the Potomac. Although McClellan insisted that the Union must be preserved, most members of his party were seeking an end to the war—almost at any price.

The fall of Atlanta in September, however, changed the situation. Suddenly, victory looked probable, even certain. War fatigue melted in the warmth of military triumph. On Election Day, Lincoln won 55 percent of the vote and overwhelmed McClellan 212 to 21 in the Electoral College. The election of 1864 guaranteed that the effort to preserve the Union would continue. Interestingly, Lincoln captured 78 percent of the recorded soldiers' vote against his former general.

Confederate Collapse

Siege of Petersburg (July 1864–March 1865)

After Grant's Cold Harbor disaster, he continued to move southward, slipped across the James River, and laid a twenty-five-mile-long siege line against **Petersburg**, Virginia. Petersburg was the major railroad junction that led into Richmond from the south. If Petersburg fell to the overwhelming Union forces, Richmond would be separated from the remainder of the CSA.

For nine months (July 1864–March 1865), the two armies eyed each other and tested each other's defenses. Battle deaths and disease took their toll on both sides, but the drain was particularly noticeable in the Confederate ranks, because no replacements were

The "Bummers"

Worse than the regular Union troops were the "bummers," a shabby collection of men on the fringes of Sherman's army. Some of the bummers were Union deserters. Under no discipline whatsoever, they committed the worst atrocities of the march—robbery, rape, and murder. Sherman's inability or unwillingness to control these men left a bitter legacy long after the war was over.

Lincoln's Second Inaugural Address

On March 4, 1865, Lincoln delivered his second inaugural speech. The war was nearing its end. In that address, he stated:

> Both read the same Bible and pray to the same God, and each invokes His aid against the other.... The prayers of both could not be answered.... The Almighty has His own purposes. "Woe unto the world because of offenses; for it must needs be that offenses come, but woe to that man by whom the offense cometh." [Then] we shall suppose that American slavery is one of those offenses which, in the providence of God, must needs come, but which, having continued through His appointed time, He now wills to remove, and that He gives to both North and South this terrible war as the woe due to those by whom the offense came.... Fondly do we hope, fervently do we pray, that this mighty scourge of war may speedily pass away. Yet, if God wills that it continue until all the wealth piled by the bondsman's two hundred and fifty years of unrequited toil shall be sunk, and until every drop of blood drawn with the lash shall be paid by another drawn with the sword, as was said three thousand years ago, so still it must be said "the judgments of the Lord are true and righteous altogether."

available. The torching of the fertile Shenandoah Valley by Union cavalry under Philip Sheridan and of East Tennessee by George Stoneman's cavalry compounded supply problems for Lee's army. Also, the situation in the Carolinas was quickly sealing the fate of the Confederates. From Savannah, Sherman marched his army north through the Carolinas, wreaking the same havoc there that he had in Georgia. As Union forces pushed north, they left destruction and bitterness in their wake.

On April 1, 1865, when the fall of Petersburg was nearing, Lee's only hope was to slip out of the siege and link with General Johnston in North Carolina. Johnston's soldiers were retreating from Sherman's advance. Davis and his cabinet abandoned Richmond for Danville in southern Virginia. The Confederate army also made a desperate attempt to reach the rail lines, first at Danville, then at Lynchburg. At every turn, Grant's encircling army stopped them. Realizing the obstacles that he faced, Lee told his men that he was "compelled to yield to overwhelming numbers and resources" and was "determined to avoid the useless sacrifice of those whose past services have endeared them to their countrymen."

Appomattox (April 1865)

On Palm Sunday, April 9, 1865, Lee met Grant at **Appomattox Court House**, Virginia, where they agreed on the terms of surrender for the Army of Northern Virginia. Grant, recalling his impression of their meeting, later wrote that he felt "sad and depressed. I felt anything rather than rejoicing at the downfall of a foe who had fought so long and valiantly." Grant's generous terms—basically that the Confederates would lay down their weapons and go home—gave Lee the opportunity to surrender with honor. Lee appreciatively accepted Grant's offer.

When word of Lee's surrender spread, the noise of celebration and gun salutes erupted throughout the Union lines. But Grant quickly ordered it stopped. "The war is over," he said. "The Rebels are our countrymen again."

Indeed, for all practical purposes the war was over. Within days, Joseph Johnston surrendered his forces to William Sherman near Durham, North Carolina. The remaining Confederate forces surrendered in May.

Bitter Harvest

The surrender at Appomattox closed the bloodiest chapter in American history. More Americans died during the Civil War than in all other wars combined from 1775 to 1975, from the Revolutionary War through Vietnam. Over 600,000 men died in the four-year war. Tens of thousands were maimed for life.

A national tragedy occurred five days after Appomattox. On Good Friday, April 14, an actor named **John Wilkes Booth** shot Lincoln in Ford's Theater in Washington, D.C. Several hours later, Lincoln died. Soldiers trapped Booth in a Virginia barn almost two weeks later. The barn was burned, and Booth either took his own life or was killed by one of his pursuers.

At his last cabinet meeting on the day he was assassinated, Lincoln had extended his hand to the fallen South. According to one cabinet member, the president had warned that "there were men in Congress who . . . possessed feelings of hate and vindictiveness in which he did not sympathize and could not participate." In

Lee surrendered to Grant in the village of Appomattox Court House. The home of Wilmer McLean (*above*) was the location for their meeting.

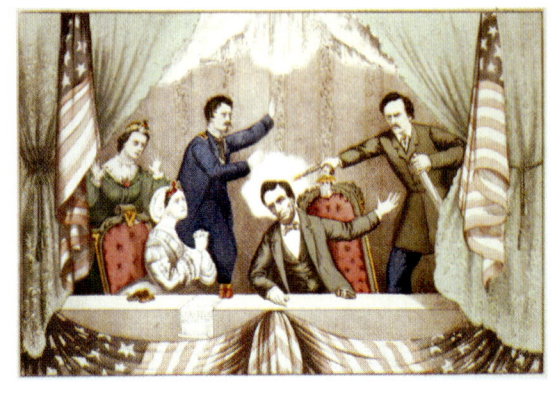

Five days after Lee surrendered to Grant, Lincoln was fatally shot while watching a play at Ford's Theater.

Eyewitness at Appomattox

By early April 1865, General Robert E. Lee recognized he had little choice but to surrender to General Ulysses S. Grant. After exchanging notes, they agreed to meet in the village of Appomattox Court House. The meeting, in the home of Wilmer McLean, lasted about two and a half hours. Lieutenant Colonel Horace Porter, an assistant to Grant, was present and wrote this description of the event.

It was then about half-past one of Sunday, the 9th of April. We entered, and found General Grant sitting at a marble-topped table in the center of the room, and Lee sitting beside a small oval table near the front window.... We walked in softly and ranged ourselves quietly about the sides of the room, very much as people enter a sick-chamber when they expect to find the patient dangerously ill....

The contrast between the two commanders was striking, and could not fail to attract marked attention as they sat ten feet apart facing each other. General Grant, then nearly forty-three years of age, was five feet eight inches in height, with shoulders slightly stooped. His hair and full beard were a nut-brown, without a trace of gray in them. He had on a single-breasted blouse, made of dark-blue flannel, unbuttoned in front, and showing a waistcoat underneath. He wore an ordinary pair of top-boots, with his trousers inside, and was without spurs. The boots and portions of his clothes were spattered with mud.... He had no sword, and a pair of shoulder-straps was all there was about him to designate his rank. In fact, aside from these, his uniform was that of a private soldier.

Lee, on the other hand, was fully six feet in height, and quite erect for one of his age, for he was Grant's senior by sixteen years. His hair and full beard were a silver-gray.... He wore a new uniform of Confederate gray, buttoned up to the throat, and at his side he carried a long sword of exceedingly fine workmanship, the hilt studded with jewels.... His top-boots were comparatively new, and seemed to have on them some ornamental stitching of red silk. Like his uniform, they were singularly clean, and but little travel-stained. On the boots were handsome spurs.... A felt hat, which in color matched pretty closely that of his uniform, and a pair of long buckskin gauntlets [gloves] lay beside him on the table....

General Grant began the conversation by saying: "I met you once before, General Lee, while we were serving in Mexico, when you came over from General Scott's headquarters.... I have always remembered your appearance, and I think I should have recognized you anywhere."

"Yes," replied General Lee, "I know I met you on that occasion, and I have often thought of it...."

The two generals talked a bit more about the Mexican War. Then they discussed the terms of surrender. Lee asked Grant to place those in writing.

"Very well," replied General Grant.... And calling for his manifold order-book, he opened it on the table before him and proceeded to write the terms.... Then he looked toward Lee, and his eyes seemed to be resting on the handsome sword that hung at that officer's side. He said afterward that this set him to thinking that it would be an unnecessary humiliation to require the officers to surrender their swords, and a great hardship to deprive them of their personal baggage and horses, and after a short pause he wrote [that officers could keep their side-arms and private horses].

After reviewing the document, Lee mentioned that the artillery men and cavalry men owned their horses. He asked that they be allowed to keep them. Grant agreed. Lee then wrote a letter formally accepting the surrender.

At a little before 4 o'clock General Lee shook hands with General Grant.... One after another [of those present] ... passed out to the porch. Lee signaled to his orderly to bring up his horse, and while the animal was being bridled the general stood on the lowest step and gazed sadly in the direction of the valley beyond where his army lay.... [He] seemed not to see the group of Union officers in the yard who rose respectfully at his approach, and appeared unconscious of everything about him. All appreciated the sadness that overwhelmed him, and he had the personal sympathy of every one who beheld him at this supreme moment of trial. The approach of his horse seemed to recall him from his reverie [meditation], and he at once mounted. General Grant now stepped down from the porch, and, moving toward him, saluted him by raising his hat. He was followed in this act of courtesy by all our officers present; Lee raised his hat respectfully, and rode off to break the sad news to the brave fellows whom he had so long commanded.

restoring the Confederate states to the Union, Lincoln called for "no persecution, no bloody work."

In Jefferson Davis's last address to his beleaguered citizens, in the final desperate days in April, he wrote, "Let us not, then, despond, my countrymen; but, relying on the never failing mercies and protecting care of our God, let us meet the foe with fresh defiance, with unconquered and unconquerable hearts." But as he wrote these words, much of the South lay in ruins. It was an impoverished land of widows and orphans where many were nursing the wounds of war. Ahead of the country lay a long and difficult road to national healing.

Wanted poster for John Wilkes Booth and his accomplices

Casualties

Union Forces	**Army**	Killed in action/mortally wounded	110,100
		Died of disease	224,580
		Died as prisoners of war	30,192
		Nonbattle deaths	24,881
		Wounded in action	275,175
	Navy	Killed in action/mortally wounded	1,804
		Died of disease/accident	3,000
		Wounded in action	2,226
Total Union Casualties			671,958
Confederate Forces	**Army**	Killed in action/mortally wounded	94,000
		Died of disease	164,000
		Died as prisoners of war	31,000
		Wounded in action	194,026
	Navy	No figures available	—
Total Confederate Casualties			483,026

Section Review

1. Why did Jefferson Davis replace Joseph Johnston as commander of the Confederate forces in Georgia?
2–3. What were Sherman's two purposes in launching the March to the Sea?
4. What military victory helped Abraham Lincoln win the election of 1864?
5. Who was Lincoln's opponent in the 1864 election?
6. Where was Lincoln when he was shot?
7. Who murdered Lincoln?
★ Evaluate the casualties in the eastern campaigns of 1864–65. Why were these more troublesome for Lee's army than for Grant's even though Union losses were greater?
★ In his second inaugural address, what does Lincoln suggest may have been God's providential purpose in the Civil War? Do you agree with Lincoln's suggestion? Why or why not?

CHAPTER REVIEW 14

Making Connections

1. Why was life on the home front more difficult in the South than in the North?
2. Why did many state governments in the South oppose conscription?
3. How did the Lincoln administration keep Maryland in the Union?
4–6. List three of the reasons South Carolina provided when it seceded from the Union.
7. Why did the South assume at first that Great Britain would come to the aid of the Confederacy?

Developing History Skills

1. Explain briefly why each side in the war thought it was right.
2. Conduct an online search for the declarations of secession of Georgia, Mississippi, and Texas. List three of the basic reasons these states provided for seceding from the Union.

Thinking Critically

1. Consider William Sherman's statement: "War is cruelty, and you cannot refine it." Is that statement true? Is there a potential danger in such an attitude?
2. Why was the Emancipation Proclamation significant even though it only applied to slaves in areas not under Union control?

Living as a Christian Citizen

1. If you were actively involved in the effort to end abortion in the United States, what lessons would you draw from Lincoln's approach to emancipation of the slaves?
2. Imagine that you are a Christian congressional representative from the North. How should your Christian faith influence your response to the conduct of Sherman?

People, Places, and Things to Remember

states' rights
Anaconda Plan
Thomas J. Jackson
First Battle of Bull Run
George B. McClellan
ironclad
USS *Merrimack*
USS *Monitor*
Robert E. Lee
J.E.B. Stuart
Second Battle of Bull Run
Clara Barton
Battle of Antietam
Battle of Fredericksburg
Battle of Chancellorsville
Pickett's Charge
Battle of Gettysburg
Gettysburg Address
Ulysses S. Grant
Battle of Shiloh
David Farragut
Vicksburg
Braxton Bragg
Battle of Chickamauga
Battle of Chattanooga
blockade runners
conscription
New York draft riot
border states
West Virginia
Copperheads
Trent affair
Emancipation Proclamation
Wilderness Campaign
William Tecumseh Sherman
Battle of Atlanta
March to the Sea
Petersburg
Appomattox Court House
John Wilkes Booth

15 RECONSTRUCTION (1865–1877)

May God forgive, unite and bless us all.

Inscription on a rocking chair given by a Union veteran to a Confederate acquaintance

The ruins that were Richmond

Big Ideas

1. How did the early plans for Reconstruction differ?
2. What were the highlights of the congressional Reconstruction period?
3. What were examples of corruption during the years Ulysses S. Grant served as president?
4. What were the long-term consequences of the Civil War and Reconstruction?

I. Presidential Reconstruction

II. Congressional Reconstruction

III. Years of Corruption

IV. A Reconstructed Nation

On March 4, 1865, Abraham Lincoln closed his Second Inaugural Address with a plea for Americans to forsake past hatreds and to unite for the healing of the nation:

> With malice toward none, with charity for all, with firmness in the right as God gives us to see the right, let us strive on to finish the work we are in, to bind up the nation's wounds, to care for him who shall have borne the battle and for his widow and his orphan, to do all which may achieve and cherish a just and lasting peace among ourselves and with all nations.

A little more than a month later, John Wilkes Booth's bullet left Americans wondering whether Lincoln could have achieved these noble goals. Instead, to **Andrew Johnson**, Lincoln's vice president, fell the task of "binding up the nation's wounds."

The period from 1865 to 1877 is usually known as the era of **Reconstruction**. In its narrowest sense, *Reconstruction* refers to the national government's attempts to rebuild the South after the war. Such recovery was not easy, and Southerners, black and white alike, struggled to make their way forward following the terrible devastation. In a broader sense, *Reconstruction* refers to changes in the whole country. The nation that went into the war in 1861 was very different from the nation that emerged from Reconstruction in 1877.

I. Presidential Reconstruction

Plans for Reconstruction

The obvious question facing the national government was how to treat and administer the Southern states after the war was won. Events soon proved that there was little agreement in the North as to what policy should be followed.

Lincoln's Ten Percent Plan

In 1863, Lincoln had formulated his **Ten Percent Plan** for restoring the South. As the Union army pushed into the South, Lincoln appointed a military governor for each captured state. Each governor was to reestablish a civilian government as soon as enough citizens, who had been eligible to vote in 1860, took an oath of allegiance to the Union. Lincoln set the required number as 10 percent of the votes cast in each state's 1860 election. Lincoln also intended to grant presidential pardons to many Confederate leaders. In many ways, this plan was fairly lenient.

Radicals' View

Opposing Lincoln in Congress was a group known as the **Radical Republicans**. Although they were only a minority within the Republican Party, they were highly influential. They set forth their view of Reconstruction in 1864 in the **Wade-Davis Bill**. It required military governors for each Southern state until a majority of all adult white males signed an oath of allegiance. The bill also demanded several provisions for new state constitutions: denial of the right of **suffrage** (the right to vote) and right to hold political office to all former Confederate leaders; abolition of slavery; and repudiation of Confederate war debts (that is, the federal government would refuse to pay the debts the Confederate states had

> ### Guiding Questions
> 1. What were the different approaches of Lincoln, Congress, and Johnson when Reconstruction began?
> 2. What was the significance of the Thirteenth Amendment?
> 3. What role did the black codes play in the course of Reconstruction?

An Old Warrior's Last Campaign

The fate of Confederate leaders after the war was uncertain. Some Northerners demanded treason trials and hangings. Jefferson Davis was imprisoned at Fort Monroe, Virginia, from 1865 until 1867. He lived for more than two decades after his release, passing away in 1889.

After Appomattox, Robert E. Lee wondered how he would support his family. Washington College in Lexington, Virginia, invited him to be their president. The school had only forty students and was in physical disrepair. Its presidency was hardly a prestigious position. Lee, however, accepted the offer.

Rebuilding the school seemed to demonstrate, in a small way, his desire to see the whole South rebuilt and reestablished. Lee oversaw the repair and restoration of the campus, broadened its curriculum, and made it more flexible in order to accommodate the changing economic needs of the South. He administered with the gentlemanly restraint and kindness for which he was well known. Under Lee's guidance, Washington College grew from forty students to four hundred.

Lee's Christian character was evident. Every day, he took his seat for morning chapel. During the war, Lee had encouraged prayer meetings and preaching among his soldiers, and he continued that emphasis among his students.

Shortly after the war ended, he had said, "I have fought against the people of the North because I believed they were seeking to wrest [take] from the South its dearest rights. But I have never cherished toward them bitter or vindictive feelings, and have never seen the day when I did not pray for them."

Five years of work on behalf of the college took its toll on Lee's health. He suffered a stroke in late September 1870 and passed away two weeks later.

The college trustees honored Lee's memory by changing the name of the school he had rebuilt. Washington and Lee College (now a university) became a memorial to *two* of the best-known sons of Virginia.

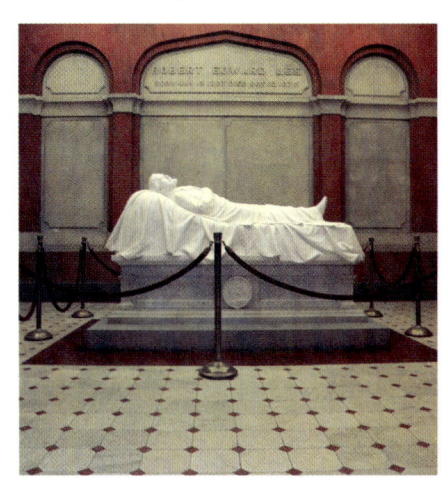

Lee's tomb at Washington and Lee University

Summary of Johnson's Life

Like Lincoln, Johnson had been born in poverty and had risen to political prominence through hard work and determination. He was barely literate until he married a schoolteacher who tutored him. He worked as a tailor before starting his political career as an alderman then as mayor of Greeneville, Tennessee. Next, he was elected to the Tennessee House of Representatives before being elected to the U.S. House in 1843. He was later elected governor of Tennessee and then to the U.S. Senate, where he was serving when the Civil War began.

Johnson remained loyal to the Union, retaining his Senate seat although Tennessee had seceded. Lincoln named him the provisional governor of Tennessee after it was captured by the Northern armies. Lincoln added Johnson to his ticket in 1864 hoping that, as a Southerner and a Democrat, Johnson would broaden the ticket's appeal and help promote unity when the war ended. However, Johnson was often short-tempered, impatient, and stubborn. Those tendencies caused great difficulties for him when he became president.

---

incurred). No state was to be readmitted until it had fulfilled those requirements. However, Lincoln vetoed the bill.

Though Lincoln and the Radical Republicans agreed that states could not legally secede, the Wade-Davis Bill showed that they had different views of the South's post-war status. Lincoln believed that the Southern states were still in the Union and that the president should oversee restoration of the rebellious members. However, the leading Radical in the House of Representatives, Pennsylvania's **Thaddeus Stevens**, viewed the Southern states as "conquered provinces" under the direct authority of Congress. **Charles Sumner**, who had survived his 1856 beating in the Senate, was that body's leading Radical. This Massachusetts lawmaker believed the Southern states had "committed suicide" and had ceased to be states. Their readmission to the Union, he argued, should be determined by Congress.

The motives of the Radicals varied. Most sincerely believed that rigorous requirements were necessary during Reconstruction to secure and protect the rights of blacks in the South. For years, they had sought equality for African Americans. But some seemed to be more concerned about simple revenge. For others, Republican control of the South and, in turn, Republican control of the nation was the highest priority.

Johnson's Plan

After Lincoln's assassination, all eyes turned to Andrew Johnson. What course would he take? He had been vice president for only a few weeks.

Johnson's plan for Reconstruction was a modification of Lincoln's. In addition, it offered **amnesty** (a pardon for offenses) to Southerners who would swear loyalty to the Union. But Johnson excluded those whose property was worth more than $20,000. Those people, mostly former large-plantation owners, had to apply to him personally for a pardon. Unpardoned Southerners could not vote, hold office, or reclaim property seized by the government.

Next, each former Confederate state was required to hold a state convention. That body would draft a new state constitution that would revoke its declaration of secession, refuse to pay Confederate debts, and ratify the **Thirteenth Amendment** (which abolished slavery).

Implementation of Johnson's Plan

Changes in Southern States

At the end of the war, the South lay devastated. Nearly 300,000 Southern men had died in battle, in prison camps, or from disease. The economy of the South was in shambles, devastated by the heavy fighting that had taken place throughout the region. Some Northern observers touring the region said that morale was so low that Southerners would accept almost any government that the North chose to impose on them. Andrew Johnson's lenient approach, however, encouraged the South. Perhaps, thought Southerners, recovery would not be as painful as they had feared.

By the winter of 1865, most of the former Confederate states had met most of Johnson's terms. As they organized their new governments and elected members to Congress, Johnson began granting pardons to thousands of Southerners.

Black Codes

The new Southern legislatures passed a series of laws known as **black codes**. These severely limited the rights of black people. Though the codes varied from state to state, all seemed intended to keep African Americans in a condition similar to slavery.

In some states, black people could work only as household servants or farmers. Some codes forbade them to live in towns or cities. The codes restricted many blacks to the same fieldwork they had done as slaves. Those who wanted to practice trades or do anything besides farming had to be apprenticed and often had to obtain costly licenses. Few black Americans had enough money to pay these fees.

Blacks who were not employed could be arrested. Those who could not pay fines could be hired out to anyone who would pay their fines. Some black codes forbade them to carry weapons and other codes limited where they could own property. In some states, they were prohibited from voting, holding office, suing whites, or serving on juries.

Southerners defended the codes by arguing that the uneducated former slaves could be easily manipulated and thus should not be granted equal rights. Many Northerners strongly disagreed and insisted that black Americans should be treated as equal members of society.

Congressional Response

When Congress gathered for its next session in December 1865, the newly elected Southern legislators arrived to take their positions. Dozens of them had been members of the Confederate

As Reconstruction progressed, African American men were given the right to vote. In this November 1867 illustration, some are doing so for the first time. Unfortunately, many Southern states later instituted laws and regulations designed to make it difficult for black men to have access to the ballot box.

Black Codes

The following codes were instituted in Opelousas, Louisiana, in 1865.

No negro or freedman shall be allowed to come within the limits of the town of Opelousas without special permission from his employers.... Whoever shall violate this provision shall suffer imprisonment and two days' work on the public streets, or shall pay a fine of two dollars and fifty cents....

No negro or freedman shall be permitted to rent or keep a house within the limits of the town under any circumstances....

No negro or freedman shall reside within the limits of the town of Opelousas who is not in the regular service of some white person or former owner....

No public meetings or congregations of negroes or freedmen shall be allowed within the limits of the town....

No freedman who is not in the military service shall be allowed to carry firearms, or any kind of weapons....

No freedman shall sell, barter, or exchange any articles of merchandise ... within the limits of Opelousas without permission in writing from his employer.

Congressman Thaddeus Stevens (*top*) and Senator Charles Sumner (*bottom*) were bitter enemies of President Andrew Johnson (*center*).

Congress, six had served in the Confederate cabinet, four had been Confederate generals, and eight had been colonels in the Confederate army. Alexander Stephens, who had served as vice president of the Confederacy, had been elected as one of Georgia's two senators. All had obtained pardons based on Johnson's Reconstruction plans.

Many in Congress were shocked and outraged that Southern voters had elected these officials. They argued that it was wrong for those who had led a hard-fought rebellion against the Union to immediately return to power. Some argued that without changes in leadership the South would not be much different than it had been before the war. As a result, Congress refused to allow the newly elected Southern members of Congress to take their offices. Instead, moderate and Radical Republicans established a Joint Committee on Reconstruction. It consisted of nine members of the House of Representatives and six senators. Among the fifteen members were Congressman Thaddeus Stevens, Senator Charles Sumner, and Senator Benjamin Wade (co-author of the Wade-Davis Bill). Congress intended to oversee Reconstruction. The disgust with the passage of black codes and the election of so many former Confederate leaders to Congress had caused many moderate Republicans to ally themselves with the Radicals.

The congressional actions outraged Johnson. He believed Congress was dealing too harshly with the Southern states. Democrats in Congress, along with some conservative and moderate Republicans, were still willing to work with the president. But Johnson, known for his fiery temper, lashed out at his opponents. As Johnson's popularity sank, more Republicans drifted into the Radical camp. Johnson refused to compromise.

Section Review

1. How did Lincoln's Ten Percent Plan differ from the Radicals' Wade-Davis Bill concerning the number of white males taking the oath of allegiance?
2. What is suffrage?
3–4. Who were the two leading Radical Republicans in Congress?
5–7. What three items were Southern states required to include in their new state constitutions?
★ Discuss the term *Reconstruction*.
★ Assess President Johnson's Reconstruction plan and its implementation. What were the key factors that caused many in Congress to oppose the president?

Guiding Questions

1. What major pieces of legislation did Congress enact regarding Reconstruction?
2. Why was President Johnson impeached?
3. What were the varying assessments of carpetbaggers and scalawags?
4. How did some Southerners react violently to Reconstruction?

II. Congressional Reconstruction

Congressional Acts

The Radicals acted quickly to limit the power of the president and to seize control of the Reconstruction process. Several pieces of legislation were soon enacted.

Freedmen's Bureau

In March 1865, Congress had passed laws to establish a short-term agency that became known as the **Freedmen's Bureau**. Officially, it was called the Bureau of Refugees, Freedmen, and

A Northern Teacher in Georgia

Sarah Chase, a Quaker from Massachusetts, traveled to the South in early 1863. She was a teacher there for the next seven years. The excerpt below is from a letter she wrote in February 1866 to a friend. At the time she was teaching in Columbus, Georgia.

We came here [to Columbus, Georgia], where a school house, built by the soldiers, had just been destroyed by the citizens and the feeling is intensely bitter against anything Northern....

And I am so satisfied with the work here that nothing in the world could make me wish to be in another place, or doing anything else. In my own day school and night school, I have 140 pupils, who have made truly wonderful progress, in the five weeks I have been teaching.

How much I wish you could see my school! A more earnest, fine looking set of scholars could not be found.... I find the people here more tidy and thrifty than in any place I am acquainted with— though many are intensely poor... [they are] cheerful and hopeful, ever anxious to improve....

I shall organize mutual relief societies in the Negro churches (Baptist and Methodist) as soon as possible. Large numbers are working for their food alone; and the white people tell them that they are not free yet. Across the river, in Alabama, several Negroes have been shot because they were free!...

No mortal is happier than I am in my work; and my success is fairly intoxicating.... knowing how useful it is my good fortune to be, to the blacks—and how truly they love me.

Courtesy, American Antiquarian Society

Abandoned Lands. Its tasks included helping former slaves and **refugees** (people who flee for refuge or safety). It issued rations of surplus army food and clothing and attempted to locate jobs for the freedmen and prevent employers from exploiting them. It also sent agents into the South to establish schools and hospitals for black people of all ages.

In February 1866, Congress voted for a bill that would extend and enlarge the bureau. The bill gave the bureau power to deal with the injustices of the black codes. It empowered the agency to help African Americans negotiate fair work contracts and allowed it to establish special courts to protect the rights of freedmen. Many Southerners objected to these courts because they had the power to overrule state courts.

President Johnson vetoed the bill. However, with the exclusion of Southern congressional representatives a few months earlier, Republicans controlled more than two-thirds of the votes in Congress. Thus, they were able to override the president's veto.

Union General Oliver O. Howard, who was often called "the Christian general" (Chapter 14), headed the Freedmen's Bureau. He believed that education was the foundation for assisting former slaves. Consequently, the encouragement and oversight of schools for blacks occupied much of the agency's time. The group coordinated the activities of various Northern societies that were committed to black education. By 1869, nearly

Freedmen school on Edisto Island, South Carolina

The Zion School in Charleston, South Carolina (*right*), enrolled more than 800 black students in 1866. Students at Hampton Institute (now called Hampton University) in Hampton, Virginia, are shown in 1870 (*left*).

Devastation in the South

As Reconstruction began, many of the South's largest cities lay devastated. The once prosperous Southern economy was in ruins.

One historian wrote, "Throughout the South, fences were down, weeds had overrun the fields, windows were broken, live stock had disappeared. The assessed valuation of property declined from 30 to 60 percent in the decade after 1860. In Mobile, business was stagnant; Chattanooga and Nashville were ruined; and Atlanta's industrial sections were in ashes."

Much of Richmond, the capital, had been destroyed by fire. One observer described Charleston, South Carolina, as the scene of "vacant houses, of widowed women, of rotting wharves, of deserted warehouses, of weed-wild gardens, of miles of grass-grown streets, of acres of pitiful and voiceless barrenness."

Charleston, SC, after the war

3,000 schools, serving over 150,000 pupils, reported to the bureau. These figures did not include many evening and private schools operated by missionary groups and blacks themselves. In addition to work in the education field, more than forty hospitals were established by the bureau.

Civil Rights Act

In March 1866 Congress, now clearly led by the Radical Republicans, passed the Civil Rights Act. It granted citizenship to African Americans. It also gave them "full and equal benefit of all laws." This was intended to protect blacks from the black codes and other discriminating laws.

Andrew Johnson also vetoed this bill. He said the federal government did not have the power to enact such legislation. He believed individual states, not the national government, had the power to determine citizenship. In April 1866, Congress overrode the veto. Fearing that the Supreme Court might rule the Civil Rights Act unconstitutional or that it might be repealed by a future Congress, the Republicans proposed the Fourteenth Amendment in June 1866.

Fourteenth Amendment

The Thirteenth Amendment freed the slaves, but questions remained about the legal status of freedmen. The **Fourteenth Amendment**, which addressed some of that matter, contained four important provisions.

1. It granted freedmen full citizenship in both the United States and the state where they resided. It prohibited any state from depriving a person of his life, liberty, or property without due process of law. A state could not deny equal protection of its laws to any person who lived there.

2. It said that a state's representation in Congress would be based on its whole population. All former slaves, not just three-fifths, were to be counted to determine the state's representation.

3. It said that people who had sworn an oath to support the Constitution and were viewed as having broken that oath by supporting the Confederacy were barred from voting or holding office. Congress (not the president) could, by a two-thirds vote, remove this restriction.

4. It said that neither federal nor state governments could pay any of the Confederate debts or provide any compensation to former slaveholders for the loss of their slaves.

When ratified, the amendment would cancel not only black codes in the South but also laws against blacks in some midwestern states. But Johnson urged Southern states to vote against it. He believed it treated former Confederate leaders too harshly and that it was wrong to enact an amendment when the representatives of the Southern states, who had been barred from Congress, had no part in its writing.

Johnson realized that he was powerless as long as the Radicals and their moderate supporters had a two-thirds majority in Congress. So he campaigned against Radical candidates in the 1866 congressional races. He traveled to the North and the Midwest, speaking against the Radicals, but his efforts backfired. His train trip from Washington, D.C., to St. Louis, to Chicago and back, was a disaster. His audiences heckled him. Instead of ignoring them, Johnson lost his temper and responded harshly. Earlier, some people had rejected his Reconstruction plan because they feared it would return former Confederates to power. Now many more became skeptical of his leadership.

In the 1866 elections, Republicans won a landslide victory over Democrats. Thus, beginning in 1867 the Radical Republicans in Congress, now exercising even greater control, enacted their program speedily and with little resistance. When the president vetoed their legislation, Congress quickly overrode his vetoes.

Reconstruction Act of 1867

Congress passed the **Reconstruction Act of 1867** (also known as the Military Reconstruction Act). It ordered the army to ensure that the South complied with congressional mandates. Black Southerners and Southern Unionists welcomed the measure, but many other Southerners resented the military occupation of the South.

The act affected the South in many ways. First, the act divided the South into five military districts, each governed by a Union general. Second, it gave black people the right to vote and hold office. Third, it said that Southern states wanting to reenter the Union had to hold conventions that included both black and white voting delegates. (Those who had taken an oath, before the Civil War, to uphold the Constitution and then supported the Confederacy were excluded from participation.) These conventions were to write new state constitutions, using the guidelines given by Congress. Fourth, the act required the Southern states to submit their new constitutions to Congress for approval. Fifth, the act required states to ratify the Fourteenth Amendment.

When a state met all of the requirements, it would be entitled to representation in Congress. Tennessee was exempt from this law because it had already ratified the Fourteenth Amendment.

Thus, the Fourteenth Amendment prohibited most former Southern leaders from holding public office. Their exclusion opened the way for Southern Unionists, Northerners, and black Americans to occupy such positions. These groups had formerly possessed little political power in the South.

Impeachment

In March 1867, Congress passed the **Tenure of Office Act**. This act made it illegal for the president to remove any appointee who had been approved by the Senate unless the Senate also approved the dismissal. The Radicals intended the law to protect Secretary of War **Edwin Stanton**, the most important Radical in the cabinet. Johnson thought that the act was unconstitutional. He viewed Stanton as a Radical spy and decided to test the act by dismissing him. Stanton responded by literally barricading himself in his office. The president's violation of the law delighted the Radicals because it gave them a potential opportunity to remove Johnson.

The Constitution provides that the House of Representatives, by majority vote, can bring charges against the president. This is called **impeachment**. After being impeached, the president must face trial in the Senate. Two-thirds of the Senate must declare the president guilty in order for him to be removed from office.

According to the Constitution, the only basis for removal of the president is "conviction of . . . treason, bribery, or other high crimes and misdemeanors" (Article II, Section 4). In February 1868, the

"Life of Former Slaves"

Frederick Douglass, a former slave, made the following comments about the problems freed slaves faced after the Civil War.

"Though slavery was abolished, the wrongs of my people were not ended. Though they were not slaves, they were not yet quite free. No man can be truly free whose liberty is dependent upon the thought, feeling, and action of others, and who has himself no means in his own hands for guarding, protecting, defending, and maintaining that liberty. Yet the Negro, after his emancipation, was precisely in this state of destitution. . . .

"And yet the government had left the freedmen in a [poor condition]. . . . It felt that it had done enough for him. It had made him free, and henceforth he must make his own way in the world. Yet he had none of the conditions for self-preservation or self-protection. He was free from the individual master, but the slave of society. He had neither money, property, nor friends. He was free from the old plantation, but he had nothing but the dusty road under his feet. He was free from the old quarter that once gave him shelter, but a slave to the rains of summer and to the frosts of winter. He was, in a word, literally turned loose, naked, hungry, and destitute, to the open sky."

Edwin Stanton, secretary of war

House voted 126–47 to impeach Johnson on eleven charges. The primary allegation was that he had violated the Tenure of Office Act by firing Stanton. The president's Senate trial began on March 13 and lasted until May 26. Johnson never attended the trial. He believed that he had done nothing wrong and that his attendance would only lend credibility to his accusers. Senators sold tickets to the affair.

Senators had varied opinions about Johnson's guilt. Was the Tenure of Office Act constitutional? Even if it was, did it apply in Stanton's case? Stanton, after all, was Lincoln's appointee before the Tenure of Office Act was passed. The real issue was that Radicals were trying to remove the president because they disagreed with him politically. Removing a president for political reasons would set a dangerous precedent (or example) for the future. Some senators were troubled by this.

Senators knew that if Johnson were removed, Benjamin Wade would become president. Wade was the president pro tempore of the Senate and one of the most extreme Radicals. (Johnson had no vice president, so according to the law at the time, the president pro tempore of the Senate was next in line. In 1948, the law was changed to make the Speaker of the House the next in line after the vice president.)

When the final vote at the Senate trial was taken, thirty-five senators voted to convict Johnson. Nineteen voted to acquit him. Seven Republicans risked their political careers to join the twelve Democrats who voted for acquittal. The Radicals were one vote short of the two-thirds needed to convict Johnson. So Johnson completed his term in March 1869. Years later, the Supreme Court declared the Tenure of Office Act unconstitutional.

This ticket enabled the recipient to attend President Johnson's trial (*top*) in 1868.

Johnson After the Presidency

After completing his term of office in March 1869, Johnson returned to Tennessee. In 1875, he was elected to represent his state in the U.S. Senate. He is the only former president to serve in the Senate after leaving the White House. However, he held that office for only a few months. On July 30, 1875, Johnson suffered a stroke and later died in Tennessee. He is buried in Greeneville, Tennessee.

Life in the South

Farming

The Southern economy, devastated by the war, did not improve much under Radical rule. The freed slaves generally returned to farming, the only occupation they knew, and agriculture remained the leading Southern industry. Land was, in fact, the most important Southern resource. To grow crops in the South, farm owners needed laborers. But, after the Civil War, few owners had money to pay such individuals. Thus, with the shortage of cash and the absence of slave labor, the **sharecropping** system became popular.

Not only blacks but also poor whites became involved in this new economic system. Sharecroppers farmed small plots owned by planters and paid an annual rent for seed, tools, a mule, a cabin, and the use of the land. Their rent was a portion, or share, of the crop they grew. That share was typically one-half, or more, of the harvest. Since share-

Picking cotton on a Southern farm

croppers had little money, especially at the beginning of the season, they borrowed money to buy provisions for their family. Often, the landlord provided the loan. Landlords sometimes also owned local stores. At harvest, each sharecropper settled his account. If the sharecropper broke even, he was fortunate. He usually started the next season still in debt since interest rates were often quite high.

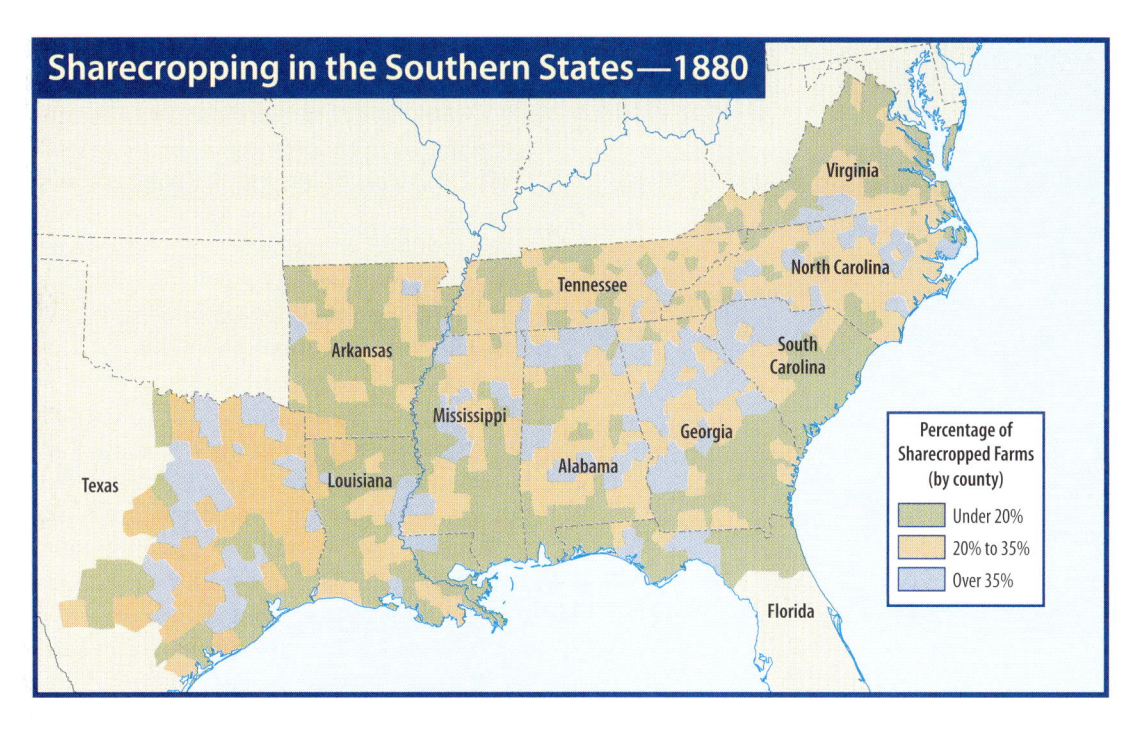

Sharecropping in the Southern States—1880

Percentage of Sharecropped Farms (by county)
- Under 20%
- 20% to 35%
- Over 35%

Because of the need for profits, landowners usually insisted that sharecroppers grow crops that provided quick cash, such as tobacco or cotton. But those crops depleted the soil of nutrients and obviously provided nothing for the sharecroppers to eat. Low prices for cotton and tobacco after the war only worsened the situation for both sharecroppers and landowners.

A sharecropper worked as hard as a slave and often received less for his efforts. As years passed, the debts increased as interest grew and further debts were incurred. Thousands of Southerners—both white and black—were trapped in the endless cycle of annual debt and were unable to save enough money to purchase their own land, even after many years. Sharecropping allowed many Southerners to survive, but it did not enable them to prosper. Most struggled just to provide food for their families.

Tenant farmers had slightly better conditions. They usually had their own tools and mule, but paid a landlord rent for farmland and a house. They owned the crops they planted and received income after harvesting the crop. However, they faced many of the same challenges of the sharecroppers.

Carpetbaggers and Scalawags

By denying the vote to many former Confederates, a coalition of blacks and white Republicans was able to control state governments in the South. The majority of white Southerners opposed those governments. They called Northerners who moved to the South "**carpetbaggers**." That term was a reference to the cheap luggage in which many of them brought all their belongings. Why did they move to the South? Some sincerely wanted to help freed slaves. Some came to make their fortunes by acquiring farmland or starting new businesses. Southerners who supported these new governments were known as "**scalawags**." That term basically meant "scoundrel" or "worthless person." Both groups were despised as treasonous, dishonest, and self-serving. However, many of them were far better than Southerners claimed. Some carpetbaggers had come south with idealistic motives, such as aiding in the region's recovery. Likewise, most scalawags had been pro-Union men since

Carpetbaggers often carried their possessions in this type of luggage.

before the war, and their behavior now was consistent with their political beliefs. But most Southerners viewed scalawags as traitors.

Many white Southerners were also angered that blacks now participated in the writing of the new state constitutions and held elective offices. Bitterness against Northern interference increased when instances of corruption and electoral fraud occurred.

How good or bad were the Reconstruction governments? Many of them were undeniably corrupt, as men sought to use political power to enrich themselves. The legislature of South Carolina, for example, voted a bonus of $1,000 to its speaker of the house after he had lost that amount betting on a horse race. The legislature of that state spent $16,000 in one year for paper and supplies. The average spent on these materials before the war was $400. Corruption, however, was not limited to the "carpetbaggers" in the South during this era. Critics failed to mention that many Democratic politicians were just as corrupt and inefficient. For example, the scandals of the Grant administration and the corruption of Tammany Hall in New York (both discussed in the next section) demonstrate that such abuses were not uncommon. Furthermore, some of the Southern state governments after Reconstruction were just as bad during this period.

The Republican governments in the South could point with pride to some accomplishments. They organized public school systems and rebuilt roads, railroads, and other transportation systems destroyed by the war. Critics argued that some of those state governments relied on military might and the **disenfranchisement** (denial of the right to vote) of many Southern whites. Over time, Southern whites regained control of their states. When the military departed, the Republican governments collapsed quickly. Unfortunately, the white majority disenfranchised the blacks.

Violence

Shamefully, some Southerners who disliked Radical rule turned to violence. Some established secret societies. The largest of these was the **Ku Klux Klan** (KKK). It was organized in 1866 by former Confederate soldiers in Pulaski, Tennessee. Many of them were determined to place black people firmly under white control. They targeted successful black businessmen and landowners. They intimidated white people who did business with black businesses. Schools and churches for blacks were burned to prevent black people from gaining the education needed to become self-sufficient.

The Klan also targeted black officeholders and white Republican leaders. Some were beaten and some were killed. Even voting made a black person a target. The violence severely damaged the Republican Party's organization in some parts of the South. Some party leaders had to flee for their safety.

The Klan included many prominent citizens—a fact that added to the Klan's power. Dressed in white hooded robes to conceal their identity, they usually terrorized at night. Many white citizens who opposed Klan violence did not voice their concerns publicly. Testifying against Klan members in court would make the witness a Klan target.

Hundreds of freedmen were **lynched** (executed, often by hanging, without a legal trial). Many of them were dragged from their homes at night and killed in the presence of their families. Because local law enforcement could not or would not deal with the Klan, Congress passed several laws in 1870 and 1871. These outlawed

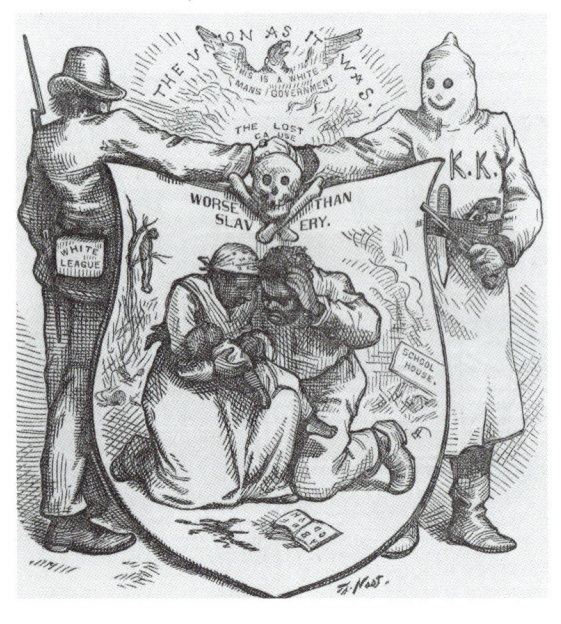

In this political cartoon, a man labeled "White League" is shaking hands with a member of another racist group, the Ku Klux Klan. In the background a man is hanging from a tree, implying he was lynched. A black family is huddled beneath a banner that indicates life after the Civil War was worse for them than slavery.

Ku Klux Klan

The following excerpt is part of a petition to Congress in 1871 by a group of Kentucky blacks.

We believe you are not familiar with the description of the Ku Klux Klans riding nightly over the country, going from county to county . . . spreading terror wherever they go by robbing, whipping, ravishing, and killing our people without provocation [reason], compelling colored people to break the ice and bathe in the chilly waters of the Kentucky River.

The [state] legislature has adjourned. They refused to enact any laws to suppress [stop] Ku-Klux [Klan] disorder. We regard them as now being licensed [approved] to continue their dark and bloody deeds under cover of the dark night. They refuse to allow us to testify in the state courts where a white man is concerned. We find their deeds are perpetrated only upon colored men and white Republicans. We also find that for our services to the government and our race we have become the special object of hatred and persecution at the hands of the Democratic Party. Our people are driven from their homes in great numbers. . . .

We would state that we have been law-abiding citizens, pay our taxes, and in many parts of the state our people have been . . . refused the right to vote. Many have been slaughtered while attempting to vote. We ask, how long is this state of things to last?

---

the use of force to prevent people from voting and gave the president the power to place federal troops to ensure compliance with this legislation. One of those laws, the Ku Klux Klan Act, imposed heavy penalties against terrorist groups, such as the Klan. Eventually thousands of Klansmen were arrested and hundreds of those were convicted for their actions. Though the Klan's power was diminished, it was not destroyed. Unfortunately, it reemerged in the twentieth century with renewed vigor.

Section Review

1. What agency was established to help former slaves and refugees?
2. Who was Oliver O. Howard?
3–6. Summarize the four major provisions of the Fourteenth Amendment.
7–8. How did Johnson violate the Tenure of Office Act? How did the Radicals respond to his action?
9. Why did some senators vote for President Johnson's acquittal at his Senate trial?
10. What is the difference between a "carpetbagger" and a "scalawag"?
11. What was the largest of the violent secret societies during Reconstruction?
* Describe some of the pros and cons of the sharecropping system.
* Assess the Ku Klux Klan. List reasons a Christian should have opposed such an organization.

Guiding Questions

1. What scandals occurred during the years Grant served as president?
2. What was the significance of the Fifteenth Amendment?
3. What conditions led to the Panic of '73?
4. Why was the election of 1876 so significant?

III. Years of Corruption

The North did not undergo a formal period of Reconstruction. It had suffered no widespread war destruction, it had no need to rebuild the state governments, and it had not faced military occupation. Nonetheless, the Reconstruction era was still a period of change in the North.

The Grant Years (1869–1877)

Election of 1868

As the nation approached the presidential election of 1868, the Republicans turned to their leading hero, General **Ulysses S. Grant**, as their candidate. Grant appeared to be the pillar of strength that the nation needed after the war and after the bitter struggle between President Johnson and Congress. Grant captured the mood of the people in his campaign slogan: "Let us have peace."

Grant won the election by defeating the Democratic candidate, former New York governor Horatio Seymour. Grant's victory in the popular vote would not have been possible without the support of the vast majority of the 500,000 Southern black men who voted in the election.

Grant lacked political experience. He soon learned that leading a nation was quite different from leading an army. He had virtually no preparation for the presidency, and the duties of the office seemed to confuse and frustrate him. One visitor to the White House said that Grant looked like "a man with a problem before him of which he does not understand the terms." But the greatest problem with Grant's administration was corruption. Although Grant himself was honest, he had friends, cabinet members, and other associates who took advantage of his position to personally enrich themselves. Many were soon involved in unethical and illegal activities. A new word, **Grantism**, became a synonym for political corruption.

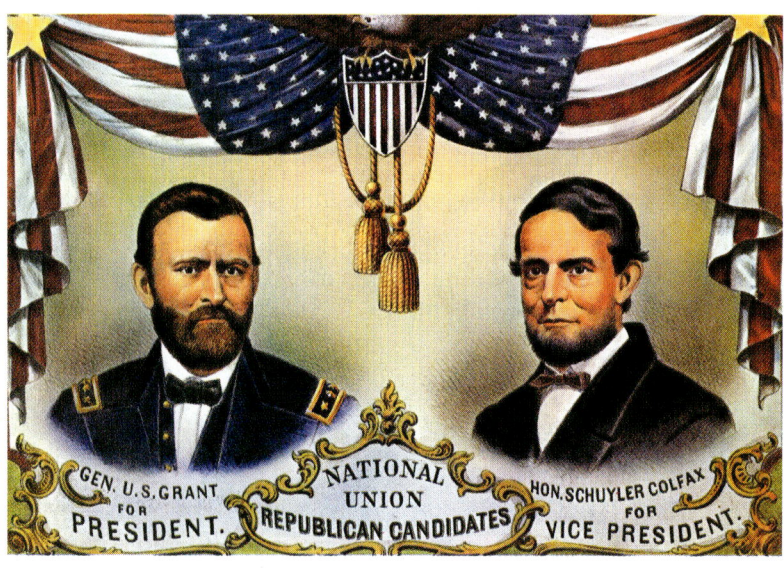

President Ulysses S. Grant

Election of 1868 campaign poster

Fifteenth Amendment

The Reconstruction Act of 1867 required that Southern states allow black men to vote and hold office in order to regain admission to the Union. However, as late as 1868, only about half of Northern states had legalized black suffrage. To prevent Southern states from possibly revoking this right in the future and to ensure that right nationwide, Congress passed the **Fifteenth Amendment**. It was adopted in 1869 and stated, "The right of the citizens of the United States to vote shall not be denied or abridged by the United States or by any state on account of race, color, or previous condition of servitude." It was ratified the following year.

Scandals

Several scandals rocked the Grant administration. One of them, the **Crédit Mobilier** (CRED-it moh-BEEL-yur) **scandal**, actually began before Grant took office. The Crédit Mobilier was a construction company controlled by promoters and officers of the Union Pacific Railway. During the construction of the transcontinental railroad (see Chapter 17), that railway company received a substantial amount of money from the federal government. Crédit Mobilier overcharged the Union Pacific for construction expenses and then paid the excesses to the stockholders, most of whom were Union Pacific officers. To discourage investigation into this illegal activity, Crédit Mobilier sold stock to congressmen and other government officials at prices far below the market value. An eventual congressional investigation in 1872 revealed that several prominent Republicans had received shares of the stock, including Vice President Schuyler Colfax.

Another scheme that cast shadows on Grant's political reputation was one in which James Fisk and Jay Gould, two unethical businessmen, tried to gain control of the gold market. They planned to buy gold on the New York Stock Exchange until the price of gold rose. They would then sell theirs and make an enormous profit. For their plan to work, however, the federal treasury had to refrain from selling any of its gold reserves, or the price of gold would drop. Fisk and Gould therefore convinced Grant that the nation would be racked with inflation if the secretary of the treasury sold any federal gold. They even convinced Grant's brother-in-law to join them to use his influence to ensure the government's cooperation. Then on September 24, 1869, which became known as "Black Friday," Fisk and Gould began to bid up the price of gold. When Grant learned of the scheme, he ordered the treasury to release gold for sale, and the Fisk-Gould plan only partially succeeded.

Some scandals reached into Grant's inner circle of cabinet members and advisers. Secretary of War William Belknap, Grant's close personal friend, received thousands of dollars in bribes in return for granting special licenses to sell goods to the Indians. After the House began impeachment proceedings, Belknap resigned in March 1876. One of the worst scandals, revealed in 1875, was the **Whiskey Ring**, a group of whiskey distillers and distributors and federal tax collectors who conspired to cheat the government out of millions of dollars in revenue from taxes. Because his private secretary, Orville Babcock, was among those accused in the swindle, Grant was hesitant to demand a thorough investigation.

There is no evidence that Grant himself personally profited from any of the fraud. However, his poor choice of friends and associates as well as his lack of good judgment resulted in widespread criticism. Sadly, the Grant administration was one of the most scandal-ridden of any American president.

Tammany Hall

The most notorious political corruption in this period was not in the Grant administration; it was in the city government of New York run by the Democratic **Tammany Hall** under the direction of **William "Boss" Tweed**. Tammany Hall was a political organization founded after the Revolutionary War. Its influence grew until it controlled most of New York's political affairs during the last half of the nineteenth century. Under the leadership of Boss Tweed, its corruption in the 1860s and 1870s reached astonishing depths.

New York City's debt increased from $36 million in 1868 to more than $136 million in 1870, largely because Tweed and other Tammany leaders diverted city funds into their own pockets. It has been estimated that fraudulent expenditures from 1865 to 1871 totaled more than $75 million. In just one of his many frauds, Tweed charged New York taxpayers about $11 million to build a courthouse that actually cost about $3 million. (Thermometers for the building, for example, were listed as costing $7,500 each.) Excess funds, entered on falsified records as expenditures, were stolen by Tweed and others in Tammany Hall. Hospitals, asylums, and other institutions that never existed except on paper received large funds from the city—money deposited into the wallets of Tweed and company.

Boss Tweed and his dishonest associates managed to stay in power by bribing people to vote for Democrats and by cheating during elections. Needing Tammany's help to win, many Democrats in New York ignored the corruption in New York City. Tammany politicians used bribes to persuade Republicans to leave them alone.

Reform efforts aimed at destroying Tammany Hall resulted in Tweed finally being arrested in 1871, although Tammany's political influence continued well into the twentieth century. Tweed's arrest and imprisonment were encouraged by the gifted political cartoonist **Thomas Nast**, who repeatedly attacked Tweed and Tammany

William "Boss" Tweed

Thomas Nast

The cartoonist known for opposing Boss Tweed was a short, bespectacled German immigrant who looked more like a bookish professor than a fearless reformer. But Thomas Nast was a man of firm principles with a fierce sense of right, and his political cartoons in *Harper's Weekly* had a sharp edge that made him the leading political cartoonist of the day.

A diehard Republican, Nast was not exactly unbiased. Even at the height of the Grant scandals, he defended the president. Yet Nast's opponents could not deny the power of his work. When Tweed died, it was discovered that he had kept every cartoon Nast had ever drawn of him.

In addition to the Tweed drawings, Nast's cartoons made popular the symbols of the two parties—the Republicans' elephant and the Democrats' donkey. He also illustrated Clement Moore's poem "A Visit from St. Nicholas," thereby popularizing the modern conception of Santa Claus as the round-bellied, red-cheeked, "jolly old elf" who is recognized today as "Saint Nick."

Hall. Tweed feared the cartoons more than any other opposition; as Tweed himself said, his uneducated supporters could not read editorials, but they could understand Nast's drawings. Tweed was eventually convicted of his crimes. Later he managed to escape prison and flee to Spain. Ironically, he was identified there through one of Nast's cartoons. He was arrested and returned to prison in New York.

Liberal Republicans

The corruption of the Grant administration and the disagreements with Radical Republicans led to the development of a splinter group within the Republican Party. Calling themselves the "**Liberal Republicans**," they decided to oppose Grant's reelection in 1872. They supported an end to military occupation of the South and an end to corruption in the national government. They had trouble finding an acceptable candidate. Eventually, they chose New York newspaper editor **Horace Greeley**.

The Democrats, still weakened by the war, decided their best hope for defeating Grant was to join forces with the Liberal Republicans. Thus, they also nominated Greeley. Although Greeley was well-known and thoroughly honest, he had long been a bitter critic of the South and aroused little excitement among many southern Democrats. (Greeley had once said, "All Democrats may not be rascals, but all rascals are Democrats.") Now, oddly, he was the Democratic nominee. Furthermore, Greeley was an eccentric, advocating such unusual (at least for the time) practices as vegetarianism and spiritualism (communication with the dead). Presidential corruption or not, most voters did not see Greeley as an improvement over Grant. The president crushed Greeley in the election and, in so doing, destroyed the Liberal Republican movement. Exhausted by the campaign, Greeley died three weeks after the election.

Economic Boom and Bust

One of the reasons Grant won reelection so easily was the general prosperity of the nation, particularly in the North. As mentioned in the last chapter, the war had spurred the growth of both agriculture and heavy industry. After the war, business continued to boom as manufacturing quickly shifted from wartime to peacetime goods. A rifle-making plant in Hartford, Connecticut, for example, converted to manufacturing sewing machines. For most voters, economic good times excused many of the failures of Grant's administration.

Prosperity came to a devastating halt during Grant's second term, however. A financial collapse called the **Panic of '73** touched off a six-year depression, the worst depression that the United States had endured up to that time. By 1875, more than 18,000 companies had collapsed. A startling 89 of the nation's 364 railroads went bankrupt. Unemployment soared to 14 percent.

One cause of the panic was a struggle over the nation's currency. At the outset of the Civil War, Congress had issued paper money called "**greenbacks**" (so called because they were printed with green ink) to help pay for the war. Unlike earlier currencies, however, the greenbacks were not backed by gold or silver, but simply by the government's promise to honor them. As a result, most Americans viewed greenbacks as less valuable than "hard money" (gold and silver or notes redeemable for gold and silver).

In this Thomas Nast cartoon, Boss Tweed's body is shown, but a moneybag replaces his head. Nast often portrayed Tweed as a man motivated by greed.

After the war, conservative financiers wanted to get rid of the greenbacks and return to money based entirely on gold. "Easy money" advocates wanted not only to continue using greenbacks but also to print more. Debtors and those on the poorer end of the economic ladder liked the greenbacks because the more money that was in circulation, the more everybody would have. Wages would rise, and it would also be easier to pay debts. Bankers and other conservative economists quickly pointed out that higher prices on goods and services would also result from an increase in the amount of currency in circulation.

Eventually a compromise of sorts was reached. More than $300 million in greenbacks was left in circulation, but the government pledged to begin redeeming them for their face value in gold. Thus, the greenbacks became "as good as gold." The government's action restricted the amount of money in circulation and thereby made the depression worse. The nation's economic problems began to stir opposition and gave the Democrats a strong political weapon.

The Redeemers

By the mid-1870s, many Northerners had lost interest in Reconstruction and conditions in the South. They were more concerned about the return to economic prosperity. Others were more interested in the West—in its opportunities for expansion and the Indian wars occurring there. Some believed that peace in the South would be better for business. The country seemed tired of scandal and controversy. Such attitudes paved the way for Democrats to retake Southern state governments from Republican rule and congressional control. Since they wanted to "redeem" (or regain) the South, this group became known as **Redeemers**.

In 1872, some Republicans convinced Congress to pass the General Amnesty Act. It pardoned all but a few hundred former Confederate leaders. Those who had held federal offices at the time of secession were among those excluded. Basically, about 150,000 former Confederates regained the right to vote and to hold office. These people would almost certainly vote for Democratic candidates. With this change, many former Confederate leaders now regained their influence in government.

During Reconstruction, some African Americans, often those from the North, participated in Southern politics. Six hundred black men served as state legislators, others were judges, and some were elected to Congress. Joseph Rainey of South Carolina was the first black man elected to the U.S. House of Representatives, while Hiram R. Revels of Mississippi was the first black man elected to the U.S. Senate.

Although black people had gained some rights, some white Southerners found it difficult to accept them as equals. Republicans were able to keep their offices for a while, but their organization in some parts of the South collapsed when some Republicans were beaten or even killed by angry white Southerners. Under these conditions, Republicans soon found they could not match the organization and experience of Southerners who sought to "redeem the South." By the 1870s, Southerners were electing white Democrats to replace black officials and white Republicans. Only in areas still occupied by federal troops did Republican governments control a bit longer. By 1876, federal troops remained only in Louisiana, Florida, and South Carolina.

Congressman Joseph Rainey from South Carolina

Hiram Revels (1822–1901)

When Congress met in January 1870, a new member drew an unusual amount of attention. He was Hiram Revels, senator from Mississippi and the first black to serve in the U.S. Congress. Revels was born to free black parents in Fayetteville, North Carolina, in 1822. Because of the lack of educational opportunities for blacks in North Carolina at the time, he moved to the Midwest. There he attended schools in Indiana, Ohio, and Illinois. Revels became a minister in the African Methodist Episcopal (AME) Church, the black denomination founded by a former slave, Richard Allen (see Chapter 11). He preached and taught in the Midwest and the border states, and at the outbreak of the Civil War was pastoring in Baltimore.

During the war, he recruited African Americans to fight for the Union and also served as a Union chaplain. Later, he preached to blacks in Mississippi and helped the Freedmen's Bureau establish schools there. He was elected to that state's senate in 1868 as a Radical Republican. He was later elected to finish the last year of an unexpired U.S. Senate term.

He served only one year in the Senate, and his legislative role was limited. However, he persuaded the War Department to hire qualified black mechanics in the U.S. Naval Yard and spoke out against segregation in the schools of Washington, D.C. Although he supported the presence of troops in the South (he believed that only the army could protect the rights of blacks in the region), he opposed efforts to deprive former Confederates of the vote. Having seen his own people deprived of the right to vote because of their race, Revels did not favor depriving others of the vote.

When his term in the U.S. Senate expired, Revels returned to Mississippi. There he served as president of Alcorn College and briefly as Mississippi's secretary of state. After retiring from the presidency of Alcorn because of health problems, Revels returned to the ministry. He spent his last years preaching. He died in 1901 while attending a church conference in Mississippi.

Redeemer rule had wide-ranging, long-term effects for black Southerners. Though black men continued to vote in significant numbers in the South into the 1880s, the effectiveness of their vote was hindered by episodes of fraud and violence. Sometimes ballot boxes were stuffed with more votes than there were voters. Sometimes Republican ballots were removed. Congressional districts were sometimes drawn in strange shapes to ensure that black voters were not in a majority. In other cases, black sharecroppers had their votes determined by the man for whom they worked. In many states black children had their access to education hindered and some of the old black codes were reestablished. Segregation, or separation of the races, was commonplace.

Though Redeemers were determined to restore the rule of white Southerners in their states, some, like Wade Hampton of South Carolina, thought that the superiority of the white race meant that white citizens had a duty to protect and care for the black race. As a result, when Hampton served as governor of his state, he sought to preserve educational opportunities and certain rights for African Americans. This approach was not followed throughout the South. Moreover, stringent efforts to keep black Americans in inferior positions were common.

Election of 1876

Campaign

Reconstruction, Republican scandals, and economic hard times were among the themes of the presidential

In this cartoon, members of the White League are intimidating black men who want to vote. The caption stated, "Every thing points to a Democratic victory this fall."

election of 1876. Republicans chose **Rutherford B. Hayes** as their candidate. He had served as a Union general in the Civil War, had been a three-time governor of Ohio, and—most important to the Republicans—possessed a reputation for unimpeachable honesty. The Democrats nominated **Samuel J. Tilden**, a railroad lawyer and former governor of New York. Tilden had gained a national reputation by successfully fighting the "Tweed ring" and by reforming the state judiciary system.

A Disputed Election

When the election returns were tallied, Tilden won the popular vote by a margin of 250,000. He had 184 of the 185 electoral votes needed to win. However, three Southern states—Florida, Louisiana, and South Carolina (all states that federal troops still occupied)—submitted conflicting election results. The Republicans claimed that Hayes had won those states; the Democrats, of course, claimed that Tilden had won them. If Tilden could capture at least one of the disputed electoral votes, he would be president. If Hayes captured all nineteen, he would be president.

Congress established a commission of fifteen men—five each from the Supreme Court, the Senate, and the House—to determine which party should receive the disputed votes. Eight of the fifteen were Republicans, while seven were Democrats. By a vote of eight to seven, divided along party lines, the commission gave all of the disputed votes to the Republicans. Thus, the final tally gave Hayes 185 electoral votes to Tilden's 184.

It is difficult to decide who—if anyone—was in the right in the disputed election. Voting corruption marked the efforts of both parties. Southern Democrats, for example, made obvious efforts through threats and fraud to prevent black Republicans from vot-

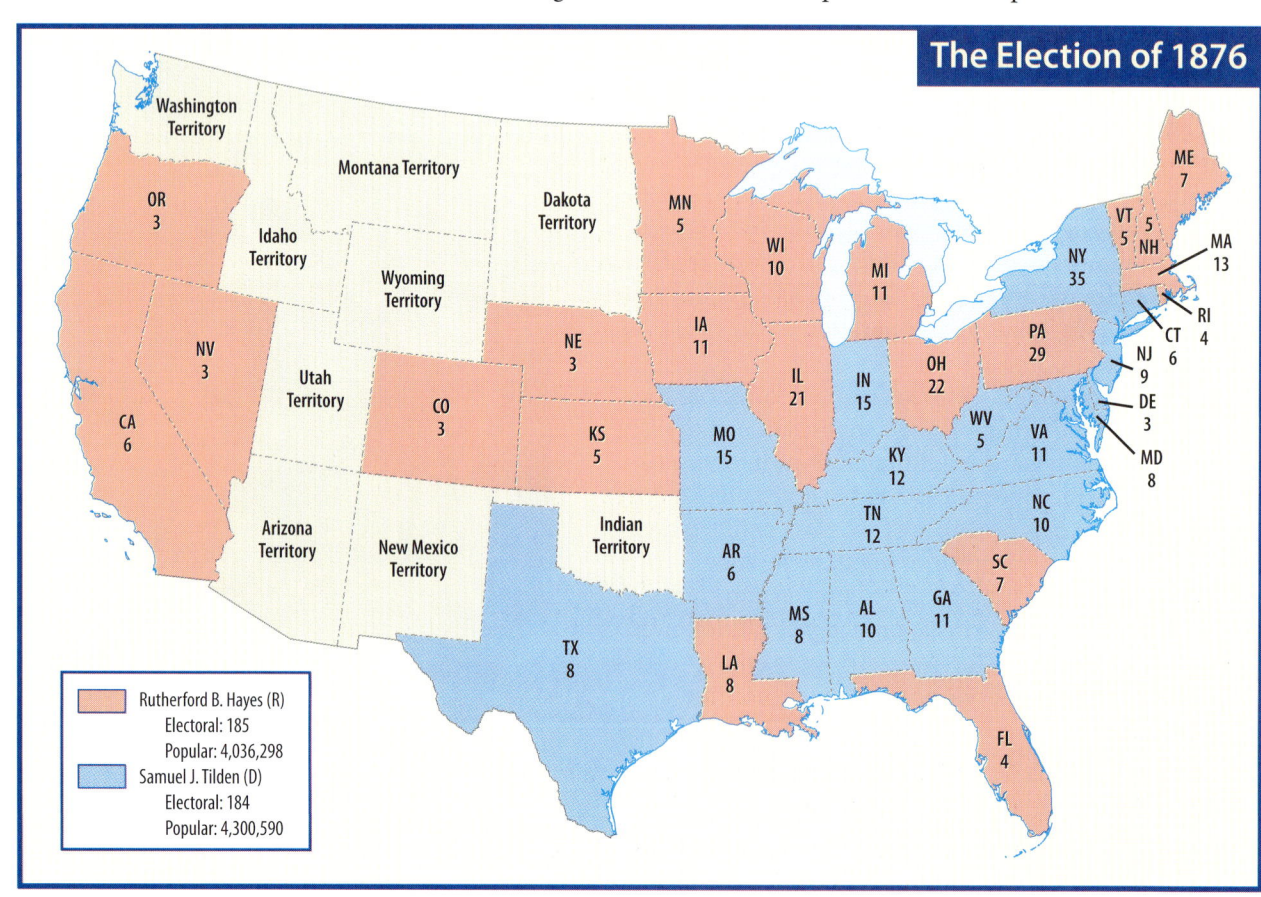

Republican campaign poster in the 1876 election

The Election of 1876

Rutherford B. Hayes (R)
Electoral: 185
Popular: 4,036,298

Samuel J. Tilden (D)
Electoral: 184
Popular: 4,300,590

When Former Confederate States Were Readmitted to the Union			
Order	State	Date of Readmission	Date on which Local Rule was Reestablished
1	Tennessee	July 24, 1866	October 4, 1869
2	Arkansas	June 22, 1868	November 10, 1874
3	Florida	June 25, 1868	January 2, 1877
4	North Carolina	July 4, 1868	November 28, 1876
5	Louisiana	July 9, 1868	January 2, 1877
6	South Carolina	July 9, 1868	November 28, 1876
7	Alabama	July 13, 1868	November 16, 1874
8	Virginia	January 26, 1870	October 5, 1869
9	Mississippi	February 23, 1870	January 4, 1876
10	Texas	March 30, 1870	January 14, 1873
11	Georgia	July 15, 1870	November 1, 1871

ing. Likewise, the Republican majority on the special congressional election commission appeared more concerned with electing its candidate than in honestly determining who had won. It might be, as some have noted, that the Democrats stole the election first and the Republicans stole it back.

Compromise of 1877

As one might expect, the Democrats contested the commission's decision. The party threatened to prevent the official counting of the electoral votes in Congress so that Hayes could not take office. No one knew what would happen if the Democrats carried out their threat, and a few people even hinted that another war might result. The deadlock was broken, however, when a group of Southern Democrats met secretly with the Republicans to make a deal. The agreement, known as the **Compromise of 1877**, was essentially a tradeoff. Southern Democrats would help Hayes by allowing the electoral votes to be counted. Hayes, in turn, would remove the last federal troops from the South. Each side kept its part of the bargain. Hayes took office on schedule, and within two months he had withdrawn the last troops from the South. Reconstruction was officially over.

Waving the Bloody Shirt

After the Civil War, Republicans sometimes used a technique called "waving the bloody shirt." It was an attempt to appeal to voters by blaming the war on Democrats and thereby urge them to vote for Republicans. The phrase originated from an incident in which a Republican supposedly waved a bloody shirt to highlight Democratic treachery.

One Republican speaker in 1876 made the following attack on the Democrats:

> Every State that seceded from the [Union] was a Democratic State.... Every man that shot Union soldiers was a Democrat.... The man that assassinated Abraham Lincoln was a Democrat.... Soldiers, every scar you have on your heroic bodies was given you by a Democrat. Every scar, every arm that is [missing], every limb that is gone, is a souvenir of a Democrat.

Section Review

1–4. List four major scandals that were directly related to the Grant administration.

5–6. Who was the corrupt politician who controlled the city government of New York during the Reconstruction era? What was his political party?

7–9. What were the three main campaign themes in the election of 1876?

10–11. What did Southern Democrats promise in the Compromise of 1877? What did the Republicans promise?

★ Evaluate President Grant's administration. What do you think were his greatest weaknesses?

Guiding Questions

1. Why were some people dissatisfied with Reconstruction?
2. How did Reconstruction impact the nation?

The Reconstruction Amendments

The Thirteenth Amendment (ratified 1865), the Fourteenth Amendment (ratified 1868), and the Fifteenth Amendment (ratified 1870) are often known collectively as the "Reconstruction amendments." With the exception of the first ten amendments (the Bill of Rights), no other amendments have proved so influential in American life. These three amendments are the most lasting heritage of the Reconstruction period.

Thomas Nast, in this cartoon and in others, used the elephant to represent Republicans and the donkey to represent the Democrats.

IV. A Reconstructed Nation

Reconstruction was one of the most difficult periods in American history. African Americans were struggling to overcome black codes and violence as they sought their place as free and equal citizens. White Southerners were upset by the changes thrust upon them and hated being treated as a conquered nation. At times, the challenges of rebuilding the devastated region appeared insurmountable. Some Northerners were dissatisfied with the results of Reconstruction.

Many argue that Reconstruction should have been more extensive. Steps were made toward granting civil rights for black Americans, but those rights did not become permanent. After white Southerners regained control of their state governments, many of the civil rights advances were eventually lost. Even in the North, few white people were willing to give black citizens significant social and political power.

Still, the impact of Reconstruction was enormous. First, one of the great legacies of the period was the adoption of three constitutional amendments—the Thirteenth, Fourteenth, and Fifteenth. With these, slaves were freed, granted citizenship, and given the right to vote. These changes were monumental for our nation. Second, a stronger, more centralized federal government emerged. Centralization occurred partly because local and state governments in the South had failed to treat newly freed blacks in a just manner. This increased power would provide both benefits and problems in the future. Third, the South, where many bitterly opposed Republicans because of the war and Radical Reconstruction, soon became known as "**the Solid South**" for its commitment to the Democratic Party. With some exceptions, the region elected only Democratic governors, state legislators, and congressmen for nearly a hundred years. Not until 1972 would a Republican candidate for president again be the victor in most southern states.

Section Review

1–3. Which three amendments to the Constitution were adopted during Reconstruction?

4. What term was applied to the states of the former Confederacy because of their consistent support of the Democratic Party?

★ Was the South ever really "reconstructed"?

CHAPTER REVIEW 15

Making Connections

1. How did Lincoln and Johnson differ with the Radical Republicans concerning the ultimate responsibility for Reconstruction?
2–6. What were the five major parts of the Reconstruction Act of 1867?
7–12. The Freedmen's Bureau helped former slaves and refugees in many ways. List six of these.
13. Why did the Liberal Republicans' choice of a candidate in 1872 harm their efforts to defeat Grant?

Developing History Skills

1. What is meant by "waving the bloody shirt," and how was it used as an election tactic?
2. Why did some say of the presidential election of 1876 that "the Democrats stole the election first and the Republicans stole it back"?

Thinking Critically

1. Why was sharecropping very common in the South after the Civil War?
2. Why were black codes written? What did they dictate in order to achieve their goal?

Living as a Christian Citizen

1. Imagine you are a congressman during Reconstruction. Construct a speech supporting the Fifteenth Amendment. Use Scripture to support your arguments.
2. Evaluate Reconstruction-era Radicals from a Christian perspective. How could a Christian worldview have improved their strengths and curbed their excesses?

People, Places, and Things to Remember

Andrew Johnson
Reconstruction
Ten Percent Plan
Radical Republicans
Wade-Davis Bill
suffrage
Thaddeus Stevens
Charles Sumner
amnesty
Thirteenth Amendment
black codes
Freedmen's Bureau
refugees
Fourteenth Amendment
Reconstruction Act of 1867
Tenure of Office Act
Edwin Stanton
impeachment
sharecropping
tenant farmers
carpetbaggers
scalawags
disenfranchisement
Ku Klux Klan
lynched
Ulysses S. Grant
Grantism
Fifteenth Amendment
Crédit Mobilier scandal
Whiskey Ring
Tammany Hall
William "Boss" Tweed
Thomas Nast
Liberal Republicans
Horace Greeley
Panic of '73
greenbacks
Redeemers
Rutherford B. Hayes
Samuel J. Tilden
Compromise of 1877
the Solid South

QUEST
1850–1920

1867
Purchase of Alaska

1869
First transcontinental railroad completed

1876
Alexander Graham Bell invents the telephone

| 1850 | 1860 | 1870 | 1880 |

1870
Rockefeller forms the Standard Oil Company of Ohio

1883
Pendleton Act creates Civil Service Commission

CHAPTERS

16 THE GILDED AGE (1877–1896)

17 AMERICA EXPANDS (1850–1900)

18 THE PROGRESSIVE ERA (1890–1920)

19 THE GREAT WAR (1914–1920)

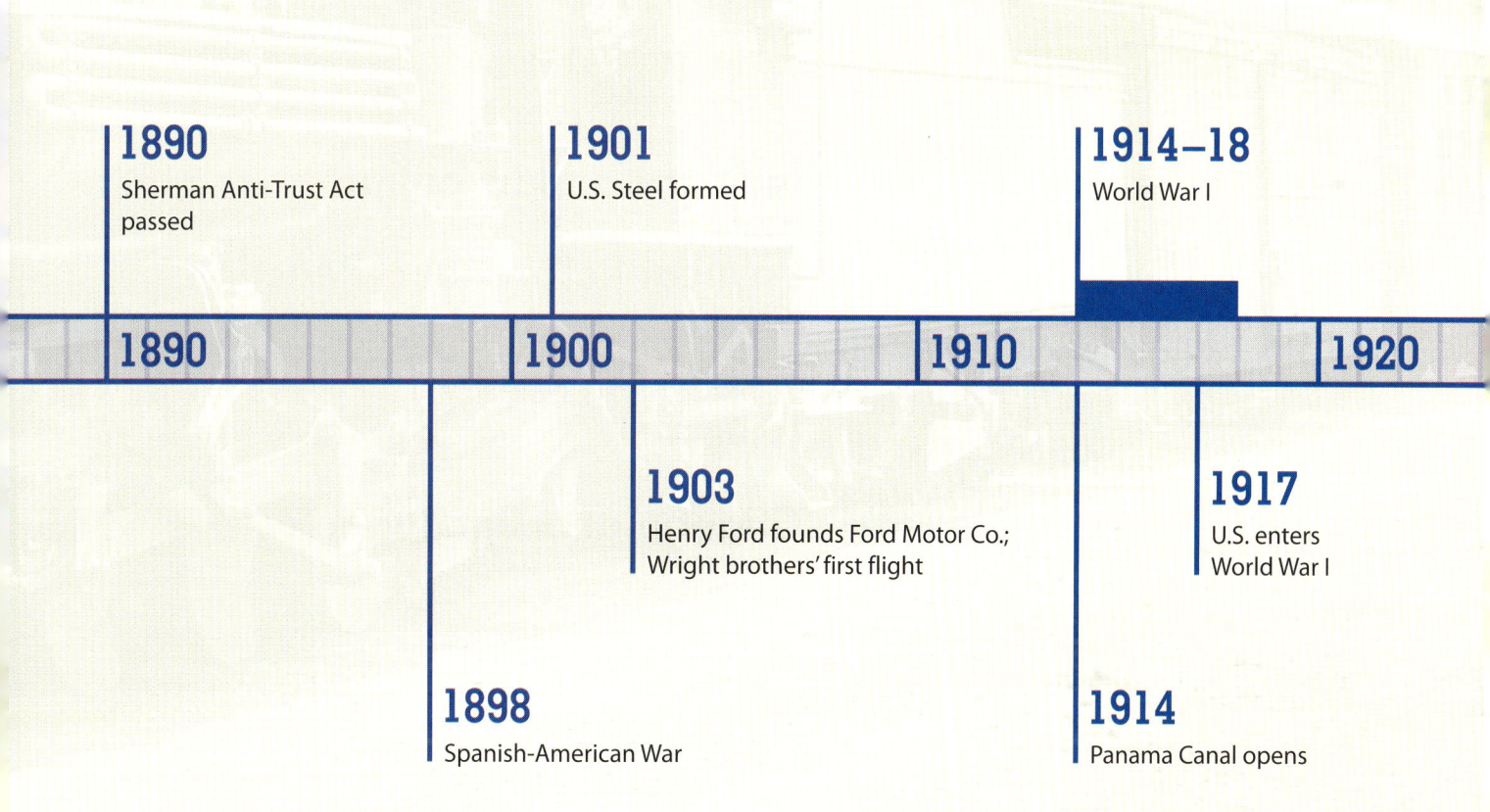

1890
Sherman Anti-Trust Act passed

1901
U.S. Steel formed

1914–18
World War I

| 1890 | 1900 | 1910 | 1920 |

1903
Henry Ford founds Ford Motor Co.; Wright brothers' first flight

1917
U.S. enters World War I

1898
Spanish-American War

1914
Panama Canal opens

16 THE GILDED AGE (1877–1896)

Well, well, my boy, things are looking pretty bright now I tell you. Speculation—my! The whole atmosphere's full of money.

Con man Colonel Beriah Sellers discussing a business venture over a dinner of water and raw turnips.
Mark Twain's *The Gilded Age* (1873)

Ellis Island Immigration Station

Big Ideas

1. Who were the key leaders of industry and technology in the United States during this period?
2. What were the political reforms in the United States during this period?
3. How did the economic goals of urban labor differ from those of rural labor?
4. What were key changes and challenges to the United States during this era?

I. Industry and Invention

II. Political Reform and Reaction

III. Labor, Rural, and Economic Issues

IV. Change and Challenge

As the country hurried headlong toward the twentieth century, the skyscraper and the smokestack replaced the steeple as the skyline's most prominent feature. Industrialization put its golden stamp of prosperity on much of society. This brief period in America after Reconstruction took its name from a novel by Mark Twain entitled *The Gilded Age: A Tale of Today*. "Gilded" refers to something that is covered with a gold veneer but is not pure gold. It describes the promise and problems of this period. Unprecedented political and economic freedom enabled a flood of inventions and innovations in almost every industry and area of life and affected everyone. The rich got richer, and even the poor got less poor. Yet behind the glitter of America's growing wealth were contrasts and divisions that would transform national life.

I. Industry and Invention

The Rise of Industrialism

The postwar period witnessed a rapid rise in the importance of industry in the United States. From a few small iron factories and oil wells in the 1850s, American industry grew until the United States was a leader in the world's industrial community.

American industrial growth occurred for several reasons. First, the nation itself grew. A modest postwar baby boom combined with immigration nearly tripled the population from about 32 million in 1860 to 92 million in 1910. Increased population led to an increased demand for products and an increased work force to produce them. It also encouraged the movement westward and the accompanying development of farmland and mining in the resource-rich West.

Second, the innovative spirit of the times fostered new machines and methods that enhanced industrial expansion. Communication capabilities improved as entrepreneurs experimented with the telegraph, telephone, and radio.

Third, industry benefited from a sympathetic government. The generally high tariff laws reduced foreign competition, and the nation's liberal immigration laws provided a vast and inexpensive work force for prospective employers.

Fourth, new sources of power sprang up to supplement or supplant the waterpower that had driven America's early industry. Whole new energy industries in oil and electricity spurred greater manufacturing and opened new markets. The success of these industries led to the development of new, more efficient ways of doing and organizing business, especially corporations and trusts. Commercial capitalism made way for industrial capitalism (factories) and then finance capitalism, in which banks and investors played the leading role.

Captains of Industry

At the top of America's growing industrial empire were men whose ideas, energy, and money dominated the age. Their lives often illustrated the best and worst aspects of industrialization. These men were the "captains of industry," and their efforts helped forge America into a prosperous and productive nation. Many historians and journalists, by calling these men "**robber barons**," imply that they were the personifications of greed and callousness. They were, indeed, aggressive, cost- and efficiency-conscious

Guiding Questions

1. How did industrial growth in the United States change following the Civil War?
2. What is the difference between a market entrepreneur and a political entrepreneur?
3. How did industrialization impact the lifestyle of many Americans during this period?

Results of Westward Expansion

The development of the West made accessible to the nation an increased supply of raw materials with which to produce goods. It also encouraged the rapid expansion of the railroads, connecting manufacturers with new markets, helping distribute resources and goods throughout the country, and binding East and West with steel rails.

Core Values During the Gilded Age

Individuals capitalized on their freedoms when inventing or improving products. Their work, combined with rapid growth across industries, resulted in a proliferation of inventions during this period and in many creative ways to lower prices for customers. Despite such growth, not all companies profited equally. Some losing competitors accused successful companies of using unfair tactics to deny them equal opportunity for success.

businessmen, but those characteristics actually accomplished enormous good for the average consumer, lowering prices on consumer goods and making available goods that once had been within reach of only the rich. Some of the industrialists were ruthless and exploited their workers. However, most created jobs by which workers could provide for their families. They made the United States the economic envy of the world and sparked a flood of immigrants seeking "the American dream." They became wealthy by providing efficiently what consumers needed and wanted. Moreover, many of them became great philanthropists, giving to numerous charitable causes, including hospitals and libraries that would benefit the common person.

Historian Burton Folsom groups the captains of industry in two categories: market entrepreneurs and political entrepreneurs. Market entrepreneurs were those who sought success by good business practices—time management, cost-cutting, improved operations, new technology. These practices resulted in more and better products and lower prices for the consumers. Market entrepreneurs made their money from volume, ingenuity, and service to the "little guy," not on the backs of others. The most efficient businesses succeeded; inefficient competitors failed.

Political entrepreneurs, on the other hand, sought success by special privileges or political advantages. They sought high tariffs to price out competitors and asked for government subsidies (taxpayer dollars) to reduce costs to themselves. In fact, some of them found that they could make almost as much money by getting government grants and subsidies as they could by producing products or providing services. They lobbied politicians to influence political decisions that might affect their businesses. Some even resorted to bribery to gain an advantage over competitors.

Entrepreneurs of both types, however, did more to shape America's future than anyone who sat in the White House or Congress at the time. Their lives illustrate a number of important trends during this formative period.

Cornelius Vanderbilt—Shipping

As a young man, **Cornelius Vanderbilt** borrowed one hundred dollars from his mother and started a ferry service. From this humble beginning, Vanderbilt gained control of much of New York's waterborne shipping through hard work and increased cost efficiency. Vanderbilt duplicated his successes throughout the Northeast and into the West. By 1860, he controlled much of the nation's shipping. Besides a fortune, Vanderbilt gained an inflated title—"Commodore."

James J. Hill—Railroads

Another entrepreneur, James J. Hill, gained his fame and fortune in railroads. His climb to fortune began with a job in a grocery store. As a young man, he determined that his future prospects lay in the westward movement. With six hundred dollars he had saved, he traveled to St. Paul, Minnesota, in 1856 to start a shipping business. He got a job as a clerk in a local shipping company and began to learn the business and make plans for his own company. He noted the "puny" railroad systems in the Great Lakes area and determined to find new and better ways of doing things. He became an expert on the economics of the upper Northwest, including the railroad industry.

Edward Collins—Political Entrepreneur

Vanderbilt's success actually began with another entrepreneur, Edward Collins. Collins wanted to compete with the British, who had a virtual monopoly on passenger and freight steamship traffic across the Atlantic. He approached Congress, claiming that he could compete with the British if the government subsidized the building of four steamships. He promised that within a year he would be showing a profit and no longer need government money. Congress voted the appropriation. Collins built the ships and began his service, but he kept coming back year after year for more subsidies, every time offering excuses as to why he could not make a profit.

Vanderbilt approached Congress, saying that he could do what Collins was doing—and actually make a profit—for half the money they were giving Collins. Congress turned him down, so Vanderbilt did it with his own and voluntary investors' money. By the end of his first year, he was turning a profit, and he continued to do so year after year.

James J. Hill, who built the Great Northern Railroad without any special privileges or finances from the government, is an example of a market entrepreneur.

In 1865, he founded the James J. Hill Company, providing warehouse facilities for products brought by steamship from the East. He provided railroad tracks directly from the warehouse to the rail line. Successful in that, he shifted his emphasis to railroads, buying up failing rail lines. He also bought land in Dakota Territory in preparation for fulfilling his dream of building a railroad across the northern part of the United States to the Pacific Northwest.

Hill innovated by shifting from wood fuel for his locomotives to coal and soon achieved stunning success in the trading of coal. He sought to get the best prices possible for not only coal but also all other purchases for his companies. For example, he demanded more accurate weighing of carloads of coal, which led to more accurate billing for freight fees, and that in turn translated into savings and greater profits.

In constructing his Great Northern Railroad, Hill applied his core principles. "What we want," he said, "is the best possible line, shortest distance, lowest grades, and least curvature that we can build. We do not care enough for Rocky Mountain scenery to spend a large sum of money developing it." His workers laid rails twice as fast as a nearby government-subsidized railroad had. He cut costs wherever he could and passed the savings on to customers in the form of lower rates. He adopted as his motto "We have got to prosper with you [the consumers and small businesses] or we have got to be poor with you." He practiced the art of building goodwill by throwing in many extras for those who used his businesses. He taught crop rotation to farmers along his route and provided free seeds and cattle to help farmers recover after a drought. He transported new immigrants to the Great Plains for a low fare if they would settle and farm along his rail lines. He even set up and operated model farms to demonstrate the latest improvements in farming science.

Hill's sharp business eye and his desire to meet the needs of consumers resulted in the Great Northern Railroad, a line that was far superior to any other lines built elsewhere in the world. Most importantly, Hill did all of that without a penny of government money or influence. He prospered immensely—and the population of the northern plains shared in that success.

Andrew Carnegie—Steel

Andrew Carnegie was born in Scotland, but hard times there forced his poor family to immigrate to western Pennsylvania in 1848. His life in America was a classic "rags-to-riches" story. His first job in America was as a bobbin boy in a textile mill, where he earned $1.20 a week. He then worked for a short time as a bookkeeper's clerk before becoming a telegraph delivery boy and then a telegrapher. As he worked hard to advance himself, he developed scorn for those whom he considered lazy, unambitious, and unwilling to work. Because he was diligent, efficient, and quick to learn about everything he undertook, Carnegie advanced rapidly to become superintendent of the Pittsburgh division of the Pennsylvania Railroad (PRR). He saved and invested heavily (eventually doubling his investments) from his PRR salary. By the early 1870s, he was focusing on the steel industry. He invested heavily in anything that involved steel: sleeping-car construction, an iron company, and

Andrew Carnegie was known as both an entrepreneur and a philanthropist.

Carnegie, the Bridge Builder

One of Carnegie's early achievements was construction of the St. Louis Bridge, which his Keystone Bridge Company built. He used pneumatic caissons to sink the piers a decade before the same method was used on the more famous Brooklyn Bridge. He bought all the iron used in the construction of the bridge from Union Iron Mills, which he owned. He also was the key investment banker for the project. By that time, Carnegie had a net worth of nearly two million dollars, but his cash on hand was only five thousand dollars.

> ### Carnegie, the Philanthropist
> Carnegie was as good as his word. Although he disdained the word *philanthropy* (giving to charitable causes) because it implied a handout, Carnegie gave millions of dollars to causes that promoted self-improvement. Carnegie's generosity built libraries, hospitals, universities, and concert halls across the country. Christians can applaud Carnegie for generously using his wealth to benefit others. Loving others is at the core of Christianity. But the greatest commandment is to love God with all our heart. As an avowed unbeliever who scorned the Scriptures, Carnegie violated this greatest of God's commands. In the end he falls under the sad condemnation of Jesus in Mark 8:36, "For what shall it profit a man, if he shall gain the whole world, and lose his own soul?"

Muckrakers portrayed John D. Rockefeller as a callous, uncaring moneygrubber. His supporters viewed him as an entrepreneur who improved the quality of life for millions of common people.

bridge building. He was always looking for better ways to organize, operate, and capitalize his various business ventures, including a telegraph company (which he eventually sold to Western Union).

Through a method known as **vertical integration**, Carnegie controlled every aspect of steel production from the mine to the market. Such a conglomerate effectively dismantled most of Carnegie's less efficient competitors, most of whom dealt with only one segment of the steel industry. Carnegie Steel soon became the largest steel company in the world, producing about half as much steel as the entire nation of Great Britain and about one-fourth of America's. When financier J. P. Morgan bought out Carnegie in 1901, the former bobbin boy's personal share was nearly $226 million.

Carnegie's companies always provided high-quality products and performance. However, he was more than a financial genius; he was also a philosopher of big business. In 1889, he published "The Gospel of Wealth," in which he reveals the influence of evolutionist Charles Darwin on his thinking. The accumulation of wealth, Carnegie believed, simply illustrated the survival of the fittest—and he considered himself among "the fittest." Wealth, however, was not an end in itself. Carnegie wrote, "The man who dies thus rich dies disgraced. . . . Surplus wealth is a sacred trust which its possessor is bound to administer in his lifetime for the good of the community."

John D. Rockefeller—Oil

America's first billionaire was **John D. Rockefeller**, the founder of Standard Oil Company (1870). In 1859, when Rockefeller was still a young businessman, oil was discovered in Titusville, Pennsylvania, and the "black gold" rush began. He saw that his future was in oil, but he realized that drilling for it involved too much risk. He determined that a safer investment and greater profits would be in oil refining, turning raw petroleum into useful products. Others saw the profit potential in refining, too, and competition was stiff and chaotic. However, Rockefeller determined that through efficiency and technological improvements he could succeed.

Historian Thomas DiLorenzo wrote that Rockefeller, reared as a Baptist, "was religious about working and saving his money." Rockefeller invested $4000 in an oil company and "paid meticulous attention to every detail of his business, constantly striving to cut his costs, improve his product, and expand his line of products. He also sometimes joined in with the manual laborers as a means of developing an even more thorough understanding of his business."

Rockefeller also waged a relentless war against waste in his company. When Rockefeller entered the oil industry, only half a typical barrel of oil was deemed useful in the production of kerosene, the source of lighting for the wealthy few who could afford it. The rest was thrown away, poured into rivers and lakes, polluting the water and surrounding lands. Through research and development, Rockefeller found ways to use that "useless" half barrel of oil and make money from it. His scientists developed petroleum jelly, paraffin, and about three hundred other useful products that increased both the quality of consumers' lives and his own profits. He continued to trim costs and improve production until he had cut the cost of refining to three cents per gallon and then to less than a penny by 1885. Rockefeller's efficiency reduced the cost of kerosene to the customer from fifty-eight cents to eight cents per gallon. (Lower costs made kerosene affordable for many more people.) By 1879, he was so successful that he controlled 90 percent

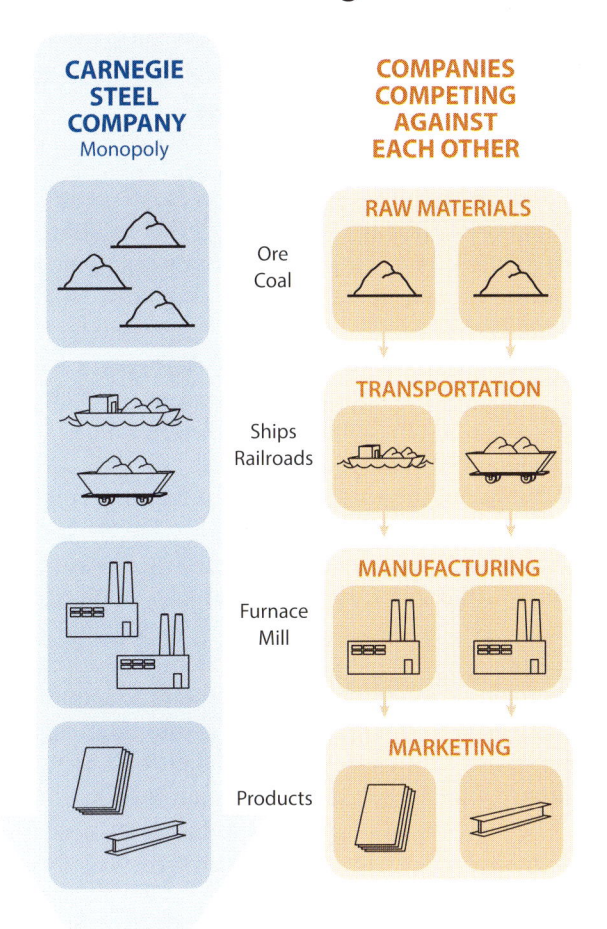

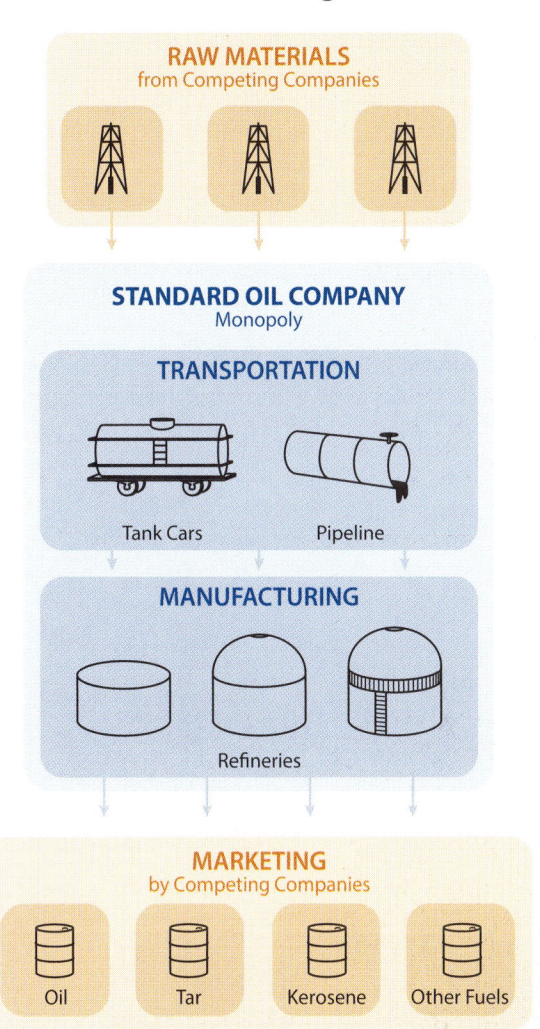

Vertical Integration

CARNEGIE STEEL COMPANY (Monopoly)
- Ore, Coal
- Ships, Railroads
- Furnace, Mill
- Products

COMPANIES COMPETING AGAINST EACH OTHER
- RAW MATERIALS
- TRANSPORTATION
- MANUFACTURING
- MARKETING

Horizontal Integration

RAW MATERIALS from Competing Companies

STANDARD OIL COMPANY (Monopoly)
- TRANSPORTATION: Tank Cars, Pipeline
- MANUFACTURING: Refineries

MARKETING by Competing Companies: Oil, Tar, Kerosene, Other Fuels

---

of the American oil market and 65 percent of the world market. Consumers in America and many other countries benefited by paying much less for the products refined from oil.

In 1879, Rockefeller organized his oil-refining empire into a **trust**. The trust was a legal device by which a board of trustees was empowered to make decisions and control the operations of a whole group of companies. As a result, the Standard Oil Trust purchased twenty-seven competing oil companies. Rockefeller's trust became the pattern for the formation of other trusts during the 1880s by businessmen who also had the means to buy up competing companies. This led to cries from competitors for the government to break up the giants and to create a so-called fair playing field. The result was the Sherman Anti-Trust Act of 1890.

The image that many people have today of Rockefeller as a callous, cutthroat competitor was primarily the work of Ida Tarbell, a journalist whose father's company was one that Rockefeller bought out. Tarbell, thinking that Rockefeller had illegally and immorally put her father out of business, produced *The History of the Standard Oil Company*. Unfortunately, the image she painted of Rockefeller has been the most lasting image of the man.

Some of the criticism of Rockefeller overlooks the role that his competitors' unwise business decisions played in their own demise and minimizes Rockefeller's efficiency and honest administration

> ### Horizontal Integration
> Unlike the vertical integration that Carnegie practiced, in which a company controlled a *part* of *all* segments of the production of a good from raw material to finished product, Rockefeller practiced **horizontal integration**, consolidation of *all* of *one* entire segment of an industry. Rockefeller controlled every aspect of the oil-refining process from barrel making to pipelines and transportation.

> **The Generosity of Rockefeller**
>
> On one occasion, Rockefeller quietly gave one thousand dollars to the American Board of Commissioners for Foreign Missions. When word leaked out, people began to oppose it, saying it was "tainted money." He later gave ten million dollars to the Euclid Avenue Baptist Church General Education Board. According to historian Allan Nevins, Rockefeller "devoutly believed that God had made him a trustee for [his] hundreds of millions, not to be kept but to be given wisely and carefully.... [W]e must not forget that Rockefeller began to give as soon as he began to earn."

of his business. Far from being uncaring toward his employees, Rockefeller set up a pension program for them thirty years before any other business did so. During the Panic of 1907, rather than cut wages or lay people off, Standard Oil increased employment in order to carry out extensive construction projects.

James Buchanan Duke—Tobacco

After the war, Southerners, as they had done for two centuries, returned to the soil for their livelihood. Nonetheless, many Southerners began to envision a "**New South**" that would match the North in economic and industrial capacity. The economic house of the New South would be built on the two *T*s—tobacco and textiles. Virginia and Carolina piedmont towns—such as Danville, Virginia, and Greensboro and Charlotte, North Carolina—had largely escaped the ravages of war. Those cities became leaders in the economic revitalization of the postwar New South. By 1900, four hundred cotton mills dotted the old Confederacy, far surpassing the textile production of New England.

Tobacco, the South's original cash crop, gained new profitability during the postwar period. Capitalizing on the popularity of a tobacco known as bright leaf, James Buchanan "Buck" Duke of Durham, North Carolina, used new marketing techniques to create a national and international market for his tobacco products.

Through the skillful use of advertising and promotion, Duke outstripped his competitors. In 1890, Duke founded the American Tobacco Company, which captured 90 percent of the nation's cigarette market. The New South's captain of industry also became a leader in developing hydroelectric power, opening the way for greater economic expansion in the South.

J. P. Morgan—Finance

John Pierpont Morgan was the leading investment banker in America during the Gilded Age. Morgan came to symbolize the power and prestige at the top of America's industrial pyramid.

Morgan's business was not an industrial product but money—buying and selling stocks on a grand scale. Morgan bought up a controlling interest in competing companies to reorganize them into streamlined corporations that could make even more money. His mergers began in the railroad industry, where he reorganized a number of major lines, such as the Northern Pacific, Union Pacific, B & O, and Southern Railroads. Morgan's biggest deal, however, was the consolidation of much of the steel industry. Through a series of mergers, culminating in the purchase of the giant Carnegie Steel, Morgan formed the first billion-dollar corporation, **United States Steel Corporation**, in 1901.

Innovations

Behind the rapid industrialization in America were new methods, ideas, and inventions that fueled expansion and created new markets. Thousands of inventions during the Gilded Age completely changed the way Americans lived.

Diet and Dress

The rising standard of living allowed changes in the American diet. Refrigerator cars brought beef and pork from the vast midwestern plains as well as strawberries, tomatoes, and oranges from the South and West to eastern cities and the waiting iceboxes of

J. P. Morgan was known as America's banker, and he was an organizer of railroads too.

middle-class homes. By 1880, the mass production of tin cans and new methods of cooking and sealing allowed the preservation of a wider variety of foods.

Americans enjoyed positive changes in their dress as well. The development of the sewing machine and its widespread use during the Civil War spawned a huge retail market for mass-produced clothing. For the first time, standardized sizes and designs were applied to clothing. Fashion and comfort became important considerations in the American wardrobe. By the turn of the century, suits of lighter weight and color were being produced for men's summer wear. The generous Victorian styles for ladies were gradually being trimmed down. By 1920, a woman's dress required only three yards of material to produce compared with ten yards in the 1890s. Mass production of high-quality, stylish clothing also decreased class distinctions. Ordering from a *Sears and Roebuck Catalog*, men and women of even modest means could dress in style.

H. J. Heinz

H. J. Heinz was an unbendingly honest food producer in Pittsburgh. A devout Methodist, he wrote in his will, "I desire to set forth, at the very beginning of this Will, as the most important item in it, a confession of my faith in Jesus Christ as my Saviour." Although Heinz pioneered much of modern billboard and newspaper advertising, he refused to allow his products to be advertised in Sunday newspapers; he believed such advertising desecrated the Lord's Day. Heinz gave liberally to Christian works, particularly Sunday school organizations, and he was an officer in various Sunday school associations.

Heinz was a leader in producing bottled and canned foods: horseradish, ketchup, pickles, and dozens of other products. His honesty was a byword in the food industry. Other producers added fillers to their products, such as mixing ground turnips or even wood pulp with their horseradish, and sold their goods in green-tinted bottles to hide the impurities. Heinz insisted on 100 percent pure products sold in clear bottles so that everyone could see the purity for themselves.

While other businesses endured strikes and labor unrest, the H. J. Heinz Company never had a single strike during Heinz's life. Heinz ensured that his employees had no reason to strike. He provided them free medical care, gyms, swimming pools, gardens, and educational opportunities, such as libraries and free concerts and lectures. Employees of other companies labored in dark, dirty, noisy factories. Heinz's workers, however, enjoyed clean, well-lit, well-ventilated plants where dining halls provided food at discount prices.

Heinz denied having any "secret" to his success other than honesty and hard work. "To do a common thing uncommonly well brings success," he often said. Another motto was "Do the best you can, where you are, with what you have today."

Communications

Industrialization also created a communications revolution during the Gilded Age. The growth of businesses across the nation resulted in increased correspondence and more sophisticated record keeping. The invention of the typewriter (1867) and an improved system of shorthand (1888) met the new demands of the business world. The development of cheap paper from wood pulp and the invention of continuous-action roller presses resulted in the birth of mass media. Inexpensive newspapers, magazines, and books became available for an increasingly literate and sophisticated society.

The crowning communications achievement of the time came in 1876 with the invention of the telephone by **Alexander Graham Bell**. Bell was a Scottish immigrant who arrived in the United States at the age of twenty-four to teach speech to the deaf. An innovative thinker who combined his interest in sound with his propensity for experimentation, Bell struggled for three years with the idea that he could "make iron talk." On March 10, 1876, he transmitted his first message over wire, calling an assistant in another room of his house: "Mr. Watson, come here, I want you." People have been answering phone calls ever since.

Electricity

America's most prolific inventor was **Thomas Alva Edison**. Although he had little formal education, Edison had a knack for new ideas and a thirst for discovery. He established an "invention factory" at Menlo Park, New Jersey, that was the forerunner of today's industrial research laboratories.

Edison was responsible for more than a thousand inventions during his lifetime, but the most influential ones were the phonograph, the motion-picture projector, and the incandescent light bulb. On September 4, 1882, after years of experimentation in developing the light bulb and the power system that could make indoor lighting practical, Edison flipped a switch that lit up New York's financial district. A new age was born in the eerie glow on Wall Street.

The contributions of George Westinghouse and Hungarian immigrant Nikola Tesla in devising alternating current generators and transformers gave electrical power long-range practicality. In 1893, for example, power generated at and transmitted from Niagara Falls lit the Columbian Exposition in Chicago. Men rightly marveled at the potential that electricity offered the world. As Harvard President Charles Eliot declared at the turn of the century, electricity is the "carrier of light and power; devourer of time and space; bearer of human speech over land and sea; greatest servant of man."

Alexander Graham Bell

Thomas Edison in his laboratory

Section Review

1–4. What were the four causes of American industrial growth in the second half of the nineteenth century?

5–9. In which industry was each of the following men a leader?
   a. Andrew Carnegie
   b. John D. Rockefeller
   c. J. P. Morgan
   d. James J. Hill
   e. Cornelius Vanderbilt

10. What was unique about the success of James J. Hill?

11–12. What was the most important invention in communications in the late nineteenth century, and who invented it?

13–14. Name two of Thomas Edison's most influential inventions.

   ✯ Freedom, individualism, equality, and growth define the values of Americans. Describe how these core values explain the rise of the market entrepreneurs.

   ✯ What core values might appear to conflict with one another during this period in American history? How can such conflict be managed?

II. Political Reform and Reaction

The rapid and far-reaching changes of the last quarter of the nineteenth century did not occur in a vacuum. They touched the lives of all Americans, from rich industrialists to ragged immigrants. The changes that produced prosperity also caused problems and spawned reform movements in a number of areas.

Four issues dominated American politics from the mid-1870s to the end of the century: government corruption, civil service reform, tariff revision, and regulation of the trusts. Debate over these issues was intensified by some of the most evenly matched party politics in American history.

The "Spoiled" System

During the early part of Rutherford Hayes's administration, reform of the spoils system (see Chapter 10) was the pressing issue. Grant's name especially had become a synonym for government corruption, and the spoils system was associated with corruption and incompetence. Changes were needed to remove the corrupting influence of politics and ensure competent, efficient government workers.

Hayes had been nominated largely because he was a reformer. He courageously attacked political "machines," groups that sought to control voters, although his action cost him political support. He particularly attacked a notorious New York Republican political machine—similar to the Democrats' Tammany Hall—controlled by Senator **Roscoe Conkling**. This machine controlled New York's tariff-collecting agency, the Customs House, where New York politicians manipulated records and siphoned off money belonging to the federal government. Hayes, hoping to check the corrupt practices, removed the Collector of the Port, future president Chester Arthur. The removal angered Conkling and other influential Republicans.

Stalwarts versus Half-breeds

The clash between Hayes and Conkling reflected a growing division within the Republican Party. On one side was Conkling's faction, the "**Stalwarts**," who favored high tariffs, hard money, and the spoils system. Opposing them were moderate Republicans, called "**Half-breeds**," who had earlier been dissatisfied with Grant, the Radical Republicans, and Reconstruction and who tended to favor reform. The struggle between Stalwarts and Half-breeds intensified over the Republican presidential nomination in 1880. When the convention deadlocked, the Republican factions eventually compromised by nominating Ohio's **James A. Garfield**, a Half-breed, for president and New York's **Chester A. Arthur**, a Stalwart, for vice president.

In the general election, Garfield faced Democratic nominee Winfield S. Hancock, who had gained fame as a Union general at Gettysburg. Garfield won the electoral vote easily, but the popular vote was extremely close; the Republican candidate won by fewer than ten thousand votes out of nine million cast.

James A. Garfield was a man of integrity and character, but his efforts at reform were short-lived. On July 2, 1881, just a few months after the inauguration, a distraught office-seeker, Charles J. Guiteau (gih TOH), shot Garfield at a railway station in Washington, D.C.,

> **Guiding Questions**
> 1. What characterized the administrations of James A. Garfield and Chester A. Arthur?
> 2. What characterized the administrations of Grover Cleveland and Benjamin Harrison?

James A. Garfield

Chester A. Arthur

Civil Service Reform

Arthur is best known for reforming the civil service (government employee) system. George H. Pendleton, a Democrat from Ohio, introduced what became the **Pendleton Act**, which established an independent **Civil Service Commission** and eliminated much of the spoils system. Garfield's death at the hands of a disappointed office-seeker had spurred interest in such an act, and Pendleton's proposal was enacted in January 1883.

The Pendleton Act authorized the president to appoint three civil service commissioners, who were to be responsible for seeing that only those who scored well on examinations held offices. The intent of the act was to prevent the awarding of political offices for no other reason than party loyalty. To some extent, it succeeded, although only about 12 percent of the federal offices were filled by the commission during Arthur's term.

Grover Cleveland was a strict constructionist who vetoed over 400 bills, more than twice the number vetoed by all previous presidents.

1884 Election "Mud"

The 1884 campaign produced such memorable political poetry as the Democratic cry "Blaine, Blaine, James G. Blaine, the continental liar from the state of Maine." The Republicans responded with a ditty of their own, alleging that the bachelor Cleveland had fathered an illegitimate child: "Ma, Ma, where's my pa?" they would wail. "Gone to the White House, ha, ha, ha."

---

shouting, "I am a Stalwart, and Arthur is now president." After enduring eleven weeks of pain and crude medical care, Garfield died on September 19, and Vice President Arthur became president.

Arthur's past attachment to New York's political machines led Conkling's supporters to rejoice and caused others to feel uneasy. But Arthur, called "the gentleman president," turned out to be a pleasant surprise. He conscientiously assumed his responsibilities as president and refused to use his high office to provide special favors for Conkling's Stalwarts. Arthur also backed civil service reform and favored lowering the tariff.

The Mongrel Tariff

Arthur also tried to revise the tariff. Because general prosperity had led to government surpluses, a commission appointed by Arthur recommended a general tariff reduction of 20 to 25 percent. Congressmen who wanted to protect the trade interests of their constituents, however, added many amendments to the proposed tariff. As a result, when the tariff passed in 1883, it was a mixture of inharmonious policies. Critics soon dubbed it the "Mongrel Tariff." This legislation completely failed to reform the tariff as had been intended. All it did was clarify party positions on the tariff issue. The Republicans, coming mainly from industrial areas, more commonly favored protective tariffs; the Democrats, representing the South and the West, favored low tariffs.

The Election of 1884

In 1884, the Republicans bypassed Arthur, who had offended some Republicans by refusing to grant party members special favors, and chose instead Maine's James G. Blaine, a long-time Republican leader tainted by an earlier railroad corruption scandal. The Democrats nominated New York's former governor **Grover Cleveland**, a courageous opponent of Tammany Hall noted for his honesty. Even many disgusted Republicans supported Cleveland. Stalwarts sneeringly called these party deserters "Mugwumps" (an Indian word meaning "big chief") because the straddling Republicans had their "mugs" on one side of the fence and their "wumps" on the other. The Mugwumps, however, took the name as a badge of honor for their stand for reform.

The 1884 election was a spirited, hard-fought affair better remembered for its mudslinging than for any issues that were debated. Cleveland won a narrow victory. Had Blaine won the extremely close race in New York—he lost there by only 1,149 votes of more than a million cast—he would have won the election. Cleveland's election was the first Democratic presidential victory in twenty-eight years.

Challenging the Trusts

During Cleveland's first term, Congress passed the first comprehensive act to provide for federal regulation of commerce. Some railroad trusts had been engaged in shady activities, such as rate-fixing schemes and discriminatory rates. The railroads were unwilling to police themselves, however, and state railroad commissions had no authority to regulate activities outside the borders of their own states. Nearly all Americans favored federal regulation of the railroads under the interstate commerce clause of the Constitution.

In February 1887, Cleveland signed the **Interstate Commerce Act**, which (1) directed that railroad rates must be "reasonable and just," (2) required that railroad companies publish all rates and make financial reports, and (3) provided for the creation of the Interstate Commerce Commission (ICC), an independent regulatory agency, to investigate and stop alleged abuses.

The Election of 1888

The Democrats renominated the popular Cleveland in 1888. The Republicans, however, abandoned Blaine and nominated Indiana's **Benjamin Harrison**, who, though somewhat colorless, was a capable, honest man. He was also the grandson of ex-president William Henry Harrison, a fact the Republicans loudly proclaimed. Some of Cleveland's aides feared that the president's insistence on lowering the tariffs might cost him the election. Cleveland retorted, "What is the use of being elected unless you stand for something?" Cleveland won more popular votes, but Harrison won more electoral votes and hence the election.

Although personally honest, Harrison was a disappointingly weak president. He appointed Blaine as secretary of state, and Blaine, in turn, dominated both the administration and the Republican Party. The Republicans sought to win favor with the voters and maintain control of the government through liberal spending. The Fifty-First Congress (1889–1891) became known as the "Billion-Dollar Congress" because, for the first time in history, the annual budget exceeded a billion dollars. Weak leadership in the White House and Congress combined with free-spending policies only squandered the Treasury surplus that Cleveland had left, without improving Republican popularity.

Benjamin Harrison, grandson of an earlier president, won the 1888 election.

The Sherman Anti-Trust Act

One law during the Harrison years, however, became influential. Congress greatly expanded its power to regulate business with the passage of the **Sherman Anti-Trust Act** in 1890. The public had become increasingly wary of the tendency of big businesses to form monopolies, or "trusts." Competitors of companies such as Rockefeller's Standard Oil claimed that large companies were driving all competition out of business or forcing small companies to merge with their larger competitors and form monopolies. The charge was that these companies then took advantage of their monopoly by raising prices to an exorbitant level. While some of these accusations were unfounded, stories in the press and popular opinion convinced many of the need for government intervention.

The Sherman Anti-Trust Act made such monopolizing illegal. It declared, "Every contract, combination in the form of trust or otherwise, or conspiracy, in restraint of trade or commerce . . . is hereby declared to be illegal." The act was difficult to enforce, however, because it offered no specific definitions of *contract*, *combination*, or *restraint of trade*. Therefore, the act was relatively ineffective until the passage of tougher federal regulations in the twentieth century.

Raising the Tariff

A major goal of the Republicans in the Fifty-First Congress was to raise the tariff again. The Republican majority in both houses of Congress was slim but was bolstered by the admission of six new predominantly Republican states: North Dakota, South Dakota, Montana, and Washington in November 1889 and Idaho and Wyoming in July 1890. The addition of Republican representatives and senators from those states enabled the party to pass the **McKinley Tariff** in 1890.

Named for Ohio representative William McKinley, who introduced the bill, the tariff imposed higher duties on manufactured and agricultural imports than had any previous tariff in history, thereby protecting American inefficiency. The high tariff also lowered revenue by radically decreasing trade. This decrease in the government's income, combined with lavish congressional spending, reduced the Treasury's reserves alarmingly. The voters demonstrated their anger at the tariff in the congressional election of 1890, reducing the Republican majority in the Senate and giving the Democrats an overwhelming 235–88 advantage in the House. Even Representative McKinley was turned out of office.

The 1890 congressional elections were only a prelude to the 1892 presidential rematch between Benjamin Harrison and Grover Cleveland. Ex-president Cleveland made an ex-president of Harrison by recapturing the White House with a clear victory. Democrats regained control of both the House and the Senate. Unfortunately for the Democrats, a financial collapse called the Panic of '93 occurred shortly after Cleveland's inauguration, plunging the nation into four years of the worst economic depression it had yet seen. The Democrats watched helplessly as banks and businesses failed and unemployment mounted to a record 20 percent.

Section Review

1–4. What four issues dominated American politics from the mid-1870s to the end of the nineteenth century?

5. How did Republicans and Democrats differ concerning the tariff in the late nineteenth century?

6. Why was the Fifty-First Congress called the "Billion-Dollar Congress"?

★ Does the civil service system reduce the corrupting influence of politics and ensure better government employees? Defend your answer.

★ Do laws like the Sherman Anti-Trust Act protect competition? Defend your answer.

III. Labor, Rural, and Economic Issues

Along with the industrial growth of the Gilded Age came labor problems. The rural areas continued to demand solutions to their unique farm-related problems. And the economy faced unprecedented challenges and unusual suggestions for solving them.

Labor

The demands of industrialization and the flood of immigration swelled the ranks of America's labor force. The rising standard of living that industrialization brought in its wake touched all Americans. Even unskilled immigrants living in difficult circumstances in most cases had better prospects for themselves and their children than they had in the "old country" with its war and poverty.

Yet industrialization had a human cost. Although workers had been accustomed to working long hours on farms, they found that six twelve-hour days or more could be trying when combined with other factors such as unsafe factories and low wages. Hard times also brought war widows and children into the factories to make ends meet, further complicating the labor system. Many people opposed child labor, not only because they considered the factory work inhumane for children but also because it left children no time for formal education.

Child Labor

According to the 1900 census, more than 1,750,000 children ages ten to sixteen worked for wages in the United States, about 20 percent of the children in that age group. An additional 250,000 workers were under ten years old. Immigrant families who assembled clothing, toys, or other items in their homes used children as young as five years old. Some boys worked on the streets as peddlers, shoeshine boys, and newspaper boys. Children as young as five worked as "breaker boys" in coal mines, picking debris, stones, and sulfur from the coal as it flowed through chutes beneath their feet. At twelve, they went down into the mines. In the seafood industry, children began working at about eight years of age. Even more children worked on their family farms, picking fruit, plowing, weeding, cultivating, caring for animals, and so forth.

During this period, many, including employers, considered child labor to be acceptable or even necessary for several reasons. One was the extensive loss of male workers in the Civil War. Another was that children were faster and more agile than adults in doing some tasks. They were also cheaper to hire. Families may not have wanted to send their children to work at dangerous jobs for small wages, but parents often found it necessary for their children to work. This was especially true for newly arrived immigrants.

However, as reformers drew attention to the plight of child workers, state governments began to enact legislation limiting child labor. In 1879, only seven states had laws limiting the age of workers in manufacturing, with the average age being eleven. But by 1909 forty-three of the forty-six states had such laws, with the average age of fourteen. These laws typically limited the age of the child who could work, the number of hours a day, and the number of hours a week. The passage of compulsory school attendance laws further restricted child labor. Businesses learned to prosper without child labor, and families' standard of living rose as a result of industrialization.

Guiding Questions

1. What labor-related problems emerged in the United States during this period?
2. How did farmers respond to changing economic conditions?
3. How did the 1896 presidential campaigns of William McKinley and William Jennings Bryan differ?

Dangers to Child Laborers

Dangers were a constant reality for child workers. Breaker boys could fall into the coal chutes and be crushed by the coal or choked by the dust. They always had a persistent cough from breathing the coal dust. Those who entered the mines faced death or injury from cave-ins, explosions, or asphyxiation from poisonous gases or lack of oxygen. Child workers in canneries, where they shucked oysters or peeled or sliced fruits and vegetables, risked slicing—or even cutting off—fingers or hands.

Labor Unions

After the war, workers occasionally held unorganized strikes in response to wage cuts, and the effectiveness and potential of labor organizations soon became apparent. Responding to the challenge and human cost of industrialization, organized labor became a powerful political and social force during the period.

The earliest significant labor union was the **Knights of Labor**, formed in 1869 as a secret society of skilled and unskilled workers from various occupations. Although weakened by the Panic of 1873, the union emerged as an effective force under the leadership of Terrence V. Powderly, former mayor of Scranton, Pennsylvania.

The Knights advocated an eight-hour workday, laws prohibiting child labor, and equal pay for men and women. However, the Knights, like most early American labor unions, tended to be much more conservative than the radical and even violent unions of Europe. In fact, Powderly favored boycotts and arbitration over strikes to settle wage disputes because strikes often resulted in violence. A number of successful strikes, however, gained the Knights new clout and new members, and the group reached a peak of 700,000 members in 1886.

A more influential labor organization was formed in 1881. The **American Federation of Labor** (AFL), a splinter group from the Knights of Labor, formed craft unions for skilled laborers. Grouping skilled workers together by profession gave union members greater bargaining power with management. Under the leadership of **Samuel Gompers**, the AFL supported higher wages, shorter working hours, safer and cleaner working conditions, and elimination of child labor. The AFL's goals, however, were not entirely humanitarian. Unions in the AFL did not oppose child labor primarily out of sympathy for children but because child labor contributed to low wage rates and reduced available jobs for adults.

> ### AFL's Most Enduring Achievement
> The most enduring achievement of the AFL was the acceptance of the eight-hour workday as a standard.

Labor Unrest

During the late 1860s and the 1870s, only scattered, poorly managed strikes occurred over labor grievances. As unions grew, however, strikes—and violence—became more common. Probably the most famous example of labor violence was the **Haymarket Riot** of 1886. Factory workers in Chicago, agitated by anarchists, went on strike, demanding an eight-hour workday. On May 4, 1886, police attempted to disperse a crowd of strikers listening to an anarchist speaker at Haymarket Square in Chicago. (An anarchist is an opponent of the established political order who seeks change through violent means.) Someone threw a bomb into a group of policemen, touching off a riot. When the unrest ended, seven policemen and four civilians had been killed and many others seriously wounded. The Haymarket Square episode discredited the Knights of Labor and ended the "eight-hour" movement for the time being.

In 1892, violence erupted during a strike at the Carnegie Steel Company in Homestead, Pennsylvania, a suburb of Pittsburgh.

The Haymarket Riot in Chicago resulted in the deaths of seven policemen (shown atop this picture) and several civilians.

Carnegie's assistant at the company, Henry C. Frick, proposed lowering the workers' wages because of the use of new labor-saving machinery. When the workers threatened to strike, Frick closed the plant, an action that became known as a "lockout." Frick then hired three hundred guards to subdue picketers. The fighting that broke out on July 6, 1892, left nine people dead. The hired guards were beaten back. Despite the temporary victory for the workers, the **Homestead Strike** gained nothing. After five months of striking, the workers agreed to Frick's proposal. The union was broken.

Another violent strike occurred at the Pullman Palace Car Company in Chicago. Although the name *Pullman* is most commonly associated with railroad sleeping cars, the company contracted to carry not only passengers but also the U.S. mail. Therefore, any labor union activity was potentially disruptive for both business owners and taxpayers.

The leader of the strike was **Eugene V. Debs**, founder of the American Railway Union and later a presidential candidate on the Socialist ticket. The **Pullman Strike** was precipitated by five successive wage reductions, totaling 25 percent, in the spring of 1894. Although these reductions were necessitated by the depression at the time, the company did not simultaneously reduce the rent on the houses it provided its employees or the cost of goods in the company stores. When the workers retaliated by striking, the Pullman Company withdrew the strikers' credit from the company stores. Facing starvation, the Pullman workers appealed to Debs's American Railway Union.

On June 26, Debs ordered union members to cut all Pullman passenger cars out of trains and leave them standing on the sidetracks. The boycott of Pullman cars affected all western railroads. When boycotters were fired, the strike became general, and traffic, including the mail between the West and Chicago, came to a virtual standstill. Strikers and unemployed ruffians destroyed engines, cars, and equipment, causing owners to demand that federal troops be sent to break the strike. They wanted the government to protect their property. President Cleveland complied to keep the U.S. mail moving. He declared, "If it takes every dollar in the Treasury and every soldier in the United States to deliver a postal card in Chicago, that postal card should be delivered."

In addition, the federal courts issued an **injunction**, or court order, forbidding Debs and other strike leaders to further encourage the strike. Debs ignored the order and promoted the general strike; consequently, he spent six months in jail. He claimed that it was while in jail that he became an avowed socialist, but his views actually had been socialistic for all of his adult life. (**Socialism** advocates government regulation or ownership of the means of production.) After Debs's release, he became the leader of the Social Democratic Party of America (later called simply the Socialist Party), a position he was to hold until the 1920s.

Rural Revolt

Industrialism and innovation caused important changes in American agriculture. Improved farm machinery and methods increased production and made agricultural commodities an important export. Yet, such innovations also created problems for farmers. They could not adjust quickly to supply and demand because of the seasonal nature of farming. They could not know

Jailbird for President!

Eugene V. Debs was a five-time candidate for president on the Socialist Party ticket. He ran in 1900, 1904, 1908, 1912, and 1920. In 1920, he became the first—and to date the only—candidate to campaign from a jail cell.

Legacy of the Unions

The violence and radicalism of the movement discredited unions for nearly half a century. Perhaps in part because of this radicalism, the government tended to side with management by providing court orders to end strikes and even troops to quell violence. Although organized labor made some gains for some workers, most union goals remained unrealized until the twentieth century.

for sure how much of a crop they would have at harvest because of changes in weather. Drought, too much rain, or the right amount of water with a sudden attack of insects or disease could affect output dramatically.

Railroads were the essential link between the farm and the market. High shipping costs siphoned off farm profits into the pockets of railroad owners and left farmers outraged. Abundant production itself became a problem because high yields kept prices low.

High tariffs also affected farmers. Whenever the United States placed a tariff on certain imports, the countries trying to sell those products to U.S. consumers usually retaliated by raising their own tariffs on American exports, often farm products. The American farmers then had a hard time finding buyers. Combining high tariffs with overproduction further complicated the farmers' plight.

The Grange

During the 1870s, protesting farmers organized under the leadership of the Patrons of Husbandry, more commonly called the **Grange**. Oliver H. Kelly founded the organization in 1867 to encourage social contacts and scientific methods of farming. Its growth and influence were negligible until farmers began to use it as a means of confronting railroads. The Granger movement made state regulation of railroads its chief goal, and it gained increasing support during the 1870s.

As a result of Grange influence, several midwestern states passed Granger Laws, legislation regulating railroads. In response, the railroads went to the Supreme Court in the case of *Munn v. Illinois* in 1877. The Court ruled against the railroads, deciding that a state through its "police powers" had the right to regulate a business that was public in nature though privately owned. Despite its success, the Grange lacked organizational strength and declined in influence.

Agricultural reform efforts resurged in the 1880s as the **Farmers' Alliance**. Taking a lesson from industrial labor, the Farmers' Alliance united farm cooperatives across the country and looked to politics to meet agrarian demands such as railroad regulation, favorable currency policies, and antitrust laws.

Populism

Independent grassroots organizations sprang up throughout the Midwest and eventually merged through the politics of discontent to form the People's or **Populist Party**. The Populist Party seemed to prove the truth of the adage that "misery loves company." The hard times in Middle America between the Great Blizzards of 1886–1887 and the Panic of '93 attracted thousands of farmers and reformers to the party's banner. Although the party only officially formed in 1891, the Populists polled more than a million votes with their presidential candidate, James B. Weaver, in 1892. In fact, the new third party carried four western states and showed remarkable strength in the otherwise solidly Democratic South.

The issue that dominated the Populist movement during the mid-nineties was currency policy. After the failure of the greenback efforts under Grant, easy-money advocates began to view coinage of silver as the answer to their problems. The Populists wanted to make both silver and gold the dual standard for American currency. Money was scarce during the depression of the 1890s, and,

Populism and Free Silver

Amid the hard times and the economic complexities of industrialism, silver became a seemingly simple solution for the down-and-out, a kind of patent medicine for all economic ills. In the Midwest, free silver became the battle cry for the Populist legions. Not even the major parties were immune from the growing Populist force. Lacking, however, the organizational, financial, and numerical strength of the major parties, the Populists decided to ally with the more sympathetic Democratic Party in the 1896 presidential election. The result was a colorful, crucial contest—part campaign, part crusade.

for a growing number of Americans who were feeling the squeeze, the solution was the unlimited coinage of silver. Such purposeful inflation would make more money available to the hard-pressed workingman. In the words of the 1894 bestseller *Coin's Financial School*, **free silver** would "make it possible for the debtor to pay his debts; business to start anew, and revivify all the industries of the country, which must remain paralyzed so long as silver as well as all other property is measured by a gold standard." For the farmers, more money in circulation would mean higher prices for crops. What farmers did not consider, however, was that having more money in circulation would also mean that prices for *all* products, including those that farmers had to buy, would increase. In the long run, they would be no better off than before.

William McKinley (*left*) and William Jennings Bryan (*right*) were presidential candidates in 1896.

Goldbugs versus Silverbugs

The Panic of '93 and the ensuing depression hounded Grover Cleveland throughout his second term and left the Democratic nomination in doubt in 1896. Republicans, however, had a candidate on the first ballot, Ohio's **William McKinley**. A likable though somber figure, McKinley was the friend of industrialists, a fitting candidate for the gold-standard, pro-tariff (having sponsored the highest tariff to that date, the McKinley Tariff), big-business platform of the Republicans.

When the Democrats arrived in Chicago for their convention, the place was abuzz with talk of silver and the inevitable question of who would get the nomination and stamp out the "goldbugs." The answer was a thirty-six-year-old Nebraskan named **William Jennings Bryan**.

Bryan, called "the Great Commoner" because of his genuine sympathy for the common man, was both a remarkable political figure and a fervent Christian. His oratory sprang from roots deep in America's heartland. In Chicago, his eloquent appeals for economic deliverance through silver sealed his nomination.

The campaign that followed was the first modern campaign and a study in contrasts. Leading a cash-poor campaign (Republicans outspent Democrats as much as twenty to one), Bryan went on a whirlwind tour of the country. He made hundreds of whistle-stops during an 18,000-mile trek and was seen and heard by audiences totaling nearly five million. McKinley, however, stayed home. In a carefully orchestrated effort, McKinley ran a "front porch campaign" from his home in Canton, Ohio. Trainloads of select audiences were given all-expense-paid trips to Canton to hear McKinley read a prepared script, while hundreds of speakers fanned out across the country to promote him.

On Election Day, Bryan polled six and a half million votes, but McKinley got more than seven million. The Great Commoner, however, was not the only casualty on Election Day. The influence of the Populist Party, which had supported Bryan's candidacy, soon withered. Other groups would take up many of its reforms, but they would be won under different labels and circumstances in later years.

Importance of the 1896 Election

The 1896 election was a turning point in American political history, the culmination of the struggle between the past and the future, between the farm and the factory—and the factory won. The rural leadership that Populism represented was growing old with the century. For good or bad, America's future lay amid her crowded city streets.

Cross of Gold

Bryan stood before the convention and declared to a sea of rapt faces, "I come to speak to you in defense of a cause as holy as the cause of liberty—the cause of humanity." The government must have a social conscience, he cried. Its voice must be the people's voice, and the people would be heard. He concluded,

"Having behind us the producing masses of this nation and the world, supported by the commercial interests, the laboring interests, and the toilers everywhere, we will answer their [the business interests'] demand for a gold standard by saying to them: 'You shall not press down upon the brow of labor this crown of thorns; you shall not crucify mankind upon a cross of gold.'"

The Election of 1896

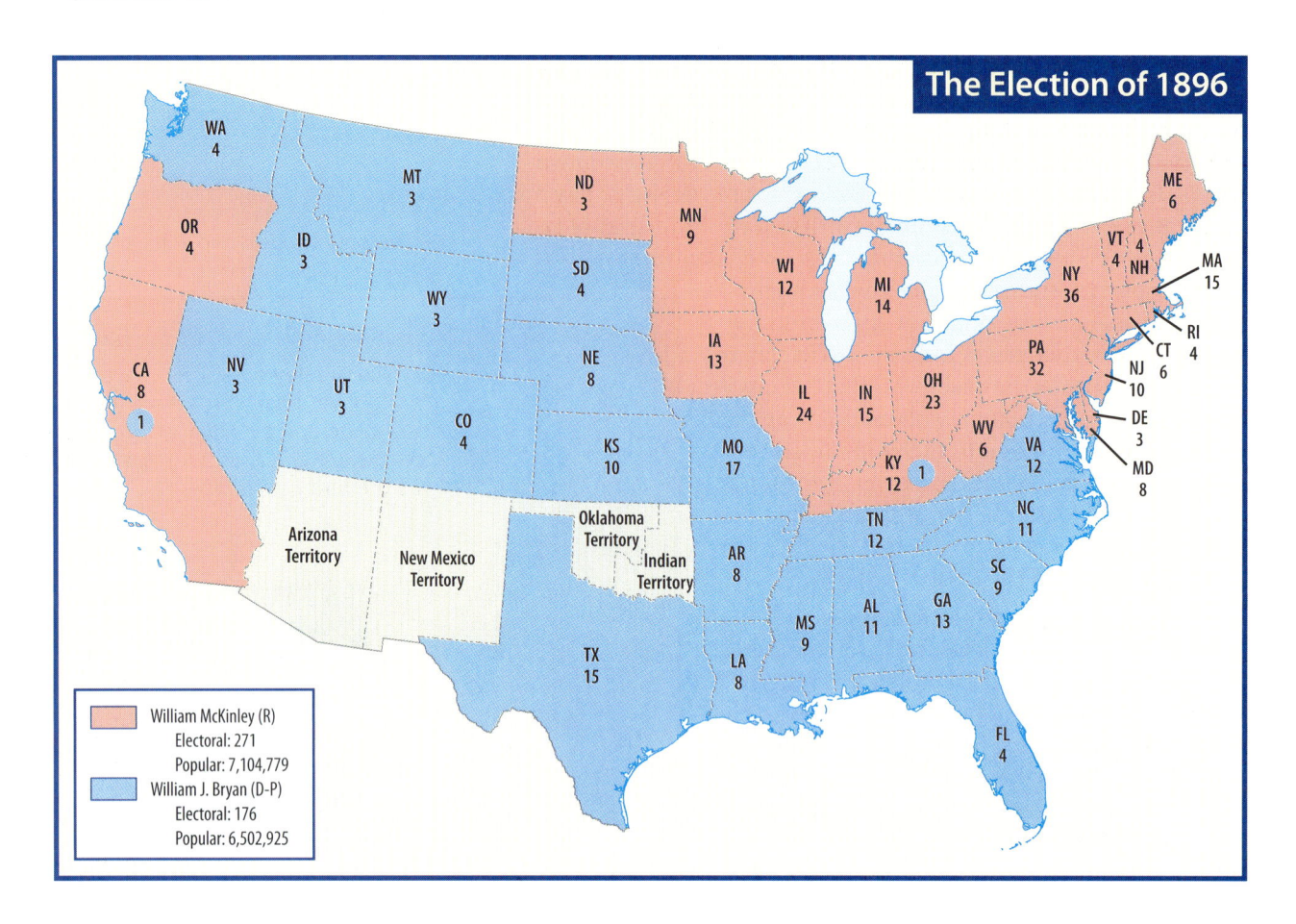

William McKinley (R)
Electoral: 271
Popular: 7,104,779

William J. Bryan (D-P)
Electoral: 176
Popular: 6,502,925

Section Review

1. What was the most enduring achievement of the American Federation of Labor?
2–3. Name two major labor strikes of the late 1800s.
4. What industry did most farmers blame for their low profits?
5. Describe the difference between the campaigns of the two candidates in the 1896 presidential election, William McKinley and William Jennings Bryan.
★ How did farmers respond to fluctuating prices and high tariffs?
★ Read Deuteronomy 24:14, Proverbs 3:27, and Malachi 3:5. Based on these passages, what should be a Christian's attitude regarding oppressing the poor in their wages?

IV. Change and Challenge

Growth of Cities

One reason the Populism revolt came up short was that many farmers had moved to the city. The 1890 census revealed that for the first time, the majority of Americans were in nonagricultural occupations. The concentrations of industry with the resulting concentrations of labor made urbanization (movement of population to the cities) the most significant social movement of the period.

Between 1860 and 1910, increases in the urban population were nearly twice the increases in the rural population. The dramatic

Guiding Questions

1. What characterized the growth of cities in the United States during this period?
2. How did American response to immigration after 1865 differ from previous periods of immigration?
3. How did the attitudes of many Americans change during the 1890s?
4. What religious responses emerged to address a changing America during this period?

shift was reflected in the size and number of cities. In 1860, only New York and Philadelphia had populations greater than 500,000. By 1910, Chicago, St. Louis, Boston, Cleveland, Baltimore, and Pittsburgh had joined the ranks of the big cities, with New York City approaching a population of nearly five million. The most phenomenal urban growth, however, was in the small cities with populations of 2,500 or more. There were 400 such cities at the beginning of the Civil War; that number jumped to 2,200 cities in the next fifty years.

What was the attraction of city dwelling? The boom in manufacturing and service industries provided jobs for both the influx of immigrants and down-and-out farm laborers who had been squeezed off the land by hard times or labor-saving machinery. And people found the services and attractions of city living alluring.

Yet to those who lived there, the "gilded metropolis" (as one wide-eyed farm boy described Kansas City) became a tinsel town. Urbanization also had an ugly side: slum squalor, high crime, and dangerous diseases. In fact, the infant mortality rate in cities was double that in rural areas. In Chicago during the 1880s, for example, only half the children born lived past their fifth birthday. People also lost their privacy, living in "dumbbell apartments" or, worse yet, living with several people in squalid, one-room apartments.

Industrialization gradually created a substantial, growing middle class. But the path to prosperity was choked with moral and industrial pollutants, and the promises offered by smoke-stacked cities often proved empty.

Greeley on Urbanization
Horace Greeley observed, "We cannot all live in cities, yet nearly all seem determined to do so. Hot and cold water, baker's bread, gas, the theatre and the streetcars . . . indicate the tendency of modern taste."

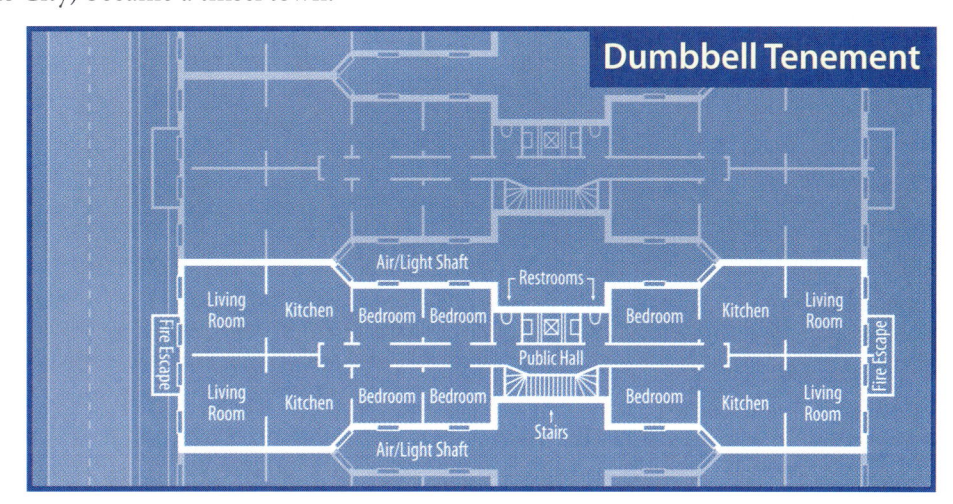

Dumbbell Tenement

Immigration

Aggravating the problems of the cities was another wave of immigration. The American continent had been receiving immigrants, of course, since the English settled at Jamestown and Plymouth. After 1865, however, came a wave of immigrants so different from those in the past that it was called the **New Immigration**. As the turn of the twentieth century neared, the percentage of British and German immigrants (who had made up most earlier immigration) shrank in contrast to new immigrants from southern and eastern European countries, such as Italy, Greece, and Russia. By 1900, for the first time in American history, immigrants from southern and eastern Europe outnumbered those from northern and western Europe. Another new element in immigration was the large number of Chinese who began to settle on the West Coast, where they provided labor for the railroads.

Some of the more fortunate immigrants, particularly those from Scandinavia and Germany, were able to move directly to the Midwest and immediately find work in farming or logging. Most of the immigrants, however, had no money or job skills to enable them to move from the cities to which they first came. New York, Chicago, Philadelphia, and other large cities swelled in population. Immigrants tended to band together in the cities so that different

The Three "A"s of Immigration
To understand immigration, one needs to know the three *A*s. The first, *adaptation*, is normally the first change that occurs after migration to a new country. Adaptation refers to the changes a person makes to fit in a new environment. Examples would include adopting a different style of dress and learning the new nation's language. The second and third *A*s are *assimilation* and *acculturation*. Assimilation is the process of adopting the customs and priorities of the new nation. Acculturation is the cultural change of a group, or individual, that results from contact with a different culture. Whether assimilation precedes or follows acculturation may be up for debate. However, successful blending of immigrants into any society involves all three of these elements.

neighborhoods often had their own distinct ethnic character—Polish, Italian, Greek, or any one of a number of others. Often illiterate and knowing little English, many of the immigrants had to take low-paying jobs in "sweat shop" factories and live in squalid tenements. American businesses actively recruited immigrant laborers in Europe and even helped them secure passage to the United States. They were willing to work at low-paying jobs to gain the freedom of opportunity that America offered, and they hoped to work their way up financially and socially. Many of them did just that, achieving a better life for themselves and their children.

As the New Immigration grew in proportion to the old, so did opposition to immigration. American labor leaders feared—rightly in some cases—that immigrant workers would take jobs from other Americans by agreeing to work longer hours for less pay. The poverty of ethnic slums created fears that immigrants would lower the nation's standard of living and breed crime and disease—although obviously no immigrant wanted to live under such conditions. The large number of Catholic, Jewish, and Eastern Orthodox immigrants raised religious fears among America's predominantly Protestant population. A tiny minority of radicals and revolutionaries among the immigrants caused many of them to be branded as potential enemies of American freedoms and institutions. Racial prejudice, especially in California against the Chinese, also motivated calls for limits to immigration. The simple fact that immigrants tended to form churches and sometimes schools where only their native language was spoken led many Americans to fear that the cultural unity of the nation was being undermined. As a result of these fears, Congress placed an increasing number of quotas and restrictions on immigration. By 1930, such restrictions had reduced immigration from southern and eastern Europe to less than a fifth of what it had been in 1910.

Despite the many cultural obstacles, immigrants continued to come, and many of them prospered. The children of immigrants, able to learn the language and American customs more easily than their parents, often rose higher economically than their elders. Immigrants provided labor for construction projects and for factories; they built rich and fertile farms in the Midwest; some became prosperous shopkeepers and small businessmen. Immigrants, in short, provided much of the backbone and muscle needed to transform the United States into an industrial giant. Assimilation into the broader American culture was not easy. The immigrants could not transform overnight. But they tried, and eventually they became fully Americanized. As they began to adopt American culture, fears of an ethnically fragmented society began to subside. The aspects of their cultures that the immigrants retained contributed to the growing diversity (especially religious diversity) of the nation. In fact, some people began to speak of the United States as a

For many immigrants, America provided new hope and opportunity.

Lady Liberty's Light

As immigrants streamed into the United States, more than a million a year passed through the immigrant reception center on Ellis Island in New York Harbor alone. There in the harbor they saw a gleaming torchbearer, a bronze lady—the Statue of Liberty. Inscribed in the statue's pedestal were the following words of welcome:

> Give me your tired, your poor,
> Your huddled masses yearning to breathe free,
> The wretched refuse of your teeming shore.
> Send these, the homeless, tempest-tossed, to me,
> I lift my lamp beside the golden door!

melting pot in which diverse ethnic cultures would blend to form a new and unified nation.

New Forces

Machines alone were not changing America; new ideas, philosophies, and attitudes were also challenging old systems. Whether these new philosophies were accepted or rejected, they had—and continue to have—a wide influence throughout society.

Darwinism

The book *On the Origin of Species* (1859) by **Charles Darwin** found a receptive audience in burgeoning industrial America. Darwin's basic theory involved "natural selection," a process through which all current species, including man, have supposedly struggled and evolved. The survival, development, and improvement of species depend upon their ability to adapt to the changes of a sometimes cruel world. Despite the faulty scientific reasoning and the clear contradiction of the biblical record, a number of Darwin's disciples came to apply his ideas to every area of a rapidly changing society. To them, **Darwinism** was the key to the riddle of life.

The chief proponent of Social Darwinism (the application of the evolutionary theory to social institutions) was Englishman Herbert Spencer, whose only memorable contribution out of eight dense volumes on the new philosophy was the phrase "survival of the fittest." In America, Spencer's Social Darwinism fit well with racism. White supremacy thrived on the concept of racial inferiority of all races other than white.

But not all Darwinists were satisfied with Spencer's conclusions. In the late nineteenth century, a movement known as Reform Darwinism emerged as a result of the work of a Washington bureaucrat named Lester Frank Ward. Ward could view the evolutionary process only from the bottom up. From that perspective, he determined that human progress was best achieved not through competition but through cooperation. Not surprisingly, Ward believed that government was best equipped to promote human progress through cooperation. As a result, government—as an active agent for social change—could remove the two great barriers to a better world: poverty and ignorance. Ward's ideas would have a tremendous impact on social thinking and public policy in the twentieth century.

Liberal theologians and pulpiteers accommodated and incorporated the new philosophy. They used evolution to explain the origin of not only the earth but also the Scriptures. According to these new thinkers, the Bible was not God-inspired (2 Tim. 3:16) but was the result of a process of human aspirations.

In addition, building on a liberal tradition, the Reform Darwinists among the evolutionists believed that man was not, as the Scriptures taught, sinful; rather, man was inherently good. Man could cure the ills of society by improving the human condition. The social gospel often grew out of a genuine concern to relieve the misery of the slums and was based on the belief that the essence of Christianity was the command "Thou shalt love thy neighbor as thyself." This love, however, was misdirected and inadequate because it embraced only the present life and not the life to come. Love for our neighbor is hardly complete if it gives him food and shelter but leaves his soul in darkness.

Charles Darwin

Literature

A number of literary styles emerged during the late nineteenth century, reflecting the changes in society and capturing the spirit of the times. Perhaps the most popular writer of the day was Samuel Langhorne Clemens, who wrote under the pen name **Mark Twain** (*The Adventures of Huckleberry Finn* and *Life on the Mississippi*). Twain's work reflected the literary school of **realism**. In contrast to the emotional, exotic character of romanticism (see Chapter 11), Twain drew a picture of simple, ordinary life colored with his captivating humor. Similarly, realist painters such as Winslow Homer and Thomas Eakins portrayed daily life from the common man's perspective, revealing both its strength and its mundaneness.

This painting by Winslow Homer is entitled *The Fog Warning*.

By the 1890s, a new literary approach known as **naturalism** developed. In some ways an extreme form of realism that was shaped by Darwinism, naturalism emphasized man's helplessness and struggle with the world. **Stephen Crane** used that style in *Maggie: A Girl of the Streets* (1893) and *The Red Badge of Courage* (1895). **Jack London** (*Call of the Wild*, 1903) also wrote from the naturalist perspective, portraying the triumph of brute force over the cruel world.

Materialism

Jefferson's phrase "the pursuit of happiness" took on a new meaning during the Gilded Age. Mass production and labor-saving machinery provided more people with more things and more time to enjoy them. America was increasingly becoming a consumer society in which people associated with each other based on what they owned. Brand names, advertising, and new mass marketing techniques took on greater importance in the economic choices of daily life. Unfortunately, materialism—the desire for worldly possessions and the belief that they can bring true happiness—became the philosophy of a growing number of Americans.

Leisure

With the increase of leisure time that mechanization provided, Americans sought new outlets for recreation and amusement. Organized sports took on the broad appeal that other "consumables" had. Baseball became the national pastime beginning in 1869 when the Cincinnati Red Stockings, the first all-professional team, toured the country. In the decades that followed, thousands of fans

---

The Move Toward Naturalism

"When it occurs to a man that nature does not regard him as important, and that she feels she would not maim the universe by disposing of him, he at first wishes to throw bricks at the temple, and he hates deeply the fact that there are no bricks and no temples. Any visible expression of nature would surely be pelleted with his jeers.

Then if there be no tangible thing to hoot, he feels, perhaps, the desire to confront a personification and indulge in pleas, bowed to one knee, and with hands supplicant, saying, 'Yes, but I love myself.'"

Stephen Crane, "The Open Boat," in *The Red Badge of Courage and Other Stories*, Oxford World's Classics, ed. Anthony Mellors and Fiona Robertson (New York: Oxford University Press, 1998), 139.

Christmas in the Gilded Age

The transformation of the celebration of Christmas perhaps best illustrates the changes that materialism brought. In 1880, F. W. Woolworth, pinching pennies for his Five and Ten Cent Store in Lancaster, Pennsylvania, cautiously ventured to spend $25 for Christmas ornaments. Surprised when eager customers snapped up the decorations, Woolworth began to pour more and more into his Christmas stock to meet the demands of the market. By 1891, Woolworth was reminding the managers of his chain of stores that Christmas "is our harvest time, make it pay." Increasingly, for retailers and consumers alike, Christmas was "good" in proportion to its gain. Somewhere amid the growing materialism, many Americans were trading away spiritual values at bargain prices.

flocked to city ballparks. In 1903, the first World Series was played; the Boston Pilgrims defeated the Pittsburgh Pirates to become the first "world champions."

Other sports—such as golf, tennis, and particularly croquet—enjoyed an even broader appeal because both men and women could play them. Throughout the entire period, croquet was the sport of choice for upper- and middle-class people. Some enterprising croquet clubs even organized night parties with candles attached to the wickets. The popularity of mixed sports prompted illustrator Charles Dana Gibson to produce the "Gibson girl," the quintessential American woman—athletic yet without the loss of feminine charm.

Other forms of entertainment popular during the period included vaudeville, Wild West shows, and circuses. Vaudeville was a variety stage show that might include such attractions as jugglers, song-and-dance routines, comical skits, and stand-up comics. Vaudevillians had to be able to do it all—sing, dance, speak, and perform physical feats. Several Wild West shows featured marksmen, equine trick riders, buffalo, cowboys, and even Indians. The most popular shows included those operated by Pawnee Bill and Mexican Joe, but by far the most famous was the Wild West Show of William "Buffalo Bill" Cody. He toured not only the United States but also Europe, featuring his stars Annie Oakley, a crack sharpshooter, and Sitting Bull, the famous Sioux chief.

Traveling circuses were even more plentiful than Wild West shows. The most famous one was begun by P. T. Barnum, who had started in the 1840s by featuring such attractions as the dwarf Tom Thumb, the Fiji mermaid, and conjoined twins. He later merged with the circus of James Bailey to form the Barnum and Bailey Circus. In the early 1900s, John and Charles Ringling bought them out to form the now-famous (and active until 2017) Ringling Bros. and Barnum & Bailey Circus.

Bicycles were immensely popular during the 1890s, with sales figures showing over a million pedal pushers by 1893. Cycle clubs were so numerous that they even became a political force, lobbying with municipal and state governments for more paved roads.

Sadly, consumption of alcoholic beverages also became a growing pastime. Drinking had been an issue since colonial days, but it grew in direct proportion to the population. Some immigrants' native cultures were especially accepting of alcohol. Saloons were plentiful. The incidence of actions associated with alcohol—drunkenness, unemployment, child and spousal abuse, and physical assaults, including murder—grew with the increased consumption and led to reform movements.

The material prosperity not only changed social conditions but also influenced spiritual conditions. For many people, financial gain became paramount. In his "Acres of Diamonds" speech, prominent lecturer Russell Conwell told an estimated thirteen million people that it was the Christian's *duty* to be prosperous. The Baptist minister exhorted, "I say, get rich, get rich." Conwell forgot Christ's message of Luke 12:15—life does not consist in the abundance of the things one possesses.

Meeting the Challenge

Christians did not let the challenges of urbanization, materialism, immigration, and class conflict go unanswered. Many

> ### New Sports
> Two new sports were introduced during this time: basketball and football. Canadian James Naismith introduced basketball as a YMCA (Young Men's Christian Association) winter sport in 1891. The Ivy League colleges began playing football—without helmets or pads—in the fall of 1869.

Barnum & Bailey poster

D. L. Moody was a famous evangelist during the Gilded Age.

How Did He Do It?

Although he was not formally educated, Moody had a gift for communicating. He spoke plainly from the heart and filled his sermons with compelling stories, jokes, and illustrations. His theme was simple but profound: God loves sinners and wants to save them. Moody also avoided denominational ties. He wanted all true Christians of all denominations to join in winning the lost to Christ.

Moody and Sankey

Moody became one of the first evangelists to use music in his campaigns as a means of attracting and winning over a crowd and of presenting "the gospel in song." He recruited baritone Ira Sankey to serve as his song leader and soloist. Sankey helped popularize the "gospel song," a sacred tune that is less formal than a hymn and has a more popular, easily sung melody. Sankey composed the tunes for such gospel songs as "A Shelter in the Time of Storm," "Hiding in Thee," and "Faith Is the Victory!" Moody and Sankey also helped establish the gospel song as part of American church life.

Christians sought to deal with those problems scripturally. Some Christians, for example, confronted the squalor of city slums by establishing rescue missions, centers located in the middle of the slums for preaching the gospel and ministering to the physical needs of city dwellers. The most widespread method of meeting those challenges with the gospel, however, was **urban evangelism**, the conducting of large, citywide campaigns in huge auditoriums or large churches in major cities. The leader of the movement during this period was Evangelist **Dwight L. Moody**.

D. L. Moody

Dwight Lyman Moody was born in Northfield, Massachusetts, in 1837. At the age of seventeen, Moody went to seek his fortune in Boston. He worked for his uncle in a shoe store and at his uncle's insistence, went to church regularly. There Moody sat in the class of a concerned Sunday school teacher, who eventually led the young man to Christ. Despite his salvation, Moody was in some ways still worldly-minded. He desired above all to be rich, and to that end he moved to Chicago in 1856, where he thought lay greater opportunities for wealth.

In Chicago, however, Moody was touched by the Prayer Meeting Revival (see Chapter 11). As a result, he became more involved in Christian work than in the search for wealth. In 1859, he began a Sunday school in the slums of Chicago that grew under his leadership to more than one thousand students. In 1860, Moody abandoned his materialistic goals, quit his high-paying job with a shoe company, and devoted himself to working with his Sunday school, the YMCA, and other Christian organizations. He began a church in Chicago, although he was not an ordained minister, and became a popular speaker at conventions and churches on subjects such as Sunday school organization and promotion.

Evangelism

In 1873, Moody began a speaking tour of Great Britain. At first it was small and little noticed. As the tour continued, however, crowds swelled, and newspapers began to report the success of the "Yankee evangelist." In four months in London alone, Moody conducted 285 meetings attended by two and a half million people. Even the English nobility, including the Princess of Wales, came to hear him.

When Moody returned to the United States in 1875, he was deluged with requests to hold citywide campaigns across the United States. Moody eagerly agreed to as many of those invitations as he could because he believed that reaching the major cities with the gospel would reach the whole nation. "Water runs down hill, and the highest hills in America are the great cities," he said. "If we can stir them we shall stir the whole country." Over the next twenty years, Moody preached to millions in the United States, Canada, the British Isles, and Mexico. Reported conversions numbered in the thousands in each campaign.

Methodology

Moody's methodology was influenced by the business world. Like successful businessmen of his time, Moody was well organized. One minister noted, "As he stood on the platform, he looked like a businessman, he dressed like a businessman; he took the meeting in hand as a businessman would." Although Moody's services were informal, he demanded order. He carefully planned and organized each element of the massive meetings. The all-important "business" of saving souls, Moody thought, certainly required at least as much care, planning, and forethought as the operation of some secular company.

Moody's combination of business practices with evangelism influenced Christians well into the twentieth century. The priority given to business practices became so pronounced that R. A. Torrey, who had served alongside Moody, warned in the 1920s against pastors becoming reliant on business methodology for results. Torrey reminded Christians that the reason for people's response to the gospel is always the moving of the Holy Spirit in the hearts of men.

Effects

Moody launched the urban evangelism movement, and scores of evangelists followed after him. Methodist **Sam Jones**, often called "the Moody of the South," was probably second only to Moody himself in popularity and success. Like Moody, Jones preached in a direct—almost blunt—and colorful manner that spoke to listeners on their own level. Led by evangelists such as Moody and Jones, the period from 1875 to 1915 was the golden age of urban evangelism.

In Moody's campaigns alone, millions of people heard the gospel and tens of thousands professed salvation through Christ. It is difficult to measure what impact those conversions had on American society, but it became clear in the 1890s and 1900s that the urban revivals gave at least a push to reform efforts such as Prohibition. For Moody and the urban evangelists, however, the salvation of the lost was clearly the most important result. Their motto was best summarized in the title of a gospel song—"Rescue the Perishing." As Moody said on one occasion, "I look upon this world as a wrecked vessel. God has given me a lifeboat and said to me, 'Moody, save all you can.'"

At the beginning of the nineteenth century, Methodist circuit riders and frontier camp meetings had been on the leading edge of American Christianity. By Moody's day, however, congregations had moved from brush arbors to big auditoriums. The nation now bridged two oceans, and half the country had moved to the city. As the twentieth century dawned, more change and new challenges lay ahead.

Fanny Crosby

The most prolific hymn writer in history was Fanny Crosby. Blinded by an incompetent doctor when she was only six months old, Fanny spent most of her life in darkness. Yet she refused to be bitter and found an outlet for her talents in writing poetry.

Christian musician William Bradbury persuaded Fanny to write the words for songs. Popularized by the Moody-Sankey campaigns, her songs (including "Pass Me Not, O Gentle Saviour," "Jesus Is Calling," "Rescue the Perishing," "Blessed Assurance," "All the Way My Saviour Leads Me," "To God Be the Glory," and "Praise Him! Praise Him!") soon filled the churches of America and Great Britain.

She was so prolific that music publishers asked her to write some songs under pseudonyms so that people would not think that *all* of their songs were by her. (She used at least ninety-four pseudonyms!) Her inspiration might come from a passing thought or an overheard comment. She reportedly wrote "Pass Me Not, O Gentle Saviour," after hearing someone in a rescue mission pray, "Savior, do not pass me by." Crosby's life spanned nearly a century (1820–1915), during which she wrote hundreds of verses, not for wealth or fame but from love and devotion to Christ.

Section Review

1–4. List two advantages and two disadvantages of living in the city in the late 1800s.

5. What is the major difference between a traditional hymn and a gospel song?

6. Who was the most prolific hymn writer of the late nineteenth century?

★ How did people use their new-found leisure during this period? How does that compare with leisure activities today?

★ Explain the ultimate reason for the success of the Moody campaigns.

People, Places, and Things to Remember

robber barons
Cornelius Vanderbilt
Andrew Carnegie
vertical integration
John D. Rockefeller
horizontal integration
trust
New South
John Pierpont Morgan
United States Steel Corporation
Alexander Graham Bell
Thomas Alva Edison
Roscoe Conkling
Stalwarts
Half-breeds
James A. Garfield
Chester A. Arthur
Pendleton Act
Civil Service Commission
Grover Cleveland
Interstate Commerce Act
Benjamin Harrison
Sherman Anti-Trust Act
McKinley Tariff
Knights of Labor
American Federation of Labor
Samuel Gompers
Haymarket Riot
Homestead Strike
Eugene V. Debs
Pullman Strike
injunction
socialism
Grange
Farmers' Alliance
Populist Party
free silver
William McKinley
William Jennings Bryan
New Immigration
Charles Darwin
Darwinism
Mark Twain
realism
naturalism
Stephen Crane
Jack London
urban evangelism
Dwight L. Moody
Sam Jones

CHAPTER REVIEW

Making Connections

1–2. With which "captain of industry" do we associate oil refining? steel production? the "New South"?

3. What crime in 1881 helped promote civil service reform by the passage of the Pendleton Act?

4–6. Give three reasons why many Americans opposed the "New Immigration" of the late nineteenth and early twentieth centuries.

7. What was the most widespread method of meeting the challenges of the city with the gospel?

Developing History Skills

1. Explain the difference between vertical integration and horizontal integration. What was the historical significance of these forms of integration?

2. Review the discussions of the spoils system in Chapter 10 and in this chapter. Then list at least one advantage and one disadvantage of the spoils system. Do you think the system is good or bad?

Thinking Critically

1. Was federal regulation of the railroads, such as the Interstate Commerce Act, necessary? Why or why not?

2. Read Matthew 6:19–21, 24–34. What do those passages teach the Christian concerning his attitude toward materialism?

Living as a Christian Citizen

1. Imagine that you are a Christian businessman in the late nineteenth century. Write out a series of biblical principles that will guide you in your business.

2. The opportunity for leisure time has only grown since the nineteenth century. What should a Christian think about leisure time, and how should he use it?

AMERICA EXPANDS (1850–1900) 17

Sod houses, such as this one in Nebraska, were common in the Great Plains.

One does not sell the earth upon which the people walk.

Crazy Horse
A Sioux warrior, September 1875

I. Western Expansion

II. Indian Affairs

III. International Expansion

Big Ideas

1. How did Americans expand to the West and what were their motivations for this expansion?
2. What was the American government's Indian policy?
3. What were the results of the international expansion of the United States in the second half of the nineteenth century?

Americans were restless and energetic. During the Gilded Age, they not only enlarged their cities and factories but also settled the continent, pushing the frontier to the Pacific and beyond.

With the climax of Manifest Destiny in the Mexican War (1848), the United States encountered a new challenge. It now faced the difficult task of developing the huge tracts of land gained from Mexico as well as large segments of the Louisiana Purchase and Oregon territory that were still relatively unsettled. Railroaders, cowboys, miners, and farmers—all pioneers—met this challenge by pushing toward the Pacific in the last great wave of westward expansion in American history.

Yet the idea of Manifest Destiny did not really end with the Mexican War. With the continent in U.S. hands from Atlantic to Pacific, some Americans began to look across the seas to other lands where they could plant the Stars and Stripes. Part of this "overseas Manifest Destiny" was economic, securing new markets for the products of a growing American economy. Part of the expansion, however, was the strong desire for territory that had helped spark the Mexican War. Much of the expansion was peaceful, although before the century closed, the United States found itself involved in its first foreign war in fifty years.

I. Western Expansion

Rails to the West

The history of the American West rode on iron rails. The railroads crisscrossed the country, uniting the eastern and the western halves of the nation. Trains carried settlers into the West, of course, but they also carried to the East the products and resources of the West. Development of the region's resources was not impossible without the railroad; the California gold rush had proved that. But without question, precious metals and rich land for grazing and agriculture became even more valuable when supply sources and markets were as close as the nearest rail junction. Railroads proved to be the main instrument of developing the American West.

The Transcontinental Idea

The California gold rush created a population explosion on the Pacific coast, and Americans began to dream of the ideal "bridge" over the intervening mountains and prairie—the railroad. But the mammoth cost of building a **transcontinental railroad** frightened potential investors. Congress passed two railroad acts that provided incentives for them. First, for each mile of track laid, the railroad company would receive land grants of alternating ten-square-mile sections of land along each side of the road. This land grant was expanded in 1864 to twenty-square-mile sections, ultimately giving the participating railroads about twenty million acres—an area nearly as large as the state of Indiana. Later, much of this land was sold by the railroad companies. Second, the government provided loans to the railroads: $16,000 for each mile of track laid in the plains, $32,000 per mile in the foothills, and $48,000 per mile in the mountains.

Two railroads received charters to build the first transcontinental railroad. The **Union Pacific** was to begin in Omaha, Nebraska, and build westward; the **Central Pacific** was to begin in Sacramento, California, and build eastward. Eventually, the two

---

Guiding Questions

1. How did the transcontinental railroads affect westward expansion?
2. What were the vast potentials and hazards of developing resources in the West?
3. How did pioneers overcome the difficulties of settling the Great Plains?

companies raced to see which could lay the most track—and therefore receive the most money. The Union Pacific, with mostly plains to cross, had an easier task than the Central Pacific, which had to cross a steep mountain range, the Sierra Nevadas. Even so, the Union Pacific still had to contend with searing heat, waterless and treeless plains, and Indian attacks. Neither company faced an easy task.

Building the Line

The Union Pacific hired mostly Irish immigrants, many of them former Union army veterans. The Central Pacific Railroad relied mainly on immigrant Chinese workers. The Central Pacific faced the major, even potentially fatal, challenge of blasting tunnels through the Sierra Nevada and the Rocky Mountains. Both companies' workers overcame tremendous obstacles and astonished their employers with the speed they laid track. An English visitor described the process of the Union Pacific track gangs:

> A light car, drawn by a single horse, gallops up to the front with its load of rails. Two men seize the end of a rail and start forward, the rest of the gang taking hold by twos until it is clear of the car. They come forward at a run. At the word of command the rail is dropped in its place, right side up. Less than thirty seconds to a rail for each gang, and so four rails go down to the minute!

Almost poetically, the observer went on to note that there were "three strokes to the spike, . . . ten spikes to the rail, four hundred rails to a mile, eighteen hundred miles to San Francisco."

But the builders soon learned the truth of the adage "Haste makes waste." Because of their rush to lay more track and thereby qualify for more subsidies, the companies often failed to prepare the roadbed properly before laying the track, so over time and under the weight of locomotives and loaded freight cars, the ties sunk or tilted, twisting and misaligning the track. In such cases, the companies had to remove and repair or replace the track. The companies returned to the government seeking more financial help when this occurred.

The climax of the work came on May 10, 1869, when the two lines joined near Promontory (PRAH mun tohr ee) Point, Utah. Officials drove in four special spikes—two gold, one silver, and one a mixture of gold, silver, and iron. On one of the gold spikes was inscribed, "May God continue the unity of our Country as this Railroad unites the two great Oceans of the world."

The Central Pacific completed 688 miles of track while the Union Pacific laid 1,086 miles. Within twenty-five years, four more transcontinental lines spanned the country: the Atchison, Topeka, and Santa Fe (finished 1881); the Southern Pacific (1883); the Northern Pacific (1883);

Workers for the Central Pacific Railroad lay track in Nevada.

Workin' on the Railroad

The Central Pacific set the single-day record for laying track. At 7:00 a.m. on April 28, 1869, 5,000 men set to work using five trains full of more than 25,000 railroad ties, 3,500 rails, 55,000 spikes, and 14,000 bolts. By the time they stopped at 7:00 p.m., the crews had laid ten miles of track.

In May 1869, the driving of the golden spike near Promontory Point, Utah, marked the completion of the first transcontinental railroad.

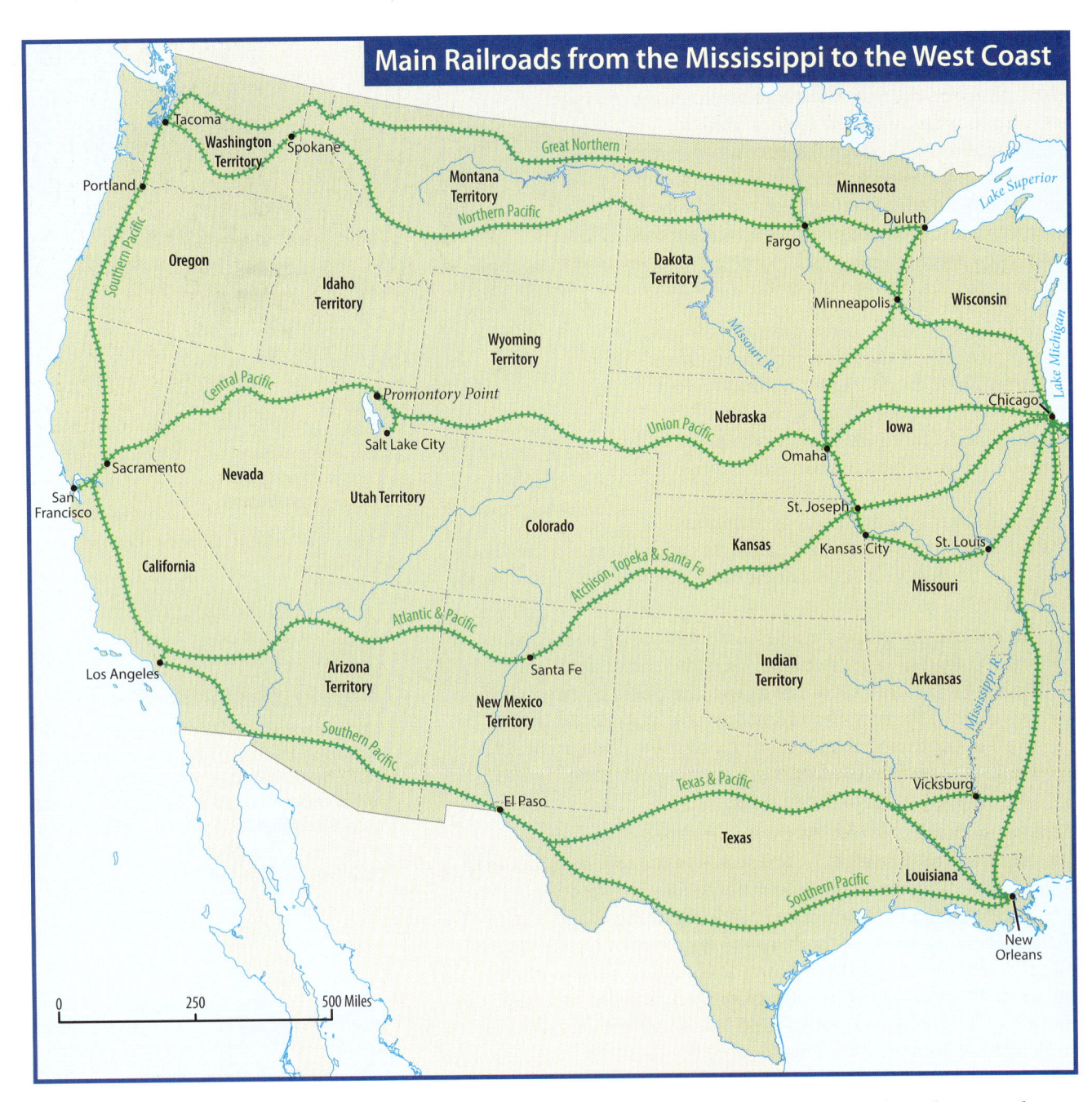

Main Railroads from the Mississippi to the West Coast

Deadwood, South Dakota, a mining town, in 1876

and the Great Northern (1893). The Great Northern line was the only one of the four that was completed without a penny of government subsidy. The railroads quickly became the vehicles for tremendous change in the West.

Resources of the West

Mining

One of the reasons for the settlement of the West and the building of the transcontinental railroad was the mining of precious metals. The California gold rush in 1849 was but the first of several western scrambles to dig wealth from the earth. One of the earliest gold strikes after California was the **Pikes Peak gold rush** in 1859, which resulted in the settlement of Colorado. Thousands of pioneers seeking to "get rich quick" streamed into Colorado, particularly the rapidly expanding "boom town" of Denver. On their wagons, gold hunters boldly advertised, "Pikes Peak or Bust!" When the gold in Colorado gave out, however, many disappointed fortune seekers rode back with a new message: "Busted!"

Miners often found more than gold in the Rockies. Leadville, Colorado, is a splendid example of the diverse resources of the region. After a gold boom in Leadville ended in the early 1860s, the town shifted its emphasis and became a center for silver and lead mining. After the silver ran out, Leadville also became a center for mining zinc and copper. Towns that could thus diversify thrived; those that could not became ghost towns. The story of Leadville and similar communities often made it seem that the mineral resources of the West were limitless.

Farther west, one of the largest and richest mines was the **Comstock Lode** in Nevada. It was named for Henry Comstock, an early prospector there. Miners eagerly dug gold out of the ground, but they were disappointed to find that it was contaminated by some other metal and therefore sold for less. Upon closer examination, the "other metal" turned out to be silver. In fact, more than half of the ore eventually mined from the Comstock Lode was silver; the rest was gold. Miners extracted some $400 million worth of gold and silver from the Comstock Lode between 1859 and 1900.

The mining of the Comstock Lode was typical of mining in the latter half of the nineteenth century. No longer was it a matter of a lone grizzled prospector with his pickaxe and shovel digging for gold in the side of a mountain; mining was big business. Large companies hired dozens of miners, sank shafts hundreds—even thousands—of feet into the earth, and brought in huge drills, pumps, and other heavy machinery to extract the precious ores. Comstock was also typical in spurring the growth of mining towns. Near Comstock was Virginia City, a metropolis of 30,000 at its height, containing only four churches but a hundred saloons. Yet, after the mine gave out, the population plummeted to fewer than a thousand permanent residents.

Other mines throughout the West attracted workers and investors to the region. Gold was always the chief attraction, but fortunes could be made in other metals as well. The Anaconda Mine in Montana, for example, began as a rather poor silver mine. But miners soon discovered that it included one of the richest veins of copper in the world. Nearby deposits of zinc and lead further enriched the region. Wealth in the West, it seemed, was there for the digging.

Cattle

One glamorized element of the American West, celebrated in numerous motion pictures and television programs, was the **cattle drive**.

With all of his equipment loaded on a single burro, a miner sets out to seek his fortune in the mineral-rich American West.

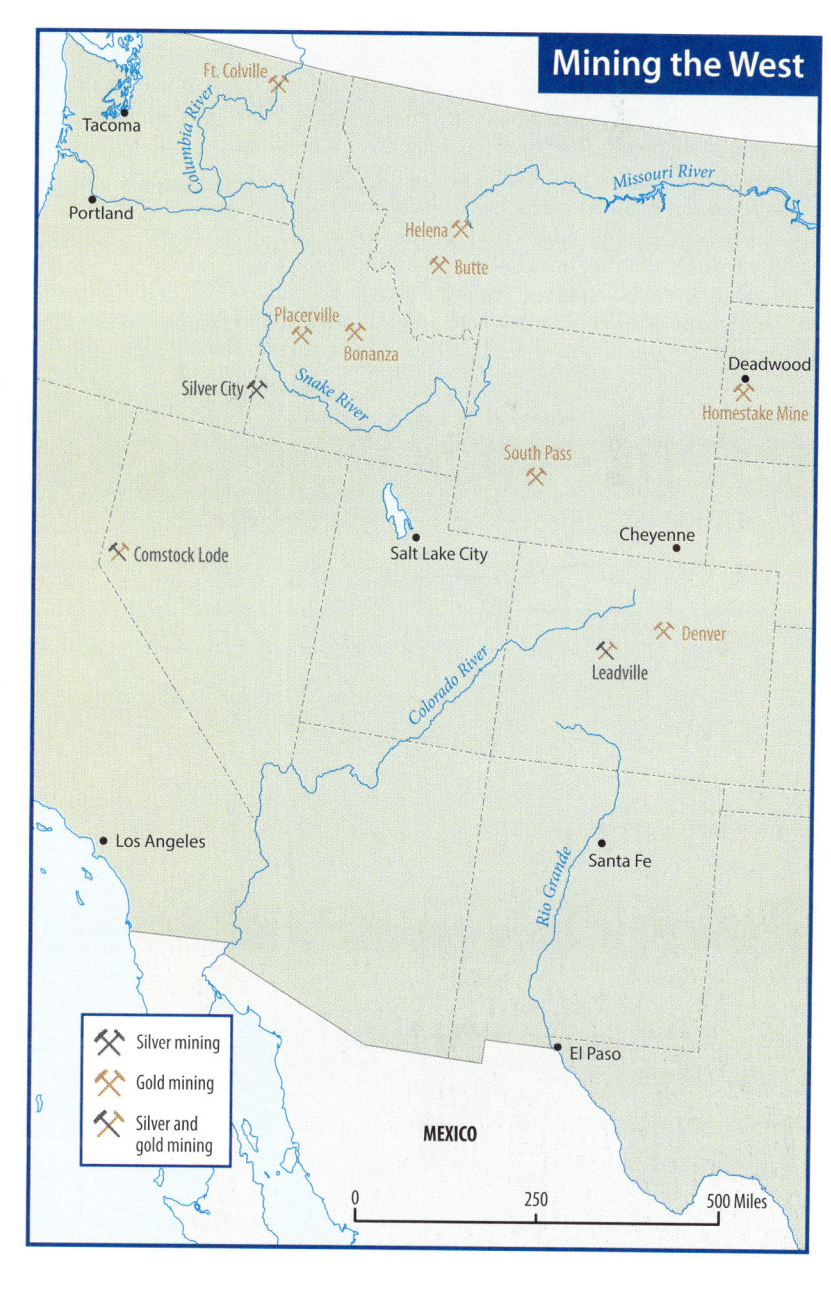

The Life of an American Cowboy on a Cattle Drive

Life on the cattle trails was strenuous. The average herd was about two thousand head of cattle. The trail crew comprised eleven men. The two who led the herd were called point men. Two others came behind the point men on the sides. Another two were on the flanks. Two others, called drag men, brought up the rear behind the herds. These two men came in at the end of the day spitting and coughing, covered with dust. The crew also included a cook, a wrangler to care for the horses, and the trail boss.

A good night's sleep was a luxury. The cowboys' day began when the cook awoke them at 3:00 a.m. and did not end until about 9:00 p.m. when they bedded down the cattle. Everyone except the cook, the wrangler, and the trail boss had to do a two-hour shift of guard duty throughout the night. If everything went well and the weather was nice, cowboys might get a total of five hours of sleep at night, but guard duty often interrupted that. When the weather was bad, they might get an hour of sleep or less. They slept on the ground with only a blanket. They pillowed their heads on their saddles. Much sleep or little, good weather or bad, the wagon rolled the next morning like clockwork.

After the war, ranchers in Texas found themselves with herds of cattle too large for nearby markets. In the East, however, there was a large demand for beef. The problem was how to get the meat to market. The answer was simple in concept but enormously difficult in practice: Cattlemen drove the herds overland to northern railroad terminals. Soon, such frontier settlements as Kansas City, Missouri, and Dodge City, Kansas, became thriving "cow towns," centers of the cattle trade. From these towns, the cattle were moved east by rail.

Driving the herds were **cowboys**, men now shrouded by myth but who were actually tough and hard-working. The cattle they drove were longhorns—stubborn, ornery, and independent. Their meat was not the best beef, but only the tough longhorns could survive the rigors of the cattle trails. Several of the trails stretched north from Texas; the Goodnight-Loving Trail and the Chisholm Trail were perhaps the most famous. The cowboys herded the cattle across the **"open ranges"** (so called because the plains were unfenced public lands) and allowed them to feed on the grasses there. Though viewed by some as an exciting and adventurous undertaking, the drives were actually grueling and dangerous work. Stampedes, cattle "rustlers" (thieves), and Indian attacks were the most dramatic threats. A more common and constant danger was simply a lack of water. If the cattle failed to reach the next watering hole in time, the entire herd could perish and leave an owner financially ruined.

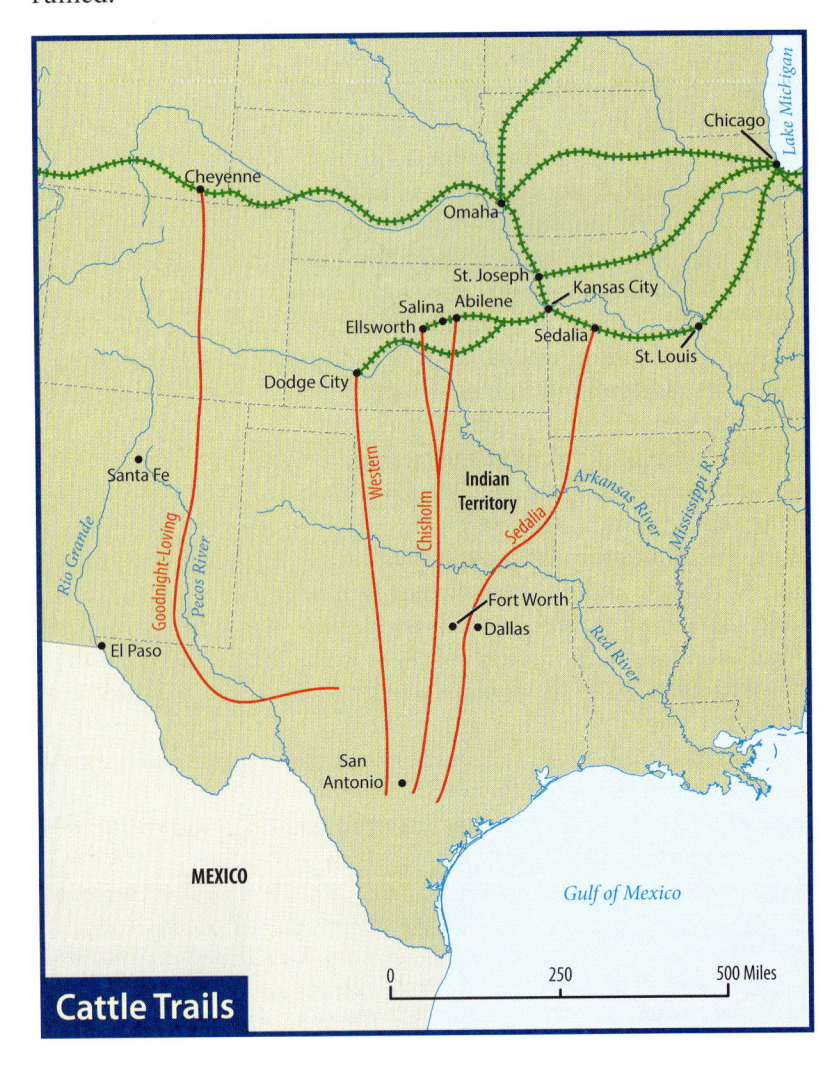

Cattle Trails

Dress of the West

The clothing we associate with the American West was worn more for practicality than for style. Hats, for example, were designed to protect the cowboys from the elements—mainly sun and rain. The "Stetson," the hat commonly considered "a cowboy hat," was one of the most popular. (Because hats were sometimes used to carry water, the ample Stetson was jokingly called "the ten-gallon hat.") Many cowboys, however, preferred the Mexican sombrero with its wide brim. Likewise the bandana, or "neckerchief," was not simply a decoration. When a cowboy was trailing a herd or caught in a dust storm, the bandana provided him with a mask to protect his mouth and nose. (Villains, of course, found the bandana a convenient way to hide their identity.)

The cowboy's boots were tight at the top to help keep rocks and dirt out. Toes of the boots were often narrow and pointed so that a rider could get his feet in and out of stirrups easily. A cowboy's clothes were usually made of wool. Although wool was warm in hot weather, cowboys appreciated it during the cool nights and found that it wore much better than fabrics such as cotton. Some cowboys wore chaps, coverings for their trousers made of leather or other animal hides. The chaps were particularly helpful for protecting a cowboy riding through thorns and brush.

The most popular clothing to emerge from the Old West was the work of a Jewish merchant, an immigrant from Germany. Levi Strauss moved west to San Francisco in 1853 and soon opened a store there. Years later, he and a customer developed sturdy trousers that could endure the demands of frontier life. Using material which he had originally planned to use for making tents, Strauss built a booming trade. He eventually began to make the trousers out of a tough cloth from Nîmes, France, *serg de Nîmes*, from which the word *denim* comes. Other tailors named the material from the French for Genoa, Italy—*Gênes*—where a similar cloth was manufactured. This name eventually became corrupted in English as "jeans." After the material was dyed blue, an American institution was born—"blue jeans."

The cattle industry owed at least part of its success to the development of a related business, meatpacking. The idea of meatpacking had first gained popularity during the Civil War when the Union army used treated meat packed in barrels or tins to feed its soldiers. After the war, city dwellers in particular found the process convenient for purchasing and storing food. Meatpacking plants opened first in Midwestern cities such as Cincinnati, Chicago, Milwaukee, and Minneapolis. At first, cattle were shipped live by train to the packing houses. The invention of the ice-cooled refrigerator railcars by meat-packer Gustavus Swift allowed meat packers to slaughter the beef in the West and then ship it to the plants. Eventually, plants opened in the West too, shortening the process even further. Meat-packers such as Swift and Philip Armour became household names as their canned meat products stocked the shelves of American pantries.

The open-range cattle industry ended in the 1880s. Cattle overgrazed much of the land, ruining it for large herds. In addition, bitterly cold winters in 1886 and 1887 killed thousands of cattle and bankrupted many cattlemen. As railroads expanded in the West, long cattle drives became unnecessary; the chief advantage of the longhorns—their ability to survive long and difficult drives—no longer mattered. Some cattlemen began fencing in their ranches and breeding smaller, meatier stock. Beef remained a profitable product, and related industries such as meatpacking continued to thrive; but the era of the cattle drive and the longhorn was over.

Settlers and Sod-busters

The most significant factor in the demise of the open range was farming. The railroads that hauled cattle to meatpacking plants also brought back settlers who farmed the land instead of using it for grazing. To help protect their crops from ranging cattle, frontier farmers fenced their properties, breaking up the open ranges and hindering trail drives. Ranchers sent cowboys to drive off the "sod-busters," as farmers were called, and "range wars" often developed between cattlemen and farmers.

The farmers were destined to win the range wars. In the first thirty years after the Civil War, more new land was settled than in all of America's previous history. By the 1880s, farmers far outnumbered cowboys, and the open ranges began to dwindle as homesteaders fenced more and more land.

Acquiring Land

Acquiring land was the farmer's first priority. Railroads sold their land grants to settlers, but the location of the lands near the tracks (hence, closer to supply sources and markets) made them much more valuable than other lands. Many settlers could not afford the railroad's prices. The federal government, eager to see the West settled, passed the **Homestead Act** in 1862. This act provided 160 acres of land to any settler who would live on the land for five years and "improve" it by building a dwelling on it and farming there. The Homestead Act proved to be a tremendous success, and by 1900 nearly a million settlers had filed for homesteads under that law.

Most of the influx of homesteaders was gradual, but the **Oklahoma land rushes** were an exception. When the government decided to open large sections of the Indian Territory (Oklahoma) to white settlement, it decided to do so in five large blows called land runs. Other lands were offered by a lottery and an auction. This opening of Indian Territory to white settlement was a violation of treaties made with the Southern Indian tribes and led to renewed conflicts with them. The U.S. government tried to justify the violation by saying that the Cherokees had fought for the Confederacy.

Developing the Land

The **Great Plains** is the region between the Mississippi River Valley and the Rocky Mountains, stretching north to south from Canada to southern Texas. Before the Civil War, Americans often called the region "the Great American Desert," not because it was really a desert but because the grassy plains were nearly treeless and suffered from infrequent rainfall. This treeless, semiarid region provided daunting challenges to settlers.

To compensate for the lack of rain, some farmers irrigated their fields from the region's rivers. Others pumped water up from the underground water table using windmills. Dry farming, the cultivation of crops by careful conservation of water, was widespread, with farmers using ground covers—such as stubble from previous crops or a top layer of powdery soil—to hold in precious moisture. Because plants use more water while growing than when mature, farmers also planted crops such as winter wheat, which grew to maturity before the heat of summer increased the rate of evapora-

Settlers rushing to claim land in Oklahoma in April 1889

Oklahoma Land Rush

Each Oklahoma land rush—three million acres thrown open in 1889 and six million in 1893—began like a race on a set day at a set time. With the sounding of a signal, a massive flood of settlers rushed across the borders to claim the land. In the 1889 rush, more than fifty thousand people entered the territory on the first day.

The effects of the rush were dramatic. The town of Guthrie, for example, was founded and immediately grew to a population of six thousand, leading residents to joke, "Rome was not built in a day, but Guthrie was."

Some settlers took control of land before it was officially opened. Because they claimed land sooner than they should have, Oklahoma became known as the "Sooner State." Today, athletic teams at the University of Oklahoma are called the "Sooners."

tion. Wheat, in fact, became the main crop of the Great Plains, making that region one of the great "breadbaskets" of the world.

The lack of trees on the plains created a major construction problem for buildings. Many early pioneers lived in **soddies**, houses built of blocks of earth and sod. Soddies were warm in the winter and cool in the summer, but they were hardly luxurious. Rain, on the rare occasions when it fell, was a particular menace to sod houses. One pioneer wife said,

> Sometimes the water would drip on the stove while I was cooking, and I would have to keep tight lids on the skillets to prevent mud from falling into the food. With my dress pinned up, and rubbers on my feet, I waded around until the clouds rolled by. Life is too short to be spent under a sod roof.

If rains were heavy or prolonged, the sod house might collapse completely. At best, a soddie lasted only a few years, usually long enough for a settler to build another soddie or to import materials such as lumber by rail and build a more permanent house.

Fencing was likewise a problem in the treeless plains. Obviously, the split-rail fences used in the East were out of the question. Some farmers experimented with hedges, but these took time to grow. The ideal invention for fencing the plains came from Joseph Glidden of Illinois. In the 1870s, he developed **barbed wire**—two twisted strands of wire studded with sharp metal barbs at measured intervals. Pioneers strung the wire along posts, thus fencing their

A sod house, such as this one, provided shelter for many early settlers in areas where trees were scarce.

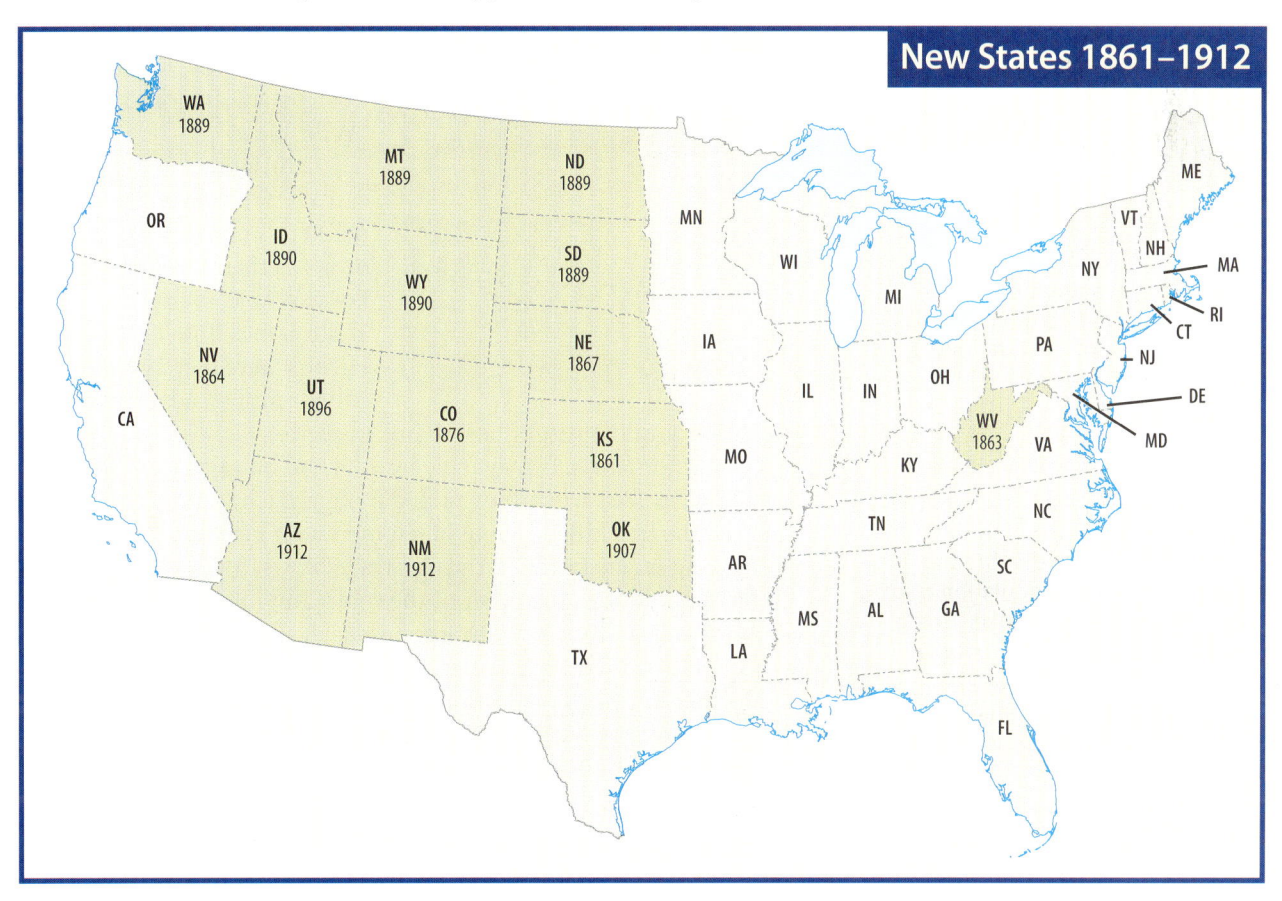

New States 1861–1912

- WA 1889
- MT 1889
- ND 1889
- OR
- ID 1890
- SD 1889
- WY 1890
- NV 1864
- UT 1896
- NE 1867
- CO 1876
- KS 1861
- AZ 1912
- NM 1912
- OK 1907
- WV 1863

property more easily and quickly than they ever could have done with rail fences. The barbs kept wary livestock away from the fence so that they would not break it down.

The innovations of dry farming and barbed wire—combined with inventions brought from the East, such as the reaper and the steel plow—allowed the plains farmer to transform the grasslands into an agricultural paradise. When traveling in the West in 1893, Wellesley College teacher Katherine Lee Bates was moved by the sight of the rich and lovely lands. After a visit to Pikes Peak, she wrote a poem celebrating that divinely blessed land:

> O beautiful for spacious skies,
>   For amber waves of grain,
> For purple mountain majesties
>   Above the fruited plain!
> America! America!
>   God shed His grace on thee
> And crown thy good with brotherhood
>   From sea to shining sea!

Law and Order

The West was big. The immense distances lawmen had to patrol often made law enforcement difficult. Some of the people who came to the West were tough, independent, and hard to control. Some of them—especially those who had already been notorious criminals back East—had little regard for law and order. Their answer to the difficult life in the West was often to steal to get what they wanted and to kill anyone who got in their way. Crime became a way of life for some of them, and the gun was the tool of their trade. The gun was also the tool used to bring law and order to the "Wild West."

Gunfighters of the American West, however, were neither as noble nor as glamorous as their legends suggest. For example, many "facts" about James Butler "Wild Bill" Hickok were merely embellished rumors, advertising gimmickry, and outright lies. In one instance, Hickok described to a reporter for *Harper's* magazine how he had handled the "McCanles Gang" in 1861 when they raided a stagecoach station. Hickok said that he had killed a gang of ten men with his rifle, Colt revolver, and bowie knife, "striking savage blows, following the devils up from one side to the other of the room and into the corners, striking and slashing until everyone was dead."

In reality, David McCanles, often described as a local bully, was the former owner of the station. He had come unarmed with his young son and two friends to collect payment on a debt from the station owner. In the argument that ensued, Hickok killed McCanles and wounded the other two men. Those two were then killed by others present at the station. Only McCanles's twelve-year-old son escaped.

Cattlemen in Nebraska cut a homesteader's wire fence in 1885 during one of the many farmer-cattleman clashes on the Great Plains. This photo shows a historical reenactment of that event.

The Colt army service revolver became a favorite weapon of gunfighters and outlaws in the West.

The author of a 1927 article in the *Nebraska History Magazine* described Wild Bill Hickok's gunfighting reputation, a description that is probably apt for most western gunfighters: "From all accounts of killings in which Hickok subsequently took part, I have been unable to find one single authentic instance in which he fought a fair fight. . . . He was a cold-blooded killer without heart or conscience. The moment he scented a fight he pulled his gun and shot to kill."

Still, a fierce reputation was no guarantee of safety for a gunfighter. The infamous James Gang, led by the brothers Jesse and Frank James, terrorized Missouri and neighboring states for fifteen years after the Civil War, staging more than two dozen raids. They were widely known and even more widely feared. Yet, Jesse was shot in the back of the head by one of his own men while at his home in St. Joseph, Missouri. Frank later turned himself in, lamenting, "I'm tired of running. Tired of waiting for a ball in the back. Tired of looking into the faces of friends and seeing a Judas."

The mild features of Jesse James disguised the heart of a killer. A former Confederate guerrilla in Missouri, he turned to robbery and murder after the war.

This group portrait shows three of the most colorful characters from the American West—"Wild Bill" Hickok (*left*), "Texas Jack" Omohundro (*standing*), and "Buffalo Bill" Cody (*right*).

Several types of lawmen operated in the Old West. The lowest in prestige was the town marshal. Next up the ladder was the county sheriff, who, like the town marshal, appointed deputies to serve under him. In addition, the U.S. government had an interest in establishing law and order in its territories. The president himself commissioned U.S. marshals and judges to enforce the law in the counties and towns. Finding qualified, honest men was difficult, however, and turnover was high. Furthermore, the lawmen were given unreasonably large territories to cover. One county marshal in Wyoming was responsible for 16,800 square miles, an area larger than several individual eastern states.

Most of the U.S. marshal's duties involved politics, tax collection, and paperwork; he usually left the field work to deputies. The town marshal's job was even less glamorous. His duties could include fire and health inspections and even shooting stray dogs. Town marshals, who rarely earned a suitable salary, often supplemented their income by running gambling operations. The potential for corruption was great.

In the absence of official justice, townspeople sometimes turned to their own brand of justice—lynching. The people of Laramie, Wyoming, once hanged their own town marshal when they found that he was drugging people and taking their money in the saloon that he managed. Vigilante groups (private citizens who enforced the law without any authority) were another force for "order," although they rarely had the sanction of the law. A few vigilante groups did manage to get quiet approval from the law, even winning legal status as stock growers' associations or homesteaders' associations.

Was the West Really so Wild?

Many people think that the American West was a truly wild place, with shootings, murders, bank robberies, and other acts of violence occurring with regularity. But was it really? The perception of the "wild" West is actually influenced by movies and television programs about the region. To keep viewer interest high, producers and directors have included a great deal of fast-paced, action-packed adventure in their productions.

Historians have determined that most people of the West were actually peaceful, polite, civil and desired progress. Conditions in the West might not have been like conditions in the big cities "back East," but neither were they as bad as we sometimes think.

Though practically every man wore or had ready access to a gun, people tended not to start fights. One historian has suggested that there are more bank robberies in a typical large modern city in a year than occurred in the entire West in a decade. The West could be rowdy and crime did occur, but it was not as wild as has been commonly believed.

"Peace Commissioners" of Dodge City, Kansas, pose for a photograph. Included are Wyatt Earp (*front row, second from left*) and Bat Masterson (*back row, on far right*).

Hanging was the most common form of execution in the Old West. In this photograph, "Black Jack" Ketchum is being prepared for "the final drop" in the New Mexico Territory, 1901.

Many businesses on the frontier also wanted to bring law and order to the West. For example, after suffering more than two hundred stagecoach robberies in one month in 1877, the Wells Fargo shipping company hired the Pinkerton National Detective Agency to supplement the work of the government lawmen. The Pinkertons developed America's first extensive "most-wanted" file on criminals, an idea that was later adopted by the Federal Bureau of Investigation. The list of criminals included such men as Black Bart, a well-dressed "gentleman bandit" who robbed twenty-eight stagecoaches but never hurt any passengers. He was finally apprehended after he dropped a handkerchief with markings on it at the scene of a crime. Pinkerton detectives traced the handkerchief to Black Bart after visiting some ninety laundries in California.

Judges in the early years were often ill trained and not respected. At first, they held court in improvised surroundings, such as a grocery store or a saloon. Eventually, judges brought a grudging respect for the law. At the local level were the justices of the peace or the police court judges. The territories were divided among district judges, who often traveled great distances to hear a wide variety of cases.

One of the most famous judges of the West was Isaac Charles Parker, better known as "the Hanging Judge." Parker's jurisdiction was a rough portion of land in western Arkansas bordering Indian Territory (modern Oklahoma). Technically, only Indians were allowed in the vast Indian Territory, but the region had become a hideout for criminals. Although the tribes were self-governing, any case involving a white man was sent to this single U.S. court judge in west Arkansas. Parker was viewed as an honest, qualified man. The thirty-six-year-old attorney, who volunteered to serve for the $3,500 annual salary, wanted to help bring justice to the territory.

Within a few days of moving to Fort Smith, Arkansas, the imposing judge opened his court. Parker hired a fearsome collection of lawmen. Their instructions were plain: "Bring them in, alive—or dead." During one of his eight-week court sessions, he condemned to death six of the ninety-one people brought before him. A huge oak gallows was erected just for the occasion. Parker kept his position, despite mounting criticism, for twenty-one years, working six days a week. He said of complaints, "If criticism is due, it should be [for] the system, not the man whose duty lies under it." By the end of his career, he had heard 13,940 cases, found 9,454 men guilty, and had sentenced 160 of them to death by hanging. Through his tireless efforts, organizational skills, and firm grasp of the law, Judge Parker brought a measure of peace to a difficult area and won for himself a reputation as the West's greatest judge.

Section Review

1–2. What two incentives did the federal government give the railroads to build a transcontinental line?
3–4. Name the two railroad companies that were given charters to build the first transcontinental railroad and the city from which each started.
5. What did the Homestead Act of 1862 provide?
★ Describe the opposing sides in the range wars. Explain which side you think was right.
★ Assess the accuracy of the term "Wild West."

II. Indian Affairs

One could wish that the story of the American West was one of unbroken triumph, of courageous settlers overcoming the obstacles they faced to build a new and better land. Unfortunately, the story has a dark side to it. As American settlers moved west, they clashed with the Indians, just as they had done since the days of the Jamestown colony in Virginia. This time the conflict would be the final, climactic struggle between white and Indian for control of the rest of the American continent.

Plains Indians

The Great Plains region was already inhabited when the settlers came. It was home to the **Plains Indians**, tribes such as the Cheyenne, the Comanche, and the **Sioux** (soo). These tribes came closer to the popular conception of Indians than did the eastern tribes. They lived in tepees, hunted buffalo on swift Indian ponies, and fought American cavalry with bows and arrows. Such superficial stereotypes, however, do not do justice to the complex culture of these people.

The key to the survival of the Plains Indians was the buffalo. The men of the tribes, riding on horses descended from those left by the Spanish centuries before, were the ones who usually hunted the buffalo that wandered in herds so huge that they blackened the Great Plains with their numbers. The Indians ate a great deal of buffalo meat, either fresh, in dried strips (jerky), or dried and mixed with berries (pemmican). Buffalo hides provided clothing, blankets, curtains, drumheads, tent coverings, and other necessities. Buffalo tendons provided bowstrings and the thread for sewing coverings together. Some Indians made dice out of buffalo bones for gambling. Even the dung of the buffalo was dried and burned as fuel in the treeless plains. Buffalo were so important to the Indians that during the Indian Wars the U.S. government quietly encouraged the slaughtering of the herds to rob the Indians of their means of livelihood. In 1867, an army colonel told a hunter, "Kill every buffalo you can. Every buffalo dead is an Indian gone." By 1900, the huge herds of the Great Plains had become nearly extinct. Some historians

Guiding Questions

1. What was the Plains Indians' way of life?
2. What were the major battles, and who were the leaders in the Indian Wars?
3. How did the federal government treat the American Indians?

The Bison

The American buffalo is more properly called a "bison." (A buffalo is native to Africa and Asia, whereas a bison is native to North America.) Experts estimate that thirty million or more bison inhabited the Great Plains when Europeans first came. The slaughter of the bison in the latter nineteenth century, however, reduced that massive number to a scant five hundred by 1900. Careful protection of the breed since that time has raised the number. Today more than three hundred thousand bison exist in the United States.

This painting is entitled The Last of the Buffalo *(detail).*

Railway passengers firing at herds of American buffalo, or bison

Chief Joseph Speaks

In the account below, Chief Joseph, one of the leaders of the Nez Perce, describes how white men erroneously claimed to own land belonging to his tribe.

> If we ever owned the land we own it still, for we never sold it. In the treaty councils the commissioners have claimed that our country had been sold to the Government. Suppose a white man should come to me and say, 'Joseph, I like your horses, and I want to buy them.' I say to him, 'No, my horses suit me, I will not sell them.' Then he goes to my neighbor, and says to him: 'Joseph has some good horses. I want to buy them, but he refuses to sell.' My neighbor answers, 'Pay me the money, and I will sell you Joseph's horses.' The white man returns to me, and says, 'Joseph, I have bought your horses, and you must let me have them.' If we sold our lands to the Government, this is the way they were bought.
>
> On account of the treaty made by the other bands of the Nez Perces, the white men claimed my lands. We were troubled greatly by white men crowding over the line. Some of these were good men, and we lived on peaceful terms with them, but they were not all good.

believe that the destruction of the buffalo was more important in the conquest of the Plains Indians than any military campaign.

Settlers soon learned that the Plains Indians were skilled warriors, dashing about on their horses and firing arrows almost as fast as a man could fire a repeating rifle. The Indians were hardy, independent fighters. One on one, few settlers could stand up to them. However, disunity among the tribes and the Indians' tendency to fight as individuals rather than as coordinated units kept them from overwhelming the soldiers they often faced.

The Plains Indians were also fiercely proud of their heritage, and they became increasingly protective of their lands as frontiersmen encroached on them. The Plains tribes did not intend simply to give their land away, and they soon learned—as other tribes had learned earlier—that the government's word was often worthless. Even when government officials intended to be fair, their lack of understanding of Indian culture sometimes caused them to make fatal errors. And even if one settler intended to abide by an agreement, other leaders could change the policy if it did not suit their desires. Whites never seemed to understand, for example, that few Indian chiefs had the authority to bind all of their people to a treaty—treaties that the chiefs themselves often did not understand. Misunderstanding, fueled by the greed of some, resulted in bloody conflict on the Great Plains.

Indian Wars

From the 1850s to the 1870s, the U.S. Army fought a series of campaigns against the Plains Indians. The army demonstrated a remarkable ability to underestimate its opponents. During the First Sioux War in the Wyoming-Montana region (1866–68), Captain William Fetterman bragged that with eighty men, he could ride through the entire Sioux nation. Ironically, Fetterman had exactly eighty men with him when he met a large Sioux war party near Fort Phil Kearny. There, he and all his troops were killed. As the conflict continued, the Sioux won every battle and forced the government to give them a treaty granting all of their demands. Unfortunately for the Indians, the government had little intention of honoring that treaty.

The goal of the Indian Wars for the American government was to force the tribes onto **reservations**, special tracts of land set aside for the Indians where they could theoretically live in peace. Some Americans undoubtedly thought this policy to be a means of helping and protecting the Indians. Many others, instead, viewed it as an opportunity to move the Indians out of the way so that they could seize rich Indian lands. The Indians, for their part, could see no reason for abandoning their tribal lands. Even some Indians who agreed to move to the reservations rebelled when they saw the poor quality of the reservation land. (The government tended to establish reservations on arid, barren land that was often useless.) Given the superior numbers and technology of the United States, the result of the Indian Wars was a foregone conclusion. However, because the Indians fought so courageously, it took long, hard fighting for the American army to emerge victorious.

The Sioux War

The climax of the Indian Wars is commonly known as the **Sioux War.** It occurred in 1876–77 and was also known as the

Second Sioux War or the Great Sioux War (to distinguish it from the conflict of 1866–68). The fame of this war lies partly in the fact that it was the last great Indian War and partly in the personalities involved: cavalry Colonel George Armstrong Custer and Indian leaders Sitting Bull and Crazy Horse.

Ohio-born **George Armstrong Custer** was a rash, dashing, and self-centered army officer. He had risen from the rank of lieutenant to major general during the Civil War as a result of his reckless daring and his constant efforts to impress his superiors. Reduced to the rank of colonel when the army shrank after the war, Custer became a renowned Indian fighter. Typical of his method was the Battle of the Washita (WASH uh tah) River (1868) in what is today Oklahoma. Coming upon an Indian camp on the banks of the river, Custer divided his force and attacked. The attack was a smashing success for the cavalry over the surprised Indians. It was later revealed that some of the Indians had been raiding white settlements, but Custer had not known that beforehand—nor did he care. To the impulsive Custer, the fact that they were Indians was enough.

During the 1870s, white settlers were overrunning Sioux lands so that they could mine gold in the Black Hills of the Dakota Territory. The U.S. Army failed to stop these prospectors. By 1876, the Sioux War was underway. Opposing Custer in the war were **Sitting Bull** and **Crazy Horse**. Although both men were Sioux chiefs, Sitting Bull was primarily a political leader of the Sioux forces. He provided moral inspiration to the Indians and led negotiations with the American government. Crazy Horse acted primarily as the commander of the Sioux warriors. Under Crazy Horse's leadership, the Sioux warriors fought one of the most unified, best-organized Indian campaigns in history.

The major battle of the Sioux War took place on June 25, 1876. Custer's cavalry regiment came upon a huge Indian camp on the banks of the Little Bighorn River in what is now Montana. Unknown to Custer, Sitting Bull and Crazy Horse had noted his approach and were prepared to meet him. Custer's scouts looked at the size of the camp and warned the colonel that the Sioux had more warriors than the soldiers had bullets. Custer brushed these warnings aside. As he had done at the Washita River eight years before, Custer divided his forces to attack the Indians from two

Crazy Horse Memorial in South Dakota

Brutal and Bloody

The Indian Wars were brutal, bloody affairs. Both sides committed horrible deeds and slaughtered without mercy. American settlers and Indians did not merely kill each other; sometimes they tortured the living and mutilated the dead, including the women and children of both sides. Frontiersmen called the Indians "savages," but the supposedly "civilized" white man proved hardly less brutal than his Indian counterpart.

Sitting Bull Speaks

One of the Sioux leaders, Sitting Bull, said:

> What treaty that the whites ever made with us red men have they kept? Not one. When I was a boy the Sioux owned the world. The sun rose and set in their lands.... They sent 10,000 horsemen to battle. Where are the warriors today? Who slew them? Where are our lands? Who owns them? What white man can say I ever stole his lands or a penny of his money? Yet they say I am a thief.
>
> What white woman, however lonely, was ever captive or insulted by me? Yet they say I am a bad Indian. What white man has ever seen me drunk? Who has ever come to me hungry and gone unfed? Who has ever seen me beat my wives or abuse my children? What law have I broken? Is it wrong for me to love my own? Is it wicked in me because my skin is red; because I am a Sioux; because I was born where my fathers lived; because I would die for my people and my country?

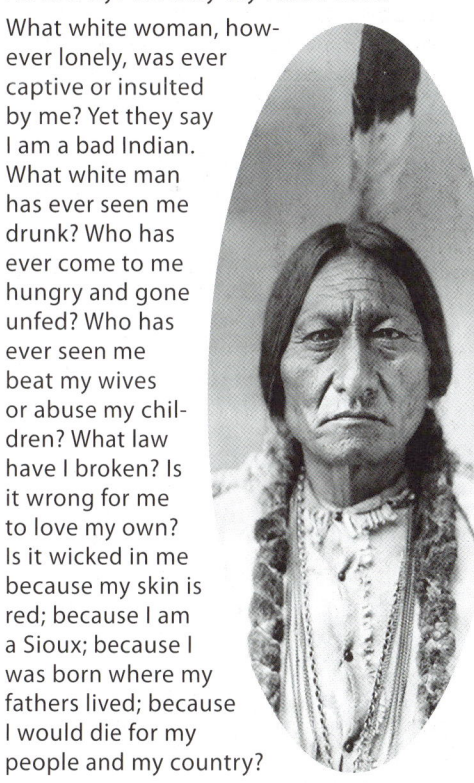

directions. One force, under Major Marcus Reno, attacked the camp head-on and was soon driven back with heavy losses. Even so, Reno's force was the fortunate one. Custer took some two hundred men and swept north of the Indian camp to launch what he thought would be a surprise attack. Instead, the Indians surprised Custer by fighting him with overwhelming numbers. Perhaps two thousand braves attacked the two hundred soldiers. Custer and all of his force lost their lives in the Battle of the Little Bighorn in less than an hour's time. That defeat became known as **Custer's Last Stand**.

This great Indian victory eventually worked to the advantage of the U.S. Army. Thinking that they had won the war, many Sioux left Sitting Bull's force. Shocked and sobered by the defeat, the U.S. government quickly sent more men and supplies west to defeat the Sioux. Within months of Custer's defeat, the army had forced the Indians to accept peace on the government's terms. Most Sioux went sadly to the reservations. Crazy Horse, after giving himself up, died in a scuffle with soldiers as they attempted to put him in a guardhouse. Sitting Bull fled to Canada for a time. He eventually returned to live on a reservation. In 1890, he was accused of encouraging Indians to rebel. The U.S. Indian agent, a government official in the area, ordered Indian police to arrest him. In doing so, a fight occurred. More than a dozen policemen and tribesmen were killed. Sitting Bull was among them.

Later Indian Affairs

The fate of the Sioux was typical of what happened to the tribes of the West. Some Indians still resisted the idea of living an impoverished life on the barren reservations. Some fought like the Apache leader Geronimo, who with a small band of Indians for several years frustrated the army's attempts to force them onto a reservation. He and his followers were finally captured. Others tried to escape. The Nez Perce (NEHZ PURS) leader Chief Joseph conducted a masterful campaign to save his tribal lands or at least lead his people to refuge in Canada, but he was forced to surrender in 1877.

Just two weeks after the death of Sitting Bull, Native American resistance came to a tragic end. On December 29, 1890, near Wounded Knee Creek in South Dakota, the army tried to disarm and capture a band of Sioux who had fled the reservation. In the

The Apache warrior Geronimo, using only small raiding parties, fought large numbers of U.S. cavalry before he finally surrendered.

Treatment of American Indians

In 1877, President Rutherford B. Hayes said, "Many, if not most, of our Indian wars have had their origin in broken promises and acts of injustice on our part."

In 1878, General Philip Sheridan commented, "We took away their country and their means of support, broke up their mode of living, their habits of life, introduced disease and decay among them, and it was for this and against this that they made war. Could anyone expect less?"

General Nelson A. Miles sent a telegram from South Dakota to Washington, D.C., on December 19, 1890. He described problems facing the Sioux, the Cheyenne, and other Indians in the area by stating, "The difficult Indian problem cannot be solved permanently at this end. . . . It requires the fulfillment of Congress of the treaty obligations that the Indians were entreated and coerced into signing. They signed away a valuable portion of their reservation, and it is now occupied by white people, for which they have received nothing.

"They understood that ample provision would be made for their support; instead, their supplies have been reduced, and much of the time they have been living on half and two-thirds rations. . . .

"The [dissatisfaction] is wide spread."

Chief Joseph, Man of War and Peace (1840–1904)

Of the Indians who fought against the U.S. Army in the nineteenth century, none won more sympathy among the American public than **Chief Joseph**, a leader of one of the bands of the Nez Perce tribe. He conducted a military campaign and march so brilliant that some newspapers compared him to Napoleon Bonaparte.

Chief Joseph and his tribe lived in the Wallowa Valley in what is now Idaho. In 1877, the government tried to force the Nez Perce onto a reservation. Joseph did not want to leave his land, but he hated war. He thought that the tribe must submit or risk destruction at the hands of the army. While he was trying to organize his people for the move, a handful of young warriors attacked and killed some white settlers. With little hope of peace now, Joseph prepared to flee and—if necessary—to fight.

Joseph took his people east, eventually deciding to escape to Canada, where Sitting Bull and his Sioux were already living. In 108 days, Joseph marched more than 700 Indians—most of them women, children, and old men—nearly 1,400 miles. In eight separate battles and skirmishes, the Nez Perce defeated contingents of four separate cavalry units.

Joseph refused to fight a savage war, however. He forbade the killing of women and children and the taking of scalps from the dead. He simply wanted to get his tribe to a place where they could live in peace. Americans followed with interest the newspaper reports describing his trek through the mountains and how he seemed to be outwitting and baffling the army at every turn.

Finally, on September 30, 1877, the U.S. cavalry, led by General Oliver O. Howard, former head of the Freedmen's Bureau, overtook Joseph's band just forty miles from the Canadian border. Outnumbered and numbed by a chilling cold, Chief Joseph surrendered. A young lieutenant present wrote that the chieftain said, "It is cold and we have no blankets. The little children are freezing to death. . . . I am tired; my heart is sick and sad. From where the sun now stands, I will fight no more forever."

Joseph was eventually settled on a reservation in Washington State. He died there on September 21, 1904. A doctor on the reservation said, "Joseph died of a broken heart."

---

process, someone fired a shot. Versions of the story vary, and it is still unclear who did so. Fighting quickly began. When it was over, 25 soldiers and more than 150 Indians (half of them women and children) were dead. The **Wounded Knee massacre** was a horrific conclusion to the Indian Wars.

In 1881, Helen Hunt Jackson published *A Century of Dishonor*, a work portraying the government's ruthless and often dishonorable dealings with the Indians. Jackson's book, combined with the decreasing threat of the Plains Indians, inspired some belated sympathy for the Indians' plight. In 1887, Congress tried to undo some of the damage by passing the **Dawes Act**, which allowed Indian lands to be parceled out to individual Indian families to use and develop as they liked. Unfortunately, the act tended to break down the unity of the tribes, and many unhappy Indians sold their allotted lands to whites and were soon more impoverished than before.

In the twentieth century, the U.S. government tried to remedy some of the wrongs done to the Indians. In 1924, Congress gave Indians full citizenship. In 1934, to preserve the remaining Indian lands, the Indian Reorganization Act halted the allotment program of the Dawes Act and gave the reservations limited self-government. Congress also made it easier for Indians to seek damages for past

Indians killed at Wounded Knee, South Dakota

violations of treaties and other agreements. These acts, however, were far too little considering the injustices done to the Indians.

Section Review

1. What was the goal of the American government in its military campaigns against the Indians?
2-4. Who was the most famous cavalry officer of the Sioux War of 1876-77? Which two chiefs were his main opponents?
5. Why did the great Indian victory at the Little Bighorn work to the advantage of the U.S. Army?
★ How do you think the conflict with the Indians might have been settled peacefully?
★ Analyze the events at Wounded Knee, South Dakota, on December 29, 1890. What is your opinion of the events?

III. International Expansion

After reaching the Pacific Ocean at the conclusion of the Mexican War (1848), the United States sought new lands to annex. The sectional conflict climaxing in the Civil War postponed most thoughts of overseas expansion, but then a surge of economic and political growth occurred. American foreign policy-makers in the last half of the nineteenth century pursued three main goals: (1) to defend the Western Hemisphere from intervention by European powers while maintaining good relations with Europe, (2) to create new economic opportunities for American trade with other countries, and (3) to extend the territory of the United States through purchase, annexation, or conquest.

Building and Mending Fences

France in Mexico

During the Civil War, France mounted one of the most serious challenges to the Monroe Doctrine in American history. France, Great Britain, and Spain sent soldiers to Mexico in the 1860s, supposedly to force Mexico to repay its debts to those nations. After Mexico repaid the debts, the British and Spanish withdrew their troops while the French remained.

Taking advantage of the distractions of the war, Napoleon III (nephew of Napoleon Bonaparte and ruler of France) installed the Austrian nobleman **Maximilian I** as the Mexican ruler in 1864. Napoleon III ignored American protests, particularly since the United States government was far too busy to do anything about it. After the Civil War, however, the United States stationed 50,000 veteran troops by the Rio Grande. Secretary of State William Seward then gave Napoleon an ultimatum to withdraw the French soldiers he had sent to Mexico. The French, worried by the troops and plagued by troubles in Europe, quietly withdrew. Maximilian lost the support of the French, and a Mexican firing squad executed him in 1867. The United States had successfully met one challenge.

Treaty of Washington

After its confrontation with France, the United States sought to settle three longstanding differences with Great Britain. First, the United States sought compensation for the damages its mer-

---

Guiding Questions

1. What were the main goals of American foreign policy in the last half of the nineteenth century?
2. What imperialistic methods did the United States use to acquire territory?
3. How did the North American foreign missions movement expand during this period?
4. What were the motives for and results of the Spanish-American War?

chant fleet had suffered from commerce raiders during the Civil War. Second, the United States and Britain had been arguing since the 1840s over who owned a group of islands between Vancouver Island and the state of Washington. Third, the United States and Canada had long disagreed over fishing rights off the coasts of North America.

The **Treaty of Washington** (1871) settled these matters by setting up international tribunals to deal with each question. One tribunal awarded the United States more than $15 million in damages from Britain in payment for the destruction caused by the commerce raiders. Another tribunal awarded possession of the islands off Vancouver to the United States. A third required the United States to pay Canada more than $5 million for special fishing privileges. The importance of the treaty was not simply in settling these individual questions; it also paved the way for greater friendship and cooperation between the United States, Britain, and Canada.

Economic Expansion

Because of improvements in transportation and technology, the United States was able by the mid-1800s to produce more goods—food, raw materials, and manufactured products—than it could use. The nation therefore sought more foreign markets in which to sell its goods.

Perry in Japan (1854)

The California gold rush and the acquisition of Mexican territories after the Mexican War had established America as a potential Pacific power and had made increased trade with Asia a major American goal. However, Japan, one of the main powers in Asia, had virtually isolated itself from the rest of the world for some two hundred years. Hoping to open a door for trade, the United States government commissioned Commodore **Matthew Perry** to take a small squadron of warships to Japan and to negotiate with Japan's rulers in 1853. Perry's four warships awed and intimidated the Japanese. They had never seen steamships. Despite opposition by many in his government, the Japanese ruler agreed to the Treaty of Kanagawa (1854). He realized Japan could not resist modern weapons.

The agreement, which the United States had essentially forced Japan to sign, opened some Japanese ports to American trade. It was also a major step in allowing western influences in the country. The Japanese soon adopted Western technology and began to industrialize. By the 1890s, they had a powerful navy and had begun to expand their territory.

Pan-Americanism

After the Civil War, the United States resumed its push for new markets abroad. One obvious potential market was Latin America. The nations south of the Rio Grande, although rich in raw materials and some foodstuffs, had little industry. The United States hoped to increase inter-American trade and decrease Latin American trade with Europe.

James G. Blaine, secretary of state during the administrations of three presidents, was a major promoter of closer relations with Latin America. He advocated **Pan-Americanism**, a movement favoring greater cooperation and unity among the nations of the Western Hemisphere. Blaine hoped to create economic unity by

Commerce Raiders
Commerce raiders were warships owned and commanded by the Confederates but built in British shipyards. The American government believed that Britain was partly responsible for the damage caused by these raiders.

Commodore Matthew Perry

A U.S. Navy squadron, commanded by Perry, visited Japan in 1853.

Uncle Sam (saying, "I'm out for commerce, not conquest!") holds back the great powers of Europe in this *Harper's Weekly* cartoon supporting the idea of free trade in China.

American troops marching in China during the Boxer Rebellion.

First Steps Toward Imperialism

While Americans had been defending and expanding their borders, the powers of Europe had been building empires. The Germans, Dutch, French, and British had established colonies around the world. The British could boast that their empire was so extensive that the sun never set on it. In that context, America was poised to take on a relatively minimal involvement in imperialism, but the consequences would be extensive.

reducing trade barriers such as tariffs among the nations. Blaine and others even dreamed of creating a loose political confederation of American nations, which the United States would dominate. With some delight, then, Blaine hosted delegates from Latin American countries at the First Pan-American Congress in 1889, but the meeting was not a resounding success. The southern nations feared political and economic domination by the United States, and most could not forget past offenses, such as the Mexican War. Furthermore, the secretary of state's own Republican Party was wary of lowering tariffs. The meeting did at least provide a precedent for further discussion and friendlier relations as the years passed.

An Open Door in China

Although the United States pioneered efforts to open Japan for trade, it found itself in the middle of intense competition when attempting to trade with China, another major nation in Asia. Each European power, along with Japan, was attempting to set up "spheres of influence" in China, regions where one foreign nation could dominate Chinese trade. Some diplomats even talked of carving up China into colonies. Because the United States was interested only in trading in China, it did not want to send a military force to establish a colony. Therefore, in 1899 Secretary of State John Hay proposed the **Open Door Policy**. Hay's policy called for all nations trading in China to refrain from interfering with one another and to allow free trade in China. Although the United States could do little to enforce such a policy, the idea fit well with what some European powers—notably Great Britain—already wanted to do in China. Because the policy suited the inclinations of the major powers, it succeeded.

Hay nearly saw his open door close as soon as it had opened. The Chinese resented attempts by foreign powers to determine the future of their country. In 1900, an antiforeign movement, the **Boxer Rebellion**, erupted in China. (The name "Boxer" comes from a leading organization in the rebellion, "the Society of Righteous and Harmonious Fists.") Chinese rioters destroyed anything foreign. Boxers killed missionaries, diplomats, foreign merchants, and Chinese converts to Christianity (which Boxers considered a "foreign" religion). They wanted foreigners and foreign influence expelled from the nation. An international military force intervened to protect foreigners in China. Among the 20,000 soldiers sent by several European nations, Japan, and the U.S. were approximately 2,500 Americans. The Boxer Rebellion was crushed.

The peace terms imposed by the victors were harsh. Secretary Hay opposed dividing China among the victors. He and British diplomats persuaded the other nations to accept payments from the Chinese rather than insist on territorial concessions. The nations involved accepted Hay's proposal. The payments totaled $333 million; the United States was promised $25 million, but Congress reduced that amount and sent what it did collect back to China with the understanding that the money would be used to educate Chinese students in America. American efforts to help China, although not free from self-interest, helped improve feelings between the two countries.

Territorial Expansion: Imperialism

As the events in China demonstrated, the nineteenth century was the great century of **imperialism**, the extension of power by one people or country over another people or country. An imperialist nation might acquire territory by purchase, annexation, or conquest.

The negative effects of imperialism were numerous. Imperialism usually meant the exploitation of weaker nations by the stronger nations. The weaker nation often lost its land, its independence, and sometimes its national identity. The economy was usually restructured to benefit those now in control. Many times, the invaders were quick to claim their own superiority.

However, imperialism sometimes brought improvements. Better medical treatment, development of natural resources, and improvements in education often came in the wake of imperial conquest. In addition, better roads, bridges, and railroads were usually constructed. Missionaries took the gospel to people who had never heard of Jesus Christ.

Seward's Folly

The single largest American acquisition after the Civil War was the **purchase of Alaska** from Russia in 1867. When Secretary of State William Seward announced the purchase, many Americans—believing Alaska to be only an empty wasteland of snow and ice—called the area "Seward's Folly" or "Seward's Icebox." Still, at a cost of only $7.2 million (less than two cents an acre), Alaska seemed a bargain, and the treaty of purchase passed the Senate easily.

Within a few years, Alaska had proved its value to the United States. First gold and then oil were discovered in the region, making it a source of enormous wealth. Furthermore, the rise of the Soviet Union in the twentieth century and its proximity to Alaska increased the value of military bases in Alaska. It vindicated the wisdom of those who wanted to take the region out of Russian hands. "Seward's Folly" proved to be a very shrewd bargain indeed. In 1959, it became the forty-ninth state.

Pacific Expansion

Trade with Japan and China was not America's only interest in the Pacific in the last half of the nineteenth century. The United States also began building a Pacific empire. Many of the areas gained would serve as bases for America's navy. The United States, for example, simply annexed (took control of) the Midway Islands in 1867. The unoccupied islands received the name because they were approximately halfway between North America and Asia.

The most important Pacific addition to the United States was **Hawaii** (also known as the Sandwich Islands). The Hawaiian Islands had been an important supply point for whalers, merchant ships, and warships since the 1700s. In the early 1800s, American missionaries had come to the islands and had enjoyed remarkable success in winning many islanders to Christ. Unfortunately, many Americans who followed the missionaries—and sadly, many sons of the missionaries—proved more interested in profits than in souls. American businessmen soon built a thriving sugar industry that dominated the economy of the islands and, indeed, helped the islands to prosper.

Until 1891, Hawaii was ruled by native kings who usually followed the businessmen's wishes. In that year, Queen Liliuokalani (lee LEE oo oh kah LAH nee) took the throne. She tried to reestablish native control of the island and limit the power of the Americans. In 1893, the business owners revolted against "Queen

In this Thomas Nast cartoon, William Seward is portrayed as a mother patting the head of her child—Andrew Johnson. Johnson was president when Alaska was purchased.

American Samoa

In 1889, the United States joined Britain and Germany in a joint protectorate of the Samoan islands. Disagreements among the three nations, however, led to the division of the islands. The United States formed the eastern islands into the U.S. territory of American Samoa.

Queen Liliuokalani

Sanford Dole

Lottie Moon was a missionary to China.

Lil." With the help of U.S. Marines, she was overthrown. The U.S. ambassador to Hawaii, who had supported the overthrow, reported to the U.S. secretary of state, "The Hawaiian pear is now fully ripe, and it is the golden hour for the United States to pluck it." The new government, led by Sanford Dole, asked to be annexed to the United States. President Grover Cleveland, however, refused to approve the uprising and blocked annexation of the islands. Like Texas after its war for independence, Hawaii was forced to exist for several years as an independent country. During its years as an independent nation, Dole served as president. He was the son of missionaries in Hawaii. His cousin established a pineapple business there known as Dole Food Company. It still exists today.

In 1898 when McKinley was president and a war with Spain was making the United States nervous about the security of the Pacific, Congress voted to annex the islands. Hawaii became an American territory. In 1959, it became the fiftieth state.

Missions

As noted earlier, one of the results of imperialism was a growth in opportunities for Christian missions. Some historians criticize missionaries as "agents of imperialism" who secretly made colonies for their homelands under the cloak of preaching the gospel. Actually, the opposite was often true. For example, Hiram Bingham, one of the first Congregationalist missionaries to go to Hawaii in 1820, clashed with Americans and others who were determined to exploit the Hawaiians. When Bingham helped end prostitution among the native women, outraged white sailors armed with knives and clubs assaulted him.

Missionaries went to all corners of the globe in the nineteenth century. One nation that attracted many was China, where Methodists took an early lead in establishing American gospel outposts. The most prominent North American leaders in Chinese work in the late nineteenth and early twentieth centuries were not from the United States but from Canada: Jonathan Goforth and his wife, Rosalind. Together, they faithfully preached to the Chinese despite major difficulties, such as the Boxer Rebellion. Another hero of Chinese missions was Lottie Moon, an American. She bravely traveled into the dangerous interior of China to minister to the Chinese people. She did more to arouse enthusiasm among Baptists for missions than anyone else since Adoniram Judson.

The latter part of the nineteenth century also saw the growth of a new kind of mission board. Up to this time, most mission boards had been tied directly to a major denomination. The denomination collected money from its member churches and, in turn, paid salaries to the missionaries so that they could continue their work. Faith missions, on the other hand, are usually independent mission boards that have no guaranteed income. Even today missionaries under "faith boards" go on "deputation" to visit local churches directly and solicit support for their work. One of the first faith mission boards in America was the Christian and Missionary Alliance (C&MA), founded by A. B. Simpson in 1887. The C&MA grew so much that it eventually became an independent denomination. Most faith missions focused on one region of the world. One example was the Central American Mission, founded in 1890 by C. I.

The Student Volunteer Movement

One of the most important movements in foreign missions was the Student Volunteer Movement (SVM). This organization began in 1886 at a Bible conference in Massachusetts hosted by D. L. Moody. Spurred by an appeal to consider foreign missions, one hundred college students pledged themselves to become missionaries. Taking as its motto "The evangelization of the world in this generation," the SVM grew rapidly. It is credited with ultimately sending twenty thousand missionaries to the mission field.

Scofield, a Congregationalist pastor in Dallas and later the editor of a famous reference Bible.

Whether American missionaries ministered under a denominational or a faith board, most labored loyally and diligently throughout the world. Some suffered martyrdom; thirty-five C&MA missionaries and their children, for example, died in the Boxer Rebellion. Because of the sacrificial labors by so many brave and faithful missionaries, many came to find Jesus Christ as their Savior.

Height of Imperialism: Spanish-American War

The height of American imperialism came in 1898, when the United States went to war with Spain in a conflict involving the Spanish colony of Cuba. Although the Cubans had periodically revolted against the Spanish government for decades, the revolt that occurred in 1895 was unusually serious. A depression with its resulting unemployment—combined with weak, corrupt Spanish rule over the colony—provided ideal conditions for an insurrection. Bands of guerrillas destroyed sugar mills, plantations, and anything else the people loyal to Spain valued. To stop the destruction, Spanish troops arrested rebels and put them in barbed-wire concentration camps, where many of them died of starvation or disease. As American newspapers sensationalized the brutal Spanish treatment of the rebels, American sympathy for the Cubans began to grow.

Causes

Sympathy alone, however, was not enough to push the United States into war. Three other factors fanned American hatred of Spain and hastened the war: (1) yellow journalism, (2) the de Lôme letter, and (3) the sinking of the USS *Maine*.

"**Yellow journalism**" is sensationalized news reporting aimed more at attracting readers than at reporting the truth. Two of the leading "yellow journals" were William Randolph Hearst's *New York Journal* and Joseph Pulitzer's *New York World*. Each paper attempted to outdo the other in reporting shocking stories that would boost sales. Hearst, for example, paid a famous illustrator, Frederic Remington, to go to Cuba to draw sketches of the revolt. When Remington arrived in Cuba and reported that conditions were not bad enough to warrant U.S. intervention, Hearst reportedly replied, "You furnish the pictures and I'll furnish the war."

American public opinion, inflamed by yellow journalism, began to favor war with Spain to establish Cuba's independence. In spite of journalistic propaganda, President McKinley intended to avoid hostilities. The situation was actually improving, and the Spanish government was willing to meet McKinley's demands for better treatment of the Cubans when two incidents gave those who supported the war new reasons to demand military action.

First, on February 9, 1898, the *New York Journal* published a stolen letter written by the Spanish ambassador in Washington, Enrique Dupuy de Lôme. In the **de Lôme letter**, as it came to be known, the ambassador denounced McKinley as, among other things, "weak and a bidder for the admiration of the crowd." This was hardly strong language. Assistant Secretary of the Navy Theodore Roosevelt, for instance, allegedly described McKinley as having "no more backbone than a chocolate eclair." Roosevelt, however, was an American citizen, whereas de Lôme was the representative

---

American Army Not Prepared

The American army was not nearly as well prepared as the navy. The army had done little to arrange for transporting and supplying troops. Many soldiers had to fight in the steaming jungles of Cuba dressed in heavy wool uniforms designed for winter campaigns against the Indians. In fact, the regular army had only 26,000 men at the outbreak of the war, but Congress voted to raise several volunteer regiments.

The USS *Maine* exploded in the Havana, Cuba, harbor in February 1898.

Newspaper reporting the sinking of the USS *Maine*

of a foreign country. Americans were outraged at the insult to their president. De Lôme resigned and the Spanish government apologized; despite this, Spanish-American relations worsened.

A second incident was even more damaging. The battleship *Maine* had been sent to Havana Harbor in Cuba in January 1898 to protect American interests on the island. On February 15, the *Maine* exploded and sank in the harbor, killing 260 Americans. An investigation at that time by the American government claimed that a mine had sunk the *Maine*. Actually, no one knows precisely what happened to the *Maine*. A careful study of the evidence by two American naval engineers in 1975, for example, concluded that the explosion resulted from an accident *inside* the ship, in the ship's coal bunkers. Yet, a 1998 analysis stated a mine might have caused the explosion.

Of course, the Spanish had no reason to destroy the battleship. But Americans believed what they *wanted* to believe and what the yellow press told them—that the explosion occurred outside the ship and was an act of Spanish treachery.

McKinley caved to political pressure and sent a war message to Congress in April 1898. Congress demanded Spain's withdrawal from Cuba and authorized the president to use force, if necessary, to establish Cuba's independence. Spain refused. As a result, the **Spanish-American War** began on April 20, 1898.

Manila Bay

The United States Navy was a powerful, modern fleet and was reasonably well prepared for war. Ironically, the war over the Caribbean island of Cuba

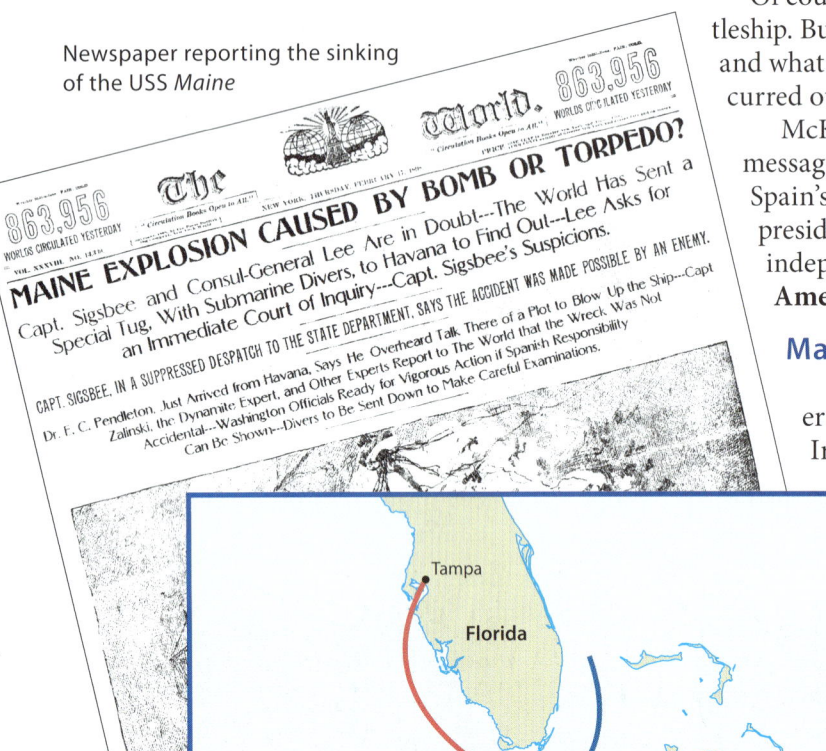

The Spanish-American War: Caribbean Theater—1898

started in the Pacific Ocean, where one of Spain's major fleets was located. America's Pacific fleet, under Commodore **George Dewey**, left Hong Kong on May 1, 1898, and fought the Spanish fleet in Manila Bay, the main harbor of the Spanish-controlled Philippine Islands. The Americans wrecked the outdated Spanish fleet, sank eight ships, and killed or wounded almost 400. American losses were slight—one warship damaged, one sailor killed (of heatstroke), and nine others wounded. The **Battle of Manila Bay** destroyed Spanish sea power in the Pacific and left the Philippines in the hands of the United States.

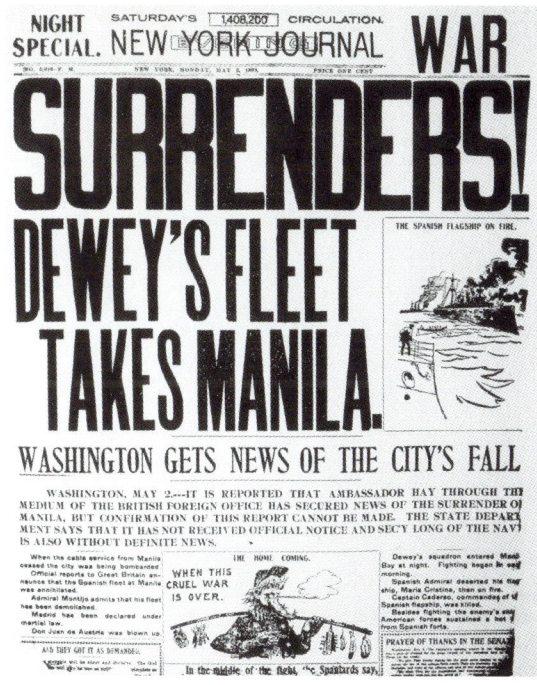

Santiago

On May 19, Spain's Atlantic fleet entered Santiago Harbor in Cuba. The American fleet quickly blockaded the harbor, and the U.S. government decided to send the army into Cuba to capture Santiago and force out the Spanish fleet. In late June, 17,000 American soldiers landed in Cuba. In a series of sharp battles, the Americans pushed back the dispirited Spaniards and encircled the city.

The most famous battle there was probably the Battle of San Juan Hill. Theodore Roosevelt and his **Rough Riders** helped storm the Spanish fortifications. Roosevelt had resigned his position as Assistant Secretary of the Navy to fight in the war. (Ironically, Roosevelt was the only Rough Rider with a horse. The others fought on foot because their horses were still in Florida.) The Rough Riders were volunteers which included cowboys, miners, college students, and adventurers from the West. They were commanded by Colonel Leonard Wood and Roosevelt, a lieutenant colonel.

On July 3, the Spanish fleet tried to escape. The resulting **Battle of Santiago Bay** was similar to Manila Bay. The American fleet suffered three warships damaged, one sailor killed, and ten others wounded. The Spanish, however, had three ships sunk, three ships run aground, and 474 sailors killed or wounded. The city of Santiago surrendered on July 17. Shortly thereafter, American forces captured the island of Puerto Rico, and the Spanish called for peace.

This May 1898 newspaper reports Commodore George Dewey's victory in Manila.

Aftermath

An American diplomat called the Spanish-American conflict "a splendid little war." Years later, Theodore Roosevelt said, "It wasn't much of a war, but it was the best war we had."

The Spanish-American War was indeed a "little war" in many ways. It lasted only four months, and fewer than 400 Americans died in battle. (Almost ten times that number died of disease either in Cuba or in unsanitary camps in the United States.) The results of the war, though, were anything but little.

At the beginning of the war, Congress had passed an amendment to a bill proclaiming that the United States wanted no territory in Cuba. That did not stop the U.S., however, from taking Puerto Rico, Guam, and the Philippines during the war (although America paid the Spanish $20 million for the Philippines). Furthermore, the United States virtually ruled Cuba for several years after the war. As mentioned earlier, the panic caused by the outbreak of

Rough Riders with Theodore Roosevelt

"Well, I hardly know which to take first", says Uncle Sam to "waiter" William McKinley as he views the "expansionist menu" in this 1898 cartoon from the *Boston Globe*.

the war had hastened American annexation of Hawaii. The United States was now widely recognized as a world power and had an empire of its own.

But the nation soon found that empires can be extremely costly. For the first time in its history, the United States had to maintain a large peacetime standing army and navy to protect the newly annexed areas. It also found that not all of the peoples liberated from Spain were eager to exchange Spanish control for American control. In the Philippines in 1899, Emilio Aguinaldo (ay-MEE-lee-oh ah-gee-NAHL-doh), a revolutionary who had aided the United States against the Spanish, led an insurrection (or rebellion) to overthrow the Americans and establish Philippine independence. He believed that after the Spanish were overthrown, the Filipinos would receive independence. He strongly opposed merely exchanging control by the Spanish for control by the Americans. For two years, the United States conducted a campaign in the islands that was costlier and far more difficult than the Spanish-American War. The revolt was finally suppressed. The war and the resulting acquisition of distant islands of which many Americans knew little challenged the United States' traditional foreign policy of isolation.

When the 1900 presidential election took place, the Democrats, once again headed by William Jennings Bryan, tried to make the election a referendum on American imperialism, which Bryan opposed. The Republicans embraced imperialism, renominating McKinley and enlisting "rough-riding" Theodore Roosevelt as their vice-presidential candidate. That ticket won an electoral landslide over Bryan and the Democrats. At the dawn of the twentieth century, America—burgeoning, energetic, and continental—was moving toward prominent leadership in the world.

Section Review

1. What was the most serious challenge to the Monroe Doctrine during this era?
2. What event almost ended John Hay's Open Door Policy for China?
3. What is the difference between a denominational mission board and a faith mission board?

4–6. What three factors hastened the United States toward war with Spain?

7. What was the central issue of the presidential election of 1900?

8–9. Who were the two leading candidates in the 1900 election? Where did each stand on the central issue of the campaign?

★ Assess news reporting during this period.

★ Contrast the political aims of imperialism and the religious aims of missions during this time.

CHAPTER 17 REVIEW

Making Connections

1. What method of transportation was most important in the development of the American West in the nineteenth century?
2–3. Name at least two actions that the United States government took in the twentieth century to alleviate the plight of the American Indians.
4–6. What were the three major goals of American foreign policy in the last half of the nineteenth century?
7. What event indirectly caused the United States to hasten to annex Hawaii?

Developing History Skills

1–4. Explain the four factors that caused the end of the open-range cattle industry.
5–7. Describe the three methods by which an imperialist nation might acquire territory. Which one of these do you think is the least ethical? Why?

Thinking Critically

1. Do you think that the Spanish-American War was justified? Why or why not?
2. In what ways are the methods of yellow journalism a tendency among some people involved in media today?

Living as a Christian Citizen

1. If you were a Christian congressman during this period of American history, what legislation would you propose to govern Indian affairs?
2. Describe your response to imperialism as if you were a missionary in this period.

People, Places, and Things to Remember

transcontinental railroad
Union Pacific
Central Pacific
Pikes Peak gold rush
Comstock Lode
cattle drive
cowboys
open ranges
Homestead Act
Oklahoma land rushes
Great Plains
soddies
barbed wire
Plains Indians
Sioux
reservations
Sioux War (1876–77)
George Armstrong Custer
Sitting Bull
Crazy Horse
Custer's Last Stand
Chief Joseph
Wounded Knee massacre
A Century of Dishonor
Dawes Act
Maximilian I
Treaty of Washington
Matthew Perry
Pan-Americanism
Open Door Policy
Boxer Rebellion
imperialism
purchase of Alaska
Hawaii
yellow journalism
de Lôme letter
USS *Maine*
Spanish-American War (1898)
George Dewey
Battle of Manila Bay
Rough Riders
Battle of Santiago Bay

18 THE PROGRESSIVE ERA (1890–1920)

> The object of government is the welfare of the people.
>
> **Theodore Roosevelt**
> August 1910

A milestone in history captured on film: Wilbur Wright watches as his brother Orville pilots their plane on its historic first flight.

Big Ideas

1. What were the origins of progressivism?
2. What attempts were made to make state and local politics more democratic?
3. How did progressivism affect everyday life in America?

I. Progressive Movement

II. Progressive Politics

III. Progressive Society

IV. Progressivism Evaluated

On September 6, 1901, President William McKinley hosted a public reception at the Pan-American Exposition in Buffalo, New York. In the Exposition's Temple of Music, the president stood in a receiving line greeting the well-wishers who filed past him. McKinley smiled, shook hands, and murmured pleasantries. One tall, thin young man in the line wore what looked like a white bandage on his right hand. Kindheartedly, McKinley stretched out his left hand toward the man's unbandaged hand. The young man, however, pushed the president's outstretched hand aside, and from the "bandage" came the sharp bang of a pistol. Two shots struck the astonished president. As guards and bystanders swarmed over the assailant, the wounded president said pitifully, "Don't let them hurt him."

Doctors could not locate the bullet that was lodged in the president's body, and infection set in. Eight days later, President McKinley died. Unknown to the doctors, in the room next to McKinley was a new invention that might have located the bullet and saved his life—an x-ray machine.

For the third time, the nation's president had been assassinated. Vice President Theodore Roosevelt took office as the nation's twenty-sixth president. The change was more than a simple switch in personnel. Two presidents of the same party could hardly have been more different. McKinley was quiet, reserved, and sedate; Roosevelt was energetic, active, and outgoing. At age forty-two, he was the youngest person ever to become president. Furthermore, McKinley was a political conservative, a cautious man who favored the tried-and-true Republican policy of supporting "big business" and advocating "little government." Roosevelt was a political progressive, an aggressive man who favored a vigorous, active government. With Roosevelt's presidency, Americans entered what historians call the Progressive Era of United States history.

These newspapers report the shooting and death of President McKinley.

I. Progressive Movement

Definition

Progressivism was a movement of the late nineteenth and early twentieth centuries that favored achieving political and social reform through education, wider political participation, and direct government action. It had its roots in several nineteenth-century movements. Some progressives, such as William Jennings Bryan, had been supporters of Populism. A few were outright Socialists. Still others were from the ranks of pro-reform Republican groups such as the Half-breeds and the Mugwumps. Many people in the movement were members of the middle and upper classes who were upset by the abuses of some industrialists, by corruption in government, and by the plight of the poor. Today, most people who identify themselves as progressives are classified as political "liberals." However, the progressivism of this time period included people with varying political ideas—liberals, conservatives, and moderates.

Progressivism represented a shift in thought by many leading Americans. In the nineteenth century, religious leaders often held influential positions in American colleges. By the progressive era, they were being replaced by scientists and social scientists. As institutions of higher learning became less spiritual, they influenced many American leaders to become more secular in their thinking.

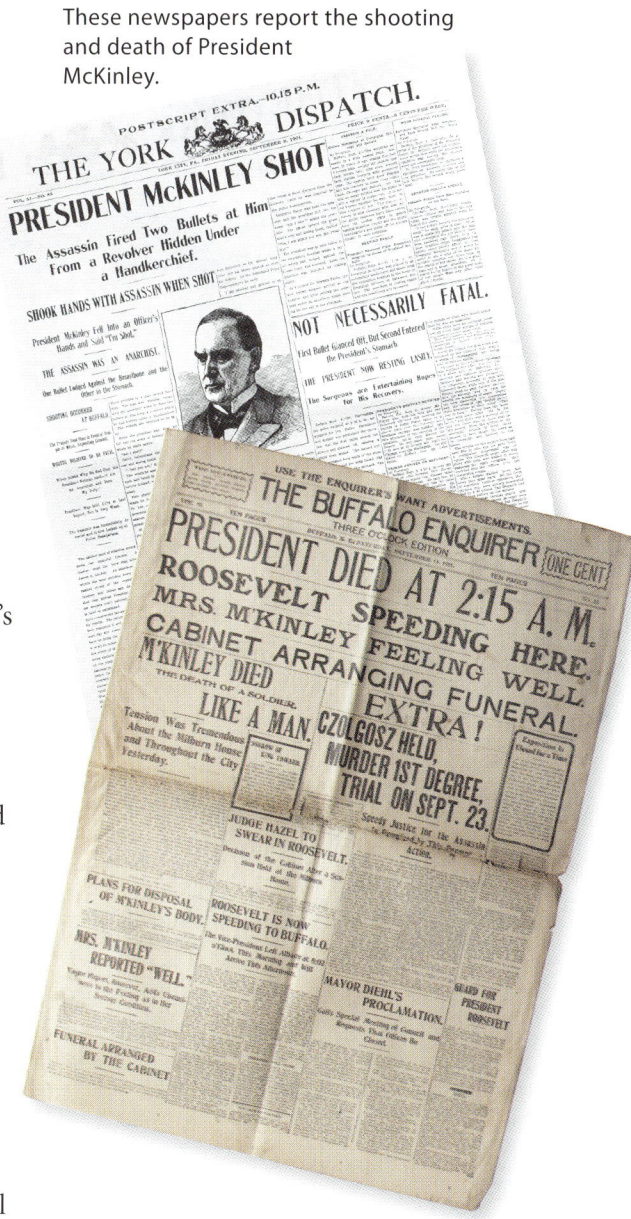

Guiding Questions

1. What was the progressive movement?
2. What progressive principles and reforms were advanced by progressive leaders?
3. What four progressive amendments were added to the Constitution?
4. Who were the muckrakers and the major political leaders of progressivism?

Progressivism was not a single organized movement. It was a collection of people and ideas. Sometimes supporters disagreed about which changes needed to be made, and they differed regarding how best to implement change. However, they all advocated reform.

The progressives' motives varied. Many of them were simply moral Americans whose sense of justice was outraged. They looked at the abuses and corruption around them and concluded that something had to be done. Some of the progressives, however, operated from an evolutionary point of view. In their view, because man supposedly had been evolving and improving from a lower form of life to a higher form, he should continue to improve and progress. To these Reform Darwinists (see Chapter 16), progress was a process of the natural order that could be aided by government intervention. Some Christians strongly opposed the unbiblical evolutionary view of progress but still supported progressive reforms. For these believers, reform was an "opportunity . . . [to] do good unto all men" (Gal. 6:10).

Principles

The progressive movement was a broad coalition of diverse interests. Generally, the progressives favored reform through (1) promoting direct democracy, (2) increasing government efficiency, and (3) advocating government intervention.

Direct Democracy

For progressives, as historian George Tindall noted, "the cure for the ills of democracy was more democracy." Partly because many had faith in the basic goodness of man, progressives believed that direct democracy or placing power in the hands of the people would naturally result in better government. William Jennings Bryan said that he favored "anything that makes the government more democratic, more popular in form, anything that gives the people more control over government."

Progressives tried to further the growth of democracy through several specific reforms. They favored the **secret ballot** for elections. Before this time, Americans had to indicate publicly which candidate they preferred as they voted. For example, they would have to request a certain ballot for their candidate or sign their names on a list for the candidate. Such a system allowed unethical political bosses to intimidate voters who favored the "wrong" candidate. The secret ballot reduced the possibility of influencing voters and also frustrated corrupt politicians who now could never be sure whether the votes they "bought" through bribery were actually cast.

Progressives also wanted to replace the nomination of candidates by party conventions and caucuses with **direct primaries**, nominating a party's candidates by popular vote. In theory, the direct primary took power from party bosses and gave it directly to the people. Progressives also called for greater popular participation in legislation through the initiative and the referendum. **Initiative** is a process in which voters initiate legislation by presenting to their legislature petitions that require the legislators to consider some action. A **referendum** allows the people to vote yes

America's burgeoning cities, typified by this scene from Mulberry Street on New York's Lower East Side, presented numerous challenges to the nation at the turn of the century.

or no in a regular election to determine whether a law should be enacted or rejected. Closely related to these two processes is **recall**, in which voters petition to hold a special election to decide whether to remove an elected official from office. Voters can also vote to recall (repeal) specific legislation or in some cases judicial decisions. Although the national government accepted none of these innovations except the secret ballot, many state and city governments embraced them.

Government Efficiency

Progressives sought to make government more efficient by putting qualified technical experts in positions of responsibility. City governments showed the greatest zeal for such improvements. Some cities abandoned rule by an elected mayor and city council and adopted the city commission form of government. This plan divided city government into several departments, each one under an expert commissioner's control. Other cities adopted the city manager form of government, under which the city council hired a qualified city manager who served as the administrator of the city government.

The emphasis on technical experts grew from the increased trust in social scientists to address difficult problems. Progressives thought experts would be guided by impartial science and would therefore develop the best policies. Yet with hindsight, experts could not provide the answers to all of society's problems. While relying on specially trained individuals was often beneficial, it was not a solution for all difficulties.

Government Intervention

The progressives strongly believed that they could best achieve reform by direct government action or government intervention. However, they did not always agree about which action to take. For instance, progressives were united in attacking the alleged abuses and corruptions of trusts. But they differed on how to deal with the problem. (As mentioned in Chapter 16, a trust controlled the operations of a whole group of companies.) Some progressives favored "**trustbusting**," breaking up the monopolies and restoring competition to the marketplace. Others favored leaving the trusts intact but regulating their operations.

For some progressives, government ownership of businesses was the answer. The most extreme progressives—the Socialists—wanted the government to take over major businesses. Most reformers, however, preferred only limited government ownership. The most widely accepted form of control was "**gas-and-water socialism**," city or state control of utilities such as gas and water companies. The progressives argued that a monopoly was the most efficient way to operate a utility and that the safest monopoly was one owned and operated by the government.

Progressives also promoted government intervention on behalf of labor. They favored legislation that was sympathetic to labor unions and wanted to force businesses to negotiate fairly with the unions. In this way, unions could provide a check to the power of big business. They favored legislation directly helping the working man. For example, progressives on the city, state, and national levels sponsored laws establishing minimum wage levels, prohibiting child labor, limiting the number of hours in a workday, and mandating safety standards for factories.

This cartoon shows President Theodore Roosevelt crushing the "bad trusts" and controlling the good ones.

Constitutional Progressivism

Four progressive ideas eventually became a part of the U.S. Constitution by the amendment process.

Sixteenth Amendment

The first such amendment was the federal income tax, established by the **Sixteenth Amendment** (ratified 1913). Progressives had two reasons for favoring the tax. First, income taxes would provide the government with funds to initiate reforms and provide the expanded social services that the progressives wanted. Second, the tax rate was *graduated*, that is, the more money one made, the higher percentage of income one must pay in taxes. Thus, the income tax took money from the very wealthy (ideally the industrialists and monopolists whom most progressives opposed) and used it, theoretically, for the benefit of all Americans.

Some people later argued that in reality, the taxes ultimately hurt people of *all* classes because they raised prices, discouraged investment in production, and removed monies from other productive endeavors. They noted that as overall economic activity declined, the income tax was gradually extended to include more people, even many who were supposed to benefit from the social services funded by the tax.

Seventeenth Amendment

The second of the "progressive amendments" was the **Seventeenth Amendment** (1913), calling for the direct election of U.S. senators. Under the constitutional procedure before that time (Article I, Section 3, Clause 1), state legislatures elected U.S. senators. Progressives charged that senatorial elections had become corrupt auctions in which the wealthy sometimes bribed legislators to elect them. Direct election, they believed, would end this abuse by giving the decision to the voters of each state. Although the reason for this change was to stop corruption, it did create a problem by removing one of the state legislatures' checks on federal power.

Eighteenth Amendment

The third reform was **Prohibition**, banning the manufacture, sale, or transportation of alcoholic beverages. Established by the **Eighteenth Amendment** (1919), Prohibition proved to be the most controversial progressive amendment and was eventually repealed by the Twenty-first Amendment (1933). The progressives saw the amendment as a simple means of solving major social problems. Social workers visiting the slums saw families in which drunken parents neglected or even abused their children and spent money on alcohol that should have been spent on food and clothing. Prison reformers spoke to inmates who blamed alcohol for leading them into crime. Progressives naturally concluded that eliminating liquor would reduce crime and poverty.

The Eighteenth Amendment also demonstrates the widespread support that reform enjoyed in that period, even beyond the progressive movement. Joining the progressives on behalf of Prohibition was a large group of Christian leaders, who denounced alcohol consumption as sinful. Perhaps the most famous of these Christian crusaders was Evangelist Billy Sunday. Although he did not show a consistent interest in progressivism, Sunday

---

Progressive Logic

Many progressives viewed government intervention as an extension of direct democracy. They argued that the people control the government, so government control of business is really the people controlling businesses. Later, many realized that true popular control of government was very difficult to achieve.

The First Income Tax

After the passage of the Sixteenth Amendment, the first income tax was 1 percent of all annual income over $3,000 ($4,000 for married couples), gradually rising to 6 percent of all income over $500,000. Since the average American income at the time was much less than $3,000, one writer joked, "It will be an exclusive circle, this income-tax class—one which the ordinary . . . man cannot hope to attain." The act nonetheless marked a significant change in American tax policies.

Capital police arrest two bootleggers who have crashed their car after leading police on a chase through the streets of Washington, D.C.

zealously championed the cause of Prohibition. In his huge city-wide evangelistic campaigns, he vigorously attacked the "damnable, hellish, vile, corrupt, iniquitous liquor business." Also joining the progressives on that issue were some businessmen. They saw Prohibition as a means of increasing production by eliminating worker absences and accidents caused by drunkenness.

When the U.S. entered World War I, Americans had another reason to support Prohibition. With shortages of grains and other agricultural products caused by the war, it seemed wasteful to use those products to manufacture alcoholic beverages.

Nineteenth Amendment

The fourth constitutional reform climaxed a movement much older than the progressive movement. The **Nineteenth Amendment** (1920) granted women suffrage (the right to vote). The drive for gaining the vote for women had begun before the Civil War (see Chapter 11). Throughout the nineteenth century "women suffragettes" had campaigned unceasingly for the right to vote. Led by women such as Elizabeth Cady Stanton and especially **Susan B. Anthony**, the crusade for women's suffrage was part of an overall campaign for equal rights for women.

Susan B. Anthony and Women's Rights

Susan B. Anthony labored for not only women's suffrage but also the right of women to control their own property and to receive custody of children in divorce cases. Her campaign for the vote, however, garnered the most attention. Although she died fourteen years before it was ratified, the Nineteenth Amendment was sometimes called the "Anthony Amendment" in her honor.

More than 20,000 suffragettes marched in this New York City parade in 1915.

Personalities

Muckrakers

The literary leaders of progressivism were writers who exposed abuse and corruption. Theodore Roosevelt nicknamed them **muckrakers** (*muck* means "filth, dirt, or mud"). He compared them to the man in John Bunyan's *Pilgrim's Progress* who ignored everything but filth.

> [He] could look no way but downwards, with a muck-rake in his hand. There stood also one over his head with a celestial crown in his hand, and [extended] him that crown for his muck-rake; but the man did neither look up nor regard, but raked to himself the straws, the small sticks, and dust of the floor (*Pilgrim's Progress*, Part II).

The muckrakers served an important purpose in informing the public. The golden age of muckraking began in 1902 when *McClure's* magazine published an exposé by Lincoln Steffens of municipal corruption in St. Louis. His work was soon followed by Ida Tarbell's *History of the Standard Oil Company* (1904), a scathing

Extreme Progressivism

The extreme wing of the progressive movement included the Socialists, who advocated government ownership of the major means of production and distribution. The leading Socialist of the era was **Eugene V. Debs**, former head of the American Railway Union (Chapter 16). Debs ran for president on the Socialist ticket five times. His highest percentage of the vote came in 1912, when he won 6 percent of the total. Debs's most interesting showing, however, was in 1920, when he won nearly a million votes while in prison for opposing American involvement in World War I. The vote totals of Debs, along with a few Socialist victories in city elections, demonstrate that the call for radical reform was present, though only among a small segment of American society.

portrait of supposed unscrupulous and dishonest methods John D. Rockefeller used to build his oil empire (mentioned in Chapter 16).

Other muckraking articles and books followed—such as attacks on insurance fraud and on impure and worthless medicines. Unlike proponents of yellow journalism, who reported sensational stories simply to boost sales, muckrakers felt genuine concern for the causes they advanced. For the most part, muckrakers did not call for any specific action; they contented themselves with describing corruption in graphic detail and trusting the disgust of the American people to motivate reforms. In many cases, their attacks resulted in legislation addressing alleged abuses. In other instances, muckrakers had a political agenda that drove their writing.

Political Progressives

Many politicians embraced the progressive movement. As mentioned earlier, William Jennings Bryan turned from Populism to progressivism and became a leader of the progressive wing of the Democratic Party. One of the major Republican leaders was **Robert La Follette** (luh FAHL-et) of Wisconsin. As a lawyer, governor, and senator, La Follette pressed for a series of reforms (such as the direct primary and railroad regulation) that made Wisconsin, as Theodore Roosevelt called it, "the laboratory of democracy."

Progressive Presidents

Three U.S. presidents governed during the Progressive Era: Theodore Roosevelt (1901–09), William Howard Taft (1909–13), and Woodrow Wilson (1913–21). Each of them endorsed progressive ideas, but **Theodore Roosevelt** was probably the president most closely associated with the movement. A member of a moderately wealthy New York family, a Harvard graduate, and an accomplished historian, Roosevelt was in some ways the most "aristo-

Teddy Bears

A fad developed during Theodore Roosevelt's presidency that shows his popularity with the American public. On a 1902 hunting trip in Mississippi, Roosevelt refused to shoot a captured bear. A reporter recounted the story, and an inspired cartoonist drew a caricature of the incident: "Drawing the Line in Mississippi."

The story caught the public's fancy. Soon, toy makers were selling stuffed bears in all sorts of attire, including one in a Rough Rider uniform. Children loved the cuddly toys.

One toy maker, Morris Michtom, wrote to Roosevelt, asking permission to market stuffed toy bears under the name "teddy bear."

Roosevelt replied, "I doubt if my name will mean much in the bear business, but you may use it if you wish." Michtom successfully marketed the teddy bears, and his business eventually became the Ideal Toy Company, a multimillion-dollar corporation.

By all accounts, Roosevelt was rather embarrassed by the teddy bear boom, but he went along with the fad. Roosevelt had one personal reason for disliking the toy, though—he had always hated the name "Teddy."

cratic" president since John Adams. Yet by living as a cowboy on his cattle ranch in the Dakotas and through his heroics with the Rough Riders in Cuba, Roosevelt shed much of his upper-class image and displayed a great appeal to the common man. As a New York state legislator, member of the U.S. Civil Service Commission, New York City police commissioner, and governor of New York, Roosevelt had a reputation as a friend of reform. As noted previously, he was elected vice-president in 1900. The stage was set for a dramatic change in American government when Roosevelt took office in September 1901.

Section Review

1–3. What were three broad means proposed by the progressives for furthering reform?

4–5. What is the difference between an initiative and a referendum?

6–7. What were the two popular forms of city government developed during the Progressive Era?

8. What was the most controversial of the four progressive amendments to the Constitution?

9. Who was a leader of the progressive wing of the Democratic Party?

★ Was Prohibition a practical solution to the ills caused by alcoholic drinks? Why or why not?

★ Assess the four constitutional amendments during the era. Which do you think had the greatest impact and why?

The boisterous Theodore Roosevelt in many ways personified the energetic, reformist tendencies of the Progressive Era.

II. Progressive Politics

Roosevelt and the Square Deal

Roosevelt approached the presidency as he did life—zealously. He planned to govern actively. He wanted to lead, instead of follow, Congress in setting the political agenda for the nation. By persuasion, intimidation, and sheer force of personality, Roosevelt shaped the policies of the government. Central to his philosophy was his belief that every man and woman should receive fair treatment and equal opportunity, a "**Square Deal**," as he put it.

Trustbusting

Early in his presidency, Roosevelt launched his attack on the abuses of the trusts by reviving the little-used Sherman Anti-Trust Act. In 1902, the federal government charged the Northern Securities Company with violating the act, and the government filed a lawsuit to break it apart. The Northern Securities Company, which controlled the powerful Great Northern and Northern Pacific Railroads, fought the suit, but the Supreme Court agreed with the government's action. The Northern Securities case was a milestone in confirming the government's authority to regulate trusts, and it encouraged Roosevelt to proceed against other monopolies. Although it is unclear how much this antitrust activity increased competition, it won Roosevelt widespread public acclaim as a "trustbuster."

Guiding Questions

1. What reform legislation did Theodore Roosevelt endorse?
2. What international actions occurred during Theodore Roosevelt's administration?
3. What characterized William H. Taft's administration?
4. What were the highlights of Woodrow Wilson's first term of office?

A Novel Prompts Novel Regulations

Passage of the Pure Food and Drug Act and the Meat Inspection Act was due in large part to the public outrage resulting from the muckraking work of Upton Sinclair. Sinclair spent weeks secretly investigating the conditions in Chicago's meatpacking plants. The publication of his book, ***The Jungle***, in 1906 shocked the nation.

When President Roosevelt read the book, he reacted quickly. He appointed officials to investigate packing plants. They issued a scathing report that confirmed most of Sinclair's disgusting account.

Sinclair's original intent in writing the book was to focus on the dreadful living conditions of immigrant packing plant employees. Though these were mentioned throughout the book, it was his graphic descriptions of how meat products were manufactured that captivated the public's attention. Sinclair later commented about the impact of his novel: "I aimed at the public's heart, and by accident, I hit it in the stomach."

Enlarging Executive Powers

Theodore Roosevelt, though a Republican, was a firm believer in a growing federal government, especially the executive branch. He used presidential executive orders extensively. These bypassed the congressional legislative process in favor of presidential decree. During his seven and one-half years as president, he signed 1,081 executive orders. By contrast, McKinley, whom Roosevelt succeeded, had issued only 185. But even with that large number, Roosevelt ranks only fourth in the number of executive orders issued. Learning from his example, Woodrow Wilson issued 1,803; Calvin Coolidge issued 1,203; and Franklin Roosevelt issued 3,522.

Regulation

Roosevelt wanted to regulate the conduct of business and industry for what he viewed as the public good. He gave the most attention to railroads, the major means of transportation and shipping in the nation. Consumers often complained that the railroads, which operated as monopolies in some areas, charged excessively high rates and granted special concessions to businesses they favored. The **Hepburn Act** (1906) was Roosevelt's most important railroad-regulating legislation. This act strengthened the Interstate Commerce Commission's (ICC) ability to set rates for railroads and provided a standard bookkeeping system that made it easier to compare and regulate those rates. Most importantly, the act shifted the burden of proof in rate setting from the ICC to the railroads. Earlier, the ICC had to take a rail company to court to enforce its rate decisions. Under the Hepburn Act, however, the railroads had to take the ICC to court to overturn the commission's decisions. Increasingly, the railroads simply followed the rates that the ICC set.

Roosevelt also pushed for regulation in the production of food and medicine. The **Pure Food and Drug Act** (1906) outlawed the interstate sale of impure food and drugs and required honest labeling of such products. The **Meat Inspection Act** (1906) required the Department of Agriculture to oversee the preparation and packaging of meat and to inspect the health of animals before they were slaughtered. The supervisory agencies established by those two acts have unquestionably benefited the public, and their powers have not been so extensive that they have seriously hampered private production, as some regulatory agencies have done. In fact,

From *The Jungle*

When *The Jungle* was published in 1906, the novel aroused the indignation of the public. Though only a small portion of the book dealt with the gruesome details of meat production, those selections created a sensation throughout the country. Below are some of those descriptions.

"There was no heat upon the killing beds.... On the killing beds you were apt to be covered with blood, and it would freeze solid.... The men would tie up their feet in newspapers and old sacks, and these would be soaked in blood and frozen, and then soaked again, and so on, until by nighttime a man would be walking on great lumps the size of the feet of an elephant. Now and then, when the bosses were not looking, you would see them plunging their feet and ankles into the steaming hot carcass of the steer....

"For it was the custom, as they found, whenever meat was so spoiled that it could not be used for anything else, either to can it or else to chop it up into sausage....

"There was never the least attention paid to what was cut up for sausage; there would come all the way back from Europe old sausage that had been rejected, and that was moldy and white—it would be dosed with borax and glycerine, and dumped into the hoppers, and made over again for home consumption. There would be meat that had tumbled out on the floor, in the dirt and sawdust, where the workers had tramped and spit uncounted billions of consumption germs. There would be meat stored in great piles in rooms; and the water from leaky roofs would drip over it, and thousands of rats would race about on it. It was too dark in these storage places to see well.... These rats were nuisances, and the packers would put poisoned bread out for them; they would die, and then rats, bread, and meat would go into the hoppers together.... the meat would be shoveled into carts, and the man who did the shoveling would not trouble to lift out a rat even when he saw one—there were things that went into the sausage in comparison with which a poisoned rat was a tidbit."

---

increased public confidence in the quality of food and drugs might have helped increase sales.

Coal Strike

Roosevelt's dedication to a "square deal" for labor and business was severely tested by a coal miners' strike in 1902. Coal was the major source of fuel for steam-operated machinery, including railroad locomotives, and the major source of heat for the nation. As winter drew near and the public grew concerned, Roosevelt tried to break the stalemate. He arranged a meeting between the owners and the union leaders at the White House, but the owners refused even to speak to the union men assembled there. Losing his patience, Roosevelt threatened to use federal troops to operate the mines. For the first time, the threat of federal force was used against owners rather than against workers. Reluctantly, the owners consented to a 10 percent pay raise and a nine-hour day. This was the first instance of the federal government's acting as the mediator in a labor dispute, and the success of the effort increased Roosevelt's popularity among labor leaders. His threat against business, however, foreshadowed even greater future government involvement.

> *Coal Strike of 1902*
> How was Roosevelt's threat to use troops to keep the mines running an action against the owners? Wouldn't the owners want the mines kept running? At the time of the strike, there was a surplus of coal, so the price of coal was quite low. As the strike hindered production, the price of coal rose, so the owners were content to let the strike continue. Using troops to keep the mines running would have stopped the increase in the price of coal.

Conservation

Nothing was more important to Roosevelt, the rugged outdoorsman, than the conservation of natural resources. The Reclamation Act, passed in 1902, set aside nearly 100 million acres of western land to be controlled by the federal government. This was in addition to the millions of acres already set aside for national forests. During his last year in office, Roosevelt established the

The National Parks President

Colorado's Mesa Verde National Park and Oregon's Crater Lake National Park are two of the five national parks established during Roosevelt's presidency. The others are Wind Cave, South Dakota; Sully's Hill, North Dakota; and Platt National Park, Oklahoma.

Yosemite became a national park before Roosevelt became president. He is shown there on a 1903 trip to California.

Eugenics

Eugenics is a set of beliefs and practices whose goal is improving the genetic quality of the human population. During the Progressive Era, faith in evolutionary ideas led to a rise in the "science" of eugenics. Progressives who embraced this idea wanted only individuals with the best genetic traits to have children. Those that were criminal, "feebleminded," or disabled were discouraged or prevented from reproducing. Because of the influence of supporters of this idea, some states passed laws that led to sterilizing Americans deemed to be "unfit." In some areas marriage between people of differing races was illegal, partly because some believed certain races were inferior to others. Furthermore, those who believed Caucasians were the superior race sometimes used eugenics to justify their support of Jim Crow laws.

Eugenics advocates believed they were using science to help society progress. Critics argued they were actually advancing injustice.

National Conservation Commission, headed by Gifford Pinchot (PIN shoh), chief of the U.S. Forest Service. The commission was assigned the task of compiling a record of the nation's water, timber, land, and mineral resources.

Discrimination and Injustice

One of the great failures of progressivism was its inability to prevent worsening discrimination. In California, resentment of the growing Asian population resulted in discrimination and even violence. In 1906, the San Francisco school board sparked an international incident when it tried to place all Asian students into a separate public school. When the Japanese government strongly protested this treatment, Roosevelt pressured the school board to reverse its decision in return for voluntary Japanese restrictions on immigration.

The situation for black people in the South (where the overwhelming majority of African Americans lived before World War I) worsened during the Progressive Era. Roosevelt stirred controversy by inviting black educator Booker T. Washington to dine with him at the White House, but progressives on the whole did little to alleviate growing discrimination. Though black Americans held elective or appointive offices during this period (for example, in every session of Congress from 1869 to 1901 except one, there was at least one black member of the House of Representatives), their number was so small, they had little influence.

Discrimination worsened in the 1890s as states began passing **"Jim Crow" laws**. This legislation required the forced **segregation**, or separation, of the races in trains, restaurants, hotels, schools, and other social settings. (Jim Crow was a stereotyped black character in a nineteenth-century minstrel show.) In fact, segregation was so extensive that whites and blacks even had separate restrooms and drinking fountains.

In addition, Southern states began to deprive black people of their right to vote by establishing **literacy tests** or requiring special taxes, called **poll taxes**, in order to vote. African Americans were often given a more difficult literacy test, to determine reading and writing ability, than whites. Black people were often too poor to pay the poll tax. Many times election officials were far less strict in collecting the poll tax or applying literacy requirements to white men. Later, many states also passed a **grandfather clause** which typically said a person who could not pay the poll tax or pass the literacy test could still vote if he or his father or his grandfather was eligible to vote before 1867. No black citizens met this requirement. As a result of these laws, the number of black voters plummeted. For example, the number of registered black voters in Louisiana was 130,000 in 1896 but only about 1,300 in 1904.

There were several factors that motivated the disenfranchisement (denial of the right to vote) of blacks. First, overtly racist politicians, who played on the fears and prejudices of white voters, gained popularity. Second, the alliance of black people with some reform groups such as the Populists caused many conservative Democrats to limit African American voting in order to dilute Populist political power. Third, the national government and the northern public generally lost interest in the cause of civil rights for African Americans.

Segregation was strengthened when the Supreme Court issued a series of decisions that gutted the enforcement of the Reconstruction civil rights legislation. The most famous of these cases was **Plessy v. Ferguson**, a case which decreed that "separate but equal" facilities for blacks and whites (in this case, on trains) were constitutional. These decisions gave state legislatures the legal justification they needed to pass whole Jim Crow law codes.

Black Americans reacted to increased discrimination in differing ways. One approach was represented by a well-known black leader of the era, **Booker T. Washington**. As described in his famous autobiography, *Up from Slavery*, Washington had risen from slavery to the presidency of Tuskegee Institute in Alabama, the nation's leading black industrial school. Washington was basically conservative; in 1895, he delivered a famous speech in Atlanta, Georgia. He urged African Americans not to risk strife by insisting

Booker T. Washington

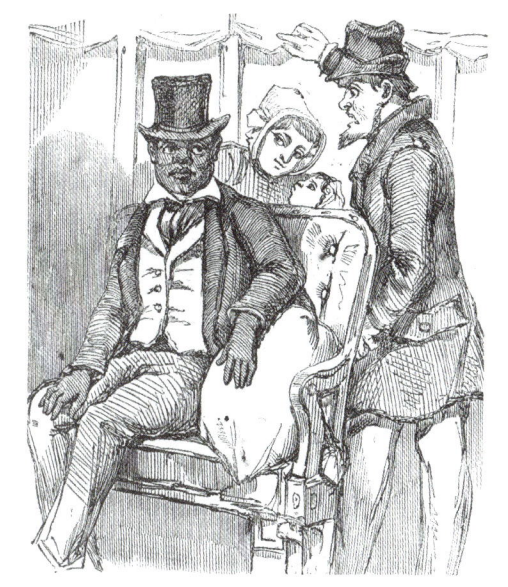

An African American forced to leave a railway car reserved for white people

Opposing Views from African American Leaders

Below is an excerpt from Booker T. Washington's 1895 speech that became the basis of the Atlanta Compromise.

"Ignorant and inexperienced [after the Civil War], it is not strange that in the first years of our new life we began at the top instead of at the bottom; that seat in Congress or the state legislature was more sought than real estate or industrial skill; that the political convention or stump speaking had more attractions than starting a dairy farm or . . . garden. . . .

"No race can prosper till it learns that there is as much dignity in tilling a field as in writing a poem. It is at the bottom of life we must begin, and not at the top. Nor should we permit our grievances to overshadow our opportunities. . . .

"The wisest among my race understand that the agitation of questions of social equality is the extremest folly, and that progress in the enjoyment of all the privileges that will come to us must be the result of severe and constant struggle rather than of artificial forcing. No race that has anything to contribute to the markets of the world is long in any degree ostracized [excluded]. It is important and right that all privileges of the law be ours, but it is vastly more important that we be prepared for the exercises of these privileges. The opportunity to earn a dollar in a factory just now is worth infinitely more than the opportunity to spend a dollar in an opera-house."

W. E. B. Du Bois (a major civil rights leader discussed on the next page) opposed Booker T. Washington's approach. Below are portions of an essay he wrote in 1903 criticizing the Atlanta Compromise.

"Mr. Washington came, with a simple definite programme [that included industrial education]. . . . and submission and silence as to civil and political rights. . . .

"To gain the sympathy and co-operation of . . . the white South was Mr. Washington's first task. . . .

"Mr. Washington represents in Negro thought the old attitude of adjustment and submission. . . . [It developed into] a gospel of Work and Money to . . . almost completely [disregard] the higher aims of life. . . . Mr. Washington's programme practically accepts the alleged inferiority of the Negro races. . . . Mr. Washington withdraws many of the high demands of Negroes as men and American citizens. . . .

"[He] asks that black people give up, at least for the present, three things,—

"First, political power,

"Second, insistence on civil rights,

"Third, higher education of Negro youth,—and concentrate all their energies on industrial education. . . . What has been the return [outcome]?

1. The disfranchisement of the Negro.
2. The legal creation of a distinct status of civil inferiority for the Negro.
3. The steady withdrawal of aid from institutions for the higher training of the Negro.

"These movements are not, to be sure, direct results of Mr. Washington's teachings; but his propaganda has, without a shadow of doubt, helped their speedier accomplishment."

W. E. B. Du Bois

on their political rights. Instead, they should concentrate on bettering themselves economically through vocational education and the establishment of black businesses and trades. As black people became more powerful economically, Washington argued, white people would be forced to accept them and grant them political equality. Booker T. Washington's approach, explained in that 1895 Atlanta speech, became known as the "Atlanta Compromise."

Opposing Washington was a group of black intellectuals led by **W. E. B. Du Bois**. Du Bois was the first African American to receive a PhD from Harvard University. He and his supporters argued that blacks could not truly improve themselves economically until they enjoyed equal participation in the political process as American citizens. They opposed Washington's emphasis on technical and industrial education over liberal arts, fearing that it would force black Americans into an economically inferior laboring class and discourage higher education among them. Where Washington sought an economic solution to the problem, Du Bois pursued a political solution.

In 1909 Du Bois and other like-minded leaders—black and white—formed the **National Association for the Advancement of Colored People (NAACP)**. Their goal was to seek equality for blacks and to focus on fighting legal battles to achieve that objective. During Washington's lifetime, his views dominated relations between blacks and whites; afterward, however, because many white people refused to recognize the equality of black people, the NAACP's approach gained strength and became the basis of the civil rights movement of the 1950s and 1960s.

Roosevelt and the "Big Stick"

Theodore Roosevelt's favorite saying was "Speak softly and carry a big stick." Just as the phrase "square deal" describes Roosevelt's domestic policy, the "big stick" describes his foreign policy. His foreign policy was vigorous and expansive and involved the United States more actively in international affairs. It was still aligned with his reformist impulses; he considered the expansion of a "civilized power," such as the United States, into world affairs to be "a victory for law, order, and righteousness."

Philippines

One major problem that Roosevelt inherited from McKinley was the situation in the Philippines. Even after the surrender of Emilio Aguinaldo and the end of the insurrection, the Filipinos were not content with American rule; they wanted independence. Roosevelt approached the Philippine problem cautiously. The governor of the islands, his friend and advisor William Howard Taft, tried to win the affection of the Filipinos by improving education, transportation, and healthcare. Railroads and bridges were built. American leaders desired to maintain a foothold in the Pacific and feared that if the islands were granted independence too quickly, they might fall prey to another major power, such as Japan.

However, a number of prominent Americans including Andrew Carnegie, William Jennings Bryan, and former president Grover Cleveland opposed maintaining control of the islands. In 1917, the U.S. adopted a law promising eventual independence for the Filipino people. Therefore, over a period of thirty years, the United States gradually gave the Filipinos increasing amounts of self-rule.

Shortly after the U.S. freed the islands of Japanese control during World War II, they were given their independence (1946).

Panama Canal

One of Roosevelt's favorite projects was the building of an American-controlled canal in Central America to link the Atlantic and the Pacific. Members of Congress, however, disagreed about the best route. Some of them favored a route through Nicaragua; others favored a route through Panama (at the time a part of Colombia), where in the 1880s a French company had gone bankrupt trying to dig a canal. The French company, needing the money from the sale of their rights of construction, sent a representative, Philippe Bunau-Varilla (fih-LEEP BOO-noh vuh-REE-yuh), to negotiate with the United States. In 1902, Congress passed an act authorizing purchase of the French rights for $40 million, and in 1903 the Senate passed a treaty with Colombia agreeing to purchase perpetual control of the Canal Zone for $10 million initially, with annual payments of $250,000 thereafter. But the Colombian senate, believing the price was too low, rejected the treaty.

Infuriated by their action, Roosevelt denounced the Colombians as "foolish and homicidal corruptionists" who were attempting to blackmail the United States. Bunau-Varilla, who was still trying to promote the sale of his company's rights, quickly pointed out to the president that a revolution in Panama was imminent; many Panamanians resented the Colombian government and wanted to break away. Officers of the French company, led by Bunau-Varilla, helped finance and organize the revolt. Roosevelt, for his part, ordered the U.S. Navy to prevent Colombian troops from landing in Panama to crush the rebellion.

Theodore Roosevelt stands tall as the Western Hemisphere's "policeman" in this 1905 cartoon. His "speak softly and carry a big stick" philosophy governed his actions in foreign affairs.

Dr. Walter Reed

Questionable Means

The circumstances under which the United States acquired the Canal Zone were at best questionable, although the canal clearly benefited most of the nations of the Western Hemisphere. Colombia was understandably resentful, and other Latin American countries expressed their fear of the United States—the "Colossus of the North," as they put it. Some congressmen raised ethical objections, but Roosevelt characteristically commented, "I took the Canal Zone and let Congress debate; and while the debate goes on the Canal does also."

President Roosevelt sitting on a steam shovel at the Panama Canal in 1906

Mainly because of that American support, Panama's revolt succeeded on November 3, 1903. Three days later, President Roosevelt recognized Panama's independence, and the Panamanians then appointed Bunau-Varilla as their minister to the United States. He and Secretary of State John Hay signed an agreement on November 18 promising Panama the same payment for the canal that the United States had offered to Colombia.

Construction of the **Panama Canal** took approximately ten years. One of the obstacles that both French and Americans faced with building the canal was outbreaks of **yellow fever** among canal workers. During the Spanish-American War, a commission of U.S. Army doctors, led by Walter Reed, proved that mosquitoes transmitted the disease. Earlier a Cuban doctor, Carlos Finlay, had theorized this. **Malaria** was also spread by mosquitoes.

In 1904, William Gorgas became chief sanitary officer of the Panama Canal project. He improved sanitary conditions in Panama by draining swamps, pouring oil on standing water where mosquitoes bred, and clearing away mosquito-infested underbrush. By the time the canal was completed, Gorgas had reduced malaria and yellow fever deaths from about forty per one thousand workers to about seven per one thousand.

As many as forty thousand Americans were employed on the project at one time, despite the many hazards. The canal cost about $400 million, but its financial benefits to world shipping outweighed the cost. In August 1914—just days after World War I had broken out in Europe—the canal opened and linked ocean to ocean.

Dr. William Gorgas

Roosevelt Corollary

Roosevelt's actions in Panama represented his general approach to affairs in Latin America. He envisioned the United States as the leader in the Western Hemisphere, protecting the region and regulating its behavior. Complicating Roosevelt's position was the conduct of some Latin American nations. In 1902, Venezuela ran afoul of Great Britain and Germany when it proved unable to repay loans from those nations. Likewise, a bloody revolution in the Dominican Republic in 1904 worried the European powers that had sizable investments in that nation. Fearing European intervention in the hemisphere, Roosevelt devised an addition to the Monroe Doctrine that became known as the **Roosevelt Corollary**.

The president told Congress in 1904, "Chronic wrongdoing . . . [may] ultimately require intervention by some civilized nation, and in the Western Hemisphere the adherence of the United States to the Monroe Doctrine may force the United States, however reluctantly, in flagrant cases of such wrongdoing or impotence [weakness], to the exercise of an international police power."

To the Monroe Doctrine's assertion that Europe could not intervene in the Americas, Roosevelt's corollary added that the United States would act as a "policeman" to maintain economic and political stability in the Western Hemisphere. Roosevelt's new doctrine placed the United States in a position of constantly intervening in Latin America to prevent European nations from intervening there. During the next decade, the United States intervened in Haiti, Honduras, Nicaragua, and the Dominican Republic in attempts to collect debts or maintain order. As a result, European and Latin American resentment toward the United States intensified.

Relations with Japan

Trade with China and American possessions in the Pacific, such as the Philippines and Guam, brought the United States into closer contact with Japan. Throughout the Roosevelt years, relations with the proud and increasingly powerful Japanese were a sensitive issue.

The Japanese were understandably offended at the discriminatory legislation directed at Asians on the West Coast of the United States. Roosevelt finally negotiated what he called the "Gentleman's Agreement" with the Japanese government. Japan agreed to refuse passports to Japanese laborers leaving for the United States; Roosevelt forbade immigration of Japanese traveling by way of other nations. In return for these concessions, Roosevelt was able to win better treatment for Asians in California. The agreement slowed Japanese immigration, and tensions eased.

Great White Fleet

Japanese-American relations also sparked the climax of Roosevelt's foreign policy, a grand display of American naval power. In December 1907, sixteen battleships, referred to as the "Great White Fleet," steamed from Virginia, heading around South America, into the Pacific, and on to Japan. Roosevelt's goal for the fleet, which got its name from the fact that the ships were painted white, was to impress the Japanese with American strength. In 1908, partly because of that "battleship diplomacy," the two countries signed an agreement in which both powers pledged to respect each other's territorial claims in the Pacific and to maintain the "open door" for trade in China. The fleet itself imitated Magellan by sailing around the world, symbolizing American power wherever it went.

Roosevelt's foreign policy did have its critics. Americans were still essentially isolationists, whereas Roosevelt was clearly an internationalist. One of Roosevelt's most vocal critics was William Jennings Bryan. But Roosevelt succeeded in convincing Congress that the nation had to be more involved internationally because of strategic concerns; it needed to expand the market for its exports. Roosevelt set the nation on the road to growing international involvement.

Taft and the Presidency

Roosevelt did not run for a third term in 1908, but he handpicked his successor, **William Howard Taft**. Taft was a huge man (more than three hundred pounds) whose pleasant nature made

This cartoon shows Roosevelt enforcing his corollary to the Monroe Doctrine with the help of his "big stick" and the U.S. Navy.

Roosevelt, Nobel Peace Prize Winner

In February 1904, war broke out between Japan and Russia over conflicts of interest in Manchuria (a province of China). The Japanese won a series of quick naval and land victories that worried the other great powers, who feared growing Japanese power in the Pacific. The war, known as the Russo-Japanese War, strained the finances of both nations, and they invited Roosevelt to mediate. In 1905, at a conference in Portsmouth, New Hampshire, Roosevelt negotiated a settlement that preserved most of Japan's gains but allowed Russia to escape with some of its honor intact.

Roosevelt later received the Nobel Peace Prize for his services. Unfortunately, both Russia and Japan were unhappy with the compromises embodied in the Treaty of Portsmouth (1905), and American relations with both nations soon cooled.

him almost instantly likable and whose physique delighted political cartoonists. Taft had enjoyed a distinguished public career mostly in appointed positions such as governor of the Philippines and secretary of war. With Roosevelt's support, Taft easily captured the Republican nomination and then comfortably defeated William Jennings Bryan in the 1908 presidential election.

Tariff Fiasco

Taft's first effort at reform was a failure. Taft wanted to lower tariff rates—a controversial issue that Roosevelt had avoided during his two terms. The House drafted a bill lowering the tariff moderately, but by the time the Senate was finished with the bill, rates remained virtually unchanged. Progressives urged Taft to veto the bill, but the president accepted it as the best he could get. When Taft tried to defend the new tariff as "on the whole . . . the best [tariff] bill that the Republican party ever passed," progressives became even more dismayed.

Congressional Reform

Many members of the House of Representatives resented the tremendous powers of the Speaker of the House, **Joseph Cannon**. As Speaker, Cannon assigned the members to the various House committees and selected the chairman for each. Furthermore, Cannon himself was chairman of the powerful Rules Committee, which controls when and how bills are debated. In 1910, a coalition of Democrats and Republicans joined forces to reduce Cannon's power. They voted to increase the membership of the Rules Committee from five to fifteen members, to remove the Speaker as a member of the committee, and to elect members of the committee by the House. In addition, they stripped Cannon of his power to appoint members to other committees. Taft, however, did not endorse all these changes. Although he had originally supported trimming Cannon's power, Taft relented when other Republican leaders warned him against antagonizing the powerful Speaker. As a result, the progressives thought that Taft had abandoned them, and another wedge was driven between the president and the progressives.

Taft's support of Speaker of the House Joe "Czar" Cannon (*second from left*) against the wishes of reform-minded representatives in Congress drove a wedge between the president and many other progressives.

Split with Roosevelt

Roosevelt, after helping Taft reach the presidency, left in 1909 for an African hunting trip. Afterwards, Roosevelt travelled to Europe.

But even overseas, he heard complaints about Taft from progressives. One issue that divided the two men was conservation. In reality, Taft was just as concerned with conservation as Roosevelt; however, Taft believed it should be accomplished through legislation rather than executive orders. He believed Roosevelt had stretched the law in his administration of public lands; the new president preferred to act only when the law was clearly and unquestionably on his side. As a result, Taft clashed with the head of the U.S. Forest Service, Gifford Pinchot, who was worried about the future of some of the public lands that Taft was returning to private use. Eventually, Pinchot so publicized his conflicts with the president that Taft dismissed him. This act, combined with Pinchot's denunciations, cast public suspicion on Taft's devotion to conservation. Furthermore, because Pinchot was also a close friend of Roosevelt's, the dismissal chilled the relationship between Taft and Roosevelt.

The final break between Roosevelt and Taft came over antitrust proceedings. Taft had an impressive record in antitrust actions and initiated more antitrust suits in one term than Roosevelt had in two. But one suit in particular upset Roosevelt. In 1907, during Roosevelt's second term, U.S. Steel had wanted to purchase the Tennessee Coal and Iron Company. The businessmen involved in the deal asked whether the government considered such a purchase too monopolistic. Roosevelt agreed that the move was acceptable and gave his unofficial blessing to the purchase. The Taft administration, however, viewed the transaction as a step in building an illegal monopoly and filed suit against U.S. Steel. Since the charges included the suggestion that Roosevelt had allowed himself to be fooled by the corporation, the former president was angry and offended. A formal split was developing, not only between Taft and Roosevelt but also between the conservatives and the progressives within the Republican Party.

Dollar Diplomacy

Taft also adopted a less confrontational foreign policy than the displays of military might that Roosevelt favored. Taft preferred to influence foreign affairs through the investment of American dollars in foreign countries, a policy that was soon nicknamed "**dollar diplomacy.**" Concerned by Japan's efforts at expansion in China, he encouraged American companies to build railroads in China and establish themselves as competitors there. Taft also backed similar efforts in Latin America, particularly in Nicaragua.

The results of dollar diplomacy were mixed. It was mildly successful in increasing trade and industry in Latin America, where foreign leaders realized that the United States might intervene militarily to protect American investments. It was less successful in regions such as China where interference was likely to bring little more than formal protests from the United States.

Taft's dollar diplomacy was a well-intentioned plan to bring mutual economic benefit and to build better foreign relations between the United States and foreign nations. Its limited success disappointed both Taft and the public and contributed to the perception that Taft was an ineffective president.

Election of 1912

Roosevelt finally concluded that Taft was not wholly committed to the progressive cause. Therefore, he "threw his hat into the ring" (announced his candidacy) for the Republican nomination in 1912. He was still popular with the voters and won nine of the twelve

---

Taft vs. Roosevelt

Taft favored reform but was more reserved and cautious than Roosevelt. His subdued manner, orderly mind, and legal background actually suited him better for a judicial career than a political one. (He eventually served as chief justice of the Supreme Court.) Taft's caution led him into conflict with the progressives of his own party and eventually to a split with Roosevelt.

The difference in temperament between Roosevelt and Taft has been described as the difference between pursuing justice and preserving law. Roosevelt, in his zealous quest of what he considered just causes, extended his presidential powers. Taft, with his love for law and orderliness, sought to achieve reform through an active legislative branch that passed unambiguous laws to accomplish change and remedy injustice.

The Bull Moose Platform

The Progressive Party platform called for strong federal regulation of business (instead of breaking up monopolies as Roosevelt had previously favored), a federal securities commission to supervise the sale of stocks and bonds, revision of the tariff, direct primary elections for nomination of candidates, easier amendment of the Constitution, and numerous social reforms, including women's suffrage and labor reforms.

Woodrow Wilson

state primaries that chose delegates for the Republican convention. However, Taft, as the incumbent president, held solid control of the nonprimary states, and he won the hard-fought campaign for the nomination.

Roosevelt declared that Taft had not only betrayed progressivism but also stolen the nomination. He and his followers formed a third party, the **Progressive Party** (popularly known as the Bull Moose Party because Roosevelt had told a reporter that he felt "as strong as a bull moose"). Roosevelt ran on a platform that he called the "New Nationalism."

The Democrats also nominated a progressive candidate, Governor **Woodrow Wilson** of New Jersey. As a historian, professor, and president of Princeton University, Wilson had both studied deeply and written intelligently about the American system of government. Elected governor of New Jersey in 1910, Wilson proved to be a zealous progressive. He initiated reforms such as the direct primary, state regulation of utilities, and legislation designed to drive monopolies out of the state. Wilson campaigned under the motto "New Freedom." His platform sounded much like the progressive principles of Roosevelt's earlier years in the presidency. For example, Wilson called for increased competition through trust-busting rather than the greater regulation for which Roosevelt was campaigning.

In the election all three candidates were actually supporters of progressivism. Roosevelt and his Progressive Party made the best third-party showing in presidential history. Roosevelt won 4.1 million votes to 3.5 million for Taft, and he won 88 electoral votes to Taft's 8. With the Republicans divided, however, Wilson won 6.3 million votes (42 percent of the total) and 435 electoral votes. Wil-

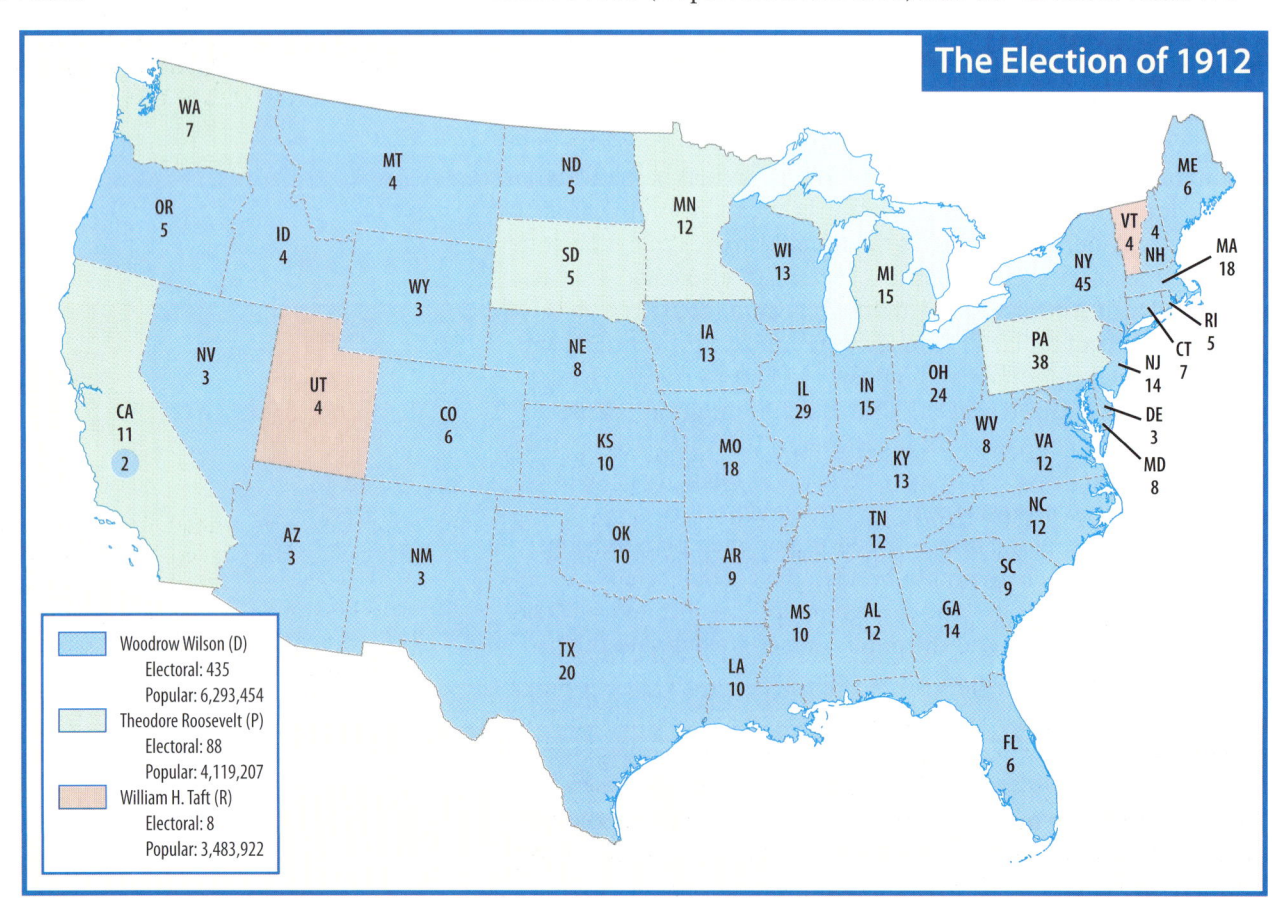

The Election of 1912

Woodrow Wilson (D)
Electoral: 435
Popular: 6,293,454

Theodore Roosevelt (P)
Electoral: 88
Popular: 4,119,207

William H. Taft (R)
Electoral: 8
Popular: 3,483,922

WA 7, OR 5, CA 11 (2), NV 3, ID 4, MT 4, WY 3, UT 4, AZ 3, CO 6, NM 3, ND 5, SD 5, NE 8, KS 10, OK 10, TX 20, MN 12, IA 13, MO 18, AR 9, LA 10, WI 13, IL 29, MS 10, MI 15, IN 15, KY 13, TN 12, AL 12, GA 14, FL 6, OH 24, WV 8, VA 12, NC 12, SC 9, PA 38, NY 45, VT 4, NH 4, ME 6, MA 18, RI 5, CT 7, NJ 14, DE 3, MD 8

son swept into office, and the Democrats captured both houses of Congress. For the first time in nearly twenty years, the Democrats controlled both Congress and the White House.

Wilson and the New Freedom

Most Americans today associate Woodrow Wilson with World War I and the complicated foreign affairs involved in that conflict (discussed in the next chapter). But Wilson's first term was the climax of the progressive movement in America. For example, three of the four "progressive amendments" to the Constitution (17–19) were ratified during Wilson's time in office. His presidency represented the crowning achievements of the Progressive Era.

Revenue Revision

One of the first important reforms of the Wilson administration was the **Underwood Tariff Act** of 1913. Unlike Roosevelt and Taft, Wilson succeeded in achieving the first genuine tariff reform since the Civil War. The new tariff slashed overall rates by about a third from what they had been. Even more important, the act compensated for the loss of tariff revenue by adopting the first income tax under the recently ratified Sixteenth Amendment.

Federal Reserve Act

In 1907, the latest in a series of financial panics left American businessmen desiring a better system of regulating currency and banking practices. These businessmen envisioned something similar to the Bank of the United States that Andrew Jackson had destroyed. They argued that the country needed a centralized, privately owned national bank that could easily set standards for banks and regulate the flow of currency throughout the country. The nation's business interests, therefore, presented this request to the leaders in Washington.

Wilson and the progressives in Congress, however, developed a different system in the **Federal Reserve Act** (1913). This legislation divided the nation into twelve banking districts, each served by a private regional Federal Reserve Bank. Over these district banks was a central, government-run organization, the Federal Reserve Board.

This system represented a compromise between a totally private banking system (as businessmen wanted) and a totally government-controlled system (as many progressives wanted).

Business and Labor

Wilson's administration passed two important pieces of legislation in 1914 concerning the regulation of business and labor. The **Clayton Antitrust Act** strengthened the Sherman Anti-Trust Act by expanding the list of practices prohibited to corporations. It also exempted labor unions from antitrust legislation and legalized practices such as strikes, picketing, and boycotts.

Even more sweeping in its effects was the **Federal Trade Commission Act**. That act established the Federal Trade Commission (FTC), a board of five men authorized to help define and halt unfair business practices. The FTC Act marked a growing tendency for government regulation of business practices. Increasingly, the determining of unfair practices, the establishment of regulations, and the enforcement of policies were being left to regulatory agencies such as the FTC instead of Congress or the courts. This

---

Assassination Attempt

"Friends, I shall ask you to be as quiet as possible. I don't know whether you fully understand that I have just been shot; but it takes more than that to kill a Bull Moose. But fortunately I had my manuscript, so you see I was going to make a long speech, and there is a bullet—there is where the bullet went through—and it probably saved me from it going into my heart. The bullet is in me now, so that I cannot make a very long speech, but I will try my best."

—Theodore Roosevelt, Address at Milwaukee, WI, October 14, 1912

On this day, John F. Schrank shot the former president when he was campaigning in Milwaukee, Wisconsin. In addition to the fifty page manuscript of his speech, the bullet was also slowed by his overcoat and a steel-reinforced eyeglass case. In spite of his comment above, Roosevelt delivered a ninety-minute speech. But at times, he spoke only in a whisper.

Later in the day, doctors located the bullet lodged against one of Roosevelt's ribs. They determined it was more dangerous to attempt to remove it than to leave it in his chest. It remained there until his death in 1919.

The man who tried to kill Roosevelt was later declared insane. He was committed to a mental asylum and remained there until he died of natural causes in 1943.

Labor's "Magna Carta"?

Samuel Gompers, head of the American Federation of Labor, called the Clayton Antitrust Act labor's "Magna Carta." His label was a bit premature, however, because later court rulings weakened or eliminated some of the act's prolabor provisions.

Section Review

1-2. What piece of muckraking literature spurred the passage of the Pure Food and Drug Act and the Meat Inspection Act? Who wrote the work?

3. Why did some Americans fear giving the Philippines their independence too quickly?

4-5. Why did Colombia reject the canal treaty with the United States in 1903? How did the U.S. acquire the canal area?

6. What method of raising revenue did the Underwood Tariff use in place of reduced tariff rates?

7-8. What two major pieces of legislation concerning business and labor were passed during Wilson's first term?

★ Contrast the views of Booker T. Washington and W. E. B. Du Bois regarding discrimination against black people. What do you think were the strengths and weaknesses of each man's view?

★ What effect do third-party candidates typically have on presidential elections? What effect did they have on the election of 1912?

III. Progressive Society

Important changes in other aspects of American life paralleled the dramatic changes in American politics during the Progressive Era. Just as politicians pushed for what they considered inevitable progress, so leaders in other areas called for progress and improvement in their fields—socially, economically, philosophically, and religiously. In some areas, particularly technical fields such as transportation and agriculture, the advances were genuine and remarkable. In education and religion, however, "progressive" sometimes proved to be regressive. Some progressives placed their faith in science and technology to solve the nation's problems and saw biblical religion as irrelevant.

Transportation Transformation

The development of two inventions in the Progressive Era—the automobile and the airplane—transformed American transportation in the twentieth century. They brought greater speed, power, flexibility, and dependability to transportation. The automobile in particular gave the average American a new mobility. Distances that would have intimidated an early American pioneer became mere inconveniences in the increasingly hurried life of twentieth-century America.

Automobiles

In 1896, **Henry Ford**, an engineer for the Edison Illuminating Company in Detroit, unveiled in his garage a contraption he had been tinkering with in his spare time—a motorized "horseless carriage." Ford did not invent the automobile; other inventors in America and Europe were experimenting with motorcars at the

---

Guiding Questions

1. What were the two Progressive Era transportation innovations?
2. How did the Progressive Movement affect American society?
3. What was the orthodox Christian response to liberalism in theology?

Henry Ford, who was once one of Thomas Edison's employees, talks with the genius inventor, who was nearly deaf.

time, and nothing distinguished Ford's car from the others. His vehicle, with its tiny two-cylinder engine, seemed little more than a novelty. However, Ford's grit, determination, and hard work—as well as generous financial support from several backers—enabled him to found the Ford Motor Company in 1903.

In 1908, Ford produced the Model T, a plain but remarkably sturdy car. Although the Model T was well designed, Ford's genius lay more in the manufacture of his vehicle than in the car itself. Drawing on the ideas of several other manufacturers, Ford perfected the **assembly line** method of production. Each car moved by stages along the assembly line, where at each stop a worker specializing in one task would attach his part or perform his process. By using standardized, interchangeable parts and the assembly line, Ford achieved a high degree of efficiency and speed in auto manufacturing. This allowed Ford to lower costs and make the Model T affordable through mass production. The price of a new Model T dropped steadily from more than $800 when it was first sold to $360 by 1916 and to $260 by 1925. By the 1920s, more than half the cars on America's roads were Fords.

"Tin Lizzies" ready for the road. Ford's assembly-line process revolutionized American manufacturing and transportation.

How to Make a Car
"The way to make automobiles," said Ford, "is to make one automobile like another automobile, to make them all alike, to make them come through the factory just alike."

Airplanes

Like the development of the automobile, the development of the airplane was the work of little-known, independent, Midwestern inventors. The **Wright brothers**—Orville and Wilbur—were not the only men of the era attempting to fly, but they were the first to succeed. The Wrights had first become interested in flight as boys when their father gave them a toy helicopter powered by rubber bands. Fascination with flying, however, was only one aspect of the Wright brothers' mechanical and inventive concerns. As young men in Dayton, Ohio, they began a weekly newspaper printed on a press that they had built themselves. Later, the popularity of bicycling led them to open a bicycle sales and repair shop that eventually became a successful bicycle-manufacturing firm.

The profits of their bicycle company enabled the Wrights to pursue their dream of flight. They read all the literature on flying they could find, and they experimented with homebuilt kites and gliders. Needing more room for their work, they established an

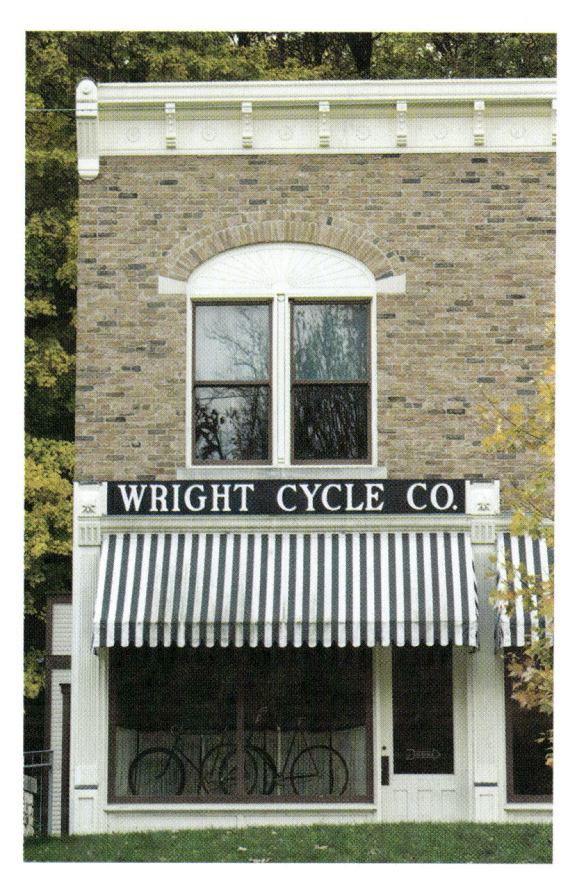

Wilbur and Orville Wright

Replica of the Wright brothers' bicycle company

experimental proving ground on the treeless, windswept dunes of Kitty Hawk, North Carolina. On December 17, 1903, after years of tiring work, Orville climbed into their flying machine, the *Flyer*. In the damp chill of the morning, the *Flyer* rolled smoothly down its track and rose into the air. The 12-second, 120-foot trip was the first powered, sustained, and controlled flight in history. From this humble beginning at Kitty Hawk, the airplane developed quickly into a faster means of shipping and transportation and a decisive military weapon.

Agriculture

The era from 1898 to 1914 is often called the "golden age" of American agriculture because the profits for American farmers skyrocketed after years of depressed prices. There were at least two major reasons for this growth. First, America's population was shifting heavily from farms to the cities. This change left increasingly fewer farmers raising food for growing cities. Farmers were able to sell as much food as they could grow, and the demand naturally drove prices up, giving farmers greater profits for their goods. Second, technology improved. Probably the most important technical advance was the development of the tractor, which provided more power and speed in sowing, cultivating, and harvesting crops. The greater speed, in turn, allowed farmers to sow and raise even more crops. Improvements in veterinary science also reduced the number of livestock that died from disease; improvements in transportation made it easier and cheaper to get foods to market. Farmers of the time saw little reason to question the progressives' claim that life for Americans was getting steadily better.

Medicine

Tremendous advances in medicine also occurred in the Progressive Era. Part of these changes involved improvements in medical organization and education. The Mayo Clinic, founded in Rochester, Minnesota, in the late 1800s, developed the concept of private group medicine (that is, creating a center for medical research and practice that brings together several doctors). Each physician contributed to the practice his strengths in medical knowledge and skill, thus providing better treatment for patients.

Likewise, the founding of Johns Hopkins Medical School in Baltimore in 1893 created, as one educator described it, "a small but ideal medical school, embodying . . . the best features of medical education in England, France, and Germany." The institution pioneered the modern medical school in which advanced research, laboratory experience, and actual hospital work are essential parts of a physician's education.

Education

What is commonly called **progressive education** actually had its greatest impact in America from the 1920s to the early 1950s. But its philosophy is rooted in the overall progressive movement. In general, progressive educators aimed at improving education by relating learning to the child's interests.

Progressive educators emphasized that they were teaching *students*, not *subjects*. Education, they said, should be based on experience rather than on simple memorization; therefore, activi-

Doctors William Mayo (*left*) and Charles Mayo (*right*) founded the Mayo Clinic.

Progressives' View of Man

Many progressives had a faulty view of the nature of man. They believed that man is basically good and that human nature could be improved. Such a belief, of course, ignored the biblical teaching that man is sinful by nature (Eph. 2:1–3). Some progressives overlooked the fact that both the men who built the corrupt institutions and the politicians and staff of the regulatory agencies were fallible men with the same sinful nature.

ties such as laboratory experiments and field trips became part of the educational process. Some progressive educators de-emphasized traditional academic subjects, such as history, and emphasized vocational education, which seemed more relevant to the student's needs.

Progressive educators rightly sought to make education more interesting and to link understanding to learning. (This is not to say that many traditional educators did *not* want to make learning interesting or that they did *not* emphasize understanding.) The

George Washington Carver

A leader in southern agriculture during and after the Progressive Era was **George Washington Carver**, a professor at Booker T. Washington's Tuskegee Institute. Born a slave in Missouri in the early 1860s, he never knew his parents. His father died when George was only two months old. Confederate guerrillas kidnapped George, his mother, and his sister during the war. George's master, Moses Carver, located George and got him back by trading the kidnappers a horse, but he never found George's mother or sister. The Carvers, devout Presbyterians, reared George in a Christian home.

Carver had an insatiable curiosity about nature with particular interest in plants. He taught himself so much about plants and soils that neighbors nicknamed him "the plant doctor." Carver wanted more than anything to get an education. Eventually, he traveled around Missouri, Kansas, and Iowa attending various schools and supporting himself by working as a cook, launderer, and common laborer. In each school, Carver stayed as long as he could learn anything from the often poorly educated teachers and then moved on.

When in his mid-twenties, Carver decided to go to college. One college quickly accepted him—but just as quickly rejected him because he was black. But Carver persevered and was able to attend and graduate from Iowa's State Agricultural College in 1894. He received his master's degree there in 1896.

Booker T. Washington offered him a teaching position at Tuskegee Institute. When Carver got there in 1896, the school had little more than its land and a few ramshackle buildings. Carver stocked his laboratory by rifling through junk piles. He cut down milk bottles to make beakers, made mortars from old coffee cups, and used fruit jars to hold chemicals. To that odd assortment of equipment, he added his own natural genius for research and experimentation.

Cotton growing had depleted the soil of the South. Carver found that certain plants—particularly peanuts—replenished the nitrogen that cotton removed from the soil. Farmers complained, however, that although peanuts might help the soil, they brought little profit to the growers. So Carver worked to find uses for peanuts. After much experimentation, he developed more than two hundred uses for the peanut, including dyes, a milk substitute, ice cream, livestock feed, fertilizer, and flour. Unfortunately, most of these did not prove to be financially profitable.

Carver's gentle spirit disarmed those who met him. Although he sometimes faced racial discrimination, Carver did not lash out at his tormentors. "No man can drag me down so low as to make me hate him," he said. He refused all offers for more prestigious, better-paying jobs. In fact, he refused even to take any raises from Tuskegee. His salary always remained what it had been when he came in 1896—$29 a week. Carver cared only that he could use his knowledge to help others.

Carver also gave his students valuable advice for life.
- "Education is the key to unlock the golden door of freedom."
- "How far you go in life depends on your being tender with the young, compassionate with the aged, sympathetic with the striving, and tolerant of the weak and strong. Because someday in your life you will have been all of these."
- "I love to think of nature as an unlimited broadcasting station, through which God speaks to us every hour, if we will only tune in."
- "Learn to do common things uncommonly well. . . . When you can do the common things in life in an uncommon way, you will command the attention of the world."
- "Ninety-nine percent of the failures come from people who have the habit of making excuses."

> **Secular Humanism in a Nutshell**
>
> Secular humanism replaces absolute standards of truth and morality with relative, pragmatic standards based on human experience (i.e., "whatever works is right"). Obviously, the Christian must reject such a system.

philosophy behind progressive methodology, however, was problematic. **John Dewey**, a professor at Columbia University and the University of Chicago, was the leading representative of progressive education and a major leader in the twentieth-century movement known as **secular humanism**. That philosophy denies the existence of God and affirms the goodness and perfectibility of man.

Ironically, public discontent over progressive education was based on the progressives' own results-oriented standard. Much of the criticism that arose in the 1950s resulted from the belief that progressive education had done a poor job of educating America's children.

Religion

Liberalism in Theology

Two closely allied religious movements grew during this period. One was a theological movement known as **modernism**. It rejected the idea that Moses wrote the first five books of the Old Testament (Genesis through Deuteronomy). Instead, modernism contended, the Israelites preserved a series of stories, legends, and myths; the priests and royal scribes gradually shaped those tales into the biblical books. Modernists did not view Christian doctrine as an expression of God's revealed Word, and thus denied biblical teachings such as the deity of Christ, His virgin birth, atonement for sin through His blood, and the inspiration of the Bible. This movement first became popular in American colleges and seminaries and soon began to spread to American pulpits through graduates who became pastors.

> **Benjamin Warfield—Opposing Modernists**
>
> Modernists claimed there were errors in the Bible; therefore, Christians should adjust what they believed. Benjamin Warfield argued that Christians must accept what the Bible teaches about itself, that it is "breathed out" by God. He noted that the prophets, beginning with Moses, repeatedly said that they were writing a message received from God and that Jesus accepted the Old Testament as being without error. Warfield then demonstrated that the Bible's authors believed that Jesus is God. By his careful scholarship, Warfield contended that modernist attempts to reinterpret the Bible were not legitimate.

The second religious movement that gained followers was the **social gospel** movement (mentioned in Chapter 16). It replaced regeneration of individuals with "regeneration" of society through social reform. They emphasized "soup and soap": feeding and cleaning people and society—rather than true salvation (spiritual regeneration). Although some of those reforms were worthwhile, advocates of the social gospel joined with the modernists in rejecting the teachings of orthodox, or traditional, Christianity.

The leader of the social gospel movement was Walter Rauschenbusch (ROU shun boosh), a New York Baptist minister and seminary professor. In 1907, he wrote *Christianity and the Social Crisis*, expounding the goals of the social gospel. Rauschenbusch denied that man has a depraved nature as the Bible teaches and believed instead that man's environment corrupts him. Improving a man's environment, therefore, would allow his natural, inherent goodness to develop. Reformers such as Rauschenbusch were sometimes justified in accusing orthodox Protestants of lacking concern for the poor, and they were also correct in saying that Christ was always touched with compassion when He saw hunger, poverty, and suffering. They were wrong, however, when they made Jesus merely a social reformer and lost sight of His more important work in the souls of men. Social reform can never suffice when man's basic need of salvation from his sin is not met.

Orthodox Defense

Orthodox Christians did not ignore these attacks on their faith; many believers responded vigorously. One of the centers for the defense of orthodox Christianity at that time was Princeton Theological Seminary. Theologians at Princeton responded pointedly and intelligently to modernist and evolutionist attacks on the Bible. Perhaps the greatest of those defenders of the Faith in both the extent of his writing and the depth of his thought was Benjamin B. Warfield, professor at Princeton from 1887 until his death in 1921. Sadly, only a few years after Warfield's death, the modernists took control of Princeton Seminary.

Some Christians opposed unbiblical teachings by thoroughly educating other believers in the truths of Scripture. One method was the Bible institute, a school similar to a college but whose curriculum usually consisted almost entirely of courses in Bible or church-related subjects, such as Sunday school work. Bible institutes normally granted certificates or diplomas instead of college degrees.

But not all Christians could attend Bible institutes, so many of them spent their vacations at Bible conferences. These sessions featured noted preachers and Bible teachers and were held in resort spots for a week or more during the summer. The two pioneer American Bible conferences were the Niagara Conference, held in Ontario, and D. L. Moody's Northfield Conference in Massachusetts. Probably the most important twentieth-century conference in size and longevity was the Winona Lake Bible Conference in Indiana.

One notable orthodox means of defending and furthering the Christian faith was the continuation of the urban revivals popularized by D. L. Moody. After Moody's death in 1899, the most important urban evangelist was William A. "**Billy**" **Sunday**. Born in Iowa in 1862, the athletic Sunday launched into a successful professional baseball career in 1883.

In 1886, while drinking with his teammates, Sunday heard a group of workers from the Pacific Garden Mission singing in the street. Reminded of the gospel songs his devout mother had sung, Sunday followed the singers back to the mission. After attending several services there, Sunday was converted. He married in 1888 and left baseball altogether in 1891 to work for the YMCA.

He later entered into a new career as an evangelist. His popular style of preaching soon brought in the crowds. When church and city auditoriums proved inadequate to hold the growing crowds at Sunday's meetings, he borrowed an idea that Moody had used in his early campaigns—the tabernacle. Tabernacles were wide, low, wooden, barn-like structures built especially for the campaigns. To reduce noise, the floors of the tabernacles were covered with sawdust. When someone came down the aisle in response to one of Sunday's altar calls, he was said to have "hit the sawdust trail."

Billy Sunday's reputation grew throughout the early twentieth century. His most famous campaign was in New York City in 1917. In that ten-week campaign, nearly one and a half *million* people attended his meetings, and almost one hundred thousand responded to his altar calls. That campaign marked the height of Sunday's career.

Early Bible Institutes

One of the earliest major Bible institutes was Nyack Missionary College, founded by A. B. Simpson of the Christian and Missionary Alliance in 1882. Another was D. L. Moody's Chicago Bible Institute (1889; renamed Moody Bible Institute after its founder's death). In 1908, the Bible Institute of Los Angeles (Biola) was established. It thrived under the leadership of R. A. Torrey from 1912 to 1924. Today it is known as Biola University.

Evangelist Billy Sunday was noted for his antics in the pulpit and his support for Prohibition.

Billy Sunday's Baseball Career

Billy Sunday spent eight seasons in the major leagues, compiling solid but not record-breaking statistics. Sunday was never an overpowering hitter; his highest batting average for one season was .291, perhaps a little better than average in that era. Sunday's first manager, "Cap" Anson of the Chicago White Stockings (now known as the Cubs), reported that Billy struck out his first thirteen times at bat.

Sunday was fast, however, and a good fielder. He won respect when he joined the Chicago team by racing their fastest man and beating him by fifteen feet in a hundred-yard race. The evangelist later said that he had set a record by rounding the bases in fourteen seconds from a standing start. While in Chicago, he had the honor of playing on pennant-winning teams in 1885 and 1886.

Throughout his evangelistic career, Sunday drew upon his baseball career for illustrations. He was known, for example, to "slide into home" on the platform in order to clinch a point. He also sprinkled his sermons with baseball terminology. Sunday, for instance, recounted the deathbed experiences of a former teammate in a style more reminiscent of a sportscaster than a preacher. "It seemed like he was trying to stretch a three-base hit into a home run, and he rounded third with all his strength, and as he leaped as if to try and make it, the Umpire leaned over the battlements of the universe and said: 'You're out!'" When criticized for such informality in his preaching, Sunday replied, "I want to reach the people so I use the people's language."

Billy Sunday's Aggressive, Popular Style

To reach the masses, Sunday added dramatic, almost athletic gestures to his sermons and spoke in a slangy vernacular. The following example is from his sermon "The Three Groups":

"I don't expect any of those ossified, petrified, dyed-in-the-wool, stamped on the cork Presbyterians or Episcopalians to shout 'Amen,' but it would do you good and loosen you up. . . . I think about half the professing Christians amount to nothing as a spiritual force. They have a kind regard for religion, but as for having a firm grip on God . . . [and a] willingness to strike hard blows against the devil, they are almost a failure."

Gradually, an orthodox alliance was forming in the United States. Orthodox theologians such as Warfield, popular preachers such as Sunday, and other Christians were finding that they had a common interest in defending the Faith against modernism. In the 1920s, a major battle would occur between orthodox Christianity and liberal religion for control of America's churches.

Section Review

1–2. What two inventions in the Progressive Era transformed American transportation?

3. What was probably the most important technological advance in agriculture during the Progressive Era?

4–5. Who was the leading representative of progressive education? In what philosophical movement was he a leader?

6–7. What two religious movements became popular with those who embraced liberalism in theology?

★ Explain the role of Princeton Theological Seminary in the defense of Christian orthodoxy.

★ Compare the social gospel movement to orthodox Christianity.

IV. Progressivism Evaluated

The progressive movement was obviously a highly influential force in American history. But were its effects generally beneficial or harmful to the nation?

Guiding Question

What were the results of Progressivism?

Many progressive reforms were worthwhile. Thanks to progressive efforts, Americans enjoyed purer food and drugs, better service from gas and water utilities, and greater participation in the political process. For example, women received the right to vote; the secret ballot was adopted; and in many areas government corruption was reduced. Furthermore, changes in transportation, particularly the development of the automobile and the airplane, vastly improved society. Conservation of natural resources was emphasized and some of the country's most beautiful national parks were established. Many medical advancements were made. The value of these advancements is evident.

However, the movement created problems. Critics noted that the reforms brought an increase in the powers of government. Additional government authority was necessary for progressives to achieve the regulation of business, industry, and government they desired. Opponents argued that the Founding Fathers designed a limited government with limited powers but that progressives encouraged a shift to an expanding government with enhanced powers. Progressives believed this was necessary for a growing nation. They did not fear the growth of government; after all, they contended, the people control the government. However, others argued that government is not so easily managed: expansion of its powers leads only to further expansion and a reduction in individual freedoms. Also, opponents said some progressive reforms actually shielded the government from public control. They said enlarging the government to oversee new requirements created a class of bureaucrats who were often immune to public pressure.

Many progressives believed in the inevitability of progress. Some based that belief on evolution. The course of world history, evolutionary progressives argued, points to ever-upward improvement. Even some in the movement who denied evolution still affirmed their faith in progress. Many Christians of the era, for example, believed that as the gospel spread throughout the world, life on earth would continue to advance until the kingdom of God was established on earth and Christ returned.

Progressives believed that through education, improved living conditions, and more equal political and economic opportunity society would improve. Though that might be true, it tended to ignore the biblical teaching that man's basic problem is not his ignorance or his environment but his sin—a problem that can be remedied only by forgiveness and cleansing through the death and resurrection of Christ.

The results of progressivism were like the results of many other movements in history—mixed. Positives and negatives can be easily cited. Historians have argued its merits and shortcomings for decades. The movement did establish a major theme of twentieth-century American history—the gradual but almost continuous growth of the power of the federal government.

Section Review

1. What did many progressives believe was inevitable?
2. Discuss the biblical teaching that some progressives ignored.
3. What major theme of twentieth-century America did the progressive movement establish?

People, Places, and Things to Remember

progressivism
secret ballot
direct primaries
initiative
referendum
recall
trustbusting
gas-and-water socialism
Sixteenth Amendment
Seventeenth Amendment
Prohibition
Eighteenth Amendment
Nineteenth Amendment
Susan B. Anthony
muckrakers
Eugene V. Debs
Robert La Follette
Theodore Roosevelt
Square Deal
The Jungle
Hepburn Act
Pure Food and Drug Act
Meat Inspection Act
Jim Crow laws
segregation
literacy tests
poll taxes
grandfather clause
Plessy v. Ferguson
Booker T. Washington
W. E. B. Du Bois
National Association for the Advancement of Colored People (NAACP)
Panama Canal
yellow fever
malaria
Roosevelt Corollary
William Howard Taft
Joseph Cannon
dollar diplomacy
Progressive Party
Woodrow Wilson
Underwood Tariff Act
Federal Reserve Act
Clayton Antitrust Act
Federal Trade Commission Act
Henry Ford
assembly line
Wright brothers
George Washington Carver
progressive education
John Dewey
secular humanism
modernism
social gospel
Billy Sunday

CHAPTER REVIEW

Making Connections

1–5. List five specific progressive reforms that expressed progressives' faith in direct democracy.

6. What connection exists between the income tax and government growth?

7. Which of the three presidents of the Progressive Era is probably most closely identified with the progressive movement?

8–10. List three problems with the ideology of the progressive movement.

Developing History Skills

1. Analyze the Roosevelt Corollary and its impact during the early twentieth century.

2. What has been the long-term result of the federal government's setting aside millions of acres of land? (You may need to go beyond the textbook to provide a complete answer.)

Thinking Critically

1. Which policy—Roosevelt's "big stick" or Taft's "dollar diplomacy"—best served U.S. interests in the long term? Support your answer.

2. An emphasis on science that excludes scriptural teaching has become more prevalent in our society. Choose either embryonic stem cell research, LGBTQ issues, or poverty reduction and explain how that is the case.

Living as a Christian Citizen

1. Should Christians have been involved in the various causes of the progressive movement? Explain your answer. Note also the potential problems in the position you take.

2. Progressives expanded the power of government to deal with social ills. Is there a biblical position on the size and kind of government a nation ought to have?

THE GREAT WAR (1914–1920)

19

Sometimes people call me an idealist. Well, that is the way I know I am an American. . . . America is the only idealistic nation in the world.

Woodrow Wilson
defending his record, 1919

American soldiers in World War I

I. Idealism

II. Intervention

III. Isolation

Big Ideas

1. What events brought the United States into the European war?

2. How did the United States help bring the war to a successful conclusion?

3. What were the competing attitudes of Americans following the war?

Macy's department store had men's summer suits on sale for $6.95. Shoppers could add straw hats for a low clearance price of $1.59. For readers of the Sunday edition of the *New York Times* on June 28, 1914, the ads were another reminder that vacation was just around the corner. Elsewhere in the paper, headlines told how the tough fists of boxing champ Jack Johnson had put yet another challenger on the canvas; the Brooklyn Dodgers made easy work of the Philadelphia Phillies in yesterday's double-header; and Kay Laurell was appearing on Broadway with the Ziegfeld Follies. The newspaper's political cartoon that day, celebrating a number of successful diplomatic initiatives, depicted a rusty sword over the caption "Another Business Depression." It was a comforting cartoon for that balmy summer morning in America. The sword, still in its case, symbolized the absence of military conflicts. Yet halfway around the world, a distant disturbance on that sleepy Sunday was destined to shake an unwary America and the world off its nineteenth-century foundation. In many ways, the twentieth century began on June 28, 1914, in an obscure little city in Central Europe called Sarajevo.

The day in the Austrian provincial capital promised to be festive, a day of parties and parades, for it was the Feast of St. Vitus. In addition, Austrian **Archduke Francis (Franz) Ferdinand**, heir to the throne of the Austro-Hungarian Empire, and his wife, Sophie, were coming for a visit. The royal couple had cause for celebration as well because that day was their fourteenth wedding anniversary.

Beneath the flags and bunting, however, a dark scene was quietly shaping. Seven Serbian youths, members of the terrorist group Black Hand, were plotting murder against the Austrians in the name of Serbian nationalism. They positioned themselves along the parade route, awaiting the archduke's motorcade. Then they launched their coordinated attack. After narrowly escaping one assassin's bomb, the chauffeur took a wrong turn into a side street, slowing the car to make the turn and coming within five feet of one of the Serbian assassins, Gavrilo Princip. Princip raised his small Belgian pistol and fired two quick shots. The world would never be the same. Franz Ferdinand was shot in the neck; Sophie, in the abdomen. As the blood ran from her husband's mouth, Sophie cried, "For heaven's sake, what's happened to you?" Slumping over his wife's body, the dying archduke rasped his answer repeatedly: *"Es ist nichts, es ist nichts."* ("It is nothing, it is nothing.")

The sun that had risen over a festive city now sank blood red over Europe. Ironically, what the archduke said was "nothing" was the "spark" that led to what was soon called the Great War or the World War. Four more summers would come and go before the bitter harvest of war was finally gathered. The body count that followed coldly quantified the death of a generation—almost ten million soldiers killed, about twenty million wounded.

The devastating results of Princip's actions were not readily apparent, however, either in Europe or in faraway America. The next day, the papers duly reported the murder, and President Wilson wired the nation's condolences to the Austrians. In the weeks that followed, though, the European powers, caught in a web of treaties and intrigues, stumbled headlong into war. The **Central Powers**—Germany and Austria—split the continent against the **Allies**—France, Britain, and Russia. Other countries later joined

Archduke Francis Ferdinand and his wife Sophie (*above*) are shown shortly before they were murdered by Gavrilo Princip (*below*).

each side; the number of nations in the war eventually exceeded thirty. Despite the broad Atlantic buffer and a long tradition of isolation, not even the United States could avoid the forces of war that pulled the world into Europe's conflict. Much of Woodrow Wilson's two terms would be occupied with avoiding the war, fighting the war, and concluding the war. By the end of the decade, America was shouldered with an ill-fitting mantle of world leadership.

I. Idealism

"It would be an irony of fate if my administration had to deal chiefly with foreign affairs," Woodrow Wilson privately remarked before his inauguration in March 1913. Such irony would indeed be his "fate." The bespectacled professor, along with his secretary of state, **William Jennings Bryan**, had limited knowledge of international affairs and no experience in diplomacy; yet there was much in Wilson's background and character that would leave an enduring mark on America's foreign policy. He sought to make the United States the moral leader among nations, believing that America's role in the world was to promote democracy and peace by example and persuasion.

Wilson saw America as having a new Manifest Destiny, not of territorial expansion but of sharing political ideals. In a key foreign policy address delivered in Mobile, Alabama, in 1913, Wilson declared:

> It is a very perilous thing to determine the foreign policy of a nation in the terms of material interest. It not only is unfair to those with whom you are dealing, but it is degrading as regards your own actions....
>
> I want to take this occasion to say that the United States will never again seek one additional foot of territory by conquest. She will devote herself to showing that she knows how to make honorable and fruitful use of the territory she has....
>
> We dare not turn from the principle that morality and not expediency is the thing that must guide us and that we will never condone iniquity because it is most convenient to do so.

Wilson wanted to expand the United States economically by promoting trade with other nations. In helping American companies make profits, he thought that he could also promote freedom and democratic ideas and help other countries improve economically. Despite his noble goals, political realities soon challenged Wilson's ability to enact his proposals. He came to view all opposition to his views as wrong.

The Mexican Muddle

Wilson's idealism was first put to the test in Mexico. From 1876 to 1911 **Porfirio Díaz** (pohr-FEE-ryoh DEE-ahz) ruled Mexico with an iron fist toward his opposition and an open palm toward foreign investors. Dictator Díaz and European and American businessmen all profited from the petroleum and mining resources of Mexico but left the Mexican people impoverished. In 1911, a popular revolt led by Francisco Madero drove Díaz out of office, but the rebellion

Guiding Questions

1. How did President Wilson's idealism differ from his international intervention?
2. How did the United States try to avoid entanglement in the war?
3. What events led many Americans to support the Allies?

Wilson's Background

Woodrow Wilson grew up in a Presbyterian home. His father, the Reverend Joseph Ruggles Wilson, instilled in his son sturdy moral convictions and a strong belief in God's sovereign direction in the universe. President Wilson brought that moral vision to his foreign policymaking.

Pancho Villa (center), shown here with General John J. Pershing (right), was a U.S. favorite in the Mexicans' struggle for control of their government.

Later, Pancho Villa became an enemy of the United States after killing American civilians in Mexico and Columbus, New Mexico. General Pershing was assigned to track him down and bring him to justice. Pershing never found him.

He Couldn't Win

To his credit, Wilson resisted the full-scale war with Mexico that many in Congress urged. Yet in the wake of his withdrawal of American troops, Wilson's heavy-handed idealism gained the president little more than ridicule at home and resentment abroad.

also unleashed violent rivals for power, groups that had previously been suppressed by Díaz's stern rule.

Just weeks before Wilson's inauguration, President Madero was murdered by his own military commander, the ruthless General **Victoriano Huerta** (WEHR tah). Many countries quickly extended diplomatic recognition to the new Mexican government in hopes of reestablishing profitable business relations as in the days of Díaz. Previously, most countries, including the United States, traditionally extended such recognition if a government simply *held* power, without concerning themselves with *how* it obtained that power. (Huerta's regime has since been described as "one of the most grotesque tyrannies in Mexican history.")

But this time it was different. Woodrow Wilson refused to recognize "government by murder." "My ideal is an orderly and righteous government in Mexico," he declared. He added, "My passion is for the submerged 85 percent of the people of that Republic who are now struggling toward liberty." The former professor later warned, "I am going to teach the South American republics to elect good men!"

Determined to drive, in Wilson's words, the "desperate brute" out of office, the president began supplying weapons to Huerta's challengers, Venustiano Carranza (vay-NOOS-tee-AH-noh kah-RAHN-zah) and **Pancho Villa** (PAHN-cho VEE-yah) while also eliminating armament shipments to Huerta. In April 1914, a group of American sailors in Tampico, Mexico, were arrested. Although they were soon released and the local commander expressed regret to the American naval commander, the U.S. government was outraged. Wilson, citing national honor, went to Congress and requested authority to use force against the Huerta regime. On April 20, 1914, Congress granted the request. American marines landed in the city of Veracruz. Following a bloody clash between U.S. troops and Mexicans there, the "ABC powers" (Argentina, Brazil, and Chile) mediated a truce between the United States and Mexico. The accumulated internal and international pressure encouraged by Wilson eventually toppled Huerta, bringing Carranza to power.

Peace, however, did not come with Huerta's exit. Villa soon rebelled against Carranza. Wilson at first supported Villa. He believed Villa wanted to improve the lives of poor Mexicans. As the fight between Villa and Carranza intensified, Wilson decided to withdraw his support. Villa was furious with the Americans.

Villa was a ruthless man. In January 1916, he had a train stopped in northern Mexico, and his men murdered eighteen Americans in cold blood. Two months later, his men led a raid into New Mexico, where his band killed seventeen more Americans and burned the border town of Columbus. In response, President Wilson sent General **John J.** ("Black Jack") **Pershing** into Mexico with eleven thousand troops to capture the bandit. After months of searching fruitlessly for the elusive Villa, and as problems with the European war loomed ever larger, Wilson ordered Pershing to cancel the expedition in early 1917.

Mexico and the Caribbean During Wilson's Presidency

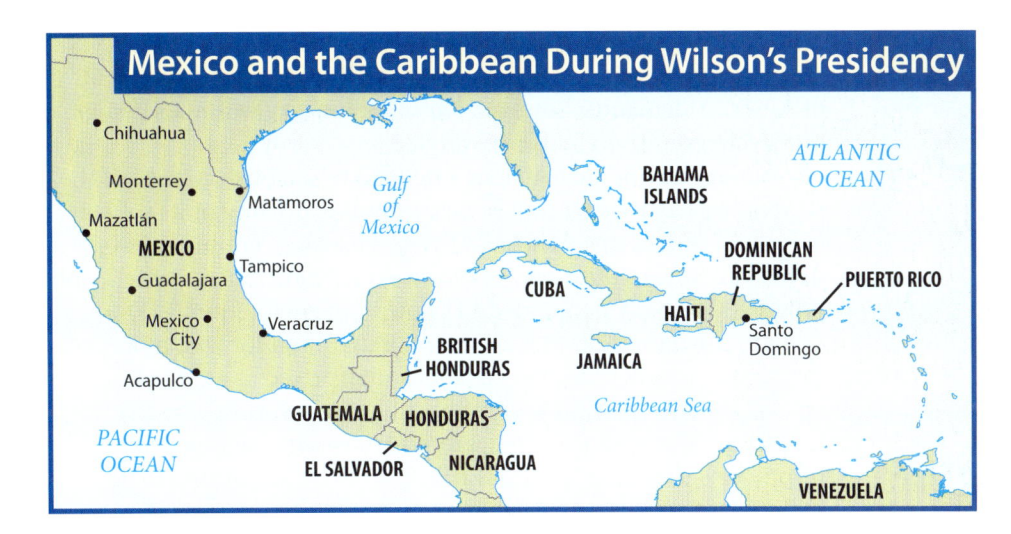

Caribbean Conflict

At the beginning of his administration, President Wilson denounced both Taft's dollar diplomacy and Roosevelt's "big stick" policies as contrary to the new moral leadership of the United States. But the desire to protect the strategic Panama Canal and Wilson's eagerness to see America's neighbors form orderly democratic governments led to a number of military interventions in the Caribbean.

More than a half-dozen presidents in Haiti were killed or overthrown between 1911 and 1915. Fearing both the loss of American lives or property and European intervention, Wilson ordered U.S. Marines to occupy Haiti. American forces were there from July 1915 until 1934. They built roads and schools and established order. Unfortunately, the U.S. dominated the government of the nation, often ignoring the opinions of the Haitian people.

Next door to Haiti, in the Dominican Republic, civil war erupted in 1916. A U.S. Marine police force occupied that area until 1924. As in Haiti, the Dominican Republic benefited materially during the U.S. occupation, but resentment of the "Colossus of the North" remained high in Latin America.

The Irony of It All

Ironically, Wilson, who set out to mend fences with America's southern neighbors, conducted more peacetime interventions than any of his predecessors. Wilson's idealism often ran afoul of strategic demands and uncontrollable events, sometimes creating sharp differences between plans and reality. Despite Wilson's nagging foreign policy questions over Mexico, Central America, and the Caribbean, a far greater crisis loomed at the same time—the threat of American involvement in a European war.

The Web of War

By the early twentieth century, several of the major nations of Europe had aligned themselves into two mutual defense alliances. The German chancellor, or prime minister, Otto von Bismarck, established the **Triple Alliance** of Germany, Austria-Hungary, and Italy in 1882. France, Russia, and Great Britain, fearing the growing German Empire, allied themselves in the **Triple Entente** (ahn TAHNT) in 1907.

After Gavrilo Princip assassinated Archduke Ferdinand on June 28, 1914, fears and friendships among the nations of Europe caused them to slide into war. The government of Austria-Hungary, believing that the Serbian government was at least passively responsible for their archduke's assassination, issued an ultimatum on July 23. It demanded that Serbia suppress all anti-Austrian sentiments in the country and allow Austria-Hungary to send

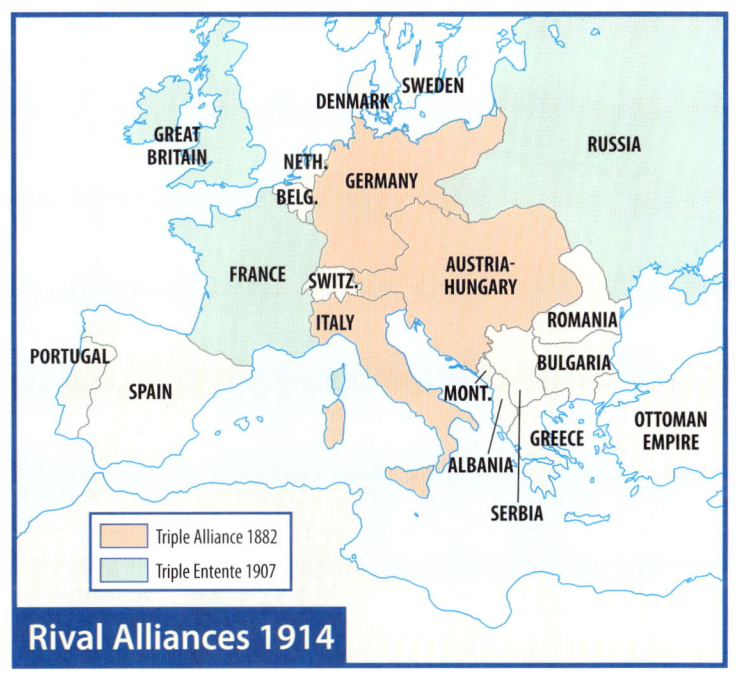

Rival Alliances 1914

Kaiser Wilhelm II

British News

Propaganda, information spread to advance a cause or damage an opponent's cause, became a major part of the war. After the British seized control of the transatlantic cables, they provided most of the war news available to Americans. After the war, many German "atrocities" that had been reported in the news were exposed as exaggerated products of British propaganda writers. The reality was bad enough. For example, German troops burned Belgian homes and historic monuments and occasionally shot unarmed civilians whom they had randomly selected.

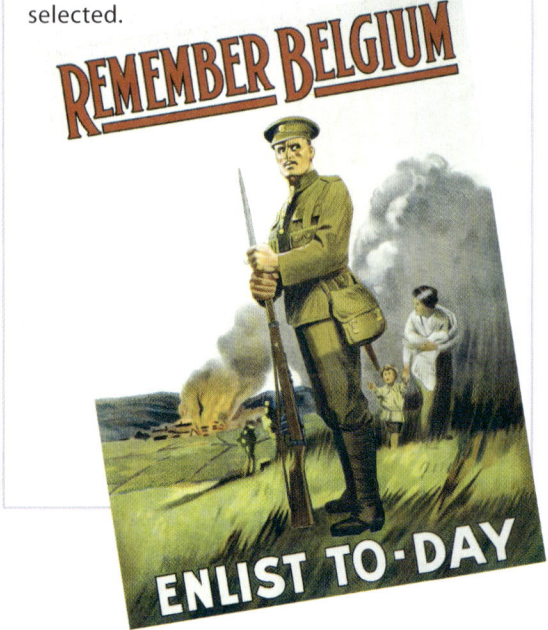

officials to investigate matters relating to the archduke's death. Surprisingly, Serbia replied that it was willing to accept almost all of Austria's demands; however, Austria-Hungary was not satisfied and declared war on Serbia on July 28.

Russia, fearing that Austria intended to establish control of the region, began **mobilization** of its troops (assembling of its soldiers) on July 30. Germany, Austria's ally, declared war on Russia two days later. Since Russia and France were both members of the Triple Entente, Germany demanded to know France's intentions. The French, concerned about Germany's preparation for war, mobilized their troops, an act that the Germans interpreted as aggressive.

Facing war with Russia and possibly France, the Germans turned to their long-standing, secret strategy for waging a two-front war—the Schlieffen (SHLEEF ehn) Plan. According to its directives, the German army had to first crush France quickly by swinging through Belgium and occupying Paris within six weeks after declaring war. German troops would then turn east to defeat the Russians, who were not expected to organize quickly. Thus, on August 2, the German ruler, Kaiser **Wilhelm II**, asked neutral Belgium for permission to pass through its country in the event of a war with France. The following day, the Belgium king denied the request. He said, "Belgium is a nation, not a road." That same day, August 3, Germany declared war on France.

But first, German troops invaded Belgium. Britain had a treaty with Belgium promising to protect the neutrality of that nation. The British demanded that Germany withdraw its troops. The German chancellor sneered at Britain's commitment to a "scrap of paper" (its treaty with Belgium) and ignored the British demand. Britain declared war on Germany on August 4. A world war began.

In the midst of the tense but vain negotiations, the British foreign minister, Sir Edward Grey, noticed the London streetlamps being extinguished. He sadly—and prophetically—observed, "The lamps are going out all over Europe; we shall not see them lit again in our lifetime." Princip's assassination of Ferdinand lit the powder keg that would blow Europe to pieces and rattle the rest of the world. Within a week of the war beginning, all members of the Triple Alliance and Triple Entente joined the war except Italy. Italians felt that Germany and Austria-Hungary had acted too hastily in declaring war.

As confident German troops marched into Belgium, the words of their kaiser rang in their ears: "You will be home before the leaves have fallen from the trees." Brave Belgian and British troops, however, offered tough resistance, buying precious time for the French. By the end of August, the Germans had approached the outskirts of Paris, where their war machine ground to a halt. The French and British made valiant but costly attempts to push back the invasion. In the first month of war, the French alone lost two hundred thousand troops in battle.

The Slippery Slope of Neutrality

When news of the war reached the United States, President Wilson issued a proclamation of neutrality. He urged Americans not to take the side of either the Allies or the Central Powers. Yet neutral sentiment was absent in much of the country. As the scope of the conflict became evident, the American people were deeply divided.

Melting Pot Problems

The New World could hardly ignore the Old World's war. Many Americans had been born in Germany or were descended from German immigrants. Many Irish immigrants and their descendants also favored Germany, mainly because they opposed Britain. Most Americans, however, had their roots in Great Britain, and Americans generally admired British law, institutions, and culture. They also favored France because of its aid in America's Revolutionary War. As poet Robert Underwood Johnson, reflecting on the assistance of Marquis de Lafayette and other Frenchmen, glowingly declared:

> Forget us, God, if we forget
> The sacred sword of Lafayette!

Americans who favored the Allies tended to view Germany as a dictatorial, militaristic aggressor—a view that British and French propaganda naturally encouraged by portraying Germans (whom they called "the Huns") as monsters.

The Trade Trigger

America's strong economic ties with the Allies increased during the war. Because of the British blockade of Germany and the British navy's control of the Atlantic, American trade with the Central Powers all but ceased. When the Allies exhausted their credit in buying American goods, Wilson allowed American banks to grant loans to the Allies. This prevented a collapse of American trade. In essence, the United States, while proclaiming its neutrality, was actually waging a *pro-Allies* neutrality. This policy would eventually help propel the United States into the war. The Germans, suffering the effects of the British blockade, unleashed a deadly weapon on the high seas that made even trade with the Allies all but impossible. The German navy was making extensive use of submarines, which were called **U-boats** (from *Unterseeboot*, a German word for a submarine).

German U-boat

Submarine Warfare

Probably the most significant factor in America's entrance into the war was the violation of American rights on the sea by German submarines. Britain had blockaded Germany, prohibiting even the importation of food. A starving Germany countered by declaring the seas around Britain to be a war zone in which any ship would be subject to submarine attack.

According to **international law**, warships could not sink a merchant or passenger ship until two conditions were fulfilled. First, the presence of war materiel aboard those vessels had to be confirmed. Second, the crew and passengers on the ships had to be evacuated. Submarines had difficulty completing these requirements because they would have to surface to do so. Surfacing would

> # NOTICE!
>
> TRAVELLERS intending to embark on the Atlantic voyage are reminded that a state of war exists between Germany and her allies and Great Britain and her allies; that the zone of war includes the waters adjacent to the British Isles; that, in accordance with formal notice given by the Imperial German Government, vessels flying the flag of Great Britain, or any of her allies, are liable to destruction in those waters and that travelers sailing in the war zone on ships of Great Britain and her allies do so at their own risk.
>
> **IMPERIAL GERMAN EMBASSY**
> WASHINGTON, D. C., APRIL 22, 1915

German warning to travellers

Lusitania

The sinking of the *Lusitania* shocked many Americans out of their neutral attitude toward Germany.

make them easy targets for deck guns aboard ships or for ramming by a larger vessel.

Thus, in February 1915, Germany announced that it intended to follow **unrestricted submarine warfare**. This meant all ships entering the war zone would be subject to attack without warning. President Wilson warned the Germans that this abandoning of international law was unacceptable. In late April 1915, the German government placed advertisements in about fifty American newspapers, including the *New York Times*, warning American citizens not to travel into the war zone.

The British passenger ship *Lusitania* left New York on May 1, 1915, with a number of Americans aboard. When the liner entered the war zone near Ireland on May 7, no British patrol boat gave it the usual escort. The commander of a German submarine spotted the ship and fired a torpedo. Within eighteen minutes, the large liner sank, and 1,198 passengers and crewmen, including 128 Americans, perished.

President Wilson was deeply moved by the tragedy but resisted the calls of some Americans to declare war. With moral idealism, he declared, "There is such a thing as a man being too proud to fight. There is such a thing as a nation being so right that it does not need to convince others by force that it is right."

Although political opponents would scorn Wilson with his own words—"too proud to fight"—the president realized that the country was too divided to enter the war. One cabinet official remarked after the *Lusitania* incident that Californians were more concerned with their citrus crop than with fighting.

Wilson demanded that the Germans apologize and provide financial compensation for American families affected by the *Lusitania*'s sinking. Germany expressed regret for the loss of life but asserted that the sinking was "just self-defense" since the passenger vessel was also carrying war materiel. Later, Secretary of State William Jennings Bryan resigned because he feared Wilson's words were too harsh and would lead to war with Germany.

Whatever the Germans' justification, the *Lusitania* incident caused a change in many Americans' attitudes toward the Germans. As one newspaper stated, "The torpedo that sank the *Lusitania* also sank Germany in the opinion of mankind."

Three months later, a German U-boat sank another British passenger ship, the *Arabic*. More than forty passengers died, including two Americans. After American protest, Germany agreed to abandon unrestricted submarine warfare. But on March 24, 1916, a German submarine attacked an unarmed French passenger ship, the *Sussex*, in the English Channel. Among those killed and injured were several Americans. The furor over the *Sussex* caused Wilson to warn the Germans that another attack on passenger or merchant vessels would mean a break in diplomatic ties and likely war. Germany issued the "**Sussex pledge**." It restated Germany's promise to follow international law.

Election of 1916

The presidential campaign of 1916 could not escape the shadow of the foreign crisis. In St. Louis, Democrats held a thunderous convention to nominate Wilson for a second term, cheering, "He kept us out of war." On the Republican side, Supreme Court Justice Charles Evans Hughes resigned his position to run for president.

In many ways, the election mirrored the nation's mood. In the East, where war fever was highest, Hughes won the states handily. However, the German-Americans and Irish-Americans of the Midwest supported Wilson, and on the Pacific coast, Wilson's neutrality was popular. Wilson's victory over Hughes on the winning slogan "He kept us out of war" seemed to indicate a mandate for his second term. Yet the slogan was in the *past tense*—it was not a pledge at all. The future remained as uncertain as it was threatening.

Section Review

1. Why did Wilson refuse to recognize the government of Huerta in Mexico?
2–3. Name two countries in the Caribbean in which the United States intervened during Wilson's presidency.
4. The German invasion of what nation brought Great Britain into World War I?
5. What was Woodrow Wilson's campaign slogan in the election of 1916?
★ Explain why it could be said that America was waging a pro-Allies neutrality in the early part of World War I.
★ Evaluate Woodrow Wilson's response to the sinking of the *Lusitania*. Was it appropriate? Explain your answer.

II. Intervention

The Great War was going badly for both sides. New technology born of industrialization gave the armies mass-produced weapons for mass-produced death. One tragic illustration of this change is the British offensive at the Somme. On the opening day, July 1, 1916, the British suffered sixty thousand casualties—the bloodiest day in modern history. By the end of the Somme campaign, the British had gained four or five miles of mud, but the price was steep, with almost half a million British soldiers killed or wounded.

Guiding Questions

1. What events led the United States to declare war on the Central Powers?
2. How did the war affect American society?
3. How did American intervention affect the outcome of the war?

> **On the Slaughter at the Somme**
>
> "Before the war it had seemed incredible that such terrors and slaughters . . . could last more than a few months. After the first two years it was difficult to believe that they would ever end."
> —Winston Churchill

In addition, there were about 700,000 German and French casualties.

On the other side of the Atlantic, Wilson feared that the war would not end before America was dragged into it. Drawing on the idealism that characterized his foreign policy goals, Wilson appeared before the Senate and issued a historic declaration. In that January 1917 speech, he warned the deadlocked nations of Europe that only "peace without victory" could provide a lasting solution. Further, Wilson urged the formation of an organization consisting of countries, later called the League of Nations, that would provide a forum for settling international disputes.

In Europe, where millions of men lay in untimely graves, Wilson's "peace without victory" was not even a consideration. A week after Wilson's speech, the Germans, sorely pressed by the British blockade, declared they would resume the unrestricted submarine warfare. *All* ships in the war zone—passenger or merchant, from a nation at war or a neutral one—would be sunk without warning.

Wilson reluctantly severed diplomatic ties with Germany on February 3, 1917. Many Americans, including the president, still hoped that war could yet be avoided. Such thinking, however, would quickly change.

Declaring War

On March 1, tensions heightened with the revelation of a secret, though clumsy, German diplomatic plot. The German foreign minister, Arthur Zimmermann, sought to gain Mexico's support in case the United States joined the Allies. He sent a telegram to Mexico offering to help that nation reconquer Texas, New Mexico, and Arizona. He also asked Mexico to influence Japan to join the Central Powers. The British intercepted and decoded the telegram and then enthusiastically forwarded it to the United States. When the details of the **Zimmermann telegram** were first revealed, they seemed so fantastic that some people thought the entire affair was a British hoax. When the message was verified, however, Americans were outraged. Interestingly, Zimmermann's scheme succeeded in arousing the western United States, an area that had been indifferent to Europe's war. Now, with their lands being "promised" to Mexico, many westerners were eager to enter the world war.

Two weeks later, German submarines sank four unarmed American merchant vessels. More than thirty civilians were killed. On April 2, the president appeared before a joint session of Congress and requested that the House and Senate formally recognize that Germany had "thrust" a state of war upon the United States. Wilson said, "The world must be made safe for democracy. Its peace must be planted upon the tested foundations of political liberty." Within days, the Senate voted 82 to 6 to declare war on Germany, the leading member of the Central Powers. The House of Representatives agreed by a vote of 373 to 50. On **April 6, 1917**, the

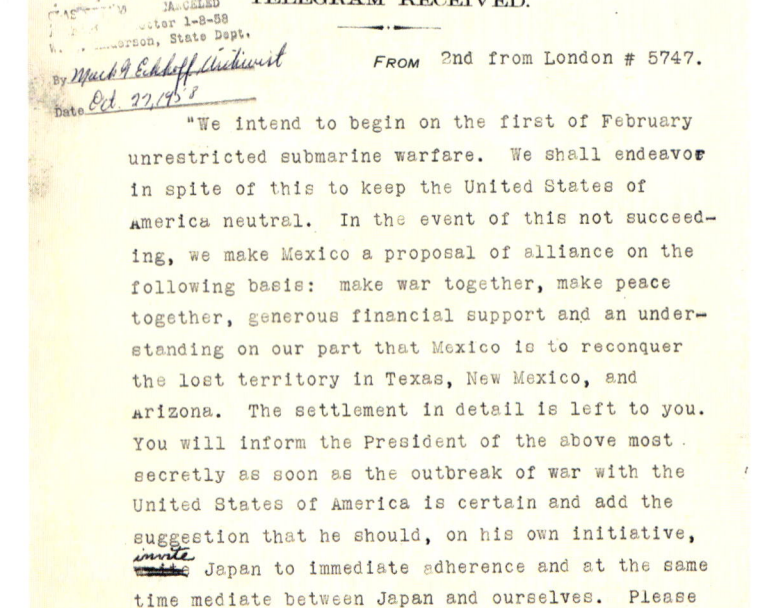

The Zimmermann telegram (*below*) outraged Americans. It was a major reason the U.S. declared war on Germany (*see newspaper bottom*) in April 1917.

Black American Soldiers in World War I

Of the more than four million Americans who served in World War I, about 350,000 were African Americans. Many of them enlisted to demonstrate their patriotism and hoped that their service would improve their opportunities at home. Unfortunately, they faced much discrimination in the military. Most were assigned to support roles, such as cooks and laborers; however, some 40,000 were involved in combat.

One of the most distinguished units was the 369th Infantry Regiment. They fought on the front lines in Europe for six months, longer than any other Americans during the war. During that time, they did not surrender any territory to the enemy nor were any of the soldiers captured. Germans, recognizing their courage and determination, nicknamed them the "Hellfighters." These New Yorkers were soon known as the "Harlem Hellfighters." The French government honored them with the prestigious Croix de Guerre (the war cross) in recognition of their bravery.

More than three thousand veterans of the 369th Infantry paraded through New York City after the war ended. An estimated two million were there to welcome them back to America. Unfortunately, little changed for black Americans after the war concluded. Prejudice was still common in much of the nation.

---

president signed the declaration—America entered World War I on the side of the Allies.

Over Here

Raising an Army

America found itself ill-prepared to answer Wilson's call to war. At the time of the war declaration, the peacetime army and National Guard numbered only 379,000 men. Remarkably, that number increased tenfold to 3.7 million by the end of the war. This rapid recruitment to meet the tremendous manpower demands of modern war was the result of a national draft through the **Selective Service Act**. In 1917, all men ages 21 to 30 were required to register for the draft, and in 1918 the bracket was expanded to include those 18 to 45 years old. Altogether, 2.8 million men were drafted into the army. The total number of Americans in the military during the conflict exceeded 4 million. About half of those were transported to France to fight.

When the recruits arrived at hastily constructed boot camps, they quickly learned just how unprepared the United States was for the war to which they were being committed. Theodore Roosevelt, a longtime—though often unheeded—champion of military preparedness, wrote disappointedly that

> the enormous majority of our men in the encampments were drilling with broomsticks or else with rudely whittled guns. . . . In the camps I saw barrels mounted on sticks on which zealous captains were endeavoring to teach their men how to ride a horse.

U.S. Navy recruiting poster

The War's Effect on the Economy

Industrial production increased by more than a third between 1916 and 1919. The Gross National Product (GNP) increased from $49.6 billion to $78.3 billion during the same period. The average full-time manufacturing worker saw his annual earnings climb from $751 to $813 in that period.

Purpose of the Wartime Agencies

The main tasks of Wilson's wartime agencies were to control prices and ensure "fair" (by the government's standards) distribution of resources. The Railroad Administration went further and basically controlled the nation's railways. Those agencies lasted only until shortly after the war, when the free market was once again allowed to function.

As head of the Food Administration, Herbert Hoover helped spread Wilson's unprecedented expansion of government into Americans' daily lives.

The draft could provide the men but not the machinery of war. It took nearly a year for the nation's industry to convert to full wartime production. The importance of the industrialization reflected the changing face of modern war. As President Wilson said, "In the sense in which we have been [conditioned] to think of armies, there are no armies in this struggle; there are entire nations armed." All across the home front, Americans enthusiastically met the challenge to war and to win.

Effect of War on the Economy

U.S. entry into the war had several profound effects, some good and some bad. For Americans young and old, the war was "fought" in backyard gardens and factory assembly lines.

Americans also saw their national government take unprecedented control of the economy. The Wilson administration did not think the free market could respond quickly or efficiently enough to meet the demands of war. The president also wanted to prevent what he considered "excessive" profiteering. Thus Wilson created numerous government agencies to control the economy. Among these were the Fuel Administration, the Railroad Administration, and the War Industries Board.

One of the key needs was an adequate food supply for both the American forces and also the beleaguered Allies. To address that need, the **Food Administration** was established. Future president **Herbert Hoover** became its leader and gained international attention for organizing methods of saving and producing food. "Hooverizing" became the byword as citizens joined in "Meatless Mondays" and "Wheatless Wednesdays." Many people, encouraged by the slogan "Food Will Win the War," raised their own food in "liberty gardens," or "victory gardens," so that more of the nation's commercial agricultural production could be sent to ease shortages in Europe.

In addition to raising food, patriotic Americans raised money. The nationwide effort to invest in war bonds, or "Liberty Loans,"

Wartime posters helped rally civilian support for bond drives and voluntary conservation measures.

reaped $17 billion in revenue. Movie celebrities such as Douglas Fairbanks and Mary Pickford appeared at huge rallies to boost bond sales. Even schoolchildren saved their pennies to fill Liberty Books with 25¢ stamps appropriately captioned "Lick a Stamp and Lick the Kaiser."

The war touched every area of life. Artists used their pens and paints in the war effort, producing posters to recruit men and raise money. And in a day before radio and television, families often gathered around the piano in the evening to sing such sentimental ballads as "I'm Hitting the Trail for Normandy, So Kiss Me Good-bye" or George M. Cohan's spirited "Over There," the unofficial anthem of the American "**doughboy**," or soldier.

Politics of Patriotism

The national zeal for the war effort contributed toward widespread anti-German sentiment. Many high schools dropped German language courses, and "liberty" replaced virtually everything connected with the hated Hun—German measles became "liberty measles," German shepherds were renamed "liberty dogs," and sauerkraut was now "liberty cabbage."

The anti-German attitude led to changed laws as well, often at the cost of constitutionally guaranteed liberties. For example, the **Espionage and Sedition Acts** made it a criminal offense to criticize the war effort in any way. Such acts must be understood in their wartime context. A number of German spy plots, including the successful sabotage of a New Jersey munitions plant, prompted lawmakers to enact stiff laws to safeguard national security. Undoubtedly though, some of the enforcement of the Espionage and Sedition Acts, which resulted in more than a thousand convictions, was the result of unfounded fears and hysteria. Despite

"Over There!"

This song, written in 1917, became popular with both the military and the public. It was used to encourage young men to enlist in the army.

Over there, over there, send the word, send the word, over there,

That the Yanks are coming, the Yanks are coming,

The drums rum-tumming ev'rywhere.

So prepare, say a prayer, send the word, send the word to beware:

We'll be over, we're coming over,

And we won't come back 'til it's over over there!

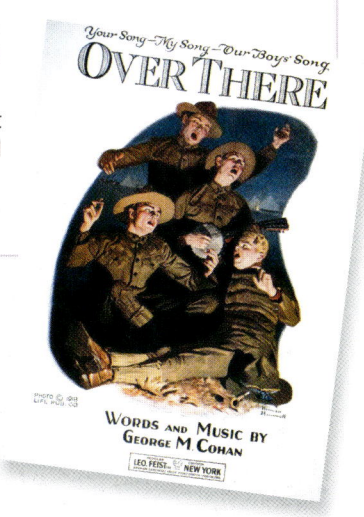

World War I in Europe

Trench Warfare

By the end of 1914, a long, bloody stalemate had settled over the frontlines as both sides dug opposing trenches that stretched from Belgium to Switzerland. **Trench warfare** became a major part of World War I. The trench system included frontline trenches, support trenches (for men and supplies to assist those on the frontlines), and communication trenches (which assisted with the movement of messages as well as supplies). Beyond the frontline trenches were barbed wire and "**no man's land**," a neutral zone that varied in size from a few yards to more than a mile. This system, as might be guessed, made advancing difficult. Direct assaults against enemy lines, poison gas, flamethrowers, and tunneling (digging under enemy lines and planting explosives) met with varying degrees of success. Stalemate was generally the result of such efforts.

Trench life was not for the fainthearted. Soldiers faced severe discomfort. Trenches were often filled with water and pests—rats and lice. In addition, food was a problem, both in availability and desirability. Beside discomfort, soldiers faced disease. Unsanitary conditions caused dysentery, a flu-like disease. Waterlogged trenches could lead to trench foot, an infection that, if left untreated, could result in gangrene. Sometimes toes or an entire foot had to be amputated because of the problem. Lice carried a disease that came to be known as trench fever, which was not life-threatening but was disabling.

The American Red Cross

The American Red Cross played a significant role during the First World War. Its members performed a variety of services for soldiers and civilians alike. They provided medical assistance for the wounded at places such as American base hospitals and hospital trains. In addition, they manned canteens that supplied food, beverages, and varied supplies and gave soldiers a place to socialize. Almost half of the eighteen thousand Red Cross nurses were active on the home front, proving especially invaluable during the influenza epidemic of 1918–19. After the war, Red Cross workers set up hospitals, convalescent homes, health centers, clinics, and mobile dispensaries to meet postwar needs around the world.

examples of excessive enforcement, however, the Supreme Court ruled in the 1919 landmark decision **Schenk v. United States** that Congress *could* limit free speech, particularly during wartime, if such speech presented "a clear and present danger" to national interests. In the ruling, Justice Oliver Wendell Holmes noted, "Free speech would not protect a man in falsely shouting fire in a theater and causing a panic."

For most Americans, support for the war came not from coercion but as a matter of patriotism and idealism. None was better at defining and focusing that idealism than Woodrow Wilson. At the outset he declared:

> We desire no conquest, no dominion. We seek no indemnities [payment] for ourselves, no material compensation for the sacrifices we shall freely make. We are but one of the champions of the rights of mankind. . . . America is privileged to spend her blood and her might for the principles that gave her birth and happiness and the peace which she has treasured. God helping her, she can do no other.

Wilson continued his theme of America's moral leadership by listing the objectives that he hoped would produce a lasting peace. His plan, known as the **Fourteen Points**, was released in January 1918. It proposed freedom of the seas, an end to secret treaties, free trade, and reduction of every nation's military. It also called for **self-determination** for the people of Europe. This meant people would decide for themselves under which governments they wished to live. Wilson's Fourteenth Point renewed his earlier idea for a **League of Nations**, urging the formation of "a general association of nations . . . for the purpose of affording mutual guarantees of political independence and territorial integrity to great and small states alike." In Wilson's idealistic—though unrealistic—thinking, a League of Nations would prevent a recurrence of the events that ignited the 1914 conflict. Wilson hoped to turn the war into a crusade for Americans. He also hoped his plans would encourage Europeans to bring an end to this conflict. Therefore, Wilson's Fourteen Points were widely published in Europe for everyone from kings to common laborers on both sides to consider.

Wilson believed that establishing a peace based on his Fourteen Points would ensure this would be the "war to end all wars." While Wilson was waging war on the diplomatic front, American troops were making a timely entrance and crucial contribution on the battlefront.

Over There

"Lafayette, We Are Here"

On July 4, 1917, U.S. troops, known as the **American Expeditionary Force** (AEF), marched through the streets of Paris. The French were delighted. An American colonel, Charles E. Stanton, recalling an old debt and capturing the timeliness of the American arrival, declared simply, "Lafayette, we are here."

The American entry was crucial for the Allies. On the Eastern Front the bloody Bolshevik Revolution, headed by Vladimir Lenin, had swept the communists to power in Russia in November 1917. Lenin negotiated a separate

Religion and World War I

Religion might not immediately come to mind when thinking about the Great War, but religious motivations were often given for young men to fight. When soldiers died, their sacrifice for the nation was often equated with sacrifice for God.

Some liberal German theologians viewed the Germans as a chosen people who could use their military to advance God's kingdom. Some Americans pointed to the rejection of orthodox Christianity by some German philosophers and argued that the kingdom of God could be advanced by fighting Germany.

These viewpoints confused cultural progress with the kingdom of God. The kingdom of God is the reign of Christ over men and cannot be identified with particular nations.

Sergeant York

A great American hero of World War I was Alvin C. York, a shy Christian man from the mountains of north central Tennessee. He earned several honors and medals, including the Congressional Medal of Honor, for his bravery in the Argonne Forest in France in 1918.

York was converted in a revival a few years before the U.S. entered the war. When drafted into the army, he underwent a crisis; his church taught that killing was always wrong—even in war. He almost registered as a conscientious objector (one who refuses to fight because of religious belief). But York wanted to serve both God and country. He later wrote, "I prayed and prayed. I prayed for two whole days and a night out on the mountainside. And I received my assurance that it was all right, that I should go."

York, one of the best marksmen in his county, impressed his superiors with his accurate shooting and soon attained the rank of corporal. He was sent to France in May 1918 as part of the 82nd Division, the All-American division (so named because it had soldiers from every state).

On October 8, 1918, York's unit was exploring an enemy position in the Argonne Forest when they found themselves behind enemy lines. They surprised a group of encamped Germans and took them prisoner. But a nearby machine gun nest opened fire on the Americans, killing several of York's companions.

York took command of the remaining seven American soldiers and began using his shooting skills. One by one, as the Germans peered over the embankment to take aim, York shot and killed them. York did this a number of times until the Germans finally surrendered.

When York, his men, and his prisoners reached the Allied lines, a lieutenant asked, "York, have you captured the whole German army?"

York answered that he had "a tolerable few." The "tolerable few" was actually 132 prisoners. In addition, York had single-handedly killed numerous other Germans and silenced the German machine guns.

York was promoted to sergeant. On returning to his native Tennessee, York devoted his life to building schools for the mountain children of his home state. He built a small non-denominational Bible college as a "school for God." When asked about his adventures in France, York replied, "We know there were miracles, don't we? Well, this was one. It's the only way I can figure it."

Four Aces

Both sides in World War I glamorized the bravery of a new breed of warrior—the fighter pilot. "Flyboys" seemed to symbolize the charm, chivalry, and daring of warfare that were lacking in the muddy slaughter of trench warfare. Most famous were the "aces," those who scored at least five "kills" (enemy planes shot down). Following are descriptions of the four major powers' top aces.

American ace Captain Eddie Rickenbacker

Manfred von Richthofen. Better known as the Red Baron because of his scarlet-red triplane (a three-wing Fokker Dr 1), von Richthofen was the most successful ace in the war, scoring eighty kills. On April 20, 1918, he scored his seventy-ninth and eightieth kills. The next day, he was mortally wounded in combat. It is still unclear whether he was killed by a Canadian pilot he was fighting or by machine gun fire from the ground (when his plane was flying at very low heights).

Paul-René Fonck. Fonck was France's premier ace, with seventy-five kills. He embodied the cocky, almost arrogant attitude that many people associated with the aces. Fonck twice shot down six enemy planes in one day and once brought down three planes in ten seconds. Fonck survived the war and worked in the aviation field afterwards. He died in 1953 at age 59.

Edward "Mick" Mannock. The chief British ace (at least sixty-one kills) was "Mick" Mannock, an altogether different kind of character—moody and restless. He was not a carefree "knight of the air." He took a grim delight in shooting down Germans, but he went to his quarters and wept when one of his mates was shot down. Mannock feared fire and was tormented by thoughts of being trapped in a burning plane. Sadly, his plane was hit in July 1918, and he died in a fiery crash.

Eddie Rickenbacker. America's "ace of aces," Rickenbacker scored twenty-six kills. He was a race-car driver before the war and once held the world land-speed record. He combined his knowledge of engines with his personal bravery to become America's leading pilot. Perhaps his most famous exploit was a solo attack on seven German planes. He downed two of them and then escaped from the others unharmed. He won the Medal of Honor for his exploits.

During World War II, he was a military consultant. In October 1942, the B-17 in which he was flying with a secret message to General MacArthur crashed at sea. He took command of the situation and helped the crewmen survive against amazing odds for twenty-four days. The men held prayer meetings, sang hymns, and read from one of the men's Bibles. He and all but one of the crewmen were rescued. In later years, he was first president and then chairman of Eastern Airlines. He died in 1973 at age 82.

peace with Germany early in 1918, freeing hundreds of thousands of German troops to join their comrades on the Western Front. The Germans hoped this would deal a final blow to the Allies.

In addition, morale among the beleaguered Allies was miserable. They had suffered seven million casualties in the war. Weary in the face of death, French troops staged mass mutinies in May and June 1917. Some French soldiers even murdered their officers before deserting. As the Allied armies teetered toward collapse, the arrival of the Americans, led by the tough "Black Jack" Pershing, revived Allied spirit. Although the arriving Yanks (Americans) were inexperienced, by the spring of 1918, the doughboys—a million strong—became a critical factor in the Allied recovery and ultimately in the Allied victory.

Holding the Line

The German commander Erich von Ludendorff knew that Germany could not prolong the war when the forces of the United States were added to those of the rest of the Allies. He decided to wage a full offensive against the British and French, forcing them to surrender before the United States could give substantial support. Germany began the British phase of the offensive in northern France and Belgium on March 20, 1918, with the heaviest artillery fire ever used. Some 6,000 German guns, answered by 2,500 British guns, pounded the front with tons of steel and explosive shells for more than four hours. Then the German infantry charged across "no man's land," (the area between the Allied and the German lines). Flamethrowers, poison gas, hand grenades, and machine guns were used by both sides. The Germans, aided by a fog cover, successfully broke through in some places, but the drive slowed and faltered. After several days of intense battle, the British, aided by recently arrived American troops, prevented a general collapse of the line.

Having failed to break the British line, the Germans opened an attack on the French line to the south on May 27. The German assault broke the lines by May 30 and reached the Marne River, only fifty miles from Paris. But on June 2 and 3, American troops rushed into the gaps, halting the German drive at **Château-Thierry** (sha-toh tyeh-REE) **and Belleau** (BEL oh) **Wood**.

"Black Jack" Pershing

Women and the War

Women also played an important role in the war effort. For the first time, some industrial jobs became open for women as men entered the military. Women also figured prominently in propaganda and recruiting posters. While remaining exempt from combat roles, many women still worked near the front lines as nurses or ambulance drivers.

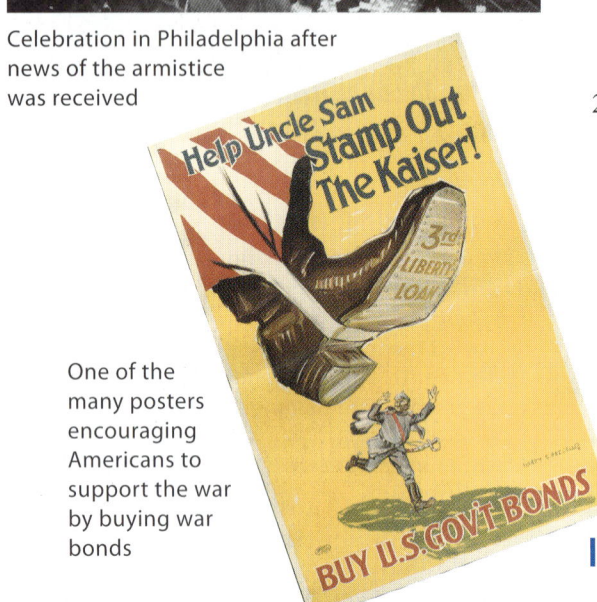

Celebration in Philadelphia after news of the armistice was received

One of the many posters encouraging Americans to support the war by buying war bonds

Guiding Questions

1. What were the differing positions of the leaders at Versailles?
2. Why did the U.S. fail to ratify the Treaty of Versailles?

Push to Victory

On July 18, the Allies began a counterattack, slowly pushing the Germans back. The doughboys won an impressive victory at Saint-Mihiel (sahn mee-YEL), but the largest effort was the American **Argonne offensive** that began on September 26. It was one of the costliest military campaigns in American history. One and a quarter million U.S. troops, concentrated on a twenty-five-mile front, fought for six weeks toward the central German rail center at Sedan. The Americans suffered 117,000 casualties, including 26,000 killed in action, but the effort turned the tide. In October, the German leadership began to negotiate for peace using Wilson's Fourteen Points. Germany's allies were withdrawing from the war. Bulgaria did so on September 29; Turkey (also called the Ottoman Empire) withdrew October 30; Austria-Hungary quit the fighting on November 3. On November 9, the kaiser fled the country; the German lines collapsed. On **November 11, 1918**—at the eleventh hour of the eleventh day of the eleventh month—an **armistice** took effect. The Great War was over.

Section Review

1. What German decision caused Wilson to break diplomatic relations with Germany?
2–4. Name three methods that Americans on the home front used to provide food and money for the war effort.
5. What conditions on the Eastern Front in early 1918 made the entry of the United States crucial to the Allies?
6. What World War I offensive was the largest and one of the costliest military campaigns in American history up to that time?
* Explain the significance of the statement, "Lafayette, we are here."
* How great was the influence of U.S. troops on the outcome of the war?

III. Isolation

With their lines collapsing, their leadership fleeing, and their people starving, the Germans had asked for an armistice. They hoped for the best peace terms possible—peace according to Wilson's Fourteen Points. After the armistice, though, hopes for a favorable settlement proved empty. The German people would not be the only ones disappointed by the results of what one writer referred to as "The Great War and the Petty Peace."

Treaty of Versailles

Five treaties were signed between the Allies and the defeated nations in 1919 and 1920. Bulgaria, the Ottoman Empire, and Germany signed separate agreements. Austria-Hungary was split into two separate nations, Austria and Hungary. Each signed a treaty with the Allies. The Treaty of Versailles, between the winning nations and Germany, was the most important of the five.

Wilson as Diplomat

Just one week after the armistice was signed, Wilson announced that he would personally lead the American peace delegation that would travel to Europe. Wilson's decision drew immediate fire from his critics, who charged that by personally negotiating the treaty the president would be more susceptible to public pressures and hasty decisions. But Wilson believed that a personal appearance, given his tremendous prestige in Europe, would best help preserve his Fourteen Points. He was particularly concerned about the establishment of a League of Nations, which he believed would ensure lasting peace.

Allied leaders met outside Paris at the Palace of Versailles on January 18, 1919. Wilson's peace mission was seriously flawed from the beginning. The Americans accompanying him did not include a single prominent Republican from the Senate, where any treaty would have to be submitted for ratification. In the November elections of 1918, the Democrats had lost their majorities in both houses of Congress to the Republicans. It was a time when Wilson desperately needed to cooperate with his opponents; yet, as he and his supporters headed for the cheering crowds of Europe, his opponents back home were feeling further alienated.

Big Four, Big Differences

The Paris Peace Conference, held from January to June 1919, was dominated by the "**Big Four**"—President Wilson, France's Premier Georges Clemenceau (clem mahn SOH), Italy's Premier Vittorio Orlando, and Britain's Prime Minister David Lloyd George. Each nation had distinct aims. Wilson made clear that the U.S. wanted no territory in return for its participation in the war. What Wilson wanted was acceptance of the Fourteen Points. He was interested in peace, but his Allied colleagues seemed more concerned about punishing the Central Powers. Clemenceau, though claiming to support the Fourteen Points, was more interested in revenge for France than in anything else. Conflicts between France and Germany over the mineral-rich coal- and iron-mining area west of the Rhine River, including the area known as Alsace-Lorraine, dated to the days of the Franks and the Gauls. Germany had taken Alsace-Lorraine in 1871, and France wanted it back. France also wanted a buffer zone, or neutral zone, east of the Rhine to ensure its future security.

Italy's Orlando represented a nation that had been Germany's ally at the beginning of the war but had then joined the Allies, in part because of British promises of territory in Austria. Orlando came expecting a large share of the "spoils of victory" to come to Italy at the peace table, although Italy had contributed little to the actual victory.

Lloyd George was a master politician, willing to do whatever was necessary to maintain British control of the seas. Although he professed to support the terms of the armistice, he had campaigned for reelection in December 1918 promising that the Germans would be made to bear the cost of the war. His party won a landslide victory just weeks before the peace conference began. His supporters used such slogans as "Make Germany Pay" and "Hang the Kaiser."

This sign, "Long Live Wilson," welcomed the American president to Paris.

The Big Four at Versailles: (*left to right*) David Lloyd George, Great Britain; Vittorio Orlando, Italy; Georges Clemenceau, France; and Woodrow Wilson, United States

Dark Clouds Over the Peace

One of the people who felt betrayed by the armistice and was still willing to fight to the death for Germany was a twenty-nine-year-old German corporal named Adolf Hitler (*below on right*). His dark mind soon burned with dreams of revenge.

Petty Peace

The **Treaty of Versailles** was signed on June 28, 1919—exactly five long years after the Black Hand triggered a war that led to the deaths of almost ten million soldiers. The treaty drastically changed the map of Europe and had far-reaching consequences.

The Germans were permitted virtually no part in the treaty negotiations. They were, in effect, forced to sign the treaty and its "**war-guilt**" **clause**. That item stated that the German nation was responsible for the war. Since Germany was responsible, then Germany must pay the bill. As a result, Britain and France demanded huge **reparations**, money a defeated nation pays for the cost of the war. The huge sum assigned to Germany, more than $30 billion, was such an unreasonable demand that it only deepened poverty and resentment in Germany.

After all the haggling among Allied leaders was over, most of Wilson's Fourteen Points were not incorporated into the Treaty of Versailles. However, concerns about self-determination did lead to the creation of the nations of Poland, Czechoslovakia, Yugoslavia, as well as the Baltic countries of Lithuania, Latvia, and Estonia. While the new national identities satisfied millions, they also created problems. Many of the new countries encompassed a number of ethnic groups whose own nationalist desires were further awakened by the changes. For example, Yugoslavia, composed of six major groups, was originally called the Kingdom of the Serbs, Croats, and Slovenes—hardly a name to inspire national unity. In addition, thousands of Germans found themselves living under foreign flags after the mapmakers in Versailles finished drawing the lines. Adolf Hitler would use that point of irritation to expand his country's borders when he gained control of Germany in the 1930s.

Wilson and others were aware of the problems of the Treaty of Versailles. But Wilson believed that the League of Nations would fix those flaws. Its establishment was one of the conditions of the Treaty of Versailles. First, however, if the U.S. were to take the lead

A large crowd assembled in the Hall of Mirrors at Versailles to watch the signing of the treaty with Germany.

in the newly formed League, Wilson would have to find enough senators to ratify the treaty. It would be the toughest fight of his life; one, some have argued, that ultimately led to his death.

Rejection and Retreat

When Wilson returned from Europe, his most formidable opponent against the Treaty of Versailles and his most cherished part, the League of Nations, was Senate majority leader **Henry Cabot Lodge** of Massachusetts. Besides stubbornness, Wilson and Lodge had one other thing in common—they strongly disliked each other.

Most Democrats in the Senate naturally sided with their party leader, President Wilson, but the Democrats were in the minority there. The focus was on the Republicans, who were divided into two groups: the "irreconcilables" opposed any entanglement in European politics, and the "reservationists," led by Lodge, would ratify the treaty but only with reservations attached that would limit U.S. commitment. The reservationists feared that unqualified support of the League could drag Americans into future European wars by tying the country to unwanted alliances. The hard-bargaining Lodge insulted Wilson's idealism by describing the Versailles Treaty as "the beautiful scheme of making mankind virtuous [honorable] by a statute or a written constitution." America's security, Lodge believed, was best protected by two oceans and a strong military force.

As the debate over treaty ratification continued, public opinion, which had initially favored the ideas behind the treaty, began to shift in Lodge's direction. Wilson, who opposed compromising on any of the treaty provisions, decided to take the issue to the people. In a marathon mission of eight thousand miles in twenty-two days, the president delivered forty speeches in favor of the treaty and membership in his brainchild, the League of Nations. The president declared, "America does not want to feed upon the rest of the world. She wants to feed it and serve it. America . . . is the only national idealistic force in the world, and idealism is going to save the world."

Wilson's crusade, however, nearly killed him. On September 25, 1919, after an enthusiastic rally in Pueblo, Colorado, the president slumped with exhaustion. His aides canceled the rest of the tour and took Wilson back to Washington, where he suffered a serious stroke that paralyzed him on one side. Wilson's wife and a few close friends shielded his condition from the public, but his fighting days were over. For seven critical months, Wilson did not meet with his cabinet. Most executive functions were performed on his behalf by his wife and closest advisors. In November, the Senate vote on the treaty fell short of the two-thirds required for ratification.

When public and administration pressure brought a reconsideration of the treaty in March 1920, it seemed that the amended treaty would finally pass. But Wilson, who had regained some of his strength, bitterly fought any changes. Ironically, Wilson sided with the irreconcilables to defeat his own treaty in the interest of keeping it intact. The stricken president, clinging to his stubbornness, became his own enemy.

The United States never joined the League of Nations nor ratified the Treaty of Versailles. Not until October 1921, after Wilson's term, did the Senate ratify a new agreement with Germany ending the official state of war between the United States and Germany. By then, Wilson had been replaced by Warren G. Harding, a Republi-

Henry Cabot Lodge

Territorial Changes in Europe After World War I

can elected in 1920. Harding was no crusader; his striking contrast to Wilson illustrated the changing mood of the country. America had helped liberate the Old World, but now it was shifting out of the uncomfortable harness of international leadership and retreating into the 1920s.

Section Review

1–4. Name the members of the Big Four and the nation that each represented.

5–6. What two provisions of the Versailles treaty were especially offensive to the Germans?

7. What was the difference between the Republican irreconcilables and reservationists concerning the Versailles treaty?

★ Was the U.S. Senate correct in rejecting the League of Nations, or should the United States have joined the League? Explain your opinion.

★ Why did the Treaty of Versailles include the war-guilt clause and the requirement that Germany pay huge reparations? What was the effect of their inclusion? What alternative courses of action were possible?

CHAPTER REVIEW 19

Making Connections

1–2. What event sparked World War I? How?

3. How did the British blockade of Germany actually bring the neutral Americans closer to the Allies?

4–5. Which nation released the *Sussex* pledge, and what did it state?

6–7. Who was the main opponent of the League of Nations in the Senate and why?

Developing History Skills

1. Place the following events in chronological order:
   a. Great Britain declares war on Germany.
   b. Germany declares war on France.
   c. Austria declares war on Serbia.
   d. Germany declares war on Russia.

2. Why did William Jennings Bryan resign as secretary of state when Wilson sent a sharp message to Germany after the sinking of the *Lusitania*?

Thinking Critically

1. Wilson said, "I am going to teach the South American republics to elect good men!" What characteristic of Wilson's foreign policy does that statement reflect? Is that characteristic necessarily a benefit in conducting foreign policy? Why or why not?

2. Wilson said, "Idealism will save the world." What truths or fallacies or both are behind that statement?

Living as a Christian Citizen

1. Should Christians try to transform their world? If yes, how do they avoid the problems of Wilsonian idealism? If not, what role should Christians play in broader society?

2. Evaluate the Treaty of Versailles from a Christian perspective.

People, Places, and Things to Remember

Archduke Francis (Franz) Ferdinand
Central Powers
Allies
William Jennings Bryan
Porfirio Díaz
Victoriano Huerta
Pancho Villa
John J. Pershing
Triple Alliance
Triple Entente
mobilization
Wilhelm II
propaganda
U-boats
international law
unrestricted submarine warfare
Lusitania
Sussex pledge
Zimmermann telegram
April 6, 1917
Selective Service Act
Food Administration
Herbert Hoover
doughboy
Espionage and Sedition Acts
trench warfare
no man's land
Schenk v. United States
Fourteen Points
self-determination
League of Nations
American Expeditionary Force
Château-Thierry and Belleau Wood
Argonne offensive
armistice (November 11, 1918)
Big Four
Treaty of Versailles
war-guilt clause
reparations
Henry Cabot Lodge

LEADERSHIP
1920–1945

1919 Red Scare

1920

1925 Scopes Trial

1925

1928 Kellogg-Briand Pact

1929 Stock Market Crash

1930

1931 Japan invades Manchuria

CHAPTERS

20 THE TWENTIES (1920–1929)

21 THE THIRTIES (1929–1939)

22 THE WORLD AT WAR (1939–1945)

1939–45
World War II

| 1935 | 1940 | 1945 |

1933
FDR's "Hundred Days"

1941
Attack on Pearl Harbor—
U.S. enters World War II

1944
D-day

20 THE TWENTIES (1920–1929)

> The chief business of the American people is business.
>
> **President Calvin Coolidge**
> January 17, 1925, to the Society of American Newspaper Editors

The "Roaring Twenties" was a period of national frivolity.

Big Ideas

1. What were the economic and political conditions in the United States following the first World War?
2. What competing ideas produced the culture wars in the United States following the first World War?
3. What conditions led to the Great Depression?

I. **Normalcy and Shortsightedness**

II. **Culture Wars**

III. **From Roar to Ruin**

It was the age of flappers, foxtrots, Freud, and all that jazz. If the country was growing up, then the 1920s was America's adolescence. "Over There" was strangely out of date; America was singing "Ain't We Got Fun?" The generation coming of age in the 1920s enjoyed postwar prosperity and passive politicians. Moral crusades were out, replaced with a sometimes mindless pursuit of frolic and frivolity. The new heroes were on the silver screen, the athletic field, and the radio waves. The roar of the twenties seemed to drown out problems both at home and abroad, but by the decade's end, the lines at America's movie palaces had turned into bread lines at soup kitchens. The party was over.

I. Normalcy and Shortsightedness

On the campaign trail in 1920, Warren G. Harding preached the political philosophy that carried the United States into the new decade: "America's present need is not heroics but healing; not nostrums but normalcy; not revolution but restoration; . . . not surgery but serenity." **Normalcy** was a new word, and whatever else it was, it became the goal of a people wishing to distance themselves from wartime pressures and problems.

Postwar Problems

In 1920, America was readjusting to the challenges of peacetime. The nation's industries and manpower were no longer demanded by the war effort. The people's energies and emotions were no longer focused on defeating a foreign enemy. The mundane activities of a workaday world replaced the drama of wartime, and the resulting changes in American life brought some unpleasant side effects.

When the war ended and the doughboys returned and the parades down main street were over, the soldiers often found that America held few opportunities for them. War industries closed, but peacetime industries did not resume production quickly because they had to retool to make consumer goods. With more than two million men returning from the American Expeditionary Force to a dismal job market, unemployment climbed to a staggering 11.9 percent in 1921. Not until after this problematic peak would business activity boom and factory jobs begin to absorb the excess workers.

If a soldier returning from the Great War decided to farm instead of seeking his fortune in the city, his prospects were no less bleak. Agriculture had been a profitable business during the war; American farms were not only feeding the nation and its soldiers but also exporting farm products to war-torn regions. With the war over, however, the agricultural market faced an upheaval.

The bountiful harvest of 1920 brought farmers calamity instead of profit. Exports of farm products declined as Europeans began to farm their own lands again, and the tremendous wartime demand for foodstuffs vanished. All that farmers could do was to sell their abundant produce for the ordinary peacetime needs of the nation. In keeping with the law of supply and demand, the huge surpluses caused food prices to plunge by the end of 1920. The meager returns for their labors devastated farmers, especially since many farmers were heavily in debt for land and equipment purchased during the years of high demand. Continued overproduction and

> **Guiding Questions**
>
> 1. How did the United States' economy change during and after World War I?
> 2. What was the foreign policy of the United States following World War I?
> 3. What characterized the administrations of Presidents Harding, Coolidge, and Hoover?

low prices kept the agricultural market depressed, not just for a year or two but for the entire decade. The farm problem remained a major domestic issue throughout the 1920s.

Another change Americans had to face once the war ended was the discarding of emotions raised by newspapers, war posters, rallies, and songs. The kaiser had been defeated, but some Americans feared that other enemies were still at large. They especially feared Communists and anarchists (people who seek to destroy governmental authority), who had talked of overthrowing the U.S. government ever since the Bolshevik Revolution had engulfed Russia in 1917. The violent activities of a few leftists stirred this fear and created a panic called the **Red Scare**.

The scare began in 1919 when a few anarchists mailed small packages containing bombs to various government officials and businessmen who had opposed their actions by breaking strikes and prosecuting suspected leftists. One of the bombs blew up in the hands of a senator's maid, injuring her and the senator's wife. Although the other mail bombs were discovered before they exploded, the violence set off a wave of leftist bombings that resulted in death and great property destruction. Even the house of Wilson's attorney general, A. Mitchell Palmer, was bombed. The terrorism led to an intense government effort to track down foreigners with objectionable political views and either prosecute them for crimes or simply deport them. When a predicted "Red revolution" did not break out on May Day (a Communist holiday) in 1920, the scare subsided, but Americans' widespread suspicions of foreign leftists occasionally resurfaced in following years.

The home of Attorney General A. Mitchell Palmer was bombed by anarchists.

Reaction Against Organized Labor

Americans feared the threat of labor violence during the Red Scare. One labor organization, the Industrial Workers of the World—or "Wobblies," as they were commonly known—tried to organize workers to achieve their socialistic goals. But in the wake of the Bolshevik Revolution, Americans did not respond to them well. Because Americans were already suspicious of dangerous radicals, organized labor did not prosper during the twenties.

Internationalism Amid Isolationism

Although isolationism was the general theme, it was by no means total. The counter-theme of internationalism was clearly evident. Examples include several efforts to secure peace among nations through arms limitations and even to outlaw war. A worldwide economic depression also forced nations to work more closely together than they might otherwise have done.

World Relations

The general theme of American foreign policy in the 1920s was **isolationism**. The taste of war had left many Americans disillusioned with idealistic efforts to change the world. Wilson's failure to persuade the United States to join the League of Nations illustrated the preference of Americans to focus on things at home rather than dabble in foreign matters. Nonetheless, America had proved itself to be a world leader, and in that role it could not avoid affecting the history of the 1920s.

The United States faced two basic foreign policy tasks in the twenties: to maintain world peace and to stabilize the world economy. Americans undertook both of those tasks with special attention to how any action would affect the peace and prosperity of the United States. Americans did not want foreign conflicts to draw their sons into battle again, and they did not want foreign economic problems and policies to endanger American business and prosperity.

Pursuit of Peace

Although America sent "unofficial observers" to meetings of the League of Nations, major American activities in pursuit of world peace were independent of that organization. The first such activity was the **Washington Naval Conference** of 1921. The buildup of sea power sparked by the war did not halt abruptly at the armistice. Japan and Britain continued strengthening their navies to acquire military advantages over potential enemies. France and Italy also were determined to enhance their naval strength. To keep these powers in check, the United States had to continue the expansion of its own navy, thereby participating in a necessary (and expensive) armament. The Washington Naval Conference brought foreign diplomats to the nation's capital to negotiate an agreement limiting the growth of naval power. The result was a plan that called for Japan, Britain, and the United States to scrap some of their vessels, curtail battleship construction, and establish a ratio for naval forces of 5 : 5 : 3 : 1.75 : 1.75. For every 5 tons of naval vessels that the United States had, Britain would maintain 5 tons; Japan, 3; and France and Italy, 1.75 each.

Idealists hailed the noble treaties devised at the Washington Naval Conference. But the agreements had some notable flaws that later led to a war in the Pacific. Although they limited the buildup of battleships, they did not restrict the buildup of cruisers, destroyers, or submarines—the vessels that would prove more valuable in future naval warfare. Also, Japan left the conference unsatisfied. Japan resented being given an inferior standing to Britain and the United States, and its militaristic goals necessitated naval expansion. For these reasons, Japan would later abandon any appearance of adhering to the treaties. Other conferences in 1927 and 1930 revived the principles established at the first conference, but cooperation among the nations soon deteriorated.

The second major peace initiative of the 1920s was set forth by President Coolidge's secretary of state, Frank B. Kellogg, and the French foreign minister, Aristide Briand. They proposed an international agreement that would outlaw war. On August 27, 1928, fourteen nations signed the **Kellogg-Briand Pact** in Paris, and most other nations assented later. The pact won great praise, but it had a severe flaw that, in effect, rendered it worthless—it had no means of enforcement. This feature, however, allowed America to maintain its isolationist stance rather than entangle itself in the web of international politics.

In addition to making these efforts to maintain peace, the United States also modified its relationship with Latin American nations to promote peace with these near neighbors. President Wilson had maintained a forceful protection of American interests in the region. Presidents Harding and Coolidge continued that policy so that in 1925 the United States had marines stationed in several of those lands and controlled the financial policies of half of the twenty countries in the region. Naturally, such interventionism created resentment toward the United States in its Latin neighbors. Eventually, many Americans began to question the wisdom of such dealings with fellow independent nations.

Coolidge's second secretary of state, Charles Evans Hughes, began softening the policies of the Roosevelt Corollary to the Monroe Doctrine, which had asserted the police power of the United States in the Western Hemisphere. Hughes also urged the withdrawal of troops from Latin American countries.

Economic Entrapment

World War I had wreaked havoc on the economy of Europe. Not only were its farms and factories devastated by warfare, but also its surviving governments were saddled with an incredible burden of debt. Although the war had depleted the economic resources

The Failure of Peace and the Cause of War

While the supporters of arms control and peace efforts of the 1920s had laudable goals, their idealism caused them to underestimate the human sinfulness that leads to wars in the first place. Though speaking of interpersonal conflicts, the book of James reveals the source of all conflict: the lusts and desires that people have but cannot fulfill (James 4:1). While Christians should try to avert war whenever possible, they should realize that the sinful urges that lead to war will exist until Christ returns and rules the world.

> ### Economic Burdens of the Treaty of Versailles
> The Treaty of Versailles demanded that Germany pay $30 billion in reparations to the Allies. Also, in the wake of the war, the United States demanded that the Allies repay $22 billion in war loans—with interest.

of Europe, the United States had escaped relatively unscathed with its finances in order and its factories intact. The Allies were appalled that America would insist on repayment, and the Germans were angered that reparations would be forcefully extracted from their nation. Nevertheless, these conditions dictated the international economic activity of the 1920s.

The Allied debt had been received in the form of war materiel and foodstuffs, yet America required that it be repaid in cash (gold). The war had depleted the Allied coffers, so the logical means for them to acquire the needed sums was by trading European goods for the needed gold. But the United States blocked that method. Intent on protecting America's own reviving industries, Congress passed the **Fordney-McCumber Tariff** in 1922. This high tariff (supplanted by an even higher tariff in 1930) established a nearly insurmountable wall restricting European trade with the United States. Despite its many disagreeable consequences, protectionism remained entrenched in American policy.

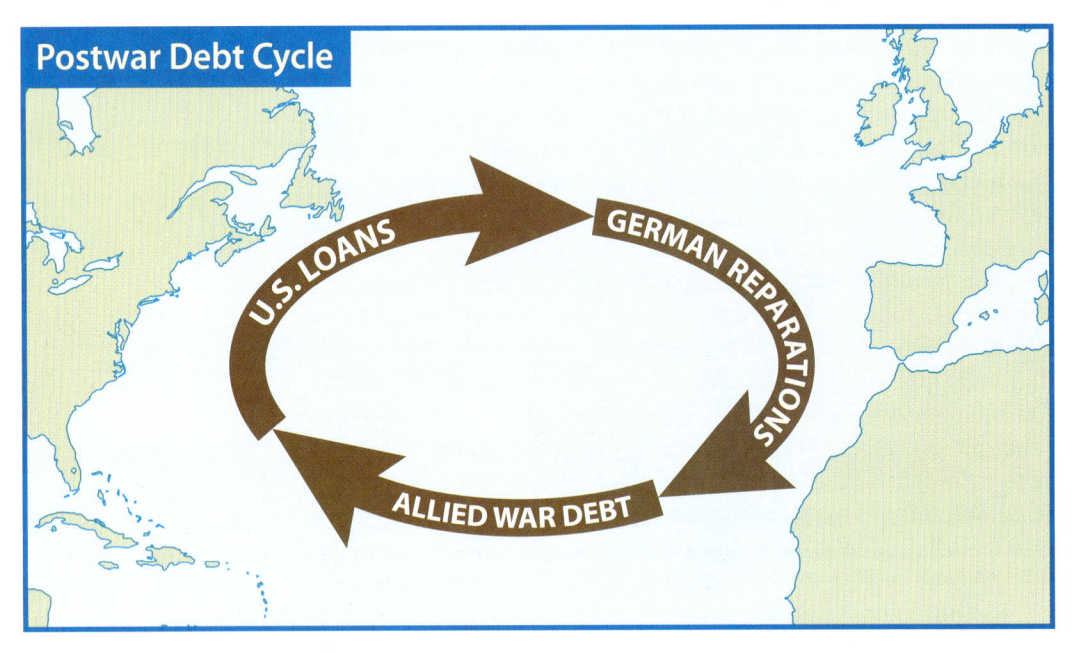

Postwar Debt Cycle

U.S. LOANS → GERMAN REPARATIONS → ALLIED WAR DEBT →

Trade with America being blocked, the Allies had only one other source for the money to pay their debt—the German reparations payments. Those payments, the Allies believed, would cover the Allied debts with extra left over for rebuilding their lands. Germany, however, was in ruins, and its economy was in shambles. The defeated foe had little with which to rebuild its industry, much less to make the colossal reparations payments. Germany had only one means of obtaining the needed cash, and that was through loans. Even so, what country in the postwar era could possibly have money to invest in loans to Germany? The answer was the United States. Thus began a dangerous circular flow of money: money lent by American financial institutions to Germany was passed on by Germany to the other Allies in reparations, which were, in turn, used to repay the United States for war debts. Money repaid to America provided investment capital to spare for more loans to Germany. In the process, Germany fell heavily into debt to the United States without having funds to improve its own economy. As the debts mounted, Germany could not meet its obligations. The Allies, deprived of reparations payments, could not make their loan

> ### Fruit of the Cycle of Debt
> The tensions resulting from the postwar cycle of debt plagued international relations throughout the twenties. Eventually, the Great Depression brought down the entire system of repayment as the world economy collapsed.

payments, and American investors were alarmed by unpaid foreign loans.

In 1924, an American banker, Charles Dawes, led a panel of economic experts from the involved countries to resolve the impending crisis. The result was the **Dawes Plan**, which reduced German reparations payments significantly and encouraged private American institutions to continue lending money to help Germany rebuild. The American government also reduced the interest charged on the Allied war debts and offered more generous terms for repayment. Despite these efforts, the financial demands in the absence of free trade continued to sustain the ominous cycle of debt.

Presidents

In an era when Americans generally wanted to mind their own business, have a good time, and make a fortune, they chose political leaders who were in tune with their desires. After Versailles, Wilson's ill health and bitterness over the rejection of his peace plans left America and the Democratic Party without a leader. Republicans easily won the White House in not only 1920 but also 1924 and 1928 as their party received credit for the apparent peace and prosperity of the decade. Those years were politically the most conservative years of the twentieth century. Government regulation and activism were minimal, and **laissez-faire** capitalism (free-enterprise economy with minimal government regulation) was thriving.

Harding

Warren G. Harding, the first of the Republican presidents of the 1920s, had been a newspaper editor in Marion, Ohio, until a state politician named Harry Daugherty took him under his wing. Daugherty thought Harding *looked* like a president, and as the leader of a group of state politicians called the Ohio Gang, he assisted the unassuming editor up the political ladder. Harding was elected to the Senate in 1914, but he was not particularly well-known at the time of the 1920 Republican convention. His old friend Daugherty wanted to change that. Several weeks before the convention, Daugherty predicted a deadlocked convention that would be overcome when, in the middle of the night, "fifteen men in a smoke-filled room" would agree to make Senator Harding the Republican candidate. His prediction came true, and Harding entered a race against the Democratic candidate, Governor James M. Cox of Ohio, and his running mate, Franklin D. Roosevelt of New York. Harding's theme of a return to "normalcy" pleased the nation, and he won decisively.

The American public generally liked Harding and approved of his policies, but some scandals in his administration brought his name into disrepute soon after his death in 1923. Most historians agree that Harding was personally honest, but he rewarded his friends in the Ohio Gang with high offices and imprudent favors. The improprieties of those friends soon put the president under extreme strain, and this, in addition to a weak heart, possibly hastened his death.

Following his death, the most infamous of the scandals became public knowledge. This incident involved his secretary of the interior, Albert B. Fall. Fall had won Harding's approval to take control of the navy's oil reserves at two locations, Teapot Dome in

Ranking the Presidents

When historians rank the best presidents, few of them include on their lists the presidents in this chapter. That is because of the false assumption on the part of many historians that only activist presidents are great whereas passive, "do-nothing" presidents are weak. Many historians rank Harding and Coolidge low because they both had a "hands-off" philosophy of government that gave great freedom to individuals and the market economy. Harding is also ranked low because of corruption in his administration. Historians rank Hoover low because they blame him for causing the Depression.

Harding was a dapper dresser but made some poor choices when selecting appointees.

> **Harding on His Scandalous Friends**
>
> "I have no trouble with my enemies. I can take care of my enemies all right. But . . . my friends, . . . they're the ones that keep me walking the floor nights!"

Wyoming and Elk Hills in California. In turn, Fall leased the oil rights on those properties to two friends, who were later found to have returned the favor to Fall in the form of sizable "loans." The **Teapot Dome scandal** also implicated various other members of the administration, but it was not the only scandal of that era. For example, Charles Forbes, head of the Veterans' Bureau, defrauded that agency of more than $200 million. And Harding's old pal, Attorney General Harry Daugherty, was brought to trial after being implicated in bribery schemes. Daugherty managed to have the case dismissed, although investigations later revealed that he had burned the records of his account in his brother's bank. Daugherty refused to give his reason for destroying the records but cannily implied that the revelation would further harm the memory of the late President Harding.

Harding was a weak president, but not because he involved the federal government in few intrusive activities. He was weak because his character was weak, and he did not appoint strong officials or deal with officials' misdeeds as soon as they occurred. However, he did allow the free market to adjust without interference. This adjustment enabled the American economy to overcome the postwar economic downturn.

Coolidge

When **Calvin Coolidge**, Harding's vice president, became president upon Harding's sudden death from a heart attack in 1923, the Harding scandals were just beginning to unfold. Coolidge immediately made clear that thorough investigations into the underhanded dealings would be conducted and that the guilty would be punished. As a result, this man of few words from rural Vermont distanced himself from the corruption and won both the praise of the American people and their votes in 1924. Coolidge had first gained national fame in 1919 as governor of Massachusetts by quelling a Boston police strike. When Samuel Gompers of the American Federation of Labor asked Coolidge to acknowledge the right of the police to express their grievances, the governor declared, "There can be no right to strike against the public safety by anybody, anywhere, anytime." That strong statement elicited the applause of the nation, which was immersed in the Red Scare at that time, and soon brought him the vice presidency.

As president, Coolidge took a hands-off approach to administration. He was content to let the market have free rein, saying, "The chief business of the American people is business." His philosophy of hard work, frugality, and simple living struck a chord with many Americans. That was what they had been taught, and Coolidge expressed what they wanted.

Calvin Coolidge, a man of few words, believed strongly in the free market economic system.

> **Coolidge, Fiscal Conservative**
>
> Under Coolidge, although the nation was experiencing unprecedented prosperity, federal spending was never more than $3.3 billion.

Encouraged by the president's approval, investors watched the prices on the stock market climb and prosperity in the country boom. In 1924, Coolidge was elected president in his own right. In light of his popularity, Coolidge surprised the nation when he announced in 1927, "I do not choose to run for president in 1928."

Hoover

That announcement opened the door for Coolidge's secretary of commerce, **Herbert Hoover**, to seek the presidential nomination.

Silent Cal

Calvin Coolidge's views on economic policies and social conversation could be summarized in one word: *economy* (i.e., frugality). He was nicknamed "Silent Cal."

One Sunday Mrs. Coolidge was unable to attend church with him. When he returned, she asked him what the minister's sermon was about.

"Sin," Coolidge replied bluntly.

"Well, what did he have to say about sin?" Grace pressed.

"He's agin it," he deadpanned.

Coolidge could give a public speech that equaled that of any other politician, but when he was elected to his fourth term in the Massachusetts senate, he gave the shortest speech in that body's history:

"My sincere thanks, I offer you. Conserve the firm foundations of our institutions. Do your work with the spirit of a soldier in the public service. Be loyal to the Commonwealth and to yourselves. And be brief, above all things, be brief."

Perhaps to remind himself not to be loquacious, he had the following embroidered quotation over his mantelpiece:

A wise old owl sat on an oak;
The more he saw, the less he spoke;
The less he spoke, the more he heard.
Why can't we be like that old bird?

Even when Coolidge made a joke, he did so with a straight face. He was infamous for pulling practical jokes on the White House staff. For example, he would push all the buttons on his desk simultaneously and then watch happily as the people came rushing from everywhere in the building to see what he wanted. He sometimes pushed the elevator button and then ran before the doors opened, leaving a baffled operator scratching his head.

He often had groups of congressmen eat breakfast with him. During one such event, the congressmen, none of whom had eaten with the president before, were on their best behavior, observing the president and following his lead to avoid any mistake in etiquette. When coffee was served, the president quietly poured cream into his saucer before sipping his coffee. The congressmen were perplexed, but they did not want to offend the president, so they did the same. Then they watched in embarrassment as Coolidge calmly placed his saucer of cream on the floor for his cat.

Coolidge's silence was often a political asset. He never spoke hastily or acted rashly, preferring to give time a chance to work out ticklish issues—which it usually did, making him look all the wiser.

He believed that political office should seek the man, so he made no effort to promote himself. But he was politically astute, leading journalist Walter Lippman to call Cal's practice "active inactivity." In his campaign speeches, he spoke of honesty and integrity, economy and industry, work and savings, patriotism and love of country. How could opponents contradict those "issues"?

Coolidge was very popular in all regions of the country, and he was considered a shoo-in for reelection in 1928. On August 2, 1927, he announced that he would hold a press conference. As the newsmen filed into the room, he handed each a two-by-nine-inch slip of paper that read, "I do not choose to run for president in nineteen twenty-eight." No explanation. No questions. Later, when pressed, Coolidge confided, "It is a pretty good idea to get out when they still want you."

(Adapted from "'Silent Cal' Coolidge" by Dennis L. Peterson, *The Elks Magazine*, Feb. 1999.)

After gaining a fortune as an engineer, Hoover had headed the Food Administration under Wilson, organized American food relief for Belgium during World War I, and served with distinction as secretary of commerce in the cabinets of both Harding and Coolidge. After winning the Republican nomination, Hoover faced New York governor **Al Smith** in the 1928 election. There were two reasons that many Americans opposed Smith—he was Roman Catholic and he opposed Prohibition. In the early twentieth century, the mainstream of American culture was Protestant. Catholicism appeared to many Americans to be foreign and contrary to the

In contrast to Harding and Coolidge, Herbert Hoover supported more government intervention in the nation's economy.

> ### Hoover's Interventionism
>
> Hoover pushed for farm subsidies when he was secretary of commerce. He urged farmers to cut production when foreign countries were increasing theirs. He supported going off the gold standard. He expanded credit the week in which the crash occurred, ensuring that the market was falsely stimulated. He pushed for higher wages, which ensured greater unemployment. His views on public relief were exactly the opposite of Harding and Coolidge's emphasis on individual initiative and local charitable relief. His administration increased the corporate income tax, the personal income tax, the estate tax, and postal rates, all of which suppressed economic growth. He revived wartime excise taxes; imposed sales taxes on gasoline, tires, automobiles, electricity, furs, jewelry, and other consumer items; and increased the gift tax. Hoover was an advocate of higher tariff rates and signed the Smoot-Hawley Tariff, the largest tariff in American history.

democratic spirit. In addition, Prohibition became a moral crusade that united all Protestants, conservative and liberal alike. Thus, Hoover's election was certain.

However, Hoover's reign over American prosperity was brief. Within a year of his inauguration, the stock market crashed, and America began to fall into the most severe economic depression in its history. Hoover is commonly blamed for the depression as an advocate of the free market who did too little too late. However, he did intervene in the nation's economy in an effort to end the depression. Unfortunately, Hoover's intrusive government interventions in the free market failed, and the Democrats swept into power. As a consequence, the Republican Party became the minority party for the next twenty years.

Section Review

1. What temporary panic concerning fears of a leftist revolution beset America in 1919?
2–3. What two major efforts to maintain world peace did the United States endorse in the 1920s?
4. Describe the circular flow of money between the United States and Europe that developed following World War I.
5. What proposal for resolving the foreign debt crisis was introduced by an American banker?
6–8. Who were the three Republican presidents that held office in the 1920s?
★ How should a Christian view attempts to ensure peace between nations?
★ What lessons can a Christian learn from the life of Calvin Coolidge?

> ### Guiding Questions
>
> 1. What new theories, art forms, and responses to societal problems emerged during this period?
> 2. What kinds of people did Americans tend to idolize in the 1920s?
> 3. How did some Americans improperly respond to immigrant and minority populations?
> 4. How influential was Fundamentalism in America beginning in the 1920s?

II. Culture Wars

The twenties was the first decade of what is considered modern America and one of the most glamorous periods in the nation's history. "The greatest, gaudiest spree in history," novelist F. Scott Fitzgerald labeled it. Behind the glitter, however, new philosophies ravaged the moral character of a generation—a society that poet T. S. Eliot characterized as a "waste land."

New Ideas

Darwinism and Marxism

Modern ideas brought about many of the changes in American society that became evident in the 1920s. Although the writings of Charles Darwin (evolution) and Karl Marx (communism) had appeared in the nineteenth century, their full impact did not become apparent in the United States until after World War I. Darwin's theory contradicted the scriptural account of Creation, and Marx's economic philosophy denied the depravity of man. Although these ideas had been too radical for most nineteenth-century Americans, evolution and socialism found widespread interest and acceptance in the 1920s. A growing disregard of scriptural truth naturally preceeded the acceptance of these views. But many people also opposed them. Americans were especially suspicious of communism, which they had seen take over Russia in 1917. They worried that it could also take over America.

Theory of Relativity

As the 1920s dawned, **Albert Einstein**, a German scientist, set forth a scientific theory that many writers and philosophers inaccurately used to cast additional doubt upon the scriptural and moral standards of Americans. Since the days of Sir Isaac Newton, scientists and philosophers had believed in an orderly world ruled by natural laws discovered by the scientific method. Using reason and common sense, man could comprehend the universe, which was certain and machinelike. This comfortable view was shattered by Einstein's **theory of relativity**—that space, time, and matter are not absolute dimensions but are relative to the location and motion of the observer. By 1929, a Harvard mathematician confessed, "The physicist thus finds himself in a world from which the bottom has dropped clean out." Seemingly, the absolutes of science were no longer absolute.

Freud

The ideas of **Sigmund Freud** became popular in the twenties. This Austrian psychologist believed that repressing sexual disturbances in childhood could explain the development of emotional problems later in life. Sex is pervasive in man's unconscious motivation, Freud believed, and he contributed to the popular sentiment that rejecting inhibitions can lead to a healthy emotional life. Thereafter, many Americans argued that self-restraint ("repression") led to emotional disorders and that psychoanalysis was the cure. For some people who had lost their moral bearings, the psychiatrist replaced the minister as counselor.

Literature and Art

Modern literature and art in the early twentieth century revealed the influence of the new ideas. In literature, as in art and music, traditional standards yielded to modern ones. Painting was abstract and depicted inner feelings rather than real images, and atonal music moved beyond normal harmony. Poetry written in free verse and novels in stream-of-consciousness form represented the modern break from the conventions of literature in the nineteenth century.

Both the themes and the techniques used in the literature of the twenties echoed the modern era. T. S. Eliot's poetry spoke of despair and disillusionment and criticized the emptiness of modern society. Novelist William Faulkner—with his creative syntax, departure from traditional narrative, and overemphasis on man's evil—created a meaningless world from which the old values had been removed.

Prohibition

One seeming victory for the forces of civic righteousness was the passage and ratification of the Eighteenth Amendment, or Prohibition. The amendment passed the Senate and the House of Representatives in 1917, and the necessary thirty-five states ratified it by 1919. The amendment prohibited the manufacture, sale, or transportation of intoxicating liquors. Unfortunately, the law resulted in an increase in illegal activity. Illegal liquor created a large and lucrative black market, and violent crime increased as gangsters competed for control of illegal alcohol trade in their territories.

Einstein Explains Relativity

"Gravitation cannot be held responsible for people falling in love. How on earth can you explain in terms of chemistry and physics so important a biological phenomenon as first love? Put your hand on a stove for a minute and it seems like an hour. Sit with that special girl for an hour and it seems like a minute. That's relativity."

Albert Einstein

Sigmund Freud

American Writers of the Twenties

The disillusionment of American writers in the twenties was evident from the number of prominent authors who chose to live and write in Europe (particularly Paris) rather than in the United States. Among them were Ernest Hemingway and F. Scott Fitzgerald. These authors are often referred to as "the lost generation."

Detroit police inspecting equipment found in an illegal brewery during Prohibition.

Congress had passed the Volstead Act (over Wilson's veto) in October 1919 to provide for the enforcement of Prohibition; it defined illegal beverages as those that contained more than half of 1 percent alcohol by volume. When enforcement of Prohibition proved to be a problem, President Hoover appointed the Wickersham Commission to investigate the lax enforcement. The commission found that Prohibition was impossible to enforce because a large part of the nation was willing to violate the law. The commission did not recommend repeal, but vocal opposition to Prohibition grew, especially among Democrats. When Franklin Roosevelt, who favored repeal, was elected in 1932, Prohibition's days were numbered. The end of the "noble experiment," as Hoover once called it, came in December 1933 with the ratification of the Twenty-first Amendment.

The Roaring Twenties

The modern ideas that gained acceptance in the 1920s led to a social revolution in America. So obvious was the new disregard for moral standards that the decade has often been called the Jazz Age, the ballyhoo years, the age of excess, or more commonly, the "Roaring Twenties."

The breakdown in morality naturally weakened the family. From 1870 to 1920, the U.S. population tripled, but divorce quadrupled. Several factors contributed to this rapid rise in divorce. Newspapers and movies were filled with stories of immorality. That emphasis often changed attitudes about purity and fidelity. In addition, women were freed from some household chores by new inventions, and families were generally smaller than in previous generations. The result was that wives often had time for work and social activities outside the home. Sometimes those interests interfered with family relationships. Some men also took advantage of changing moral standards and neglected their responsibilities as husbands and fathers.

In addition to moral and family breakdown, the 1920s witnessed the incredible popularity of the frivolous and the sensational. Many young Americans rushed to follow the latest fads, such as wearing raccoon coats, marathon dancing, and flagpole sitting. Tabloids and radio informed a nation craving the details of scandalous love affairs, murders, and dramatic true-life stories. In a world where standards had been broken down, people tended to seek thrills and adventure to fill the void in their lives.

Flappers and "Flaming Youth"

The young people caught up in the moral vacuum of the twenties were known as "flaming youth," and they captured attention by their rebellious behavior. Before World War I, police arrested women in towns and cities for smoking or for dressing immodestly, but during the twenties some young women in the cities flaunted their newfound freedom by drinking and smoking openly and by shortening their hemlines. Bobbed hair and the boyish look were fashionable for these "flappers." Immorality became glamorous, and virtue was too old-fashioned for many of the pleasure-seeking young people of the era.

Heroes and Villains

The twenties was certainly a colorful time in American history. The spread of daily newspapers, the advent of radio, and the shift from vaudeville to movies allowed people in every corner of the nation to keep tabs on not only rising stars in sports, entertainment, and politics, but also notorious criminals. Movies became the biggest source of entertainment for many Americans. Movies were big moneymakers and in many ways reflected the changing

America's Air Ambassador

The Lone Eagle, Charles Lindbergh, poses with his plane, Spirit of St. Louis, *ten days after his history-making flight.*

At 7:52 a.m. on May 20, 1927, one man in a small silver airplane named *Spirit of St. Louis* took off from Roosevelt Field on Long Island. The single-engine craft rose into the morning haze and carried its pilot into the headlines and history books.

That man was twenty-five-year-old **Charles A. Lindbergh**. He was trying to become the first person to fly solo nonstop across the Atlantic Ocean, from New York to Paris.

Although he was relatively unknown before his historic flight, Lindbergh captured the attention of both the United States and western Europe as they awaited news of his fate. Then, at last, word came that "the Lone Eagle" had reached his destination on the night of May 21. The next day, the *New York Times* proclaimed in its headline, "LINDBERGH DOES IT! TO PARIS IN 33½ HOURS; FLIES 1,000 MILES THROUGH SNOW AND SLEET; CHEERING FRENCH CARRY HIM OFF FIELD."

A ticker-tape parade and numerous awards, including the Distinguished Flying Cross from President Calvin Coolidge, awaited Lindbergh in New York City and St. Louis. Lindbergh's flight received more publicity in American newspapers than did the Armistice of 1918 and sparked a great number of commemorative items, including a postage stamp.

Although he modestly claimed to be only a stunt flyer, Lindbergh riveted the world's attention on the potential of air power. America showered him with acclaim and fondly remembered "Lucky Lindy's" heroic flight for years to come.

---

values of the culture. They also changed the way the world viewed America.

American Idols

Organized sports became major entertainment in the twenties. In 1921, fans overflowed a sixty-thousand-seat stadium near Jersey City to watch boxer Jack Dempsey knock out the French boxer Georges Carpentier. It was the first "million-dollar gate" for sports in the United States and the first major sports event to be broadcast by radio. Babe Ruth, "the Sultan of Swat," thrilled huge crowds at baseball games in Yankee Stadium, and in the 1927 season he hit sixty home runs. Fans filled college football stadiums to thrill in the exploits of athletes such as Red Grange of Illinois and the Four Horsemen of Notre Dame, coached by the legendary Knute Rockne. Newsreels before their movie may have given fans a glimpse of their favorite athlete off the field.

By the end of the 1920s, about a hundred million Americans, almost the entire population, were going to the movies weekly to see famous comedians such as Charlie Chaplin and Laurel and Hardy or dramatic stars such as Rudolph Valentino, Clara Bow, and Gloria Swanson. "Talkies" replaced silent films in 1927, and the more than twenty thousand movie palaces in the nation rivaled churches as the most important downtown buildings. By the twenties, many middle-class Americans had become obsessed with Hollywood, not only by the world of luxury and immorality portrayed on the screen but also by the promiscuity and glamour of the stars' offscreen lives, as reported by the nation's tabloids. Concerned about the public image of Hollywood, moviemakers hired Will Hays, Harding's postmaster general and a Presbyterian lay leader, to censor the films.

Babe Ruth, "the Sultan of Swat"

Champions of Their Sport

Other sports heroes gained wealth, fame, and admiration during the 1920s while popularizing their sports for the enjoyment of millions of Americans. Bobby Jones became the king of the golf links, and William Tilden aspired to the heights of the tennis world. Golf courses and tennis courts multiplied across the land as their popularity soared.

Pride and Prejudice

Around the turn of the century, American culture became more diverse with the increased "New Immigration" (discussed in Chapter 16). From 1900 to 1910, almost nine million immigrants entered this country, the highest number for any one decade. Most of them were from southern and eastern Europe. The first generation of these immigrants often retained their languages, religions, and cultures and usually lived in crowded neighborhoods of the same nationality in the nation's major cities. Many middle-class Protestant Americans, who had long been predominant in the population, perceived the large numbers of Roman Catholics and people of Jewish descent in this wave of immigration as a threat. Many of the foreigners were poor and uneducated, and some had radical political ideas.

The Red Scare of 1919 encouraged the public to associate crime with immigrants, and this association was evident in the famous **Sacco-Vanzetti case**. In 1920, Nicola Sacco and Bartolomeo Vanzetti allegedly murdered two men during a robbery in South Braintree, Massachusetts. After their case received mounting publicity, the two men were convicted and in 1927 were executed. Their defenders argued that they had been convicted because they were Italian-born aliens and anarchists, not because of the evidence, which many people viewed as doubtful.

During World War I and the 1920s, another trend altered American cities as black Americans migrated from the South to the North. With the reduction in immigrants following the National Origins Act, northern industries needed workers, and the one million African Americans who moved to northern cities between 1910 and 1930 helped fill that need. The northern urban setting offered political opportunities for black Americans. Oscar DePriest from Chicago became the first black congressman from the North. **Marcus Garvey** of New York City, with his Universal Negro Improvement Association, organized urban African Americans into a potent force. Touting racial pride, he enrolled six million members by 1923. Culturally, African Americans gained even greater visibility. With the **Harlem Renaissance**, black intellectuals and writers including James Weldon Johnson, Alain Locke, and Langston Hughes achieved prominence. Entertainers such as trumpeter Louis Armstrong and singer Paul Robeson saw their appeal grow from core black audiences to mainstream America. Several fashionable night spots in the twenties featured black performers playing popular jazz music, but African Americans remained excluded from the audiences.

The rapid social changes of the 1920s caused some Americans to react with violence. Fear of immigrants and African Americans led in 1915 to the revival of the **Ku Klux Klan**, a secretive, ritualistic group patterned after the organization founded during Reconstruction. It promoted "100% Americanism" and limited membership to native-born white Protestants. Through skillful promotion, the Klan expanded nationally through the early 1920s, becoming a strong social and political force in many northern cities, where immigrant and black populations were rising. In 1924, for example, 40 percent of the Klan's total membership was located in the states of Ohio, Indiana, and Illinois, and a Klan-backed write-in candidate nearly won a three-way race for mayor of Detroit. Feeding on bigotry and racism, the Klan's organizers

---

The National Origins Act

The suspicion of foreigners combined with the surge in immigration after the war resulted in congressional restrictions. The **National Origins Act** (1924) set quotas to restrict immigration. It limited immigration of a nationality to 2 percent of that nationality living in the United States as of the 1890 census. In addition, it totally prohibited Japanese immigration. Clearly the government wanted to preserve America from a perceived threat to its Anglo-Saxon heritage.

In September 1926, the Ku Klux Klan conducted a march in Washington, D.C., against blacks, Catholics, and Jews.

Scarface

Chicago was headquarters for a man who was probably the most infamous gangster of the twenties—**Al Capone**.

Several gangs entered the bootlegging business in Chicago during the 1920s. Johnny Torrio led one of those gangs with the help of a strong man, barely out of his teens, named Alphonse Capone. Growing up in New York, Capone was slashed in a knife fight, receiving three prominent scars on the left side of his face (hence the nickname "Scarface," which he hated).

Torrio brought Capone to Chicago in 1920 as a bodyguard, but Capone quickly proved to be clever and effective in operating the illegal businesses of the gang. After Torrio was wounded in a gangland attack in 1925, he left town and gave Capone command of his crime ring. Capone soon established himself as the king of Chicago's underworld. People who stood in his way were killed. The most famous example of gang violence was the "Saint Valentine's Day Massacre" in 1929, when members of Capone's gang, disguised as policemen, gunned down members of a rival gang in a garage.

Despite Capone's lifestyle, which was obviously the result of illegal gain, authorities struggled to find evidence that would put him behind bars. His subordinates were too well paid, too loyal, or too afraid to testify against him. He was careful to leave no written evidence of his ill-gotten gains. Finally, federal investigators uncovered evidence of about $1 million in income on which Capone had paid no taxes. Prosecutors brought Capone to trial for income tax evasion in 1931. The court found him guilty and sentenced him to eleven years in prison, part of which was spent in Alcatraz. While Capone was in prison, venereal disease ravaged his brain. At age forty-eight, the kingpin of Chicago died in 1947.

---

resorted to intimidation and violence against African Americans, Roman Catholics, and people of Jewish descent.

While the evils of the Klan are now obvious, Klan members in the 1920s sought to justify their movement by appropriating the symbol of the cross and the cause of moral reform. In addition to attacking African Americans, immigrants, and Roman Catholics, Klan targets included bootleggers, wife-beaters, and immoral movies. In some communities, the Klan achieved a degree of respectability, indicating that many were accepting or at least tolerant of its racism. The 1924 Democratic National Convention refused, by a narrow margin, to condemn it by name. Because of its secretive nature, precise statistics on membership are elusive, but the Klan's membership may have reached several million. That number declined after the mid-1920s, partly because the 1924 immigration law reduced the number of immigrants. Also, the Klan's use of violence alienated mainstream America, and a sex scandal among the Indiana Klan leaders made a mockery of the Klan's so-called moral crusade.

Fighting for the Faith

Rise of Fundamentalism

One religious movement reacted strongly to the modern trends of the 1920s. As was mentioned in Chapter 18, several orthodox movements in the Progressive Era resisted the theological errors of modernism, the social gospel, and the inroads of Darwinian evolution into Christian denominations. Some Christian leaders were willing to make peace with advocates of these ideas in the name of

> ### Role of Premillennialism
>
> Another influence on American Christianity at that time was premillennialism. Premillennialists rejected the liberals' unfounded faith in progress, and they contended that the world was actually growing worse. Most importantly, premillennialists emphasized that Christ could return at any time to establish His millennial kingdom. After World War I, various conservative movements (such as premillennialism) from several denominations joined forces to form what became known as Fundamentalism.

Christian unity. These leaders were indifferent to the compromise that would result. Another group of Christians argued that theological modernism was a different religion from Christianity and that the social gospel was no gospel at all. They insisted that there could be no Christian unity with those who promote a false gospel. These Christians fought to remove modernists from their denominations or, if that failed, left and founded denominations, churches, and schools that were faithful to the gospel. These Christians became known as Fundamentalists.

The origin of the term *Fundamentalism* lies in the belief of some Bible-believing Christians that certain "fundamental" doctrines exist that no one can deny and still be a Christian—doctrines such as the authority of Scripture, Christ's deity and vicarious atonement, the Resurrection, and the Second Coming. In 1910, two Christian businessmen sponsored the publication of a series of essays by some of the leading Christian scholars of the day to defend key doctrines. They sent these essays, called *The Fundamentals*, at no cost, to pastors, professors, and laymen all over the country. In 1920, a Christian editor wrote, "We suggest that those who still cling to the great fundamentals and who mean to do battle royal for the fundamentals be called 'Fundamentalists.'"

The Fundamentalist-Modernist Controversy

In the North, Fundamentalism developed into a theological battle with modernists. This battle, called the **Fundamentalist-Modernist controversy**, raged over doctrine and the control of the major denominations' schools, mission boards, and institutions. Such men as William Bell Riley fought for the faith in the Northern Baptist Convention. J. Gresham Machen and others battled the liberals for the historic Christian faith in the northern Presbyterian church. Machen's book *Christianity and Liberalism*, written in 1923, forcefully pointed out that modernism was not Christianity but another religion.

For a time, orthodox Christians remained the majority in the denominations. However, those who remained indifferent to the compromise were unwilling to expel modernists from their denominations if such action risked a major split. By siding with modernists, compromising Christians prevented Fundamentalists from removing false teachers from key leadership positions within denominations. Militant Fundamentalists, therefore, began to leave the major denominations and form their own associations. Fundamentalists in the Northern Baptist Convention left to form the General Association of Regular Baptist Churches (GARBC) in 1932. Machen led a group of Presbyterian Fundamentalists to form the Orthodox Presbyterian Church in 1936.

Antievolution Crusade

In the South—where the major Baptist, Methodist, and Presbyterian denominations were generally sound in the twenties—one of the Fundamentalist efforts focused on removing the teaching of evolution from the public schools. As these Christians pointed out, evolution not only was irreconcilable with the biblical account of Creation but also directly assaulted the authority of Scripture. With leaders such as former secretary of state and presidential candidate William Jennings Bryan, they pushed for laws banning the teaching of evolution but succeeded in doing so in only a few Southern states, one of which was Tennessee. Wanting to put their town on

> ### The Term *Fundamentalist* Today
>
> After the Fundamentalist-Modernist controversy, many social scientists lifted the term *Fundamentalist* out of its historical context. They began to apply it to any traditionalist religious group, whether Christian or not. The term particularly became associated with extremism as not only scholars but also the media used the label for groups such as the "fundamentalist Muslims" that toppled the government of Iran in the 1970s or the terrorist attack on the Twin Towers on September 11, 2001. Those Christians who self-identify as Fundamentalists, however, stand in the mainstream of the orthodox Christian tradition with all its rich intellectual heritage.

Bryan: "He Kept the Faith"

William Jennings Bryan was one of the dominant figures of his era. He was a three-time candidate for president, secretary of state under Wilson, and a political crusader and reformer. Bryan also had a clear Christian testimony. He recalled, "At the age of fourteen, I reached one of the turning points in my life. I attended a revival that was being conducted in a Presbyterian church and was converted." That event, Bryan said, "has had more influence in my life for good than any other experience."

Bryan's reputation as a political progressive sometimes confuses those who associate conservative religious beliefs with conservative political beliefs. Some Christians of Bryan's day supported progressive political reforms as a means of allowing the government to be "the minister of God . . . for good" (Rom. 13:4). Some Christians continue to embrace this use of political reforms.

Bryan devoted himself to Christian causes, especially in the last ten years of his life. The defense of Christianity took him to the Scopes trial in Dayton, Tennessee. He told the court, "I want the Christian world to know that any atheist, agnostic, unbeliever, can question me any time as to my belief in God, and I will answer him." Bryan faced cynical questions from the scoffing Darrow, questions that Bryan frankly was neither scientist nor theologian enough to answer adequately. But his courage was beyond doubt.

Following his death only days after the Scopes trial, Bryan was buried in Arlington National Cemetery. On his tomb is a simple and powerful epitaph: "He Kept the Faith."

---

the map, some town leaders of Dayton, Tennessee, coaxed a high school teacher, **John T. Scopes**, to challenge the law.

The resulting trial became a media event as national attention focused on the town for the summer of 1925. The American Civil Liberties Union hired Clarence Darrow, a famous trial lawyer and an agnostic, to defend Scopes. Bryan, who helped the prosecution, was also a witness, called by the defense as an authority on the Bible. Although Bryan showed courage in his defense of the faith, he was no Bible scholar and did not make the best case for the cause. While Scopes was convicted, Bryan and the other antievolutionists lost the publicity battle.

Fundamentalist Successes

In a larger sense, Fundamentalists in the twenties were battling the modern culture that aggressively assaulted the old-time religion. Philosophers, writers, and even liberal ministers trusted science as the true source of knowledge and extolled the virtues of men like Freud and Darwin. American society had become increasingly secular, as revealed in movies, magazines, radio, literature, jazz, and urban lifestyles. Fundamentalists fought the increasingly irreligious mood in America. The failure of World War I to bring peace and the corruption in government and society gave credibility to the Fundamentalists' message.

Despite the Scopes trial debacle, Fundamentalism flourished in the twenties. By 1930, more than fifty Bible colleges and seminaries offered training for those who could no longer trust their denominational colleges and seminaries. Fundamentalists also took to the airwaves. In 1932, *Sunday School Times* listed more than four hundred evangelical programs on eighty different radio stations in the country.

Premature Obituary for Fundamentalism

Bryan died only a few days after the Scopes trial. For many wishful critics, Fundamentalism died with Bryan in Tennessee. But the movement was still very much alive, as it demonstrated in 1928 when it assisted in defeating the anti-Prohibition, Roman Catholic, Democratic candidate Al Smith in the presidential election. In addition, Fundamentalist institutions prospered.

Section Review

1–4. Name four men whose philosophical and scientific theories were used to reshape the moral attitudes of the 1920s in ways detrimental to Christianity.

5. What term describes the young people of the 1920s who lacked moral values?

6–7. In what two occupational groups did Americans of the 1920s find many of their heroes?

8–9. What were two major evidences of American resentment toward immigrants and black Americans in the 1920s?

10–11. What two groups were involved in a major religious controversy during the 1920s?

★ Does the failure of Prohibition demonstrate that it is impossible to legislate morality?

★ How did William Jennings Bryan's motivation for progressive legislation differ from some modern supporters of progressivism?

III. From Roar to Ruin

As the 1920s progressed, Americans grew accustomed to the economic prosperity of the era. It was the most prosperous decade in American history to that point. Businesses thrived and living standards improved, making life more comfortable for most Americans. The widespread prosperity created a growing middle class and improved the lives of even the lower class through new jobs, new inventions, and expanding opportunities. A new service industry developed as well as a new classification of workers—the managerial class.

The economy was improving so much that when Herbert Hoover accepted the Republican nomination in 1928, he even predicted a total eradication of poverty in the land. Hoover's rosy prediction must have seemed legitimate at the time, but events would soon prove that material prosperity is fleeting.

We've Got the Goods

If America was on the road to ruin, it was certainly driving there in style. America was fast becoming a consumer society that was spending without counting the cost. In 1920, there had been only about nine million automobiles in the United States. During the decade, that number nearly tripled. Henry Ford had made his black Model T affordable and commonplace, but it was dull and drab in contrast to the sleek styles and colors introduced by other automakers in the twenties. Chevrolet and other competitors attracted buyers who wanted something different, forcing Ford to introduce the Model A in 1927. Chevy and Ford also set up credit corporations to help consumers who did not have the money for a car to buy one on credit. With advertising to make the product known and **installment plans** (making small monthly payments until the item is paid for) available to finance the price, Americans eagerly stepped into the driver's seat and sped away in debt.

The automobile had social as well as economic influence. Good roads improved transportation and gave rise to the suburbs, as

---

Guiding Questions

1. What two inventions had a great impact on the United States during this period?
2. What roles did advertising and speculating play on the American economy during this period?
3. What events led to the Great Depression?

Hoover's Ill-Fated Prediction

"One of the oldest and perhaps the noblest of human aspirations has been the abolition of poverty. . . . We in America today are nearer to the final triumph over poverty than ever before in the history of any land. The poorhouse is vanishing from among us. We have not yet reached the goal, but, given a chance to go forward with the policies of the last eight years, we shall soon with the help of God be in sight of the day when poverty will be banished from this nation."

Technological "Firsts"

Station KDKA in Pittsburgh broadcasted the first election returns over radio on November 2, 1920. Harding's was the first inauguration to use a public address system for amplification. And Harding became the first president to make a speech over radio when he dedicated the Francis Scott Key Memorial at Fort McHenry on June 14, 1922.

workers no longer had to live within walking distance of their jobs. Rural families could visit the city often rather than just a few times a year, and tourism boomed as the average family could travel for vacations. Also, with cars, young couples had opportunities for unchaperoned dates.

Radio was another influential item of the 1920s. From the time the first commercial station (KDKA) went on the air in Pittsburgh, Americans began to tune in to the news, music, sports, and other entertainment that it offered. At first, the enthralled listeners built crude crystal sets to receive the radio broadcasts, but during the decade those archaic radios gave way to bigger and better professionally manufactured receivers, many of them in the form of fine pieces of furniture. Rural and urban Americans alike gathered around these prized possessions to listen to the songs of their favorite crooners, to thrill to stories of adventure, to laugh at the jokes of popular comedians, and to hear religious songs and sermons.

In addition to cars and radios, Americans acquired many more new material possessions in the 1920s. With electricity becoming increasingly available in both small towns and large cities, electric appliances multiplied. Phonographs, refrigerators, irons, and other devices brought pleasure, comfort, and more leisure time into many homes. Telephone wires spread to many more homes, allowing people to communicate more easily with one another. A seemingly unlimited array of desirable possessions was available to catch the eye of the American consumer and make modern life more enjoyable.

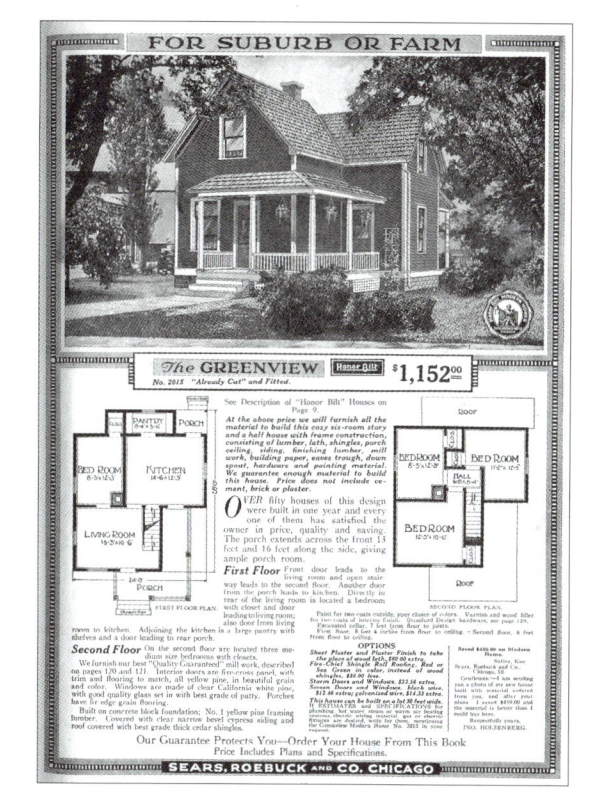

Mail-order catalogs sold all sorts of merchandise, including several models of Sears, Roebuck and Company homes.

The Golden Age of Radio

The 1920s and 1930s have been called "the golden age of radio." During that time, many "firsts" were accomplished. In the process, many radio personalities—musicians, comedians, advertisers, and news reporters—became household names.

In the 1920s, radio became the major medium of news and entertainment for the nation, a dominance that radio did not lose until the advent of television after World War II.

Some of the "Firsts"

The first religious broadcast—1921, Calvary Episcopal Church, KDKA, Pittsburgh

The first World Series baseball game—1922 (New York Giants defeated New York Yankees in five games), KDKA

First commercial ad time sold—1922, $9 for a 30 sec. spot, WEAF, Albany, NY

First business-sponsored program—"The Ever-Ready Hour," a variety show, WEAF, 1923

First network broadcast—1923

First government regulation of radio broadcasting—1925, Federal Radio Commission

Some Popular Radio Shows

"National Barn Dance"—1924, WLS, Chicago

"Grand Ole Opry"—1925, WSM, Nashville

"Amos 'N' Andy"—1928, WMAQ, Chicago

> **Diving into Debt**
> Two-thirds of all cars sold in 1927 were sold on the installment plan. By 1929, credit purchases for all sorts of major products, not just cars, made consumer loans the tenth largest industry in the nation.

On a Spending Spree

The materialism of the twenties was widely evident, but other elements were corrupting American society in more subtle ways. Advertising began to coax the public to buy things even if they did not need the products or have the money. Mass production was providing greater and greater numbers of products that needed to be sold. Therefore, mass consumption was also necessary. Through increased newspaper, magazine, and radio advertisements, businesses promoted goods ranging from cigarettes to soap and automobiles to mouthwash. Advertising appeals emphasized youth, sex, happiness, luxury, and keeping up with one's neighbors. Celebrity endorsements added glamour to products. Consumers were encouraged to spend, not to save; to enjoy the present, not to think about future needs or emergencies; to pamper themselves, not to practice self-denial. Materialism replaced biblical values as advertisers persuaded Americans to be better consumers of goods than producers of them. Buying on credit through installment plans made that possible.

Perpetually in debt for their purchases, Americans searched for ways to acquire the money they needed to maintain their comfortable lifestyles. Some resorted to fraud, bootlegging, and other illegal means; others turned to **speculation**, buying something with the hope of selling it later at a profit. Land in Florida, especially around Miami, became a popular item for speculation in the 1920s. Billed as a tropical paradise, acreage there began to sell, and the more buyers expressed interest, the higher land prices climbed. Speculators bought large tracts of land and subdivided them for sale. As the land boom progressed, they sold and resold the properties for higher and higher amounts. Much of the land was marshland or otherwise undesirable, but promises of future golf courses, shopping areas, and other developments tempted many people to buy a lot nearby for $20,000 or more. Then in 1926 a severe hurricane hit the Miami area, killing four hundred people and destroying thousands of houses. The disaster brought a sudden end to the land boom as people awoke to the hazards of their speculation. The credit that had sustained the boom collapsed as land prices plummeted. Many fortunes made in the boom were lost overnight, and thousands of unwary Americans were left with heavy debts and worthless land deeds.

As a great **bull market** (a stock market characterized by optimism and rising stock prices) began in 1927, stock became a prime target for American speculation. Wall Street had prospered throughout the decade as public infatuation with business grew and as ordinary people who had gained experience buying war bonds now became aware of the promising securities market.

> **The Federal Reserve's Role in Producing an Overheated Stock Market**
> During the late 1920s, Americans watched stock prices climb dramatically and almost steadily. The Federal Reserve flooded the market with cheap credit that encouraged many people to make unwise investments and to buy on the margin. They hoped to sell at a huge profit, pay off their stockbrokers, and pocket a tidy sum without ever risking a large amount of their own money.

Easy credit also fueled an interest in owning shares of corporations as investors were allowed to buy stock "**on the margin**." In this process, investors would purchase stock through a broker but pay only about 10 percent of the purchase price. The broker would finance the remaining amount for the investor with money he had borrowed from a bank or other sources. As long as the stock's value remained constant or increased, the broker was assured of collateral to cover the loan. However, if the stock price dropped, he would call in the investor's loan and force him to increase his margin or pay for the stock immediately.

From March 1928 to September 1929, prices of many favored stocks doubled, and nearly every stock rose. The possibilities of profits from stock speculation fueled tremendous activity on Wall Street and created even greater admiration and expectations of American business. President Coolidge disapproved of speculation, but he had encouraged American faith in business; Hoover's election helped to prompt the amazing stock market flourish that followed for several months. Republicans reveled in the prosperity that seemed to abound.

Boom Goes Bust

While Wall Street was booming, many Americans focused their attention on the excitement and affluence that resulted. However, the nation's economic condition was dependent on far more than the price of corporate stock. Besides, most Americans were not even involved in the stock market. Several fundamental problems had been developing through the decade, but optimistic Americans brushed aside the possible dangers until October 1929.

In the middle of that month, stock prices began to sag, and investors began to grow wary. On October 24 ("Black Thursday"), fear began to fuel panic selling. Millions of shares were offered for sale, but virtually no one bought. Prices dropped dramatically until New York's leading financiers pooled their resources to buy stock and halt the devastating decline. The attempt to prop up the market worked for that day, but not before stock prices had taken a significant fall. Banks began to pressure brokers, and brokers began to pressure investors who had bought stock on the margin to pay up. Because most of these speculators did not have the extra cash, they opted to sell the stock, which resulted in a new wave of selling at the stock exchange and an accompanying drop in prices. On **Black Tuesday**, October 29, the bottom fell out of the market. More than sixteen million shares were dumped on the market, and investors lost $30 billion in the process. Americans hoped that the **stock market crash** was only a temporary "readjustment" of the inordinately high stock prices caused by speculation. Instead, a **bear market** (a stock market characterized by pessimism and declining stock prices) dominated the economy for the next few years.

Headlines report the Wall Street crash

What Really Caused the Depression?

In reality, the Depression consisted of four consecutive depressions that are collectively known as the Great Depression. Many problems caused, contributed to, or aggravated the Depression, leading to business decline, unemployment, and hardship for the people. Economic historians, however, have identified three major factors as causes of the Depression.

First were the cumulative consequences following World War I and the economic problems of European powers. Many of the Allies were heavily in debt from the war—this debt included money owed

> ### How the Federal Reserve Helped Bring about the Depression
> The Federal Reserve System raised interest rates four times in 1928–29, thereby slowing and discouraging economic growth.

> ### Unintended Consequences
> The Smoot-Hawley tariff is a good illustration of how an action done with perhaps good intentions can have unintended negative consequences. The tariff was intended to protect selected American industries, but it actually hurt other leading industries. Historian Burton Folsom Jr. wrote, "The tariff on tungsten, for example, hurt steel; the tariff on linseed oil damaged the paint industry." It also "increased the duty on over eight hundred items used in making cars." Furthermore, foreign manufacturers "slapped retaliatory tariffs on the United States." As a result, American cars became more expensive, and U.S. car sales "plummeted from over 5.3 million in 1929 to 1.8 million in 1932."
>
> [Burton Folsom Jr. in *New Deal or Raw Deal? How FDR's Economic Legacy has Damaged America* (New York: Threshold Editions, 2008), 31–32.]

to the United States. But when Germany could not pay reparations to them, those European countries could not repay the United States. The United States was also in debt, and the Allies' failure to pay their loans only increased economic difficulties for the United States.

Another cause was the Federal Reserve's pursuit of reckless monetary policies. In the early 1920s the Federal Reserve System began to expand credit and to pump more money into the economy. This inflation of the monetary supply initiated a new but artificial economic boom. The Fed did this again in 1927, dramatically increasing the volume of farm and personal mortgages. State and local governments also increased their own indebtedness. Consequently, prices of real estate and stocks rose. The Fed finally abandoned its easy-money policy in mid-1929, and the economy began to readjust itself to match the true economic situation. The resulting collapse of credit devastated America's financial market.

A third cause, which came after the stock market crash but before Hoover's term ended, was the Smoot-Hawley Tariff of 1930. It was the highest tariff in American history, and it practically closed off all American foreign trade. Supposedly designed to protect American domestic manufacturers and farmers, in reality it hurt everyone because foreign nations retaliated with their own tariffs against American goods. In a very real sense, the tariff sowed the seeds of another world war because, as has been said, "If goods don't cross borders, armies will."

Although many histories of the period blame unwise stock speculation for the Depression, that was only one of many problems. In fact, most Americans did not own stock; stock speculation was available to only a small percentage of the population. Instead, a leading cause behind the recklessness on Wall Street was the Fed's easy-money policy. Buying stock on credit had resulted in more than $8 million in loans from banks to brokers by October 1929. All that credit was based on the presumed value of stocks in a speculative market. The worth of many stocks had not increased during the bull market because few American industries had become more prosperous during that decade. Neither their profits nor the dividends they paid shareholders had increased significantly. The stock market crash ended the speculative inflation.

Americans, now mired in debt and pessimistic about their future, tightened their belts in an attempt to regain their own economic security. Unfortunately, as the Depression deepened, the proposed—and implemented—solutions only made the problem worse, prolonging the Depression and opening the nation to demands for more government interference in the free market.

Section Review

1–2. What two inventions in particular had a tremendous effect on American life in the 1920s?

3–4. Name two practices that encouraged Americans to spend money extravagantly during the 1920s.

5. In what year did the stock market crash?

★ What dangers does a consumer culture hold for a Christian?

CHAPTER REVIEW 20

Making Connections

1. Why was there a "farm problem" in the years following World War I?
2. Why did President Harding's reputation become tarnished after his death?
3. What trends in the ethnic and racial make-up of America's population disturbed many people in the 1920s?
4–5. What was one of the main focuses of Fundamentalist efforts in the North? in the South?
6–8. List three effects of the automobile upon American society in the 1920s.

Developing History Skills

1. How did immigration impact the United States in the 1920s?
2. What techniques did businesses use in the 1920s to change Americans' spending habits?

Thinking Critically

1. What are some potential dangers of hero worship? Illustrate your answer with examples from the 1920s and today.
2. What are some biblical principles to guide one's involvement in installment buying or speculation in economic endeavors?

Living as a Christian Citizen

1. Imagine that you are a Fundamentalist pastor in the 1920s. Write a brief paragraph arguing for the removal of modernists from your denomination. Use Galatians 1:8–9; 2 Corinthians 6:14–7:1; Romans 16:17–18; and 2 John 1:7–11.
2. Immigration was a concern for Americans in the early part of the twentieth century, and it is again a concern for Americans in the early part of the twenty-first century. How should Christians view immigration, especially the immigration of those with other religions?

People, Places, and Things to Remember

normalcy
Red Scare
isolationism
Washington Naval Conference
Kellogg-Briand Pact
Fordney-McCumber Tariff
Dawes Plan
laissez-faire
Warren G. Harding
Teapot Dome scandal
Calvin Coolidge
Herbert Hoover
Al Smith
Albert Einstein
theory of relativity
Sigmund Freud
Charles A. Lindbergh
Sacco-Vanzetti case
National Origins Act
Marcus Garvey
Harlem Renaissance
Ku Klux Klan
Al Capone
Fundamentalism
Fundamentalist-Modernist controversy
John T. Scopes
installment plans
speculation
bull market
on the margin
Black Tuesday (October 29, 1929)
stock market crash (1929)
bear market

21

THE THIRTIES
1929–1939

> I can't. This is my sister's day to eat.
>
> A little girl's response to a teacher's suggestion that she go home and eat something

Out-of-work Americans line up for assistance during the Great Depression.

Big Ideas

1. How did Herbert Hoover's administration differ from those of his immediate predecessors?
2. What characterized FDR's administration?
3. How did Americans respond to the Depression?

I. Hoover Gets the Blame
II. FDR and the New Deal
III. Life in the Thirties

The jobless stood on city street corners, hoping to sell apples for 5¢ each. The homeless rode the rails from freight yard to freight yard, often camping in "hobo jungles." Down-and-out "Okies" (Oklahoma residents) left their dust-choked farms on the Great Plains, looking for work in the fruit and vegetable fields of California. Poor teachers in Chicago prepared little meals from their meager resources to feed their hungry students.

A nation that had become one of the wealthiest and most powerful in the world was thrown into a confusing economic quagmire, trapping millions of its people in poverty and despair. Although most Americans escaped severe deprivations, few of them passed through the 1930s without some hardship and anxiety. All around were unwanted reminders that the prosperity of the 1920s was gone and that the future was doubtful. Franklin Roosevelt, during his 1932 campaign, described the prevalent despair when he commented, "I have looked into the faces of thousands of Americans. . . . They have the frightened look of lost children." Hard times and great challenges gripped the nation during the **Great Depression**.

"Okies" traveling to California

I. Hoover Gets the Blame

During the 1928 election campaign, Herbert Hoover had promised the nation "a chicken in every pot and a car in every garage." The Republicans gladly accepted credit for the prosperity of the 1920s and promised more, a promise that the American people wanted to believe. Most Americans gave their support to Hoover, expecting him to extend their carefree existence for another four years. But when the stock market crash of 1929 hit, blame for the end of prosperity began to fall on the shoulders of one man: Herbert Hoover.

Call It a Depression

Contrary to popular assumptions, America's economic prosperity did not evaporate overnight in October 1929. The conditions that led to the market's crash had been developing during the twenties, and their impact was compounded in the months of uncertainty that followed the crash. The problems of unemployment, poverty, and despair began to surface but did not become widespread until about a year after the collapse on Wall Street. Even so, the economic decline could not be ignored. Because Hoover was intent on keeping Americans' morale high, he avoided the standard historical terms for an economic decline—*panic* or *crisis*—and instead chose to call the downturn by a title that, at the time, evoked less emotion. He called it a "depression." Although that economic term seemed less alarming at the time, the word came to strike fear in the hearts of Americans in the decades that followed and would bring to mind painful memories for the remainder of the century.

Hoover's Efforts

On October 25, 1929, the day after Black Thursday, Hoover declared that "the fundamental business of the country, that is production and distribution of commodities, is on a sound and prosperous basis." His intent was to restore American confidence and thereby avoid a financial panic, but his words of encouragement were not enough. As noted in Chapter 20, Black Thursday was soon

Guiding Questions

1. What was Hoover's response to the Depression?
2. How did the nation respond to the Depression?

This "Hooverville" above was in Seattle while the one below was in New York City.

followed by Black Tuesday, and the nation began a downward economic spiral. Nonetheless, the president continued trying to convince Americans that matters were not as grim as many believed. When a group asked for more government works projects in June 1930, he told them it was unnecessary because the Depression had ended. It was not so easy, Hoover found, to convince the nation that this was true.

The easiest response for many people in the 1930s was to blame Hoover for the Depression. His name was soon linked with the hardships of the era because he was the president when the crisis began. As conditions grew bleaker, cardboard shacks sheltering homeless people in parks and vacant lots of American cities were called "**Hoovervilles**." Newspapers used for covering on cold nights were "Hoover blankets," and empty pockets turned inside out became "Hoover flags."

The frayed sacks in which the jobless carried their belongings were called "Hoover bags." Broken-down cars pulled by horses or mules were "Hoover carts," and the jackrabbits that farmers killed for food were "Hoover hogs." A popular joke of the day was that Hoover went to Secretary of the Treasury Andrew Mellon one day and asked him for a nickel to phone a friend. Mellon replied, "Here's a dime; telephone both of them." Hoover, saddened by the animosity of the nation expressed toward him, commented, "Democracy is not a polite employer."

It has often been implied that Hoover made little effort to combat the Depression beyond assuring the nation that everything was going to be all right. This

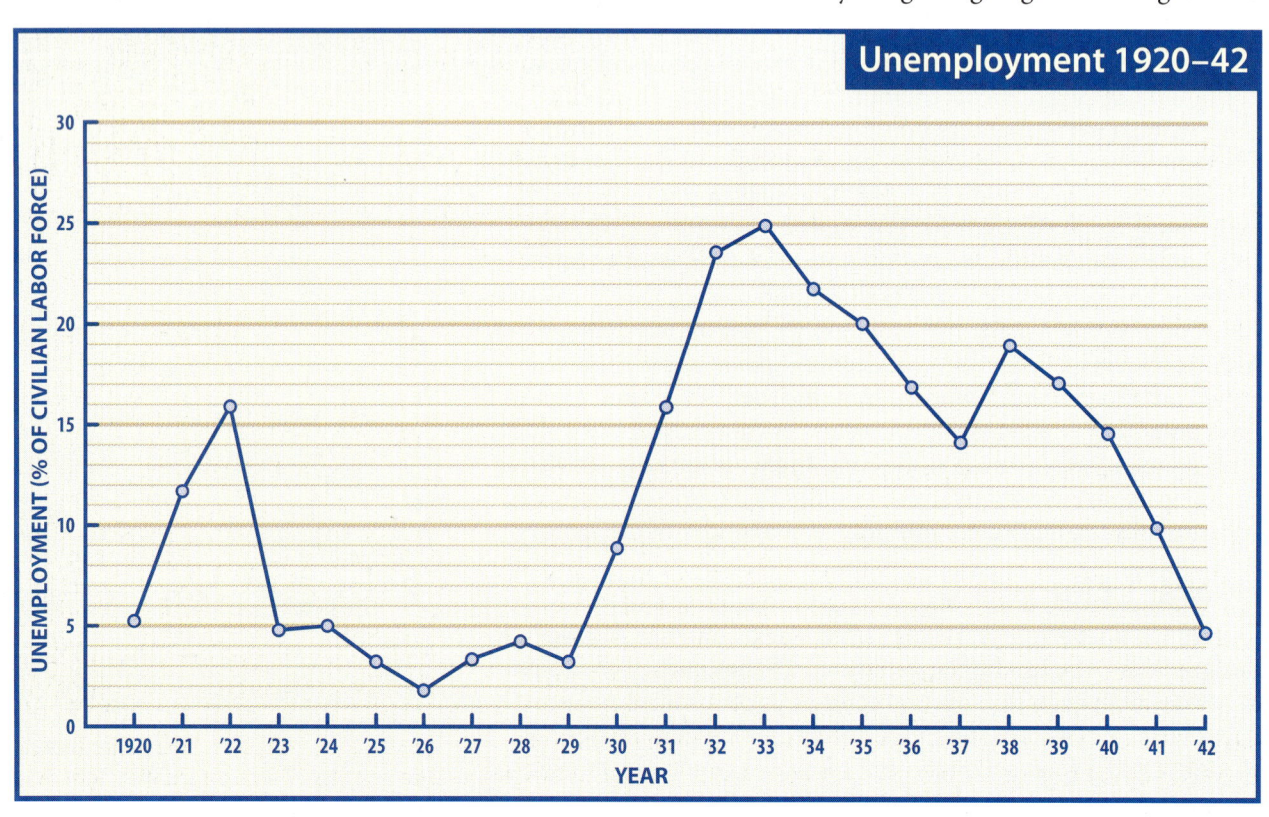

Unemployment 1920–42

In the U.S., nonfunctioning cars that were pulled by horses were called "Hoover carts." In Canada, they were named for the prime minister there, Richard Bennett, and were called "Bennett buggies."

reputation for inaction, however, is not deserved. Hoover was a progressive Republican who was willing to make changes, including getting government involved where it had never been involved. He took federal action to deal with the situation quickly. By the end of 1929, he had signed legislation to cut taxes by $160 million and to provide an increase of $420 million in spending for federal **public works** (government-financed construction of public facilities) to create jobs. These were not small steps, but they gained little notice and, unfortunately, provided few immediate substantial results.

Early in 1932, Hoover reversed course and pressed Congress to pass the Revenue Act. Hoover was worried because the federal debt was quickly rising. This law revived many taxes from World War I and imposed a sales tax on gasoline, tires, cars, electricity, and other items. It taxed stock transfers and phone, telegraph, and radio messages. It raised the personal income tax, the corporate income tax, and the gift tax. Hoover also expanded credit, which stimulated the economy. Many economists believed Hoover was making a mistake by increasing taxes. As people argued about the president's actions, conditions in the country worsened.

Voluntary Cooperation

Hoover also launched a major campaign for "voluntary" cooperation in the fight against the Depression. In December 1929, the president called a meeting of four hundred of the nation's leading business executives. He urged them to voluntarily keep their workers and maintain satisfactory wage levels. He also asked that they continue to invest in new construction and equipment rather than cut industrial growth. Although the businessmen tried to cooperate, by the end of 1930 economic realities made support impossible. To abide by the agreement would have sent many firms into bankruptcy. So unemployment grew, wages declined, and industrial expansion virtually ceased.

Unemployed people in bread lines (*above*) and soup kitchens (*below*) were a familiar sight during the Great Depression.

This unemployed man is selling apples near the Capitol during the Great Depression.

Even before the stock market crash, Hoover had directed Congress to create the Federal Farm Board. This agency, intended to relieve the prolonged hardships of American farmers, instituted public stabilization corporations chartered by the states rather than by the federal government. These corporations were supposed to bolster the prices of farm products by buying surpluses while also trying to persuade farmers to cut back production voluntarily. When the Depression began and needs increased, Hoover hoped that these efforts would ease the farm problems. But the plan quickly collapsed as overproduction continued and funds for stabilizing farm prices were depleted. The price for wheat fell from $1.03 a bushel in 1929 to 66¢ in 1930 and 38¢ in 1931. Other farm prices dropped similarly, throwing farmers deeper into debt and despair.

Other voluntary efforts initiated by the Hoover administration included the President's Emergency Committee for Employment (PECE), formed in October 1930. This committee tried to coordinate the efforts of public and private charities as they provided assistance to the poor and funneled information about relief conditions back to the government. About a year later, the President's Organization for Unemployment Relief (POUR) replaced PECE, but it never had the resources to deal effectively with the growing crisis. Another program was the National Credit Corporation (NCC). Facing increasing bank failures (from 651 in 1929 to almost 2,300 in 1931), Hoover wanted banks to cooperate to maintain their own stability. He expected the nation's prosperous banks to help establish a credit reserve fund to provide assistance to banks in danger of failing. By helping each other in this way, they might avoid further panic in the banking industry. This idea also met a humiliating end. Years later, Hoover said that the effort quickly "became ultra-conservative, then fearful, and finally died."

Hoover believed that it was the duty of private individuals, not the government, to help the needy. However, he reluctantly agreed to give federal money to state governments to provide some assistance to the unemployed and other needy individuals. But by the autumn of 1931, in the face of an uncertain future and continued economic decline, the public outcry for even more government action was mounting rapidly.

Government Involvement

When voluntary cooperation did not seem to provide the desired results quickly enough, Hoover initiated government measures to hasten recovery. Although he adamantly opposed any form of dole (an unearned government handout) to meet the needs of impoverished Americans, he believed that **work relief** was acceptable. Employment in a government relief job would at least discourage idleness and preserve the self-respect of the needy. Hoover also wanted to keep most of the relief efforts under the control of state and local government rather than creating large federal relief agencies. That way the measures taken could be adapted more easily to the specific needs in each local area.

Hoover also was determined to keep the federal budget in balance, even if it required tax increases. He declared that "the course of unbalanced budgets is the road to ruin." Most Americans shared Hoover's view that **deficit spending** (spending more money than is received) would jeopardize confidence in the nation's financial stability and further discourage industrial recovery.

In June 1930, Hoover signed the **Smoot-Hawley Tariff**, which pushed tariffs on foreign industrial and agricultural products to their highest level in the nation's history. The high protectionist tariff was intended to help American producers and stabilize prices. However, many foreign countries responded by raising their tariffs; thus, it actually reduced the market for American goods in other nations. It is impossible to measure the total effect of the tariff revision on the economy, but it did not help bring recovery to the depressed nation.

The increase in the tariff undoubtedly helped to precipitate an economic collapse in Europe in 1931. Hoover was especially concerned about this international crisis because he believed that America's foreign economic ties contributed to the Depression. He soon declared an unpopular but unavoidable moratorium, or suspension, of European debt payments to the United States. He also called for an international economic conference to solve international economic problems. Even so, no action was taken to lower the tariff until 1934.

By 1932, unemployment in the country was approaching 25 percent. In 1929, the rate was less than 5 percent. Although Hoover had rejected many of the proposals that Congress scrambled to enact, in 1932 he approved the Emergency Relief and Construction Act, which established the **Reconstruction Finance Corporation (RFC)**. This agency was his most significant measure. Patterned after the War Finance Corporation of World War I, the RFC was authorized to lend $2 billion to struggling banks, railroads, life insurance companies, and other large businesses. Although this move helped stabilize the banking industry and a few other economic concerns temporarily, it did not inspire the expansion of credit and return of confidence that Hoover wanted. Furthermore, some criticized the RFC for helping the wealthy—bankers and businessmen—rather than the needy. However, Hoover believed the RFC loans to businesses that were about to fail would help average Americans by providing jobs and higher wages.

Although Hoover's efforts to overcome the Depression did not return the nation's economy to prosperity, his actions set a precedent for a significant increase in federal government involvement in America's economic affairs. In 1930, he asked for a $25 million loan to the Department of Agriculture for the provision of seed and feed to impoverished farmers. He began the expansion of public works, spending unprecedented amounts of money for "make-work" projects; provided the first (though meager) federal funds for relief; established some pioneer programs in home financing and public housing; and established the Reconstruction Finance Corporation, a major lending agency that would become an integral part of his successor's relief efforts. The next administration would embrace and greatly expand such federal activity. Whether such expansion was positive or negative has been debated for decades.

A Demand for Change

Although Hoover did not neglect the mounting economic crisis, the spread of poverty and despair was beginning to take a toll on the American people, and many began to cry for action to stop their suffering. In 1932, the situation was bleak. The nation's measure of productivity, its GNP (gross national product, the annual value of all goods and services that a nation produces) fell to

$41 billion, down from $104 billion in 1929. More than five thousand American banks had failed, eighty-six thousand businesses had closed, and a quarter of a million families had been evicted from their homes. In September of that year, *Fortune* magazine estimated that 28 percent of the population—about 34 million men, women, and children—were without any income whatsoever. As the hardships of the Depression spread, many Americans began to clamor for help and change.

The Bonus Army

A major episode in the Hoover administration's struggle with the Depression took place in mid-1932. In 1924, Congress had passed legislation providing a bonus, averaging about $1,000, to each World War I veteran. Payment would be made in 1945. In the spring and summer of 1932, a large group of unemployed veterans made their way to Washington, D.C., to ask for an early payment of that bonus. These veterans of the American Expeditionary Force now called themselves the Bonus Expeditionary Force or **Bonus Army**. The House of Representatives approved partial early payment, but the Senate defeated the measure. Veterans turned to Hoover for help, but he would not meet with them. Most of the 15,000–20,000 veterans returned home. Congress provided money for the protestors to do so. Dismayed but unwilling to concede defeat, about 2,000 of the veterans, some with their wives and children, remained in a hastily built shantytown (consisting of huts and crudely built cabins) on the edge of the city. Others occupied some vacant buildings near the Capitol. As weeks passed, Hoover became more and more frustrated by their embarrassing presence in the capital city.

The Bonus Army in Washington, D.C.

On July 28, the situation reached a boiling point. Government agents informed the Bonus Army that they must move out of the downtown buildings, but they refused. Police with nightsticks in hand were sent to force the illegal occupants from the buildings, but the veterans, reinforced by men from the main camp, met the officers with a volley of bricks. In the clash, some of the policemen began to fire on the veterans, killing two and wounding two others. Hoover learned of the trouble and sent troops under General Douglas MacArthur to quell the disorder and destroy the shantytown. MacArthur, contrary to Hoover's orders, determined to use all necessary force to drive the veterans completely from the capital city. After an hour's warning, the general's forces marched in with tear gas, tanks, and bayonets. Once the downtown buildings were cleared, MacArthur moved on to the main camp, driving out the veterans who remained and burning their shacks.

Tanks and soldiers clearing out the Bonus Army

Although the action had been much harsher than he intended, Hoover took full responsibility for the affair. In doing so, he seemed more heartless than ever to the needs of struggling Americans. A desire for change was leading many people to look elsewhere for relief. Some began to embrace various socialistic plans, even praising the communist Soviet Union. Benito Mussolini's Fascist government in Italy also won admiration for dealing with economic difficulties. Such extreme political views were not the norm, but people without income, food, and other necessities were becoming desperate.

Election of 1932

As the 1932 presidential election approached, Republican prospects for reelection were bleak. Hoover had lost his appeal to the impatient public, but no other bright stars were on the Republican horizon that year. Republican congressmen and governors had generally fallen out of favor along with Hoover as voters held the whole party responsible for the continuing Depression. As a result, though Hoover won renomination easily, the Republicans entered the fall campaign with little confidence.

The Democrats, however, did have a popular candidate to offer in the 1932 campaign. For some time, **Franklin Delano Roosevelt (FDR)** had desired the office once held by his Republican cousin Theodore, but that ambition seemed to be shattered in August 1921 when polio struck him, paralyzing him from the waist down for life. Nonetheless, Roosevelt's courageous struggle to overcome his disability added appeal to his public image. In 1928, Roosevelt won the governorship of New York, despite overwhelming public support for Republicans in that year. With the rising public disapproval of the Republicans in 1930, the governor won reelection easily.

Roosevelt entered the Democratic convention in 1932 as the front-runner for the nomination. The governor met some stiff opposition from several factions of the party, including conservatives and Tammany Hall, but he managed to appease the conservatives with his vice-presidential pick, John Nance Garner of Texas. Roosevelt won on the fourth ballot, and, on notification of that fact, he flew from Albany to Chicago to make his acceptance speech in person at the convention. This unprecedented but calculated action helped to portray the candidate as a daring man who was willing to challenge tradition.

That perceived defiance of traditional actions proved to be the central issue of the campaign between Hoover and Roosevelt. Hoover pointed out that theme when he said, "My countrymen! The fundamental issue that will fix the national direction for one hundred years to come is whether we shall go in fidelity to American traditions or whether we shall turn to innovations." Because many needy Americans were critical of Hoover's insistence on tradition, they were ready to turn to innovations. Roosevelt promised them action, and they believed him. Even his campaign song, "Happy Days Are Here Again," renewed hope in a change for the better. Republicans, caught in the crossfire of events, were not in a singing mood.

Roosevelt was in an enviable position throughout the race against Hoover. Because so many Americans wanted something different in their new president, Roosevelt would be an easy winner unless he foolishly antagonized the public. Therefore, he carefully avoided explaining the details of his economic plans. He spread hope and assurance of action to meet the crisis.

In his July acceptance speech at the Chicago convention, Roosevelt stated, "I pledge you, I pledge myself, to a new deal for the American people." That promise of a "**New Deal**" (a name that would soon be permanently attached to his efforts to conquer the Depression) was what the people wanted to hear, regardless of his lack of specifics on the particulars. The people were willing to trust that he would help the nation overcome its serious difficulties.

Campaign buttons for Roosevelt and Hoover

The Election of 1932

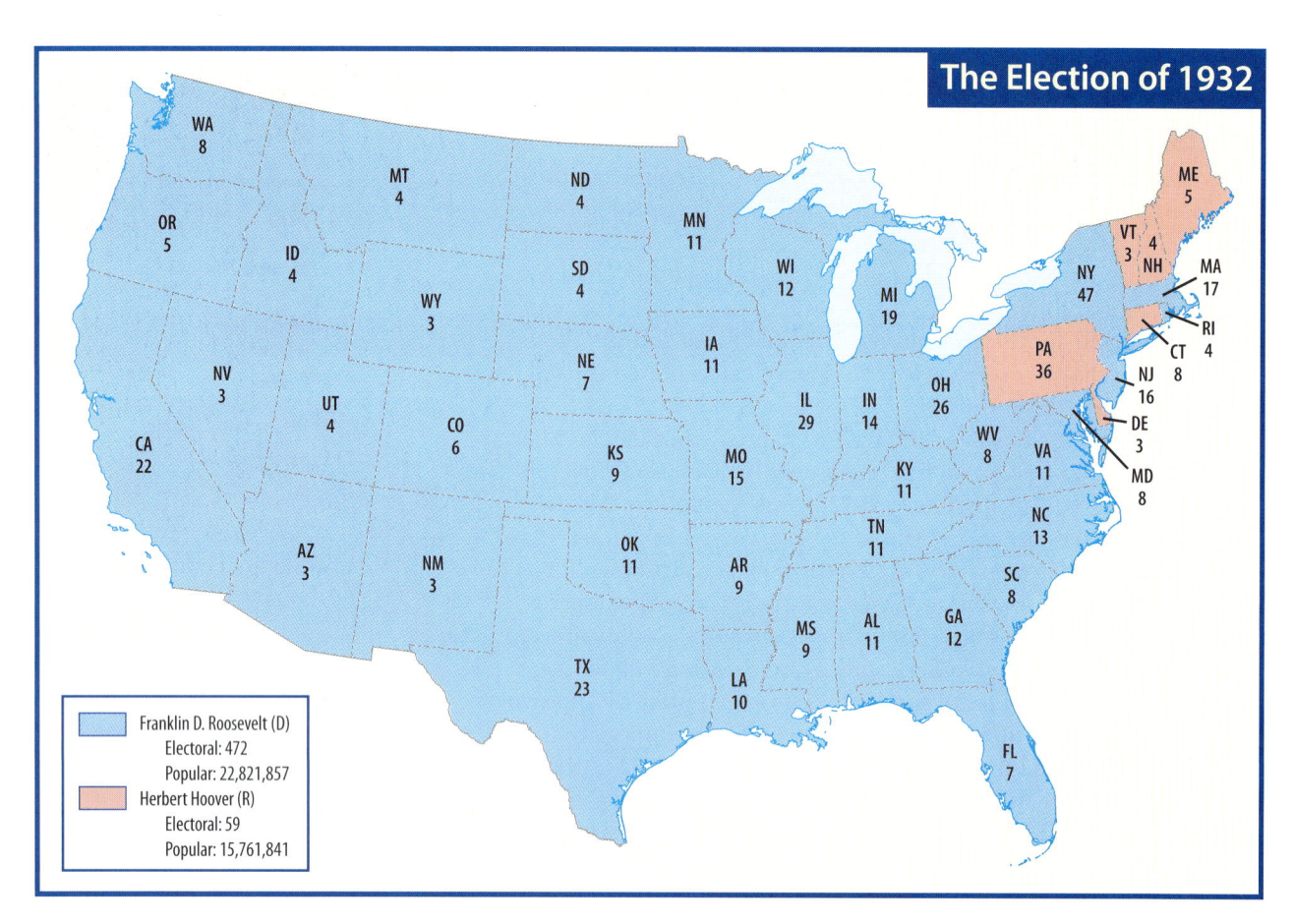

Franklin D. Roosevelt (D)
Electoral: 472
Popular: 22,821,857

Herbert Hoover (R)
Electoral: 59
Popular: 15,761,841

They heard in his speeches what they *wanted* to hear. Conservatives heard "balance the budget"; liberals heard "innovations" and "action now." Surprisingly, even the poor identified with the wealthy and aristocratic Roosevelt. Such popularity, coupled with the deepening Depression, resulted in a decisive victory for the New York governor. Roosevelt won more than 57 percent of the popular vote in November and 472 electoral votes to Hoover's 59.

Final Desperate Days

During the months between the November election and the March 4 inauguration of Roosevelt, the defeated president was left to struggle with the continuing problems of the Depression. The Twentieth Amendment, which moved presidential inaugurations from March 4 to January 20, was not ratified until early 1933; thus it did not take effect until the 1936 election.

Hoover was not only somewhat bitter about his fate but also deeply concerned that Roosevelt would take government intervention too far. He blamed Roosevelt, with some legitimacy, for scaring businesses with vague references to economic planning and deliberate inflation.

Nonetheless, Hoover tried to enlist Roosevelt's help in a cooperative effort to deal with the difficulties arising in the early weeks of 1933. For any new effort to gain acceptance, Hoover believed it must have the approval of the popular president-elect. Roosevelt, however, avoided approving any of Hoover's programs for fear that the people would transfer the blame for any failures to him. Roosevelt wanted to start his job without any ties to the unpopular moves of the outgoing administration. This position was politically wise for Roosevelt, but it meant the nation endured much continued uncertainty during those intervening weeks.

Despite the efforts of the Reconstruction Finance Corporation and other Hoover initiatives, a terrible **banking crisis** began to sweep the country. The nation's banking system was on the brink of total collapse. Depositors across the land were rushing to their banks to withdraw their money before it was too late, but panic only hastened the failure of many of these institutions and jeopardized the savings of other depositors. As the hours passed before Roosevelt's inauguration, the nation seemed to be slipping into even deeper economic chaos. By the time Hoover's term ended, 80 percent of the nation's banks were closed. Governors in some states had ordered closures, which they hoped would be temporary, until the problems of the banking crisis could be addressed.

A crowd gathers in front of one of the many banks that closed during the Depression.

Section Review

1. Why did Hoover call the economic decline a "depression"?
2–3. What two federal actions did Hoover quickly take to combat the Depression?
4. What kind of assistance to the poor did Hoover favor over a dole?
5. What episode involving World War I veterans in Washington, D.C., became a problem to the Hoover administration?
6–7. Who were the two major party candidates for the presidency in 1932?
★ How did the Smoot-Hawley Tariff affect the U.S. and world economies?
★ FDR pledged to increase direct federal relief to the poor while promising to cut government expenditures and balance the budget. Is it possible to do all of this at the same time? If so, how? If not, why not?

II. FDR and the New Deal

The drama of the banking crisis provided an emotional setting for the inauguration of the new president. Because of the sense of imminent danger, Roosevelt sought to calm apprehensions by stating in his inaugural address: "First of all, let me assert my firm belief that the only thing we have to fear is fear itself."

Guiding Questions

1. What were FDR's first actions upon becoming president?
2. What kind of resistance did FDR encounter?
3. Did FDR's actions produce an economic recovery?

President Hoover and president-elect Roosevelt ride to the inauguration (*left*).

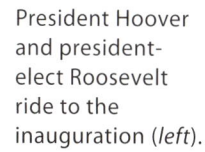

Franklin Roosevelt delivered his first inauguration speech on March 4, 1933 (*right*).

> **New Deal?**
> Although FDR coined the phrase, President Hoover had already moved the country in the direction of increased government planning and federal intervention. President Roosevelt just greatly expanded upon what Hoover had begun.

Frances Perkins, FDR's secretary of labor, was the first female cabinet member.

FDR delivering a fireside chat

Fighting Fear

Immediately after assuming office, Roosevelt took two important steps. He called Congress into special session and declared a "**bank holiday**." The banking crisis had brought the financial markets of the nation to a virtual standstill. Order and confidence needed to be restored. Therefore on March 6, just two days after taking office, Roosevelt called for a temporary closing of all banks to calm the fears of a nervous public. The banks that proved to be basically sound would be allowed to reopen. This action renewed the people's confidence in banks and greatly reduced panic withdrawals.

The First Hundred Days

Congress convened on March 9 and remained in an emergency session until June 16. In those crucial one hundred days, Congress passed Roosevelt's New Deal programs one after another. The support that the president had won in the election, along with the many newly elected Democratic congressmen, guaranteed smooth passage for most New Deal legislation. Rarely has a president enjoyed such cooperation in accomplishing his agenda. The nation watched in approval of the quick action.

Besides his cabinet members (which included the first female to hold a cabinet position—Frances Perkins, his secretary of labor), Roosevelt had recruited a group of advisors to help him formulate his plans for combating the Depression. This group, called the "**Brain Trust**," was composed mostly of professors from Columbia and other major universities who could offer opinions regarding economic policies and legislation. Roosevelt used many of their ideas to frame his legislative agenda.

On the first day of the emergency session, Congress approved the Emergency Banking Act, a measure that endorsed Roosevelt's bank holiday and authorized measures to deal with an impending currency shortage due to the bank closures and hoarding. That action was followed by a dozen more significant pieces of New Deal legislation. These laws took the nation off the gold standard, established the Civilian Conservation Corps (CCC), provided nearly $4 billion in federal relief, and created the Agricultural Adjustment Administration (AAA) to deal with farm problems. They also legalized beer (a measure which was followed within a few months by the national repeal of Prohibition), provided insurance for bank deposits, established regulations for the financial activities of Wall Street, provided for the refinancing of home mortgages, attempted to provide some regulation for the nation's industries, and approved the Tennessee Valley Authority (TVA).

To keep the nation informed and inspired, and to ensure that public support remained behind him, Roosevelt used the radio. He began his frequent "**fireside chats**" on March 12. About half of all American families owned radios in 1933, and many of those who did not made their way to the homes of neighbors or to local businesses to hear the president's messages. His personal charm and fatherly manner carried over the airwaves and persuaded most Americans that they could trust him to make the government work for their benefit.

In his first fireside chat, some sixty million Americans heard him say, "I assure you it is safer to keep your money in a reopened bank than under the mattress." When banks began reopening the following day, deposits far exceeded withdrawals. Over the next few weeks many Americans returned their savings to banks.

Alphabet Agencies

New Deal legislation created a vast array of programs and agencies that came to be known by their initials. The nation's conversations were soon filled with talk of the CCC, the AAA, the NRA, the TVA, and other "alphabet agencies." Former Democratic presidential candidate Al Smith said of those labels, "It looks as if one of the absent-minded professors had played anagrams [a game] with the alphabet soup."

The goal of Roosevelt's New Deal involved the "three Rs"—*relief*, *recovery*, and *reform*. The major role that the New Deal played in broadening the activities and authority of the federal government warrants a brief survey of some of the most important programs.

Providing work relief to furnish income to the millions of needy unemployed was a responsibility that several new agencies assumed. One was the **Civilian Conservation Corps (CCC)**. The CCC put young, unmarried men (ages 18 to 25) to work in planting trees, building roads, developing parks, and assisting with soil conservation projects under the supervision of the army. It proved to be one of the most popular New Deal agencies, lasting until after American entry into World War II. About three million young men were part of the CCC. It emphasized rigid discipline and team effort. They wore uniforms and marched like soldiers, carrying not rifles but shovels, rakes, and hoes.

Another provider of work relief was the **Public Works Administration (PWA)**, which built schools, courthouses, hospitals, bridges, and other public facilities all over the country. The PWA also built ships and planes for the nation's military. Similarly, the short-lived Civil Works Administration (CWA) put the jobless to work building roads, playgrounds, and airports. It also supported teachers, artists, and writers in public enrichment activities. The Federal Emergency Relief Administration (FERA) carried on some CWA projects and created others.

All of these programs combined, however, were unable to provide enough jobs to eliminate the dole. Therefore, one other major program, the **Works Progress Administration (WPA)**, was created in 1935. The WPA employed almost anyone in almost any kind of job. More than eight million jobs were created by the time it was disbanded in 1943. It built and repaired roads; constructed public buildings and recreational areas; supported actors, directors, writers, and artists in art programs; and manufactured a wide variety of other jobs. Many people considered the WPA "make-work"—unnecessary jobs done with lackluster efforts. This vast effort, costing almost $11 billion, was not enough to eradicate unemployment.

The New Deal launched two major measures to attack the widespread problems in American agriculture and industry, both under the control of Secretary of Agriculture (and later Progressive presidential candidate) Henry A. Wallace. The **Agricultural Adjustment Act (AAA)** and its supplements established a new method of subsidizing farm products and aided debt-ridden farmers who were in danger of losing their farms to foreclosure. To reduce the huge farm surpluses expected in the 1933 harvest, the AAA offered benefit payments to farmers who plowed up cotton and slaughtered pigs. Farmers responded by slaughtering six million piglets and

Just Do Something!

The nation was eager for action when FDR became president. "The whole country is with him," commented the popular humorist Will Rogers about FDR. "Just so he does something. If he burned down the Capitol, we would cheer and say, 'Well, we at least got a fire started anyhow.'"

Millions of Americans worked for the Civilian Conservation Corp (*top*), the Public Works Administration (*center*), and the Works Progress Administration (*bottom*).

The Four Horsemen of Reaction

In the early years of the New Deal, the Supreme Court consisted of four conservatives, four liberals, and a "swing" justice (one who sometimes voted with conservative members and sometimes with liberal ones). Because the four conservatives frequently ruled against FDR, they became known as "the Four Horsemen of Reaction." But just who were those four men—and the fifth swing justice—who were able to slow FDR's programs?

Willis Van Devanter was a lawyer whose interests lay in cattle and railroads. William McKinley had appointed him assistant attorney general, and Theodore Roosevelt nominated him for the Eighth Circuit U.S. Court of Appeals. William Howard Taft nominated him for the U.S. Supreme Court, where he served for twenty-six years.

Willis Van Devanter

James Clark McReynolds, a lifelong Democrat, was a corporate lawyer appointed assistant attorney general by President Theodore Roosevelt, a Republican. Democrat Woodrow Wilson nominated him for the Supreme Court. His opinions emphasized protection of private property and the freedoms of contract and speech. As he saw the New Deal programs unfolding, he concluded that FDR was an "utter incompetent."

James Clark McReynolds

Pierce Butler was a lawyer whom Taft enlisted to help his administration prosecute antitrust cases, especially those involving the meatpacking and railroad industries. Butler argued several such cases before the Supreme Court. Warren Harding later nominated him for the Supreme Court. Butler seems to have loved individualism and free enterprise.

Pierce Butler

George Sutherland believed that the most important function of law was to protect individual liberty by restraining government power. He was especially concerned about protecting economic liberties. Although a lawyer, he had more practical political experience than the others, having served in both the U.S. House and the U.S. Senate. As a senator, he had introduced the "Anthony Amendment," the constitutional amendment to give women the right to vote. He was an advisor to Harding, and Harding nominated him for the Supreme Court.

George Sutherland

The swing justice was Chief Justice Charles Evans Hughes. He sometimes voted in favor of New Deal measures but joined the Four Horsemen in opposing other such programs when he thought FDR's proposals were attacks on economic freedom. He later returned to supporting the New Deal measures.

Charles Evans Hughes

destroying ten million acres of cotton. That policy, however, was despised by many in a nation where thousands of children wore rags and remained undernourished, and it brought rampant criticism of the entire program.

The **National Industrial Recovery Act** (**NIRA**) attempted to organize guidelines for industries to increase employment, maintain wages, and reduce unwanted competition. Businesses that complied with the codes were allowed to display the blue eagle symbol of the **National Recovery Administration** (**NRA**), the agency designed to carry out the activities prescribed by the NIRA.

The NRA established about 540 specific codes, all of which tended to raise prices and wages, reduce hours, and remove competition. It also included some unusual code provisions, such as the following:

- Lumber companies were required to keep a list of all customers' names.
- Investment securities analysts were fined for sending letters to prospective clients without their prior permission.
- Jewelers could not advertise watch-repair prices.
- Dry cleaners who operated in low-traffic areas could not charge lower prices to compete with cleaners operating in high-traffic areas.
- Businesses could not offer discounts to customers.

This government attempt at industrial planning met opposition and ultimate elimination. The NIRA—and later the AAA—was declared unconstitutional by the Supreme Court.

Another large group of New Deal programs was intended to provide security, improve conditions, and supply other benefits for large groups of Americans. A banking act led to the formation of the **Federal Deposit Insurance Corporation** (**FDIC**), an agency devised to insure the bank deposits of millions of Americans against loss. Because deposits up to a certain amount were protected, the FDIC greatly increased public confidence in the banking system. The **Tennessee Valley Authority** (**TVA**) undertook an extensive project to build dams along the Tennessee River that would provide navigation, flood control, and cheap electricity for the valley residents.

Congress passed the **Social Security Act** in 1935, instituting old-age pensions and unemployment insurance for American workers. Social Security was essentially a pay-as-you-go system by which benefits were to be paid to beneficiaries from the taxes paid into the system by younger workers. The designers of this social program assumed that there would always be more workers paying in than retirees withdrawing benefits. But today, as the number of workers is decreasing and the number of retirees is increasing, the program is threatened with the possibility of insufficient funds to pay Social Security recipients. Another program was the Rural Electrification Administration (REA), which offered funds to farmer cooperatives for extending electricity to the many rural areas still lacking that utility.

Who Set the Guidelines?

A group of government officials and representatives of the largest industrial leaders set the NIRA guidelines. Their fixed prices and so-called codes of fair competition ensured NIRA-compliant businesses a large profit. This led to higher costs for the customer and financially burdened many who struggled to survive during the Depression.

A waitress installs the NRA blue eagle emblem in the window of a restaurant.

Norris Dam, north of Knoxville, TN, was the first dam completed in the TVA system.

President Roosevelt, pictured as the doctor, is trying a variety of medicines for the ailing Uncle Sam.

Roadblocks and Pitfalls

Roosevelt's extensive New Deal activities sought to meet the nation's demand for change. He had stated during his 1932 campaign that

> the country needs and, unless I mistake its temper, the country demands bold, persistent experimentation. It is common sense to take a method and try it: If it fails, admit it frankly and try another. But above all, try something.

Because he was taking action, he received widespread praise from many Americans, especially the poor, regardless of whether their lives were improved. One woman wrote Roosevelt in 1935 to tell him of the undernourishment of her children, but she did not neglect to add, "you are the best president we ever had." Such praise for FDR was not uncommon, but then, neither was criticism.

Opposition from the Right

People to the political right of Roosevelt, including most Republicans and a few Democrats, found much in the New Deal to criticize. First was its great expense. The government was spending billions of dollars to support the various programs, sending the nation heavily into debt in the process. Also, many of the programs were bringing increased government regulation of American businesses and a corresponding loss of freedom, a tendency that looked suspiciously socialistic. For instance, the NRA was a significant step toward the government control of industry, and the TVA was simply government ownership and control of a large electricity-producing industry. Finally, the New Deal was not bringing recovery. American businesses were still in the doldrums, and millions of people were still unemployed.

Roosevelt's opponents rejoiced in 1935 when the Supreme Court, still dominated by conservative Republican appointees, began to reject some New Deal legislation. Until that time, the Court had not found occasion to strike down popular measures, especially in light of the "national emergency." But after two years of compliance, it began to question certain New Deal actions and even to strike down some minor pieces of legislation. Then, on May 27, 1935, the court declared unanimously that the National Industrial Recovery Act was unconstitutional. Roosevelt denounced the decision, but his NRA was doomed. Early in 1936, the Supreme Court, in a 6–3 decision, struck down the Agricultural Adjustment Act. Clearly, that phase of the New Deal was losing its momentum.

Opposition from the Left

In addition to those who thought the president was doing too much were others who complained that he was not doing enough. Three different men gained wide followings by advocating bolder governmental moves to combat the Depression. One was Senator **Huey Long**, a flamboyant, loud, plain-spoken former governor

Louisiana senator and former governor Huey Long attacked FDR and promoted his "Share Our Wealth" scheme.

of Louisiana. His "Share Our Wealth" scheme proposed that the government heavily tax the rich and redistribute that wealth to the poor. The idea was alarming, not to mention impractical, but it became popular among the uneducated poor who desperately wanted assistance. Long seemed to be stealing some support from Roosevelt prior to the 1936 election, but the rise of the Louisiana "Kingfish" ended suddenly with his assassination in September 1935.

Another popular plan, especially among older Americans, was espoused by Dr. **Francis Townsend**. He proposed that the government pay a pension of $200 a month to each citizen over sixty, provided that they agreed to hold no job and to spend every penny they received. This pension would be financed, supposedly, by a 2 percent national sales tax. Thousands joined Townsend clubs, and many began to buy merchandise on credit in expectation of receiving the monthly checks. The plan's supporters, however, failed to recognize that it would simply rob younger Americans of their purchasing power to give that power to the elderly.

Another challenger who promoted his own brand of government action during the 1930s was Father **Charles Coughlin**, a Roman Catholic priest from Royal Oak, Michigan. Coughlin turned his weekly radio program of sermons into a national political broadcast. At one point, over thirty million people were listening to his radio program. By 1934, the eloquent priest was telling his huge audience that the nation needed to abandon the "pagan god of gold" and coin large amounts of silver, thereby inflating the money supply. He also began to propose that capitalism be replaced with his own system of "social justice." (He published a weekly magazine titled *Social Justice*.) Eventually, he lost many followers because of his increasingly anti-Semitic (anti-Jewish) views.

Coughlin allied with Townsend briefly in 1936 to help support a third-party candidate for the presidency. Many supporters of the deceased Huey Long joined them. The effort did not fare well, and their candidate garnered less than 2 percent of the popular vote that year.

Although the radical opposition to the New Deal was ultimately unsuccessful, the wide popularity evoked by those socialistic schemes posed a threat to America's economic foundations. The New Deal, by contrast, was certainly less extreme.

"A Switch in Time Saves Nine"

Roosevelt believed that his overwhelming election victory had given him a clear mandate to proceed with his New Deal. The decisions of the Supreme Court in 1935 and 1936 declaring various New Deal measures unconstitutional, however, disturbed the president greatly. At first, he thought about pushing for a constitutional amendment to protect New Deal legislation but dismissed the strategy because it could be defeated easily and would take too long. On February 5, 1937, he announced instead a plan to enlarge the Court. For each justice over age seventy who did not retire, he wanted the right to appoint an additional justice up to a maximum of six. Roosevelt argued that the new members would make the Court more efficient.

Huey Long died two days after being shot in the Louisiana State Capitol.

Dr. Francis Townsend also thought the New Deal did not go far enough and proposed his own pension scheme.

Father Charles Coughlin used his fiery oratory to promote his version of "social justice."

In this political cartoon, even the Democratic donkey kicks in opposition to FDR's court-packing plan.

The president's proposal generated a storm of opposition from many directions and for many reasons. Many people attacked the plan because it threatened the American tradition of an independent judicial system. Conservatives argued that efficiency was not the issue; having more justices would actually delay Court proceedings. Rather, they pointed out, Roosevelt wanted to "pack the Court" with liberal New Dealers. Politicians who before had not dared oppose Roosevelt publicly because of his popularity spoke out against the **court-packing plan** because they sensed that the public was on their side.

Because of the extensive opposition to the plan, Court reform failed to win approval even in the Democrat-controlled Congress, but Roosevelt won the "war." One of the justices announced his retirement from the Court, giving the president the opportunity to replace him with a liberal appointee. Meanwhile, another justice left the conservative bloc on the Court and voted with a new majority that approved New Deal programs in several decisions. Newspapers characterized it as a "switch in time saves nine." Roosevelt eventually was able to nominate several members of the Supreme Court because of deaths or retirements of justices. By 1940, five of the nine justices were his appointees. In the end, however, Roosevelt did pay a price. The fight over the Court divided his party and strengthened the enemies of the New Deal.

Elusive Recovery

Despite the criticisms Roosevelt faced during his first term in office, his popularity remained widespread. Millions of Americans had received some form of government aid through the CCC, the WPA, or other federal programs, making those people as grateful to Roosevelt as they had been bitter toward Hoover. On the surface, economic conditions seemed to be improving, ensuring the New Deal some credit in the upcoming election.

1936 Election

In 1936, the Republicans had only one viable candidate to offer in the race against Roosevelt—**Alfred Landon**. As one of only seven Republican governors at the time and the only one to have won re-election in 1934, Landon was the "most available" man. Being from Kansas, he was free of the image of Wall Street and big business, an image that had plagued the Republican Party since the Depression began.

Although Landon had a progressive record and supported much of the New Deal, Republicans hoped that he would be "the Kansas Coolidge," bringing a return of business prosperity to the nation. Unfortunately for Landon, the big business interests launched a major effort to elect the Kansas governor, thereby linking him with that unpopular segment of society after all. Roosevelt jumped at the chance to lash out at the forces of "organized money," thereby solidifying his support from the poorer classes.

Nevertheless, Landon maintained hopes of winning the election when a poll conducted by the *Literary Digest* predicted a decisive Republican victory. This straw vote, however, was based on

Republican Kansas governor Alf Landon ran a losing campaign against FDR in 1936.

The Election of 1936

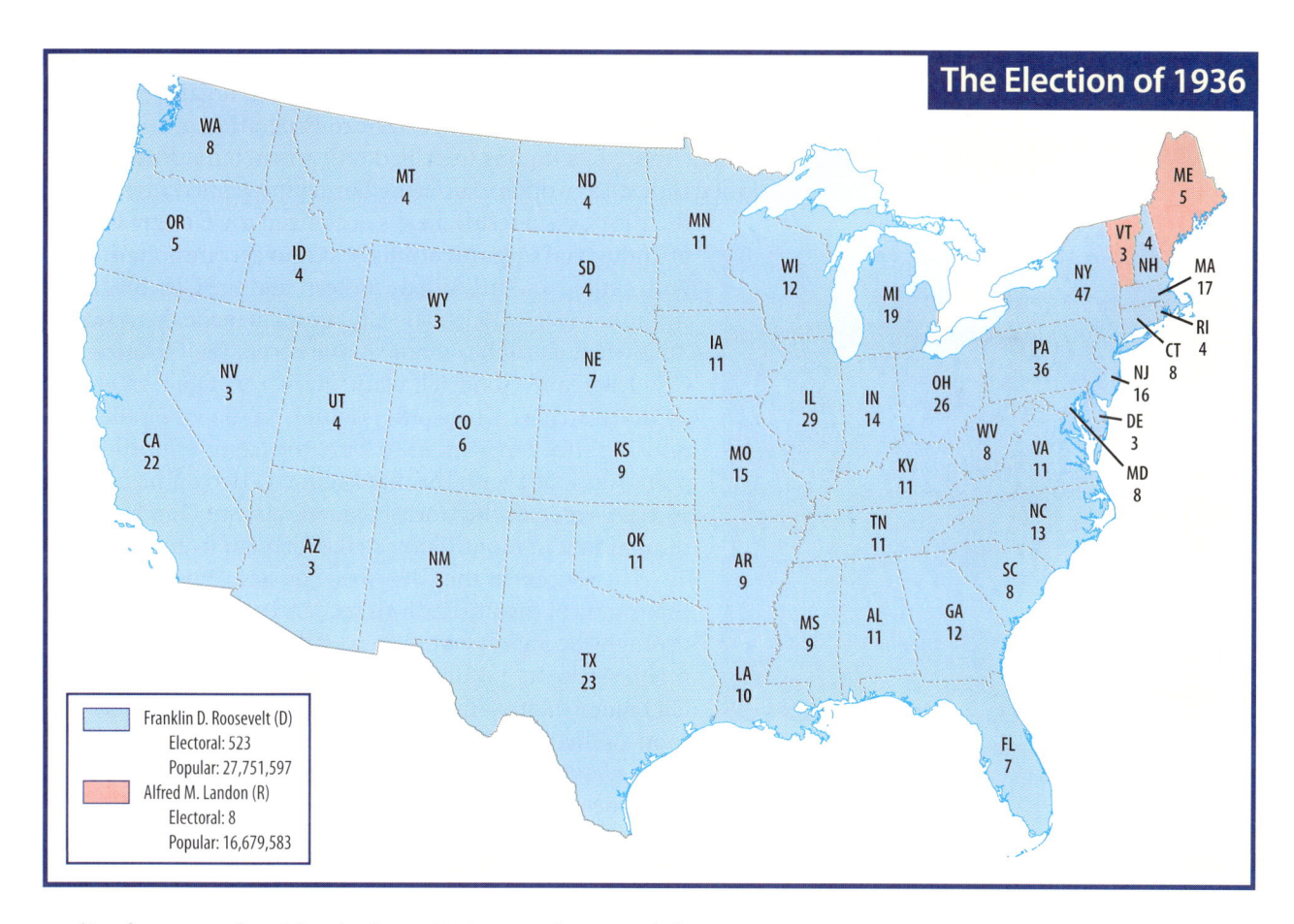

- Franklin D. Roosevelt (D)
  - Electoral: 523
  - Popular: 27,751,597
- Alfred M. Landon (R)
  - Electoral: 8
  - Popular: 16,679,583

replies from people with telephone listings and automobile registrations, thereby entirely overlooking the preferences of the poor, who lacked those luxuries. On Election Day, the votes of the poor were not overlooked, and Roosevelt won by a landslide. Landon won only two states—Maine and Vermont—and garnered only 8 electoral votes to Roosevelt's 523. Republicans were only able to keep less than one-quarter of the seats in the Senate and the House of Representatives, and the future of their party was in doubt. The Democrats and their leader, FDR, were clearly in control of the nation's political machinery.

No Way Out

Despite his impressive victory in the 1936 election, Roosevelt still faced major problems. Four years after he took office and initiated his numerous New Deal programs, the nation was still beleaguered by a severe economic depression—despite his having spent enormous sums of government money. When Roosevelt took his oath of office again in 1937, he said, "I see one-third of a nation ill-housed, ill-clad, ill-nourished."

What is more, in that year the nation experienced another sharp economic decline. It was a depression within the Depression. Many gains that had been credited to the New Deal were washed away. The government was pumping billions of dollars into the economy and plunging the nation ever deeper into debt only to find that recovery was as elusive as ever and that millions of Americans were still in need. Furthermore, as mentioned earlier in this chapter, Roosevelt's reputation was badly damaged by the court-packing episode.

Adding to the other problems of the time, labor unions were gaining strength and using strikes to cripple big industries. John L.

Lewis, president of the United Mine Workers, recognized that recent legislation had provided the opportunity to organize the workers in large industries. The American Federation of Labor (AFL) had limited its unions to skilled craftsmen, but millions of unskilled industrial workers suffering hardships wanted more from their jobs. As a result, Lewis organized the **Congress of Industrial Organizations** (**CIO**) to accommodate both skilled and unskilled workers, and the CIO broke from the AFL in 1936. The CIO quickly made the headlines when its rubber industry workers at the Firestone, Goodyear, and Goodrich plants in Akron, Ohio, staged sit-down strikes. The workers simply sat down on the job, refusing either to work or to leave the factories until their point was made with the management. Two of the companies gave in to the workers' demands, but Goodyear refused until a month-long strike forced it to concede.

The success of the CIO in Akron gave new hope to thousands of dissatisfied workers and sent a shudder through the nation's employers. Later in 1936, the automobile industry began to feel the pressure of increased CIO membership among its workers. The CIO's ranks soon swelled to 400,000, and with the increase, sit-down strikes multiplied as well. Not all labor disagreements were peaceful. Violence came on Memorial Day 1937 when, in response to a barrage of rocks and sticks, police killed ten striking workers at the Republic Steel mill in South Chicago. Besides their dismay at the violence, some middle-class Americans were alarmed by the sit-down tactic, which endangered private property rights. (The strikers sometimes abused, destroyed, or pilfered company property during such strikes.) Finally, the Supreme Court outlawed the sit-down strike in 1939. This decision eliminated the CIO's most effective weapon, but the union remained powerful, eventually reuniting with the AFL to become the AFL-CIO.

Many domestic problems plagued the United States during the later years of the Depression. However, the focus would soon shift to foreign concerns. The unemployment, poverty, and despair of the Depression would ultimately give way to the fear, excitement, and activity of World War II.

Union members stage a sit-down strike at this automobile plant in Flint, Michigan.

Did War End the Depression?

Many argue that U.S. entry into World War II ended the Depression. They point to such statistics as unemployment and the GDP (gross domestic product).

Evidence does show that unemployment fell dramatically when war occurred (see chart earlier in this chapter) because men were transferred from unemployment lines in the United States to the front lines in Europe or the Pacific. The nation's GDP, the total value of goods produced by a country, certainly grew during World War II.

Section Review

1–2. What were the first two actions that Roosevelt took to deal with the Depression?

3. What was the name for Roosevelt's radio talks that were used to inspire confidence and approval for New Deal measures?

4. What was the common purpose of the CCC, the PWA, and the WPA?

5. What New Deal program involved the government in ownership and control of a large electric power industry?

6. How did Roosevelt attempt to make the Supreme Court support the New Deal?

★ Evaluate FDR's use of radio talks.

★ Explain indications that by 1937 the New Deal had not resolved the problems of the Depression.

III. Life in the Thirties

The 1930s was a bewildering decade for Americans. They often did not understand the reasons for their plight, and they sometimes found it difficult to believe that there was any hope of something better in the future. Too many dreams had been shattered when the crash and Depression hurled financiers, factory workers, and farmers alike into unemployment, bankruptcy, and desperation. Yet in the midst of the Depression, life continued in the nation, and the people found ways to cope and even laugh in the face of difficulty.

The Family

Once the Depression struck, almost anything that President Hoover said was used to mock him, especially when he told reporters, "Nobody is starving. The hoboes [beggars, drifters], for example, are better fed than they have ever been. One hobo in New York got ten meals in one day." Soon a flood of newspaper headlines refuted the president's point. Ninety-five cases of starvation were reported in New York City during 1931. That report is probably inflated because substantiated reports were few, but some starvation did occur and lack of food was commonplace among the poor. In 1932, the New York City Health Department declared that more than 20 percent of the city's public school children were suffering from malnutrition. Jobless men who happened to find work were sometimes too weak from hunger to labor.

In May 1939, FDR's trusted secretary of the treasury Henry Morgenthau lamented, "We have tried spending money. We are spending more than we have ever spent before, and it does not work. . . . We have never made good on our promises. . . . I say after eight years of this Administration we have just as much unemployment as when we started. . . . And an enormous debt to boot!" Morgenthau was clearly frustrated. In 1933, the year FDR became president, the unemployment rate was 25 percent. Though it had dropped to 14 percent in 1937, it was now nearing 20 percent again.

Private charities had maintained rescue missions and soup kitchens for the down and out in the past, but they were not prepared to continue helping the vast numbers of the unemployed. The federal funds given to states for relief were partly used to provide needed extra provisions for the hungry. Soon "**bread lines**" formed along city streets as the desperate sought food in the soup kitchens. Local agencies were established to provide some cash for relief to those who applied and met all the requirements. Even then, the sums given were hardly enough to feed a family, much less clothe and house them. A FERA representative in North Carolina reported that a good relief payment to help support a family of five totaled $5.25 per week. The amount was $2.39 in New York City. When New Jersey's relief funds were exhausted, that state decided to issue licenses for legal begging.

Often it was the parents' concern for their children that finally brought the family to apply for relief, but that concern could not cover the sense of humiliation that the adults felt. Husbands and fathers who had trudged from business to business trying to find work blamed themselves for their inability to gain and hold a job. Wives struggled with their own cares, trying to keep the ragged clothes that their families wore from falling apart and even searching for housecleaning jobs or other employment that might bring in some money.

Guiding Questions

1. How did the Depression affect everyday life in American society?
2. How did Americans entertain themselves during this period?

Begging Directly to the President and Mrs. Roosevelt

Thousands of people wrote letters to President Roosevelt, and even more wrote to his wife, Eleanor, telling them of their trials and needs and asking for some help. An uneducated, disabled man wrote, "My family is barfooted and naked and an suferns and we all are a goin to purish if I cannot get some help some way." Some women pleaded with Mrs. Roosevelt to send them clothing for their children or old clothes discarded by the first lady for themselves. Many such petitioners added a final request, asking that their letters be kept private so that no one else would know of their disgrace.

Migrant workers, such as those shown here, suffered greatly during the Depression. They often lived in makeshift tents (*bottom*).

> **Looking for a Place to Live**
>
> As renters were evicted and homes and farms foreclosed, thousands of families were left to scramble for a place to live. Some people moved in with relatives; others built their own shacks in a Hooverville; and still others found new landlords with more patience.

Hobos traveling by train was a common sight during the Great Depression.

Homelessness

About two million people were uprooted from their homes in the 1930s. A few of them had deliberately fled from the torment of watching their families suffer, but many were simply young, unmarried men and teenage boys who had lost hope of finding a job and settling down. They rode in, on, or even under boxcars on freight trains from place to place, eating in soup kitchens, sleeping in city parks, camping in "hobo jungles," and perhaps dreaming that the next stop might hold promise for a job.

Countless thousands of families faced the threat of homelessness. Some of them had mortgages on modest homes, but now, without income, they could not make their payments. Banks were seldom quick to foreclose, but many institutions eventually had to repossess the houses. Other people rented houses or apartments for which they now had no money to pay. Rent in those days was typically low (often around $10 to $12 per month), but even that was beyond the means of many families.

Minority Groups

The hardships of the Depression fell heavily on black Americans, although economic struggles were not new to them. In 1932, about half of all African American workers were unemployed, a rate of joblessness double that of the general population. Farm

The Dust Bowl

In the opening decades of the twentieth century, farmers poured into the Great Plains region. They plowed the tough prairie sod, sowed wheat, and met with enough success to build a respectable life for themselves and their families. In the process, they converted millions of acres from prairie grassland to fields of fertile, powdery soil. In the late 1920s, abundant rains brought bountiful crops and temporary prosperity to the farmers.

But soon came the Depression with its falling farm prices combined with a devastating drought that began in 1932. For four years, rainfall was rare, and the region's produce all but vanished. Adding to the woes that the farmers were experiencing, the prairie winds began to pick up the powdery dust from the plains and carry it across the land. Billowing black clouds of dust sometimes engulfed the region, the dirt sifting through every crack in a farmer's house, piling in huge drifts against buildings and fences, obscuring sunlight, and nearly suffocating anyone who ventured outdoors. Even indoors the people often slept with wet cloths over their faces to keep from breathing the dust. This was the "**Dust Bowl**," a term coined by a newspaper reporter in 1935.

The Dust Bowl reached as far north as Colorado and Kansas and as far south as Texas and New Mexico, but its most brutal effects were felt in Oklahoma. Some of the stricken farmers resorted to relief through WPA jobs and various agencies while trying to reclaim their farms.

Others gave up and moved away. Called "Okies," thousands of them loaded their cars or trucks with all their possessions and headed west to California. There they sought jobs as migrant farm workers, harvesting various crops as they came in season. The uprooted farm families generally remained in poverty until the end of the Depression, but at least they had opportunities for work.

Those who remained on the land soon learned to adjust their farming methods to the needs of their arid land. Much acreage was returned to grassland and used as pasture for livestock, and soil conservation techniques prevailed on the remaining fields. Those efforts continue today to keep the dust of the plains settled, thereby averting any recurrence of the Dust Bowl.

problems and government policies drove sharecroppers in the South, many of them black, off the land. Many moved to cities in the North and West, continuing the migration of African Americans that had begun with World War I. With unemployment wracking America's cities, the North was hardly a promised land for jobless black people.

Government relief efforts were slow to reach needy black Americans. At first, Roosevelt was reluctant to press for needed steps for fear of angering Southern Democrats, and some aspects of his AAA and NRA were actually harmful to the interests of black citizens. However, Eleanor Roosevelt helped to turn attention to problems of discrimination by openly befriending African American leaders. FDR then began to try to prohibit racial discrimination in some federal programs, beginning in 1935 with the WPA. The PWA also constructed a large share of its public housing projects for black Americans.

The most noticeable effect of Roosevelt's policies was the winning of African American voters to the Democratic Party. This group had strongly supported Republicans ever since they had achieved the right to vote—even voting for Herbert Hoover in 1932. But while they believed Republicans offered little hope for efforts to relieve the problems of black people, the actions of FDR and the Democrats seemed encouraging. Thus in 1936, Roosevelt gained more than 70 percent of the black vote, initiating a long-term political trend of black Americans voting for Democrats.

Hispanic families in the Southwest who were not U.S. citizens generally returned to Mexico when the Depression hit, or they were deported. Jobs were not available for Americans, much less immigrants. Those who remained faced the same problems that other Depression-era families encountered, but they also had to deal with prejudice and even violence because they were competing for jobs. Most migrated to urban areas, hoping to find employment as unskilled workers.

Entertainment

Although the 1930s witnessed a quarter or more of the population in want, 80 million Americans (of a population of about 123 million) did *not* experience great deprivations. They likely experienced some hardships because of the departure of the prosperous Roaring Twenties, but they still had jobs, food on their tables, clothes on their backs, and roofs over their heads.

Americans often seemed intent on forgetting their troubles during the rough times. Many of them found escape from their cares in reading books such as Margaret Mitchell's epic Civil War novel *Gone with the Wind*, which appeared in 1936 and became a popular movie in 1939. Hollywood produced more than five thousand feature films of fantasy and drama, providing escape and entertainment for millions of Americans. Walt Disney's first full-length animated presentation, *Snow White*, debuted in 1938, and many new movie stars began to draw wide admiration, among them a little girl named Shirley Temple, who became the darling of the nation.

Radio became the most popular medium of home entertainment in America. Old and young alike laughed at the comedy "Amos and Andy," swooned to the songs of crooner Bing Crosby, and thrilled to the adventures of the Lone Ranger. Children listened

Jesse Owens

In the 1936 Olympics in Berlin, Germany, an African American named **Jesse Owens** won four gold medals in track events. His performance was an irritation to Adolf Hitler, the leader of the host country. Hitler believed that Germans (he called them Aryans) were the master race.

Owens won his first gold medal in the 100-meter dash with a time of 10.3 seconds. In his next event, the long jump, he competed with German Luz Long. Owens won by landing a jump of 26 feet and 5 1/2 inches, gaining his second gold medal. Defying Hitler's racist beliefs, Long congratulated Owens warmly, and the two walked arm-in-arm around the track. Owens's third gold medal came in the 200-meter race and the fourth in the 4x100 relay. In 1984 a street in Berlin was named for Jesse Owens (Jesse-Owens-Allee).

Why the War of the Worlds Broadcast Was So Believable

Americans had become enthralled with radio during the twenties. By the thirties, they were used to radio programs being interrupted occasionally to announce breaking news. That is why so many people believed the dramatized news broadcast of Orson Welles reporting invaders from outer space on October 30, 1938.

Rehearsal of the War of the Worlds

Depression Comic Relief

During the Great Depression, Americans wanted some escape, no matter how brief, from their pressing problems. Some sought relief through destructive means, such as alcohol. Most, however, found harmless diversion through popular entertainment. One source of drama, adventure, and comedy was as near as the daily newspaper—the comic strip.

Comic strips had been appearing in newspapers since the 1890s. The 1930s, however, proved to be a golden age of comics. Whether in the black-and-white strips found in the daily papers or in the four-color "funny papers" found in Sunday editions, comics provided millions of readers (children *and* adults) with an avenue to adventure.

One of the most popular strips was *Little Orphan Annie*. Along with her dog Sandy, Annie, an orphan, overcame the challenges of the Depression with backbone and courage. Adopted by a wealthy weapons manufacturer (appropriately named Daddy Warbucks), Annie was a reflection of her creator's philosophy. Harold Gray, who began the strip in 1924, was a conservative Republican and dedicated opponent of FDR's New Deal. Through Annie and her friends, Gray advocated his views of self-help through hard work. As Daddy Warbucks says in one early strip, "Annie doesn't need charity—just give her an even break and she'll do the rest—Charity!!—BAH!"

The lawlessness of the 1920s and 1930s also gave birth to one of the toughest detectives comics have ever seen—Dick Tracy. Created by Chester Gould in 1931, *Dick Tracy* brought a realism to police comics never before seen. In the best "crime does not pay" tradition, villains in *Dick Tracy* often died realistically (and sometimes gruesomely). The police used the most advanced scientific methods of crime detection, such as "two-way wrist radios" (miniature walkie-talkies).

Tracy's grotesque rogues' gallery of such villains as Flattop, Pruneface, the Mole, and Mumbles was an important part of the comic strip's appeal.

Those who wanted to escape the problems of the 1930s could travel by comic strip to exotic, faraway places. *Tarzan* took the readers to "deepest, darkest Africa" with "the adventures of Edgar Rice Burroughs's famous hero." Or readers could follow the Stone Age exploits of *Alley Oop*. Other similar adventure strips were *Captain Easy*, *Terry and the Pirates*, *Joe Palooka*, *Prince Valiant*, and *The Phantom*. Two popular science fiction strips were *Flash Gordon* and *Buck Rogers*. But the ultimate superhero was *Superman*.

For pure humor, one could read *Popeye*, *Krazy Kat*, *Blondie*, *Li'l Abner*, *Our Boarding House*, or *Nancy*. The "funnies" became one small means of facing the Depression with a smile.

Radio was the major source of news and entertainment during the thirties, especially for rural families.

devotedly to the tales of Little Orphan Annie and cowboy hero Tom Mix. Clarinetist and band leader Benny Goodman introduced "swing music" in 1935, and soon a host of big bands were broadcasting jazzy orchestra numbers on popular radio programs. Radio created one of the most dramatic and yet comic episodes of the 1930s when Orson Welles presented his radio dramatization of H. G. Wells's *War of the Worlds* on a major network in 1938. So realistic was his version of the story of invasion from Mars that thousands of listeners who tuned in to the program as it was in progress were terrified, unaware that the frightening account of a spaceship landing in New Jersey was only fiction. Radio stations and public officials hastened to quell the growing panic, but several days passed before emotions were entirely calmed.

Sports continued to attract many fans, and fads such as miniature golf and Chinese checkers gained momentary popularity. World's fairs also became a big attraction in the decade. Chicago hosted one on its lakeshore in 1934. It featured, among other "Century of Progress" innovations and wonders, an exhibit of premature babies in incubators and the Burlington Route's *Zephyr*, a streamlined diesel locomotive that set the record for a Denver-to-Chicago trip. The Chicago fair was surpassed by the spectacular New York

World's Fair in 1939. From its opening to its closing two years later, the New York fair attracted 45 million visitors to its 1,500 exhibits. People marveled at the technological innovations on display at this event christened "The World of Tomorrow," and they delighted in the breathtaking carnival rides. One of the most popular attractions, General Motors' "Futurama," carried fairgoers on a fifteen-minute tour of America in 1960. The 1939 prophets provided breathless audiences with a fast-lane future of 100-mph highways traveled by Americans in radio-controlled, raindrop-shaped cars, who enjoyed their two months of vacation each year. In retrospect, the forecasters provided a good example of man's inability to predict the future.

Crime

Real-life drama also captured the nation's attention during the 1930s. One of the biggest headlines was the 1932 kidnapping of the infant son of aviation hero Charles Lindbergh. All across the nation, people were eager to hear of any developments in the case, and they grieved when word finally came that the child had been found dead. The search for the murderer required more than two years of intense detective work and ended in the conviction and execution of Bruno Hauptmann, a German immigrant.

Other crimes gained wide attention during the Depression, particularly those of bank-robbing gangs. Although those desperate criminals sometimes were portrayed as modern-day Robin Hoods, they were brutal. John Dillinger topped the "most wanted list," but

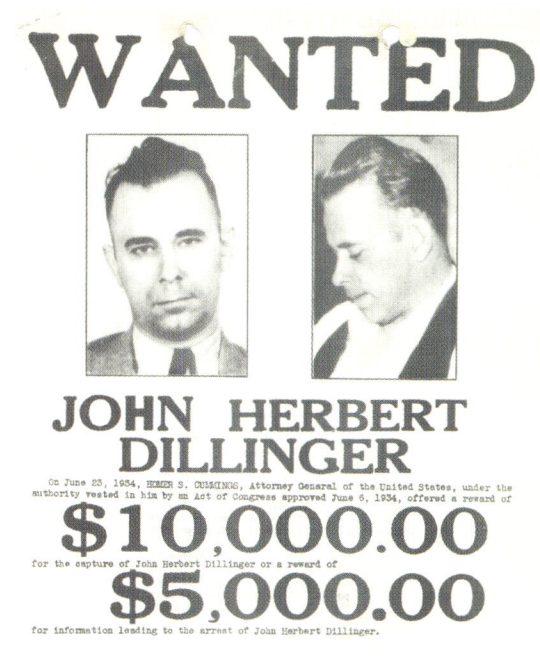

Wanted poster for John Dillinger

The Crime of the Century

Baby Charles A. Lindbergh Jr. disappeared on the evening of March 1, 1932. His mother, Anne Lindbergh, and a nurse had put the toddler to bed earlier that evening after giving him some medication for a cold. Around 10:00 p.m., the nurse discovered that the twenty-month-old baby was gone and immediately notified the family. Charles Lindbergh Sr. rushed to the room to find the window open and a note on the windowsill. It informed the Lindberghs that their baby was fine, but they would have to pay $50,000 for his safe return. They would be informed of a drop-off time and location.

News of the kidnapping spread quickly, and soon the whole nation tuned in to hear news of the baby's whereabouts. Police received several reports of sightings, but they were all false. Al Capone, who was incarcerated, even offered to find the kidnapper—if he were set free. That never happened.

Charles Lindbergh Sr. personally oversaw the investigation, but because of his inexperience he was of little help. One man claimed to be in contact with the kidnappers, and in a cemetery meeting the ransom was exchanged for information on the baby's location. The information was false.

Then, seventy-two days after the disappearance, a dead baby was found in the woods near the Lindbergh's house. An autopsy confirmed that it was the Lindberghs' baby. He had died of a fractured skull and had been dead since the night of the kidnapping.

In September 1934, more than two years after the crime, police arrested Bruno Hauptmann. They later found part of the ransom money at his home. He claimed he was holding it for the real kidnapper who had since died. Despite his claims of innocence, Hauptmann was executed by electric chair on April 3, 1936. The **Lindbergh kidnapping** case was so famous, it has sometimes been called "the crime of the [20th] century."

Wanted poster for Bonnie and Clyde

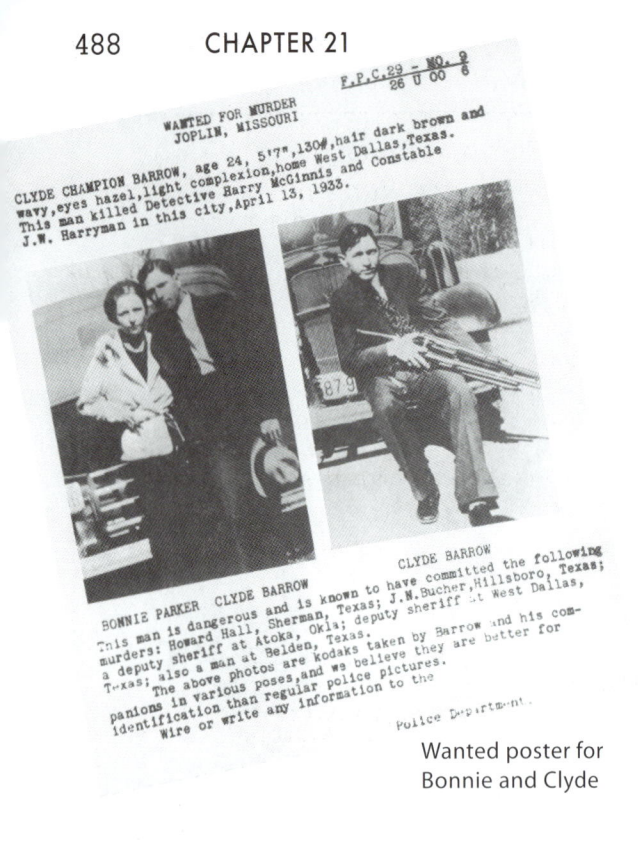

On May 6, 1937, the hydrogen-filled *Hindenburg* mysteriously exploded as it attempted to land in Lakehurst, NJ, after a transatlantic flight.

he was joined by desperados such as "Pretty Boy" Floyd, "Machine Gun" Kelly, "Baby Face" Nelson, and a couple-in-crime, Bonnie Parker and Clyde Barrow. Most of these criminals died in a hail of gunfire or spent long stints in jail. Lawmen, especially agents of the newly formed **Federal Bureau of Investigation (FBI)**, led by director J. Edgar Hoover, became heroes as they tracked down criminals. FBI agent Melvin Purvis gained fame as the top "G-man" (as "government men" in the FBI were sometimes called) when he led the team that cornered and killed Dillinger.

Flight

Amelia Earhart became America's flying heroine when, in 1932, she became the first female pilot to fly solo across the Atlantic. But in 1937, during an adventurous round-the-world flight, the aviator disappeared somewhere in the Pacific. Hers was not the only air tragedy of the 1930s, however. Popular humorist Will Rogers perished in an airplane crash while on a tour of Alaska with Wiley Post, the first man to fly solo around the world.

Amelia Earhart

The most dramatic of the 1930s air tragedies was the explosion and crash of the zeppelin *Hindenburg*. As the giant, blimp-like craft approached Lakehurst, New Jersey, in 1937, it suddenly burst into flames. A radio announcer watching the landing described the catastrophe for the nation with uncontrollable emotion:

> Oh, flames four or five hundred feet into the sky, it's a terrific crash, ladies and gentlemen, the smoke and the flames now and the crashing to the ground, not quite to the mooring, oh the humanity, and I told you, I can't even talk, mass of smoking wreckage, I can, I can hardly breathe!

Thirty-five of the airship's ninety-seven passengers perished.

New Decade Dawning

In 1939 the United States, and much of the world, continued its struggle with the Depression. By that year undercurrents of war were also stirring the world's already troubled waters. Soon, the tides of war would reach America's shore and invigorate the nation's weak economy. Bread lines were transformed to assembly lines. The nation would assume a new role of world leadership in the decade to come.

Section Review

1. In what way did black Americans change their voting patterns during the Depression?
2. What was the most popular means of home entertainment during the Depression?
3. What 1930s kidnapping case captured national attention?
★ How did Americans try to relieve their minds of worries about economic troubles that were beyond their control?

CHAPTER REVIEW

Making Connections

1. Why was Hoover blamed for the Depression?
2. What American governmental action in 1930 helped precipitate a European economic collapse in 1931 by dealing a harmful blow to world trade?
3. What problematic situation arose to heighten economic tensions in the final days before Roosevelt's inauguration?
4–5. What two major pieces of New Deal legislation were struck down by the Supreme Court?
6–8. Name three left-wing leaders who denounced Roosevelt's New Deal for not doing enough to combat the Depression's problems, and briefly state their proposals for solving the Depression.
9. What proposal made by President Roosevelt following the 1936 election alarmed many Democrats as well as Republicans?

Developing History Skills

1. Examine Hoover's efforts to end the Depression, and compare them with Roosevelt's programs.
2. How did Roosevelt's effort to pack the Supreme Court place the integrity and power of the Supreme Court at risk?

Thinking Critically

1. In what ways was the increased role of government that resulted from the New Deal beneficial to America? In what ways was it harmful?
2. How were the American core values of growth and freedom sometimes in conflict during the Depression?

Living as a Christian Citizen

1. The Bible contains passages such as Deuteronomy 15:7–11 that command generosity to the poor. How should this affect Christian support for government programs to assist the poor? Refer to Deuteronomy 14:28–29 in your answer.
2. In what ways can an individual Christian help the poor today?

People, Places, and Things to Remember

Great Depression
Hoovervilles
public works
work relief
deficit spending
Smoot-Hawley Tariff
Reconstruction Finance Corporation (RFC)
Bonus Army
Franklin Delano Roosevelt (FDR)
New Deal
banking crisis
bank holiday
Brain Trust
fireside chats
Civilian Conservation Corps (CCC)
Public Works Administration (PWA)
Works Progress Administration (WPA)
Agricultural Adjustment Act (AAA)
National Industrial Recovery Act (NIRA)
National Recovery Administration (NRA)
Federal Deposit Insurance Corporation (FDIC)
Tennessee Valley Authority (TVA)
Social Security Act
Huey Long
Francis Townsend
Charles Coughlin
court-packing plan
Alfred Landon
Congress of Industrial Organizations (CIO)
bread lines
Dust Bowl
Jesse Owens
Lindbergh kidnapping
Federal Bureau of Investigation (FBI)
Amelia Earhart

22

THE WORLD AT WAR
1939–1945

"Not in vain" may be the pride of those who survived and the epitaph of those who fell.

British Prime Minister Winston Churchill
September 28, 1944

U.S. Marines raise the American flag atop Mount Suribachi on Iwo Jima.

Big Ideas

1. How did the dictators seize power, and what territories did each conquer?
2. How did the United States transition from a neutral state to an active participant in the war?
3. What role did American forces play in Europe?
4. What role did American forces play in the Pacific?

I. A Time of Tyrants

II. Isolation and Infamy

III. The Fight for Fortress Europe

IV. Pushing Back the Axis

It's a long one down to around the three-yard line....

The radio announcer's voice crackled across the airwaves. The New York Giants, the champs of the National Football League's Eastern Division, were getting a surprise beating from the Brooklyn Dodgers at the Polo Grounds in New York.

Ward Cuff takes it....
Coming up to his left ... he's over the 10....
Nice block by Leemans! Cuff still going....

Listeners across the country edged up in their seats.

He's up to the 25....
And now he's hit and hit hard about the 27-yard line!
Bruiser Kinard made the tack—
We interrupt this broadcast to bring you this important bulletin from the United Press:
FLASH Washington:
The White House announces Japanese attack on Pearl Harbor....

The announcement on that Sunday afternoon of December 7, 1941, did more than interrupt a football game; it shattered America's uneasy peace. The nation had been plunged into the largest, costliest war in history. Isolation was over; the heroic effort to liberate the Pacific from the Japanese military leaders and Europe from Hitler and Mussolini was soon underway. The global conflict changed the face of the world for the rest of the century and gave America a superpower role in that new world.

I. A Time of Tyrants

Clouds on the Horizon

In the early 1920s, Americans celebrated their return to normalcy and enjoyed the ease of isolation. Meanwhile, storm clouds were building on the world horizons in both Europe and Asia. The Communist Party had gained control of Russia during World War I and consolidated its power in the 1920s under dictator Joseph Stalin. Then two forms of fascism reared their heads in Italy and Germany; yet another form of militant nationalism grew in Japan.

Guiding Questions

1. How did tyrants seize power in four important nations before the war?
2. What events led to the war?
3. What were the early successes of the Axis powers?

Italy: Benito Mussolini

The **Fascist Party** came to power in Italy in 1922 when **Benito Mussolini** was appointed prime minister. It was a nationalistic, militaristic, totalitarian movement that profited from the discontent created by difficult economic conditions. Mussolini, who soon became dictator, promised the masses that he would restore Italy to the greatness that existed in the days of Roman Caesars. His black-shirted followers pronounced him *Il Duce* (DOO chay), "the leader," and they crushed their opposition. Mussolini declared all political parties, except the Fascists, illegal.

If Italy were to have power and prestige in the world, Mussolini reasoned, the country would need to acquire foreign territories and markets. In search of victims, Mussolini moved against backward, but resource-rich, Ethiopia in 1935. Sword- and stone-wielding Ethiopian tribesmen bravely yet vainly fought machine guns and tanks. Mussolini quickly conquered and annexed Ethiopia. The League of Nations

Benito Mussolini (*left and below*)

Mein Kampf, Hitler's autobiography, outlines his political ideas.

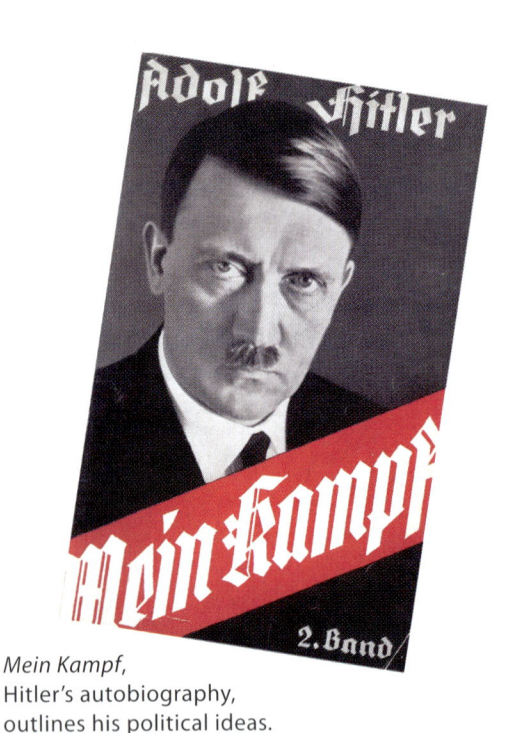

condemned Italy and banned the sale of some materials to that nation; however, that did not deter Mussolini. Later, Italy initiated an alliance with its Fascist friends to the north, the Nazis.

Germany: Adolf Hitler

In 1923, a German World War I veteran sought to avenge Germany's earlier defeat by using radical politics. **Adolf Hitler** tried to overthrow the government in Munich, Germany. The failed attempt landed him in jail. While imprisoned, he wrote an autobiography filled with hatred, *Mein Kampf* (My Struggle), in which he set forth his ideas for a new Germany. He advocated abandoning the League of Nations, ridding Germany of the "weakening" influence of democracy, uniting all Germans, and eliminating all Communists and Jews. After his release from prison, he preached his doctrines to growing audiences of all classes. Hitler and his National Socialist German Workers' Party, or **Nazi Party**, came to power in Germany in 1933 when he was appointed chancellor, the equivalent of prime minister, of the nation. He used his new power to eradicate opponents and establish himself as the *Führer* (FYOOR ur) or "the leader." He called the Nazi regime the "Third Reich" (meaning third empire) and promised that it would last a thousand years.

Fascism

Fascism is a political movement that promotes extreme nationalism, or patriotism, and places great emphasis on militarism (a strong military). Italy's Fascist Party, led by Benito Mussolini, and Germany's Nazi Party, led by Adolf Hitler, both embraced Fascism. The system is characterized by dictatorial, one-party rule.

Fascists believe that the government is more important than individuals. They justify this by saying that the common good (interests of the country) supersedes individual interests.

Both Hitler and Mussolini permitted the ownership of private property, but under each the government heavily regulated, controlled, and restricted how that property could be used and what the individual could do with any profits from using it. All individual or business activity had to fit within the interest of the state. These systems justified such control by claiming to provide economic equality for all, but to deliver on that pledge, they used force, taking from the "haves" to give to the "have nots." When they could not deliver the equality they promised, they provided scapegoats on whom to heap the blame—another nationality, another ethnic group, or another economic class. That, in turn, led to suppression of and violence against the targeted group.

Adolf Hitler

Mussolini organized industries into categories called syndicates. He insisted that the government plan, or coordinate, all economic activity in so-called partnership with the syndicates. The stipulation was that the government was the "senior partner" in such arrangements and therefore had the final say regarding policy. This was based on the idea that government knows best.

The Nazis in Germany governed much like the Fascist Party in Italy. But, as economist Ludwig von Mises wrote, "The main difference was that the [Italian] Fascists were less efficient and even more corrupt than the Nazis."

As dictator, Hitler instituted a government of blind nationalism, anti-Semitism (anti-Jewish feelings), and **totalitarianism** (a government that regulates every aspect of life). For years, in violation of the Versailles agreement, he secretly rebuilt the German navy, army, and air force. This military used all the latest technological improvements and proved a fearful instrument in Hitler's hands.

Japan: Military Leaders

The Japanese, who had come recently to the scene of industrialism and world trade, found that the European nations that had carved out Asian "spheres of influence" during the last century had established many trade barriers against Japan. With growing militarism, the Japanese sought to extend their power through direct conquest. Their first show of force was the invasion of Manchuria, a province of China, in 1931. In 1937, the Japanese launched a full-scale war against China, a war that would not end until 1945.

Japanese soldiers fighting in China

Beginning in the 1930s and continuing until the end of World War II, Japan was controlled by military leaders. General **Hideki Tojo**, the most important of these, was prime minister from 1941 to 1944. **Hirohito** had become emperor in 1926. His degree of involvement in the government remains controversial among historians. Some believe he exercised much control over the military and was actively involved in making decisions. Others say his role was limited.

With the distraction of the Great Depression at home and an ongoing desire to remain isolated from the rest of the world, the United States took little action to stop Japanese aggression. In 1934, Japan canceled the Washington Naval Treaty, and relations with Japan continued to deteriorate during Roosevelt's first term. Encountering no real opposition from America or the other world powers and desiring to gain resources through military force, Japan continued to lay plans for greater gain. As U.S. trade policies tightened in an effort to halt the Japanese brutalization of China, Japanese leaders developed an animosity toward their chief rival in the Pacific—the United States. In 1940, Japan joined Italy and Germany to form an alliance called the **Rome-Berlin-Tokyo Axis**. During World War II, the three nations would join together to form the **Axis Powers**.

Soviet Union: Joseph Stalin

In Russia, the decades of the twenties and thirties were among the most brutal years in human history. **Joseph Stalin** oversaw systematic terror and bloodshed and became one of the most savage tyrants of all time. Most historians estimate that he was responsible

Hideki Tojo

Hirohito, the Japanese emperor

Joseph Stalin

> **Soviet Collectivization**
> This program involved the Communist government's seizing all private land and crops and forcing farm workers to labor wherever they were told. Any who resisted the seizure of their property or refused to work where ordered were imprisoned or killed.

for the deaths of ten to twenty million of his own countrymen during those two decades.

Stalin eliminated those who disagreed with him, both in and out of the Communist Party. In 1928, he ordered the destruction of all resistance to his agricultural "reforms," or collectivization. Millions were shot, starved, or died from brutal treatment in labor camps. Throughout the 1930s, Stalin continued to push Russia into the industrial age and fortify his own power with a chilling ruthlessness. Stalin also trampled any perceived threat by organized religion. Many Christians suffered and died simply because of their loyalty to Christ. During the 1920s, Russia officially became known as the **Union of Soviet Socialist Republics (USSR)**. It was also called the Soviet Union.

Meanwhile, Americans watched events unfold. Things were bad, they agreed; still, it was not America's business to get involved. But the dictators in Italy, Germany, Japan, and the Soviet Union would soon take the world, including the United States, into the turmoil known as World War II.

The Coming of War

Hitler was neither a skilled diplomat nor, as later blunders would prove, a military genius. But he was a master politician who could assess other leaders, predict their responses, and outmaneuver them. Despite Hitler's open violations of the Treaty of Versailles and the growing threat he represented to Europe, the rest of Europe did virtually nothing. In fact, they allowed Hitler to make numerous territorial gains unopposed. He assured other nations that he was interested only in consolidating German territory and reestablishing German control over areas "stolen" by the World War I victors through the Treaty of Versailles.

Easy Successes

In March 1936, German troops moved into the **Rhineland**, an industrial region of Germany near Alsace-Lorraine that, under the Versailles Treaty, was to remain demilitarized (free of soldiers and military equipment). The League of Nations protested Hitler's action, but the Nazis had little concern for world opinion.

The Germans then began building the Siegfried Line in this area. It was a series of fortifications along the German bank of the Rhine River from the Swiss border to the North Sea. Hitler claimed that the Siegfried Line was a response to the Maginot (MAZH eh noh) Line, a similar French line of fortifications on the west side of the river; however, his actions were another violation of the Versailles Treaty. Winston Churchill, a member of the British Parliament, was one of the few who protested.

Hitler next moved against Austria. He had long dreamed of union, or *Anschluss* (AHN schloos), with Austria, a German-speaking land and Hitler's birthplace. Despite explicit prohibitions against such unification in the World War I peace treaties,

The Siegfried Line (*above*) was built by Germany, and the Maginot Line (*three images below*) was built by France.

in March 1938, Hitler took control of Austria. When his soldiers marched into the country, Britain and France did nothing.

The Munich Conference

Czechoslovakia was next on Hitler's agenda. He declared that Germany had a right to annex the **Sudetenland** (soo DATE un land), a predominantly German area in western Czechoslovakia. Czech leaders appealed to the British and French to protect them from such blatant aggression.

In September 1938, Britain's prime minister, **Neville Chamberlain,** and France's premier, Édouard Daladier, agreed to meet with Hitler in Munich, Germany. Benito Mussolini, Hitler's ally, was also present. Czechoslovakia, whose fate was the topic of discussion, was not allowed to send a representative. Hitler was determined to get the Sudetenland, even if it meant going to war. To "preserve the peace," Chamberlain and Daladier agreed to allow Hitler to take the Sudetenland—but nothing more. Hitler promised, "This is the last territorial claim I have to make in Europe." The French and British leaders believed him. Chamberlain returned to England proclaiming that this meant "peace for our time." At the Munich Conference, Chamberlain and Daladier followed a policy of **appeasement** (yielding to the demands of an aggressor in order to preserve peace). Churchill observed bitterly, "The German dictator, instead of snatching his victuals [food] from the table, has been content to have them served to him course by course." In March 1939, Hitler openly violated his promise and annexed the remainder of Czechoslovakia. Public outrage over Hitler's betrayal of his promise forced the British and French leaders to act. Anticipating Hitler's next move, they promised to protect Poland and Romania if those nations were attacked.

Chamberlain and Hitler

Chamberlain overestimated his charm and his ability to deal with Hitler. He confided in a letter to his sister, "Hitler definitely liked me and thought he could do business with me." Historian William Manchester commented acidly, "This was true in the sense that an armed robber thinks he can do business with a bank teller."

Tyrants' Prey

Hitler knew that to continue his expansion eastward, he would have to deal with the Soviet Union. On August 23, 1939, the surprising announcement of a **Nazi-Soviet nonaggression pact** was published. The agreement stated that the Soviet Union and Germany would not attack each other for a period of ten years. Secretly, the two nations agreed that Stalin could control the Baltic countries (Lithuania, Latvia, Estonia), Finland, and a slice of eastern Poland. In exchange, Hitler would invade Poland from the west.

Hitler lost little time taking advantage of the secret clauses. The Munich Conference had emboldened the Führer to ignore British and French threats to intervene. War began on **September 1, 1939,** when sixteen hundred *Luftwaffe* (Nazi air force) aircraft bombed military and civilian targets while 1.5 million German soldiers rolled across the Polish border. The swift assault was called ***blitzkrieg***, "lightning war." Forty-eight hours after the assault began, the brave Polish defenders had suffered one hundred thousand casualties, and by the end of September, Hitler's conquest of Poland

Germany attacked Poland in September 1939 (*left and below*).

was complete. On September 17, Russian troops attacked Poland from the east. By war's end, the Germans and Russians would kill six million Poles, half of them Jews.

On September 3, Britain and France declared war on Germany. They became known as the **Allies**, or Allied Powers, but those hesitant nations did little. Americans watched with growing concern but did nothing. In their minds, it was not their affair.

More German Victories

Denmark and Norway

In April 1940, Hitler attacked again. Once more using *blitzkrieg*, powerful German armored divisions, or *panzers*—assisted by fighters, bombers, and paratroopers—occupied neutral Denmark in a matter of hours. That same day, Germany attacked neutral Norway to gain naval bases and access to iron-rich Sweden. Norway, however, resisted fiercely, fighting for sixty-two days before they were betrayed. German destroyers sailed under land-based guns that could have sent them to the bottom. The guns, though, had been rendered useless by sabotage because of a prominent Norwegian political official named Vidkun Quisling. Acquisition of Denmark and Norway secured the northern border of the Third Reich. The securing of the southern border was next.

The Fall of France

On May 10, Germany launched a coordinated attack on the countries on its western border from southern France to the North Sea. Against the overwhelming German force, resistance was short-lived. Luxembourg fell after only a day, Holland in five days, and Belgium in eighteen days.

In May 1940, the French army, reinforced by the British, was trapped by the German army in northern France. The *Luftwaffe* destroyed French fortifications far ahead of German armored divisions and infantry. Millions of refugees scattered, trying to escape their doomed cities. German Stuka dive-bombers dominated the air. These new weapons and tactics were a total departure from the trench warfare of World War I. For the French, who relied on the old methods of the last war, *blitzkrieg* was disastrous.

The German forces drove the British and French forces northward to the French port of **Dunkirk** on the English Channel and surrounded them. But before the Germans could move to destroy the Allied army, a dense fog settled over the Channel, making it difficult for the *Luftwaffe* to bomb. Shortly before, Hitler had ordered his land armies to stop their advance and allow the *Luftwaffe* to destroy the enemy. The German army continued to wait even though the air force was grounded. The usually efficient Nazi war machine ground to a halt.

The Allies, encouraged by what was apparently divine intervention on their behalf, moved to rescue their men. Using a fleet of 850 fishing boats, yachts, lifeboats, and almost anything else that would float, British citizens crossed the twenty-two-mile-wide English Channel to rescue some 338,000 of the 400,000 trapped men.

Norway's Benedict Arnold

Vidkun Quisling assisted German agents for months before the invasion. As a reward for his treason, the Nazis made him the leader of Norway during World War II. Like the name Benedict Arnold, the name Quisling became a synonym for traitor. After the war, Quisling was arrested, tried, and sentenced to death. He was executed by a firing squad on October 24, 1945.

Thousands of British and French troops lined the beaches of Dunkirk awaiting evacuation.

France soon accepted the inevitable. In the same railroad car in which the Germans had signed the humiliating armistice terms on November 11, 1918, France accepted the German terms of surrender on June 22, 1940.

The fall of France stunned the world, especially America, and left Britain on the brink of destruction. Several weeks earlier, Neville Chamberlain had been replaced with a new prime minister, **Winston Churchill**. The new leader inspired the Britons with his grand defiance and fighting spirit: "I have nothing to offer but blood, toil, tears, and sweat. . . . You ask, what is our policy? I can say: It is to wage war, by sea, land, and air, with all our might and with all the strength God can give us. . . . You ask, what is our aim? I can answer in one word: It is victory."

Britain Alone

Britain now faced the Nazi menace alone. Hitler planned to bomb the island extensively, hoping to "soften" it before landing troops. Throughout the late summer and fall of 1940, the **Battle of Britain** took place in the skies above southern England and the Channel. Bombing during the daylight hours, however, became too costly for the *Luftwaffe*. The Germans lost many more planes than the British and many more pilots. The *Luftwaffe* later changed its tactics and began night bombing with incendiaries, or fire bombs.

London, Plymouth, Manchester, Birmingham, Dover, Portsmouth, and Coventry were heavily damaged, and tens of thousands of Britons were killed or injured. Yet British resolve in the face of the enemy was firm. During those fearful days when the fate of Britain hung in the skies above them, the British were inspired by Churchill. On June 18, 1940, he declared:

> Hitler knows that he will have to break us on this island or lose the war. If we can stand up to him all Europe may be free and the life of the world may move forward into broad, sunlit uplands. But if we fail, then the whole world, including the United States, including all that we have known and cared for, will sink into the abyss of a new Dark Age. . . . Let us therefore brace ourselves to our duty, and so bear ourselves that, if the British Empire and its Commonwealth lasts for a thousand years, men will still say: "This was their finest hour."

During the Battle of Britain, Germany lost 1,733 aircraft while Britain's Royal Air Force (RAF) lost 915 planes. In August 1940, Churchill declared, referring to the RAF, "Never in the field of human conflict was so much owed by so many to so few." In late 1940, Hitler indefinitely postponed his intended invasion of Britain.

Barbarossa

In the wake of the fall of France, continued bombing of Britain, and conquests in the Mediterranean, Hitler again seized the initiative, launching a massive surprise attack on the Soviet Union. In doing so, he violated the non-aggression pact signed less than two years earlier. On June 22, 1941, three million troops of the *Wehrmacht* (the German army) rolled deep into Russia, covering five hundred miles of territory within two months on a front that stretched from the Black Sea to the Arctic. In an operation

---

Churchill on Dark Days

In an October 1941 speech, Churchill said, "Do not let us speak of darker days: let us speak rather of sterner days. These are not dark days; these are great days—the greatest days our country has ever lived; and we must all thank God that we have been allowed, each of us according to our stations, to play a part in making these days memorable in the history of our race."

A London bus lies in a large crater after an attack by the *Luftwaffe*.

code-named "Barbarossa," the Germans launched attacks at three strategic cities—Leningrad to the north, Moscow in the center, and Stalingrad to the south—engulfing the Soviet heartland in some of the fiercest, costliest fighting of the war.

By September 1941, the Russians were suffering enormous losses, and England was badly battered. Just two years after launching his *blitzkrieg* against Poland, Hitler was virtually master of Europe. Americans watched with growing unease. But still they felt it was not their fight.

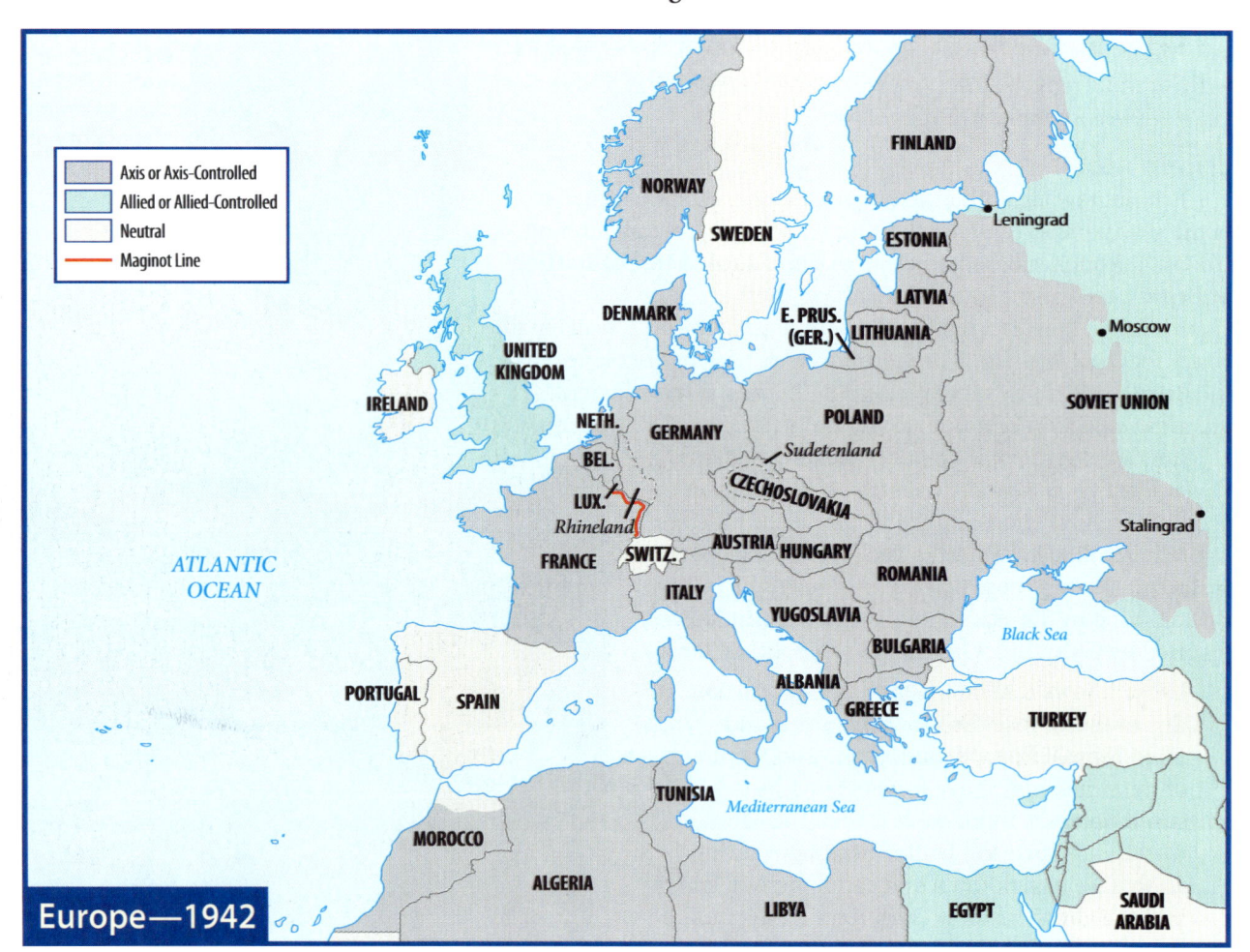

Europe—1942

Section Review

1–3. Name the dictators who rose to power in Italy and the Soviet Union in the 1920s and in Germany in the 1930s.

4. What African nation did Italy conquer in the 1930s?

5. What was *Anschluss*?

6–7. What nation was forced to surrender one region of its land to Germany at the Munich Conference? What was the name of that region?

8. Place the following nations in the proper chronological order in which they fell to Germany: Belgium, Denmark, France, Norway, Poland.

★ Compare and contrast fascism and communism.

★ What lessons can one learn about appeasement and totalitarian, expansionist regimes from the events in this section?

II. Isolation and Infamy

While war was devastating much of Europe, America sat safe behind its ocean walls. Three major forces kept the United States on the sidelines as war clouds gathered over Europe and Asia. First, tradition held America to an isolationist foreign policy. Rejection of membership in the League of Nations was an indication of returning to pre–World War I attitudes. Franklin Roosevelt had begun his political career as an outspoken supporter of Wilson's League in 1920. Yet, in the 1932 election, Roosevelt opposed the League.

Second, isolationism was spurred by the war debt problem (see Chapter 20), which created resentment on both sides of the Atlantic. Americans viewed the huge war loans to the Allies during World War I, which totaled $22 billion, as just that—*loans*. About half was owed to U.S. banks and other investors, and about half was owed to the U.S. government. Payment from the debtor nations, however, was difficult not only because of the slowness of their postwar recovery but also because trade with the United States, which would have helped pay their bill, was effectively cut off by America's high protective tariffs. In addition, Europeans took a different view of their debts. The old Allies observed that much of the American credit was used to purchase American goods, which fueled the American economy. Europeans viewed settling their American debt with about as much enthusiasm as they would have when making a funeral payment. After bitter losses of millions killed and maimed, the British and French pointed to miles of graves as payment enough. By 1933, most of America's former allies were paying little or none of their war debts.

Third, the Great Depression kept most Americans focused on domestic rather than international concerns. Leaders in Washington were too occupied with economic recovery to take more than a sideline role in European and Asian politics.

Despite the drift to isolationism, the sympathies of most Americans were with the Allies. As in the days before U.S. entry into World War I, Americans felt strong cultural ties to Britain. They also felt a natural sympathy for the nations devastated by the vicious Nazi war machine. Yet, Americans wanted no part of the war itself, if they could avoid it. They hoped that the Allies would crush the German aggressions without direct U.S. military support. They based those hopes on a number of inaccurate beliefs. Many Americans, like the French, believed that France's Maginot Line would stop Hitler's tanks. They believed that the Germans could not sustain their war effort for long without additional oil, rubber, and food—supplies that Germany could not easily acquire in adequate amounts. And many people hoped that the German people themselves would not long support their mad dictator's bloody ambitions.

> **Guiding Questions**
>
> 1. How did America initially try to avoid participation in the war?
> 2. How did America support the Allied cause without declaring war?
> 3. How did Americans view the war prior to the attack on Pearl Harbor, and how did they change following that attack?
> 4. How did America transition to a nation at war?

This 1930s political cartoon ridiculed America's policy of isolationism.

Nervous Neutrality

Changing with the Times

In September 1939, while the Germans were trampling Polish resistance and the Russians were devouring the Baltic states and eastern Poland, President Roosevelt called Congress into special

Charles Lindbergh speaking at an America First rally

Campaign buttons used in the 1940 election

session to consider changes to the Neutrality Act of 1937. That law had cut American military supplies to belligerents—nations engaged in war. Ironically, the Neutrality Act had not greatly affected Germany because Hitler had been rearming for years using German factories and had little need for U.S. arms. It had, however, seriously hurt democratic nations because the law prohibited them from purchasing military supplies from the United States when they needed them most.

After intense debate, Congress passed the **Neutrality Act of 1939**, which provided that belligerents could purchase weaponry from the United States but only on a cash basis. It further stipulated that the buyers must transport the weapons in their own ships. This "cash-and-carry" policy was a help to England, which had a large navy. In addition, the act prohibited U.S. ships and passengers from entering the ports of belligerent nations. That unwittingly helped Germany by ensuring that U.S. ships would not be traveling into the ports of Germany's enemies; thus, Hitler could use unrestricted submarine warfare with less fear of becoming involved with the United States.

The more vocal isolationists and pacifists (those who condemn all wars) organized the **America First Committee**. Famed pilot Charles Lindbergh was one of their leading spokesmen. These organizations, many of them in the Midwest, were watchdogs to oppose American involvement in the war.

1940 Election

Despite preparedness measures, the American public and leaders vacillated between preparedness and pacifism. During the election of 1940, Roosevelt, running for an unprecedented third term, promised, "I have said this before, but I shall say it again and again and again: Your boys are not going to be sent into any foreign wars."

FDR's opponent was Republican **Wendell Willkie**. The former Democrat had never held political office, but he attracted enthusiastic crowds across the country. Willkie had recognized the Nazi menace early and urged preparedness and support of the Allies, but he was careful not to seem to support U.S. intervention. He received twenty-two million votes in the November election, while more than than twenty-seven million Americans chose Roosevelt as their candidate. The next four years for FDR and the nation would be among the most demanding in American history.

The Arsenal of Democracy

Despite the isolationist tendencies of most Americans, there was an increasing sense of the need for preparedness. In addition to changes in the neutrality laws, Congress instituted a peacetime draft—the first in American history—in September 1940.

Roosevelt's reelection in 1940 ensured further aid to England and the other Allies. America had become the "arsenal of democracy," and the Allies were to use that aid to guarantee what Roosevelt called the "Four Freedoms": freedom of speech and of worship, and freedom from want and from fear.

Aid to the Allies

Backed by a growing belief that the United States would have to fight the enemies of free people alone if England were destroyed, FDR asked for and received from Congress "all-out aid" to the Allies. "They do not need manpower," the president stated. "They do need billions of dollars' worth of weapons of defense." On March 11, 1941, he signed the **Lend-Lease Act** to provide supplies for the embattled nations. Under the provisions of the act, Roosevelt was empowered to supply any Allied nation with war materiel on almost any terms he desired. Eventually, the United States distributed nearly $50 billion worth of military supplies to thirty-eight Allied countries. In addition, U.S. forces were stationed in Iceland and Greenland to protect the vital shipping lanes of the North Atlantic as American supplies were ferried to Britain.

The United States also sent China one hundred P-40 Tomahawk fighter planes. Claire Chennault, a retired Army Air Force captain, served as an advisor to the Chinese air force. He helped organize a group of pilots known as the American Volunteer Group (AVG), more commonly called the "**Flying Tigers**." Although always outnumbered, the Flying Tigers became a formidable foe of Japanese pilots, downing almost 300 Japanese planes in the seven months the group existed. In mid-1942, the AVG became part of the U.S. military. Chennault rejoined the army with the rank of colonel. By that time, the U.S. had entered World War II.

The Flying Tigers helped China fight the Japanese during World War II.

The Atlantic Charter

The alliance between the United States and Britain was energized in August 1941 when Churchill and Roosevelt secretly met at Placentia Bay, Newfoundland. In an exchange of meetings aboard the American cruiser *Augusta* and the British battleship *Prince of Wales*, the two leaders devised the **Atlantic Charter**, a list of "common principles" such as self-determination, freedom of the seas, and economic cooperation. It was essentially a list of the goals of the anti-Axis nations. It sought to provide "a better future for the world" and expressed America's moral commitment to the Allied cause. Increasingly, President Roosevelt's statements against Germany and massive supplies to the Allies were making America, as one newspaper editor observed, "as unneutral as possible without getting into war." By late September, more than a dozen additional anti-Axis nations signed the charter.

Hitler was aware of America's "unneutral" neutrality. In May 1941, a German submarine attacked and sank an American merchant vessel in the waters off Brazil. In September, the U.S. destroyer *Greer* was fired on by a German submarine, after which Roosevelt ordered the fleet to "shoot on sight" German or Italian attack vessels. In October, another U.S. destroyer, the *Kearny*, was torpedoed, and eleven sailors were killed in the attack. Later that same month, the destroyer *Reuben James* was sunk west of Iceland with the loss of more than a hundred Americans. In the waning days of 1941, escalating tensions in the Atlantic brought America to the verge of war. Yet, surprisingly, when the blow finally came, it fell not in the Atlantic, but in the Pacific.

Another Perspective on the Greer and Kearny Incidents

The USS *Greer* had chased the German submarine for three hours and was radioing information about the U-boat's position to the British. The sub turned and fired two torpedoes. The *Greer* responded with depth charges (an explosive device used for attacking submarines). The USS *Kearny* had sighted the German sub with which it was involved and fired on it first. In both cases, the U.S. ships had provoked the attacks.

"Remember Pearl Harbor!"

Japan's desire for territory placed increasing strain on U.S.-Japanese relations. The decade-long domination of China extended in the summer of 1941 to the Japanese seizure of the strategic oil fields and rubber plantations of French Indochina in Southeast Asia

Damages at Pearl Harbor

U.S. Losses:
8 battleships—sunk or heavily damaged
13 other warships—destroyed or damaged
188 planes—destroyed
159 planes—damaged
2,403—killed
1,178—wounded

Japanese Losses:
29 of 344 planes—destroyed
64—killed
5 midget submarines—sunk or disabled

A memorial stands atop the sunken USS *Arizona* at Pearl Harbor.

(present day Vietnam, Laos, and Cambodia). Roosevelt responded by placing an oil embargo (a refusal to sell oil) on the Japanese and freezing Japanese assets. He named General **Douglas MacArthur** commander of all American forces in the Far East.

The Japanese, though, had bigger plans than simply taking French Indochina. With England being pounded by Hitler and the Netherlands under Nazi occupation, the Japanese eyed the resource-rich British and Dutch colonies of the Pacific. First, however, the Japanese would have to deal with the chief naval threat in the Pacific—the United States.

The Attack on Pearl Harbor

Shortly before 8:00 a.m. on Sunday, **December 7, 1941**, Japanese warplanes swept across the blue Hawaiian sky over Pearl Harbor. Commander Mitsuo Fuchida signaled, "*Tora! Tora! Tora!*" ("Tiger! Tiger! Tiger!") to indicate that Americans had been caught by surprise. A second wave of Japanese aircraft attacked an hour later. The Japanese sank or damaged eight battleships and thirteen other warships. Within two hours, most American air power in Hawaii had been destroyed as Japanese planes damaged or destroyed over 300 aircraft. The two-hour attack took a heavy toll in American lives as well, with 2,403 killed and about 1,200 wounded.

In their broader whirlwind attack, Japanese forces conquered many other U.S. and British bases throughout the South Pacific during the rest of December, including Guam, Hong Kong, Wake Island, and the Gilbert Islands.

Despite the heavy American losses, Pearl Harbor was not a complete success for the Japanese. First, they had missed the American aircraft carriers, which were at sea rather than at port, at the time of the attack. In the war that had begun, the carrier, not the battleship, would be the most decisive factor in the region. Second, by not sending a third wave of planes to attack, Japan failed to completely destroy the American naval base. The Americans would rebuild with the facilities that remained. Third, with one blow, the Japanese had done what Hitler's accumulated atrocities and aggressions had not—united the American nation to enter the war.

The day after the Pearl Harbor attack, President Roosevelt addressed a joint session of Congress, declaring that December 7, 1941, would be a date that would "live in infamy." Congress quickly declared war on Japan, as did Britain that same day. On December 11, Germany and Italy declared war on the United States, which responded by declaring war on them. Pearl Harbor had triggered war on a global scale.

Fall of the Philippines

In the Philippines, the Japanese forced the American and Philippine forces to retreat to the Bataan Peninsula by early January 1942. Slowly, the huge Japanese force advanced in the face of stiff American resistance. In March, to prevent the capture of General Douglas MacArthur, Roosevelt ordered him to leave. MacArthur, vowing "I shall return," left for Australia, where he laid plans for stopping the Japanese advance and reversing Japanese gains in the

Pacific. In April, the surviving American defenders on Bataan surrendered to the Japanese. The Japanese, who had not planned for dealing with so many prisoners, forced the American and Filipino prisoners to make a brutal sixty-five-mile march to prison camps. They shot or bayoneted anyone who fell behind, paused for water or rest, or tried to help those who did. Approximately 10,000 of the 78,000 prisoners died in what became known as the Bataan Death March. On May 6, the last American troops, holding out on the island fortress of Corregidor, surrendered. The conquest of the Philippines was complete.

First Strike Against Japan

With American forces suffering one defeat after another, the American people badly needed positive news. They needed to know that U.S. forces were fighting back. Military planners considered an air attack on Japan, but the range of typical navy planes was limited, and aircraft carriers could not get close enough to Japan to allow the planes to operate. Army bombers could travel farther but required longer takeoff distances.

The solution to the dilemma was modifying the B-25, a medium bomber that was compact enough to take off at sea. After intense special training, volunteer crews under Lieutenant Colonel Jimmy Doolittle set out with sixteen B-25 bombers from the United States aboard the carrier USS *Hornet*, which joined Task Force 16 at sea under the command of Vice Admiral "Bull" Halsey.

The original plan was for the B-25s to take off when the task force was 400 miles off Japan's coast. But the force was spotted by a Japanese fishing ship, which an American warship promptly sank. The possibility that the fishermen had radioed a warning of the task force to Japan required takeoffs at 625 miles instead.

The raid was successful in bombing Tokyo and three other Japanese cities. But bad weather and other circumstances foiled the landings on the Chinese mainland that the American raiders had planned. Eleven crews had to parachute out, and four crash-landed. Of the eighty men involved in the raid, three men were killed and eight were captured by the Japanese (four of those died in captivity). One plane landed in the Soviet Union, where the crew was imprisoned for thirteen months.

Although the raid did little damage to the factories, military installations, and oil storage facilities that the Americans hit, it encouraged Americans and surprised the Japanese, who were bewildered as to where the planes had originated. They knew that American forces were within striking range, which forced the Japanese to keep some military personnel and equipment on the home islands.

Battle of Midway

With the fall of Corregidor in May 1942, the Japanese controlled a huge Pacific empire stretching from Burma to the Bering Sea. Yet, May 1942 was the greatest extent of the Japanese advance. A naval and air battle in the Coral Sea that month stopped the Japanese advance toward Australia. Japanese expansion was again halted at Midway Island in the northern Pacific in June. The **Battle of Midway** was a critical battle—a major turning point of the war in the Pacific. By breaking the Japanese radio codes, the U.S. intercepted war messages and anticipated Japanese moves. U.S. Admiral **Chester W. Nimitz** skillfully directed carrier forces

The Death March in the Philippines

Japanese Internment Camps

Early in 1942, the U.S. government feared that some Japanese Americans might be spies or might somehow assist the Japanese war effort from within the U.S. and began relocating all Japanese living on the U.S. West Coast. This group of more than 120,000 people, most of whom were born in the U.S. and were American citizens, was moved to inland internment camps. President Reagan formally apologized for that mistreatment in 1988. The United States paid $1.6 billion to internees or their families as reparations. The following table shows the names of the major camps, their locations, and the maximum number of internees that were held in each camp.

Manzanar	CA	10,046
Tule Lake	CA	18,789
Poston	AZ	17,814
Gila River	AZ	13,348
Granada	CO	7,318
Heart Mountain	WY	10,767
Minidoka	ID	9,397
Topaz	UT	8,130
Rohwer	AR	8,475
Jerome	AR	8,497

Minority Groups in World War II

Nisei

After the attack on Pearl Harbor, many Americans feared anyone of Japanese ancestry, even other Americans. The fear was especially great on the West Coast, where most Nisei (people of Japanese descent that were born in America) lived. Early in 1942, the former attorney general of California asked Congress to restrict the freedom of Japanese Americans because "they are not of an assimilable race and they are strangers to our customs, our way of life. . . . If they are permitted to live at large among us, the possibility of disaster cannot be reckoned."

Responding to that wartime hysteria, President Roosevelt on February 19, 1942, authorized the War Department to restrict Japanese Americans. Some 120,000 were forced from their homes in California, Oregon, and Washington and placed in highly undesirable detention camps farther inland. None was ever charged with or convicted of treason or espionage.

In 1976, President Gerald Ford marked the thirty-fourth anniversary of Roosevelt's action by issuing a proclamation, which ended with these words: "We have learned from the tragedy of that long-ago experience forever to treasure liberty and justice for each individual American, and resolve that this kind of action shall never be repeated." In 1988, a formal apology and financial redress were offered to the Japanese Americans who had been interned as a result of what a congressional commission called "race prejudice, war hysteria, and a failure of political leadership."

Despite the gross violations of their civil liberties during internment, 30,000 Nisei demonstrated their patriotism by serving in combat units in Europe. The first all-Nisei unit formed was the 100th Infantry Battalion, which became known as the "Purple Heart Battalion" because so many of its men were wounded in combat. The most famous unit was the 442nd Regimental Combat Team, which became the most decorated combat unit in the war.

Navajo

Another group that received little recognition until well after the war was the Navajo Indians. They became famous as the "code talkers" who, by using their native language, frustrated Japanese code breakers throughout the entire war. Japanese intelligence forces were never able to "decode" the language. The idea for using Navajo for code work came from Philip Johnston, the son of a missionary.

The code talkers became famous for their speed, skill, and accuracy. About 540 Navajos served in the U.S. Marines, 375 to 420 of them as code talkers. Other Native Americans served in the U.S. Army, most of them Cherokees, Choctaws, and Comanches. Several Native Americans received the Medal of Honor for their bravery in the war.

African Americans

More than 2.5 million black Americans registered for the draft in World War II. Although blacks served in every branch of the service, about 909,000 of them served in the U.S. Army. No matter in which branch they served, they were segregated from white soldiers, reflecting the practice in the broader civilian society.

The first black U.S. Marine to report for training was Howard Perry. The first 1,200 black enlistees were organized into an all-black unit called the 51st Composite Defense Battalion.

Brigadier General Benjamin Davis was the first black general in the U.S. Army. Also, his son commanded the all-black Tuskegee Airmen of the U.S. Army Air Corps.

No black Americans received the Medal of Honor during World War II, but President Clinton presented Medals of Honor to seven black soldiers on January 13, 1997, six of them posthumously (that is, awarded after the death of the recipient).

---

against the Japanese, destroying four Japanese carriers, a cruiser, and about 250 airplanes. More than 3,000 Japanese died. American losses included one aircraft carrier, one destroyer, and about 150 airplanes. Some 300 Americans died. The outstanding victory at Midway, combined with the Battle of the Coral Sea, turned the tide of Japanese conquest. Despite those victories, Tokyo was far away; the road to victory would be long and very bloody.

Home Front

The idea that "each citizen should be a soldier" was born in the French Revolution, but it had its greatest demonstration during the Second World War. Victory was not merely the result of one army defeating another in battles. Rather, the war was won on both the field and in the factory. This war would impact everyone. The price for that united mobilization for war was the surrendering of some individual freedoms and an enormous expansion of federal power over the entire economy through regulation.

Under Roosevelt's generous Lend-Lease program, the economic output of the United States had already been critical to sustaining both Britain and the Soviet Union, which were teetering on the brink of defeat by the Nazis. Now America's tremendous production capability would be a crucial factor in bringing victory over the Axis.

Mobilizing the Economy

The new War Powers Act of 1941 authorized President Roosevelt, as commander in chief, to get the nation's economy ready for war. The **War Production Board** (WPB), which began operation in January 1942, immediately halted nearly all domestic building construction to conserve materials for war production. Production of many consumer goods was discontinued through much of the war because the WPB ordered massive industrial conversion from civilian to military production.

For example, civilian automobiles were not produced from February 1942 to July 1945. Instead, the government ordered Ford Motor Company to build B-24 bombers, General Motors to produce tanks, and its Cadillac division to build P-51 fighter planes and engines for tanks. Clothing manufacturers made uniforms, blankets, and parachutes. Even small manufacturers, such as the maker of Hoover vacuum cleaners, switched to producing helmets and bomb fuses.

Conserving vital goods such as foodstuffs, rubber, and gasoline for diversion to the war effort required a system of nationwide **rationing**. The government issued every man and woman ration books containing stamps needed to purchase various goods such as meat, sugar, coffee, and shortening. Even the purchase of shoes was limited to three pairs a year. Ladies' nylon stockings were almost nonexistent; the nylon was needed for parachutes. A new generation of "Victory Gardens" also sprang up in backyards across America to offset the shortages created by the war. By 1943, those gardens produced one-third of the nation's vegetables. Gasoline was rationed; motorists received a monthly allowance in relation to the importance of their vehicle to the war effort. In addition, several states established a "Victory Speed" of 35 mph to conserve fuel.

Besides conservation measures, recycling was an important part of the national war effort. Boy Scouts went through their neighborhoods collecting cooking grease and discarded metal and rubber goods. Farm boys scoured the fields for old plow tips and even junk cars, doing their part to help "scrap" the Axis.

Manpower and Womanpower

The war also created massive changes in the labor force and as a result, dramatic changes in American society. Fifteen million men and women served in the military during the course of the

---

Dorie Miller, Hero

Doris "Dorie" Miller was one of many heroes at Pearl Harbor on Sunday, December 7, 1941. He was an African American mess attendant aboard the battleship *West Virginia* at the time. He was awarded the Navy Cross for his courageous actions that fateful day. The citation reads in part, "While at the side of his Captain on the bridge, Miller, despite enemy strafing and bombing and in the face of a serious fire, assisted in moving his Captain, who had been mortally wounded, to a place of greater safety, and later manned a machine gun directed at enemy Japanese attacking aircraft until ordered to leave the bridge."

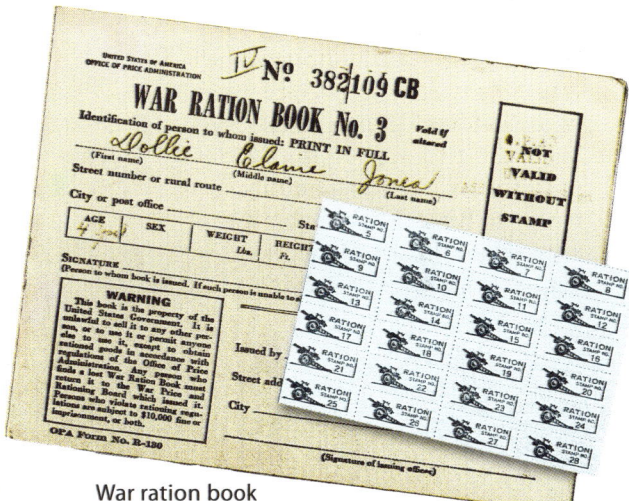

War ration book

Precedent for Restricted Liberties

Recall from Chapter 19 how the government either took control of or heavily regulated much of the economy during World War I through the Food Administration, the Fuel Administration, the Railroad Administration, and the War Industries Board. Those restrictions set the stage for extensive government controls over the economy and reduction of individual freedoms during World War II.

war. Although the overwhelming majority of those in the military were men, about 268,000 women joined the various women's auxiliary units of the service branches. The largest such unit was the Women's Army Corps (WAC), which enlisted 150,000 women. The Navy enlisted 86,000 women in its WAVES (Women Accepted for Volunteer Emergency Service) program. The Coast Guard also had a unit called the SPARs, named for the Coast Guard motto, "*Semper Paratus*, Always Ready," which about 10,000 women joined. The 2,000 WASPs (Women Air Service Pilots) flew new warplanes to their frontline bases for the Army Air Corps. About 20,000 women also joined the marines' auxiliary unit. The war increased the production needs of industry but at the same time subjected every able-bodied man between the ages of eighteen and forty-five to the draft. Consequently, it created a huge demand for workers. Women filled many of those jobs.

The number of women in the job market jumped from 25 percent in 1941 to 36 percent by 1944. In addition, female workers filled many traditionally male-oriented jobs, particularly in the defense industry. Working on the assembly line and in the shipyard, women played a vital role in the war on the home front.

The contribution that women made in the work force was not without its cost, however. During the war, the number of married women who worked outnumbered single women workers for the first time. Working mothers faced new problems including concerns about childcare. Women also became more financially independent, which, in some cases, led to marital tensions when husbands returned after the war.

Axis Taxes

Paying for the war posed an enormous challenge. It had long-term effects on both the taxed and the taxer alike. America's war bill totaled about $350 billion, a figure that Roosevelt believed should be paid with increased taxes rather than allowing the nation to lapse into debt. Congress, however, was less enthusiastic about raising taxes. With elections looming in 1942, Congress supported only half the tax increase that FDR recommended. Altogether, only about 45 percent of the war's cost was paid through taxation, and thus the national debt increased sixfold. The government not only imposed new taxes but also developed new means of collecting them. Congress introduced payroll deductions for income tax nationally in 1943 to help improve the government's tax flow. In 1939, only 5 percent of the workforce were required to pay income tax. By the end of the war, that percentage was ninety.

But for most Americans the war was about far more than taxes and ration books. With the mobilization of millions of men, nearly every family had an intense personal interest in the news from the war front. Blue star banners proudly hung in windows

Women put the finishing touches on B-25 bomber nose cones (*top*).

Female pilots ferried bombers for the Army Air Force, including B-17s (*bottom*).

The woman on the poster was called "Rosie the Riveter."

across America, representing a son gone to war. "Gold star mothers" replaced the blue banner with a gold one in memory of a fallen son who would not be coming home. The war required the courage, patriotism, sacrifice, and oftentimes grief of millions of Americans.

Section Review

1–3. What three forces kept the United States out of the war until late 1941?

4. Who was one of the leading spokesmen for the isolationist America First committees?

5–7. What three actions did FDR take in response to Japan's seizure of French Indochina?

8. What was a major turning point of the Pacific war in 1942?

9. What action did several states take during World War II to conserve gasoline?

★ Was complete national isolation a realistic position for the United States before the bombing of Pearl Harbor? Why or why not? Is it realistic today? Why or why not?

★ In your opinion, was the U.S. government justified in requiring that 120,000 Japanese Americans move to internment camps? Read Exodus 23:9; Leviticus 24:22; Proverbs 17:15; and Romans 13:3–4 as you consider your answer.

III. The Fight for Fortress Europe

Hitler's occupation of Europe was imposing and seemingly invincible. Yet by 1942 faint cracks in his empire could be detected. The eastern "wall" of "Fortress Europe," deep within Russia, was locked in bitter cold and bitter fighting. German casualties had mounted to a million since the invasion was launched. Westward, Hitler's defenses, which ranged from the Aegean Sea to the Arctic Ocean, did not invite attack. Yet the Führer underestimated his enemy. The British, led by Churchill, had much determination in them, and Hitler's latest enemy, the United States, loomed beyond the Atlantic. Hermann Goering, leader of Hitler's *Luftwaffe*, dismissed the now-awakened industrial giant by reportedly saying, "All the Americans can make are razor blades and refrigerators." But Americans turned their plowshares into swords and soon showed their eagerness to fight against Hitler's Fortress Europe.

Desert War

Mussolini, seeking to expand his African empire beyond his Ethiopian conquest, moved to annex more territory in North Africa. The British, who controlled Egypt and the Suez Canal, sent troops to halt the Italian advance. By February 1941, the British had defeated the Italian army in Libya and taken 130,000 prisoners.

The British triumph was short-lived: the British had exhausted their resources, and German panzers led by the famed General **Erwin Rommel** arrived by the end of February. Rommel took command of the Axis forces in North Africa at Tripoli. With the superb military strategy that earned him the nickname "the Desert Fox," Rommel moved his *Afrika Korps* (an elite armored division) eastward toward the Suez Canal. For months, the tank war in the

Guiding Questions

1. What Allied strategies were designed to liberate Europe?
2. What role did D-day play in defeating the Axis powers in Europe?
3. How did the Allies respond to the German offensive at the Battle of the Bulge?

General Erwin Rommel

World War II (1942–44)

desert moved back and forth from Egypt to Libya. At times, the fall of Egypt seemed imminent. After a string of stinging British defeats at the hands of Rommel, Churchill ordered Field Marshal **Bernard Montgomery** ("Monty") to take command in August 1942. In November, Montgomery's forces won a decisive victory over Rommel at the Battle of El Alamein. The Allies then began to push the Axis army westward.

On November 8, 1942, **Operation Torch**, commanded by U.S. General **Dwight D. Eisenhower** (or "Ike," as his men called him), used 850 ships to land troops on the west coast of Africa at Casablanca, Oran, and Algiers. In a three-day advance, the American tanks raced eastward toward Tunisia. With Montgomery coming west, the German and Italian tank corps were caught in the middle. After suffering repeated defeats and numerous shortages, the last German outpost at Tunis fell on May 13, 1943. The Axis Powers had been conquered in Africa.

General Bernard Montgomery

Italian Campaign

Casablanca Conference

In January 1943, while the desert war was raging far to the east in Tunisia, Franklin Roosevelt and Winston Churchill met with French General **Charles de Gaulle**. After France surrendered in June 1940, de Gaulle and thousands of Frenchmen who had escaped the country became known as the "Free French." The three leaders met in **Casablanca** to develop an Allied strategy for the assault on Hitler's Europe. Stalin, who had been invited but was not present because of the ongoing Nazi siege of Stalingrad, had been urging a second front in France to relieve German pressure on the Russian front. Both Roosevelt and Churchill refused to commit themselves to such an invasion, citing a lack of troops and preparedness for such a grand assault. They did agree, however, to open a front in southern Europe against Mussolini's Italy, which Churchill described as Europe's "soft underbelly." A successful invasion there would not only thrust into the heart of Europe but also reopen Mediterranean sea lanes.

Up the Boot

The invasion of Italy began with an attack on Sicily, the island just off the Italian coast. In Operation Husky, three thousand ships and landing craft carried troops and equipment to Sicily in July 1943. Although suffering heavy casualties, the Allied forces defeated the Italian army and forced the German army off the island. By the end of the summer, Sicily was an Allied base. From there, the Allies, led by General Mark Clark, landed at Salerno and Anzio, Italy.

Mussolini had been removed from power by the Italian king shortly after the Allies attacked Sicily. When Allied soldiers landed on the Italian mainland in September 1943, Italy surrendered. However, the Germans refused to recognize the surrender and fought furiously to stop the Allied advance northward. Germans declared Mussolini was still the leader, and he "ruled" from northern Italy rather than Rome.

Allied troops faced stiff German resistance as they slowly fought northward toward Rome. They finally marched into Rome on June 4, 1944. Most Romans viewed the conquest of their city as a deliverance. An American soldier, viewing the ancient ruins of the Forum for the first time, reportedly whistled and said with amazement, "I didn't know our bombers had done *that* much damage in Rome."

Despite the successful capture of Rome, the Italian campaign was far from over. The push into northern Italy continued to be costly as the "soft underbelly" was the scene of intense, deadly fighting because of tough Nazi resistance. Not until the closing days of the war did the Allies finally cross the Po River at the foot of the Alps.

D-Day

On June 4, 1944, Erwin Rommel looked at the impressive coastal defenses on the French side of the English Channel and glanced at the threatening skies. (After the Axis loss of North Africa, Hitler had assigned Rommel to defend France from the expected Allied invasion across the English Channel.) Based on the weather forecasts, he thought no Allied invasion was possible

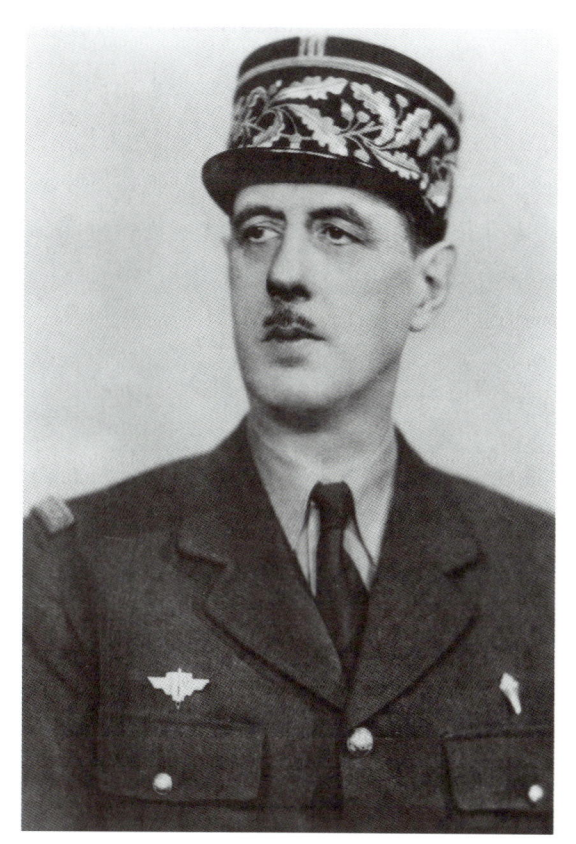

General Charles de Gaulle

Allied troops wade ashore under heavy enemy fire during the D-day invasion.

in the next few days. He traveled to Germany to celebrate his wife's fiftieth birthday which was on June 6.

In January 1944, General Eisenhower had been appointed Supreme Allied Commander and tasked with coordinating a cross-channel invasion into occupied France. Eisenhower was not only a strategist but also an organizer who had demonstrated in Africa and Italy his ability to work with the multinational Allied army. The fifty-three-year-old Midwesterner now faced his greatest challenge ever—an amphibious assault on the "Atlantic Wall of Fortress Europe." Three million Allied soldiers, sailors, and airmen—half of them Americans—were readied in southern England for the grand invasion.

The invasion, code-named Operation Overlord, began on the morning of "**D-day,**" **June 6, 1944**. In spite of the bad weather and deadly opposition, the Allied Expeditionary Force (AEF) estab-

Paratroopers in Normandy

Eisenhower speaking to paratroopers

American General Maxwell Taylor, commander of the 101st Airborne Division, combined integrity, courage, duty, and creativity with practical concern for his men. He did not command from the rear but fought alongside his soldiers on the front lines.

As he and his soldiers prepared to parachute into Normandy on D-day, he grew concerned about scattered paratroopers' ability to distinguish between friend and foe in the darkness. His solution was both simple and original: he ordered thousands of toy "crickets." Each man received one of the clicking tin noisemakers as a signaling device. Whenever a soldier heard an approaching person, he would click his cricket. If the unknown person responded with a similar click, he knew it was a friend. If he got no click in return, it was an enemy. During that difficult Normandy night, many lives were spared, and the operation was expedited by General Taylor's "crickets."

Taylor later recalled his own experience during that nighttime jump into France.

> At this moment, the plane was flying low at about 500 feet to avoid ground fire and to allow us parachutists to land more or less together. The latter did not occur in my case. My chute opened with a jerk and I floated toward the top of a tall tree. Not eager to become hung up in it and an easy target for a German rifleman, I made every effort to avoid branches and succeeded in landing inside a small field. . . . While there was considerable firing in the neighborhood, I was all alone except for three cows that were casting suspicious eyes at this man from Mars.
>
> My first problem was to get out of my tightly buckled parachute, work my way from this field, and then locate such troops as we might have nearby. To speed things up, I cut away my parachute and equipment with my jump knife, drew and cocked my pistol, readied my identification cricket and moved cautiously toward a nearby gate. . . . I suddenly heard the welcome sound of a cricket. I responded in kind and jumped around the gate. There in the moonlight stood a parachute infantryman, bareheaded but with his rifle ready and the bayonet fixed. I have often said in later years that he was the finest looking soldier I had ever seen in my career. We slapped backs reciprocally and proceeded in silence to look for our misplaced division.

Cemetery in Normandy, France

lished a beachhead along a sixty-mile stretch of the Normandy coast of France, taking beaches code-named Gold, Sword, Juno, Utah, and Omaha in fierce fighting. The invaders encountered mines and pilings along the beaches and under the water level. On the shore, the Germans had assembled miles of fortifications with barbed wire, machine guns, and heavy artillery. Before the beach assault began, over 20,000 paratroopers and soldiers in gliders landed behind German lines in the darkness. They cut vital transportation and communication lines and captured key bridges and roads for miles around the invasion site. Allied bombers pounded the Nazi defenses while battleships, cruisers, and destroyers hurled tons of high explosives onto the same areas. More than 150,000 troops in landing crafts raced through the surf and landed on the beaches under intense enemy fire.

The Nazis resisted fiercely but could not stop the surprise invasion. They were outplanned, outequipped, and outnumbered. The Allies controlled the skies and bombed roads, bridges, and supply depots to prevent German reinforcements from reaching the front. This invasion, the largest in history, was a crucial success.

After intense fighting inland and throughout the countryside, the Allied forces pushed toward Paris. The determined American General George Patton led the rapid advance to Paris, which Allied soldiers liberated on August 25, 1944. Another invading army landed in southern France, opening new ports and supply bases. The troops pushed quickly up the Rhône Valley to join the forces in northern France. By the end of 1944, France, Holland, and much of Luxembourg and Belgium had been freed of German armies. The three-million-man Allied force was at Germany's border, ready to break the famous Siegfried Line and move on to Berlin.

Battle of the Bulge

As snow fell in early December, mounting victories and thoughts of home had many Allied soldiers believing that the war would be over by Christmas. But the Germans had other plans. At 5:00 a.m. on December 16, 1944, Hitler unleashed a stunning counteroffensive out of Belgium's Ardennes Forest in a bold drive to divide the Allied forces in two.

The massive Nazi spearhead against the weakest point in the Allied line surprised Allied troops. The thrust created a "bulge" fifty miles deep into the Allied lines, giving the battle its name—the **Battle of the Bulge**. By Christmas Day, the Germans had captured thousands of troops and had surrounded American forces in the city of Bastogne. When the German commander ordered the American commander, General Anthony McAuliffe, to surrender his outnumbered army, the defiant American sent a one-word reply—"Nuts!"

Elsewhere along the Allied lines, the same fighting spirit prevailed. Eisenhower ordered Montgomery to attack from the northern portion of the bulge while he sent Patton against the southern part to free Bastogne. Together, they squeezed the bulge back by the middle of January 1945. Hitler's last gamble had cost him one hundred thousand casualties, nearly one thousand aircraft, and eight hundred tanks. American troops, who had borne the brunt of the attack, suffered heavy losses too, but they had recovered lost territory and were ready to cross the Rhine River for the final push into the German heartland.

A German Soldier's Impression of the D-Day Invasion

A German soldier manning the beach defenses at Normandy recalled his impression of the scene on June 6, 1944. "When it started to get light, I saw ships through the haze. When the fog lifted, it looked like a city out there. Between the ships you couldn't see any water. It was unbelievable—terrifying to behold."

George Patton

George Smith Patton Jr. (1885–1945), who graduated from West Point in 1909, served under General Pershing in the search for Pancho Villa and as a tank commander in France during World War I. Hard-driving and flamboyant, Patton was a brilliant strategist. In World War II, he distinguished himself in North Africa, Sicily, France, and Belgium. After D-day, he became famous as his armored division charged across Europe. Ironically, Patton, who fought in every major campaign in Africa and Europe, was fatally injured in a car accident in December 1945. He is buried in an Allied cemetery in Luxembourg.

Americans fought desperately in snow, cold, and the dense woods of the Ardennes Forest during the Battle of the Bulge.

Section Review

1. What was the name for the attack on western North Africa?
2. At their conference at Casablanca, where did FDR and Churchill agree to open another front against the Axis?
3. What was the name for the sixty-mile-long region in France where the landings in Operation Overlord took place?
4. What battle was Hitler's attempt to cut the Allied forces in two in December 1944?
* Describe the disagreement among Allied leaders (Churchill, Roosevelt, and Stalin) regarding where an invasion in Europe should occur in 1943.
* Assess the significance of the Battle of the Bulge.

IV. Pushing Back the Axis

While war raged in Europe and North Africa against Hitler's *Wehrmacht*, the United States also had the necessary task of defeating the Japanese in the Pacific. The Americans had halted Japan's expansion at Midway in June 1942. However, victory for America came only after many costly battles at sea and on tiny islands known only because they were the scenes of some of the most desperate fighting of the entire war.

In broad terms, the Pacific war consisted of a two-pronged drive, with General Douglas MacArthur of the U.S. Army heading the southern force from New Guinea and Admiral Chester Nimitz of the U.S. Navy commanding the Central Pacific force. These two separate campaigns would converge to reclaim the Philippines and then plan for the invasion of the Japanese home islands.

Island Hopping

In August 1942, the drive to defeat Japan began when U.S. Marines landed on **Guadalcanal** (gwad ul kuh NAL), a jungle island in the Solomon Islands, three thousand miles from Tokyo. After several sea battles and months of bloody jungle fighting, Japanese troops abandoned the island in February 1943. Because it was impossible to capture all of the thousands of Pacific islands, American forces began "**island hopping**" toward Tokyo. They bypassed heavily fortified islands and established air bases after securing less-fortified ones. Launching from runways on these islands, bombers such as the B-17 Flying Fortress and the B-29 Superfortress attacked Japanese fortifications on other islands and cut supply lines.

For the next year, U.S. forces slowly reduced the area of Japanese control in the South and Central Pacific. The United States also retook the western Aleutian Islands that the Japanese had occupied. Early in 1944, U.S. troops captured the Marshall Islands and in April attacked New Guinea.

The Marianas

The Japanese resistance became desperate and bitter during the summer of 1944. The most significant fight of the summer was the taking of the Mariana Islands, including Saipan and Guam. While the amphibious assault on Saipan was under way, a massive air battle took place between carrier-based fighters. The F6-F Hellcats, new U.S. fighter planes, knocked 346 Japanese warplanes from the

---

Guiding Questions

1. How did the Allies combat Japanese plans to protect their territory?
2. How did the Allies plan for victory and for dealing with liberated nations?
3. How did the Allies win the war?

PT Boats in World War II

Small, motorized torpedo boats were used extensively in World War II, especially in the Pacific theater. Called PT (patrol torpedo) or "mosquito" boats, they usually operated in squadrons called "mosquito fleets." They were built mainly of mahogany plywood and ranged from 70 to 80 feet long. They were amazingly sturdy and could withstand major damage while remaining afloat. Powered by three Packard twelve-cylinder, 1500 horsepower engines, they were sleek and built for speed.

Armament on PT boats varied, but they typically had two to four one-ton torpedoes; two to four depth charges, which rolled off racks; two twin .30- or .50-caliber machine guns; and sometimes a 40 mm cannon. They also boasted smoke-generating machines for laying smoke screens. By the end of the war, PT boats had more "firepower per ton" than any other vessel in the U.S. Navy.

sky, a victory that Americans quickly dubbed "the Great Marianas Turkey Shoot." The capture of the Marianas enabled Allied bombers to target both the Japanese home islands and the Japanese bases in the Philippines.

Fight for the Philippines

By the fall of 1944, U.S. forces were ready to attack the Philippines. The first major assault on the heavily fortified area began around the central island of Leyte (LAY tee). The **Battle of Leyte Gulf** was the largest naval battle in history and a critical blow to Japanese naval and air forces. The Japanese lost three battleships,

World War II in the Pacific

Legend:
- Japanese Occupied Territory
- Extent of Japanese Control (1942)

MacArthur returned to the Philippines at Leyte Gulf.

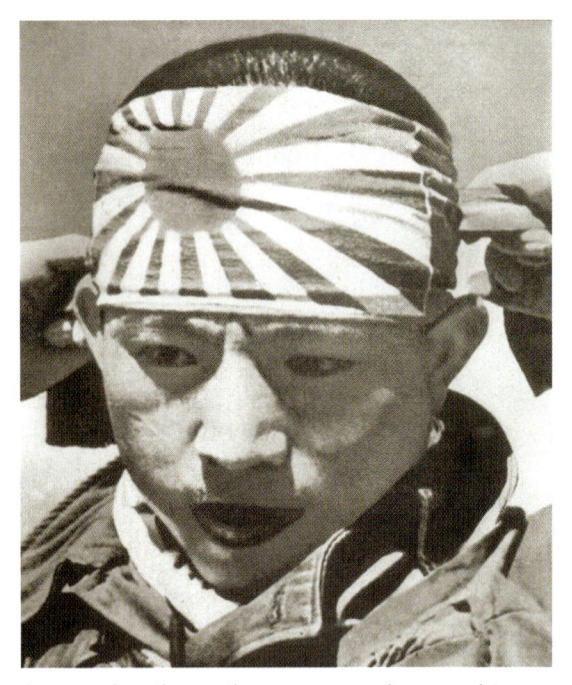

A young kamikaze pilot prepares to leave on his suicide mission.

This American aircraft carrier was one of the hundreds of ships damaged by kamikaze attacks.

nine cruisers, ten destroyers, and one hundred eighty aircraft to American firepower. This victory was the first step in a process that would require months of fighting and eventually lead to the recapture of Manila and the liberating of the Philippines.

During the Battle of Leyte Gulf, the Japanese, in dire need due to their losses, organized squadrons of suicide pilots, or **kamikazes** (kah mih KAH zeez). Their mission was simply to crash their bomb-laden planes into American warships. The Japanese word *kamikaze* means "divine wind," a term first applied to the typhoon in 1281 that destroyed Kublai Khan's huge navy sailing for an invasion of Japan. Although American gunners, by concentrated antiaircraft fire, stopped most of the fanatical missions, too many still succeeded. Kamikazes sank or crippled over three hundred U.S. ships in the final ten months of the war and inflicted about ten thousand casualties.

Iwo Jima

While MacArthur's forces pushed toward Manila, American strategists looked ahead to the next target—Okinawa (oh kih NAH wah)—and eventually the invasion of Japan itself. The planners determined that they needed a secondary foothold, a place where damaged B-29s could land as they returned from bombing raids over Japan. Scanning the map, they chose a small volcanic island called **Iwo Jima** (EE-woh JEE-muh). It was 750 miles from Tokyo.

U.S. Marines landed on Iwo Jima on February 19, 1945, beginning what would become the toughest, costliest battle of their illustrious history. On the cave-riddled island, 70,000 marines fought against 21,000 entrenched Japanese defenders for every foot of black sand. More than 6,800 American soldiers were killed, and 20,000 were wounded before they crushed Japanese resistance.

Okinawa

The grim victory at Iwo Jima opened the way to **Okinawa**, the bloodiest single campaign in the Pacific. Both sides, knowing the importance of the island to the final stages of the war, fought fiercely. For the Americans, a victory on Okinawa would provide a base for intensive bombing raids and a launch site for an amphibious assault on the Japanese home islands. For the Japanese, a victory at Okinawa (just 350 miles south of the main islands) would mean keeping their enemy at a defensible distance.

The Americans launched the invasion of Okinawa on Easter Sunday, April 1, 1945, beginning a fierce two-and-a-half-month battle. While the infantry fought for the island, the U.S. Navy found itself locked in combat with an equally determined aerial foe. Nearly two thousand kamikazes attacked the American fleet, killing five thousand American sailors and sinking thirty-eight U.S. ships. But by mid-June, Okinawa had been conquered.

Victory on Okinawa came at a high price: 12,000 American servicemen killed and 50,000 wounded. The Japanese casualty figures underscored their suicidal resistance. Of their estimated 117,000 casualties, 110,000 were killed. Committed to fighting to the death, most of the Japanese captives were those so seriously wounded as to be unable to kill themselves.

In addition to the military losses, tens of thousands of Okinawan civilians died. Survivors testified that before the invasion began, Japanese soldiers distributed grenades to civilians, ordering them to throw all but one at the American soldiers and to use the last one to commit suicide. Other Okinawans jumped from cliffs onto jagged rocks or into the sea to escape surrender.

The grim tale of Okinawa was an indication of the difficulty America would face when invading Japan. As the war neared an end in Europe, U.S. leaders feared hundreds of thousands of Americans would die in such an endeavor. Those problems weighed heavily on the mind of President Roosevelt as he met with fellow Allied chiefs Churchill and Stalin to discuss the future of war and peace.

Planning for Victory

A week before the assault on Iwo Jima in February 1945, the Big Three—Roosevelt, Churchill, and Stalin—met at the Soviet Union's Black Sea resort of **Yalta**. Much had happened since their first meeting at Tehran, Iran, in November 1943. There they had discussed plans for the opening of a second front in Europe. Now, with Allied forces pushing Hitler's crumbling army from both the east and the west, the Big Three laid plans for postwar Europe.

Roosevelt came to Yalta enjoying the wide support of the American people. The previous November, he had won an unprecedented fourth term, defeating New York governor Thomas Dewey. Most Americans agreed with the Democratic slogan that year: "Don't switch horses in the middle of the stream." In other words, now was not the time to elect a new president. In fact, one of the biggest fights for FDR during the 1944 election was not with the Republicans but with his own party over his vice president, Henry Wallace (elected in 1940). Southern conservatives did not like Wallace's strong liberal views, and political bosses in the North did not like his ties to labor. As a result, Roosevelt tapped a little-known U.S. senator from Missouri named **Harry Truman** for vice president. Just as he had handled a split in his own party, Roosevelt came to Yalta expecting to handle the growing rift between the Western nations and their at-arm's-length ally, the Soviet Union.

Confidently, Roosevelt came to the Yalta Conference believing that if the United States corrected the mistake, as he saw it, of not joining the League of Nations, then the postwar world would be secure. As a result, formation of an international organization for peace, known as the United Nations, was a major part of his Yalta agenda.

Roosevelt believed he could work effectively with Stalin. FDR thought that he could deal with Stalin as one politician to another. A number of historians have argued that FDR failed to understand the difficulties and challenges of dealing with a tyrant. Others have suggested FDR's declining health played a role in his interchanges with Stalin. They point to photographs that indicated FDR's physical condition was deteriorating.

The Big Three agreed to support democratic elections and government in all the liberated nations of Europe. Stalin gave the appropriate answers that FDR wanted on the issue, but the Soviet army destroyed democratic forces in Eastern Europe and set up Communist governments there. Wherever the Red Army advanced, Nazi control was simply replaced by Communist control.

Roosevelt was aware of the gulf between Soviet promises and practices, but because Stalin promised to join the war against Japan within three months of Germany's defeat, FDR did not press the issue. With Americans bogged down in costly fights in the South Pacific and the atomic bomb still in development, Roosevelt wanted

A Japanese soldier, blood pouring from his head, surrenders to Americans at Okinawa.

Winston Churchill, Franklin Roosevelt, and Joseph Stalin (*left to right on front row*) met at Yalta in February 1945.

FDR's funeral procession passing through the streets of Washington, D.C.

Russia's help in defeating the Japanese. Stalin agreed to join the fight, but he wanted additional Asian territory in return. Roosevelt agreed.

The conference participants also agreed to divide Germany, as well as its capital city of Berlin, into four zones. The Soviet Union, the U.S., Britain, and France would administer these divisions.

Just eight weeks after Yalta, on April 12, Roosevelt died of a cerebral hemorrhage at Warm Springs, Georgia. After fewer than three months as vice president, Harry Truman was the new commander in chief.

The Holocaust

As Allied forces freed Europe from Nazi tyranny, they came across unexpected horrors. In Nazi prison camps they found evidence of mass murder. The astounding massacre of millions of people became known as the **Holocaust**.

Nazis believed in the doctrine of "Aryan" (German) superiority over all other "lesser" peoples. Hitler used his ruthless Gestapo (secret police) and SS (*Schutzstaffel*, special security) forces to control, isolate, and exterminate "undesirable" elements in Germany and the countries that Nazi forces conquered. "Undesirables" included political opponents, Jews, prisoners of war, Poles, Romanies, the disabled, and others, but Jews had Hitler's special attention.

The first concentration camp was opened at Dachau in March 1933, less than two months after Hitler was appointed chancellor of Germany. Two weeks later, the Reichstag began passing laws against Jews. Eventually, these laws included forcing Jewish government workers to retire, excluding Jews from the army, defining "Jew" as anyone with two Jewish grandparents, revoking citizenship rights for Jews, and requiring Jews to wear yellow triangles or stars of David.

The Nazis encouraged Germans to boycott all Jewish businesses. On November 9, 1938, the Nazis vandalized thousands of Jewish businesses, burned scores of synagogues, and robbed, shamed, and arrested thousands of Jews all across Germany. That night became known as *Kristallnacht*, "the night of broken glass."

Next, Hitler ordered that all Jews be segregated into areas called **ghettos**. There they lived in crowded, unsanitary conditions, often with several families in one apartment. They had little food or fuel for warmth. The Warsaw ghetto was the most infamous.

In May 1940, the Nazis opened a concentration camp at Auschwitz, Poland, and began to transport thousands of Polish Jews there by train in filthy, unheated, and overcrowded cattle cars. Hundreds died en route. As the war progressed and began going against the Nazis, Hitler ordered the "Final Solution" implemented—the mass extermination of all Jews.

Execution in gas chambers was commonly used to carry out the Nazi plan. The guards expelled the gas with ventilators and then removed the bodies. Other prisoners shaved the heads of the corpses and removed any gold fillings from their teeth before shoving the bodies into ovens for cremation.

Concentration camps and extermination camps existed all across Nazi-controlled areas. The most notable ones were in Germany, Poland, and Austria. Auschwitz, Bergen-Belsen, Ravensbrück, Buchenwald, Dachau, Treblinka, Sobibor, Belzec, Chelmno, Mauthausen, and other such camps revealed their own gruesome secrets. One American soldier related that as U.S. troops neared Dachau, they "could smell the camp from at least five miles away."

An estimated 6 million Jews alone were killed in Hitler's program of state-supported mass murder. Combining this number with the number of non-Jews killed, an estimated 11 to 17 million people died at the hands of the Nazis.

Victory Achieved!

Victory in Europe

On April 20, 1945, Hitler celebrated his fifty-sixth birthday in his bunker more than fifty feet beneath Berlin. He had been living there for three months. Soviet artillery shells were exploding throughout the city. Allied forces to the west under Eisenhower had pushed as far as the Elbe River in central Germany, where Ike ordered them to halt while the Soviets advanced to Berlin.

On April 27 as the Germans were fleeing northern Italy, a group of anti-Fascist Italians stopped a German convoy of trucks. They found Mussolini disguised as a German soldier. He was arrested, and the following day, they shot him. His body was hung upside down in Milan for crowds to view.

By April 30, the Battle of Berlin raged less than a quarter mile from Hitler's underground headquarters. The Führer had ordered his favorite dog, Blondi, be fed cyanide, a poison. That afternoon, he and his bride of less than two days, Eva Braun, committed suicide. (Eva took cyanide and Hitler shot himself, perhaps after taking the poison, in the right temple with his pistol.) The Third Reich was no more. On May 7, the Nazis surrendered. News of victory in Europe triggered joyous celebrations. V-E Day (Victory in Europe Day) was commemorated from Times Square in New York City to Red Square in Moscow.

In his victory address to the nation, President Truman pointed to the unfinished task.

> We must work to bind up the wounds of a suffering world—to build an abiding peace, a peace rooted in justice and law. We can build such a peace only by hard, toilsome, painstaking work—by understanding and working with our Allies in peace as we have in war.

Truman would soon learn that "working with our Allies," particularly the Soviet Union, would be the hardest work of all.

V-E Day in New York City

Potsdam Conference

Truman traveled to Berlin in July 1945 to meet with Churchill and Stalin to plan the conclusion of the war in the Pacific. The meeting lasted from July 17 to August 2. Truman was not the only new face among the Big Three at **Potsdam**, just outside Berlin. Elections in Britain during the conference had swept Churchill's party out of power. Churchill returned to Britain during the meeting and was replaced by a new prime minister, **Clement Attlee**.

In other ways, the Potsdam Conference underscored changes in the alliance. Stalin had installed **puppet governments** (a government that is supposedly in control but is actually dominated by an outside power) throughout much of the area his armies occupied. Truman could do little more than remind Stalin of his promises to support free elections in Eastern Europe. But Stalin's problem was not memory loss. In the spring, shortly after Yalta,

Clement Attlee, Harry Truman, and Joseph Stalin (*left to right on front*) met at the Potsdam Conference.

Little Cost but a Great Return

The problem with Stalin's promise to fight against Japan was that the Russians did not declare war on Japan until early August 1945. That was just days before Japan surrendered. By that time, the U.S. had developed the atomic bomb. So the Russians had little, if any, impact on the outcome of the war against Japan. Yet they insisted on receiving what had been promised to them.

Explosion of the first atomic bomb at Hiroshima

the dictator had boasted, "This war is unlike all past wars. Whoever occupies a territory imposes his own social system . . . as far as his army can advance."

One item on which the Big Three at Potsdam could agree was the demand for Japan's unconditional surrender. Behind that declaration was perhaps the biggest event to occur during the conference. Shortly after arriving at Potsdam, Truman received the following message:

TOP SECRET

PRIORITY WAR 33556

TO SECRETARY OF WAR FROM HARRISON. DOCTOR HAS JUST RETURNED MOST ENTHUSIASTIC AND CONFIDENT THAT THE LITTLE BOY IS AS HUSKY AS HIS BIG BROTHER. THE LIGHT IN HIS EYES DISCERNIBLE FROM HERE TO HIGHHOLD AND I COULD HAVE HEARD HIS SCREAMS FROM HERE TO MY FARM.

The coded words meant that the test of the **atomic bomb** on July 16 had been successful; the noise of the blast could be heard for over a hundred miles. The "big brother" mentioned was the bomb that had been tested in the New Mexico desert. The "little boy" was a second atomic bomb that was ready, if approved by Truman, to be used against Japan.

"These Proceedings Are Closed"

The Allies issued an ultimatum to Japan—surrender or face destruction. No mention was made of the secret weapon, the atomic bomb. The Japanese premier refused to surrender. On the morning of August 6, Colonel Paul Tibbets piloted a B-29 (named the *Enola Gay* in honor of his mother) over the sun-drenched city of **Hiroshima** (hir uh SHEE muh) and dropped the first atomic bomb. The extraordinary weapon destroyed half the city in a single blast. It is estimated that more than 70,000 of 280,000 residents died that day. Tens of thousands later died from injuries and the results of radiation exposure.

Yet, the Japanese refused to surrender. Three days later, Charles Sweeney, piloting a B-29 named *Bocks Car*, dropped the second bomb on **Nagasaki** (NAH guh SAH kee). About 40,000 of the 200,000 residents were killed that day. On August 14, the Japanese agreed to surrender. On September 2, 1945, proclaimed as V-J Day (Victory over Japan), the official ceremony took place aboard the USS *Missouri* anchored in Tokyo Bay. General MacArthur stood on deck and addressed victor and vanquished alike:

> We are gathered here, representatives of the major warring powers, to conclude a solemn agreement whereby peace may be restored. The issues, involving divergent ideals and ideologies, have been determined on the battlefields of the world and hence are not for our discussion or debate. Nor is it for us here to meet, representing as we do a majority of the people of the earth, in a spirit of distrust, malice, or hatred. . . . It is my earnest hope . . . that from this solemn occasion a better world shall emerge . . . a world dedicated to the dignity of man. . . . Let us pray that peace be now restored to the world, and that God will preserve it always. These proceedings are closed.

Japanese representatives signed official surrender documents aboard the USS *Missouri* on September 2, 1945.

Silent Guns

While victory celebrations erupted around the world, in lands where the victory occurred, survivors searched for food in the rubble of what had once been their homes. There were millions of destitute refugees, particularly in Europe. Throughout the world the wounds of war ran deep. The grim tally was simply overwhelming: fifty million men, women, and children killed, with millions more disabled for life.

The United States, separated from the fighting by oceans, suffered no direct civilian loss, but 400,000 American soldiers, sailors, and airmen gave their lives for the cause of freedom. Victory placed the heavy mantle of world leadership on the shoulders of the United States. As the shadow of communism hung over the ruined cities of Europe and the wasted fields of Asia, America would soon learn that vigilance in peace is as important as vigilance in war.

The Japanese announced their surrender on August 14, 1945.

Should the Atomic Bombs Have Been Used?

Aftermath of the bombing of Nagasaki

For more than seventy years, historians and others have debated whether or not the atomic bombs should have been dropped on Japan. Some have argued that Japan could have been defeated by continued use of traditional bombing, blockading the coast of Japan, and with the help of Soviet troops who would be entering the war in August 1945. Others have noted that a demonstration of the bomb could have been staged over an unpopulated area so that the Japanese could see the enormous destruction that one bomb could produce without loss of any lives.

Those that support the decision to use the atomic bomb point to the near-fanatical resistance the Japanese had demonstrated. They note the use of kamikaze pilots and the number of Japanese soldiers who fought to their deaths, even when defeat was inevitable, on Iwo Jima, Okinawa, and in other Pacific battles. They mention that by August 1945, some 400,000 Americans had died in World War II. If U.S. soldiers invaded Japan, the projected death total was an additional 350,000 to 800,000 Americans (some say even higher). Many more would be wounded. Thus, supporters say the bomb was justified because it saved the lives of so many American soldiers.

How many Japanese would have died if the atomic bombs had not been used? Though estimates vary widely, it is commonly accepted that between 400,000 to 2,000,000 Japanese might have died if the fighting continued for many months. The number might have been even higher. Thus, more Japanese would likely have died if traditional fighting had continued and the atomic bombs had not been used.

The following excerpt is from a radio speech made by President Truman on August 9, 1945.

I realize the tragic significance of the atomic bomb.

Its production and its use were not lightly undertaken by this Government. But we knew that our enemies were on the search for it. We know now how close they were to finding it. And we knew the disaster which would come to this Nation, and to all peace-loving nations, to all civilization, if they had found it first....

We won the race of discovery against the Germans.

Having found the bomb we have used it. We have used it against those who attacked us without warning at Pearl Harbor, against those who have starved and beaten and executed American prisoners of war, against those who have abandoned all pretense of obeying international laws of warfare. We have used it in order to shorten the agony of war, in order to save the lives of thousands and thousands of young Americans.

Section Review

1–2. Who was the military commander of each of the two prongs of the Allied strategy in the Pacific war?

3. What was the largest naval battle in history?

4. What island located 350 miles from Japan did American forces capture as a launching point for the final assault on Japan?

5–6. What two cities were the sites of the first uses of the atomic bomb in warfare?

★ Explain and evaluate the strategy of island hopping.

CHAPTER REVIEW 22

Making Connections

1. Place the following events in their correct chronological order.
   a. Battle of Britain
   b. Germany's invasion of France
   c. Operation Barbarossa
   d. invasion of Denmark and Norway
   e. invasion of Poland
   f. evacuation of Dunkirk
2. Why was the United States called "the arsenal of democracy"?
3–5. Who were the three leaders present at the Yalta Conference?
6–9. Who were the four leaders present at the Potsdam Conference? (One country had two representatives.)

Developing History Skills

1. Could President Roosevelt have made the outcome of the Yalta Conference more beneficial to the United States? Why or why not?
2. With your parent's and/or teacher's permission, use Emory University's Holocaust Denial on Trial website (or a similar site) to identify a Holocaust denial argument and related debunking of that argument. What fallacies of historical research are exhibited by the Holocaust denial claim?

Thinking Critically

1. Was President Truman right to use the atomic bomb against Japan? Defend your answer.
2. Compare the actions of kamikaze pilots to suicide attacks by terrorists. What are the similarities and differences?

Living as a Christian Citizen

1. How should a Christian in a country governed by a tyrant obey Christ's command to "love your enemies" and "do good to them which hate you" (Luke 6:27)? Could a Christian obey that command and participate in armed resistance?
2. Imagine you are a German pastor in Nazi Germany. Develop the outline of a sermon that critiques the racial policies that led to the Holocaust. Use Acts 17:26; Zechariah 2:8–9; Romans 10:12; and Revelation 5:9–10.

People, Places, and Things to Remember

Fascist Party
Benito Mussolini
Adolf Hitler
Mein Kampf
Nazi Party
totalitarianism
Hideki Tojo
Hirohito
Rome-Berlin-Tokyo Axis
Axis Powers
Joseph Stalin
Union of Soviet Socialist Republics (USSR)
Rhineland
Sudetenland
Neville Chamberlain
appeasement
Nazi-Soviet nonaggression pact
September 1, 1939
blitzkrieg
Allies
Dunkirk
Winston Churchill
Battle of Britain
Neutrality Act of 1939
America First Committee
Wendell Willkie
Lend-Lease Act
Flying Tigers
Atlantic Charter
Douglas MacArthur
December 7, 1941
Battle of Midway
Chester W. Nimitz
War Production Board
rationing
Erwin Rommel
Bernard Montgomery
Operation Torch
Dwight D. Eisenhower
Charles de Gaulle
Casablanca
D-day (June 6, 1944)
Battle of the Bulge
Guadalcanal
island hopping
Battle of Leyte Gulf
kamikazes
Iwo Jima
Okinawa
Yalta
Harry Truman
Holocaust
ghettos
Potsdam
Clement Attlee
puppet governments
atomic bomb
Hiroshima
Nagasaki

CHALLENGE
1945–2017

1950–53 Korean War

1954 *Brown v. Board of Education*

1961 First American in space

1964 Gulf of Tonkin Resolution

1969 First man on the moon

1974 President Nixon resigned

1950 — 1960 — 1970 — 1980

1949 NATO formed

1948 European Recovery Program (Marshall Plan)

1964 Civil Rights Act of 1964

CHAPTERS

23 **THE POSTWAR ERA (1945–1963)**

24 **THE SHATTERED SOCIETY (1963–1973)**

25 **A NATION WITH CHALLENGES (1973–1980)**

26 **RESURGENCE OF CONSERVATISM (1981–1992)**

27 **FACING A NEW MILLENNIUM (1993–2017)**

1989–91
Communist governments in Eastern European nations collapsed

2001
Major terrorist attacks on United States

1991
Persian Gulf War

2009
Barack Obama, first black U.S. president, inaugurated

2017
Donald Trump inaugurated

23 THE POSTWAR ERA (1945–1963)

> Let every nation know, whether it wishes us well or ill, that we shall pay any price, bear any burden, meet any hardship, support any friend, oppose any foe, to assure the survival and success of liberty.
>
> **President John F. Kennedy**
> Inaugural Address, January 20, 1961

America continues the dangerous atomic age: a test explosion of the atomic bomb in the South Pacific, 1946.

Big Ideas

1. How did the United States respond to the threat of communism?
2. What was the political climate in the United States after World War II?
3. What major changes occurred in American culture in postwar America?

I. Cold War Begins

II. Domestic Reform

III. Life in Postwar America

On April 12, 1945, the day Franklin Roosevelt died, **Harry Truman** took the presidential oath of office. "Boys, if you ever pray, pray for me now," the overwhelmed Truman confided to reporters the next day. "I don't know whether you fellows ever had a load of hay fall on you, but when they told me yesterday what had happened, I felt like the moon, the stars, and all the planets had fallen on me." Truman indeed seemed unprepared for the White House. Taking office after serving less than three months as vice president, Truman had little experience in foreign policy. He was told nothing about the project to develop the atomic bomb until he became president. Little in his background seemed to foreshadow greatness. Only a high school graduate, Truman failed in the clothing business; then, largely due to the assistance of an influential political leader in Missouri, he was elected county judge. In 1934, he won a U.S. Senate seat and there gained praise for his work as chairman of a committee to investigate war mobilization. As the 1944 election approached, President Roosevelt was seeking a new vice presidential candidate. Wanting to replace his very liberal vice president, Henry Wallace, he selected Truman, a moderate.

Prepared or not, Truman proceeded to make his mark on American policy at home and in the world. Aided by his own toughness, common sense, and the best advice he could get, the president charted a course unknown to America for peacetime. After involvement in wars, past presidents typically had resumed an isolationist position. Truman, however, led the United States into membership in, and even sponsorship of, international organizations such as the United Nations and the North Atlantic Treaty Organization (NATO). Furthermore, in a departure from tradition, he pushed for a peacetime buildup of America's armed forces, a buildup anchored by atomic weapons. He established the **Central Intelligence Agency (CIA)** to gather and analyze information, often through the use of spies, regarding foreign affairs.

Truman was followed as president by Dwight Eisenhower and John Kennedy, two men who exhibited a different style from the lively Truman. Eisenhower was a former commanding general and grandfather-like figure; Kennedy was a handsome young senator and war hero. Both Eisenhower and Kennedy, however, pursued Truman's goal of American leadership in international affairs. They followed Truman to a lesser extent in domestic affairs, particularly in the gradual increase in the size and power of government.

I. Cold War Begins
Trials for War Crimes

After World War II, the Allies placed many leaders of the Axis powers on trial. They faced such charges as conspiring to commit crimes against peace, planning and waging wars of aggression, and committing war crimes and crimes against humanity.

The trials of many Nazi war criminals were held in Nuremberg, Germany. Some of the highest officials, including Adolf Hitler, had escaped prosecution because they had committed suicide. Robert Jackson, the chief United States prosecutor present, observed in his opening statement, "The wrongs which we seek to condemn and punish have been so calculated, so malignant and so devastating, that civilization cannot tolerate their being ignored because it cannot survive their being repeated."

Harry S. or Harry S?

When Harry Truman was born, his parents wanted to avoid offending either of his grandfathers, Anderson Shippe Truman and Solomon Young. The parents compromised by giving young Harry the middle initial *S* but no middle name, so each grandfather could claim that Harry was named for him. (Truman personally preferred the name *Shippe* and occasionally used it.)

But when Truman was sworn in as president, Chief Justice Harlan Stone administered the oath of office by saying, "I, Harry Shippe Truman . . ." Truman responded, "I, Harry S. Truman . . ." Since the president's middle name was really simply *S*, shouldn't the period be omitted? Many newspapers, deciding that it should, referred to him as "Harry S Truman." Although the omission was sensible, it looked too much like a mistake, so one style manual devised a special rule: "For convenience and consistency, . . . it is recommended that all initials given with a name be followed by a period." The president, incidentally, agreed.

Guiding Questions

1. Where did trials for World War II war criminals occur?
2. Which two major agencies constitute the United Nations?
3. What did the United States do to restrain the advance of communism?
4. Where did the United States fail to prevent the spread of communism?

In the first of the **Nuremberg Trials**, twenty-four individuals were charged. Twelve were sentenced to death, seven received prison sentences ranging from ten years to life, three were found innocent, one committed suicide early in the proceedings, and one was released without going to trial.

Similar proceedings were held in Tokyo for important Japanese officials. Of the twenty-eight defendants, two died of natural causes during the lengthy trial, one was declared insane, seven were sentenced to death, and eighteen received prison sentences. Hideki Tojo was among the seven executed. One of the terms of the peace settlement was that Hirohito would remain emperor and would not be charged with any crimes; however, he was required to renounce a longstanding Japanese tradition—the belief that the emperor was divine. He remained the emperor until his death at age 87 in 1989, more than four decades after the war ended.

In later trials, thousands of other individuals faced charges. These included Japanese prison camp guards who had brutalized Allied soldiers they supervised as well as ruthless guards at the Jewish concentration camps in Europe.

After World War II, leading Nazi war criminals were tried in Nuremberg, Germany.

Japanese war criminals, including Hideki Tojo (*above*), were placed on trial in Tokyo.

United Nations

One effort to maintain peace was the formation of the **United Nations** (UN). Born out of wartime cooperation among the Allies, the UN began on April 25, 1945, in San Francisco with delegates from fifty nations meeting to write a charter for the organization. The United States Senate ratified the UN charter in 1945 by an overwhelming margin, and eventually the UN made its permanent home in New York City.

The UN includes two major agencies. The **General Assembly** consists of delegates from all member nations and provides a forum in which those nations can express their views. The **Security Council** currently includes five permanent members—the United States, Russia, Britain, France, and China—and ten members elected by the General Assembly for two-year terms. Permanent members have veto power. This means that if any of those five members votes against a Security Council resolution, it does not pass. The highest official in the UN is the Secretary-General.

Proponents of the United Nations hoped that the body would provide an avenue for rational discussion and a means of furthering world peace. Good intentions lay behind the founding of the United Nations, but its record as a mediator and preserver of the peace has seen a mixture of both successes and failures.

Battling Communism

The Cold War

The failures of the United Nations in the postwar era are highlighted by the struggle of the free world against the aggres-

The United Nations was another attempt to achieve world peace through discussion rather than war.

sive policies of the Soviet Union. This hostility between the two superpowers—the United States and the Soviet Union—and their allies became known as the "**Cold War**." The United States and the Soviet Union entered a period of tension and intense competition which occasionally flared into actual military conflict (i.e., a "hot war"). The relationship between the two countries had never been cordial. The United States government did not officially recognize the Communist government of the Soviet Union until 1933. Even when fighting their common enemy, Hitler, during World War II, Roosevelt and Stalin disagreed about the location and timing of the opening of a second front and other matters. What really launched the Cold War, however, was the realization that the USSR intended to spread its power throughout the world. The Cold War was waged as the forces of democracy and communism confronted each other in nation after nation.

Winston Churchill's "iron curtain" speech marked the symbolic beginning of the Cold War.

Eastern Europe

The first campaign of the Cold War took place in Eastern Europe as the Soviets established pro-Soviet governments there. Before World War II ended, the Soviet Union had installed "puppet" governments in Poland and Romania. Soon, East Germany, Hungary, Bulgaria, Albania, and Yugoslavia fell to Communist control. In 1948, Czechoslovakia was the last Eastern European country to succumb to Soviet conquest. All of this was contrary to Soviet guarantees at the Yalta Conference of free democratic elections in those nations. Winston Churchill described the unfolding events in Europe as the descent of an "**iron curtain**" separating Communist Eastern Europe from the free nations of Western Europe. Soon the term *East* or *Eastern* was used to refer

The Iron Curtain

In 1946, former British prime minister Winston Churchill visited the United States. In March, he and President Truman traveled to Fulton, Missouri, where Churchill delivered a speech at Westminster College. He told the audience that an "iron curtain" had fallen across Europe.

> A shadow has fallen upon the scenes so lately lighted by the Allied victory. . . .
>
> From Stettin in the Baltic to Trieste in the Adriatic, an iron curtain has descended across the Continent. Behind that line lie all the capitals of the ancient states of Central and Eastern Europe. Warsaw, Berlin, Prague, Vienna, Budapest, Belgrade, Bucharest and Sofia, all these famous cities and the populations around them lie in what I must call the Soviet sphere, and all are subject in one form or another, not only to Soviet influence but to a very high and, in many cases, increasing measure of control from Moscow. . . .
>
> The Communist parties, which were very small in all these Eastern States of Europe, have been raised to pre-eminence and power far beyond their numbers and are seeking everywhere to obtain totalitarian control. . . .
>
> I do not believe that Soviet Russia desires war. What they desire is the fruits of war and the indefinite expansion of their power and doctrines.

Iron Curtain in Europe

to Communist-controlled areas throughout the world, and *West* or *Western* referred to democratic nations. The term **Third World** referred to nations that did not align themselves with either the East or West. (Today that term refers to underdeveloped, or developing, nations—especially those with widespread poverty.)

President Truman responded to the Soviet presence in Eastern Europe with the policy of **containment**. Though unhappy with the expansion of communism, he feared that trying to force the Communists to withdraw from Eastern Europe might cause another war, perhaps World War III. Truman declared, however, that further Communist aggression would be resisted; in other words, communism must be contained to its new boundaries. In 1945, for example, the combative Truman confronted Soviet foreign minister Molotov about Poland. "I have never been talked to like that in my life," Molotov said. "Carry out your agreements and you won't get talked to like that," Truman shot back. Faced with the growing Communist menace, Truman was intent on pursuing the containment policy by providing military and economic support to halt Soviet expansion.

Middle East and Mediterranean

The goal of stopping the spread of communism achieved some successes. In 1946, the Soviets withdrew their forces from Iran. More critically, that same year civil war erupted in Greece, where Communists tried to take over the country. The Soviet Union also pressured Turkey for territory and the right to establish naval bases on the Bosporus, the strategic waterway providing access between the Black Sea and the Aegean Sea. To prevent the spread of Soviet influence in the Mediterranean, Truman asked Congress for $400 million in economic aid for Greece and Turkey. Both Greece and Turkey successfully pushed back Communist threats. This policy of aiding countries in fighting Communist takeovers became known as the **Truman Doctrine**.

Western Europe

After 1945, American attention focused on Western Europe, where economic ruin from the war created an opportunity for Communist advances. France and Italy, for example, already had strong left-wing parties that could lay a foundation for a Communist takeover. To reduce the appeal of the Soviets, Secretary of State George C. Marshall in 1947 offered a plan for massive economic aid to all European countries. The Soviet Union and its puppet governments in Eastern Europe refused the aid, but Western Europe welcomed it. In 1948, Congress passed this European Recovery Program, better known as the **Marshall Plan**. By 1951, the United States had spent $13 billion on restoring the economies of Western Europe. The Marshall Plan stabilized the region and thereby diminished the appeal of communism. It also restored those European countries as trading partners with the United States.

Reacting to the Soviet military threat to the West, the Western nations forged a military alliance to defend themselves. In April 1949, representatives from ten Western European countries, the United States, and Canada formed the **North Atlantic Treaty Organization (NATO)**. The twelve nations agreed to provide military support for any member that was attacked. (Later in the Cold War, additional nations joined.) In 1955, the Communist countries of Eastern Europe reacted by creating their own military alliance, the **Warsaw Pact**, to counter NATO.

Former General George C. Marshall (*left*) served as secretary of state during the Truman administration.

Supplies arrive in France in 1948 (*below*) as a part of the Marshall Plan, named in his honor.

Occupation of Germany After World War II

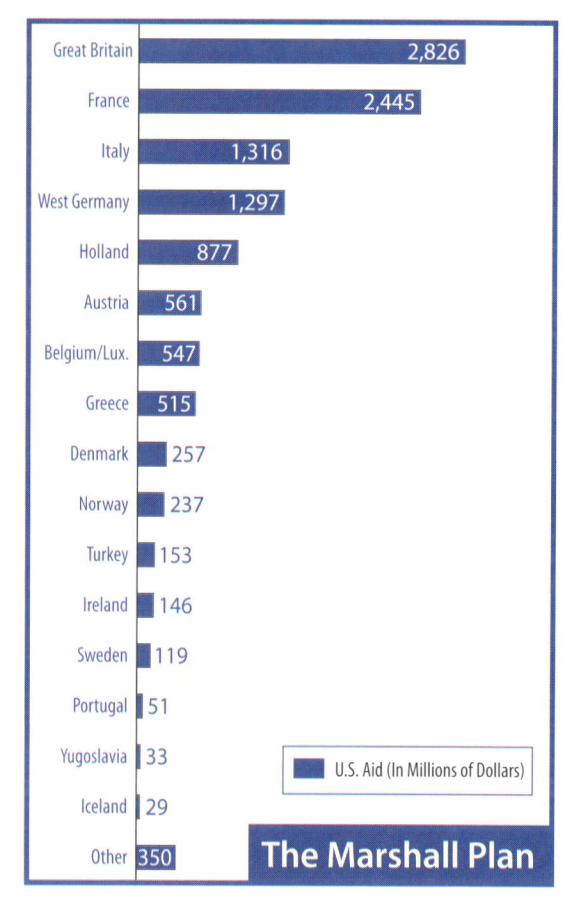

The Marshall Plan

Country	U.S. Aid (In Millions of Dollars)
Great Britain	2,826
France	2,445
Italy	1,316
West Germany	1,297
Holland	877
Austria	561
Belgium/Lux.	547
Greece	515
Denmark	257
Norway	237
Turkey	153
Ireland	146
Sweden	119
Portugal	51
Yugoslavia	33
Iceland	29
Other	350

The division of Germany after the war into a Soviet zone in the East and French, British, and American zones in the West also created tensions. In 1948, the Americans, the British, and the French consolidated their occupied zones in western Germany and began the process of forming a government. Threatened by the prospect of a unified West Germany, the Soviets blocked highway, water, and rail traffic into West Berlin. Berlin, located deep in East Germany, had been divided into a Communist East and a free West after the war. Surrounded by the Communist East, Berlin was especially vulnerable. By blocking all access to that area, Stalin hoped to take over the entire city or force the West to stop the unification of West Germany. Truman responded quickly with a massive airlift of food and supplies to West Berlin. The **Berlin airlift** continued for eleven months. British and American planes departed and landed every few minutes. Some 277,000 flights brought food, fuel, medicine, and other essentials to the city. In May 1949, the Soviet Union ended the blockade. Afterward, the Soviets reacted to the formation of the Federal Republic of Germany (West Germany) by fashioning East Germany into a Communist state, called the German Democratic Republic. Germany would remain divided until 1990.

The Berlin Airlift (*above and right*) rescued West Berliners from Soviet efforts to isolate their city.

Cold War—1982

"Year of Shocks"

For the free world, 1949 was a "year of shocks." Since the 1920s, China had endured civil war between the Nationalists led by **Chiang Kai-shek** (CHANG KYE-SHEK) and the Communists led by **Mao Zedong** (MOU DZUH-DONG). World War II interrupted their fighting as they both battled the Japanese, but after 1945 civil war resumed. The United States supported the Nationalists with $2 billion in aid from 1945 to 1949, but it was not enough. In 1949, Communist forces gained control of mainland China. Nationalist forces fled to the island of Taiwan (Formosa) about a hundred miles off the coast of China, and there they established their government. The United States and the UN continued to recognize the Nationalists in Taiwan as the "real" China. Only in the 1970s did both officially recognize Mao Zedong, on the mainland, as the legitimate leader of China.

The existence of nuclear weapons heightened Cold War tensions. In August 1949, the Soviet Union successfully tested its first atomic bomb and forced Truman to reevaluate America's defense policy. He called first for increasing conventional military forces since the Soviets possessed "the bomb." He also ordered development of a more powerful weapon, the hydrogen bomb. When the "H-bomb," as it was popularly known, was finally developed in 1952, it had an explosive power hundreds of times greater than the bomb dropped on Hiroshima. Within a year, the Soviet Union revealed that it, too, had developed a hydrogen bomb.

The Nationalist Chinese led by Chiang Kai-shek (*left*) failed to defeat the Communists led by Mao Zedong (*right*) in the long Chinese civil war that ended in 1949.

The Korean War

The most serious military conflict of the early Cold War occurred in Asia on the Korean peninsula. Freed from Japanese control after World War II, Korea had been divided along the **38th parallel** of latitude into Communist North Korea and non-Communist South Korea. The Communists, however, failed to fulfill their promises to allow free elections that would unite the country. Then on June 25, 1950, more than eighty thousand North Korean soldiers invaded the South in an attempt to unite the peninsula under Communist rule. President Truman, rather than ask Congress for a declaration of war, worked through the UN Security Council to respond to this act of aggression. The USSR, which could have vetoed the action, was boycotting UN meetings in protest of America's refusal to recognize the government of Communist China. Although sixteen other nations sent troops, the United States contributed the most men, and General **Douglas MacArthur**, America's hero of the Pacific in World War II, was placed in charge of the UN military forces.

Initially, the North Korean forces penetrated deeply into the South, easily brushing aside both disorganized South Korean resistance and the first American units sent to Korea. Within three months, North Korea controlled 90 percent of the peninsula and was on the verge of making all Korea Communist.

MacArthur, however, reversed the situation by taking advantage of his superior air and naval power to launch an amphibious invasion behind North Korean lines at **Inchon,** a seaport halfway up the western coast of Korea. In that September 1950 attack, MacArthur cut the North Korean supply lines and began destroying the North Korean forces. Soon, the UN forces had pushed the Communists back across the 38th parallel and into the North, hoping to unify the peninsula under a non-Communist government.

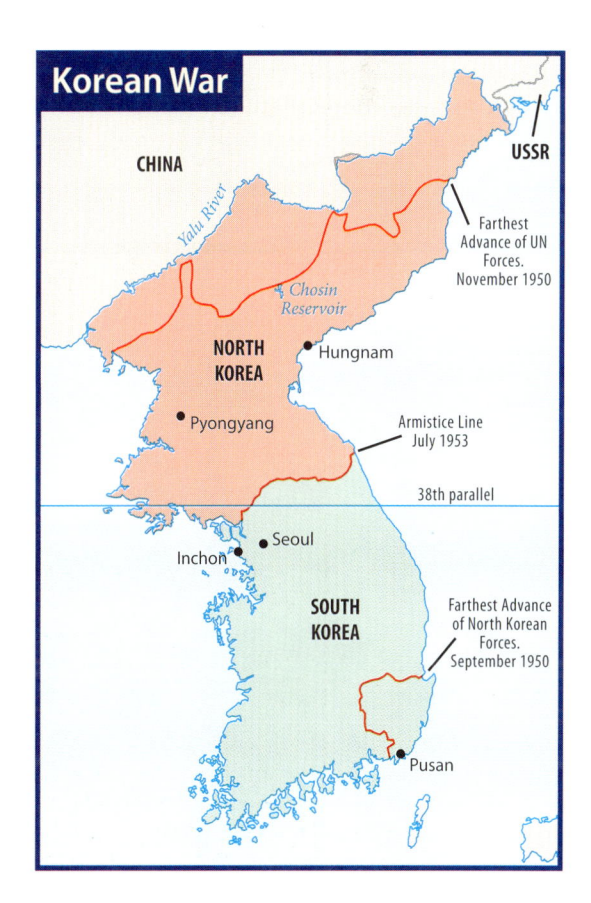

Frozen Chosin

The influx of Communist Chinese forces into the Korean War surprised MacArthur's army. The U.S. 1st Marine Division, holding a position by the Chosin Reservoir not far from the Yalu River (the boundary between North Korea and China), was nearly surrounded by the oncoming Chinese. The division's only hope of escape was to break out to the south toward the seaport of Hungnam.

One colonel told his men, "The enemy is in front of us, behind us, to the left of us, and the right of us. They won't escape *this* time." The commanding general of the division, Oliver P. Smith, denied that the action was a retreat. "We are simply attacking in another direction," he said. The marines' escape involved combat just as fierce as any offensive operation.

Bitterly cold weather complicated the situation. Marines joked that *Chosin* rhymed with *frozen*, but the subzero temperatures were no laughing matter. Something as simple as tossing a grenade meant removing a glove and risking frostbite. Weapons froze. (One ingenious soldier found that lubricating his gun with hair cream kept it in operation.)

The breakout produced countless individual acts of bravery. One sergeant, his legs paralyzed from a bullet wound, died holding off the enemy on a hilltop for ten minutes while his comrades escaped. Others used shovels like baseball bats to return grenades that the enemy tossed at them. A private was being treated for severely frostbitten feet when he discovered his unit was in danger. Without hesitation, he ran toward his buddies, his feet leaving bloody footprints in the snow. A sergeant holding back the Chinese in one gap was hit twice but refused medical attention. "There isn't time," he said. "They're only small holes anyway." The sergeant died of blood loss, but his unit held the line.

Fox Company deserved special commendation. The company had to hold the heights of Toktong Pass south of Chosin Reservoir against overwhelming odds or the enemy would stop the withdrawal. The unit would have to fight to the last man if necessary; there could be no retreat. For five days, Fox Company survived the waves of attacking Chinese soldiers. Of the company's 240 men, 115 of them were killed or wounded, including all but one of its officers. Even when relief arrived, the rest of the unit stayed until the last truck was safely through Toktong Pass. The peak they defended was thereafter known as Fox Hill.

The withdrawal took fourteen days, and the Chinese contested almost every foot of the more than fifty miles from the reservoir to Hungnam. The marines suffered nearly 13,000 casualties from both battle and the bitter cold; the Chinese took even heavier losses—37,500 casualties. The Marine Corps added the men of "Frozen Chosin" to its roll call of valor.

Soldiers of the Frozen Chosin

American soldiers during the Korean War

But MacArthur's success had an unexpected effect. In October Communist China sent 260,000 troops into North Korea to rescue the North's Communist government. Soon the Chinese forces sent the UN forces reeling back down the peninsula. MacArthur, who had downplayed the possibility of Chinese intervention, now admitted, "We face an entirely new war." Communist forces pushed the UN troops back to the 38th parallel. Soon, the two well-entrenched sides were fighting each other desperately for a few square miles of worthless land. The Korean conflict had become a stalemate.

MacArthur—declaring, "There is no substitute for victory"—argued for breaking the deadlock by expanding the war into China. He mentioned the possibility of dropping atomic bombs on some Chinese cities. Truman, however, held to the principle of **limited war,** a war with a limited objective short of total victory over the enemy. Calling war with China a "gigantic booby trap," Truman refused to expand the conflict. Joseph Stalin and Mao Zedong had signed a mutual assistance treaty in February 1950. Truman feared if UN forces attacked China that Russia might enter the war and that the conflict might even cause a third world war.

MacArthur disagreed publicly with the president's views. He voiced his opposition to the press and to members of Congress. He stated that limited war was a mistake and was nothing more than appeasement. Despite repeated warnings, MacArthur continued to criticize Truman. In early April 1951, Truman fired MacArthur as commander.

Many Americans were outraged that MacArthur had been dismissed. A public opinion poll showed that 69 percent of Americans opposed the president's action. MacArthur returned to the U.S. for the first time since 1937. On April 19, 1951, he gave an address to Congress during which he was interrupted by applause fifty times.

Later, Congress investigated MacArthur's dismissal. The Truman administration sent numerous witnesses to testify to Congress and present the idea of limited war in Korea. One of them was General Omar Bradley, the chairman of the Joint Chiefs of Staff. He said an all-out conflict with China would have been "the wrong war, at the wrong place, at the wrong time, and with the wrong enemy." Though the discharge of MacArthur remained controversial, eventually many Americans began to change their views about the matter.

Peace talks began in July 1951. Fighting continued for two years until a truce was signed on July 27, 1953. More than 54,000 Americans died in the war. The agreement reached left the boundary between North and South Korea about where it was before the war began (see map on p. 531). In part because of the unpopularity of the Korean War, Truman did not seek reelection in 1952. His successor, Dwight Eisenhower, was elected to two terms. In

MacArthur's Speech to Congress

After his dismissal by Truman, General MacArthur spoke to a joint session of Congress on April 19, 1951. His speech, in part, was as follows:

Once war is forced upon us, there is no other alternative than to apply every available means to bring it to a swift end. War's very object is victory, not prolonged indecision.

In war there can be no substitute for victory.

There are some who for varying reasons would appease Red [Communist] China. They are blind to history's clear lesson, for history teaches with unmistakable emphasis that appeasement but begets new and bloodier wars. It points to no single instance where this end has justified that means, where appeasement has led to more than a sham [phony] peace. Like blackmail, it lays the basis for new and successively greater demands until, as in blackmail, violence becomes the only other alternative....

I am closing my 52 years of military service. When I joined the Army, even before the turn of the century, it was the fulfillment of all of my boyish hopes and dreams. The world has turned over many times since I took the oath at West Point, and the hopes and dreams have all since vanished, but I still remember the refrain of one of the most popular barracks ballads of that day which proclaimed most proudly that old soldiers never die; they just fade away. And like the old soldier of that ballad, I now close my military career and just fade away, an old soldier who tried to do his duty as God gave him the light to see that duty.

Good Bye.

1960, John F. Kennedy was elected president. Containing communism continued to be a foreign policy goal for presidents.

Indochina

Another Cold War trouble spot was Indochina. France had controlled that area (present-day Vietnam, Laos, and Cambodia) from the middle of the nineteenth century until Japan captured it during World War II. After the war, France attempted to reclaim its former colony. Communists in Vietnam, the largest part of Indochina, used the anti-French sentiment of the people to organize a revolution. The Communist leader, **Ho Chi Minh** (HOE CHEE MIN), successfully conducted a guerrilla war against the French that climaxed in 1954 with the defeat of the French at the Battle of Dien Bien Phu.

In 1954, an international conference in Geneva, Switzerland, recognized that Laos and Cambodia were independent nations. It divided Vietnam between the Communist North and the non-Communist South. Ho Chi Minh imposed a totalitarian government in the North, and tens of thousands who opposed it were executed. In the South **Ngo Dinh Diem** (dee EM), who was strongly anti-Communist, became president. The South Vietnamese constitution gave Diem almost absolute power. With the establishment of a Communist government in the North, more than a million people moved to the South in the years 1954–56. There was a smaller movement in the opposite direction as some 130,000 supporters of communism moved to the North.

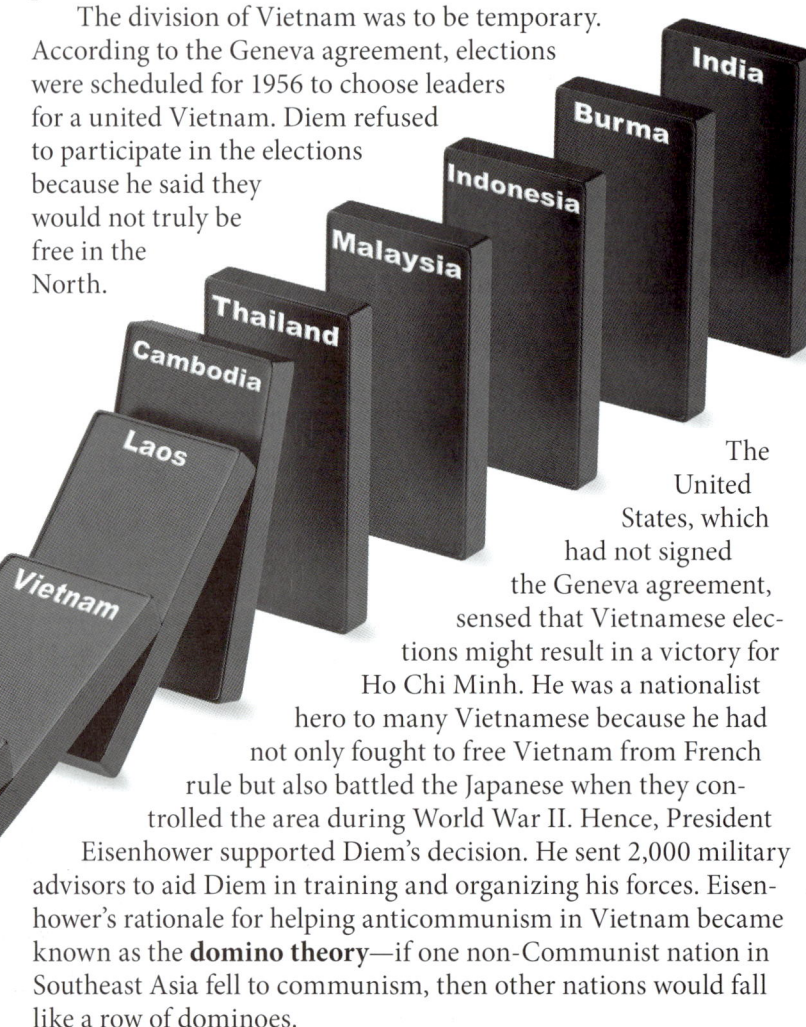

The division of Vietnam was to be temporary. According to the Geneva agreement, elections were scheduled for 1956 to choose leaders for a united Vietnam. Diem refused to participate in the elections because he said they would not truly be free in the North.

Ho Chi Minh

Eisenhower feared that if Communists continued to gain territory that all of Southeast Asia would fall under their control.

The United States, which had not signed the Geneva agreement, sensed that Vietnamese elections might result in a victory for Ho Chi Minh. He was a nationalist hero to many Vietnamese because he had not only fought to free Vietnam from French rule but also battled the Japanese when they controlled the area during World War II. Hence, President Eisenhower supported Diem's decision. He sent 2,000 military advisors to aid Diem in training and organizing his forces. Eisenhower's rationale for helping anticommunism in Vietnam became known as the **domino theory**—if one non-Communist nation in Southeast Asia fell to communism, then other nations would fall like a row of dominoes.

President Kennedy increased the number of American advisors in Vietnam to 16,000 by 1963, but the situation there was worsening. The Communists were determined to take over the South, and Diem's government became even more unpopular. Diem was a Roman Catholic in a predominately Buddhist nation, his government had grown increasingly corrupt, and many wanted him to implement land reforms. Several South Vietnamese generals plotted against Diem and in November 1963 launched a coup, or overthrow, of his government. He was executed shortly afterwards. However, the new government, though anti-Communist, was unstable. Meanwhile, the Communists increased their guerrilla warfare in the South. The stage was set for massive American military intervention in South Vietnam under Kennedy's successor, Lyndon Johnson. Vietnam soon replaced Korea as the Cold War's hottest conflict.

Cuba

In 1959, **Fidel Castro** overthrew Fulgencio Batista, the corrupt dictator on the island of Cuba. Many hoped that conditions within that nation would improve; instead, they soon worsened. Castro proved to be another harsh dictator. He refused to allow elections, imprisoned or executed opponents, and placed restrictions on the press. In addition, he confiscated foreign-owned property and signed a trade agreement with the Soviet Union. Instead of installing the democratic government that many Cubans had anticipated, he announced he was Communist and established a totalitarian government only ninety miles from Florida. President Eisenhower responded by restricting trade with Cuba, breaking diplomatic relations with the nation, and secretly authorizing the CIA to plan an attack to overthrow Castro.

The CIA project culminated during the Kennedy administration when some fourteen hundred Cuban exiles (Cubans who had fled the nation after Castro came to power) invaded their homeland. Assisted by the CIA, they landed at a place called the **Bay of Pigs** on April 17, 1961. The operation was a disaster. Some of the invading ships ran aground on coral reefs; Kennedy canceled the air force support for the attack; Castro had learned the "secret" attack was forthcoming and had begun preparing his troops for it; and an anticipated uprising against Castro never occurred. Within two days, almost all of the invaders were killed or captured. One American newspaper writer commented, "We looked like fools to our friends, rascals to our enemies, and incompetents to the rest." The incident was a great embarrassment for John Kennedy, who had been president for only three months.

An even more dramatic confrontation over Cuba occurred a little more than a year later. The Soviets, upset that America had supported a plan to overthrow Castro, began secretly installing missiles in Cuba that were capable of carrying nuclear warheads. Such missiles would be able to reach the United States within minutes. On October 22, 1962, after American spy planes confirmed that missile sites were under construction, President Kennedy described the situation to Americans in a televised speech. He demanded that the Soviets dismantle the sites immediately and then established a naval blockade around the island to prevent the arrival of any more missiles. Kennedy also stated that any missile attack from Cuba would result in

Cuban dictator Fidel Castro

More than a thousand anti-Castro Cubans were captured at the Bay of Pigs.

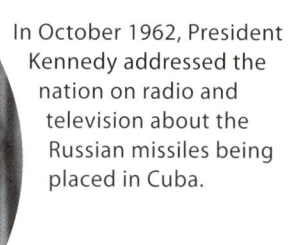

In October 1962, President Kennedy addressed the nation on radio and television about the Russian missiles being placed in Cuba.

the U.S. launching a full-scale nuclear attack on the Soviet Union.

Nikita Khrushchev, who was now the Soviet leader, denounced the blockade as illegal and said his ships would not stop for it. Both the U.S. and USSR placed their military forces on high alert. For several days, the world faced the possibility of nuclear war in what became known as the **Cuban missile crisis**.

After intense, secret negotiations, an agreement was reached. Khrushchev agreed to remove the missiles in exchange for Kennedy's public promise not to invade Cuba. In addition, the president privately pledged to remove American missiles from Turkey, near the Russian border. An extremely stressful week ended.

Berlin Wall

Joseph Stalin died in 1953. After a power struggle among the Communist party officials, Nikita Khrushchev emerged as the new Soviet leader. While visiting Britain in 1956, he seemed to indicate a softening of Stalin's aggressive and expansionist policies. Khrushchev said, "You don't like communism. We do not like capitalism. There is only one way out—**peaceful coexistence**." The idea of Communist and democratic nations existing side by side without constant conflict was a stark contrast to the past decade. The Berlin Airlift, the Korean War, the formation of NATO and the Warsaw Pact, and other incidents had produced enormous tensions. Unfortunately, the idea of peacefully coexisting was threatened on numerous occasions after Khrushchev made his comments. Even before the Cuban missile crisis, the Soviets and Americans again clashed over Berlin.

Just as Americans resented a Communist dictator controlling Cuba, Communists were embarrassed by the situation in West Berlin. That city was a "showcase of democracy" and a haven for refugees fleeing from East Germany. By 1961, almost three million East Germans had fled communism by crossing into West Berlin. That huge number, which represented more than 15 percent of East Germany's population, clearly showed that Communist boasts that they provided a better life for Germans were groundless. Most of those who departed East Germany were under age forty-five. Such a loss of workers dramatically weakened the nation's economy.

In 1961, just two months after the disaster at the Bay of Pigs, Khrushchev and Kennedy held a summit in Vienna, Austria. Evidently, Khrushchev viewed Kennedy as young and incompetent; the president was determined to prove otherwise.

Khrushchev wanted Britain, France, and the U.S. to withdraw their troops from West Berlin. Kennedy, fearing this would merely be the first step in a Communist takeover of the city, refused. The Soviet leader then threatened to restrict access to West Berlin, just as Stalin had done in 1948.

In August 1961, just two months after the Vienna meeting, the Communists began erecting the **Berlin Wall**. It prevented movement between the two parts of the city. Soon, the wall was topped with barbed wire and accompanied by guard towers and minefields. The wall solved the East German refugee problem but clearly demonstrated the failure of communism—an immense barrier had to be constructed to keep people from leaving.

Nikita Khrushchev (*left*) meeting with President Kennedy (*right*)

The Communists in East Berlin built the Berlin Wall in 1961.

This photo shows East Germans escaping into West Germany by hiding in a car.

Section Review

1. What was the last Eastern European nation to fall to Soviet domination after World War II?
2–3. Name the two countries whose resistance to communism caused Truman to announce the Truman Doctrine.
4. What action by the Allies led Stalin to blockade West Berlin?
5. In addition to calling for stronger conventional forces, what did Truman do in reaction to the Soviet development of the atomic bomb?
6. Why were the Soviets unable to veto the UN's decision to intervene in Korea?
7. What country became a Communist foothold in the Western Hemisphere by the early 1960s?
★ Read the last two sentences in the excerpt of Winston Churchill's speech on p. 527. Assess Churchill's viewpoint.
★ Who do you think was right in the disagreement between MacArthur and Truman? Why?

II. Domestic Reform

Each U.S. president during this period not only dealt with Cold War affairs but also pursued a policy of domestic reform. The "Fair Deal" (Truman), "Dynamic Conservatism" (Eisenhower), and the "New Frontier" (Kennedy) were the slogans that America's postwar presidents used to describe their policies.

In 1951 the Twenty-Second Amendment to the Constitution was adopted. It declared that no one could be elected president more than two times. Many supported it because they felt that Roosevelt had set a dangerous example by being elected to a third and fourth term. Previously, no president had been elected more than two times following George Washington's precedent.

Guiding Questions

1. What characterized the Truman administration?
2. What were the main aspects of the Eisenhower administration?
3. What were the highlights of the Kennedy administration?

Truman and the Fair Deal

Shortly after the war, President Truman sent Congress a list of proposals signaling that his domestic program would be an expansion of the New Deal. By 1949, he was calling his legislative goals the **Fair Deal**. Truman sought a government commitment to full employment (federal spending designed to ensure jobs for the unemployed), but conservative opposition killed it. Truman settled instead for the Employment Act of 1946, which created the Council of Economic Advisers to advise the president on the economy. That year Congress also created the Atomic Energy Commission, which gave control over atomic energy to civilian rather than military authorities.

Truman faced economic problems as well as foreign policy setbacks. There were also allegations that Communists held government positions. As a result, Truman's approval ratings sank, and Democrats lost public support. The wife of a leading Republican senator captured the mood when she quipped, "To err is Truman." "Had enough?" was an effective Republican slogan. In the 1946 elections, Republicans captured both houses of Congress for the first time since 1928. With control of Congress, Republicans pushed through the Taft-Hartley Act of 1947. This antiunion measure, passed over Truman's veto, permitted states to pass "right-to-work" laws banning the union shop, which required union membership as a condition for hiring. The act also required an eighty-day cooling-off period for strikes in businesses that the president thought were crucial to maintaining the health and safety of the nation. It also required union officials to swear that they were not Communists. In another matter of national security in 1949, Congress changed the American military establishment with the **National Security Act**. World War II, especially the Pearl Harbor disaster, had revealed the need for greater coordination among the armed forces. This act created the post of secretary of defense, a civilian cabinet position that supervised the army, navy, and air force. The position of secretary of war was eliminated. The National Security Council and CIA were also created to assist the president in foreign policy matters.

Election of 1948

When Truman faced the voters in the 1948 election, prospects for victory looked dim. The left wing of the Democratic Party was enraged over the president's firing of Secretary of Commerce **Henry A. Wallace** because of his criticism of Truman's policies. These extreme liberals bolted the party and supported Wallace, who had served as FDR's second vice president, on the Progressive ticket. (This was a far different Progressive Party from the one in 1912 that had nominated Theodore Roosevelt.) Conservative southern Democrats, upset over Truman's support of civil rights for black Americans, walked out of the Democratic National Convention and eventually nominated Governor **Strom Thurmond** of South Carolina on a States' Rights Party ticket, more commonly known as "**Dixiecrats**." Confident because of the disarray among Democrats, Republicans chose **Thomas Dewey**, the popular governor of New York, as their candidate.

Truman campaigned vigorously against the odds. He called the Republican-controlled Congress back into a special session. When it refused to act on several of his proposals, he dubbed it the "do-nothing" Congress and used it as a campaign issue. Truman targeted his appeals to labor union members and African Americans in the cities as well as to farmers in the Midwest and West in hopes of keeping the old New Deal coalition alive. On a 31,000-mile "whistle-stop" train tour, Truman continued his attacks on the Republicans. Many Americans went to bed on election night thinking that Dewey had won, but the ballot count the next morning revealed that Truman had beaten Dewey in one of the biggest upsets in the history of presidential elections. After his election, Congress passed many of the president's Fair Deal proposals, which basically updated the New Deal. Congress raised the minimum wage, extended Social Security coverage, and gave more aid to farmers. Congress, however, rejected civil rights bills, federal aid to education, and national health insurance. Like most presidents, Truman got only part of what he wanted from Congress.

Thomas E. Dewey was the Republican nominee for president in 1944 and 1948.

Displaying the *Chicago Daily Tribune*'s premature headline, an elated Harry Truman celebrates his upset victory over Thomas Dewey.

The Election of 1948

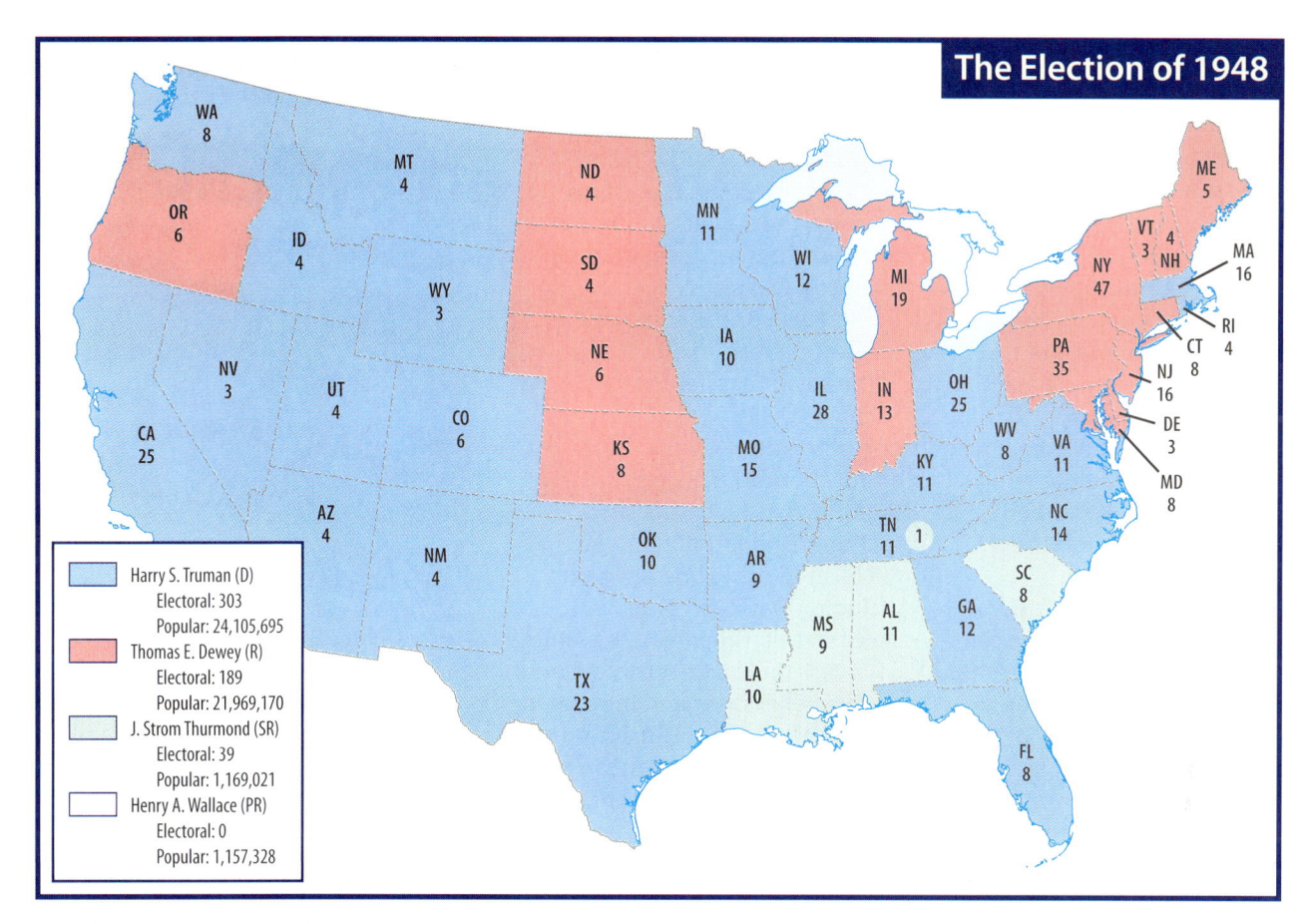

■ Harry S. Truman (D)	Electoral: 303 / Popular: 24,105,695
■ Thomas E. Dewey (R)	Electoral: 189 / Popular: 21,969,170
■ J. Strom Thurmond (SR)	Electoral: 39 / Popular: 1,169,021
☐ Henry A. Wallace (PR)	Electoral: 0 / Popular: 1,157,328

Anticommunism in America

One important domestic issue throughout the postwar era was a growing anti-Communist crusade in the United States. Just as a "Red Scare" (widespread fear of communism) followed World War I in the United States, so a second **Red Scare** followed World War II. Many Americans blamed Communist supporters in their own government for Soviet advances, and several events in the postwar era gave credibility to the charge. The most sensational case involved **Alger Hiss**, a former State Department official. In 1948, Whittaker Chambers, a former Communist, testified before Congress and accused Hiss of passing secret documents to him ten years earlier when Chambers was a Soviet spy. Hiss could not be tried for espionage since the statute of limitations had expired (meaning the actions had occurred too many years earlier). Hiss was convicted of perjury (or lying) because he denied the accusations under oath. The Hiss case also launched the political career of Congressman **Richard Nixon**, whose aggressive work eventually sent Hiss to jail. In addition to the charges against Hiss, the government in 1950 revealed the existence of a spy ring in America. Two members of that ring, Julius and Ethel Rosenberg, were convicted of passing atomic secrets to the Soviets during World War II. They were executed in 1953 for their treason.

The government reacted quickly to these threats. In 1947, President Truman instituted a loyalty program to check federal employees. The House Un-American Activities Committee (HUAC) in Congress conducted extensive investigations, such as those for the Hiss case and an in-depth study of Communist activity in the entertainment industry. Fearful of other Communist supporters within the government, Congress in 1950 passed, over Truman's

A Couple of Spies

No incident better illustrates the reality of the Communist threat to America during and after World War II than the theft of the secrets relating to the atomic bomb.

Julius Rosenberg had been reared in a Jewish home and had even considered becoming a rabbi. In college, however, Rosenberg turned to communism. He later married a Communist, Ethel Greenglass. A talented engineer, Rosenberg secured a civilian job with the U.S. Army during World War II.

Keeping his Communist ties secret, Rosenberg became the center of a Soviet spy ring. His recruits included David Greenglass, his brother-in-law, who worked at the top-secret atomic bomb research center in Los Alamos, New Mexico. In 1944 and 1945, Rosenberg, with his wife's knowledge and support, helped funnel classified information concerning the atomic bomb to the Soviets, helping to speed Russia's development of atomic weapons.

In 1950, British investigators uncovered a major figure in the spy ring, scientist Klaus Fuchs (FYOOKS), who had been one of the developers of the atomic bomb. Fuchs confessed that he was a spy. Using information gained from him, the FBI located other Soviet agents, including David Greenglass. To save himself, Greenglass became a witness for the government and turned in his sister and brother-in-law, Ethel and Julius Rosenberg.

The Rosenbergs were arrested, tried, and convicted of espionage (or spying). They were sentenced to death in the electric chair and were executed in 1953. Supporters insisted that the Rosenbergs were innocent. The facts, though, reveal that the Rosenbergs were guilty of one of the greatest acts of treason in American history—they had helped a totalitarian nation develop the most destructive weapon in history.

---

veto, the McCarran Internal Security Act. The act made it easier for the government to combat espionage. One provision of this act required Communists and their organizations to register with the Justice Department.

The man most closely associated with the Red Scare in the 1950s was Senator **Joseph McCarthy** of Wisconsin. In a 1951 speech in West Virginia, McCarthy declared boldly that the State Department had over two hundred Communists working there. He insisted he had a list of their names. A Senate committee investigated the charges and concluded that the charges were "a fraud and a hoax." McCarthy continued his attacks, however, and he headed a Senate subcommittee that looked into the presence of Communists in government. His political power was greatest during the Korean War, when no one dared attack him for fear of being suspected of holding Communist sympathies. Republicans encouraged McCarthy, some because they believed him but others simply because fighting Communists was a winning political issue.

Senator Joseph McCarthy points to a map during televised hearings on alleged Communist involvement in the U.S. Army. On the left sits an emotionally drained Boston attorney, Joseph Welch. Only shortly before, Welch—in response to McCarthy's reckless charge that a member of Welch's staff was a Communist—had demanded in anger, "Have you no sense of decency, sir, at long last?"

Despite his well-publicized investigations, the senator never found a single Communist in the government. (His failure was due in part to Truman's previous success in removing security risks from the government.) By the end of 1954, McCarthy's charges had become increasingly irresponsible, and his Senate colleagues passed a vote of censure, or formal disapproval, against McCarthy. His opponents coined a new word, "**McCarthyism**," to describe his alleged use of lies, distortion, and innuendo. What was often ignored in the outrage over McCarthy's methods was the reality of the Communist threat in America.

Eisenhower and "Dynamic Conservatism"

With his popularity at a low ebb, due mainly to the Korean War, Truman declined to run for reelection in 1952. Republicans, frustrated by their defeat in 1948, looked for victory with **Dwight Eisenhower**. He had served as Allied commander in Europe during World War II and later was the commander of NATO. The popular war hero balanced the Republican ticket by choosing thirty-nine-year-old Senator Richard Nixon, a conservative, as his vice-presidential running mate. The Democrats nominated the governor of Illinois, **Adlai Stevenson**, for president. Though an intellectual, Stevenson could not match the popularity and charm of Eisenhower, captured in the slogan "I like Ike." Eisenhower promised to end corruption in Washington and the war in Korea. Elected in a landslide, Eisenhower was the first Republican president since Herbert Hoover. The new president described his philosophy as "**Dynamic Conservatism**," calling himself "conservative when it comes to money and liberal when it comes to human beings." In 1954, his new budget cut expenditures by nearly 10 percent. Eisenhower abolished the Reconstruction Finance Corporation, a holdover from the Depression, and reduced farm price subsidies. Furthermore, the presence of businessmen in the cabinet gave the administration a strong conservative image. Because several cabinet members were from the auto industry, Adlai Stevenson quipped that the New Dealers had been replaced by the "car dealers."

Like the Truman administration, however, Eisenhower expanded government programs in many ways, much to the frustration of many conservatives. Congress broadened Social Security to cover professionals, domestics, farm workers, armed services personnel, and other groups that had previously been excluded. In 1955, Congress increased the minimum wage from 75¢ to $1 an hour. The federal bureaucracy grew as the government created a new cabinet department in 1953—Health, Education, and Welfare (renamed Health and Human Services in 1979)—to coordinate federal social programs. Eisenhower supported the National Defense Education Act, which provided large sums of federal money for education.

Eisenhower proved to be very popular with Americans. He and Vice President Nixon were easily reelected in 1956. In that election the Democratic candidate, Adlai Stevenson, was defeated for a second time. One of Eisenhower's most enduring projects was a new federal highway act that committed the national government to pay for 90 percent of an extensive **interstate highway system**. These limited-access "interstates," as they are commonly known, have become the main arteries of highway transportation in the United States.

Kennedy and the New Frontier

In the election of 1960, two World War II veterans competed for the leadership of a new generation of Americans. **John F. Kennedy**—youthful, handsome, and witty—skillfully promoted himself as an author and war hero. He had served fourteen years in the House of Representatives and Senate. Kennedy won a close

Conservatives

Many people were politically conservative during this period after World War II, and the reasons for embracing conservative ideas varied. One group of conservatives focused their attention on the threat of communism at home and abroad. Another group was more concerned about economic issues; their highest priority was limiting the government's role in the economy. Yet another group consisted of traditional conservatives. They emphasized the need for strong moral principles and believed that society would only prosper if these ideas were followed. While many American conservatives identified with all three of these elements, others emphasized one aspect in particular. Sometimes there was tension between the groups. Nevertheless, conservatives in this era worked together toward common goals.

The ticket of Eisenhower and Nixon brought the Republicans two presidential election victories in the 1950s.

Construction of the interstate highway was one of the major accomplishments of the Eisenhower presidency.

The Election of 1960

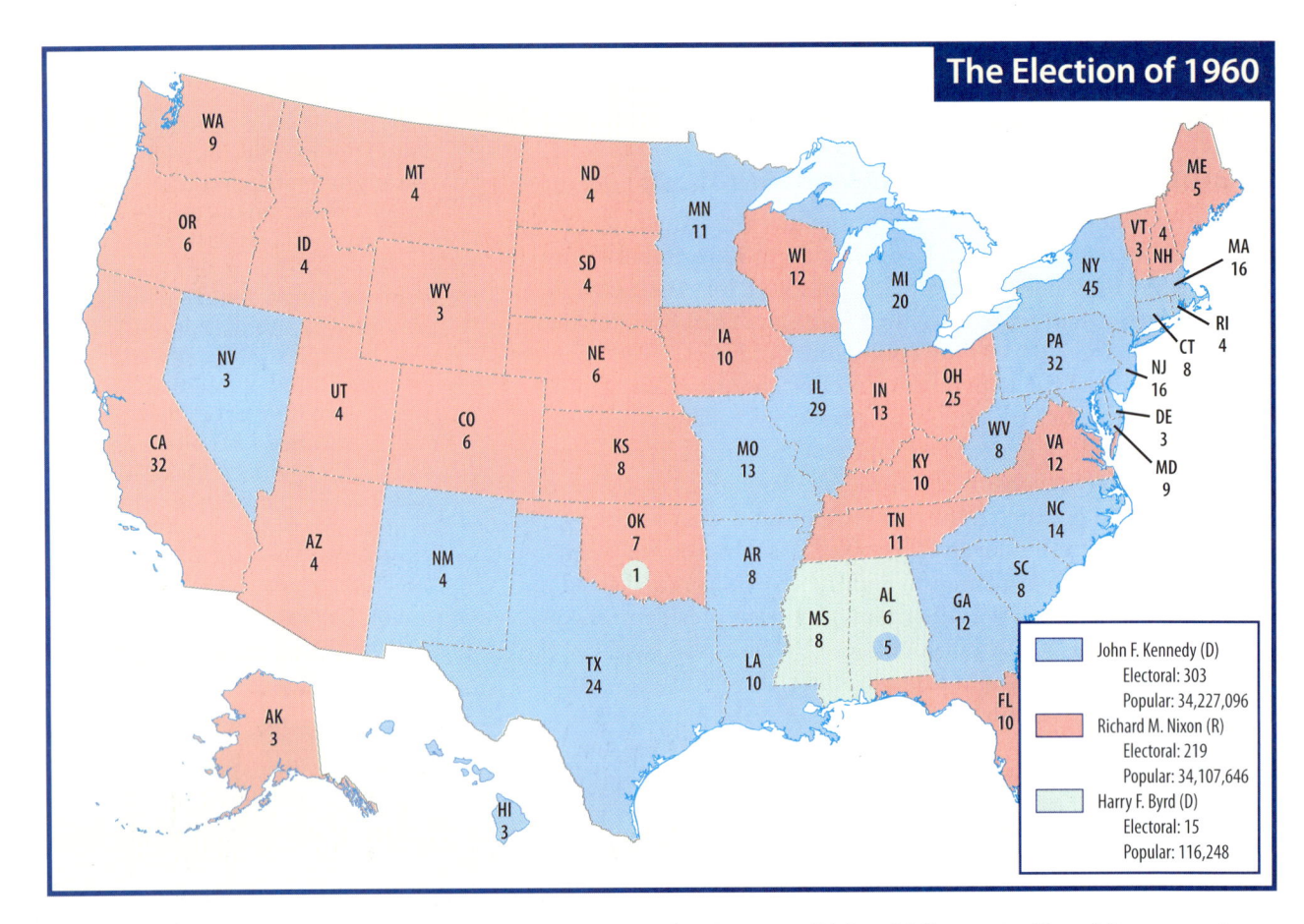

	John F. Kennedy (D)	Richard M. Nixon (R)	Harry F. Byrd (D)
Electoral	303	219	15
Popular	34,227,096	34,107,646	116,248

Richard Nixon (*left*) and John Kennedy (*right*) participated in the first televised debates between presidential candidates.

election over Richard Nixon, the Republican nominee. Nixon had served six years in the House of Representatives and Senate and eight years as Eisenhower's vice president. Kennedy impressed the voters with a vigorous campaign. He also used television as a new political tool. Poised and charismatic, Kennedy outshined Nixon—at least in image—in four televised presidential debates. At age forty-three, Kennedy was the youngest person ever elected president. He became the first Catholic to serve as president.

Because of his youth and vigor, Kennedy seemed to embody a dramatic change in government. People admired the handsome, articulate Kennedy; his lovely young wife, Jacqueline, became a model and trendsetter for women's fashion. The sight of the young president romping with his children in the White House presented a pleasing picture to most Americans. Kennedy himself proclaimed a change in emphasis. In his inaugural speech the president said,

> Let the word go forth from this time and place, to friend and foe alike, that the torch has been passed to a new generation of Americans—born in this century, tempered by war, disciplined by a hard and bitter peace, proud of our ancient heritage—and unwilling to witness or permit the slow undoing of those human rights to which this nation has always been committed, and to which we are committed today at home and around the world.

Kennedy appealed to American patriotism, as demonstrated by the famous line from his inaugural address: "And so, my fellow Americans: ask not what your country can do for you—ask what you can do for your country." He gave his legislative program the inspiring name the **New Frontier**. One of Kennedy's most popular programs, the **Peace Corps** was a government project designed to send skilled volunteers overseas to help underdeveloped nations. To deal with the threat of a Communist economic foothold in Latin America, Kennedy initiated the Alliance for Progress in 1961. Through it, the United States granted economic aid in the hope of strengthening economic cooperation between North and South America. The program aimed at increasing the income of Latin Americans, decreasing illiteracy, establishing democratic governments, and avoiding extremes of inflation and deflation. Although some of the economic goals were reached in some countries, politically the Alliance failed to achieve many goals. For example, during the 1960s, about a dozen governments became dictatorships.

Critics said Kennedy's administration differed from previous ones more in style than in substance. Entering office in 1961, Kennedy faced one of the worst recessions in the postwar period. The government sharply increased its spending to stimulate the economy; Congress expanded public works, appropriated almost $5 billion for housing, gave financial aid to distressed areas, increased Social Security benefits, and raised the minimum wage. Yet some of Kennedy's agenda reflected a more conservative approach. Business owners endorsed his 1962 Trade Expansion Act, which stimulated trade with several European nations. The Telstar satellite system aided the communications industry. Kennedy's challenge to put a man on the moon by the end of the decade expanded the space program and was a boon to aerospace companies. In 1962, the Revenue Act gave $1 billion in tax credits to business. Later that year, Kennedy proposed a drastic tax cut in an address that a liberal economist called "the most Republican speech since William McKinley." Congress enacted it a few months after Kennedy's death.

Liberals criticized Kennedy not only for pro-business policies but also for a lack of leadership in federal aid to education, medical care for the elderly, and civil rights. Kennedy's defenders argued that his narrow victory over Nixon dictated caution in the White House. Following Kennedy's assassination in Dallas, Texas, in November 1963, Lyndon Johnson became president.

President Kennedy claps as his daughter, Caroline, and son, John Jr., play in the Oval Office.

Jackie Kennedy, the First Lady

Section Review

1. What is a "right-to-work" law?
2–5. Name the four major candidates and their parties in the 1948 presidential election.
6–8. Give three examples of how Eisenhower expanded federal programs.
9. What new political tool was important in helping Kennedy defeat Nixon in 1960?
★ Why was Truman's victory in the 1948 election so surprising?
★ Read the feature box entitled "A Couple of Spies." Why do you think the Rosenberg case attracted so much attention?

Guiding Questions

1. What were some of the long-term changes in American society after World War II?
2. How did the typical American family change after World War II?
3. How did the civil rights movement affect postwar America?
4. How did religion influence postwar America?

JACK ROOSEVELT "JACKIE" ROBINSON
Brooklyn Dodgers—2nd Base
Major League Statistics
10 years (1947–56)

Games	Avg.	AB	R	H	2B	3B	HR	RBI
1,382	.311	4,877	947	1,518	273	54	137	734

SB	BB	SO	HBP	BA	OBP	SLG
197	740	291	72	.311	.409	.474

Born: January 31, 1919, Cairo, Georgia
Died: October 24, 1972, Stamford, Connecticut

III. Life in Postwar America

An Affluent Society

After World War II, many Americans feared another economic decline because the war demand, which had stimulated the economy, had ended. However, the postwar era brought unprecedented economic prosperity. The biggest reason for the economic improvement was defense spending, a necessary expense given the challenges of the Cold War. With Europe and Japan devastated by the war, America had little competition as a major supplier of industrial goods to the world. With newer industries (such as aerospace, electronics, and chemicals) and technological improvement in automation, industry output jumped dramatically. Also, many American consum-

Televisions were an important household item in the 1950s.

Jackie Robinson

Professional sports, like most areas of American life before the 1950s, were racially segregated. Baseball, one of America's national pastimes, was no exception. The best white players joined the major league teams of the National and American Leagues. Black players participated in leagues composed of all-black teams. But a brave and talented ballplayer, Jackie Robinson, broke that color barrier.

Robinson was born in Georgia but moved with his family to California while still a child. A gifted athlete, Robinson earned a scholarship to UCLA, where he starred in football, basketball, track, and baseball. After serving in the army during World War II, Robinson joined the Kansas City Monarchs, a team in one of the black leagues. There he came to the attention of Branch Rickey, president of the Brooklyn Dodgers.

Rickey was determined to integrate the major leagues. But the first player to do so would have to be special. He not only had to be talented but also had to have the strength of character to withstand intense public scrutiny and even open bigotry. Rickey observed Robinson and became convinced that Robinson met the requirements to become baseball's black pioneer.

Robinson joined the Dodgers in 1947 as their second baseman. Rickey had not overestimated the challenge Robinson faced. From his first time at bat, he heard racial slurs and insults from not only hecklers in the crowd but also opposing players. Some players tried to start fights with him or, when sliding into second, purposely tried to injure him with the spikes on their shoes. In many cities, Robinson had to stay in a separate hotel from his white teammates.

Aware that the nation's eyes were on him, Robinson curbed both his natural competitiveness and his resentment of the treatment he received. He knew that—fairly or not—many Americans would judge black Americans by his behavior. For Robinson, Branch Rickey later wrote, "there could be but one direction of dedication—the doctrine of turning the other cheek. There came in the greatness of Jackie Robinson."

In his first season, Robinson won Rookie of the Year. In 1949, his .342 batting average and 37 stolen bases helped him win the league's Most Valuable Player Award. In Robinson's ten seasons with Brooklyn, the Dodgers won six pennants and one World Series. After his retirement, he was elected to baseball's Hall of Fame. In 1997, as a permanent acknowledgement of Robinson's achievements, Major League Baseball retired his uniform number, 42, across all major league teams.

ers, after sacrificing and saving during the war, went on an unrestrained buying spree. They bought automobiles, homes, washing machines, televisions, refrigerators, and numerous other items for their new homes. The number of homeowners in the United States increased significantly between 1945 and 1960. People were making money and spending it to improve their standard of living. By the mid-1950s the number of Americans in the middle class was about twice as many as before World War II. Never before had Americans been so well off.

The economic growth altered American culture as well. With extra money earned, Americans turned their attention to consuming, buying the latest goods in the marketplace. Businesses carefully orchestrated the "consumer culture." Borrowing from the 1920s, advertisers taught the public to forget the problems of the Depression and war years and to spend. Manufacturers continually offered different models and styles so that earlier models were outdated or out of style. Such "planned obsolescence," or purposely making items obsolete quickly, fueled the urge to buy. Marketing specialists appealed to self-gratification, social status, and materialism. With televisions in 90 percent of American homes by 1960, almost no one was immune to such appeals.

In 1950, Diners Club released the first credit card, and by 1965 more than a million people had one. Other cards, such as American Express, soon equaled the success of Diners Club. Consumers, less thrifty and less concerned about debt, readily used their credit cards when they did not have the money. Retail activity in the postwar period shifted from the downtown to the suburban malls, and the number of malls mushroomed from eight in 1945 to almost four thousand by 1960. Shopping—drudgery for previous generations—became a leisure activity for millions.

Young people also became avid consumers. When rock music exploded on the scene in the 1950s, businessmen capitalized on the craze by marketing transistor radios, phonographs, and records. The pop culture also included magazines and movies that featured all of the teen idols. Many, such as actor James Dean and singer Elvis Presley, came to symbolize rebellion against traditional values.

Family

Baby Boom

Postwar America witnessed enormous changes in the family. Young adults had postponed marriage and children during the war; after 1945, they married and started families. Americans had one of the highest marriage rates in the world for the period 1944 to 1948. Most of the fifteen million returning soldiers became new fathers, contributing to the **baby boom**, a massive rise in the birth rate lasting until 1964. Between 1945 and 1960, America's population increased by almost 30 percent. With the prosperity of the 1940s and 1950s, more couples were having more children.

Television, which replaced movies as the major source of entertainment, celebrated the American middle-class family. The

This 1950s kitchen is filled with modern appliances.

Danny Kaye, a well-known actor, is holding a Diners Club credit card.

Automobile ads like this appealed to Americans' desires for new things, stylish cars, and travel for leisure.

Andersons of *Father Knows Best,* the Cleavers of *Leave It to Beaver,* and the Nelsons of *Ozzie and Harriet* were models of the ideal family, presided over by a patient and dutiful father who had all the answers. Jackie Gleason's *The Honeymooners* carried the theme of a bickering but devoted working-class husband and wife. Lucille Ball's *I Love Lucy* program gave a comic dimension to family life.

However, many argued that television, magazines, and music were often negative influences in society. Rather than challenging Americans intellectually, they usually focused on entertaining.

The American family faced some serious threats in the post–World War II era. Divorce rates climbed in 1946, leveled off for several years, and then increased substantially in the 1970s. The 1950s also produced national concern over juvenile delinquency. Some people blamed television, movies, and crime comic books; others cited the breakdown of discipline in the home and the school. Dr. Benjamin Spock's book *Baby and Child Care* might have contributed to underlying permissiveness, according to his conservative critics, by advocating less structured methods of child-rearing. Spock, popularizing theories of psychologist Sigmund Freud and philosopher John Dewey, wanted children to become well-adjusted, guilt-free adults. His child-care book sold twenty-three million copies between 1946 and 1976. Only the Bible outsold it during that same period.

Women at Work

The role of women changed after World War II. According to the popular ideal, women married, had children, and reigned over the middle-class suburban household as "queens of domesticity." Mothers, wives, and family managers, they juggled numerous tasks—ranging from cooking, gardening, and club meetings to Little League and piano lessons—all with a self-sacrificing spirit. The family was still important to society in the 1950s, and being a housewife was considered a rewarding career for a woman.

Much in the postwar society, however, contradicted the image of the ideal housewife. More women than ever worked outside the home. Government policy had encouraged it during the war because of the shortage of workers in the defense industries. When "Rosie the Riveter" came marching home, she was accustomed to the income and independence and often continued to work, not just in traditional female jobs but in male ones as well. By the 1970s, a large percentage of married women were in the work force. The increase in divorce posed another issue—the number of single-parent heads of household rose dramatically, an unfortunate trend for American families.

Emergence of Minority Rights

The push for equal treatment for all people gained momentum after World War II with the rise of the **civil rights movement**. A *civil right* is a basic right that is granted because of one's citizenship and that the government is responsible for actively protecting from both government and individual interference. Discrimination occurs when the civil rights of an individual are denied or lessened because of their membership in a particular group or class. In modern American history, the phrase *civil rights movement* refers primarily to attempts by black Americans to secure the exercise and protection of their basic civil rights as citizens.

The Cleaver family from the '50s television show *Leave It to Beaver*

The cast of the *I Love Lucy* television show

Truman was the first twentieth-century president to give considerable attention to civil rights for African Americans. He stated, "No citizen of this great country ought to be discriminated against because of his race, religion, or national origin. This is the essence of the American idea, and the American Constitution." He appointed black judges and territorial governors and ordered the end of discrimination in the armed forces.

The first great victory of the modern civil rights movement was the Supreme Court decision **Brown v. Board of Education of Topeka, Kansas** (1954). In Topeka, a young African American girl named Linda Brown was not allowed to attend the all-white school in her neighborhood. Instead, she was assigned to attend an all-black school across town. With the help of the NAACP, her parents and the parents of other black students sued the Topeka school board. Citing sociological evidence, the court concluded that segregated public schools treated black students as inferior and that such institutions had no place in American society. *Brown* overturned an earlier court ruling, *Plessy v. Ferguson* (1896), which approved the doctrine of "separate but equal" schools. In the 1954 case, the Supreme Court unanimously declared that "separate educational facilities were inherently unequal" and then ordered an end to segregated schools.

Compliance came slowly, however, because some states resisted. A dramatic incident occurred in 1957 in Little Rock, Arkansas. Governor Orval Faubus used the Arkansas National Guard to block nine black students from entering Central High School, an all-white school with 2,000 students. Later, a court ordered him to withdraw the troops. Afterwards, violence occurred when the black students tried to attend. President Eisenhower sent more than 1,000 soldiers, from a paratrooper division, to protect the black students; to keep order in the school; and to enforce obedience to the *Brown* decision.

In late 1955, the civil rights struggle had gained national attention with the **Montgomery bus boycott**. At that time, black passengers were required to sit in the back of all city buses in Montgomery, Alabama, and had to give their seats to white customers and stand if the buses

Soldiers escort African American students at Central High School in Little Rock, Arkansas.

Governor Orval Faubus, of Arkansas, angrily displays a newspaper detailing the army's involvement in desegregating Central High School.

became crowded. On December 1, 1955, a black seamstress named **Rosa Parks** refused to relinquish her seat to a white male. She was arrested and fined for disobeying the bus driver's order to stand. Her small act of defiance energized the black community of Montgomery. The city's black citizens joined a boycott of the city's bus system which continued for 381 days. The boycott financially devastated the Montgomery city bus system. But the fight did not end until a Supreme Court decision forbade discrimination in public transportation in December 1956.

During the boycott, a popular and charismatic figure in the civil rights movement emerged. He was the Baptist pastor **Martin Luther King Jr.**, and he became the leader of the fight against Montgomery's bus system. King was convinced that black churches could become the vehicles of such reform in the United States, and the Montgomery effort seemed to confirm his ideas.

In 1957, King and his associates organized the Southern Christian Leadership Conference (SCLC). King and the SCLC encouraged nonviolent marches and protests against laws that violated the rights of African Americans. King had long been an admirer of the ideas of Mohandas Gandhi, who had used nonviolence, including civil disobedience (peaceful refusal to obey unjust laws), effectively in India during the 1930s and 1940s.

King's appeal was not limited to the black population; many middle-class white citizens also found his oratory compelling. He was a pastor and employed biblical terminology and the cadence of a preacher. They also liked his efforts to achieve equal rights without resorting to violence when many activists were calling for the use of any necessary means, including bloodshed.

The early 1960s brought even greater exposure to the civil rights movement. Black young people staged "sit-ins" at restaurants and lunch counters in 1960 in several southern states to focus more attention on social equality for minorities. Testing the effect of Supreme Court decisions prohibiting discrimination in interstate transportation, black and white "freedom riders" traveled in buses across the Deep South in 1961 to challenge segregated buses and terminals. In 1962, James Meredith enrolled as the first black student at the University of Mississippi after federal marshals and troops overcame a defiant governor and mob. Television also became an ally of the civil rights movement. As news cameras showed police dogs, tear gas, and fire hoses being used against protesters, many middle-class Americans began to realize the need to protect the rights of black Americans.

In August 1963, more than two hundred thousand people—both black and white—gathered in the nation's capital for a huge civil rights protest known as the **March on Washington**. The highlight for the protestors was Martin Luther King's speech in front of the Lincoln Memorial. King said,

> I have a dream that one day this nation will rise up and live out the true meaning of its creed, "We hold these truths to be self-evident, that all men are created equal." I have a dream that one day on the red hills of Georgia, sons of former slaves and the sons of former slave owners will be able to sit down together at the table of brotherhood.... I have a dream that my four little children will one day live in a nation where they will not be judged by the color of their skin, but by the content of their character.

Rosa Parks refused to give her seat to a white passenger on the Montgomery bus she was riding.

Rosa Parks being fingerprinted after her arrest

Montgomery Bus Boycott

A few days after Rosa Parks's arrest, Martin Luther King spoke to a crowd of more than five thousand African Americans who had gathered to hear more about the bus boycott. He said,

> There comes a time when people get tired of being trampled over by the iron feet of oppression....
>
> We are here ... because we're tired.... We are not here advocating violence.... We are Christian people.... The only weapon that we have ... is the weapon of protest....
>
> We're going to work ... to gain justice on the buses in this city....
>
> We are not wrong in what we are doing. If we are wrong, the Supreme Court ... is wrong.... If we are wrong, God Almighty is wrong.... If we are wrong, justice is a lie.

Martin Luther King Jr. addressing the crowd at the March on Washington in 1963. His "I Have a Dream" speech, delivered that day, became famous throughout the world.

Two months before the March on Washington, President Kennedy had presented a historic civil rights bill to Congress. The march focused more attention on the issue. The legislation was not passed, however, until the following year. By that time, President Kennedy had been assassinated.

Religion

Americans displayed a renewed interest in religion after World War II. Membership in religious groups rose significantly. In 1953, President Eisenhower joined a church for the first time in his public life. He promoted religion with comments such as "In other words, our form of government has no sense unless it is founded in a deeply felt religious faith, and I don't care what it is. With us of course it is the Judeo-Christian concept, but it must be a religion that all men are created equal." Congress, in 1954, added "under God" to the pledge of allegiance. The following year, President Eisenhower signed a law mandating that the phrase "In God We Trust" be printed on all paper currency. It had first appeared on coins during the Civil War. In 1956, the president signed a bill making the statement the national motto. However, these actions were not necessarily a sign that Americans were embracing orthodox Christian beliefs. This was the Cold War period, and the nation was engaged in a bitter struggle with communism, which identified itself with atheism. Some actions were motivated by a desire to contrast American religious values with those of our enemy.

The ecumenical movement also became popular during the postwar period. It promoted universal, or ecumenical, Christian unity. The goal was to develop understanding and cooperation among Christian churches. For many supporters of this idea, the long-range objective was to unite Christian denominations into a single church. Though that did not occur, some denominations with similar backgrounds united. American Methodists, for example, had healed their 1844 North-South split in 1939, and in 1968 they merged with the Evangelical United Brethren to form

Martin Luther King Jr. and his wife, Coretta Scott King

President Eisenhower signed legislation that added "In God We Trust" to all paper currency.

the United Methodist Church. Work toward greater cooperation was also facilitated by organizations like the National Council of Churches and the World Council of Churches. These groups—which included representatives from various denominations—met, dialogued, and often sought to reach agreement on debated issues. Unfortunately, these two groups embraced liberal theology rather than traditional Christian beliefs.

Conservative Christian groups also grew in the 1940s and 1950s. Known as fundamentalists or evangelicals, these Protestants expanded through large local churches and other ministries. Charles E. Fuller preached to millions on his popular *Old Fashioned Revival Hour* radio program. Youth rallies during the war led to the creation in 1944 of a large evangelistic outreach called Youth for Christ. **Billy Graham** was the first full-time evangelist of Youth for Christ and, in his own ministry, soon received national attention during his 1949 Los Angeles crusade. Graham became the world's most prominent evangelical. He preached to millions in crusades that were conducted and televised around the world.

Billy Graham

Section Review

1. During the postwar era, what replaced the downtown area in most cities as the center of retail business activity?
2. What replaced movies as the major source of entertainment?
3. Technically, what is a "civil right"?
4. What action sparked the Montgomery bus boycott?
5. Who emerged as the leader of the Montgomery bus boycott?

★ Reread the excerpt from the speech Martin Luther King delivered at the time of the Montgomery bus boycott in December 1955. It is in the margin box on page 548. Summarize what is stated there.

★ Reread the excerpt from the speech Martin Luther King delivered at the time of the March on Washington in August 1963. Consider the location, the event, and the words of the speech and then give some reasons you believe this speech has become so famous.

CHAPTER REVIEW

Making Connections

1–2. What are the two major agencies of the United Nations?

3–5. Name three nations that were split into Communist and non-Communist divisions after World War II.

6. Which of the two Chinese governments did the United States recognize as the "real" China from 1949 to the 1970s?

7. What event caused MacArthur to say that the Korean conflict had become "an entirely new war"?

8. What did the Communists do to stop the escape of refugees to West Berlin?

9. Under which president was the interstate highway system begun?

Developing History Skills

1. How does the career of Joseph McCarthy illustrate the danger of pursuing a worthy cause in an unworthy manner?

2. What lessons can one learn from the history of the Berlin Wall?

Thinking Critically

1. Was the Korean War a success or a failure for the United States? Why?

2. Review the map of the presidential election of 1960 (on p. 542) and offer some reasons why the states in certain sections of the nation voted for Kennedy rather than Nixon.

Living as a Christian Citizen

1. During the postwar era, some Christians were reluctant to support the civil rights movement, in part, because it was supported by theological and political liberals. Evaluate this stance from Scripture (see Gen. 1:26–27; Prov. 31:4–5, 8–9; Phil. 2:3–4).

2. How should a Christian view the rise of consumerism (see Gen. 1:28; Prov. 15:16–17; 16:19; 31:18, 24; Rom. 13:8; I Tim. 6:6–10)?

People, Places, and Things to Remember

Harry Truman
Central Intelligence Agency (CIA)
Nuremberg Trials
United Nations
General Assembly
Security Council
Cold War
iron curtain
Third World
containment
Truman Doctrine
Marshall Plan
North Atlantic Treaty Organization (NATO)
Warsaw Pact
Berlin airlift
Chiang Kai-shek
Mao Zedong
38th parallel
Douglas MacArthur
Inchon
limited war
Ho Chi Minh
Ngo Dinh Diem
domino theory
Fidel Castro
Bay of Pigs
Nikita Khrushchev
Cuban missile crisis
peaceful coexistence
Berlin Wall
Fair Deal
National Security Act
Henry A. Wallace
Strom Thurmond
Dixiecrats
Thomas Dewey
Red Scare
Alger Hiss
Richard Nixon
Joseph McCarthy
McCarthyism
Dwight Eisenhower
Adlai Stevenson
Dynamic Conservatism
interstate highway system
John F. Kennedy
New Frontier
Peace Corps
baby boom
civil rights movement
Brown v. Board of Education of Topeka, Kansas
Montgomery bus boycott
Rosa Parks
Martin Luther King Jr.
March on Washington
Billy Graham

24

THE SHATTERED SOCIETY (1963–1973)

> The Great Society has become the sick society.
>
> **Democratic Senator William Fulbright**
> 1968

The Vietnam War was the defining event of the presidencies of both Johnson and Nixon.

Big Ideas

1. What characterized the Johnson administration?
2. Why did the United States see a rise in radicalism during this period?
3. What was the significance of the year 1968 for the United States?
4. What important events occurred during the first term of President Nixon?

I. Johnson and the Great Society

II. Upheaval

III. 1968

IV. Nixon and the Silent Majority

On the afternoon of November 22, 1963, millions of Americans were watching the afternoon soap operas when, suddenly, an announcer interrupted with a shocking news bulletin: "In Dallas, Texas, three shots were fired at President Kennedy's motorcade in downtown Dallas. The first reports say that President Kennedy has been seriously wounded by the shooting." Soon came the horrifying news—President Kennedy was dead. Only two days later, Kennedy's alleged assassin, Lee Harvey Oswald, was gunned down by a Dallas nightclub owner in front of seventy policemen and a national television audience.

Over the next ten years, Americans endured a series of similar news bulletins flashing over their TVs and radios. Civil rights leader Martin Luther King Jr. was slain on the balcony of a motel in Memphis by a sniper's bullet. Senator Robert Kennedy was assassinated in a California hotel during his presidential campaign. Democratic presidential hopeful Governor George Wallace of Alabama was shot and paralyzed in a mall parking lot in Maryland.

These acts of violence were but the individual highlights in a decade of massive civil unrest. The nation witnessed urban riots punctuated by looting and killing, student protests often climaxing in bloody clashes between protesters and police, and, above all, scenes of the frustrating carnage of the seemingly endless war in Vietnam. The war in Southeast Asia might have been far away in miles, but every night television brought it into the living rooms of America.

In the midst of apparent chaos, many Americans looked to their political leaders for guidance—and deliverance. The presidents during the era were two of the shrewdest, most experienced politicians in America—Democrat Lyndon B. Johnson and Republican Richard M. Nixon. Yet both men found that America's problems defied their best efforts to solve them. Johnson's presidency was wrecked by his inability to deal with violence at home and the quagmire of American involvement in Vietnam. Nixon finally ended the war, and domestic violence at last subsided, but serious divisions remained. From 1963 to 1973, the United States was shattered by hatred and conflict. More than a few people wondered whether the social fabric could stand the strain.

Headed for Collapse

"We just seem to be headed toward a collapse of everything."

—A California newspaper editor reviewing the unrest in the United States during the 1960s

I. Johnson and the Great Society

Although he lacked Kennedy's charisma, **Lyndon Johnson** of Texas was well prepared for political leadership. He was one of the country's most experienced, energetic, and crafty politicians. He had spent twelve years in the Senate, including five years as majority leader. Few other presidents have known how to work as well with Congress as Johnson did. He also came to the presidency with a clear vision of what he thought the United States must accomplish. Johnson believed that the government had the power and resources to eliminate poverty and inequality, to create a "**Great Society**" in which government would help all citizens gain the opportunity to better themselves politically, socially, and economically.

Building the Great Society

Civil Rights

Ethnic tensions over unequal treatment had been increasing since the late nineteenth century. During the 1960s, more and more

Guiding Questions

1. How did President Johnson's administration differ from those of previous twentieth-century presidents?
2. How did the United States become more deeply involved in Vietnam?
3. What was the impact of military action in Vietnam on Johnson's popularity?

> **The Civil Rights Act of 1964**
> This act established fairer procedures for voter registration, forbade racial discrimination in public buildings such as restaurants and stores, promoted the desegregation of public schools, authorized withholding federal funds from projects or institutions that discriminated against minorities, and created the Equal Opportunity Commission to ensure that job seekers did not encounter discrimination.

An assembly of politicians and civil rights leaders, including Martin Luther King Jr., watches as Lyndon Johnson signs the Civil Rights Act of 1964.

> **Spur for Passage of the Voting Rights Act**
> President Johnson used the murder of three voting rights advocates in Selma, Alabama, to spur Congress to approve the Voting Rights Act.

> **Inconvenient Reality**
> In 1965, Daniel Moynihan produced a report on poverty in the black community. While noting that opposition to black civil rights had damaged the black family, his report also confirmed that intact families are vital to bringing people out of poverty. The second conclusion met with strong resistance from the far left. Critics argued that the report was judging poor black people for having a different family structure. As a result, the War on Poverty did not include efforts to sustain the intact family.

Americans supported the legitimate demand for equal rights for all. Black Americans often led the way, and a growing number of white Americans stood with them in their effort to secure rights that included improved educational opportunities for their children and the right to vote.

Opponents of the civil rights movement often used violence against nonviolent protestors. Early protest marches and demonstrations sometimes ended with assaults on the demonstrators by mobs of angry whites or even by policemen using tear gas and police dogs. In 1964 in Mississippi, members of the Ku Klux Klan brutally murdered three civil rights workers who were trying to help black Americans register to vote. Likewise, during a voting rights protest in Selma, Alabama, three white civil rights advocates died in separate incidents at the hands of Klansmen and other extremists.

Soon after becoming president, Johnson pressed for legislation to guarantee the rights of black Americans. He ensured passage by dedicating civil rights legislation to recently slain President Kennedy. Congress responded by passing the **Civil Rights Act of 1964**.

Following the murders in Selma, Johnson motivated Congress to pass the **Voting Rights Act of 1965**, which sent federal officials into states to help register blacks to vote and outlawed literacy tests for voters. Such tests were often administered only to African Americans to prevent their voting. This measure augmented the provisions of the **Twenty-fourth Amendment**, ratified in January 1964, which outlawed the use of poll taxes, similarly used to prevent black suffrage. The intent of both the amendment and the Voting Rights Act was to help black Americans acquire more nearly equal treatment by giving them a greater political voice.

War on Poverty

In his first State of the Union message, Johnson also declared a "**War on Poverty**." Through the newly formed Office of Economic Opportunity (OEO), the government attacked poverty through job-training and job-placement programs; Head Start (a preschool program for children in poor families); and Volunteers in Service to America (VISTA), a sort of domestic Peace Corps in which thousands of enthusiastic young people volunteered to work in government programs helping the poor. The programs of the War on Poverty did succeed in raising thousands of people above the poverty level (although the general economic prosperity of the Johnson years might have had much to do with that success).

1964 Election

A factor that further helped Johnson push his program through Congress was his landslide victory in the 1964 presidential election. Even before Kennedy's assassination, many political observers had predicted a Democratic victory in 1964. The shock of the president's death made Americans even less likely to change leaders again in under a year. Johnson was further helped by the Republican nomination of Senator **Barry Goldwater** of Arizona. Goldwater was an honest, unbending conservative, and he rejected the usual political practice of tailoring his message to please his audience. He denounced the Social Security system in front of senior citizens in

Florida, for example, and suggested in a speech in Knoxville, Tennessee, that the government sell the Tennessee Valley Authority.

Goldwater fought a losing battle from the beginning. Black Americans objected to Goldwater's vote against the civil rights bill, and liberal Republicans refused to support him. Besides representing a minority party, Goldwater frightened many voters by his indiscreet statements about how he would conduct the war in Vietnam, including possible use of nuclear weapons. Johnson, on the other hand, soberly committed himself to "no wider war" in Vietnam. He tried to scare voters by running a TV ad showing a little girl in a field plucking petals from a daisy, a voice-over giving a countdown, which was followed by a photo of a nuclear explosion. On Election Day, Johnson scored an overwhelming victory with 61 percent of the vote. He garnered 486 electoral votes to only 52 for Goldwater, who won just his home state plus five states in the Deep South. Johnson believed that he had an unquestioned mandate for the Great Society.

A Flood of Legislation

The 1964 elections also gave the Democrats huge majorities in Congress, 68–32 in the Senate and 295–140 in the House. In the first session of Congress, Johnson used his victory and lopsided majorities to push no fewer than eighty-nine bills through the legislature, including a bill increasing federal aid to education ($1.5 billion).

The program having the widest reach, perhaps, was **Medicare**, a government health insurance program established in 1965 to help elderly people pay for medical care. Medicare was designed to ensure that the nation's elderly would be able to afford proper medical treatment. The federal government paid for this program by taxing the wages of all Americans.

The Warren Court

Even before the Johnson years, the Supreme Court had followed the same approach that Johnson advocated. Led by Chief Justice **Earl Warren**, the Warren Court (1953–69) pursued a policy of **judicial activism**, interpreting the law and the Constitution broadly to address what the judges perceived as major social problems.

The Warren Court is probably best known for its civil rights decisions, beginning with *Brown v. Board of Education of Topeka, Kansas* (1954). As noted in the last chapter, that decision ordered an end to segregated schools. The court also handed down decisions touching *all* areas of American life. The court placed tighter restrictions on law enforcement officials and gave greater protection to accused criminals in cases such as *Gideon v. Wainwright* (1963), which required the state to provide an attorney for defendants who could not afford one, and *Miranda v. Arizona* (1966), which required that criminal suspects be informed of their constitutional rights before they could be questioned.

In *Engel v. Vitale* (1962), the court banned state-sponsored prayers in public schools as an alleged violation of the First Amendment. In *Roth v. United States* (1957) the Supreme Court ruled that obscenity was not protected by the First Amendment's guarantee of freedom of speech, but it defined *obscenity* so narrowly that the decision actually struck down many obscenity laws. As a result, an underground pornography industry flourished in the United States in the 1960s.

Barry Goldwater, Republican candidate in the 1964 presidential election

Philosophical Differences Between the Candidates

Goldwater advocated a philosophy of government almost diametrically opposite to that of Johnson. The Arizona senator believed that less government activity and regulation would benefit the nation. Goldwater opposed anything that gave the federal government more power to interfere in the private lives of citizens. Johnson, on the other hand, was committed to more government and more regulation.

What Is the Difference Between Medicare and Medicaid?

Medicare: Everyone over age 65 (younger if disabled) qualifies, regardless of income. A monthly premium is required for some parts, as is a co-pay. It is federally administered.

Medicaid: All ages qualify. It is income based. It is state administered with federal regulation.

The court ordered the redrawing of legislative districts in a series of "one man, one vote" decisions. In these cases, the justices ruled that districts that were unequal in population violated the guarantees for "equal protection of the law" in the Fourteenth Amendment. The court eventually extended the "one man, one vote" principle all the way to city councils and local school boards.

Not all of the justices agreed with the court's policy. In a dissenting opinion in 1964, Justice John Harlan warned:

> The Constitution is not a panacea for every blot upon the public welfare, nor should this Court, ordained as a judicial body, be thought of as a general haven for reform movements.... This Court... does not serve its high purpose, when it exceeds its authority even to satisfy justified impatience with the slow workings of the political process.

However, a majority of Harlan's associates did not heed his warning.

Johnson and Vietnam

America's commitment to maintaining the non-Communist government in South Vietnam had begun under President Eisenhower (see Chapter 23). From the 2,000 military advisers that Eisenhower had sent to the 16,000 under Kennedy, that commitment had increased. Ostensibly, the troops were there to train and advise the South Vietnamese army and to protect American personnel. However, the situation in Asia, as one historian noted, proved to be like a "tar baby": the more the United States tried to free itself, the more entangled it became. Under Johnson, the

American soldiers in Vietnam

"advisers" became combatants, and the United States became engaged in a full-fledged war.

Escalation

During his campaign against Goldwater, Johnson had said, "We are not about to send American boys nine or ten thousand miles away from home to do what Asian boys ought to be doing for themselves." Yet an incident occurred off the coast of Vietnam during the campaign that changed the complexion of the war. In the summer of 1964, the American destroyer *Maddox* reportedly repulsed an attack by North Vietnamese patrol boats in the Gulf of Tonkin. Although the affair was relatively minor, Johnson denounced the attack and asked Congress to pass a joint resolution giving him authority to respond to Communist aggression in Vietnam. Congress overwhelmingly approved the **Gulf of Tonkin Resolution**, approving "the determination of the President . . . to take all necessary measures to repel any armed attack against the forces of the United States and to prevent further aggression."

Armed with this resolution, Johnson began to *escalate* the war in Vietnam, increasing the number and expanding the role of American troops. Americans began to take over a large part of the fighting from the South Vietnamese army. By 1968, U.S. forces there numbered more than 500,000. Johnson also ordered American bombers to extend the war to North Vietnam by bombing supply lines and military sites in that nation.

Several factors made the war far more difficult to win than American politicians and generals had imagined. First, the war was not a clear-cut conflict between two separate nations, as the Korean War had been. Americans were fighting both the North Vietnamese and pro-Communist South Vietnamese guerrillas called the **Viet Cong**. The war was fought mainly within South Vietnam between the cities (held by the government of South Vietnam) and the countryside (controlled by the Viet Cong). At the same time, both China and the Soviet Union supplied North Vietnam and the Viet Cong.

Second, supplies for the Communist forces from North Vietnam flowed not only across the north-south border but also through the neighboring and supposedly neutral countries of Laos and Cambodia on the west. Such supply lines would be impossible to cut without attacking those nations, and American political leaders were hesitant to do so.

Third, the government of South Vietnam—although non-Communist—was corrupt, undemocratic, and unstable. The only advantage it offered to Americans was that it was "better than the Communists."

Fourth, the civilian leadership in both the executive and legislative branches wanted to micromanage the war rather than set broad strategy and let the military professionals determine the tactics appropriate for executing the strategy. The civilian leaders tended

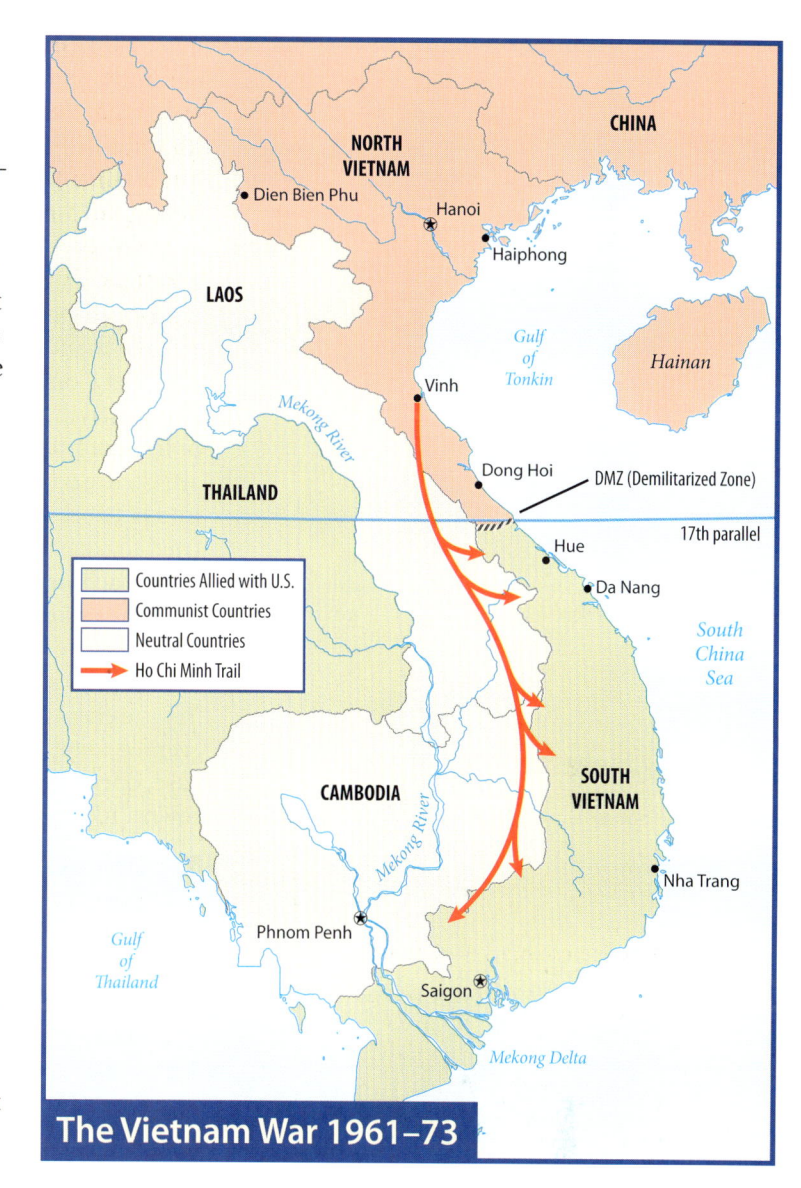

The Vietnam War 1961–73

to let politics and how their decisions might affect the next election determine how the war was conducted.

Fifth, and most importantly, Johnson was committed to the idea of a limited, defensive war. He did not want to risk an outright war against North Vietnam—a war that might draw in the Soviet Union or Communist China, divert dollars from the Great Society at home, and prove politically damaging. He wanted to "have both guns and butter," to conduct a war but not allow it to affect economic prosperity or his social agenda.

For many soldiers, the war took on an unreal, nightmarish hue. The Viet Cong looked, dressed, and acted just like the South Vietnamese civilians—until they opened fire. There were no clear fronts or lines of battle; enemy forces emerged suddenly from the jungle, attacked, and then faded out of sight, into the thick forests or even into networks of tunnels that honeycombed some areas. Americans tried to cope by using their superior technology. Helicopters armed with machine guns and carrying troops swooped like war birds over the jungles; napalm, Agent Orange, and other chemical defoliants burned away the jungle cover in which the enemy hid; American fighter planes and bombers pounded their opponents' positions. Yet the enemy kept coming back. The American military at times seemed to be trying to win the war by sheer firepower. In an extreme case, one American officer reportedly said after a fierce battle for one town, "It became necessary to destroy the town to save it."

Tet Offensive

Grumblings about the war began to arise among the American people, and a student protest movement was growing. The large majority of Americans, however, tended to support the war. Unfortunately, that support was partially the result of misrepresentation and outright deception by the government. President Johnson feared that if Americans knew how deeply committed the United

Ruins of a Saigon street after the Tet Offensive

States was to the war and how the war was actually going, they would stop supporting the programs of the Great Society. Therefore, he disguised the number of U.S. troops involved in the conflict and covered up setbacks. All that the American people generally heard from the government were optimistic reports of how well the war was going. However, the media began to tell a different story.

Support for the war changed dramatically after the Communists launched the **Tet Offensive** in January 1968. During the South Vietnamese celebration of Tet, the lunar new year (January 30), the Viet Cong infiltrated the major cities in the South. They smuggled in arms, for example, by carrying them into the cities in coffins during funeral processions. On the first day of the new year, 60,000 Viet Cong troops launched attacks on nearly every major city and strategic point in South Vietnam. One force even captured part of the U.S. embassy for a time. In the weeks that followed the attacks, American and South Vietnamese forces drove back the enemy, recapturing what had been lost and inflicting massive casualties on the enemy.

Militarily, the Tet Offensive was a major failure for the Communists, but it had a dramatic effect on the American public. Television newscasts emphasized only the negative aspects—the suddenness of the attack and the heavy losses—leading many Americans to believe that Tet was a Communist victory. The U.S. government, to some extent, reaped what it had sown. Having misled the American people and media about the course of the war, the government now faced the wrath of a public who wanted to know how things could come so close to disaster so suddenly. After Tet, many Americans no longer looked to win the war; they only wanted a way out.

Paris Peace Talks

In May 1968, the North Vietnamese offered to hold peace negotiations, and the United States accepted. The **Paris Peace Talks** began with a heated discussion over a critical topic: what shape of table to use. After that unpromising start, the peace talks dragged on for nearly five years while the fighting continued. The United States wanted out but also wanted to preserve South Vietnam as a non-Communist nation. North Vietnam wanted the reunion of the two nations under Communist rule. The talks droned on while casualties mounted.

Protests against the Vietnam War were one of the major expressions of the rebellion of the counterculture in the late 1960s and early 1970s.

Section Review

1. What methods of keeping African Americans from voting were outlawed by the Twenty-fourth Amendment and the Voting Rights Act of 1965?
2. What incident did Johnson use to motivate Congress to pass the Voting Rights Act of 1965?
3–5. List three factors that made the Vietnam War harder to win than American politicians and military leaders expected.
6. What event caused the American people to begin doubting government reports of progress in the Vietnam War?
★ Evaluate the success or failure of the Great Society.
★ Should the United States have escalated its involvement in the Vietnam War under Lyndon Johnson? Why or why not?

The Space Race

On October 4, 1957, the Russians successfully launched **Sputnik I**, a satellite, into space. Americans were shocked to learn that it was orbiting the earth at 18,000 miles per hour and circling the globe every 96 minutes. How far behind the Communists were Americans in developing such technology?

Today, satellites are a vital part of communications, travel, and our everyday life. Among other things, they transmit television and cell phone signals and assist in the navigation of ships, airplanes, and cars. However, in 1957, Americans were trailing the Russians in what was soon called the space race. A month after the launch of *Sputnik I*, a second Soviet rocket carried the first living creature into orbit, a dog named Laika. In April 1961, cosmonaut Yuri Gagarin became the first person to orbit the earth.

In December 1957, America attempted to place a U.S. satellite into orbit. The launch was a humiliating failure when the rocket exploded. Nevertheless, the following month an attempt succeeded. Shortly afterwards, Congress established the **National Aeronautics and Space Administration (NASA)** to conduct the new space program. Rising to the challenge, NASA scientists overcame many of the complex problems of space travel in a series of projects.

Space shuttle, Challenger

In May 1961, the Mercury project succeeded in sending the first American, Alan Shepard, into space. In February 1962, it reached another milestone when John Glenn became the first American to orbit the earth. In an address to Congress, President Kennedy declared, "I believe that this nation should commit itself to achieving the goal, before this decade is out, of landing a man on the moon." In a later speech he said, "We choose to go to the moon in this decade and do the other things, not because they are easy, but because they are hard."

After the Mercury project, the Gemini missions tested the technology needed to dock two craft in outer space. The third program, Apollo, culminated in beating the Soviets in the race to the moon. On July 20, 1969, Neil Armstrong, the commander of Apollo 11, stepped from the ladder of the *Eagle* lunar module to become the first person to set foot on the moon. As he did so, he said, "That's one small step for a man, one giant leap for mankind." Over the next few years, a dozen Americans walked on the moon, but the space program soon turned to such projects as Skylab, the International Space Station, and the Hubble telescope. In addition, the space shuttle program, from its beginning in April 1981 until its end in July 2011, completed 135 missions.

First man lands on the moon

The space race has seen some tragedies. In 1967, three astronauts were killed during a simulated launch of Apollo I. In 1986, the space shuttle *Challenger* exploded seventy-three seconds after liftoff, killing its seven-person crew. And in 2003, the space shuttle *Columbia* burst into flames upon reentry, killing all seven people aboard. Despite the dangers, NASA continues to pursue unknowns in space, going far beyond Kennedy's wildest dreams.

Alan Shepard Jr.

John Glenn Jr.

Neil Armstrong

II. Upheaval

The sense of harmony that had developed during and following World War II and the early days of the Cold War was shattered during the 1960s. Violence at home paralleled the fighting in Vietnam as the United States endured some of the worst civil disturbances in its history. Even Americans who lived nowhere near the unrest often saw it in graphic detail on their television sets. As the violence and bloodshed increased, many citizens felt a sense of despair and helplessness. One Democratic senator moaned, "The Great Society has become the sick society."

Racial Conflict

Despite federal legislation in the 1960s to ensure the equality of all Americans, violence against civil rights workers continued. As the civil rights movement moved north, the violence spread. Many northerners who had approved implementing desegregation in the South resisted calls for desegregated schools and neighborhoods in the North.

As a result, the civil rights movement failed to bring about the needed change as quickly as many Americans had hoped. The combination of this disappointment and increasing violence among the counterculture of the 1960s in general led to **urban riots** during the summers of 1965, 1966, and 1967. The first of these riots began in a predominantly black section of Los Angeles known as Watts. Only days after Congress passed the Voting Rights Act, a white policeman in Watts tried to arrest a young black man for drunk driving. Angry crowds began to gather in the summer heat, and wild tales of police brutality began to circulate. Finally, the tension exploded as mobs roamed Watts, burning and looting. Police, and eventually the National Guard, tried to restore order. In six days of violence, thirty-four people died, nearly nine hundred others were wounded, and rioters destroyed $45 million in property. More than thirty other riots occurred across the nation after the Watts riot. The worst riot was in Detroit in 1967. Forty-three people died there while looters ransacked shops and arsonists set hundreds of fires. Again the National Guard was called in. Detroit took on the appearance of Vietnam as tanks rolled through streets that were filled with smoke from smoldering ruins of buildings. Troops exchanged fire with snipers on buildings.

The effect of the violence was traumatic. Tragically, black Americans felt the brunt of the destruction; their homes and businesses suffered most of the damage, and most of the casualties were black. When the televisions showed nonviolent demonstrators being brutally treated

Guiding Questions

1. Why was there a growing ethnic struggle during this decade?
2. How significant was the threat of radicalism in the United States during this period?

Watts became a symbol of urban violence in the late 1960s.

by police, most Americans realized the need for black Americans to receive justice and equal rights with all other Americans. But violence caused white Americans to become increasingly suspicious of, rather than sympathetic to, the protesters. Even Martin Luther King Jr. began to lose ground among white Americans. By the end of the 1960s, ethnic tensions had reached a new high. As a result, progress on civil rights issues slowed considerably.

Many groups such as the Student Nonviolent Coordinating Committee (SNCC) had originally formed with a commitment to nonviolent methods in securing black rights. The riots contributed to the rise of "**black power**" advocates, many of whom had lost faith that the government would protect their rights. They determined to defend their rights "by any means necessary." While some went so far as to proclaim black supremacy over white people, most wanted to protect and strengthen self-determination for African Americans.

Radical Youth

The radicalization of many young African Americans was but one aspect of a general radicalization of youth. By the late 1960s, half of the population of the United States was under the age of twenty-five. Many of these young people had grown up in the midst of prosperity and affluence, but some began to question and then rebel against the materialistic values of the day—the constant striving after material possessions and luxuries. They became dissatisfied and disillusioned when they found that materialism did not satisfy spiritual needs. Unfortunately, they often turned for satisfaction to things that were even more destructive than their parents' materialism.

Antiwar Movement

The rallying point for disaffected youth was opposition to the Vietnam War. Antiwar demonstrations grew in proportion to the number of troops Johnson was sending overseas. Demonstrators held rallies to protest the war; antiwar radicals seized control of college buildings, barricaded themselves inside, and dared police to come after them; a number of young men fled to Canada to avoid being drafted into the army.

One force behind the antiwar movement was the "**New Left**," radical groups that hoped to use resentment of the war as a means of overthrowing established American institutions. The Students for a Democratic Society (SDS) was the largest New Left group, with more than five thousand members on more than two hundred campuses. An even more radical group, the Weathermen, actually engaged in terrorist bombings of buildings to "bring the war home." Some demonstrators went beyond protesting U.S. involvement in the war and actually supported the enemy. The North Vietnamese and Viet Cong flags became common symbols at antiwar demonstrations even as protestors burned the American flag. Others waved Mao's "little red book" of Communist maxims. Many men burned their draft cards.

Left-wing sympathies, however, were not sufficiently powerful to motivate the whole antiwar movement. Much of the energy for the movement came from the resistance to authority that is always present in sinful human nature. The New Left merely harnessed that discontent. Antiwar sentiment began to spread to older age

---

"Aid and Comfort" to the Enemy?

Jane Fonda, a popular actress of the sixties, traveled to North Vietnam and had her picture taken on an antiaircraft gun used to down American planes, thereby encouraging the Communists there and demoralizing American POWs housed in the nearby prison known as the "Hanoi Hilton." Even today, more than forty years later, many Americans resent Fonda's actions.

Disrespect for Authority

The antiwar movement directed its rage at the president, the ultimate symbol of human authority. Johnson became the object of verbal attacks, such as when thousands of demonstrators in Washington chanted, "Hey! Hey! LBJ! How many kids did you kill today?"

groups, and the number of protesters multiplied. By the end of Johnson's term, military bases were the only places the president could speak without being heckled.

Counterculture

The antiwar movement was itself only a part of an overall youth movement known as the **counterculture**. More an attitude than an ideology, the counterculture of the 1960s and early 1970s had its roots in rebellion, specifically a rejection of the materialism, morals, and values of the previous generation. Proponents of the counterculture believed that the solution to society's problems included self-expression and espousing a philosophy of love and sharing. "Do your own thing" and "All you need is love" were simplistic expressions of the counterculture creed. The counterculture also praised youth as having the answers to society's problems, as illustrated by the popular saying "Don't trust anyone over thirty."

The popular expression of the counterculture was the "hippie" movement (derived from the slang term *hip*, "approving of current tastes and attitudes"). Hippies made a virtue of nonconformity. In place of the neat clothing and appearance of their parents, most wore jeans and t-shirts that were dirty, patched, and garishly colored. Young men grew their hair and beards long as a sign of protest. Rejecting traditional standards, hippies repudiated marriage and advocated unrestricted sexual activity. They embraced rock music, which, with its provocative lyrics and heavy beat, symbolized their rebellion. Hippies were also leaders in the drug culture. They experimented with numerous illegal hallucinogenic drugs, notably LSD (lysergic acid diethylamide). The most popular drug was marijuana, a product of the hemp plant. The American Medical Association estimated that by the late 1960s eight million people had experimented with marijuana.

Much within the counterculture was ungodly—the illicit sex, drug use, and other immoral behavior. Indeed, many hippies embraced the counterculture lifestyle simply so that they could live without assuming any responsibility for their actions. Their philosophy provided a license to sin. Even when they were sincere, however, the hippies were wrong. Their belief that merely expressing "love" as the answer to man's problems was naive and simplistic; they did not realize that genuine love requires sacrifice and discipline. Furthermore, they believed that material possessions and moral restrictions corrupted people rather than people being corrupt by their sinful nature.

Radicalism in Perspective

One can make too much of the radicalism and domestic violence of the 1960s. Even among young people, the radicals were a minority, and the United States came nowhere near equaling the death and destruction through civil disorder that occurred in other nations in the decade. (In Nigeria in the late 1960s, for example, a civil war resulted in the deaths of tens of thousands of people.) The violence shocked Americans, however, especially after the relative calm of the Eisenhower and Kennedy years. They wondered how a nation so advanced and so wealthy could suddenly be convulsed with such disorder. As 1968 neared—a presidential election year—Americans began looking for a leader who could cure the country's ills.

Countering the Counterculture

The Bible teaches that all are born corrupt (Ps. 58:3; Rom. 5:12) and that forsaking possessions or breaking restrictions does nothing to free one from the power of sin. Curing humanity's ills requires changing our sinful nature through the power of God in salvation.

Robert Indiana's "pop art" painting, *Love*, commemorated on an 8-cent U.S. postage stamp, aptly captures the emphasis of the counterculture's professed faith in love as a remedy for society's problems—a faith that ultimately proved vain as it left the nature of that love undefined.

Guiding Questions

1. What significant events occurred in 1968?
2. What political events led to a Republican victory in the presidential election in 1968?

The burdens and controversy of the Vietnam War contributed to Johnson's decision not to seek reelection in 1968.

Civil rights colleagues of Martin Luther King Jr., on the motel balcony where an assassin felled King, point in the direction from which the bullet came.

Section Review

1. What city was the site of the worst urban riot in the United States in the 1960s?
2. What was the rallying point for disaffected young people in the 1960s and early 1970s?
3. What was the popular expression of the counterculture?
4. What was the most widely used illegal drug of the 1960s?
★ What were some of the factors that tended to encourage heavy involvement of college-aged young people in the civil disruptions of the 1960s?
★ How did the civil rights movement become a model for other rights movements, including women's rights and gay rights?

III. 1968

The violence and conflicting ideologies of the decade of 1963 to 1973 are encapsulated in one year: 1968. Against the background of presidential politics and in a campaign marred by bloodshed, American leaders offered their respective answers to the nation's problems.

Johnson Bows Out

Johnson bemoaned the failure of his Great Society to solve America's problems. Despite his unpopularity, he was favored to win renomination by the Democrats. His only challenger was an antiwar Democrat, Minnesota senator **Eugene McCarthy**, but Johnson's staff did not take McCarthy's threat seriously. Then the Tet Offensive in January reinvigorated the Vietnam issue. In the New Hampshire primary in March, the underdog McCarthy nearly upset the president. New York senator **Robert Kennedy**, a younger brother of the slain president, suddenly announced that he, too, would challenge Johnson. After Johnson's advisers warned him that he could lose badly to McCarthy in the upcoming Wisconsin primary, Johnson stunned the nation by withdrawing from the race.

Johnson's withdrawal created a scramble among the Democrats, setting a wide-open race for the nomination. Kennedy and McCarthy competed for the antiwar vote. Vice President **Hubert H. Humphrey** also joined the race, more or less representing Johnson's positions. Humphrey ignored the primaries, depending instead on Johnson's still formidable power and prestige within the Democratic Party organization to win delegates in nonprimary states. McCarthy and Kennedy battled it out in the primaries to win the right to challenge Humphrey at the convention in Chicago.

Two Tragedies

In April 1968, while the candidates fought over the nomination, Martin Luther King Jr. went to Memphis to support a strike by garbage workers. A sniper shot and killed King while he stood on the balcony of his motel. His death sparked a new wave of urban violence. Sadly, the death of King, who had advocated nonviolence, led to fighting, looting, and bloodshed.

As the campaign continued, Kennedy pulled ahead of McCarthy, threatening to wrest the nomination from Humphrey. After Kennedy won a major victory in the California primary, he was greeting scores of supporters in a Los Angeles hotel corridor as he made his way to speak to the press. Suddenly, a young Arab nationalist who opposed Kennedy's support of Israel thrust forward a revolver and fired. Kennedy fell, mortally wounded. Within a period of two months, two major American leaders had died violently.

Nixon Takes the Center

The Republican race narrowed to one question: Could anyone stop **Richard Nixon**? In spite of his losses to John Kennedy in 1960 and in the California governor's race in 1962, the former vice president remained heavily involved in politics. In 1968, he won a series of primaries that made him front-runner for the Republican nomination.

Nixon tried to take the "middle of the road" on political issues. Only that way, he thought, could he appeal to the general public and win the fall election. At the Republican convention in Miami, he beat back challenges by both liberal Nelson Rockefeller and conservative Ronald Reagan to win the nomination.

Nixon sensed the dismay of the American electorate with the violence that racked the country and their sense of helplessness in the face of apparently uncontrollable unrest. So he hit a sympathetic nerve when he called for "law and order" and a firm response to the anarchy. One of the biggest boosts to Nixon's "law and order" message was the contrast provided by the Democratic convention.

Richard Nixon and Spiro Agnew were nominated to carry the Republican banner in 1968.

Democratic Disarray

With the death of Robert Kennedy, Humphrey easily captured the nomination at the party's Chicago convention. But some Democrats wondered if the nomination would be worth anything. As Americans watched on television, police and radical demonstrators battled outside the convention hall. Inside the hall the Democratic mayor of Chicago shouted obscenities at a Democratic senator who was denouncing what he called the "Gestapo tactics" of Chicago's police. Another weight on Humphrey's candidacy was Johnson's unpopular Vietnam policy, which Humphrey, as vice president, was virtually bound to defend.

The Wallace Factor

Another element in the confusion-filled campaign was the third-party candidacy of Alabama governor **George Wallace**, who ran as the candidate of the newly formed American Independent Party. The fiery Wallace had risen to fame as a pro-segregation governor during the civil rights struggles of the early 1960s. He sought to draw on popular discontent with the civil rights movement, urban violence, rampant immorality, rising crime rates, and the seemingly endless war in Vietnam. Wallace's political pronouncements were generally conservative but couched in tough, pugnacious language.

Wallace did not really believe that he could win the election, but he hoped that in the three-way contest he could win enough

The third-party candidacy of Alabama governor George Wallace further complicated the election. He told voters that there was "not a dime's worth of difference" between the Republicans and Democrats.

> **Wallace's Popular Message in the Popular Language**
>
> Wallace attacked the "pointy-headed intellectuals" who ran the government bureaucracy. "When I get to Washington," he said, "I'll throw all these phonies and their briefcases into the Potomac." Scorning antiwar protestors, he told cheering audiences, "If any demonstrator ever lays down in front of my car, it'll be the last car he'll ever lay down in front of."

electoral votes to throw the election into the House of Representatives. He believed that a strong showing would "send a message" to Washington that a bloc of conservative Americans existed that the politicians could not afford to ignore, thereby forcing them to take more conservative positions.

Election: Nixon's the One

The election reflected the fragmented state of American society. Nixon got 31,785,480 votes (43.4 percent) to Humphrey's 31,275,166 (42.7 percent). Nixon's lead in the Electoral College, however, was more substantial, 301–191. Wallace won nearly ten million votes (13.0 percent) and 46 electoral votes. The voters repudiated Johnson's policies but did not give Nixon an overwhelming mandate.

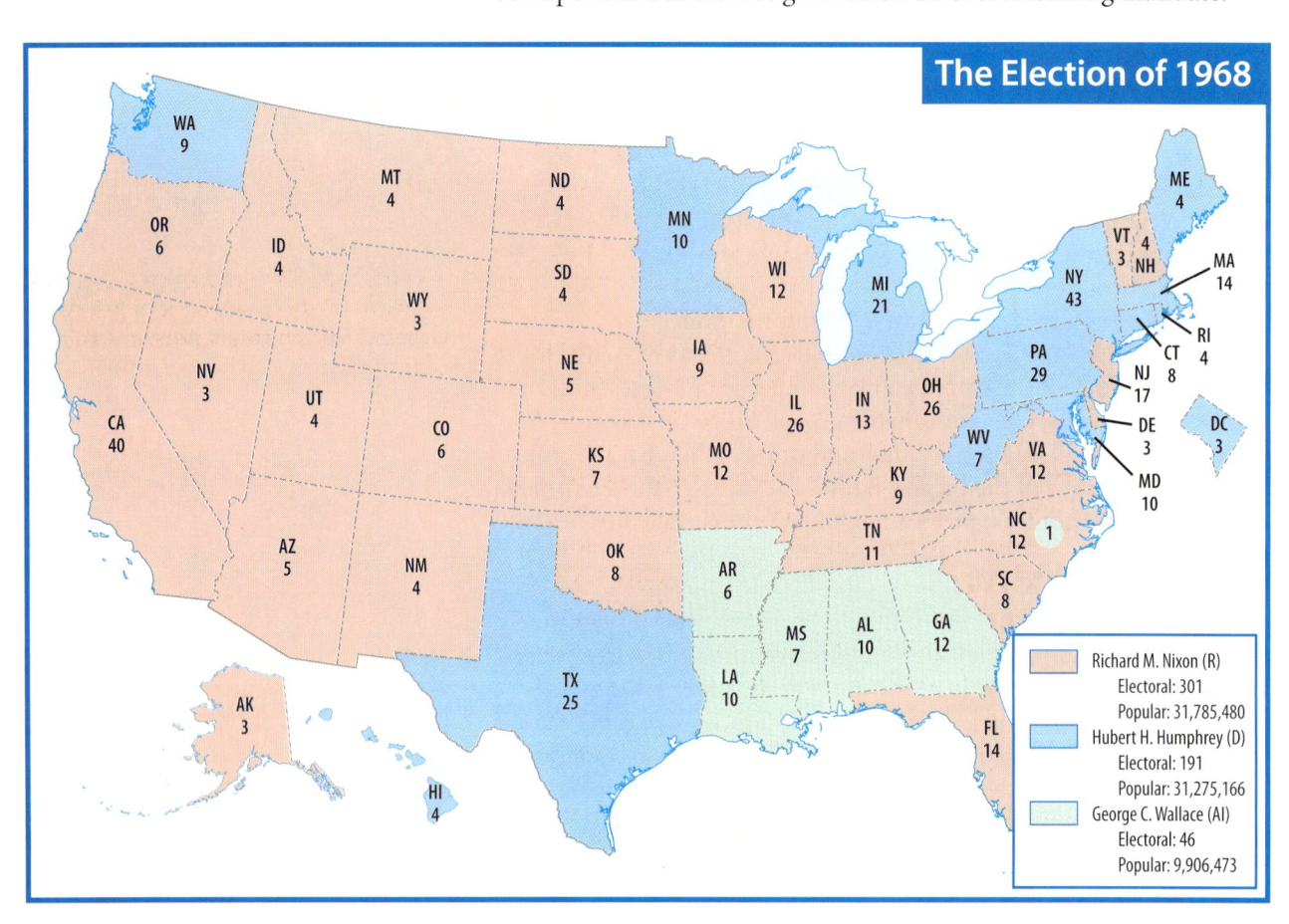

The Election of 1968

Richard M. Nixon (R) — Electoral: 301, Popular: 31,785,480
Hubert H. Humphrey (D) — Electoral: 191, Popular: 31,275,166
George C. Wallace (AI) — Electoral: 46, Popular: 9,906,473

Section Review

1. Who was the first antiwar Democrat to challenge the renomination of Lyndon Johnson?
2. After the withdrawal of Johnson in the 1968 campaign, which Democratic candidate best represented the incumbent president's policies?
3–4. Which two major American leaders died violently in 1968?
5–7. Name the Republican nominee, the Democratic nominee, and the major third-party candidate in the presidential election of 1968.
★ Explain the factors in the 1968 presidential election that led to the election of Richard Nixon.

IV. Nixon and the Silent Majority

In a speech during his first year in office, Richard Nixon appealed to "the great silent majority of . . . Americans" for support. With the term *silent majority*, the president affirmed his belief that most Americans were not violent radicals wholly discontent with the status quo. The bulk of the population, he believed, were quiet, decent, respectable, and hard-working citizens who wanted only peace and order. Nixon claimed that he represented the interests of that silent majority and that his administration would represent their values. Many writers called Nixon's statement an appeal to "Middle America," the views of the dominant middle class.

Guiding Questions

1. What were President Nixon's domestic and diplomatic policies?
2. How did Nixon strive to end the Vietnam War?
3. How did the two political campaigns differ leading up to the 1972 presidential election?

Domestic Problems

Busing

Nixon confronted a highly emotional issue early in his presidency, one that outraged many Americans. Despite Supreme Court orders for the desegregation of schools since the 1950s, the integration of schools had proceeded slowly. One of the main obstacles to integration was that nearly all schools drew their students from surrounding neighborhoods. Most neighborhoods, however, tended to be segregated by ethnic group. As a result, African Americans went to predominantly black schools in their own neighborhoods, and whites went to predominantly white schools in their own neighborhoods. To overcome this fact, the courts ordered the **busing** of students out of their neighborhoods to other schools until all schools reflected the overall ethnic makeup of the community as a whole.

Forced busing was controversial. Some parents opposed busing simply because they opposed racial integration. Other parents thought that it was senseless to bus children to a school miles away when they had a perfectly good one right in their own neighborhood. Angry protesters—mostly blue-collar and middle-class white Americans—demonstrated against court-ordered busing. Sometimes violence resulted, as in Pontiac, Michigan, where protesters fire-bombed empty school buses. Nixon tried to placate antibusing forces by slowing the process of integration. The courts, however, pressed the issue, and busing continued. In time, many neighborhoods became more integrated and the practice of forced busing declined.

Divided Government for a Divided Country

Nixon was the first president since Zachary Taylor to begin his first term with both houses of Congress in the hands of the opposing party.

Economic Problems

Nixon inherited a deteriorating economic situation. Johnson had tried to pay for both the Great Society and the Vietnam War without raising taxes. The result was a growing budget deficit which, in turn, led to inflation. When Nixon tried to control inflation by trimming the federal budget and supporting the raising of interest rates, inflation remained unchanged but unemployment rose and a recession set in. Nixon then responded with what he called his **New Economic Policy** (NEP). First, he imposed a ninety-day freeze in 1971 on all wages and prices. Then he established a board to regulate all wage and price increases. Finally, in 1973, he replaced the mandatory guidelines with voluntary ones.

Results and Consequences

Nixon's freeze and mandatory regulations seemed to slow inflation, but they did not reduce unemployment. Also, once the guidelines became voluntary, prices rose again. All of his actions in the NEP were departures from the free market economics supported by his "silent majority." They resembled more the policies of his liberal opponents than those of a fiscal conservative.

Diplomatic Successes

China

Nixon scored his most notable triumphs in foreign affairs. Probably his biggest breakthrough was establishing relations with

President and Mrs. Nixon visit the Great Wall during their historic trip to Communist China in 1972.

Nixon's Plan Backfired
Contrary to Nixon's wishes, the United Nations expelled Taiwan when it admitted Communist China in 1971.

the Communist People's Republic of China. Since the flight of Chiang Kai-shek's Nationalist government to the island of Taiwan in 1949 (see Chapter 23), the United States had recognized the Nationalist government as the legitimate government of China rather than that of the Communists on the mainland. Nixon hoped to exploit dissension between Communist China and the Soviet Union by currying favor with the Chinese. In 1971, the president announced that he would visit the People's Republic the following year, and he endorsed the admission of Communist China to the United Nations as an equal of Taiwan.

Nixon's visit was an enormous public relations success. Television cameras followed the president as he toured the Great Wall and other sites long closed to foreigners. He banqueted with Communist leaders and exchanged messages of good will with them. The visit portrayed Nixon as an astute diplomat and able statesman. He laid the groundwork for resuming trade with mainland China and for the possible reunification of the mainland with Taiwan. He did not abandon Nationalist China, however, by granting full diplomatic recognition to the Communist government. President Carter did that in 1978 when he formally recognized the People's Republic and severed official ties with Nationalist China.

Soviet Union

At least in part because of his overtures to China, Nixon was able to win some concessions from the Soviet Union. Through the influence of Nixon and **Henry Kissinger**, his secretary of state, the United States entered a period of **détente** (day TAHNT), a relaxation of the tension that had existed between the two nations since World War II. In the Strategic Arms Limitations Talks (SALT), the United States and the USSR agreed to limit the number of missiles and warheads each nation had. Nixon also arranged the sale of large amounts of grain to the Soviets. Americans watched in surprise as Nixon, the former anti-Communist "cold warrior," did more to improve relations between the United States and Communist nations than any other president. Under Nixon, the United States government actively sought to develop friendly relationships with repressive Communist regimes.

Secretary of State Henry Kissinger

Nixon and Vietnam

De-escalation and Expansion

In a reversal of Johnson's Vietnam policy, Nixon de-escalated the war by bringing American troops home and leaving the bulk of the fighting to the South Vietnamese. Nixon called his policy of reducing American forces and increasing the role of the South Vietnamese the **Vietnamization** (VYET nah muh ZAY shun) of the war.

Vietnamization by the Numbers
Nixon gradually reduced American forces in Vietnam from more than 500,000 when he took office to fewer than 140,000 by the beginning of 1972.

While he was reducing the number of American soldiers, however, Nixon took other steps that expanded the war. In an effort to force the North Vietnamese to make peace, the president authorized raids into neutral Cambodia in 1970 and Laos in 1971 to destroy enemy bases. In 1972, he approved massive bombing of North Vietnam, the mining of Haiphong Harbor, and the blockading of North Vietnam.

Dissent at Home

The antiwar movement entered a lull when Nixon took office; protesters waited to see what the new president would do. The bombing of North Vietnam and the expansion of the war into Cambodia and Laos, however, revitalized the movement. At least three traumatic events at home further divided the country over the war.

The first such event was the court-martial of Lieutenant **William Calley**. In March 1968, Calley led C Company into the South Vietnamese village of **My Lai** (MEE LYE). The company had suffered many casualties from Viet Cong in the area, and they were angry and on edge. In My Lai, they killed more than three hundred apparently unarmed civilians whom they suspected of aiding the Viet Cong. When news of the massacre leaked out, the army launched an investigation and a series of courts-martial lasting from 1969 to 1971. Only Calley was convicted of murder; he received a sentence of life in prison. Nixon first reduced Calley's sentence to twenty years and then, in 1974, placed him under a mild form of house arrest.

The second event took place in May 1970 at **Kent State** University near Cleveland, Ohio. Demonstrators protesting the invasion of Cambodia rioted on and near the campus and even burned an ROTC building at the university. The governor of Ohio called out the National Guard. On May 4, a group of protesters taunted the guardsmen and hurled rocks at them. A few of the soldiers panicked and fired. Four students, two of whom were simply walking to class and had nothing to do with the protest, were killed.

The Kent State incident revealed the deep divisions in the nation over the war. One faction considered the slain students martyrs for peace. Another faction, angered at what they considered a lack of patriotism by the antiwar movement, claimed that the students "had it coming to them." Peace seemed no closer at home than it did in Vietnam.

The third event was the publication of the **Pentagon Papers** in 1971. Pentagon staff analyst Daniel Ellsberg stole a number of confidential documents concerning the progress of American involvement in Vietnam and released them to the *New York Times*. The Nixon administration tried vainly to block publication in the interest of "national security." But the documents were more embarrassing to the government than they were dangerous to the nation. They revealed the blunders and deceptions of primarily the Kennedy and Johnson administrations in the conduct of the war. Readers learned, for example, that Johnson had drafted what became the Gulf of Tonkin

Limited Success of the Expansion

Although Nixon's raids into Laos and Cambodia destroyed some enemy bases and strained the resources of North Vietnam, they did not end the war. In fact, with those two nations drawn directly into the conflict, the fighting was even more widespread.

Public Perception of My Lai

Americans were appalled that American troops could commit such a slaughter, but many sympathized with Calley. They believed that either the army was making him a scapegoat to cover for other officers or the antiwar movement was persecuting him in anger over the whole war effort.

A girl screams in horror as she kneels by the body of a student killed by a stray bullet fired by National Guardsmen at Kent State University.

Resolution months before the actual incident in the Gulf of Tonkin took place. These revelations of government deceit prompted even more antiwar sentiment.

"Peace"

Although Nixon's Vietnam policy was unpopular at home, it was wearing down North Vietnam. The North Vietnamese were not near defeat, but the constant casualties and bombings were draining the Communists' resources. After an extremely heavy "Christmas bombing" late in 1972, the war-weary Americans and North Vietnamese reached an agreement at the Paris Peace Talks early in 1973. The United States recalled its troops, and North Vietnam released most U.S. prisoners of war. The United States gave South Vietnam huge amounts of arms to protect itself, but North Vietnam still maintained troops and guerrillas in the South. Nixon hoped that the supply of arms and the threat of future American intervention would protect South Vietnam. Secretary of State Kissinger hinted, however, that all the United States wanted was a "decent interval" between the removal of American forces and the fall of South Vietnam.

Aftermath

In spring 1975, North Vietnam launched a massive offensive, and South Vietnamese resistance collapsed with astonishing speed. Nixon was no longer in office, and President Ford was unable to persuade Congress to help South Vietnam. With no outside help and torn by internal dissension and corruption, the South fell. Vietnam was finally united and at "peace"—under Communist rule.

The results of the war at least partially proved Eisenhower's "domino theory" (Chap. 23). One after the other, South Vietnam, Laos, and Cambodia fell to the Communists. Fears of Communist atrocities in the fallen nations also proved justified. The worst example was the cruel Communist regime in Cambodia called the Khmer Rouge. Led by dictator Pol Pot, the Khmer Rouge slaughtered 1.2 million Cambodians—one-fifth of the nation's population. Relief came to the Cambodians in 1979 when Vietnam invaded the nation, toppled the murderous Khmer Rouge government, and installed its own totalitarian rule.

In America, the result was a wave of isolationism. Citizens wanted "no more Vietnams," which usually meant almost no commitment of any U.S. troops to fight anywhere for any reason. Upset at how American presidents—particularly Johnson and Nixon—had run the war on their own authority, Congress passed a series of acts, including the War Powers Act of 1973, limiting the president's power to use American troops abroad.

Why did America lose in Vietnam? Liberal critics argued that, given the unpopularity and corruption of the South Vietnamese government, the war was unwinnable; Communist domination was inevitable. Conservative critics, however, charged that an earlier commitment of larger forces, or even an invasion of North Vietnam, would have won the war; only the halfhearted concept of limited war prevented victory. Conservatives also accused the American media of sapping American support for the war by unsympathetic and even distorted reporting. Such questions are, of course, ultimately unanswerable. What was certain was that the American people were deeply wounded by the trauma of the Vietnam experience and would not soon recover.

The War Powers Act of 1973

The War Powers Act requires that the president notify Congress within forty-eight hours of his committing U.S. troops to military action and withdraw such troops after sixty days unless Congress specifically approves continued use of those forces.

LeMay's Plan for Victory

General Curtis LeMay, George Wallace's vice-presidential running mate, proposed a plan to guarantee U.S. victory in Vietnam. LeMay, who had led the American bombing of Japan, advocated bombing the North Vietnamese "back to the Stone Age." Because it had worked in defeating the Japanese, he thought it would work again when used against the North Vietnamese. He was even willing to use atomic weapons.

1972 Election

In the 1972 presidential election, Nixon's chances of reelection, strengthened by his trip to China and the de-escalation of the Vietnam War, looked good. His opposition for the Republican nomination was minor: a liberal congressman who accused the president of being too conservative and a conservative congressman who accused him of being too liberal. The Democrats, furthermore, were again divided. George Wallace campaigned for the Democratic nomination and, by crusading against busing, was able to win primaries not only in the South but also in northern industrial states such as Massachusetts and Michigan. A would-be assassin shot him in Maryland, cutting short his campaign and leaving him paralyzed and in pain for life.

The Democratic nomination eventually went to a candidate who was almost the exact opposite of Wallace, the zealously liberal South Dakota senator **George McGovern**. His campaign, though, was almost hopeless. He was far to the left of most American voters, and he managed to botch his best issue—discontent with the war in Vietnam—by saying that he would "crawl" to North Vietnam if necessary for peace. Then word leaked that his running mate, Thomas Eagleton, had twice undergone electroshock treatments for depression. At first, McGovern announced that he was "1,000 percent" behind Eagleton, but a week later he forced him off the ticket. Five leading Democrats turned McGovern down before he could find someone else to run with him.

The election was much like that of 1964: the incumbent president crushed an unpopular challenger. Nixon won 61 percent of the popular vote and captured every state except Massachusetts and the District of Columbia for a 520–17 edge in the Electoral College. It proved to be like 1964 in another respect: the winner would be discredited—even hated—before the next presidential election. Within two years of his triumph, Nixon would be disgraced and out of office.

The Democratic nominee in 1972 was the very liberal senator from South Dakota, George McGovern.

McGovern's Eventual Running Mate
The man who agreed to be McGovern's running mate was Sargent Shriver, John F. Kennedy's brother-in-law.

Section Review

1–3. What were the three components of Nixon's New Economic Policy?
4. What was Nixon's greatest triumph in foreign affairs?
5–7. What three actions did Nixon take in 1970, 1971, and 1972 to force the North Vietnamese to make peace?
8–9. What two other Southeast Asian nations fell to communism after the fall of South Vietnam?
★ Evaluate court-ordered busing as a method for integration.
★ Although Nixon had positioned himself as a conservative and an anti-Communist in 1968, which policies of his administration contradicted his claims?

CHAPTER REVIEW 24

People, Places, and Things to Remember

Lyndon Johnson
Great Society
Civil Rights Act of 1964
Voting Rights Act of 1965
Twenty-fourth Amendment
War on Poverty
Barry Goldwater
Medicare
Earl Warren
judicial activism
Gulf of Tonkin Resolution
Viet Cong
Tet Offensive
Paris Peace Talks
Sputnik I
National Aeronautics and Space Administration (NASA)
urban riots
black power
New Left
counterculture
Eugene McCarthy
Robert Kennedy
Hubert H. Humphrey
Richard Nixon
George Wallace
silent majority
busing
New Economic Policy
Henry Kissinger
détente
Vietnamization
William Calley
My Lai
Kent State
Pentagon Papers
George McGovern

Making Connections

1–2. Give two reasons for Barry Goldwater's unpopularity with most American voters in 1964.

3–5. Match each of the following slogans with the tenet of counterculture philosophy that it describes.

    a. "Do your own thing."

    b. "All you need is love."

    c. "Don't trust anyone over thirty."

    (1) the ability to work out society's problems in a spirit of cooperation

    (2) the belief that youth alone has the answer to society's problems

    (3) the importance of nonconformity

Developing History Skills

1. Why were the results of the 1968 election a repudiation of Johnson but not a mandate for Nixon?

2. What is the danger of the isolationist philosophy illustrated by the postwar phrase "no more Vietnams"?

Thinking Critically

1. Why is a policy of judicial activism such as that pursued by the Warren Court dangerous?

2. Why is a philosophy inadequate that simply espouses "love" as the solution to humanity's problems?

Living as a Christian Citizen

1. Leviticus 19:9–10 instructs the Israelites to leave behind produce so that the poor could come and glean it. This law does not directly apply in the New Testament era, and the United States is no longer primarily a nation based on agriculture. But the principle of helping the poor remains (Luke 14:13–14). What are ways that Christians can help the poor today? What are some dangers to avoid?

2. Select a current or proposed law and evaluate it in terms of how its goals, methods, and likely outcome align with scriptural principles. In areas in which it falls short, offer alternatives.

A NATION WITH CHALLENGES (1973–1980)

25

President Gerald Ford working in the Oval Office in the White House

> I did not take the sacred oath of office to preside over the decline and fall of the United States of America.
>
> **President Gerald Ford**
> September 1975

I. The Embattled Presidency

II. Domestic Difficulties

III. The Carter Years

IV. The Rising Conservative Tide

Big Ideas

1. What events led to the resignation of Richard Nixon?
2. What economic and philosophical challenges occurred during this period?
3. What characterized the administrations of Gerald Ford and Jimmy Carter?
4. What factors led to the growth of conservatism during this period?

An average American watching the *CBS Evening News* in 1980 would have noticed a difference from earlier broadcasts on that network. Each night, Walter Cronkite, anchor of the program, still closed with his trademark line "And that's the way it is...." But after Muslim extremists seized more than fifty American hostages in the American embassy in Tehran, Iran, viewers heard Cronkite add a final phrase to his remarks. By January he was saying: "... on the eightieth day of captivity for the American hostages in Iran." Each night Cronkite added another day to the total—ninety, one hundred, two hundred, and still more with no end in sight. The nightly broadcasts became a reminder of the inability of the nation to resolve the Iranian situation. Cronkite continued the demoralizing count until the 444th day, the day on which the hostages were freed. That same day, Americans inaugurated a new president that their frustration, in part, had led them to elect.

The departing president on January 20, 1981 (day 444 of the hostage crisis), was Jimmy Carter. He was the latest in a series of presidents that had become unpopular with many Americans. For much of the 1970s, some believed the United States suffered a "leadership crisis." It began when one president (Nixon) was forced to resign. Although Gerald Ford tried to unite the nation, he had been named but not elected vice president, and he had never been elected outside his own congressional district in Grand Rapids, Michigan. It ended with Carter, a man elected in part because of the failures of his predecessors, being voted from office.

Guiding Questions

1. What led to the decline in popularity of Nixon during his second term of office?
2. What were the highlights of the Ford administration?

The Watergate building was the scene of a famous burglary in 1972.

I. The Embattled Presidency

The Fall of Richard Nixon

Watergate Affair and Other Scandals

In the early hours of June 17, 1972, during the heat of the presidential campaign, police arrested five burglars, carrying electronic listening devices, who had broken into the headquarters of the Democratic National Committee. That event, at the Watergate Office Complex in Washington, D.C., caused little stir at the time. The White House vigorously denied any connection with this "third-rate burglary," and George McGovern's campaign was already in such deep trouble that few listened to his charges of criminality and corruption against Nixon.

After the election, however, more about the **Watergate affair** began to leak out. One of the convicted burglars alleged to the trial judge that authorities "higher up" were behind the break-in and were trying to cover up the fact. Further investigation revealed a pattern of questionable and illegal activities organized by Nixon's Committee to Re-elect the President (CRP).

During the Nixon administration, there were numerous other incidents of misconduct. For example, some aides sent letters to newspapers, accusing Democratic candidates of racism and sexual immorality. Others burglarized the office of Daniel Ellsberg's psychiatrist (Ellsberg had released the *Pentagon Papers* to the *New York Times*), trying to find material with which to discredit Ellsberg. In 1973, investigations by both Congress and a federal court resulted in the firing or resignation of several members of Nixon's staff and cabinet. The controversy did not disappear with those dismissals, however; people wondered whether the president himself was involved and, if so, how deeply.

Resignation of Agnew

Another problem that plagued Nixon's administration was the allegation that Vice President **Spiro Agnew** had taken bribes as the governor of Maryland and as vice president. By negotiating an agreement with prosecutors, Agnew was allowed to plead *nolo contendere* (which meant he did not plead guilty or not guilty), and he received only a fine and probation. He also resigned as vice president in October 1973, becoming the second person to relinquish that office. (John C. Calhoun had resigned for political—not criminal—reasons in 1832.) Although Agnew's crimes were unrelated to Watergate, they increased the perception that the Nixon administration was thoroughly corrupt.

Using the procedure outlined by the Twenty-fifth Amendment (ratified 1967), President Nixon nominated House minority leader (leader of the Republicans in the House of Representatives) **Gerald Ford** of Michigan to succeed Agnew. Both houses of Congress confirmed the nomination by overwhelming margins. Nixon hoped that Ford's popularity in Congress and reputation for honesty would help deflect criticism from his administration. But, Ford seemed aware of his own limitations. Upon becoming vice president in December 1973, he commented, "I am a Ford, not a Lincoln."

Resignation of Nixon

Despite all the charges and investigations, no evidence had come to light that implicated Nixon himself in the Watergate scandal. That situation changed in the middle of 1973 when a White House aide revealed that Nixon had installed a secret recording system in the Oval Office that taped every conversation there. Immediately, both the courts and Congress pressed Nixon to release the tapes. The president refused, claiming that national security and the separation of powers were at stake. His refusal began a long struggle over control of the tapes. Nixon tried to satisfy investigators by first releasing edited transcripts of the tapes and then by releasing just some of the tapes. Meanwhile, he maintained his complete innocence of wrongdoing. The president's approval rating plummeted. The tapes and wrenching judicial and congressional inquiries exposed a disturbing side of the Nixon administration—the political "dirty tricks," subtle lies, and outright deceit that Nixon and his aides had practiced. They also revealed Nixon's crude and offensive language.

The Watergate affair became a national trauma. For months, the government seemed paralyzed by the accusations and rumors that swirled about. Televised congressional hearings kept the scandal constantly before the public eye. Finally, in July 1974, the Supreme Court ruled unanimously that Nixon must release all the tapes. Though the tapes did not indicate Nixon knew about the Watergate break-in beforehand, they proved that he participated in attempts to cover up the involvement of his White House subordinates. With impeachment by the House a virtual certainty and conviction (and removal from office) by the Senate likely, Nixon resigned on August 9. In his resignation speech, Nixon said that some of his judgments were wrong, but

Vice President Spiro Agnew

Senator Howard Baker (R-TN; *left*) and Bible-quoting Senator Sam Ervin (D-NC; *center*) directed the nationally televised Senate Watergate hearings.

Nixon boarded a helicopter (*above*) and left the White House after becoming the only U.S. president to resign (*right*).

A President Resigns

Richard Nixon was the only president to resign. His resignation speech was broadcast live on radio and television at 9 p.m. on August 8, 1974. The following is an excerpt from his remarks. Note that the president did not admit to breaking any laws; however, it was increasingly clear that he was guilty of obstructing justice and probably other offenses.

This is the 37th time I have spoken to you from this office, where so many decisions have been made that shaped the history of this Nation....

In all the decisions I have made in my public life, I have always tried to do what was best for the Nation. Throughout the long and difficult period of Watergate, I have felt it was my duty to persevere, to make every possible effort to complete the term of office to which you elected me....

From the discussions I have had with Congressional and other leaders, I have concluded that because of the Watergate matter I might not have the support of the Congress that I would consider necessary to back the very difficult decisions and carry out the duties of this office in the way the interests of the Nation would require....

Therefore, I shall resign the Presidency effective at noon tomorrow. Vice President Ford will be sworn in as President at that hour in this office....

I regret deeply any injuries that may have been done in the course of the events that led to this decision. I would say only that if some of my judgments were wrong, and some were wrong, they were made in what I believed at the time to be the best interest of the Nation....

I shall leave this office with regret at not completing my term, but with gratitude for the privilege of serving as your President for the past five and a half years....

To have served in this office is to have felt a very personal sense of kinship with each and every American. In leaving it, I do so with this prayer: May God's grace be with you in all the days ahead.

---

he never admitted that he was guilty of crimes. Eventually, about two dozen members of the Nixon administration were convicted and jailed for offenses relating to Watergate.

The New President

Gerald Ford, in his first speech as president, said, "My fellow Americans, our long national nightmare is over." Ford enjoyed a flood of goodwill when he took office. The American people indeed wanted to put the "long national nightmare" behind them. Furthermore, Ford's reputation as a decent, honest man was a welcome contrast to Nixon and his bitter struggle with Congress. But after only a month in office, Ford dashed his popularity with one stroke: he granted Nixon a full pardon for any crimes he might have committed while in office. The president maintained that his action would put the Watergate affair behind the nation and would save the United States the agony of a trial of the former president.

The **Nixon pardon** was widely denounced. Many critics thought it unfair that Nixon should escape punishment while his subordinates suffered. As a result, Ford's popularity fell dramatically.

Ford also faced several other obstacles that hampered his effectiveness. For instance, he was the first person to serve as president who had never been elected as president or vice president during a presidential election. He owed his elevation to the nation's highest office not to a national election but to an appointment and a resignation. Complicating the situation for the Ford administration, the man whom Ford nominated to be vice president, Nelson Rockefeller, also had not been elected by the people. For the first time in history, neither of the nation's top two officials had been elected.

Headline reporting Ford's controversial pardon of Nixon

Another obstacle was the public's increasingly critical perception of Ford. Despite Ford's athletic ability (which included a stint as a star center for the University of Michigan's football team), a series of public accidents gave people the impression that he was clumsy. For example, he stumbled as he descended the ramp of the presidential jet, and he accidentally hit spectators with balls when he played golf.

Ford's greatest obstacle, however, was a hostile Congress. The Democrats held comfortable majorities in both houses, and they were determined to control the government after the excesses of the Nixon administration. Ford's main weapon against them was the veto; he vetoed sixty-six bills in fewer than three years in office while attempting to limit government spending and protect the powers of the presidency. Congress, however, overrode twelve of his vetoes, one of the highest percentages of overrides since the troubled presidency of Andrew Johnson. The standoff between Ford and Congress often created a legislative deadlock.

Other factors also damaged his reputation. In 1975, America tasted final defeat in Southeast Asia as South Vietnam, Cambodia, and Laos fell to the Communists. A sluggish national economy also worried voters. Under Nixon and Ford, the presidency had sunk to its lowest level of prestige since the era of Warren G. Harding.

Gerald Ford became president during a time of great uncertainty following President Nixon's resignation.

Section Review

1. Why did the release of the presidential tapes cause President Nixon to resign?
2. What event early in Ford's administration drastically lowered his popularity with the American people?
3. What was Ford's greatest obstacle to effectiveness in his presidency?
★ Was Gerald Ford an ineffective president as his critics claimed, or was he merely the victim of circumstances?

II. Domestic Difficulties

The problems of the 1960s—urban violence, student unrest, and racial conflict—gave way to problems in the 1970s that were less dramatic but no less important. Despite all its difficulties, the 1960s had been economically prosperous; in the 1970s, however, economic conditions became the nation's primary concern. Also, the success of the civil rights movement in the 1960s spurred other groups to seek their "rights"—some legitimate, some not—in the new decade.

Economic Woes

Energy Crisis

In October 1973 Arab nations, led by Egypt and Syria, launched a surprise attack on the neighboring Jewish nation of Israel. Israel, which became a country in 1948, was supported by the United States. In retaliation, the Organization of Petroleum Exporting Countries (OPEC)—which included the Arab nations that produced the greatest amounts of oil—announced an **oil embargo** against the United States (and other nations that supported Israel), prohibiting

Guiding Questions

1. What complex economic issues challenged the nation during this period?
2. What "rights" movements arose during this period?

The OPEC oil embargo led to long lines and higher prices at American gas stations.

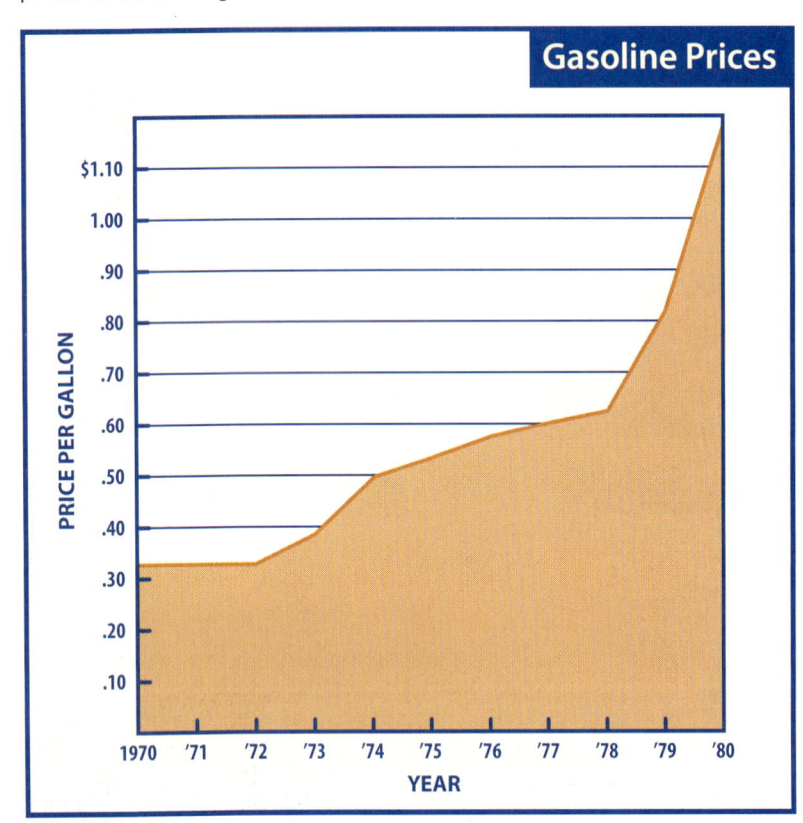

Christians and the Environment

The Creation Mandate in Genesis 1:26–28 requires humans to exercise dominion over God's creation. Proper stewardship would include taking reasonable steps to protect the environment. Since pollution harms nature and humans, Christians should combat it to obey both the Creation Mandate and Christ's command to love one's neighbor.

the sale of any oil to America. When the embargo started, the United States was still under President Nixon's wage and price controls. With a shrinking supply of gasoline, gas stations stayed open fewer hours and limited the amount of gas each customer could buy. Motorists often waited in long lines to buy the gas that was available. When price controls were finally lifted, the price of gasoline shot from about 35¢ a gallon at the beginning of 1973 to well over a dollar a gallon by 1980.

The gasoline shortages were only part of an overall **energy crisis**, a combination of higher prices for and shortages of American energy resources. Until the 1970s, Americans had assumed that there would be enough cheap fuel resources to power any project that American industry undertook. They began to realize, however, that America's energy sources were not inexhaustible and would not always be inexpensive. Petroleum production had already begun to drop before the embargo, and the embargo itself simply heightened the shortages and increased prices more quickly. Even when the Arabs lifted the oil embargo, they increased their prices for oil fourfold. The prices for all petroleum products—from heating oil and fuels to asphalt and plastics—rose even more.

During this time, a growing number of people voiced concern about the effects of industrial development on the environment. Beginning in the 1960s, the **environmental movement** began to sound warnings about industrial pollution of the water and air.

Severe smog, particularly in large cities, posed health risks to many Americans. By the late 1970s tests showed that air quality in Los Angeles was unhealthy for the majority of the year. Automobile emissions were also a serious concern in many parts of the nation.

Water quality issues due to pollution existed in every region of the country. The Great Lakes, because of the discharge of large amounts of waste (from factories and cities), were seriously affected. Many rivers were not safe for swimming or fishing.

Due to increased concerns and with pressure from environmentalists, Congress passed a number of laws regulating pollution. In 1970, Congress established the Environmental Protection Agency to oversee and coordinate environmental regulations. The main acts to combat pollution were the Clean Air Act (1963; amended 1970, 1977, and 1990) and the Clean Water Act (1972; amended 1977 and 1987).

Those actions helped reduce pollution of the environment, but they also increased demands on the nation's energy resources. Many industries, for example, began to switch from highly pollutant coal to oil as a power source, further straining American oil resources. Likewise, regulations to reduce air pollution by cars required adding emission-control devices, which reduced pollution but also lowered fuel efficiency. Additional costs led many industries to plead for delays in implementing the environmental regulations to give them time to make the adjustments.

Stagflation

Normally, when inflation is high, unemployment is low; and when unemployment is high, inflation is low. During much of the 1970s, however, the United States experienced high inflation and high unemployment at the same time, a condition that economists called **stagflation**.

Three key factors contributed to the stagflation. First, the energy crisis created a scarcity of many products and thus caused price increases. Second, Johnson had created a large budget deficit by attempting to pay for both the Vietnam War and the Great Society without major tax increases. As a result, the government had to print more money to cover the deficit, further fueling inflation. The third cause was increased competition in international trade. In 1971, the United States suffered its first **trade deficit** (meaning the nation imported more goods than it exported) of the twentieth century.

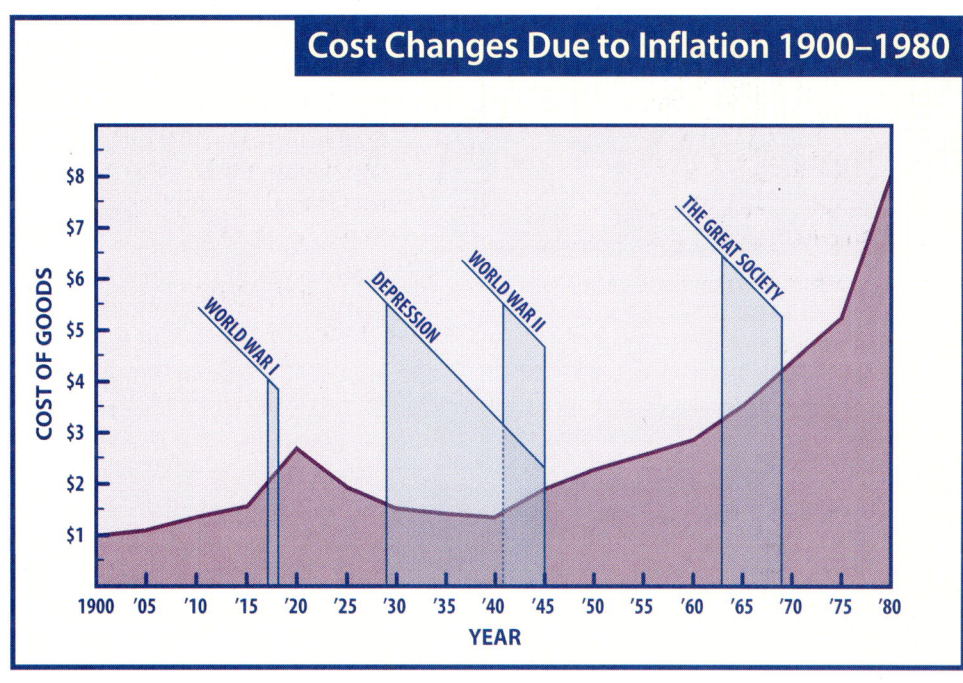

Cost Changes Due to Inflation 1900–1980

Stagflation left Congress in a dilemma. Attacking inflation by cutting government spending added to the already high unemployment because many jobs depended on federal funds. On the other hand, attacking unemployment through increased government spending added to the already alarming inflation rate and increased the nation's debt. No action seemed to work. As the 1970s ended, most Americans listed economic issues—primarily inflation—as their main concern.

Rights Movements

While African Americans were making gains in securing their civil rights, many other minorities attempted, with varying degrees of success, to broaden their legal rights. American Indians, for example, protested to reveal their plight: a high rate of unemployment and lower life expectancy. One of the most publicized protests was at Wounded Knee, South Dakota, in 1973, on the hundredth anniversary of the Wounded Knee massacre (see Chapter 17). Some Indian groups sued the government for violating numerous treaties with the Indians, and the courts often granted the Indians financial compensation and sometimes returned lands they had lost.

One of the largest and most influential movements in the 1970s was the **women's rights movement**. Although not a numerical minority, women as a group suffered from various forms of discrimination. For instance, women often received less pay than men working at the same job. In some states, a married woman could not own property in her own name. In addition, widows sometimes discovered after the death of a spouse that the excellent credit rating they had built with their husbands no longer existed; however, a widower's credit rating continued unimpaired. With such injustices

Protesters at Wounded Knee

After *Roe v. Wade,* abortion became an even more prominent social and political issue. Pro-life supporters (*above*) and abortion rights advocates (*below*) participated in demonstrations.

as illustrations, advocates of women's rights successfully appealed to the public's sense of fairness to address these problems.

The radical element within the women's movement became known as the **women's liberation movement**. Some within this group portrayed modern American marriage as a form of slavery in which wives labored in the "demeaning" roles of mother and homemaker. Betty Friedan became a leader in making these arguments. In 1963 her book, *Feminine Mystique*, was a best-selling but controversial work. She argued that many middle class homes had become "a comfortable concentration camp" for women. She and others in the women's liberation movement wanted to "free" women from such "slavery" and looked down on women who preferred the role of housewife—being a wife and mother in the home. To achieve their vision of equality, some women's liberationists advocated a platform of bold immorality: "free love" (premarital and extramarital sex), easier divorce laws, recognition of lesbian marriages, and, above all, a woman's unquestioned "right" to abortion on demand.

State laws had long restricted or even prohibited abortion. In the landmark case **Roe v. Wade** (1973), however, the Supreme Court declared that most state laws that restricted abortion were unconstitutional. Women's liberationists celebrated the decision. Consequently, the death of unborn children by abortion rose to more than one million a year by 1977.

Although radicals in the movement seized much of the public's attention, the real strength of the women's movement lay in the basic justice of its demands in the marketplace. Many women who were uninterested in or even opposed to the demands of the liberationists were very interested in economic equality. Both higher inflation and rising divorce rates were forcing more women out of the home and into the workplace simply to survive. Those women desired the opportunity to make a living and support their families. In addition, a large number of women were pursuing career opportunities. Therefore, Congress and the states began to address economic inequality by passing legislation to give women equal access to employment and equal pay for performing the same jobs as men.

The most controversial and divisive piece of pro-feminist legislation was the **Equal Rights Amendment (ERA)** passed by Congress in 1972. Section 1 of that proposed amendment said briefly, "Equality of rights under the law shall not be denied or abridged

Opponents (*left*) and supporters (*right*) of the ERA were active during the 1970s and early 1980s.

The Woman Who Stopped the ERA

The leader of the fight against the Equal Rights Amendment was a determined woman named Phyllis Schlafly. She worked her way through college during World War II, test-firing bullets in an ammunition plant. She earned her master's degree from Radcliffe College, a prestigious women's school. After marrying, she was a homemaker, rearing six children. She also was a candidate for Congress twice, served as a delegate to the Republican National Convention eight times, and eventually wrote twenty-seven books.

Schlafly first made headlines in 1964 when she published *A Choice Not an Echo*, an examination of Republican national politics that is often credited with helping Barry Goldwater win the 1964 presidential nomination. After Congress sent the ERA to the states for ratification in 1972, Schlafly visited the states that had not ratified it to stress the dangers of the amendment to the traditional rights of women.

She took abuse from many reporters, radical feminists, and other opponents. When opponents ridiculed her for speaking out on legal and constitutional issues without being a lawyer, she entered law school and earned her law degree.

"The claim that American women are downtrodden and unfairly treated is the fraud of the century," Schlafly said. She pointed to her own success. "I've achieved my goals in life and I did it without sex-neutral laws." She continued throughout her life to be vocal about politics and issues that concerned her. In September 2016, Schlafly passed away at age ninety-two.

---

by the United States or by any state on account of sex." Proponents of the amendment claimed that it would reinforce the basic rights as citizens that women held under the Constitution. Opponents claimed that sufficient laws were already in effect to guarantee those rights. Opponents also feared that the amendment would break down the traditional protections that women enjoyed, such as exemption from the military draft, and might result in the banning of single-sex bathrooms. A bitter fight regarding the ERA ended in 1982 when the amendment failed to garner the necessary approval of three-fourths of the state legislatures before its deadline for ratification expired. It had been approved by thirty-five of the needed thirty-eight state legislatures. However, by 1979, five of those thirty-five had revoked earlier support.

In addition to the movements for Indian rights and women's rights, the **gay rights movement** increased in size. One of its goals was to remove the many legal prohibitions to practicing homosexuality. Later, a major objective was to redefine marriage to include same-sex unions.

The push for homosexual rights gained supporters because it was presented as a struggle for freedom. Proponents compared the issue to the civil rights struggle of African Americans. Whereas African Americans faced discrimination because of their skin color, they claimed homosexuals were victims of bigotry because of their sexuality. They insisted that homosexuality was not an illness, as some claimed. In the early years of the movement, supporters argued homosexuality was a "sexual preference." Later, many asserted it was not a preference or choice but that it was a "sexual orientation" that was biologically determined.

Opponents of the gay rights movement voiced a number of concerns. Conservative Christians said that homosexuality was immoral. They observed that the Bible forbids homosexual practice (Leviticus 18:22; Romans 1:27; and Jude 1:7) and noted that from

Creation God had ordained marriage to be a heterosexual institution. While some Christians insisted homosexual desires must be a choice since homosexuality is a moral matter, other Christians contended that orthodox Christian theology has always taught that everyone is born with differing sinful desires. According to Christian teaching, sinful desires should always be resisted.

Christians and many non-Christians pointed to the need for children to have both a mother and father. They noted that this traditional family structure had been an important part of most civilizations and that it was a foundation of American society. Critics of the gay rights movement also highlighted differences between the civil rights struggle for black Americans and the gay rights movement. They stated that a person's ethnicity or skin color are not moral matters and that neither can be changed. However, sexual behavior is a moral issue, and sexual conduct is a matter of choice.

Section Review

1. Why did Arab nations place an oil embargo on the United States in 1973?
2–4. Name the agency and two major acts that were part of Congress's plans to protect the environment from pollution.
5–7. What were three key factors that contributed to stagflation in the 1970s?
8. What is the name for the radical wing of the women's rights movement?
★ Why do you think the Equal Rights Amendment failed to achieve sufficient support to become part of the Constitution?
★ Evaluate the impact of Phyllis Schlafly's political involvement.

III. The Carter Years

1976 Election

Gerald Ford entered the 1976 presidential race burdened by numerous weights. Although he was the incumbent, he was an unelected incumbent. The high unemployment rate, the Nixon pardon, and the public perception of Ford as a good-natured bumbler all hampered the president's election efforts. Furthermore, Ford was not even the preferred choice of many members of his own party. Former California governor **Ronald Reagan**, the hero of the Republican conservatives who dominated the party, mounted a strong challenge to Ford in the primaries. The president won the Republican nomination but only by a narrow margin after a bruising fight.

The Democrats' candidate proved unusual. **Jimmy Carter** was a successful peanut farmer. His political experience consisted of service as a local school board member, four years in the Georgia state senate, and one term as governor of Georgia. But he surprised the experts by winning the Democratic nomination. Carter's strategy was clever. He placed himself in the political center where he could attract the most voters—to the right of a host of liberal Democratic candidates but to the left of Democratic firebrand George Wallace. He also ran as an "outsider," a candidate untainted by the corruption in Washington and therefore supposedly better able to clean it up.

Guiding Questions

1. What were the issues and who were the candidates in the 1976 presidential election?
2. What characterized Carter's foreign policy?
3. What characterized Carter's domestic policy?

The 1976 election looked at first as though it would be an easy victory for Carter. Ford, however, fought back. The incumbent hammered away at Carter's vagueness on the issues. "Jimmy Carter will say anything anywhere to be president of the United States," Ford said. "He wavers, he wanders, he wiggles, and he waffles." But Ford hurt himself by proclaiming in a televised debate that he did not believe Eastern Europe was under Soviet domination, despite the presence of Soviet-imposed governments in those nations. This blunder merely reinforced the perception of some people that Ford was the weaker candidate.

As a further contrast to the dishonesty of the Nixon years, Carter campaigned as a "born-again" Christian who wanted a government "as filled with love as are the American people." After the trauma of Watergate, Americans were attracted to a candidate who said plainly, "I will never tell a lie to the American people."

In the end, Carter won narrowly—50.1 percent to 48 percent in the popular vote. The vote in the Electoral College, 297 to 240, was the closest since Woodrow Wilson defeated Charles Evans Hughes in 1916.

Carter (*above left*) and Ford (*above right*) participating in one of their televised political debates

1976 campaign buttons

The Carter Style

Carter entered office professing his desire to be a "people's president" with an open, honest, and compassionate administration. He surprised and delighted the American people by abandoning his armored limousine and walking down Pennsylvania Avenue after his inauguration. Later, he made some televised addresses wearing a sweater instead of a suit, and many photographs showed him relaxing in blue jeans. He calculated that all of these "down-home" images would endear him to the public as "one of them."

Carter appointed record numbers of women and minorities to government positions. But not all his "healing" gestures were appreciated. When he granted amnesty (a general pardon) to those who fled the country or failed to register for the draft to avoid fighting in Vietnam, Carter felt the wrath of veterans who had loyally fulfilled their obligation and fought in the war. Mercy to "draft dodgers" was not popular with many veterans.

Carter also had some negative characteristics. Like James Polk, he was a compulsive worker who seemed to micromanage the government; as a result, he was often bogged down by details that could have been delegated to subordinates. Carter's "outsider" status in Washington made it hard for him to work with Congress, despite large Democratic majorities in both houses. These flaws eventually damaged Carter's reputation, causing many Americans to become disenchanted with his policies and causing many to view him as an ineffective leader.

Foreign Affairs

Carter tried to pursue a foreign policy based on fairness and morality, much as Woodrow Wilson had tried to do. The cornerstone of Carter's foreign policy was the defense of **human rights**, protecting people from government oppression and ensuring that people had basic freedoms. While Carter's goals were commendable, the United States could influence only friendly nations concerning human rights. Communist nations, among the worst

President and Mrs. Carter walk down Pennsylvania Avenue after his inauguration.

violators of human rights, resisted Carter's pressures and continued to mistreat their people.

Panama Canal Treaty

Carter's first great challenge in foreign affairs concerned the Panama Canal. Panamanians had resented American control of the canal for many years. The United States had helped Panama win its independence from Columbia and paid Panama for control of the Canal Zone, according to the original treaty, "in perpetuity" (i.e., essentially forever). The Nixon and Ford administrations had begun negotiations to give the canal to Panama; Carter merely completed the process. He signed the **Panama Canal Treaty** in 1977, and the Senate narrowly ratified it the following year. The new treaty allowed Panama and the United States to operate the canal jointly until December 31, 1999, when Panama would take over the operation completely.

The treaty created controversy in the United States. Administration officials, numerous leading Democrats, and even some Republicans, such as Gerald Ford and Senator Howard Baker, defended the treaty. They claimed that the canal's narrow width and the growth of air power made the canal less important (militarily and economically) to the United States. They noted, for example, that aircraft carriers and oil tankers were too wide to use the canal. Supporters also hoped that the U.S. action would improve relations with Latin America.

Opponents of the treaty claimed that the waterway was still vital to American interests and should not be handed over to the authoritarian and sometimes unstable government of Panama. As for its narrowness, it could be widened to accommodate larger ships. (Panama did complete a decade-long widening project in 2016.)

Camp David Accords

President Carter's greatest triumph in diplomacy came in the Middle East. After becoming a nation in 1948, Israel was in constant conflict with its Arab neighbors. The nation fought four brief wars, and the region suffered from constant unrest and violence. But Egypt, one of Israel's most powerful opponents, was tired of the fighting, which had brought it no gain and much loss. In 1978 Carter invited the president of Egypt, Anwar Sadat (AHN-wahr sah-DAHT), and the prime minister of Israel, Menachem Begin (mehn-AH-kehm BAY-gihn), to meet with him at Camp David, the presidential retreat in Maryland.

After thirteen days of difficult negotiations, the three men reached an uneasy agreement known as the **Camp David Accords**. In return for Egypt's recognition of Israel's right to exist (which no other Arab nation had done) and a guarantee of peace, Israel returned to Egypt the Sinai Peninsula, which it had taken in the Six-Day War (1967). The agreement marked one of the greatest advances for peace in the Middle East since World War II. Egypt and Israel have yet to go to war since that agreement.

Anwar Sadat paid a heavy price for signing the Camp David Accords. On October 6, 1981, he was assassinated by Muslim

Carter (left) and the leader of Panama (right) signing the Panama Canal Treaty

President Carter (center) enjoyed his greatest foreign affairs triumph in negotiating the Camp David Accords between Egypt's president, Anwar Sadat (left), and Israel's prime minister, Menachem Begin (right).

extremists who opposed Sadat's agreement to recognize Israel's right to be a nation. During a military review, the assassins jumped from a military vehicle in front of the reviewing stand and opened fire. Sadat and several others were killed.

Soviet Union

Carter's success with the Camp David Accords, however, was overshadowed by several setbacks in foreign policy. His dealings with the Soviet Union are one example. Like Nixon and Ford before him, Carter pursued a policy of *détente* with the Soviet Union. The key to good relations, Carter decided, would be passage of the **SALT II Treaty**. This treaty was the result of Strategic Arms Limitation Talks (SALT) between the Soviets and the Americans to limit the number and kinds of nuclear weapons of each superpower. The president signed the treaty in June 1979, but he faced a stiff challenge getting it ratified by the Senate. Conservatives charged that the treaty would put the Soviet Union ahead of the United States in nuclear weaponry and that, given the Communists' consistent treaty violations, the United States could not be sure that the Soviets would maintain the agreement.

In late December 1979, all chance of passing the treaty vanished with the **Soviet invasion of Afghanistan**. The Soviets claimed that they were going to help the pro-Communist ruler of that neighboring country, but he was quickly assassinated and replaced by a Soviet puppet. Furious, Carter soon announced an embargo (or ban) on all sales of grain to the Soviets and an American boycott of the 1980 summer Olympic Games in Moscow. He also withdrew the SALT II Treaty from the Senate's consideration and called for a new registration of young men for the discontinued draft (although he did not revive the draft itself). In his State of the Union address for 1980, he announced the "Carter Doctrine," that the United States would resist by military force if necessary any Soviet attempt to push farther south to the Persian Gulf.

Afghan fighters celebrating atop a destroyed Russian helicopter

Carter's actions brought a storm of criticism. Liberals described the Carter Doctrine, draft registration, and withdrawal of the SALT II Treaty as harsh, provocative overreactions that threatened world peace. Farmers complained about their financial losses from the grain embargo. Conservatives claimed that Carter's response was weak—too much talk and too little action.

Iran

The Camp David Accords gave Carter his greatest triumph, but the Middle East also gave him his worst defeat when revolution erupted in Iran. The shah (king) of that nation, **Mohammed Reza Pahlavi** (known as the Shah of Iran), was long known to be pro-West in his outlook but dictatorial in his rule. In January 1979, after months of violent disorder, the Shah fled the country, and a fanatical Islamic extremist, the **Ayatollah Ruhollah Khomeini** (koh MAY nee), took power. Khomeini denounced everyone who

Mohammed Reza Pahlavi

Ayatollah Ruhollah Khomeini

Iranian radicals held more than fifty Americans hostage for 444 days. One hostage is shown blindfolded.

Carter's attempt to rescue the hostages failed tragically.

was not as zealous as he and his followers were—the Shah, other Arab nations, the Soviet Union, and especially "the great Satan" who had supported the Shah, the United States. In November, when Carter allowed the exiled Shah to enter the United States to receive medical treatment for cancer, enraged Muslims stormed the American embassy in Tehran, Iran. They took more than fifty Americans hostage. They offered to free the Americans in exchange for the Shah's return to Iran. They wanted to place him on trial. Carter refused to accept their conditions.

The **Iranian hostage crisis** became Carter's foreign policy nightmare. American citizens raged helplessly as television networks almost daily broadcast footage of Iranians burning American flags and chanting anti-American slogans. Iranians threatened to kill the hostages or place them on trial as spies. Carter, with few options open to him short of military invasion, tried vainly for months to use economic sanctions, negotiations, and world opinion to move the Iranians to release the hostages.

As the weeks dragged on, the American public's frustration and anger partially turned from Iran to the president himself. Many in the nation seemed to be asking, "Why doesn't the president do something?" Carter's inaction—which was perhaps not entirely his fault, considering his limited choices—made him seem weak, indecisive. In April 1980 an attempted military rescue of the hostages was a disaster. An American helicopter collided with an American transport plane in the desert of Iran, and eight American soldiers died without ever getting near the hostages.

The crisis continued and became a major issue in the 1980 presidential election. Many Americans voted against Carter because of his inability to obtain freedom for the hostages. Release finally came after 444 days of captivity on January 20, 1981—the day Americans inaugurated a new president, Ronald Reagan.

Domestic Problems

Carter's foreign problems were matched by his domestic difficulties. The economy was the primary problem. Ford had managed

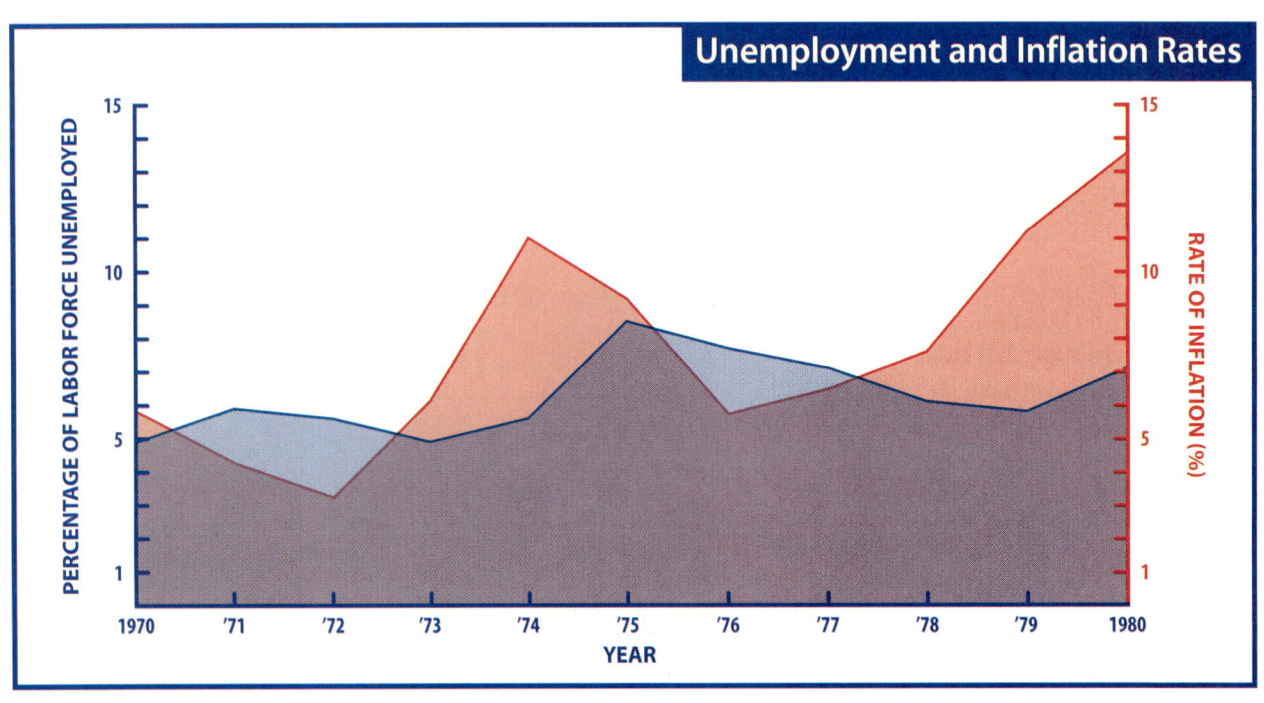

Unemployment and Inflation Rates

to get the rate of inflation down to about 5.5 percent, but the result was a recession and an unemployment rate of almost 8 percent by the time he left office. In his four years in office, Carter was able to lower unemployment only slightly. Inflation, however, soared. By 1980, the annual inflation rate rose to over 13 percent. Depositors and investors worried about how inflation was devastating their hard-earned savings. Consumers complained loudly about rising prices for food, clothing, fuel, and other necessities. The American economy seemed out of control, and Carter appeared helpless.

Carter's inability to get along with Congress aggravated matters. Congress's determination to be independent tide after the excesses of Watergate often paralyzed legislation. A growing number of Americans became frustrated as President Carter and a Democratic majority in Congress could not agree on how to help the nation. In addition, the Iranian revolution in 1979 diminished oil supplies in the United States again, reviving the long lines and high prices at gas stations that had characterized the early 1970s.

As American anger rose, Carter's popularity dropped. By December 1979 only 19 percent of the American people approved of Carter's performance—a rating lower than that of Richard Nixon during the depths of the Watergate affair. Many Americans—fed up with the failures of Nixon, Ford, and Carter—were looking for bold, new leadership.

Section Review

1–4. Name four difficulties President Ford faced in the 1976 presidential election.

5. What act did Carter perform at his inauguration to symbolize his desire to be a "people's president"?

6. Why was the narrow width of the Panama Canal an argument against its value to the United States?

7. What was President Carter's greatest diplomatic triumph?

8. What event virtually eliminated all chance of the Senate ratifying the SALT II Treaty?

★ Analyze the Camp David Accords (the negotiations and the agreement). Why was this so significant?

★ Knowing what we do now, how was the hostage crisis in Iran near the end of Carter's term a warning to the United States of further dangers to come?

IV. The Rising Conservative Tide

Thunder on the Right

Among the people who were unhappy with the course that America was taking in the 1960s and 1970s were political conservatives, typified by Republicans Barry Goldwater and Ronald Reagan. Traditional conservatives held to a firm ideology of limited powers for the national government and staunch opposition to the growth of communism. They opposed increased government spending, especially since the nation's budget deficit was growing at an alarming rate. Such conservatives feared particularly that the United States was falling behind the Soviet Union in military power and

Guiding Questions

1. What led to the resurgence of political conservatism in the United States?

2. How did the message of the political parties differ leading up to the 1980 presidential election?

therefore opposed initiatives such as President Carter's SALT II Treaty. They also denounced Carter's decision to break relations with Nationalist China on Taiwan to establish full relations with Communist China. Such an action was to them a betrayal of a long-time friend and anti-Communist force to accommodate a Communist government. Likewise, most political conservatives opposed the Panama Canal Treaty as symbolic of America's declining power and prestige. Those events energized conservatives as a political force.

New Right

Joining the old-line conservatives was a faction called the **New Right**. Those conservatives shared many beliefs of the traditionalists, notably opposition to communism and belief in limited government. But the New Right was also motivated by numerous social and moral issues, and some New Right groups focused on a single overriding issue. The *Roe v. Wade* decision legalizing most abortions, for example, spurred a **Right-to-Life movement** that opposed abortion and sought to use such means as a constitutional amendment to overturn the *Roe* decision. Other New Right activists emphasized the need to reduce the increasingly heavy burden of taxation by national, state, and local governments. The campaign to defeat the ERA gained much support from the New Right.

The Supreme Court decision legalizing abortion sparked a groundswell of opposition and launched a Right-to-Life movement dedicated to finding legal means to overturn the decision.

Religious Right

An important component of the New Right was the **Religious Right**, various conservative Christian leaders and organizations that were concerned primarily with moral issues. The Religious Right grew in reaction to immoral trends in the United States, such as widespread drug abuse, the legalization of abortion, the increasing secularization of American culture, and increased toleration and even advocacy of homosexuality. The Religious Right hoped to stem the tide of immorality through political action that would reestablish America's traditional standards of morality, standards that reflected the unique contribution of the Christian faith to American history.

Some of the most prominent leaders of the Religious Right were television evangelists. They motivated many Christians to become active politically. One such leader was **Pat Robertson**, who established the first Christian television station in the United States in 1961. From that start, he built the Christian Broadcasting Network (CBN) and became host of a prominent Christian talk show, *The 700 Club*.

Another leader was Baptist pastor **Jerry Falwell** of Virginia, who, like Robertson, used television to promote his cause. Falwell founded a religious political action group called the Moral Majority to help elect conservative candidates and to further conservative causes.

Falwell drew heated criticism from liberals, who attacked him for breaking down the alleged wall of separation between church and state. They accused him of attempting to force his religious views on the general public and also criticized him for using a religious organization to achieve political ends. Many of those liberals

George H. W. Bush (*left*), who served as vice president and later president, shakes hands with Jerry Falwell (*right*).

were silent, however, when liberal politicians used liberal churches to register voters and advance liberal causes.

The Religious Right also benefited as more Americans were turning from theologically liberal churches to more doctrinally conservative ones. In a 1977 survey, seventy million Americans described themselves as "born-again" Christians. Although definitions of "born again" did not always agree with the scriptural doctrine of regeneration, those numbers meant that a large portion of the American population was at least sympathetic to conservative religious views. The Religious Right included not only Protestants, such as Robertson and Falwell, but also Catholics and Mormons.

The Religious Right feared that the government was undercutting the nation's traditional religious freedoms. The 1963 Supreme Court decisions against prayer and Bible reading in public schools were major examples of government interference. Another fear was government control of Christian schools. Since the 1960s, many Christians had placed their children in private Christian day schools to protect them from secular influences and declining public school educational standards. Some state and federal authorities began to call for intense regulations for Christian schools. Religious conservatives, realizing that growing governmental power could threaten all constitutional religious freedoms, began to fight back with their dollars and their ballots.

Some Christians who supported many of the goals of the Religious Right were concerned about some of its methods. In an attempt to bring Catholics and Mormons together for political purposes, there were efforts to downplay differences in the religious teachings of these groups. Other Christians wanted to focus on the major cultural issues from a biblical worldview rather than a political one. They emphasized loving their neighbor, influencing society through living a consistent Christian life, and the need to reach non-believers with the gospel.

Election of 1980

Nomination of Reagan

Riding the surge of conservatism to the Republican nomination was Ronald Reagan. Reagan had been a leading and persuasive advocate of conservative causes. With extensive experience in radio broadcasting and as a Hollywood actor, Reagan used his vocal skills to rouse conservatives with his defense of free enterprise. He called for shrinking the federal government and steadfastly opposed Communist expansion.

Reagan rose to fame politically by giving a persuasive television address on behalf of Barry Goldwater in 1964. In 1966, he was elected governor of California by a huge margin and was reelected in 1970. Reagan made two attempts at the Republican presidential nomination—a brief attempt to halt Richard Nixon in 1968 and a nearly successful bid to wrest the nomination from Gerald Ford in 1976. By 1980, Reagan was certainly the best-known and most popular Republican in the nation.

Reagan brushed aside his competition in the 1980 primaries and won the nomination. To unify the party, he chose one of his politically moderate opponents, George H. W. Bush, to be his running mate. With Reagan at the head of the ticket and the nation in a conservative mood, Republicans believed that they could win back the presidency that they had lost four years earlier.

1980s campaign buttons

Carter's Problems

Carter had political concerns in addition to Reagan. Some of his policies did not please the liberal wing of the Democratic Party. Liberals rallied behind Massachusetts senator **Edward Kennedy**, the younger brother of John and Robert. Eventually Kennedy realized that he had almost no chance to beat Carter, but he stubbornly remained in the campaign, hoping to force the president to pursue more liberal policies. This divisive candidacy hampered Carter's attempts to unify the party behind him.

Carter and Reagan faced another opponent. Republican Congressman **John Anderson** of Illinois, proclaiming that both Reagan and Carter were too conservative, announced that he would run as an independent third-party candidate. Anderson had no chance to win, but he was more likely to draw votes from Carter, whose policies were moderate to liberal, than from the staunchly conservative Reagan.

The Campaign

Conservative zeal alone was not enough to win a national election. The Republicans hoped that popular discontent with Carter and the Democrats would help them. Many voters viewed Carter's failure to obtain the release of hostages in Iran as a major foreign policy failure. An even more immediate problem was the state of the economy, mainly the dangerously high inflation rate. Reagan shrewdly perceived public sentiment. In his closing statement during a televised debate with Carter only a week before the election, Reagan turned to the camera and asked the American people,

> Are you better off than you were four years ago? Is it easier for you to go and buy things in the stores than it was four years ago? . . . Is America as respected throughout the world as it was? . . . I would like to have a crusade today, and I would like to lead that crusade with your help. And it would be one to take government off the backs of the great people of this country and turn you loose again to do those things that I know you can do so well, because you did them and made this country great.

Carter (*left*) and Reagan (*right*) shake hands at one of their televised debates.

The Misery Index
Republican economists combined the unemployment rate with the inflation rate to create the "misery index." Whereas the index had been 2.97 percent in July 1953, in June 1980 it was 21.98 percent.

Ronald Reagan won the presidency by a landslide in the 1980s election.

The Election of 1980

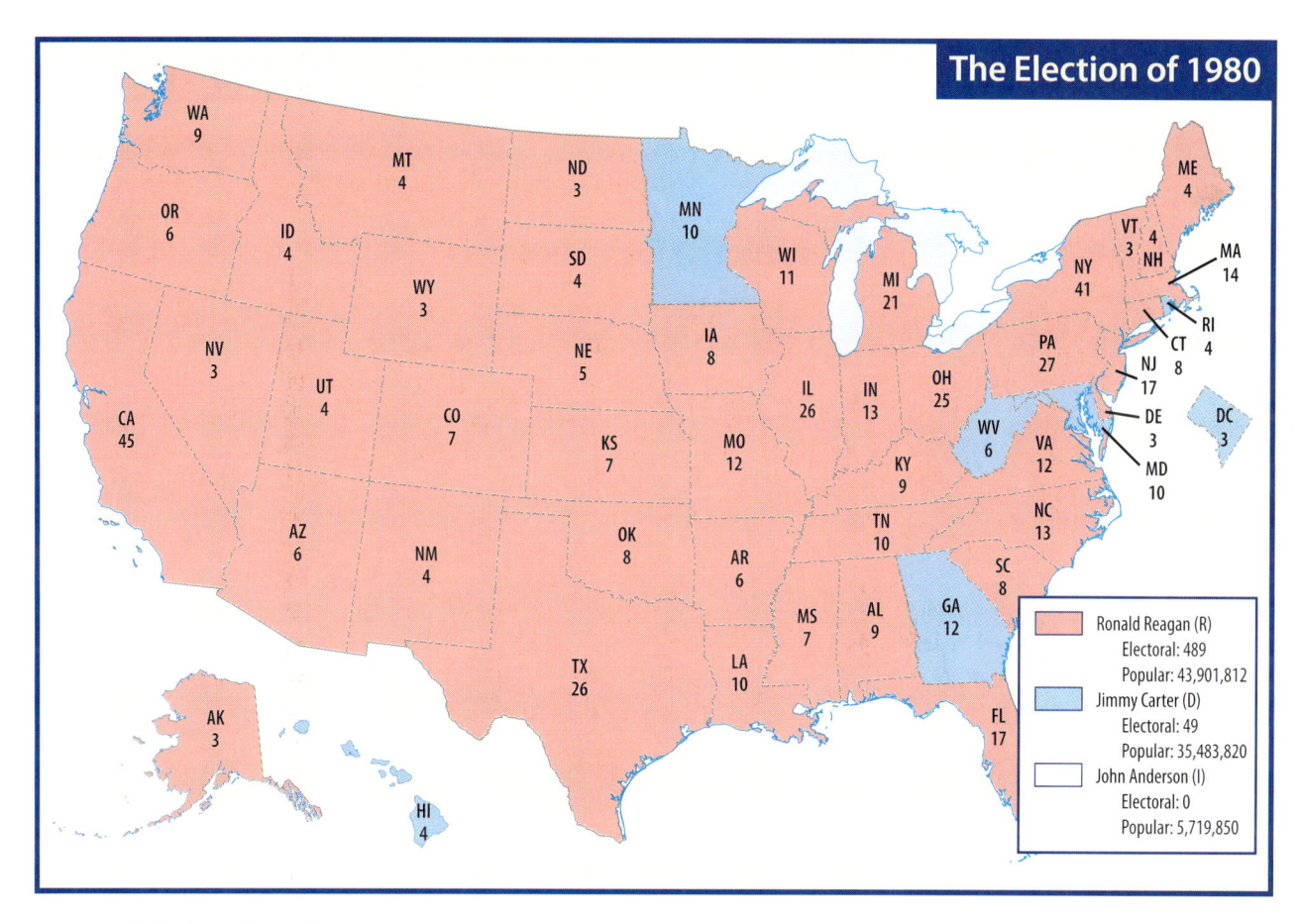

■ Ronald Reagan (R)	Electoral: 489 Popular: 43,901,812
■ Jimmy Carter (D)	Electoral: 49 Popular: 35,483,820
□ John Anderson (I)	Electoral: 0 Popular: 5,719,850

Until the last days of the campaign, the polls predicted a close race. It was not. On Election Day, Reagan won 50.7 percent of the popular vote to Carter's 41 percent and John Anderson's 6.6 percent. In the Electoral College, Reagan carried forty-four states for a massive 489–49 landslide victory. Furthermore, the Republicans won twelve additional seats in the Senate, capturing control of that body for the first time since Eisenhower's first term. The nation had decisively rejected not only Jimmy Carter but also his party. Now Ronald Reagan and the Republicans had the task of handling the nation's many challenges.

Section Review

1. What was the goal of the Right-to-Life movement?
2–3. Name two important political leaders of the Religious Right.
4–5. Who was the major third-party candidate of the 1980 presidential election? Why did he run?
6–7. What foreign policy issue hurt Carter most in the 1980 election? What domestic issue?

★ List the factors that led to the emergence of the Religious Right. In your opinion, was political involvement an appropriate way to address these concerns?

★ What factors made Reagan a popular leader among conservatives?

People, Places, and Things to Remember

Watergate affair
Spiro Agnew
Gerald Ford
Nixon pardon
oil embargo
energy crisis
environmental movement
stagflation
trade deficit
women's rights movement
women's liberation movement
Roe v. Wade
Equal Rights Amendment (ERA)
gay rights movement
Ronald Reagan
Jimmy Carter
human rights
Panama Canal Treaty
Camp David Accords
SALT II Treaty
Soviet invasion of Afghanistan
Mohammed Reza Pahlavi (Shah of Iran)
Ayatollah Ruhollah Khomeini
Iranian hostage crisis
New Right
Right-to-Life movement
Religious Right
Pat Robertson
Jerry Falwell
Edward Kennedy
John Anderson

CHAPTER REVIEW

Making Connections

1–2. Under the provisions of what amendment did Gerald Ford become vice president? Whom did he replace?

3–4. What is OPEC? What did it do in 1973?

5. What was the most controversial piece of legislation that emerged from the women's movement?

6. Describe the events that occurred in Iran in January 1979.

Developing History Skills

1. How can some extreme "rights movements," such as the gay rights movement, undermine genuine civil liberties?

2. Analyze the charts in this chapter that deal with gasoline prices and inflation. What was true regarding these two items in the 1970s?

Thinking Critically

1. Why did conservatives oppose the SALT II Treaty?

2. Some political observers in the late 1970s claimed that the presidency had grown too large for one man to handle. Why would they think so? Do you agree or disagree with their claim? Why?

Living as a Christian Citizen

1. If you had influence among the early leaders of the Religious Right, would you have attempted to reshape their approach in any way? If not, why not? If so, why and how?

2. If you were a Christian journalist during the time of Watergate, to what lessons would you focus the American public's attention? Compose a brief essay for your answer.

RESURGENCE OF CONSERVATISM (1981–1992)

26

President Reagan and Soviet Premier Mikhail Gorbachev converse at the White House.

It's morning again in America.

The opening line of Ronald Reagan's most famous 1984 campaign commercial

I. The Reagan Revolution

II. Reagan's Foreign Policy

III. The Presidency of George H. W. Bush

Big Ideas

1. What were the most important parts of Reagan's domestic policies?
2. What were the key aspects of Reagan's foreign policy?
3. What characterized the George H. W. Bush administration?

Reagan's inauguration on January 20, 1981 (*left*)

Confusion reigns as police and Secret Service agents respond to the attempt on Reagan's life. A Secret Service agent has just shoved Reagan to safety inside the limousine, which is about to race to the hospital (*right*).

The bullet stopped about an inch from his heart. For the man and the times, it was one critical, providential inch. **Ronald Reagan**, looking up from an operating room table into the worried faces of the physicians, smiled weakly and said, "Please tell me you're Republicans." Their faces brightened. "Today, Mr. President, we're all Republicans," one doctor replied.

Reagan survived the March 30, 1981, assassination attempt. To many, his resilience and determination symbolized the national spirit he hoped to awaken.

Guiding Questions

1. Why was Reagan's presidency called the Reagan Revolution?
2. What were Reagan's economic policies?

I. The Reagan Revolution

The Reagan years marked a clear shift in the nation's leadership, policies, and attitudes. Many Americans welcomed the new president's strong presence and inspiring rhetoric. But Reagan brought more than a polished image to the White House; he also brought new and substantive policy changes. As Reagan himself observed near the end of his tenure, "A revolution of ideas became a revolution of governance on January 20, 1981."

Reagan believed that with Communist threats from Central America to Central Asia, the United States had no choice but to maintain a firm grip on the reins of free-world leadership. He also believed that America's economic strength must be unleashed by reducing the size of government and the amount of taxes. He believed that both hindered growth and opportunity. According to his ideals, Reagan wanted to restore and strengthen traditional American values by curbing government intrusion into the home, the church, and the school.

Those ambitious goals of strength and freedom answered a need that many Americans keenly felt. Critics noted that those goals were never fully achieved and that Reagan's rhetoric often fell short of reality. But, others believed that a revolution of spirit was spreading as America saw the dawn of its third century.

Reaganomics

First on Reagan's agenda was tackling the nation's economic woes. Frustration over the economic recession, with its double-digit inflation and high unemployment, had helped elect him, and Reagan was determined to address the problem quickly. In his inaugural address, he declared an end to a "tax system which penalizes successful achievement and keeps us from maintaining full productivity." In that speech, he also promised that the days of big government-spending sprees were numbered. Reagan declared:

> For decades we have piled deficit upon deficit, mortgaging our future and our children's future for the temporary convenience of the present. To continue this long trend is to guarantee tremendous social, cultural, political, and economic upheavals.... We must act today in order to preserve tomorrow. And let there be no misunderstanding: We are going to begin to act, beginning today.

Reagan's prescription for America's inflation ills was **supply-side economics** (or **Reaganomics**, as it was called by his opponents). The supply-side approach seeks to lower inflated prices by enhancing productivity and increasing the supply of goods. Higher productivity and a larger supply of goods help lower prices and energize the economy by providing fuller employment. This approach depended on a limited-government agenda: cut taxes so that citizens will have incentive to earn, save, and invest; and encourage economic expansion by reducing government regulations on business and by providing corporate tax breaks.

Critics of Reaganomics called it "trickle-down economics." They argued that Reagan's approach would help wealthy Americans and large businesses but that little money would "trickle down" to middle- or lower-class Americans.

The Law of Supply and Demand

According to the law of supply and demand, the more of a good that is produced, the lower the price will be for each one of that good. The lower the price is, the more of the product will be sold. Similarly, the greater the demand for a good is, the higher its price will be. Conversely, when demand for a good drops, so will its price. For example, the price of gold is high because the supply is relatively low but demand is high. Conversely, the price of apples is generally low because, although demand might be high, the supply is also high.

Reagan Leadership

After a decade of Vietnam, Watergate, Iran, and economic turmoil, Ronald Reagan sought to revive hope, pride, and patriotism. During his years in office, supporters saw Reagan as the commander in chief of the American spirit, marshaling national emotion with a skill that few leaders have been able to master. When Reagan came to Washington, many critics dismissed him as a has-been, B-grade actor clearly out of his element in the rough-and-tumble national scene and the world of politics.

Reagan's greatest talents were not those of an administrator or of an economist; they lay in his ability to inspire many Americans. In his inauguration speech in January 1981, he said:

> It is time for us to realize that we're too great a nation to limit ourselves to small dreams. We're not, as some would have us believe, doomed to an inevitable decline. I do not believe in a fate that will fall on us no matter what we do. I do believe in a fate that will fall on us if we do nothing. So ... let us begin an era of national renewal. Let us renew our determination, our courage, and our strength. And let us renew our faith and our hope.
>
> We have every right to dream heroic dreams. Those who say that we're in a time when there are not heroes, they just don't know where to look. You can see heroes every day going in and out of factory gates. Others, a handful in number, produce enough food to feed all of us and then the world beyond. You meet heroes across a counter.... There are entrepreneurs with faith in themselves and faith in an idea who create new jobs, new wealth and opportunity. They're individuals and families whose taxes support the government and whose voluntary gifts support church, charity, culture, art, and education. Their patriotism is quiet, but deep. Their values sustain our national life.

Reagan went directly to the people to enlist support for his tax cuts.

The Tax Axe

Central to Reagan's economic policy was tax cuts. Using his skills of persuasion, Reagan took his cause both to Congress and directly to the taxpayers. Congress, fearful of a popular backlash, mustered majorities in both houses to pass the Economic Recovery Tax Act of 1981. It cut income taxes by about 25 percent over three years, reduced maximum tax rates for upper incomes from 70 to 50 percent, and lowered business taxes.

Budget Battles

Another important part of Reagan's economic plan was budget cuts. In 1981 Congress approved cuts of $35 billion, reducing funding for some highway programs and education, welfare, and arts assistance. Opponents claimed such cuts unfairly affected the poor. For example, forced cutbacks in Aid to Families with Dependent Children (AFDC) ended the benefits for four hundred thousand homes.

One budget area that did receive a boost by the Reagan administration was defense. The administration added $12 billion to defense programs in 1982, and the buildup continued through the end of the decade. Critics of the defense buildup, altering a famous remark of humorist Will Rogers, charged that President Reagan had never met a weapons system he did not like. However, Reagan supporters argued that in the post-Vietnam era of the 1970s, America's military had declined in both morale and modern materiel. Given Communist expansion in Asia, Africa, and Central America and the need to protect vital oil interests in the Middle East, Reagan continued throughout his administration to advocate military spending.

Deficit Debacle

Tax cuts, increases in defense spending, and the unwillingness of Congress and the White House to make more serious budget cuts produced a huge deficit problem. Each year the government continued to spend more money than it received. This borrowing of huge amounts of money led to enormous increases in the national debt. At the end of the 1970s, the debt had been $827 billion. A decade later, the figure soared to $2.9 trillion. By then, interest payments alone on the debt reached more than $200 billion, effectively wiping out any savings gained by budget cuts. The huge debt presented a continuing threat to America's strength.

The president and Congress were not the only ones lacking the will to deal with the debt. Americans representing many interests supported the *idea* of budget cuts as long as those cuts did not affect programs *they favored*. Public outcries occurred when spending reductions threatened popular programs.

Recession and Recovery

During the 1980 campaign, while the country was experiencing a deep recession, Carter had argued with candidate Reagan over the challenger's assertion that the country was in an actual depression. Reagan responded, "I'm talking in human terms and he is hiding behind a dictionary. If he wants a definition, I'll give him one. A recession is when your neighbor loses his job. A depression is when you lose yours. A recovery is when Jimmy Carter loses his."

Deficits and Debt

What is a **budget deficit**? It is the amount by which expenditures exceed income. For example, if the U.S. has $4.2 trillion in revenue, or income, for a year, but it spends $4.7 trillion, the budget deficit would be $500 billion.

What is the **national debt**? It is the amount of money that the government owes. Every year in which there is a budget deficit, the U.S. government borrows more money and thus the national debt increases.

Candidate Reagan's joke brought a good laugh in 1980, but by 1982 President Reagan found that a recession was no laughing matter. That year, the economy slumped along with the president's approval rating, and unemployment grew to more than 10 percent. The president's response was mixed. Abandoning his antitax policies, Reagan pushed through a tax increase aimed mainly at businesses, hoping to calm anxiety concerning the budget deficit. At the same time, Reagan urged Americans to "stay the course" while the Reaganomics tax cuts on individual incomes and pro-business policies reduced unemployment.

By 1983 America's economy rebounded. In the growth that followed, the nation enjoyed lower unemployment, lower interest rates, and lower oil prices. Eighteen million new jobs were created during the 1980s, and unemployment dropped to about 5 percent. In some parts of the nation, unemployment figures were even lower, reflecting a labor shortage rather than a job shortage. The housing market, an important indication of American economic strength, mushroomed.

Reagan had a personal charm that enabled him to work with his political opponents, such as Speaker of the House Tip O'Neill.

Section Review

1–2. In addition to cutting taxes for all citizens, what two actions did supply-side economics propose for business in order to promote economic expansion?

3. What was a central aspect of Reagan's economic policies?

4–6. What three factors helped to dramatically increase the budget deficits in the 1980s?

★ Why do voters often eagerly vote for someone who pledges to cut wasteful government spending but then, after that candidate wins, often oppose him when he tries to keep his promise?

II. Reagan's Foreign Policy

America faced challenges abroad and at home. From the beginning, Reagan demonstrated his determination to confront Communist aggression. The Soviet invasion of Afghanistan in December 1979 had ended the era of détente. During his first month in office, Reagan characterized the Communist leaders as those who "reserved unto themselves the right to commit any crime, to lie, to cheat" and were still bent on "world domination." Reagan later referred to the Soviet Union as an "evil empire." Critics groaned that Reagan's harsh words were renewing and worsening Cold War tensions.

In keeping with America's tough stance toward the Soviets, one of the key aspects of Reagan's foreign policy was the **Reagan Doctrine**, which pledged America's support to groups fighting Communists in the Third World. As a result, military and economic aid flowed to anti-Communist fighters in Latin America, Africa, and Asia. The Reagan Doctrine also sparked battles on the home front as Congress struggled with the White House over the new direction in foreign policy.

Central America

In 1981, Communist rebels and the government of El Salvador were involved in a civil war. True to his doctrine, Reagan responded

Guiding Questions

1. How did Reagan's foreign policy differ from that of his predecessors?
2. What factors led to a thaw in the Cold War?
3. What was the Iran-Contra affair?

to the aggression of the Soviet- and Cuban-backed rebels by supplying arms, military advisors, and economic aid to the Salvadoran government.

American support for the government of El Salvador led to further U.S. involvement in Central America. In 1979 rebels, known as Sandinistas, had taken control of Nicaragua. After establishing a Communist government there, the Sandinistas began sending military supplies to the Communists in El Salvador. Under the direction of the Central Intelligence Agency (CIA), groups of anti-Sandinista guerrillas known as **Contras** (from the Spanish word for counterrevolutionary) were organized in Nicaragua to fight communism there.

Reagan's support for anti-Communist forces in Nicaragua ignited fierce debates in Congress. Critics warned that reviving "big stick" policies would renew anti-Americanism throughout the region. They urged compromising with the Sandinistas and increasing economic aid to the region. Reagan, however, believed that the Sandinistas posed a threat to not only the democratic elements within Nicaragua but also the security of all Central America. With the Soviets supporting Nicaragua's Communist government, Reagan argued that U.S. support of the Contras also represented a vital test of American commitment to the Monroe Doctrine.

By 1983, the government of Grenada, a tiny Caribbean island, was increasingly influenced by Communists who had close ties with Cuba. Fearing a second Cuba in the Caribbean and respond-

Contras in Nicaragua

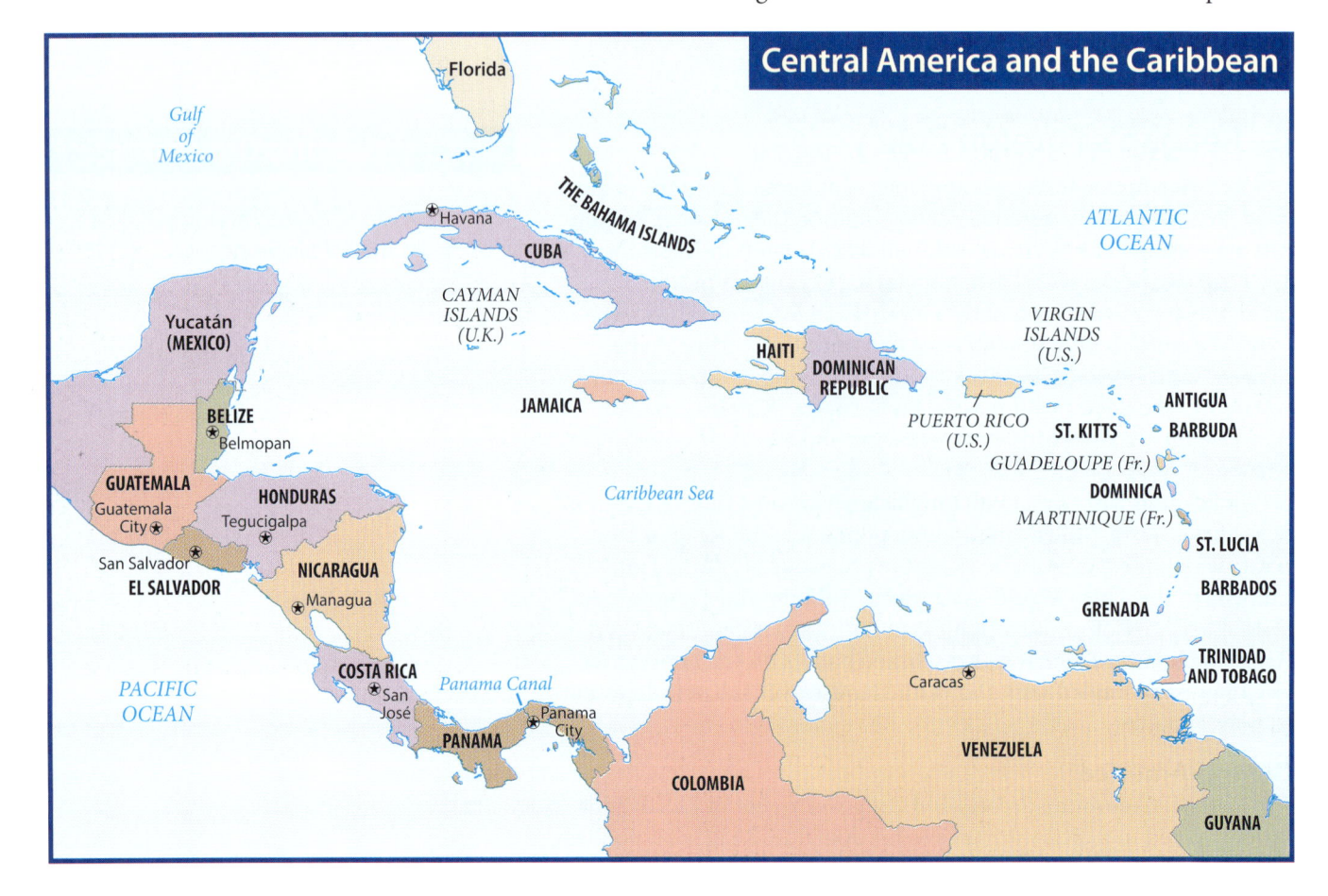

Central America and the Caribbean

ing to calls for help from the governments of neighboring islands (who also feared the spread of communism), President Reagan sent nearly 2,000 U.S. troops to Grenada. The October 1983 invasion defeated the Cuban and Grenadian soldiers there. A new, anti-Communist government was established. Reagan hoped that his actions in El Salvador, Nicaragua, and Grenada would send a clear message to Communists regarding his desire to stop their expansion.

Afghanistan

The frontline of the Reagan Doctrine was in Soviet-occupied Afghanistan. Since their 1979 invasion, the Soviet army had waged a brutal war against both the Afghan guerillas, known as *mujahideen* (moo JAH heh DEEN), and Afghan civilians of all ages.

Reagan supplied military advisors and state-of-the-art weapons, including surface-to-air missiles, to the mujahideen. American support, combined with determined rebel resistance, dealt a stunning blow to Moscow's troops. After ten years of fighting, the Soviet army withdrew in the spring of 1989, leaving Afghanistan bloodied and battered. Many Americans viewed the Soviet retreat as a great triumph for the Reagan Doctrine. Because it was costly and inconclusive, the war in Afghanistan was often referred to as "Russia's Vietnam."

Sadly, the United States did not commit resources to rebuild Afghanistan and form strong alliances in this region following the defeat of the Soviets. Instead, radical elements filled the power vacuum. Future U.S. administrations would expend immense human and financial resources to combat this rise of Muslim radicalism in Afghanistan.

Terrorism

In contrast to Reagan's successes in Afghanistan, terrorism was a persistent problem that produced setbacks. Lebanon had been in a state of war since the 1970s. Eventually, Reagan ordered American troops into that nation to join a multinational peacekeeping force there. However, there was little peace to keep; fighting continued to boil over into the streets of Beirut, the capital city. After repeated Arab attacks on American positions, the U.S. Navy began shelling terrorist bases. On October 23, 1983, a terrorist driving a bomb-laden truck crashed through barricades and into the U.S. Marines barracks in Beirut, killing 241 Americans.

Several U.S. citizens, some working in Beirut as teachers and journalists, were taken hostage during the 1980s. The American public watched in helpless anger. Eventually some hostages were released, but others died in captivity.

Four More Years

Forty-Nine-State Landslide

As the 1984 election approached, Democrats renewed some of their earlier criticisms of Ronald Reagan: the president's trigger-happy foreign policy, as the Democrats characterized it, was an embarrassment in the international community; and his social policies isolated the poor, ignored the working class, and insulted women. Even though Reagan had appointed the first woman

The Evil Empire

In March 1983, President Reagan spoke to a group of religious leaders. As part of his speech, he stated the following about the Soviet Union.

"Yes, let us pray for the salvation of all of those who live in that totalitarian darkness—pray they will discover the joy of knowing God. But until they do, let us be aware that while they preach the supremacy of the [government], declare its omnipotence [power] over individual man, and predict its eventual domination of all peoples on the earth, they are the focus of evil in the modern world. . . . [they have the] aggressive impulses of an evil empire."

The U.S. Marines barracks in Lebanon after the October 1983 attack

Democrats Mondale and Ferraro lost to Reagan in a landslide in 1984.

Mikhail Gorbachev was the Soviet leader from 1985 to 1991.

Cooperating with Dictators
During the Cold War, the U.S. government made alliances with some leaders who did not always share America's views on human rights or the importance of free elections. Our government viewed these alliances as necessary to prevent the spread of communism. However, many Americans were critical of supporting any dictators.

Supreme Court justice, Sandra Day O'Connor, in 1981 and had named a number of women to important government posts, feminists in the Democratic Party charged that he had ignored the female half of the electorate.

Walter Mondale, former vice president under Jimmy Carter, won the Democratic nomination. Mondale chose New York congresswoman **Geraldine Ferraro** as his running mate. She was the first female vice-presidential candidate for a major party. Reagan's personal popularity and a strong economy brought him one of the greatest landslides in U.S. history on Election Day. Reagan lost only Mondale's home state of Minnesota and the District of Columbia.

Reagan's second term was plagued by few of the domestic economic issues that confronted his first term. Despite mounting deficits, the continuing slide in oil prices helped keep the economy strong. Much of the focus of Reagan's second term was on foreign policy: improving relations with the Soviet Union and, after 1986, dealing with the political fallout from a matter known as the Iran-Contra affair.

Cold War Thaw

The Soviet Union had a succession of dictators during the Reagan years as death took its toll on the old leadership. Leonid Brezhnev died in 1982; his successor, Yuri Andropov, served only fifteen months and died in 1984; and Andropov's successor, Konstantin Chernenko, died in 1985. When a reporter criticized Reagan for not making progress with the Soviet leaders, Reagan quipped in frustration, "Well, they keep dying on me!"

Mikhail Gorbachev (mik-HEL GOR-buh-CHOF) became the new leader in 1985. In contrast to his recent predecessors, he presented a new, polished style. As he took control, the Russian economy was experiencing enormous difficulties, and the Red Army was stuck in the quagmire of Afghanistan. In confronting those problems throughout the late 1980s, Gorbachev called for *perestroika* (PEHR ih STROY kuh), or "restructuring," of the stagnant Communist economy, shifting to more free-market policies and some private ownership. Gorbachev also advocated **glasnost** (GLASS nost), or "openness," in Soviet society. He allowed more freedom of speech, press, and religion.

Gorbachev spoke of new ideas, but he clung to old, failed ones. Perestroika was actually a series of half-measures that raised Soviet expectations rather than the standard of living. Yet in contrast to the slow progress of perestroika, glasnost was perhaps *too* successful. Giving the Russian people a taste of freedom only awakened their desire for more; nationalism replaced Marxism. The diverse ethnic groups of the Soviet Empire, bound together by military force and a failed Marxist philosophy, called for greater freedom from government control. Gorbachev and the Red Army responded to those stirrings of independence and nationalism with tear gas and bullets. Glasnost was more successful on the fringes of the iron curtain as, one by one, Eastern European countries ousted their Communist governments between 1989 and 1991. Germany—divided since World War II—reunited in 1990.

During his second term, Ronald Reagan made a dramatic shift in Soviet relations. During his last three years in office, Reagan met with Gorbachev five times to improve diplomatic ties. The summit meetings between the two leaders were called Strategic Arms Reduction Talks (START). START aimed primarily at reaching an

The Berlin Wall Crumbles

Reagan visited Berlin in June 1987 and delivered a speech beside the Berlin Wall. He issued a public challenge to Gorbachev: "General Secretary Gorbachev, if you seek peace, if you seek prosperity for the Soviet Union and Eastern Europe, if you seek liberalization: Come here to this gate! Mr. Gorbachev, open this gate! Mr. Gorbachev, tear down this wall!"

Two years later, revolutions were sweeping through the Communist nations in Eastern Europe. On November 9, 1989, the Communist-controlled East German government announced that it would begin allowing its citizens to freely cross from East Berlin into West Berlin the following day. When word spread, crowds rushed to the Berlin Wall. That night guards watched, and took no action, as Germans chipped away at the twenty-eight-year-old structure with picks and hammers.

Reagan's speech occurred two years before the Berlin Wall was dismantled.

---

agreement to substantially reduce the number of nuclear weapons the two nations possessed.

Gorbachev knew that reducing his nation's military spending would help solve some of the economic difficulties it faced. Reagan also favored weapons reductions but wanted to ensure that Soviets did not publicly agree to changes and then privately violate them. Thus, throughout negotiations, Reagan emphasized the principle of "trust—but verify." He insisted that all treaties include enforcement procedures.

At the Washington Summit in 1987, Reagan and Gorbachev signed the Intermediate Nuclear Forces (INF) Treaty, which eliminated most medium-range missiles from Europe. The superpowers' agreement was heralded as a symbol of friendlier relations.

While Reagan continued negotiations, he proposed developing the **Strategic Defense Initiative (SDI)**. First announced by Reagan in 1983, SDI—or "Star Wars" (after the popular series of science fiction movies), as opponents mockingly called it—was a proposed space-based defense shield of satellites, missiles, and lasers designed to safeguard the country from nuclear attack. Although SDI was many years, many billions of dollars, and many technological hurdles away from reality, the program seriously affected the nuclear arms issue. Gorbachev knew that SDI would force the Soviet Union to develop its own defense shield—a long and costly endeavor. With the Soviet economy on the verge of collapse, as evidenced by empty store shelves throughout the country, Reagan's SDI development brought increased pressure on Gorbachev's government as the 1990s began.

Iran-Contra

In November 1986, an underground newspaper in Beirut, Lebanon, reported that the Reagan administration had secretly sold

Vice President Bush, President Reagan, and Soviet Premier Gorbachev meet in New York City, in December 1988.

weapons to Iran in exchange for its help in obtaining the release of American hostages in Lebanon (those captives were held by terrorist groups sympathetic to Iran). As the story unfolded, it revealed that members of the White House National Security Council (NSC)—principally NSC chief John Poindexter, his aide U.S. Marine Lt. Col. Oliver North, and CIA director William Casey—had established this arrangement. At the time, Iran was locked in a costly war with neighboring Iraq and needed missiles and other military supplies.

Investigations into what happened to the money from the arms sales to Iran widened the scandal. The funds, funneled through Swiss banks, were used to supply the Nicaraguan Contras battling the Communist Sandinistas, giving the matter the name **Iran-Contra affair**.

The support to the Contras came at a time when Congress, under the provisions of a law known as the Boland Amendment, had cut off military aid to that group. The Reagan White House was already embarrassed about the disclosure that it sold weapons to Iran, as part of the attempt to obtain freedom for hostages, in violation of the president's long-stated policy of not negotiating with terrorists. Congress conducted televised hearings regarding the issue. Reagan initially distanced himself from his subordinates, but the whole matter raised questions about Reagan's management of the White House. The president's public approval rating dropped significantly. On March 4, 1987, in a speech to the nation, the President took responsibility for the actions of those who served in his administration.

Throughout 1987, the investigations and congressional hearings continued to uncover more details of the Iran-Contra affair. Much of the responsibility for the events was placed on Reagan's loose management style and his failure to properly supervise subordinates.

The White House insisted that the Boland Amendment did not apply to the NSC; congressional investigators disagreed. Though President Reagan had approved the weapons sales to Iran, no evidence was found that he knew about the money being sent to the Contras. However, North and Poindexter were found guilty of criminal charges, though their convictions were later overturned. Nevertheless, the scandal tainted Reagan's second term and his reputation.

Section Review

1. What Central Asian country's resistance to a ten-year Soviet occupation was viewed by many as a great triumph for the Reagan Doctrine?
2. To which Caribbean nation did the U.S. send troops in 1983?
3. Terrorism in what Middle Eastern nation caused setbacks in the Reagan administration's foreign policy?
4. Who was the first female Supreme Court justice?
5. What was the official name for the "Star Wars" project?
* Explain the Reagan Doctrine and describe when that doctrine was first implemented.
* Explain the terms *perestroika* and *glasnost* and assess their impact on Soviet society.

RESURGENCE OF CONSERVATISM

III. The Presidency of George H. W. Bush

One More for the Gipper

Despite the problems with Iran-Contra during Reagan's last two years in office, the president remained strong and popular. But as the election of 1988 approached, Democrats and Republicans alike sought his job.

Several Republicans claimed the right to Reagan's mantle, from Jack Kemp, one of the architects of Reaganomics, to newcomer Pat Robertson of the Religious Right. The nominee who emerged, however, was Reagan's vice president, **George H. W. Bush**. Having been in the shadow of a strong president for nearly eight years, Bush struggled to establish his own identity. Governor **Michael Dukakis** of Massachusetts survived a crowded field of contenders and emerged to win the Democratic nomination.

Republicans gathered in New Orleans for their national convention. Reagan, in an emotional farewell to his faithful supporters, urged them

Guiding Questions

1. Why was the Bush administration more successful abroad than domestically?
2. What factors led to Bush's defeat in the election of 1992?

Bush and Quayle, his running mate, celebrate their nomination at the 1988 Republican National Convention.

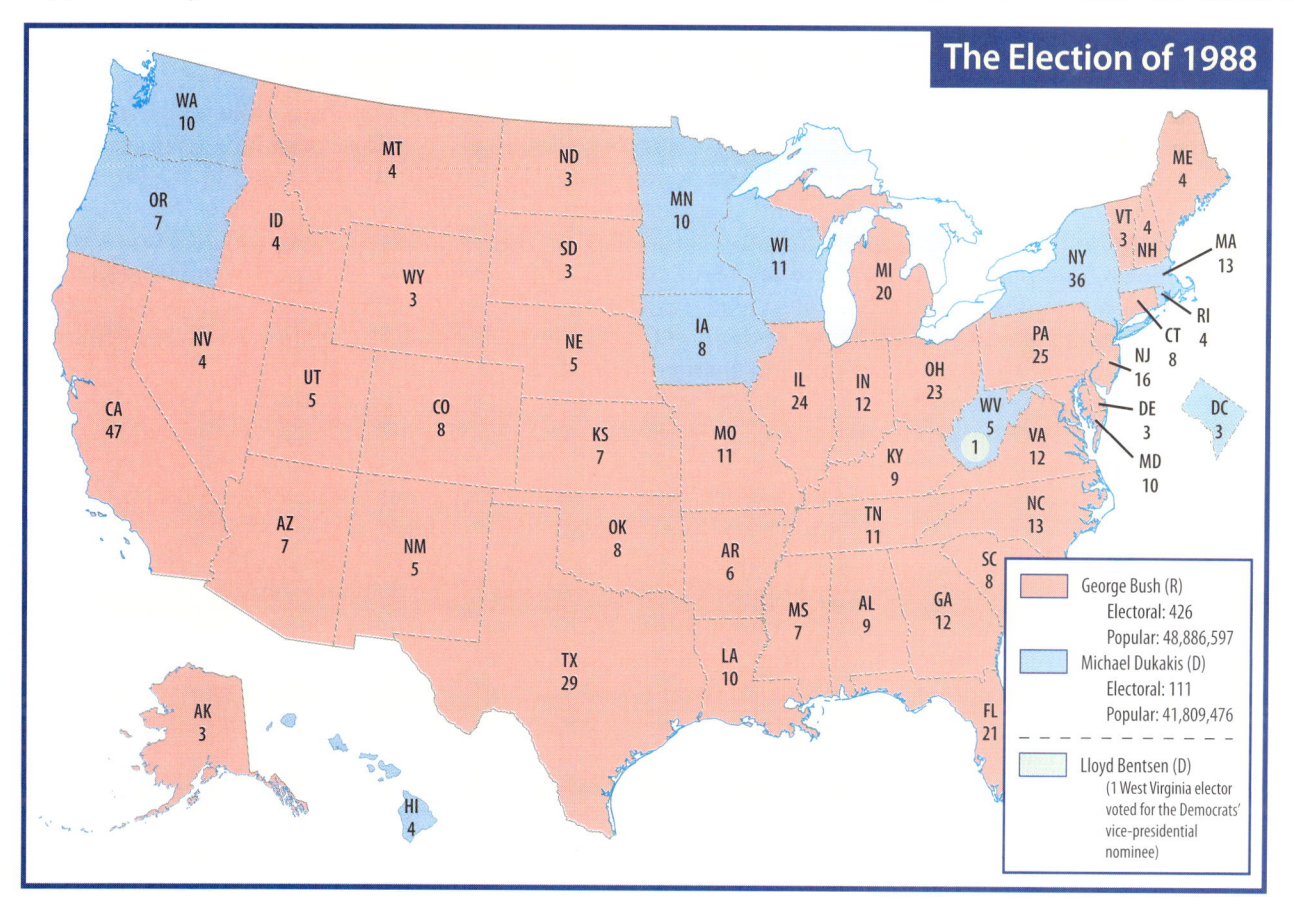

The Election of 1988

State	Electoral Votes
WA	10
OR	7
MT	4
ND	3
MN	10
ME	4
ID	4
SD	3
WI	11
VT	3
NH	4
MA	13
WY	3
MI	20
NY	36
RI	4
NV	4
NE	5
IA	8
PA	25
CT	8
UT	5
IL	24
IN	12
OH	23
NJ	16
CA	47
CO	8
KS	7
MO	11
WV	5
VA	12
DE	3
DC	3
KY	9
MD	10
AZ	7
NM	5
OK	8
AR	6
TN	11
NC	13
MS	7
AL	9
GA	12
SC	8
TX	29
LA	10
FL	21
AK	3
HI	4

George Bush (R)
Electoral: 426
Popular: 48,886,597

Michael Dukakis (D)
Electoral: 111
Popular: 41,809,476

Lloyd Bentsen (D)
(1 West Virginia elector voted for the Democrats' vice-presidential nominee)

> **"The Gipper"**
> The nickname "the Gipper" recalled a character and a familiar story from an old movie in which Reagan played George Gipp of Notre Dame, a dying football hero whose name became a rallying cry when his team was losing. Reagan—as Gipp—told his coach, Knute Rockne, "Rock, some day when the team's up against it—the breaks are beatin' the boys—ask them to go in there with all they've got and win just one for the Gipper." In the 1988 election opinion polls, the Republican team was down, and they resurrected the saying: "Win one for the Gipper"—Reagan.

again to "go out there and win one for the Gipper." After a shaky start, Bush rallied support largely by promoting strength at home and abroad and by promising no new taxes. The election provided a decisive win for Bush and his running mate, Dan Quayle. Bush's victory was in many ways a final vote of approval of Reagan. Bush won forty states and became the first vice president since Martin Van Buren in 1836 to be elected president immediately after serving as vice president.

Unfortunately for Bush, he also followed in the footsteps of Van Buren in other ways. After eight years under a popular president, Bush inherited problems of economic decline. Furthermore, foreign challenges demanded immediate attention. He proved astonishingly successful in his greatest foreign policy challenge, but domestic difficulties weakened his presidency.

Triumph Abroad

The Bush administration, which lasted from January 1989 until January 1993, saw the final collapse of the Iron Curtain and the end of the Cold War. By the time Bush left office, the Soviet Union no longer existed—in December 1991, the fifteen republics became fifteen separate nations. Eastern Europe was free of Communist domination. Despite the decline of communism, however, tyranny did not vanish. The United States soon faced a new challenge in an old hot spot, the Middle East.

1989—When the Walls Came Tumbling Down

One by one, the Iron Curtain countries cast off communism and opened their borders to Western influence. The amazing developments that year not only captured the attention of sympathetic Americans but also presented the United States with new foreign policy questions to be answered in the decades to come. The following simplified chronicle recounts some of the many startling events of those memorable days.

April 18—Poland legalized the Solidarity union and opened the way for the first free elections in Poland in forty years.

May 2—Hungarians began to tear down the fences along their Austrian border.

June 4—Solidarity candidates won stunning victories over Communists in Poland's parliamentary elections.

August 25—Poland's new non-Communist government took power.

September 10—Hungary opened its western borders. Many East Germans and Romanians began to use Hungary as an escape route to the West.

October 11—Hungary's Communist Party abandoned communism and changed its name to compete better in free elections.

October 18—East German Communist leader Erich Honecker resigned under pressure, later to be arrested and charged with criminal acts.

October 24—Hungary declared itself a republic.

October 25—Soviet leader Gorbachev told the West that his nation would no longer use force to keep the governments of Eastern Europe under Communist control, thereby opening the way for greater change in the region.

November 9—East Germany opened its borders. The Berlin Wall was no longer a barrier for East Germans as the gates swung open. The Wall, the symbol of Cold War division, began to be dismantled, and East Germany and West Germany were on the road to reunification.

November 24—The Communist leaders in Czechoslovakia resigned, leaving the nation to hold free elections. Bulgaria's Communist leader was ousted, and thousands of demonstrators in Sofia, the capital, chanted for democracy and free elections.

December 22—A popular uprising led to the capture, trial, and execution of Romania's oppressive Communist dictator, Nicolae Ceausescu, and his wife.

In 1990 and 1991, the Communist governments in East Germany, Albania, Yugoslavia, and the Soviet Union were also dissolved.

"Communist Dominoes Are Falling"

The year after leaving the White House, Ronald Reagan gave a speech in which he described the moral high ground that America occupies in the struggle between free and totalitarian states and the collapse of communism. On May 18, 1990, he said,

Let me tell you the basis of my optimism for our future. What has made the United States great is that ours has been an empire of ideals. The ideals of freedom, democracy, and a belief in the remarkable potential of the individual. Power isn't simply wealth or troops. Power is also spirit and ideas. And these we have in abundance....

We wanted to establish the best government on Earth. We wanted to put a man on the moon. This is the spirit we set loose. This is the passion that invented revolutionary technologies and a culture young people everywhere envy.

And this is the attitude that has defeated communism. At some dark, lonely moment during the last decade, a terrible realization set in upon the leaders of the Soviet Union. They realized that their system could not take them where the United States and the rest of the free world was going....

Our communications technology sailed over the barbed wire and concrete walls, letting their citizens know what democracy could offer, what free markets could provide. Our computer technology left them bewildered and behind, paper societies in an electronic age....

Children rest on a statue of Stalin that had been toppled in Moscow.

Communist dominoes are falling all over the world. We must continue to give Communist dominoes a good push whenever and wherever we can. There are still those that must fall—China, North Korea, North Vietnam, North Yemen, and of course, Cuba. Cuba is next in democracy's sweep. And let me say directly to Fidel Castro—like Honecker [the Communist leader] in East Germany, like Ceausescu [the Communist leader] in Romania . . . like all the other has-been dictators of despair, you cannot fight democracy's destiny. Fidel, you're finished! . . .

We should not be timid in our embrace of democracy. We should be as bold and brash in our democratic ideals as ever in our history. The Golden Age of Freedom is near because America has remained true to her ideals.

Used by permission of the Reagan Foundation

Confrontation

On August 2, 1990, Iraq, led by dictator **Saddam Hussein** (sah-DAHM hoo-SANE), launched a military attack that overwhelmed its neighbor Kuwait. On a number of occasions, Hussein had claimed that the tiny, oil-rich nation actually belonged to Iraq. By sending a force of nearly one hundred thousand soldiers, Hussein quickly captured Kuwait and stood poised for potential further conquest with his troops located on the border of Saudi Arabia.

Opposing this aggression and fearing that much of the world's oil supply might fall under the control of Hussein (Iraq, Kuwait, and Saudi Arabia contain almost half of the world's known oil reserves), Bush vowed, "This shall not stand." Working through the United Nations Security Council, the United States coordinated a defensive operation. Code-named **Operation Desert Shield**, the plan sent allied forces (chiefly American) to Saudi Arabia to prevent further Iraqi aggression.

Storm in the Desert

The United Nations overwhelmingly passed a resolution authorizing the use of military force to push the Iraqis out of Kuwait if they did not withdraw voluntarily by January 15, 1991. It did not, however, authorize the removal of Hussein from power.

The allies (the United States, Kuwait, Saudi Arabia, Egypt, Great Britain, France, and several other nations) gathered a force of 700,000 in Saudi Arabia. Before launching a military attack, the allies exhausted every possible diplomatic effort to get the Iraqis to withdraw. Finally, on January 12, 1991, Congress voted to authorize Bush to use force if necessary to get Iraq out of Kuwait.

The January deadline became a line in the sand as the Iraqi forces defiantly refused to withdraw. On January 16, Bush ordered a massive military assault on Iraqi military targets. Code-named **Operation Desert Storm**, the liberation of Kuwait began. The allied commander, American general Norman Schwarzkopf, told his forces, "Now you must be the thunder and lightning of Desert Storm."

The war began with more than five weeks of massive, around-the-clock bombing and air strikes on military targets in Iraq and Kuwait. Allied cruise missiles, bombers, and fighters, including the new stealth fighters (aircraft that use technology to avoid detection), pounded enemy installations. Enjoying almost complete air superiority, the U.S.-led forces destroyed much of Iraq's military capability—communications networks, airfields, bridges, roads, and missile launch sites. Then the attacks targeted Iraq's ground forces, demolishing tanks and artillery and relentlessly pounding Hussein's entrenched troops.

The 100-Hour War

The second stage of the war was a ground attack on the Iraqis. On February 24, a coalition of American, Arab, and British troops assaulted enemy positions in southern Kuwait, pinning down the Iraqis, who thought this attack was the main thrust. But while the battle was raging, American and British forces, supported by French units, moved into southern Iraq west of Kuwait. With amazing speed, armored and infantry forces encircled and entrapped the main Iraqi force in Kuwait and southern Iraq. Dispirited by the weeks of bombing and because they were virtually surrounded, thousands of Iraqi soldiers deserted and surrendered to the coalition army. Some Iraqi units fought fiercely but, with lines of communication severed, ineffectively. The allies destroyed them. On February 27—just one hundred hours after the ground war began—Bush addressed a television audience:

> Kuwait is liberated. Iraq's army is defeated. Our military objectives are met.... No one country can claim this victory as its own. It was not only a victory for Kuwait but a victory for all the coalition partners. This is a victory for the United Nations, for all mankind, for the rule of law, and for what is right.

Aftermath

The **Persian Gulf War** was an intensive American military effort. Allied planes flew more than 100,000 missions during the six-week war, losing about 75 aircraft. The American-led coalition wrecked nearly 4,000 enemy tanks and killed between 20,000 and 35,000 Iraqi soldiers. It destroyed the effectiveness of an enemy force numbering more than 500,000. Only about 300 allied soldiers died.

Allied bombs rain down on Baghdad during the air phase of the Gulf War.

Much of the Persian Gulf War involved fighting in the desert areas.

A War of Precision

Allied forces had lost about 300 men and women in the Persian Gulf War. Because of the technological advances in weaponry, military and civilian casualties and "collateral damage" were less than in any other war on that scale. The United States used precision-guided missiles and "smart bombs" that pinpointed targets to within a few feet. Numerous videos released by the Defense Department show pilots placing such camera-carrying bombs right into air ducts of targeted military installations.

General Schwarzkopf, commenting about allied losses, said, "The loss of one human life is intolerable to any of us who are in the military. But ... casualties of that order of magnitude, considering the job that's been done and the number of forces that are involved, is almost miraculous."

Gulf War: Operation Desert Storm

February 25–27, 1991

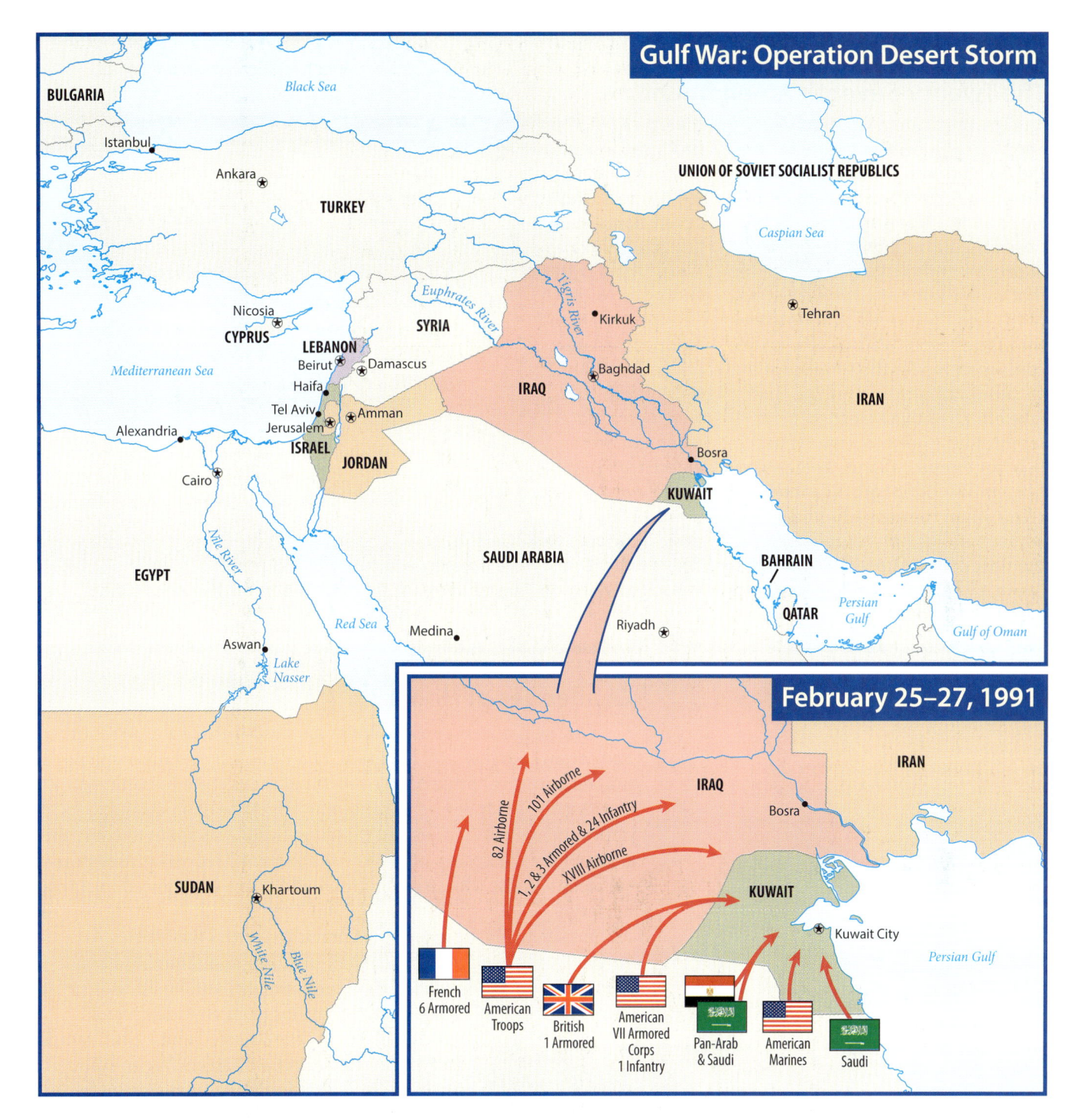

However, the long-term results were far less positive. Although defeated, Saddam Hussein still ruled Iraq and threatened the stability of the Middle East. He resisted efforts by UN officials to inspect his military sites and defied the economic sanctions that the victors imposed on him.

Among the allies, differences forgotten in war were soon remembered in peace. Trouble continued to simmer in the Middle East long after Desert Storm ended. Many Muslims resented the presence of U.S. troops in Saudi Arabia, a nation with some of Islam's holiest sites. This resentment led to terrorist attacks by radical Muslims on American targets throughout the world.

Victory in the war was a great achievement for George H. W. Bush. Unfortunately for the president, it was soon followed by a bitter political defeat.

The Twenty-Seventh Amendment

The Bush administration saw the adoption of a new amendment to the Constitution—one drafted more than two hundred years earlier! When James Madison originally proposed the Bill of Rights, he offered twelve amendments, not just the ten that we are familiar with today. One of the two that were not adopted by the states reads, "No law, varying the compensation for the services of the senators and representatives, shall take effect, until an election of representatives shall have intervened." In other words, changes in the salary of members of Congress cannot take effect when they are adopted. The adjustment cannot occur until after the next congressional election. Because it was not adopted along with the other ten, the proposed amendment remained in legal limbo. Only seven states had ratified it by 1792. Ohio joined them by ratifying it in 1873.

The old amendment gained new life in the 1980s. Many taxpayers were outraged when Congress voted itself pay raises, even when the national economy was in a downturn. The resulting furor gave a fresh push to the old Madison amendment. In May 1992, the thirty-eighth state ratified the amendment, thus making it a part of the Constitution.

27th Amendment

No law, varying the compensation for the services of the senators and representatives, shall take effect, until an election of representatives shall have intervened.

Challenges at Home

One sign of economic trouble was the failure of a number of the nation's savings and loan (S&L) banks. Unsound investments and declining oil prices drove several of the S&Ls into bankruptcy. Because the federal government guarantees the deposits in banks, approximately $125 billion in taxpayer funds was spent to cover the debts of the collapsing institutions. Voters and federal prosecutors wanted to know why so many troubled S&Ls were allowed to stay afloat for so long.

President Bush signed the **Americans with Disabilities Act** in 1990. This legislation prohibited job discrimination based on disabilities. It also required local governments and businesses to improve and alter their accommodations (e.g., provide special parking places for the disabled and install ramps for wheelchairs) for the disabled. When some opposed the legislation as an intrusion by the federal government on local governments and private citizens, the bill's supporters labeled them as uncompassionate.

Probably the most damaging action George H. W. Bush took was breaking a campaign promise. During the 1988 presidential election campaign, he had declared, "The Congress will push me to raise taxes, and I'll say no, and they'll push, and I'll say no, and they'll push again, and I'll say, 'Read my lips, no new taxes.'" But budget deficits, worsened by the S&L crisis, and pressure from Congress made him rethink his vow. The president signed a budget deal, passed by Congress, that sought to tame the

President George H. W. Bush signed the Americans with Disabilities Act in 1990.

federal deficit by increasing taxes. Consequently, many voters were upset with Bush, and some voted against him in 1992 because he broke his promise.

The 1992 Election

In the glow of the triumph immediately following the Persian Gulf War, George H. W. Bush looked unbeatable as he prepared to run for reelection. His approval rating was 87 percent. As a result, some major Democratic candidates hesitated to enter the presidential race and endure what looked to be certain failure. Their hesitancy opened the door for a little-known politician to capture the nomination—**Bill Clinton**.

Clinton, the governor of Arkansas, surprised many experts by winning the Democratic nomination. A shrewd politician with a strong popular appeal, Clinton sidestepped and deflected charges concerning his past behavior. First his Democratic opponents and then the Republicans leveled charges concerning Clinton's alleged sexual immorality, marijuana use, draft dodging during the Vietnam War, and shady financial transactions as governor of Arkansas. Clinton shrugged off these attacks and marketed himself as a "New Democrat." He said he would not promote big government and would end the tax-and-spend policies that many Democrats had supported in the past.

Complicating the campaign was an unusual third-party candidate. Billionaire **Ross Perot** financed his own campaign for the presidency. A small, folksy man with the spirit and blunt speaking of a Texas maverick, Perot promised to put an end to "politics as usual" and to trim the budget deficit. He made a virtue of the fact that he was no politician. Many Americans—tired of the candidates of the major parties and what they saw as dirty Washington politics—warmed to a candidate who was a true outsider. Even his wealth, which might have offended some voters, made Perot seem independent and self-sufficient. He said no special interests could "buy" him in return for their financial support.

George H. W. Bush (*left*), Ross Perot (*center*), and Bill Clinton (*right*) at one of the presidential debates

The campaign was confusing. Perot first dropped out of the race and then returned. Bush focused on Clinton's moral failings and tried, unsuccessfully, to label him as just another "tax-and-spend" liberal like those Reagan had defeated. Responding to the recession that followed the Gulf War, Clinton shrewdly made the economy his central issue. With the Cold War won and no immediate foreign threats facing the country, Americans worried about domestic issues such as education, health care, and especially the economy. Clinton's campaign advisors placed signs in their offices reminding themselves, "It's the economy, Stupid!"

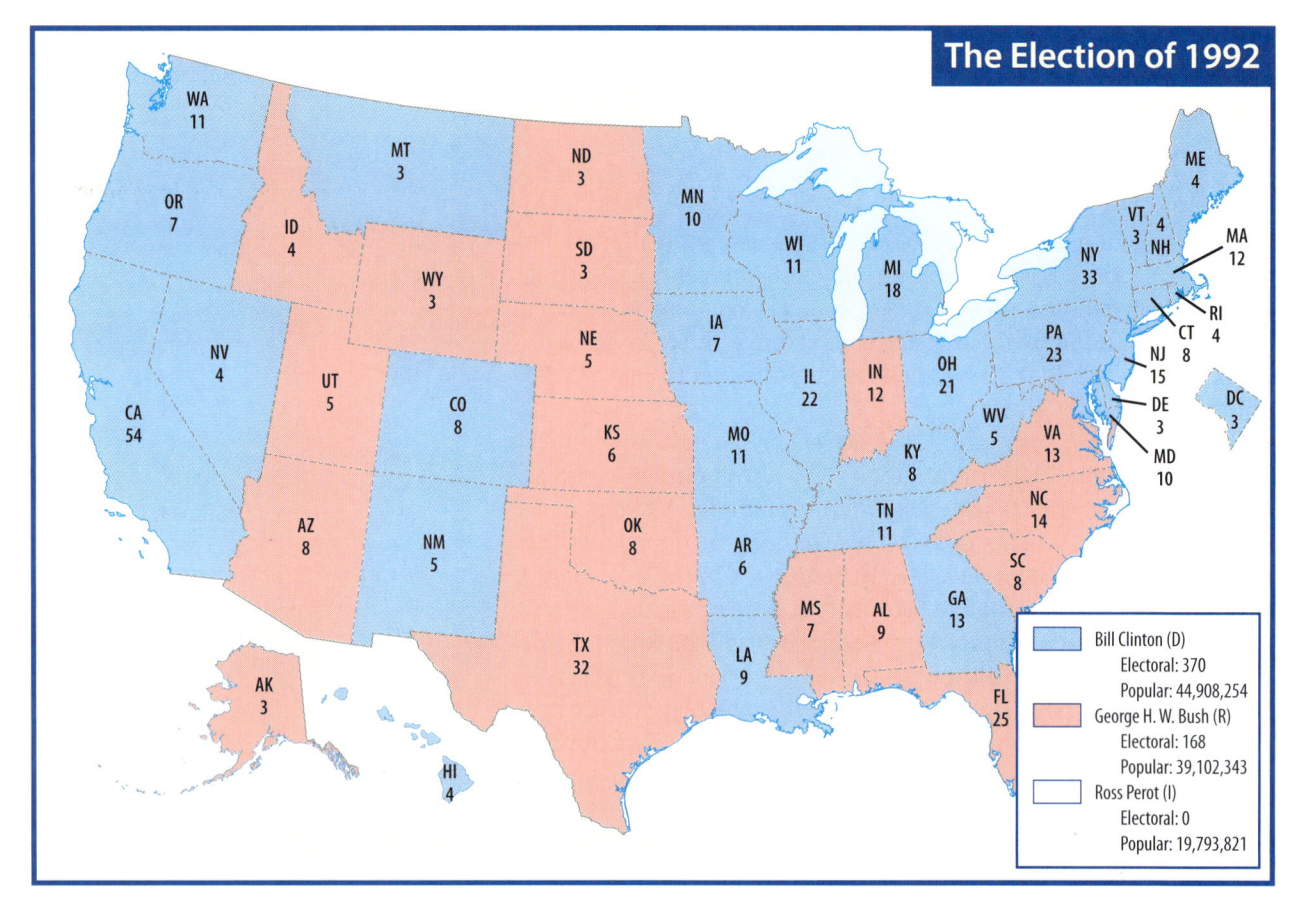

The Election of 1992

	Electoral	Popular
Bill Clinton (D)	370	44,908,254
George H. W. Bush (R)	168	39,102,343
Ross Perot (I)	0	19,793,821

Bill Clinton became president in January 1993.

By Election Day 1992, Bush's approval rating had dropped to less than 40 percent. American voters decidedly rejected Bush and slightly endorsed Clinton. Democrats lost some ground in Congress but retained control of both chambers. In the presidential race, Perot won 19 percent of the popular vote, the largest total for a third-party candidate since Theodore Roosevelt in 1912, but he won no electoral votes. Clinton defeated Bush by only a plurality, 43 to 37 percent, but in the Electoral College, he won by a landslide of 370 to 168. Clinton became the new president and brought an end to the Reagan era.

Section Review

1–2. The invasion of what country sparked a war in the Middle East during the early 1990s? What country invaded it?

3. Through what organization did the United States coordinate its efforts in the Persian Gulf War?

4–5. What amendment was added to the Constitution during the Bush administration? What issue did it address?

6. What decision by President Bush was probably the most damaging to his reelection campaign?

7. Who was the significant third-party candidate in the election of 1992?

★ Why did the Bush administration not push for removal of Saddam Hussein at the conclusion of the Persian Gulf War?

★ Compare Reagan's comments about "Communist dominoes" in his May 1990 speech to Eisenhower's domino theory (discussed in Chapter 23).

CHAPTER REVIEW

Making Connections

1. Who were the Contras?
2–3. Whom did the Democrats nominate for president and vice president in 1984?
4. What was the difference between Operation Desert Shield and Operation Desert Storm?
5–7. Name the three major candidates in the election of 1992.

Developing History Skills

1. What factors contributed to the large increase in the national debt during the 1980s?
2. The Reagan Doctrine, as well as the defense buildup of the 1980s, was said to exhibit "peace through strength." What do you think this slogan means?

Thinking Critically

1. Review the Twenty-seventh Amendment. Why would such an idea be popular with voters?
2. Is the United States right to involve itself in military efforts, such as the Persian Gulf War, in which its own territory is not threatened? Why or why not?
3. Do you agree or disagree with the Americans with Disabilities Act? Why?

Living as a Christian Citizen

1. The influence of the Religious Right (Chapter 25) increased during the Reagan Revolution. What are the benefits and the dangers of organized Christian involvement in politics?
2. Some people, including some Christians, argued that the military buildup of the 1980s was immoral, especially because it included nuclear armaments. Were Ronald Reagan's policies wrong? Why or why not?

People, Places, and Things to Remember

Ronald Reagan
supply-side economics (Reaganomics)
budget deficit
national debt
Reagan Doctrine
Contras
mujahideen
Walter Mondale
Geraldine Ferraro
Mikhail Gorbachev
perestroika
glasnost
Strategic Defense Initiative (SDI)
Iran-Contra affair
George H. W. Bush
Michael Dukakis
Saddam Hussein
Operation Desert Shield
Operation Desert Storm
Persian Gulf War
Americans with Disabilities Act
Bill Clinton
Ross Perot

27 FACING A NEW MILLENNIUM (1993–2017)

> There is a religious war going on in our country for the soul of America. It is a cultural war, as critical to the kind of nation we will one day be as was the Cold War itself.
>
> **Pat Buchanan**
> August 17, 1992, at the Republican National Convention

Presidents (*left to right*) George H.W. Bush, Barack Obama, George W. Bush, Bill Clinton, and Jimmy Carter pose in the Oval Office in 2009.

Big Ideas

1. What characterized the Clinton administration?
2. What were the main aspects of the George W. Bush administration?
3. What typified the Obama administration?
4. How has American culture changed in the last twenty-five years?

I. The Clinton Administration

II. The George W. Bush Administration

III. The Obama Administration

IV. American Culture in a New Era

In honor of Presidents' Day (February 21, 2000), a cable television network invited a team of historians to rank America's presidents from best to worst. Abraham Lincoln ranked first, just ahead of Franklin Roosevelt and George Washington. Lincoln's predecessor, James Buchanan, came in last, just behind Lincoln's successor, Andrew Johnson.

Another poll of presidential scholars was released in 2010. FDR, Teddy Roosevelt, and Abraham Lincoln ranked first, second, and third respectively. George Washington was ranked in fourth place, and Thomas Jefferson placed fifth. James Buchanan had advanced one position, and Andrew Johnson had slipped to last place.

Evaluating presidents is a difficult and controversial task. Often it is impossible to properly assess a person's tenure until years after the individual leaves the White House. In this chapter, we will discuss recent presidents—Bill Clinton, George W. Bush, Barack Obama, and Donald Trump.

I. The Clinton Administration

Bill Clinton had a difficult start in life. Three months before his birth, his father died in a car accident. He was raised by an alcoholic and sometimes abusive stepfather. Yet he graduated from Yale Law School, went on to become attorney general of Arkansas, and in 1978, at age 32, became governor of that state. At that time, he was the country's youngest governor. After a two-year term as governor, however, Clinton lost a reelection bid. This event caused him to revamp his political philosophy. Clinton pursued more moderate policies and kept a close ear tuned to public opinion. He recaptured the governor's office in 1982 and won successive reelection until he assumed the presidency. He became a major leader in the Democratic Party's moderate faction, which opposed the liberal extremes that had led to so many Republican victories.

Guiding Questions

1. What were Clinton's domestic policy initiatives?
2. What characterized Clinton's foreign policy?
3. Why did the House of Representatives bring charges of impeachment against President Clinton?
4. How was the presidential election of 2000 different from previous elections?

First Term

Defeats and Victories

The new president experienced both defeats and victories as he pursued his legislative agenda. Shortly after his inauguration, Clinton presented a proposal that would allow open homosexuals to serve in the armed forces. Though he had promised to do so if he were elected, the plan still roused an uproar of opposition from the military, Congress, and the public at large. Quickly, Clinton backed down and adopted a policy of "don't ask, don't tell" for homosexuals in the military: they were not to declare their homosexuality, and no one was to ask them about it. It was an uneasy compromise.

Bill Clinton was inaugurated on January 20, 1993. On the left is his daughter, Chelsea, and on the right is his wife, Hillary.

Past controversies also dogged Clinton. For example, a series of women from the president's past accused him of sexual immorality. In addition, the "Whitewater" scandal was a major problem for him. It took its name from the president's earlier investment in the failed Whitewater Development Corporation, a resort in northeastern Arkansas. Rumors surfaced that Governor Clinton had unethically used his influence to promote the Whitewater scheme for his private benefit. Eventually, the federal justice department hired an independent counsel (an attorney not under the control of the executive branch) to investigate the Whitewater affair. This investigation

The Brady Bill initially required a five-day waiting period and a background check for all buyers. Later, an instant background check replaced this waiting period.

continued throughout the Clinton administration and eventually led to the president's greatest humiliation late in his second term.

Despite these distractions and with a Democratic majority in Congress, Clinton was able to enact significant legislation. The **Family and Medical Leave Act** required businesses to give employees up to twelve weeks of unpaid leave to care for newborn children or seriously ill family members. The **Brady Bill** (named for a top Reagan administration staffer wounded in the assassination attempt on President Reagan) mandated that before a gun shop could sell a gun to an individual, the buyer had to wait five days and undergo a background check. The National Voter Registration Act, commonly called the "Motor Voter Act," required states to allow voters to register to vote when they applied for or renewed a driver's license. Also, with the help of Republicans and over the objections of many in his own party, the president herded the **North American Free Trade Agreement** (**NAFTA**), which opened free trade with Mexico and Canada, through Congress.

Health-Care Fumble

When he undertook to reform American health care, Clinton found that even a Democratic Congress was no guarantee of legislative victory. Joining the president in that effort (and in the blame for its defeat) was the First Lady, **Hillary Rodham Clinton**.

The president appointed his wife as the leader of a task force to plan the best way to implement health-care reform. In late 1993, she presented a massive 1,342-page plan addressing what her husband had called a health-care crisis during his presidential campaign. The plan promised to pay for the health care for the millions of Americans who had insufficient (or no) medical insurance and to hold down rising costs.

At first, the promises of universal insurance coverage and low costs for medical care appealed to many Americans. Then, as details of the plan emerged, many argued that the plan was too expensive and complicated and that it was giving the government too much power over health care. The First Lady suggested raising taxes to pay for the plan. She added further controversy by insisting that the plan provide tax money to pay for abortions. Critics noted that the Clinton health-care plan would create a new government bureaucracy and many new government regulations. Because of intense disagreements, Congress never voted on the proposal. Eventually the plan died.

Hillary Rodham Clinton appealed to Congress to support new health-care legislation.

Conservative Backlash

The Clinton health-care plan collapse was due to opposition from Republicans, many medical professionals, and even some Democrats who were lukewarm to the plan. The battle over health care also revealed the power of a new and surprising force in America: "talk radio." Radio had not been a great political force since the 1950s, when television displaced it as America's favorite source of entertainment and information. Radio became mostly a medium

replaced music. Aggressive and impassioned radio hosts expressed their usually conservative views and took phone calls on the air; listeners heatedly voiced their protests about conditions in America.

Also displaying new political muscle was the Religious Right. The Moral Majority (see Chapter 25) had gradually weakened and dissolved in the late 1980s, and new conservative religious organizations took its place. Probably the most important one was the **Christian Coalition**. Religious broadcaster Pat Robertson had begun this organization after his failed attempt to win the Republican presidential nomination in 1988. Robertson revitalized the Religious Right by putting together a grassroots network of people who identified themselves as Christians and were united on moral issues such as opposition to abortion and homosexuality. The coalition mailed and distributed voter guides in churches, showing how candidates had voted on various issues.

As the 1994 congressional elections approached, Republicans in the House of Representatives issued what they called a "**Contract with America**." House Republicans presented ten bills they promised to introduce—if they were elected—in their first hundred days in office. This legislation included such issues as term limits and a balanced federal budget. Displeasure with the Clinton health-care plan, opposition to Democratic policies, the efforts of the Religious Right, and the Contract with America all contributed to a stunning defeat of the president's party in the fall elections. The Republicans captured control of both houses of Congress for the first time since Eisenhower's first term. Some Republicans confidently predicted that Clinton would be a one-term president like George H. W. Bush. But as those opponents would soon learn, the president was only down, not out.

"The Comeback Kid"

Throughout his career, Bill Clinton was often called "the Comeback Kid." After his defeat in the 1980 Arkansas governor's race, he came back to recapture that office two years later. After allegations of sexual immorality led to his defeat in the 1992 New Hampshire presidential primary, he rebounded to capture the Democratic nomination. Faced with embarrassing defeats involving his health-care plan and the 1994 congressional elections, Clinton began another comeback.

Battling with Congress

Under the aggressive leadership of House Speaker **Newt Gingrich**, House Republicans kept their Contract with America by pushing through votes on the promised legislation. Though the House of Representatives passed almost all of the Contract, the Senate defeated several proposals, and Clinton vetoed others.

Meanwhile, Clinton chose his battles with Congress shrewdly. Despite the defeat of his party in the 1994 congressional elections, he still retained his popularity with the public. He also proved to be more skilled than the Republicans in shaping public opinion. He showed these strengths in a battle over the

The Christian Coalition, founded by Pat Robertson, was a leading voice of religious political conservatives.

Newt Gingrich orchestrated the "Contract with America" that helped Republicans win control of Congress in the November 1994 election. A few months later, he and other Republican members of the House of Representatives celebrated passage of many aspects of that contract.

federal budget. The new Republican Congress insisted on spending cuts that addressed the government's budget deficit. Clinton and the Democrats opposed cuts that they said would hurt the poor and needy. A group of determined Republicans refused to pass any budget if it did not deal with the deficit. As a result, twice (in November 1995 and in December/January 1995–96) the government technically ran out of money and shut down "nonessential" federal agencies, such as national parks. Unfortunately for Republicans, the Democrats and some in the media portrayed the Republicans as irresponsible and coldhearted. Under public pressure, Congress passed a budget more to the president's liking.

Republicans nominated Bob Dole for president and Jack Kemp for vice president in 1996. Democrats supported the reelection of Bill Clinton and Al Gore.

Move to the Middle

In addition to outmaneuvering Republicans, the president also made a sharp shift toward the middle of the political spectrum. Aware that many voters had begun to view him as too liberal, Clinton moved to the moderate, middle-of-the-road stance that had gotten him elected. In his 1996 State of the Union address, Clinton presented himself again as a New Democrat—tough on crime, supportive of family values, and ready to reform welfare. He declared, "The era of big government is over."

But the president did more than talk. Despite his endorsement of homosexual rights, he signed the **Defense of Marriage Act (DOMA)**, which secured federal benefits, such as health insurance, for spouses in traditional marriages only, denying any status to homosexual unions. Then he signed the **Welfare Reform Act of 1996**. This Republican-sponsored legislation required welfare recipients to go back to work within two years and set a lifetime maximum of five years for assistance. It also gave blocks of federal funds to the states to address welfare reform as they saw fit. It was an attempt, as Clinton said, to "end welfare as we know it." The new law reduced federal guarantees for the poor for the first time since FDR's New Deal. Many within the president's own party opposed it.

Election of 1996

The success of Clinton's comeback became evident in the 1996 presidential election. The Republicans nominated Senate Majority Leader **Bob Dole** of Kansas. Dole was a decorated World War II veteran with a conservative voting record. He was also an experienced legislator with a thorough knowledge of Washington politics. Ross Perot was on the ballot again with his Reform Party, splitting the votes of Clinton's opponents.

Clinton cruised to reelection. Although he failed again to get a majority of the popular vote, he had 49 percent to Dole's 41 percent and Perot's 8 percent. In the Electoral College, the president swamped Dole 379–159; however, the Republicans retained control of Congress. Bill Clinton "came back," but his party remained in the minority in Congress.

Bill Clinton debating Bob Dole in 1996

Second Term

Economic Prosperity

One of the reasons for Clinton's easy reelection was the nation's booming economy. In 1992, the motto "It's the economy, Stupid!"

reminded candidate Clinton to hammer Bush on economic issues, which were the greatest concern of American voters. By the dawn of Clinton's second term, the United States was enjoying extraordinary economic growth, and citizens generally credited the president for their prosperity. A strong economy bolstered the president's popularity as most Americans remained generally satisfied, even optimistic, about the nation's financial status.

Inflation remained low. Unemployment fell steadily to its lowest level in thirty years. Businesses had to offer higher salaries and benefits not only to attract but also to retain skilled employees. The stock market soared to record levels. By Clinton's second term, the government was actually showing a budget surplus instead of the deficits that had characterized the federal budget since the Vietnam War.

Foreign Affairs

In Haiti, brutal military leaders overthrew a democratically elected president in 1991. When he took office, Clinton began to pressure the Haitian regime to allow the ousted president to return to office. When Clinton gathered a military force off the island and threatened armed intervention, the Haitian military backed down. The United States succeeded in putting the former president back in office.

Probably the most significant American involvement overseas in the Clinton years was in the Balkans (see map). During the Cold War, the strong Communist government in Yugoslavia held the many different ethnic groups together. But in 1991, after communism collapsed, the country split apart. In the region called Bosnia, a brutal civil war erupted between Orthodox Christian Serbs, Catholic Croatians, and Muslims. The Serbs practiced **ethnic cleansing**—the killing or expelling of an ethnic group from an area—in their attempt to control the area.

American diplomats took a leading role in trying to negotiate a peaceful settlement in the area. Finally, all the parties met together at Wright-Patterson Air Force Base in Dayton, Ohio, and hammered out the Dayton Accords. In 1995, that fragile agreement fashioned Bosnia into a confederation in which the Serbs, Croats, and Muslims shared power. In 1996, some 60,000 NATO troops, including 20,000 Americans, entered Bosnia to enforce the plan. An uneasy peace settled over the bitterly divided nation.

In 1998, another war began in the area. In the province of Kosovo, the two major ethnic groups there—Serbs and Albanians—clashed. The U.S. and its NATO allies intervened to stop the fighting. Afterwards, U.S. soldiers were part of a peacekeeping force there.

Impeachment

No other event dominated Clinton's second term as did the **Lewinsky scandal** and the historic impeachment trial that followed. The investigation of the Whitewater affair continued into the president's second term, and although it led to the trials and convictions of several friends of the president, including the governor of Arkansas who succeeded Clinton, the evidence never

Bill Clinton was the second U.S. president to be impeached.

touched the president himself. Then in January 1998, while digging deeper into Whitewater, Kenneth Starr, the independent counsel, found evidence that the president had been having a sexual relationship with a young White House intern named Monica Lewinsky and that Clinton and his staff were trying to cover it up. The president asked Lewinsky to lie by denying their relationship. When the matter became public, the president declared, "I did not have sexual relations with that woman. . . . I never told anybody to lie." He had issued the same denial, under oath, in an earlier investigation.

As details emerged, it was clear that the president had committed perjury (lying under oath) about his relationship with Lewinsky. He was likely guilty of obstruction of justice in not only this matter but also a separate investigation in which a woman had accused him of sexual harassment. As a result, the House of Representatives conducted an investigation marked by bitter conflict between Republicans and Democrats. Finally, in December 1998, the House voted to impeach (to formally charge) the president. For the second time in American history, a president would be tried by the U.S. Senate. If convicted, Clinton would be removed from office. Andrew Johnson, the only other president to have been impeached, faced a Senate trial in 1868. He barely avoided removal from office when the Senate acquitted him by a single vote. (President Nixon resigned in August 1974 when it was clear that he would soon be impeached for his actions in the Watergate scandal.)

In contrast to Johnson, Clinton was in little danger of losing his position. Before a president can be removed, two-thirds of the senators must vote to convict. The support of the Senate Democrats for the president almost guaranteed that Clinton would be acquitted. Furthermore, polls indicated that the majority of the American public did not want him removed from office. Many Americans apparently considered his behavior a private matter. Other Americans were disgusted with what the president had done, but even some of those individuals did not think that "lying about sex" was sufficient grounds for removing him from office.

The trial before the Senate took place in January and February 1999. Members of the House of Representatives served as prosecutors while Chief Justice William Rehnquist presided. The Senate weighed two charges against the president: perjury and obstruction of justice. The vote was tied 50–50 on the charge of obstruction of justice. On the perjury charge, 45 senators voted guilty while 55 voted not guilty. Not a single Democrat voted against Clinton on either charge. Thus, the votes were not even close to the 67 votes needed to remove him from office. Bill Clinton, "the Comeback Kid," had survived again, and he claimed that the vote vindicated him.

Though Clinton remained in office, his reputation suffered serious damage. Christian leaders expressed concern about the moral impact on the nation. Though not agreed about whether impeachment was the right course of action for Congress, they noted that the integrity of America's system of government requires that its officials be principled people. Even some of the president's supporters denounced his actions as immoral.

Election of 2000

The presidential election of 2000 developed into a referendum on the Clinton presidency. The Democrats nominated Clinton's vice president, **Al Gore**, as their candidate. As a leading member of the Clinton administration, Gore represented the Clinton policies and approach. The vice president was not involved in the Lewinsky scandal, but he had loyally stood by the president during the impeachment. Thus, he represented the Clinton heritage.

Joseph Lieberman and Al Gore in the 2000 election (*left*)

George W. Bush and Richard Cheney in the 2000 election (*right*)

The Republicans turned to the son of the man whom Clinton had defeated in 1992. Texas governor **George W. Bush** ran on a theme of "compassionate conservatism." He promised educational reforms and swore that he would restore honor and dignity to the White House.

The two sides ran the closest presidential campaign in a generation. Each man chose a running mate who buttressed his weaknesses. Since Bush had little experience in Washington politics, he selected **Richard Cheney**, a former Wyoming congressman who had served as chief of staff for President Gerald Ford and as secretary of defense under the elder Bush during the Gulf War. Gore, needing to distance himself from the scandals of the Clinton presidency, chose Connecticut senator Joseph Lieberman. He was the first practicing Jewish man to serve as a candidate on a major party's ticket. Lieberman had denounced Clinton's behavior in the Lewinsky scandal (though he did not vote to impeach the president). Lieberman also had severely criticized the entertainment industry for the deplorable behavior portrayed in film and on television. He added a moral tone to the Democratic ticket.

Bush and Gore differed significantly on some issues. Governor Bush was pro-life, for example, and Vice President Gore was pro-abortion. But both candidates tried to appeal to the undecided, middle-of-the-road voters. Both wanted tax cuts, for example, but of a different nature. Gore wanted tax cuts for select groups whereas Bush favored cuts for all taxpayers. Many of the dominant issues focused on personality. The Gore team tried to portray Bush as an "intellectual lightweight" who was incapable of handling the job of president. The Bush forces responded by highlighting the vice president's numerous exaggerations, including his remarks suggesting that he had played a role in inventing the Internet.

The election was the most unusual since the disputed 1876 election in which Rutherford B. Hayes defeated Samuel Tilden (see

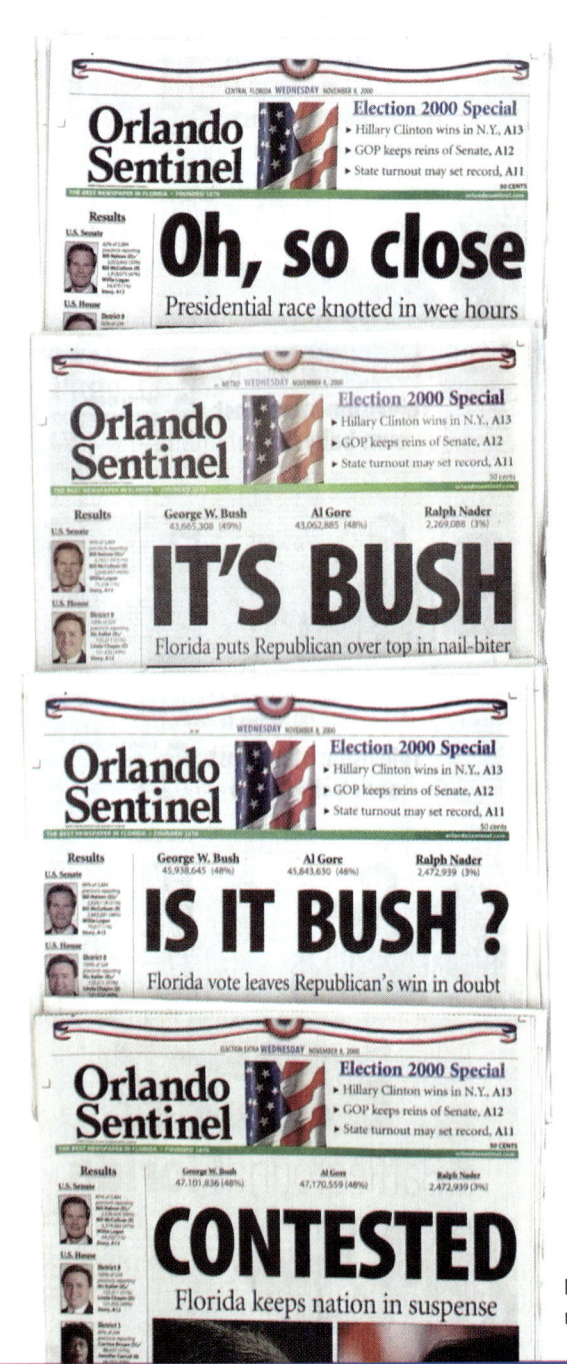

Chapter 15). It was a virtual tie. Gore narrowly won the popular vote by a little more than five hundred thousand votes out of more than one hundred and five million cast, a margin of about one-half of one percent of the vote. In the twentieth century, only John F. Kennedy's margin over Richard Nixon in 1960 was smaller.

The Electoral College, however, not the popular vote, decides the presidency. The candidate who could win enough states to garner 270 electoral votes would be president. Gore won 267 electoral votes and Bush won 246, but the crucial state of Florida (with 25 electoral votes) was the subject of much controversy. Bush led after the initial count in that state by only about eighteen hundred votes out of some six million cast. A recount of the votes in Florida (required by Florida law because the result was so close) cut Bush's lead to about 300 votes.

With the presidency at stake, both sides began to plead their cases before the American people and especially before the courts. The Democrats claimed that many of the computer-read ballots should be recounted by hand, but they initially asked for those recounts only in heavily Democratic counties where the results would favor Gore. Republicans replied that such hand-counting was done by arbitrary standards and therefore was unfair. Some counties began recounting the ballots.

A flood of sometimes contradictory court decisions from Florida state courts, federal courts, and the U.S. Supreme Court interrupted the recount. Weeks dragged by as some court decisions favored Bush and others favored Gore. Finally, on December 12—exactly five weeks after Election Day—the Supreme Court ruled for Bush, halting all recounts and, by default, making him the victor in Florida (by 537 votes) and therefore the winner of the presidency.

This dramatic contest illustrated divisions within the government. The two candidates had almost equal support in the nation. Republicans controlled both houses of Congress, but only by narrow margins. During his campaign, Bush had promised to bring a spirit of cooperation to Washington, saying, "I'm a uniter, not a divider." A divided Congress and a slender electoral mandate would give Bush the opportunity to prove his claim.

Newspaper headlines changed as the close presidential race in Florida perplexed the nation.

Popular Vote or Electoral Vote?

On five occasions the candidate who won the popular vote did not become president. In 1824, Andrew Jackson received the most popular votes, but neither Jackson nor any of the other three major candidates had a majority of the electoral votes. Thus, as is stipulated in the Constitution, the election was decided by the House of Representatives. John Quincy Adams was chosen there (Chapter 10). In 1876, Rutherford B. Hayes lost the popular vote, to Samuel Tilden, but won the electoral vote (Chapter 15). In 1888, the Electoral College chose Benjamin Harrison as president, while Grover Cleveland won the popular vote (Chapter 16). As noted in this chapter, George W. Bush was chosen by the Electoral College in 2000, while Al Gore narrowly won the popular vote. In the 2016 election, Donald Trump was the electoral vote winner while his opponent, Hillary Clinton, had more popular votes.

Some Americans believe the Electoral College should be abolished and the winner of the popular vote should become president. Others believe the Electoral College serves many useful purposes. For example, they note that it helps prevent the domination of smaller states and rural areas by larger states and urban areas.

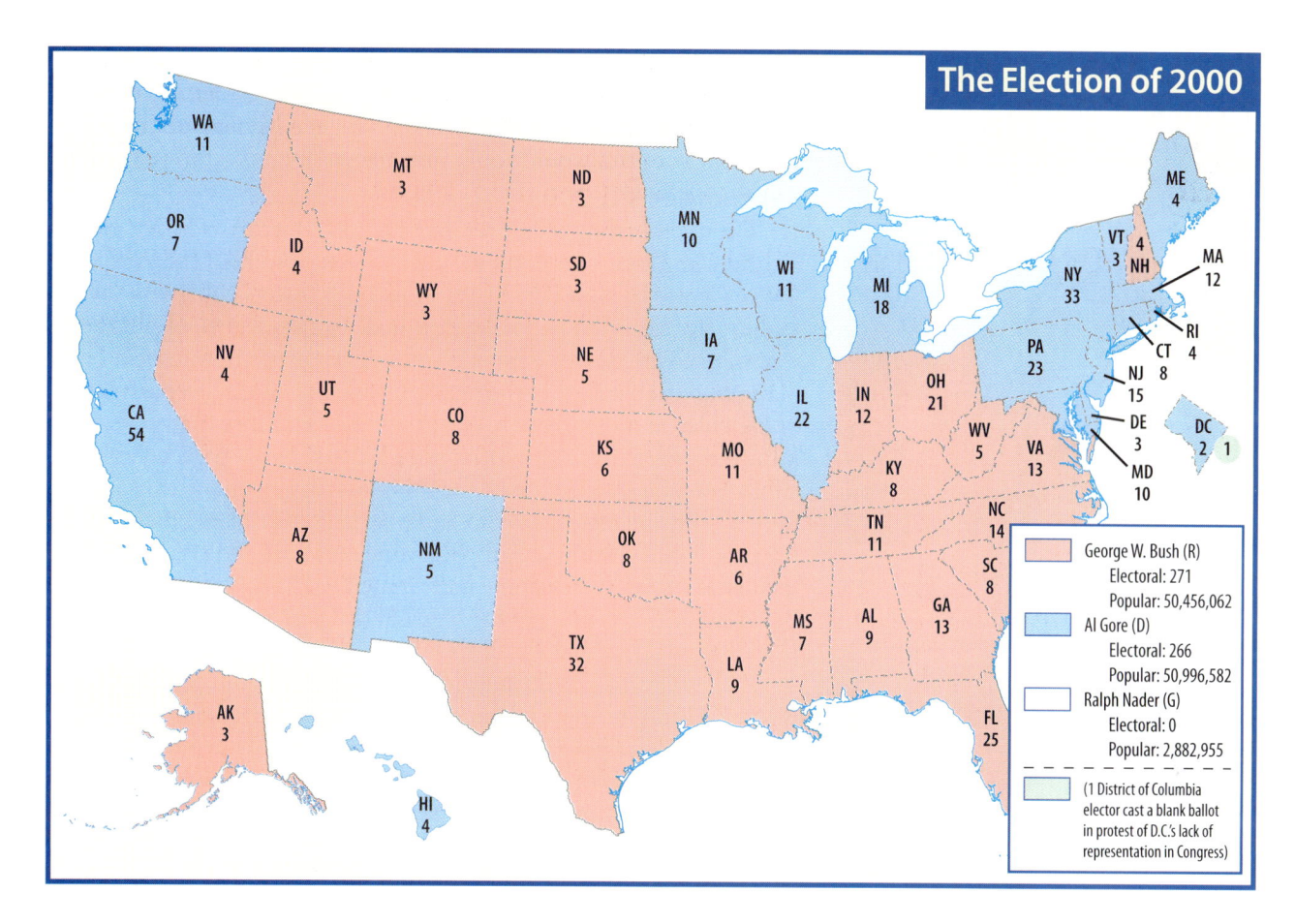

The Election of 2000

▇	George W. Bush (R) Electoral: 271 Popular: 50,456,062
▇	Al Gore (D) Electoral: 266 Popular: 50,996,582
▢	Ralph Nader (G) Electoral: 0 Popular: 2,882,955

(1 District of Columbia elector cast a blank ballot in protest of D.C.'s lack of representation in Congress)

Section Review

1. What ambitious legislative effort by the Clinton administration was never approved by Congress?
2. What were the provisions of the Welfare Reform Act passed during the Clinton administration?
3–5. Who was the Republican candidate in the 1996 presidential election? Who was the significant third-party candidate? What was his political party?
6. The splintering of what nation in the Balkans led to deep unrest in the region?
7–8. Who were the presidential candidates of the Democratic and Republican parties in the presidential election of 2000?
9. The electoral votes of which state ultimately decided the presidential election of 2000?
★ Why were the Senate votes on the articles of impeachment so partisan (that is, heavily determined by political party affliation)?
★ The disputed election of 2000 renewed efforts to abolish the Electoral College in favor of the direct popular election of the president. Is that a good or a bad idea? Why?

II. The George W. Bush Administration

First Term

When Bush took office in 2001, he called for a major tax cut of $1.6 trillion to stimulate the economy. Democrats opposed it,

Guiding Questions

1. How did President George W. Bush respond to the attack on the United States on September 11, 2001?
2. What characterized Bush's second term of office?
3. What were the political and economic conditions just prior to the 2008 election?

George W. Bush takes the oath of office as the forty-third president of the United States.

A war with Islamic radicalism began with the terrorist attacks on the World Trade Center (*above*) and the Pentagon (*right*).

Remains of Flight 93 that crashed on 9/11/2001

arguing that the plan favored the wealthy and would reduce the budget surplus. Compromising, Bush and Congress agreed on a $1.35 trillion tax cut over eleven years. Yet events beyond the new president's control would soon force him to focus on foreign affairs.

September 11, 2001

On the morning of **September 11, 2001**, terrorists hijacked four airliners and flew two of them into the twin towers of the World Trade Center in New York City. Soon, both towers collapsed. Over twenty-five hundred people were killed, and several blocks of the city were covered with dust and smoke. Terrorists flew a third plane into the Pentagon, the headquarters of the U.S. Department of Defense, in metropolitan Washington, D.C. More than one hundred people in the building were killed. Heroic passengers in a fourth plane learned about the other attacks by phone calls and fought with the terrorists who had hijacked their plane. It crashed in rural Pennsylvania, killing everyone on board. It is likely that the terrorists in the fourth plane had wanted to crash it into the Capitol Building or the White House. The hijackers aboard the four airplanes were all radical Muslims.

The 9/11 attack was the worst terrorist attack in the nation's history, killing or injuring about three thousand people. The terrorists purposely targeted many innocent civilians. They intentionally struck at symbols of America—a major financial complex in New York City and the government in the nation's capital. More Americans were killed by the 9/11 attacks than the number of Americans who died at Pearl Harbor or on D-day during World War II.

In response, Americans generously donated money and time to help the victims, especially those at the World Trade Center. American flags appeared on front porches and on cars. Members of both political parties attended public ceremonies all across the country in demonstrations of unity. Baseball fans sang "God Bless America" during the seventh-inning stretch. Bush pledged to achieve victory over the terrorists when he visited "Ground Zero" at the World Trade Center crash site. People around the globe publicly sympathized with America. But in some places in the world, radical Muslims rejoiced, even dancing in the streets. A *jihad*, or holy war, against "the Great Satan," the United States, was occurring.

Intelligence experts and the FBI learned that the nineteen hijackers were members of an international terrorist network called **al-Qaeda**, led by **Osama bin Laden**, a radical Muslim from Saudi Arabia. The organization was linked to several other terrorist attacks. Such Muslim extremists hated the Jews, Israel, and America, considering them obstacles to the expansion of Islam. Al-Qaeda members trained for terrorist activities at bases in Afghanistan. The government of that nation was controlled by a group of Muslim extremists known as the **Taliban**. They protected bin Laden and his supporters as he commanded al-Qaeda's worldwide network.

Osama bin Laden

The War on Terrorism Begins

For a growing minority of Muslims, hatred of the West, especially America, fueled a network of terrorist groups in some sixty countries, most of them in the Middle East, Africa, and Asia. They operated secretly. No tactic—even the slaughter of civilians—was deemed too violent if it helped achieve their goals. A few nations protected such terrorists, but the terrorists were not officially part of those governments. Consequently, fighting the terrorist groups proved difficult.

In the Cold War, potential enemies had been restricted by the very threat of nuclear force. Muslim extremists, however, were bound by no such restraints. They followed no traditional rules of war. They resorted to suicide bombings, targeted innocent civilians, and even threatened to use weapons of mass destruction (such as biological or chemical weapons).

After the September 11 attacks, the U.S. began a real war against terrorism, both at home and in foreign countries. Bush warned that the war would be neither short nor conventional. Some of the warfare would be publicly visible; other aspects would be highly secretive.

The Taliban refused Bush's demands to turn over bin Laden and his supporters to the U.S. and to shut down all terrorist camps. The president's first task was to assemble a multinational coalition to oust the Taliban controlling Afghanistan. On October 7, those allied forces invaded Afghanistan, using "smart" weapons to minimize military and civilian casualties. The coalition received help from the anti-Taliban Northern Alliance in Afghanistan and from Pakistani volunteers. Within two months, Taliban forces fled into the mountains on the Afghan-Pakistani border. Afghan leaders of several anti-Taliban factions met in Germany in December and signed a peace agreement. They established a temporary government and began working to rebuild their country. Unfortunately, bin Laden had escaped capture. Almost ten years would pass before he was located.

Americans drove the Taliban from power in Afghanistan.

To protect Americans at home, Bush created the **Office of Homeland Security**. It later became a cabinet-level department.

It regulated security issues related to U.S. borders, transportation (especially at airports), and preparations for emergencies. To screen for potential terrorists, Americans faced longer delays and lines for check-in at airports. Congress also overwhelmingly passed the Patriot Act, making it easier for law enforcement officials and the courts to catch, convict, and imprison terrorists. Most Americans agreed with Bush's approach. But critics contended that the government, in its zeal to protect citizens from terrorism, had gone too far and was infringing on the rights of Americans. The Supreme Court later declared some provisions of the Patriot Act unconstitutional.

The War with Iraq

President Bush was greatly concerned about the government of Iraqi dictator Saddam Hussein. Hussein continued to threaten peace in the Middle East, and rumors abounded of his development of chemical and biological **weapons of mass destruction (WMDs)**. He had used chemical weapons against the Kurds, citizens of his own country, in the late 1980s.

One of the conditions of the cease-fire at the end of the Persian Gulf War in 1991 was that Iraq would get rid of its WMDs. Furthermore, it would not build any additional ones and would allow UN weapons inspectors to verify its adherence to these agreements. Throughout the 1990s, Iraq only partly cooperated with UN weapons inspectors, and by December 1998, it was no longer allowing UN inspectors into the country. In September 2002, President Bush gave a speech to the United Nations in which he demanded that Hussein surrender his WMDs, readmit inspectors, provide more freedoms for Iraqi citizens, and stop supporting terrorism. The UN later adopted a resolution supporting Bush's demands.

Iraq admitted that it had WMDs before the Persian Gulf War but stated they no longer had them. Hussein agreed to allow the resumption of UN inspections. Unfortunately, Hussein did not fully cooperate with the inspection process. American, British, and Spanish officials then pushed for a UN resolution authorizing force against Iraq. Germany, France, Russia, China, and other countries opposed military action.

Saddam Hussein was the dictator of Iraq from 1979 until 2003.

On March 19, 2003, a "**coalition of the willing**" (consisting of the United States and other nations who were willing to participate) invaded Iraq, defeating that country's military forces in only two weeks. But some Iraqis, aided by extremists from other Muslim countries, continued the fight as guerillas, launching terrorist attacks, encouraging suicide bombings, and setting improvised explosive devices (IEDs) beside roads.

As the war dragged on, Muslim factions clashed. Members of the major divisions within Islam, Sunnis and Shiites, attacked each other. Ethnic conflicts also occurred as the Arabs, the vast majority of Iraqis, fought the Kurds. Amid the chaos, some Iraqis, desiring freedom, held elections and approved a constitution.

Americans were deeply divided over the Iraq War. Many were upset when the U.S. military found no evidence of the much-discussed WMDs. They noted that the invasion made radical Muslims hate America more. Supporters of the war argued that the war in Iraq was part of the war on terror.

In April 2003, Saddam Hussein had gone into hiding. He was finally captured in December of that year. He was charged with crimes against humanity and other offences. His trial began in October 2005. He was convicted and on December 30, 2006, was executed by hanging.

American troops (*left*) pulling down a statue of Saddam Hussein in 2003

Saddam Hussein (*right*) was tracked down and captured by Americans. He was convicted by an Iraqi court and later executed.

The Election of 2004

The Democratic nominee for president was Massachusetts senator **John Kerry**. Republicans renominated Bush. Bush continued to oppose abortion and called for a constitutional amendment to ban same-sex marriages. Kerry opposed those positions. Bush continued to support tax cuts while Kerry endorsed raising taxes on those with the highest incomes.

Although John Kerry was a decorated Vietnam veteran, he had opposed the war after he returned home. That opposition led many veterans to oppose him in the 2004 election. Kerry also seemed indecisive. For example, after voting for the Iraq War, he later opposed measures necessary for fighting it. His effort to defend his actions—"I actually voted for the war before I voted against it"—only cemented his image, in the eyes of his opponents, as a "flip-flopper."

Bush's reelection campaign was influenced by mixed economic news, violence and mounting casualties in Iraq, and a scandal over U.S. mistreatment of Iraqi prisoners of war at Abu Ghraib prison in that country. Consequently, his approval ratings were falling. However, when the votes were counted, Bush won by 3.3 million votes. His support came from southern and central states and evangelical voters.

George W. Bush and John Kerry debating in 2004

Second Term

Domestic Matters

When Bush took office in 2001, the economy was sluggish, but his tax cuts that year—and two other cuts over the next two years—spurred economic activity. Yet the government did not cut

Embryonic Stem Cell Research

One of the pressing moral issues that President Bush faced was what to do about embryonic stem cell research. An embryo is a baby in its first eight weeks of development. A stem cell can be grown into different kinds of cells, such as nerve or muscle cells. Scientists said that embryonic stem cells could be used to treat diseases like Alzheimer's—but they would have to kill the embryo to get the stem cells.

Many people wanted the federal government to pay for scientific work using embryonic stem cells. President Bush, however, believed that killing an embryo was killing a human. He later wrote, "My faith and conscience led me to conclude that human life is sacred. God created man in His image and therefore every person has value in His eyes."

Nevertheless, Bush did allow for federal funding to research stem cells from embryos that had already been destroyed. Though their destruction was wrong, it had already occurred.

---

spending; instead, expenditures increased. As a result, the annual budget deficits soared. After the eight years of the Bush presidency, the national debt had grown by almost $5 trillion to reach a total of $10.6 trillion.

Unemployment was 4.2 percent when Bush became president in January 2001. It rose to 6.3 percent by June 2003 but decreased thereafter. It dropped to 4.8 percent in February 2006 and remained below 6 percent until the last few months of his presidency. By that time a financial crisis was occurring. It had begun in 2006 when millions of Americans began defaulting on their home mortgages. Too many banks had made risky loans. Further complicating economic matters was the fact that by the summer of 2008 the price of gasoline was nearly double what it had been in 2006.

During his White House years, Bush personally made religion a more prominent issue. He openly shared his faith in Christ. Soon after becoming president, he had embraced a greater role for evangelical Christians by enlisting pastors from varying ethnic groups to help administer government social programs that put into practice what he called "compassionate conservatism." These programs, known as **faith-based initiatives**, became an important part of his domestic plan to combat problems in the inner cities. Those efforts continued throughout his second term. But some conservative Christians questioned the wisdom of those initiatives. They worried that government regulations that accompanied these programs would limit the religious aspects.

A natural disaster led to further problems for Bush. **Hurricane Katrina**, a Category 3 storm, hit the Gulf Coast of Louisiana, Mississippi, and Alabama on August 29, 2005. Floodwaters broke the levees in New Orleans, which protected the low-lying areas there, and soon 80 percent of the city was under water. Gulf residents suffered greatly from the hurricane, and at least twelve hundred people were killed. About $100 billion in damages occurred, making it the costliest hurricane in American history.

Bush received much of the blame for the disaster. The Federal Emergency Management Administration (FEMA) was rightly criticized for its slowness to respond. But faulty decisions by local officials and local residents and the crime that swept the area in the aftermath of the hurricane were also to blame for some of the loss. For example, residents were warned to evacuate New Orleans well before the hurricane hit, but thousands failed to leave. School buses could have been used to evacuate people who had no other means of transport. But city officials ignored this option, and the buses sat unused until they were stranded in floodwaters. Unfortunately, many New Orleans police officers simply walked away from their jobs, leaving the city at a time their assistance was sorely needed.

But Hurricane Katrina also brought out the best in some people. Aid workers risked their lives to help victims, other Americans gave generous financial support, and cities throughout the nation offered to house refugees in shelters. Schools, church groups, and other nonprofit organizations went to the Gulf region to help rescue and rebuild. Christians had the opportunity to show love to fellow citizens and live the truth that Paul described in 1 Corinthians 13—the greatness of love.

Devastation in New Orleans after Hurricane Katrina

The Supreme Court

During the previous decades, the Supreme Court had issued a number of liberal rulings. For example, the Court removed prayer and Bible reading from public schools in the 1960s, and it granted women the "right" to an abortion in the 1970s.

In 2005 and 2006 Bush nominated two conservative justices to the Court. Sandra Day O'Connor, the first woman to serve on the Supreme Court and a moderate, retired in 2005. The president nominated **John G. Roberts Jr.** to replace her. Before the Senate could vote on the nomination, however, Chief Justice William Rehnquist died. Bush chose Roberts to replace Rehnquist, and Roberts was confirmed. He was sworn in as the seventeenth chief justice of the United States in September 2005.

Bush then chose **Samuel Alito Jr.** to replace O'Connor. The Senate confirmed Alito in January 2006. Alito and Roberts were both Catholics. For the first time, the Supreme Court had a Catholic majority, represented in Justices Alito, Roberts, Antonin Scalia, Anthony Kennedy, and Clarence Thomas.

John Roberts, a Bush nominee, became chief justice of the U.S. Supreme Court following the death of William Rehnquist.

Diplomatic Successes and Problems

Bush toppled Saddam Hussein and convinced Pakistan to cooperate in the war on terror. He forged closer economic and diplomatic ties with China and negotiated with China, Japan, and the Koreas to ensure stability in East Asia.

But Bush also faced problems with North Korea and Iran as they both sought to develop nuclear weapons. Furthermore, like every president since Israel had become a nation in 1948, Bush was concerned about the tensions between Israel and the Arab nations. Progress toward peace was hindered by several events. Yasir Arafat, a longtime Arab leader, died. Israeli prime minister Ariel Sharon was incapacitated when he went into a coma. Hamas, an Arab terrorist group, gained influence in the region. Peace in the Middle East remained elusive.

Samuel Alito joined Roberts on the Supreme Court.

Election of 2008

The Democrats narrowed their field of candidates for the presidency to former First Lady Hillary Clinton and a U.S. senator from Illinois, **Barack Obama**. Clinton seemed to be the frontrunner, but Obama did well in the primaries and later captured the nomination. He chose as his vice-presidential running mate, Delaware senator **Joe Biden**.

Republicans had a large number of contestants, but Arizona senator **John McCain** emerged as the nominee. He had been a

Barack Obama and Joe Biden during the 2008 election (*left*)

John McCain and Sarah Palin during the 2008 election (*right*)

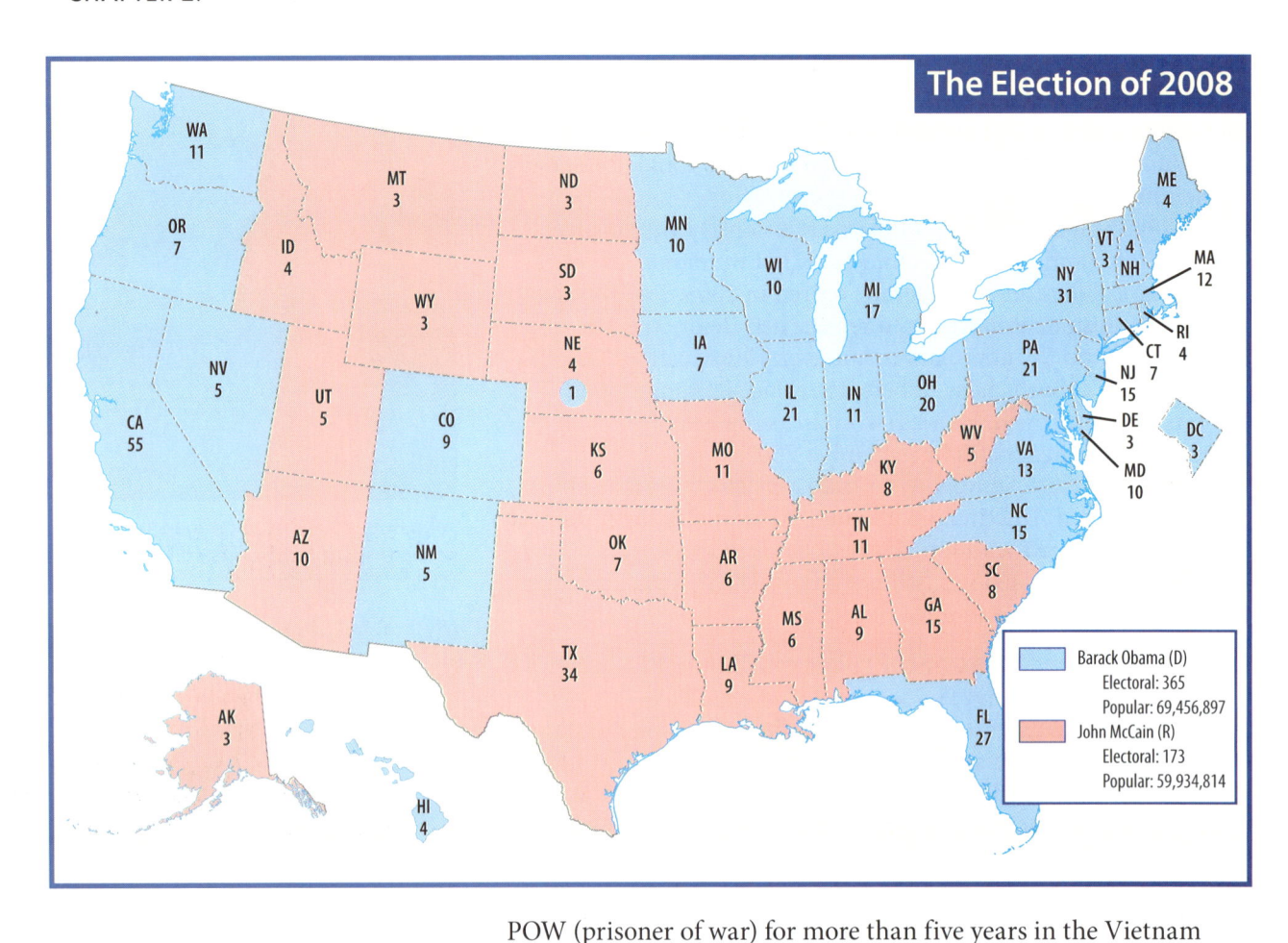

The Election of 2008

Barack Obama (D) — Electoral: 365, Popular: 69,456,897
John McCain (R) — Electoral: 173, Popular: 59,934,814

Barack Obama with his wife and two daughters in December 2011

POW (prisoner of war) for more than five years in the Vietnam War and had served as U.S. senator from Arizona since 1982. McCain chose Alaska governor Sarah Palin as his running mate. The Republican campaign focused on Obama's lack of administrative experience or accomplishment.

As Election Day neared, the economy continued to weaken. The nation was in a recession, and it was worsening. In early October, after two weeks of intense discussions, Congress passed a controversial bill called the Troubled Asset Relief Program (TARP). It provided $700 billion in government assistance to prevent some of the nation's financial institutions from collapsing. Bush signed the bill. It drew criticism from those who believed the huge expenditure was an inappropriate use of government funds. Others applauded it as a brave and necessary move to prevent economic catastrophe.

Obama was a tough campaigner. He was able to create an image of himself as powerful, authoritative, and hopeful. Many viewed him as an optimist who was better able to handle the economic crisis than McCain. People, of various races, were pleased at the prospect of his becoming the nation's first African American president.

Although critics argued that his speeches lacked substance or specifics, he was elected president on November 4, 2008. He defeated McCain by several million popular votes and by 365–173 in the Electoral College vote. He was sworn in as president on January 20, 2009.

Section Review

1. What happened on September 11, 2001?
2–3. Who were the two Supreme Court justices appointed by George W. Bush?
4. Why did the United States and other nations invade Afghanistan in October 2001?
★ Explain why fighting Muslim terrorists is often more difficult than fighting a traditional war.
★ Do you think the United States was right to lead the attack on Iraq in March 2003? Explain your answer.

III. The Obama Administration

A short time after winning the election, Barack Obama announced that he was appointing Hillary Clinton, his former opponent for the Democratic nomination, as his secretary of state. Thus, she would be his chief representative in issues relating to foreign affairs. But domestic matters would soon occupy most of the new president's attention. The country was involved in an intense economic downturn that became known as the "**Great Recession**."

First Term

Economic Issues

By early 2009, unemployment passed 8 percent and was continuing to climb. More than five million Americans had lost their jobs in the past two years. President Obama called for drastic action. Less than a month after his taking office, Congress passed, and Obama signed, the American Recovery and Reinvestment Act. This provided approximately $800 billion in federal funds to attempt to stimulate the economy. The measure included money for distribution to the states, additional funds for food stamps and unemployment benefits, and financing construction projects (such as bridges, roads, and government buildings). In addition one-fourth, or $200 billion, was designated to pay for tax reductions for individuals and businesses. Supporters praised this legislation, though some thought the amount allocated should have been larger. Opponents, which included almost every Republican member of Congress, argued that the bill was too expensive and that it called for too much government intervention in the economy.

Next, Obama tackled the nation's health-care system. His goal was to make health insurance affordable and to make health care accessible for everyone. Throughout 2009, government officials worked to develop a plan. The result was the **Patient Protection and Affordable Care Act (PPACA)**, which spanned over twenty-five hundred pages. The legislation, which also became known as **Obamacare**, required all Americans to either obtain health insurance or pay a fine.

Guiding Questions

1. What characterized Barack Obama's domestic policy?
2. What were the major foreign policy issues during the Obama administration?
3. Why did the 2016 presidential election turn out so differently than most predicted?

Our Soaring National Debt

As noted earlier, during the eight years that George W. Bush served as president the debt grew by more than $5 trillion to total about $10.6 trillion.

The national debt continued to skyrocket during the years President Obama was in office. At the end of his eight years in the White House, the debt was nearly $20 trillion.

Controversies During the Obama Administration

Fast and Furious—the federal government secretly allowed criminals to buy guns in order to track them; several shootings of law enforcement officers have been traced back to these guns

IRS—agents were authorized to discriminate against conservative groups regarding tax exemption

Veterans Administration—mismanagement of care for veterans and falsification of records to conceal extremely long delays in patients seeing doctors

Benghazi—death of American diplomats in Libya

In December 2009, the controversial bill was passed in the Senate, although no Republicans voted for it. In March 2010, it was approved by the House of Representatives by a vote of 219–212, with 34 Democrats joining all Republicans in voting against it. President Obama signed it into law later that month. The president praised the bill as a huge step toward providing insurance for the millions of uninsured Americans and improving health care for everyone. Critics warned of future problems similar to those being experienced by Canada and Great Britain, both of which have socialized health-care systems. They predicted that health insurance costs would rise dramatically. Eventually, the government-issued regulations for implementing PPACA exceeded twenty thousand pages. As the disagreements continued, Obamacare became a major topic of debate among political candidates.

The Supreme Court

During the first eighteen months of Obama's administration, two Supreme Court justices announced their retirements—David Souter and John Paul Stevens. Obama nominated **Sonia Sotomayor** to replace Souter and **Elena Kagan** to replace Stevens.

Most conservatives and strict constructionists opposed the president's two nominees. They argued that both were liberals who embraced a broad, or loose, interpretation of the Constitution. Nevertheless, both received Senate approval. When Sotomayor took office in August 2009, she became the first Hispanic justice to serve on the court. Kagan joined the court in August 2010.

The 2010 Elections

As the 2010 elections neared, many Americans viewed them as a referendum on the Obama administration and the Democrat-controlled Congress. Large rallies were staged by conservative groups that became known as the **Tea Party**. Like participants in the Boston Tea Party of 1773, from which this group derived its name, members protested against the power of the government. They called for a significant reduction in its size and scope. The record of the Obama administration, they said, indicated that the era of big government was *not* over. Tea Party supporters argued that although government had continued to grow under both Clinton and Bush, it had expanded at an even more alarming pace during Obama's administration.

Republicans, many backed by the Tea Party movement, won numerous victories in the November elections. They regained control of the House of Representatives by winning more than sixty seats. They won six additional Senate seats but fell short of winning control of that chamber. President Obama later commented that the Democrats "took a shellacking."

The sweep was even more dramatic on the state level as the Republicans won most of the governorships that were contested. They also took control of a dozen state legislatures that had been controlled by the Democrats.

Sonia Sotomayor (*top*) and Elena Kagan (*bottom*) were appointed to the Supreme Court by President Obama.

Repeal of Don't Ask Don't Tell

This compromise made by President Clinton in 1994 proved to be unpopular, and its overturn became the goal of the ACLU and other progressive groups. After much debate in Congress and despite serious concerns raised by many in the military, President Obama signed into law the repeal of this policy on December 22, 2010. Gays, bisexuals, and lesbians were now free to serve openly in the military. This became a campaign issue during the 2012 election.

Foreign Policy

Following a build-up of troops under President George W. Bush in 2007, the American military had achieved great successes in Iraq and Afghanistan by the time Barack Obama became president. President Obama promised to complete the defeat of enemy forces in Afghanistan, a war he considered just, and withdraw American forces from Iraq, a war he considered unjust. Despite the warning of many military leaders and members of Congress, the president fulfilled his pledge regarding Iraq and oversaw the withdrawal of virtually all American forces by December 2011. An ongoing power struggle between Sunni and Shiite groups in Iraq, accompanied by the withdrawal of American forces, resulted in a power vacuum. Radical Muslims, that were members of a group known as the Islamic State of Iraq and Syria (**ISIS**), rushed to seize this opportunity. Following the capture of key Iraqi cities by ISIS and many reports of atrocities against the Iraqi people, President Obama reluctantly began to send special forces back to Iraq, with their stated mission being to train Iraqi forces.

The Death of Osama bin Laden

For almost a decade after the attacks of 9/11, the American military had sought Osama bin Laden, head of the al-Qaeda terrorist network. In the dark hours of Sunday, May 1, 2011, two combat helicopters bearing about two dozen specially trained commandos descended on a compound in Abbottabad, Pakistan. Based on highly credible information that indicated bin Laden was hiding there, President Obama gave his approval to the mission. The soldiers were part of the U.S. Navy SEALs. One of their helicopters had mechanical problems and was damaged as it landed. The other chopper landed successfully, and SEALs sped from both in a well-rehearsed operation to capture or kill bin Laden.

A firefight erupted as bin Laden and his lieutenants tried to avoid capture, but bin Laden fell to a SEAL bullet. The SEALs seized bin Laden's body as well as extensive documentation found in the compound and departed into the night aboard the functioning helicopter, after destroying the damaged one. The operation had taken only about forty minutes, and there were no American casualties. Safely back at a U.S. military base in Afghanistan, DNA and facial recognition tests confirmed bin Laden's identity. Afterwards, the body was flown to a U.S. aircraft carrier in the Arabian Sea. Bin Laden's remains, which had been washed and wrapped in a white sheet (in accordance with Islamic practice), were placed in a weighted plastic bag and buried at sea.

News of bin Laden's death sparked joyous demonstrations throughout the United States. In a televised speech late Sunday evening, President Obama stated, "To those families who have lost loved ones to al-Qaeda's terror: Justice has been done." Crowds gathered outside the White House, at the site of the World Trade Center in New York City, in New York's Times Square, and numerous other places to celebrate the news.

The compound in Abbottabad, Pakistan, where Osama bin Laden was killed

Afghanistan proved to be a more difficult conflict to end, despite the expenditure of billions of dollars and the continued loss of American lives. Radical Muslims demonstrated resilience and the ability to reconstitute their military forces.

Beginning in December 2010 protests erupted in the nation of Tunisia. The demand for major political and economic change spread across the Arab world into countries such as Iraq, Libya, Syria, Yemen, and Egypt. This movement became known as the **Arab Spring**, a series of legitimate protests concerning political corruption and oppression. In many of these countries Muslim radicals took advantage of the unrest to incite violence and to expand their control over citizens.

In 2012, on the anniversary of the 9/11 attacks, four Americans in Benghazi, Libya, were murdered when the U.S. diplomatic compound there was attacked. Many Americans viewed this as a tragic example of Islamic radicals taking advantage of perceived American weakness. Many people blamed the Obama administration for not protecting American diplomats abroad. The Benghazi tragedy was an issue in both the 2012 and 2016 presidential elections.

Mitt Romney and Barack Obama talk in the Oval Office after Obama's reelection in 2012.

Vice-presidential debate between Paul Ryan and Joe Biden

Election of 2012

Barack Obama ran on the slogan "Forward" and challenged the American people to continue supporting his policies. With Joe Biden continuing as his running mate, President Obama mounted a formidable campaign.

Initially a dozen men and one woman entered the race for the Republican nomination in 2012. After several struggles during the primaries, former Massachusetts governor **Mitt Romney** emerged as the candidate and selected Congressman Paul Ryan from Wisconsin as his running mate. Romney's opponents sought every opportunity to describe him as a wealthy and out-of-touch elitist.

On November 6, 2012, Obama was reelected with 51 percent of the popular vote and 332 electoral votes. Romney received 47 percent of the popular vote and 206 electoral votes. Barack Obama easily won a second term as president of the United States.

Second Term
Domestic Policy

At the beginning of President Obama's second term, he emphasized several issues. Included in his list were climate change, immigration, and gun control. He also addressed "wealth inequality" and promised to work with Congress when possible, or bypass Congress using **executive orders**. (Executive orders have historically been issued to "help officers and agencies of the executive branch" carry out the intentions of existing law.) However, many were offended by Obama's statement in 2014 that he had a "phone and a pen" and that he could use that pen "to sign executive orders and take executive actions." Opponents saw the president's broad use of executive orders as a means to push his political agenda by circumventing congressional restraint. The weakness of this policy was that what one president can accomplish through executive orders, the next president can revoke.

With the election of the first African American president to a second term of office, many Americans hoped that racial conflict would diminish. Many viewed President Obama as a role model to black young people as a husband and father and as someone whose hard work enabled him to succeed. However, despite President Obama's call for racial harmony, his eight-year term of office saw an intensification of racial discord. Several controversial shootings of black men led to protests, some of which were violent and destructive with black communities bearing the brunt of most of the destruction. Groups such as **Black Lives Matter** (BLM) sharpened the divide between police and citizen, and black and white, with divisive rhetoric. Mixed messages from the Obama administration, the Department of Justice in particular, seemed to increase the racial discord.

Decisions by the Obama administration regarding immigration led to tensions as well. In spite of his previous announcement that he was powerless to change immigration regulations, Obama issued executive orders that effectively ended the enforcement of existing law and restricted the ability of local, state, and federal officials to apprehend, detain, or deport thousands of violent illegal aliens. He also ignored the growing number of cities that violated federal law by providing sanctuary to illegal aliens. Contrasting views of immigration became a major theme during the 2016 presidential election.

Foreign Policy

Opponents criticized President Obama's foreign policy decisions. For example, Secretary of State Hillary Clinton met with **Vladimir Putin**, the Russian president, in 2009 and proposed a "reset," or new beginning, for Russian and American relations. Yet, in 2014 Russians seized the Crimea (part of Ukraine) and then made several military intrusions into Ukraine and largely ignored protests from the United States and its allies. Many Americans argued that little had changed regarding the tense relationship between the two nations.

Negotiations with Iran that began while George W. Bush was president concluded during the Obama administration. In 2015, Obama reached an agreement with that nation. He argued that it would prevent Iran from producing nuclear weapons. Critics stated that it lacked the necessary conditions to ensure enforcement.

In December 2014, President Obama and Cuban president Raul Castro, brother of Fidel Castro, announced that their two nations would restore full diplomatic ties for the first time in more than a

Supporters of Black Lives Matter (*top*) and pro-police movement Blue Lives Matter (*middle*) sought to raise awareness of their beliefs.

Vladimir Putin

half century. In March 2016, Obama made a historic trip to Cuba to meet with the Cuban president. That November, Fidel Castro, who had retired several years earlier, died.

Election of 2016

Hillary Clinton entered the 2016 presidential race with many advantages. She touted her time as First Lady, senator from New York, and secretary of state as uniquely qualifying her to be president. However, she received strong competition from Vermont senator Bernie Sanders, a self-identified socialist. Her path to the nomination became complicated as she made conflicting statements regarding the death of Americans in Benghazi, Libya (2012), and the growing controversy regarding her use of a private email server while secretary of state. Even though a thorough FBI investigation into the server and transmission of highly classified documents did not lead to prosecution, the investigation resulted in a high "unfavorable" rating for Clinton and a very low "trustworthy" rating. However, her campaign raised huge sums of money and assembled a team of thousands across America who labored to assure Clinton's selection as the Democratic nominee.

The Republican field began with seventeen candidates. Most had political experience, but two men sought the office with no such background: neurosurgeon Dr. Ben Carson and entrepreneur **Donald Trump**. While the campaign became heated and resorted to name-calling at times, a growing number of Americans began

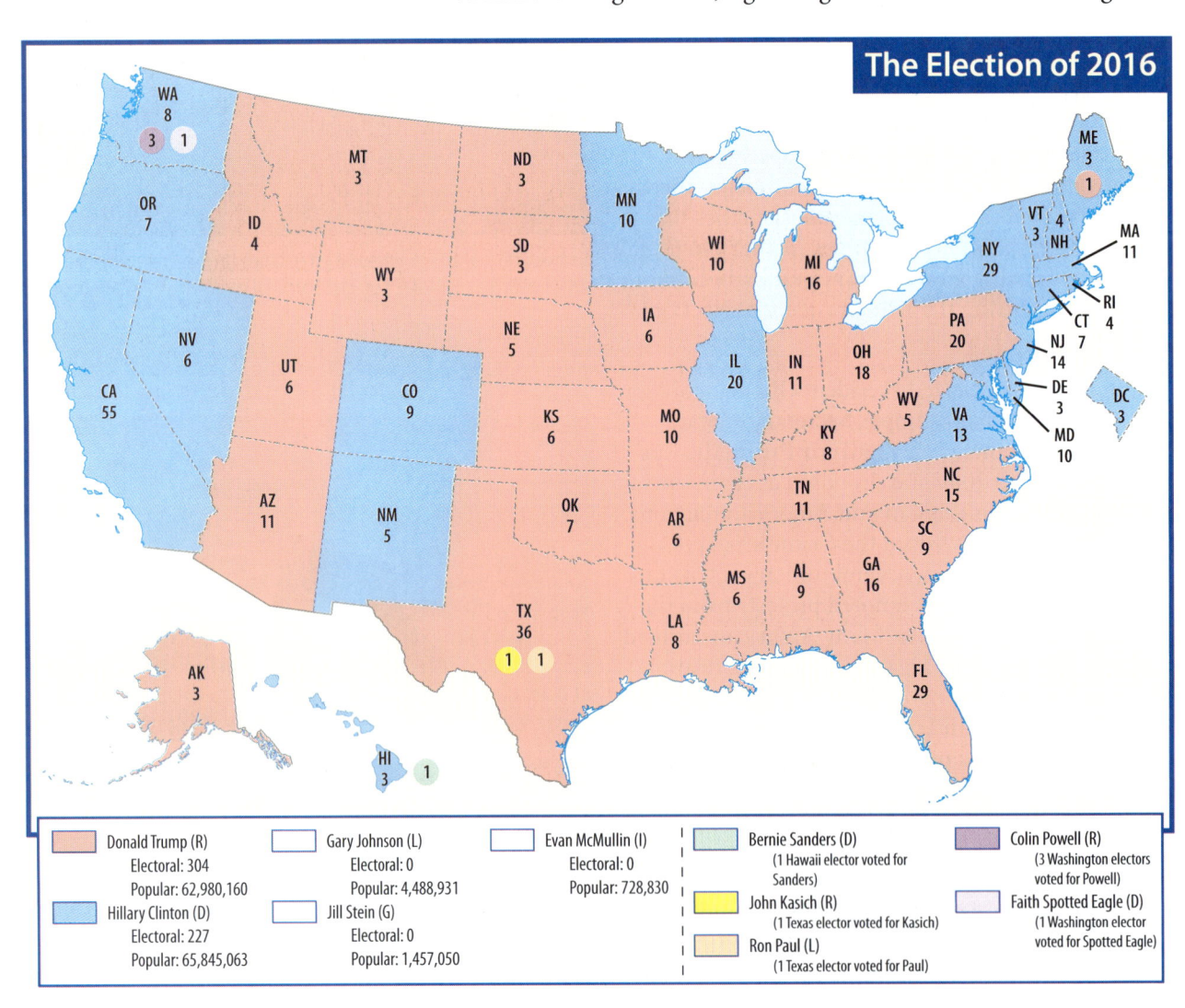

The Election of 2016

Donald Trump (R)
Electoral: 304
Popular: 62,980,160

Hillary Clinton (D)
Electoral: 227
Popular: 65,845,063

Gary Johnson (L)
Electoral: 0
Popular: 4,488,931

Jill Stein (G)
Electoral: 0
Popular: 1,457,050

Evan McMullin (I)
Electoral: 0
Popular: 728,830

Bernie Sanders (D)
(1 Hawaii elector voted for Sanders)

John Kasich (R)
(1 Texas elector voted for Kasich)

Ron Paul (L)
(1 Texas elector voted for Paul)

Colin Powell (R)
(3 Washington electors voted for Powell)

Faith Spotted Eagle (D)
(1 Washington elector voted for Spotted Eagle)

to watch the debates and campaign speeches with great interest. Trump's sometimes crude remarks and his earlier liberal positions on social issues concerned many, including a large number of evangelical Christians. But his populist positions and his later embrace of more conservative social views echoed with enough voters for him to outpoll his opponents during the primaries. As contestants yielded to the seemingly unstoppable Trump campaign, some gave their support to Trump while others remained outspoken critics.

After becoming the Republican nominee, Trump selected Indiana governor **Mike Pence**, who described himself as a "born-again, evangelical Catholic," as his running mate. That choice was popular among conservatives and evangelicals.

The campaign was intense. Clinton had the advantages of more money and strong support from President Obama. However, Trump's campaign appealed to segments of the population that felt abandoned—such as factory workers and rural voters. As the election neared, polls and political observers overwhelmingly predicted a Clinton victory. But Election Day brought stunning results. Although Clinton received about 48 percent of the popular vote to Trump's 46 percent, Trump won in the Electoral College. Furthermore, Republicans maintained control of the legislative branch.

On January 20, 2017, Donald Trump took the oath as the nation's forty-fifth president. With two branches of government in Republican hands, carefully selecting judicial appointments became a major priority for Republicans.

Presidential debate between Donald Trump and Hillary Clinton (*top left*)

The Democratic nominee for vice president, Tim Kaine (*above on left*), and Republican Mike Pence (*above on right*) debate

Donald Trump was inaugurated on January 20, 2017.

Section Review

1. During his first month in office, how did Obama and the Democrat-controlled Congress address the economic downturn that was occurring?
2. What was the Patient Protection and Affordable Care Act (PPACA) often called?
3. In what country was Osama bin Laden living when he was killed?
4. What tool did President Obama use frequently to bypass legislative restraints?
5. What protest group arose following the controversial deaths of several African Americans?
★ Evaluate the passage of the Patient Protection and Affordable Care Act (PPACA) and its regulations.
★ Assess the impact of the Tea Party movement.

Guiding Questions

1. What major shifts in science and technology are occurring during this era?
2. What are some major contemporary moral shifts?

IV. American Culture in a New Era

Major Shifts in Science and Technology

The United States has historically been a nation of inventors. The government has maintained a patent system that protects the investments of those who have improved technology. During the last several decades, science and technology have combined to produce inventions that make the lives of most Americans and many across the world more comfortable and safer.

Technology has transformed communication, health, transportation—nearly every area of our lives. The benefits are obvious. They are part of the reason that new technologies are adopted. The disadvantages they bring are often less obvious but nevertheless real.

Advantages

One of the most noticeable advances in technology is the increased speed and reduced size in computing devices. Computers have changed from room-sized behemoths used primarily by governments and universities to desktop machines that individuals could purchase to smartphones that can be carried in a pocket. When combined with the Internet, these devices enable instant worldwide communication via text, voice, or video. Increased computing power combined with sensor technology and the Internet allow researchers to collect and process massive amounts of data. Many hope that this data can be used to solve problems in the fields of medicine, business, and education.

In medicine, advances include robotic surgery and greater use of laparoscopic procedures that reduce the size of the incision and the time of recovery. The uses of 3D-printing are expanding with developments such as printed robotic hands. Experiments to grow human tissue and even entire organs hold great promise for the future.

Automobile manufacturers are working to produce self-driving cars and to devise technology to help avoid collisions. The goal is to reduce car accidents and fatalities caused by human error.

Concerns

Technology is beneficial to people because it extends human capacities. For instance, a person can walk only so far in a day, but an automobile or an airplane can vastly expand the range of human travel. But what people do with the additional abilities that technology provides depends on their character. The Internet makes possible the easy access of educational information, but it also has made possible easy access to pornography. The human heart is bent to lust after evil things; technology can make it easier to nourish those lusts.

Cultural observers have also begun to question how technology is constructed. Technology is not neutral. For instance, many believe that online social media sites, such as Facebook, Instagram, and Twitter, can serve to distract people, and some have raised the concern that the Internet itself is a distraction engine. Many believe there is a direct link between the shortening of the attention

One of Uber's self-driving cars

Virtual reality headset

span and the diminishing of reading skills with increased use of the Internet.

Finally, it is important to realize technology is not the solution to all of society's problems. To some, technology has turned from being a tool to being an ideology and an idol. In contrast to technology as savior, Neil Postman observed, "Where people are dying of starvation, it does not occur because of inadequate information. If families break up, children are mistreated, crime terrorizes a city, education is impotent, it does not happen because of inadequate information. Mathematical equations, instantaneous communication, and vast quantities of information have nothing whatever to do with any of these problems. And the computer is useless in addressing them."

Champions of technology typically embrace the question "can we?" The question "should we?" is often dismissed as a moral or religious obstacle to progress. But since technologies embody worldviews, the question "should we?" remains necessary.

Moral Cultural Shifts

Attacks on the traditional family and biblical Christianity are not new; however, the intensity has increased in recent years. Although many examples could be listed to demonstrate this, a review of the demise of the Defense of Marriage Act (DOMA) provides a timely example. Furthermore, some recent Supreme Court cases have had a major impact on American culture.

Attack on the Family

As previously mentioned, during the 1990s Congress responded to the attack on the traditional definition of the family by passing DOMA. President Clinton signed that bill into law. Also mentioned was President George W. Bush's endorsement of a proposed constitutional amendment restricting marriage to opposite-sex couples, as a means of supporting the principles of DOMA.

The attack on traditional marriage increased during the 2008 presidential campaign when Barack Obama advocated the repeal of DOMA. In 2011 Obama's attorney general, Eric Holder, announced that his department would no longer defend DOMA in the growing number of court cases seeking to declare it unconstitutional. In 2015, in the case of **Obergefell v. Hodges**, the Supreme Court declared key sections of DOMA to be unconstitutional. The court decreed that the 14th Amendment to the Constitution required all U.S. state laws to recognize same-sex marriages.

By a vote of five to four, this Supreme Court decision created a new right for same-sex couples to marry. It was praised by President Obama and many on the Left. Many other Americans viewed this sweeping decision with dismay. The dissenting opinions of Supreme Court Justices John Roberts, Antonin Scalia, Clarence Thomas, and Samuel Alito reflected the thoughts of many by noting the questionable basis for and drastic effect of this decision on the traditional, and many would say biblical, view of the family.

The nine Supreme Court justices are shown in this June 2017 photograph.

Amendment XIV

Section 1. All persons born or naturalized in the United States, and subject to the jurisdiction thereof, are citizens of the United States and of the State wherein they reside. No State shall make or enforce any law which shall abridge the privileges or immunities of citizens of the United States; nor shall any State deprive any person of life, liberty, or property, without due process of law; nor deny to any person within its jurisdiction the equal protection of the laws.

Supreme Court building

The Supreme Court

Antonin Scalia unexpectedly passed away in February 2016 after serving for almost thirty years as a Supreme Court justice. At the time, the 2016 presidential race was in progress, and the selection of a replacement quickly became a heated political issue. Which president would appoint Scalia's successor, the current one or the next? Democrats wanted President Obama to name a new justice, while Republicans hoped to regain control of the White House and have the new president make the selection.

A month after Scalia's death, President Obama nominated a candidate. The Constitution requires that federal judges be approved by the U.S. Senate. Republicans, who controlled that body, never scheduled hearings to discuss Obama's choice.

Eleven days after Donald Trump was inaugurated in January 2017, he nominated Neil Gorsuch, a U.S. Court of Appeals judge, to fill the vacancy. Gorsuch was widely praised by conservatives as a capable and distinguished choice while liberal politicians voiced concerns. In April, the Senate approved his nomination with a 54–45 vote.

Gorsuch (left) is shown with his wife (right) and President Trump

Assault on Christianity

The catalog of instances in which Christianity has been attacked seems to grow by the day. Three Supreme Court cases provide recent examples of the growing animosity. Fortunately, each was a victory for Christian groups. However, this came only after prolonged legal battles.

In 2004 a teacher left her job at a Christian school in Redford, Michigan, due to health issues and began to receive disability payments. When she tried to return to her teaching position in 2005, the school informed her that her position had been filled. She responded by suing the school for unlawful dismissal under the Americans with Disabilities Act. The case made its way to the Supreme Court as *Hosanna-Tabor Evangelical Lutheran Church & School v. Equal Employment Opportunity Commission*. In an unusual show of unanimity, the Court voted nine to zero against the plaintiff. Chief Justice John Roberts wrote that "the Establishment Clause prevents the Government from appointing ministers, and the Free Exercise Clause prevents it from interfering with the freedom of religious groups to select their own."

In 2014 the Supreme Court ruled 5–4 that the rights of privately owned, for-profit companies should be protected from a law their owners find objectionable if there is a less restrictive way of carrying out the legislation's requirements. Known as *Burwell v. Hobby Lobby*, this case prevented the Obama administration from forcing Hobby Lobby to purchase insurance that provided some controversial contraceptives to its employees. While the court remained narrowly divided, it provided much publicity to the pressure by the federal government to force Christians who own businesses to comply with federal mandates that violate their conscience.

Another case that generated much attention, and took on the tenor of a David versus Goliath story, was the case of the Obama administration against a Catholic order known as the Little Sisters of the Poor. The issue again was the contraceptive mandate in the Affordable Care Act. When the Little Sisters refused to submit, they were threatened with fines that would have totaled $70 million per year. When the Supreme Court heard the case *Little Sisters of the Poor v. Burwell* in 2016, the justices voted unanimously to overturn the lower court rulings against the Little Sisters. Though this case and the earlier ones noted were obvious victories for religious freedom, Christians continue to face hostility because of their beliefs.

Section Review

1–3. List three positive advancements in science and technology that are mentioned in the chapter.

4. What question should Christians ask about potential scientific and technological developments?

5. What amendment to the Constitution was used by the Supreme Court to create a right for same-sex couples to marry?

★ Considering the previous question, how did the court's interpretation of the amendment depart from its original purpose?

★ What role do you think the federal government should play in providing and regulating health insurance?

CHAPTER REVIEW 27

Making Connections

1. What was President Clinton's "don't ask, don't tell" policy for homosexuals in the military?

2–5. List four indications of the strength of the economy during the Clinton administration.

6–7. What two charges did President Clinton face when he was impeached?

8. Based on the information in this chapter and in Chapter 22, what are similarities and differences between the Japanese attack on Pearl Harbor and the terrorists' attack on the United States on 9/11?

Developing History Skills

1. In light of the circumstances facing George W. Bush, evaluate his presidency. Rank him in relation to the other presidents before him. Support your assessments.

2. List at least three events that have occurred since the beginning of the school year that you think will be included in future history books. Support your answers.

Thinking Critically

1. Is it right for the United States to intervene militarily in the internal affairs of other areas, as it did in Haiti, Bosnia, and Kosovo? Why or why not?

2. Do you think the Senate was right to acquit President Clinton? Explain your answer.

Living as a Christian Citizen

1. When Christians vote or otherwise participate in the political process, they should consider the Bible's direction regarding specific areas of life. Evaluate the following policies from a biblical perspective: the Welfare Reform Act of 1996, recognition of homosexual marriage, and government health care.

2. Identify a social media site that you use or would like to use. Identify its benefits and problems. Create a plan for making use of the benefits while avoiding the problems. If the problems are severe enough, propose an idea for an alternative site.

People, Places, and Things to Remember

Family and Medical Leave Act
Brady Bill
North American Free Trade Agreement (NAFTA)
Hillary Rodham Clinton
Christian Coalition
Contract with America
Newt Gingrich
Defense of Marriage Act (DOMA)
Welfare Reform Act of 1996
Bob Dole
ethnic cleansing
Lewinsky scandal
Al Gore
George W. Bush
Richard Cheney
September 11, 2001
al-Qaeda
Osama bin Laden
Taliban
Office of Homeland Security
weapons of mass destruction (WMDs)
coalition of the willing
John Kerry
faith-based initiatives
Hurricane Katrina
John G. Roberts Jr.
Samuel Alito Jr.
Barack Obama
Joe Biden
John McCain
Great Recession
Patient Protection and Affordable Care Act (PPACA)
Obamacare
Sonia Sotomayor
Elena Kagan
Tea Party
ISIS
Arab Spring
Mitt Romney
executive orders
Black Lives Matter
Vladimir Putin
Donald Trump
Mike Pence
Obergefell v. Hodges

States of the Union

Order of Admission	State	Admitted	Capital	Nickname
1	Delaware	1787	Dover	Diamond State, First State
2	Pennsylvania	1787	Harrisburg	Keystone State
3	New Jersey	1787	Trenton	Garden State
4	Georgia	1788	Atlanta	Empire State of the South, Peach State
5	Connecticut	1788	Hartford	Constitution State, Nutmeg State
6	Massachusetts	1788	Boston	Bay State, Old Colony
7	Maryland	1788	Annapolis	Old Line State, Free State
8	South Carolina	1788	Columbia	Palmetto State
9	New Hampshire	1788	Concord	Granite State
10	Virginia	1788	Richmond	Old Dominion State
11	New York	1788	Albany	Empire State
12	North Carolina	1789	Raleigh	Tar Heel State, Old North State
13	Rhode Island	1790	Providence	Little Rhody, Ocean State
14	Vermont	1791	Montpelier	Green Mountain State
15	Kentucky	1792	Frankfort	Bluegrass State
16	Tennessee	1796	Nashville	Volunteer State
17	Ohio	1803	Columbus	Buckeye State
18	Louisiana	1812	Baton Rouge	Pelican State
19	Indiana	1816	Indianapolis	Hoosier State
20	Mississippi	1817	Jackson	Magnolia State
21	Illinois	1818	Springfield	Land of Lincoln, Prairie State
22	Alabama	1819	Montgomery	Heart of Dixie, Camellia State
23	Maine	1820	Augusta	Pine Tree State
24	Missouri	1821	Jefferson City	"Show Me" State
25	Arkansas	1836	Little Rock	Natural State, Razorback State
26	Michigan	1837	Lansing	Wolverine State, Great Lakes State
27	Florida	1845	Tallahassee	Sunshine State
28	Texas	1845	Austin	Lone Star State
29	Iowa	1846	Des Moines	Hawkeye State
30	Wisconsin	1848	Madison	Badger State
31	California	1850	Sacramento	Golden State
32	Minnesota	1858	St. Paul	North Star State, Gopher State
33	Oregon	1859	Salem	Beaver State
34	Kansas	1861	Topeka	Sunflower State
35	West Virginia	1863	Charleston	Mountain State
36	Nevada	1864	Carson City	Sagebrush State, Silver State, Battle Born State
37	Nebraska	1867	Lincoln	Cornhusker State
38	Colorado	1876	Denver	Centennial State
39	North Dakota	1889	Bismarck	Peace Garden State
40	South Dakota	1889	Pierre	Coyote State, Mt. Rushmore State
41	Montana	1889	Helena	Treasure State
42	Washington	1889	Olympia	Evergreen State
43	Idaho	1890	Boise	Gem State
44	Wyoming	1890	Cheyenne	Equality State, Cowboy State
45	Utah	1896	Salt Lake City	Beehive State
46	Oklahoma	1907	Oklahoma City	Sooner State
47	New Mexico	1912	Santa Fe	Land of Enchantment
48	Arizona	1912	Phoenix	Grand Canyon State
49	Alaska	1959	Juneau	The Last Frontier
50	Hawaii	1959	Honolulu	Aloha State

Presidents of the United States

President	Term(s)	Political Party	Home State	Vice President(s)
George Washington	1789–1797	None	Virginia	John Adams
John Adams	1797–1801	Federalist	Massachusetts	Thomas Jefferson
Thomas Jefferson	1801–1809	Republican **	Virginia	Aaron Burr George Clinton
James Madison	1809–1817	Republican **	Virginia	George Clinton Elbridge Gerry
James Monroe	1817–1825	Republican **	Virginia	Daniel D. Tompkins
John Quincy Adams	1825–1829	Republican **	Massachusetts	John C. Calhoun
Andrew Jackson	1829–1837	Democrat	Tennessee	John C. Calhoun Martin Van Buren
Martin Van Buren	1837–1841	Democrat	New York	Richard M. Johnson
William H. Harrison	1841	Whig	Ohio	John Tyler
John Tyler	1841–1845	Whig	Virginia	
James K. Polk	1845–1849	Democrat	Tennessee	George M. Dallas
Zachary Taylor	1849–1850	Whig	Louisiana	Millard Fillmore
Millard Fillmore	1850–1853	Whig	New York	
Franklin Pierce	1853–1857	Democrat	New Hampshire	William R. King
James Buchanan	1857–1861	Democrat	Pennsylvania	John C. Breckinridge
Abraham Lincoln	1861–1865	Republican	Illinois	Hannibal Hamlin Andrew Johnson
Andrew Johnson	1865–1869	Democrat; National Union	Tennessee	
Ulysses S. Grant	1869–1877	Republican	Illinois	Schuyler Colfax Henry Wilson
Rutherford B. Hayes	1877–1881	Republican	Ohio	William A. Wheeler
James A. Garfield	1881	Republican	Ohio	Chester A. Arthur
Chester A. Arthur	1881–1885	Republican	New York	
Grover Cleveland	1885–1889	Democrat	New York	Thomas A. Hendricks
Benjamin Harrison	1889–1893	Republican	Indiana	Levi P. Morton
Grover Cleveland	1893–1897	Democrat	New York	Adlai E. Stevenson
William McKinley	1897–1901	Republican	Ohio	Garret A. Hobart Theodore Roosevelt
Theodore Roosevelt	1901–1909	Republican	New York	Charles W. Fairbanks
William H. Taft	1909–1913	Republican	Ohio	James S. Sherman
Woodrow Wilson	1913–1921	Democrat	New Jersey	Thomas R. Marshall
Warren G. Harding	1921–1923	Republican	Ohio	Calvin Coolidge
Calvin Coolidge	1923–1929	Republican	Massachusetts	Charles G. Dawes
Herbert Hoover	1929–1933	Republican	California	Charles Curtis
Franklin D. Roosevelt	1933–1945	Democrat	New York	John N. Garner (two terms) Henry A. Wallace Harry S. Truman
Harry S. Truman	1945–1953	Democrat	Missouri	Alben W. Barkley
Dwight D. Eisenhower	1953–1961	Republican	Pennsylvania	Richard M. Nixon
John F. Kennedy	1961–1963	Democrat	Massachusetts	Lyndon B. Johnson
Lyndon B. Johnson	1963–1969	Democrat	Texas	Hubert H. Humphrey
Richard M. Nixon	1969–1974	Republican	California	Spiro T. Agnew Gerald R. Ford
Gerald R. Ford	1974–1977	Republican	Michigan	Nelson A. Rockefeller
Jimmy Carter	1977–1981	Democrat	Georgia	Walter F. Mondale
Ronald Reagan	1981–1989	Republican	California	George H. W. Bush
George H. W. Bush	1989–1993	Republican	Texas	Dan Quayle
Bill Clinton	1993–2001	Democrat	Arkansas	Al Gore
George W. Bush	2001–2009	Republican	Texas	Richard Cheney
Barack Obama	2009–2017	Democrat	Illinois	Joe Biden
Donald Trump	2017–	Republican	New York	Mike Pence

** The Republicans during this period were also called Democratic-Republicans. The group developed into today's Democratic Party. The present-day Republican Party originated in 1854.

Map of the United States

innesota
Lake Superior
Saint Paul
Wisconsin
Lake Michigan
Lake Huron
Michigan
Madison
Lansing
Lake Ontario
Lake Erie
White Mountains
Vermont
Montpelier
Green Mountains
Maine
Augusta
Concord
New Hampshire
Albany
New York
Boston
Massachusetts
Providence
Hartford
Rhode Island
Connecticut
Iowa
Des Moines
Pennsylvania
Harrisburg
Trenton
New Jersey
Ohio
Columbus
Indiana
Indianapolis
Illinois
Springfield
Missouri
Missouri R.
Ohio R.
West Virginia
Charleston
Dover
Annapolis
Delaware
Washington, D.C.
Maryland
Richmond
Virginia
peka
Jefferson City
Frankfort
Kentucky
Appalachian Mtns.
Great Smoky Mtns.
Raleigh
North Carolina
ATLANTIC OCEAN
Nashville
Tennessee
Arkansas
Little Rock
Mississippi R.
Columbia
South Carolina
Atlanta
Alabama
Georgia
Mississippi
Louisiana
Jackson
Montgomery
Tallahassee
Baton Rouge
Florida
Gulf of Mexico
N
W
E
S
0
250
500 Miles
Above 12,000 ft.
9,000–12,000 ft.
6,000–9,000 ft.
3,000–6,000 ft.
0–3,000 ft.

The Declaration of Independence of the United States

In CONGRESS, July 4, 1776.

The unanimous Declaration of the thirteen united States of America.

When in the course of human events, it becomes necessary for one people to dissolve the political bands which have connected them with another, and to assume among the powers of the earth, the separate and equal station to which the laws of nature and of nature's God entitle them, a decent respect to the opinions of mankind requires that they should declare the causes which impel them to the separation.

We hold these truths to be self-evident, that all men are created equal, that they are endowed by their Creator with certain unalienable rights, that among these are life, liberty and the pursuit of happiness.—That to secure these rights, governments are instituted among men, deriving their just powers from the consent of the governed,—That whenever any form of government becomes destructive of these ends, it is the right of the people to alter or to abolish it, and to institute new government, laying its foundation on such principles and organizing its powers in such form, as to them shall seem most likely to effect their safety and happiness. Prudence, indeed, will dictate that governments long established should not be changed for light and transient causes; and accordingly all experience hath shewn, that mankind are more disposed to suffer, while evils are sufferable, than to right themselves by abolishing the forms to which they are accustomed. But when a long train of abuses and usurpations, pursuing invariably the same object evinces a design to reduce them under absolute despotism, it is their right, it is their duty, to throw off such government, and to provide new guards for their future security. — Such has been the patient sufferance of these colonies; and such is now the necessity which constrains them to alter their former systems of government. The history of the present king of Great Britain is a history of repeated injuries and usurpations, all having in direct object the establishment of an absolute tyranny over these states. To prove this, let facts be submitted to a candid world.

He has refused his assent to laws, the most wholesome and necessary for the public good.

He has forbidden his governors to pass laws of immediate and pressing importance, unless suspended in their operation till his assent should be obtained; and when so suspended, he has utterly neglected to attend to them.

He has refused to pass other laws for the accommodation of large districts of people, unless those people would relinquish the right of representation in the legislature, a right inestimable to them and formidable to tyrants only.

He has called together legislative bodies at places unusual, uncomfortable, and distant from the depository of their public records, for the sole purpose of fatiguing them into compliance with his measures.

He has dissolved representative houses repeatedly, for opposing with manly firmness his invasions on the rights of the people.

He has refused for a long time, after such dissolutions, to cause others to be elected; whereby the legislative powers, incapable of annihilation, have returned to the people at large for their exercise; the state remaining in the meantime exposed to all the dangers of invasion from without, and convulsions within.

He has endeavoured to prevent the population of these states; for that purpose obstructing the laws for naturalization of foreigners; refusing to pass others to encourage their migrations hither, and raising the conditions of new appropriations of lands.

He has obstructed the administration of justice, by refusing his assent to laws for establishing judiciary powers.

He has made judges dependent on his will alone, for the tenure of their offices, and the amount and payment of their salaries.

He has erected a multitude of new offices, and sent hither swarms of officers to harass our people, and eat out their substance.

He has kept among us, in times of peace, standing armies without the consent of our legislatures.

He has affected to render the military independent of and superior to the civil power.

He has combined with others to subject us to a jurisdiction foreign to our constitution, and unacknowledged by our laws; giving his assent to their acts of pretended legislation:

For quartering large bodies of armed troops among us:

For protecting them, by a mock trial, from punishment for any murders which they should commit on the inhabitants of these states:

For cutting off our trade with all parts of the world:

For imposing taxes on us without our consent:

For depriving us in many cases, of the benefits of trial by jury:

For transporting us beyond seas to be tried for pretended offences:

For abolishing the free system of English laws in a neighboring province, establishing therein an arbitrary government, and enlarging its boundaries so as to render it at once an example and fit instrument for introducing the same absolute rule into these colonies:

For taking away our charters, abolishing our most valuable laws, and altering fundamentally the forms of our governments:

For suspending our own legislatures, and declaring themselves invested with power to legislate for us in all cases whatsoever.

He has abdicated government here, by declaring us out of his protection and waging war against us.

He has plundered our seas, ravaged our coasts, burnt our towns, and destroyed the lives of our people.

He is at this time transporting large armies of foreign mercenaries to complete the works of death, desolation and tyranny, already begun with circumstances of cruelty and perfidy scarcely paralleled in the most barbarous ages, and totally unworthy the head of a civilized nation.

He has constrained our fellow citizens taken captive on the high seas to bear arms against their country, to become the executioners of their friends and brethren, or to fall themselves by their hands.

He has excited domestic insurrections amongst us, and has endeavored to bring on the inhabitants of our frontiers, the merciless Indian savages, whose known rule of warfare, is an undistinguished destruction of all ages, sexes and conditions.

In every stage of these oppressions, we have petitioned for redress in the most humble terms: our repeated petitions have been answered only by repeated injury. A prince whose character is thus marked by every act which may define a tyrant, is unfit to be the ruler of a free people.

Nor have we been wanting in attentions to our British brethren. We have warned them from time to time of attempts by their legislature to extend an unwarrantable jurisdiction over us. We have reminded them of the circumstances of our emigration and settlement here. We have appealed to their native justice and magnanimity, and we have conjured them by the ties of our common kindred to disavow these usurpations, which, would inevitably interrupt our connections and correspondence. They too have been deaf to the voice of justice and of consanguinity. We must, therefore, acquiesce in the necessity, which denounces our separation, and hold them, as we hold the rest of mankind, enemies in war, in peace friends.

We, therefore, the representatives of the united states of America, in general congress, assembled, appealing to the Supreme Judge of the world for the rectitude of our intentions, do, in the name, and by authority of the good people of these colonies, solemnly publish and declare, that these united colonies are, and of right ought to be free and independent states; that they are absolved from all allegiance to the British Crown, and that all political connection between them and the state of Great Britain, is and ought to be totally dissolved; and that as free and independent states, they have full power to levy war, conclude peace, contract alliances, establish commerce, and to do all other acts and things which independent states may of right do. And for the support of this declaration, with a firm reliance on the protection of divine Providence, we mutually pledge to each other our lives, our fortunes and our sacred honor.

The Constitution of the United States

We the People of the United States, in order to form a more perfect union, establish justice, insure domestic tranquility, provide for the common defence, promote the general welfare, and secure the blessings of liberty to ourselves and our posterity, do ordain and establish this Constitution for the United States of America.

Article I: The Legislative Branch

Section 1

All legislative powers herein granted shall be vested in a Congress of the United States, which shall consist of a Senate and House of Representatives.

Section 2

1. The House of Representatives shall be composed of members chosen every second year by the people of the several states, and the electors in each state shall have the qualifications requisite for electors of the most numerous branch of the state legislature.

2. No person shall be a representative who shall not have attained to the age of twenty-five years, and been seven years a citizen of the United States, and who shall not, when elected, be an inhabitant of that state in which he shall be chosen.

3. *Representatives and direct taxes shall be apportioned among the several states which may be included within this Union, according to their respective numbers, which shall be determined by adding to the whole number of free persons, including those bound to service for a term of years, and excluding Indians not taxed, three-fifths of all other persons.* The actual enumeration shall be made within three years after the first meeting of the Congress of the United States, and within every subsequent term of ten years, in such manner as they shall by law direct. The number of representatives shall not exceed one for every thirty thousand, but each state shall have at least one representative; *and until such enumeration shall be made, the state of New Hampshire shall be entitled to choose three, Massachusetts eight, Rhode-Island and Providence Plantations one, Connecticut five, New-York six, New Jersey four, Pennsylvania eight, Delaware one, Maryland six, Virginia ten, North Carolina five, South Carolina five, and Georgia three.*

4. When vacancies happen in the representation from any state, the executive authority thereof shall issue writs of election to fill such vacancies.

5. The House of Representatives shall choose their speaker and other officers; and shall have the sole power of impeachment.

Section 3

1. The Senate of the United States shall be composed of two senators from each state, *chosen by the legislature* thereof, for six years; and each senator shall have one vote.

2. Immediately after they shall be assembled in consequence of the first election, they shall be divided as equally as may be into three classes. The seats of the senators of the first class shall be vacated at the expiration of the second year, of the second class at the expiration of the fourth year, and of the third class at the expiration of the sixth year, so that one third may be chosen every second year; *and if vacancies happen by resignation, or otherwise, during the recess of the legislature of any state, the executive thereof may make temporary appointments until the next meeting of the legislature, which shall then fill such vacancies.*

3. No person shall be a senator who shall not have attained to the age of thirty years, and been nine years a citizen of the United States, and who shall not, when elected, be an inhabitant of that state for which he shall be chosen.

4. The vice president of the United States shall be president of the Senate, but shall have no vote, unless they be equally divided.

5. The Senate shall choose their other officers, and also a president pro tempore, in the absence of the vice president, or when he shall exercise the office of president of the United States.

6. The Senate shall have the sole power to try all impeachments. When sitting for that purpose, they shall be on oath or affirmation. When the president of the United States is tried, the chief justice shall

[Note: Sections in *italics* are sections of the Constitution that are no longer in force.]

preside: And no person shall be convicted without the concurrence of two-thirds of the members present.

7. Judgment in cases of impeachment shall not extend further than to removal from office, and disqualification to hold and enjoy any office of honor, trust or profit under the United States: but the party convicted shall nevertheless be liable and subject to indictment, trial, judgment and punishment, according to law.

Section 4

1. The times, places and manner of holding elections for senators and representatives, shall be prescribed in each state by the legislature thereof; but the Congress may at any time by law make or alter such regulations, except as to the places of choosing senators.

2. The Congress shall assemble at least once in every year, *and such meeting shall be on the first Monday in December, unless they shall by law appoint a different day.*

Section 5

1. Each house shall be the judge of the elections, returns and qualifications of its own members, and a majority of each shall constitute a quorum to do business; but a smaller number may adjourn from day to day, and may be authorized to compel the attendance of absent members, in such manner, and under such penalties as each house may provide.

2. Each house may determine the rules of its proceedings, punish its members for disorderly behaviour, and, with the concurrence of two-thirds, expel a member.

3. Each house shall keep a journal of its proceedings, and from time to time publish the same, excepting such parts as may in their judgment require secrecy; and the yeas and nays of the members of either house on any question shall, at the desire of one-fifth of those present, be entered on the journal.

4. Neither house, during the session of Congress, shall, without the consent of the other, adjourn for more than three days, nor to any other place than that in which the two houses shall be sitting.

Section 6

1. The senators and representatives shall receive a compensation for their services, to be ascertained by law, and paid out of the Treasury of the United States. They shall in all cases, except treason, felony and breach of the peace, be privileged from arrest during their attendance at the session of their respective houses, and in going to and returning from the same; and for any speech or debate in either house, they shall not be questioned in any other place.

2. No senator or representative shall, during the time for which he was elected, be appointed to any civil office under the authority of the United States, which shall have been created, or the emoluments whereof shall have been increased during such time; and no person holding any office under the United States, shall be a member of either house during his continuance in office.

Section 7

1. All bills for raising revenue shall originate in the House of Representatives; but the Senate may propose or concur with amendments as on other bills.

2. Every bill which shall have passed the House of Representatives and the Senate, shall, before it become a law, be presented to the president of the United States; If he approve he shall sign it, but if not he shall return it, with his objections to that house in which it shall have originated, who shall enter the objections at large on their journal, and proceed to reconsider it. If after such reconsideration two-thirds of that house shall agree to pass the bill, it shall be sent, together with the objections, to the other house, by which it shall likewise be reconsidered, and if approved by two-thirds of that house, it shall become a law. But in all such cases the votes of both houses shall be determined by yeas and nays, and the names of the persons voting for and against the bill shall be entered on the journal of each house respectively. If any bill shall not be returned by the president within ten days (Sundays excepted) after it shall have been presented to him, the same shall be a law, in like manner as if he had signed it, unless the Congress by their adjournment prevent its return, in which case it shall not be a law.

3. Every order, resolution, or vote to which the concurrence of the Senate and House of Representatives may be necessary (except on a question of adjournment) shall be presented to the president of the United States; and before the same shall take effect, shall be approved by him, or being disapproved by him, shall be repassed by two-thirds of the Senate and House of Representatives, according to the rules and limitations prescribed in the case of a bill.

Section 8

The Congress shall have power

1. To lay and collect taxes, duties, imposts and excises, to pay the debts and provide for the common defence and general welfare of the United States; but all duties, imposts and excises shall be uniform throughout the United States;

2. To borrow money on the credit of the United States;

3. To regulate commerce with foreign nations, and among the several states, and with the Indian tribes;

4. To establish an uniform rule of naturalization, and uniform laws on the subject of bankruptcies throughout the United States;

5. To coin money, regulate the value thereof, and of foreign coin, and fix the standard of weights and measures;

6. To provide for the punishment of counterfeiting the securities and current coin of the United States;

7. To establish post offices and post roads;

8. To promote the progress of science and useful arts, by securing for limited times to authors and inventors the exclusive right to their respective writings and discoveries;

9. To constitute tribunals inferior to the Supreme Court;

10. To define and punish piracies and felonies committed on the high seas, and offences against the law of nations;

11. To declare war, grant letters of marque and reprisal, and make rules concerning captures on land and water;

12. To raise and support armies, but no appropriation of money to that use shall be for a longer term than two years;

13. To provide and maintain a navy;

14. To make rules for the government and regulation of the land and naval forces;

15. To provide for calling forth the militia to execute the laws of the Union, suppress insurrections and repel invasions;

16. To provide for organizing, arming, and disciplining, the militia, and for governing such part of them as may be employed in the service of the United States, reserving to the states respectively, the appointment of the officers, and the authority of training the militia according to the discipline prescribed by Congress;

17. To exercise exclusive legislation in all cases whatsoever, over such district (not exceeding ten miles square) as may, by cession of particular states, and the acceptance of Congress, become the seat of the government of the United States, and to exercise like authority over all places purchased by the consent of the legislature of the state in which the same shall be, for the erection of forts, magazines, arsenals, dock-yards, and other needful buildings;—and

18. To make all laws which shall be necessary and proper for carrying into execution the foregoing powers, and all other powers vested by this Constitution in the government of the United States, or in any department or officer thereof.

Section 9

1. The migration or importation of such persons as any of the states now existing shall think proper to admit, shall not be prohibited by the Congress prior to the year one thousand eight hundred and eight, but a tax or duty may be imposed on such importation, not exceeding ten dollars for each person.

2. The privilege of the writ of habeas corpus shall not be suspended, unless when in cases of rebellion or invasion the public safety may require it.

3. No bill of attainder or ex post facto law shall be passed.

4. No capitation, or other direct, tax shall be laid, *unless in proportion to the census or enumeration herein before directed to be taken.*

5. No tax or duty shall be laid on articles exported from any state.

6. No preference shall be given by any regulation of commerce or revenue to the ports of one state over those of another: nor shall vessels bound to, or from, one state, be obliged to enter, clear, or pay duties in another.

7. No money shall be drawn from the Treasury, but in consequence of appropriations made by law; and a regular statement and account of the receipts and expenditures of all public money shall be published from time to time.

8. No title of nobility shall be granted by the United States: and no person holding any office of profit or trust under them, shall, without the consent of the Congress, accept of any present, emolument, office, or title, of any kind whatever, from any king, prince, or foreign state.

Section 10

1. No state shall enter into any treaty, alliance, or confederation; grant letters of marque and reprisal; coin money; emit bills of credit; make any thing but gold and silver coin a tender in payment of debts; pass any bill of attainder, ex post facto law, or law impairing the obligation of contracts, or grant any title of nobility.

2. No state shall, without the consent of the Congress, lay any imposts or duties on imports or exports, except what may be absolutely necessary for executing its inspection laws: and the net produce of all duties and imposts, laid by any state on imports or exports, shall be for the use of the Treasury of the United States; and all such laws shall be subject to the revision and control of the Congress.

3. No state shall, without the consent of Congress, lay any duty of tonnage, keep troops, or ships of war in time of peace, enter into any agreement or compact with another state, or with a foreign power, or engage in war, unless actually invaded, or in such imminent danger as will not admit of delay.

Article II: The Executive Branch

Section 1

1. The executive power shall be vested in a president of the United States of America. He shall hold his office during the term of four years, and, together with the vice president, chosen for the same term, be elected, as follows:

2. Each state shall appoint, in such manner as the legislature thereof may direct, a number of electors, equal to the whole number of senators and representatives to which the state may be entitled in the Congress: but no senator or representative, or person holding an office of trust or profit under the United States, shall be appointed an elector.

The electors shall meet in their respective states, and vote by ballot for two persons, of whom one at least shall not be an inhabitant of the same state with themselves. And they shall make a list of all the persons voted for, and of the number of votes for each; which list they shall sign and certify, and transmit sealed to the seat of the government of the United States, directed to the president of the Senate. The president of the Senate shall, in the presence of the Senate and House of Representatives, open all the certificates, and the votes shall then be counted. The person having the greatest number of votes shall be the president, if such number be a majority of the whole number of electors appointed; and if there be more than one who have such majority, and have an equal number of votes, then the House of Representatives shall immediately choose by ballot one of them for president; and if no person have a majority, then from the five highest on the list the said house shall in like manner choose the president. But in choosing the president, the votes shall be taken by states, the representation from each state having one vote; a quorum for this purpose shall consist of a member or members from two-thirds of the states, and a majority of all the states shall be necessary to a choice. In every case, after the choice of the president, the person having the greatest number of votes of the electors shall be the vice president. But if there should remain two or more who have equal votes, the Senate shall choose from them by ballot the vice president.

3. The Congress may determine the time of choosing the electors, and the day on which they shall give their votes; which day shall be the same throughout the United States.

4. No person except a natural born citizen, *or a citizen of the United States, at the time of the adoption of this Constitution,* shall be eligible to the office of president; neither shall any person be eligible to that office who shall not have attained to the age of thirty-five years, and been fourteen years a resident within the United States.

5. *In case of the removal of the president from office, or of his death, resignation, or inability to discharge the powers and duties of the said office, the same shall devolve on the vice president, and the Congress may by law provide for the case of removal, death, resignation or inability, both of the president and vice president, declaring what officer shall then act as president, and such officer shall act accordingly, until the disability be removed, or a president shall be elected.*

6. The president shall, at stated times, receive for his services, a compensation, which shall neither be increased nor diminished during the period for which he shall have been elected, and he shall not receive within that period any other emolument from the United States, or any of them.

7. Before he enter on the execution of his office, he shall take the following oath or affirmation:—"I do solemnly swear (or affirm) that I will faithfully execute the office of president of the United States, and will to the best of my ability, preserve, protect and defend the Constitution of the United States."

Section 2

1. The president shall be commander in chief of the army and navy of the United States, and of the militia of the several states, when called into the actual service of the United States; he may require the opinion, in writing, of the principal officer in each of the executive departments, upon any subject relating to the duties of their respective offices, and he shall have power to grant reprieves and pardons for offences against the United States, except in cases of impeachment.

2. He shall have power, by and with the advice and consent of the senate, to make treaties, provided two thirds of the senators present concur; and he shall nominate, and by and with the advice and consent of the Senate, shall appoint ambassadors, other public ministers and consuls, judges of the Supreme Court, and all other officers of the United States, whose appointments are not herein otherwise provided for, and which shall be established by law: but the Congress may by law vest the appointment of such inferior officers, as they think proper, in the president alone, in the courts of law, or in the heads of departments.

3. The president shall have power to fill up all vacancies that may happen during the recess of the Senate, by granting commissions which shall expire at the end of their next session.

Section 3

He shall from time to time give to the Congress information of the state of the Union, and recommend to their consideration such measures as he shall judge necessary and expedient; he may, on extraordinary occasions, convene both houses, or either of them, and in case of disagreement between them, with respect to the time of adjournment, he may adjourn them to such time as he shall think proper; he shall receive ambassadors and other public ministers; he shall take care that the laws be faithfully executed, and shall commission all the officers of the United States.

Section 4

The president, vice president and all civil officers of the United States, shall be removed from office on impeachment for, and conviction of, treason, bribery, or other high crimes and misdemeanors.

Article III: The Judicial Branch

Section 1

The judicial power of the United States, shall be vested in one Supreme Court, and in such inferior courts as the Congress may from time to time ordain and establish. The judges, both of the Supreme and inferior courts, shall hold their offices during good behavior, and shall, at stated times, receive for their services, a compensation, which shall not be diminished during their continuance in office.

Section 2

1. The judicial power shall extend to all cases, in law and equity, arising under this Constitution, the laws of the United States, and treaties made, or which shall be made, under their authority;—to all cases affecting ambassadors, other public ministers and consuls;—to all cases of admiralty and maritime jurisdiction;—to controversies to which the United States shall be a party;—to controversies between two or more states;— *between a state and citizens of another state,*—between citizens of different states,—between citizens of the same state claiming lands under grants of different states, and between a state, or the citizens thereof, and foreign states, citizens or subjects.

2. In all cases affecting ambassadors, other public ministers and consuls, and those in which a state shall be party, the Supreme Court shall have original jurisdiction. In all the other cases before mentioned, the Supreme Court shall have appellate jurisdiction, both as to law and fact, with such exceptions, and under such regulations as the Congress shall make.

3. The trial of all crimes, except in cases of impeachment, shall be by jury; and such trial shall be held in the state where the said crimes shall have been committed; but when not committed within any state, the trial shall be at such place or places as the Congress may by law have directed.

Section 3

1. Treason against the United States, shall consist only in levying war against them, or in adhering to their enemies, giving them aid and comfort. No person shall be convicted of treason unless on the testimony of two witnesses to the same overt act, or on confession in open court.

2. The Congress shall have power to declare the punishment of treason, but no attainder of treason shall work corruption of blood, or forfeiture except during the life of the person attainted.

Article IV: Interstate Relations

Section 1
Full faith and credit shall be given in each state to the public acts, records, and judicial proceedings of every other state. And the Congress may by general laws prescribe the manner in which such acts, records and proceedings shall be proved, and the effect thereof.

Section 2
1. The citizens of each state shall be entitled to all privileges and immunities of citizens in the several states.

2. A person charged in any state with treason, felony, or other crime, who shall flee from justice, and be found in another state, shall on demand of the executive authority of the state from which he fled, be delivered up, to be removed to the state having jurisdiction of the crime.

3. *No person held to service or labour in one state, under the laws thereof, escaping into another, shall, in consequence of any law or regulation therein, be discharged from such service or labour, but shall be delivered up on claim of the party to whom such service or labour may be due.*

Section 3
1. New states may be admitted by the Congress into this Union; but no new state shall be formed or erected within the jurisdiction of any other state; nor any state be formed by the junction of two or more states, or parts of states, without the consent of the legislatures of the states concerned as well as of the Congress.

2. The Congress shall have power to dispose of and make all needful rules and regulations respecting the territory or other property belonging to the United States; and nothing in this Constitution shall be so construed as to prejudice any claims of the United States, or of any particular state.

Section 4
The United States shall guarantee to every state in this Union a republican form of government, and shall protect each of them against invasion; and on application of the legislature, or of the executive (when the legislature cannot be convened), against domestic violence.

Article V: Amending the Constitution

The Congress, whenever two-thirds of both houses shall deem it necessary, shall propose amendments to this Constitution, or, on the application of the legislatures of two-thirds of the several states, shall call a convention for proposing amendments, which, in either case, shall be valid to all intents and purposes, as part of this Constitution, when ratified by the legislatures of three-fourths of the several states, or by conventions in three-fourths thereof, as the one or the other mode of ratification may be proposed by the Congress; provided that *no amendment which may be made prior to the year one thousand eight hundred and eight shall in any manner affect the first and fourth clauses in the ninth section of the first article; and that* no state, without its consent, shall be deprived of its equal suffrage in the Senate.

Article VI: Constitutional and National Supremacy

1. All debts contracted and engagements entered into, before the adoption of this Constitution, shall be as valid against the United States under this Constitution, as under the Confederation.

2. This Constitution, and the laws of the United States which shall be made in pursuance thereof; and all treaties made, or which shall be made, under the authority of the United States, shall be the supreme law of the land; and the judges in every state shall be bound thereby, any thing in the Constitution or laws of any state to the contrary notwithstanding.

3. The senators and representatives before mentioned, and the members of the several state legislatures, and all executive and judicial officers, both of the United States and of the several states, shall be bound by oath or affirmation, to support this Constitution; but no religious test shall ever be required as a qualification to any office or public trust under the United States.

Article VII: Ratifying the Constitution

The ratification of the conventions of nine states, shall be sufficient for the establishment of this Constitution between the states so ratifying the same....

Done in convention by the unanimous consent of the states present the seventeenth day of September in the year of our Lord one thousand seven hundred and eighty-seven and of the independence of the United States of America the twelfth. In witness whereof we have hereunto subscribed our names,

George Washington, president and deputy from Virginia

New Hampshire: John Langdon, Nicholas Gilman

Massachusetts: Nathaniel Gorham, Rufus King

Connecticut: William Samuel Johnson, Roger Sherman

New York: Alexander Hamilton

New Jersey: William Livingston, David Brearley, William Paterson, Jonathan Dayton

Pennsylvania: Benjamin Franklin, Thomas Mifflin, Robert Morris, George Clymer, Thomas Fitzsimons, Jared Ingersoll, James Wilson, Gouverneur Morris

Delaware: George Read, Gunning Bedford Jr., John Dickinson, Richard Bassett, Jacob Broom

Maryland: James McHenry, Daniel of St. Thomas Jenifer, Daniel Carroll

Virginia: John Blair, James Madison Jr.

North Carolina: William Blount, Richard Dobbs Spaight, Hugh Williamson

South Carolina: John Rutledge, Charles Cotesworth Pinckney, Charles Pinckney, Pierce Butler

Georgia: William Few, Abraham Baldwin

Amendments to the Constitution

Amendment I: Foundational Freedoms

Congress shall make no law respecting an establishment of religion, or prohibiting the free exercise thereof; or abridging the freedom of speech, or of the press; or the right of the people peaceably to assemble, and to petition the Government for a redress of grievances.

Amendment II: The Right to Bear Arms

A well regulated militia, being necessary to the security of a free state, the right of the people to keep and bear arms, shall not be infringed.

Amendment III: No Quartering of Troops

No soldier shall, in time of peace be quartered in any house, without the consent of the owner, nor in time of war, but in a manner to be prescribed by law.

Amendment IV: No Unreasonable Searches

The right of the people to be secure in their persons, houses, papers, and effects, against unreasonable searches and seizures, shall not be violated, and no warrants shall issue, but upon probable cause, supported by oath or affirmation, and particularly describing the place to be searched, and the persons or things to be seized.

Amendment V: Rights of the Accused

No person shall be held to answer for a capital, or otherwise infamous crime, unless on a presentment or indictment of a grand jury, except in cases arising in the land or naval forces, or in the militia, when in actual service in time of war or public danger; nor shall any person be subject for the same offence to be twice put in jeopardy of life or limb; nor shall be compelled in any criminal case to be a witness against himself, nor be deprived of life, liberty, or property, without due process of law; nor shall private property be taken for public use, without just compensation.

Amendment VI: Rights of the Accused in Criminal Trials

In all criminal prosecutions, the accused shall enjoy the right to a speedy and public trial, by an impartial jury of the state and district wherein the crime shall have been committed, which district shall have been previously ascertained by law, and to be informed of the nature and cause of the accusation; to be confronted with the witnesses against him; to have compulsory process for obtaining witnesses in his favor, and to have the assistance of counsel for his defence.

Amendment VII: Rights of Citizens in Civil Trials

In suits at common law, where the value in controversy shall exceed twenty dollars, the right of trial by jury shall be preserved, and no fact tried by a jury, shall be otherwise reexamined in any court of the United States, than according to the rules of the common law.

Amendment VIII: Cruel, Unusual, and Unjust Punishments

Excessive bail shall not be required, nor excessive fines imposed, nor cruel and unusual punishments inflicted.

Amendment IX: Unspecified Rights

The enumeration in the Constitution, of certain rights, shall not be construed to deny or disparage others retained by the people.

Amendment X: Unlisted Rights Go to States or to the People

The powers not delegated to the United States by the Constitution, nor prohibited by it to the states, are reserved to the states respectively, or to the people.

Amendment XI: Suing States

(Passed by Congress March 4, 1794; ratified February 7, 1795)

The judicial power of the United States shall not be construed to extend to any suit in law or equity, commenced or prosecuted against one of the United States by citizens of another state, or by citizens or subjects of any foreign state.

Amendment XII: Separate Ballots for President and Vice President

(Passed by Congress December 9, 1803; ratified June 15, 1804)

The electors shall meet in their respective states and vote by ballot for president and vice president, one of whom, at least, shall not be an inhabitant of the same state with themselves; they shall name in their ballots the person voted for as president, and in distinct ballots the person voted for as vice president, and they shall make distinct lists of all persons voted for as president, and of all persons voted for as vice president, and of the number of votes for each, which lists they shall sign and certify, and transmit sealed to the seat of the government of the United States, directed to the president of the Senate; — the president of the Senate shall, in the presence of the Senate and House of Representatives, open all the certificates and the votes shall then be counted; — The person having the greatest number of votes for president, shall be the president, if such number be a majority of the whole number of electors appointed; and if no person have such majority, then from the persons having the highest numbers not exceeding three on the list of those voted for as president, the House of Representatives shall choose immediately, by ballot, the president. But in choosing the president, the votes shall be taken by states, the representation from each state having one vote; a quorum for this purpose shall consist of a member or members from two-thirds of the states, and a majority of all the states shall be necessary to a choice. *And if the House of Representatives shall not choose a president whenever the right of choice shall devolve upon them, before the fourth day of March next following, then the vice president shall act as president, as in case of the death or other constitutional disability of the president.*—The person having the greatest number of votes as vice president, shall be the vice president, if such number be a majority of the whole number of electors appointed, and if no person have a majority, then from the two highest numbers on the list, the Senate shall choose the vice president; a quorum for the purpose shall consist of two-thirds of the whole number of senators, and a majority of the whole number shall be necessary to a choice. But no person constitutionally ineligible to the office of president shall be eligible to that of vice president of the United States.

Amendment XIII: Slavery

(Passed by Congress January 31, 1865; ratified December 6, 1865)

Section 1. Neither slavery nor involuntary servitude, except as a punishment for crime whereof the party shall have been duly convicted, shall exist within the United States, or any place subject to their jurisdiction.

Section 2. Congress shall have power to enforce this article by appropriate legislation.

Amendment XIV: Citizenship

(Passed by Congress June 13, 1866; ratified July 9, 1868)

Section 1. All persons born or naturalized in the United States, and subject to the jurisdiction thereof, are citizens of the United States and of the state wherein they reside. No state shall make or enforce any law which shall abridge the privileges or immunities of citizens of the United States; nor shall any state deprive any person of life, liberty, or property, without due process of law; nor deny to any person within its jurisdiction the equal protection of the laws.

Section 2. Representatives shall be apportioned among the several states according to their respective numbers, counting the whole number of persons in each state, *excluding Indians not taxed.* But when the right to vote at any election for the choice of electors for president and vice president of the United States, representatives in Congress, the executive and judicial officers of a state, or the members of the legislature thereof, is denied to any of the *male* inhabitants of such state, being *twenty-one years of age*, and citizens of the United States, or in any way abridged, except for participation in rebellion, or other crime, the basis of representation therein shall be reduced in the proportion which the number of such *male* citizens shall bear to the whole number of *male* citizens *twenty-one* years of age in such state.

Section 3. No person shall be a senator or representative in Congress, or elector of president and vice president, or hold any office, civil or military, under the United States, or under any state, who, having previously taken an oath, as a member of Congress, or as an officer of the United States, or as a member of any state legislature, or as an executive or judicial officer of any state, to support the Constitution of the United States, shall have engaged in insurrection or rebellion against the same, or given aid or comfort to the enemies thereof. But Congress may by a vote of two-thirds of each house, remove such disability.

Section 4. The validity of the public debt of the United States, authorized by law, including debts incurred for payment of pensions and bounties for services in suppressing insurrection or rebellion, shall not be questioned. But neither the United States nor any state shall assume or pay any debt or obligation incurred in aid of insurrection or rebellion against the United States, or any claim for the loss or emancipation of any slave; but all such debts, obligations and claims shall be held illegal and void.

Section 5. The Congress shall have the power to enforce, by appropriate legislation, the provisions of this article.

Amendment XV: Black Voting Rights

(Passed by Congress February 26, 1869; ratified February 3, 1870)

Section 1. The right of citizens of the United States to vote shall not be denied or abridged by the United States or by any state on account of race, color, or previous condition of servitude.

Section 2. The Congress shall have the power to enforce this article by appropriate legislation.

Amendment XVI: Income Tax

(Passed by Congress July 2, 1909; ratified February 3, 1913)

The Congress shall have power to lay and collect taxes on incomes, from whatever source derived, without apportionment among the several states, and without regard to any census or enumeration.

Amendment XVII: Direct Election of Senators

(Passed by Congress May 13, 1912; ratified April 8, 1913)

The Senate of the United States shall be composed of two senators from each state, elected by the people thereof, for six years; and each senator shall have one vote. The electors in each state shall have the qualifications requisite for electors of the most numerous branch of the state legislatures.

When vacancies happen in the representation of any state in the Senate, the executive authority of such state shall issue writs of election to fill such vacancies: provided, that the legislature of any state may empower the executive thereof to make temporary appointments until the people fill the vacancies by election as the legislature may direct.

This amendment shall not be so construed as to affect the election or term of any senator chosen before it becomes valid as part of the Constitution.

Amendment XVIII: Prohibition

(Passed by Congress December 18, 1917; ratified January 16, 1919. Repealed by Amendment 21.)

Section 1. *After one year from the ratification of this article the manufacture, sale, or transportation of intoxicating liquors within, the importation thereof into, or the exportation thereof from the United States and all territory subject to the jurisdiction thereof for beverage purposes is hereby prohibited.*

Section 2. *The Congress and the several states shall have concurrent power to enforce this article by appropriate legislation.*

Section 3. *This article shall be inoperative unless it shall have been ratified as an amendment to the Constitution by the legislatures of the several states, as provided in the Constitution, within seven years from the date of the submission hereof to the states by the Congress.*

Amendment XIX: Women's Suffrage

(Passed by Congress June 4, 1919; ratified August 18, 1920)

Section 1. The right of citizens of the United States to vote shall not be denied or abridged by the United States or by any state on account of sex.

Section 2. Congress shall have power to enforce this article by appropriate legislation.

Amendment XX: Lame Duck Amendment

(Passed by Congress March 2, 1932; ratified January 23, 1933)

Section 1. The terms of the president and the vice president shall end at noon on the 20th day of January, and the terms of senators and representatives at noon on the 3rd day of January, of the years in which such terms would have ended if this article had not been ratified; and the terms of their successors shall then begin.

Section 2. The Congress shall assemble at least once in every year, and such meeting shall begin at noon on the 3rd day of January, unless they shall by law appoint a different day.

Section 3. If, at the time fixed for the beginning of the term of the president, the president elect shall have died, the vice president elect shall become president. If a president shall not have been chosen before the time fixed for the beginning of his term, or if the president elect shall have failed to qualify, then the vice president elect shall act as president until a president shall have qualified; and the Congress may by law provide for the case wherein neither a president elect nor a vice president elect shall have qualified, declaring who shall then act as president, or the manner in which one who is to act shall be selected, and such person shall act accordingly until a president or vice president shall have qualified.

Section 4. The Congress may by law provide for the case of the death of any of the persons from whom the House of Representatives may choose a president whenever the right of choice shall have devolved upon them, and for the case of the death of any of the persons from whom the Senate may choose a vice president whenever the right of choice shall have devolved upon them.

Section 5. Sections 1 and 2 shall take effect on the 15th day of October following the ratification of this article.

Section 6. *This article shall be inoperative unless it shall have been ratified as an amendment to the Constitution by the legislatures of three-fourths of the several states within seven years from the date of its submission.*

Amendment XXI: Repeal of Prohibition

(Passed by Congress February 20, 1933; ratified December 5, 1933)

Section 1. The eighteenth article of amendment to the Constitution of the United States is hereby repealed.

Section 2. The transportation or importation into any state, territory, or possession of the United States for delivery or use therein of intoxicating liquors, in violation of the laws thereof, is hereby prohibited.

Section 3. *This article shall be inoperative unless it shall have been ratified as an amendment to the Constitution by conventions in the several states, as provided in the Constitution, within seven years from the date of the submission hereof to the states by the Congress.*

Amendment XXII: Presidential Terms

(Passed by Congress March 21, 1947; ratified February 27, 1951)

Section 1. No person shall be elected to the office of the president more than twice, and no person who has held the office of president, or acted as president, for more than two years of a term to which some other person was elected president shall be elected to the office of the president more than once. *But this article shall not apply to any person holding the office of president when this article was proposed by the Congress, and shall not prevent any person who may be holding the office of president, or acting as president, during the term within which this article becomes operative from holding the office of president or acting as president during the remainder of such term.*

Section 2. *This article shall be inoperative unless it shall have been ratified as an amendment to the Constitution by the legislatures of three-fourths of the several states within seven years from the date of its submission to the states by the Congress.*

Amendment XXIII: Voting for Washington, D.C.

(Passed by Congress June 16, 1960; ratified March 29, 1961)

Section 1. The District constituting the seat of government of the United States shall appoint in such manner as the Congress may direct:

A number of electors of president and vice president equal to the whole number of senators and representatives in Congress to which the district would be entitled if it were a state, but in no event more than the least populous state; they shall be in addition to those appointed by the states, but they shall be considered, for the purposes of the election of president and vice president, to be electors appointed by a state; and they shall meet in the district and perform such duties as provided by the twelfth article of amendment.

Section 2. The Congress shall have power to enforce this article by appropriate legislation.

Amendment XXIV: No Poll Tax

(Passed by Congress August 27, 1962; ratified January 23, 1964)

Section 1. The right of citizens of the United States to vote in any primary or other election for president or vice president, for electors for president or vice president, or for senator or representative in Congress, shall not be denied or abridged by the United States or any state by reason of failure to pay any poll tax or other tax.

Section 2. The Congress shall have power to enforce this article by appropriate legislation.

Amendment XXV: Presidential Succession

(Passed by Congress July 6, 1965; ratified February 10, 1967)

Section 1. In case of the removal of the president from office or of his death or resignation, the vice president shall become president.

Section 2. Whenever there is a vacancy in the office of the vice president, the president shall nominate a vice president who shall take office upon confirmation by a majority vote of both houses of Congress.

Section 3. Whenever the president transmits to the president pro tempore of the Senate and the Speaker of the House of Representatives his written declaration that he is unable to discharge the powers and duties of his office, and until he transmits to them a written declaration to the contrary, such powers and duties shall be discharged by the vice president as acting president.

Section 4. Whenever the vice president and a majority of either the principal officers of the executive departments or of such other body as Congress may by law provide, transmit to the president pro tempore of the Senate and the Speaker of the House of Representatives their written declaration that the president is unable to discharge the powers and duties of his office, the vice president shall immediately assume the powers and duties of the office as acting president.

Thereafter, when the president transmits to the president pro tempore of the Senate and the Speaker of the House of Representatives his written declaration that no inability exists, he shall resume the powers and duties of his office unless the vice president and a majority of either the principal officers of the executive department or of such other body as Congress may by law provide, transmit within four days to the president pro tempore of the Senate and the Speaker of the House of Representatives their written declaration that the president is unable to discharge the powers and duties of his office. Thereupon Congress shall decide the issue, assembling within forty-eight hours for that purpose if not in session. If the Congress, within twenty-one days after receipt of the latter written declaration, or, if Congress is not in session, within twenty-one days after Congress is required to assemble, determines by two-thirds vote of both houses that the president is unable to discharge the powers and duties of his office, the vice president shall continue to discharge the same as acting president; otherwise, the president shall resume the powers and duties of his office.

Amendment XXVI: Eighteen-Year-Old Vote

(Passed by Congress March 23, 1971; ratified July 1, 1971)

Section 1. The right of citizens of the United States, who are eighteen years of age or older, to vote shall not be denied or abridged by the United States or by any state on account of age.

Section 2. The Congress shall have power to enforce this article by appropriate legislation.

Amendment XXVII: Congressional Pay Raises

(Passed by Congress September 25, 1789; ratified May 7, 1992)

No law, varying the compensation for the services of the senators and representatives, shall take effect, until an election of representatives shall have intervened.

Glossary

A

abolitionism: The movement to eliminate slavery

A Century of Dishonor: Published by Helen Hunt Jackson; portrayed the government's ruthless and often dishonorable dealings with the Indians

Adams-Onis Treaty: Under this treaty, the U.S. took possession of Florida in 1821 at a cost of $5 million.

Agricultural Adjustment Act (AAA): Act that established a new method of subsidizing farm products and aided debt-ridden farmers in danger of losing their farms to foreclosure

Alamo: An abandoned Catholic mission in San Antonio that was used by Texans in a futile stand against the Mexican army. The defeat there rallied Texans to defeat the Mexicans later at San Jacinto.

Albany Congress: An attempt to unite the English colonies in America during the French and Indian War

Alien and Sedition Acts: Four laws passed by a Federalist-controlled Congress and signed by John Adams that were designed to protect the country during the threat of war but that the Federalists tried to use to silence the Republicans

Allies: World War I alliance between Great Britain, France, Russia, Italy, and (later) the United States; World War II alliance between Great Britain, France, (later) Russia, and the United States

al-Qaeda: Terrorist group led by Osama bin Laden, who was responsible for numerous attacks on American targets, including foreign embassies, the USS *Cole*, and the World Trade Center. The greatest attack came on September 11, 2001.

amendments: Changes to the Constitution

America First Committee: Committee organized by vocal isolationists and pacifists; watchdogs to oppose American involvement in World War II

American Expeditionary Force: U.S. troops that came to France in 1917 during World War I

American Federation of Labor: A more influential labor organization than the Knights of Labor; a splinter group from the Knights of Labor; formed craft unions for skilled laborers

Americans with Disabilities Act: Legislation that prohibited job discrimination based on disabilities

American System: A national economic system advocated by Henry Clay that included protective tariffs, renewal of the National Bank, and internal improvements

Amish: A more conservative branch of the Mennonites

amnesty: A pardon for offenses

Anaconda Plan: The Northern press's derisive term for Union General Winfield Scott's plan to win the war

Annapolis Convention: Only five states sent representatives to this trade convention under the confederation government.

The Anti-Federalist Papers: The collected writings and speeches by opponents of the new Constitution

Anti-Federalists: Members of ratification conventions in each state who were opponents of the proposed Constitution; included George Clinton, Patrick Henry, and George Mason

appeasement: The policy of Neville Chamberlain in dealing with the demands of Hitler; yielding to the demands of an aggressor in order to preserve peace

Appomattox Court House: The town where Lee surrendered the Army of Northern Virginia to Grant

April 6, 1917: Date on which the United States entered World War I

Arab Spring: A series of legitimate protests concerning political corruption and oppression. Many Muslim radicals took advantage of the unrest to incite violence and to expand their control over citizens.

Argonne offensive: The largest American effort in the Allied counterattack; one of the costliest military campaigns in American history

armistice (November 11, 1918): Agreement signed to end World War I

Articles of Confederation: The first plan of government of the United States, in force from 1777 until ratification of the U.S. Constitution in 1789. It constituted a unicameral national legislature, a weak national government, and strong state governments.

assembly line: Method of production by which a worker specializing in one task would attach his part or perform his process at a partial stop along the assembly line

assumption: Part of Hamilton's plan to deal with debt; the national government's takeover of all state debts

astrolabe: An instrument that enabled sailors to determine the latitude of their location at sea

Atlantic Charter: Compact that was the result of a secret meeting between FDR and Churchill; a list of "common principles" such as self-determination, freedom of the seas, and economic cooperation

atomic bomb: Secret weapon used against Japan to end World War II

Axis Powers: Alliance of Germany, Italy, and Japan during World War II

B

baby boom: Massive rise in the birth rate lasting until 1964

Baltimore & Ohio Railroad: The first economically successful railroad in America

bank holiday: Temporary closing of all banks declared by President Franklin Delano Roosevelt to calm the fears of the jittery public about the banking situation

banking crisis: Point at which the nation's banking system was on the brink of total collapse

Bank of the United States: National bank proposed and established by Alexander Hamilton; also known as the National Bank

Baptists: Emphasize the practice of baptism by immersion for professing believers; practice congregational polity and believe that only the regenerate should be church members

Barbary States: Muslim states in North Africa that provided safe haven for pirates

barbed wire: Two twisted strands of wire studded with sharp metal barbs at measured intervals

Battle of Antietam: The bloodiest one-day battle in American history. Technically, Antietam was a Union victory because the Confederates had withdrawn; the battle was a draw in reality. Lincoln used news of this battle to announce the Emancipation Proclamation.

Battle of Atlanta: Confederate surprise attack on General Sherman from which the Union recovered quickly

Battle of Bladensburg: Battle in which the British scattered a large force of American militia and cleared a path to the American capital, causing the president and government leaders to leave in haste

Battle of Britain: Battle in the skies above southern England between the German *Luftwaffe* and the British Royal Air Force

Battle of Chancellorsville: Confederate victory in which Stonewall Jackson was wounded and later died

Battle of Chattanooga: Union victory after which Confederate General Bragg resigned

Battle of Chickamauga: Major Confederate victory; the Union avoided complete disaster through the courage of General George Thomas

Battle of Fallen Timbers: Battle in which "Mad Anthony" Wayne's forces routed the Indians; so called because most of the fighting occurred in a maze of tangled trees knocked down by a storm

Battle of Fredericksburg: Confederate victory in which the new Union General Ambrose Burnside was defeated

Battle of Gettysburg: The two sides suffered about 50,000 casualties between them. The South never recovered from the Confederate loss there on July 1–3.

Battle of Kings Mountain: American victory in the Carolinas that strengthened Patriot resolve; battle where the "over-mountain men" defeated the Tory army (almost all were killed, wounded, or captured)

Battle of Lake Erie: Battle in which Perry defeated the British fleet and gained control of Lake Erie

Battle of Leyte Gulf: The largest naval battle in history and a critical blow to Japanese naval and air forces

Battle of Manila Bay: Destroyed Spanish sea power in the Pacific and left the Philippines in the hands of the United States

Battle of Midway: A major turning point during World War II in the Pacific

Battle of New Orleans: The most stunning victory of the War of 1812; fought after the war was over

Battle of Quebec: Brief but decisive battle in which the British routed the French

Battle of San Jacinto: Battle between Texans, led by Sam Houston, and the Mexican army, led by Santa Anna, on April 21, 1836. The Texans routed the Mexicans with the battle cry, "Remember the Alamo!"

Battle of Santiago Bay: Battle in which the Spanish fleet tried to escape but suffered defeat

Battle of Saratoga: Turning point of the Revolutionary War after which France recognized United States sovereignty and joined the war against Britain

Battle of Shiloh: Technically a Union victory but a costly one. After this battle Lincoln refused to dismiss Grant, though angry newspapers and politicians called for it.

Battle of the Bulge: Battle given its name due to the "bulge" fifty miles deep into the Allied lines. Allies achieved victory.

Battle of Tippecanoe: Clash between William Henry Harrison's forces and the Prophet's forces. Prophetstown was destroyed, but Harrison's forces sustained heavy losses.

Bay of Pigs: Operation in Cuba that ended in total failure because Castro had learned of the "secret" attack and had begun preparing his troops for it while U.S. aid was withdrawn at the last minute

Bear Flag Republic: Established by settlers in California that revolted from Mexico

bear market: A stock market characterized by pessimism and declining stock prices

Bering Strait: Narrow waterway between Russia and Alaska thought by some to be the passage that brought the ancestors of the American Indians to the Western Hemisphere

Berlin airlift: Massive airlift of food and supplies to West Berlin; forced the Soviet Union to end the blockade

Berlin Wall: Wall built by the Soviets that split East and West Berlin

bicameral: Having two houses in a legislature

Big Four: Leaders of the major Allied powers during World War I: David Lloyd George of Great Britain, Vittorio Orlando of Italy, Georges Clemenceau of France, and Woodrow Wilson of the United States

Bill of Rights: The first ten amendments to the Constitution that protect citizens' democratic rights by limiting the power of government

black codes: Codes that attempted to regulate the conduct of the former slaves; severely limited the rights of black people

Black Hawk War: A brief but bloody war between the Sauk and Fox Indians led by Chief Black Hawk and the Illinois militia and regular soldiers. The Indians were seeking to reclaim land in northern Illinois, but lost the war.

Black Lives Matter: Group that sharpened the divide between police and citizen, and black and white, with divisive rhetoric; began after several controversial shootings of black men

black power: Groups that wanted to protect and strengthen self-determination for African Americans; some proclaimed black supremacy over whites, determined to gain supremacy "by any means necessary," including violence

Black Tuesday (October 29, 1929): The name for the day of the stock market crash

Bleeding Kansas: The name for the dissension-torn Kansas Territory

blitzkrieg: "Lightning war"; simultaneous attacks by air power and armored forces in sudden and fast-moving spearheads; the military strategy of Hitler's war machine at the beginning and early years of World War II

blockade runners: Daring merchant ships that risked the wrath of the Union navy to bring supplies into Southern ports, where those goods were sold for enormous profits

Bonus Army: Unemployed veterans of the American Expeditionary Force that came to Washington, D.C., to ask for an early payment of the bonus promised to them

border states: Slave states that did not secede from the Union (Missouri, Kentucky, Maryland, and Delaware)

Boston Massacre: The outbreak of violence between colonists and British troops on March 5, 1770, resulting in the deaths of five people and the wounding of others

Boston Tea Party: A protest, by colonists disguised as Indians, against the Tea Act of 1773 during which the colonists threw tea from British ships into Boston Harbor

Boxer Rebellion: An antiforeign movement that broke out in China

boycotts: Refusal to buy another's goods; in the colonies' case, refusal to buy British goods

Brady Bill: Act that mandated that before a gun shop could sell an individual gun, a buyer had to wait five days and undergo a background check

Brain Trust: Group composed primarily of college professors to whom FDR turned for advice in solving the nation's economic problems.

bread lines: Name for the lines formed along city streets as the desperate sought food in the soup kitchens

Breed's Hill: Site where most of the fighting took place on June 16, 1775; see **Bunker Hill**

Brown v. Board of Education of Topeka, Kansas: First great victory of the modern civil rights movement, overturning *Plessy v. Ferguson.* The Supreme Court concluded that segregated public schools stamped blacks as inferior and that such institutions had no place in American society.

budget deficit: The amount by which expenditures exceed income

bull market: A stock market characterized by optimism and rising prices

Bunker Hill: A major battle on the Charlestown peninsula north of Boston; a costly victory for the British

Burr-Hamilton duel: Event that occurred after Burr lost the race for governor of New York and resulted in the death of Alexander Hamilton

busing: Transporting students out of their neighborhoods to other schools until all schools reflected the overall racial makeup of the city or community as a whole

C

cabinet: The name for an advisory body that regularly meets with the president to discuss policy decisions

Calhoun Resolutions: Resolutions which demanded that new territories be open to slavery

California gold rush: The lure of wealth that drew several hundred thousand men after the discovery of gold in California

Camp David Accords: Agreement between Egypt and Israel that was brokered by President Carter in 1978

camp meeting: A series of religious services lasting several days and often held outdoors

Cane Ridge: One of the significant camp meetings of the Second Great Awakening, held in Cane Ridge, Kentucky, in 1801, where thousands of people attended

caravel: A Portuguese sailing vessel that had two or three triangular sails, which made it extremely maneuverable at sea. They could be heavily equipped with cannons, making them formidable adversaries in battles between ships on water.

carpetbaggers: Northerners who came South during Reconstruction

Casablanca: Location of a meeting between FDR, Winston Churchill, and Charles de Gaulle of the Free French to forge an Allied strategy for the assault on Hitler's Europe

"Cato": New York governor George Clinton, who denounced the Constitution in an article penned under this pseudonym

cattle drive: Name for the process by which cattle were brought overland to northern railroad terminals

caucus: A closed meeting of party leaders

Central Intelligence Agency (CIA): Established to gather and analyze information, often through the use of spies, regarding foreign affairs

Central Pacific: Received a charter to build the first transcontinental railroad; railroad line that began building in Sacramento, California, and built eastward to meet the Union Pacific railroad line

Central Powers: World War I alliance between Germany, Austria-Hungary, Bulgaria, and Turkey

charter colony: A colony that was governed by a charter granted to a trade company by the king

Château-Thierry and Belleau Wood: German assault on British and French lines. Germans broke the French line but were halted by American soldiers.

checks and balances: The principle of keeping each branch of government in check through the power of another branch of government, with the goal of hindering the concentration of power and thus protecting personal liberty.

***Chesapeake* affair:** Resulted in an American call for retaliation due to a British attack on an American warship that involved impressment

Christian Coalition: Important conservative religious organization that was involved in politics

Christian Science: A religion begun by Mary Baker Eddy

Church of England: England's official church, also known as the Anglican Church

circumnavigate: Sail completely around

Civilian Conservation Corp (CCC): Agency that put young, unmarried men to work in reforestation, building roads, developing parks, and soil conservation projects under the supervision of the army; one of the most popular New Deal agencies, lasting until after American entry into World War II

Civil Rights Act of 1964: The first of President Johnson's civil rights legislation; established fairer procedures for voter registration, forbade racial discrimination in public places, promoted desegregation of public schools, authorized withholding federal funds from projects or institutions that practiced discrimination, and created the Equal Opportunity Commission

civil rights movement: Movement that pushed for the equality of races; attempts by blacks to secure the exercise and protection of their basic civil rights as citizens

Civil Service Commission: Responsible for seeing that only men who scored well on examinations held offices

Clayton Antitrust Act: Act that strengthened the Sherman Anti-Trust Act by expanding the list of practices prohibited to corporations

coalition of the willing: Name for the force that invaded Iraq in 2003, defeating that country's military forces in only two weeks

Coercive Acts: A series of four acts that were intended to punish the troublesome colony of Massachusetts

Cold War: Hostility that developed between the Soviet Union and the other Allies, especially the United States, after World War II; a period of tension and intense competition

colonial style architecture: Also known as "Williamsburg style" architecture; steep gabled roofs, tall brick chimneys, brick arches over doors and windows, and interiors with exposed beam ceilings

Committee of Correspondence: Under the guidance of Samuel Adams, this committee provided information on British threats to liberty to other areas of the colony.

***Common Sense*:** Pamphlet published by Thomas Paine; put Patriot ideas into words that fired their will

compass: An instrument that enabled sailors to know the direction they were traveling

Compromise of 1850: An attempt to resolve the dispute over slavery whereby California entered the Union as a free state, the slave trade—but not slavery itself—be abolished in the District of Columbia, slavery was protected in the District of Columbia, a strict Fugitive Slave law was passed, and the new territories of New Mexico and Utah would be organized and the slavery question would be decided by popular sovereignty in those territories

Compromise of 1877: A tradeoff that helped Hayes by allowing the electoral votes to be counted. In turn, Hayes would remove the last federal troops from the South.

Compromise Tariff of 1833: Tariff agreement proposed by Henry Clay that substantially, though gradually, reduced the Tariff of 1832, making it acceptable to South Carolina

Comstock Lode: One of the largest and riches mines. More than half the ore eventually mined was silver and the rest was gold.

Confederate States of America (CSA): The group of states that seceded from the Union

confederation: A close alliance of sovereign states

congregational form of government: System of church government in which each individual congregation is independent of other churches and where the members of each congregation elect their own officials

Congregationalists: Eventually became the name of most Puritans in America

Congress of Industrial Organizations (CIO): Organized by John L. Lewis for both skilled and unskilled workers; quickly made headlines when its rubber industry workers at Firestone, Goodyear, and Goodrich plants in Akron, Ohio, staged a simultaneous sit-down strike

conquistadors: Spanish conquerors who explored much of Central and South America

conscription: The "drafting," or compulsory enrollment of men into military service

Constitutional Convention: A special meeting of state delegates to correct weaknesses in the Articles of Confederation, thereby strengthening the United States. It is sometimes called the Philadelphia Convention. The delegates met in the Pennsylvania State House, today called Independence Hall, in Philadelphia (1787).

Constitutional Union Party: The coalition of conservative Southerners and Northerners, including many former Whigs, that formed a third party for the election of 1860

containment: The U.S. policy to prevent the spread of Communism; further Communist aggression would be resisted; communism must be contained to its new boundaries

Contract with America: Proposal by House Republicans that laid out ten popular bills that House Republicans promised to bring up to vote in their first hundred days of office if elected

Contras: Groups of anti-Sandinista guerilas; from the Spanish word for counterrevolutionary

Copperheads: Northerners who were sympathetic to the South

corrupt bargain: The allegation made by supporters of Andrew Jackson that John Quincy Adams won the election of 1824 by promising Henry Clay the position of Secretary of State if Clay would support Adams for president when the election was thrown into the House of Representatives, where Clay was the Speaker.

cotton gin: A machine invented by Eli Whitney containing a series of metal teeth mounted on rollers that separated the cotton from the seeds fifty times faster than slaves working by hand

counterculture: A youth movement that had its roots in rebellion, specifically a rejection of the materialism, morals, and values of the previous generation; believed the solution to society's problems included self-expression, love, and sharing

court-packing plan: FDR's plan to add six more justices to the Supreme Court; plan never became a reality

covenant: A legally binding relationship

cowboys: Men now shrouded by myth but were actually tough, hard-working ranch hands

Crédit Mobilier Scandal: Scandal involving the financial practices of the Union Pacific Railway

Cuban missile crisis: Crisis in 1962 between the United States and the Soviet Union resulting from placement of missiles in Cuba by Soviet forces

Custer's Last Stand: Another name for the Battle of Little Bighorn where Custer and all his force lost their lives

D

dame schools: A village school open to boys and girls, generally taught by women

dark horse: A nominee who is not a serious candidate before the nominating convention and about whom little is usually known by the general public

Darwinism: A name given to evolutionary theory that involved "natural selection"

Dawes Act: A law passed in 1887 which allowed Indian lands to be parceled out to individual Indian families; detrimental effects included the breakdown of unity of the tribes and the sale of the land, leaving the Indians impoverished

Dawes Plan: Effort that reduced German reparation payments significantly and encouraged private American institutions to continue lending money to help Germany rebuild

D-day (June 6, 1944): Code-named Operation Overlord; allied invasion of France along a sixty-mile stretch of the Normandy coast of France, taking beaches code-named Gold, Sword, Juno, Utah, and Omaha in fierce fighting

December 7, 1941: Date of Japanese attack on American naval forces at Pearl Harbor in Hawaii

Declaration of Independence: Document approved by the Second Continental Congress; listed the grievances that Americans had against the king and stated the universal principles that would shape the character and direction of the emerging nation (July 4, 1776)

Declaratory Act: Stated that Parliament had the right to pass any law regarding the colonies that it desired

Defense of Marriage Act (DOMA): Secured federal benefits, such as health insurance, for spouses in traditional marriages only, denying any status to homosexual "unions"

deficit spending: Spending more money than is received

deism: Belief that reason rather than Scripture was the way men came to know God and that God created the world but rarely if ever became personally involved in its affairs

delegated powers: Powers specifically given to the national government by the Constitution; define the limits of the government's authority

de Lôme letter: Letter written by the Spanish Ambassador to the United States in which he insulted President McKinley

Democratic Party: Originally Democratic-Republican, but eventually dropped the Republican part of the name; Andrew Jackson's wing of the Democratic-Republicans

détente: An easing of tensions between the United States and the Soviet Union during the 1970s

direct primaries: Nominating a party's candidates by popular vote

disenfranchisement: Denial of the right to vote

Dixiecrats: Another name for the States' Rights Party. Strom Thurmond ran as their candidate in the 1948 election.

dollar diplomacy: The view that rather than relying solely on military might, the United States could use the promise of foreign aid and business development to influence foreign countries

domino theory: The belief that if one country in a region fell to Communism, a neighboring country also would soon succumb to Communism, and then another, and another, until the entire region was controlled by Communism

doughboy: Another name for the American soldier

***Dred Scott v. Sandford*:** Supreme Court decision that declared that a slave was not a citizen and could not sue in court, that a slave did not become free simply because his master took him into a free territory, and that the Missouri Compromise was unconstitutional

Dunkirk: French port on the English Channel where the English and French troops escaped the Germans under cover of a dense fog

Dust Bowl: Term coined by a newspaper reporter to describe the area affected by massive dust storms

Dynamic Conservatism: President Eisenhower's philosophy, calling himself "conservative when it comes to money and liberal when it comes to human beings"

E

Eastern Woodlands Indians: Indians along the Atlantic coast who were probably the first Indians settlers encountered in the New World

Eighteenth Amendment: Amendment that prohibited the manufacture, sale, or transportation of alcoholic beverages; later repealed by the Twenty-First Amendment

Electoral College: The indirect means by which the president is elected. Each state has a number of electors equal to the state's representation in Congress.

Emancipation Proclamation: Declaration by President Lincoln that slaves in Confederate-held territory were free. This declaration was unenforceable, but it did prevent European nations from recognizing the South because those nations opposed slavery.

Embargo Act: Banned all American trade with the rest of the world

energy crisis: A combination of higher prices for and shortages of American energy resources

environmental movement: Group that warns about industrial pollution of water and air

Equal Rights Amendment: This amendment was passed by Congress but failed to garner the necessary approval of three-fourths of the state legislatures before its deadline for ratification passed. It stated, "Equality of rights under the law shall not be denied or abridged by the United States or by any state on account of sex."

Era of Good Feelings: The period from 1817–25, during which James Monroe was president and the major parties did not clash

Erie Canal: The most famous canal in early America, connecting Albany, New York, to Lake Erie; also called the "Big Ditch"

Espionage and Sedition Acts: Made it a criminal offense to criticize the war effort in any way

established denominations: Denominations that enjoy state (government) support and protection

ethnic cleansing: The killing or expelling of an ethnic group from an area

executive orders: An order given by the president that bypasses Congress

F

Fair Deal: President Truman's name for his legislative goals

faith-based initiatives: Part of President George W. Bush's domestic program that involved Christians in administering government social programs that put into practice his "compassionate conservatism"

Family and Medical Leave Act: Act that required businesses to give employees up to twelve weeks of unpaid leave to care for newborn children or seriously ill family members

Farmers' Alliance: United farm cooperatives across the country and looked to politics to meet agrarian demands such as railroad regulation, favorable currency policies, and antitrust laws

Fascist Party: A nationalistic, militaristic, totalitarian movement that profited from the discontent created by difficult economic conditions

Federal Bureau of Investigation (FBI): Organization of lawmen that became heroes as they tracked criminals

Federal Deposit Insurance Corporation (FDIC): An agency devised to insure the bank deposits of millions of Americans against loss

federalism: The division of power between national and state levels of government

***The Federalist*:** Also known as *The Federalist Papers*; answered Anti-Federalist objections by carefully explaining and forcefully defending constitutional provisions of power; also predicted dangers and dismemberment for the nation if the Constitution were rejected

Federalists: Originally referred to supporters of the proposed Constitution's ratification, including Alexander Hamilton, James Madison, and John Jay. Later the name of one of the two original political parties that developed in the government. Federalists believed in having a strong, though limited, central government, weaker state governments, and a national bank.

Federal Reserve Act: The act setting up twelve banking districts under a national board each served by a private regional Federal Reserve Bank; has power to set standards for banks and regulate the flow of currency throughout the country in an effort to manage the economy

Federal Trade Commission Act: Act that established the Federal Trade Commission (FTC), a board of five men authorized to help define and halt unfair business practices

Fifteenth Amendment: Gave freedmen the right to vote

Fifty-four-forty or fight!: Expansionist slogan that described the boundary they wanted between U.S. and British territory

fireside chats: Radio talks that FDR used to influence public opinion in favor of his New Deal programs

First Battle of Bull Run: Also known as First Battle of Manassas; a Confederate victory

First Continental Congress: Meeting of representatives from all colonies except Georgia; gathered in Philadelphia's Carpenter Hall

Flying Tigers: The group of pilots in the American Volunteer Group; became the scourge of Japanese pilots

Food Administration: Designed to address the need of an adequate food supply for the American forces and the beleaguered Allies

Force Bill: Gave the president war powers against South Carolina

Fordney-McCumber Tariff: High tariff that established a nearly insurmountable wall restricting European trade with the United States

Fort Duquesne: French fort during the French and Indian War

Fort McHenry: Well-designed fort that, along with a disciplined force, protected the city of Baltimore

Fort Sumter: Federal fort in Charleston Harbor where the first shots of the War Between the States were fired

Fort Ticonderoga: British-held fort in New York that fell to Patriot forces from Vermont known as the "Green Mountain Boys" under the command of Ethan Allen and Benedict Arnold

forty-niners: The first wave of gold hunters that came as part of the California gold rush in 1849

Fourteen Points: Woodrow Wilson's objectives that he hoped would produce lasting peace following World War I

Fourteenth Amendment: Gave freedmen citizenship and equal protection under the law; all former slaves, not just three-fifths, were to be counted to determine the state's representation; those who swore an oath to defend the Confederacy could not vote or hold office unless approved by a two-thirds vote of Congress; federal and state governments could not pay any Confederate debts or provide slaveholders any compensation for former slaves.

Freedmen's Bureau: Government agency that was supposed to look out for the interests of former slaves during Reconstruction

Freeport Doctrine: Stated that a territory could still prohibit slavery by refusing to adopt laws establishing and protecting it

free silver: The unlimited coinage of silver

Free-Soilers: Those who favored keeping slavery where it already existed but opposed its extension into the territories

Free Soil Party: The joined forces of the antislavery and Free-Soil groups that formed a third party in the 1848 election

French and Indian War: War that erupted between England and France and lasted from 1754 to 1763. The French were helped by various Indian tribes. It was known in Europe as the Seven Years' War.

French Revolution: Violent overthrow of monarchy in France that resulted in political turmoil and dictatorship

Fugitive Slave Act: A law that required the return of runaway slaves to bondage

Fundamentalism: 1920s movement started by Christians who believed that the Bible was to be taken literally and was verbally inspired, and that church discipline should be exercised toward erring believers; fought in the 1920s to remove modernists from their denominations and, having failed at that, founded new denominations, churches, and schools that remained faithful to the fundamentals of the Christian faith

Fundamentalist-Modernist controversy: Battle that raged over doctrine and the control of major denominations' schools, mission boards, and institutions

funding: Part of Hamilton's plan to deal with debt; proposed that the federal government give bonds paying six percent to those to whom the Continental Congress owed money for goods or military services provided during the war

G

Gadsden Purchase: Land bordering the southwestern United States purchased from Mexico for $10 million; needed for the path of a transcontinental railroad

gas-and-water socialism: City or state control of utilities such as gas and water companies

***Gaspee*:** An armed British customs ship that ran aground near Providence, Rhode Island. Local citizens boarded this ship, captured and removed its crew, and burned the ship.

gay rights movement: Movement with goals to remove the legal prohibitions to practicing homosexuality and to redefine marriage to include same-sex unions

General Assembly: Consists of delegates from all member nations of the United Nations and provides a forum in which those nations can express their views

Gettysburg Address: The address President Lincoln gave four months after the Battle of Gettysburg at the dedication of the cemetery

ghettos: Special segregated areas where Jews were forced to live in crowded, unsanitary conditions without adequate food, clothing, facilities, and medical care; often considered as holding cells for the inhabitants' ultimate transfer to concentration, or death, camps

Gibbons v. Ogden: Case in which the Supreme Court ruled that the delegated powers given to the national government by the Constitution could not be limited by state boundaries

glasnost: A policy encouraging more "openness" with the West, resulting in a greater degree of freedom for the Soviet citizenry

grandfather clause: Allowed those who could not pay the poll tax or pass the literacy test to vote if he or his father or grandfather was eligible to vote before 1867; no black citizens met this requirement

Grange: Another name for the group of protesting farmers under the leadership of the Patrons of Husbandry; founded by Oliver H. Kelly to encourage social contacts and scientific methods of farming

Grantism: A synonym for political corruption

Great Awakening: A powerful spiritual revival that swept through the colonies beginning in the 1720s; a social, political, and religious force that permanently altered the course of American history

Great Compromise: The agreement, also known as the Connecticut Compromise, reached concerning how states would be represented in the new government. The compromise was for a bicameral Congress with states represented equally in the Senate and by population in the House of Representatives.

Great Depression: Severe economic downturn that occurred worldwide during the 1930s

Great Plains: The region between the Mississippi River valley and the Rocky Mountains, stretching north to south from Canada to southern Texas

Great Recession: An intense economic downturn during the early 2000s

Great Society: The legislative program of Lyndon Johnson, the primary focus of which was a "war on poverty"

Great Wagon Road: An old Iroquois Indian trail that was an avenue through the wilderness; provided the chief access to backcountry settlements from Virginia to Georgia

greenbacks: Paper money issued by Congress during the Civil War, so called because they were printed with green ink

Guadalcanal: A jungle island in the Solomon Islands, three thousand miles from Tokyo; began the drive to defeat Japan

guerrilla warfare: Sudden surprise attacks by small, hidden groups

Gulf of Tonkin Resolution: Resolution approved by Congress that gave the president the ability to take all necessary measures to repel any armed attack against the forces of the United States and to prevent further aggression in Vietnam

H

Half-breeds: Moderate Republicans who had earlier been dissatisfied with Grant, the Radical Republican, and Reconstruction, and who tended to favor reform

Half-Way Covenant: Scheme by which outwardly moral church members who had not owned the covenant could have their children baptized; designed to keep more people under the influence of the church, though it really only weakened the church

hard money: Silver and gold

Harlem Renaissance: Movement in which black intellectuals and writers including James Weldon Johnson, Alain Locke, and Langston Hughes achieved prominence; included entertainers such as trumpeter Louis Armstrong and singer Paul Robeson

Harpers Ferry: The location of John Brown's attack on a federal arsenal, from which he planned to supply weapons for a spontaneous slave revolt

Hartford Convention: Meeting of a group of Federalists who opposed the War of 1812 and hinted that New England might secede from the Union if its demands were not met. After the Treaty of Ghent and the Battle of New Orleans, its main reason for existence was removed.

Harvard College: Established by the Puritans near Boston to train young men for the ministry

Haymarket Riot: In probably the most famous example of labor violence, factory workers in Chicago, agitated by anarchists, went on strike, demanding an eight-hour work day.

headrights: Land grants of fifty-acre tracts to those who paid for their passage to America or fulfilled an indenture

Hepburn Act: President Theodore Roosevelt's most important railroad-regulating legislation

Hessians: German mercenaries who were hired to fight for the British in the colonies

high-church Anglicans: Held that the church's traditional practices, notably its rule by bishops, were divinely ordained; differed doctrinally among themselves, but were more liberal in their beliefs and less opposed to Catholicism than the Puritan and low-church parties

Hiroshima: Japanese city on which the first atomic bomb was dropped

Holocaust: The name given to Hitler's efforts to exterminate Jews, his enemies, and all whom he and the Nazis considered "inferior" persons. An estimated six million Jews alone were murdered during this time.

Homestead Act: Provided 160 acres of land to any settler who would live on the land for five years and "improve" it by building and farming

Homestead Strike: Strike that occurred after Carnegie's assistant, Henry C. Frick proposed lowering the workers' wages because of the use of new labor-saving machinery. After five months of striking, the workers agreed to Frick's proposal.
Hoovervilles: Name some gave to the areas of cities where people lived in cardboard shacks in parks and vacant lots during the Depression
horizontal integration: Consolidation of all of one entire segment of an industry
hornbook: A child's first "book," a board shaped like a paddle. On its face was a card containing the alphabet and the Lord's Prayer, and it was covered with a thin sheet of horn for durability.
House of Burgesses: The legislative government of colonial Virginia; the first self-governing assembly in America
Huguenots: Religious group that originated in France
human rights: Standards of acceptable behavior toward humans
Hurricane Katrina: Category 3 storm that hit the Gulf Coast of Louisiana, Mississippi, and Alabama; put eighty percent of New Orleans under water; costliest hurricane in American history

I

impeachment: To bring formal charges against an elected or appointed official. Andrew Johnson was the first president to be impeached.
imperialism: The extension of one's way of life to other nations by taking control of or heavily influencing other countries
implied powers: Powers that are derived from powers expressly granted by the Constitution and that the government has by virtue of being a government
impressment: Practice of seizing American sailors and forcing them into British naval service
Inchon: Seaport halfway up the western coast of Korea; site of MacArthur's amphibious invasion
indenture: A work contract for a specified period, usually between four and seven years
Indian removal policy: The government policy that forced the removal of Indians from their lands in the 1830s
initiative: Process in which voters initiate legislation by presenting to their legislature petitions that require the legislators to consider some action
injunction: A court order that forbids certain actions; used extensively in labor conflicts
installment plans: Financing a purchase by making small monthly payments until the item is paid for
internal improvements: Construction and maintenance of roads, canals, and harbors, paid for by government funds

internal tax: A tax on goods produced and consumed entirely within the colonies
international law: Laws that governed interactions between countries; violated by Germany's unrestricted submarine warfare
Interstate Commerce Act: (1) directed that railroad rates must be "reasonable and just"; (2) required that railroad companies publish all rates and make financial reports; and (3) provided for the creation of the Interstate Commerce Commission (ICC), an independent regulatory agency, to investigate and stop alleged abuses
interstate highway system: The main arteries of highway transportation in the United States
Intolerable Acts: Name Americans gave the "Coercive Acts" passed by Parliament to punish Boston for the Tea Party
Iran-Contra affair: Action in which money from arms sales to Iran was funneled though Swiss banks and used to supply the Nicaraguan Contras battling the Communist Sandinistas
Iranian hostage crisis: President Carter's foreign policy nightmare where Americans were held hostage for 444 days of captivity
ironclad: An iron-plated warship
iron curtain: The symbolic wall that separated the free nations of Western Europe from the Communist countries of Eastern Europe
ISIS: Group of radical muslims called the Islamic State of Iraq and Syria
island hopping: The American strategy of bypassing and isolating heavily fortified islands and securing air bases on less fortified islands to be used for launching air attacks and staging further invasions of islands progressively closer to Japan's main islands
isolationism: American desire to avoid foreign entanglements and wars; contributed to the United States not joining the League of Nations
Iwo Jima: Toughest, costliest American victory in the U.S. Marines' history

J

Jamestown: Colony founded by the London Company in 1607; the first permanent English settlement in the New World
Jay Treaty: Treaty between the United States and Great Britain in 1794 that averted war
Jeffersonian Republicanism: The political principles held by supporters of Thomas Jefferson and his successors, James Madison and James Monroe, during what is known as the Jeffersonian Era (1801–25)
Jim Crow laws: Laws that required forced segregation, or separation, of the races in trains, restaurants, hotels, schools, and other social settings

joint resolution: An action that requires only a simple majority in both houses of Congress

joint-stock companies: Companies whose investors shared profits; provided a means whereby enterprises could obtain large monetary resources and remain free from the government control that accompanied government-sponsored projects

judicial activism: The practice of some judges, especially those on the Supreme Court, of interpreting the Constitution very broadly, reading into it meanings that were not intended by the Founders, to address what they consider major social problems; also known as "legislating from the bench"

judicial review: The judicial branch's power to review the constitutionality of laws passed by the legislative branch or of actions taken by the executive branch and to declare them unconstitutional

Judiciary Act of 1789: Act that organized thirteen district courts (one for each of the states), established three circuit courts to handle appeals, and set the number of Supreme Court justices at six

Judiciary Act of 1801: Act which increased the number of federal judges

The Jungle: Novel by Upton Sinclair that focused attention on conditions under which the nation's food (specifically meat) was prepared

K

kamikazes: Japanese suicide pilots who crashed their bomb- and fuel-laden planes into U.S. naval vessels during the closing months of World War II

Kansas-Nebraska Act: Proposed organizing two territories from a region—the Kansas Territory west of Missouri and the Nebraska Territory west of Iowa; gave those in the territories the option of popular sovereignty; repealed the provision of the Missouri Compromise that banned slavery north of 36°30′ latitude

Kellogg-Briand Pact: International agreement that outlawed war by international law; had absolutely no means of enforcement

Kent State: Location of a demonstration protesting the invasion of Cambodia, in which the National Guard was called in. Four students, not all of whom were involved in the protest, were killed in the ensuing encounter.

Kentucky Resolutions: An attempt by Thomas Jefferson to overrule the Alien and Sedition Acts; declared that the states have the right to judge the constitutionality of a law because the central government exists only by the consent of the states and could be dissolved—or its laws declared null—by the states

Kitchen Cabinet: An informal group of Andrew Jackson's friends whom he consulted about governmental matters

Knights of Labor: The earliest significant labor union; secret society of skilled and unskilled workers from various occupations

Know-Nothings: Also known as the American Party, this movement arose in reaction to increasing immigration from Europe in the 1840s and 1850s. The movement turned out to be a passing fad.

Ku Klux Klan: A group formed by former Confederate soldiers in 1866 to oppose Radical Reconstruction and frighten freedmen and whites sympathetic to the freedmen to prevent them from voting; a secretive, ritualistic group patterned after the organization founded during Reconstruction

L

laissez-faire: Free-enterprise economy with minimal government regulation

Land Ordinance of 1785: Ordinance that focused on the settlement of the Northwest Territory; divided the new lands into orderly townships for sale and development

League of Nations: The last of Wilson's Fourteen Points; an organization of cooperating nations that would discuss and solve problems peacefully

Lend-Lease Act: Act that appropriated billions to provide supplies for the embattled nations; empowered FDR to supply any Allied nation with war materiel on almost any terms he desired

Lewinsky scandal: Scandal that dominated Clinton's second term as president

Lexington and Concord: The villages where colonists skirmished with British troops on April 19, 1775, firing the first shots of what became the War for Independence

Liberal Republicans: A splinter group of the Republican party that decided to oppose Grant's reelection in 1872; called for an end to military occupation in the South and the purging of corruption from the national government

limited government: A constitutional principle that limits government to only those powers granted by law

limited war: A war with a limited objective short of total victory over the enemy

Lincoln-Douglas debates: Became a platform for not only the Illinois election but also the national debate on slavery

Lindbergh kidnapping: Famous case in the 20th century that involved the kidnapping of baby Charles A. Lindbergh Jr.

literacy tests: Tests that often deprived black people of their right to vote

loose constructionists: Those who take a broad and flexible approach to constitutional interpretation

Lost Colony: Raleigh's colony that mysteriously disappeared

Louisiana: The vast region at the mouth of the Mississippi that La Salle claimed for France

Louisiana Purchase: The 1803 purchase by the United States from France of land stretching from the Mississippi River to the Rocky Mountains. The purchase price for the nearly 530 million acres was $15 million.

low-church Anglicans: Agreed doctrinally with the Puritans but saw no problem with the church's ceremonies and structure

Loyalists: Colonists who supported the British king; also known as Tories

Lusitania: British passenger liner that also carried military arms and ammunition and was sunk by a German submarine at the cost of 128 Americans. The event convinced many Americans of the need for American involvement in the European war on the Allied side.

Lutherans: Followers of the teachings of the great German reformer Martin Luther

lynched: Executed, often by hanging, without a legal trial

M

Macon's Bill Number Two: Abolished the non-intercourse policy and restored all trade; stated that if either Britain or France would repeal its antitrade regulations, the United States would restore trade with that side in the war and refuse to trade with the other

malaria: A disease transmitted to humans by mosquitoes

Manifest Destiny: The belief that God intended for Americans to possess the North American continent; term coined by newspaperman John L. O'Sullivan

Marbury v. Madison: A Supreme Court ruling that established the principle of judicial review of acts of Congress

March on Washington: Event in which more than two hundred thousand people—both black and white—gathered in the nation's capital for a huge civil rights protest

March to the Sea: General Sherman's destructive push from Atlanta to Savannah

Marshall Plan: U.S. program that spent billions of dollars to help rebuild European countries ravaged by World War II; named for Secretary of State George C. Marshall

Mayflower: Ship that carried the Pilgrims to the New World where they landed at Cape Cod, Massachusetts, rather than their intended destination of Virginia

Mayflower Compact: The agreement that the Pilgrims made for setting up a self-governing civil government for the Plymouth colony; first document of self-government in America

McCarthyism: A new word coined to describe McCarthy's alleged use of lies, distortion, and innuendo

McCulloch v. Maryland: Perhaps the most far-reaching decision of the Marshall Court, in which the Supreme Court overruled the state of Maryland's attempt to tax the Baltimore branch of the national bank out of existence

McKinley Tariff: Imposed higher duties on manufactured and agricultural imports than had any previous tariff in history, thereby protecting American inefficiency

Meat Inspection Act: Required the Department of Agriculture to oversee the preparation and packing of meat and to inspect the health of animals before they were slaughtered

Medicare: A government health insurance program established in 1965 to help elderly people pay for medical care

Mein Kampf: Hate-filled autobiography of Adolf Hitler, which outlines his political ideas

Mennonites: Followers of the Dutch teacher Menno Simons; the largest Anabaptist group

mercantilism: An economic system whereby national wealth was measured by how much gold and other precious metal a nation possessed and that used wealth produced by colonies to enrich itself

Methodists: Followers of the teachings of English minister John Wesley

Mexican War (1846–48): The war between the United States and Mexico during the push for Manifest Destiny

middle colonies: Segment of the colonies that reflected cultural diversity; English, Dutch, Germans, French, Finns, Scots, and Swedes all settled here; included New York, New Jersey, Pennsylvania, and Delaware

Middle Passage: Name for the Africans' journey to the New World on slave ships

midnight appointments: Judges appointed by John Adams the night before Jefferson's inauguration

militia: "Citizen soldiers"; part-time fighters who left their farms and businesses to fight during emergencies

minutemen: Colonial militiamen who were ready to defend their colony at a moment's notice

Missouri Compromise: An agreement brokered in Congress by Henry Clay whereby Maine was admitted to the Union as a free state and Missouri was admitted as a slave state, thereby ensuring a continued balance between slave states and free states in Congress

mobilization: A country's assembling of its soldiers; can be interpreted as aggressive

modernism: A theological movement that rejected many Christian doctrines; first became popular in American colleges and seminaries and soon began to spread to American pulpits through graduates who became pastors

Monroe Doctrine: An 1823 foreign-policy statement by James Monroe that declared that the United States would not tolerate interference in the Western Hemisphere by European powers

Montgomery bus boycott: Started by Rosa Parks when she refused to give up her seat on the bus to a white male.

The boycott financially devastated the Montgomery city bus system.

Moravians: Followers of preacher John Huss of Bohemia

Mormonism: A religion begun by New Yorker Joseph Smith

Mormon Trail: Blazed by the Mormons when they fled from Nauvoo, Illinois, to Salt Lake City

Mound Builders: Indians in the Midwest who were noted for the hundreds of large burial mounds they built

muckrakers: Writers who exposed abuse and corruption

mujahideen: Afghan guerilla soldiers

My Lai: Vietnamese village that was massacred by Lieutenant William Calley and his company

N

Nagasaki: Japanese city on which the second atomic bomb was dropped after which Japanese emperor Hirohito accepted defeat

National Aeronautics and Space Administration (NASA): Established by Congress to conduct the new space program

National Association for the Advancement of Colored People (NAACP): Formed by W.E.B. Du Bois and other like-minded leaders—black and white—to fight legal battles on behalf of blacks

National Bank: Institution founded by Congress to provide a standard currency and financial stability for the young nation

national convention: Meeting where state delegates gathered to nominate the party's presidential and vice-presidential candidates; since 1832 has become a standard part of the American political process

national debt: The amount of money the government owes

National Industrial Recovery Act (NIRA): Act that attempted to organize guidelines for industries to increase employment, maintain wages, and reduce unwanted competition

National Origins Act: Act that set quotas to restrict immigration

National Recovery Administration (NRA): The agency designed to carry out the activities prescribed by the NIRA

National Republicans: John Quincy Adams's wing of the Republican party, which was distinguished by its nationalist thrust

National Road: A graveled road that was begun during Jefferson's administration and continued during Madison's administration; Cumberland, Maryland, to Vandalia, Illinois

National Security Act: Act that created the post of Secretary of Defense, a civilian cabinet position set over the army, navy, and air force; also created the National Security Council and Central Intelligence Agency (CIA) to assist the president in foreign policy matters

naturalism: Emphasized man's helplessness and struggle with the world

Nazi Party: National Socialist German Workers' Party; came to power in Germany in 1933 when Hitler was appointed chancellor of the nation

Nazi-Soviet nonaggression pact: An agreement between Hitler and Stalin to avoid aggression against each other for a period of ten years

Neutrality Act of 1939: Provided that belligerents of World War II could purchase weaponry from the United States but only on a cash basis and transported in their own ships

Newburgh Conspiracy: According to this plan, the officers intended to force Congress and the states to grant their back pay. George Washington diffused the situation, and the plan collapsed.

New Deal: Program of President Franklin Roosevelt that tried to control the economy through government action rather than through the free market

New Economic Policy: Nixon's effort to fix economic problems; imposed a ninety-day freeze in 1971 on all wages and prices, established a board to regulate all wage and price increases, and replaced the mandatory guidelines with voluntary ones in 1973

New England: Name given by John Smith to the coast far to the north of Jamestown. Smith's account of this land stimulated interest in this region. It includes Massachusetts, Connecticut, Rhode Island, Vermont, New Hampshire and Maine.

New England Primer: Served as the standard textbook throughout the colonial period; provided basic grammar and vocabulary accented with moral lessons; also included a short catechism

New France: Name for the location of the sparse French settlements in Canada; largely dependent on the mother country for their success

New Frontier: Kennedy's proposed legislative program for exploring space, helping underdeveloped countries, and dealing with Communist threats to Latin America with economic aid

New Immigration: A wave of immigrants different from those in the past; many came from eastern European countries

New Jersey Plan: The plan of the small states for equal representation of all states in Congress

New Left: Radical groups that hoped to use resentment over the Vietnam War as a means of overthrowing established American institutions

New Netherlands: Name for New York when the Dutch settled the area

New Right: Group of conservatives that shared many beliefs of the traditionalists; also motivated by numerous social and moral issues

New South: An economically revitalized South that developers, promoters, and businessmen hoped would revive the South and make it match the North as an economic force

New York draft riot: A riot by those resisting the draft in which mobs attacked government officials and the city's black population

Nineteenth Amendment: Amendment that gave women the right to vote

Nixon pardon: President Ford granted Nixon a full pardon for any crimes he might have committed while in office; this action was widely denounced and Ford's popularity was dashed.

no man's land: A neutral zone beyond the frontline trenches that varied in size from a few yards to more than a mile

non-established denominations: Denominations that do not have state (government) support and protection

normalcy: A new word that became the goal of a people wishing to distance themselves from wartime pressures and problems

North America Free Trade Act (NAFTA): The North American Free Trade Agreement; designed to increase free trade among Mexico, Canada, and the United States

North Atlantic Treaty Organization (NATO): Military alliance between Western European countries, the United States, and Canada

Northwest Ordinance of 1787: Ordinance that focused on government of the Northwest Territory

Northwest Territory: All the lands north of the Ohio River that passed into the hands of the national government

no taxation without representation: The rallying cry for many American colonists

nullification: The doctrine that states could nullify, or reject, congressional acts they deemed unconstitutional. This position had been put forth in the Virginia and Kentucky Resolutions.

Nuremberg Trials: Trials of many Nazi war criminals

O

Obamacare: Name for the Patient Protection and Affordable Care Act (PPACA)

Obergefell v. Hodges: The Supreme Court declared key sections of DOMA to be unconstitutional; the Supreme Court decreed that the 14th Amendment to the Constitution required all U.S. state laws to recognize same-sex marriages.

Office of Homeland Security: Established by President Bush to protect Americans at home; later became a cabinet-level department

oil embargo: Prohibited the sale of any oil from OPEC to America and other nations that supported Israel

Okinawa: The bloodiest single campaign in the Pacific; American victory

Oklahoma land rushes: Rapid influxes of homesteaders on large sections of the Indian Territory

Olive Branch Petition: A pledge of loyalty to King George III that delegates to the Second Continental Congress presented to the king along with a request that the king intervene to curb Parliament's abuse of power over the colonies; a final plea for a peaceful resolution

on the margin: Purchasing stock through a broker but only paying a percentage of purchase price while the broker finances the remaining amount for the investor with money borrowed from the bank or other sources

Open Door Policy: Secretary of State John Hay's policy that called for all nations trading in China to refrain from interfering with one another and to allow free trade in China

open ranges: Unfenced public lands where the cowboys herded cattle

Operation Desert Shield: Plan that deployed allied forces (chiefly American) in Saudi Arabia to prevent further Iraqi aggression

Operation Desert Storm: A brief, 100-hour war in 1991 to oust Iraq's forces under dictator Saddam Hussein from Kuwait

Operation Torch: The Allied invasion of North Africa

Ordinance of Secession: Document drafted and ratified by each state that seceded from the Union

Ordinance of 1784: Ordinance written by Thomas Jefferson that never went into effect; proposed creating ten new states out of the Northwest Territory, banning slavery in the region, and giving the land to settlers rather than selling it

Oregon Trail: Important westward trail that led to Oregon and had branches that reached California

P

Panama Canal: American-built canal that links the Atlantic and Pacific Oceans; signed over to Panama in 1977

Panama Canal Treaty: Treaty signed and ratified during Carter's presidency whereby the United States returned control of the Panama Canal to Panama

Pan-Americanism: A movement favoring greater cooperation and unity among the nations of the Western Hemisphere

Panic of 1819: The first peacetime economic crisis in the United States

Panic of 1837: The name of a five-year depression in the United States starting in 1837

Panic of 1873: Financial collapse that touched off a six-year depression, the worst depression that the United States had endured up to that time

Paris Peace Talks: Talks between the United States and North Vietnam that dragged on for nearly five years while the fighting continued

Patient Protection and Affordable Care Act (PPACA): Healthcare legislation, also known as Obamacare, which required all Americans to either obtain health insurance or pay a fine

Patriots: Colonists who supported the cause of independence and were willing to fight for it

Paxton Boys: A large group of Scots-Irish living in the backcountry of Pennsylvania near present-day Harrisburg who formed a vigilante group and took out their frustrations on the nearest Indians

Peace Corps: A government project designed to send skilled volunteers overseas to help underdeveloped nations

peaceful coexistence: Public policy whereby the Soviet Union and the United States sought to settle tensions between them without allowing it to break into military confrontation

Pendleton Act: Established an independent Civil Service Commission and eliminated much of the spoils system

Pennsylvania Dutch: German immigrants who settled primarily in Pennsylvania

Pentagon Papers: A number of confidential documents that were stolen by Pentagon staff analyst Daniel Ellsberg and released to the *New York Times*; were more embarrassing to the government than dangerous to the nation; prompted even more antiwar sentiment

perestroika: The restructuring of the stagnant Soviet economy, shifting to more free-market policies and some private ownership

Persian Gulf War: An intensive American-led military effort that destroyed the effectiveness of an enemy force numbering more than 500,000 but still left Saddam Hussein in power

pet banks: Name that Jackson's enemies gave to the state banks where Secretary of the Treasury Roger B. Taney placed federal deposits after removing them from the Bank of the United States

Petersburg: Location of a siege conducted by General Grant and the Union forces in 1864–65

Pickett's Charge: Confederate charge at the Battle of Gettysburg in which approximately half of the division was decimated

Pikes Peak gold rush: One of the earliest gold strikes after the California rush; resulted in the settlement of Colorado

Pilgrims: Separatists who left Europe and went to the New World, establishing the Plymouth colony

Plains Indians: Tribes such as the Cheyenne, the Comanche, and Sioux who lived in the Great Plains region

platform: A written statement describing where a party stands on various issues

Plessy v. Ferguson: A Supreme Court case which decreed that "separate but equal" facilities for blacks and whites (in this case, on trains) were constitutional

poll taxes: A special tax required to vote; often prevented black people from voting

Poor Richard's Almanack: Written by Benjamin Franklin and published from 1733 to 1758. In addition to the usual astronomical and weather predictions, it was filled with sayings that emphasized thrift, honesty, and diligence.

popular sovereignty: The idea that the ultimate source of governmental power lies in the people; a constitutional principle that is evident in several areas of the Constitution; a system whereby the people of a given state or area would determine the slavery issue in their area for themselves

Populist Party: Formed from independent grassroots organizations that sprang up throughout the Midwest and eventually merged through the politics of discontent

Potsdam: Location of meeting between Stalin, Truman, and Churchill (eventually replaced by Clemet Attlee); agreed on the demand for Japan's unconditional surrender

Pottawatomie Massacre: Occasion when John Brown's men butchered five proslavery settlers

power of the purse: Power given to some assemblies that meant that salaries for royal officials, military appropriations, and taxes had to pass the approval of elected officeholders

Prayer Meeting Revival: Called by some the "third great awakening"; began shortly after a serious financial crisis, the Panic of 1857

Preamble: The introduction to the Constitution

Presbyterians: Denomination that originated in the British Isles; like the Puritans, many came to the American colonies seeking religious freedom

Princeton: American victory following Trenton

Proclamation of Neutrality: President Washington's response to the French Revolution

Proclamation of 1763: Document issued by the British Parliament that prohibited the colonists from settling beyond the Appalachian Mountains

progressive education: Aimed at improving education by relating learning to the child's interests; the problematic philosophy of secular humanism was behind progressive methodology

Progressive Party: Third party in the 1912 election; popularly known as the Bull Moose Party because Roosevelt had told a reporter that he felt "as strong as a bull moose"

progressivism: Reform movement that favored achieving political and social reform through education, wider political participation, and direct government action

Prohibition: Banning the manufacture, sale, or transportation of alcohol by the eighteenth amendment

propaganda: Information spread to advance a cause or damage an opponent's cause

proprietary colony: A colony given by a king to an individual or group

protective tariff: An unusually high tariff designed to shield a nation's manufacturers from foreign competition

Protestant Reformation: Movement that pressed for changes in the Roman Church and society

public works: Government-financed construction of public facilities

Public Works Administration (PWA): Another agency that provided work relief; built school buildings, courthouses, hospitals, bridges, and other public facilities all over the country; also built ships and planes for the nation's military

"Publius": Alexander Hamilton, the lone New York delegate, responded to the Anti-Federalist articles under this pseudonym

Pueblo Indians: Southwest Indians who lived in small villages made up of two or three family groups or clans; some lived in caves and became know as cliff dwellers

Pullman Strike: Precipitated by five successive wage reductions, totaling twenty-five percent, in the spring of 1894. Though the reductions were due to the depression, rent on company houses and goods in company stores remained the same price.

puppet governments: A government that is supposedly in control but is actually dominated by an outside power

purchase of Alaska: The largest single American acquisition after the Civil War

Pure Food and Drug Act: Outlawed the interstate sale of impure food and drugs and required honest labeling of such products

Puritans: Members of the Anglican Church who hoped to purify the church of various Roman Catholic practices and ceremonies

Q

Quakers: The Society of Friends; originated with Englishman George Fox; teach that an "Inner Light" in man is some kind of "spark of divinity" and that man is saved through obeying its leading rather than through the atonement of Christ

Quartering Act: Act which officially subjected the colonies to a standing army in peacetime and further required that the colonists help supply provisions for it

Quasi War: A conflict resembling war in nearly every particular except a formal declaration

Quebec Act: Act that set up a rigid political system, made Roman Catholicism the official religion of Quebec, and extended the territorial boundaries of Quebec southward to the Ohio River

R

Radical Republicans: Republicans in Congress who opposed Lincoln's plans for a benevolent Reconstruction. They favored, instead, a much stricter form of Reconstruction.

rationing: System for conserving vital goods such as foodstuffs, rubber, and gasoline for diversion to the war effort

Reagan Doctrine: One of the key aspects of Reagan's foreign policy; pledged America's support to insurgent groups battling Communist governments in the third world

realism: Contrasted the emotional, exotic character of romanticism; drew a picture of simple, ordinary life

recall: Process in which voters petition to hold a special election to decide whether to remove an elected official from office; can also be used to repeal specific legislation or even judicial decisions

Reconstruction: The period of rebuilding of the South from 1865 to 1877, when the last Union troops left the South

Reconstruction Act of 1867: Legislation that imposed military occupation of the South, like an army of a conquering nation occupying a defeated foe

Reconstruction Finance Corporation (RFC): Patterned after the War Finance Corporation of World War I; was authorized to lend $2 billion to struggling banks, railroads, life insurance companies, and other large businesses

Redeemers: Group of people during Reconstruction that desired to "redeem" (or regain) the South

Red Scare: Term used to describe the panic in the United States started by the violent activities of a few leftists following World War I; later also used to refer to the widespread fear of communism

referendum: Allows the people to vote yes or no in a regular election to determine whether a law should be enacted or rejected

refugees: People who flee for refuge or safety

regulars: Professional, full-time soldiers who made the military their career

Regulators: Residents of western North Carolina who were dissatisfied with the colony's wealthy, upper-class leaders, whom they considered cruel and corrupt and who imposed high taxes on the colonials; rose up in armed rebellion with the goal of setting up an honest government and reducing taxes

Religious Right: Important component of the New Right; various conservative Christian leaders and organizations that were concerned primarily with moral issues

reparations: Demanded by Britain and France from Germany to pay for war damages and the entire cost of the war

Republican Party: The successor to the Whig party

Republicans (Democratic-Republicans): Also known as Democratic-Republicans; political opponents of the Federalists; believed in having strong state governments but a weaker central government and opposed a national bank

Republic of Texas: The name for Texas during the ten-year span of time that Texas was independent from Mexico but not yet a U.S. state; also known as the "Lone Star Republic"

reservations: Tracts of land set aside for Indians to live on

Rhineland: An industrial region of Germany near Alsace-Lorraine that, under the Versailles Treaty, was to remain demilitarized

Right-to-life movement: Opposed abortion and sought to use such means as a constitutional amendment to overturn the *Roe* decision

Roanoke Island: Location of a new-world settlement funded by Sir Walter Raleigh. The second settlement here disappeared and became known as the Lost Colony.

robber barons: Derogatory name referring to capitalists who built industries and acquired great wealth

Roe v. Wade: Supreme Court ruling in 1973 that declared that most state laws that restricted abortion were unconstitutional

Rome-Berlin-Tokyo Axis: An alliance of the dictator states Italy, Germany, and Japan

Roosevelt Corollary: Added to the Monroe Doctrine that the United States would act as a "policeman" to keep Latin American nations in line; resulted in intensified European and Latin American resentment toward the United States

Rough Riders: A collection of cowboys, miners, college students, and adventurers from the West, commanded by Colonel Leonard Wood and Lieutenant Colonel Theodore Roosevelt

royal colony: Colony over which the king had direct control

S

Sacco-Vanzetti case: Case of alleged murder. Some thought the two men had been convicted of murder because they were Italian-born aliens and anarchists, not because of the evidence.

sack of Lawrence: Time when a town in Kansas that was a center of free-state strength was attacked by an army of border ruffians

Salem witch trials: A period in 1692 of hysteria over witchcraft allegedly being practiced in Salem, Massachusetts; resulted in the executions of at least twenty people and ruined reputations before it ended

SALT II Treaty: Treaty that would limit the number and kinds of nuclear weapons for the United States and the Soviet Union; was never passed by Congress

Santa Fe Trail: An important commercial westward trail; closed by the Mexican government due to fear of growing American activity in Texas

scalawags: Southerners who cooperated with carpetbaggers during Reconstruction

Schenk v. United States: Supreme Court ruling that Congress could limit free speech, particularly during wartime, if such speech presented "a clear and present danger" to national interests

Scots-Irish: Presbyterian Scots from the Protestant colony of Ulster in Northern Ireland, many of whom came to America, settling primarily in the middle colonies

Sea Dogs: Group of mariners including Sir Francis Drake who led attacks on Spanish shipping in the New World

secede: The action of a state to leave the Union

Second Battle of Bull Run: Sent the Union army reeling back to Washington

Second Continental Congress: The gathering of delegates in Philadelphia on May 10, 1775

Second Great Awakening: A spiritual revival that swept through the nation shortly after the Constitution was ratified

secret ballot: System by which only the one voting knows who he votes for; reduces the possibility of influencing voters who favor the "wrong" candidate

secular humanism: Philosophy that denies the existence of God and affirms the goodness and perfectibility of man

Security Council: Includes five permanent members—the United States, Russia, Britain, France, and China—and ten members elected by the General Assembly for two-year terms; permanent members have veto power in the agency of the UN

segregation: Separation of races in a variety of situations

Selective Service Act: Congress's response to Wilson's call for war; a peacetime military draft to prepare America to enter World War I

self-determination: Principle under which people would decide for themselves under what governments they wished to live

Seminole War: War between the Seminole Indians led by Osceola and American troops. Most Seminoles were rounded up and sent west, but some held out in Florida until the government gave up and left them to live in peace.

separation of powers: The principle of dividing national power among three different branches of government (the legislative, executive, and judicial branches) to prevent any group or individual from gaining too much control

Separatists: A group of dissenters who did not believe that the Anglican Church could be purified; chose to separate themselves from the church and held their own worship services

September 1, 1939: The beginning of World War II; started with Germany's invasion of Poland

September 11, 2001: Date of the terrorist attack on America that targeted the World Trade Center towers, the Pentagon, and a fourth unknown target

Seventeenth Amendment: Amendment that took away the right of the state legislatures to elect U.S. senators and changed it to direct popular election. This did create a problem by removing one of the state legislatures' checks on federal power.

Seven Years' War: Name for the French and Indian War in Europe

siege of Charleston: British strategy to conquer Charleston; resulted in America's worst defeat of the war

silent majority: Term that Nixon used to refer to the belief that most Americans were not violent radicals but quiet, hard-working people who wanted peace and order

Sioux: Tribe of the Plains Indians

Sioux War (1876–77): The climax of the Indian Wars; known as the Second Sioux War and the Great Sioux War to distinguish it from the conflict of 1866–68

Sixteenth Amendment: Amendment that instituted the federal income tax

Shakers: Unorthodox group who took their name from the shaking or dancing that accompanied their worship; also practiced celibacy and owned property in common; eventually died out because of its practice of celibacy

sharecropping: Developed as an answer to the economic deprivations of the South. Farming system in which laborers leased the land, provided their own tools and seeds, grew what they wanted, and then paid their rent with cash or crops, or simply provided the labor while the landowner provided land, tools, and supplies. Farm laborers often remained constantly in debt.

Shays's Rebellion: An insurrection of farmers against the courts in the western part of Massachusetts led by Daniel Shays; uprising crushed by the militia

Sherman Anti-Trust Act: Made the monopolizing of businesses illegal

Smoot-Hawley tariff: Pushed tariffs on foreign industrial and agricultural prices to their highest level in United States history

social gospel: Applied its social-reform ethic to religion; replaced regeneration of individuals with regeneration of society through social reform. Social salvation was the only salvation.

socialism: Government regulation or ownership of the means of production; involves the forced redistribution of wealth by taking it from those who have it and giving it to those who do not

Social Security Act: Act that instituted old-age pensions and unemployment insurance for American workers

soddies: Houses built of blocks of earth and sod

Solid South: Name for the South due to its commitment to the Democratic Party

Sons of Liberty: Opponents of British rule in the colonies

southern colonies: Colonies of Virginia, Maryland, the Carolinas, and Georgia

Soviet invasion of Afghanistan: Aggressive Soviet action that removed all chance of the Senate passing the SALT II Treaty

Spanish-American War: A war fought between the United States and Spain in 1898; fought mainly in Cuba and the Philippines

Spanish Armada: Fleet of Spanish ships defeated by the English and mostly destroyed in a storm (1588)

speculation: Buying something with the hope of selling it later at a profit

spoils system: The practice, used extensively by Andrew Jackson, of giving government jobs to friends and supporters

Sputnik I: A Russian satellite that was successfully launched into space on October 4, 1957, orbiting the earth at 18,000 miles per hour and circling the globe every 96 minutes

Square Deal: President Theodore Roosevelt's name for his philosophy that every man and woman should receive fair treatment and equal opportunity

stagflation: An economic condition in which inflation and unemployment are both high, causing the economy to be stagnant

Stalwarts: Conkling's faction of the Republican Party that favored high tariffs, hard money, and the spoils system

Stamp Act: Law of Parliament that required the purchase of special stamps and their use on taxed items, such as legal documents, newspapers, and calendars

Stamp Act Congress: Delegates from nine colonies met in New York for this congress; formally denounced the Stamp Act and the seizure of colonial rights that it represented

starving time: Name for the winter of 1609–10 in Jamestown. About ninety percent of the colony died during this time.

states' rights: According to this view, each state was largely an independent entity joined in a voluntary compact of union—but a union in which they maintained their identity and were not subservient to a centralized national authority.

St. Augustine: The oldest permanent city settled by Europeans in the present United States

stock market crash: The day in October 1929 when more than sixteen million shares were dumped on the stock market, and investors lost $30 billion in the process

Strategic Defense Initiative (SDI): Initiative that proposed a space-based defense shield of satellites, missiles, and lasers designed to safeguard the country from nuclear attack

strict constructionists: Those who emphasize the importance of a close reading of the Constitution's text and believe that any interpretation should be kept to a minimum

Sudetenland: A predominantly German area in western Czechoslovakia that Germany annexed; as Hitler promised, "This is the last territorial claim I have to make in Europe."

suffrage: The right to vote

Sugar Act: Act that placed a tariff, or tax, on certain goods imported into the colonies, such as sugar, molasses, and coffee

Sumner-Brooks episode: Violent attack on Charles Sumner by Preston Brooks in the Senate following a fiery speech by Sumner regarding abolition and Kansas

supply-side economics (Reaganomics): Economic policy of the Reagan administration based on tax cuts and depended on a limited-government agenda: cut taxes so that citizens will have incentive to earn, save, and invest; and encourage economic expansion by reducing government regulations on business and by providing corporate tax breaks. Critics called it "trickle-down economics," "Reaganomics," or "voodoo economics."

***Sussex* pledge:** Restated Germany's promise to follow international law; issued after a German submarine attacked an unarmed French passenger ship, the *Sussex*, in the English Channel

T

Taliban: A group of Muslim extremists that controlled the government of Afghanistan; protected bin Laden and his supporters

Tammany Hall: A political organization founded after the Revolutionary War that soon grew in influence until it controlled most of New York's political affairs during the last half of the nineteenth century

tariff: A tax on imports; can be for revenue or to protect a domestic industry from foreign competition

Tariff of Abominations: A new, higher protective tariff with rates of up to fifty percent on some imports

Tariff of 1816: America's first protectionist legislation

Tea Act of 1773: Act that granted the East India Company a monopoly on shipment and sale of English tea in America

Tea Party: Conservative groups that protested against the power of the government and called for a significant reduction in its size and scope

Teapot Dome scandal: Scandal involving President Harding's Secretary of the Interior, Albert B. Fall

tenant farmers: Farmers with slightly better conditions than sharecroppers

Tennessee Valley Authority (TVA): Agency that undertook the extensive project to build dams along the Tennessee River that would provide navigation, flood control, and cheap electricity for the valley residents

Ten Percent Plan: President Lincoln's plan for restoring the South

Tenure of Office Act: Forbade the president from dismissing cabinet members who had been approved by the Senate without the consent of the Senate

Tet Offensive: North Vietnamese offensive that was a major failure for the Communists but had a dramatic effect on the American public, who now wanted a way out of the war

theory of relativity: Theory that space, time, and matter are not absolute dimensions but are relative to the location and motion of the observer

third party: A political party that is in addition to the two predominant parties at any given time

Third World: In the past, referred to nations that did not align themselves with either the East or West. Today the term refers to underdeveloped, or developing, nations—especially those with widespread poverty.

Thirteenth Amendment: Abolished slavery

38th parallel: Latitude dividing Communist North Korea and non-Communist South Korea

Three-Fifths Compromise: Under this settlement, three-fifths of the total slave population of a state would be included for representation purposes in the House, but slave states would also have to pay taxes on slaves at the same rate.

Tories: Pro-British American colonists; named after the political party in Parliament that supported the king; also know as Loyalists

totalitarianism: A government that regulates every aspect of life

Townshend Acts: Acts which placed taxes on glass, paint, paper, and tea and were in direct conflict with the traditional "power of the purse" that many colonial assemblies had maintained for nearly a century

trade deficit: Situation in which more goods are imported than are exported

Trail of Tears: The forced removal in 1838 of the Cherokee Indians from Georgia and Tennessee to Oklahoma

transcontinental railroad: A continuous rail line that reached the entire width of the continent; completed on May 10, 1869

Treaty of Ghent: Signed December 24, 1814; returned conditions largely to what they had been in 1812

Treaty of Guadalupe Hidalgo: Treaty between Mexico and the Americans in which Mexico recognized American claims to Texas southward to the Rio Grande and ceded New Mexico and California to the United States. In turn, the United States paid Mexico $15 million and assumed all debts that Mexico owed American citizens.

Treaty of Paris (1763): Treaty that ended the French and Indian War

Treaty of Paris (1783): Signed on September 3, 1783, it ended the War for Independence and marked Britain's granting of independence to the former colonies.

Treaty of Versailles: Treaty forced upon Germany after World War I; forced Germany to accept full blame for causing the war and imposed severe reparation payments that contributed to the coming of World War II

Treaty of Washington: Settled disputes between the United States, Britain, and Canada by setting up international tribunals to deal with each question

trench warfare: Major part of World War I; the trench system included frontline trenches, support trenches, and communication trenches

***Trent* affair:** Event in which the U.S. Navy forced the British mail ship, the *Trent*, to surrender Confederate agents that were going to Europe to negotiate for aid. The British were outraged, but Secretary of State Seward was able to satisfy them and thus narrowly avoid British intervention.

Trenton: Location of surprise attack by Washington's forces where nearly one thousand Hessians were killed or captured

Triple Alliance: Alliance of Germany, Austria-Hungary, and Italy formed by Otto von Bismarck in 1882

Triple Entente: Alliance of France, Russia, and Great Britain formed in 1907

Truman Doctrine: President Truman's intention to provide aid to any country that was fighting to prevent its takeover by Communists. This policy was first applied to Greece and Turkey, both of which were able to prevent Communist takeovers.

trust: A legal device by which a board of trustees was empowered to make decisions and control the operations of a whole group of companies

trustbusting: Breaking up monopolies and restoring competition to the marketplace

Twelfth Amendment: Enabled electors to cast separate ballots for president and vice president

Twenty-fourth Amendment: Outlawed the use of poll taxes, which had been used to prevent black suffrage

U

U-boats: Name for submarines; from *Unterseeboot*, a German word for a submarine

***Uncle Tom's Cabin*:** Novel written by Harriet Beecher Stowe that drew greater attention to the evils of slavery

Underground Railroad: The escape route for fugitive slaves that consisted of a secret network of people who assisted the escaping slaves

Underwood Tariff Act: Slashed overall tariff rates in 1913 by about a third from what they had been

unicameral: Having only one house in a legislature

Union of Soviet Socialist Republics (USSR): Also known as the Soviet Union; became the official name of Russia during the 1920s

Union Pacific: Received a charter to build the first transcontinental railroad; railroad line that began building in Omaha, Nebraska, and built westward to meet the Central Pacific railroad line

Unitarianism: One of the most prestigious unorthodox religions; denies the Trinity and the deity of Christ

United Nations: International organization that began with delegates from fifty nations writing a charter for the organization; includes two major agencies—General Assembly and Security Council

United States Steel Corporation: Formed by John Pierpont Morgan; the first billion-dollar corporation

unrestricted submarine warfare: German policy that all ships in the war zone—passenger or merchant, belligerent or neutral—would be sunk without warning

urban evangelism: The conducting of large, citywide campaigns in huge auditoriums or large churches in major cities

urban riots: Riots that occurred in areas such as Los Angeles and Detroit as a result of disappointment over the lack of progress in the area of civil rights and increasing violence among the counterculture in the 1960s

USS *Constitution* ("Old Ironsides"): A particularly effective American vessel that defeated British ships in combat

USS *Maine*: American warship sunk in Havana Harbor; event blamed on Spain and contributed to the start of the Spanish-American War

USS *Merrimack*: The Confederate ironclad; built on the damaged hull of an abandoned Union warship; the CSS *Virginia*

USS *Monitor*: The Union ironclad

utopian reformers: Sought to establish small, perfect communities that would serve as models for the reform of society at large

V

Valley Forge: The headquarters of the continental army during the winter of 1777–78

vertical integration: When a company controls a part of all segments of the production of a good from raw material to finished product

Vicksburg: An important river port in the south; a key to Confederate supply and the Mississippi campaign; starved into submission by Union General Grant's siege

Viet Cong: North Vietnamese and pro-Communist South Vietnamese guerrillas

Vietnamization: Nixon's effort to increase the role of the South Vietnamese in fighting their war while gradually withdrawing American troops

Virginia Plan: James Madison's plan that favored the large states for representation in Congress according to population

Virginia Resolutions: An attempt by James Madison to overrule the Alien and Sedition Acts; declared that the states have the right to judge the constitutionality of a law because the central government exists only by the consent of the states and could be dissolved—or its laws declared null—by the states

Voting Rights Act of 1965: Act that sent federal officials into states to help register blacks to vote and outlawed literacy tests for voters

W

Wade-Davis Bill: Set forth the Radical Republicans' view of Reconstruction

war-guilt clause: Stated that Germany was responsible for World War I

War Hawks: House representatives led by Henry Clay of Kentucky and John C. Calhoun of South Carolina; pushed for war with Britain

War on Poverty: Declared by President Johnson in his first State of the Union message

War Production Board: Immediately halted nearly all domestic building construction to conserve materials for war production; ordered massive industrial conversion from civilian to military production

Warsaw Pact: Military alliance created by the Communist countries of Eastern Europe to counter NATO

Washington Naval Conference: Brought foreign diplomats to the nation's capital to negotiate an agreement limiting the growth of naval power; resulted in a plan that called for Japan, Britain, and the United States to scrap some of their vessels, curtail battleship construction, and establish a ratio for naval forces

Washington's Farewell Address: In this address, Washington urged Americans to lay aside partisan divisions and encouraged the cultivation of commercial ties with Europe while warning against political ties.

Watergate affair: A political break-in by Nixon aides in 1972 that the president tried to help cover up; resulted in Nixon's near impeachment and his resignation in 1973

weapons of mass destruction (WMDs): Chemical and biological weapons that Saddam Hussein used against the Kurds

Welfare Reform Act of 1996: Rolled back federal guarantees for the poor for the first time since FDR's New Deal

West Virginia: Originally part of Virginia but did not secede along with it; recognized by the federal government and admitted to the Union on June 20, 1863

Whig Party: A political alliance of anti-Jackson forces; derived their name from the British party that traditionally opposed royal tyranny

Whiskey Rebellion: Rebellion of farmers who wanted to avoid the tax on whiskey; crushed by President Washington in command of thirteen thousand troops

Whiskey Ring: A group of whiskey distillers and distributors and federal tax collectors who conspired to cheat the government out of millions of dollars in revenue from excise taxes

Wilderness Campaign: Resulted in the costliest and most desperate fighting of the Civil War; nicknamed a continuous "funeral procession"

Wilmot Proviso: An amendment to a bill stipulating that the United States prohibit slavery in any territory acquired from Mexico; passed the House but was rejected by the Senate

women's liberation movement: Radical element of the feminist movement that portrayed modern American marriage as a form of slavery in which wives labored in the "demeaning" roles of mother and homemaker

women's rights movement: Movement that appealed to a sense of fairness to address problems such as unequal pay for men and women

work relief: Assistance program that requires the one receiving assistance to work in return for the aid

Works Progress Administration (WPA): Program created in an attempt to eliminate the relief doles; employed almost anyone in almost any kind of job

Wounded Knee Massacre: A sad and bloody epilogue to the Indian Wars; occurred when the army tried to disarm and capture a band of Sioux who had fled the reservation

X

XYZ Affair: An affair involving French agents who brought the message from French foreign minister Charles Maurice Talleyrand that he would negotiate with Americans for a price

Y

Yahweh: Name for God used in the Hebrew Bible

Yalta: Site of a meeting between FDR, Churchill, and Stalin where they laid plans for postwar Europe

yellow fever: A disease transmitted to humans by mosquitoes

yellow journalism: Reporting of sensational stories, even bending the truth or twisting news to make it more exciting to sell more newspapers

Yorktown: The site of the defeat and surrender of the British army in the American colonies (October 19, 1781)

Z

Zimmerman telegram: German telegram that British intelligence intercepted and forwarded to the United States; promised Mexico part of the United States if Mexico would go to war with the United States, in the event that the United States decided to enter World War I

Index

A

abolition/abolitionists, 220–21, 261–62, 264, 266, 270, 280
abortion, 580, 588, 614–15, 619, 625, 627
aces, 432
Adams, John, 52, 90, 96, 104–105, 117, 121, 134, 152–53
    presidency of, 149–52
    vice presidency of, 135, 149
Adams, John Quincy, 177, 181, 186–87
Adams, Samuel, 87, 88, 93, 95–96, 98
Adams-Onis Treaty, 177
Affluent Society, 544
Afghanistan, 585, 597, 599, 623, 632
AFL-CIO, 482
African Methodist Episcopal (AME) Church, 221–22, 327
Agent Orange, 558
Agnew, Spiro, 575
Agricultural Adjustment Act (AAA), 475, 478
Agricultural Adjustment Administration (AAA), 474
Agriculture, Department of, 396, 469
Aguinaldo, Emilio, 386, 400
Aid to Families with Dependent Children (AFDC), 596
airplanes, 409–10
Alabama, 174, 181, 273
Alamo, the, 236–37
Alaska,
    purchase of, 381
Albania, 527, 617
Albany Congress, 79
Albemarle, 34
Alcatraz, 455
alcoholic beverages, 213, 357, 392–93
Alcott, Louisa May, 212
Algonquin Indians, 65, 75
Alien and Sedition Acts, 151–52, 161
Alito, Samuel Jr., 627, 637
Allen, Ethan, 102, 110
Allen, Richard, 221, 327
Alliance for Progress, 543
Allied Expeditionary Force (AEF), 510–11
Allies (WWI), 418
Allies (WWII), 496
al-Qaeda, 623, 631
Amendment I, 141
Amendment II, 141
Amendment III, 141
Amendment IV, 141
Amendment V, 141
Amendment VI, 141
Amendment VII, 141
Amendment VIII, 141
Amendment IX, 141
Amendment X, 141
Amendment XII, 153, 161
Amendment XIII, 313
Amendment XIV, 316–17, 556, 637
Amendment XV, 322–23
Amendment XVI, 392, 407
Amendment XVII, 392, 407
Amendment XVIII, 213, 392–93, 407, 451
Amendment XIX, 393, 407
Amendment XX, 472
Amendment XXI, 392, 452
Amendment XXII, 537
Amendment XXIV, 554
Amendment XXV, 575
Amendment XXVII, 608
America First committees, 500
American Board of Commissioners for Foreign Missions (ABCFM), 226, 233
American Expeditionary Force, 431, 470
American Federation of Labor (AFL), 348, 407, 482
American Independent party, 565
American Recovery and Reinvestment Act, 629
American Samoa, 381
American Spelling Book, 212
Americans with Disabilities Act, 608, 638
American System, 181–83
American Volunteer Group (AVG), 501
Amish, 61–62
amnesty, 313, 583
Anabaptists, 61–62
Anaconda Plan, 283–84
An American Dictionary of the English Language, 212
anarchists, 348, 444
Anderson, John, 590
Anderson, Robert, 275
André, John, 110
Andropov, Yuri, 600
Anglican Church. *See* Anglicanism
Anglicanism,
    elements of Roman Catholicism in, 20, 25–26
    forming of, 55
    in America, 59–60, 70, 97, 224
Annapolis Convention, 126
Anschluss, 494
Anthony, Susan B., 393
Antietam, Battle of, 288–89
Anti-Federalist Papers, The, 134
Anti-Federalists, 133–35
Anti-Masonic Party, 194
anti-Semitic, 479, 492
Anzio, 509
Apache Indians, 376
Apollo, 560
Apollo I, 560
Appalachian Mountains, 39, 84, 165
appeasement, 495
Appomattox Court House, 306–307
April 6, 1917, 426–27
Arabic, 425
Arab Spring, 632
Arafat, Yasir, 627
architecture
    colonial style (Williamsburg style), 43
    Federalist style, 216
    Greek revival, 216
Argonne offensive, 434
Arizona, 13, 426
Arkansas, 275, 613
armistice, 434
Armour, Philip, 367
Armstrong, Louis, 454
Armstrong, Neil, 560
Army of Northern Virginia, 287, 292
Army of the Potomac, 286, 292
Arnold, Benedict, 102, 109–10, 496
art
    Federalist style, 215–16
    modern, 451
Arthur, Chester A., 343–44
Articles of Confederation, 120–26
Asbury, Francis, 221, 224
Ashburton, Lord, 240
assembly line, 409
assumption, 142
astrolabe, 4
astronauts. *See* space program
Atlanta, Battle of, 304
Atlanta Campaign, 304
Atlantic Charter, 501
Atlanta Compromise, 400
atomic bomb, 518, 520. *See also* nuclear weapons

Attlee, Clement, 517
attorney general, 139, 444, 448, 613, 637
Attucks, Crispus, 90
Auschwitz, 516
Austin, Stephen F., 234–35
Australia, 502, 503
Austria, 494–95
automobiles, 408–9
Axis powers, 493
Aztec Indians, 9, 12

B

Babcock, Orville, 323
baby boom, 545
Baker, Howard, 575, 584
Balkans, 617
Baltic countries, 496
Baltimore, 211
Baltimore, Lord. See Calvert, Cecilius
Baltimore & Ohio (B & O) Railroad, 210
bank holiday, 474
banking crisis, 473
Bank of the United States. See National Bank
Baptists, 135, 226
    General Association of Regular Baptist Churches (GARBC), 456
    form of church government, 57, 60
    in the colonial era, 40, 60
Barbary pirates, 125, 162–63
Barbary states, 163
barbed wire, 369
Barnum, P.T., 357
Barnum and Bailey Circus, 357
Barré, Isaac, 85, 88
Barrow, Clyde, 488
Barton, Clara, 288
Bataan, 502–3
Bataan Death March, 503
Bates, Katherine Lee, 370
Batista, Fulgencio, 535
battleship diplomacy, 403
Bay of Pigs, 535
Bay Psalm Book, 64
Beanes, Williams, 174
Bear Flag Republic, 248
bear market, 461
Beauregard, Pierre G.T., 275, 285
Bee, Barnard, 285–86
Begin, Menachem, 584
Belgium, 422, 496
Belknap, William, 323
Bell, Alexander Graham, 342
Bell, John, 272
Belleau Wood, 433
Benghazi, 629, 632, 634
Bering Strait, 9

Berlin airlift, 530
Berlin, Battle of, 517
Berlin Wall, 536, 601
Bible conferences, 413
Bible institutes, 413
Biddle, Nicholas, 194–95
Biden, Joe, 627, 632
Big Four, 435
big stick policy, 400–401, 403
Big Three, 515, 517–18
Billion-Dollar Congress, 345
Bill of Rights, 135, 139–40
Bingham, George Caleb, 215
Bingham, Hiram, 382
bin Laden, Osama, 623, 631
Biola University, 413
Birney, James, 241
bison, 373
Black Bart, 372
Blackbeard. See Teach, Edward
Black Codes, 313
Black Hand, 418
Black Hawk War, 195
Black Lives Matter, 633
black power, 562
Black Thursday, 461, 465
Black Tuesday, 461, 466
Bladensburg, Battle of, 173
Blaine, James G., 344, 379
blitzkrieg, 495–96
blockade (of Southern ports), 283
blockade runners, 298
Blue Lives Matter, 633
Bocks Car, 518
Boland Amendment, 602
Bolívar, Simón, 177
Bolshevik Revolution, 431
Bonhomme Richard, 113
Bonus Army, 470
Boone, Daniel, 148, 209
Booth, John Wilkes, 306
border states, 299–300
Bosnia, 617
Boston, Massachusetts, 29
Boston Massacre, 88–90
Boston Massacre engraving, 89
Boston, siege of, 102–3
Boston Tea Party, 94–95
Bow, Clara, 453
Bowie, Jim, 237
Boxer Rebellion, 380
boycotts, 88
Bradbury, William, 359
Braddock, Edward, 79
Braddock's Road, 79, 209
Bradford, William, 27–28
Bradley, Omar, 533
Brady Bill, 614

Bragg, Braxton, 295–96
Brainerd, David, 65
Brain Trust, 474
Brandywine, Battle of, 109
bread lines, 483
Breckinridge, John C., 272
Breed's Hill, 103
Brezhnev, Leonid, 600
Briand, Aristide, 445
Britain, 526, 606. *See also specific wars with America*
    colonial wars with France, 75–81
    colonization, 6, 15–17, 20–36
    in Civil War, 301
    in World War II, 497–98
Britain, Battle of, 497
Brooks, Preston, 266
Brown, John, 266, 270–71
Brown University, 69
Brown v. Board of Education of Topeka, Kansas, 547, 555
Bryan, William Jennings, 351, 386, 394, 403–4, 419, 424, 456–57
Buchanan, James, 265, 272–73
budget deficit, 596
Buena Vista, Battle of, 247
buffalo, 373–74
Buffalo Bill Cody's Wild West Show, 357
Bulfinch, Charles, 216
Bulgaria, 527
Bulge, Battle of the, 511
bull market, 460
Bull Moose Party, 406
Bull Run, First Battle of, 285–86
Bull Run, Second Battle of, 287–88
Bummers, 305
Bunau-Varilla, Philippe, 401–2
Bunker Hill, Battle of, 102–3
Burgoyne, John, 109
Burke, Edmund, 102
Burnside, Ambrose, 289
Burr, Aaron, 149, 152–53, 166
Burr-Hamilton duel, 166
Burroughs, Edgar Rice, 486
Burwell v. Hobby Lobby, 638
bus boycott, 547–48
Bush, George H. W., 589, 603–4, 607–10
Bush, George W., 619–21, 621–27, 637
busing, 567
Butler, Andrew, 266
Butler, Elizur, 196
Butler, Pierce, 476

C

Cabinet—first, 139–40. *See also separate departments*
Cabot, John, 6

Calhoun, John C., 171, 181, 183, 188, 191–93, 245, 256, 259–60, 575
Calhoun Resolutions, 256
California, 243–44, 248, 249, 257–59
California gold rush, 257–58, 364
Calley, William, 569
Calvert, Cecilius (Lord Baltimore), 34
Calvin, John, 8, 102
Cambodia, 502, 534, 557, 569, 570
Camden, Battle of, 112, 115
campaigns, presidential. *See* elections
Camp David Accords, 584–85
camp meetings, 225
Canada, 16, 75–76, 172, 562
canals, 209–10
Canal Zone, 401–2, 584
Cane Ridge, 225
Cannon, Joseph, 404
Capone, Al, 455
caravel, 4
Caribbean, 5, 421
Carnegie, Andrew, 337–38
Carnegie Steel, 338
Carolina colonies, 34–35. *See also* North Carolina; South Carolina
carpetbaggers, 319–20
Carranza, Venustiano, 420
Carson, Ben, 634
Carter, Jimmy, 568, 574, 582–88, 590–91
Carter Doctrine, 585
Cartwright, Peter, 190
Carver, George Washington, 411
Carver, Moses, 411
Casablanca, 509
Casey, William, 602
Cass, Lewis, 256
Castro, Fidel, 535, 633–34
Castro, Raul, 633
catechism, 44
Cato, 133–34
cattle drive, 365–66
caucus, 186
Cayuse Indians, 234
Ceausescu, Nicolae, 604–5
Central America, 9, 258, 401, 421, 594, 597–99
Central American Mission, 382–83
Central High School, 547
Central Intelligence Agency (CIA), 525, 535, 538
Central Pacific Railroad, 362–63
Central Powers, 418
Century of Dishonor, A, 377
Challenger, 560
Chamberlain, Neville, 495
Chambers, Whittaker, 539
Champlain, Samuel de, 75

Chancellorsville, Battle of, 289
Chaplin, Charlie, 453
Charles I, 24, 34
Charles II, 32
Charleston (Charles Town), S.C., 38, 45, 51, 210, 316
   Siege of, 114–15
charter colony, 24
Chase, Sarah, 315
Château-Thierry, 433
Chattanooga,
   Battle for, 296
checks and balances, 131
Cheney, Richard, 619
Chennault, Claire, 501
Chernenko, Konstantin, 600
Cherokee Indians, 11, 195–96
Chesapeake affair, 170
Chesapeake Bay, 21, 116, 174
Chesapeake, USS, 173
Cheyenne Indians, 373
Chiang Kai-shek, 531, 568
Chickamauga, Battle of, 295–96
Chickasaw Indians, 11
child labor, 347
China, 493, 526
   Communist, 531, 567–68, 588
   Nationalist. *See* Taiwan
Chisholm Trail, 366
Choctaw Indians, 11
Chosin, 532
Christian and Missionary Alliance, 382
Christian Broadcasting Network (CBN), 588
Christian Coalition, 615
Christian Science, 228
Christian Science Monitor, 228
Christmas, 356
church buildings, colonial, 63–64
Churchill, Winston, 39, 494, 497, 509, 515, 517, 527
Church of England, 20, 25, 55, 224. *See also* Anglicanism
Church of Jesus Christ of Latter-Day Saints, 228
Cincinnati, 167
circuit riding, 224
circumnavigate, 7
city commission, 391
city manager, 391
Civilian Conservation Corps (CCC), 474–75
civil rights, 546, 553–54
Civil Rights Act, 316
Civil Rights Act of 1964, 554
civil rights movement, 546–49, 561
Civil Service Commission, 344

civil service reform, 343–44
Civil War, 249, 282–306
   casualties, 308
   causes, 279–81
   names of, 279
   Northern/Southern comparisons, 282–83
Civil Works Administration (CWA), 475
Clark, George Rogers, 113, 164
Clark, Mark, 509
Clark, William, 164–65
Clay, Henry, 171, 181, 184, 186–87, 193–94, 240, 259
Clayton Antitrust Act, 407
Clean Air Act, 578
Clean Water Act, 578
Clemenceau, Georges, 435
Clemens, Samuel Langhorne. *See* Twain, Mark
Cleveland, Grover, 344–45, 351, 382
Clinton, Bill, 609–610, 613–19
Clinton, DeWitt, 176, 209
Clinton, George, 134–35
Clinton, Hillary Rodham, 614, 627, 629, 633–35
clipper ships, 211
coalition of the willing, 624
Cody, William "Buffalo Bill," 357
Coercive Acts. *See* Intolerable Acts
Coffin, Levi, 262
Coker, Daniel, 222
Cold Harbor, Battle of, 303
Cold War, 525, 527–31, 535–36, 568, 585, 604
Cole, Thomas, 216
Colfax, Schuyler, 323
Collectivization, 494
Collins, Edward, 336
Colombia, 401–2
Colonies, Thirteen 20–36. *See also* individual colonies
   French threat to, 75–81
   growing rift with Britain, 84
Colorado, 364–65
Colt, Samuel, 204
Columbia, 560
Columbia River, 165, 242
Columbia University, 141, 412
Columbus, Christopher, 5
Comanche Indians, 373
comic strips, 486
commerce raiders, 379
Committees of Correspondence, 93–94
Common Sense, 104, 134
communications, 341–42
Communism/Communists, 450, 491, 570, 594

during the Cold War, 526–32, 534–36, 604
during World War II, 494
compass, 4
Compromise of 1850, 259–60
Compromise of 1877, 329
Compromise Tariff of 1833, 193
Comstock Lode, 365
Concord, Battle of, 98–100
Confederacy, 275
Confederate army/forces, 284, 290
Confederate States of America. *See* Confederacy
Confederation. *See* government: Confederation
Congregationalists, 57, 226, 227
   See also Congregational form of church government
Congregational form of church government, 57
Congress of Industrial Organizations (CIO), 482
Conkling, Roscoe, 343–44
Connecticut,
   colonization, 29–30
Connecticut Compromise. *See* Great Compromise
conquistadores, 12
conscription. *See* draft
conservation, 397–98
Constitution, 120, 129–32, 300
   amendments, 132. *See also individual amendments*
   flexibility, 131–32
   ratification, 133–36. *See also* government, Federal
Constitutional Convention, 126–32, 139, 142
Constitutional Union Party, 272
Constitution, USS, 172
containment, 528
Continental Congress, 102
   First, 96–97
   Second, 102, 120
Continental dollars, 124
Contract with America, 615
Contras, 598, 602
Conwell, Russell, 357
Coolidge, Calvin, 448–49
Cooper, James Fenimore, 216
Cooper, Peter, 210
Copperheads, 300
Coral Sea, Battle of, 503–4
corduroy roads, 209
Cornwallis, Charles, 115–17
Coronado, Francisco de, 12–13
Corregidor, 503

corrupt bargain, 186–87
Cortés, Hernando, 12
cotton, 206–7, 282, 301
cotton gin, 207
Coughlin, Charles, 479
counterculture, 563
Countess of Scarborough, 113
County Election, The, 215
covenant, 29
cowboys, 366
cowcatcher, 210
Cowpens, Battle of, 116
Cox, James M., 447
Crane, Stephen, 356
Crater Lake National Park, 398
Crawford, William H., 186–87
Crazy Horse, 375–76
Crédit Mobilier Scandal, 323
Creek Indians, 11, 190
Crimea, 633
Crittenden, John J., 274
Croatoan, 16, 20
Crockett, Davy, 236–37
Cronkite, Walter, 574
Crosby, Bing, 485
Crosby, Fanny, 359
Cross of Gold, 351
Cuba, 12, 383–85, 535–36, 598–99, 633–34
Cuban missile crisis, 535–36
Cumberland Gap, 148, 232
Cumberland Road. *See* National Road
Custer, George Armstrong, 375–76
Custer's Last Stand, 376
Czechoslovakia, 495, 527

D

Daladier, Édouard, 495
dame schools, 44
Dare, Virginia, 16
dark horse, 240
Darrow, Clarence, 457
Dartmouth College, 69
Darwin, Charles, 355, 450
Darwinism, 450
   Reform Darwinism, 355
   Social Darwinism, 355
Daugherty, Harry, 447–48
Davies, Samuel, 86
David, General Benjamin, 504
Davis, Jefferson, 273, 275, 287, 298, 304, 308, 312
Dawes, Charles, 447
Dawes, William, 98
Dawes Act, 377
Dawes Plan, 447
Dayton Accords, 617

D-day, 509–11
Debs, Eugene V., 349, 394
Decatur, Stephen, 175
December 7, 1941, 502
Declaration of American Rights, 97
Declaration of Independence, 102, 105, 218
Declaratory Act, 87
Deere, John, 205
Defense, Department of, 622
Defense of Marriage Act (DOMA), 616, 637
deficit spending, 468
de Gaulle, Charles, 509
de Grasse, Admiral, 116–17
deism, 224
de Kalb, Baron, 112
de Lasalle, Robert, 75
Delaware, 299
   colonization, 34
delegated powers, 162
De Lôme, Enrique Dupuy, 383–84
De Lôme letter, 383
democracy, 124
Democratic Party/Democrats, 187, 198, 272
   progressivism in, 394, 406
Democratic-Republicans, 144, 187
Democratization. *See* Government, Federal
Dempsey, Jack, 453
Denmark, 496
Denver, 364
Depression, Great. *See* Great Depression
depressions. *See* economic conditions
DePriest, Oscar, 454
Description of the World, 3
desegregation. *See* segregation
de Soto, Hernando, 14
détente, 568, 585
Detroit, 173, 408, 561
Dewey, George, 385
Dewey, John, 412, 546
Dewey, Thomas, 515
Dias, Bartholomeu, 5
Díaz, Porfirio, 419–20
Dickinson, John, 120, 128
Diem, Ngo Dinh, 534–35
Dien Bien Phu, Battle of, 534
Dillinger, John, 487, 488
Diners Club, 545
direct democracy, 390–91
Directory, 150
direct primaries, 390
diseases. *See* epidemics
disenfranchisement, 320, 398
Disney, Walt, 485

District of Columbia–slave trade, 259
Dix, Dorothea, 213
Dixiecrats, 538
Dodge City, 366
Dole, Bob, 616
Dole, Sanford, 382
dollar diplomacy, 405
Dominican Republic, 421
domino theory, 534, 570
Donner, George, 238
Doolittle, Jimmy, 503
doughboys, 429
Douglass, Frederick, 220–21, 317
Douglas, Stephen A., 256, 263, 267–68, 272–73
draft,
    Civil War, 298–99
    World War I, 427–28
    World War II, 500
Drake, Francis, 14–15
Dred Scott decision, 267
drug abuse, 588
dry farming, 368
Du Bois, W.E.B., 399–400
Dukakis, Michael, 603
Duke, James Buchanan, 340
Dunkers, 40
Dunkirk, 496
Dust Bowl, 484
Dutch. *See* Netherlands
Dutch Reformed, 62
Dwight, Timothy, 224–25
Dynamic Conservatism, 541

E

Eagle lunar module, 560
Eagleton, Thomas, 571
Eakins, Thomas, 356
Earhart, Amelia, 488
Earp, Wyatt, 372
Eastern Europe, 353, 527–28, 601, 604
Eastern Woodlands Indians, 11
East India Company, 94
Eclectic Readers, 213
economic conditions,
    Cold War era, 529, 536–37, 543–45
    Great Depression, 461–62, 465–71, 499
    World War I, 428–29
    World War II, 505
Economic Recovery Tax Act of 1981, 596
ecumenical movement, 549
Eddy, Mary Baker, 228
Edison, Thomas Alva, 342
education,
    in the colonies, 29, 44–45
    in Northwest Territory, 123

progressive education, 410–12
public education, 212–13
Edward VI, 55
Edwards, Jonathan, 55, 65, 66, 67–68, 166
effigy, 87
Egypt, 584, 606, 632
Einstein, Albert, 451
Eisenhower, Dwight D., 508–9, 525, 533–34, 541, 591
El Alamein, Battle of, 508
elections, of 1796, 149–50; of 1800, 152–53; of 1824, 186–87; of 1828, 187–88; of 1832, 194; of 1836, 197–98; of 1840, 199–200; of 1844, 240–41; of 1848, 256–57; of 1852, 260–61; of 1856, 265; of 1860, 272–73; of 1864, 305; of 1868, 322; of 1872, 325–26; of 1876, 327–28; of 1880, 343–44; of 1884, 344; of 1888, 345; of 1892, 346; of 1896, 351–52; of 1900, 386; of 1908, 403–4; of 1912, 405–7; of 1916, 425; of 1920, 437–38, 447; of 1924, 448; of 1928, 449–50; of 1932, 465, 471–72; of 1936, 480–81; of 1940, 500; of 1944, 525; of 1946, 537; of 1948, 538–39; of 1952, 541; of 1960, 541–42; of 1964, 554–55; of 1968, 564–66; of 1972, 571; of 1976, 582–83; of 1980, 589–91; of 1984, 599–600; of 1988, 603–4; of 1992, 609–10; of 1996, 616–17; of 2000, 619–21; of 2004, 625; of 2008, 627–28; of 2010, 630; of 2012, 632; of 2016, 634–35; progressive changes, 390–91
Electoral College, 132, 185, 620
electricity, 342
Eliot, Charles, 342
Eliot, John, 65
Eliot, T. S., 450, 451
Elizabeth I, 15
Ellis Island, 354
Ellsberg, Daniel, 569, 574
Ellsworth, Oliver, 129
El Salvador, 597–98
Emancipation Proclamation, 289, 301–2
Embargo Act, 170, 181
embryonic stem cell research, 626
Emergency Banking Act, 474
Emergency Relief and Construction Act, 469
Emerson, Ralph Waldo, 214, 216
energy crisis, 577–78
Engel v. Vitale, 555
England. *See* Britain
Enlightenment, 99, 102, 160
Enola Gay, 518
entertainment, 485–87

    colonial era, 50–52
    films, 485
    Gilded Age, 356–57
    movies, 485
    radio, 485–86
    sports: baseball, 356–57; basketball, 357; bicycling, 357; croquet, 357; football, 357; golf, 357; tennis, 357;
    television, 544–46
environmental movement, 578
Environmental Protection Agency, 578
epidemics, 41–42
Equal Opportunity Commission, 554
Equal Rights Amendment, 580–81
Equiano, Olaudah, 24
Era of Good Feelings, 176–78, 185
Erie Canal, 209–10
Espionage and Sedition Acts, 429
established denominations, 55
Ethiopia, 492
eugenics, 398
evangelism. *See* missions
Everett, Edward, 291
evolution. *See* Darwinism
Ewell, Richard, 290
executive orders, 632

F

Fair Deal, 537–38
Fair Oaks, Battle of, 287
faith-based initiatives, 626
faith missions, 382
Fall, Albert B., 447–48
Fallen Timbers, Battle of, 167
Falwell, Jerry, 588–89
Family and Medical Leave Act, 614
Farmers' Alliance, 350
Farragut, David G., 294
fascism, 470, 491–92
Fascist Party, 491
Fast and Furious, 629
Faubus, Orval, 547
Faulkner, William, 451
Federal Bureau of Investigation (FBI), 372, 488, 634
Federal Deposit Insurance Corporation (FDIC), 477
Federal Emergency Management Administration (FEMA), 626
Federal Emergency Relief Administration (FERA), 475, 483
Federal Farm Board, 468
Federalism, 131–32
Federalist, The, 130, 134
Federalist Papers, The, 134
Federalist Party/Federalists, 144–45, 176
Federalists (constitutional), 133–34

Federal Reserve Act, 407
Federal Reserve, 460, 462
Federal Trade Commission Act, 407–8
Feminine Mystique, 580
feminists, 580–81
Ferdinand, Archduke Francis (Franz), 418, 421
Ferguson, Patrick, 115–16
Ferraro, Geraldine, 600
Fifty-four-forty or fight!, 242
Fillmore, Millard, 260, 265
Finland, 496
Finlay, Carlos, 402
Finney, Charles, 212, 226–27
Fire-Eaters, 261–62
fireside chats, 474
Fisk, James, 323
Fitzgerald, F. Scott, 450, 451
flaming youth, 452
flappers, 452
Florida, 13, 81, 273, 460
    Spanish rule, 177, 190
Floyd, "Pretty Boy", 488
Flying Tigers, 501
Fonck, Paul-René, 432
Fonda, Jane, 562
Food Administration, 428
Foote, Andrew, 297
Forbes, Charles, 448
Force Bill, 193
Ford, Gerald, 570, 574–76, 582–83, 589
Ford, Henry, 408–9
Ford Motor Company, 409
Fordney-McCumber Tariff, 446
Forest Service, U.S., 398
Forrest, Nathan Bedford, 283
Fort Donelson, 292–93
Fort Duquesne, 78–79, 80. *See also* Pittsburgh
Fort Greenville, Treaty of, 167
Fort Henry, 292–93
Fort Leavenworth, 247
Fort McHenry, 173–74
Fort Necessity, 78, 79
Fort Sumter, 274–75
Fort Ticonderoga, 102, 110
Fort Washington, 167
forty-niners, 257–58
Foster, Stephen, 217
Fourteen Points, 430–31
Fox, Charles James, 102
Fox, George, 60–61
Fox Indians, 195
France, 526
    colonial wars with Britain, 75–81
    during French Revolution, 112, 145
    Indochina, 501–2, 534

Mexico, 378
New World, 16
World War I era, 421, 431, 433, 435
World War II era, 494, 496–97, 509
Franklin, Benjamin, 47, 51, 68, 79, 95, 105, 117, 133, 135, 139
Fredericksburg, Battle of, 289
Freedmen's Bureau, 314–16
Free Market, 4
Freeport Doctrine, 267
Free-Soilers, 257
Free-Soil Party, 257
Frelinghuysen, Theodore, 66
Frémont, John C., 248, 265
French and Indian War, 78–81
French Reformed. *See* Huguenots
French Revolution, 145–46
Freud, Sigmund, 451, 546
Frick, Henry C., 349
Friedan, Betty, 580
Fuchs, Klaus, 540
Fugitive Slave Act, 261
Führer, 492
Fuller, Charles E., 550
Fulton, Robert, 209
Fundamentalism, 455–57
Fundamentalist-Modernist controversy, 456
Fundamentalists, 456
Fundamental Orders of Connecticut, 29–30
funding, 142

G

Gadsden, James, 250
Gadsden Purchase, 249–50
Gagarin, Yuri, 560
Gage, Thomas, 96–98, 102
Gama, Vasco da, 5
Garfield, James A., 343–44
Garner, John Nance, 471
Garrison, William Lloyd, 220, 262
Garvey, Marcus, 454
gas-and-water socialism, 391
Gaspee, 93
Gates, Horatio, 109
gay rights movement, 581
Gemini missions, 560
General Amnesty Act, 326
General Assembly, 526
Genêt, Citizen Edmond Charles, 146
George II, 77
George III, 81, 86, 95, 104, 117, 120
Georgia, 273, 303
    colonization, 35
German Reformed Church, 62
Germantown, Battle of, 109

Germany,
    in World War I, 421–25, 433–34, 436
    in World War II, 492–98, 502, 511, 516–17
    war reparations, 436
    See also German settlers/immigrants
Germany, East, 527, 530, 536
Germany, West, 529–30
Geronimo, 376
Gerry, Elbridge, 133
Gettysburg Address, 291
Gettysburg, Battle of, 290–91
Ghent, Treaty of, 175
ghettos, 516
Gibbons v. Ogden, 162
Gibson, Charles Dana, 357
Gibson girl, 357
Gideon v. Wainwright, 555
Gilbert Islands, 502
Gilded Age, 335–59
Gingrich, Newt, 615
glasnost, 600
Glenn, John, 560
Glidden, Joseph, 369
Goforth, Jonathan and Rosalind, 382
gold,
    in Alaska, 381
    in California, 257–58
    in New World, 4, 12
goldbugs, 351
gold standard, 351
Goldwater, Barry, 554–55, 581, 587, 589
Gompers, Samuel, 348, 407
Goodman, Benny, 486
Goodnight-Loving Trail, 366
Gorbachev, Mikhail, 600–601
Gore, Al, 619–21
Gorgas, William, 402
Gorsuch, Neil, 638
Gould, Jay, 323
government,
    bicameral, 127–28
    bureaucracy/regulation, 396–97
    centralization/decentralization of, 120, 139, 330
    Colonial, 24
    Confederation, 120–26
    democratization, 185
    Federal authority increased during the Cold War era, 541; increased during Great Depression/FDR's Presidency, 468–69, 475, 477; increased by Progressivism, 391; increased during Reconstruction, 330; increased during World War II, 505–6
    unicameral, 120

gradual emancipation, 221
Graham, Billy, 550
Graham, Sylvester, 212
Grand Canyon, 13
grandfather clause, 398
Grange, the, 350
Grant, Ulysses S., 244, 249, 292–96, 302–3, 306–7, 322–25
Grantism, 322
Great Awakening,
 First, 66–70, 83, 185
 Second, 223–27
Great Britain. *See* Britain
Great Compromise, 127–28
Great Depression, 461–62, 465–71, 499
Great Lakes, 121, 166, 177
Great Northern Railroad, 337, 364
Great Plains, 165, 368–69, 465
Great Recession, 629
Great Society, 553–55, 579
Great Wagon Road, 39
Great War. *See* World War I
Great White Fleet, 403
Greece, 353, 528–29
Greeley, Horace, 325, 353
Green Mountain Boys, 102
greenbacks, 325–26
Greene, Nathanael, 116
Greenglass, David, 540
Greenland, 501
Greer, 501
Grenada, 598–99
Grenville, George, 85
Grimké sisters, 220
gross national product (GNP), 469
Guadalcanal, 512
Guadalupe Hidalgo, Treaty of, 249
Guam, 7, 385, 502, 512
guerilla warfare, 79, 80
Guilford Court House, 116
Guiteau, Charles J., 343
Gulf of Tonkin resolution, 557, 569–70

H

Haiti, 421, 617
Half-breeds, 343–44
Half-Way Covenant, 57, 59, 66, 69
Hamas, 627
Hamilton, Alexander, 126, 128, 134–35, 139, 141–42, 144, 149–50, 166
Hampton, Wade, 327
Hancock, John, 88, 98, 134
Hancock, Winfield S., 343
Harding, Warren G., 437–38, 443–45, 447–48
hard money, 124
Harlan, John, 556

Harlem Hellfighters, 427
Harlem Renaissance, 454
Harmony Society, 214
Harpers Ferry, 270–71
Harrison, Benjamin, 345
Harrison, William Henry, 167–69, 173, 197, 199–200, 239
Hartford Convention, 176, 192
Harvard College, 29, 59, 69, 227
Hauptmann, Bruno, 487
Hawaii, 381–82, 386, 502
Hawthorne, Nathaniel, 217
Hay, John, 380, 402
Hayes, Rutherford B., 328–29, 376, 619
Haymarket Riot, 348
Hayne, Robert Y., 192
Hays, Mary. *See* Molly Pitcher
headrights, 20
Head Start, 554
Hearst, William Randolph, 383
Heinz, H. J., 341
Hemingway, Ernest, 451
Henry, Patrick, 85–86, 96–98, 134–35
Henry VIII, 55
Hepburn Act, 396
Hessians, 101–2, 107
Hickok, James Butler "Wild Bill," 370–71
High-church Anglicans, 56, 60
Hill, James J., 336–37
Hindenburg, 488
hippies, 563
Hirohito, 493, 526
Hiroshima, 518, 520
Hispaniola, 11–12
Hiss, Alger, 539
Hitler, Adolf, 436, 485, 492, 494–95, 497, 500, 501, 507, 517, 525
hoboes, 465, 483–84
Ho Chi Minh, 534
Holland, 496
Holmes, Oliver Wendell, 430
Holocaust, 516
Homeland Security, Office of, 623–24
Homer, Winslow, 356
Homestead Act, 368
Homestead Strike, 348–49
Honduras, 403
Honecker, Erich, 604–5
Hong Kong, 502
Hood, John B., 304
Hooker, Joseph "Fighting Joe," 289
Hooker, Thomas, 29
Hoover, Herbert, 428, 448–50, 465–71
Hoover, J. Edgar, 488
Hooverizing, 428
Hoovervilles, 466
horizontal integration, 339

hornbook, 44
Hornet USS, 503
Horseshoe Bend, Battle of, 174–75
Hosanna-Tabor Evangelical Lutheran Church & School v. Equal Employment Opportunity Commission, 638
House of Burgesses, 23, 85, 96
House of Representatives, 128
House Un-American Activities Committee, 539
Houston, Sam, 235–37, 241
Howard, Oliver, 304, 315, 377
Howard University, 304
Howe, Elias, 204
Howe, William, 106, 109
Hubble telescope, 560
Hudson, Henry, 16, 31
Hudson River school, 215–16
Huerta, Victoriano, 420
Hughes, Charles Evans, 425, 445, 476
Hughes, Langston, 454
Huguenots, 62
humanism, secular, 412
human rights, 583–84
Humphrey, Hubert H., 564–66
Hungary, 527
Hunt, Robert, 59
Hurricane Katrina, 626
Huss, John, 62
Hussein, Saddam, 605, 607, 624–25, 627
Hutchinson, Anne, 31
hymns and gospel songs, 217

I

Idaho, 232–33, 346
idealism,
 under Wilson, 419
Il Duce, 491
Illinois, 181, 300
immigrants/immigration,
 German, 39–40
 Irish, 39–40
 New, 353–54, 454
 restrictions, 354, 403
impeachment, 317, 618
imperialism, 380–81
implied powers, 162
impressment, 146, 170
Inca Indians, 9
Inchon, 531
income taxes. *See* taxes
indenture, 20
indentured servants, 20, 23, 36
Independence Hall, 93
independent treasury, 199, 242
Indiana, 181, 300

Indian removal, 195–96
    Policy, 195
Indian Reorganization Act, 377
Indians. *See also* individual tribal names
    and diseases, 11, 12
    and English colonists, 22, 27, 30, 75
    and Thanksgiving, 28
    at Horseshoe Bend, 174–75
    during Revolution, 110
    French alliances with, 75, 79
    in Kentucky, 148
    in Northwest Territory, 167
    Jackson's policies toward, 174–75, 177, 190, 195–96
    missionary efforts to, 64–65
    named by Columbus, 5
    removal of. *See* Indian removal
    rights movement, 579
    sale of Manhattan, 32
Indian Territory, 196, 368, 372
Indian Wars, 82, 374–78
Indochina. *See* Southeast Asia
industrialism, 335–42. *See also* economic conditions
industry/industrial development, 203–5, 280, 335–42. *See also* industrialism
infant mortality, 353
inflation, 579, 587
initiative, 390
injunctions, 349
installment plans, 458
interchangeable parts, 204
Intermediate Nuclear Forces (INF) Treaty, 601
internal improvements, 182–83
internal tax, 85
international law, 423
International Space Station, 560
Interstate Commerce Act, 345
Interstate Commerce Commission (ICC), 396
interstate highway system, 541
Intolerable Acts, 95–96
Iran, 528, 574, 585–86, 633
Iran-Contra affair, 601–2
Iranian hostage crisis, 574, 586
Iraq, 605–7, 624, 631–32
ironclads, 286–87
iron curtain, 527, 604
Iroquois Indians, 75
Irving, Washington, 216
Isabella, queen of Spain, 5
Islamic State of Iraq and Syria (ISIS), 631
island hopping, 512
isolationism, 444, 499
Israel, 577, 584–85, 623, 627
Italy, 163, 353, 491–92, 509
Iwo Jima, 514

J

Jackson, Andrew, 174–75, 177, 181, 185–97, 235, 237
Jackson, Robert, 525
Jackson, Thomas J. "Stonewall," 249, 283, 285, 287–90, 297
Jacksonian democracy, 188, 215, 227
James I, 21, 23
James II (duke of York), 32
James, Frank, 371
James, Jesse, 371
Jamestown, 21–23, 116
Japan, 379, 403, 491, 493
    called Cipango, 5
    in World War II, 493, 501–4, 512–15, 518
Japanese internment camps, 503
Japanese-Nisei, 504
Jarratt, Devereaux, 45
Jay, John, 117, 134, 146–47, 161
Jay Treaty, 146–47
Jefferson, Thomas, 105, 122, 126, 134, 139, 144, 149–50, 152–53, 186, 216
    presidency, 159–64, 170
    religious views, 160
Jeffersonian Republicanism, 159–60
Jews, 516, 623
jihad, 623
Jim Crow laws, 398–99
Johns Hopkins Medical School, 410
Johnson, Andrew, 311–18, 618
Johnson, James Weldon, 454
Johnson, Lyndon B., 535, 553–58, 564, 579
Johnston, Albert Sidney, 293–94, 304
Johnston, Joseph E., 287, 296, 297, 306
joint resolution, 241
joint-stock companies, 21
Jones, John Paul, 113
Jones, J. W., 297
Jones, Sam, 359
Joseph, Chief (Nez Perce), 374, 377
judicial activism, 555
judicial review, 161
Judiciary Act of 1789, 140
Judiciary Act of 1801, 153, 160–61
Judson, Adoniram, 226, 382
June 6, 1944, 510
Jungle, The, 396–97
Justice, Department of, 540, 633

K

Kagan, Elena, 630
kamikazes, 514
Kanagawa, Treaty of, 379
Kansas, 366
    Bleeding Kansas, 265–66

Kansas City, 366
Kansas-Nebraska Act, 263
Kaskaskia, Illinois, 113
KDKA, 458–59
Kearny, 501
Kearny, Philip, 304
Kearny, Stephen, 247
Kellogg-Briand Pact, 445
Kellogg, Frank B., 445
Kelly, "Machine Gun," 488
Kelly, Oliver H., 350
Kemp, Jack, 603
Kennedy, Anthony, 627
Kennedy, Edward, 590
Kennedy, Jacqueline, 542–43
Kennedy, John F., 525, 534, 535, 541–43, 549, 553, 560, 620
Kennedy, Robert, 553, 564–65
Kent State, 569
Kentucky, 114, 148, 295, 299
Kentucky Resolutions, 152, 192
Kentucy-Tennessee Campaign, 295–96
Kerry, John, 625
Key, Francis Scott, 174
Khmer Rouge, 570
Khomeini, Ayatollah Ruhollah, 585–86
Khrushchev, Nikita, 536
King George's War, 77, 83
King, Martin Luther, Jr., 548–49, 553, 562, 564
Kings Mountain, Battle of, 115–16
King William's War, 77
Kissinger, Henry, 568, 570
Kitchen Cabinet, 191
Kitty Hawk, N.C., 410
Knights of Labor, 348
Know-Nothings, 264–65
Knox, Henry, 103, 139
Korea,
    North, 531–32
    South, 531–32
Korean War, 531–33
Kosovo, 617
Ku Klux Klan, 320–21, 454–55, 554
Kuwait, 605–6

L

labor unions, 348–49, 538
Lafayette, Marquis de, 112, 116, 423, 431
La Follette, Robert, 394
laissez-faire capitalism, 447
Lake Champlain, 109, 173
Lake Erie, 78, 173, 209–10
Lake Erie, Battle of, 173
Lake Michigan, 210
Landon, Alfred, 480–81
Land Ordinance of 1785, 122–23

Lanphier, Jeremiah, 229
Laos, 502, 534, 557, 569, 570
Latin America, 177, 402–3, 543
Latrobe, Benjamin, 216
Lawrence (Kansas), sack of, 265–66
Leadville, 365
League of Nations, 426, 430–31, 437, 515
    during World War II, 491–92, 494
Lebanon, 599, 601
Lee, Henry "Light-Horse Harry," 282
Lee, Mother Ann, 228
Lee, Richard Henry, 105
Lee, Robert E., 249, 271, 282, 283, 287–91, 297, 302–3, 306–7, 312
Leland, John, 135
LeMay, Curtis, 570
Lend-Lease Act, 501, 505
Lenin, Vladimir, 431
Lewinsky scandal, 617–18
Lewis and Clark Expedition, 164–65
Lewis, John L., 481–82
Lewis, Meriwether, 164–65
Lexington, Battle of, 98–100
Leyte Gulf, Battle of, 513–14
Liberal Republicans, 325
Liberator, 220
Liberty Party, 241
Libya, 632
Lieberman, Joseph, 619
Lightning, 211
Liliuokalani, Queen, 381–82
limited government, 130
limited war, 558
Lincoln, Abraham, 245, 267–70, 272–75, 291, 300–302, 305–6, 311
Lincoln, Benjamin, 114–15, 117
Lincoln-Douglas debates, 267–69
Lindbergh, Charles A., 453, 487, 500
Lindbergh, Charles A. Jr., 487
Lindbergh kidnapping, 487
literacy tests, 398, 554
literature, 216–17, 356, 451
Little Bighorn, Battle of, 376
Little Rock, Arkansas, 547
Little Sisters of the Poor v. Burwell, 638
Livingstone, Robert, 105, 163
Lloyd George, David, 435
Locke, Alain, 454
Locke, John, 101–2, 105
Lodge, Henry Cabot, 437
Logan, John, 285
log cabin campaign, 199–200
Log College, 67
London, Jack, 356
London Company, 21
Long, Huey, 478–79
Long Island, Battle of, 106

Long, Luz, 485
loose constructionists, 143
Los Angeles, 248, 413, 561
Lost Colony, 16
Louis XIV, 62, 75
Louis XVI, 145
Louisiana, 181, 273
    French, 75
Louisiana Purchase, 162–65
Low-church Anglicans, 56, 59
Loyalists, 95, 101, 121
Ludendorff, Erich von, 433
Luftwaffe, 495–97
Lusitania, 424–25
Luther, Martin, 7, 61
Lutherans, 61
Luxembourg, 496
lynched, 320, 371

M

MacArthur, Douglas, 470, 502, 512, 518, 531–33
Machen, J. Gresham, 456
Macon's Bill Number Two, 171
Maddox, 557
Madero, Francisco, 419–20
Madison, Dolley, 173
Madison, James, 130, 134–35, 141–42, 161, 186
    "Father of the Constitution," 126, 171
    presidency of, 170–75
    Virginia Plan, 127
Magellan, Ferdinand, 6
Maginot Line, 494, 499
Maine, 181, 184, 213, 240
Maine, USS, 384
malaria, 402
Manassas. *See* Bull Run
Manchuria, 403, 493
Manhattan Island, 32, 106
Manifest Destiny, 232, 362
Manila Bay, Battle of, 385
Mann, Horace, 212–13
Mannock, Edward "Mick," 432
Mao Zedong, 531, 532
Marbury, William, 161
Marbury v. Madison, 161
March on Washington, 548–49
March to the Sea, 304–5
Mariana Islands, 512–13
Marion, Francis ("Swamp Fox"), 115
market entrepreneurs, 336
Marshall, George C., 529
Marshall, John, 132, 153, 161–62, 166, 196
Marshall Islands, 512
Marshall Plan, 529

Marx, Karl, 450
Mary (Queen of England), 56
Maryland, 299
    colonization, 34
Mason, George, 129, 133, 134–35
Mason, James, 301
Mason, Lowell, 217
Massachusetts, 25–29
    Bay Colony, 28–29, 56
    colonization, 25–29
Massachusetts Bay Company, 28, 30
Masterson, Bat, 372
materialism, 57, 356, 562
Mather, Cotton, 41
Maximilian I, 378
Mayan Indians, 9
Mayflower, 26
Mayflower Compact, 26
Mayo Clinic, 410
McAuliffe, Anthony, 511
McCain, John, 627–29
McCanles, David, 370
McCarthy, Eugene, 564
McCarthy, Joseph, 540–41
McCarthyism, 540–41
McClellan, George B., 286–88, 300, 305
McCormick, Cyrus, 205
McCulloch v. Maryland, 162
McDowell, Irvin, 285–86
McGovern, George, 571, 574
McGready, James, 225
McGuffey, William H., 213
McKay, Donald, 211
McKinley, William, 346, 351, 383, 386, 389
McKinley Tariff, 346
McReynolds, James Clark, 476
Meade, George, 290–91
Meat Inspection Act, 396
meat-packing industry, 367
Medicaid, 555
Medicare, 555
medicine, 410, 636
Mediterranean, 528–29
Mein Kampf, 492
melting pot, 423
Mennonites, 61–62
mercantilism, 3–4,
Mercury project, 560
Meredith, James, 548
Merrimack, USS, 286–87
Mesa Verde National Park, 398
Methodists, 224, 227, 549–50
Mexican War (1846–48), 243–50
Mexico, 235, 243, 255
    conquered by Cortés, 12
Michigan, 122, 168

middle colonies,
    founding of, 31–34. *See also* individual colonies
Middle East, 528–29
Middle Passage, 24
midnight appointments, 153, 161
Midway, Battle of, 503–4
Midway Islands, 381
Military Reconstruction Act. *See* Reconstruction Act of 1867
militia, 97
Miller, Dorie, 505
Millerites, 227–28
Miller, William, 227–28
Mills, Samuel, 226
miners/mining, 364–65
Minnesota, 240
Minuit, Peter, 32
Minutemen, 97
Miranda v. Arizona, 555
Missionary Ridge, 296
missions, 64–65, 225–26, 382–83
Mississippi, 174, 181, 273
Mississippi River, 14, 76, 163, 205, 233–34, 283
    Civil War Campaign, 292–95
Missouri, 181, 184, 299, 366
Missouri Compromise, 184–85
Missouri River, 165
mobilization, 422
Model T, 409
modernism, 412
Molotov, Vyacheslav, 528
Mondale, Walter, 600
Mongrel Tariff, 344
Monitor, USS, 286–87
Monmouth, Battle of, 111–12
Monroe, James, 134, 163, 176–78, 185–86
Monroe Doctrine, 177–78, 402
Montana, 165
Montcalm, Marquis de, 80–81
Monterrey, Battle of, 246
Montezuma, 12
Montgomery, Bernard, 508
Montgomery bus boycott, 547–48
Monticello, 153, 216
Moody, Dwight L., 206, 297, 358–59, 382, 413
Moody Bible Institute, 413
Moon, Lottie, 382
Moral Majority, 615
Moravians, 35, 62, 101
Morgan, Daniel, 109, 116
Morgan, John Pierpont, 338, 340
Morgenthau, Henry, 483
Mormonism/Mormons, 228, 589
Mormon Trail, 228, 238

Morse, Samuel F. B., 211, 215
Mound Builders, 10–11
Mount Vernon, 126
muckrakers, 393–94
Mugwumps, 344
mujahideen, 599
Munich Conference, 495
Munn v. Illinois, 350
music, 217, 295. *See also* hymns and gospel songs
    rock, 545
Muslims, 3, 4
    merchants to China, 5
Mussolini, Benito, 470, 491–92, 495, 507, 509, 517
My Lai Massacre, 569

N

NAFTA, 614
Nagasaki, 518, 520
Napoleon III, 378
Napoleon Bonaparte, 151, 163–64, 170–71, 177
Nashville, 190
Nast, Thomas, 324–25
National Aeronautics and Space Administration, 560
National Association for the Advancement of Colored People (NAACP), 400
National Bank,
    first, 142–43, 161, 162
    second, 181–83, 193–95
National Conservation Commission, 398
National Council of Churches, 550
National Credit Corporation (NCC), 468
national debt, 596, 629
National Defense Education Act, 541
National Guard, 427, 561, 569
National Industrial Recovery Act (NIRA), 477–78
nationalism, 181
National Origins Act, 454
National Parks, 398
National Recovery Administration (NRA), 475, 477–78
National Republicans, 187
National Road, 39, 183, 209
National Security Act, 538
National Security Council, 538, 602
National Socialist German Workers' Party. *See* Nazism
National Voter Registration Act, 614
Naturalism, 356
Navajo code talkers, 504
Navy, Department of, 151

Navy, U.S.,
    in Spanish-American War, 384
    in World War II, 506, 512
Nazi Party, 492
Nazism/Nazis, 492
Nazi-Soviet nonaggression pact, 495
Nelson, "Baby Face," 488
Netherlands, 26, 62
Neutrality Act of 1939, 500
New Amsterdam. *See* New Netherland
Newburgh Conspiracy, 125
New Deal, 471, 473–75, 477–78
New Democrat, 609
New Economic Policy, 567
New England,
    Puritans in, 25, 28–29, 56–59
    settlement of, 25–31. *See also* individual colonies
New England Primer, 44
New France, 16, 75. *See also* Canada
New Freedom, 406–7
New Frontier, 541–43
New Guinea, 512
New Hampshire, 30
    colonization, 31
New Harmony, 214
New Jersey, 107
    College of. *See* Princeton
    colonization, 32
    Great Awakening in, 66
New Jersey Plan, 128
New Left, 562
New Measures, 226
New Mexico, 247, 249
New Nationalism, 406
New Netherland, 16–17, 31
New Orleans, 81, 163, 174–75, 294, 626
    Battle of, 175, 203
New Right, 588
New South, 340
newspapers, 217
    inciting the Spanish-American War, 383
New Sweden, 61
Newton, Sir Isaac, 451
New World colonization,
    Separatists in, 26
New York,
    colonization, 16–17, 31–32
    Revolutionary era, 106–7
New York City, 17, 32, 106, 526
New York draft riot, 299
New York World's Fair, 486–87
Nez Perce Indians, 233
Niagara Conference, 413
Niagara Falls, 172

Nicaragua, 598
Nimitz, Chester W., 503, 512
Nine-eleven. *See* September 11, 2001
Nixon, Richard M., 539, 541–42, 553, 565–71, 574–76, 589, 620
    pardon of, 576
Nobel Peace Prize, 403
"no man's land," 430
non-established church, 60
Normalcy, 443
Normandy invasion, 510–11
North American Free Trade Act (NAFTA), 614
North Atlantic Treaty Organization (NATO), 525, 529, 541, 617
North Carolina, 275
    colonization, 34
    colony, 35
    Revolutionary era, 116
North Dakota, 165
Northern Baptist Convention, 456
Northern Securities case, 395
North, Lord, 88
North, Oliver, 602
Northwest Ordinance of 1787, 123
Northwest Ordinances, 123, 260
Northwest Territory, 122–23, 167–68, 205
Norway, 496
no taxation without representation, 88
Notre Dame, 453, 604
November 11, 1918, 434
nuclear weapons, 531, 568, 585
nullification, 152, 191–92
    Virginia and Kentucky Resolutions, 152
Nuremberg trials, 525–26

O

Oakley, Annie, 357
Obama, Barak, 627–34, 637
Obamacare, 629–30
Obergefell v. Hodges, 637
Oberlin College, 226
O'Connor, Sandra Day, 599, 627
Office of Economic Opportunity (OEO), 554
Of Plymouth Plantation, 27
Oglethorpe, James, 35
Ohio, 167, 300
Ohio Gang, 447
Ohio River, 78, 166
oil embargo, 502, 577–78
Okies, 465, 484
Okinawa, 514–15
Oklahoma, 196
    land rushes, 368
Old Deluder Satan Act, 45

Old Ironsides, 172
Olive Branch Petition, 104
one man, one vote decisions, 556
"on the margin," 460
Open Door Policy, 380
open ranges, 366
Operation Barbarossa, 497–98
Operation Desert Shield, 605
Operation Desert Storm, 606
Operation Husky, 509
Operation Overlord, 510
Operation Torch, 508
Ordinance of 1784, 122
Ordinance of Secession, 273
Oregon, 232–34, 242–43
Oregon Territory, 177, 232
Oregon Trail, 238
Organization of Petroleum Exporting Countries (OPEC), 577
organized labor, 348, 444
Origin of Species, On the, 355
Orlando, Vittorio, 435
Orthodox Presbyterian Church, 456
Osceola, 195
O'Sullivan, John Louis, 232
Oswald, Lee Harvey, 553
"Over There!," 429
Owen, Robert, 214
Owens, Jesse, 485

P

Pacific Garden Mission, 413
Pahlavi, Mohammed Reza, 585–86
Paine, Thomas, 104
Palin, Sarah, 627–28
Palmer, A. Mitchell, 444
Panama, 401–2, 584
Panama Canal, 401–2, 421
Panama Canal Treaty, 584
Pan-Americanism, 379–80
Panic of 1819, 183
Panic of 1837, 198–99
Panic of 1857, 229
Panic of '73 (1873), 325–26
Panic of '93 (1893), 350
panzers, 496
Paris, Treaty of (War for Independence), 117, 121, 240
Paris, Treaty of (1763), 81
Paris Peace Talks, 559, 570
Parker, Bonnie, 488
Parker, Isaac Charles, 372–73
Parker, John, 98
Parks, Rosa, 548
Parliament, 85, 88
patents, 204
Paterson, William, 128, 134

Patient Protection and Affordable Care Act (PPACA), 629–30
Patriot Act, 624
Patriots, 100–101
Patton, George, 511
Paxton Boys, 95
Peace Corps, 543
peaceful coexistence, 536
Pearl Harbor, 491, 501–2
Pence, Mike, 635
Pendleton Act, 344
Pendleton, George, 344
Peninsular Campaign, 286
Penn, William, 32–33
Pennsylvania, 205
    colonization, 32–33
Pennsylvania Dutch, 40
Pentagon, 622
Pentagon Papers, 569, 574
People's Republic of China. *See* China, Communist
Pequot Indians, 30
perestroika, 600
perjury, 618
Perkins, Frances, 474
Perot, Ross, 609–10, 616
Perry, Matthew, 379
Perry, Oliver Hazard, 173
Pershing, John J. "Black Jack," 420, 433, 511
Persian Gulf, 606–7, 624
pet banks, 194
Petersburg, siege of, 305–6
Petition of Right, 85
Philadelphia, 96, 109, 126
philanthropy, 338
Philip II, 14
Philippines, 7, 385–86, 400–401, 502–3, 513
Pickett, George, 291
Pickett's Charge, 291
Pierce, Franklin, 261, 263, 265
Pike, Zebulon, 165
Pikes Peak, 165, 370
Pikes Peak gold rush, 364–65
Pilgrims, 25–28
Pinchot, Gifford, 398, 405
Pinckney, Charles Cotesworth, 129, 150, 152–53, 170
Pinckney, Thomas, 149–50
Pinkerton National Detective Agency, 372
Pinkertons, 372
pirates,
    Barbary, 125, 162–63
Pitcairn, John, 98–99
Pitcher, Molly, 111

Pitt, William, 80, 81–82, 102
Pittsburgh, 80, 84
Plains Indians, 373–74
Plains of Abraham, 80
plank roads, 209
platform, party, 194
Platt National Park, 398
Plessy v. Ferguson, 399, 547
Plymouth Colony, 26–28
Pocahontas, 22, 23, 65
Poe, Edgar Allan, 217
Poindexter, John, 602
Poland, 495–96, 527
political entrepreneurs, 336
political parties,
　emergence of, 143–44
　national conventions, 194
　nominating conventions, 194
Polk, James K., 240–43, 244
poll taxes, 398
Polo, Marco, 3
Ponce de León, Juan, 13
Pontiac/Pontiac's War, 82
Pony express, 211
Poor Richard's Almanack, 47, 113
Pope, John, 287–88
popular sovereignty, 132, 256, 265
Populism/Populists, 350–51, 398
Populist Party, 350–51
Portsmouth, Treaty of, 403
Portugal, 5
Portuguese explorers, 5
Post, Wiley, 488
Potomac River, 126, 142
Pot, Pol, 570
Potsdam, 517–18
Pottawatomie Massacre, 266
Poverty, War on, 554
Powdery, Terrence V., 348
Power of the purse, 84, 88, 93
Powhatan, 22
Prayer Meeting Revival, 229, 358. *See also* Religion, Revivals/Evangelism
Preamble, 132
Premillennialism, 227, 456
Presbyterians,
　in the colonial era, 62
Prescott, Samuel, 98, 102
President's Emergency Committee for Employment (PECE), 468
President's Organization for Unemployment Relief (POUR), 468
Princeton, Battle of, 107–8
Princeton Theological Seminary, 412–13
Princeton University, 69, 166
Princip, Gavrilo, 418, 421
Proclamation Line of 1763, 84

Proclamation of Neutrality, 146
Progressive Era, 389–415
Progressive Party, 406
Progressive Party (1948), 538
Progressivism/Progressive, 389–90. *See also* Progressive Era
Prohibition, 213, 392–93, 451–52
Promontory Point, 363
propaganda, 422
Prophet, the, 168–69
proprietary colony, 24
protective tariff, 181–82, 499
Protestant Reformation, 7–8, 44
Providence, Rhode Island, 30, 93, 204
Prussia, 78, 80
public works, 467
Public Works Administration (PWA), 475
Publius, 134
Pueblo Indians, 10
Puerto Rico, 12, 385
Pulaski, Count Casimir, 112
Pulitzer, Joseph, 383
Pullman Strike, 349
puppet governments, 517, 527
Pure Food and Drug Act, 396
Puritans,
　and education, 29, 44
　and founding of Massachusetts Bay Colony, 28–29
　beliefs of, 25–26, 56–57
　sermons of, 64
Purvis, Melvin, 488
Putin, Vladimir, 633
Putnam, Ann, 58

Q

Quakers, 32, 60–61, 101
Quartering Act, 85, 96
Quasi War, 150–51
Quayle, Dan, 604
Quebec, 75, 80–81
Quebec Act, 96
Quebec, Battle of, 80–81
Queen Anne's War, 76–77
Quisling, Vidkun, 496

R

racial discrimination, 561–62
　during the 1920s, 454–55
　during the Cold War era, 546–49
　during the Great Depression, 485
　during World War II, 504
　in Reconstruction, 313–17, 320–21
　in the Progressive Era, 398–400
racism. *See* racial discrimination
Radical Republicans, 311–12

radio, 459, 475
　talk, 614–15
railroads, 210, 283
　regulation of, 396, 428
　transcontinental, 362–63
Rainey, Joseph, 326
Raleigh, Sir Walter, 15, 21
Randolph, Edmund, 127, 133, 134–35, 139
range wars, 368
Rapp, George, 214
rationing, 505
Rauschenbusch, Walter, 412
Reagan, Ronald, 565, 582, 587, 589–91, 594–603
Reagan Doctrine, 597
Reaganomics, 594–95
Reagan Revolution, 594–97
Realism, 356
recall, 391
Reclamation Act, 397
Reconstruction, 311
　Congressional Reconstruction, 314–21
　Presidential Reconstruction, 311–14
Reconstruction Act of 1867, 317
Reconstruction amendments, 313, 316, 322–23, 330
Reconstruction Finance Corporation, 469, 541
Red Cross, 288, 430
Redeemers, 326–27
Red Scare, 444, 539–40
Reed, Walter, 402
referendum, 390–91
Reform Darwinism. *See* Darwinism
reform movements,
　Progressivism, 389–95
refugees, 315
regulars, 97
Regulators, 95
Rehnquist, William, 627
Reign of Terror, 145
relativity, theory of, 451
religion. *See also* individual denominations, groups, and movements
　American churches and slavery, 219
　church and State, 28, 30, 97, 588
　Cold War era, 549–50
　Gilded Age, 357–59
　in World War I, 431
　Jacksonian Era, 185
　persecution, 34, 45, 60, 62, 76, 96, 99
　Progressive Era, 412–14
　revivals, 66–70, 223–27, 229
　salvation, 7–8
　unorthodox, 227–28
Religious Right, 588–89, 615

Remington, Frederic, 383
Reno, Major Marcus, 376
reparation payments. *See* reparations
reparations, 436
Report on Public Credit, 142
Republic, 136
Republican Party/Republicans, 263–65
Republicans (Jeffersonians). *See* Democratic-Republicans
rescue missions, 358–59, 483
reservations, Indian, 374
Reuben James, 502
Revels, Hiram, 326–27
Revenue Act, 467
revenue tariff, 182
Revere, Paul, 83, 98
Revolution/Revolutionary War, 70, 127
  compared to French and Russian revolutions, 99. *See also* War for Independence
Rhineland, 494
Rhode Island, 127
  colony, 30–31
Rice, Luther, 226
Richmond, Virginia, 283–84, 287, 316
Richthofen, Manfred von, 432
Rickenbacker, Eddie, 432
Rickey, Branch, 544
Right of Rebellion, 105
Right-to-Life movement, 588
Riley, William Bell, 456
Ringling Bros., 357
Ringling, Charles, 357
Ringling, John, 357
Rio Grande, 244
road building, 209
Roanoke Colony, 15–16, 20
Roanoke Island, 15–16, 20
Roaring Twenties, 452
robber barons, 335–36
Roberts, John G., 627, 637–38
Robertson, Pat, 588–89, 603, 615
Robeson, Paul, 454
Robinson, Jackie, 544
Rockefeller, John D., 338–40
Rockefeller, Nelson, 565, 576
Rocky Mountains, 165, 363
Roe v. Wade, 580, 588
Rogers, Will, 475, 488, 596
Rolfe, John, 22, 23
Roman Catholicism, 7
  elements in Anglican Church, 20, 25–26
  Henry VIII's break from, 55
  in Canada, 96
  in Maryland, 34, 62
Romania, 495, 527

Romanticism, 216–17, 356
Romanticism (literature), 216–17
Rome-Berlin-Tokyo Axis, 493
Rommel, Erwin, 507–8, 509
Romney, Mitt, 632
Roosevelt, Eleanor, 485
Roosevelt, Franklin Delano, 447, 465, 471–75, 477–81, 500, 509, 515, 525
Roosevelt, Theodore, 386, 389, 394–98, 400–406
Roosevelt Corollary, 402–3
Rosecrans, William, 295–96
Rosenberg, Julius and Ethel, 539–40
Roth v. United States, 555
Rough Riders, 385
Royal Air Force (RAF), 497
royal colony, 24
Rural Electrification Administration (REA), 477
Rush-Bagot Treaty, 177
Russell, James Lowell, 244
Russell, William, 211
Russia, 353, 491, 493–94, 526. *See also* Soviet Union
Russian Revolution. *See* Bolshevik Revolution
Russo-Japanese War, 403
Rutgers, 69
Ruth, Babe, 453
Ryan, Paul, 632

S

Sacagawea, 165
Sacco, Nicola, 454
Sacco-Vanzetti case, 454
Sadat, Anwar, 584–85
Saipan, 512
Salem witch trials, 58–59
Salt II Treaty, 585
Salt Lake City, 228
Samoset, 27
Sanders, Bernie, 634
Sandinistas, 598
San Francisco, 211, 526
San Jacinto, Battle of, 235, 237
Sankey, Ira, 358
San Martín, José de, 177
Santa Anna, Antonio López de, 236–37, 247, 248–50
Santa Fe Trail, 39, 238, 247
Santiago Bay, Battle of, 385
Sarajevo, 418
Saratoga, Battle of, 109–10
Saudi Arabia, 605–7, 623
Savannah, Georgia, 35, 305
Scalawags, 319–20
Scalia, Antonin, 627, 637–38

Schenk v. United States, 430
Schlafly, Phyllis, 581
Schlieffen Plan, 422
Schrank, John F., 407
Schwarzkopf, Norman, 606
Scofield, C. I., 282–83
Scopes, John T., 457
Scopes trial, 457
Scots-Irish, 39
Scott, Dred, 267
Scott, Winfield, 245, 247–48, 261, 283
Sea Dogs, 15
secede. *See* secession
secession, 273, 275–76, 279–81
secret ballot, 390
Secret Six, 270
secular humanism, 412
Security Council, 526, 531, 605
segregation/desegregation, 399, 561, 567
Selective Service Act, 427
self-determination, 430
Seminole Indians, 11, 190, 195
Seminole War, 195
Senate, 128
Seneca Falls Convention, 214
separation of powers, 130–31
Separatists, 26, 56. *See also* Pilgrims
September 1, 1939, 495
September 11, 2001, 622
Sequoyah, 195
Serapis, 113
Seven Days' Battles, 287
Seventh-day Adventists, 228
Seven Years' War. *See* French and Indian War
Sewall, Samuel, 58, 59
Seward, William, 255, 265, 274–75, 378, 381
Shakers, 228
shantytown, 470
sharecropping, 318–19
Sharon, Ariel, 627
Shawnee Indians, 166
Shays, Daniel, 125
Shays's Rebellion, 125
Shenandoah Valley, 39, 287, 306
Shepard, Alan, 560
Sheridan, Philip, 306, 376
Sherman, Roger, 105, 128
Sherman, William Tecumseh, 249, 303–5
Sherman Anti-trust Act, 345–46, 395, 407
Shiloh, Battle of, 293–94
Shoshone Indians, 165
Siegfried Line, 494
Sierra Nevada, 238, 363
silent majority, 567

silver,
    free silver, 350–51
silverbugs, 351
Simons, Menno, 61
Simpson, A. B., 382, 413
Sinclair, Upton, 396
"Sinners in the Hands of an Angry God," 55, 67
Sioux Indians, 373
Sioux War, 374–76
Sitting Bull, 357, 375–76
Six-Day War, 584
Skylab, 560
Slater, Samuel, 203–4
slaves/slavery, 217–23
    abolishing of, 129, 313
    in England's colonies, 23–24
    in the Civil War, 280–81
    issue at Constitutional Convention, 129
    Lincoln's position on, 269–70, 274, 302
    Spanish and Portuguese trade, 13, 14, 24
Slidell, John, 301
smallpox, 41
Smith, Al, 449
Smith, Captain John, 22, 25, 59
Smith, Joseph, 212, 228
Smith, Oliver P., 532
Smoot-Hawley tariff, 450, 462, 469
Social Darwinism. *See* Darwinism
social gospel, 412
Socialism/Socialists, 349
    World War II era, 492, 494
Socialist Party, 349, 394
Social Security Act, 477
Society of Friends. *See* Quakers
soddies, 369
sod houses. *See* soddies
Solid South, 330
Somme campaign, 425–26
Sons of Liberty, 85, 87, 90, 95
Sotomayor, Sonia, 630
soup kitchens, 443, 465, 483–84
Souter, David, 630
South, the,
    during Civil War, 282–83. *See also* individual battles
    during Reconstruction, 313, 316, 318–21
    during War of 1812, 174–75
    solid, 330
South Carolina, 273
    colonization, 34
    colony, 35
    Revolutionary era, 115

South Dakota, 165
Southeast Asia, 501–2, 577
Southern Christian Leadership Conference (SCLC), 548
Southern colonies, 34–36. *See also* individual colonies
Soviet Union,
    Cold War era, 527–31, 535–36, 568, 585, 604
    invasion of Afghanistan, 585, 597
    World War II era, 494, 497–98
space program, 560
space race, 560
Spain,
    exploration, 5, 11–14
Spalding, Henry and Eliza, 233–34
Spanish-American War, 383–86
Spanish Armada, 15
Specie Circular of 1836, speculation, 460
Spencer, Herbert, 355
Spirit of St. Louis, 453
Spock, Benjamin, 546
spoils system, 190–91, 343
Sputnik I, 560
Squanto, 27
Square Deal, 395
stagflation, 579
Stalin, Joseph, 491, 493–94, 509, 515, 530, 532, 536, 605
Stalwarts, 343–44
Stamp Act, 85, 87–88, 95
Stamp Act Congress, 87
standard gauge, 210
Standard Oil Company, 339
Stanton, Charles E., 431
Stanton, Edwin, 317–18
Stanton, Elizabeth Cady, 393
Starr, Kenneth, 618
Star-Spangled Banner, The, 174
starving time, 23
State, Department of, 139
States' rights, 280
Statue of Liberty, 354
St. Augustine, 13–14
steamships, 211
steel, 205
Steffens, Lincoln, 393
Stephens, Alexander, 314
Steuben, Baron von, 111
Steven, John Paul, 630
Stevenson, Adlai, 541
Stevens, Thaddeus, 312, 314
St. Joseph, 211
St. Louis, 165
stock market crash, 461
Stone, Harlan, 525

Stones River, Battle of, 285, 295
Stowe, Harriet Beecher, 264
Strategic Arms Limitations Talks (SALT) treaties, 568, 585
Strategic Arms Reduction Talks (START), 600
Strategic Defense Initiative (SDI), 601
Strauss, Levi, 367
Strict constructionists, 143
strikes, 348–49, 397
Stuart, Gilbert, 215
Stuart, James Ewell Brown, (J.E.B.), 271, 283, 287–88, 290
Student Nonviolent Coordinating Committee (SNCC), 562
Students for a Democratic Society (SDS), 562
Student Volunteer Movement (SVM), 382
Stump Speaking, 215
Stuyvesant, Peter, 17
submarine warfare, 423–25
    unrestricted, 424
Sudetenland, 495
suffrage, 311
    blacks, 323, 554
    universal manhood, 185
    women's, 214, 393
Sugar Act, 85
Sully's Hill National Park, 398
Sumner, Charles, 266, 312, 314
Sumner-Brooks Episode, 266
Sunday, Billy, 392, 413–14
supply-side economics (Reaganomics), 594–95
Supreme Court, 131, 140, 627, 630
    Burwell v. Hobby Lobby, 638
    court-packing plan, 479–80
    during FDR's presidency, 480
    Marshall court, 161–62
    Warren Court, 555–56
Supreme Court decisions
    Brown v. Board of Education of Topeka, Kansas, 547, 555
    Dred Scott v. Sandford, 267
    Engel v. Vitale, 555
    Gibbons v. Ogden, 162
    Gideon v. Wainwright, 555
    Hosanna-Tabor Evangelical Lutheran Church & School v. Equal Employment Opportunity Commission, 638
    Little Sisters of the Poor v. Burwell, 638
    Marbury v. Madison, 161
    McCulloch v. Maryland, 162
    Miranda v. Arizona, 555
    Munn v. Illinois, 350

Northern Securities case, 395
Obergefell v. Hodges, 637
Plessy v. Ferguson, 399, 547
Roe v. Wade, 580, 588
Roth v. United States, 555
Schenk v. United States, 430
Sussex, 425
Sussex pledge, 425
Sutherland, George, 476
Sutter, John, 257–58
Sweden/Swedes, 496
Sweeney, Charles, 518
Swift, Gustavus, 367
Syria, 632

T

Taft, William Howard, 394, 400, 403–6
Taft-Hartley Act, 537–38
Taiwan, 531, 568, 588
Taliban, 623
Talleyrand, Charles Maurice, 150
Tallmadge Amendment, 184
Tallmadge, James, 184
Tammany Hall, 324–25, 471
Taney, Roger B., 194, 267
Tarbell, Ida, 339, 393
tariffs, 147, 181, 280, 346, 404
    of Abominations, 191
    of 1816, 181
Tarleton, Banastre, 116
taxes, 467, 596, 608–9
    colonial, 84–85
    Confederation era, 121
    federal income tax, 392, 506
    internal, 85
    World War II era, 506–7
Taylor, Maxwell, 510
Taylor, Zachary, 244, 245–46, 256–57, 260
Tea Act of 1773, 94
Teach, Edward "Blackbeard," 35
Tea Party, 630
Tea Party. *See* Boston Tea Party
Teapot Dome scandal, 447–48
technology, 636–37
Tecumseh, 166–69, 173
teddy bears, 394
telegraph, 211
telephones, 342
television, 542, 544–46
Temple, Shirley, 485
tenant farmers, 319
Tennent, Gilbert, 66–67
Tennent, William, Sr., 67
Tennessee, 115–16, 148, 275
Tennessee Valley Authority (TVA), 474–75, 477–78

Ten percent plan, 311
Tenure of Office Act, 317–18
terrorism, 599, 622–24
Tesla, Nikola, 342
Tet Offensive, 558–59
Texan War for Independence, 235–36
Texas, 234–37, 244–45, 273, 366
    annexation of, 241
    Republic of, 237
textile industry, 203–4, 340
Thames, Battle of the, 173
Thanksgiving, 28
The American Crisis, 104
Third party, 194
Third Reich, 492, 496
Third World, 528
38th parallel, 531
Thomas, Clarence, 627, 637
Thomas, George, 295–96
Thoreau, Henry David, 214
Three-Fifths Compromise, 129
Thumb, Tom, 357
Thurmond, Strom, 538
Tibbets, Paul, 518
Tilden, Samuel J., 328, 619
Tippecanoe, Battle of, 169, 199
tobacco, 23, 340
Tojo, Hideki, 493, 526
Toleration Act of 1649, 34
toll roads, 209
Tom Thumb, 210
Tories. *See* Loyalists
Torrey, R. A., 359, 413
totalitarianism, 492
Townsend, Francis, 479
Townshend, Charles, 88
Townshend Acts, 88
trade deficit, 579
Trade Expansion Act, 543
Trail of Tears, 196
transatlantic cable, 211
Transcendentalism, 214
transportation, 208–11, 408
    highway, 541
Travis, William, 237
Treasury, Department of, 139
Treaty of Alliance, 145, 151
trench warfare, 430
Trent affair, 301
Trenton, Battle of, 107
tribute, 163
Triple Alliance, 421
Triple Entente, 421
Tripoli, 163
Troubled Asset Relief Program (TARP), 628
Truman, Harry, 515, 517, 525, 531–33, 537–38, 547

Truman Doctrine, 529
Trumbull, John, 215
Trump, Donald, 634–35, 638
trustbusting, 391, 395
trusts, 339
Tubman, Harriet, 219, 262
Tunisia, 632
Turner, Nat, 219
turnpikes, 209
Turkey, 529
Tuskegee Institute, 399, 411
Twain, Mark, 335, 356
Tweed, William "Boss," 324–25
Tyler, John, 199–200, 239–40

U

U-boats, 423
Ukraine, 633
Uncle Tom's Cabin, 264
Underground Railroad, 218–19, 262
Underwood Tariff Act, 407
unemployment, 579, 587, 626, 629
    during the Great Depression, 467, 470, 483
Union army/forces, 283, 284
Union of Soviet Socialist Republics (USSR), 494, 527, 568
Union Pacific Railroad, 323, 362–63
Unitarianism, 214, 227
United Kingdom. *See* Britain
United Mine Workers, 482
United Nations, 515, 526, 605, 624
United States Steel Corporation, 340
University of Chicago, 412
University of Virginia, 160, 216
Urban evangelism, 358
Urbanization, 205, 353
urban riots, 561
Utah, 228, 365
utopia, 214
Utopian reformers, 214–15

V

Vallandigham, Clement, 300
Valley Campaign, 287
Valley Forge, 110–11, 125
Van Buren, Martin, 188, 191, 194, 197–99, 240, 257
Vanderbilt, Cornelius, 336
Van Devanter, Willis, 476
Vanzetti, Bartolomeo, 454
Vaudeville, 357
V-E Day, 517
Vermont, 148
Versailles,
    Treaty of, 434–37, 446, 494
vertical integration, 338–39

Vespucci, Amerigo, 6
Veterans Administration, 629
Veterans' Bureau, 448
Vicksburg,
　siege of, 294–95
Viet Cong, 557–59, 569
Vietnam, 502, 534–35, 556–59
Vietnamization, 568–69
Vietnam War, 556–59, 568–70
　antiwar movement, 562–63, 569–70
vigilantes, 95, 371
Villa, Pancho, 420, 511
Vincennes, Indiana, 113–14
Virginia, 275, 300
　colonization, 21–24, 56
　religion in, 59–60
　Revolutionary era, 116
Virginia Company, 20, 21, 23, 24, 26. *See also* London Company
Virginia, CSS. *See Merrimack*, USS
Virginia Plan, 127–28
Virginia Resolutions, 152, 192
V-J Day, 518
Volstead Act, 452
Volunteers in Service to America (VISTA), 554
Voting Rights Act of 1965, 554, 561

W

Wade, Benjamin, 314, 318
Wade-Davis Bill, 311–12
Wake Island, 502
Wallace, George, 553, 565–66, 570–71
Wallace, Henry A., 475, 515, 538
War, Department of, 139
Ward, Lester Frank, 355
Warfield, Benjamin B., 412–14
War for Independence, 100, 102, 120
war-guilt clause, 436
War Hawks, 171–72
War of 1812, 169–175, 181
War of Austrian Succession. *See* King George's War
War of Jenkins' Ear. *See* King George's War
War of the League of Augsburg. *See* King William's War
War of the Spanish Succession. *See* Queen Anne's War
War of the Worlds, 485–86
War on Terror, 623–25, 627
War Powers Act of 1973, 570
War Production Board, 505
Warren, Earl, 555
Warsaw Pact, 529
Washington and Lee University, 312
Washington, Booker T., 398–400

Washington College, 312
Washington, D.C., 142, 152, 159, 211
Washington, George,
　Farewell Address, 148–49
　in Constitutional Convention, 127
　in First Continental Congress, 96
　in French and Indian War, 78–79
　in Newburgh Conspiracy, 125
　in War for Independence, 102–4, 106–12, 114, 116–17
　presidency of, 120, 135–36, 139
Washington, March on, 548
Washington Naval Conference/Treaty, 444–45, 493
Washington, Treaty of, 378–79
Watergate affair, 574–76
Watts, Isaac, 217
Watts riot, 561
waving the bloody shirt, 329
Wayne, "Mad Anthony," 167
weapons of mass destruction (WMDs), 624
Weathermen, 562
Weaver, James B., 350
Webster, Daniel, 123, 181, 192, 197, 240, 259–60
Webster, Noah, 212
Webster-Ashburton Treaty, 240
Wehrmacht, 497
Weld, Theodore, 220
Welfare Reform Act of 1996, 616
Welles, Orson, 485
Wells, H. G., 486
Wesley, Charles, 35, 65
Wesley, John, 35, 62, 65, 224
West, Benjamin, 215
western lands,
　confederation era, 121–23
　conservation, 397–98
Westinghouse, George, 342
West Point, 110, 249, 275, 283, 296, 304, 511, 533
West Virginia, 300
West Virginia, 505
Whig Party/Whigs, 197–98, 239–40, 263–64
Whiskey Rebellion, 147
Whiskey Ring, 323
Whitefield, George, 68, 86, 97
White, Hugh, 197
Whitewater scandal, 613, 617–18
Whitman, Marcus and Narcissa, 233–34
Whitman, Walt, 214, 216
Whitney, Eli, 204, 207
Wickersham Commission, 452
Wilderness campaign, 303
Wilderness Road, 148, 209

Wilhelm II, Kaiser, 422
William III, 77
William and Mary College, 59
Williams College, 225–26
Williams, John, 76
Williams, Roger, 30–31, 60, 65
Williamsburg, Virginia, 96
Willkie, Wendell, 500
Wilmot, David, 255
Wilmot Proviso, 255
Wilson, Woodrow, 394, 406–7, 418–28, 430–31, 434–38
Wind Cave National Park, 398
Winona Lake Bible Conference, 413
Winthrop, John, 28–29
Wolfe, James, 80–81
women
　in World War I, 433
　in World War II, 505–06
　post-World War II, 546
women's liberation movement, 580
women's rights movement, 213–14, 579–80
Wood, Leonard, 385
Woodmason, Charles, 51
Woolworth, F.W., 356
Worcester, Samuel, 196
Worcester v. Georgia, 196
work relief, 468
Works Progress Administration (WPA), 475
World Council of Churches, 550
World Trade Center, 622
World War I,
　African American soldiers, 427
　posters, 427–28, 434
World War II,
　African American soldiers, 504
　in North Africa, 507–8
　in the Pacific, 501–3, 512–15
　Italian Campaign, 509
　Normandy Invasion, 510–11
Wounded Knee Massacre, 377, 579
Wright Brothers (Wilbur and Orville), 409
Wyoming, 148, 232, 346

X

XYZ Affair, 150–51

Y

Yale, 67, 69, 224–25
Yalta, 515, 527
yellow fever, 402
yellow journalism, 383
Yellowstone National Park, 165

Yemen, 632
York, Alvin C., 431
Yorktown, 116–17
Yosemite National Park, 398
Young, Brigham, 228
Young Men's Christian Association (YMCA), 229, 357
Youth for Christ, 550
Yugoslavia, 527, 617

Z

Zimmermann telegram, 426

Photograph Credits

Key

(t) top; (c) center; (b) bottom; (l) left; (r) right; (bg) background

Cover

front © iStock.com/endriashz; **back** Library of Congress

Front Matter

v t Joseph Sohm/Shutterstock.com; **v** b AP Photo/Joe Rosenthal, File; **vi** t Science History Images / Alamy Stock Photo; **vi** bl "Portrait of John Paul Jones" by George Bagby Matthews/Wikimedia Commons/Public Domain; **vi** br "NH 56464 KN"/National Museum of the U.S. Navy/Flickr/Public Domain; **vii** t Library of Congress, LC-USZC4-3156; **vii** c SuperStock / SuperStock; **vii** b Science History Images / Alamy Stock Photo; **viii** Universal History Archive/Universal Images Group/Getty Images

Unit Openers

x–1 Joseph Sohm/Shutterstock.com; **72–73** "Scene at the Signing of the Constitution of the United States" by Howard Chandler Christy/The Indian Reporter/Wikimedia Commons/Public Domain; **156–57** Bruce Ellis/Shutterstock.com; **252–53** Rob Hainer/Shutterstock.com; **332–33** Paul Dempsey/Shutterstock.com; **440–41** Library of Congress; **522–23** J. Bicking/Shutterstock.com

Chapter 1

2 Stocktrek Images/Getty Images; **3** Science History Images / Alamy Stock Photo; **4** © Ricardo Sousa /Fotolia; **5t** Universal Images Group / Superstock; **5b** "Christopher Columbus"/Wikimedia Commons/Public Domain; **6** Iberfoto / Superstock; **7t**, **8** Imagno/Hulton Fine Art Collection/Getty Images; **7b**, **13**, **15b**, **16c** Stock Montage/Archive Photos/Getty Images; **9l** "Lefferts Wigwam jeh" by Jim.hendersen/Wikimedia Commons/Public Domain; **9r** "Oglala girl in front of a tipi"/Wikimedia Commons/Library of Congress/Public Domain; **10t** Richard T. Nowitz/The Image Bank/Getty Images; **10c** MyLoupe/Universal Images Group/Getty Images; **10b** John Kropewnicki/Shutterstock.com; **11** Mark Burnett / Alamy Stock Photo; **12** DEA/G. DAGLI ORTI/De Agostini/Getty Images; **14t** "Castillo de San Marcos"/Wikimedia Commons/Public Domain; **14c** DEA/G. NIMATALLAH/De Agostini/Getty Images; **14b** © Sharpshot/Fotolia; **15t** "Elizabeth1England" by The Hatfield House/Wikimedia Commons/Public Domain; **16t** "Welcome to Roanoke Island" by Jimmy Emerson, DVM/Flickr/CC By NC-ND 2.0; **16b** GraphicaArtis/Archive Photos/Getty Images; **17** © iStock.com/HultonArchive

Chapter 2

19 MPI/Archive Photos/Getty; **20** "A Chronicle of England - Page 226 - John Signs the Great Charter"/Wikimedia Commons/Public Domain; **21** Richard Cummins / Alamy Stock Photo; **22t**, **31** Bettmann/Getty Images; **22b** Library of Congress, LC-USZC4-3368; **23** © spiritofamerica/Fotolia; **24** Everett Historical/Shutterstock.com; **26l** © iStock.com/Kenneth Wiedemann; **26r** "Robert Walter Weir - Embarkation of the Pilgrims - Google Art Project"/Wikimedia Commons/Public Domain; **27l** "The Mayflower Compact 1620 cph.3g07155"/LOC/Wikimedia Commons/Public Domain; **27r** Susan Pease / Alamy Stock Photo; **28**, **30** Stock Montage/Archive Photos/Getty Images; **29** © iStock.com/Pglam; **33t** Library of Congress, LC-USZC4-12141; **33b** "The Treaty of Penn with the Indians" by Benjamin West/Pennsylvania Academy of Fine Arts, Philadelphia/Wikimedia Common/Public Domain; **35t** Fototeca Storica Nazionale/Hulton Archive/Getty Images; **35bl, br** Photos.com/Getty Images Plus/Getty Images

Chapter 3

38 "The Copley Family" by John Singleton Copley/Wikimedia Commons/Public Domain; **40t** Library of Congress; **40b** Courtesy, American Antiquarian Society; **41** Stock Montage/Archive Photos/Getty Images; **42** North Wind Picture Archives; **43t** "Van-cortland-house-bronx" by Dmadeo/Wikimedia Commons/CC By-SA 3.0; **43ct** age fotostock / SuperStock; **43cb** HLPhoto/Bigstock.com; **43b** © iStock.com/Jan Tyler; **44t** "Front of horn book, STC 13813.5."/Folger Shakespeare Library/CC By-SA 4.0; **44b**, **48b** Public Domain; **46t** Courtesy of Middleton Place Foundation, Charleston, SC; **46b** AP Photo/Bruce Smith; **47l** John Parrot/Media Bakery; **47r** *Poor Richard, 1733: An Almanack For the Year of Christ 1733 . . .*/Public Domain; **48t** North Wind Picture Archives via AP Images; **49** Lee Snider/Media Bakery; **50** "Portrait of George Washington" by Gilbert Stuart/Wikimedia Commons/Public Domain; **51l** Collection of the Massachusetts Historical Society.; **51r** "Pennsylvania Gazette (May 9, 1754), page 1" by Benjamin Franklin/Library of Congress/Wikimedia Commons/Public Domain; **52** "Official Presidential portrait of John Adams" by John Trumbull/Wikipedia/Public Domain

Chapter 4

54 SuperStock / SuperStock; **55t**, **65l**, **68t** North Wind Picture Archives via AP Images; **55bl** Hans Holbein the Younger/Dover Publications, Inc./Public Domain; **55br** "Edward VI of England c. 1546"/Wikimedia Commons/Public Domain; **56l** Pantheon / SuperStock; **56r** "Portrait of Elizabeth I of England" by George Gower/Wikimedia Commons/Public Domain; **58** © Peabody Essex Museum, Salem, Massachusetts, USA / Bridgeman Images; **59** © Massachusetts Historical Society, Boston, MA, USA / Bridgeman Images; **60** "Religious denominations of the world- comprising a general view of the origin, history, and condition, of the various sects of Christians, the Jews and Mahometans, as well as the pagan forms of (14803203463)"/Wikimedia Commons/Public Domain; **61** Robert F. Leahy/Shutterstock.com; **62** "Old Salem-1" by David Bjorgen/Wikimedia Commons/CC By-SA 3.0; **64t** LEE SNIDER PHOTO IMAGES/Shutterstock.com; **64b** 1640 Bay Psalm Book/Rosenbach Museum/Public domain; **65r** "David Brainerd on horseback"/Wikimedia Commons/Public Domain; **67** "Sinners in the Hands of an Angry God by Jonathan Edwards 1741"/Library of Congress/Public Domain; **68bl** John Collet/The Bridgeman Art Library/Getty Images; **68br** DEA PICTURE LIBRARY/De Agostini Picture Library/Getty Images; **70** "Old Ship Church" by Timothy Valentine/Flickr/CC By-SA 2.0

Chapter 5

74 "The Death of General Wolfe" by Benjamin West/Wikimedia Commons/Public Domain; **77** Bank of England, London, UK / Photo © Heini Schneebeli / Bridgeman Images; **78** "Portrait of George Washington" by Charles Willson Peale/Wikimedia Commons/Public Domain; **79**, **80c**, **87b**, **90** Library of Congress; **80t** Courtesy Lilly Library, Indiana University, Bloomington, Indiana.; **80b** "Duquesne outline" by Kevin Myers/Wikimedia Commons/CC By-SA 3.0; **82l, r**, **87r** North Wind Picture Archives via AP Images; **83** "King George III in coronation robes" by Allan Ramsay/Wikimedia Commons/Public Domain; **85t** "Proof sheet of one penny stamps Stamp Act 1765" by Board of Stamps/Wikipedia/Public Domain; **85b** "Patrick henry" by George Bagby Matthews/Wikimedia Commons/Public Domain; **86** Fotosearch/Archive Photos/Getty Images; **87tl** ACME Imagery / SuperStock; **89** "Boston Massacre high-res"/Library of Congress/Wikimedia Commons/Public Domain

Chapter 6

92, **102**, **103**, **107** SuperStock / SuperStock; **93** © Boris Hudak | Dreamstime.com; **94t** "The Bostonians Paying the Excise-man, or Tarring and Feathering." by Philip Dawe/Wikimedia Commons/Public Domain; **94b** Library of Congress, LC-DIG-ds-03379; **96**, **97** Granger, NYC; **98t** Ed Vebell/Archive Photos/Getty Images; **98b** DeAgostini / SuperStock; **104l** DEA PICTURE LIBRARY/De Agostini Picture Library/Getty Images; **104r**, **110b** Library of Congress; **105t** "Writing the Declaration of Independence, 1776" by Jean Leon Gerome Ferris/Library of Congress/Wikimedia Commons/Public Domain; **105bl** "Declaration independence" by John Trumbull/US Capitol/Wikipedia/Public Domain; **105br** Public Domain; **109** North Wind Picture Archives via AP Images; **110t** © iStock.com/shyflygirl; **111** Artist - Edwin Austin Abbey / 3LH-Fine Art / SuperStock; **112** "Portrait of Marquis de La Fayette (1757-1834)" by Jean-Baptiste Weyler/Wikimedia Commons/Public Domain; **113l** "Portrait of John Paul Jones" by George Bagby Matthews/Wikimedia Commons/Public Domain; **113r** "NH 56464 KN"/National Museum of the U.S. Navy/Flickr/Public Domain; **114** Indiana Historical Bureau, State of Indiana; **116t** MPI/Archive Photos/Getty Images; **116b** DEA PICTURE LIBRARY/De Agostini/Getty Images; **117** "Surrender of Lord Cornwallis" by John Trumbull/Wikimedia Commons/Public Domain

Chapter 7

119, **125**, **128**, **135t** North Wind Picture Archives via AP Images; **121** NPS/Public Domain; **124** Courtesy of Tim Keesee; **126** "James Madison" by Gilbert Stuart/National Gallery of Art/Wikimedia Commons/Public Domain; **131** "Scene at the Signing of the Constitution of the United States" by Howard Chandler Christy/The Indian Reporter/

PHOTO CREDITS

Wikimedia Commons/Public Domain; **134t** Stock Montage/Archive Photos/Getty Images; **134b** "Federalist Papers"/Wikipedia/Public Domain; **135b** Bettmann/Getty Images; **136** "George Washington" by Gilbert Stuart/Clark Art Institute/Wikipedia/Public Domain

Chapter 8
138 Donna Neary/National Guard; **139l** Bettmann/Getty Images; **139r** "George Washington (Lansdowne portrait, 1796)" by Gilbert Stuart/Wikipedia/Public Domain; **140** "The Washington Family" by Edward Savage/Wikimedia Commons/Public Domain; **141** © iStock.com/AleksandarNakic; **143** Gary Whitton/Shutterstock.com; **144l, r** John Parrot/Media Bakery; **145t** The Brooklyn Museum/Public Domain; **145c** SuperStock / SuperStock; **145b, 149r** Everett - Art/Shutterstock.com; **146, 147t, 151** Granger, NYC; **147b** Science Source; **148t** Stock Montage/Archive Photos/Getty Images; **148b** Carolyn M Carpenter/Shutterstock.com; **149l** ACME Imagery / SuperStock; **150** Archives du Ministere des Affaires Etrangeres, Paris, France / Archives Charmet / Bridgeman Images; **153t** "ThomasJeffersonStateRoomPortrait" by Charles Willson Peale/Diplomatic Reception Rooms, U.S. Department of State/Wikimedia Commons/Public Domain; **153b** "Vanderlyn Burr"/Wikimedia Commons/Public Domain; **154** Library of Congress, LC-DIG-ppmsca-09502

Chapter 9
158 Library of Congress; **159t, 174b** Everett Historical/Shutterstock.com; **159b** "Monticello - path to house" by AgnosticPreachersKid/Wikimedia Commons/CC By-SA 4.0; **160** "Thomas Jefferson by Rembrandt Peale, 1800"/White House Historical Association/Wikimedia Commons/Public Domain; **161t** Stock Montage/Archive Photos/Getty Images; **161b** Rembrandt Peale, Collection of the Supreme Court of the United States; **163** "The Emperor Napoleon in his study at the Tuileries." by Jacques-Louis David/Wikimedia Commons/Public Domain; **164t** "Meriweather Lewis-Charles Willson Peale"/Wikimedia Commons/Public Domain; **164b** "William Clark-Charles Willson Peale"/Wikimedia Commons/Public Domain; **165t** neftali/Shutterstock.com; **165c** © 2009 JupiterImages Corporation/Stockxpert Image; **165b** American Philosophical Society, Lewis and Clark Journals; **166** North Wind Picture Archives via AP Images; **167** Chicago History Museum/Archive Photos/Getty Images; **168** Private Collection / Peter Newark American Pictures / Bridgeman Images; **169** Library of Congress, LC-USZC4-782; **170t** The Mariners' Museum, Newport News, VA; **170b** Granger, NYC; **171t** "James Madison" by John Vanderlyn/Wikimedia Commons/Public Domain; **171b** "Dolley Madison" by Gilbert Stuart/White House Historical Association/Wikimedia Commons/Public Domain; **172** Boston Globe/Getty Images; **173** National Park Service; **174t** Stock Montage / SuperStock; **175t** Classic Vision / age foto stock / SuperStock; **175b** "The Signing of the Treaty of Ghent, Christmas Eve, 1814" by Amédée Forestier/Smithsonian American Art Museum, Washington D.C./Wikimedia Commons/Public Domain; **176** "Portrait of James Monroe" by John Vanderlyn/Daderot/Wikimedia Commons/Public Domain; **178** Bettmann/Getty Images

Chapter 10
180 North Wind Picture Archives / Alamy Stock Photo; **181** DEA PICTURE LIBRARY/De Agostini/Getty Images; **182** Zack Frank/Shutterstock.com; **183** Jason O. Watson / historical-markers.org / Alamy Stock Photo; **185** BJU Photo Services; **186t** "John Quincy Adams" by George Peter Alexander Healy/Wikipedia/Public Domain; **186bl** "WilliamHCrawford" by John Wesley Jarvis/Wikimedia Commons/Public Domain; **186bc** "Portrait of Henry Clay" by John Neagle/Wikimedia Commons/Public Domain; **186br** "Andrew Jackson" by Thomas Sully/Wikipedia/Public Domain; **188** "Election Day 1815 by John Lewis Krimmel"/Wikimedia Commons/Public Domain; **189, 195** Library of Congress; **190** "Portrait of Rachel Donelson Jackson" by Ralph Eleaser Whiteside Earl/Tennessee Portrait Project/Wikimedia Commons/Public Domain; **191t, 193t, 197t** Granger, NYC; **191b** U.S. Senate Collection.; **192t** © iStock.com/HultonArchive; **192b** © Chicago History Museum, USA / Bridgeman Images; **193b** © Philadelphia History Museum at the Atwater Kent, / Courtesy of Historical Society of Pennsylvania Collection, / Bridgeman Images; **194** Unusual Films; **196t** Library of Congress, LC-USZC4-3156; **196b** SuperStock / SuperStock; **197b** "Mvanburen" by G.P.A. Healy/Wikimedia Commons/Public Domain; **199** Private Collection / Peter Newark American Pictures / Bridgeman Images

Chapter 11
202 © Collection of the New-York Historical Society, USA / Bridgeman Images; **203** © Daniel Logan | Dreamstime.com; **204** © iStock.com/JerryBKeane; **209, 220b** Stock Montage/Archive Photos/Getty Images; **210** Vintage Images / Alamy Stock Photo; **213t** Image courtesy of Stanford University Libraries; **213b** "Samuel Bell Waugh - Dorothea Lynde Dix - Google Art Project-crop"/Wikimedia Commons/Public Domain; **215t** "The Death of General Wolfe" by Benjamin West/Wikimedia Commons/Public Domain; **215b** "George Washington (The Athenaeum Portrait)" by Gilbert Stuart/Wikimedia Commons/Public Domain; **216t** "A View of the Mountain Pass Called the Notch of the White Mountains (Crawford Notch)" by Thomas Cole/Wikimedia Commons/Public Domain; **216b** William England/Hulton Archive/Getty Images; **217** Foster Hall Collection, Center for American Music, University of Pittsburgh Library System; **220t** "William Lloyd Garrison by Southworth and Hawes, c1850"/Wikimedia Commons/Public Domain; **221** Hulton Archive/Archive Photos/Getty Images; **224, 228b** Library of Congress; **226** "Charles g finney"/Wikimedia Commons/Public Domain; **228t** Universal Images Group / SuperStock

Chapter 12
231 Courtesy, Special Collections, The University of Texas at Arlington Libraries, Arlington, Texas.; **232** "Daniel Boone escorting settlers through the Cumberland Gap" by George Caleb Bingham/The Bridgeman Art Library/Wikimedia Commons/Public Domain; **233** North Wind Picture Archives via AP Images; **234t** © iStock.com/HultonArchive; **234b** The State Preservation Board, Austin, Texas; **235t** "Sam Houston" by Thomas Flintoff/Wikimedia Commons/ Public Domain; **235b** © iStock.com/Dean_Fikar; **236t** Bettmann/Getty Images; **236b** MPI/Archive Photos/Getty Images; **238** Richard Cummins/Corbis Documentary/Getty Images; **239** "Official White House portrait of John Tyler" by George Peter Alexander Healy/Wikimedia Commons/Public Domain; **241t** "James Knox Polk by George Peter Alexander Healy, 1846 - DSC03258"/Wikimedia Commons/Public Domain; **241b** © 33ft /Fotolia; **242** "Picturesque America58"/Wikimedia Commons/Public Domain; **245** "Zachary Taylor 2" by James Reid Lambdin/Wikipedia/Public Domain; **247t** Public Domain; **247b** The Jay Robert Nash Collection; **248t** "Original Todd bear flag"/Wikimedia Commons/Public Domain; **248c** © Elswarro | Dreamstime.com; **248b** Library of Congress, LC-DIG-pga-02526; **249lt, 249rt** Library of Congress; **249lb** "Robert E Lee Signature" by Connormah/Wikimedia Commons/Public Domain; **249ct** © iStock.com/Steven Wynn; **249cb** "Ulysses S Grant Signature" by Connormah/Wikimedia Commons/Public Domain; **249rb** "TJ Stonewall Jackson Signature" by Connormah/Wikimedia Commons/Public Domain

Chapter 13
254 Cincinnati Art Museum, Ohio, USA / Subscription Fund Purchase / Bridgeman Images; **255** "David Wilmot"/Wikimedia Commons/Public Domain; **257t, 264b, 267c, 271t** Everett Historical/Shutterstock.com; **257b** World History Archive / SuperStock; **258** Collection of the Oakland Museum of California, Oakland Museum of California Founders Fund; **260t, 265b** North Wind Picture Archives via AP Images; **260b** "ZacharyTaylor small" by John Vanderlyn/Wikimedia Commons/Public Domain; **262t, b, 267br** Library of Congress; **264t** "Harriet Beecher Stowe" by Alanson Fisher/Wikimedia Commons/Public Domain; **265t** Stock Montage/Archive Photos/Getty Images; **265c** "James Buchanan, Fifteenth President (1857-1861)" by Cliff/Flickr/CC By 2.0; **266l** Hulton Archive/Getty Images; **266c** © iStock.com/HultonArchive; **266b** Granger, NYC; **267t** "DredScott" by Louis Schultze/Missouri History Museum/Wikimedia Commons/Public Domain; **267bl** "Stephen Arnold Douglas"/Library of Congress/Public Domain; **269** Bettmann/Getty Images; **271b** "The Last Moments of John Brown" by Thomas Hovenden/Wikimedia Commons/Public Domain; **272t** "Stephen Douglas by Whitehurst Gallery"/Wilson Family Photographic Collection/Wikimedia Commons/Public Domain; **272c** Encyclopaedia Britannica/Universal Images Group/Getty Images; **272b** Library of Congress, LC-DIG-cwpbh-02532; **274** "Abraham Lincoln O-27 by Hesler, 1860-crop"/Library of Congress/Wikimedia Commons/Public Domain; **275** Library of Congress, LC-USZC4-528

Chapter 14
278 Library of Congress, LC-USZ62-134479; **279** Granger, NYC; **280t** Jay Robert Nash Collection; **280b** Provided by BACM; **281t** Library of Congress, LC-DIG-ppmsca-19204; **281b** Library of Congress, LC-DIG-cwpbh-00879; **282t** "Confederate General Robert E. Lee poses in a late April 1865" by Mathew Brady/National Archives/Wikimedia Commons/Public Domain; **282b** Library of Congress, LC-DIG-cwpb-03461; **283** "Gen.

PHOTO CREDITS

Winfield Scott" by Mathew Brady/NARA/Wikimedia Commons/Public Domain; **286t, 291t** Private Collection / Bridgeman Images; **286b, 308** Library of Congress; **287t** Library of Congress, LC-DIG-ppmsca-31277; **287c** Library of Congress, LC-USZ62-103202; **287b** "Abraham Lincoln and men of wartimes" by Alexander K. McClure/Internet Archive Book Image/Flickr/Public Domain; **288t** Getty Images/Photos.com/Thinkstock; **288b** Library of Congress, LC-DIG-cwpb-01099; **289t, 301c, 305** Everett Historical/Shutterstock.com; **289b** Library of Congress, LC-DIG-cwpb-05368; **290** "Thomas Jonathan 'Stonewall' Jackson" by J. W. King/Cliff/Flickr/CC By 2.0; **291b** Library of Congress, Prints & Photographs Division; **294** H -D Falkenstein/ima / imageBROKER / SuperStock; **296t** National Archives; **296b** Library of Congress, LC-USZ61-903; **297** Unusual Films; **298** Library of Congress, LC-DIG-cwpbh-03386; **299t** Library of Congress, LC-DIG-cwpb-03950; **299b** "New York Draft Riots - fighting" by The Illustrated London News/Wikimedia Commons/Public Domain; **300t** Library of Congress, LC-DIG-ppmsca-33101; **300b** Library of Congress, LC-DIG-ppmsca-34253; **301t** Library of Congress, LC-DIG-ppmsca-18444; **301b** Bettmann/Getty Images; **303** Library of Congress, LC-DIG-cwpb-04324; **304t** Library of Congress, LC-DIG-cwpb-06583; **304c** "Destroying CW railroads"/US Army Military History Institute/Wikimedia Commons/Public Domain; **304b** Library of Congress, LC-DIG-cwpb-06989; **306t** Steve Heap/Shutterstock.com; **306b** Library of Congress, LC-USZC4-1155; **307** National Geographic Creative / Bridgeman Images

Chapter 15

310 © 2008 by Dover Publications, Inc.; **312** Bruce Yuanyue Bi/Lonely Planet Images/Getty Images; **313** Science History Images / Alamy Stock Photo; **314t** "Thaddeus Stevens, Representative from Pennsylvania"/Flickr/Public Domain; **314c** "Andrew Johnson photo portrait head and shoulders, c1870-1880-Edit1" by Mathew Brady/Library of Congress/Wikimedia Commons/Public Domain; **314b** Library of Congress, LC-DIG-cwpbh-00477; **315t** Library of Congress, LC-DIG-ppmsca-11194; **315bl, br** North Wind Picture Archives; **316** "Ruins in Charleston, S.C - NARA - 525149" by Mathew Brady/National Archives/Wikimedia Commons/Public Domain; **317t** National Archives; **317b** Library of Congress, LC-DIG-cwpbh-00958; **318t** Granger, NYC; **318c** Library of Congress; **318b** Christie's Images / SuperStock; **319** "Carpetbag" by Sobebunny/Wikipedia/CC By-SA 3.0; **320** Library of Congress, LC-USZ62-128619; **321** Harper's Weekly/Public Domain; **322t** "Ulysses Grant 1870-1880"/Library of Congress/Wikimedia Commons/Public Domain; **322b** Interfoto / SuperStock; **324t** Art Archive, The / SuperStock; **324bl** "Thomas Nast - Brady-Handy" by Mathew Brady/Library of Congress/Wikimedia Commons/Public Domain; **324br** "1881 0101 tnast santa 200" by Thomas Nast/Wikimedia Commons/Public Domain; **325** Library of Congress, LC-USZ6-787; **326** "Joseph Rainey - Brady-Handy" by Mathew Brady or Levin Handy/Library of Congress/Wikimedia Commons/Public Domain; **327t** "Hiram Rhodes Revels Brady-Handy2" by Mathew Brady/Library of Congress/Wikimedia Commons/Public Domain; **327b** Library of Congress, LC-USZ62-127754; **328** Library of Congress, LC-DIG-ppmsca-07604; **330** Library of Congress, LC-USZ62-112163

Chapter 16

334, 336, 340, 344, 348, 357 Library of Congress; **337** Library of Congress, LC-DIG-ggbain-14523; **338** SuperStock / SuperStock; **341** Bettmann/Getty Images; **342t** World History Archive / SuperStock; **342b** Library of Congress, LC-USZ62-41756; **343 t, b, 351r** Everett Historical/Shutterstock.com; **345** "Benjamin Harrison" by Eastman Johnson/Wikimedia Commons/Public Domain; **351l** "Mckinley"/Wikimedia Commons/Public Domain; **354** "Immigrant-children-ellis-island" by Brown Brothers/Records of the Public Health Service/US GOV National Archives/Wikimedia Commons/Public Domain; **355** "Darwin - John G Murdoch Portrait restored"/Wikimedia Commons/Public Domain; **356** "The Fog Warning" by Winslow Homer/Wikimedia Commons/Public Domain; **358** AP Photo

Chapter 17

361 Nebraska State Historical Society, RG2608PH-1189 (cropped); **363t** MPI/Archive Photos/Getty Images; **363b** "East and West Shaking hands at the laying of last rail Union Pacific Railroad - Restoration"/Wikimedia Commons/Public Domain; **364, 374, 384b** Public Domain; **365** Library of Congress, LC-USZ62-19414; **368** Underwood Archives/Archive Photos/Getty Images; **369** "Rawding family sod house" by Solomon D. Butcher (1856-1927)/Wikimedia Commons/Public Domain; **370t** Nebraska State Historical Society, RG2608PH-2430 (cropped and text removed); **370b** Unusual Films/Courtesy of Terry Rude; **371l** Library of Congress, LC-USZ62-3854; **371r** Print Collector/Hulton Archive/Getty Images; **372t** "WyattEarp-andothers"/Wikimedia Commons/Public Domain; **372b** National Archives; **373t** Corcoran Collection (Gift of Mary Stewart Bierstadt [Mrs. Albert Bierstadt])/Courtesy National Gallery of Art, Washington; **373b, 379t** North Wind Picture Archives via AP Images; **375l** Biosphoto / Superstock; **375r** "Sitting Bull" by David F. Barry/Library of Congress/Wikimedia Commons/Public Domain; **376** "Goyathlay"/Wikimedia Commons/NARA/Public Domain; **377t** "Chief Joseph, Nez Perce, when young - NARA - 523607"/Wikimedia Commons/Public Domain; **377b** Library of Congress, LC-USZ62-44458; **379b** North Wind Picture Archives / Alamy Stock Photo; **380t** The Ohio State University Billy Ireland Cartoon Library & Museum; **380b** Bettmann/Getty Images; **381t** "Nast on Alaska" by Thomas Nast/Harper's Weekly/Wikimedia Commons/Public Domain; **381b** Library of Congress/Corbis Historical/Getty Images; **382t, 384t, 385t** Everett Historical/Shutterstock.com; **382b** "Lottie Moon-1"/ Wikimedia Commons/Public Domain; **385b** "RoughRiders"/Library of Congress/Wikimedia Commons/Public Domain; **386** Library of Congress/Wikimedia Commons/Public Domain

Chapter 18

388 "First flight2" by John T. Daniels/Library of Congress/Wikipedia/Public Domain; **389t, b** Public Domain; **390, 392b, 395, 399l, 400, 404, 409t, bl** Library of Congress; **391** Corbis Historical/Getty Images; **392t** Timothy Hughes Rare & Early Newspapers; **393l** Library of Congress, LC-USZ62-50393; **393r, 399r** Everett Historical/Shutterstock.com; **394t** "1904socialist"/Wikimedia Commons/Public Domain; **394b** "Drawing the Line in Mississippi" by Clifford Berryman/Public Domain; **396l** Bettmann/Getty Images; **396r** "Upton Sinclair cph.3c32336"/Library of Congress/Public Domain; **397** Library of Congress, LC-USZ62-55730; **398** Library of Congress, LC-DIG-ppmsca-37579; **401** Library of Congress, LC-DIG-ds-05213; **402lt** PhotoQuest/Archive Photos/Getty Images; **402lb** "Roosevelt and the Canal"/Wikimedia Commons/Public Domain; **402r** "William Crawford Gorgas" by Harris & Ewing/Library of Congress/Wikimedia Commons/Public Domain; **403** Granger, NYC; **406** Stock Montage/Archive Photos/Getty Images; **408** National Archives; **409br** Panoramic Images / Alamy Stock Photo; **410** Used with permission of Mayo Foundation for Medical Education and Research. All rights reserved.; **411** Alpha Historica / Alamy Stock Photo; **412** Historical Center of the Presbyterian Church in America, Photo collection- http://www.pcahistory.org; **413** Library of Congress, LC-USZ62-108493; **414** National Baseball Library/Public Domain

Chapter 19

417, 422b, 428bl, 428br, 430t Everett Historical/Shutterstock.com; **418t, 426b** Bettmann/Getty Images; **418b** STR/AFP/Getty Images; **419** Library of Congress, LC-USZ62-9981; **420t** Science History Images / Alamy Stock Photo; **420b** Library of Congress, LC-DIG-ggbain-09255; **422t, 435b, 437** Library of Congress; **423** "German U-boat UB 14 with its crew"/SMU Central University/Wikimedia Commons/Public Domain; **424t** "RMS Lusitania coming into port, possibly in New York, 1907"/Library of Congress/Wikimedia Commons/Public Domain; **424b** BJUP Files; **426t** National Archives and Records Administration; **427tl** Library of Congress, LC-DIG-ppmsca-18640; **427tr** "369th 15th New York"/National Archives/Wikimedia Commons/Public Domain; **427b** Library of Congress, LC-USZC4-8890; **428t** Library of Congress, LC-DIG-hec-10538; **428bcl** Library of Congress, LC-USZC4-9868; **428bcr** Courtesy of Tim Keesee/Public Domain; **429** Universal History Archive/Universal Images Group/Getty Images; **430b** "Cheshire Regiment trench Somme 1916" by John Warwick Brooke/Wikimedia Commons/Public Domain; **431** neftali/Shutterstock.com; **432t, b** National Archives; **433** "John Pershing" by 2d Lt. L J. Rode./Wikimedia Commons/Public Domain; **434t** PhotoQuest/Archive Photos/Getty Images; **434b** World War Poster collection (Mss036), Literary Manuscripts Collection, University of Minnesota Libraries, Minneapolis, Minnesota.; **435t** "Parisians Greet Wilson"/Woodrow Wilson Presidential Library Archives/Wikimedia Commons/Public Domain; **436t** Hulton Archive/Archive Photos/Getty Images; **436b** "Interior of Versailles"/Woodrow Wilson Presidential Library Archives/Flickr/Public Domain

Chapter 20

442 Hulton Archive/Getty Images; **444** Library of Congress, LC-USZ62-111661; **447** Library of Congress, LC-USZ62-91485; **448** Library of Congress, LC-USZ62-93287; **449** Library of Congress, LC-USZ62-111716; **451t** Library of Congress, LC-DIG-hec-31012; **451b**

PHOTO CREDITS

Leemage/Corbis Historical/Getty Images; **452** "Detroit police inspecting equipment found in a clandestine underground brewery during the prohibition era"/NARA/Wikimedia Commons/Public Domain; **453t** Library of Congress, LC-USZ62-22847; **453b** Culver Pictures, Inc. / SuperStock; **454** Library of Congress, LC-DIG-npcc-16220; **455** "AlCaponemugshotCPD"/US Department of Justice/Wikimedia Commons/Public Domain; **457** Library of Congress; **459t** "SearsHome2015"/Sears, Roebuck & Co./Wikimedia Commons/Public Domain; **459c** © iStock.com/fstop123; **459b** Archive Holdings Inc./Archive Photos/Getty Images; **461** Underwood Archives/Archive Photos/Getty Images

Chapter 21
464 Franklin D. Roosevelt Library; **465** "Farm Security Administration: farmers whose topsoil blew away joined the sod caravans of "Okies" on Route 66 to California"/NARA/Wikimedia Commons/Public Domain; **466t, 473bl** Universal Images Group/Getty Images; **466b, 468** Everett Historical/Shutterstock.com; **467t** Glenbow Archives (NA-2256-1); **467c** "Unemployed men queued outside a depression soup kitchen opened in Chicago by Al Capone, 02/1931"/NARA/Wikimedia Commons/Public Domain; **467b** Archive Photos/Getty Images; **470t** Library of Congress, LC-DIG-hec-36872; **470b** PhotoQuest/Archive Photos/Getty Images; **471t** Blank Archives/Hulton Archive/Getty Images; **471b** Independent Picture Service/Universal Images Group/Getty Images; **473t** AP Photo; **473br** Hulton Archive/Getty Images; **474t, 487bl** Bettmann/Getty Images; **474b** Stock Montage/Archive Photos/Getty Images; **475t** "CCC crew clearing a roadside, Boise National Forest, Idaho (3226091593)" by U.S. Forest Service/Oregon State University Archives/Wikimedia Commons/Public Domain; **475c** "PWA Construction Site in Washington, D.C"/NARA/Wikimedia Commons/Public Domain; **475b, 485t** Photo Researchers/Science Source/Getty Images; **476l** Library of Congress, LC-DIG-npcc-26426; **476ct** Library of Congress/Corbis Historical/Getty Images; **476cb** Library of Congress, LC-DIG-npcc-07526; **476rt** Library of Congress, LC-DIG-hec-20296; **476rb** Library of Congress, LC-DIG-hec-28983; **477t** Courtesy of the Franklin D. Roosevelt Library website; version date 2009; **477b** "Norris"/Tennessee Valley Authority/Flickr/CC By 2.0; **478t** MPI/Archive Photos/Getty Images; **478b** "HueyPLongGesture"/Library of Congress/Wikimedia Commons/Public Domain; **479t** Timothy Hughes Rare & Early Newspapers; **479c** Library of Congress, LC-DIG-hec-24268; **479b, 488r** Fotosearch/Archive Photos/Getty Images; **480t, 484t** Granger, NYC; **480b** Library of Congress, LC-USZ62-106389; **482** Sheldon Dick/Hulton Archive/Getty Images; **483t** "Edison, Kern County, California. Children of young migratory parents. They originally lived in Texas." by Dorothea Lange/NARA/Wikimedia Commons/Public Domain; **483c** GraphicaArtis/Archive Photos/Getty Images; **483b** "Migrant family looking for work in the pea fields of California"/NARA/Wikimedia Commons/Public Domain; **484b** Library of Congress/Science Faction/Getty Images; **485b, 487** Universal History Archive/Universal Images Group/Getty Images; **486t** H. Armstrong Roberts/Retrofile/Getty Images; **486b** Library of Congress, LC-USF34-050311-E; **487br** Sueddeutsche Zeitung Photo / Alamy Stock Photo; **488lt** Everett Collection / SuperStock; **488lb** Arthur Cofod/The LIFE Picture Collection/Getty Images

Chapter 22
490 AP Photo/Joe Rosenthal, File; **491l** Culture Club/Hulton Archive/Getty Images; **491r** Fox Photos/Hulton Archive/Getty Images; **492t, 515b** Universal History Archive/Universal Images Group/Getty Images; **492b** Roger Viollet Collection/Getty Images; **493l, rt** AP Photo; **493rc** Fox Photos/Hulton Royals Collection/Getty Images; **493rb** Sovfoto/Universal Images Group/Getty Images; **494lt, 515t** Keystone/Hulton Archive/Getty Images; **494lc** © bluesky6867/Fotolia; **494lb** "Maginot line 1" by John C. Watkins V/Wikimedia Commons/Public Domain; **494r** ZYLBERYNG Didier / Hemis.fr / SuperStock; **495t** Hulton Archive/Archive Photos/Getty Images; **495c** Pictorial Parade/Archive Photos/Getty Images; **495b** ullstein bild/Getty Images; **496** Hulton Deutsch/Corbis Historical/Getty Images; **497t** National Portrait Gallery / SuperStock; **497b** William Vandivert/The LIFE Picture Collection/Getty Images; **499, 510c** Library of Congress; **500t, 514t** Bettmann/Getty Images; **500ct** Blank Archives/Hulton Archive/Getty Images; **500cb** The New York Historical Society/Archive Photos/Getty Images; **500b** Courtesy of Busy Beaver Button Museum; **501** 502 collection / Alamy Stock Photo; **502t** "Burning ships at Pearl Harbor" by U.S. Navy/Wikimedia Commons/Public Domain; **502b** © iStock.com/400tmax; **503t** Corbis Historical/Getty Images; **503b** Eliot Elisofon/The LIFE Picture Collection/Getty Images; **504tl, 504b, 510t, 516bl, br** National Archives; **504tr** "Tuskegee airmen 2" by Toni Frissell/Library of Congress/Wikimedia Commons/Public Domain; **505t** Naval Historical Foundation; **505b** BJU Photo Services/Courtesy of Tim Keesee; **506tl** ClassicStock.com / SuperStock; **506tr** Provided by BAC software; **506b** PhotoQuest/Archive Photos/Getty Images; **507, 509** adoc-photos/Corbis Historical/Getty Images; **508** War Archive / Alamy Stock Photo; **510b** pedrosala/Shutterstock.com; **511t** "GeorgeSPatton" by U.S. Army Signal Corps/Wikimedia Commons/Public Domain; **511b** Tony Vaccaro/Archive Photos/Getty Images; **512** "PT-140 underway off Melville (Rhode Island) in 1943"/U.S. Navy/Wikimedia Commons/Public Domain; **514c** fototeca gilardi/Marka/SuperStock; **514b** Edward Steichen/The LIFE Picture Collection/Getty Images; **516t** New York Daily News Archive/New York Daily News/Getty Images; **517t, 518** SuperStock / SuperStock; **517b** Underwood Archives/Archive Photos/Getty Images; **519t** U.S. National Archives and Records Administration; **519b** John Frost Newspapers / Alamy Stock Photo; **520** Everett Historical/Shutterstock.com

Chapter 23
524, 536b, 538b National Archives; **525, 526t, 533, 543b, 545t, 546t, 547b** Bettmann/Getty Images; **526c** Archive Photos/Getty Images; **526b** Kametaro/Shutterstock.com; **527** Popperfoto/Getty Images; **529t** "George C. Marshall"/Wikimedia Commons/Public Domain; **529b, 538t, 541t, 542** AP Photo; **530** Walter Sanders/The LIFE Picture Collection/Getty Images; **530b** US Air Force; **531** Jack Wilkes/The LIFE Picture Collection/Getty Images; **532t** "Chosin" by Corporal Peter McDonald, USMC/Wikimedia Commons/Public Domain; **532b** US Army/Getty Images; **534t** Hulton Archive/Getty Images; **534b** Phonlamai Photo/Shutterstock.com; **535t** Keystone-France/Gamma-Keystone/Getty Images; **535c** MIGUEL VINAS/AFP/Getty Images; **535b** Courtesy The History Place (www.historyplace.com); **536t** Paul Schutzer/The LIFE Picture Collection/Getty Images; **536c** picture-alliance/dpa/AP Images; **540t, 547t** Granger, NYC; **540b** The Senate Historical Office; **541b** George Marks/Retrofile/Getty Images; **543t** Estate of Stanley Tretick LLC/Corbis Premium Historical/Getty Images; **544t** Found Image Holdings Inc/Corbis Historical/Getty Images; **544b** Afro American Newspapers/Gado/Getty Images; **545c** Heritage Image Partnership Ltd / Alamy Stock Photo; **545b** Apic/Getty Images; **546t** Michael Ochs Archives/Getty Images; **548t** Library of Congress, LC-USZ62-111235; **548b** Underwood Archives/Getty Images; **549t, c** AFP/Getty Images; **549b** FrameAngel/Shutterstock.com; **550** BJU Photo Services

Chapter 24
552 "Boeing B-52 dropping bombs" by USAF/Wikimedia Commons/Public Domain; **554** LBJ Library photo by Cecil Stoughton; **555, 560t, 560bc** Bettmann/Getty Images; **556, 558** Tim Page/Corbis Historical/Getty Images; **559** Wally McNamee/Corbis Premium Historical/Getty Images; **560c** NASA / SuperStock; **560bl** Ralph Morse/The LIFE Picture Collection/Getty Images; **560br** "Neil Armstrong pose" by NASA/Wikimedia Commons/Public Domain; **561** Everett Collection / SuperStock; **563** © iStock.com/Denise Roup; **564t** LBJ Library photo by Jack Kightlinger; **564b** Joseph Louw/The LIFE Images Collection/Getty Images; **565t** Rolls Press/Popperfoto/Getty Images; **565b** Hudson Library & Historical Society; **568t** National Archives; **568b** Mondadori Portfolio/Getty Images; **569** John Filo/Getty Images; **571** Wally McNamee/Corbis Historical/Getty Images

Chapter 25
573 White House Photograph Courtesy Gerald R. Ford Library; **574** Hulton Archive/Getty Images; **575t** PhotoQuest/Getty Images; **575ct** The Senate Historical Office; **575cb, 580bl, br, 581, 586b, 590t** Bettmann/Getty Images; **575b** "Letter of Resignation of Richard M. Nixon, 1974"/U.S. National Archives/Wikipedia/Public Domain; **576** Timothy Hughes Rare and Early Newspapers; **577** Wally McNamee/Corbis Historical/Getty Images; **578** Smith Collection/Gado/Getty Images; **579** SLADE Paul/Paris Match Archive/Getty Images; **580t** Mikki Ansin/Getty Images; **580c** Barbara Freeman/Hulton Archives/Getty Images; **583t, 585bl, 586t** AP Photo; **583cl, cr, 588b, 589b** Terry Ashe/The LIFE Images Collection/Getty Images; **583b** Ron Galella/WireImage/Getty Images; **584t** Everett Collection Inc / Alamy Stock Photo; **584b** Wally McNamee/Corbis Premium Historical/Getty Images; **585t** Alain Dejean/Sygma Premium/Getty Images; **585br** JOEL ROBINE/AFP/Getty Images; **588t** Suzanne R. Altizer; **589t** Unusual Films; **590b** Courtesy Ronald Reagan Library

Chapter 26
593, 594r, 596, 597, 602 Courtesy Ronald Reagan Library; **594l** AFP/Getty Images; **595**

"Reagan on horseback"/National Archives/Wikimedia Commons/Public Domain; **598** AP Photo/Michael Stravato; **599** AP Photo/Jim Bourdier, File; **600**t Bettmann/Getty Images; **600**b ullstein bild/Getty Images; **601** MIKE SARGENT/AFP/Getty Images; **603** The White House/Pete Souza; **605** AP Photo/Dieter Endlicher; **606**t Laurent VAN DER STOCKT/Gamma-Rapho/Getty Images; **606**b Georges MERILLON/Gamma-Rapho/Getty Images; **608**t © iStock.com/DNY59; **608**b AP Photo/Barry Thumma; **609** Wally McNamee/Corbis Historical/Getty Images; **610** The White House

Chapter 27
612, **630**t AP Photo/J. Scott Applewhite; **613** Ira Wyman/Sygma/Getty Images; **614**t Rob Nelson/The LIFE Images Collection/Getty Images; **614**b AP Photo/John Duricka; **615**t Wally McNamee/Corbis Historical/Getty Images; **615**b RICHARD ELLIS/AFP/Getty Images; **616**t, c Courtesy of Busy Beaver Button Museum; **616**b AP Photo/Susan Sterner, pool; **618**t New York Daily News Archive/New York Daily News/Getty Images; **618**b WILLIAM PHILPOTT/AFP/Getty Images; **619**l Mark Wilson/Hulton Archive/Getty Images; **619**r AP Photo/Eric Draper; **620** AP Photo/Peter Cosgrove, File; **622**t The White House/John Ficaro; **622**cl Spencer Platt/Getty Images News/Getty Images; **622**cr "Pentagon on 9.11 - 2" by Tech. Sgt. Cedric H. Rudisill/Wikimedia Commons/Public Domain; **622**b DAVID MAXWELL/AFP/Getty Images; **623**t Getty Images News/Getty Images; **623**b Official USMC photo by Lance Cpl. James Patrick Douglas; **624** INA/AFP/Getty Images; **625**tl Gilles BASSIGNAC/Gamma-Rapho/Getty Images; **625**tr Department of Defense; **625**b Joe Raedle/Getty Images News/Getty Images; **626** "FEMA - 19187 - Photograph by Jocelyn Augustino taken on 09-02-2005 in Louisiana"/Wikimedia Commons/Public Domain; **627**t AP Photo/Susan Walsh; **627**c Mark Wilson/Getty Images News/Getty Images; **627**bl Bloomberg/Getty Images; **627**br © Traceywood | Dreamstime.com; **628** © bupole maweja | Dreamstime.com; **630**b Pool/Getty Images News/Getty Images; **631** MCT/Tribune News Service/Getty Images; **632**t "Mitt Romney and Barack Obama Oval Office meeting 2012-11-29" by Pete Souza/Wikimedia Commons/Public Domain; **632**b Justin Sullivan/Getty Images News/Getty Images; **633**t AAraujo/Shutterstock.com; **633**c Pacific Press/LightRocket/Getty Images; **633**b Evgenii Sribnyi/Shutterstock.com; **635**tl Win McNamee/Getty Images News/Getty Images; **635**tr SAUL LOEB/AFP/Getty Images; **635**b Drew Angerer/Getty Images News/Getty Images; **636**t AFP/Getty Images; **636**b © Brphoto | Dreamstime.com; **637** Alex Wong/Getty Images News/Getty Images; **638**t Steven Frame/Shutterstock.com; **638**b Alex Wong/Getty Images News/Getty Images

Back Matter
640–41 dibrova/Shutterstock.com; **644–56** bg locote/Shutterstock.com

All maps from Map Resources